The Cambridge Handbook of the Imagination

The human imagination manifests in countless different forms. We imagine the possible and the impossible. How do we do this so effortlessly? Why did the capacity for imagination evolve and manifest with undeniably manifold complexity uniquely in human beings? This handbook reflects on such questions by collecting perspectives on imagination from leading experts. It showcases a rich and detailed analysis on how the imagination is understood across several disciplines of study, including anthropology, archaeology, medicine, neuroscience, psychology, philosophy, and the arts. An integrated theoretical-empirical-applied picture of the field is presented, which stands to inform researchers, students, and practitioners about the issues of relevance across the board when considering the imagination. With each chapter, the nature of human imagination is examined – what it entails, how it evolved, and why it singularly defines us as a species.

ANNA ABRAHAM is the E. Paul Torrance Professor of Creativity and Gifted Education, and the Director of the Torrance Center for Creativity and Talent Development in the College of Education at the University of Georgia, Athens, USA.

D1158728

The Cambridge Handbook of the Imagination

Edited by

Anna Abraham
University of Georgia, Athens, GA, USA

CAMBRIDGE
UNIVERSITY PRESS

CAMBRIDGE
UNIVERSITY PRESS

University Printing House, Cambridge CB2 8BS, United Kingdom

One Liberty Plaza, 20th Floor, New York, NY 10006, USA

477 Williamstown Road, Port Melbourne, VIC 3207, Australia

314–321, 3rd Floor, Plot 3, Splendor Forum, Jasola District Centre,
New Delhi – 110025, India

79 Anson Road, #06–04/06, Singapore 079906

Cambridge University Press is part of the University of Cambridge.

It furthers the University's mission by disseminating knowledge in the pursuit of
education, learning, and research at the highest international levels of excellence.

www.cambridge.org
Information on this title: www.cambridge.org/9781108429245
DOI: 10.1017/9781108580298

First published 2020

Printed in the United Kingdom by TJ International Ltd. Padstow Cornwall

A catalogue record for this publication is available from the British Library.

ISBN 978-1-108-42924-5 Hardback
ISBN 978-1-108-45342-4 Paperback

For Marius

Contents

Figures

Contributors

ANNA ABRAHAM is the E. Paul Torrance Professor in Creativity and Gifted Education at the University of Georgia, Athens, GA. She employs a cross-disciplinary lens in exploring creativity and other aspects of the imagination including the reality-fiction distinction, mental time travel, and mental state reasoning. Her publications include *The Neuroscience of Creativity* (2018).

DONNA ROSE ADDIS holds a Canada 150 Research Chair at the Rotman Research Institute at Baycrest Health Sciences. She is a Professor of Psychology at the University of Toronto and a Fellow of the Royal Society of New Zealand. Her research focuses on the neurocognitive substrates of memory and imagination.

EVAN D. ANDERSON is a graduate student in the Decision Neuroscience Laboratory and a member of the Neuroscience Program at the University of Illinois. His research focuses on the neural dynamics of intelligence, studying the relationship between properties of brain networks and intelligent behavior.

JESSICA R. ANDREWS-HANNA is an Assistant Professor of Psychology and Cognitive Science at the University of Arizona, where she directs the Neuroscience of Emotion and Thought (NET) Laboratory. Her research centers on understanding the neuroscience of imagination and spontaneous thought across the lifespan, in both healthy and clinical populations.

SHAHAR ARZY is a cognitive neurologist at the Hadassah Hebrew University Medical School in Jerusalem. His research aims to conceptualize the cognitive system as an interplay of the experiencing self within a multidimensional representation of the environment, ranging from the spatial environment to the temporal (memories) and social (people) planes, as well as more conceptual domains.

LINDEN J. BALL is a Professor of Cognitive Psychology and the Dean of the School of Psychology at the University of Central Lancashire, Preston, UK. He conducts both laboratory-based and real-world studies of thinking, reasoning, problem-solving, and creativity. He is the co-editor of the *Routledge International Handbook of Thinking and Reasoning* (2018).

ARON K. BARBEY is a Professor of Psychology, Neuroscience, and Bioengineering at the University of Illinois. He is also Director of the Center for Brain Plasticity and the Decision Neuroscience Laboratory and conducts research on the neural foundations of human intelligence and decision-making.

CHRISTOPHER C. BERGER is a postdoctoral scholar at the California Institute of Technology. He received his PhD from the Karolinska Institute and his research focuses on the interaction and integration of the senses and crossmodal plasticity. This work also examines the role of mental imagery in multisensory perception.

SIMON E. BLACKWELL is a postdoctoral researcher at Ruhr-Universität Bochum, Germany. He trained as a clinical psychologist in Oxford, UK, and worked as a full-time clinician before entering research. His work focuses on positive mental imagery, and spans both basic and applied clinical research.

KHATEREH BORHANI is an Assistant Professor at the Institute for Cognitive and Brain Sciences in Shahid Beheshti University, Iran. She received her PhD in Cognitive Neuroscience from the University of Bologna, Italy, and her research focuses on the processing of emotions in human body postures and faces.

ALAN ROBERT BOWMAN is an academic tutor for the Teesside University Doctorate in Clinical Psychology, UK. He also works in the UK National Health Service (NHS) as a Highly Specialist Clinical Psychologist, with expertise in long-term health conditions. His research interests include mechanisms of visual hallucinations, chronic pain, and psychological adjustment to long-term health problems.

ADAM BULLEY is the C. J. Martin postdoctoral fellow in psychology at Harvard University and the University of Sydney, Australia. His research focuses on the role of foresight in decision-making and emotion. He obtained his PhD from the University of Queensland, Australia.

RUTH M. J. BYRNE is Professor of Cognitive Science in the School of Psychology and Institute of Neuroscience at Trinity College Dublin, University of Dublin, Ireland. She is the author of *The Rational Imagination: How People Create Alternatives to Reality* (2005) and carries out experimental and computational investigations of reasoning and imaginative thought.

JULIA F. CHRISTENSEN is a senior postdoctoral researcher at the Max Planck Institute for Empirical Aesthetics, Germany. Her research focuses on psychophysiological aspects of emotions related to watching dance, dance expertise, and functions of human dance. She is also a popular science writer (e.g. *Dance is the Best Medicine*, 2018).

DANIEL COLLERTON is a retired clinical psychologist with a long-standing interest in visual hallucinations, especially in older people. He has published on why they occur and why they have such differing effects on different people, along with their relationships to consciousness, and the clinical treatment of distressing hallucinations.

BERNARD J. CRESPI is a Canada Research Chair in Evolutionary Genetics and Psychology at Simon Fraser University, Canada. He studies social evolution at scales from genes, to brains, to human groups. He has won numerous awards, including the Dobzhansky Prize, the E. O. Wilson Award, a Killam Fellowship, and election to the Royal Society of Canada.

ARNAUD D'ARGEMBEAU is an Associate Professor at the University of Liège and Senior Research Associate for the Fund for Scientific Research (F.R.S.-FNRS), Belgium. His primary research interest is in the cognitive and neural bases of autobiographical memory and future-oriented thinking.

AMNON DAFNI-MEROM is an MD-PhD candidate at the Hadassah Hebrew University Medical School, Israel. He investigates the brain mechanisms underlying the relations between the behaving self and its cognitive representation of the world. He is specifically interested in how these cognitive functions deteriorate in neurodegenerative disorders such as Alzheimer's disease.

DAVID DAVIES is a Professor of Philosophy at McGill University, Canada. He has written *Art as Performance* (2004), *Aesthetics and Literature* (2007), and *Philosophy of the Performing Arts* (2011). He works on metaphysics and epistemology of art, on issues relating to individual arts, and on topics in analytic metaphysics, mind, and language.

JIM DAVIES is a Professor at Carleton University's Institute of Cognitive Science, Canada, and Director of the Science of Imagination Laboratory, which does computer modeling of the human visual imagination. He also cohosts the podcast *Minding the Brain* and is the author of *Imagination: The Science of Your Mind's Greatest Power* (2019).

PAIGE E. DAVIS is a Senior Lecturer in Developmental Psychology at York St. John University, UK. Her research centers on imaginary companions and various developmental correlates relating to the childhood creation of imaginary companions. She also investigates private speech and social-cognitive development, and recently expanded her focus to infant feeding and transition to parenthood.

ÖRJAN DE MANZANO is a senior lab manager at Karolinska Institutet, Sweden. He uses a broad array of scientific methods, from behavioral experiments to psychophysiology, and from neuroimaging to epidemiological modeling, to conduct research on the psychobiological mechanisms underpinning creativity, intelligence, personality, and expertise.

OPHELIA DEROY is the Chair of Philosophy of Mind and Neuroscience at the Ludwig Maximilian University, Munich, Germany. She has widely published both in philosophy and scientific journals, and works with several cultural institutions, such as the Tate Galleries and the Getty Foundation, to work on "applied aesthetics."

ARNE DIETRICH is the Chair and Professor of Psychology at the American University of Beirut, Lebanon. He is the author of *Introduction to Consciousness* (2007) and *How Creativity Happens in the Brain* (2015), and numerous research articles on creativity, altered states of consciousness, and the psychological effects of exercise.

G. WILLIAM DOMHOFF is a Distinguished Professor Emeritus and Research Professor at the University of California, Santa Cruz. His authored books include *The Mystique of Dreams* (1985), *Finding Meaning in Dreams* (1995), *The Scientific*

Study of Dreams (2003), and *The Emergence of Dreaming: Mind-Wandering, Embodied Simulation, and the Default Network* (2018).

AGUSTÍN FUENTES is a Professor of Anthropology at Princeton University, NJ. He has trained in Zoology and Anthropology and his research delves into the how and why of being human. Fuentes's most recent book is *Why We Believe: Evolution and the Human Way of Being* (2019).

GIORGIO GANIS is an Associate Professor in Cognitive Neuroscience at the University of Plymouth, UK. He received his PhD from the University of California at San Diego, CA, and his research focuses on the neuroscience of visual and social cognition.

VLAD GLĂVEANU is an Associate Professor and Head of the Department of Psychology and Counseling at Webster University Geneva, Switzerland. He is also the Director of the Webster Center for Creativity and Innovation (WCCI), Switzerland, and an Associate Professor II at SLATE at the University of Bergen, Norway. He has published widely in the area of creativity and culture.

AYMERIC GUILLOT is a Professor at the University Claude Bernard Lyon 1 in France. His research delves into the effects of motor imagery on motor performance and motor recovery following different types of injury and motor impairments. He also explores the neurophysiological substrates and correlates of the imagery experience.

HANA HAWLINA is a PhD candidate at the University of Neuchâtel, Switzerland, and works at the Research Center in Sociocultural Psychology (CURIOUS). Her research interests are centered on collective imagination and sociogenesis, exploring the formation and transformation of societies through the prism of imagining collective futures.

NOAH HUTTON is a writer and filmmaker, who has presented work at the Venice Biennale, the Society for Neuroscience, the Wellcome Collection, the Rubin Museum of Art, and elsewhere. He directed the documentary films *Crude Independence* (SXSW 2009) and *Deep Time* (SXSW 2015). Noah studied art history and neuroscience at Wesleyan University, CT.

MUIREANN IRISH is an Australian Research Council Future Fellow and Associate Professor of Psychology at the Brain and Mind Centre, University of Sydney, Australia, where she leads the MIND research team. Her research program explores alterations in memory, imagination, and mind-wandering in neurological disorders, and their underlying neural substrates.

KELLY JAKUBOWSKI is an Assistant Professor of Music Psychology at Durham University, UK, where she serves as Co-Director of the Music and Science Lab (musicscience.net). Her research interests include musical imagery and "earworms," music-evoked autobiographical memories, and timing and synchronization in music performance.

MAX JONES is a Teaching Associate at the University of Bristol, UK, and lectures in philosophy of psychology, philosophy of mind, metaphysics, and epistemology. His research focuses on exploring the implications of embodied cognition and the predictive processing framework for our understanding of imagination and abstract thought.

REX E. JUNG is an Assistant Professor of Neurosurgery at the University of New Mexico, and a practicing clinical neuropsychologist in Albuquerque, NM. He has published over 100 research articles, addressing brain-behavior relationships in traumatic brain injury, lupus, schizophrenia, intelligence, and creativity. He co-edited *The Cambridge Handbook of the Neuroscience of Creativity* (2018).

AMY KIND is the Russell K. Pitzer Professor of Philosophy at Claremont McKenna College in Claremont, CA. She has authored the introductory textbook *Persons and Personal Identity* (2015) and has edited several books including *Philosophy of Mind in the Twentieth and Twenty-First Centuries* (2018).

ANNE CAROLYN KLEIN is a Professor of Religion at Rice University, TX, and co-founding teacher of Dawn Mountain Tibetan Buddhist Temple. She has studied, practiced, and translated in three of Tibet's five traditions. Her Dzogchen-related books include Strand of Jewels (2016), *Heart Essence of the Vast Expanse* (2009), and *Meeting the Great Bliss Queen* (1995).

MARIA DANAE KOUKOUTI is a research assistant in the Institute of Archaeology at the University of Oxford, UK. Her research interests are in visual anthropology, narratives, materiality, and the anthropology of self and the body. She is a co-author of *An Anthropological Guide to the Art and Philosophy of Mirror Gazing* (2020).

LAMBROS MALAFOURIS is a Senior Research Fellow at the Institute of Archaeology and Keble College, University of Oxford, UK. His research interests lie in the archaeology of mind, philosophical anthropology, and semiotics of material culture. He directs the European Research Council Consolidator Grant (HANDMADE, Horizon 2020) and is the author of *How Things Shape the Mind* (2013).

RAYMOND A. MAR is a Professor of Psychology at York University, Canada. He received his PhD from the University of Toronto and his research focuses on the real-world influence of imaginative experiences. This includes engagement with fictional narratives across various forms of media (e.g. novels, films, and video games).

KOURKEN MICHAELIAN is a Professor at Grenoble Alpes University, France, where he directs the Centre for Philosophy of Memory. He is the author of *Mental Time Travel: Episodic Memory and Our Knowledge of the Personal Past* (2016) and co-editor of several volumes on the philosophy of memory.

BENCE NANAY is a BOF Research Professor of Philosophy at the Centre for Philosophical Psychology at the University of Antwerp, Belgium, and a

Senior Research Associate at Peterhouse College, University of Cambridge, UK. His books include *Between Perception and Action* (2013), *Aesthetics as Philosophy of Perception* (2016), and *Seeing Things You Don't See* (forthcoming).

JENNY NISSEL is a graduate student in psychology under the advisement of Professor Jacqueline Woolley in the Imagination and Cognition Lab at the University of Texas at Austin. Her research explores the development of imagination and children's engagement with pretense and fictional worlds.

DAVID A. OAKLEY is an Emeritus Professor in the Division of Psychology and Language Sciences at University College London and Honorary Professor in the School of Psychology at Cardiff University, UK. He is also a chartered clinical psychologist. His interests are in consciousness, the nature of hypnosis and suggestion, and their relevance to clinical conditions.

NIGEL OSBORNE is a composer and former Reid Professor of Music at Edinburgh University, UK. He has pioneered methods for using music to support children who are victims of conflict in the Balkans, Caucasus, Middle East, East Africa, and Southeast Asia, and has contributed to developing musical-medical technologies that are now applied in health care.

JOEL PEARSON is a National Health and Medical Research Council Fellow and Professor of Cognitive Neuroscience at the University of New South Wales, Australia. He is also the Founder and Director of the Future Minds Lab, a multidisciplinary research group for fundamental and clinical research that consults with companies, artists, and designers on brain science.

DENIS PERRIN is a Professor at Grenoble Alpes University, France. His research partly focuses on the philosophy of memory and he has co-edited volumes in the area, including *New Directions in the Philosophy of Memory* (2018) and a special issue of the *Review of Philosophy and Psychology* (2014).

ELAINE PERRY is an Emeritus Professor of Neurochemical Pathology at Newcastle University, UK, and Curator of Dilston Physic Garden in Northumberland, UK. Her research focuses on the human brain and therapy for its disorders: Alzheimer's and Parkinson's disease, aromatherapy, autism, cholinergic system, consciousness, dreaming, dopamine, Lewy body dementia, medicinal plants, phyto-therapy.

JOSHUA A. QUINLAN is a PhD candidate at York University, Canada. His current research focuses on the propensity for video games to promote changes in beliefs and attitudes. This research also examines whether these changes in attitude are moderated by the video game's genre and level of engagement.

QUENTIN RAFFAELLI is a graduate student in the Department of Psychology at the University of Arizona. His scientific interests and work mainly concern spontaneous cognition, creativity, and imagination, including new ways to assess these processes.

CHAKRAVARTHI RAM-PRASAD is a Fellow of the British Academy, and Distinguished Professor of Comparative Religion and Philosophy at Lancaster University, UK. He has written more than fifty papers and seven books on a range of topics.

JONATHAN REDSHAW is a postdoctoral research fellow at the University of Queensland, Australia. His research focuses on the nature, development, and evolution of foresight and metacognition. He is particularly interested in how humans come to recognize and compensate for the limits of their own foresight capacities.

ANDRÉ SANT'ANNA is a postdoctoral researcher in the Centre for Philosophy of Memory at Grenoble Alpes University, France. He has published articles on the philosophy of memory and perception in journals including *Synthese*, *Review of Philosophy and Psychology*, *Frontiers in Psychology*, and *Philosophia*.

DANIEL L. SCHACTER is the William R. Kenan, Jr. Professor of Psychology at Harvard University, MA, and has authored numerous scientific publications concerning memory and imagination. He has won several research awards, most recently the Distinguished Career Contributions Award from the Cognitive Neuroscience Society. He is also a member of the National Academy of Sciences.

MICHAEL SHANKS is an archaeologist and Professor of Classics at Stanford University, CA. He received his PhD from the University of Cambridge, UK, and is the author of nearly 200 books and papers on prehistory, Graeco-Roman antiquity, and archaeological theory and method.

THOMAS SUDDENDORF is a Professor of Psychology and Director of the Early Cognitive Development Centre at the University of Queensland, Australia. He has pioneered research on mental time travel, and investigates mental capacities in young children and animals to answer fundamental questions about the nature and evolution of the mind.

DEVIN B. TERHUNE is a Reader (Associate Professor) in the Department of Psychology at Goldsmiths, University of London, UK. His primary research interests include the neural bases of time perception and the use of suggestion to regulate awareness.

STHANESHWAR TIMALSINA is a Professor at San Diego State University, CA. He works in the areas of consciousness studies, classical Indian philosophy, and tantric studies. His books include *Seeing and Appearance* (2006), *Consciousness in Indian Philosophy* (2008), *Tantric Visual Culture: A Cognitive Approach* (2015), and *Language of Images: A Cognitive Approach* (2015).

OSHIN VARTANIAN is the co-editor of *Neuroscience of Creativity* (2013) and *The Cambridge Handbook of the Neuroscience of Creativity* (2018), as well as the journal *Psychology of Aesthetics, Creativity, and the Arts*. He is a Defence Scientist at Defence Research and Development Canada.

GERARDO VIERA is a postdoctoral research fellow at the Centre for Philosophical Psychology at the University of Antwerp, Belgium. He researches the philosophy of cognitive science, focusing on theories of mental representation, particularly the mental representation of time, and cognitive architecture.

RAMSEY WILCOX is a graduate student in the Neuroscience of Emotion and Thought Laboratory at the University of Arizona. His research interests lie at the intersection between cognition, emotion, and mental health.

SAM WILKINSON is a Lecturer at the University of Exeter, UK. He works on perception, action, and emotion, and pathologies thereof, as viewed from predictive processing and embodied perspectives. He is also interested in the way that the mind harnesses social and cultural context to enhance and shape cognition.

JENNIFER M. WINDT is a Lecturer in philosophy at Monash University, Australia. Her research focuses on dreaming, sleep, and mind-wandering. She is the author of *Dreaming: A Conceptual Framework for Philosophy of Mind and Empirical Research* (2015) and, together with Thomas Metzinger, edited *Open Mind: Philosophy and the Mind Sciences in the Twenty-First Century* (2016).

JACQUELINE D. WOOLLEY is a Professor of Psychology and Director of the Imagination and Cognition Lab at the University of Texas at Austin. Her research addresses how people decide what to believe, with a specific focus on how children make the fantasy-reality distinction, and the ontogenesis of supernatural beliefs.

DAHLIA W. ZAIDEL teaches and conducts research on the human brain and behavior at the University of California, Los Angeles. She focuses on brain structure and function, facial beauty, the biology of neuroaesthetics, and the distant origins of art practice. Her publications reflect the intersection of neurology, archaeology, biology, and evolution.

SANDRA ZAKKA has a Master of Arts in Psychology from the American University of Beirut, Lebanon. She carries out experimental research on the effects of acute aerobic exercise on higher-order cognition. Her research also examines whether these effects are moderated by gender and the level of cognitive task difficulty.

ADAM ZEMAN is a Professor of Cognitive and Behavioural Neurology at the University of Exeter, UK. His main research interests are memory disorders in epilepsy, especially Transient Epileptic Amnesia, and the neurology of visual imagery. He is the author of *Consciousness – A User's Guide* (2002) and *A Portrait of the Brain* (2008).

TANIA ZITTOUN is a Professor of Sociocultural Psychology at the University of Neuchâtel, Switzerland. She studies imagination across the lifespan, and has co-authored *Imagination in Human and Cultural Development* (2016) with Alex Gillespie and co-edited the *Handbook of Imagination and Culture* (2018) with Vlad Glăveanu.

Acknowledgments

I thank Cambridge University Press and affiliated organizations for the opportunity to securely transport this handbook from the hypothetical space of my imaginings to the actual space of the real world. Special thanks to Charles Phillips for the meticulous and thoughtful copyediting.

I thank Gerald Cupchik – fellow cross-disciplinary explorer of the imagination – for reaching out to commence an open and generous conversation on this beautifully complex topic.

I thank Will Glover for the magical gift of Starobinski and for being such excellent company.

And I thank the contributors to this handbook for saying yes.

1 Surveying the Imagination Landscape

Anna Abraham

> O Imagination, you who steal men so
> From outer things that they would miss the sound
> Should in their ears a thousand trumpets blow,
>
> What moves you then, when all the senses drown?
> A light moves you, that finds its form in heaven,
> By itself, or by the will that guides it down.[1]

Let us reflect on the image presented in Figure 1.1. It shows a fragment, the remains of a statue from circa 1353–1336 BCE.[2] Although several key features are missing, we readily recognize a human face. If asked to imagine what the rest of the head might look like, we have little trouble undertaking this mental reconstruction. We can alter the features of the summoned image to fit the description of a man or woman, belonging to the peasantry or royalty. We can imagine a different headdress accompanying a queen of ancient Egypt compared to a goddess of ancient India. Indeed, we could go much further into the realm of hypotheticals by contemplating the potential musings of the creator of this work, its subject, and its audience.

This ability to conjure up images, ideas, impressions, intentions and the like: This is the imagination at work. The conceptual space it spans is stupendously vast, stretching across the real and the unreal, the possible and the impossible. Its workings are spontaneous and deliberate, ordinary and extraordinary, conscious and unconscious, deriving from the outer world external to our bodies as well as our inner world. The word "imagination" is therefore a particularly curious one. Because if "words are really the history of people's agreement about things,"[3] then what we apparently agree on is that this word is one that can be imbued with an exuberance of disparate meanings that emerge from across the incalculable breadth and depth of human experience that constitutes our mental lives. A key point to note right at the outset is that "we use imagination in our ordinary perception of the world. This perception cannot be separated from interpretation. Interpretation can be common to everyone, and in this sense ordinary, or it can be inventive, personal and revolutionary ... So imagination is necessary to enable us to recognize things in the world as familiar ... but it is also necessary if we are to see the world as significant of something unfamiliar" (Warnock, 1976: 10).

---

1 Dante (Purgatorio XVII, 25) as quoted in *Six Memos for the Next Millennium* (Calvino, 2016).
2 Available online: www.metmuseum.org/art/collection/search/544514.
3 Quote from Edwin Schlossberg speaking with Debbie Millman on the *Design Matters* podcast on March 5, 2018.

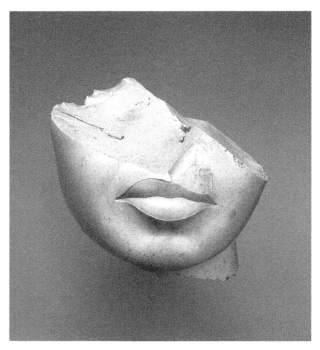

Figure 1.1 *Fragment of a queen's face. Metropolitan Museum of Art. Accession Number: 26.7.1396. CC0 1.0. Geography: From Egypt. Date: ca. 1353–1336 B.C. Period: New Kingdom, Amarna Period. Medium: Yellow jasper.*

Domains of the Imagination

In extolling the wonders of the imagination, Eva Brann (1991) charted the territory as follows: "First it represents the appearances, clarified, within its own space; it absorbs them, beautified into its own visions; it projects them back as rectifying transparencies upon the world. And then it proceeds to captivate thought, inciting it to pierce these imaginative panoramas and to transcend them in search of their unseen core" (Brann, 1991: 786). This captivating statement speaks to the sheer heterogeneity associated with the concept, which poses a considerable problem for scholars of the imagination who seek to define it. This is because defining something necessitates grasping its true nature, verbalizing this understanding accurately and comprehensively, and, in doing so, delimiting the expanse of this idea – a formidable challenge for a concept as expansive as the imagination. Most scholars tend to shy away from doing this and instead restrict their focus to one or another specific facet of the imagination. The option of leaning on the work of lexicographers is therefore warranted and, fortunately, is also particularly useful in the present circumstance, given the meticulous record on hand. The Oxford English Dictionary currently attributes five meanings to the word "imagination"[4]:

4 "imagination, n." OED Online, Oxford University Press, March 2018, www.oed.com/view/Entry/ 91643.

1 (a) "The power or capacity to form internal images or ideas of objects and situations not actually present to the senses, including remembered objects and situations, and those constructed by mentally combining or projecting images of previously experienced qualities, objects, and situations. Also (esp. in modern philosophy): the power or capacity by which the mind integrates sensory data in the process of perception." (b) "An inner image or idea of an object or objects not actually present to the senses; often with the implication that the idea does not correspond to the reality of things. Also: †the action or an act of forming such an image or idea (obs.)."

2. "The mind considered as engaged in imagining; a person's mind, or a part of it, represented as the place where images, ideas, and thoughts are produced and stored, or in which they are contained. Formerly also: †the inner operations of the mind in general, thinking; thought, opinion (obs.)."

3. "The mental consideration of future or potential actions or events." (a) "The scheming or devising of something; a plan, scheme, plot; a fanciful project. Obs." (b) "A person's impression as to what is likely; expectation, anticipation. Obs."

4. "The tendency to form ideas which do not correspond to reality; the operation of fanciful, erroneous, or deluded thought. Also: an individual's fanciful, erroneous, or deluded thinking."

5. "The mind's creativity and resourcefulness in using and inventing images, analogies, etc.; poetic or artistic genius or talent. Also: an individual's poetic or artistic genius or talent."

The categories of meanings detailed in this entry bear striking overlaps with many of the connotations evoked in Leslie Stevenson's twelve conceptions of imagination (Stevenson, 2003) (Figure 1.2).[5] This philosophical classification is particularly useful because it gives us a tangible overview of the many states that can be said to exemplify operations of the imagination. Our imaginations aid our perception of the current external reality as perceived through our sense organs. Our imaginations allow us to conceive of our former external realities. Our imaginations render it possible to fabricate alternative realities and fictional realms that we have never experienced in quite the same manner before. Our imaginations facilitate our ability to reconstruct events from the real past, the counterfactual past, and the potential future. Our imaginations enable us to fantasize aimlessly and problem-solve purposefully. Our imaginations impel us toward creative labor in the service of beauty, truth, and wonder. Through our imaginations, we can savor the fruits of creative labor. And so on.

The advantage of having such a classification is that it captures much of what is vital about the immense complexity that is the imagination in a manner that stands to be of value to theorists across academic traditions. The disadvantage is that it may be deemed too wide to be of immediate utility to empiricists who are seeking to bridge different aspects of the imagination. Such a classification also sidesteps the fact that there are several discrepancies in our understandings of the nature and the workings of the imagination.

---

5 An infographic depicting the twelve conceptions of imagination, published by the Open University, can be accessed at tinyurl.com/12conceptions.

"The ability to think of something that is not presently perceived but is, was or will be spatio-temporally real."	"The ability to think of whatever one acknowledges as possible in the spatio-temporal world."	"The liability to think of something which the subject believes to be real, but which is not real."
"The ability to think of things that one conceives of as fictional, as opposed to what one believes to be real, or conceives of as possibly real."	"The ability to entertain mental images."	"The ability to think of (conceive of, or represent) anything at all."
"The non rational operations of the mind, that is, those kinds of mental functioning which are explicable in terms of causes rather than reasons."	"The ability to form beliefs, on the basis of perception, about public objects in three-dimensional space which can exist unperceived, with spatial parts and temporal duration."	"The sensuous component in the appreciation of works of art or objects of natural beauty without classifying them under concepts or thinking of them as practically useful."
"The ability to create works of art that encourage such sensuous appreciation."	"The ability to appreciate things that are expressive or revelatory of the meaning of human life."	"The ability to create works of art that express something deep about the meaning of life, as opposed to the products of mere fantasy."

Figure 1.2 *Leslie Stevenson's twelve conceptions of the imagination. Text quoted from Stevenson (2003), Twelve Conceptions of the Imagination,* The British Journal of Aesthetics, *43(3), 238–259.*

Disagreements About the Imagination

Our construals of what the imagination does and does not entail differ across academic traditions. Some of the factors that may explain this misalignment include that (a) some disciplines have devoted much study to the imagination for centuries (e.g. philosophy, see Kind, 2016) whereas others are recent additions to the playing field (e.g. neuroscience), (b) there is relatively little cross-talk between disciplines on most topics of the imagination, and (c) some aspects of imagination are better studied than others. To take the disciplines of psychology, philosophy, and neuroscience as examples, the topic of mental imagery is a subject of concerted engagement and effort across all three disciplines (e.g. Hubbard, 2010; Pearson and Kosslyn, 2015; Thomas, 2014), and it has been commensurately associated with the most progress. Other topics of the imagination have had less luck. The topic of engaging with fiction, for instance, is studied widely in philosophy (e.g. Nichols, 2006), narrowly in psychology (e.g. Taylor, 2013), and only sparsely in neuroscience (e.g. Abraham, von Cramon, and Schubotz, 2008). Interest in some topics is also mainly confined to single disciplines. For instance, episodic future thinking is an actively studied topic chiefly within neuroscience (e.g. Schacter, 2012), and, until fairly recently, creativity was largely limited to the corridors of psychological study (e.g. Sternberg, 1999).

This lopsided distribution of focus means that there are several differences in our understandings of what constitutes the imagination. For instance, in the philosophi-cal tradition (Gendler, 2013) mental states of the imagination are often framed as being distinct from other mental states like remembering, conceiving, believing, and desiring. However, such distinctions are not held in quite the same manner in other disciplines. For instance, abundant psychological and neuroscientific evidence has indicated that the distinction between remembering and imagining is far more blurred than is typically assumed. (Re)constructive processes are held to commonly occur when thinking about a personal event (e.g. having a baby) that could take place in the future (episodic future thinking or prospection), that could have taken place in the past (episodic counterfactual thinking), and that did actually take place in the past (episodic memory or retrospection) (Schacter, 2012). Interpretive distortions are well documented in the context of eyewitness testimonies and these demonstrate that memory retrieval processes critically impact the fidelity of recall – creating a gap between the reality or truth of what occurred during an event and one's own belief of what transpired (Loftus, 1992). The content of one's thoughts during daydreaming and mind-wandering are often reflective of desired mood states, social goals, and the like (Poerio et al., 2015). And within the domain of mathematical reasoning, which necessitates conceiving of abstract relations, both "inventive" and "imagistic" aspects of the imagination are considered crucial for good reasoning (Perkins, 1985). Comparative claims have been made for the connection between reason and inventiveness in literature, in that "the keener and clearer is the reason, the better the fantasy will it make" (Tolkien, 2006: 144).

Differentiations additionally emerge when considering conceptualizations of the overarching purpose of the human imagination, with many scholars emphasizing mental simulation as the key role (Currie and Ravenscroft, 2002; Markman, Klein, and Suhr, 2009), while others hand that honor to novel idea generation (Gerard, 1946). The expansive conceptualization of the imagination also means that it is necessarily intertwined with several other illustrious constructs of the human psyche. Language is one example: Speech is held to bridge the gap between one's inner world of "visionary creativity" and the outer "object-ridden" world (Shulman, 2012: 8). The same is true of consciousness. Take this statement by the philosopher Nigel J. T. Thomas: "Imagination is what makes our sensory experience meaningful, enabling us to interpret and make sense of it, whether from a conventional perspective or from a fresh, original, individual one. It is what makes perception more than the mere physical stimulation of sense organs. It also produces mental imagery, visual and otherwise, which is what makes it possible for us to think outside the confines of our present perceptual reality, to consider memories of the past and possibilities for the future, and to weigh alternatives against one another. Thus, imagination makes possible all our thinking about what is, what has been, and, perhaps most important, what might be" (2004, as cited in Manu, 2006: 47).

Compare it with the first lines of the Mandukya Upanishad,[6] which outlines four states of consciousness (Eknath and Nagler, 2007: 203):

---

6 One of the ancient Sanskrit texts on Hindu philosophy. The exact chronology of this upanishad is still uncertain (dated between the fifth century BCE and the second century CE).

AUM stands for the supreme Reality.
It is a symbol for what was, what is,
And what shall be. AUM represents also
What lies beyond past, present, and future.

The similarities in the essence of what is being conveyed are undeniable.

Weaving a Common Thread

So how do the components of imagination relate to one another? Several scholars have proposed theoretical frameworks that highlight emergent properties that bind together different aspects of the imagination. These accounts differ considerably in the degree to which they are "strictly argumentative or systematic-analytical" compared to "loosely ruminative and comparative-historical" (nomenclature from Strawson, 1982: 87). Examples of contemporary postulations include (a) that pretense is a precursor to understanding fiction (Harris, 2000), (b) that engagement with paintings, novels, films, and children's games has its root in the representational capacity to make believe (Walton, 1990), and (c) that imaginative "what if" operations spring from semantic "what" and spatial-episodic "what-where-when" processes (Abraham and Bubic, 2015).

The purpose of this handbook is to follow in the spirit of such approaches by bringing together a range of academic and applied perspectives on the human imagination from diverse traditions of study and practice. No single volume to date has showcased a multidisciplinary snapshot of our understandings of this vast and heterogeneous knowledge domain. The objective of arriving at a point from which we will be able to develop a more systemic understanding of this singularly complex capacity would be too ambitious. But aspiring toward this goal could be the wind in the sails that will, at the very least, bring us several steps forward from where we currently find ourselves. After all, in entering a shared diverse communicative space, we come face-to-face with ideas and approaches from unfamiliar yet potentially informative perspectives. And understanding the specific questions that drive each field, as well as the subtle connotations of the jargon employed in their discourse, will enable more efficacious cross-talk between disciplines. In channeling this exploration, the structure of this handbook is guided by a recently proposed neurophilosophically informed framework that aims to deliver a holistic understanding of the workings of the human imagination (Abraham, 2016) (Figure 1.3).

Under this framework, the different experiential and cogitative states of the imagination are allocated to one of five thematically cohesive clusters organized around central operational features. The category of "mental imagery-based forms of the imagination" includes perceptual (visual, auditory, etc.) and motor forms of imagery that, owing to the strong overlaps with perception and action, draw their impressions from the external milieu. In contrast, our internal milieu, in the form of interoceptive and emotional awareness, is the source material for processes that belong to the category of "phenomenology-based forms of the imagination" that are

Mental imagery (perceptual/motor)	Intentionality (recollective)	Novel combinatorial (generative)	Phenomenology (emotion)
Visual imagery Auditory imagery Musical imagery Gustatory imagery Tactile imagery Olfactory imagery Motor imagery …	Mental state reasoning/theory of mind Moral decision-making Mental time travel/future thinking Autobiographical/ episodic memory	Creative thinking Hypothetical reasoning Counterfactual thinking Hypothesis generation …	Aesthetic engagement Visual art-related aesthetic response Music-related aesthetic response Literature-related aesthetic response …

Altered States
Dreams, hypnosis, drug-induced states, meditative states, hallucinations, out-of-body experiences, delusions, confabulations …

Figure 1.3 *A neurophilosophically informed classification of the imagination. Adapted from Abraham (2016), The Imaginative Mind,* Human Brain Mapping*, 37(11), 4197–4211.*

involved in the aesthetic response during the appreciation of visual arts, music, literature, and so on.

The underlying commonality across operations that fall under the category of "intentionality-based forms of the imagination," such as mental state reasoning and mental time travel, is that they trigger processing that is primarily recollective in nature in order to arrive at the most plausible explanation of a given situation from the standpoint of what fits best with what one knows to be true. In contrast, when a context necessitates moving beyond what is known to seek new solutions, explanations, or expressions, processes belonging to the category of "novel combinatorial forms of the imagination" such as creativity, counterfactual reasoning, and hypothesis generation are called into play. The final category is that of "altered states of the imagination," which encompass ordinary states, such as those experienced during dreaming and meditation, as well as atypical states that come about via temporary or permanent neurological insult, such as out-of-body experiences, delusions, and hallucinations.

The five latter sections of the handbook (Parts II–VI) are organized in line with this classification. Each section features several expert contributors showcasing their unique ideas and perspectives on themes that are of direct relevance to each thematic category.

We commence our exploration of the imagination (fittingly) with the world of ideas in Part I, where theoretical frameworks on the imagination from a range of different disciplines are presented. The ten chapters cover perspectives from evolution (Fuentes: Chapter 2), anthropology (Koukouti and Malafouris: Chapter 3), archaeology (Shanks: Chapter 4), Western philosophy (Kind: Chapter 5), and Eastern philosophy (Ram-Prasad: Chapter 6). Perspectives from psychology and neuroscience place emphasis on prediction (Jones and Wilkinson: Chapter 7), memory (Schacter and Addis: Chapter 8), creativity (Dietrich and Zakka: Chapter 9), and sociocultural factors

(Zittoun, Glăveanu, and Hawlina: Chapter 10). The final chapter in this part covers developments in the field of artificial intelligence that are of potential relevance to the imagination (Davies: Chapter 11).

The seven chapters in Part II of the handbook explore key questions and issues of interest in mental imagery-based forms of the imagination. The domains covered include visual imagery (Pearson: Chapter 12), musical imagery (Jakubowski: Chapter 13), motor imagery (Guillot: Chapter 14), temporal imagery (Viera and Nanay: Chapter 15), emotional imagery (Blackwell: Chapter 16), and multisensory imagery (Berger: Chapter 17; Deroy: Chapter 18).

Part III is devoted to intentionality-based forms of the imagination. The eight chapters in this section cover philosophical perspectives on memory and imagination (Michaelian, Perrin and Sant'Anna: Chapter 19), neuroscientific and psychological perspectives on self-referential and social imagination (Arzy and Dafni-Merom: Chapter 20; Raffaelli, Wilcox, and Andrews-Hanna: Chapter 21; D'Argembeau: Chapter 22), developmental roots of mental state reasoning and the phenomenon of imaginary friends (Davis: Chapter 23), the dynamics of moral reasoning (Ganis: Chapter 24; Anderson and Barbey: Chapter 25), and prospective future-directed thought processes (Bulley, Redshaw, and Suddendorf: Chapter 26).

The seven chapters of Part IV cover perspectives on novel combinatorial forms of the imagination. These include an integrated model for episodic and semantic retrospective and prospective thought (Irish: Chapter 27), the role of the imagination in the construction and comprehension of fictional narratives (Quinlan and Mar: Chapter 28), developing the understanding of the distinction between reality and fantasy (Woolley and Nissel: Chapter 29), using Buddhist practices in exerting the imagination for novel perception of deep realities (Klein: Chapter 30), hypothetical reasoning and mental simulations (Ball: Chapter 31), counterfactual thinking and its impact on morality (Byrne: Chapter 32), and a summary of influential neuroscientific theories on creative thinking (Jung: Chapter 33).

Part V showcases seven chapters that cover features central to phenomenology-based forms of the imagination. They include understanding the aesthetic experience from the perspectives of philosophy (Davies: Chapter 34), psychology and neuroscience (Vartanian: Chapter 35; Zaidel: Chapter 36), and art history and society (Hutton: Chapter 37). Also featured are practitioner accounts of the role of the imagination in dance (Christensen and Borhani: Chapter 38) and music in the context of child development and community healing (Osborne: Chapter 39).

Part VI casts the spotlight on altered states of the imagination. Its eight chapters explore cross-disciplinary perspectives on dreaming (Windt: Chapter 40; Domhoff: Chapter 41), aphantasia (Zeman: Chapter 42), hypnosis (Terhune and Oakley: Chapter 43), hallucinations (Collerton, Perry, and Bowman: Chapter 44), psychiatric disorders of the imagination (Crespi: Chapter 45), meditative states (Timalsina: Chapter 46), and the experience of flow (de Manzano: Chapter 47).

The final chapter of the handbook seeks to identify the patterns, themes, and concerns that emerge from the forty-six feature chapters across the six parts (Abraham: Chapter 48). The hope is to attempt this while being cognizant of an overwhelming tendency typical of empiricists and theoreticians in the traditions of the social sciences and life sciences, which is just as true today as it was when articulated by Jean Starobinski in this astute observation published in his essay on "The Empire of the Imaginary" (Starobinski, 2001)[7]: "Contemporary psychology does not much like the notion of depth. When it does happen to resort to it, it is immediately to flatten depth into a readable and structured surface. According to this, there is in principle no mystery, no essential shadow. Yet, when it explores the behavior of men, it cannot fail to clash with this ascertainment: man is a strange being who likes to hide behind masks, and who constantly calls to the prestige of the hidden."

References

Abraham, A. (2016). The Imaginative Mind. *Human Brain Mapping*, *37*(11), 4197–4211. doi .org/10.1002/hbm.23300.

Abraham, A., and Bubic, A. (2015). Semantic Memory as the Root of Imagination. *Frontiers in Psychology*, *6*. doi.org/10.3389/fpsyg.2015.00325.

Abraham, A., von Cramon, D. Y., and Schubotz, R. I. (2008). Meeting George Bush versus Meeting Cinderella: The Neural Response When Telling Apart What Is Real from What Is Fictional in the Context of our Reality. *Journal of Cognitive Neuroscience*, *20*(6), 965–976. doi.org/10.1162/jocn.2008.20059.

Brann, E. T. H. (1991). *The World of the Imagination: Sum and Substance*. Savage, MD: Rowman & Littlefield.

Calvino, I. (2016). *Six Memos for the Next Millennium*. Translated by Geoffrey Brock. London, UK: Penguin Classics.

Currie, G., and Ravenscroft, I. (2002). *Recreative Minds: Imagination in Philosophy and Psychology*. Oxford, UK; New York, NY: Clarendon Press; Oxford University Press.

Eknath, E., and Nagler, M. N. (eds.) (2007). *The Upanishads*. 2nd edition. Tomales, CA: Nilgiri Press.

Gendler, T. (2013). Imagination. In E. N. Zalta (ed.), *The Stanford Encyclopedia of Philosophy* (Fall). plato.stanford.edu/archives/fall2013/entries/imagination/.

Gerard, R. W. (1946). The Biological Basis of Imagination. *The Scientific Monthly*, *62*(6), 477–499.

Harris, P. L. (2000). *The Work of the Imagination*. Oxford, UK; Malden, MA: Blackwell Publishers.

Hubbard, T. L. (2010). Auditory Imagery: Empirical Findings. *Psychological Bulletin*, *136* (2), 302–329. doi.org/10.1037/a0018436.

Kind, A. (ed.) (2016). *The Routledge Handbook of Philosophy of Imagination*. London, UK; New York, NY: Routledge.

Loftus, E. F. (1992). When a Lie Becomes Memory's Truth: Memory Distortion After Exposure to Misinformation. *Current Directions in Psychological Science*, *1*(4), 121–123. doi.org/10.1111/1467-8721.ep10769035.

---

7 Unpublished translation by William Glover (reproduced with permission). Excerpt (page 220) from Jean Starobinski, *L'oeil vivant* (Tome 2) – *La Relation Critique*. Paris: Éditions Gallimard (digital edition published in 2013).

Manu, A. (2006). *The Imagination Challenge: Strategic Foresight and Innovation in the Global Economy*. San Francisco, CA: New Riders.

Markman, K. D., Klein, W. M., and Suhr, J. A. (eds.) (2009). *Handbook of Imagination and Mental Simulation*. New York, NY: Psychology Press.

Nichols, S. (ed.) (2006). *The Architecture of the Imagination: New Essays on Pretence, Possibility, and Fiction*. Oxford, UK: Clarendon Press.

Pearson, J., and Kosslyn, S. M. (2015). The Heterogeneity of Mental Representation: Ending the Imagery Debate. *Proceedings of the National Academy of Sciences of the United States of America*, *112*(33), 10089–10092. doi.org/10.1073/pnas.1504933112.

Perkins, D. N. (1985). Reasoning as Imagination. *Interchange*, *16*(1), 14–26. doi.org/10.1007/BF01187588.

Poerio, G. L., Totterdell, P., Emerson, L.-M., and Miles, E. (2015). Love Is the Triumph of the Imagination: Daydreams about Significant Others Are Associated with Increased Happiness, Love and Connection. *Consciousness and Cognition*, *33*, 135–144. doi.org/10.1016/j.concog.2014.12.011.

Schacter, D. L. (2012). Adaptive Constructive Processes and the Future of Memory. *The American Psychologist*, *67*(8), 603–613. doi.org/10.1037/a0029869.

Shulman, D. D. (2012). *More than Real: A History of the Imagination in South India*. Cambridge, MA: Harvard University Press.

Starobinski, J. (2001). *La relation critique*. Paris, France: Editions Gallimard.

Sternberg, R. (1999). *Handbook of Creativity*. Cambridge, UK; New York, NY: Cambridge University Press.

Stevenson, L. (2003). Twelve Conceptions of Imagination. *The British Journal of Aesthetics*, *43*(3), 238–259. doi.org/10.1093/bjaesthetics/43.3.238.

Strawson, P. F. (1982). Imagination and Perception. In R. C. S. Walker (ed.), *Kant on Pure Reason*. Oxford, UK; New York, NY: Oxford University Press.

Taylor, M. (ed.) (2013). *The Oxford Handbook of the Development of Imagination*. Oxford, UK; New York, NY: Oxford University Press.

Thomas, N. J. T. (2014). Mental Imagery. In E. N. Zalta (ed.), *The Stanford Encyclopedia of Philosophy* (Fall 2014). plato.stanford.edu/archives/fall2014/entries/mental-imagery/.

Tolkien, J. R. R. (2006). On Fairy-Stories. In C. Tolkien (ed.), *The Monsters and the Critics and Other Essays*. London, UK: HarperCollins. 109–161.

Walton, K. L. (1990). *Mimesis as Make-Believe: On the Foundations of the Representational Arts*. Cambridge, MA: Harvard University Press.

Warnock, M. (1976). *Imagination*. London, UK: Faber and Faber.

PART I

Theoretical Perspectives on the Imagination

2 The Evolution of a Human Imagination

Agustín Fuentes

In the introduction to this volume, Anna Abraham suggests that our ability to imagine can be seen in our capacity to conjure up images, ideas, impressions, intentions, and more. She argues that the conceptual space the human imagination spans is "stupendously vast, stretching across the real and the unreal, the possible and the impossible." She describes it as "spontaneous and deliberate, ordinary and extraordinary, conscious and unconscious, deriving from the outer world external to our bodies as well as our inner world." She also quotes Nigel J. T. Thomas to emphasize that "imagination makes possible all our thinking about what is, what has been, and, perhaps most important, what might be."

By moving beyond simple dictionary definitions, such as "The mind's creativity and resourcefulness," Abraham lays out a model wherein we can envision the human imagination as having five modes/arenas of operation: mental imagery (perceptual and motor), phenomenological (emotional), intentionality (recollective), novel combinatorial (generative), and in altered states. This classification resonates with the possibilities for the action of imagination listed in the overview offered in Leslie Stevenson's twelve conceptions of imagination (Stevenson, 2003). Conceptualizing imagination as active in these arenas enables us to connect it to specific cognitive, behavioral, and material processes, as well as outcomes in human lives present and past – a critical step if we are to attempt to examine its evolutionary history.

I have recently argued (Fuentes, 2017a, 2018), following many others (Coward and Grove, 2011; Deacon, 2016; Hodder, 1998; Montagu, 1965) that it is the human capacity to move between the worlds of "what is" and "what could be," and its material indications in the fossil and archaeological record, that identifies the emergence of a particular evolutionary context, and history, for the genus *Homo* (humans). I argue that it is the human capacity to imagine, to be creative, to hope and dream, to infuse the world with meaning(s), and to cast our aspiration far and wide, limited neither by personal experience nor material reality, that has enabled our lineage to develop a particular niche – a niche that has proven remarkably successful in an evolutionary sense, and one wherein imagination plays a central role.

A niche, in the contemporary ecological and evolutionary view, is a dynamic, multidimensional space in which organisms exist – the totality of the biotic and abiotic factors that make up organisms' main context for their interactions with the world and thus with evolutionary processes (Hutchinson, 1957; Wake et al., 2009). As with all organisms, the human niche consists of the spatial, ecological, and social sphere, including social partners, structural ecologies, other species, and the larger population. However, in considering the human niche we must also include the contexts created by particular perceptual/behavioral patterns and characteristic of humans, including: hyper-complex manipulation of extra-somatic materials/ecologies, a particularly information-rich (and malleable) communication system, and the full range of complex pressures/affordances introduced by the patterns and modalities of human cultural, cognitive, and behavioral diversity (Fuentes, 2016, 2017b).

Humans represent an infinitesimally small percentage of living things on Earth. However, despite this, humans have become one of the most significant forces affecting all other life on this planet (Steffen et al., 2011). I suggest that the human ability to imagine responses to pressures (material, perceived, existential, etc.), and to convert those imaginings into material items or actions, has become a major tool in human evolutionary success. There is no denying that, today, the human imagination and our reliance on the symbolic, the political, the potential, and the practical are all central facets of a global ecosystem (Fuentes, 2016, 2018). Human action and perception, meaning, imagination, and hope, are as central to human evolution as are bones, genes, and ecologies.

The human capacity for imagination emerges from our neurobiologies, bodies, and ecologies interacting as dynamic agents in evolutionary processes. This distinctively human capacity shapes, structures, and alters our daily lives, our societies and the world around us.

Humans in Context

The ability for human imagination evolved as a central factor in the human niche. We better understand the evolution of the human imagination if we recognize the increasingly central roles of niche construction, systemic complexity, semiotics, and an integration of the cognitive, social, and ecological in communities of the genus *Homo* during the Pleistocene epoch (from ~2.6–.01 million years ago) (Barnard, 2012; Bloch, 2016; Fogarty et al., 2015; Fuentes, 2014, 2016, 2017a, 2017b).

However, in assessing the evolution of human beings we need not only to explain our bodies and ecologies but also to develop a theoretical approach that can describe an effective tool kit for an evolving system that facilitated the production of: simple stone tools 2 million years ago; more complex stone tools and widening geographic spread 1 million years ago; the use and control of fire, complex hunting, and communications by 400,000 years ago; art and increasingly complex multicommunity social networks by 60–120,000 years ago; agriculture and early cities by 5,000 years ago; and the megacities, global religions, and world economies of today. Part of this tool kit includes a robust imagination, and a landscape and perceptual reality wherein everything, material or not, is infused with multifaceted meaning (Fuentes, 2017a, 2017b).

Humans are not unique in our capacity to innovate, experiment, and respond creatively to life's challenges. Many animals innovate in problem-solving, both socially and materially, and experts argue that this reflects either incipient creativity or the building blocks for developing creativity. Behavioral flexibility and innovation in the face of environmental and/or social challenge is seen in many groups of mammals, birds, and some fish and other types of taxa, and is often associated with increased patterns of encephalization and or gregariousness/social complexity (but not always) (Fogarty et al., 2015; Laland, 2017; Reader and Laland, 2003). Imagination, per se, on the other hand, is much more difficult to demonstrate in nonhuman animals. Partly, this is due to the dominant definitions of imagination, which refer to inner states and particular patterns of cognitive processes that we can demonstrate humans have, but are generally unable to determine whether other organisms have.

Tool use is often the main way of assessing innovation, creativity, and the potential for an imagination in other animals (Fogarty et al., 2015). The use of tools is common in many lineages of mammals and birds (Sanz et al., 2014). Crows use rocks to break open snails, tits (small songbirds) use sticks to puncture milk caps in bottles on the doorsteps of homes, dolphins use sponges to help them catch fish, and some primates regularly use rocks, sticks, and other items to crack nuts, fish for termites, drink water, and even, on occasion, hunt other animals.

The most creative tool use, outside of the human lineage, is found in the other primates. For example, chimpanzees select specific rocks in order to crack nuts, fold leaves into cups in order to drink from streams, and take the leaves off small twigs and break the twigs to the right lengths for termite fishing. Macaques use shells and rocks to collect and open shellfish and capuchin monkeys use rocks to open a range of foodstuffs. Chimpanzees also demonstrate the ability to innovate by combining multiple tools, in sequence, for a single task (Sanz et al., 2014).

Chimpanzees are quite skilled in using lightly modified sticks and unmodified stones as tools. Using tools in this manner is not something that an individual just invents each generation; it is learned through exposure to others of the group, a kind of social facilitation, and maybe even a bit of teaching. Research demonstrates that young chimpanzees spend years with their mothers and during that time pay very close attention to adult tool use (and a whole range of other behaviors) and slowly, with lots of trial and error, acquire the tool-using skills (Sanz et al., 2014). The fact that chimpanzees will strip the leaves of a good termite-fishing twig and even break it to a specific length, or that they will leave a large stick at a site for future use, demonstrates that they have the capacity to understand that there are differences in the shapes and sizes of the sticks that translate to better or worse tools – and that this is both an individually and socially learned ability. This assessment capacity is not confined to primates; we also see it in crows and other birds in the size and shape of the rocks and sticks they use. Animals that use tools tend to select rocks or sticks of sizes and shapes that work well for the intended task, or lightly modify them (sticks, not rocks) to do so.

However, for young chimpanzees it can take years to learn, through observation, how to fish effectively for termites or crack nuts with rocks. But no other animal, not even chimpanzees, can look at a rock, and demonstrate (through reshaping it for the creation of a tool) an understanding that inside that rock is another more useful shape, and then use other rocks or wood or bone to modify that rock – and then share that information with the members of her group. This is exactly what began to happen ~3 million years ago, in groups of hominins, just before the emergence of the genus *Homo*. Making and using stone tools involves much more information, collaboration, and creativity than selecting a rock, as it is, to use: and it is material evidence of an imagination. Using stones or sticks as tools, especially in the search for food, is not uncommon in the animal kingdom, but significantly altering stones or sticks to make better tools is.

Fogarty et al. (2015: 750) state that creativity, including the invention and combination of ideas, "is the original source for cultural evolution and accumulation, introducing new artworks, new technology, and new social norms." They see a distinctively human imagination (e.g. Fuentes, 2014; Whiten and Erdal, 2012) reflected in the creativity they define as the capacity to generate ideas that are "both novel and useful in a particular social setting" (Fogarty et al. 2015: 736). They separate the human capacity for creativity from other animals' abilities to be innovative and inventive and connect it specifically to the development and aug- mentation of human culture. To set the stage fully for thinking through the evolution of a human imagination we need to clarify what we mean by a "human culture."

A Note on Human Culture

Given what we know about other organisms, it is important to note that if "culture" is defined as behavior transmitted via social facilitation and learning from others, which endures for long enough to generate customs and traditions, then many species have culture (Ramsey, 2013; Whiten et al., 2012). Culture and cultural evolution are significant phenomena for many species in that they emerge from processes of biological evolution but can develop such that they supplement genetic transmission with social transmission and can play central roles in shaping the behavior, ecology, and even biology, of populations.

Over the past fifty to sixty years researchers have effectively documented the presence of social traditions in other animals (Whiten et al., 2012). Social traditions are behavioral practices acquired through social exposure and facilitation, but not clearly rooted in specific genetic/biological causes. Recently, scholars from multiple disciplines, focusing on these social traditions in other animals and their related behavioral and cognitive processes, have urged a broader consideration of the possibility that in at least a few other species, particularly highly social mammals such as other primates and cetaceans, culture exists (Whiten et al., 2012; 2017).

There is ample evidence that primates, especially chimpanzees, and cetaceans, particularly orcas, demonstrate social complexity in a range of behavioral patterns that can fit general definitions of culture (Whiten et al., 2017). There is substantial variation between chimpanzee communities in how they live their lives, what kinds of social patterns they have, and how they greet one another – in addition to varying tool technologies and use patterns. These patterns constitute multigenerational social traditions. These social traditions, these ways of behaving that are socially learned and acquired, are central to chimpanzee society. We also know that in orcas styles of hunting are a social tradition inherited via matriarchs, the older females within pods. These older females determine which hunting pattern pods use and over centuries, if not millennia, this has had effects on the body size and shape and even the genetic structure of different geographic populations. There is good evidence that behavioral inheritance and social traditions of orcas has changed their morphology and genetic patterns (Foote et al., 2016).

However, when considering human culture we have to focus specifically on patterns and processes that characterize human behavior and society, and this includes many processes that are measurably different in scale and impact than in most other species (Fuentes, 2017a, 2018; Laland, 2017; Whiten et al., 2017). For humans, cultural elements include massive extra-somatic material creation, manipulation and use (tools, weapons, clothes, buildings, towns, etc.) and extensive ratcheting (expansion and augmentation of cultural processes based on accumulation and innovation) on scales and with a level of structural and material complexity greater than in other organisms.

Humans are born into a suite of inherited ecologies, cultural patterns, and social contexts that are inextricably intertwined with our biological structures, initiating our process of development. It is a process of development that involves a complex and intricate entanglement of the body, the social, the perceptual, and the experiential that create and shape, and are shaped by, our lives and philosophies (Downey and Lende, 2012; Fuentes, 2016). The webs of action and perception, memory and history, and materials and ideas in which humans are entangled are dynamic and fundamental constituents of a human culture (Ingold, 2000, 2004).

Culture is not just the regional "flavors" of humanity. Nor is culture the "nurture" to a biological "nature." Culture is both a product of human actions and something that shapes those actions; culture is the context, the framework, the milieu that helps give meaning to our experiences of the world and to embody them, physiologically, neurobiologically, emotionally, and philosophically (Downey and Lende, 2012; Fuentes, 2017b, 2018, 2019; Tomasello, 2014). Culture is, as the biologist Kevin Laland (Laland, 2017) recently wrote, what makes the human mind possible. For humans, culture is simultaneously the ecosystem we navigate (Deacon, 1997, 2016; Tomasello, 2014) and the embodied and perceived substance that facilitates our actions and thoughts.

To talk about culture in humans is to speak of a different, but somewhat overlapping, suite of experiences, processes, and patterns compared to what we might term "culture" in other organisms. Yes, chimpanzees have a range of fascinating social traditions (stone tool nut-cracking, leaf cup using, termite fishing, etc.) and incredible capacities (complex social hierarchies, deep social relationships, complex group conflict with other communities of chimps, etc.). However, they don't have cash economies and political institutions, arrest and deport each other, create massive systems of material and social inequity, change planet-wide ecosystems, build cities and airplanes, drive thousands of other species toward extinction, or write scientific articles. But humans do – and this stems, in large part, from the reality that human culture, and the human niche, involve a distinctively human imagination (Fuentes, 2014, 2018).

The Evolution of a Human Imagination

"Many cognitive capacities are not intrinsic; they are not strongly genetically canalized. Minds are powerfully shaped by material culture and social environment. Social learning does not just store information in our brains that we would not otherwise have; it stores skills, including cognitive skills"
                    (Sterelny, 2017: 239; see also Downey and Lende, 2012; Ingold, 2000)

Current paleoanthropological, archaeological, and biological data make it abundantly clear that the human lineage underwent specific morphological changes (bipedalism, increased brain size, reduced molar teeth, etc.) alongside less easily measurable, but significant, behavioral and cognitive shifts as it forged, and was shaped by a new niche, a highly distinctive way of being in the world – a human niche (Foley, 2016; Fuentes, 2017a, 2017b, 2018; Whiten and Erdal, 2012). Across the more than 2 million-year history of the genus *Homo* we see substantial material and fossil evidence for the development of this niche (Figure 2.1).

The density of material evidence for creativity and imagination emerges slowly at first, starting with critical innovations such as the development of consistent stone toolmaking and use, the transition to more complex tool forms from the Oldowan to the Acheulean technologies, an extension into use of wood and bone for tool production, and a rapid and extreme expansion in geographic range (demonstrating a capacity for successful interface with new ecologies). Following these are the first glimmerings and subsequent ubiquity of the use of fire, more complex foraging strategies, and the creation of meaning-laden objects. Fossil remains from across the time period from 2 million years ago to 1 million years ago demonstrate changes in overall brain size, in the inner ear structures, and in neurobiological structure. Evidence for lengthening neonatal development and altered life history patterns (extended childhoods), including cooperative parenting behavior, are also found. Additionally, fossils reveal evidence of increased care, potentially compassion, for others at a level beyond that seen in most social mammals (Spikins, 2015). It is inferred that all these patterns are accompanied by an increasingly high intensity of cooperation and increasingly complex information transfer (Foley, 2016; Fuentes 2017a, 2017b; Sterelny, 2012; Tomasello, 2014).

These patterns pick up in pace and density in the last 300,000–400,000 years and combine with what appear to be increasingly complex and dynamic demographic and social processes (Foley, 2016; Fuentes, 2017b; Sterelny, 2017). Such patterns expand dramatically in the last 80,000–125,000 years (Wadley, 2013), and explode in complexity over the last 12,000 years. Here I sidestep the issue of taxonomic nomenclature ("modern humans," "Neanderthals," "archaic sapiens," etc. – see Wood, 2010) as many populations of the genus *Homo* contributed behaviors, genes, ways of life, and other aspects to contemporary humans (*Homo sapiens sapiens*) (Ackermann et al., 2015, Scerri et al., 2018). Their physical, physiological, ecological, and behavioral legacies contributed to components underlying multiple biological and possibly cognitive processes in contemporary humanity. Thus it is by understanding the niches that populations of the genus *Homo* co-constructed, shaped, and were shaped by through our evolutionary history, that we can gain insight into the patterns and processes of the contemporary human niche (and understand the role of imagination in it). This

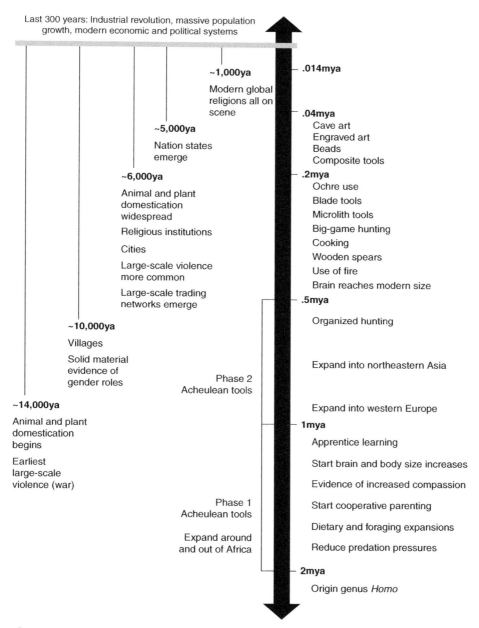

Figure 2.1 *The development of the human niche. The emergence of key patterns in behavioral, ecological, and material contexts for populations of the genus* Homo *across the Pleistocene and into the Holocene (the last ~2 million years). From Fuentes (2018),* How Humans and Apes Are Different, and Why It Matters, *Journal of Anthropological Research, 74(2), 151–167.*

dynamic mode of developing in, and engaging with, the world forms the central core of the contemporary human capacity for creating, for destroying, and for imagining (Fuentes, 2017a, 2018; Ingold and Paalson, 2013).

Here I offer examples from two, of many, of these processes to illustrate the role of imagination: changes in innovation of tool manufacture and use; and the emergence and diversification of the creation of meaning-laden artifacts. I use these two examples to illustrate the ways in which the developing dynamics of the human niche facilitated, and were facilitated by, the evolution of a robust human imagination and how such an imagination itself is a central aspect of feedback systems in human evolutionary processes.

Stone Tools

The earliest tool technology associated with the genus *Homo* is the Oldowan. This is a critical advance on the earlier hominin tool technologies (e.g. the Lomekwian: Harmand et al., 2015) that were developed by hominin lineages before the emergence of the genus *Homo*. The quality and consistency of Oldowan manufacture provides evidence of some degree of learning and instruction/social facilitation, and implies a bandwidth of information transfer that is broader and with higher density of content than is available for most other organisms (Sterelny, 2012; Stout et al., 2015).

Making even these basic stone tools involves the capacity to envision alternative and useful shapes in a stone and offers initial evidence of imaginative capacities, especially in the areas of perceptual and generative mental processes (Abraham, 2016). It also necessitates the ability to develop and share the procedures for creating new shapes via modifying the stone and demonstrating how to use them (a complex form of shared intentionality, Tomasello, 2014). Stone toolmaking involves the ability to assess the variances in characteristics and quality of stones (not all types of rock are good for tool manufacture) and an ability to consistently find, and transport, the raw materials (stones) for their use. Such toolmaking capacities, including the source selection and sharing of the manufacturing techniques, co-develops with a suite of social learning processes more intensive than we see in most other social animals (including all other nonhuman tool-using animals today) (Sterelny, 2012; Stout et al., 2015).

A significant ratcheting up of complexity in types of stone tool technology with the development of the technologies called "Acheulean," emerges and becomes more complex between ~1.5 million years ago and 400,000–500,000 years ago. Generally divided into two "phases," the Acheulean stone tool technology requires substantially more training/learning/teaching to produce than the Olduwan (Sterelny, 2012; Stout et al., 2015). Its tools are more varied and dynamic in their forms and usage, complex in their sequences of manufacture and in their structure, and enable a wider array of food processing and material manipulation than earlier stone tool types.

By about 500,000 years ago there is evidence that many types of the classic form of Acheulean tool, called a hand axe (due to its teardrop form and bifacial creation process), are being worked/crafted to a level of extreme symmetry, more so than is necessary for function. This is suggested, possibly, to be an aesthetic choice. If so, then the manufacture of these hand axes is clearly an act requiring significant imaginative capacities (given the physical, social, cognitive, and instructional requirements of their production). There is also evidence that such tools are being distributed (in some locales) across the landscape as if they were made and cached or possibly as if they were being left/used as markers of some geographical/cultural significance (Pope and Roberts, 2005). There is robust evidence that Acheulean tools are both functional tools that *Homo* used to tackle the challenges of the world and imaginatively created materials reflecting something about, and for, their makers (Fuentes, 2017a; Sterelny and Hiscock, 2014; Wadley, 2013).

This creativity in stone (and other) tool production enhanced the capacity for flexibility in behavior (more options for foraging, for manipulating extra-somatic items), diet (increased processing capacities and thus enhanced nutritive value of foraging and opening up additional foraging targets, enhancing dietary breadth) and habitat manipulation. The tools themselves and their usage enabled changes in the cognitive and social processes of the *Homo* niche and the resultant feedback into the system dynamics opened novel opportunities – behavioral, physiological, and perceptual – for populations of the genus *Homo*.

There is mounting evidence that such feedback processes affected the ways in which *Homo* neurobiology functioned: the cognitive prospecting (imagination/creativity) involved in the manufacture and use of such tool technologies appears to exert specific influences on particular areas of the brain (Hecht et al., 2014; Stout et al., 2015; Stout and Chaminade, 2012). Specifically, the instruction/social modeling and learning involved in the creation of these tool technologies can facilitate novel interconnections across neurobiological systems, focused in specific areas of the brain, which are likely related to a restructuring of the cognitive system and to developing what the neurobiologist Michael Arbib (2011: 259) calls "the language-ready brain." Cultural innovation and accumulation (and the implicated socio-cognitive processes) in the interaction between tool manufacture, use, and neurological dynamics involve the development of high intensity and broad bandwidth of information transfer and a particularly engaged interface between mental imagery, intentionality, and generative processes (Grove and Coward, 2008; Stout and Chaminade, 2012). From at least the Acheulean phase II forward (~500,000 years ago) acquisition and reliable replication of the toolmaking skills requires an intensive feedback loop between these parameters.

By the last third of the Pleistocene the niche of the genus *Homo* includes, as a central process, a complex component of lithic production that involved the development of learning environments with scaffolded structures; these had substantive social, material, ecological, and neurobiological feedback loops that facilitated the development and transmission of increasingly complex processes for the creation and manipulation of tools (Fuentes, 2015; Hiscock, 2014; Sterelny, 2017). In this niche, central social and material skills are acquired by combining information from the social world and the material-biological world. Individuals learn by "doing," and imagining, in an environment seeded with informational resources, even in the absence of explicit or formalized instruction or formalized institutions (Sterelny, 2012). Incremental construction, emulation, and passive and active information transfer in the context of a highly social cooperative group, along with expanding cognitive complexity and increasingly intensive shared intentionality (Deacon, 1997; Tomasello, 2014) can generate high-fidelity replication and broad-bandwidth information transfer (Sterelny, 2012, 2017; Wadley, 2013). The capacity for, and use of, imagination is a central, and necessary, feature of such processes.

The Material Record of Meaning-Making

Kim Sterelny and Peter Hiscock (2014: 2) suggest "stone tools were material symbols long before the ochre and jewelry." This may be the case; however, although it is universally assumed that some degree of imaginative and creative capacity was in play, even for the early stone tools, it is very difficult to demonstrate that those tools, their shape, and the stone from which they were constructed "meant" something more than "object with which to accomplish something" to their makers. However, the mid- to later Pleistocene does offer a range of evidence for the construction of other, more directly identifiable, meaning-laden (and imagination-inspired) materials.

In the archaeological record the items held up as material evidence of meaning-making are often referred to as "symbols." However, by its very definition a "symbol" (something that stands for something else and whose meaning is agreed on by the community constructing it) can only be accurately perceived and interpreted within a particular set of culturally accepted meanings, those under which it was created (Kissel and Fuentes, 2017a). Therefore, without access to the cultural context of the meaning-makers (who lived in the Pleistocene in this case) we cannot accurately know the meaning of the symbol. For example, despite our ability to imagine many possibilities, we cannot truly know what the Venus of Willendorf meant to the people who made her.

However, Marc Kissel and I (Kissel and Fuentes, 2017a) offer an alternative approach to the reliance on "symbol" in assessing meaning-making in the past. Drawing on the semiotics theory of the philosopher Charles Sanders Peirce (Peirce, 1998), we bypass his often-used sign trichotomy of "symbol, icon, index" (and Saussure's notion of symbol) and use Peirce's second proposed trichotomy of sign vehicles: qualsign, sinsign, and legisign.

A qualsign signifies something through the quality it has (like the "redness" of a red cloth). A sinsign uses essential facts to convey meaning. For example, a weather vane that shows the direction in which the wind is blowing is a sinsign. However, a legisign is a sign vehicle based on convention. That is, if there are multiple examples of the same type of human-created material item that conveys or contains and/or evokes similar or identical sensations, then we can say that it reflects a convention among the group or groups making them in that they are intentionally replicating the making of a material item with the same or similar characteristics, and thus likely, with the same intended impact. That the legisign did mean something to those who made it is evident via the repeated creation of items that evoke specific sensory responses, across space and time. This is not an assertion that we know what the actual meaning of the legisign was – in all likelihood we cannot know that (i.e. we cannot understand it as a symbol). The presence of legisigns in the archaeological record represents active meaning-making and thus specific deployment of the imagination in the perceptual, intentional, and generative modes – as well as very likely in the phenomenological mode (intentional evocation/engagement with emotional meaning and responses) (e.g. Abraham, 2016).

So, to return to our example of the Venus figurine, we can note that ~18,000–30,000 years ago, across much of western, southern and eastern Europe, multiple instances of very similar figurines are found. The figurines are not identical but share a great many features in shape, texture, size, and style of creation. They are replicas of a legisign. They offer an indication that multiple groups of people were intentionally creating material objects that represented a set of shared sensations and/or mutually understood meaning (or set of meanings). Presence of legisigns offers material evidence of meaning-making, whether symbolic or not, and of a shared intentionality (Tomasello, 2014), a sharing of imaginative possibilities, and the explicit use of the imagination in the construction of human material and perceptual worlds.

But how far back do we have evidence of legisigns, indicating the possibility of shared systems of meaning-making and thus clear material evidence of a human imagination?

The earliest occurrences of potential legisigns are at about 1 million years ago: a bovine shinbone with what appear to be a series of parallel engravings and two pieces of yellow ocher (an earthy clay with ferric oxide that can be yellow, red, or orange-brown in color) that may have been modified to extract ocher powder (for pigment-making?). At ~350,000–400,000 years ago, in Southeast Asia, we find a clamshell with a carved zigzag image, like a doodle, and in northern Africa and the Middle East we find the Berekhat Ram and Tan-Tan figurines, which are stones naturally shaped like a human that were then modified to look even more human-like (Kissel and Fuentes, 2017b; Wadley, 2013).

While these early examples of meaning-making in *Homo* are relatively rare, it is argued that they are best seen as "glimmerings," rare and potentially isolated occurrences in early human groups, which demonstrate that those early humans had the capacity to create meaning but that the context and the right set of circumstances and abilities for shared and sustained meaning-making (as evidenced by material legisigns) was not yet present (Kissel and Fuentes, 2017b, 2018). But they were just around the corner.

Between ~100,000–300,000 years ago we find multiple examples of bones with etchings on them, evidence of ochers being used, and evidence that some human groups are modifying small stones for use as beads. It is extremely likely that language, of some form, and the developing imaginations of, and increasing interaction between, *Homo* groups provide fuel for the fire of creativity and innovation in all aspects of their lives. It is in this time period that we have increasing examples of legisigns: carved ostrich eggshells, beads, ocher and pigments used to paint on bodies and tools, and many more. By 65,000 years ago we see cave art and by 40,000 years ago, figurines. The human niche becomes progressively filled with the creation of meaning-laden objects (Kissel and Fuentes, 2017b, 2018; Wadley, 2013).

The context for these processes is critical. By 200,000–400,000 years ago *Homo* brain size was the same as in modern humans and its functional capacity close to ours if not nearly identical (Anton et al., 2014; Sherwood and Gomez-Robles, 2017). At the same time the inner ear and vocal apparatus for language had developed, and the neurobiology for speech is likely to have been in place (Martinez et al., 2004; Staes et al., 2017). In this time period we see evidence for a substantial uptick in the complexity of tools and lifeways in *Homo* populations across Africa and Eurasia. Fire use becomes ubiquitous; there is evidence for the creation of glues, the manufacture and use of increasingly complex tools, and even the first possible burials of the dead. We see evidence of increased interactions, possibly trade, between groups and of the possibilities for more social and material connections across wider geographies (Brooks et al., 2018; Fuentes, 2017a; Kissel and Fuentes, 2018). More connections, more materials, more abilities and modes to communicate all act to solidify the core role of imaginative processes in the human niche as they feed back in on themselves and related cognitive processes, augmenting the capacity to engage with more than the "here and now," to develop novel ideas and concepts, share them, and convert them into material reality.

The increasingly prominent appearances of meaning-laden objects, of legisigns, in the archaeological record, especially over the past 300,000–400,000 years, suggested an enhanced ability to imagine and act on those imaginings in ways that previous populations of *Homo* were not able to (with regularity). There were glimmerings of these capacities earlier, as they developed and evolved, in the human niche. However, this terminal Pleistocene time period is when multiple contexts of these capacities and their relationships mature into a ubiquitous process of the human niche. Many of the items, even the early human-shaped rocks, use of ochers, and etchings on bones, reflect the translation of inner sensations/perceptions to material items. They are novel imaginings made material, influenced by the world around members of the genus *Homo* and their experiences.

This is part of a niche constructive pattern in human evolution, from the cognitive, behavioral, and material complexes of early stone toolmaking to that of the clearly imaginative aspects of legisigns. These increasingly complex material items, and the cognitive processes and behaviors (skills) and social ecologies associated with making, using, and sharing them, change the landscape of human sensation and perception. They change human ecologies and thus the details of evolutionary processes acting within them. This process is one of niche construction and feedback loops, wherein an enhanced complexity in material and behavioral worlds interfaces with *Homo* capacities for offline thinking. By 200,000–300,000 years ago it is extremely likely that early language, enhanced cognitive processes, and the developing imaginations of *Homo* groups provide fuel for the ratcheting up of creativity and innovation in all aspects of their lives.

The density and connectivity of ideas, materials, and groups continued to increase over the millennia. By 20,000–30,000 years ago there is deep material evidence of meaning-making and evidence that the social and ecological lives of human groups are generating greater complexity of social structures and densities; shortly thereafter, domestication begins and flourishes, altering tool kits and lifeways and ushering in the first glimpses of firm evidence of what we can identify as symbol and ritual (central facets of the human imagination) (Fuentes 2017a, Wadley 2013, Zeder 2017). The more complex and interconnected humans' lives became, the more frequent and dense the evidence of imagination as central to the human niche becomes.

Human Neurobiology, Cognition, and Imagination

Meaning, imagination, and hope, are as central to the human evolutionary story as are bones, genes, and ecologies (Deacon, 1997; Fuentes, 2017a; Tomasello, 2014). The developmental processes of the human body and brain evolve as a system that is always in concert with, and mutually co-constitutive of, the linguistic, socially mediated and constructed structures, institutions, and beliefs that make up key aspects of the human niche (Fuentes, 2016, 2017a). Specifically, via neurobiology and the endocrine system, the human learns to orchestrate herself within a cultural context and a range of individual experiences (Downey and Lende, 2012). Cultural concepts and meanings become embodied neurobiologically, physiologically, cognitively, and experientially, co-shaping our anatomy and behavior, which in turn interfaces with, and potentially reshapes, the very cultural processes shaping it.

It is worth summarizing the facets of the human niche that enable imagination to be a central feature of it (from Fuentes, 2019).

Neurobiological and endocrine systems develop as humans learn to orchestrate themselves within a cultural context. Through this process social concepts and meanings shape anatomy, an anatomy that in turn interfaces with, and potentially reshapes, those very social concepts and meanings. Skills, the specific patterns of how humans use bodies and minds, are grown, incorporated into the human organism through practice and training in a given environment. They are thus simultaneously biological and cultural and are contingent on the capacities and constraints of the development of our bodies and our relationships with one another and the cultural and material environments we are developing and living in. This processing cycle has an evolutionary history, one that can be gleaned in specific patterns and processes in the fossil and archaeological record.

Because of these particular evolutionary histories of neurobiological development and expansion of the *Homo* brain structure and function, in concert with the processes and structures of human culture, contemporary members of the genus *Homo* have developed the capacity for extensive detached mental representations, for teaching, for learning, and for sharing information. This history and its products demonstrate that a particularly powerful capacity for imagination as identified in the four key arenas proposed by Abraham (2016; Chapter 1) is a central feature of humanity. Humans evolved a robust imagination as a core component of their niche and thus this human imagination has played, and continues to play, a significant role in our species' evolutionary success.

Areas in Need of Further Investigation

(1) An examination, specifically, of how the use of various areas of the brain related to imagination could act as a feedback loop affecting other neurological functions and development in the context of creating stone tools and early meaning-laden objects.

(2) The creation of testable models and hypotheses for the appearance and evolutionary impact of imagination, given the limits on available evidence the further back we go into the Pleistocene.

(3) The continued and enhanced integration of neurobiology, paleoanthropology, and archaeology in order to develop better models for the possible cognitive dynamics of the human niche.

(4) Revisiting the details and patterns in the creation of earlier stone tools in order to examine in greater detail just how much imagination was needed to develop and replicate them.

(5) Increased engagement between philosophers of the imagination and anthropologists to develop better cross-disciplinary tool kits and shared vocabularies.

Bibliography

Abraham, A. (2016). The Imaginative Mind. *Human Brain Mapping, 37*(11), 4197–4211. doi .org/10.1002/hbm.23300.

Ackermann, R. R., Mackay, A., and Arnold, M. L. (2015). The Hybrid Origin of "Modern" Humans. *Evolutionary Biology, 43*, 1–11.

Anton, S. C., Potts, R., and Aiello, L. C. (2014). Evolution of Early Homo: An Integrated Biological Perspective. *Science, 345*(6192), 45.

Arbib, M. A. (2011). From Mirror Neurons to Complex Imitation in the Evolution of Language and Tool Use. *Annual Review of Anthropology, 40*, 257–273.

Barnard, A. (2012). *Genesis of Symbolic Thought*. Cambridge, UK: Cambridge University Press.

Bloch, M. (2016). Imagination from the Outside and from the Inside. *Current Anthropology, 57*(Supplement 13), S80–S87.

Brooks, A. S., Yellen, J. E., Potts, R., et al. (2018). Long-Distance Stone Transport and Pigment Use in the Earliest Middle Stone Age. *Science, 360*(6384), 90–94.

Coward, F. and Grove, M. (2011). Beyond the Tools: Social Innovation and Hominin Evolution. *PaleoAnthropology, 2011*, 111–129. doi:10.4207/PA.2011.ART46

Deacon, T. (1997). *The Symbolic Species: The Co-Evolution of Language and the Brain*. London, UK: Penguin Books.

(2016). On Human (Symbolic) Nature: How the Word Became Flesh. In T. Fuchs and C. Tewes (eds.), *Embodiment in Evolution and Culture*. Tübingen, Germany: Mohr Siebeck, 129–149.

Downey, G., and Lende, D. H. (2012). Evolution and the Brain. In D. H. Lende and G. Downey (eds.), *The Encultured Brain*. Cambridge, MA: MIT Press, 103–138.

Fogarty, L., Creanza, N., and Feldman, M. W. (2015). Cultural Evolutionary Perspectives on Creativity and Human Innovation. *Trends in Ecology and Evolution, 30*(12), 736–754.

Foley, R. A. (2016). Mosaic Evolution and the Pattern of Transitions in the Hominin Lineage. *Philosophical Transactions of the Royal Society B, 371*, 20150244.

Foote, A. D., Nagurjan, V., Ávila-Arcos, M. C., et al. (2016). Genome-Culture Coevolution Promote Rapid Divergence of Killer Whale Ecotypes. *Nature Communications, 7*, 11693.

Fuentes, A. (2014). Human Evolution, Niche Complexity, and the Emergence of a Distinctively Human Imagination. *Time and Mind, 7*(3), 241–257.

   (2015). Integrative Anthropology and the Human Niche: Toward a Contemporary Approach to Human Evolution. *American Anthropologist, 117*(2), 302–315.

   (2016). The Extended Evolutionary Synthesis, Ethnography, and the Human Niche: Toward an Integrated Anthropology. *Current Anthropology, 57*(Supplement 13), 13–26.

   (2017a). *The Creative Spark: How Imagination Made Humans Exceptional.* New York, NY: Dutton/Penguin.

   (2017b). Human Niche, Human Behaviour, Human Nature. *Interface Focus, 7*, 20160136.

   (2018). How Humans and Apes Are Different, and Why It Matters. *Journal of Anthropological Research, 74*(2), 151–167.

   (2019). *Why We Believe.* New Haven, CT: Yale University Press.

Grove, M., and Coward, F. (2008). From Individual Neurons to Social Brains. *Cambridge Archaeological Journal, 18*, 387–400.

Harmand, S., Lewis, J. E., Feibel, C. S., et al. (2015). 3.3-Million-Year-Old Stone Tools from Lomekwi 3, West Turkana, Kenya. *Nature, 521*, 310–315.

Hecht, E. E., Gutman, D. A., Khreisheh, N., et al. (2014). Acquisition of Paleolithic Tool-Making Abilities Involves Structural Remodeling to Inferior Fronto-Parietal Regions. *Brain Structure and Function, 220*, 2315–2331.

Hiscock, P. (2014). Learning in Lithic Landscapes: A Reconsideration of the Hominid "Toolmaking" Niche. *Biological Theory, 9*(1), 27–41.

Hodder, I. (1998). Creative Thought: A Long-Term Process. In S. Mithen (ed.), *Creativity in Human Evolution and Prehistory.* London, UK: Routledge, 61–77.

Hutchinson, G. E. (1957). Concluding Remarks. *Cold Spring Harbor Symposium on Quantitative Biology, 22*, 415–427.

Ingold, T. (2000). *The Perception of the Environment: Essays on Livelihood, Dwelling and Skill.* Abingdon, UK: Routledge.

   (2004). Beyond Biology and Culture: The Meaning of Evolution in a Relational World. *Social Anthropology, 12*(2), 209–221.

Ingold, T., and Paalson, G. (eds.) (2013). *Biosocial Becomings: Integrating Social and Biological Anthropology.* Cambridge, UK: Cambridge University Press.

Kissel, M. and Fuentes, A. (2017a). Semiosis in the Pleistocene. *Cambridge Archaeological Journal, 27*(3), 1–16.

   (2017b). A Database of Archaeological Evidence for Representational Behavior. *Evolutionary Anthropology, 26*(4), 1490150.

   (2018). "Behavioral Modernity" as a Process, not an Event, in the Human Niche. *Time and Mind, 11*(2), 163–183.

Laland, K. N. (2017). *Darwin's Unfinished Symphony: How Culture Made the Human Mind.* Princeton, NJ: Princeton University Press.

Martinez, I., Rosa, M., Arsuaga, J. L., et al. (2004). Auditory Capacities in Middle Pleistocene Humans from the Sierra de Atapuerca in Spain. *Proceedings of the National Academy of Sciences, 101*(27), 9976–9981.

Montagu, A. (1965). *The Human Revolution*. New York, NY: Bantam Books.

Peirce, C. (1998). *The Essential Peirce. Volume 2*. Bloomington, IN: Indiana University Press.

Pope, M. I., and Roberts, M. B. (2005). Observations on the Relationship Between Individuals and Artefact Scatters at the Middle Palaeolithic Site of Boxgrove, West Sussex. In C. Gamble and M. Porr (eds.), *The Hominid Individual in Context: Archaeological Investigations of Lower and Middle Palaeolithic Landscapes*. London, UK: Routledge, 81–97.

Ramsey, G. (2013). Culture in Humans and Other Animals. *Biology and Philosophy*, *28*, 457–479.

Reader, S. M., and Laland, K. N. (2003). *Animal Innovation*. Oxford, UK: Oxford University Press.

Sanz, C. M., Call, J., and Boesch, C. (2014). *Tool Use in Animals: Cognition and Ecology*. Cambridge, UK: Cambridge University Press.

Scerri, E., Thomas, M. G., Manica, A., et al. (2018). Did Our Species Evolve in Subdivided Populations across Africa, and Why Does It Matter? *Trends in Ecology & Evolution*. doi.org/10.1016/j.tree.2018.05.005.

Sherwood, C. C., and Gomez-Robles, A. (2017). Brain Plasticity and Human Evolution. *Annual Review of Anthropology, 2017*(46), 399–419.

Spikins, P. (2015). *How Compassion Made us Human*. Barnsley, UK: Pen and Sword Press.

Staes, N., Sherwood, C. C., Wright, K., et al. (2017). FOXP2 Variation in Great Ape Populations Offers Insight into the Evolution of Communication Skills. *Scientific Reports*, *7*(1), 16866.

Steffen, W., Grinevald, J., Crutzen, P., and McNeil, J. (2011). The Anthropocene: Conceptual and Historical Perspectives. *Philosophical Transactions of the Royal Society A*, *369*, 842–867.

Sterelny, K. (2012). *The Evolved Apprentice: How Evolution Made Humans Unique*. Cambridge, MA: MIT Press.

  (2017). Artifacts, Symbols, Thoughts. *Biological Theory*, *12*:236–247.

Sterelny, K., and Hiscock, P. (2014). Symbols, Signals, and the Archaeological Record. *Biological Theory*, *9*(1), 1–3.

Stevenson, L. (2003). Twelve Conceptions of Imagination. *The British Journal of Aesthetics*, *43*(3), 238–259.

Stout, D., and Chaminade, T. (2012). Stone Tools, Language and the Brain in Human Evolution. *Philosophical Transactions of the Royal Society B*, *367*(1585), 75–87.

Stout, D., Hecht, E., Khreisheh, N., et al. (2015). Cognitive Demands of Lower Paleolithic Toolmaking. *PLoS ONE*, *10*(4), e0121804.

Tomasello, M. (2014). *The Natural History of Human Thinking*. Cambridge, MA: Harvard University Press.

Vale, G. L., Dean, L., and Whiten, A. (2016). Culture in Nonhuman Animals. In H. Callen (ed.), *Wiley International Encyclopedia of Anthropology*. New York, NY: Wiley-Blackwell.

Wadley, L. (2013). Recognizing Complex Cognition through Innovative Technology in Stone Age and Palaeolithic Sites. *Cambridge Archaeological Journal*, *23*(2), 163–183.

Wake, D. B., Hadley, E. A., and Ackerly, D. (2009). Biogeography, Changing Climates, and Niche Evolution. *PNAS*, *106*(2), 19631–19636.

Whiten, A., and Erdal, D. (2012). The Human Socio-Cognitive Niche and its Evolutionary Origins. *Philosophical Transactions of the Royal Society B: Biological Sciences 367*, 2119–2129.

Whiten, A., Ayala, F. J., Feldman, M. W., and Laland, K. N. (2017). The Extension of Biology through Culture. *Proceedings of the National Academy of Sciences of the United States of America*, *114*(30), 7775–7781.

Whiten, A., Hinde, R. A., Stringer, C. B., and Laland, K. N. (2012). *Culture Evolves*. Oxford, UK: Oxford University Press.

Wood, B. (2010). Reconstructing Human Evolution: Achievements, Challenges, and Opportunities. *Proceedings of the National Academy of Sciences of the United States of America*, *107*(S2), 8902–8909.

Zeder, M. A. (2017). Domestication as a Model System for the Extended Evolutionary Synthesis. *Interface Focus*, *7*, 20160133.

3 Material Imagination: An Anthropological Perspective

Maria Danae Koukouti and Lambros Malafouris

He had prepared his death much earlier, in his imagination, unaware that his imagination, more creative than he, was planning the reality of that death.

Umberto Eco (2007: 594).

Introduction

Imagination goes too far, too fast. It has a tremendous potency that seems to unfailingly serve us: Whatever we might imagine is "given" to us immediately and in a deceitful completeness. Sartre argued that because of the human ability of imagination, we are ontologically free (Sartre, 2017). William Blake enthusiastically proclaimed: "The Imagination is not a state: it is the Human Existence itself" (Blake, 1965: 131). Certainly, imagination is as important as it is complex and its thorough study requires a multidisciplinary approach. But what has anthropology to offer to the study of imagination? What, if anything, is unique about the understanding of the process of imagination in anthropological terms?

In this chapter, we would like to step back from the traditional cognitivist view that occupies the dominant perspective on human imagination to take up some broader anthropological questions about imagination's place in human life and creativity. Our aim is to provide a more integrative and critical perspective that will allow us to explore the material bases and enactive character of imagination – and, above all, to challenge a disembodied, purely representational way of thinking about imagination. Clearly we view imagination as entangled with matter and the affordances of things. We focus more on what imagination "does" than on what it is, exploring the process of imagination and what it can include. This kind of imagination, defined through its dynamic relation with the material and relieved of the connotation of the "dreamlike," summons a different attention: It cannot be reduced to nothing. Imagination, of course, can take many meanings and invite different modes of investigation. Different elements guide different scholars in their study of the imagined. Here, we emphasize what anthropology in particular has to offer to the study of imagination. After reviewing the relevant anthropological and philosophical literature, we shall be focusing on the example of pottery-making and use this example to shed some light on the phenomenon of material imagination.

Social Being, Imagination, and Time

We do not define imagination or think of it in a fixed manner. The first thing we have to acknowledge is that, at different times or places we refer and respond to imagination in different ways, we attribute to it negative or positive qualities, we give it more or less credit. To help us understand how our appreciation of imagination changes, psychologist Douwe Draaisma uses the example of Thomas Aquinas and Albert Einstein. Widely recognized as two of the most influential thinkers of all time, they were – Draaisma writes – mainly celebrated for two different qualities. Einstein was praised for his originality and creativity, attributed mostly to his remarkable imagination. People recognized imagination to be the greater force behind Einstein's ability to break through convention and explore new scientific territories. That was all in the twentieth century. When Thomas Aquinas died in 1274, his excellence was credited to his unfailing memory. Aquinas was said to have been able to memorize texts that he had read years ago and to dictate simultaneously to more than two people on different subjects from memory. In the testimony of the fellow-members of his order, Aquinas was praised for a completely different quality from that attributed to Einstein seven centuries later. Even though passionate admiration has been expressed for both intellectual figures, the focus of that admiration is, for Einstein, his "intuition and imaginative power, qualities that allowed him to break free from what had been thought before him. Thomas's genius, in contrast, seemed to be based on a majestic memory in which knowledge was gathered in a slow and cumulative process" (Draaisma, 2000: 31). The value we assign to different instruments of thought as responsible for the generation of knowledge and creativity influences not only how we analyze and evaluate human intellect, but also our ideas about the workings of the mind or the very architecture of the brain. According to Draaisma, for instance, in the Middle Ages when memory was valued the most it was believed to be located deep in the brain, particularly in the third ventricle. Imagination, on the other hand was placed in the foremost ventricle, right behind the senses (Draaisma, 2000: 31).

Even before the Middle Ages, Aristotle proposed two types of imagination: the "sensitive imagination," which is stimulated by our senses – seeing, hearing, smelling, tasting, and touching; and the "deliberate imagination," which is superior to the other and more involved in cognitive processes and the understanding of social life and located in the mind and absent from the body (Elliott and Culhane, 2016: 14). Aristotle's line of thought was famously followed by Rene Descartes, who argued for a total separation between mind and body. In this view, known as "Cartesian dualism," an immaterial mind and a material body became two conceptually opposed and ontologically divided entities. Reason is located in this "nonphysical" mind, whereas passions and irrationalities are seated in the physical/material human body. Imagination, as a mental phenomenon, resisting fixed definitions and unruly by nature, is often thought of as an abstract, disembodied mental function, detached not only from the human body but also from its material surrounding – the things through and with which we think and create: the raw material for imagination to turn the absent into material form.

In *Anthropology and the Cognitive Challenge*, Maurice Bloch associates imagination with the element of time. He refers to what psychologists call "time travel" (Bloch, 2012: 108) – that is, the capacity to recall past events in our lives and imagine future events and our possible roles in them. Humans have this capacity because we are able to make up, in our brains, different situations from the ones that we are actually living in. "Time," of course, is complicated. We do not share the same notion of and understanding of time all over the world. In fact, different concepts of time may exist within the same culture. The Nuer, for instance, an East African people living in the open savannah of the River Nile, have two concepts of time that influential anthropologist Edward E. Evans-Pritchard specified to be ecological and structural (1951). Ecological time appears to be cyclical. It relates to the environment and the changes that cause the movement of people: rain, drought, movement of birds, fish. Structural time refers to changes in the relationships between social groups. A man's life in this culture, for instance, is centered on certain periods and rites of passages he must undergo as a boy for his status to change in the social system. A man's structural future, therefore, can in a way be foreseen. This, according to Evans-Pritchard, gives a sense (or better still, an illusion) of progressive time.

Evidently, not all of us think of time in the same way, and therefore, not all of us engage in time travel in a similar manner. Yet, according to Bloch, all of us may experience this imaginary time travel without confusing past, present, and future. Even very young children, Bloch suggests, are able to differentiate stories of imaginary heroes from reality; furthermore, these stories can assist in our understanding of time. "Imagination thus enables us to live in other worlds while knowing that these are not the here and now" (Bloch, 2012: 109). People use this capacity to write fiction and poetry and take other forms of creative action, but what is most important for anthropologists, Bloch writes, is that our capacity to imagine other worlds is at the very heart of human social life.

One especially important aspect of understanding imagination in relation to human society is, according to Bloch, the human ability of pretend play – the ability to pretend that one thing is another that starts as early as eighteen months of age. Bloch claims that children, regardless of culture, have the ability to engage in pretend play and control their imagination without confusing fantasy with reality. Malagasy girls and boys engage in pretend play – girls using corn-cobs as babies and boys using clay models of cattle – without believing that corn-cobs are babies or confusing clay models of cattle for real animals. In Madagascar, Bloch claims to have seen and photographed children playing together in mock rituals while they understand that what they are doing exists in the sphere of the imagination. As children grow older, this pretend play becomes a shared activity that involves other children and sets the ground for the acquisition of more complex social skills, and most importantly, for the appreciation of different social roles such as that of the parent, the teacher, etc. The imaginative activity of playing "teacher" means understanding the existence of a social role separated from any individual identity and, consequently, realizing that a social role is something that can be attributed. For Bloch, the idea of social roles is a matter of imagination since it does not refer to any empirical aspects of the person carrying the role. Being French, for instance, is an imagined membership; an imaginary phenomenon that carries no marks on the body of any person.

Bloch emphasizes that engaging in the social imagination of the adult world has very little to do with a lone child playing roles because it involves the coordinated imagination of many individuals. The "social imaginary," then, becomes the collective means through which social groups identify and fulfill their roles, as well as make sense of themselves and of the world (Gaonkar, 2002; Strathern, Stewart, and Whitehead, 2006; Taylor, 2004). Imagination, viewed in this light, provides a setting for individuals to realize their place and purpose among other individuals in a specific social and temporal space. Especially in our modern times, where images and individuals travel and come in contact with each other with unprecedented speed, imagination is considered to have a new power on social life. Imagination is associated with many aspects of modernity and has even been theorized by anthropologists as a force behind globalization (Appadurai, 1996; Gaonkar, 2002).

Imagination: The Challenge for Anthropology

The study of imagination has always been challenging. In their work, David Sneath, Martin Holbraad and Morten Axel Pedersen identify three major hazards in relation to the anthropological study of imagination. The first is the analogy of imagination with culture. More precisely, in recent writings, anthropologists tend to "enlarge" the concept of imagination, making it appear similar to wider concepts like culture or identity. Such writings, even though appealing, disregard the consideration of novelty in the study of imagination. In reality "a fixed totality of explicit meanings ('culture') has been substituted with a fluid totality of implicit ones ('the social imaginary'). In other words, the imagination is not 'a whole' in the same way as 'culture' once was, but it is just as holistic" (Sneath et al., 2009: 8).

A second difficulty is what the writers call the tendency toward "instrumentalism." For some anthropologists imagination is something with a specific purpose and tuned to a "social-psychological function" like that of "making sense of the world" (Sneath et al., 2009: 8). In this line of thought, the writers consider Benedict Anderson and his influential *Imagined Communities*, in which he claims that nations emerged imaginatively as "emotive-cum-political entities" resulting from practices like maps and printed texts. Imagination, therefore, need not be presented metaphysically as a source of meaning but can be explored empirically. All communities, he writes, are imagined and should be distinguished according to the style in which they are imagined. Anderson's approach is acknowledged for its preoccupation with the heterogeneous processes through which concrete imaginings come about and for allowing for the possibility of considering imagination not as holistic horizon but as "a set of emergent effects" (Sneath et al., 2009: 9). He is, however, criticized for his "Durkheimian agenda," which sets imagination in terms of basic concerns such as the need to forge a communal identity. Posited like that, imagination only interests social scientists as far as it is shown to fulfill a specific purpose, either a social function or existential potential. Sneath, Holbraad, and Pedersen also enlist Cornelius Castoriadis (1997) in their criticism. Castoriadis, indeed, claimed that, under this light, the imaginary is "constantly shifting towards something other than itself" (Sneath et al., 2009: 9).

They identify the third and final difficulty as the attempt to assign positive connotations to imagination. As an example of this "romantic tendency" the writers cite Vincent Crapanzano's (2004) notion of "imaginative horizons" as the most ambitious attempt so far by an anthropologist to theorize imagination. His work, they claim, is a "literary experiment within the tradition of hermeneutic anthropology" (Sneath et al., 2009: 9). Crapanzano offers the idea of imaginary "frontiers" that – in contrast to borders – cannot be crossed. He also opens up a "genuinely ethnographic engagement with the imagination as a social and cultural phenomenon that can be investigated empirically" (Sneath et al., 2009: 10). What he does not offer, however, is a methodological framework for carrying out such analysis. He also fails to present a negative aspect of imagination, or the possibility of imagination being mainly a European ideological concept founded in the Romantic reaction to the Industrial Revolution. In addition, the writers suggest that Crapanzano's view displays a Romanticism like that of the nineteenth-century theories of imagination, similar to Coleridge, who saw imagination as an unrestrained and transcendental source of poetic creativity.

What Does it Mean to Imagine?

But if we accept that imagination, as Castoriadis suggested, is easily absorbed by something that is not itself, then what is it? What does it mean to imagine something? To understand imagination, Tim Ingold asks us to think of a composer composing a symphony: Like a bird on the wing, he writes, music flies ahead in the composer's imagination. The composer struggles to catch the music before it is irretrievably lost beyond the horizon of his recollection (Ingold, 2013: 71). The task would be easier if music did not seem to outpace its score, its material inscription. The same, Ingold continues, goes for the writer, the painter, the performer. It seems that the difficulty with imagination is to be able to follow it, to pin it down, and to "catch" its contents.

The painter must hurry to catch the fleeting visions; the writer should dash behind untamed thoughts. One must be fast to catch the "phantom" of the imaginary before it escapes (Baudelaire, in Ingold, 2013: 72). But the hand, according to Ingold, can be hesitant, and the body and weight of material may hinder the process of putting imagination into words, notes, drawings. "It seems that composer, performer, architect, writer, draughtsman and painter alike are continually caught between the anticipatory reach of imaginative foresight and the tensile or frictional drag of material abrasion – whether of pen on paper, bow on strings, or brush on canvas" (Ingold, 2013: 72).

Finding the right distance between oneself and what one imagines also seems to be important. For instance, one should feel close enough to an imaginary landscape in order to paint it, but not so close, not so fully immersed, as to lose sight of it. Ingold uses Rane Willerslev's observations to draw a parallel between hunting and chasing things of the imagination (Willerslev, 2006). Hunters, in particular the Upper Kolyma Yukaghirs of Siberia that Willerslev describes in his ethnography, attribute great importance to acquiring knowledge through experiencing the world, especially the world of the forest. Now, in that world, dreams, imagination, and reality often interact and mingle with each other. Imagination is, in Willerslev's writings, associated with the knowledge of the world. The ability to imagine yourself as another, to overcome the boundaries of self and the world – a boundary created by language – is of great validity and is considered knowledge in itself. That is why the Yukaghirs, when they are teaching their children, avoid giving specific instructions and prefer for them to attain knowledge by engaging with the world. That is also why before they go hunting they refrain from talking in human language. The purpose is to overcome the divide between themselves and their prey. What the Yukaghir hunter strives to achieve is to "transcend the symbolic order of language, whose principle of negation is to divide and differentiate all identities and (re)enter the realm of the 'imaginary'" (Willerslev, 2007: 70).

In that imaginary realm, the Yukaghir hunter may try to deceive an animal by imitating its appearance and movement. The purpose is for the deer or elk to perceive the hunter as its mirroring and move toward him and toward its death. In that mimetic act, however, the hunter may also lose his human identity and, believing his own performance, lose touch with himself and be lost into the world of his prey. Willerslev provides two stories in which a true metamorphosis occurs and, as a result, the borders between animal and human fade. The first one belongs to a hunter named Nikolai Likhachev. Nikolai was hunting a herd of reindeer, following it around for six hours. He made a fire by the Popova river, where he tried to sleep after drinking tea. The hunter said that he was cold, tired, and hungry. Still, at dawn, he started following the herd again. As he was searching for their tracks, Nikolai had a feeling that somebody was watching him. An old man appeared in front of him in old-fashioned clothing and, without answering Nikolai's questions, gestured for Nikolai to follow him. As Nikolai did so, in the hope that the stranger would provide some food, he noticed that the old man's footprints had the same form as those of a reindeer. Nikolai thought he was hallucinating because of his hunger and kept on following the man. After they walked up a hill they reached a camp with more than thirty tents. The Yukaghir hunter noticed children playing around, women cooking, and old men sitting and smoking. The old man drove him to his tent but when he spoke to his wife, instead of speaking in the human language, the old man grunted at his wife like a reindeer and she grunted back. Nikolai was served food that he thought was lichen. He sat in the tent with the strange couple, noticing that he was starting to forget things – like the name of his wife, who was waiting for him back at home. When he fell asleep, he dreamed that he was surrounded by reindeer. Then, someone said to him "You do not belong here. Go away" (Willerslev, 2007: 90). Nikolai followed the advice. He snuck out of the tent and managed to find his way back into his village. There, the people were very surprised to see him, as they thought he had died. When Nikolai protested that he had only been away for a week, the people in his village informed him that he had been absent for more than a month. It was then that Nikolai realized what had happened to him: He reported to Willerslev that the old man he followed up the hill and the people he met in the camp were all reindeer.

The Yukaghir hunter, Willerslev explains, saw the reindeer as human beings instead of prey. At the same time, the reindeer saw the hunter not as a predator but as one of its own species. This confusion, the possible risk of identity loss, always lurks in the strange, imaginary place where human and nonhuman identities mix. To support this claim, Willerslev writes about his encounter with Old Spiridon, a Yukaghir hunter disguised as an elk. Willerslev starts by describing the hunter: "Watching Old Spiridon rocking his body back and forth, I was puzzled whether the figure I saw before me was a man or an elk. The elk-hide coat worn with its hair outward, the headgear with its characteristic protruding ears, and the skis covered with an elk's smooth leg skins, so as to sound like the animal when moving in snow, made him an elk" (Willerslev, 2007: 1). But Willerslev also notices the lower part of his human face and the rifle in his hands, which made Spiridon a man. Then, a female elk with her offspring appeared close to the hunter. In the beginning the elk stood still, puzzled by the appearance of the hunter. But as Spiridon began to move mimicking the elk, the animal was convinced by his performance, and, trusting the disguised man, it walked toward him along with her calf. Spiridon then shot both animals dead. Willerslev quotes the explanation given to him by the hunter: "I saw two persons dancing towards me. The mother was a beautiful woman and while singing she said: 'Honored friend. Come and I'll take you by the arm and lead you to our people.' At that point I killed them both. Had I gone with her, I myself would have died. She would have killed me" (Willerslev, 2007: 1).

What the Yukaghir hunter describes is the danger of losing one's identity by pretending to be an elk for too long. Here, we notice the similarity of this notion with an idea we have mentioned above – the right distance that Ingold claims one should have with what one imagines: the painter should not be too close to the imaginary landscape he or she is trying to paint so as to not lose sight of it, while the hunter should not remain for long in the "imaginary" realm so as to not lose his humanity. Imagination, then, is something we can be lost in, something that can take the best of us; at the same time, it is something we ceaselessly chase after and something we use to chase our prey. It is best to clarify that Willerslev borrows the word "imaginary" from French psychoanalyst Jacques Lacan. It describes a condition of no absolute distinction between subject and object, self and world. Anthropology, through Willerslev's writings, incorporates the "imaginary" in an effort to develop a dialogue between different theories of knowledge. Thus, the "imaginary" makes an attempt to escape the "as if"; dreams, also, try to escape their immaterial and unreal qualities: They acquire weight.

Anthropologist Eduardo Kohn in his study of the Runa of Ecuador's Upper Amazon, speaks of dreams that are not just commentaries on the world but partici-pate in it. During sleep the soul separates from the body of the owner and interacts with other spirits and beings. Most of the dreams of the Runa are associated with hunting. They warn them of dangers, or they can give away the locations of animals. Sleeping in Ávila, a Runa village, is not the solitary and sensory-deprived experience it has become for the Western world, Kohn writes. People sleep in the company of other people, in open thatch houses without electricity, surrounded by the outdoors. Sleeping, therefore, is continuously interspersed with wakefulness. People interrupt their sleep to get warm by the fire, to drink tea, to take notice of sounds coming from the forest. "Thanks to these continuous disruptions, dreams spill into wakefulness and wakefulness into dreams in a way that entangles both" (Kohn, 2013: 13).

In Willerslev's ethnography we also see that dreams and waking life constitute an equal means of acquiring knowledge and experience. Willerslev cites an instance in which a company of hunters, experiencing bad luck, were looking for answers. Yura, a hunter in this company, failed to kill an elk that simply walked away from him. Yura later had a dream. He dreamt that "a woman with a child approached him. Both were clothed in dog fur and a tiny stream of blood was running from the eye of the child" (Willerslev, 2007: 154). All the hunters in the group knew that Vasili, a Russian man among them, had killed a pregnant dog before going to the forest to hunt. After the dream, everybody was convinced that this act was behind their failures in hunting. They believed that the revelation was made to Yura in his dream by a spirit and that Vasili was polluted; as long as Vasili was among them there would be no success in their hunting. Willerslev claims that nobody explained that to Vasili or asked him to leave. The hunters, nevertheless, alienated him and stopped paying any attention to him until Vasili left them and the forest of his own accord, to live in the village. So, dreams in the land of the Yukaghir are to be taken seriously, as part of living experience. They escape the fate described by Gaston Bachelard who wrote that dreams, when described objectively, are diminished, interrupted, and reduced to nothing but oneirism (Bachelard, 2014: 171). On the contrary, dreams appear to be a vital part of the Lacanian "imaginary" described by Willerslev, where self and world are at the same time like and not like, same and different from each other: The Yukaghir chase animals also in their dreams.

According to Ingold, artists, composers, writers, and architects are also dream hunters, in the manner of catching the elusive insights of imagination and pinning them down into material engagement. Human endeavor, Ingold writes, seems to involve constant vacillation between negotiating materials and catching dreams, rather than any opposition concerning cognitive intellection and mechanical execution. Humans live their lives where "the reach of the imagination meets the friction of materials, or where the forces of ambition rub up against the rough edges of the world" (Ingold, 2013: 73).

Even though we agree on the wrongly assumed tension between cognitive intellection and execution, we notice that, fully accepting that view presupposes a "clear" point of collision – a place where imagination ends and reality begins, where the "dream-animal" and the "real animal," to use the hunting metaphor, are able to exist at a clear ontological distance from each other, or where what is intended by the craftsman or the artist before the moment of creation and what is produced exist as two different designs – the artist chasing after the desired image as one chases a butterfly.

The question, then, that permeates this article is what can anthropology do differently to demonstrate the "intimacy" between real things and the imagined?

On Material Imagination

As mentioned, from a cognitivist perspective, imagination is primarily associated with the ability to form and manipulate mental representations in the absence of corresponding visual or other stimuli (Ganis and Schendan, 2011). On this construal, what differentiates imagination from other mental processes is that it happens "offline," or disengaged from immediate reality. Still, from an anthropological perspective, our human ways of imagining cannot be separated from their relevant socio-material and cultural environment. Human persons imagine inside their world. Whatever "absence" they discover, create or re-enact, must be "present" in that world and must be understood as a situated, context-sensitive process.

Clearly, there are not only many different types of imagination but also many ways of describing the experience of bringing to presence something that is absent.[1] Our main concern in the last section of this chapter is creative imagining, which refers broadly to those imaginary processes that support human creative thinking. As with the study of human creativity at large, so with the process of creative imagining, the dominant approach has been to reduce it to a collection of internalized mental representations. However, from an anthropological perspective, such a narrow approach, focusing on private internalized representational states, minimizes the important links between creativity and imagination and their socio-material constitution.

We would like to advance a notion of material imagination and to propose an alternative way of looking at creative imagining, drawing on enactive cognitive science (Gallagher, 2017; Hutto, 2017) and material engagement theory (Malafouris, 2004, 2013, 2019; Renfrew, 2004). Put simply, the suggestion is as follows: instead of thinking about imagination as the kind of decontextualized mental sculpting of internally stored re-presentations of the world, it may be more productive to view it as a situated dynamic sculpting of heterogeneous resources and processes (both internal and external). According to the former view, imagination happens inside the head, confined to an inner realm of mental representations. According to the latter, imagination happens inside the world, achieved through processes of creative material engagement. For the material engagement approach, the basic commitment and methodological aspiration is to change the way we think about creative imagining by bringing materiality – that is, the world of things and material signs – into the cognitive fold (Malafouris, 2013, 2019; Poulsgaard, 2019; Poulsgaard and Malafouris, 2017; Walls and Malafouris, 2016). Creative material engagement is broadly defined as *"the discovery of new varieties of material forms, so far as it is possible in a given historical situation, through a saturated, situated engagement of thinking and feeling with things and form-generating materials"* (Malafouris, 2014: 144). A central claim that the material engagement approach shares with enactivism and the so-called distributed cognition framework is that the proper unit of analysis

---

1 For instance, Abraham broadly differentiates five types of imagination: (i) mental imagery-based imagination, (ii) intentionality-based imagination, (iii) novel combinatorial-based imagination, (iv) phenomenology-based imagination, and (v) altered states of imagination. (See discussion in Abraham, 2016.)

for imagination "should be responsive to the nature of the phenomena under study" (Hutchins, 2010b: 426).

That also implies that no rigid distinction between the real and the imaginary can be set *a priori*. The boundaries between the imaginary and the real, if and when they exist, must be drawn in real time and space – that is, in relation to specific creative activities. This is not to deny that imagination originates in the human mind; rather, it changes the temporal and spatial boundaries of imagining in a way that collapses the internal/external divide between mind and the material world. In that sense, the geography of human imagination changes. Acts of imagination are no longer strictly defined, or explained away by reference to internal mental states. Imagination is a "mental" process not in the "internalist" sense but in the "enactivist" sense. In the enactivist sense, lower and higher cognition are continuous, mind and action are one (Gallagher, 2017; Malafouris, 2018; Newen et al., 2018). Imagination no longer needs to be insulated from the agent's body and the environment. Rather, it is spread out into the world, and can be now observed in the wild.

How can this be? Is not imagination that special "mental" place in which all things can happen (imagined) free from any material or sensorial constraints? Is it not the ability to imagine "possible" worlds rather than to sense and to perceive the "real" world that constitutes what is special about human phantasia? Contrary to other forms of "online" perception and thinking, the term imagination has been used to describe precisely those aspects of human thought that are happening "offline," meaning, not caused by or related in any direct sense to the immediate reality of the world that surrounds us.

We agree that the ability to "see" something that does not exist seems to be a fundamental feature of imagination. It does not follow, nonetheless, that the capacity to imagine presupposes material disengagement – although this may seem to be the case from certain timescales and types of mental imagery (visual, auditory, or motor). Human imagination is much broader. Imagination cannot be captured solely by means of mental representations or described as a unified private experience. On the one hand, many other processes (cognitive, affective, and social) are intimately linked with imagination. On the other, there is currently ongoing debate on the value and meaning of mental representations, their ontology, and their material bases in the brain. Even if we agree to define imagination in pure "representational terms," the neural trace of those representations cannot be delimited in a clear way. Available neuroscientific evidence indicates a substantial overlap between the neural networks associated with task-unrelated facets of imagination and their related task-specific non-imaginative facets. For instance, it is now well accepted that, to a large extent, visual mental images rely on the same representations that support visual perception (Kosslyn et al., 2001) (see also Chapter 42). Moreover, a common brain network underlies both memory and imagination, revealing striking similarities between remembering the past and imagining the future (Schacter, et al. 2012) (see also Chapter 8).

In any case, if the role of imagination is to free us from the confines of our present perceptual reality, that can only happen by reaching out and beyond the spatial and temporal horizon of individual experience. Imagination is mind-wandering that crisscrosses past, present, and future and leads both inward and outward. The anthropologist Tim Ingold uses the example of walking to express a similar idea: "Do we not, in walking, continually place ourselves at risk by falling forward, tumbling ahead of ourselves into the void, only to regain our footing in a skilled adjustment of body posture to the irregularities of the ground? Imagination sets us loose to fall; perception restores our grip so we can keep on going. One is aspirational, the other prehensile. It is in their alternation that all life is lived" (Ingold, 2018: 43).

Indeed, as with many other aspects of human cognitive life, imagination is not confined to an inner realm of mental representations: It happens inside the world, rather than inside the head, achieved through processes of creative material engagement.

With material imagination our focus falls precisely on the imaginary ways in which humans actually relate to aspects of their material environment in the course of specific creative activities. To illustrate this idea of enactive material imagination we draw, in particular, on our anthropological study of people who make their living primarily by making ceramic forms (Malafouris, 2008, 2018; Malafouris and Koukouti, 2017, 2018; March, 2019).

Take the example of the potter forming a vase on the wheel. It is common to assume that the actual form of the vase, the details of the shape, the width and the lines of the object that the potter produces must originate in an act of imagination. What is more difficult is to try to situate those acts of material imagination inside the broader ecology of creative material engagement and to understand the role that they play in the process of making. How do acts of imagination relate to acts of making?

Let us focus on one specific act of material imagination – for instance, on the moment that the potter creates a line that runs around the pot (Figure 3.1). According to the cognitivist view,[2] if there is an element of imagination involved in this part of the creative process, this should be conceptualized as a mental image (or a combination of mental images) formed inside the head of the potter giving rise to the experience of "seeing the line with the mind's eye." This mental representation ("stand-in" for the real line) is constructed offline and ahead of the actual making of the line on the surface of the clay vase. This imaginary line (lucid or vague) can only be partial, carrying some relevant but general information about lines (e.g. about their possible width, size, color, and texture – or the skills and tools needed to produce them). Nonetheless, this imaginary line relates to (or anticipates), in ways that are yet to be properly understood, the form of the actual line to be produced with or on the surface of clay.

It makes good sense to think that the potter needs to imagine where exactly to place that line and to visualize what form the line will take: is it going to be painted, engraved in, or standing out? Probably the potter will also have to decide how thick that line should be and what kind of instrument he or she will need to use to achieve

---

2 "Cognitivism" broadly denotes the view that there is in general a strict division between perception, action, and cognition, and seeks to explain human cognitive processes solely by appeal to computations and content-carrying representational states in the head (e.g. Fodor, 1983; Adams and Aizawa, 2010).

Figure 3.1 *The making of a line with clay.*

that thickness or flatness. Will it be a line that runs around the pot evenly? Will it finish exactly where it starts, or perhaps spiral slightly? Those are situated projections (Suchman, 1987) or anticipations (van Dijk and Rietveld, 2018) that blend aesthetic and functional/practical considerations. The making of those lines tests as well as extends and challenges the potter's skills, the "cans" and "cannots" of the potter's body and the affordances of clay. The way a line travels on the surface of clay will affect people in different ways and will produce different aesthetic results (some lines being more interesting or pleasing than others).

On the cognitivist account, if there is an imaginary component in the process of making, this must be located in the potter's mind/brain and it must precede the process of making as well as the various creative, perceptual, and kinesthetic experiences that this process entails. As mentioned, the orthodox way of thinking is that the line, like any other material form produced by the potter, is imagined ahead of the action as the mental representation of a line. On this construal the form of a vase precedes in a "mental," imaginary form its "material" manifestation in clay, realized through the creative synergy of mind and matter brought about by the potter's actions and movements (Gosden and Malafouris, 2015; Malafouris, 2008, 2014; Malafouris and Koukouti, 2017). However, the description above imposes an unwanted artificial barrier between the imaginary potential of the brain and the form-generating potential of the materials, the tools, and other environmental scaffolds that make possible the process of enactive discovery that lies at the heart of material imagination. We propose that perhaps a better way to think about this process is to see imagination as immanent in the creative process. As has also been argued for many other cognitive processes that play an important role in human imagination (e.g. memory), any neural simulation and re-enaction of past events inside the brain needs to be understood within a broader cognitive ecology of action (Malafouris and Koukouti, 2017). The brain is crucial but is only a part of the process. Other important constituents of imagination remain "unrepresented" and on the "outside."

Those elements preserve stable physical material anchors for imaginary conceptual blends (Hutchins, 2010a, 2010b). The typical mistake here is to disregard those elements. A major challenge for the anthropology, philosophy, and the cognitive science of imagination is to develop theories and methods that take into consideration the cultural specificity and material ecology of imagination.

Our description of material imagination here resembles, somehow, that of the philosopher Gaston Bachelard who finds it "in the instinctive materialism of the child's play, encountering the world not as gestalt but as flux, or in the movement of the potter's hand, plying the as yet amorphous clay, drawing forth form out of formlessness, less by a movement of abstraction, than by infusing the very imagination of forms with an always prior experience of the richness and density of matter" (Bachelard, 1983: 4). Moreover, like Gilbert Simondon (2005) and Tim Ingold (2012, 2013), we are suspicious of the *hylomorphic*[3] model that imposes preformed ideas on matter. Ideas are shaped with and worked into clay, not just imposed on the clay. Of course, ideas can be turned into molds but the construction of the mold is again a form of material imagination. The purity or abstraction of the mental image can hardly account for the process of making. The actual relationship between matter and form remains unsettled. It is here that Material Engagement Theory (MET) and enactive cognitive science can help, as we set about explaining and clarifying what material imagination means. This *hylonoetic* process[4] allows the potter to anticipate and partially visualize possibilities of form-making that lie beyond the reach of the immediate here and now of the potter's perception. Whatever the final form of that vase might be, it was absent (as a real material object) during those early imaginary stages. Perhaps this also explains why during the actual process of making potters rarely say that they "see." Rather, the expression they mostly use is that they are "beginning to see." By the same token, pots and forms are more often "near to finish" than "finished." We said that imaginary objects or places are absent or quasi-present; that means they are also incomplete.

There is a feeling of natural rhythm and balance emerging from the creative tension that connects potter and clay, especially during those rare cases where the potter's hand seems to be pushing clay as far as the material will go, shaping and giving form to the potter's imagination. Even though the series of events we describe have a clear and to some extent traceable neural dimension, they cannot be reduced to those patterns of neural activation/simulation. Imagination matters because it refers to a creative process that enacts or brings forth a sequence of anticipations that often recruit different forms of mind-stuff (internal and external). Thus, imagination takes the form of a creative gesture that enables the objectification and physical handling of things absent or quasi-present. This form of material imagination is no longer disconnected and immune from the wider material ecology of creative action but rather inseparable from it – connected through the movement of the potter's brain and body. One implication of that is that outside this context of creative material engagement there is very little that the potter's brain and body can imagine. It is not

3 The term comes from Aristotle's ontology, potentiality and actuality, matter (*hyle*) and form (*morphe*).
4 Comes from the Greek words (*hyle*) for matter and (*nous*) for mind. See discussion in Malafouris (2016).

the brain that carries within it, on the inside, the imaginary act; rather, it is the actual engagement with clay that offers an opportunity to imagine. The term material imagination describes this open but skillful synergy of mind and matter. We argue that imagination is how the brain handles the world. It should be seen as the brain's creative gesture. Imagination allows the brain to reach out.

Conclusion

Our initial attitude to the study of imagination influences the way we look at and think about the world in reference to our relationship with it. To say that imagination involves only abstract mental images of one kind or another is to accept that we imagine alone – that is, in the absence of the imagination of the material. In this view, imagination entails a mental image that "aims" at an object but never comes into contact with it. The image of the object, let's say the image of a clay pot, fills the "space" in our mind, while the object itself forever remains "outside," severed both from our mind and our imagination. On the contrary, if we open up to a concept in which the imagined mingles and interacts with the material world, then, "imagining" becomes a process through which the perception of an imaginary object in our mind and the material form that exists or is produced in the world are experienced together. It becomes imaginative praxis, an enactment of possibilities. The reason this view is still debated is not the lack of realization of the sensual experience of the imaginative praxis on behalf of the potter making things on the wheel (the feeling, thinking, and moving together with the material) but the lack of a language to describe and an approach to study the unity of the experience of the imagined and the material: It is this lack of methodology that anthropology now has to tackle.

Acknowledgments

The research and writing of this chapter was supported by the European Research Council (ERC) Consolidator Grant, HANDMADE (No 771997 European Union Horizon 2020) awarded to Lambros Malafouris.

References

Abraham, A. (2016). The Imaginative Mind. *Human Brain Mapping*, *37*(11), 4197–4211. doi .org/10.1002/hbm.23300.

Adams, F., and Aizawa, K. (2010). The Value of Cognitivism in Thinking about Extended Cognition. *Phenomenology and the Cognitive Sciences*, *9*(4), 579–603.

Appadurai, A. (1996). *Modernity at Large: Cultural Dimensions of Globalization*. Volume 1. Minneapolis, MN: University of Minnesota Press.

Bachelard, G. (1983). *Water and Dreams: An Essay on the Imagination of Matter*. Dallas, TX: Pegasus Foundation.

(2014). *The Poetics of Space*. London, UK: Penguin Classics.

Benedict, A. (1983). *Imagined Communities: Reflections on the Origin and Spread of Nationalism*. London, UK: Verso.

Blake, W. (1965). *The Complete Poetry and Prose of William Blake*. Edited by David V. Erdman. Commentary by Harold Bloom. Berkeley, CA: University of California Press.

Bloch, M. (2012). *Anthropology and the Cognitive Challenge*. Cambridge, UK: Cambridge University Press.

Castoriadis, C. (1997). *The Imaginary Institution of Society*. Cambridge, MA: MIT Press.

Crapanzano, V. (2004). *Imaginative Horizons: An Essay in Literary-Philosophical Anthropology*. Chicago, IL: University of Chicago Press.

Draaisma, D. (2000). *Metaphors of Memory: A History of Ideas About the Mind*. Cambridge, UK: Cambridge University Press.

Eco, U. (2007). *Foucault's Pendulum*. Boston, MA: Houghton Mifflin Harcourt.

Elliott, D., and Culhane, D. (eds.) (2016). *A Different Kind of Ethnography: Imaginative Practices and Creative Methodologies*. Toronto, Canada: University of Toronto Press.

Evans-Pritchard, E. E. (1951). *Kinship and Marriage Among the Nuer*. Oxford, UK: Clarendon Press.

Fodor, J. (1983). *The Modularity of Mind*. Cambridge, MA: MIT Press.

Gallagher, S. (2017). *Enactivist Interventions: Rethinking the Mind*. Oxford, UK: Oxford University Press.

Ganis, G., and Schendan, H. E. (2011). Visual Imagery. *Wiley Interdisciplinary Reviews: Cognitive Science*, *2*(3), 239–252.

Gaonkar, D. P. (2002). Toward New Imaginaries: An Introduction. *Public Culture*, *14*(1), 1–19.

Gosden, C., and Malafouris, L. (2015). Process Archaeology (P-Arch). *World Archaeology*, *47*(5), 1–17.

Hutchins, E. (2010a). Cognitive Ecology. *Topics in Cognitive Science*, *2*, 705–715.

(2010b). Enaction, Imagination, and Insight. In J. Stewart, O. Gapenne, and E. A. Di Paolo (eds.), *Enaction: Toward a New Paradigm for Cognitive Science*. Cambridge, MA: MIT Press, 425–450.

Hutto, D. D. (2017). *Evolving Enactivism: Basic Minds Meet Content*. Cambridge, MA: MIT Press.

Hutto, D., and Myin, E. (2013). *Radicalizing Enactivism: Basic Minds without Content*. Cambridge, MA: MIT Press.

Ingold, T. (2012). Toward an Ecology of Materials. *Annual Review of Anthropology*, *41*(1), 427–442.

(2013). *Making: Anthropology, Archaeology, Art and Architecture*. London, UK: Routledge.

(2018). Back to the Future with the Theory of Affordances. *HAU: Journal of Ethnographic Theory*, *8*(1–2), 39–44.

Kohn, E. (2013). *How Forests Think: Toward an Anthropology Beyond the Human*. Berkeley, CA: University of California Press.

Kosslyn, S. M., Ganis, G., and Thompson, W. L. (2001). Neural Foundations of Imagery. *Nature Reviews Neuroscience*, *2*(9), 635.

Lacan, J. (2001). *Ecrits: A Selection*. London, UK: Routledge.

Malafouris, L. (2004). The Cognitive Basis of Material Engagement: Where Brain, Body and Culture Conflate. In E. DeMarrais, C. Gosden, and C. Renfrew (eds.), *Rethinking*

Materiality: The Engagement of Mind with the Material World. Cambridge, UK: The McDonald Institute for Archaeological Research, 53–62.

(2008). At the Potter's Wheel: An Argument for Material Agency. In C. Knappett and L. Malafouris (eds.), *Material Agency: Towards a Non-Anthropocentric Perspective*. New York, NY: Springer, 19–36.

(2013). *How Things Shape the Mind: A Theory of Material Engagement*. Cambridge, MA: MIT Press.

(2014). Creative Thinging: The Feeling of and for Clay. *Pragmatics and Cognition*, *22*(1), 140–158.

(2016). Hylonoetics: On the Priority of Material Engagement. In K. Grigoriadis (ed.), *Mixed Matters: A Multi-Material Design Compendium*. Berlin, Germany: Jovis Verlag, 140–146.

(2018). Bringing Things to Mind: 4Es and Material Engagement. In A. Newen, L. de Bruin, and G. Shaun (eds.), *The Oxford Handbook of 4E Cognition*. Oxford, UK: Oxford University Press, 755–771.

(2019). Mind and Material Engagement. *Phenomenology and the Cognitive Sciences*, *18*(1), 1–17.

Malafouris, L., and Koukouti, M. D. (2017). More than a Body. In C. Meyer, J. Streeck, and J. S. Jordan (eds.), *Intercorporeality: Emerging Socialities in Interaction*. Oxford, UK: Oxford University Press, 289–303.

(2018). How the Body Remembers its Skills: Memory and Material Engagement. *Journal of Consciousness Studies*, *25*(7–8), 158–180.

March, P. L. (2019). Playing with Clay and the Uncertainty of Agency: A Material Engagement Theory Perspective. *Phenomenology and the Cognitive Sciences*, *18*(1), 133–151.

Newen, A., de Bruin, L., and Gallagher, S. (eds.) (2018). *The Oxford Handbook of 4E Cognition*. Oxford, UK: Oxford University Press.

Poulsgaard, K. S. (2019). Enactive Individuation: Technics, Temporality and Affect in Digital Design and Fabrication. *Phenomenology and the Cognitive Sciences*, *18*(1), 281–298.

Poulsgaard, K. S., and Malafouris, L. (2017). Models, Mathematics and Materials in Digital Architecture. In S. Cowley and F. Vallée-Tourangeau (eds.), *Cognition Beyond the Brain: Computation, Interactivity, and Human Artifice*. Cham, Switzerland: Springer International Publishing, 283–304.

Renfrew, C. (2004). Towards a Theory of Material Engagement. In E. DeMarrais, C. Gosden, and C. Renfrew (eds.), *Rethinking Materiality: The Engagement of Mind with the Material World*. Cambridge, UK: The McDonald Institute for Archaeological Research, 23–31.

Sartre, J. P. (2017). *L'imaginaire. Psychologie phénoménologique de l'imagination*. Paris, France: Éditions Gallimard.

Schacter, D. L., Addis, D. R., Hassabis, D., et al. (2012). The Future of Memory: Remembering, Imagining, and the Brain. *Neuron*, *76*, 677–694.

Simondon, G. (2005). *L'Individuation à la lumière des notions de forme et d'information*. Grenoble, France: Millon.

Sneath, D., Holbraad, M., and Pedersen, M. A. (2009). Technologies of the Imagination: An Introduction. *Ethnos*, *74*(1), 5–30.

Strathern, A., Stewart, P. J., and Whitehead, N. L. (2006). *Terror and Violence: Imagination and the Unimaginable*. London, UK: Pluto Press, 1–250.

Suchman, L. A. (1987). *Plans and Situated Actions: The Problem of Human-Machine Communication.* New York, NY: Cambridge University Press.

(2006). *Human-Machine Reconfigurations: Plans and Situated Actions.* 2nd edition. Cambridge, UK: Cambridge University Press.

Taylor, C. (2004). *Modern Social Imaginaries.* Durham, NC: Duke University Press.

van Dijk, L., and Rietveld, E. (2018). Situated Anticipation. *Synthese*, 1–23.

Walls, M., and Malafouris, L. (2016). Creativity as a Developmental Ecology. In V. P. Glaveanu (ed.), *The Palgrave Handbook of Creativity and Culture Research.* Basingstoke, UK: Palgrave Macmillan, 553–566.

Willerslev, R. (2006). "To Have the World at a Distance": Reconsidering the Significance of Vision for Social Anthropology. In C. Grasseni (ed.), *Between Apprenticeship and Standards.* Oxford, UK: Berghahn.

(2007). *Soul Hunters: Hunting, Animism, and Personhood Among the Siberian Yukaghirs.* Berkeley, CA: University of California Press.

4 The Archaeological Imagination

Michael Shanks

Archaeologists Work with What Remains

Imagining past lives experienced through ruins and remains: telling the story of a prehistoric village through the remains of the site and its artifacts. And more: dealing with the return of childhood memories, or designing an archive for a corporation. The archaeological imagination is a creative capacity mobilized when we experience traces and vestiges of the past, when we gather, classify, conserve, and restore, when we work with such remains, collections, archives to deliver narratives, reconstructions, accounts, explanations, or whatever. The archaeological imagination involves a particular sensibility, an affective attunement to the dynamic interplay of the presence of the past in remains, and the past's absence, simultaneously witnessed by such remains. The archaeological imagination and its associated sensibility are intimately associated with the social and cultural changes of the evolution of modernity since the seventeenth and eighteenth centuries (Thomas, 2004), the growth, quite spectacular since the 1970s, of the Heritage Industry, that sector of the culture industry associated with the concept of heritage (Harrison, 2013).

Let me begin with how we understand archaeology. Archaeologists work with what remains. It is a common misconception, very much propagated in popular characterizations (Holtorf, 2005, 2007), that archaeologists discover the past in their excavations and fieldwork, and establish knowledge of the past in their laboratory science. This misconception is even supported in many academic accounts that, understandably, emphasize disciplinary practices (Renfrew and Bahn, 2016). A pragmatic understanding of archaeological work or process, in contrast, stresses engagement, that archaeological work is a mode of production connecting past and present with a view to the future (Hodder, 1999; Lucas, 2001; Olsen et al., 2012; Preucel and Mrozowski, 2010; Rathje et al., 2012; Shanks and McGuire, 1996). There is a productive aspect to such work: Remains are resources for constructing stories, accounts, exhibitions, academic papers, movies, artworks. And also a reproductive aspect: Remains re-produce or reiterate the past, refreshing, introducing the past into the present, just as archaeologists may return to rework those remains with hindsight, in the light of new discoveries of sites and finds, or in new models, with new theories.

A conjectural faculty or capacity to piece together remains into meaningful forms, the archaeological imagination is a key component of our experiences of the past, our engagements with remains, sensory, cognitive, and emotional or evaluative (Shanks, 1992). We may call this affective and embodied attunement to remains, to decay and persistence, to the possibility of recollection and reconstruction, an archaeological sensibility. We encounter the past, excavate, observe, clean and restore, gather and classify: Imagination is a necessary component of this creative process or mode of cultural production that is also well-conceived as the design of pasts-in-the-present (Shanks, 2013). The creative engagement with fragmentary remains, working with them, means that we should deny a radical separation of a past that happened from our representations made of that past. The archaeological imagination, conceived pragmatically and processually as working with what remains, does not deliver things that are made up, fictive, illusory, that stand in opposition to a "real" past; it is the very faculty through which past worlds are made real to us. The archaeological imagination frames our engagement with remains of the past, frames our perception of the past, frames the possibility of making sense of the past.

Consider how time and temporality are involved. Archaeological work certainly involves chronology and chronometry, establishing and measuring dates of sites and things, and considerable effort has been made in organizing archaeological remains, sites and artifacts, according to date and provenance (see section 3: A Genealogy of Archaeological Experiences). But prior to establishing dates and periods are two other temporal aspects of archaeological experience: duration and encounter. Any archaeological experience, any archaeological work requires duration, the persistence of remains from the past into the present, and actuality, the encounter with the remains of the past in the present. With a view to the future: Archaeologists seize the opportunity to intervene in the inevitable decay and loss of remains, through recovery, preservation, conservation, restoration. That archaeologists care to seize an opportunity to work with what remains is a particular kairotic aspect of the actuality of the past: Kairos is the term that refers to the temporary circumstances involving the past in the present that afford opportunity to act archaeologically through excavation, survey, conservation, and mediation or representation in text and image, for example. Kairos typically might designate the moment of discovery, a kind of archaeological decisive moment (Shanks and Svabo, 2013).

Archaeological experiences extend far beyond the academic discipline. In working through remains and their dynamic of presence/absence, archaeology is a type of memory practice, recollecting, connecting pasts and presents (Olivier, 2012). Given the considerable importance of memory, as recollection, to senses of belonging and identity, the archaeological imagination is thereby implicated in the construction of collective, and also personal, identities. Archaeologists have long been involved in creating accounts of the origins and evolution of nation states, ethnic groups, and more (Diàz-Andreu, 2007; Kohl and Fawcett, 1995; Trigger, 1984), telling of how the French became the French, or the origins of indigenous Americans, for example. This association of the archaeological imagination with social and cultural change since the seventeenth century will be further sketched in section 3 of this chapter: A Genealogy of Archaeological Experiences.

In working with what remains, we are all archaeologists. Or potentially: Not everyone can engage in archaeological practices, working with what remains, with the same agency. So while academic archaeologists are few and subscribe to a narrow disciplinary discourse, they have access to resources and funding far beyond those of ordinary people. State agencies, such as ministries of culture, and international agencies such as UNESCO, have extraordinary capacity to manage engagements with the past. A small community may have very limited sovereignty over its past outside the remit of state agencies. This matter of agency cuts to the heart of the cultural and personal politics of memory, identity, and representation of hegemonic and marginalized interests.

Archaeological Experiences

Archaeological experiences share a distinctive set of features that, taken together, make them uniquely archaeological (González-Ruibal 2013). Here are three examples to illustrate this.

An Archaeological Landscape

The upper valley of the River Coquet just south of the English-Scottish border is a remarkable archaeological landscape, a palimpsest of traces. Circles, channels, and cups were carved several thousand years ago into outcrops of the fell sandstone in and around Lordenshaws, a prehistoric defended hilltop that was remodeled as a farmstead in Roman times, or so it would seem from the earthworks and style of houses. Looking north, more hill forts, some excavated by a local archaeological society, occur every few miles, and the line of a Roman road runs west-east, crossing the river at Holystone, a sacred spring, site of baptisms from the days of the early Christian kingdom of Northumbria: Saint Paulinus of York is said to have baptized 3,000 during Easter week 627. Clennell Street, a medieval drover's road, can be seen leaving the valley for Scotland; now deserted, it was renowned when the borders were embroiled from 1300 in three hundred years of raiding and warfare between England and Scotland.

The valley appears in Walter Scott's historical novel *Rob Roy* (1817) and its archaeology, history, folklore, and natural history were described by a local antiquarian, David "Dippie" Dixon, at the beginning of the twentieth century (Dixon and Dixon, 1903). He was sponsored by Lord Armstrong, a wealthy inventor and industrialist. Cragside, his grand house, little changed since he died, was donated to the state in lieu of taxes and is now cared for and managed by the National Trust, a nongovernment heritage agency and one of the largest landowners in the UK. It is a major tourist attraction.

An Archaeological Artwork

Anselm Kiefer is a contemporary artist who explores the archaeological imagination. *Die Ordnung der Engel* ("The Hierarchy of Angels") (1985–1987), for example, is a massive, wall-sized canvas of thick layers of paint, shellac, chalk, and cardboard. A large airplane propeller, worn, broken, made from sheets of lead, sits on a dark, blasted, eroded, and barren landscape, from which hang nine rocks. In a text of the fifth century entitled *The Celestial Hierarchy*, attributed to Dionysius the Areopagite, angels were divided into nine categories or choirs, grouped into three hierarchies, navigating the twisting space between heaven and earth. The propeller, spiraling through the air, the airpower of Germany's Third Reich, or any twentieth-century military might, now brought down to burned earth, references Dionysius's vision of heaven as a vast spiral, a topological folding in which time and space move in all directions. The rocks, as meteorites, as angels, bring heaven to earth, to a wasted utopia in this representation of a different kind of celestial hierarchy.

Since the 1970s Kiefer has dealt in the cultural landscapes of postwar Germany, with mixed-media works manifesting the transmutation of materials, through references to burning and devastation, death and decay, erosion and ruin, the metamorphosis of substance, lead into gold, in the celestial models of alchemy. In some of Kiefer's works grand architectural and public monuments – ancient, Egyptian, classical, industrial – signal imperial ambition, the nation state; other locales remind us of the architectures of the Holocaust. Several series of books, with pages of text often eroded and undecipherable, of faded anonymous photographs, of empty pages, burned books, seem to be a melancholic kind of literary antiquarianism. All his work embodies complex allegories that draw on Jewish mysticism, Christian symbolism, and folk legend; and, as in *Die Ordnung der Engel,* Kiefer displays his fascination with the alchemical systems of thought that obsessed so many great minds before the triumph of an enlightenment will to knowledge – worlds of faith, superstition, ritual, and hope.

An Archaeological Collection

The Revs Institute, in Naples, Florida, comprises a museum of the Collier Collection of vintage automobiles, restoration and maintenance workshops, a library and archive of photographs, documents and ephemera focused on automotive archaeology, the evolution of automobile design, the place of automobility in modern culture. The Institute attends car shows like the annual Pebble Beach Concours in California, where it runs its cars; it hosts conferences, welcomes visitors, enthusiasts, and volunteers into its mission to promote awareness of the significance of the automobile to the shape of recent history. Conscious of the long history of collection and connoisseurship (specialist knowledge of material culture), the Institute explicitly raises questions of how to conserve "active matter," complex artifacts like automobiles, how to represent their affective character and appeal, how to supply adequate context for their understanding. The Institute is at a leading edge of the emergence of a new sector in the heritage industry, as the hobby of collecting cars matures into a manifold of professionally managed institutions, developed academic apparatuses of research, conservation expertise, and a system of values applied to distinguish automobiles (historical worth, cultural significance, for example).

Archaeological experiences span matters of tradition and legacy, of heritage, of roots, memories and remains, of entropy and loss, the material transformation of

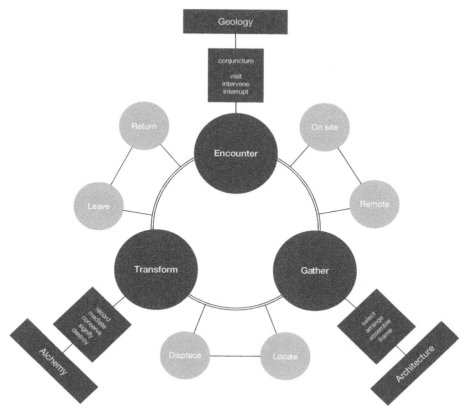

Figure 4.1 *The archaeological circuit.*

decay and ruin, connections between the past, its contemporary reception, and future prospect, the place of the past in a modern society, ethical and indeed political issues regarding respect for the past and the conservation of its remains, archives, agency, and the shape of history, but also judgment of responsibility in assessing what to do with what is left of the past. Such features of archaeological experience are summarized in Figure 4.1.

Encounter

An archaeological experience typically involves encounter, the actuality of the past, engaging remains. Visiting a ruin, handling an artifact, excavating a site: Encounters may be more or less passive and active, may occur at site, or remotely, mediated, for example, through a postcard, a video, a technical publication. Geology is suggested as a frame for the actuality of encounter, referring to processes of site formation, sedimentation of the past, faulting, polytemporal folding.

Here are some specific features of archaeological encounter.

Sense of place: Genius Loci. Engagement with place is often a complex affective experience. This can relate to the polytemporality of place, the topological folding of time inherent in our perception of site or place, as old things mingle with new, an ancient field boundary abuts a new housing development.

Place/event. This involves a fascination with the connection between place and event and is captured in the notion – "this happened here."

Forensic suspicion. An archaeological encounter often involves a particular forensic and suspicious attitude towards place in that we seek evidence that might help us piece together a story to make sense of the place and its remains.

Pattern recognition. A forensic connection between place and event involves a task of distinguishing and sorting evidence from irrelevancy, what is significant from what is garbage, signal from noise, figure from ground. Sometimes this is a kind of cryptography, seeking to decipher remains, figure out what might have happened at this place, in the ruins.

We may choose to leave the site or collection and move on, or we may return to revisit in a new encounter.

Gather

Collections are made, items sorted and classified, put in boxes, framed in different ways. The framing, containing and scaffolding involved in gathering suggests we think of architectural processes.

Sorting things out. Archaeological experiences are often concerned with classification, choosing what goes with what, in sorting finds, in making a significant collection, in deciding what matters over what is irrelevant (cf. pattern recognition).

Identity and recognition. What is it that remains and of what is it the remainder? Is this the way we were? There is a crucial component of identity and identification, questions of recognition in archaeological experiences. We might ask – Are these our ancestral traces? There may be involved an uncanny sense of a haunting past, recognizing something that was lost.

Mise-en-scène. We put things (back) in place, set things up. *Mise-en-scène* refers to the arrangement of things to fit the interest of viewing and inspection, a key component of archaeological work, whether it be a trench section cleaned for scrutiny, a reconstruction of a building, or an assemblage of artifacts in a museum. Consider also the idea of landscape as a way of looking and arranging things in place.

Transform

Items may be kept where they were found, at their origin, or displaced, moved elsewhere to a storeroom or museum, for example. Sites and artifacts fall into ruin and decay, are subject to entropy. Archaeological excavation actually destroys the past in its selection of what to preserve or conserve. Remains are transformed in conservation techniques that arrest decay, and also through their representation and description, through mediation, turning them into text and image, or into an exhibited display. The wide scope of processes of metamorphosis and transformation suggests we think of the prediscinary field of alchemy.

Here are some features of archaeological metamorphosis.

Entropy. Ruin and decay and other metamorphic processes – what becomes of what was. Sometimes archaeological experience involves an active negative entropy: People, for example, can maintain and care for things so that they resist decay.

Ruin and phantasm. Archaeology works through remains and vestiges; bits remaining of the past as well as traces or tracks, impacts, footprints, imprints. It deals in a past that is not so much over and done, no longer present, as both present in ruins and remains and uncannily non-absent phantasms, hauntingly present.

Representation. How can materiality – site, practice and thing – be documented?

Displacement. The shift from past to present, the circulation of text and image beyond the findspot, beyond the site from which the photo was taken, the re-location, citation, quotation of the image, document and account.

Mortality and our abject materiality. Archaeological objects can never be completely captured in a description. There is always more to be said. Just as there is always an uneasy sense of ultimate mortality in archaeological experiences, that we, too, will one day be the dust of decay.

Aftermath. What comes after the event? To document, repair, restore, conserve, replicate?

Alchemy and technology. The magic of past reappearing in the present. Archaeological experiences have long included a technical fascination with recovery and reconstruction, with the technology of reproduction/documentation. This may even verge on technophilia – a love of the technology of recovery and reconstruction for its own sake.

The archaeological imagination works in and through such archaeological experiences.

A Genealogy of Archaeological Experiences

We can track the evolution of an archaeological sensibility through three phases since the seventeenth century. Such a genealogical perspective offers insight into the scope of the archaeological imagination, into current and potential agendas.

One: to the middle of the nineteenth century. I have argued elsewhere (Shanks, 2012) that the contemporary archaeological imagination is a version of a longer-standing *antiquarian* imagination. Antiquarians were key representatives in the development of experimental and field sciences from the sixteenth through nineteenth centuries (Schnapp, 1996; Sweet, 2004). Their prediscinplinary, premodern outlook was focused through an interest in a description and account of regions, in exploring a sense of place (chorography), collection, survey, a systematic encounter with ancient monuments and artifacts in the sense of empirical experience, treated as the foundation for secure knowledge. Two shifts at the end of the eighteenth century opened up space for an expanded exploration of the antiquarian, the archaeological imagination. The first involved challenges to senses of history based upon religious teaching, biblical chronologies, and Graeco-Roman historiography. The establishment in geology of the deep antiquity of the earth meant that most of human history was not covered by religious and classical texts but appeared newly empty and only accessible through the archaeological remains of prehistory, or through analogy with contemporary simpler and traditional societies.

The second shift was the development of the nation states of Europe and their focus upon constructing senses of national identity in legitimating these new polities, especially given the undercutting of religious tradition, effected as well by geological sciences. Archaeological remains offered a powerfully affective means of articulating identity, especially in association with historical narratives (see the seminal work on the invention of tradition gathered by Hobsbawm and Ranger, 1983). Darwin's perfection of an evolutionary paradigm threw even more emphasis upon temporal process and mutability, key components of the archaeological imagination.

Both shifts brought an end to the experience of secure tradition, in the sense that the past is experienced no longer as a guarantor of contemporary order and security, in the sense that individuals are increasingly held responsible for their own security in a world experienced as more and more subject to risks to self, family, and community (after Giddens, 1991 and Beck, 1992; Harrison, 2013, Shanks and Witmore, 2010 for archaeology). And this includes experiences of risk to the past itself, with impulses to protect and conserve.

Two: to the 1970s. From the second half of the nineteenth century especially, archaeological fieldwork has delivered enormous amounts of material evidence, remains of past and present peoples, that was gathered and systematized in a growing number of museums. This can be taken as the second phase in the development of the archaeological imagination. The challenge has been how to handle this historical debris: a question of responsibility to gather, order, and comprehend, in order to protect a past that cannot be taken for granted. Museologists, from Thomsen and Worsaae in the 1840s onwards, adopted a solution that connected well-established but hitherto conjectural histories of humankind (evolutionary sequences from primitive stone age through bronze- and iron-using complex societies) with administrative technologies.

An architecture was built, a time-space systematics for locating and dating material remains. Databases and inventory systems mobilize schemes of historical development and change, and organize, literally, through bureaucracy: the drawers, cupboards, cases, and tables of museum galleries and storerooms offer ordered containers for the remains of the past, a frame within which can be located the stories, conceived fascinating, of the discovery of lost civilizations, the reconstruction of ruins, the rescue of forgotten times.

We can follow Foucault here in seeing how the archaeological imagination was translated into knowledge-building practices, often in the service of administration and government (Harrison, 2018). A state-sponsored inventory of archaeological sites and remains, embodied in archives and museums, authorized by legislation, can be used to establish their relative value and how significant they are in human history, and so inform urban planning – for example, by suggesting what is worth preserving, and what is disposable; archaeological and anthropological collections have offered the means of classifying people into social, cultural, class, ethnic, and gender categories that could again be used as the basis for bureaucratic administration.

So archaeological remains have come to be organized in a global time-space systematics of timelines and distribution maps rooted in universally applicable systems of classification and categorization and embodied in the fittings and architecture of museums. UNESCO, for example, has institutionalized since 1972 (after the Convention Concerning the Protection of the World's Cultural and Natural Heritage) a suite of universal human values applied to cultural property and experiences, manifested in the list of World Heritage Sites. These places are held to represent the pinnacle of human achievement and civilization: the human experience captured in what are often monumental ruins. And tourists flock to see them.

This system of ordering and managing remains has nevertheless, indeed necessarily, come with a growing awareness of threats both to the remains of the past and to the possibility of creating any kind of meaningful knowledge of what happened in history. Every nation state now has legislation to protect ancient sites and artifacts, under a not inappropriate perception that the remains of the past are at risk from urban expansion; looting, fueled by a market for antiquities; war; too many tourist visitors; and sheer neglect. Ruin and loss are key aspects of the contemporary archaeological imagination.

Here we experience a threat or risk to the past itself, as well as to the possibility of creating rich histories in the future. Systems for administering the remains of the past introduce a new dynamic between presence and absence, between the presence of the remains of the past gathered in museums, and the absence of past lives themselves, between archaeological finds and vast aeons of human history begging to be filled with what has been lost or is forever gone. In contrast to societies that experience the security of tradition, a past that serves as a reference for the present, the past in contemporary society is conspicuously not a secure given at all. It is subject to contemporary interests and concerns, infused with the interests of knowledge, a will to knowledge, and also with erosive threatening interests. We have become aware that we need to work on the past simply to have it with us; if nothing is done, it may well disappear, especially when some want to break it up and sell it off to collectors or to build a new shopping mall. The natural environment is not now seen as a given, but as a thoroughly socialized and institutionalized habitat, a hybrid under the threat of human-induced climate change, pollution and overdevelopment, raising concerns of culpability and blame, responsibility on the part of humanity to care and curate. So, too, the remains of the past are a matter of concern, demanding planning and foresight, another risk environment affecting whole populations' needs and desires for history, heritage, memories that offer orientation as much on the future as the past.

Three: archaeological experiences in contemporary "super modernity" (González-Ruibal 2018). The third phase in the evolution of archaeological experiences since the seventeenth century begins in the 1970s. The sense of risk and threat to the past is part of the massive growth in the heritage and tourist industries over the last fifty years, with archaeological and historical sites and museums the center of cultural tourism, by far the biggest fraction of this multibillion dollar economy (Harrison, 2013). The dual temporality of archaeological experiences, matters of fragile persistence and duration, and actuality, the connection between past and present, here stand in contrast to senses of tradition. The paradox or contradiction is that the control that systematic knowledge affords, for example, in managing the erosive impact of development or of the trade in illicit antiquities on the possibility of a past in the future, comes at the cost of a sense of *ontological* security. It is not just that the past (in the present) is threatened; senses of personal and community identity are threatened, when the continuity of the past is the source of such identity. The growth of systems of calculation, management, and control is intimately connected with growing political, social, cultural, and, indeed, ontological insecurity.

The security threat that individuals face today is, at base, a threat to their very identity because of the ways in which these abstract systems of knowledge work. When who you are, including your history, is no longer given by traditional institutions and cultures, but is constantly at risk, if who and what you are is subject to changing expert research, to loss of employment, to war, to displacement from where your family traditionally belonged, the challenge to individuals is to constantly construct and reconstruct their own identity. The growing absence of traditional sources of authority, a durable and persistent past, in answering who we are, accompanies a growing pressure upon the individual to take responsibility for self and decisions, to monitor their self, to self-reflect and to assert their own agency, exercise discipline in being who they are, project their identity in and through social media. This responsibility is, of course, full of risk. You might not get it right. You might not even be able to create a coherent and secure sense of self-identity, not least because you may not have the resources: The possibility of asserting individual agency is seriously circumscribed by horizontal and vertical divisions in society, by class, gender, and ethnicity.

The cultural politics of identity and representation, with regard to inclusivity and exclusivity, dominate political agendas, and accompany crises in governance, the legitimation of nation states. The universalizing perspective on the remains of the past, associated with globalizing developments especially since the 1970s, accompanies concerns to establish authentic and distinctive local and personal identities, a prominent feature of the contemporary archaeological imagination (González-Ruibal, 2018; Shanks, 1992).

Such concerns do also find early expression in works of the archaeological imagination associated with the first modern industrial nation states in the nineteenth century, which is why the evolution of an archaeological sensibility is well seen as a genealogy. The Gothic and historical fictions of the likes of Ann Radcliffe and Walter Scott, through to Edgar Allan Poe, for example, explored the ruin of great families, supernatural terror, haunting pasts, the shape of history, the fundamental uncertainty and mystery of personal experience and identity. The next section turns to this wide scope of reference of the archaeological imagination.

The Scope of the Archaeological Imagination

Where do we typically encounter works of the archaeological imagination? In museums, in collections and archives of all kinds, in the application by government and nongovernment agencies of legislation to protect the archaeological past, tangible and intangible, in the ways that memory reaches back to connect traces of the past with something in the present that has sparked the effort of recollection, in efforts to preserve and conserve the past, whether this be a site or an artifact, in reconstructions and reenactments of the past, whether this be in photorealistic virtual reality or in the performances of enthusiasts in medieval costume and character at a Renaissance Fair.

The archaeological imagination is much more pervasive culturally, offering, for example, a suite of powerful metaphors: digging deep through layers to find an answer, with the human mind being organized, according to Freud, a passionate collector of antiquities, in stratified layers, just like an archaeological site (Barker, 1996); fieldwork as forensic detection; ruin and decay as cultural decline and loss; the haunting remains of the past as a core to one's identity, personal and cultural.

Jennifer Wallace (Wallace, 2004) has sensitively explored treatments of excavation, death, and the sepulchral in an eclectic selection of literature and writing mainly from the English romantic tradition and the nineteenth century. Under her guiding topic of "digging," Wallace finds the following themes in the poems and literature she studied:

• The politics of depth, and authenticity
• Stones in the landscape, monumentality
• Bodies unearthed
• Excavation and desire
• Seeking epic origins (especially Troy)
• Digging into despair
• Holy ground
• Landfill and garbage.

David Lowenthal (Lowenthal, 2013) has gathered a miscellany of literary reflections on history, heritage, and the reception of the past. Here are his themes:

• Revisiting and reliving the past: dreams and nightmares
• Benefits and burdens of the past
• Ancients and Moderns: tradition and innovation
• The look of age: decay and wear
• Knowing the past: experience and belief, history and memory
• Changing the past: display, protection, reenactment, commemoration
• Creative anachronism: contemporary pasts.

Cornelius Holtorf (Holtorf, 2005, 2007) has analyzed the perception and representation of archaeological experiences in popular culture, and notes that the predominant image is that of the archaeologist as adventurer, as a maverick cowboy of science, exploring, often in exotic locations, digging, solving mysteries, and finding treasure.

These surveys of archaeological themes indicate the wide valencies in perceptions of archaeology and the archaeological (see also Andreassen et al., 2010; Bailey, 2018; Finn, 2001, 2004; Hauser, 2007; Neville and Villeneuve, 2002; Olsen and Pétusdottir, 2014; Russell and Cochrane, 2013; Tringham, 2019; Zielinski, 2006 and Parikka, 2012 on media archaeology). We might ask *why* and *how* these themes associated with archaeology interact and work together (after, for example, the exploration of archaeological modernisms and modernity in Schnapp et al., 2004). In keeping with an understanding of the archaeological imagination as a conjectural faculty or capacity to piece together remains into meaningful forms, an aspect of archaeological experiences of working with what remains, a dynamic model will be offered here. Holtorf outlines variations of a scenario associated with the character types of the archaeologist, with settings (from lab to the field), and possible lines of narrative or plot (exploration, discovery, mystery dispelled). Let us pursue such a conception of archaeology as performance (Pearson and Shanks, 2001).

Consider three key aspects of the working of the archaeological imagination: personae, scenographies, and dramaturgies. All imply a narratology, an investigation of narrative form associated with archaeological experiences. Together, these concepts can be used to map the scope of the archaeological imagination in relation to thematics offered by Lowenthal and Wallace and the qualities of archaeological experiences outlined in section 2: Archaeological Experiences.

Archaeological personae include the collector, the detective, the connoisseur, the curator, the restorer, the psychotherapist, and all manner of variations thereof (Holtorf, 2005; Shanks, 1992). All work with fragments. The settings, scenarios, stagings associated with an archaeological scenography, are those appropriate to such personae; the same applies to archaeological dramaturgy, the plot dynamics involved in working with remains. A narratology (Shanks 2012: Chapter 3) investigates the topics that run through the scenography and dramaturgy, exploring, for example, shifts between presence and absence, evidence and conjecture, place and event, destruction and restoration, surface and sedimentation, mimetic representation of remains and active intervention to conserve or restore, fakes and the genuine article, artworks and garbage, seeking meaningful signal in the chaos of the entropic noise of the garbage that is the overwhelming remnant of history.

So the archaeological imagination answers questions such as the following. Where do we encounter remains of the dead, of the past, and under what circumstances? In graveyards, in haunting memories. What are the affective qualities of such experiences of remains? Rot, melancholy, haunting, conjecture, hope? What might be done with such remains, and to what end? Restoration? Reincarnation? Reanimation? Destroy and forget? Glueing together a pot, or reviving the dead. Reenactment? Recounting a story that the past might live again? That we might lay to rest the ghosts of the past? Might we discover who we truly are in such work upon fragmentary traces? What if what is found is quite alien, so abject, distant and fragmentary that we can make no sense?

Such scenography and dramaturgy can encompass scientific fieldwork, crime-scene investigation, photography (persisting actualities), seeking pattern in huge piles of data, storytelling, building utopian or dystopian worlds, of fantasy, or in order to inspire hope and action. As so well illustrated by Lowenthal and Wallace, the archaeological imagination connects poems about bog bodies by Seamus Heaney with Piranesi's fantastical ruins, National Geographic's archaeological tourism with HBO's *Game of Thrones* or Tolkien's Middle Earth, M. R. James's tales of ghosts and the uncanny (Moshenska 2006, 2012) with the fictions of H. P. Lovecraft, in which deep and sometimes alien pasts return to haunt the present, where minds are lost in the encounter with horrific remains (the scope of the archaeological imagination even accounts for Lovecraft's racist anthropological types).

Personae, scenography and dramaturgy: These performative features offer a kind of repertoire of options for the conjectural leaps and associations applied in the working of the archaeological imagination, mobilized to make sense of fragmentary remains, of the persistence of the past and its actuality.

Agency, Creativity, and the Archaeological Imagination

What is on the agenda in contemporary debates about the archaeological imagination? What future for the archaeological imagination?

The growth of the heritage industry has accompanied the changing shape and forces of imperial reach, power, and international relations in a globalist world that is not so much postcolonial, with the breakup of the old European empires after World War II, as neocolonial, subject to the growing influence of corporate and financial power, the hegemony of the United States, the rise of East Asian economic strength and "soft power" since the 1990s. This is the context for what remains the key focus for concern in the academic and professional fields that service and offer commentary on and critique of the contemporary heritage industry, including its mobilization of the archaeological imagination. The debates are predominantly about representation and agency, and, in the academy have taken the form of ideological critiques of vested interests (Harrison, 2013 for an overview; Shanks and Tilley, 1987 for an inception of archaeological critique). Who gets to explore the archaeological imagination, with whose remains, and to what ends? Whose pasts are featured? In what narratives of origin (answering questions of where one belongs)? Advocacy for the rights of minority interests to exercise the archaeological imagination in their own way, constructing spiritual narratives of the past, for example, that run counter to "authorized heritage discourse" (Smith, 2006) comes from academics working in critical heritage studies (Harrison, 2013; see also, generally, the *International Journal of Heritage Studies*), and is openly embraced by professional associations such as the World Archaeology Congress and the European Association of Archaeologists.

The identification of the archaeological imagination presented in this chapter connects with four shifts of attention in contemporary archaeology and heritage.

Archaeological and heritage conservation long focused upon sites and artifacts, *material* remains. The orthodoxy is now that intangible cultural values and customs are equally deserving of respect and attention, especially since this was acknowledged by UNESCO (1972) and in the Council of Europe's Faro Convention on the Value of Cultural Heritage for Society (2005). This is a significant challenge to the separation of people and their artifacts that seems so fundamental to archaeology, when, in actuality, this is not the case (a posteriori, the argument of this chapter).

The temporal scope of archaeology has expanded markedly since the 1970s. In particular, beginning with "garbology," the study of garbage (Rathje and Murphy 1992), an archaeology of the contemporary past applies archaeological thinking and method, and thereby the archaeological imagination to all aspects of the contempor-ary world (Buchli, Lucas, and Cox, 2001; Graves-Brown et al., 2013; Harrison and Schofield, 2010; Holtorf and Piccini, 2009; Schnapp, 1997).

The academic fields of Material Culture Studies and Design Studies have, since the 1970s, addressed the character of things and likewise have come to explore the rich heterogeneous associations, the (im)materialities, the interplay of maker and material, agent and objecthood at the heart of making, creativity, and cultural experiences. Joining the challenge to the radical Cartesian separations of mind and matter, culture and nature, subjective experience and the natural physical world, person and artifact, present interests and the remains of the past, archae-ologists have asked how artifacts can have agency, proposing a fundamental symmetry between human and artifact, orienting their archaeological interests on objects themselves (in object-oriented ontologies). Some archaeologists are less interested now in seeking the maker *behind* the artifact, in determining the human intentions, values *expressed* or *represented* in and by an artifact (a representative selection: Hodder, 2012; Knappett and Malafouris, 2008; Malafouris, 2013; Olsen, 2010; Olsen et al., 2012; Shanks, 1998; Witmore, 2007).

Also since the 1970s the field of Science Studies has shifted from philosophy of scientific method to establishing an understanding of science and technology as situated practices; scientific knowledge, a social achievement rather than a discovery of the way things have always been; technology, a mobilization of resources around people's perceived needs and desires as much as an application of science in the service of innovation and to engineer solutions to problems (consider the works of Bruno Latour as exemplary of these trends).

These shifts are part of the current resurgence of support for a process-relational paradigm, associated with American Pragmatists, James, Dewey through to Rorty, A. N. Whitehead, Gilles Deleuze, Michel Serres, Isabelle Stengers. Two propositions or theses summarize this paradigm and inform the treatment of the archaeological imagination in this chapter.

First: Look to practices and processes, dynamic flows of energy and resources, if you wish to understand any phenomenon. This thesis challenges the primacy that is often given to representation, in the premise, for example, that scientific knowledge *represents* the essential qualities of timeless nature. Instead, focus upon iterative relations and engagements, capacities to produce, make, design. In this regard, the archaeological imagination concerns creative processes that constantly rearticulate pasts and presents, producing all manner of things without necessarily *representing* the past in a mimetic fashion.

Second: Always begin *in medias res*, with (human) experience conceived relationally as engagement. This thesis is post-phenomenological in that it questions the primacy of a self-contained human subject with an essential identity experiencing an external world, and treats identities as constantly reimagined, reperformed, recreated, distributed through ongoing experiences, engagements, relationships, assemblages of people, and all manner of things. This thesis directs attention to (cognitive) information processing, affective qualities of things and environments, inherent evaluative (emotional and embodied) dispositions towards things, bodily engagement in experiencing and making.

In this regard the archaeological imagination is about thinking, sensing, feeling, with remains.

The archaeological imagination is the only means of forging a bigger picture within which we have a chance of understanding the shape of history, and contemporary challenges of inequality, our cultural ecologies, sustainability, framing our understanding of where we've come from, where we are, and where we are heading (González-Ruibal, 2018). And more: The archaeological imagination is all about our shared creative agency. We are part of what we seek to understand, are part of the past, are part of the world in its constant creative remaking of itself.

References

Andreassen, E., Bjerck, H. B., and Olsen, B. (2010). *Persistent Memories: Pyramiden – A Soviet Mining Town in the High Arctic.* Trondheim, Norway: Tapir Academic Press.

Bailey, D. (2018). *Breaking the Surface: An Art/Archaeology of Prehistoric Architecture.* New York, NY: Oxford University Press.

Barker, S. (1996). *Excavations and Their Objects: Freud's Collection of Antiquity.* Albany, NY: State University of New York Press.

Beck, U. (1992). *Risk Society: Towards a New Modernity.* London, UK: Sage.

Buchli, V., Lucas, G., and Cox, M. (2001). *Archaeologies of the Contemporary Past.* London, UK; New York, NY: Routledge.

Díaz-Andreu García, M. (2007). *A World History of Nineteenth-Century Archaeology: Nationalism, Colonialism, and the Past.* Oxford, UK: Oxford University Press.

Dixon, D. D., and Dixon, J. T. (1903). *Upper Coquetdale: Its History, Traditions, Folklore and Scenery.* Newcastle-upon-Tyne, UK: Robert Redpath.

Finn, C. (2001). *Artifacts: An Archaeologist's Year in Silicon Valley.* Cambridge, MA: MIT Press.

  (2004). *Past Poetic: Archaeology in the Poetry of W. B. Yeats and Seamus Heaney.* London, UK: Duckworth.

Giddens, A. (1991). *Modernity and Self-Identity: Self and Society in the Late Modern Age.* Cambridge, UK: Blackwell Polity.

González-Ruibal, A. (ed.) (2013). *Reclaiming Archaeology: Beyond the Tropes of Modernity.* Abingdon, UK; New York, NY: Routledge.

  (2018). *An Archaeology of the Contemporary Era.* London, UK: Routledge.

Graves-Brown, P., Harrison, R., and Piccini, A. (eds.). (2013). *The Oxford Handbook of the Archaeology of the Contemporary World.* Oxford, UK: Oxford University Press.

Harrison, R. (2013). *Heritage: Critical Approaches.* Milton Park, Abingdon; New York, NY: Routledge.

  (2018). On Heritage Ontologies: Rethinking the Material Worlds of Heritage. *Anthropological Quarterly*, 91, 1365–1383.

Harrison, R., and Schofield, A. J. (2010). *After Modernity: Archaeological Approaches to the Contemporary Past.* Oxford, UK: Oxford University Press.

Hauser, K. (2007). *Shadow Sites: Photography, Archaeology, and the British Landscape, 1927–1955.* Oxford, UK: Oxford University Press.

Hobsbawm, E., and Ranger, T. (eds.) (1983). *The Invention of Tradition*. Cambridge, UK: Cambridge University Press.

Hodder, I. (1999). *The Archaeological Process: An Introduction*. Oxford, UK: Blackwell.

(2012). *Entangled: An Archaeology of the Relationships Between Humans and Things*. Malden, MA: Wiley-Blackwell.

Holtorf, C. (2005). *From Stonehenge to Las Vegas: Archaeology as Popular Culture*. Walnut Creek, CA: Altamira Press.

(2007). *Archaeology Is a Brand: The Meaning of Archaeology in Contemporary Popular Culture*. Walnut Creek, CA: Left Coast Press.

Holtorf, C., and Piccini, A. (eds.) (2009). *Contemporary Archaeologies: Excavating Now*. Frankfurt am Main, Germany: Peter Lang.

Knappett, C., and Malafouris, L. (2008). *Material Agency: Towards a Non-Anthropocentric Approach*. Berlin, Germany: Springer.

Kohl, P. L., and Fawcett, C. (1995). *Nationalism, Politics and the Practice of Archaeology*. Cambridge, UK: Cambridge University Press.

Lowenthal, D. (2013). *The Past Is a Foreign Country – Revisited*. Revised and updated edition. Cambridge, UK: Cambridge University Press.

Lucas, G. (2001). *Critical Approaches to Fieldwork: Contemporary and Historical Archaeological Practice*. London, UK; New York, NY: Routledge.

Malafouris, L. (2013). *How Things Shape the Mind: A Theory of Material Engagement*. Cambridge, MA: MIT Press.

Moshenska, G. (2006). The Archaeological Uncanny. *Public Archaeology*, 5(2), 91–96.

(2012). M. R. James and the Archaeological Uncanny. *Antiquity*, 86(334), 1192–1201.

Neville, B., and Villeneuve, J. (eds.) (2002). *Waste-Site Stories: The Recycling of Memory*. Albany, NY: State University of New York Press.

Olivier, L. (2012). *The Dark Abyss of Time: Archaeology and Memory*. Lanham, MD: AltaMira Press.

Olsen, B. (2010). *In Defense of Things: Archaeology and the Ontology of Objects*. Lanham, MD: AltaMira Press.

Olsen, B., and Petusdottir, Þ., (eds.) (2014). *Ruin Memories: Materiality, Aesthetics and the Archaeology of the Recent Past*. Abingdon, UK; New York, NY: Routledge.

Olsen, B., Shanks, M., Webmoor, T., and Witmore, C. (2012). *Archaeology: The Discipline of Things*. Berkeley, CA: University of California Press.

Parikka, J. (2012). *What is Media Archaeology?* Cambridge, UK: Polity Press.

Pearson, M., and Shanks, M. (2001). *Theatre/Archaeology*. London, UK: Routledge.

Preucel, R. W., and Mrozowski, S. A. (2010). *Contemporary Archaeology in Theory: The New Pragmatism*. 2nd edition. Oxford, UK: Wiley-Blackwell.

Rathje, W., Shanks, M., and Witmore, C. (eds.) (2012). *Archaeology in the Making: Conversations Through a Discipline*. London, UK: Routledge.

Rathje, W. L., and Murphy, C. (1992). *Rubbish!: The Archaeology of Garbage*. New York, NY: HarperCollins.

Renfrew, C., and Bahn, P. (2016). *Archaeology: Theories, Methods, and Practice*. 7th edition. London, UK: Thames and Hudson.

Russell, I., and Cochrane, A. (2013). *Art and Archaeology: Collaborations, Conversations, Criticisms*. New York, NY: Springer.

Schnapp, A. (1996). *The Discovery of the Past: The Origins of Archaeology*. Translated by I. Kinnes and G. Varndell. London, UK: British Museum Press.

Schnapp, A. (ed.) (1997). *Une archéologie du passé récent.* Paris, France: Maison des Sciences de l'Homme.

Schnapp, J., Shanks, M., and Tiews, M. (2004). Archaeologies of the Modern. *Modernism/Modernity, 11*(1), 1–16.

Shanks, M. (1992). *Experiencing the Past: On the Character of Archaeology.* London, UK: Routledge.

   (1998). The Life of an Artifact. *Fennoscandia Archaeologica, 15,* 15–42.

   (2012). *The Archaeological Imagination.* Walnut Creek, CA: Left Coast Press.

   (2013). *Let Me Tell You About Hadrian's Wall: Heritage, Performance, and Design.* Amsterdam, Netherlands: Reinwardt Academie.

Shanks, M., and McGuire, R. (1996). The Craft of Archaeology. *American Antiquity, 61,* 75–88.

Shanks, M., and Svabo, C. (2013). Archaeology and Photography: A Pragmatology. In A. González-Ruibal (ed.), *Reclaiming Archaeology: Beyond the Tropes of Modernity.* London, UK: Routledge.

Shanks, M., and Tilley, C. (1987). *Reconstructing Archaeology: Theory and Practice.* Cambridge, UK: Cambridge University Press.

Shanks, M., and Witmore, C. (2010). Memory Practices and the Archaeological Imagination in Risk Society: Design and Long-Term Community. In S. Koerner and I. Russell (eds.), *The Unquiet Past: Theoretical Perspectives on Archaeology and Cultural Heritage.* Farnham, UK: Ashgate.

Smith, L. (2006). *Uses of Heritage.* London, UK; New York, NY: Routledge.

Sweet, R. (2004). *Antiquaries: The Discovery of the Past in Eighteenth-Century Britain.* London, UK: Hambledon.

Thomas, J. (2004). *Archaeology and Modernity.* London, UK: Routledge.

Trigger, B. (1984). Alternative Archaeologies: Nationalist, Colonialist, Imperialist. *Man, 19,* 355–370.

Tringham, R. (2019). Giving Voices (Without Words) to Prehistoric People: Glimpses into an Archaeologist's Imagination. *European Journal of Archaeology, 22*(3), 338–353.

Wallace, J. (2004). *Digging the Dirt: The Archaeological Imagination.* London, UK: Duckworth.

Witmore, C. (2007). Symmetrical Archaeology: Excerpts of a Manifesto. *World Archaeology, 39*(4), 546–562.

Zielinski, S. (2006). *Deep Time of the Media: Toward an Archaeology of Hearing and Seeing by Technical Means.* Cambridge, MA: MIT Press.

5 Philosophical Perspectives on Imagination in the Western Tradition

Amy Kind

Philosophers in the Western world have long theorized about imagination – about what it is and how it is to be distinguished from related mental states. But such philosophers have also long relied upon imagination in their theorizing about other matters – that is, imagination itself has played an important methodological role for philosophers. In this chapter, I focus on these two topics in an effort to provide an introduction to, and an overview of, philosophical perspectives on imagination within the Western tradition. Moreover, as one can only cover so much in an essay of this sort, my focus here is almost solely on the Western *analytic* tradition.[1]

Philosophical Theorizing About Imagination

Consider Sophie, an eight-year-old girl who is visiting Paris for the first time, and who has just taken the lift to the summit of the Eiffel Tower. She is both excited and a little bit scared. She believes, correctly, that she is well over 1,000ft (300m) above the ground. She believes, incorrectly, that she is atop the tallest building in the world. As she enjoys the warmth of the sun on her skin and hears the distant sounds of the vehicular traffic below, she looks out at the city and takes in the magnificent view. Catching sight of various landmarks such as the Arc de Triomphe and the Grand Palais, she remembers her visits there earlier in the week. Finally, caught up in the sheer magic of the moment, she imagines a friendly dragon appearing suddenly alongside the observation deck, and she then imagines that the dragon invites her to climb aboard its back and gently flies her all the way down to the ground.

While there's much to think about philosophically when considering all of the different aspects of this brief snapshot of Sophie's mental life, for our purposes what's most important are the similarities and differences between the last mental activity mentioned – her imaginative exercises – and all that's been described previously. We'll here focus primarily on two specific comparisons: first, between imagination and belief and next, between imagination and perception.

---

1 Philosophical perspectives on imagination from the Eastern tradition are covered in Chapters 6 and 30. While there are various other aspects to philosophical investigations into imagination in the Western tradition that will unfortunately be left out here, many of these will be covered in other chapters of this handbook. To give just one example, though I don't here discuss the role that imagination has played in philosophical aesthetics, this is taken up in Chapter 34.

Imagination and Belief

Consider the proposition *the gorillas have escaped from the Los Angeles zoo*. There are many different attitudes that one might take towards this proposition. One might believe that the gorillas have escaped from the Los Angeles zoo, desire that the gorillas have escaped from the Los Angeles zoo, fear that the gorillas have escaped from the Los Angeles zoo, and so on. In addition to these other attitudes, however, one might also imagine that the gorillas have escaped from the Los Angeles zoo. Along with mental states like belief, desire, and fear, philosophers thus generally treat imagination as a *propositional attitude*.

In discussions of propositional attitudes, philosophers often characterize them in terms of their *direction-of-fit*. Beliefs aim at the truth. In forming our beliefs, we take ourselves to be representing the world correctly. That's not to say that all of our beliefs are true, of course. Recall that Sophie believes falsely that the Eiffel Tower is the tallest building in the world. But when we discover that one of our beliefs is false, we generally think that it should be discarded – that is, we think that we should change our minds to conform to the truth. Beliefs are thus said to have *mind-to-world* direction of fit. Desires, on the other hand, do not aim at the truth. In forming our desires, we do not take ourselves to be representing the world correctly. Rather, we are representing the world as we want it to be. The discovery that some desired state of affairs is not actually the case thus does not suggest that the desire should be discarded. Unlike with beliefs, where we aim to conform our mind to the world, with desires, we aim to conform the world to our mind. Desires are thus said to have *world-to-mind* direction of fit.

What, then, about imagination? Does imagination have mind-to-world or world-to-mind direction of fit? At first glance, it doesn't seem to fit well into either category.[2] Unlike beliefs, imaginings need not aim to represent the world as we take it to be, nor are they appropriately described as true or false. But they also need not aim to represent the world as we want it to be. On further thought, however, we can see that there is a way in which imaginings might be said to be belief-like with respect to direction-of-fit.[3] In line with a distinction drawn by Shah and Velleman (2005), we might distinguish between attitudes that treat their contents as *true* and attitudes that treat their contents as something that is *to be made true*. Imaginings, like beliefs and unlike desires, treat their contents as true – not actually true, of course, but true for the purposes of the relevant imaginative exercise. In the context of her imaginings while atop the Eiffel Tower, for example, Sophie regards it as true that the friendly dragon has invited her to climb aboard his back. In this way, she aims to conform her imagining to the (imaginary) world she is representing rather than aiming to have that world conform to the representational states in her mind.

---

2 Indeed, some philosophers have denied that imagination has a direction of fit (e.g. Humberstone, 1992).

3 Recently, some philosophers have argued that there is also a desire-like kind of propositional imagining (Currie and Ravenscroft, 2002; Doggett and Egan, 2007). According to proponents of this view, just as we can make believe that something is the case, we can also make desire that something is the case. Whether there really is such a phenomenon as desire-like imagining has been the subject of considerable debate. For an overview, see Kind (2016).

But while imagination shares with belief its direction of fit, our discussion thus far has already suggested an important way in which imagination differs from belief, namely, with respect to its aim. As we have noted, belief aims at truth. Indeed, this is generally taken to be constitutive of belief, i.e. part of its very nature. Imagining, in contrast, need not aim at truth. That's not to say that imaginings can never be true, nor is it to say that they can never be aimed at the truth. Not every imagining is as fanciful as Sophie's. The zookeeper searching for the escaped gorillas may well try to imagine where they have gone, and in doing so, she will be aiming to get things right. Likewise for the interior decorator who employs her imagination in an effort to determine what configuration of furniture will work best for the space she is designing or the guidance counselor who employs her imagination in an effort to discern what the troubled teenager in her office is feeling. These kinds of imaginative exercises employ what Kind and Kung (2016) call the *instructive use* of imagination. Yet even though instructive uses of imagination show us that imagination *can* aim at truth, it is differentiated from belief by the fact that it does not do so by nature.

Is there something that imagining, by its nature, does aim at? One natural suggestion invokes possibility. In aiming at truth, belief aims at what's actually true, i.e. what's true in the actual world. Analogous to this, we might take imagination to aim at what's possibly true, i.e. what's true in some possible world. This connection between imagination and possibility has led many philosophers to think it can play an important role in *modal epistemology*, that it can provide us with epistemic access to possibility the way that perception provides us with epistemic access to actuality. We return to this issue below when we turn to the philosophical employment of imagination.

The difference in aims between imagination and belief connects to another important way that they differ, namely, with respect to their relation to action. Someone who believes that it's raining outside will typically put on a raincoat or take an umbrella when they leave the house. In contrast, someone who imagines that it's raining outside will not typically take actions of these sorts. That's not to say that imagining is entirely disconnected from action. In the context of pretense, for example, someone who imagines that it's raining may well go get an umbrella. But their imagining may also lead to a different kind of action – that of pretending that they're holding an umbrella – and this is not the kind of action that would likely be taken by someone who believes that it's raining. The fact that imagination and belief have different relations to action is often captured by saying that imagination and belief have different *functional profiles*, or that they play different *functional roles* (e.g. Nichols, 2004).

The functional profiles of imagination and belief are not entirely different, however. Here we will take note of just two important similarities. First, our emotional reactions to events that we imagine often mirror our emotional reactions to events that we believe have actually occurred. Imagining a scary scenario can prompt fear, and imagining a tragic scenario can prompt sadness. Perhaps the most obvious cases come from consideration of our emotional responses to fiction, as when a reader cries upon reading the death scene of a beloved character. Second, the inferential profile of imagination often mirrors the inferential profile of belief.[4] Someone who believes they are playing tennis against Serena Williams will likely infer that the ball will be coming at them with a great degree of force; someone who imagines they are playing tennis against Serena Williams will likely also imaginatively infer that the ball will be coming at them with a great degree of force. As this point also shows, there are generally important interactions between our beliefs and our imaginings. What we believe can affect what we imagine. For example, it's because I believe that Serena Williams has a powerful shot that, when I imagine playing tennis against her I also imagine that the ball will be coming at me with a great degree of force. Likewise, what we imagine can affect what we believe. When two tennis players who have never faced each other before are about to play in the final of the Wimbledon Tennis Championships, I might engage in various imaginative exercises in an effort to determine who will win.

Finally, it's worth noting that several philosophers have recently claimed that the philosophical orthodoxy that treats belief and imagination as two distinct attitudes is mistaken. Rather, belief and imagination should be seen as the two different ends of a continuum, and there can be intermediate states that are belief-imagination hybrids. Though this view has several prominent proponents (Currie and Jureidini, 2004; Egan, 2008; Schellenberg, 2013), it is at present still a minority position.

Imagination and Perception

In discussing the contrast between belief and imagination, we focused on propositional imagining. Not all imaginings seem propositional in nature, however. In addition to imagining that the gorillas have escaped from the zoo, one might also simply imagine the gorillas themselves. This kind of imagining is often referred to as *objectual imagining.*

When characterizing objectual imagining, philosophers often take it to involve the production of mental imagery. "Imagery" is here meant in an expanded sense so as to capture not only visual imagery but also auditory imagery, tactile imagery, and so on. One locus of disagreement in contemporary philosophical discussions of imagination concerns the precise relationship between imagination and mental imagery. Most philosophers agree that the production of mental imagery is insufficient for some mental exercise to be an exercise of imagination, since mental imagery can also be involved in memory. More controversial is the necessity claim: While some philosophers have claimed that mental imagery is essential to imagination (e.g. Brann, 1991: 5; Kind, 2001), others claim that imagination can occur without mental imagery (e.g. Stock, 2017 ; van Leeuwen, 2013; Walton, 1990). Van Leeuwen, for example, argues:

> When I imagine, on reading *Lord of the Rings*, that elves can live forever, I'm fictionally imagining a proposition that I couldn't imagine using mental imagery. It would take too long. (van Leeuwen, 2013: 222)

4 For discussion supporting this claim, see Currie and Ravenscroft (2002: 12–13), and Weinberg and Meskin (2006: 178–180). In a recent discussion of imagination, Kathleen Stock argued that there are some situations – most notably with respect to our engagement with fiction – in which imagination does not share the inferential profile of belief; see Stock (2017: 175–182).

This kind of example can be generalized. Philosophers generally assume that we engage with works of fiction by imagining the text. Relying on this assumption, Stock notes that "some fictional passages describe wholly abstract and nonexperienceable states of affairs, which therefore could not be sensorily or phenomenally imagined" (Stock, 2017: 25). In support of this claim, she points specifically to the abstract descriptions of a mathematical system laid out by Borges in his short story, "Tlön, Uqbar, Orbis Tertius," but there are presumably many similar examples.

Of course, there are various responses that can be made by the defender of the necessity claim (see e.g. Kind, 2001), and we can't hope here to be able to adjudicate the debate. Note, however, that all of these purported examples of imageless imagination concern propositional imaginings. Thus, while the claim that imagination is always imagistic in nature is highly controversial, the claim that objectual imagination is always imagistic in nature is considerably less so.[5] For this reason, it's perhaps unsurprising that objectual imagining is often referred to as *imagistic* or *sensory imagination.*

Just as propositional imagining can be usefully understood in comparison with belief, objectual imagination can be usefully understood in comparison with perception. Objectual imaginings are often characterized in terms of the various sensory modalities, in that we speak of visual imagination, auditory imagination, and so on. These modifiers point to similarities between objectual imagination and perception, most notably, to phenomenological similarities. The experience of visually imagining a gorilla feels something like the experience of seeing a gorilla – and if you do a particularly good job of imagining the gorilla, it may seem a lot like the experience of seeing a gorilla. The same point holds true for the other sensory modalities. Auditorily imagining the gorilla's grunts resembles the experience of hearing the gorilla's grunts.

The phenomenological similarity is further highlighted by the fact that imagination can be mistaken for perception. Someone who is especially caught up in an imaginative episode might take themselves to be seeing what they are really imagining. Interestingly, there is some evidence that perception can be mistaken for imagination as well. In a famous experiment from the early twentieth century, subjects who were seeing a very faint image of a banana projected on a screen took themselves to be imagining the banana rather than perceiving it (Perky, 1910; for further discussion and examples, see Currie and Ravenscroft, 2002: 72–73).

These sorts of cases seem rare, however. Despite the phenomenological similarities between imagination and perception, we can almost always tell whether we are engaged in an instance of perceiving or imagining – and, indeed, we can do so both effortlessly and spontaneously. To convince us of this point, Sartre suggests that we each consult our own inner experience. As he reports of his own inner experience, "I am seated, writing, and see the things around me. Suddenly I form an image of my friend Peter. All the theories in the world are helpless against the fact that I *knew*, the

---

5 That's not to say that this claim about objectual imagination is universally accepted. For example, Alan White has suggested that one can "as easily imagine a difficulty or an objection as . . . an elephant or a bus. But only for the latter would the presence of imagery be at all plausible" (White, 1990: 88–89).

very instant of the appearance of the image, that it was an image" (Sartre, 1936/1962: 96). For Sartre, this is best explained by the fact that objects we perceive seem to have a sense of presence that is lacked by objects that we imagine; on his view, the object of imagining is presented to us as absent. (See e.g. Sartre, 1940/2010: 14.) Hume offers a different sort of explanation for how we can so easily distinguish our imaginings from our perceptions. In his view, sensory impressions typically seem to have a "degree of force and vivacity" that imaginings lack (Hume, 1739/1985).[6] Hume also invoked considerations of force and vivacity to characterize the phenomenological difference between imagination and memory.

In addition to these phenomenological differences between imagination and perception, there is at least one other important dimension of difference between them – namely, their relation to the will. Given that there are no gorillas in my immediate vicinity, I cannot make myself see an actual gorilla right now, no matter how hard I try. Granted, there are things I can do to facilitate my seeing an actual gorilla. I can go to the zoo or to an animal sanctuary, or I can take a trip to Uganda or somewhere else that gorillas exist in the wild. But I cannot come to see a gorilla simply by an act of will. Matters are different with respect to imagination. Generally speaking, all I need to do to imagine a gorilla is to decide to do so. As this suggests, imagination is under an agent's control in a way that perception is not.

To say this, however, is not to imply that an agent has complete and unconditional control over her imaginings. As Christopher Peacocke has noted, "it is a common experience for visual or auditory imaginings to come to a thinker wholly unbidden – they may even interrupt his thinking" (Peacocke, 1985: 26). Someone who is bored at work might find herself imagining the beautiful beaches of Hawaii, while someone who is hungry might find herself imagining her favorite chocolate soufflé. Moreover, not only might these imaginings arise without any conscious effort on the imaginer's part, but it might even be the case that the imaginer is powerless to stop imagining them once they have started:

> Often after seeing a particularly gruesome murder scene in a horror movie, I keep imagining the murder again and again. In such a case, I usually want the imagining to stop, I might even will myself to stop it, but I typically find myself quite powerless to stop the imagining. Analogously, after awakening to a catchy tune on the radio, the tune often runs through my head for quite awhile; I might even be unable to keep from imagining it, in this way, all day long. (Kind, 2001: 91).

Having traced these similarities and differences between imagination and perception, I'll close this section by noting one more consideration about these two mental activities that has been important philosophically. In discussing the relation between belief and imagining, we noted that there are important interactions between them; what we believe can affect what we imagine, and what we imagine can affect what we believe. Perhaps unsurprisingly, there are also important interactions between imagination and perception. Writing in the

---

6 For concerns about the use of the notion of vivacity or vividness in this context, see Kind, 2017. For additional discussions of the phenomenology of imagining, and how that phenomenology compares to and contrasts with perception, see Kind (forthcoming), McGinn (2004), and Kriegel (2015).

nineteenth century, Immanuel Kant saw imagination as responsible for synthesizing and transforming raw perceptual inputs into unified and continuous wholes. Within his system, then, imagination is fundamentally involved in every perceptual experience; as he put it, "imagination is a necessary ingredient of perception" (Kant, 1787/1998; for discussion see Strawson, 1970). Working within a broadly Kantian spirit, Church has recently argued that imagination makes possible our experience of objectivity: it's because we actively imagine alternative perspectives of the objects we're perceiving that we experience them as objective entities (Church, 2010: 648–649). Finally, imagination has been invoked to explain cases of *amodal completion*. When someone sees a cat standing on the other side of the picket fence, the cat is visually experienced as a continuous, complete entity even though various parts of its body are hidden by the fence posts. To explain how we are able to have a unified experience in these sorts of cases, philosophers such as Nanay (2010) have claimed that we represent the occluded parts by way of imagination.

Philosophical Employment of Imagination

Over the past several decades, imagination has been called upon to do explanatory work in a great variety of philosophical contexts. To name just a few of these contexts: Imagination has been thought to play a role in fiction and our engagement with it (Currie, 1990; Stock, 2017; Walton, 1990), counterfactual reasoning (Byrne, 2005), our ability to predict and explain the behavior of others (Goldman, 2006), scientific discovery (Polanyi, 1966/2009), scientific modeling (Toon, 2012), and so on. In addition to relying on the notion of imagination in these various contexts, however, philosophers have themselves put their imaginative capacities to use in their own philosophical theorizing. In this section, we discuss the key role that imagination has long played – and continues to play – in the development of philosophical theories and the arguments for such theories.

To start, we need to return to an issue we touched upon briefly above: the connection between imagination and possibility. As Hume famously wrote in his *Treatise on Human Nature*, "Tis an establish'd maxim in metaphysics, *that whatever the mind clearly conceives includes the idea of possible existence,* or in other words, *that nothing we imagine is absolutely impossible*" (1739/1985: 32). Of course, many of the scenarios that we imagine are *physically* impossible. We can imagine a talking mirror, or a flying broomstick, or a goose who lays golden eggs – all of which are impossible given the scientific laws that govern our world. But, so Hume's thought goes, even if these scenarios are physically impossible, the fact that they are imaginable shows that they are logically possible. Though they may violate the laws of physics, if they are imaginable, then they must not violate the laws of logic.

This principle, that whatever can be imagined is possible, is often referred to by Hume scholars as his *conceivability principle*, but given Hume's identification of conceiving and imagining, one might just as reasonably think of it as his *imaginability principle* – and that's how I'll refer to it here.[7] In the course of the *Treatise*, Hume goes on to use his imaginability principle to justify many of the conclusions that he draws. To give just one example, in arguing against the proposition *whatever has a beginning has also a cause of existence*, Hume relies on the fact that the idea of a cause and the idea of a beginning of existence are separable in imagination. The fact that they can be separated in imagination shows that "the actual separation of these objects is so far possible, that it implies no contradiction nor absurdity" (1739/1985: 80). He thus concludes that the original proposition must be false.

The underlying form of Hume's argument looks something like this:

1. Scenario S is imaginable.
2. If a scenario is imaginable then it is possible. (The imaginability principle.)
3. Therefore, scenario S is possible.
4. But if scenario S is possible, then theory T is false.
5. Therefore, theory T is false.

Arguments with this general structure have been widely used by philosophers across a variety of different subfields – from philosophy of mind to metaphysics to ethics. In the remainder of this section, we will explore the philosophical reliance on imagination by looking at specific examples of this kind of argumentation in more detail. First, we will survey a few common exemplars of this basic form of argument drawn from debates about the nature of mind. We will then consider the plausibility of the imaginability principle in more detail. In doing so, we will also discuss the relationship between imagining and conceiving.

Imaginability Arguments

At the heart of philosophy of mind lies a debate between two different theories of the nature of mind – physicalism, a view that sees mental processes as reducible to physical processes, and dualism, a view that sees mental processes as something over and above the physical. According to the dualists, even if we see a perfect correlation between physical processes and mental processes in actuality, that would not establish the truth of physicalism. Take some mental process M that is perfectly correlated with some physical process P. Even the existence of the perfect correlation does not show that it's *impossible* for M to exist without P. Though all actual occurrences of M are correlated with P, it may still be possible for M to exist in absence of P – or even to exist in the absence of any physical process whatsoever. This possibility, claims the dualist, is incompatible with physicalism (e.g. Gertler, 2007). But how do we know that this is really a possibility that needs to be ruled out? Here the dualists employ their imagination – and ask that we all employ our imagination – via the consideration of various hypothetical scenarios known as *thought experiments*.

---

7 That Hume equates conceiving and imagining was evident in the quoted passage above. As we will see below, not all philosophers treat these two mental activities as equivalent.

Several different thought experiments have been put forward in the literature. Most of these scenarios owe in some way to the insights of seventeenth-century French philosopher Descartes. Often considered to be the father of dualism, Descartes famously proposed in his *Meditations* that we could conceive of the mind existing without the body. In this Cartesian spirit, Brie Gertler has recently proposed a thought experiment concerning disembodiment (Gertler, 2007). Gertler asks her readers to pinch themselves, consider the pain that results, and then consider whether they can imagine themselves experiencing *that very pain* while disembodied. If we can imagine experiencing that very pain in the absence of any brain states, indeed any physical states altogether, then in line with Hume's imaginability principle, it would be possible for that very pain to exist in the absence of any physical states. Hence, physicalism would be false.

A different dualist thought experiment that has recently occupied considerable philosophical attention concerns zombies, although not the type that populate Hollywood movies! In his book *The Conscious Mind*, David Chalmers introduces the notion of a philosophical zombie – a being who is functionally, behaviorally, and even microphysically identical to its human "twin" but who is entirely lacking in phenomenally conscious states. To use a locution made famous by Thomas Nagel (Nagel, 1974), there is *nothing that it is like* to be a zombie. Though the zombie can think to itself, "That's a beautiful yellow tulip" or "This brownie has a rich chocolatey flavor," the zombie does not have a phenomenal experience of yellowness or chocolateness. But given that the zombie and its human twin are microphysically identical, and given that the human has phenomenally conscious states, those states must be something over and above the physical. Thus, if zombies are possible, then it looks like physicalism is false. In defense of the claim that zombies are indeed possible (and here it may be helpful to remember that the relevant sense of possibility is *logical possibility*), dualists point to the fact that they can be coherently imagined.

Another influential thought experiment offered to support dualism concerns a hypothetical color scientist named Mary and has hence become known as *the Mary case.* As described by Frank Jackson, who first proposed the thought experiment in a paper published in 1982, Mary is a scientist who has spent her entire life in a black and white room and who has never had color sensations of any sort. While inside the room, by way of textbooks and lectures, and so on, Mary learns absolutely everything that color science has to teach – and we are supposed to imagine that Mary lives at some point in the future when color science has been completed. Now imagine that one day Mary is released from her black and white room and is shown a ripe tomato. Upon having the experience of a red sensation for the first time, what happens? In imagining this case, most people have the strong intuition that Mary learns something new. Though she knew all the physical facts about color while she was in the room, she didn't know what seeing red was like. The imaginability, and hence possibility, of this scenario is usually taken to show that the physicalist story about color leaves something out, i.e. it is taken to show that physicalism is false (Jackson, 1982).

Outside of philosophy of mind, imaginability arguments have been used to support claims about the nature of personal identity (see e.g. Parfit, 1984), the nature of knowledge (see e.g. Gettier, 1963), the moral permissibility of abortion (see e.g. Thomson, 1971), and the configuration of a just society (see e.g. Rawls, 1971), to give just a few examples among many. Though in some of these contexts the reliance on claims about imaginability is made explicit, in other cases the role of imagination has not always been fully fleshed out.

The Imaginability Principle

Although imaginability arguments are common in philosophical contexts, there is considerable disagreement about their efficacy. Criticisms of such arguments tend to take two different (but related) lines of attack. On the first line, worries are raised about whether the scenario proposed is really imaginable. On the second line, worries are raised about whether the imaginability of a given scenario really entitles us to draw conclusions about possibility.[8]

To see one example of a worry of the first sort, consider the response the staunchly physicalist philosopher Daniel Dennett has given to the Mary case. In his view, those who think that Mary will learn something new when she leaves her black and white room have not really imagined what they were instructed to imagine. Indeed, if one really were to imagine that Mary knew *all* the physical facts about color before leaving the room – and not just lots and lots of them – one would be led to see her as having a very different reaction to her encounter with the ripe tomato – namely, she would have been able to predict perfectly in advance what her experience would be like (Dennett, 1991: 398–400).

This sort of worry presents the proponent of the imaginability principle with a further problem. The imaginability principle is silent about what conclusion should be drawn in cases where a scenario is unimaginable. The principle under consideration claims only that imaginability implies possibility, and not that unimaginability implies impossibility. But when we have disputes about whether a given scenario is imaginable or not, how are such disputes to be settled? For example, if one person claims to be able to imagine a philosophical zombie and another person claims not to be able to do so, we need some guidance as to how the dispute should be settled. The imaginability principle itself has nothing to say on this score.

In addressing this problem, the proponent of the imaginability principle might first note that not everyone is equally skilled with respect to their imaginative capacities. We see this very clearly in cases of scientific discovery. It's precisely because a scientist like Einstein was able to imagine scenarios that were previously considered unimaginable that he was able to advance our understanding of spacetime. It thus seems that we should judge whether a scenario is imaginable on the basis of the

---

8 Additionally, worries are also sometimes raised about whether the possibility of a given scenario really entitles us to the further conclusions that are drawn. For example, in the debate about zombies, some opponents of Chalmers's argument dispute whether the logical possibility of zombies is really inconsistent with physicalism. As these worries do not relate directly to imagination, we will not consider them here.

best imaginers – perhaps even ideal imaginers – rather than on the basis of ordinary, potentially flawed imaginers. The problem is that this simply pushes the issue back a step, for now we are faced with the task of determining who counts as an ideal imaginer.

However ideal imagination is specified, it must take into account not only one's imaginative capabilities, but also how well placed one is to engage in an imagining concerning a given subject. Someone might be an excellent imaginer, yet because of their ignorance of certain facts, they might make imaginative mistakes. To use an example drawn from Patricia Churchland, someone who does not know much about thermodynamics might think they can imagine "a possible world where gases do not get hot, even though their constituent molecules are moving at high velocity" (Churchland, 1998: 39). Given that temperature is identical to mean molecular kinetic energy, however, it seems that something must have gone awry in the imaginative process. To get around this problem, the proponent of the imaginability principle might try to restrict the relevant imaginings to those that are clear, where clarity requires one to have adequate grasp of the concepts being employed in the imagining. But of course, this, too, might seem just to push the issue back a step, for we are now faced with the task of determining what counts as having an adequate grasp of the relevant concepts.

Returning to Churchland's example, however, note that one could draw a different moral from the apparent imaginability of the non-heated gases scenario. Instead of concluding that something has gone wrong with the imaginative process, one might grant that such a scenario is imaginable, even clearly, and even by an ideal imaginer, and instead deny that we should draw any conclusions about possibility from claims about what's imaginable. Such a move constitutes the second of the two lines of attack against the imaginability principle that we distinguished at the start of this section.

In supporting this second line of attack, one might point to relatively uncontroversial cases of imagining the impossible. Consider the famous picture *Ascending and Descending* by M. C. Escher.[9] In this drawing, Escher depicts a group of monk-like figures on a circular staircase. For every ascending monk, it appears that if he continues climbing the staircase, he will return to his starting point without ever having to descend (and likewise, every descending monk can apparently return to his starting point without ever having to ascend). It seems uncontroversial that one cannot eternally climb a staircase without making upward progress, i.e. that such a staircase is impossible. But it also seems uncontroversial that one can imagine such a staircase – after all, one can simply imagine the staircase as depicted in the Escher drawing. In this kind of case, there don't seem to be any grounds to suggest that the imagining is not sufficiently clear, or that it would only be produced by someone whose imagination is not fully ideal. The Escher-imagining thus suggests that we can imagine the impossible and, as a result, that the imaginability principle must be false – or at least, it must be significantly restricted.[10]

---

9 Many of Escher's drawings are reproduced in Hofstadter (1979). In addition to *Ascending and Descending* (p. 12), see also *Relativity* (p. 98) and *Drawing Hands* (p. 690). Tidman (1994) also discusses Escher drawings to make a similar point.

10 For a discussion of how we might restrict the imaginability principle to only a subclass of imaginings, see Kung (2010).

Cases like this have suggested to some philosophers that we should look to conceiving, rather than imagining, as the mental capacity that can provide us with a guide to possibility (e.g. Tidman, 1994). Although Hume equated imagining and conceiving, as we saw above, many other philosophers treat them as distinct mental activities. Descartes, for example, differentiated them on the grounds that imagination is an imagistic capacity and conception is an activity of pure understanding. More recently, Balcerak Jackson (Jackson, 2016) has argued that imagination and conception are different kinds of perspective taking. While imagining takes up the perspective of the subject as the subject of phenomenal experiences, conceiving takes up the perspective of the subject as the subject of rational belief.

The question of whether conceivability entails possibility is beyond the scope of this essay.[11] But it's worth noting that many of the problems that arise for the imaginability principle will rearise for the conceivability principle. For example, just as ignorance may affect what we can seem to imagine, so, too, will it affect what we can seem to conceive. In response to Descartes' reliance on conceivability in his arguments for dualism, Arnauld famously argued in the Fourth Set of Objections printed with the *Meditations* that someone who is ignorant about geometry may take themselves to be able to imagine a right-angled triangle for which the Pythagorean theorem does not hold (Descartes 1641/1986: 109). In response, Descartes attempted to restrict the relevant conceivings to those that are "clear and distinct" (Descartes 1641/1986: 110–111), but here again, there is a difficulty assessing how this criterion is meant to be employed.

Despite the worries raised about the imaginability principle, philosophers continue to rely on imagination in their philosophical theorizing, and it is hard to see how it could be entirely excised from philosophical methodology. Given that philosophical theories need to address the merely possible along with the actual, and given that we cannot directly perceive possibilities, imagination seems to be an indispensable part of theoretical development and justification. Perhaps for this reason, many philosophers discussing the imaginability principle take it to be only a *fallible* or *prima facie* guide to imagination (see e.g. Balcerak Jackson, 2016). Here it may be useful to compare imagination to visual perception. There are some cases in which visual perception is unreliable, e.g. when the objects being perceived are very small or very far away, when it is dark, when the perceiver is under the influence of hallucinogenic drugs, and so on. That perception is in this way fallible, however, does not prevent us from relying on it. Though it may occasionally lead us astray, visual perception is still a very good guide to the nature of reality. In a similar way, though there may be cases in which imagination leads us astray, we can still rely on it as a guide to possibility.

---

11 For discussion of the relationship between conceivability and possibility, see the papers collected in Gendler and Hawthorne (2002). The editors' substantive introduction provides an excellent overview of the relevant issues.

Concluding Remarks

Our discussion thus far has suggested several loci of disagreement, and as such, it points to several avenues that are ripe for further philosophical exploration. In these brief concluding remarks, I outline three questions that could usefully guide future philosophical research into imagination.

Question 1: *What is the relation between different kinds of imagining?*

As of yet, philosophers have not been successful at providing a unifying theory that captures the different kinds of imagination discussed in the literature. Indeed, many philosophers discussing imagination consider this task so difficult or futile that they have not even attempted it. To give just one example, having laid out many dimensions on which imaginings differ, Kendall Walton has noted in a much quoted passage: "[S]houldn't we now spell out what they have in common? Yes, if we can. But I can't" (Walton 1990: 19).

Above we discussed propositional vs. objectual imagination, but there are further debates about recreative vs. creative imagination, about experiential vs. non-experiential imagination, and so on. The debate about the relationship between imagination and conception is also relevant here. To make progress on our philosophical understanding of imagination, more attention needs to be paid to the question of whether the different kinds of imagination posited in the philosophical literature have something in common and, if so, what it is. If they do have something in common, then we should be able to ferret it out. And if they don't, then we should turn to the question of why – and indeed, whether – they should all be considered kinds of imagination.

Question 2: *In what contexts is imagination really involved, and how can we tell?*

We noted above that imagination has been invoked to do explanatory work in a great variety of philosophical contexts. In the absence of a clearer conception of what imagining is, however, it's hard to know whether the kind of mental activity doing explanatory work in one context is the same as that doing explanatory work in another. Is the mental activity involved when we engage with philosophical thought experiments the same mental activity that's involved in games of pretense? Is it the same mental activity as the one that's involved in our engagement with fiction and in acts of creativity? (See Kind 2013 for a development of this worry.) Moreover, the frequent invocation of imagination leads to further stretching of the notion. To give just one example, some philosophers have recently suggested that we can best explain delusions by developing an account of them that sees them as kinds of imagining. But since delusions seem in some sense more belief-like than the typical imagining, these same philosophers have been led to suggest that we should think of imagining and belief as on a continuum, where there is no sharp distinction between the two. Perhaps this is right, i.e. perhaps there is no sharp distinction between belief and imagination, but it is difficult to know exactly how to adjudicate the issue. One might wonder, for example, whether one would be better off abandoning the commitment to invoking imagination in this context rather than adopting a belief-imagination continuum account. Analogous issues arise in many other contexts. Progress on Question 1 may help to alleviate this problem, but what is also needed is some attention to laying out a set of principled considerations for the invocation of imagination in different contexts.

Question 3: *How does skill play a role in imagining?*

It's only very recently that philosophers in the Western analytic tradition have started to think seriously about skill; previously, this topic had been largely ignored or marginalized (e.g. Pavese, 2016; Stanley and Williamson, 2017). Understanding more clearly the notion of skill – and, more specifically, what it would be for imagination to be conceived as a skill – might help us make progress on questions about imaginability. Doing so could help us better understand why some scenarios have seemed unimaginable to some yet imaginable to others, and it could also help us adjudicate these debates. This in turn could lead to philosophical progress on the connection between imagination and possibility.

References

Balcerak Jackson, M. (2016). On the Epistemic Value of Imagining, Supposing, and Conceiving. In A. Kind and P. Kung, (eds.), *Knowledge Through Imagination.* Oxford, UK: Oxford University Press, 41–60.

Brann, E. (1991). *The World of Imagination.* Lanham, MD: Rowman & Littlefield Publishers.

Byrne, R. M. J. (2005). *The Rational Imagination: How People Create Alternatives to Reality.* Cambridge, MA: MIT Press.

Church, J. (2010). Seeing Reasons. *Philosophy and Phenomenological Research, 80*(3), 638–670.

Churchland, P. S. (1998). The Hornswoggle Problem. In J. Shear (ed.), *Explaining Consciousness: The Hard Problem.* Cambridge, MA: MIT Press, 37–44.

Currie, G. (1990). *The Nature of Fiction.* Cambridge, UK: Cambridge University Press.

Currie, G., and Jureidini, J. (2004). Narrative and Coherence. *Mind & Language, 19,* 409–427.

Currie, G., and Ravenscroft, I. (2002). *Recreative Minds.* Oxford, UK: Oxford University Press.

Dennett, D. (1991). *Consciousness Explained.* Boston, MA: Little, Brown and Company.

Descartes, R. (1641/1986). *Meditations on First Philosophy with Selections from the Objections and Replies.* Translated by John Cottingham. Cambridge, UK: Cambridge University Press.

Doggett, T., and Egan, A. (2007). Wanting Things You Don't Want: The Case for an Imaginative Analogue of Desire. *Philosophers' Imprint, 7*(9), 1–17.

Egan, A. (2008). Imagination, Delusion, and Self-Deception. In T. Bayne and J. Fernandez (eds.), *Delusion and Self-Deception: Affective Influences on Belief-Formation.* New York, NY: Psychology Press, 263–280.

Gendler, T., and Hawthorne, J. 2002. *Conceivability and Possibility.* Oxford, UK: Oxford University Press.

Gertler, B. (2007). In Defense of Mind-Body Dualism. In J. Feinberg and R. Shafer-Landau (eds.), *Reason and Responsibility*. Boston, MA: Wadsworth, 312–324.

Gettier, E. (1963). Is Justified True Belief Knowledge? *Analysis*, *23*(6), 121–123.

Goldman, A. I. (2006). *Simulating Minds: The Philosophy, Psychology, and Neuroscience of Mindreading*. New York, NY: Oxford University Press.

Hofstadter, D. (1979). *Gödel, Escher, Bach: An Eternal Golden Braid*. New York, NY: Random House Books.

Humberstone, I. L. (1992). Direction of Fit. *Mind*, *101*(401), 59–83.

Hume, D. (1739/1985). *A Treatise of Human Nature*. Edited by P. H. Nidditch. Oxford, UK: Oxford University Press.

Jackson, F. (1982). Epiphenomenal Qualia. *Philosophical Quarterly*, *32*, 127–136.

Kant, I. (1787/1998). *Critique of Pure Reason*. Translated by P. Guyer and A. Wood. Cambridge, UK: Cambridge University Press.

Kind, A. (2001). Putting the Image Back in Imagination. *Philosophy and Phenomenological Research*, *62*(1), 85–109.

(2013). The Heterogeneity of the Imagination. *Erkenntnis*, *78*(1), 141–159.

(2016). Desire-Like Imagination. In A. Kind (ed.), *The Routledge Handbook of Philosophy of Imagination*. London, UK; New York, NY: Routledge, 163–176.

(2017). Imaginative Vividness. *Journal of the American Philosophical Association*, *3*(1), 32–50.

(Forthcoming). Imaginative Experience. In U. Kriegel (ed.), *The Oxford Handbook of the Philosophy of Consciousness*. Oxford, UK: Oxford University Press.

Kind, A., and Kung, P. (eds.) (2016). *Knowledge Through Imagination*. Oxford, UK: Oxford University Press.

Kriegel, U. (2015). *The Varieties of Consciousness*. Oxford, UK: Oxford University Press.

Kung, P. (2010). Imagining as a Guide to Possibility. *Philosophy and Phenomenological Research*, *81*, 620–663.

McGinn, C. (2004). *Mindsight*. Cambridge, MA: Harvard University Press.

Nagel, T. (1974). What is it like to Be a Bat? *Philosophical Review*, *83*(October), 435–450.

Nanay, B. (2010). Perception and Imagination: Amodal Perception as Mental Imagery. *Philosophical Studies*, *150*, 239–254.

Nichols, S. (2004). Imagining and Believing: The Promise of a Single Code. *The Journal of Aesthetics and Art Criticism*, *62*(2), 129–139.

Parfit, D. (1984). *Reasons and Persons*. Oxford, UK: Oxford University Press.

Pavese, C. (2016). Skill in Epistemology I. *Philosophy Compass*, *11*, 642–649.

Peacocke, C. (1985). Imagination, Experience and Possibility: A Berkeleian View Defended. In J. Foster and H. Robinson (eds.), *Essays on Berkeley*. Oxford, UK: Clarendon Press, 19–35.

Perky, C. W. (1910). An Experimental Study of Imagination. *American Journal of Psychology*, *21*, 422–452.

Polyani, M. (1966/2009). Creative Imagination. Reprinted in K. Bardsley, D. Dutton, and M. Krausz (eds.), *The Idea of Creativity*. Leiden, Netherlands: Brill, 147–163.

Rawls, J. (1971). *A Theory of Justice*. Cambridge, MA: Harvard University Press.

Sartre, J. (1936/1962). *Imagination*. Translated by Forrest Williams. Ann Arbor, MI: The University of Michigan Press.

(1940/2010). *The Imaginary*. Translated by Jonathan Webber. London, UK: Routledge.

Schellenberg, S. (2013). Belief and Desire in Imagination and Immersion. *Journal of Philosophy*, *110*(9), 497–517.

Shah, N., and Velleman, J. D. (2005). Doxastic Deliberation. *Philosophical Review, 114*(4), 497–534.

Stanley, J., and Williamson, T. (2017). Skill. *Noûs, 51*(4), 713–726.

Stock, K. (2017). *Only Imagine*. Oxford, UK: Oxford University Press.

Strawson, P. F. (1970). Imagination and Perception. In L. Foster and J. W. Swanson (eds.), *Experience and Theory*. Amherst, MA: University of Massachusetts Press, 31–54.

Thomson, J. J. (1971). A Defense of Abortion. *Philosophy and Public Affairs, 1*(1), 47–66.

Tidman, P. (1994). Conceivability as a Test for Possibility. *American Philosophical Quarterly, 31*(4), 297–309.

Toon, A. (2012). *Models as Make-Believe: Imagination, Fiction, and Scientific Representation*. Basingstoke, UK: Palgrave Macmillan.

van Leeuwen, N. (2013). The Meanings of "Imagine" Part I: Constructive Imagination. *Philosophy Compass, 8*(3), 220–230.

Walton, K. (1990). *Mimesis as Make Believe*. Cambridge, MA: Harvard University Press.

Weinberg, J. M., and Meskin, A. (2006). Imagine That! In M. Kieran (ed.), *Contemporary Debates in Aesthetics and the Philosophy of Art*. Oxford, UK: Blackwell, 222–235.

White, A. R. (1990). *The Language of Imagination*. Oxford, UK: Basil Blackwell.

6 Imagination in Classical India: A Short Introduction

Chakravarthi Ram-Prasad

This essay is not so much an addition to the philosophical essays in this volume as an alternative: It offers a glimpse of another historical articulation of the concept, sufficient to suggest that if contemporary thinking on imagination had been derived from this rather than the early modern Western tradition, this collection of essays might have looked somewhat (but not altogether) different.

I will offer here a very brief outline of some of several strands of thought about imagination over two and a half thousand years in some areas of Hinduism expressed in the Sanskrit language. I am not able to do justice to the metaphysical role of "imagination" in several Hindu and Buddhist philosophical systems, where it is understood broadly as the instinctive generation of endless interpretations of experience that block the calming of consciousness required to have ultimate insight into reality. This gnoseological framing of imagination is important in contemplative practices, but also plays a critical role in the epistemological tradition, where imagination is located within a broader discussion of the relationship between concepts and perceptual activity (Matilal, 1986). This area of discussion has a distinct set of concerns that I do not have the space to treat here.

I am also compelled for reasons of space and coherence to set aside many important developments in Pali (the language of the Buddha), Ardha-Magadhi (the primary language of the Jain religio-philosophical texts), Tamil, and other languages that also had a dynamic and interactive presence in the cultural world within which Sanskrit was dominant but by no means hegemonic.

This essay has four sections. The first looks at the articulation of ideas recognizably centered on imagination in the performative aspects of early or Vedic texts (1500–300 BCE). The second presents various terms that approach different aspects of "imagination," and looks at some of the genres within which these terms were thematized. The third section surveys some influential contemplative practices in which imagination was carefully explored as a disciplined way of cultivating and expanding awareness. The final section very briefly considers the philosophical question of the cognitive status of imagination at least in aesthetic production (although it has wider implications about the reality of what is imagined that we cannot pursue here).

In an important book that has influenced the way I have laid out key concepts in this essay, David Shulman has suggested that various technical terms, across varied contexts, can be brought together under the rubric of "imagination" (Shulman,

2012). This is a conceptual breakthrough that has helped subsequent efforts such as this essay to view under one formal English term a constellation of ideas that, especially because they have been translated in a variety of ways (with more or less lexical justification), have seldom been thematized as "imagination" as such. In discussing these terms together in a single essay, one must find a balance between (1) presenting each term in its own specific context, and (2) indicating how each might constitute one aspect of imagination in its own way. I have done this by using an established and conventional translation for each term when discussing the way it occurs in particular texts or genres, while letting the reader over the course of this essay see how each such term might equally well be translated as "imagination."

Before I begin this exploration, an important point should be made about imagination in these classical Indian contexts. It is not free-form fantasy or loose ruminations on desirable things, but a disciplined and structured way of thinking with a highly detailed and often systematically theorized teleology. All the ideas of imagination we will now encounter have this purposive function, and we can hazard the generalization that this is a defining feature of the imagination in classical India.

Early Imagination

The first texts we have, from the orally transmitted corpus that are called the Vedas, indicate that imagination is utilized in broadly two ways: to explore reality beyond the ambit of the senses, and to structure reality through mapping it on to what is available to the senses. Of course, these are not fixed and explicitly theorized in this way, but they indicate awareness of two crucial aspects of imagination. First, imagination is a capacity to generate meaning, making sense of the world as it seems to be found by us. Second, and dramatically, it is an act, upon the world but also within it, that does something to order and change the world as it is found. The latter requires an arduous regime of concentration, so that this second capacity can affect the first. Both seek to explicate truths that are either hidden from or only glimpsed by the senses. Consequently, this distinctive feature of imagination in classical India as both disciplinary and teleological is evident from the very beginning.

As Brian K. Smith has carefully laid out, ritual in early India, in the Vedic texts, was built through a principle that he calls "resemblance" between the planes of the macrocosmos ("relating to the godly"), the ritual itself (called, broadly, "sacrifice" [*yajña*], whose meaning we cannot explore here), and the microcosmos (inward-directed awareness [*adhyātman*]) (Smith, 1998). These resemblances permit the constructive activity of ritual sacrifice, in which a whole reality is constituted through the integration of these elements. Ritual imagination is systematic: It must take place between impoverished reduplication (*jāmi*) in which elements from different realms are mechanically assigned to each other, and an excess of diversification (*pṛthak*), the arbitrary assignation of elements to each other in which imagination runs riot and maps without discipline. The result of properly trained yet skillfully productive ritual imagination is discovery of the template of how to act between seen and unseen realms: "the ancient seers discovered in their hearts the binding connection of that which is *(sat)* and that which is not *(asat),*" says the *Ṛg Veda* (c. 1200 BCE) at 1.129.4. So the preservation of cosmic order itself requires the imagination to discover the order's components and perform the integration of those components into the whole.

The most widely used principle by which the equivalencies are enacted is through "substitution" of elements by their symbolic stand-ins, in common with the nature of ritual in other religious traditions. So the sacrificer (and implicitly, the deity) is substituted by animals, which in turn transmit their sacrificial quality to vegetable matter; this is a form of "homological" thinking (Smith, 1998: 53). Substitutions multiply, as when rare sacred plants are replaced with more common ones. The substitutions are not arbitrary, but imaginatively formed, "the result neither of the reduplication of the same nor of the radical differentiation of the dispersed many but is the consequence of the construction of an integrated unity out of distinct but interrelated parts" (Smith, 1998: 53). Imaginative substitutions lead to an integrated view of reality, and gradually, these substitutions move ever more abstractly away from the cosmic resemblances that they seek to capture, until they culminate in the "interiorization" of ritual. Here sacrifice becomes the renunciation of psychological values, rather than any objects in the world. Imagination takes the activity of ritual from the world into the imagination itself, in an act of ultimate reflexivity. This inaugurates a whole series of disciplined self-cultivation and pursuit of insightful distance from the conditions of the world that marks later classical Indian religious thought (Heesterman, 1985).

The systematic expansion of the mind beyond where the senses reach is the birth of that distinctively classical Indian notion of disciplined imagination. For example, during the ancient Vedic symposium (1500–1000 BCE), poems were composed in enigmatic terms to articulate visions of sacred knowledge:

> A firm light placed for vision – a mind *(manas)*
> most fleet of all that fly!
> All the gods, one-minded, single-intentioned,
> go directly beyond to this
> one inspiration *(kratu)*!
> Far beyond soar my ears, far beyond
> my eyes, far away to this light which is
> set in my heart!
> Far beyond wanders my mind, its
> spirit to remote distances.
>
> *(Ṛg Veda 6.9.5–6)* (Johnson, 1980).

In this demonstration of a self-consciously creative and ritually disciplined imagination in the earliest texts, we find the articulation of the source of such imagination, located in that elusive term *manas* that really cannot be translated any other way than as "mind" (Proto Indo-European *men-*, as in Greek *ménos*). It must be noted, however, that from the beginning Indian traditions always treated this as a functional organ of some sort, clearly distinguished from the principle of the unitary subject or "self" *(ātman)* to which it could belong in some way; the distinction being so clear from early on that the Buddha in the sixth century BCE could utilize the functional aspects of *manas* in his teachings while dispensing with any commitment to an *ātman*. So the terms are not to be used interchangeably, as has usually (although not by all scholars) been thought to be the case with Descartes' use of *anima* and *mens*.

This identification of some sort of operating capacity in the subject as the place of imagination is found, for example, in the *Śatapata Brāhmaṇa* 10.5.3.1–3 (eleventh century BCE), which says that the mind (*manas*) is neither that which is (*sat*) nor that which is not (*asat*); for it is created (*sṛṣṭa*). It is articulated (*niruktatara*) and it is coagulated (*mūrtatara*). Its operations (*vṛtti*) happen every day of life (like "36,000 [sacrificial] fires"). For its performance it requires the breathing, bodily self (*ātman*). The notion that imagination occurs in a way that cannot be ontologically collapsed into either something that is part of the furniture of the world or something fictive is one that echoes down the centuries, as we will see.

Following a fine-grained structuration of the features of what is to be done, imagination is seen as having a particular power, for out of its liminal position between what is and what is not it brings events and entities into a certain type of being; one might say, it fills in a certain ontological category with them.

Imagination, then, was understood from early on as conferring freedom on consciousness to deliberately wander beyond the environment of the person:

> If he wants the world of the fathers [mothers . . . friends, perfumes . . . food . . .] by his willed intention (*saṅkalpa*) alone the fathers will arise, and the world of the fathers will be his (*Chāndogya Upaniṣad*, seventh century BCE).

This is a person who has come to know (*anuvidya*) the self (*ātman*) and its true desires (*satyān kāmān*). This insight permits the tradition to negotiate around fruitless questioning about whether imagination is belief-like in orientation to what there is or desire-like in wanting what there is not (or not yet). Rather, imagination, by seeking what there is, in its radically expansive capacity as both exploratory self-consciousness and reflexive understanding that it so seeks, has both aspects.

Poetic and Philosophical Imagination: Some Terms and Their Varied Uses

In this section, we will look very briefly at three key words whose ramifying uses spread across poetics, philosophy of language, aesthetics, and philosophy of mind. I will begin with a set of interrelated polysemic terms – *saṃkalpa*, *kalpanā*, and *vikalpa* – whose implication for our understanding of imagination in these Sanskrit sources is rather general. I will then look at *bhāvanā* ("bringing into being"), the word whose uses most naturally lead to its being translated as "imagination"; and finally, *pratibhā* ("inspiration"), which has a rather different set of ideas associated with it but has also often been equated with imagination, especially that of the artist, poet, or writer. Together, they present us with how imagination can be understood in different, although not incompatible ways.

Saṃkalpa/Vikalpa/Kalpanā

These three words are derived from the verbal root √klp, to produce, make, intend, or fashion. To reduce the translation of each to a core meaning, *kalpanā* refers to creative doing; and *vikalpa* basically stands for "thought," so that a related word *vikalpita* means, "thought up." Finally, *saṅkalpa* generally means will, determination, or intention, but slides into implying the force that directs the will toward an outcome. Bimal Matilal (1986) points out that *kalpanā/vikalpa* can quite naturally mean "imagination" in both the "ordinary meaning" of "an inventive" "application of concepts to things" and having "a philosophically technical sense" as "concept-application and object-identification in perceptual judgement." There is broad agreement that *vikalpa* is conceptualization that structures sensory input, but this then leads to major disputes amongst different Hindu and Buddhist systems that offer competing metaphysics and epistemologies. Some systems maintain that this conceptual structuration of perceptual states is a sort of "contamination" of the "pristine purity of primary perception," while others argue that it is the necessary process for the "true construction" of "the structure of reality" in perception (Matilal, 1986: 313–314).

This area of Indian philosophy requires such technical treatment that I forbear to go into it in this broad-ranging introduction. In any case, these terms only distantly relate to imagination: Some systems such as the Buddhist Mahāyāna school of Yogācāra use these terms with negative connotations, treating them as standing for a misleading construction of experience out of pure sensory states, the stripping away of which will lead to an awareness free of the bonds of ordinary life. In such a context, the erroneousness of conceptual construction of experience can be signified by seeing it as an act of imagination, where imagination is the construal of what is not real (howsoever "real" is defined in a system).

Let us now turn to two terms that are more easily associated with "imagination."

Bhāvanā

In its narrowest sense, *bhāvanā* is "generativity," an intralinguistic process (*vyāpāra*) that provides semantic coherence by connecting elements in order to proliferate meaning in thinking and speaking a thought. It has the sense of "makes"; whereas strict lexical meaning is available just through knowledge of the words in a language, this generativity adds something further.[1] As such, it is cognition above and beyond that lexical meaning, since it adds a performative dimension that is not merely referential. The important theorist of the Mīmāṃsā system, Kumārila (sixth century) says that lexical meaning (*dhātvartha*) "colors" (*anurarañjana*) *bhāvanā* (Ollett, 2013: 244). His commentator, Pārthasārathi (tenth century) expatiates in his commentary, the *Śāstra Dīpikā*, ". . . being conducive to the production of some other thing is a quality that belongs to every lexical meaning, which is the form of 'bringing into being'

---

1 With regard to *bhāvanā* in the philosophy of language presented by the Mīmāṃsā system of thought I mainly present here ideas usefully marshalled in Ollett (2013).

(*bhāvanā* – actualization)" (Ollett, 2013: 248, translation modified). So, in the famous injunction that expresses the motivation to perform Vedic ritual, "one who desires heaven performs sacrifice" (*svargakāmo yajeti*), it is not as if there are the words and there is the action, brought together by a projection of meaning from one to the other; rather "the act is itself the meaning of the words" (Ollett, 2013: 251). The actualization of the injunction is an imaginative rendering of the lexical meaning of the injunction. To understand the injunction is to actualize its meaning through action; full understanding itself is an imaginative act, rather than a mere reception of pre-given semantic content.

The ritualists did not, however, explicitly thematize *bhāvanā* in ways that easily lend themselves to a cross-cultural understanding of imagination; their focus was on the technical question of how the injunctive nature of sacred text manifests itself in the capacity to act according to what the text is taken to command. So *bhāvanā* was the term they gave to that mysterious link between sentences, meaning, understanding, and action in accordance with the understanding of the meaning of the injunctions contained in the sacred sentences.

This implicit notion of generativity was taken up in a quite radically expanded way in poetics. A key figure in this adaptation was Bhaṭṭa Nāyaka (tenth century) (Pollock, 2010). Seizing on the notion of *bhāvanā*, he presents it as the production or bringing into being (*bhāvakatva*) of an experience of pleasure in the spectator through language and performance. It is a state of absorbed restfulness (*viśrānti*), a looking inward (*antar-mukhatva*), and the tasting (*āsvāda*) of the aesthetic essence (*rasa*) of that experience. Pollock uses the neologism "experientializing" (for Bhaṭṭa Nāyaka's own neologism, *bhogī-kṛttva*) for the spectator's process of undergoing in a unified experience the various analytic elements of language and performance in an ordered aesthetic. The result is a "generalization" (*sādhāraṇī-karaṇa*) of that aesthetic, that is to say, the reception of the particular condition of characters in a play as the emotional content of the human condition itself. When Rāma is grief-stricken because he has to comply with the moral duty (*dharma*) of the perfect king and banish his beloved wife Sītā, the audience does not merely sympathize nor even just identify with Rāma. Rather, the grief that wells up with the clash of duties and feelings occurs in consciousness as the reflexively available yet irresistible aesthetic core of the tragic (*karuṇa*). Imagination is what generates this aesthetic response; without it, the audience would be mere observers of the events and experiences of a king and queen long ago.

This transfer of *bhāvanā* from the ritual context as response to injunction, into literary-dramatic theory as an account of the reception of creativity is expatiated upon by the eleventh-century polymath Abhinavagupta (Shulman, 2012: 66–69). In ritual context, there are statements such as "the gods performed a sacrifice." The straightforward understanding of the content of such a statement is infused with "an additional apprehension," in which the past tense is discarded and a desire forms, "I shall myself perform the sacrifice." It is this additional apprehension that is called, variously, *pratibhā*, *bhāvanā*, and *udyoga* (activity). And this additional apprehension is precisely what occurs in the "qualified" (*adhikāra*) reader or spectator (Walimbe, 1980: 18–19).

In an aesthetic moment (especially, of a narrative that 'everyone knows'):

(1) The story teller makes an event occur anew
(2) Characters become "real" and "present"
(3) They are palpable in how their narrative presence is felt
(4) This feeling becomes the prompt for the generation of a typologically structured aesthetic awareness of what is essential to that moment.

The inspired imagination here goes in the opposite direction to that in ritual. Whereas the ritualist moves from the general statement on sacrifices to imagining himself specifically as the sacrificer, thereby motivating action, the connoisseur moves from the specificity of the characters and their emotions depicted in the literary production to an imaginative wonder at the quite general – indeed, universal – aesthetic essence (*rasa*) of what is being depicted.

There are two ways of interpreting what aesthetic imagination is doing here. One way of looking at it is that imagination is a typologized abstraction that, when primed, frees consciousness from all contingent particularities and enables it to experience some universal aesthetic state. Another interpretation is that imagination is the bridge between the highly particular experience represented in a play or poem and the intrinsic capacity that any (properly primed and trained) onlooker has to understand and feel what it is to have that experience. Either way, *bhāvanā* is a powerful explanatory concept at the heart of artistic production. The plastic arts and music are only occasionally, and in much later texts, assimilated explicitly into what is primarily an account of poetry and plays; but it is clear that they are always implicitly part of these aesthetic theories.

Some technical philosophers also took up *bhāvanā*, in a way related to its use by the theorists of aesthetics and poetics, but more narrowly located within a philosophy of mind. Śrīdhara (ninth century) of the Nyāya school of realist metaphysics understood *bhāvanā* to derive from (1) impressions in memory (*smṛti*) and (2) attention (*ādara*). That is to say, it is a focused attention that brings something into being by cognizing it as a particular thing, drawing on what has been learned and remembered.

The late (seventeenth-century) Nyāya text the *Bhāṣāpariccheda* of Viśvanātha is oblique in its definition: The natural tendency (*saṃskāra*) called imagination (*bhāvanā*) is a state of a person (*jīvavṛtti*), not perceptible to the senses. Its cause (*kāraṇa*) is an inquisitive certainty (*niścaya*) that is not basically unconcerned (*upekṣānātmaka*) (Viśvanātha, 1940: 160). That is to say, an indifferent person has no inclination or tendency toward something; and so, too, a person in doubt. So for the tendency toward imagination to manifest itself, one should be neither indifferent nor doubtful, but have a certain purpose toward which to think about. It is inquisitiveness and imagination that make inquisitiveness possible.

Pratibhā

If *bhāvanā* in poetics and aesthetics was primarily about the role of imagination in the reception of art, *pratibhā* concerns its role in creation.

This concept – usually translated as "illumination," "inspiration," "intuition," or even "genius" – begins as a term in the philosophy of language and is subsequently extended into literary theory and aesthetics.[2] The hugely influential thinker Bartṛhari (fifth century) and his commentator Helarāja (twelfth century) of the Grammarian school read *pratibhā* in two ways. One, it is a "flash of light" by which ever newer forms of knowledge, not born of the senses, become present in a person's innermost consciousness (Kaviraj: 1924/1966: 17). But this metaphysical sense devolves into a more specific processual understanding, too, as the source of all daily activity (*sarvavyavahārayoniḥ*). Bartṛhari says it is established by one's internal functioning (*pratyātmavṛttisiddhā*) (Bartṛhari's *Vākyapadīya* 2.146); (Christie, 1979: 174–175). It appears to be spontaneous (*ayatnaja*) when it occurs, but in fact derives from continuous effort (*abhyāsa*) (Kaviraj: 1924/1966: 19–20). Since the Grammarians think it is found in animals, too (Bartṛhari's *Vākyapadīya* 2. 148–9) (Christie, 1979: 174–175), the meaning of *pratibhā* lies somewhere between intuition and instinct.

It is in aesthetics and poetics that *pratibhā* becomes something like inspired imagination, although here, too, it partakes of the Grammarians' sense that it combines spontaneity and cultivation. An important early formulation is in the work of Ānandavardhana (ninth century). He is drawn to the uncanny nature of *pratibhā*: It is like something otherworldly (*alokasāmānyam*), shimmering (*pratisphurantam*) in awareness. In his commentary, Abhinavagupta (eleventh century) defines it in more functional terms: It is "an insight capable of creating something novel" (*apūrvavastunirmāṇakṣamā prajñā pratibhā*) (Ingalls, Masson, and Patwardhan, 1990: 120–121). Imagination in this context is both something mysterious and something immediately recognizable; phenomenologically elusive yet identifiable in its felt outcome.

The theoreticians of literary production also acknowledge the balance between the instinctive and the disciplined aspects of *pratibhā* mentioned by the Grammarians. Rājashekara (tenth century), in the fourth chapter of his *Kāvyamīmāṃsā*, says that the agent's capacity for literary composition (*kāvyaśakti*) manifests itself in the twinned processes of inspiration (*pratibhā*) and training (*vyutpatti*) (Parashar, 2000: 43–44). *Pratibhā* is what makes the meaning and the various literary figures and forms that constitute a text manifest in the heart of a person. Without it, even perceptible objects do not seem immediately present, while with it, even what is unseen becomes directly perceptible (Parashar, 2000: 44). He goes on to say that such literary inspiration is both (1) active (*kārayitri*) and (2) receptive (*bhāvayatri*).

(1) When active, it can be (a) natural/congenital (*sahaja*); (b) adventitious (*āhārya*); and/or (c) learned (*aupadeśikī*)

(2) But the truly excellent inspiration is that which is vindicated by reception: "it brings the poet's effort and intention into existence" (Parashar, 2000: 46).

Counterintuitively, the theoretician places the cultivated imagination – defined as imagination that seeks out the ways in which literary power can be expressed – below that imagination which is just open to illumination. Here we can see how *pratibhā* as "inspiration" offers a particular reading of imagination: It is what is nearest to animal

---

2 Again, it is Shulman who points out how the detailed but often separate discussions of *bhāvanā* and *pratibhā* ought to be studied together under the rubric of imagination (Shulman, 2012: 80–108). He refers to Sreekantaiya (1980), who explicitly identifies *pratibhā* with "imagination."

capacity, an instinct lying deep and naturally within a person. It is an openness to what constitutes creative excellence.

Note that this is not imagination in the sense of free-floating fantasy, for its presence is detectable only afterward, in the brilliance of what results from it. Rather, the point Rājaśekhara makes is that, while imagination can be cultivated in the search for creativity, the imagination that produces the greatest art occurs organically in the consciousness of the artist (the poet, the dramatist). As such, this aspect of imagination as mysterious occurrence is somewhat different in orientation from other ideas that also come under the formal range of "imagination," and which are much more given to discipline and the cultivation of the capacity to render real. We turn now to perhaps the most influential reading of imagination in these Indian materials, one that plays a role to this day in Hindu worship (as, too, in Buddhist and Jain practices that we have not been able to examine here). Here, imagination is highly formalized and rigorously structured to achieve its ends.

Imagination and the Construction of Reality

If the epistemological debate over conceptuality (*vikalpa*) is over whether concepts are fundamentally misleading constructions of an experiential world (as Yogācāra Buddhism would have it) or whether they enable a subject to interpret perception accurately (as the Nyāya school argues), we also have a tradition that maintains both that conceptualization constructs experience and that what is thus experienced is real in some ontologically profound sense. This tradition develops in what are called the "yoga *upaniṣad*s." They claim the mystical and pedagogic authority of the ancient *upaniṣad* texts (900–100 BCE) but through a set of arcane and highly structured disciplinary practices of the imagination, place the willed intention to create worlds at the heart of those practices. The culminating example of this textual and practical tradition is the *Yogavāsiṣṭha* (eighth to twelfth century), which also explicitly presents a metaphysics that is consistent with the worldview of this tradition. For this text, the world is a latticework of concepts (*vikalpa-jālikā*), of the nature of manifestation; it is also fashioned of fierce (*ugraiḥ*), tough (*dṛḍha*), purposive, and willed intention (i.e. "imagination" as *saṅkalpa*) (Shulman, 2012: 111–112). The world as it occurs to and in consciousness is always conceptual. It can be intractable, impinging upon the subject in various ways both pleasurable and painful. But precisely because the world's phenomenal manifestation is irreducibly conceptual – always experienced through our structured ideas of how and what things are – the deliberate manipulation of concepts can alter that world itself. By resisting a divide between world and conceptual grasp, this tradition holds that the careful and rigorous working through of our conceptual repertoire is itself a transformation of the world. In the *Yogavāsiṣṭha*, a teacher talks of how his very highly trained subjectivity infuses the experiential world, dissolving what seems to the untrained person as the borders between the world and consciousness:

> When I experienced space, I knew what earth was. I became earth. In that earth
> I experienced the existence of countless universes, without ever abandoning the
> awareness that I am the infinite consciousness. I saw the most amazing earthly
> phenomena and events within that earth (within me). In fact, I experienced even the
> farmer ploughing me (the earth), and I experienced the burning heat of the sun and the
> cool flow of rainwater. I became the fearful space in which the Lokāloka Mountains
> (the boundaries of the world) exist, and I explored the actions and movements of
> countless beings ... I experienced the weeping and wailing of those who had lost their
> dear and near ones, here I experienced the joy of dancing girls; there were cries of the
> hungry, the joy of the affluent, drought and earthquake, war and destruction, beautiful
> birds and lakes, suffering worms, flourishing forests, meditating sages. O Rāma, in this
> earth-body of mine all these took place (*Yogavāsiṣṭha*, 1984: V:2.87, 88).

Here, imagination is not about what is not real, it is not even the creative detection of
what is hidden, it is an extension of the capacity of consciousness to redraw the
boundaries of reality. What the teacher here undergoes is a more profound experience than the untrained student might have of what is taken to be the world (although
in this case, the student, Rāma, turns out to be God descended to earth as human, thus
to rediscover that the world is ultimately contained in and generated by divine
imagination).

This tradition of imagination was not only about narrative and creative profundity,
but also about disciplinary practices, and the yoga *upaniṣad*s were primarily concerned to guide the training of the imagination for the construction of a deeper reality
than encountered in ordinary life:

> In the middle of the heart is a fleshy, red lump. In it a small, fine white lotus
> blooms spreading its petals in different directions, like the red lotus. There are ten
> openings in the heart. In them are established the vital breaths. When the meditator is
> yoked to the life breath, he sees rivers and towns. When yoked to the suffusive
> breath he sees gods and sages. When yoked to the downward breath he sees nymphs,
> spirits, demigods. When yoked to the upward breath he sees the world of the
> heavens ... (*Subāla Upaniṣad* 4.1, adapted from Mahoney, 1998).

Obviously, the guidance implies what the practice eventually brings, for we do not
see heaven by simply breathing in. But we glimpse here the connection between the
most natural aspects of life – here, breathing – and the rigorous structuration of
imagination that, in this tradition, generates insight into reality, a reality that is both
constructed in experience and is irreducibly real for all that.

The notion that imagination is key to the inhabitation of a reality that is not
otherwise accessible to us, a reality that is simultaneously constructed in the
manipulation of our awareness and causally efficacious upon that awareness itself,
has a ramifying presence in religious practices to this day. Kashmiri Shaivism has
a continuous history over twelve centuries, and its roots lie in the threefold (*trika*)
doctrinal commitment to the all-pervasive and world-constituting divine consciousness, Śiva; the potency, Śaktī, by which this consciousness constitutes
reality; and the self that normally feels conscious of its own individuality. In
religio-philosophical systems such as the Trika, imagination plays a vital role in
the process by which daily worship of Śiva becomes a transformative discipline
through disciplined imagination.

To begin with, we can note that imagination plays a thematically defined role in the ritual of offering (*pūja*) that constitutes a great deal of daily Hindu worship: The image of the form in which the deity is viewed and can view the worshipper (the reciprocal seeing called *darśana*) (Eck, 1998) is enlivened in an imaginative act, and approached as a living being that can be pleased by offerings. But Trika practices develop particularly precisely a shift to the practice of "mental offering" (*mānasa-pūja*), in which the image, the objects of ritual offering, and the entire ecology of worship no longer correspond to objects in the worshipper's environment. As a final, dramatic, and demanding transition, this imaginative rendering is itself replaced by an intensified self-consciousness of identity with the deity, in which imagination vanishes into itself, leaving only conscious presence, the ultimate and irreducible reality of a non-dual God, a universal consciousness into which the sense of individuality that marks the worshipper dissolves.

The pivot of this practice is the sharply delineated and self-consciously articulated imagination of the ritual act of offering. The opening verses of the *Śivamānasapūjastotra* ("The Eulogium on Mental Offering to Śiva") has the worshipper think thus in fine-grained, visceral, phenomenally rich detail:

> "I offer you this seat of gems, cool water for a bath, robes adorned with jewels, lotion of musk, jasmine and *campaka* flowers, applewood-leaves, flame and incense! I have prepared with my mind sweet rice . . . milk and yoghurt, bananas, vegetables, camphor-scented water, and betel leaves. I offer this willed creation (*saṃkalpa*) of canopy, two yak-hair whisks, a fan, a spotless mirror, music from lute, drums . . .
> I offer you songs, dance, prostrations . . . You are myself, your consort is my intellect, my senses your attendants, my body your temple. My sleep is intense attention (*samādhi*), all my speech is prayer to you . . . " (adapted from Timalsina, 2013: 63)

Once more, we know that the locution in itself does not bring transformative awareness. But it describes on the surface the carefully developed imagination that eventually becomes trained to bring about a robust and detailed experience, one that gradually builds from the focus on the features of the ordinarily occurrent elements of worship to somatic performance to a theologically radical transformation of consciousness itself. Imagination becomes limitless. Today this practice is continuous, as we have seen, with the very beginnings of the history of disciplinary imagination in India, even if its metaphysical implications have changed over time and between systems and disciplines.

The Cognitive Status of the Moment of Imagination

Although we have glimpsed the possibility of sweeping and revisionary views of the relationship between imagination and the reality of what is imagined, we cannot study them further without detailed examination of texts and arguments. However, in order to give an indication of the philosophical interest in the status of what is "in" imagination, I will conclude this essay with a quick look at how some theoreticians of aesthetics and poetics approached the narrower issue of imagination's place in the cognitive economy of a person.

In the eleventh century, Mammaṭa attempts to answer the question: What is the nature of awareness in that aesthetic moment?

> The [imaginative] apprehension is distinct from cognitions that are accurate (*samyak*), false (*mithyā*), dubious (*saṃśaya*) or similar (*sādṛśya*), e.g. respectively, "He [the actor] is indeed Rāma"; "He is Rāma", where a subsequent cognition overrules the first and shows he is not Rāma; "He might or might not be Rāma"; and "He is like Rāma". Instead, it is rather like looking at a painting of a horse (Mammaṭa, 1967: 53) (my translation).

The commentator Vidyācakravartin says that, whereas the four options occur in ordinary life, something different happens in the awareness of the spectator at a dramatic performance: in a cognition "dense with wonder" (*camatkāraikaghana*), the meaning, or generalized implication of what is seen is filled in. Imagination is not exactly belief-like; it is not a matter for truth-claims (Shulman, 2012: 63). Abhinavagupta also makes a similar point. The wonder-filled cognition of the spectator is that "this is that (*asavayam*)" but not "this is indeed that (*asāvevāyam*)" (Gnoli, 1968: 5). That is to say, there is a provisional identification in imagination between what the actor is doing and what he represents in so doing; but this is not the identification that collapses other possibilities in order to generate a truth-statement. The imaginative identification in the reception of a performance (*mutatis mutandis*, in the reception of any art) does not have a judgment to contradict it. It is a direct experience and therefore cannot be invalidated by an epistemic procedure (*pramāṇa*). Nonetheless, it is causally effective (in the way even erroneous cognitions can be) (this is Shulman's summary of Abhinavagupta's representation of the lost work of Śrī Śankuka [eighth century] [Shulman, 2012: 62–63]). Imaginative cognition therefore has a sort of belief-like structure, too. In the section Poetic and Philosophical Imagination above, we saw how, from the ritualists to the aestheticians, imagination was also crucially seen as having a desire-like structure.

Abhinavagupta is well aware of this curious status of imagination, its quasi-doxastic nature that also carries a dimension of desire and memory. Whether as immediate experience, thought, imaginative determination (*saṃkalpa*), or memory, *pratibhā* "flashes out as truth" (*tathātvena sphurati*). Here, what occurs as remembrance – as when a happy person still grows anxious with intimations of lost love in another life – is not understood by logicians (*na tārkikaprasiddhā*) (in *Abhinavabhāratī* 6 [Kuanpoolpol, 1991: 215]). Abhinavagupta sums up the way in which aesthetic awareness – the core trope of imagination in which he is interested – is not ordinary apprehension such as sensory perception:

(1) It is not inapplicable to the assessment of things because it is false (*mithyā*)
(2) Since it is precisely what drives artistic production and reception, it is not ineffable (*anirvācya*)
(3) It is not comparable to quotidian things (*laukika-tulya*) that one deals with through perception and inference
(4) It is not the mistaken superimposition of one concept on another, such as in errors of judgment, because it is deliberately done to conjure up specific images in the mind of the reader or spectator.

To describe it positively, it has an aesthetically phenomenal flavour (*rasanīya*), with the intensification of the conditions (*upacayāvasthā*) of the phenomenon. This intensification spills out of ordinary modes of dealing with the world (in the classical Indian tradition, these are perception and inferential reasoning). What is understood in imagination defies epistemic categories even while partaking of their structures – for intentionality, tracking, variability, changing propositional content, and so on are all found in the process and act of imagination. It is this mysterious yet ever-present feature of our conscious lives that captivated the classical Indian tradition in ways that are only just beginning to be explored.

Final Remarks

Although it would be a different and exacting task to imagine a counterfactual history of a modern understanding of imagination that might have arisen from this alternative classical past, we could speculate briefly on some of its broad features. It is likely that we would more naturally have thought of imagination organically as slightly different aspects of different human cognitive functions. Practices of disciplined cultivation might have played a larger role in our understanding of how we think and live. Imagination might not have been conceptualized as a capacity fundamentally contrastable with others such as reason. It may well be that we might not have been drawn into thinking of the existence of a single such category at all! These idle thoughts are not meant to imply any judgment as to whether this would have been a good thing or bad. I merely wish to draw the reader into thinking about how the conceptualization of imagination is not the discovery of a scientific category arising in the perfect purity of philosophical analysis, but a mode of reflexivity embedded in the sophisticated concerns of different premodern cultural traditions. Arguably, while the analytic distinctions between such categories as "mind," "body," and "world" can be seen to have been available from the most ancient texts here, we do not find that particular structuration of the human being through the duality of mind and body that we find in Western thought, from Plato himself but given a particular epistemological foundation in Descartes. If the advances of contemporary psychology come from an uneasy conceptual oscillation between a physicalist reduction of dualism and its folk-language retention, then one may wonder what its discursive and experimental practices would have been if they had arisen from this classical Indian tradition. It may well be that the very phenomenology of imagination, along with other ways of carving up the same human reality, will have been somewhat different (Ram-Prasad, 2018).

Bibliography

Christie, E. (1979). Indian Philosophers on Poetic Imagination (*pratibhā*). *Journal of Indian Philosophy*, *7*, 153–207.

Eck, D. L. (1998). *Darśan: Seeing the Divine Image in India*. New York, NY: Columbia University Press.

Gnoli, R. (1968). *The Aesthetic Experience According to Abhinavagupta*. Varanasi, India: Chowkhamba Sanskrit Series.

Heesterman, J. C. (1985). Brahmin, Ritual and Renouncer. In *The Inner Conflict of Tradition: Essays in Indian Ritual, Kinship, and Society*. Chicago, IL: University of Chicago Press.

Ingalls, D. H. H, Masson, J. M., and Patwardhan, M. V. (1990). *The Dhvanyāloka of Ānandavardhana with Abhinava's Locana*. Cambridge, MA: Harvard University Press.

Johnson, W. (1980). *Poetry and Speculation of the Ṛg Veda*. Berkeley, CA: University of California Press.

Kaviraj, G. N. (1924/1966). The Doctrine of Pratibhā in Indian Philosophy. In *Aspects of Indian Thought*. Calcutta, India: University of Burdwan, 1–44.

Kuanpoolpol, P. (1991). *Pratibhā: The Concept of Intuition in the Philosophy of Abhinavagupta*. Cambridge, MA: Harvard University Department of Sanskrit and Indian Studies, PhD Thesis.

Mahoney, W. K. (1997). *The Artful Universe. An Introduction to the Vedic Religious Imagination*. Albany, NY: State University of New York Press.

Mammaṭa (1967). *Kāvyaprakasha*. Edited and translated by Ganganatha Jha. Revised edition, reprint. Varanasi, India: Bharatiya Vidya Prakashan.

Matilal, B. K. (1986). *Perception: An Essay on Classical Indian Theories of Knowledge*. Oxford, UK: Clarendon Press.

Ollett, A. (2013). What is Bhāvanā? *Journal of Indian Philosophy*, 41, 221–262.

Parashar, S. (2000). *Rājaśekara's Kāvyamīmāṃsā. Text and Translation with Explanatory Notes*. New Delhi, India: D. K. Printworld.

Pollock, S. (2010). What was Baṭṭa Nāyaka Saying? The Hermeneutical Transformation of Indian Aesthetics. In S. Pollock (ed.), *Epics and Argument in Sanskrit Literary History: Essays in Honor of Robert P. Goldman*. Delhi, India: Manohar.

Ram-Prasad, C. (2018). *Human Being, Bodily Being: Phenomenology from Classical India*. Oxford, UK: Oxford University Press.

Shulman, D. D. (2012). *More Than Real: A History of the Imagination in South India*. Cambridge, MA: Harvard University Press.

Smith, B. K. (1998). *Reflections on Resemblance, Ritual, and Religion*. Delhi, India: Motilal Banarsidass.

Sreekantaiya, T. N. (1980). *Imagination in Indian Poetics and Other Literary Studies*. Mysore, India: Geetha Book House.

Timalsina, S. (2013). Imagining Reality: Image and Visualization in Classical Hinduism. *Southeast Review of Asian Studies 35*, 50–69.

Viśvanātha Nyāya-Pañcāna (1940). The *Bhāṣāpariccheda with Siddhānta-Muktāvalī*. Translated by Swami Madhavananda. Calcutta, India: Advaita Ashrama.

Walimbe, Y. S. (1980). *Abhinavagupta on Indian Aesthetics*. Delhi, India: Ajanta Publications.

Yogavāsiṣṭha (1984). Translated by Swami Venkatesananda. Albany, NY: State University of New York Press.

7   From Prediction to Imagination

Max Jones and Sam Wilkinson

There is an increasingly popular framework for thinking about what the brain is fundamentally in the business of doing. We call this the predictive processing framework (PPF), and it takes the brain to be a hierarchically arranged prediction machine (Clark, 2013, 2016; Hohwy, 2013). In this chapter, we explore the consequences that this framework has for our understanding of imagination. In other words, we ask: "If you buy into this framework, what account of imagination should you give?"

In one sense, the PPF can be seen to demystify the imagination. One of the seemingly anomalous features of the imagination, from a naïve perspective, is its capacity for endogenously and creatively generating content, for conjuring up worlds in the mind. Yet, in the PPF approach, our basic worldly interactions through perception and action are already essentially dependent on imagination-like generative processes. However, the PPF's commitment to the ubiquity of imagination-like processes in our more mundane worldly interactions may also give rise to problems in identifying and explaining imagination as a distinct process in its own right. In particular, the PPF may struggle to explain the distinctive imaginative capacity for deliberately departing from immediate reality in a constrained and purposeful manner.

We proceed as follows. We start by introducing the PPF (section 1: Introducing the Predictive Processing Framework). Arguably, the PPF is most intuitively appealing as an account of perception and perceptual cognition, but it has also been extended to an understanding of action, through the notion of active inference. We then (in section 2: Predictive Processing and Imagination) present a first attempt at accounting for imagination within the PPF in terms of perceptual inference, which has been assumed by several theorists to be rather straightforward. We then (in section 3: Imaginative Agency and Imaginative Constraints) argue that this first attempt faces problems in accounting for the purposeful and constrained nature of deliberate imagination, which sets it aside from processes like dreaming, hallucination, or mind-wandering. We then consider (in section 4: Imagination as Mental Action) an alternative PPF account of imagination that focuses more on active inference and takes imagination to be based on action simulation. Although this account is more promising, it fails, on its own, to fully account for more drastic imaginative departures from reality. With this in mind, we gesture toward a possible way forward that focuses on the role of language in cueing and shaping imagination.

Introducing the Predictive Processing Framework (PPF)

The PPF is introduced and explained in a number of different ways by different people (see Clark, 2013 for a classic formulation). Our favorite way is to think about two things. The first is the *ambiguity* inherent in the information that we get from the world (including, crucially, ourselves as part of that world). The second is the *efficiency* with which the brain ought to operate.[1] Let's examine these two things in turn.

Bayesian Resolution of Ambiguity

The world is a noisy and *ambiguous* place. For any system trying to make sense of the world, which we can gloss roughly as trying to come up with hypotheses about the world, there is always more than one hypothesis compatible with any given piece of data. How, then, in the face of this ambiguity, does any such system pick a hypothesis out of those with equally good fit? According to the PPF the answer to this question is the same as the one that Thomas Bayes gave to it more than 250 years ago (Bayes, 1763): The system needs to use background knowledge, namely, knowledge about the probabilities of each hypothesis independently of (prior to) the evidence (the data). This is called the "prior probability," or "prior" for short, and it serves to bias hypothesis selection in the face of equal (or near-equal) fit.[2] A consequence of this idea is that a hypothesis can be selected even though it has relatively bad fit, as long as it has a high enough prior probability. Conversely, a hypothesis with a relatively good fit might not be selected if its prior probability is too low.

Let us illustrate this Bayesian story with an example (borrowed from Pezzulo, 2014). Suppose you are in a bedroom, and you hear a downstairs window creak. And suppose for simplicity's sake that two hypotheses present themselves: "That's the wind blowing the window" or "That's a burglar climbing in through the window." Both have adequate fit in the sense that, if they were true, that is the sound that might plausibly be produced. However, the probability of each hypothesis independently of the squeak (viz. the prior probability) might be quite different. Suppose you know that you live in a neighborhood with a very low crime rate, and you know that it's a windy night. That would give the wind hypothesis a higher prior probability, and that is the hypothesis that ought to be selected.

At this point it is crucial to emphasize that this example involves a person (you) dealing with experiential information (the window squeak) in a Bayesian manner. The PPF intends this to apply to even the lowest levels of neural inference. To use this same example, by the time that you have experienced the qualitative features of

---

1 By "efficiency" we mean an optimal trade-off between speed, accuracy, and energy expenditure. By "ought to" we don't mean anything robustly normative, but rather an expectation that evolutionary pressures will lead to efficient systems.

2 Where these priors come from is theoretically up for grabs. What we know is that at least some are the result of statistical learning from past experience (exposure to the world). Some might be innate in some sense (whether what counts as innate is the priors themselves or the propensity to acquire certain priors).

a squeak (even prior to recognizing it as a *window* squeak) your nervous system has already made countless earlier Bayesian inferences based on the raw (preconscious, pre-experiential) sensory input.

Efficient Neural Implementation Through Predictive Processing

According to the PPF, this is the Bayesian strategy that the brain adopts in the face of an ambiguous world. But how is it implemented in the brain? The answer here is: in a way that is *efficient*, which is to say, both *anticipatory* and *energy-saving*. Given that the human nervous system has a wealth of background knowledge that it brings to bear on an ambiguous world, we can think of each encounter with the world as already being anticipatory. As energy impacts on your sensory surfaces, it is already being greeted by expectations on the part of the system. This, one might argue, is simply a physiological extrapolation of the notion of Bayesian priors. It also paves the way for a tremendously energy-saving information-processing strategy. To see why, think about the fundamental principle underlying data compression. When passing a message between a sender-receiver pair, you optimize bandwidth by leaving out the message that the receiver can fill in for itself. This principle translates to the human brain in that the relevant senders and receivers are parts of the cortical hierarchy. In perceptual processing, say, visual processing, as light hits the retina, it is already being greeted by expectations. But what gets passed up the processing chain? The part of the signal that hasn't already been predicted, namely, prediction error (Feldman and Friston, 2010). What we end up with is a rich but hugely efficient and proactive system in which only newsworthy aspects of the nervous system are explicitly neurally represented. Furthermore, what you experience at any given time is not primarily determined by sensory input, but rather by the hypothesis that your brain has adopted to best predict (explain away/quash) that sensory input.

Two Tweaks: Hierarchy and Precision

We have in place the basic picture: the Bayesian strategy, and its neural implementation through prediction error minimization. However, there are two crucial tweaks to this picture. The first is the notion of a hierarchy of predictive hypotheses; the second, the notion of precision.

According to the PPF, predictive hypotheses are *hierarchically organized*, with the hypotheses of one level feeding into the level below (and prediction error feeding into the level above). "Higher" parts of the hierarchy are, roughly, those parts that are further away from the sensory stimulus. These tend to be at slower temporal time-scales, and a higher level of abstraction. At the very top they might correspond to relatively stable beliefs. "Lower" parts of the hierarchy are closer to the sensory stimulus. These tend to be at faster temporal frequencies, and at low levels of abstraction (i.e. concrete and specific). These, for example, might correspond to early stages of visual processing: your brain's early statistically driven attempts to make sense of noisy inputs. Of course, in order to express these neurally encoded predictions we need to use rough-and-ready descriptions in natural language, but there is nothing linguistic about the priors/hypotheses (e.g. "light tends to come from above" / "This is a face") themselves.

Let us return to the case of the squeaking window. At the stage where those two hypotheses (burglar vs. wind) are competing, a great deal of ambiguity has already been resolved, in a Bayesian fashion, at lower levels of the hierarchy. For example, in early stages of auditory processing, the qualities of the sound will have been settled upon, giving rise to the conscious experience being a certain way, qualitatively speaking. Higher up the hierarchy, that sound gets interpreted as a creaking window, as opposed to, say, a screeching cat. The direction of causation is from the (events represented in the) lower regions of the hierarchy, to the (events represented in the) higher regions of the hierarchy. However, the direction of the Bayesian inference is from the effects to the causes.

So much for *hierarchy*, now for *precision*. Although incoming signals are always ambiguous, in different contexts the degree of ambiguity will differ. To maximize its predictive success, the brain needs to accurately estimate how much ambiguity (uncertainty) there will be. In other words, it needs to make second-order predictions, namely, predictions about how much it should rely on its predictions (which amounts to how much it should pay heed to the prediction-error).

In contexts where low ambiguity is expected (high signal-to-noise ratio), higher precision will be demanded, and the prediction error will be taken more seriously. Conversely, when there is high ambiguity (or, through some top-down influence, there is no interest in the stimulus), low precision is demanded, and the prediction error will be taken less seriously. This is called "precision weighting" (Hohwy, 2013), it amounts to adjusting "the gain" on prediction error, and is taken to be modulated by neurotransmitters such as dopamine (Corlett et al., 2010).

It has been hypothesized that the turning up of precision is the mechanism that underlies attentional focus. Take visual attention as an example. If you are attending to a particular part of your visual field, you have turned the precision right up on your perceptual hypothesis. The result is more precise and informationally rich, but also (other things being equal) higher-risk in terms of error. Thankfully, in appropriate contexts, say, good lighting conditions, you can afford to take that risk because the environment is informationally reliable. If, however, you are walking through the woods at dusk, excessive levels of precision-weighting might lead you to mistake tree-stumps for lurking individuals.

The turning down of precision is also seen as equally important. It corresponds to perceptual decoupling from the world; it allows your brain to hold on to hypotheses that do not adequately predict the world (since the prediction error is down-modulated to the point of being ignored). In the context of *active inference*, which we are about to introduce now, the turning down of precision is central to the inhibition of overt action.

From Perception to Action

So the main business of brains like ours, according to the PPF, is the minimization of errors in the prediction of sensory inputs. However, the minimization of prediction error isn't only achieved by the brain updating its predictions about the world (which results in perception and belief), it is sometimes achieved by bringing the world, usually the body, in line with the predictions (Clark, 2016: Chapter 4; Feldman and Friston, 2010). The result of this is bodily action. To use a specific example, when I see someone with their hand up, my brain has adopted the hypothesis that someone has their hand up: My brain responds to the world. However, when I move to raise my hand, my nervous system adopts the proprioceptive prediction that my hand is raised. That prediction is then fulfilled by my subsequent hand-raising. Thus an organism's capacity for endogenous bodily movement is just another manifestation of prediction error minimization. It just happens that the relevant prediction in the case of action is a self-fulfilling prophecy.

This distinction between the updating of the hypothesis to fit the world and the updating of the world to fit the hypothesis amounts to the distinction between *perceptual inference* and *active inference*. Although in theory these are two quite distinct manifestations of the predictive processing apparatus, in practice organisms are constantly doing a bit of both. For example, when you are looking through a rainy windscreen, you might perform exploratory movements from side to side to see what is beyond the droplet-covered glass. Here your nervous system is effortlessly toggling between active and perceptual inference to generate an optimal hypothesis of what's in the world, including the intricate subtleties of your place in it. The central mechanism behind this toggling is precision. Precision is down-modulated during the formation of the proprioceptive prediction (the functional equivalent of what in more classical architectures is known as the motor command), otherwise it couldn't be formed at all (since it would be immediately updated to fit the world) and then increased in such a way as to bring the body in line with it.

Predictive Processing and Imagination

How does the PPF accommodate imagination? What is going on in our predictive brains when we imagine something? Here we go through a number of options.

Imagination as the Fundamental Building Block of Experience

Several theorists have taken this to be rather unproblematic, seeing the PPF as especially suited to accounting for imagination. For example, Andy Clark states that the PPF "means that perception (at least, as it occurs in creatures like us), is co-emergent with (something quite like) imagination" (Clark, 2015: 26). And as Michael Kirchhoff (Kirchhoff, 2018: 752) puts it, there is a "deep unity" in the idea, central to the PPF, that "perception and imagination are the psychological results of the brain generating its own sensory inputs top-down." This notion of the "brain generating its own input top-down," though striking, is perhaps a little misleading, at least insofar as it holds on to the idea that what we experience, our phenomenology, at a given time is determined or constituted by "input." A more complete embracing of the PPF and an understanding of how radically it departs from predominantly bottom-up views leaves us with the notion that our phenomenology at any given time is not determined – still less constituted by – an input (whether self-generated or not) that predates (even fractionally) the experience. Instead, the story goes, it is a forward-looking projection, leaving the role of input as one of correction and constraint: The difference between the imagining mind (or indeed the hallucinating mind) and the perceiving mind is much less great than in standard views, since the role of in-the-moment environmental information is much smaller. What is needed in order to take cognition offline, to break the link with the world, is to turn down the precision in a way that makes model-building (often deliberately, in the case of imagination, and accidentally in the case of hallucination) unconstrained by, and unresponsive to, *sensory input*.

In a sense, this amounts to a revisionist metaphysics of perceptual experience. Contrary to what we might think, perception *actually* involves imagination. On this view, the oft-cited dictum that "perception is controlled hallucination" is almost right. But the word "hallucination" already implies that there is no correspondence to reality. What works better is: "Perception is constrained imagination." Hallucination, on the other hand, is imagination unconstrained by sensory input. This construes imagination as a fundamental building block of PPF: the raw material of all experience, whether offline or online.

Imagination as (a Subspecies of) Offline Cognition

This interpretation of the relationship between the PPF and imagination effectively equates the mind's selected predictive hypothesis (which determines the experience at any given time) with imagination. On this view, any conscious experience – perception, hallucination, dreaming etc. – involves imagination. But one might argue that this seems like an unorthodox terminological stipulation, and an unhelpful one at that. Isn't it more apt to say that the online version of this should be called perception and the offline version (or a subset thereof at least) called imagination? If this is indeed the case, one might think (*pace* Clark) that there is no reason that they would co-emerge. Indeed, one might think that the ability to decouple from the sensory flow is a later achievement, both phylogenetically and ontogenetically (Pezzulo, 2011; Pezzulo and Castelfranchi, 2009). In contrast to the idea that imagination is basic, perception would, in this view, emerge long before imagination, and it is the latter that reuses the resources used for the former and not the other way around.

To put this another way, while our experience at any given time is determined by the multilevel predictive model that our brains have selected, sometimes this is in order to make sense of imminent sensory input, and what we are talking about in this case is *online* cognition, which gives rise to *perceptual* experience. At other times, the story goes, the link to the outside world is broken. This would be achieved through a down-regulation of precision, and what we are talking about here is *offline* cognition. The natural thing to say, one might argue, is that one subspecies of such offline cognition is *imaginative* experience. Other subspecies might include, for example, dreaming (Hobson and Friston, 2012), mind-wandering (Metzinger, 2018), hallucination (Wilkinson, 2014), or inner speech (Wilkinson and Fernyhough, 2017). Some might construe these as forms of imagination, or as involving imagination, others not.[3] In what follows we will focus on a more restricted notion of deliberate imagination as a distinct form of offline cognition.[4]

This overall approach views imagination proper, not so much as an all-pervasive building block of experience, but as a particular subspecies of offline cognition, that, yes, has a lot in common with, say, perception, but is to be sharply distinguished from it in a number of ways. The main challenge for accounts of imagination then becomes what the precise nature of that distinction is.

But even what perception and imagination have in common is qualitatively different, and this reflects a real virtue of the PPF in explaining a feature of imagination (and related mental episodes). Because the hypothesis-building in the imaginative (decoupled) instance is not driven by an attempt to minimize incoming prediction error, it is not hypothesis-building at the very bottom of the hierarchy (namely, at or near the organism's sensory surfaces), and hence the corresponding experience has certain phenomenological features. For example, in imagining a blue car, you might not imagine necessarily, as you do in perception, that particular shade of blue. In the broadest terms, imaginative experience tends to be less vivid and determinate, and more abstract, and the PPF has a convincing explanation of these differences.[5]

Departing from Reality Without Surprise

An immediate apparent worry arises for the PPF account of imagination. According to the PPF, our experiential content arises from the interaction between top-down predictions and error signals from our sensory contact with *reality*. One of the most obvious problems for accommodating imagination within the PPF is that the purpose of imagination is, in most cases, to envisage a *departure* from reality. This raises the worry of how we are able to *maintain* imagined content despite its conflict with the incoming sensory signal. One would expect predictions of content that departs from reality to generate significant error signals and thus be quickly extinguished as the relevant error signals propagate through the hierarchy. After all, the predictive hierarchy works to minimize overall surprise and imaginative departures from reality are often, in the technical sense, surprising. Thus, the question arises as to how imaginative content can be maintained despite conflicting with our sensory input. If our minds are made to model and track reality, how do we accomplish the sustained suspension of disbelief? It is hard to explain how we can foster a state of what Keats called "negative capability ... when man is capable of being in uncertainties, mysteries, doubts, without an irritable reaching after fact" (Keats, 1958: 193–194).

---

3 For example, Wilkinson and Fernyhough (2017) have argued that it is misleading to think of inner speech as involving imagination.
4 We will henceforth refer to this simply as "imagination," but this does not indicate that we see this as the only mental process worthy of the name.
5 Imagination doesn't *have* to be less vivid or determinate than perception, as we can conceive of super-imaginers who can imagine with perceptual vivacity. However, this would be an exceptional case.

This worry can potentially be assuaged by taking account of the role of precision-weighting according to the PPF. Earlier we saw how turning down the precision on incoming error signals was central to explaining action in PPF. However, it may also play a central role in explaining how we are able to maintain imaginative content that is mismatched with the immediate environment. When we are engaged in an imaginative exercise, we should expect there to be a large discrepancy between the imagined content being predicted by higher levels in the hierarchy and incoming sensory signals. As such, we expect the incoming sensory signals to be extremely imprecise with respect to our *departure* from reality. Therefore, by assigning a low precision-weighting to error-signals coming from the sensory periphery, the errors can be down-modulated to the extent that they do not perturb the imagined content. Just as in action control, where precision-weighting allows one to maintain content of an action that has not yet happened in order to bring that action about, in the case of imagination, precision-weighting allows one to maintain content pertaining to circumstances that are not (yet) occurring in one's immediate environment and that may never actually occur.

However, while this explains how imagination can be *maintained*, it does not explain how it can be *constrained*. Our imaginative episodes tend to be relatively coherent, so one would expect there to be something playing the error-correcting role of inputs from the external world and thereby constraining the *development* of imaginative activity.

Imaginative Agency and Imaginative Constraints

An upshot of this appeal to precision-weighting is that imagination is just like perception but without being constrained by incoming sensory input. However, this immediately gives rise to the question of what, if anything, *constrains* imagination. The deliberate act of imagining can be distinguished from dreaming, hallucination, and mind-wandering by the fact that it is a product of our personal-level agency. Imagination is often *voluntary* and *goal-directed*, and must therefore be *constrained*.

Imaginative Agency

Imagining is something we often do voluntarily, usually to serve a particular purpose. One way of appreciating this phenomenon is to carefully contrast imagination with imagery. In contrast to imagery, imagination is a personal-level phenomenon: People are engaged in acts of imagination, people imagine things, and, although they do all manner of things that *involve* imagery, they don't do imagery, or engage in imagery *tout court*. Acts of imagination enable people to appreciate, in potentially many different ways, non-actual scenarios, and, when they are engaged in such acts, they may be motivated to do so by a number of different things. These acts of imagination will often recruit or make use of imagery in many modalities, but there will also be aspects to the imaginative experience that aren't imagistic (Langland-Hassan, 2015; Yablo, 1993).[6]

Imagination is often within the control of our intentions; it is something that we do for a reason (Langland-Hassan, 2016). We use our imagination to serve a variety of different purposes. We may be trying to remember the color of someone's hair, judge whether we could jump over a stream, reason about a social situation, or simply entertain fantastical scenarios for the pleasure of it. The potential aims of imagination include (but are not limited to) (1) knowledge-acquisition, (2) creativity, and (3) comprehension of others' creative outputs. In short, imagination is goal-directed.

Imaginative Constraints

Understanding imagination as a goal-directed activity immediately gives rise to issues regarding how we are able to keep the imagination under control so that it reaches its goals. If imagination were just the free association of ideas, then it's hard to see how we could ever plot a stable course to the goal that we are aiming for. Imagination must be constrained in some way so that we can pursue a given goal. However, all of the goals that we put imagination to require that it is in some sense *generative*. To serve any useful purpose it must give us more than we already started with. Thus, in order for imagination to serve its purpose, it cannot be too constrained by our intentions. If we could only imagine exactly what we intend to imagine, then imagination couldn't give us any new content (Langland-Hassan, 2016). To explain the balance between the goal-directed and generative nature of imagination, the PPF needs to explain how imagination is constrained to just the right extent.

This is particularly pertinent when one focuses on cases in which the imagination is used to generate knowledge. The imagination often *seems* unbounded and without constraint. However, if this were the case then it would be *more* likely to generate falsehoods than truths. Imagination must be constrained in order to provide knowledge (Balcerak Jackson, 2018; Kind, 2016; Williamson, 2016). On the other hand, if we want to generate any new knowledge, what we imagine cannot be entirely "up to us," as it must go beyond what we already know (Balcerak Jackson, 2016, 2018; Langland-Hassan, 2016). The knowledge-generating capacity of the imagination can be explained by suggesting that some constraints on the imagination are fixed and within our control, allowing for exploratory activity within these constraints. For example, if one wants to know whether a sofa will fit through a door, one must constrain one's imagination to keep the relevant shapes and sizes and the laws of physics fixed, while allowing for exploration of various possible ways of manipulating the sofa. Van Leeuwen refers to this kind of imaginative process as "*exploratory constraint satisfaction*" (van Leeuwen, 2013: 229).

Imagination does not only serve to provide us with knowledge, it also plays a central role in creative activity, for example in the development of art and fiction for others' consumption. As with the case of knowledge-directed imagination,

---

6 It should be noted that some take imagination to be inherently imagistic (Kind, 2001); however, this does not preclude a distinction between imagination and imagery, as there can be imagery that is not the product of imagination.

creative imagination must be constrained. The structures, situations, or narratives that play out in our minds are not wild free-associations of concepts, they are coherent, in some sense that is akin to the coherence of perceptual experience, albeit with room for departures from reality. Again, the notion of imaginative exploration within chosen constraints seems apt to capture this activity. Creative imaginers explore what is possible within well-defined constraints that behave in accordance with certain (natural or narrative) expectations.

A further role for imagination lies in our ability to engage with others' creative outputs. When we engage with a fiction, our imaginative episodes are, again, constrained in various ways. First, our imaginative episodes tend to try to conform to our beliefs about reality as much as possible (Weisberg and Goodstein, 2009), although not necessarily the immediately experienced environment. Second, imaginative engagement with fiction is constrained by expectations determined by genre-specific narrative conventions (van Leeuwen, 2013).

Where are the Constraints in PPF?

The problem for the PPF account of imagination lies in explaining where the voluntary constraints on imagination come from. How can the imagination be constrained to achieve its goals without being kept in check by the outside world, when, according to the PPF, the constraints on perceptual inference come from error signals from the world? Both perception and action are dynamic processes, with experiential content unfolding over time in a relatively coherent manner. In the case of the former, this coherence can be explained by the fact that the content is constantly being entrained to reality by an incoming error signal. However, in the case of imagination, where the precise aim is a departure from reality, there is no error signal coming from a merely possible world to keep the content in check. In line with this concern, even Clark admits that "it seems very likely that for most creatures acts of deliberate imagining . . . are simply impossible" (Clark, 2016: 94). Yet acts of deliberate imagining are precisely the target explanandum.

This problem is not limited to accounts of the imagination. It is equally problematic in accounting for any departure from one's immediate reality. The PPF should be able to account for how we are able to accurately remember the past despite the sensory signals having long departed, and how we are able to predict and plan for distant future events taking place in environments different than those from which one's current sensory stimulation is coming.[7] In these cases, as with imagination, the question arises as to where the relevant error signals for constraining one's departure from immediate reality come from.

The PPF can arguably explain these capacities for "mental time travel" in terms of dampening the error signals from sensory inputs by lowering the expected sensory precision, so that error signals from *within* the generative hierarchy, rather than the sensory periphery, play the primary role in constraining content (see Clark, 2016:

---

7 There is some evidence to suggest that memory, planning, and imagination may have more in common than is often assumed, suggesting that all of these processes that call for departures from reality may be mediated by the same underlying mechanisms (De Brigard, 2014, 2017).

102–108). In this way, content can be constrained by past occurrences, since the hierarchy has been shaped by experiences, and more distant future predictions can be kept in check by the inbuilt assumption that the future will resemble the past that has sculpted the hierarchy.

Returning to the case of imagination, for situations that are similar to those that we have encountered in the past, imagination may similarly be constrained by error signals from within the hierarchy in the same manner as in cases of memory or longer-term prediction. Intra-hierarchical error signals may explain our ability to imagine scenarios that are closely related to our immediate situation or those that closely mirror our own past experiences. Imagination is thus likely to work in a similar fashion to memory or planning when the goals of imagination are closely aligned with those of these other activities. However, it seems unable to account for our ability to purposefully engage with imaginative content that drastically departs from reality, either for gaining knowledge of more distant possibilities or for engaging in more fantastical creative or recreational imaginative episodes.

Imagination as Mental Action

So far, we have considered accounts that conceive of imaginative experiences as grounded in sensory hypotheses. Although this speaks to the sensory phenomenology present in much (although arguably not all) imagining, it generates problems with accounting for how these hypotheses can be purposeful and constrained. However, an alternative way of understanding imagination within the PPF is in terms not so much of perception as of action.

Active Inference and Mental Action

Imagination, in this view, emerges as predicted consequences of anticipated possible actions. In order to explain how actions are selected from a range of options, proponents of the PPF arguably need to include *counterfactual* representations (Burr and Jones, 2016; Friston et al., 2012; Seth, 2014), i.e. predictions of what the sensory consequences *would* be if one *were* to engage in a particular action. For example, in order to decide whether to look left or right, one must predict the likely sensory consequences of each option. Since many actions will be mutually exclusive, many such representations will inevitably be about merely fictional circumstances, representing possible sensory consequences of actions that never occur. The fact that action may already require representing non-actual states may provide a clue as to the basis of imagination, for which representation of merely possible or non-actual states is central (Pezzulo, 2011; Pezzulo and Castelfranchi, 2009). Imagination may emerge from active inference with "suppression of overt sensory and motor processes" (Pezzulo, 2012: 1; see also Pezzulo, 2017).

This reliance on action may seem like a perplexing move, since action is usually *contrasted* with sensory, perception-like events. Thus, at this point, it is vital to distinguish between two different senses of "action." In one sense (most commonly used in the cognitive sciences), "action" simply means motor activity, the endogenous bringing about of bodily movement. But this is neither sufficient, nor is it necessary, for "action" in the second sense (most commonly used in philosophy), which is tied not so much to the *motoric,* but to the *agentive.* Roughly, something is an action if it is intentional (or, to be more precise, has a description under which it is intentional). If you deliberately imagine a red triangle (maybe you've been offered a large sum of money to do so), that counts as an action in the agentive sense, but not (at least not obviously) in the motoric sense.[8]

What is the relationship between these two senses of "action" within the PPF? We said in the section "From Perception to Action" (above) that motor activity is understood within the PPF in terms of *active inference* (where this is contrasted with perceptual inference). In active inference, the world (in this case the body) is brought in line with predictions (in this case proprioceptive predictions), instead of the other way around, as it is with perceptual inference. However, if precision is turned down, the prediction doesn't have to be fulfilled, the bodily movement doesn't ensue, and you end up with motor imagination or rehearsal. But although active inference is usually thought of in the context of explaining motor activity via proprioceptive predictions, there is nothing special or different about proprioception, and the same can apply to the sensory domain. In other words, the organism can generate sensory predictions that also don't need to be fulfilled, and the result here would be sensory imagination.

Note that, although this looks like a view of imagination as merely decoupled perception, it is grounded in active inference, not in perceptual inference. In relying on active inference, these events, both proprioceptive and sensory, have to be potential events. More specifically, they are decoupled versions of potential actions (in the philosophical sense), both practical and epistemic. And this provides constraints that you wouldn't get from freewheeling perceptual inference: Proprioceptive and sensory imagination in this view is constrained by potential bodily actions, by potential acts of listening and looking. Note that, in being active, visual imagination is best thought of as decoupled looking, rather than seeing; and auditory imagination is best thought of as decoupled listening, rather than hearing. We do not get our attention passively grabbed by what we imagine (as we do with a worldly event like a bang or a flash). We bring it actively (and often effortfully) into being. It is driven by our agency.

This core idea, that imagination involves possible actions and experiences, generates constraints that come from two main sources. The first is bodily constraints that are the result of the organism's phenotype. The second is constraints from past experience. Some of the ways in which actions affect sensory input are relatively stable, both throughout one's lifetime and over recent evolutionary history, since they are determined by the shape of one's body. These stable relationships between action and sensation are known as sensorimotor contingencies (O'Regan and Noë, 2001; Seth, 2014). Given this stability, they are likely also to be stable features of one's predictive model of the world (Burr and Jones, 2016). As a result, when one

---

8 That is why the latter is not always necessary for the former, and indeed, there is a great deal of action (motor activity) that is not action (intentional/agentive).

engages in merely imagined action, the content of one's imagination will be constrained by the sensorimotor contingencies for the kind of body that one possesses.

However, some constraints on the predicted sensory consequences of action derive from stable structure in the world rather than one's own body. For example, by engaging in the action of eating an apple on several occasions, we may come to associate this action with a certain gustatory consequence: the taste of an apple. These kinds of stable relationships can also be modeled by the predictive hierarchy, allowing the predicted consequences of actions to be constrained by the way the world is. As a result, the merely simulated action involved in imagination can also be suitably constrained by past experience.

Distant Fantasies and the Role of Language

The active-inference-based account improves upon the purely perceptual-inference-based account of imagination by accommodating the purposive nature of imagination, as well as the idea that imagination can be constrained. By deliberately simulating actions that never actually take place we can generate content that departs from our immediate circumstances, yet which is constrained by the brain's model of how actions impact on sensation.

However, one concern goes, in doing so, does this not still tie imagination too closely to the real world? The active-inference-based accounts can explain how we are able to simulate the kinds of actions that we tend to engage in with the kinds of bodies that we possess and the kinds of lives we have led, and this may account for a wide range of the kinds of imaginative activity that we engage with in everyday circumstances. However, even a cursory reflection on the phenomenology of imagination suggests that not all of our imaginative episodes are quite this mundane.

Thus far, neither a perceptual-inference-based nor an active-inference-based PPF account seems apt to explain the full range of our imaginative competences. Neither approach seems able to walk the tightrope between imagination being entirely unconstrained and freewheeling, on the one hand, and too closely tied to reality, on the other. A potential solution may lie in exploring the role that language plays in structuring our imaginative episodes.

Although Clark is skeptical about the possibility of deliberate imagination in most creatures, he takes deliberate imagination to be possible in humans as a result of "the use of self-cueing via language" (Clark, 2016: 94). In many cases, our ability to generate imaginative episodes is closely tied to our consumption and production of *narrative*. Perhaps language helps to steer attention when we engage in offline imagination, much as it can do in our online interactions with the world (Lupyan, 2012; Lupyan and Clark, 2015).

As humans, we develop in a linguistically saturated environment. Language serves as more than just a medium for communicating thought; it is also central to the development of our cognitive capacities and to shaping and steering our thoughts (Clark, 2006). The hierarchical generative model that we build up through our interactions with the environment models more than just the natural causal structure of the world around us: It is also likely to encompass associations between words and their contents. Simply hearing, reading, or merely entertaining a word or sentence about a particular content is likely to impact the predictions regarding perceiving or acting on instances of that content. Words create "artificial contexts" in which one is biased toward expecting to perceptually encounter their content (Lupyan and Clark, 2015: 282–283). For example, merely hearing the word that corresponds to a stimulus that would otherwise remain invisible to subjects can boost the stimulus into visual awareness (Lupyan and Ward, 2013).

In more mundane imaginative exercises, such as imagining whether a sofa will fit through the door, we tend not to engage in drastic fantastical departures from reality, and that is a very good thing. It wouldn't help if one suddenly imagined the sofa turning into a hippopotamus. Notice, however, that as you read the previous sentence, it was hard not to imagine the aforementioned fantastical transformation, despite it being far from our usual bodily interactions with the world. This suggests that the interaction between language and imagination may provide a route for the PPF proponent to account for our ability to imagine more distant fantasies. Linguistic cues may bias our offline simulations in a similar way to how they bias perception, bringing particular content to awareness. Furthermore, the compositional and thus productive nature of language may explain how we are able to combine contents in imagination of which we have no experience and that we are vanishingly unlikely ever to experience.

The idea that language has a significant role to play in a PPF account of imagination seems promising. However, much more work needs to be done to fully flesh out this idea. At first sight, the proposal seems to suffer from a "chicken-and-egg" problem. We tend to see narrative linguistic expression as the product of creative imaginative endeavors, so it is hard to see how language could be both the product of the process and the precursor that needs to already be in place to guide and constrain it. Moreover, the precise details of how complex linguistic abilities are realized according to PPF and how such abilities impact on other mental processes within the PPF remain to be worked out in detail. Thus, exploring the way in which language engenders the capacity for drastic imaginative departures from reality is a fruitful line for further research.

Concluding Remarks

On the one hand, PPF has the potential to demystify the imagination, as it frames the imagination as much more similar and closely tied to perception and/or action. On the other hand, a PPF account of the imagination faces problems of its own. In particular, as things stand, PPF must do more to account for how the imagination can be both suitably constrained and sufficiently generative without the relevant constraints being imposed by the world. How can our predictions be constrained by mere fictions and fantasies, when the main task of the brain is to predict reality rather than departures from it?[9] If the PPF can overcome these issues,

---

9 Answering this question could also provide insight into cases in which the mind is detrimentally constrained by fiction and fantasy in atypical contexts (e.g. delusions and hallucinations in schizophrenia). In particular, it might be that imaginative episodes in these contexts are, for whatever reason, not recognized as such by the subject.

perhaps by appealing to the role of language, and provide an account of the imagination, then it can come one step closer to fulfilling its promise of providing a grand, unified approach to the mind.

References

Balcerak Jackson, M. (2016). On Imagining, Supposing and Conceiving. In A. Kind and P. Kung (eds.), *Knowledge Through Imagination*. Oxford, UK: Oxford University Press, 42–60.

(2018). Justification by Imagination. In F. Macpherson and F. Dorsch (eds.), *Perceptual Imagination and Perceptual Memory*. Oxford, UK: Oxford University Press, 209–226.

Bayes, T. (1763). LII. An Essay Towards Solving a Problem in the Doctrine of Chances. By the Late Rev. Mr. Bayes, FRS Communicated by Mr. Price, in a Letter to John Canton, AMFR S. *Philosophical Transactions of the Royal Society of London*, *53*, 370–418.

Burr, C., and Jones, M. (2016). The Body as Laboratory: Prediction-Error Minimization, Embodiment, and Representation. *Philosophical Psychology*, *29*(4), 586–600.

Clark, A. (2006). Language, Embodiment, and the Cognitive Niche. *Trends in Cognitive Sciences*, *10*(8), 370–374.

(2013). Whatever Next? Predictive Brains, Situated Agents, and the Future of Cognitive Science. *Behavioral and Brain Sciences*, *36*(3), 181–204.

(2015). Perception as Prediction. In D. Stokes, M. Matthen, and S. Biggs (eds.), *Perception and its Modalities*. New York, NY: Oxford University Press, 23–43.

(2016). *Surfing Uncertainty: Prediction, Action and the Embodied Mind*. Oxford, UK: Oxford University Press.

Corlett, P. R., Taylor, J. R., Wang, X. J., Fletcher, P. C., and Krystal, J. H. (2010). Toward a Neurobiology of Delusions. *Progress in Neurobiology*, *92*(3), 345–369.

De Brigard, F. (2014). Is Memory for Remembering? Recollection as a Form of Episodic Hypothetical Thinking. *Synthese*, *191*(2), 155–185.

(2017). Memory and Imagination. In A. Kind (ed.), *The Routledge Handbook of Philosophy of Imagination*. London, UK; New York, NY: Routledge, 127–140.

Feldman, H., and Friston, K. (2010). Attention, Uncertainty, and Free-Energy. *Frontiers in Human Neuroscience*, *4*, 215.

Friston, K., Adams, R., Perrinet, L., and Breakspear, M. (2012). Perceptions as Hypotheses: Saccades as Experiments. *Frontiers in Psychology*, *3*, 151.

Hobson, J. A., and Friston, K. J. (2012). Waking and Dreaming Consciousness: Neurobiological and Functional Considerations. *Progress in Neurobiology*, *98*(1), 82–98.

Hohwy, J. (2013). *The Predictive Mind*. Oxford, UK: Oxford University Press.

Keats, J. (1958). *The Letters of John Keats, 1814–1821*. Edited by H. E. Rollins. Cambridge, MA: Harvard University Press.

Kind, A. (2001). Putting the Image Back in Imagination. *Philosophy and Phenomenological Research*, *62*(1), 85–109.

(2016). Imagining Under Constraints. In A. Kind and P. Kung (eds.), *Knowledge Through Imagination*. Oxford, UK: Oxford University Press, 145–159.

Kirchhoff, M. D. (2018). Predictive Processing, Perceiving and Imagining: Is to Perceive to Imagine, or Something Close to it? *Philosophical Studies*, *175*(3), 751–767.

Langland-Hassan, P. (2015). Imaginative Attitudes. *Philosophy and Phenomenological Research*, *90*(3), 664–686.

(2016). On Choosing What to Imagine. In A. Kind and P. Kung (eds.), *Knowledge Through Imagination*. Oxford, UK: Oxford University Press, 61–84.

Lupyan, G. (2012). Language Augmented Prediction. *Frontiers in Psychology*, *3*, 422.

Lupyan, G., and Clark, A. (2015). Words and the World: Predictive Coding and the Language-Perception-Cognition Interface. *Current Directions in Psychological Science*, *24*(4), 279–284.

Lupyan, G., and Ward, E. J. (2013). Language Can Boost Otherwise Unseen Objects into Visual Awareness. *Proceedings of the National Academy of Sciences*, *110*(35), 14196–14201.

Metzinger, T. (2017). The Problem of Mental Action: Predictive Control Without Sensory Sheets. In T. Metzinger and W. Wiese (eds.), *Philosophy and Predictive Processing*. Mainz, Germany: Johannes Gutenberg-Universität.

(2018). Why is Mind-Wandering Interesting for Philosophers? In K. Christoff and K. C. R. Fox (eds.), *The Oxford Handbook of Spontaneous Thought: Mind-Wandering, Creativity, and Dreaming*. Oxford, UK: Oxford University Press, 97–111.

O'Regan, J. K., and Noë, A. (2001). A Sensorimotor Account of Vision and Visual Consciousness. *Behavioral and Brain Sciences*, *24*(5), 939–973.

Pezzulo, G. (2011). Grounding Procedural and Declarative Knowledge in Sensorimotor Anticipation. *Mind & Language*, *26*(1), 78–114.

(2012). An Active Inference View of Cognitive Control. *Frontiers in Psychology*, *3*, 478.

(2014). Why Do You Fear the Bogeyman? An Embodied Predictive Coding Model of Perceptual Inference. *Cognitive, Affective, & Behavioral Neuroscience*, *14*(3), 902–911.

(2017). Tracing the Roots of Cognition in Predictive Processing. In T. Metzinger and W. Wiese (eds.), *Philosophy and Predictive Processing*. Mainz, Germany: Johannes Gutenberg-Universität.

Pezzulo, G., and Castelfranchi, C. (2009). Thinking as the Control of Imagination: A Conceptual Framework for Goal-Directed Systems. *Psychological Research PRPF*, *73*(4), 559–577.

Seth, A. K. (2014). A Predictive Processing Theory of Sensorimotor Contingencies: Explaining the Puzzle of Perceptual Presence and its Absence in Synesthesia. *Cognitive Neuroscience*, *5*(2), 97–118.

van Leeuwen, N. (2013). The Meanings of "Imagine" Part I: Constructive Imagination. *Philosophy Compass*, *8*(3), 220–230.

Weisberg, D. S., and Goodstein, J. (2009). What Belongs in a Fictional World? *Journal of Cognition and Culture*, *9*(1–2), 69–78.

Wilkinson, S. (2014). Accounting for the Phenomenology and Varieties of Auditory Verbal Hallucination Within a Predictive Processing Framework. *Consciousness and Cognition*, *30*, 142–155.

Wilkinson, S., and Fernyhough, C. (2017). Auditory Verbal Hallucinations and Inner Speech: A Predictive Processing Perspective. In Z. Radman (ed.), *Before Consciousness: In Search of the Fundamentals of the Mind*. Exeter, UK: Imprint Academic, Limited, 372–397.

Williamson, T. (2016). Knowing by Imagining. In A. Kind and P. Kung (eds.), *Knowledge Through Imagination*. Oxford, UK: Oxford University Press, 113–123.

Yablo, S. (1993). Is Conceivability a Guide to Possibility? *Philosophy and Phenomenological Research, 53*(1), 1–42.

8 Memory and Imagination: Perspectives on Constructive Episodic Simulation

Daniel L. Schacter and Donna Rose Addis

Questions concerning the relation between memory and imagination have occupied a prominent place in cognitive psychology and cognitive neuroscience during the past several decades. Johnson and Raye's (1981) reality monitoring framework brought the issue into prominence by portraying the relation as constituting a fundamental problem that must be addressed by any cognitive model. Johnson and Raye's framework provided the inspiration for subsequent cognitive and neuroimaging studies concerning the mnemonic qualities of perceived and imagined events, and the underlying psychological and neural processes that allow us to distinguish between them (for an update, see Simons, Garrison, and Johnson, 2017).

A little more than a decade ago, a related line of research emerged that focused on striking neural and cognitive similarities that occur when people remember past experiences and imagine or simulate future and hypothetical experiences. The foundation of this work was set in the 1980s and 1990s by clinical observations that an amnesic patient with a severe deficit in recalling past experiences also had comparable difficulties imagining future experiences (Tulving, 1985; see also, Klein, Loftus, and Kihlstrom, 2002) and that suicidally depressed patients showed similar reductions in the specificity of autobiographical memories and future imaginings (Williams et al., 1996). Observations that remembering past experiences and imagining future experiences show similar neural correlates (Okuda et al., 2003), phenomenological characteristics (D'Argembeau and van der Linden, 2004) and individual differences (D'Argembeau and van der Linden, 2006) heightened interest in the relation between the two. This growing interest was galvanized by the publication in 2007 of several papers that strengthened the case for a link between remembering and imagining by revealing strong overlap in the brain regions engaged when people remembered past experiences and either imagined future experiences (Addis, Wong, and Schacter, 2007; Szpunar, Watson, and McDermott, 2007) or imagined novel scenes (i.e. *scene construction*: Hassabis, Kumaran, and Maguire, 2007a). This evidence from functional magnetic resonance imaging (fMRI) was complemented by neuropsychological evidence showing that several amnesic patients with medial temporal lobe damage exhibit scene construction deficits (Hassabis et al., 2007b).

Based on these and related observations, Schacter, Addis, and Buckner (2007; see also, Buckner and Carroll, 2007) pointed to the existence of a core neural network, comprised of medial temporal and frontal lobes, posterior cingulate and retrosplenial cortices, and lateral parietal and temporal areas, that supports both remembering and imagining – a network that overlaps substantially with the well-known default mode network (for review, see Buckner, Andrews-Hanna, and Schacter, 2008; Raichle, 2015). Other papers published in 2007 delineated theoretical implications of this emerging line of research for a variety of issues in psychology and neuroscience, including the nature of constructive memory (Schacter and Addis, 2007a, 2007b) and the evolution of mental time travel (Suddendorf and Corballis, 2007).

Since 2007, there has been a vast amount of research exploring the relation between memory on the one hand and imagination, simulation, and scene construction on the other. This rapidly growing literature has been thoroughly reviewed in a number of publications (e.g. Klein, 2013; Michaelian, 2016; Michaelian, Klein, and Szpunar, 2016; Mullally and Maguire, 2014; Schacter et al., 2012; Schacter, Benoit, and Szpunar, 2017; Szpunar, Spreng, and Schacter, 2014; Ward, 2016).

In the present chapter, we do not seek to provide yet another comprehensive review regarding the relation between memory and imagination. Instead, we provide a more focused theoretical discussion motivated by an idea that we initially advanced in 2007 that we refer to as the *constructive episodic simulation hypothesis* (Schacter and Addis, 2007a, 2007b). This hypothesis focuses on the important role of episodic memory (Tulving, 2002) in generating simulations of imagined future events, which we have referred to as *episodic simulation* (Schacter, Addis, and Buckner, 2008). As stated in our initial formulation of the constructive episodic simulation hypothesis, a key function of episodic memory is to support the construction of imagined future events by allowing the retrieval of information about past experiences and the flexible recombination of elements of past experiences into simulations of possible future scenarios. We suggested that remembering past events and simulating future events draw on similar kinds of information in episodic memory and rely on a number of shared processes, including the capacity for relational processing (i.e. linking together disparate bits of information; Cohen and Eichenbaum, 1993). We further argued that the flexible, constructive nature of episodic memory makes it well suited to supporting simulations of ways in which future experiences might play out: The future is rarely an exact repetition of the past, so it is important that information stored in memory can be accessed flexibly and recombined to form simulations of novel upcoming events that are informed by past experiences. However, we suggested that this same flexible, constructive character of episodic memory can produce memory errors that result from miscombining elements of past experiences or confusing imagined and actual events.

More than a decade has passed since we advanced the constructive episodic simulation hypothesis, and there is now a great deal more pertinent experimental work available. In this chapter, we discuss how the constructive episodic simulation hypothesis has fared during the past decade, and how we think about the hypothesis now compared with the original formulation in 2007. We believe that such discussion can help to bring out a number of key theoretical issues regarding the nature of the cognitive and neural mechanisms that underpin the relation between memory and imagination (for related discussions, see Addis, 2018; Schacter and Madore, 2016).

The chapter consists of four main sections. First, we consider cognitive/behavioral studies that have tested the constructive episodic simulation hypothesis. Second, we discuss some of the cognitive neuroscience research on remembering and imagining published since 2007 that has informed our understanding of the neural underpinnings of the constructive episodic simulation hypothesis. Third, a key idea in our 2007 formulation was that the flexible recombination processes that are critical for constructing episodic simulations of imagined future events can also contribute to memory errors. No direct evidence on this point was available at the time, but over the past few years relevant evidence has emerged that we review here. Fourth, we clarify ways in which the conceptual focus of the constructive episodic simulation hypothesis has changed over the past decade.

Assessing the Constructive Episodic Simulation Hypothesis: Cognitive/Behavioral Evidence

One line of cognitive/behavioral evidence that has generally supported the constructive episodic simulation hypothesis comes from studies showing that various patient populations characterized by episodic memory deficits show similar impairments when asked to imagine future or hypothetical events (for reviews, see Hallford et al., 2018; Schacter, Addis, and Buckner, 2008; Schacter et al., 2012; Ward, 2016). Similarly, individual, cultural, and gender differences in level of detail and specificity for remembered past events are paralleled in imagined future events (e.g. Cao et al., 2018; D'Argembeau and van der Linden, 2006; Palombo et al., 2013; Wang et al., 2011).

A related line of evidence comes from studies of normal aging. Addis, Wong, and Schacter (2008) presented young and older adults with a series of word cues, and instructed them to either remember a past experience or imagine a future experience related to the cue word in as much detail as possible. The resulting transcripts were scored using the Autobiographical Interview (AI) that had been previously developed by Levine et al. (2002). The AI distinguishes between two major kinds of details: *internal* or episodic, including who, what, where, and when information, and *external*, including semantic knowledge, related facts, commentary, or references to other events including general events. Replicating earlier work by Levine et al. (2002), Addis, Wong, and Schacter (2008) found that when remembering past experiences, older adults produced fewer internal and more external details than did young adults. Importantly, Addis, Wong, and Schacter (2008) also documented the same pattern for imagined future events. In a subsequent study, Addis et al. (2010) reported an identical pattern of results when using an *experimental recombination procedure* in which participants initially provide autobiographical memories, comprised of a person, place, and object, and the experimenter then recombines the three elements across memories to generate novel stimuli for imagination trials. In a later session, participants imagine a novel event involving the recombined person, place, and object elements, or remember some of the original episodes. Once again, older adults produced fewer internal and more external details for both remembered and imagined events than did young adults, and were less able to integrate all three elements together into a coherent episode.

We initially interpreted the striking parallels between episodic memory and simulation in the Addis, Wong, and Schacter (2008) and Addis et al. (2010) studies as direct support for the constructive episodic simulation hypothesis, theorizing that age-related impairments in retrieving and/or recombining episodic details are responsible for the similar age-related reductions in internal details for remembered past and imagined future events. However, the results of a subsequent study by Gaesser et al. (2011) raised questions about this interpretation. Gaesser et al. (2011) provided pictures of complex scenes to young and older adults, and in conditions comparable to earlier studies instructed participants to generate either memories or imagined future events that were related to the cues. Extending previous results, Gaesser et al. (2011) found parallel age-related declines in internal details (and increases in external details) for both past and future events, pointing again toward an age-related decline in episodic retrieval as the common mechanism. Importantly, however, Gaesser et al. (2011) also included a third condition in which participants were asked to simply describe each picture cue in as much detail as possible (internal details for this task were defined as details present in the depicted scene; external details were defined in the same way as on the memory and imagination tasks). If age-related episodic retrieval impairments are entirely responsible for the reduced internal details by older adults in memory and imagination, then no such reduction should be observed for picture description, because the task should not involve any episodic retrieval. However, Gaesser et al. (2011) observed the same pattern of reduced internal details and increased external details on the picture description task as in the memory and imagination tasks.

Because episodic memory should not impact the picture description task, these results challenged our interpretation of parallel age-related declines in memory and imagination as support for the constructive episodic simulation hypothesis. The results suggested instead that non-episodic factors that are common to the memory, imagination, and description tasks may be primarily responsible for the similar effects of aging on the three tasks. These non-episodic factors could include age-related differences in narrative style or increased off-topic speech in older adults (for further discussion, see Abram et al., 2014; Schacter, Gaesser, and Addis, 2013) that would produce decreased internal and increased external details among older adults on memory, imagination, and description tasks. Moreover, these observations raised the possibility that the aforementioned similarities between remembering and imagining documented in other studies might be produced partly or entirely by non-episodic rather than episodic influences.

Distinguishing Between Episodic and Non-Episodic Influences: Episodic Specificity Induction

The foregoing considerations highlight the critical need to distinguish between episodic and non-episodic influences in order to properly evaluate the constructive episodic simulation hypothesis. Madore, Gaesser, and Schacter (2014) attempted to do so by giving participants brief training in recalling episodic details of a recent experience – an *episodic specificity induction* (ESI) – and examining the downstream effects of such training on subsequent tasks. The ESI is adapted from the Cognitive Interview, which was initially developed as a forensic protocol for increasing retrieval of episodic details of a recent experience from eyewitnesses (Fisher and Geiselman, 1992). The logic of this approach holds that an ESI should increase performance on a subsequent cognitive task only if that task relies on episodic retrieval processes. According to the constructive episodic simulation hypothesis, both remembering past experiences and imagining future experiences in response to picture cues recruit episodic retrieval, and thus should be impacted by a prior ESI, but describing a picture does not involve any episodic retrieval and thus should not be influenced by a prior ESI.

In the study by Madore, Gaesser, and Schacter (2014), participants viewed a brief video of people performing various tasks in a kitchen, and then either received an ESI that directed them to recall the video in as much detail as possible, or a control induction in which they provided their general impressions of the video. Consistent with predictions, Madore, Gaesser, and Schacter (2014) found that following ESI compared with the control induction, both young and old adults produced more internal details during memory and imagination tasks. By contrast, the ESI had no effect on the number of external details on these tasks, or on the number of internal or external details that participants produced on a picture description task (this pattern of results was replicated in a subsequent experiment using a more neutral control induction in which participants simply completed math problems instead of the general impressions control). Madore and Schacter (2016) replicated and extended these results in a young adult sample using words instead of pictures as cues for memory and imagination.

These experiments demonstrate that an episodic retrieval process that is common to remembering past experiences and simulating future experiences can be dissociated from semantic retrieval and narrative description, and therefore supports the constructive episodic simulation hypothesis. More recent studies have extended this approach to other aspects of future simulations, and to related domains in which there are reasons to suppose that episodic retrieval and simulation play an important role in task performance. For example, in studies of social problem-solving, participants perform a *means-end problem-solving* task (MEPS; Platt and Spivack, 1975) in which they are given hypothetical social problems, such as difficulties with friends or handling a situation at work, and attempt to generate means or steps that can solve the problem. Several studies have reported that MEPS performance is positively correlated with the specificity and detail of autobiographical memories in depressed and anxious patients (e.g. Raes et al., 2005) as well as in older adults (Sheldon, McAndrews, and Moscovitch, 2011), suggesting that MEPS performance draws on episodic retrieval and simulation abilities. Consistent with this idea, Madore and Schacter (2014) reported that ESI boosts MEPS performance in young and older adults: Both groups generated more steps that were deemed relevant to solving a social problem, but not more irrelevant steps, after ESI vs. an impressions control induction. Jing, Madore, and Schacter (2016) extended these findings to the domain of personally worrisome future experiences, and found that ESI also boosted the number of alternative positive outcomes that participants imagined regarding standardized or personal negative future events. McFarland et al. (2017) recently documented similar ESI effects on MEPS, remembering, and imagining in a sample of depressed adults.

A parallel line of research has used ESI to reveal that episodic retrieval contributes to aspects of divergent creative thinking, a form of simulation that is analogous in some respects to imagining future events (Roberts and Addis, 2018). Based on several kinds of evidence suggesting the possibility of such a link (for review, see Beaty et al., 2016), Madore, Addis, and Schacter (2015) administered ESI and control inductions (either impressions or math problems) prior to performance of a standard test of divergent thinking that requires generating novel but appropriate uses of common objects (Alternate Uses Task or AUT), or an object association task (OAT) that requires generation of object characteristics related to a cue object, but places little demand on divergent thinking. Madore, Addis, and Schacter (2015) found that ESI (vs. a control induction) boosted measures of generative output on the AUT (e.g. measures of novel and appropriate object uses such as fluency and flexibility) while having no effect on OAT performance. We replicated this effect in a second experiment that also revealed that ESI had no detectable impact on a measure of convergent thinking, and later extended the main findings to a different divergent thinking task and to an older adult population (Madore, Jing, and Schacter, 2016). The novel uses generated on the AUT following ESI were not rated as any more original than those generated after a control induction; there were simply *more* novel uses of approximately equal originality generated after an ESI than a control induction.

In summary, studies of autobiographical remembering, future imagining, social problem-solving, and divergent thinking using ESI have established a role for episodic retrieval in these tasks, which all involve some type of mental simulation. ESI allows the influence of episodic retrieval to be distinguished from other, non-episodic influences that may be operating in parallel with episodic retrieval on these tasks, and critically, the results of the ESI studies have provided support for the constructive episodic simulation hypothesis.

Additional Cognitive/Behavioral Tests

While the evidence we have considered so far has focused on the *processes* shared by memory and imagination, the constructive episodic simulation hypothesis also makes claims about shared *content*, namely, that imagined events are constructed, at least in part, by recombining elements of specific past personal experiences. Several cognitive/ behavioral studies have reported evidence that is generally consistent with this claim by showing that, for example, phenomenological features of remembered and imagined events are affected similarly by such variables as temporal distance from the present (D'Argembeau and van der Linden, 2004) and contextual familiarity (Szpunar and McDermott, 2008). Further evidence along these lines comes from a study that examined perspective or vantage point for remembered past and imagined future events (i.e. first- vs. third-person perspective; McDermott et al., 2016). Both remembered past and imagined future events were experienced predominantly from a first-person perspective.

Perhaps most strikingly, McDermott et al. (2016) examined the spatial distribution of third-person perspectives adopted (e.g. "seeing" one's self from behind, in front, above, below, etc.), and found that they were nearly indistinguishable during episodic memories and future thoughts, a finding that the authors noted fits well with the constructive episodic simulation hypothesis.

More recently, Thakral, Madore, and Schacter (2019) attempted to provide a strong test of the claim that simulated future events rely on the recombined contents of past episodes by assessing whether content-specific episodic information, such as people or locations from particular past episodes, is retrieved and used when people simulate an imagined future experience. Participants initially recalled past episodes that each contained two critical episodic details: a location and person, and then imagined future episodes using pairs of person and location details that were recombined from different memories. Participants rated the vividness with which they experienced each location and person in both remembered and imagined events. To examine whether the content associated with individual episodic details is shared across remembered and imagined events, Thakral et al. (2019) examined whether vividness ratings for person and location details given during the memory task could be used to predict the vividness ratings assigned to the two kinds of event details during the simulation task. If imagined future events are based upon the recombined contents of particular episodic memories, as maintained by the constructive episodic simulation hypothesis, then vividness of individual imagined details should covary with the vividness of those same details in the episodic memories from which they were drawn. This is exactly what was found. To address the possibility that details used to construct a novel episode are based on general knowledge of, or familiarity with, the person or location rather than specific episodic information, participants also rated their knowledge of/familiarity with each person or location in everyday life, ranging from not very familiar to very familiar (on a scale of 1 to 5). Critically, even when the level of familiarity was accounted for, a significant relationship between vividness of remembered and imagined person details and place details remained.

Of course, not all cognitive/behavioral evidence reveals similarities between remembered past and imagined future experiences; numerous differences have been documented (see Schacter et al., 2012). Importantly, our initial formulation of the constructive episodic simulation hypothesis attributed some of these differences to "the more intensive constructive processes required by imagining future events relative to retrieving past events" (Schacter and Addis, 2007b: 782). We will elaborate on this point in the next section when we turn our attention to neural evidence that bears on the constructive episodic simulation hypothesis.

Assessing the Constructive Episodic Simulation Hypothesis: Neural Evidence

Neuroimaging of the Core Network

Neuroimaging has provided compelling support for the constructive episodic simulation hypothesis by demonstrating extensive overlap between patterns of activity associated with memory and simulation (Addis, Wong, and Schacter, 2007; Okuda et al., 2003; Szpunar, Watson, and MacDermott, 2007; Thakral, Benoit, and Schacter, 2017b). For example, Addis, Wong, and Schacter (2007) had participants remember past or imagine future events in response to word cues, press a button when the event was in mind, and elaborate for the remainder of the twenty-second trial. This construction-elaboration paradigm enabled separation of activity associated with the initial generation of events from the subsequent fleshing out of the event representation, revealing maximal neural overlap during the elaboration phase. Subsequent studies have also reported overlap of memory-related brain activity with activity during other forms of simulation, including imagining hypothetical scenes (Axelrod, Resse, and Bar, 2017; Hassabis, Kumaran, and Maguire, 2007a), past events that never occurred (Addis et al., 2009) and counterfactual events (De Brigard et al., 2013). Importantly, the common activity associated with memory and simulation cannot be explained as an artifact of a simulation task that allows participants to simply recast a remembered past event as occurring again in the future. Specifically, Addis et al. (2009) experimentally recombined key details (people, places, objects) to be included in imagined events and still observed considerable neural overlap with remembered events. A recent meta-analysis of twelve studies (Benoit and Schacter, 2015) localized overlapping activity primarily within the default mode network, including regions such as medial prefrontal cortex, lateral temporal and parietal cortices, posterior cingulate and retrosplenial cortices, and the medial temporal lobes (including the hippocampus). These results provide strong support for the designation of this set of regions as the *core* network mediating both memory and simulation, reflecting recruitment of a fundamental constructive process both when remembering and imagining (Hassabis, Kumaran, and Maguire, 2007a; Hassabis et al., 2007b; Schacter, Addis, and Buckner, 2007). Note that despite their extensive overlap, the default mode network is broader than the core network; it contains some cortical regions (e.g. parts of the superior frontal gyri) that are not part of the core network (see Benoit and Schacter, 2015).

Neuroimaging has also revealed differences between memory and simulation. Specifically, relative to remembering past events, imagining future events is associated with greater activity in a number of core network regions; of particular interest is differential simulation-related activity in the hippocampus, initially observed by Addis, Wong, and Schacter (2007) during event construction, and evident in a meta-analysis of eleven studies (Benoit and Schacter, 2015). We have investigated potential explanations for increased hippocampal activity during simulation (for detailed discussion and a multicomponent model, see Addis and Schacter, 2012; for a meta-analysis, see Viard et al., 2012; and for recent related evidence, see Thakral, Benoit, and Schacter, 2017a). In part this activity is related to the successful encoding of simulated events (Martin et al., 2011; Thakral, Benoit, and Schacter, 2017a), but the balance of evidence suggests that it largely reflects the *construction* of novel simulations (e.g. Addis and Schacter, 2008; Campbell et al., 2018; Gaesser et al., 2013; van Mulukom et al., 2013; for discussion, see Schacter, Addis, and Szpunar, 2017; Sheldon and Levine, 2016). Findings of higher activity during memory relative to simulation are less commonly reported (e.g. Gilmore, Nelson, and McDermott, 2016), but have been observed in the hippocampus when the imagined events, having been "pre-simulated" earlier, are retrieved rather than constructed during scanning (see Addis et al., 2011, for discussion).

Despite the consistency of the neuroimaging evidence, the nature of the fundamental constructive process that underpins memory and simulation remains a topic of debate (cf. Palombo et al., 2018; Roberts, Schacter, and Addis, 2018). The scene construction theory (Hassabis, Kumaran, and Maguire, 2007a; Hassabis et al., 2007b; Mullally and Maguire, 2014) posits that the hippocampus is commonly engaged by the construction of a scene that forms the basis of both remembered and imagined events. Indeed, any realistic event representation is highly likely to be played out within a scene (Robin, Wynn, and Moscovitch, 2016) given that space is intrinsic to our experience of reality. However, scene construction theory does not adequately explain differences between memory and imagination, including why the hippocampus is more intensively engaged during imagination. In contrast, the constructive episodic simulation hypothesis emphasizes the centrality of relational processing (Cohen and Eichenbaum, 1993) common to both memory and simulation, while also outlining the ways in which relational processing is more intensive during imagination. Specifically, while the reconstruction of an episodic memory requires the reactivation and reintegration of *existing relations* between details, the construction of a novel imagined event necessitates the *formation of novel relations* by recombining and integrating details retrieved from disparate episodic memories into a coherent event representation (Addis and Schacter, 2012; Schacter and Addis, 2007b). This perspective is not mutually exclusive with scene construction theory; the (re)constructed relations include spatial relations comprising scenes. Importantly, however, we go beyond spatial context to include the other perceptual and conceptual components comprising these often multifaceted and dynamic event representations (e.g. objects, people, actions, time, and emotions). As such, the constructive episodic simulation hypothesis offers a more general theory of memory and simulation that also addresses core network activity beyond the hippocampus (see also Addis, 2018).

Recruitment of extra-hippocampal aspects of the core network reflect recruitment of other processes involved in both memory and imagination, such as attention to and maintenance of event representations (inferior lateral parietal cortex; e.g. Cabeza, Ciaramelli, and Moscovitch, 2012; Thakral, Benoit, and Schacter, 2017b) and mental imagery (precuneus; e.g. Cavanna and Trimble, 2006). Moreover, regions within and beyond the core network mediate particular types of content that typically comprise event representations (Addis, 2018), including contextual information (parahippocampal gyrus, retrosplenial cortex; Bar and Aminoff, 2003), as well as lower-level perceptual content (e.g. visual network; Binder et al., 2009). There is behavioral evidence to suggest that remembered events tend to be more vivid than imagined events (e.g. D'Argembeau and van der Linden, 2004) and in line with these observations, Addis et al. (2009) found that relative to imagined events, remembered events were associated with greater activity in visual cortices. Therefore, the degree to which these different processes and types of content contribute differentially to memory and imagination will influence the spatial distribution of activity across the core network and related networks (Addis, 2018).

Although the focus of the constructive episodic simulation hypothesis has been on the role of episodic memory in the imagining of hypothetical events, it is also important to consider semantic memory processes. Indeed, Schacter and Addis (2007b) suggest that anterior temporal activity evident during both remembering and imagining likely reflects the personal semantic content (e.g. knowledge of familiar people, common activities) inherent to autobiographical event representations. Subsequent findings from patient and neuroimaging studies have indicated that, relative to remembering, simulating novel events may be more reliant on semantic processes. Specifically, semantic dementia patients who are able to retrieve episodic memories in similar detail as healthy controls, and can recast past events into the future, are nevertheless unable to simulate novel future events (Irish et al., 2012). This differential impairment suggests that a schematic framework may be a critical component of an imagined event; once generated, the framework can be fleshed out with relevant episodic and semantic content. Consistent with this idea, neuroimaging studies have reported differential activity for imagining relative to remembering in regions mediating schematic and semantic knowledge (medial prefrontal and lateral temporal cortices, respectively; e.g. Addis, Wong, and Schacter, 2007; Addis et al., 2009; Okuda et al., 2003; see also, Abraham, Schubotz, and von Carmon, 2008). It is likely that the degree to which a schematic framework is required during imagination exists along a continuum, with recasting a past event into the future at one end and imagining novel – and even implausible – events at the other (Addis, 2018; Szpunar, Spreng, and Schacter, 2014). Indeed, semantic information is particularly important when imagining events that fall outside of one's own experience. In a recent fMRI study (Roberts et al., 2017), we had participants imagine events involving a set of congruent details (e.g. "Mum," "living room," "handbag") or incongruent details (e.g. "Dad," "conference poster," "gym"). When constructing a simulation was more challenging, as in the incongruent condition, the anterolateral prefrontal cortex was differentially recruited, likely reflecting an increased reliance on semantic processes such as conceptual expansion to support the construction of a plausible event framework from disparate details.

Manipulating episodic retrieval

Although the foregoing evidence is broadly consistent with the constructive episodic simulation hypothesis, because of its correlational nature, interpretive caution is required. We have recently taken two new approaches in an attempt to provide stronger evidence bearing on the neural substrates of constructive episodic simulation. First, we have attempted to *manipulate* the involvement of episodic retrieval during fMRI scanning by using the aforementioned ESI procedure. Madore et al. (2016) scanned participants after an ESI or control induction while they imagined a future event that could happen to them within the next few years in response to a verbal object cue. We used the construction-elaboration paradigm (Addis, Wong, and Schacter, 2007), in which participants press a button to indicate when they have constructed an imagined event, and then elaborate the details of that event for the remainder of the twenty-second trial. Participants also performed an object comparison control task in which they generated two objects that were related to each object cue and put them together in a size sentence (e.g. "X is larger than Y is larger than Z"). Similar to the future imagining task, participants were told to press a button once they had constructed the size sentence, and to then elaborate on a semantic definition of each object for the remainder of the trial.

Results revealed increased activity throughout the core network during the future imagining task compared with the object comparison task following both ESI and the control induction, thus replicating and extending earlier results. Critically, following ESI compared with the control induction, there was significantly increased activity in core network regions previously linked with retrieval of episodic detail, notably left hippocampus and right inferior parietal lobule/angular gyrus. Resting-state connectivity analyses using these hippocampal and inferior parietal lobule areas as seed regions revealed significantly stronger coupling with other core network regions after ESI compared with the control induction. Because the involvement of episodic retrieval was experimentally manipulated via ESI, these findings provide strong evidence for a role of episodic retrieval processes in future imagining, in line with the constructive episodic simulation hypothesis.

Madore et al. (2019) took a similar approach to investigating the contribution of episodic retrieval to divergent creative thinking: after receiving ESI or a control induction, participants were scanned while they completed either the AUT task described earlier, which draws on divergent thinking, or the OAT control task, which makes little demand on divergent thinking. Similar to the previous results, ESI produced increased hippocampal activity during the AUT vs. the OAT. Moreover, a multivariate ICA (independent components analysis) revealed that following ESI there was stronger connectivity during the AUT between the core network and a frontoparietal brain network previously linked to cognitive control, and this increased coupling extended to a subsequent resting-state scan. The increased connectivity between core and frontoparietal control networks following ESI is notable because coupling between these two networks has been linked to creative cognition in previous research (see Beaty et al., 2016).

Another approach that goes beyond purely correlational evidence to assess the constructive episodic simulation hypothesis entails using transcranial magnetic stimulation (TMS) to manipulate the activity of a region thought to be critical for both episodic memory and simulation by temporarily disrupting it. Thakral, Madore, and Schacter (2017) examined the effects of applying inhibitory TMS to the left angular gyrus, a key node of the core network associated with retrieval of episodic detail, on subsequent tasks in which word cues were presented and participants (a) remembered a past experience, (b) imagined a future experience, or (c) generated semantic associates. Compared with a condition in which TMS had been applied to a control region not thought to be important for retrieving episodic details (the vertex), TMS to the left angular gyrus produced a selective reduction in internal/episodic details during remembering and imagining, while having the opposite effect on external details and no effect on generating semantic associates. Again, the results provide empirical support for the constructive episodic simulation hypothesis by showing selective and similar effects of TMS to the left angular gyrus on episodic memory and simulation.

Constructive Episodic Simulation and Memory Errors

A key theme in our initial articulation of the constructive episodic simulation hypothesis (Schacter and Addis, 2007a, 2007b) was that the same flexible retrieval and recombination processes that render episodic memory useful for simulating future events could also make the system prone to error (for related ideas, see Dudai and Carruthers, 2005; Suddendorf and Corballis, 2007). Only recently, however, has directly relevant experimental evidence appeared.

One line of evidence comes from Devitt et al. (2016), who adapted the experimental recombination procedure described earlier. Participants initially generated person-place-object autobiographical memories, and the experimenter then recombined elements of the episodes: either partial recombinations (one element of a memory changed) or full recombinations (two elements changed). In a second session, participants imagined the recombined items as events that might have occurred in the past. Finally, in a third session, participants judged whether recombined detail sets and "real" detail sets (i.e. original person-place-object combinations) belonged to a real event, an imagined event, or was a novel recombination they had not seen previously. In two experiments, Devitt et al. (2016) found that imagining partial or full recombination modestly but significantly boosted the number of "real" judgments assigned to recombined events. These autobiographical memory conjunction errors were more frequent for partial than full recombinations, likely reflecting greater similarity of imagined past events to an actual event for the partial recombinations.

More recently, Carpenter and Schacter (2017) linked flexible recombination with memory errors that result from mistakenly combining elements of distinct but related episodes. They attempted to isolate the influence of flexible recombination processes on memory errors by adapting an *associative inference* paradigm (e.g. Zeithamova and Preston, 2010). In this paradigm, participants are required to combine information from separate episodes involving people, objects, and contextual settings in order to make associative inferences about individuals who are linked to one another because each is paired with the same object in distinct settings (i.e. scenes depicting the individual, object, and a background setting or context). Carpenter and Schacter (2017) found that participants are more susceptible to making memory errors that are attributable to mistakenly combining contextual details from related episodes when they made *correct* inferences about the relations between the people in these episodes (i.e. judged correctly that the individuals were linked by a common object) than when they made *incorrect* inferences. Of key theoretical importance, this increase in memory errors for correct inferences occurred only when contextual details were probed *after* an associative inference test that engaged flexible recombination processes; there was no difference in memory errors for correct vs. incorrect inferences when memory for contextual details was probed *before* the associative inference test (i.e. before flexible recombination processes were engaged). Carpenter and Schacter (2018) extended this phenomenon to the domain of value memory and reward processing in a paradigm in which individuals who were designated high, low, or no value were linked to one another via a common object. Participants mistakenly attributed high value to a low- or no-value individual more often when they made correct vs. incorrect inferences about the relation between these individuals (i.e. judged correctly that the individuals were linked by a common object). Critically, however, once again this increase in memory errors was observed only when memory for value details was probed after the associative inference test that engaged flexible recombination processes.

Carpenter and Schacter's (2017, 2018) data provide clear evidence linking flexible recombination and memory errors, in line with the constructive episodic simulation hypothesis. However, Carpenter and Schacter's paradigm did not involve any future thinking. The same can be said of Devitt et al.'s (2016) experiments, in which participants imagined events that might have occurred in the past (for related evidence, see Gerlach, Dornblaser, and Schacter, 2014). Yet in our initial articulation of the constructive episodic simulation hypothesis, we emphasized not only that flexible recombination processes could result in memory errors, but also that such errors might arise as a consequence of using flexible recombination to simulate possible *future* experiences. Several recent studies provide relevant evidence. Dewhurst et al. (2016) had participants encode lists of semantically related words by thinking about how the list items might be used in a future situation that requires planning, with reference to a past event, or by rating each item's pleasantness. Encoding with reference to a future situation produced higher levels of subsequent false recall and false recognition of a non-presented, semantically related "critical lure" word (Roediger and McDermott, 1995) than did the other two encoding conditions. Dewhurst et al. (2018) extended this pattern of increased false recognition following future-related encoding to schema-related lure items. Devitt and Schacter (2018) found that when participants simulated positive or negative outcomes of hypothetical future events before learning the actual outcomes of those events, neutral outcome events were later remembered more positively because of a liberal response bias for positive information. Devitt and Schacter (2018) also found the same positivity bias after participants simulated positive outcomes to imagined past events, suggesting that biased remembering in this paradigm reflects the qualities of episodic simulations in either temporal direction.

Overall, this evidence supports a key assertion of the constructive episodic simulation hypothesis that flexible recombination and episodic simulation, including but not limited to future-oriented simulation, can contribute to memory errors (for further discussion of conceptual issues related to episodic simulation and memory errors, see Devitt and Addis, 2016; Mahr and Csibra, 2018; Schacter, 2012; Schacter et al., 2018).

Conceptual Development of the Constructive Episodic Simulation Hypothesis

Our initial articulation of the constructive episodic simulation hypothesis emphasized that imagining future experiences relies on episodic memory as conceived by Tulving (2002). However, this broad-brush invocation of episodic memory requires refinement. For example, Tulving (2002) emphasized the importance of "autonoetic consciousness" – awareness of self in time – as a defining feature of episodic memory. Yet there is little evidence that such autonoetic consciousness is critically involved in all the forms of imagination that we have linked to episodic memory, including simulation of future experiences, means-end problem-solving, and divergent creative thinking. In our initial papers (Schacter and Addis, 2007a, 2007b), we discussed the role of flexible recombination processes in future imagining, and over the years we have placed increased theoretical emphasis on these kinds of episodic retrieval processes in the construction of various kinds of mental events, with little theoretical emphasis on autonoetic consciousness. In a related vein, Schacter and Madore (2016) have proposed that the ESI procedure discussed earlier primarily impacts an *event construction* process that supports assembling a mental event with details related to people, places, objects, and actions. We think that it is this kind of constructive retrieval process that is central to the various manifestations of imagination discussed here.

Related to this point, although we initially emphasized that imagination and simulation rely on episodic memory, episodic memory itself can be thought of as a form of mental simulation (for detailed articulations of this view, see Addis, 2018; De Brigard, 2014; Michaelian, 2016). Although memories contain original elements of experiences, these details are woven together with imagined content (Michaelian, 2016). Memories are embellished and gaps "filled in" with relevant semantic and schematic knowledge as well as details from other events, so that remembering is not only reconstructive but constructive (Bartlett, 1932). That we can remember events from unexperienced visual perspectives (e.g. seeing ourselves) is compelling evidence of an imaginative process during remembering. Moreover, St. Jacques et al. (2018) recently reported that prefrontal and parietal regions recruited when remembering past events from novel visual perspectives overlapped more with the neural correlates of an imagination task (imagining counterfactual past events) than veridical remembering, further supporting the notion that remembering can be similar to imagination and so can be thought of as a kind of simulation.

Remembered and imagined events rely on the same cognitive processes (reactivation of pre-existing schemas to guide construction, reactivation of relevant semantic and perceptual content, relational processing, as well as attention to, and encoding of, the constructed representations) and the same brain networks (i.e. the core network), albeit to varying degrees. Together, the utilization of the same content and cognitive processes explains both the neural overlap and neural differences between memory and imagination. We have previously argued that while both memory and imagination rely on relational processing, there are nevertheless critical differences in the degree and types of relational processes recruited by the two tasks: the re-integration of previously associated details during remembering places lower demands on relational processing than recombining details to create new associations during imagination (Schacter and Addis, 2007b). However, given that remembering also involves some amount of imaginative construction (Bartlett, 1932), it follows that some degree of recombining also occurs even during remembering. Moreover, when imagining events, some level of reintegration occurs (e.g. chunks of related content are incorporated with novel information; entire memories are reintegrated and recast into the future with minimal changes). Thus, Addis (2018) suggests that the contribution of relational processes to simulation may be better conceptualized as "associative history" of the composite elements: While veridical memories comprise the most preassociated elements, novel imaginings comprise the least. It is possible that the overall associative strength is manifest as fluency (Michaelian, 2016), explaining why memories are typically brought to mind more quickly and with less difficulty than imagined events (e.g. Anderson, Dewhurst, and Nash, 2012).

Concluding Comments: Big Questions

During the past decade, various kinds of evidence have provided empirical support for key components of the constructive episodic simulation hypothesis, namely that episodic retrieval contributes to simulations of various kinds, that imagined and remembered events draw on similar episodic contents, and that flexible recombination processes used to support episodic simulation can contribute to memory errors. The hypothesis has also evolved, with increased emphasis on attempting to understand core constructive retrieval processes underlying simulations that occur during both imagining and remembering. For each of the key components of the hypothesis, some major questions remain to be investigated: Does episodic retrieval contribute differently to different kinds of simulations, such as simulations that support future imagining, atemporal scene construction, divergent thinking, and counterfactual simulation? How do episodic contents interact with semantic and schematic processes during various forms of simulation? Can we identify neural markers of the flexible recombination processes that contribute to both episodic simulation and memory errors? We think that deeper analyses of all these questions will be essential to achieving a better understanding of the relation between memory and imagination.

Acknowledgments

We thank Aleea Devitt, Kevin Madore, and Preston Thakral for comments on an earlier draft of the manuscript, and thank Jyotika Bindra and Ethan Harris for help with its preparation. DLS was supported by National Institute of Mental Health grant R01 MH060941 and National Institute on Aging grant R01 AG008441. DRA was supported by a Rutherford Discovery Fellowship RDF-10-UOA-024 and a Grant-in-Aid from the Faculty of Science at The University of Auckland.

References

Abraham A., Schubotz, R. I., and von Cramon, D. Y. (2008). Thinking About the Future versus the Past in Personal and Non-Personal Contexts. *Brain Research*, *1233*, 106–119.

Abram, M., Picard, L., Navarro, B., and Piolino, P. (2014). Mechanisms of Remembering the Past and Imagining the Future: New Data from Autobiographical Memory Tasks in a Lifespan Approach. *Consciousness and Cognition*, *29*, 76–80.

Addis, D. R. (2018). Are Episodic Memories Special? On the Sameness of Remembered and Imagined Event Simulation. *Journal of the Royal Society of New Zealand*, *48*(23), 1–25.

Addis, D. R., Cheng, T., Roberts, R. P., and Schacter, D. L. (2011). Hippocampal Contributions to the Episodic Simulation of Specific and General Future Events. *Hippocampus*, *21*, 1045–1052.

Addis, D. R., Musicaro, R., Pan, L., and Schacter, D. L. (2010). Episodic Simulation of Past and Future Events in Older Adults: Evidence from an Experimental Recombination Task. *Psychology and Aging*, *25*, 369–376.

Addis, D. R., Pan, L., Vu, M. A., Laiser, N., and Schacter, D. L. (2009). Constructive Episodic Simulation of the Future and the Past: Distinct Subsystems of a Core Brain Network Mediate Imagining and Remembering. *Neuropsychologia*, *47*, 2222–2238.

Addis, D. R., and Schacter, D. L. (2008). Constructive Episodic Simulation: Temporal Distance and Detail of Past and Future Events Modulate Hippocampal Engagement. *Hippocampus*, *18*, 227–237.

(2012). The Hippocampus and Imagining the Future: Where Do We Stand? *Frontiers in Human Neuroscience*, *5*, 173.

Addis, D. R., Wong, A. T., and Schacter, D. L. (2007). Remembering the Past and Imagining the Future: Common and Distinct Neural Substrates During Event Construction and Elaboration. *Neuropsychologia*, *45*, 1363–1377.

(2008). Age-Related Changes in the Episodic Simulation of Future Events. *Psychological Science*, *19*, 33–41.

Anderson, R. J., Dewhurst, S. A., and Nash, R. A. (2012). Shared Cognitive Processes Underlying Past and Future Thinking: The Impact of Imagery and Concurrent Task Demands on Event Specificity. *Journal of Experimental Psychology: Learning, Memory, and Cognition*, *38*, 356–365.

Axelrod, V., Rees, G., and Bar, M. (2017). The Default Network and the Combination of Cognitive Processes that Mediate Self-Generated Thought. *Nature Human Behaviour*, *1*, 896–910. doi.org/10.1038/s41562-017-0244-9.

Bar, M., and Aminoff, E. (2003). Cortical Analysis of Visual Context. *Neuron*, *38*, 347–358.

Bartlett, F. C. (1932). *Remembering*. Cambridge, UK: Cambridge University Press.

Beaty, R. E., Benedek, M., Silvia, P. J., and Schacter, D. L. (2016). Creative Cognition and Brain Network Dynamics. *Trends in Cognitive Sciences*, *20*, 87–95.

Benoit, R. G., and Schacter, D. L. (2015). Specifying the Core Network Supporting Episodic Simulation and Episodic Memory by Activation Likelihood Estimation. *Neuropsychologia*, *75*, 450–457.

Binder, J. R., Desai, R. H., Graves, W. W., and Conant, L. L. (2009). Where is the Semantic System? A Critical Review and Meta-Analysis of 120 Functional Neuroimaging Studies. *Cerebral Cortex*, *19*, 2767–2796.

Buckner, R. L., Andrews-Hanna, J. R., and Schacter, D. L. (2008). The Brain's Default Network: Anatomy, Function, and Relevance to Disease. *The Year in Cognitive Neuroscience, Annals of the New York Academy of Sciences*, *1124*, 1–38.

Buckner, R. L., and Carroll, D. C. (2007). Self-Projection and the Brain. *Trends in Cognitive Sciences*, *11*, 49–57.

Cabeza, R., Ciaramelli, E., and Moscovitch, M. (2012). Cognitive Contributions of the Ventral Parietal Cortex: An Integrative Theoretical Account. *Trends in Cognitive Sciences*, *16*, 338–352.

Campbell, K. L., Madore, K. P., Benoit, R. G., Thakral, P. P., and Schacter, D. L. (2018). Increased Hippocampus to Ventromedial Prefrontal Connectivity during the Construction of Episodic Future Events. *Hippocampus*, *28*, 39–45.

Cao, X., Madore, K. P., Wang, D., and Schacter, D. L. (2018). Remembering the Past and Imagining the Future: Attachment Effects on Production of Episodic Details in Close Relationships. *Memory*, *26*, 2040–2050.

Carpenter, A. C., and Schacter, D. L. (2017). Flexible Retrieval: When True Inferences Produce False Memories. *Journal of Experimental Psychology: Learning, Memory, and Cognition*, *43*, 335–349.

(2018). False Memories, False Preferences: Flexible Retrieval Mechanisms Supporting Successful Inference Bias Novel Decisions. *Journal of Experimental Psychology: General*, *147*(7), 988–1004. dx.doi.org/10.1037/xge0000391.

Cavanna, A. E., and Trimble, M. R. (2006). The Precuneus: A Review of Its Functional Anatomy and Behavioural Correlates. *Brain*, *129*, 564–583.

Cohen, N. J., and Eichenbaum, H. (1993). *Memory, Amnesia, and the Hippocampal System*. Cambridge, MA: MIT Press.

D'Argembeau, A., and van der Linden, M. (2004). Phenomenal Characteristics Associated with Projecting Oneself Back into the Past and Forward into the Future: Influence of Valence and Temporal Distance. *Consciousness and Cognition*, *13*, 844–858.

(2006). Individual Differences in the Phenomenology of Mental Time Travel. *Consciousness and Cognition*, *15*, 342–350.

De Brigard, F. (2014). Is Memory for Remembering? Recollection as a Form of Episodic Hypothetical Thinking. *Synthese*, *191*, 1–31.

De Brigard, F., Addis, D. R., Ford, J. H., Schacter, D. L., and Giovanello, K. S. (2013). Remembering What Could Have Happened: Neural Correlates of Episodic Counterfactual Thinking. *Neuropsychologia*, *51*, 2401–2414.

Devitt, A. L., and Addis, D. R. (2016). Bidirectional Interactions Between Memory and Imagination. In K. Michaelian, S. B. Klein, and K. K. Szpunar (eds.), *Seeing the Future: Theoretical Perspectives on Future-Oriented Mental Time Travel*. New York, NY: Oxford University Press.

Devitt, A. L., Monk-Fromont, E., Schacter, D. L., and Addis, D. R. (2016). Factors that Influence the Generation of Autobiographical Memory Conjunction Errors. *Memory*, *24*, 204–222.

Devitt, A. L., and Schacter, D. L. (2018). An Optimistic Outlook Creates a Rosy Past: The Impact of Episodic Simulation on Subsequent Memory. *Psychological Science*, *29*, 936–946. dx.doi.org/10.1177%2F0956797617753936.

Dewhurst, S. A., Anderson, R. J., Grace, L., and Howe, D. (2018). Simulation, False Memories, and the Planning of Future Events. *Journal of Experimental Psychology: Learning, Memory & Cognition*, *45*(1), 26–36. doi.org/10.1037/xlm0000575.

Dewhurst, S. A., Anderson, R. J., Grace, L., and van Esch, L. (2016). Adaptive False Memories: Imagining Future Scenarios Increases False Memories in the DRM Paradigm. *Memory & Cognition*, *44*, 1076–1084.

Dudai, Y., and Carruthers, M. (2005). The Janus Face of Mnemosyne. *Nature*, *434*, 823–824.

Fisher, R. P., and Geiselman, R. E. (1992). *Memory-Enhancing Techniques for Investigative Interviewing: The Cognitive Interview.* Springfield, IL: Charles C. Thomas Books.

Gaesser, B., Sacchetti, D. C., Addis, D. R., and Schacter, D. L. (2011). Characterizing Age-Related Changes in Remembering the Past and Imagining the Future. *Psychology and Aging, 26,* 80–84.

Gaesser, B., Spreng, R. N., McLelland, V. C., Addis, D. R., and Schacter, D. L. (2013). Imagining the Future: Evidence for a Hippocampal Contribution to Constructive Processing. *Hippocampus, 23,* 1150–1161.

Gerlach, K. D., Dornblaser, D. W., and Schacter, D. L. (2014). Adaptive Constructive Processes and Memory Accuracy: Consequences of Counterfactual Simulations in Young and Older Adults. *Memory, 22,* 145–162.

Gilmore, A. W., Nelson, S. M., and McDermott, K. B. (2016). The Contextual Association Network Activates More for Remembered than Imagined Events. *Cerebral Cortex, 26,* 611–617.

Hallford, D. J., Austin, D. W., Takano, K., and Raes, F. (2018). Psychopathology and Episodic Future Thinking: A Systematic Review and Meta-Analysis of Specificity and Episodic Detail. *Behaviour Research and Therapy, 102,* 42–51.

Hassabis, D., Kumaran, D., and Maguire, E. A. (2007a). Using Imagination to Understand the Neural Basis of Episodic Memory. *Journal of Neuroscience, 27,* 14365–14374.

Hassabis, D., Kumaran, D., Vann, D. S., and Maguire, E. A. (2007b). Patients with Hippocampal Amnesia Cannot Imagine New Experiences. *Proceedings of the National Academy of Sciences USA, 104,* 1726–1731.

Irish, M., Addis, D. R., Hodges, J. R., and Piguet, O. (2012). Considering the Role of Semantic Memory in Episodic Future Thinking: Evidence from Semantic Dementia. *Brain, 135,* 2178–2191.

Jing, H. G., Madore, K. P., and Schacter, D. L. (2016). Worrying About the Future: An Episodic Specificity Induction Affects Problem Solving, Reappraisal, and Well-Being. *Journal of Experimental Psychology: General, 145,* 402–418.

(2017). Preparing for What Might Happen: An Episodic Specificity Induction Impacts the Generation of Alternative Future Events. *Cognition, 169,* 118–128.

Johnson, M. K., and Raye, C. L. (1981). Realty Monitoring. *Psychological Review, 88,* 67–85.

Klein, S. B. (2013). The Complex Act of Projecting Oneself into the Future. *Wiley Interdisciplinary Reviews – Cognitive Science, 4,* 63–79.

Klein S. B., Loftus, J., and Kihlstrom, J. F. (2002) Memory and Temporal Experience: The Effects of Episodic Memory Loss on an Amnesic Patient's Ability to Remember the Past and Imagine the Future. *Social Cognition, 20,* 353–379.

Levine, B., Svoboda, E., Hay, J. F., Winocur, G., and Moscovitch, M. (2002). Aging and Autobiographical Memory: Dissociating Episodic from Semantic Retrieval. *Psychology and Aging, 17,* 677–689.

Madore, K. P., Addis, D. R., and Schacter, D. L. (2015). Creativity and Memory: Effects of an Episodic-Specificity Induction on Divergent Thinking. *Psychological Science, 26,* 1461–1468.

Madore, K. P., Gaesser, B., and Schacter, D. L. (2014). Constructive Episodic Simulation: Dissociable Effects of a Specificity Induction on Remembering, Imagining, and Describing in Young and Older Adults. *Journal of Experimental Psychology: Learning, Memory, and Cognition, 40,* 609–622.

Madore, K. P., Jing, H. G., and Schacter, D. L. (2016). Divergent Creative Thinking in Young and Older Adults: Extending the Effects of an Episodic Specificity Induction. *Memory & Cognition*, *44*, 974–988.

Madore, K. P., and Schacter, D. L. (2014). An Episodic Specificity Induction Enhances Means-End Problem-Solving in Young and Older Adults. *Psychology and Aging*, *29*, 913–924.

(2016). Remembering the Past and Imagining the Future: Selective Effects of an Episodic Specificity Induction on Detail Generation. *The Quarterly Journal of Experimental Psychology*, *69*, 285–298.

Madore, K. P., Szpunar, K. K., Addis, D. R., and Schacter, D. L. (2016). Episodic Specificity Induction Impacts Activity in a Core Brain Network During Construction of Imagined Future Experiences. *Proceedings of the National Academy of Sciences USA*, *113*, 10696–10701.

Madore, K. P., Thakral, P. P., Beaty, R. E., Addis, D. R., and Schacter, D. L. (2019). Neural Mechanisms of Episodic Retrieval Support Divergent Creative Thinking. *Cerebral Cortex*, *29*(1), 150–166. doi:10.1093/cercor/bhx312.

Mahr, J., and Csibra, G. (2018). Why Do We Remember? The Communicative Function of Episodic Memory. *Behavioral and Brain Sciences*, *41*, e1.

Martin, V. C., Schacter, D. L., Corballis, M. C., and Addis, D. R. (2011). A Role for the Hippocampus in Encoding Simulations of Future Events. *Proceedings of the National Academy of Sciences of the United States of America*, *108*, 13858–13863.

McDermott, K. B., Woolridge, C. L., Rice, H. J., Berg, J. J., and Szpunar, K. K. (2016). Visual Perspective in Remembering and Episodic Future Thought. *Quarterly Journal of Experimental Psychology*, *69*, 243–253.

McFarland, C. P., Primosch, M., Maxson, C. M., and Stewart, B. T. (2017). Enhancing Memory and Imagination Improves Problem-Solving Among Individuals with Depression. *Memory & Cognition*, *45*, 1–8.

Michaelian, K. (2016). *Mental Time Travel: Episodic Memory and our Knowledge of the Personal Past*. Cambridge, MA: MIT Press.

Michaelian, K., Klein, S. B., and Szpunar, K. K. (eds.) (2016). *Seeing the Future: Theoretical Perspective on Future-Oriented Mental Time Travel*. New York, NY: Oxford University Press.

Mullally, S. L., and Maguire, E. A. (2014). Memory, Imagination, and Predicting the Future: A Common Brain Mechanism? *Neuroscientist*, *20*, 220–234.

Okuda, J., Fujii, T., Ohtake, H., et al. (2003). Thinking of the Future and the Past: The Roles of the Frontal Pole and the Medial Temporal Lobes. *NeuroImage*, *19*, 1369–1380.

Palombo, D. J., Hayes, S. M., Peterson, K. M., Keane, M. M., and Verfaellie, M. (2018). Medial Temporal Lobe Contributions to Episodic Future Thinking: Scene Construction or Future Projection? *Cerebral Cortex*, *28*, 447–458.

Palombo, D. J., Williams, L. J., Abdi, H., and Levine, B. (2013). The Survey of Autobiographical Memory (SAM): A Novel Measure of Trait Mnemonics in Everyday Life. *Cortex*, *49*, 1526–1540.

Platt, J., and Spivack, G. (1975). *Manual for the Means-End Problem-Solving Test (MEPS): A Measure of Interpersonal Problem-Solving Skill*. Philadelphia, PA: Hahnemann Medical College and Hospital.

Raes, F., Hermans, D., Williams, J. M. G., et al. (2005). Reduced Specificity of Autobiographical Memory: A Mediator Between Rumination and Ineffective

Social Problem-Solving in Major Depression? *Journal of Affective Disorders*, *87*, 331–335.

Raichle, M. E. (2015). The Brain's Default Network. *Annual Review of Neuroscience*, *38*, 433–447.

Roberts, R. P., and Addis, D. R. (2018). A Common Mode of Processing Governing Divergent Thinking and Future Imagination. In R. Jung and O. Vartanian (eds.), *The Cambridge Handbook of the Neuroscience of Creativity* (Cambridge Handbooks in Psychology). Cambridge, UK: Cambridge University Press, 211–230.

Roberts, R. P., Schacter, D. L., and Addis, D. R. (2018). Scene Construction and Relational Processing: Separable Constructs? *Cerebral Cortex*, *28*, 1729–1732.

Roberts, R. P., Wiebels, K., Sumner, R. L., et al. (2017). An fMRI Investigation of the Relationship Between Future Imagination and Cognitive Flexibility. *Neuropsychologia*, *95*, 156–172.

Robin, J., Wynn, J., and Moscovitch, M. (2016). The Spatial Scaffold: The Effects of Spatial Context on Memory for Events. *Journal of Experimental Psychology: Learning, Memory, and Cognition*, *42*, 308–315.

Roediger, H. L., and McDermott, K. B. (1995). Creating False Memories: Remembering Words not Presented in Lists. *Journal of Experimental Psychology: Learning, Memory, and Cognition*, *21*, 803–814.

Schacter, D. L. (2012). Adaptive Constructive Processes and the Future of Memory. *American Psychologist*, *67*, 603–613.

Schacter, D. L., and Addis, D. R. (2007a). Constructive Memory: The Ghosts of Past and Future. *Nature*, *445*, 27.

(2007b). The Cognitive Neuroscience of Constructive Memory: Remembering the Past and Imagining the Future. *Philosophical Transactions of the Royal Society of London B*, *362*, 773–786.

Schacter, D. L., Addis, D. R., and Buckner, R. L. (2007). Remembering the Past to Imagine the Future: The Prospective Brain. *Nature Reviews Neuroscience*, *8*(9), 657–661.

(2008). Episodic Simulation of Future Events: Concepts, Data, and Applications. *The Year in Cognitive Neuroscience, Annals of the New York Academy of Sciences*, *1124*, 39–60.

Schacter, D. L., Addis, D. R., Hassabis, D., et al. (2012). The Future of Memory: Remembering, Imagining, and the Brain. *Neuron*, *76*, 677–694.

Schacter, D. L., Addis, D. R., and Szpunar, K. K. (2017). Escaping the Past: Contributions of the Hippocampus to Future Thinking and Imagination. In D. E. Hannula and M. C. Duff (eds.), *The Hippocampus from Cells to Systems: Structure, Connectivity, and Functional Contributions to Memory and Flexible Cognition.* New York, NY: Springer, 439–465.

Schacter, D. L., Benoit, R. G., and Szpunar, K. K. (2017). Episodic Future Thinking: Mechanisms and Functions. *Current Opinion in Behavioral Sciences*, *17*, 41–50.

Schacter, D. L., Carpenter, A. C., Devitt, A., Roberts, R. P., and Addis, D. R. (2018). Constructive Episodic Simulation, Flexible Recombination, and Memory Errors. *Behavioral and Brain Sciences*, *41*, e32.

Schacter, D. L., Gaesser, B., and Addis, D. R. (2013). Remembering the Past and Imagining the Future in the Elderly. *Gerontology*, *59*, 143–151.

Schacter, D. L., and Madore, K. P. (2016). Remembering the Past and Imagining the Future: Identifying and Enhancing the Contribution of Episodic Memory. *Memory Studies*, *9*, 245–255.

Sheldon, S., and Levine, B. (2016). The Role of the Hippocampus in Memory and Mental Construction. *The Year in Cognitive Neuroscience, Annals of the New York Academy of Sciences, 1369*, 76–92.

Sheldon, S., McAndrews, M. P., and Moscovitch, M. (2011). Episodic Memory Processes Mediated by the Medial Temporal Lobes Contribute to Open-Ended Problem-Solving. *Neuropsychologia, 49*, 2439–2447.

Simons, J. S., Garrison, J. R., and Johnson, M. K. (2017). Brain Mechanisms of Reality Monitoring. *Trends in Cognitive Sciences, 21*, 462–473.

St. Jacques, P. L., Carpenter, A. C., Szpunar, K. K., and Schacter, D. L. (2018). Remembering and Imagining Alternative Versions of the Personal Past. *Neuropsychologia, 110*, 170–179.

Suddendorf, T., and Corballis, M. C. (2007). The Evolution of Foresight: What is Mental Time Travel and is it Unique to Humans? *Behavioral and Brain Sciences, 30*, 299–313.

Szpunar, K. K., and McDermott, K. B. (2008). Episodic Future Thought and its Relation to Remembering: Evidence from Ratings of Subjective Experience. *Consciousness and Cognition, 17*, 330–334.

Szpunar, K. K., Spreng, R. N., and Schacter, D. L. (2014). A Taxonomy of Prospection: Introducing an Organizational Framework for Future-Oriented Cognition. *Proceedings of the National Academy of Sciences USA, 111*, 18414–18421.

Szpunar, K. K., Watson, J. M., and McDermott, K. B. (2007). Neural Substrates of Envisioning the Future. *Proceedings of the National Academy of Sciences of the United States of America, 104*, 642–647.

Thakral, P., Benoit, R. G., and Schacter, D. L. (2017a). Characterizing the Role of the Hippocampus During Episodic Simulation and Encoding. *Hippocampus, 27*, 1275–1284.

(2017b). Imagining the Future: The Core Episodic Simulation Network Dissociates as a Function of Timecourse and the Amount of Simulated Information. *Cortex, 90*, 12–30.

Thakral, P., Madore, K. P., and Schacter, D. L. (2017). A Role for the Left Angular Gyrus in Episodic Simulation and Memory. *Journal of Neuroscience, 37*, 8142–8149.

(2019). Content-Specific Phenomenological Similarity Between Episodic Memory and Simulation. *Memory, 27*(3), 417–422.

Tulving, E. (1985). Memory and Consciousness. *Canadian Psychologist, 26*, 1–12.

(2002). Episodic Memory: From Mind to Brain. *Annual Review of Psychology 53*, 1–25.

van Mulukom, V., Schacter, D. L., Corballis, M. C., and Addis, D. R. (2013). Re-Imagining the Future: Repetition Decreases Hippocampal Involvement in Future Simulation. *PLoS One, 8*, e69596.

Viard, A., Desgranges, B., Eustache, F., and Piolino, P. (2012). Factors Affecting Medial Temporal Lobe Engagement for Past and Future Episodic Events: An ALE Meta-Analysis of Neuroimaging Studies. *Brain and Cognition, 80*, 111.125.

Wang, Q., Hou, Y., Tang, H., and Wiprovnick, A. (2011). Travelling Backwards and Forwards in Time: Culture and Gender in the Episodic Specificity of Past and Future Events. *Memory, 19*, 103–109.

Ward, A. M. (2016). A Critical Evaluation of Episodic Future Thinking. *Neuropsychology, 30*, 887–905.

Williams, J. M. G., Ellis, N. C., Tyers, C., et al. (1996). The Specificity of Autobiographical Memory and Imaginability of the Future. *Memory and Cognition, 24*, 116–125.

Zeithamova, D., and Preston, A. R. (2010). Flexible Memories: Differential Roles for Medial Temporal Lobe and Prefrontal Cortex in Cross-Episode Binding. *Journal of Neuroscience, 30*, 14676–14684.

9 Capturing the Imagination

Arne Dietrich and Sandra Zakka

Introduction

The human imagination is vast and unknown. It is vast in its scope and unknown in its structure. What's more, we have little understanding of its purpose or the brain mechanisms involved. Efforts to capture it, whole or in part, have been either brave or foolhardy, depending on your point of view. But in our quest to understand the human condition, psychologists, neuroscientists, and philosophers, among many others, must embrace this challenge. We spend a great deal of time "in our heads" and it is certainly true that no theory or general framework of the mind is complete without the imagination occupying a central role.

In philosophy, the imagination has been an item of discussion for centuries (Gendler, 2013), but the topic is also generally considered so broad and complex that no common classification has emerged. A key ingredient that is widely accepted, however, is that the imagination involves mental representation that differs from perception or memory (Gendler, 2013). One often-cited framework for structuring and categorizing aspects of the imagination comes from Stevenson (2003). It outlines twelve types of imagination that are primarily descriptive and based on content or domain. One important short-coming of this and other such approaches is that it does not consider mechanisms or processes, which should inform any classification of the imagination.

For this reason, an interdisciplinary approach is likely to yield more useful results. Extending early work in psychology on facets of the imagination – daydreaming (Singer, 1975) or mental imagery (Shepard and Metzler, 1971), for instance – brain imaging technology has revived interest in this area, leading psychologists and neuroscientists to study specific operations of what can broadly be termed non task-specific mental activities, such as spontaneous thought, stimulus-independent thought, aesthetic experience, and mind-wandering (e.g. Chatterjee and Vartanian, 2014; Christoff, 2012). Recently, Abraham (2016) has organized this work into a framework of the imagination. Although interdisciplinary, the framework comes from a perspective of cognitive neuroscience and the large-scale brain network terminology of functional MRI. It proposes five thematically cohesive clusters or categories of the imagination – mental imagery, phenomenology, intentionality, novel combinatorial, and altered states (for details, see Abraham, 2016). This organization is as good as any to act as a springboard for further exploration.

The present chapter considers differences and similarities among Abraham's categories in terms of evolutionary algorithms or EAs. We start by focusing on creative imagination – the main component of the novel-combinatorial category – which is generally acknowledged to operate by way of EAs. We then contrast this with all other, or noncreative, aspects of imagination. They can be said to primarily differ from creativity in that they occur in a known problem space, which is what makes them noncreative. Still, the way we "walk through" imagined spaces that have a known topography, or fitness function, can be also described by EAs, albeit different EAs from those involved in creativity.

In the wilderness of the human imagination, problem spaces are rarely fully unknown or known. Given that the imagination deals inherently with hypotheticals, simulations, future scenarios, or the unpredictability of other agents, there are always degrees of uncertainty or unknowns involved. That is why it gets more interesting, especially in terms of EAs, when we consider partially known problem spaces, that is, imagined spaces in which we have degrees of sightedness of the fitness landscape. Based on this analysis, this chapter argues that creative thinking is best subsumed as part and parcel of all forms of the imagination rather than separated out as a distinct thing in its own category. In other words, creativity should be fully embedded and distributed, as it can occur in all aspects of the imagination.

Before we can comfortably proceed, it might be useful to disentangle a common confusion that often surfaces when thinking about creativity and imagination. Many use these concepts interchangeably, but this conflation is demonstrably false. Either can occur without the other. While it is somewhat obvious that creativity is but one form of the imagination, this is also true the other way around – that is, imagination is not necessary for creativity. Biological evolution, for instance, creates without imagination. In human creativity, or cultural evolution, there are also several examples. The easiest is perhaps serendipitous discoveries (e.g. the accidental discovery of the microwave oven by Percy Spencer, for instance); they can result in a creative product, that is, something novel, useful, and surprising, which is the standard definition of creativity. Another is the flow experience. A flow experience ensues when one becomes so deeply focused on a task and pursues it with such passion that all other content, imagined or otherwise, disappears. The mind is, in a word, empty. The essence of flow is the merging of perception and action, the smooth, rapid-fire integration of sensory input and motor output that cleanly bypasses consciousness. This meshes well with the notion that flow emanates from the implicit system (Dietrich, 2004, 2019), which possesses a concrete-operational setup and thus lacks the computational capacity to imagine a hypothetical world.

Kinds of Evolutionary Algorithms

There are different kinds of EA. This section brings to the fore what is for our purposes the key dimensions on which EAs differ, starting with the two most prominent ones: Darwinian and Lamarckian EAs (Figure 9.1). This is necessary

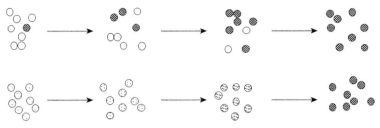

Figure 9.1 *Patterns of change (adapted from Medawar, 1953). The upper panel shows a Darwinian variational pattern of change. Individuals in such a system are unique. They vary. Evolution occurs because different types have different survival rates, which shifts their relative distribution in the population. The lower panel shows a Lamarckian transformation pattern of change. This system has no variation and no selection. Change acts on every individual in the same way. Evolution occurs because the entire population is transformed together, pulled into the direction of complexity under the guidance of the environment. Culture is obviously not a transformational system because it does not act on every individual in the same way. Adapted from Medawar (1953), A Commentary on Lamarckism, reprinted in P. Medawar (1981),* The Uniqueness of the Individual, *New York, NY: Dover, 63–87.*

because any lack of clarity here, at this level, is prone to lead to confusions once we push for the application of EAs in the realm of the human imagination.

Cultural evolution is a hotly contested domain but, to a first approximation, the following is unanimously agreed upon: (1) Culture is an evolutionary system (Dawkins, 1976; Gould, 1979; Smith, 2013); (2) Culture is a system with a variational or variation-selection pattern of change (Lewontin, 1991; Medawar, 1953); and (3) Culture exhibits some coupling between variation and selection or degrees of sightedness (Richerson and Boyd, 2005) – that is, the brain's EAs are not blind (Dietrich, 2015; Kronfeldner, 2010). It follows that human creativity, which is the source of cultural change, is neither a Neo-Darwinian system[1] with all the added parameters of the new synthesis nor a Lamarckian system that is based on a transformational pattern of change and thus on adaptation-guaranteeing instruction.

Traditionally, three dimensions (explained in detail below) have been used to define and classify EAs: (1) the pattern of change at the population level, (2) the degree of sightedness or coupling, and (3) the method of inheritance. Based on these, Neo-Darwinism is variational, blind, and digital; Lamarckism is transformational, directed, and blended (Dennett, 1995; Mayr, 1981).[2] A critical insight is that these dimensions need not come grouped together like this. An EA can consist of a different mix (Kronfeldner, 2007). To jump before being pushed, this is the case for cultural EAs. Bracketing the third dimension of a digital or blended (or both) copying mechanism, a matter that can only be settled by the neuroscientific counterpart of genetics, is a hybrid system with (1) a variational pattern of change that has

1 In this chapter, the term Neo-Darwinian is used to denote the more specific theory of evolution that describes biological evolution, while the term Darwinian is used for the general idea of a variation-selection EA.
2 In Mendelian inheritance, genes do not mix together but pair up and thus stay distinct.

(2) some sightedness, and for which (3) we do not yet know the mechanism(s) of inheritance, a matter that can only be settled by the neuroscientific counterpart of genetics, as it is in the brain that information replication occurs.

To get a clearer picture of this, we can start by looking at the overall pattern of change that is produced by Darwinian and Lamarckian EAs. A (Darwinian) variational system is based on the variation-selection method. The constituent units of the system vary naturally and a sorting process biases their survival. Evolution occurs because different units have different copying rates, which shifts their relative distribution in the system. At the population level, this appears as a statistical change that alters the proportions of the different variants over time (Lewontin, 1970, 1991). A (Lamarckian) transformational system is not based on variation but on adaptation-guaranteeing instruction. The change is sure always to march toward ever greater complexity. This system knows no individuality, no variability, and no waste. Variation does exist, but it is treated as noise and thus evolutionarily irrelevant. And without variation, a selection process is superfluous as there is nothing it could work on. Evolution occurs because all units of the system are transformed in lockstep, pulled into the direction of adaptation by instructions provided by the environment (Lewontin, 1991). For example, Lamarck believed that the long necks of giraffes evolved because preceding generations of giraffes reached for higher and higher leaves found in their environment. From this population-level view, the (Lamarckian) transformational pattern of evolution is not an accurate description of cultural change. Cultural evolution is essentially a (Darwinian) variational system and this much is not contentious.

The second dimension (blind/directed) was the eye of the storm for many years in the cultural evolution debate, particularly in psychology where this issue was framed in terms of the expert-novice paradigm in human creativity (see Campbell, 1960; Simonton, 1999; Schooler and Dougal, 1999; Sternberg, 1998). But this issue has recently given way to a broad consensus (see Dietrich, 2015; Kronfeldner, 2010; Weisberg and Hass, 2007). In the fully blind, Neo-Darwinian EA of the biosphere, the twin subprocesses of variation and selection are discontinuous, with selection only imposing a direction on variation *ex post facto*. Blind in this undirected sense means that there is zero correlation between the factors causing variation and those that sort it; they are uncoupled. The Lamarckian EA, by contrast, is not based on variation, so blindness plays no role in it. It is a transformational or instructional system in which adaptation is guaranteed from the start. The probability that any change in it is adaptive is, therefore, 100 percent. Lamarckian evolution is *fully* directed. A totally different way of seeing this is using the language of engineering. In engineering terms, the environment would be a controller. A controller guides – from the back, so to speak – the possible forward steps of the evolving (or developing) system. Since the target is known, the forward steps are guided or sighted. Think of it in terms of a climber whose upward moves are directed by someone already standing at the top and shouting down instructions to the ascending climber. The weight of the evidence shows that human creating and designing is neither totally blind nor totally sighted. It is not blind because the occurrence of novel ideas (variation) is informed by the kind of problem as well as the knowledge of the problem solver (selection), and it is not sighted, otherwise creative thinking would not be necessary in the first place. Due to the brain's cognitive coupling, cultural EAs possess *degrees of sightedness* (Dietrich, 2015; Dietrich and Haider, 2017).

The third dimension (method of inheritance) is unsettled and will likely remain so for some time. This is because neuroscience cannot tell us how brains represent and store information. And with no knowledge of the brain's coding scheme or copying mechanism, we cannot say if cultural transmission is a case of Neo-Darwinian hard (digital) or Lamarckian soft (blended) inheritance, or indeed both, as it is entirely possible that both methods coexist (Dietrich, 2015). Famously, Darwin was in the same fix. With no knowledge of particulate Mendelian genetics, the fundamental unit and mechanism of biological heredity was an intractable problem for him. Luckily, we do not need to settle the copying parameter of EAs either in order to proceed. As such, this paper leaves the inheritance issue to one side – any discussion of memetics included.

This short analysis also exposes just how pointless the discussion over the Darwinian or Lamarckian label is when it comes to creativity, and, by extension, human culture. The issue of classifying either one as Darwinian depends primarily on whether you are a lumper or a splitter (Dietrich, 2015).

Evolutionary Algorithms in the Imagination

For understanding mechanisms and processes in the imagination, the critical dimension here is sightedness. EAs in the imagination can have all degrees of sightedness from zero or blind (Neo-Darwinian) to 100 percent or sighted (Lamarckian). It is a continuum. In general, when we imagine something, we can be said to navigate or explore a given imaginary landscape. We try out several different options or paths in this landscape (variation) and pursue one but not the others (selection). Mathematically, this can be described as a variation-selection algorithm with, again, the difference to the biological EA being that we do not do so in a manner deemed blind (Dietrich and Haider, 2017). Our trajectory is (partially) informed. The degree to which it is informed or the degree of sightedness we have of the topography of this imagined landscape is determined mostly by how much we know or can possibly predict about it.

Naturally, we can also imagine things that need not exist or correspond to anything in the real world. But if the content of what is being imagined is to relate to reality in any form, fitness criteria matter. Consider a few mundane examples. To imagine the next few possible moves in a game of chess we cannot disregard the rules (fitness function) of the game. Neither can we do this when we plan out in our heads all the errands we might have to run the next day. Whether it is an artistic pursuit, problem-solving, thinking through various scenarios during moral decision-making, or anticipating someone else's behavior, in all these cases we do a variation-selection walk through an imaginary landscape that has a certain fitness function. In some landscapes, such as creative thinking or trying to predict the behavior of people we do not know well, our EAs have less sightedness because less is known about the fitness function. In others, such as chess or strategic planning, we have a much higher degree of sightedness because the topography is, in principle, known. From an EA point of view, the difference among these domains is in degrees rather than categorical.

Once we accept that imaginary thinking involves variable degrees of sightedness, we can ask what brain mechanisms underlie this sightedness evolutionary upgrade. How do brains manage to accomplish this partial coupling of variation to selection and generate thought trials that have a higher probability of adaptation? We need a sound mechanism to explain what otherwise would look like clairvoyance.

In a known problem space (KPS) the basic answer is straightforward. It is memory or the knowledge we have about the problem space. Since the problem space has been traversed before, we know its rules, shape, or structure and our imaginary walks through this landscape can be guided because that knowledge can act as an adaptive target or controller. In terms of EAs, this is best described by a fully sighted Lamarckian EA. The evolving or developing thought process is instructed by the environment. Trial and error, at least as far as finding out about the landscape itself, is thus unnecessary. There is no variation-selection process.

A couple of examples might help. Imagining the execution of a well-learned movement – motor imagery, in other words – is a case of a KPS. The problem space is already mapped out. For all possible forward steps or predictors, there are principally known consequences or controllers (Wolpert, Doya, and Kawato, 2003). Another example would be most instances of counterfactual thinking – say, imagining alternative scenarios to a decision taken in life. What would have happened to me had I decided to become a cook rather than an academic? Since such an exercise of the imagination operates in the real world as we know it, we would have controllers for most simulated alternative scenarios. The knowledge of most consequences that are possible in each scenario would then guide the imaginary thinking process in a Lamarckian fashion. The main idea here is that alternative scenarios, or counterfactual thoughts, explore problem spaces that have already been mapped out.

Before we get to the more interesting and complicated cases of partially known problem spaces, we can outline the very different instance of a fully unknown problem space (UPS). In a UPS, the very essence of creativity one might argue, an EA must proceed via a variation-selection process to find out about the fitness landscape. This is because the adaptive value of any given step is not known at any level that is accessible to the evolving or developing system. There are no known controllers, in other words. The EA of the biosphere explores such terrain fully blind. This Neo-Darwinian EA then produces, at the population level, a variational pattern of change. Human creative thinking, on the other hand, has brain mechanisms available to gain some sightedness even in the case of a UPS.

The Brain's Prediction System

The brain's prediction system has recently been proposed as the neural mechanism of partial sightedness in a UPS (Dietrich, 2015). Predictive processing is an emerging paradigm in neuroscience that presumes that the brain has evolved, fundamentally, to make predictions (Bar, 2007, 2009; Grush, 2004). The claim here is not that the business of anticipating events is one of the brain's important chores, it is *the* main reason for having a (big) brain in the first place (Dietrich,

2015). The main idea is this. We can interact with the complex world around us in an infinite number of ways. Such complexity can quickly overwhelm us. For behavior to be purposeful and timely in such a high-dimensional environment, there must be a restricted set of possible choices. We accomplish this by continuously, automatically, and, importantly, unconsciously generating expectations that meaningfully inform (or constrain) perception and action at every moment in life (Llinás, 2001). Even when we daydream and do not engage in a specific activity, the brain does not idle but actively produces predictions that anticipate future events. Prediction, as such, is not only useful during instances when one must attend to a stimulus or solve a problem – it is the brain's basic operating principle. In this view, the ability to create expectations of the future is considered the ultimate of all global brain functions (Llinás, 2001). The prediction imperative has long been established as a critical element in learning and motor control, but it is now also recognized as a central organizing theme for other cognitive domains, such as memory, attention, perception, and social interaction (Barsalou, 2009; Wolpert, Doya, and Kawato, 2003).

Memory is of particular interest in the present context. The idea that memory has evolved for prediction might sound counterintuitive at first sight. We think of memory as being about the past and prediction about the future. But the new ways of thinking turn this on its head. Contrary to what you might think is just plain old common sense, the point of memory is not to remember what was before but to be better at predicting what happens next. In other words, we form memories of the events in our lives to have information available with which to simulate the future (Bar, 2009; Fisher, 2006). Think about it in terms of adaptation. What else would memory be for? What good accrues to you by reminiscing about the past? Seen from this angle, memory is an epistemic device for simulation. What is more, psychologists have long known that memory is reconstructive and associative in nature, which makes it in a very important sense the same process as imagination. It is a database that can be used to reconstruct the past. But, again, that is not its function; its function is to shuffle the information you possess about the past so as to better imagine the future and function optimally in the present. Memory, in short, serves to enable prediction based on prior experience.

Some of the knowledge in our memory is intuitive or hardwired. Over the eons, brains have extracted good design principles – folk physics, folk psychology, etc. – from the environment and, given the adaptive advantage of these common solutions to common problems, they have become integrated into the neural hardware as a result (Dennett, 1995). We know, for instance, not to put a big heavy object on top of a small light object. However, we share many of these design principles with many of our animal relatives, and, at any rate, they cannot account for the counterintuitive creative thinking of humans (Dietrich, 2015). A second source of knowledge is all the knowledge we learn during our lifetime. The fact that we can activate this knowledge during the thought trials of imaginary thinking causes a coupling effect; adaptive variants occur more readily because the environment helps guide the thought-generating process. In other words, expert knowledge facilitates the finding of a solution. In a KPS, this sightedness is very high indeed since the problem space is mapped out, at least in principle. We can, therefore, feed a lot of this KPS information into our neural simulators and, together with the brain's higher-cognitive functions such as working memory, executive attention, or inhibition processes, our brains can run simulations that have a high probability of accurately representing the future (Dietrich, 2015).

But the brain's prediction system has the ability to constrain a variation process *a priori* even when the problem space is not mapped out. This extends some sightedness to UPSs and boosts the *ex-post-facto* EA of the biosphere by orders of magnitude. Predictive computations can generate a goal representation – an educated guess, essentially – that contains useful fitness information with which to direct the occurrence of thoughts in advance. In essence, prediction internalizes part of the selection process, and it is by virtue of having both of the twin processes of EAs operating in the same computational system that one, the predicted fitness criteria, can guide the other, the production of variants. These targets, or projected controllers, have been called ideational RPGs or Representations of Predicted Goals (Dietrich, 2015). They are like a signal flare launched into the dark to get a glimpse of the unfamiliar territory ahead and have our immediate next step be informed by the topography in the distance. In contrast to the EA of nature, RPGs generate unique properties that change the way the brain's EAs can move in a UPS as well as the type of artifacts they can bring into existence. First, the sightedness upgrade makes EAs faster and more efficient, and reducing the wasteful business of having to explore all options is likely the reason for the higher rate of change in cultural evolution. Second, for the variation-selection process to work in an imaginary landscape, a fitness function must also be modeled, and ideational RPGs can provide these merit criteria. Third, ideational RPGs make scaffolding possible. In nature, every variation-selection cycle must be a viable form in its own right. Brains, however, can breed multiple generations in a hypothetical manner. This produces a striking effect. Because some artifacts require elements that cannot be realized without a temporary scaffold, a mechanism that includes an instant payoff requirement, such as the biological EA, can also not build them. The scaffolding property of cultural EAs can keep impossible intermediates in play and create a plethora of higher-order, discontinuous designs. Fourth, ideational RPGs can account for the experiences of foresight and intention accompanying human creativity, as these experiences are also understood as the outcome of the brain's predictive processing (Frith, 1992; Wolpert, Doya, and Kawato, 2003).

Inherent Unknowns

There is an important aspect to all this that we have kept aside so far. In the imagination, we rarely face known or unknown problem spaces but rather partially known problem spaces.

For one thing, a UPS is never really fully unknown. Consider the case of a reigning paradigm in science. The big local peak of the topography has been climbed but that does not mean that all the lesser peaks of the landscape – all solutions within that paradigm – are known. Newton's three laws of motions, for instance, stem from the early 1700s, but clever solutions using Newtonian physics are still found today. RPGs projected into the unknown parts of this topography are sighted to a significant degree since we know already so much about the overall layout of this topography. Coming up with new solutions in the imagination here is a case of a well-sighted EA in a UPS – an EA at the Lamarckian end of the sightedness spectrum, in other words – and it counts as creativity in the sense that the solutions are novel, useful, and surprising.

A different situation presents itself when a paradigm shift is involved. The start of quantum physics in 1900 is perhaps the closest recent example of a relatively pure UPS. At the time, the fitness landscape of that problem space was so alien to the imagination that there was likely not much relevant prior knowledge that could be used by the brain's prediction system to compute ideational RPGs with some adaptive values. As such, early explorers of that landscape had to use EAs that probably were near the blind or Darwinian end of the sightedness spectrum (Dietrich, 2019). But this is an unusual case. Typically, the brain's higher-cognitive functions can run predictive computations of some sort in a UPS, generating ideational RPGs that contain fitness information with which to predict the location of solutions with a probability greater than zero (Dietrich, 2015).

On the other hand, it is also the case that there is rarely such a thing as a fully known problem space. When dealing with simulations, in the imagination or otherwise, there are always factors that are unknown. Whether we contemplate hypothetical scenarios or alternative futures, make probability assessments, or ponder the degrees of freedom presented by other agents, the path we take, even through a KPS, can never be imagined with total accuracy. This reintroduces the necessity of a variation-selection process. Take an example we described earlier. In chess, the game itself is a case of a KPS. The landscape is well-trotted territory and when knowledgeable players imagine a game, they are not discovering the rules of the game. All possible consequences of a given move are, in principle, mapped out. There is nothing novel or surprising about it in the sense that this has never ever been seen before. Like the planning out of one's morning chores, these are cases of strategic planning or effective decision-making in which the brain runs simulation chains that reason through a series of choice points in the future. It is essentially a mapping process that, in evolutionary language, can be navigated by a near fully sighted Lamarckian EA in which the forward steps are directed or instructed by their known adaptive values.

However, in an actual game of chess, simulating the back-and-forth between you and an opponent player cannot be described by a fully sighted Lamarckian EA. This is because the other player is a somewhat unpredictable factor who may not take the path you anticipate or indeed may make a move that is not at all adaptive. You simply do not have full sightedness of the consequences of a given move, even with the full knowledge of all permissible moves and their approximate adaptive values. This inherent uncertainty makes a variation-selection component an integral part of the EAs operating in the imagination, even when we navigate a KPS. Sure, the variation-selection process exists at a different level – that is, at the level of the actual path we take through the problem space rather than at the level of discovering the problem space itself. But a variation-selection process is involved nevertheless. And it is at this point that a chess game can also be creative.

We can summarize this by saying that the imagination in general involves variation-selection EAs with various degrees of sightedness. It is thus a common mechanism or process in the imagination. From an EA point of view, then, there is nothing fundamentally unique about creative imagination as compared to other aspects of the imagination. An argument could perhaps be made that creativity involves instances with fewer degrees of sightedness but an argument on a gradient or continuum might not be solid grounds to support a categorial distinction.

In the framework proposed by Abraham (2016), creativity is the main component of the novel-combinatorial category. It is its own thing, a distinct part of the imagination, separated from other parts. But the other members of this category – hypothetical reasoning, counterfactual thinking, and hypothesis generation – can all be creative as well. At the level of EAs, they proceed on the same basic mechanism. This argument can also be extended to the other four categories of Abraham's framework – mental imagery, intentionality, phenomenology, and altered states. Each contains aspects of the imagination that can also be creative, such as visual imagery, mental time travel, aesthetic engagement, or dreams – to pick one example from each of the four categories. Seen from this angle, creativity might not be a distinct category of the imagination but be best dissolved and embedded into all forms of the imagination.

References

Abraham, A. (2016). The Imaginative Mind. *Human Brain Mapping, 37*, 4197–4211.

Bar, M. (2007). The Proactive Brain: Using Analogies and Associations to Generate Predictions. *Trends in Cognitive Science, 11*, 280–289.

(2009). The Proactive Brain: Memory for Prediction. *Philosophical Transactions of the Royal Society B, 364*, 1235–1243.

Barsalou, L. W. (2009). Simulation, Situated Conceptualization, and Prediction. *Philosophical Transactions of the Royal Society B: Biological Sciences, 364*, 1281–1289.

Campbell, D. T. (1960). Blind Variation and Selective Retention in Creative Thought as in Other Knowledge Processes. *Psychological Review, 67*, 380–400.

Chatterjee, A., and Vartanian, O. (2014). Neuroaesthetics. *Trends in Cognitive Science, 18*, 370–375.

Christoff, K. (2012). Undirected Thought: Neural Determinants and Correlates. *Brain Research, 1428*, 51–59.

Dawkins, R. (1976). *The Selfish Gene*. Oxford, UK: Oxford University Press.

Dennett, D. C. (1995). *Darwin's Dangerous Idea*. New York, NY: Simon & Schuster.

Dietrich, A. (2004). The Cognitive Neuroscience of Creativity. *Psychonomic Bulletin & Review, 11*, 1011–1026.

(2015). *How Creativity Happens in the Brain*. London, UK: Palgrave Macmillan.

(2019). Types of Creativity. *Psychonomic Bulletin & Review, 26*(1), 1–12.

Dietrich, A., and Haider, H. (2017). A Neurocognitive Framework for Human Creative Thought. *Frontiers in Psychology: Cognitive Science, 7*, 2078–2085.

Fisher, J. C. (2006). Does Simulation Theory Really Involve Simulation? *Philosophical Psychology, 19*, 417–432.

Frith, C. D. (1992). *The Cognitive Neuropsychology of Schizophrenia*. Hove, UK: Lawrence Erlbaum.

Gendler, T. (2013). Imagination. In E. N. Zalta (ed.), *The Stanford Encyclopedia of Philosophy* (Fall). plato.stanford.edu/entries/imagination/.

Gould, S. J. (1979). Shades of Lamarck. *Natural History*, *88*, 22–28.

Grush, R. (2004). The Emulation Theory of Representation: Motor Control, Imagery, and Perception. *Behavioral and Brain Sciences*, *27*, 377–396.

Kronfeldner, M. E. (2007). Is Cultural Evolution Lamarckian? *Biology and Philosophy*, *22*, 493–512.

(2010). Darwinian "Blind" Hypothesis Formation Revisited. *Synthese*, *175*, 193–218.

Lewontin, R. C. (1970). The Units of Selection. *Annual Review of Ecology and Systematics*, *1*, 1–18.

(1991). *Biology as Ideology*. New York, NY: Harper.

Llinás, R. R. (2001). *I of the Vortex: From Neurons to Self*. Boston, MA: MIT Press.

Mayr, E. (1981). *The Growth of Biological Thought: Diversity, Evolution, and Inheritance*. Cambridge, MA: Harvard University Press.

Medawar, P. M. (1953). A Commentary on Lamarckism. Reprinted in P. Medawar (1981), *The Uniqueness of the Individual*. New York, NY: Dover, 63–87.

Richerson, P. J., and Boyd, R. (2005). *Not by Genes Alone: How Culture Transformed Human Evolution*. Chicago, IL: University of Chicago Press.

Schooler, J. W., and Dougal, S. (1999). Why Creativity Is Not like the Proverbial Typing Monkey. *Psychological Inquiry*, *10*, 351–356.

Shepard, R. N., and Metzler, J. (1971). Mental Rotation of Three-Dimensional Objects. *Science*, *171*, 701–703.

Simonton, D. K. (1999). Creativity as Blind Variation and Selective Retention: Is the Creative Process Darwinian? *Psychological Inquiry*, *10*, 309–328.

Singer, J. L. (1975). Navigating the Stream of Consciousness: Research in Daydreaming and Related Inner Experiences. *American Psychologist*, *30*, 727–738.

Smith, E. A. (2013). Agency and Adaptation: New Directions in Evolutionary Anthropology. *Annual Review of Anthropology*, *41*, 103–120.

Sternberg, R. J. (1998). Cognitive Mechanisms in Human Creativity: Is Variation Blind or Sighted? *Journal of Creative Behavior*, *32*, 159–176.

Stevenson, L. (2003). Twelve Conceptions of Imagination. *The British Journal of Aesthetics*, *43*(3), 238–259.

Weisberg, R. W., and Hass, R. (2007). We Are All Partly Right: Comment on Simonton. *Creativity Research Journal*, *19*, 345–360.

Wolpert, D. M., Doya, K., and Kawato, M. (2003). A Unifying Computational Framework for Motor Control and Social Interaction. *Philosophical Transactions of the Royal Society Series B*, *358*, 593–602.

10 A Sociocultural Perspective on Imagination

Tania Zittoun, Vlad Glăveanu, and Hana Hawlina

> Imagination is the basis of all human activity and an important component of all aspects of cultural life. Absolutely everything around us that was created by the hand of man, the entire world of human culture, as distinct from the world of nature, all this is the product of human imagination and of creation based on this imagination.
>
> (Vygotsky, 1930/2004: 4)

Imagination can be conceived of as a deeply sociocultural phenomenon that includes a large range of psychological processes enabling us to draw on past experiences, recombined in unique ways, so as to create new alternatives and possible futures. In contrast to a view of the imagination considering it as "private" or intra-psychological, and treating its processes as different from (even opposed to) what is "real," imaginative processes grow out of social interactions, use cultural resources, and build on our experiences of the world while constantly transforming and expanding them. Such an understanding is currently being explored by sociocultural research in psychology. In this chapter, we first review classical philosophical debates grounding most of the current debates on imagination, a discussion that allows us to position the original theoretical propositions of Lev Vygotsky. These are still inspirational for current cultural or sociocultural psychology, a tradition of research that takes the mutual constitution of human development and culture as its point of departure. On this basis, we present current studies in the sociocultural psychology of imagination following the four themes identified by Abraham (see Chapter 1). We then show how an integrative model of imagination may actually consider these four aspects of imagination as variations on the same fundamental dynamic. We conclude the chapter by suggesting that such an integrative view of imagination may help us reflect on the conditions of emergence of new collective futures.

Classical Debates and Divisions on Imagination

Imagination is an old theme in Western reflection and theorization, as old as philosophy itself. Given the philosophical roots of psychology, classical divisions in philosophy have found direct echoes in the ways in which psychologists have conceived of imagination (for historical accounts, see Cornejo, 2017; Hviid and Villadsen, 2018). Classical debates have addressed the creative vs. reproductive nature of imagination, the fact that it may be an inferior or incomplete form of reasoning, its representational nature, as well as whether it is an individual or a social and cultural process. In what follows, we briefly revisit the two last of these debates, which are especially relevant for our discussion (see also Zittoun and Gillespie, 2016: Chapter 2).

Many theoreticians consider imagination as "having a mental image," that is, consider that it is related to representation, though some postulate non-visual components. The distinction can be found, for instance, in Descartes, for whom imagination demands to "see in the mind's eye" (e.g. a triangle), while reason enables us to conceive ideas that are not visible such as "chiliagon" (a polygon with 1,000 sides, perceptually indistinguishable from a circle); here, reason is considered to be superior (Descartes, 1641: 85–87). In psychology, imagination as a phenomenon based on images – which usually implies that it is reproductive in nature – was taken on by Wundt and Bartlett. In contrast, and during the same period as Descartes, Giambattista Vico (Vico, 1725/1993a, 1710/1993b, 1728/2004) conceived of imagination as an embodied experience, which enables people – individuals and collectives – to confer meaning, and therefore stability, on events that otherwise escape their understanding. Hence, Vico saw myths as reflecting people's attempt to make sense of scary events, such as thunderstorms, with their noise, lightning, and actual dangers, and imagining that these were due to the anger of gods. These imaginative acts enabled them to render their environment meaningful. Imagination thus appeared to be more than merely representational; it is a creative act, filling the gap left by our incomplete knowledge and rationality.

A second important division concerns the individual vs. collective or cultural nature of imagination. Descartes, and many after him, saw imagination as something experienced or engaged at the level of the single individual, in his or her mind. Similar views can be found in a large part of the psychological literature (e.g. Byrne, 2005; Harris, 2000; Piaget, 1945/1992). In contrast, Vico's propositions were that imagination is linked to the social and cultural creation of meaning and the production of cultural artifacts, and that these cultural artifacts guide and enrich further individual imaginings. Again, scared of thunders, humans invented myths about the wrath of gods, which were then transmitted orally, as well as through the arts; these artifacts subsequently became resources for other people to imagine gods in the sky causing thunder. In this sense, imagination is at the origin of culture, and is nourished by it; it is a sociocultural process. Similarly, Sigmund Freud (1959, 1963, 2001) showed how people use material from books they read or artworks they know in their dreams, and Frederic Bartlett demonstrated that they also do so when asked to see shapes in the clouds (Bartlett, 1916, 1928). Hence, culture appeared early as a theme in the reflection on imagination – as one of its core constituents, rather than merely as a variable.

In this chapter, we will propose a view of imagination as developing across the life course, as creative, multimodal (that is, not only related to images), and, above all, as a sociocultural phenomenon. In order to do so, we will first present the assumptions we work with as sociocultural psychologists, which set the stage for such an approach to imagination.

What is Sociocultural Psychology?

Sociocultural psychology, or cultural or cultural-historical psychology, is a domain in psychology that aims at capturing the "cultural" nature of human experience. It is a field that emerged at the conjunction of various disciplines of the humanities and social sciences (see Valsiner, 2012; Valsiner and van der Veer, 2000). One may say that it developed out of three movements: first, Western psychologists explored the lands visited by anthropologists and they realized, seeing the "culture" of the others, that they had one, too (Cole, 1996; Rogoff, 2003); they had to rethink the very notion of culture. The second stems from sociology, which examines the underpinnings of social groups, movements, narratives, and values; such a "societal" nature of human experience is closely related to the "cultural" one (e.g. Hedegaard et al., 2008; Valsiner, 1998). A third movement, starting among psychologists studying the process of "socialization" in the form of close interactions in the family, at school, and so on, noticed that what mattered for development was not only *what* was done and said, but also *how* things were done and said. Shirley Brice Heath (1983) has thus shown how children from different US communities learned contrasting "ways with words" to tell a story or share experience with others. Infinite variations could be observed and cause misunderstanding, among others, when the child moved from family to school – here again, invisible differences appeared to be linked to "culture" (Nelson, 2007; Valsiner, 1997). One way or another, these movements invited authors to admit that, if culture is to humans what the water is for the eyes of fish (Bruner, 1990), as psychologists we had to understand this water *and* the eye *as well as* their mutual relations. These streams of thought found their grounds and roots in American pragmatism (Valsiner and van der Veer, 2000), dialogism (Marková, 2016), German *Ganzheit* psychology (Diriwächter and Valsiner, 2008), and Russian historico-cultural psychology (Ratner, 2012; Zavereshneva and van der Veer, 2018). In all these streams of research, culture was soon considered a central condition of human development (Cole, 1996; Rosa and Valsiner, 2018; Wertsch, 1998) and, with it, perception, reasoning, interactions, emotions and imagination, among others, gained a sociocultural origin and dynamic.

Currently, sociocultural psychologists work with a number of assumptions. Key among them are: a) the mutual constitution between mind and culture, psychological functions and their sociomaterial contexts; b) the importance of studying the "person in context"; c) the fundamental role played by actions and interactions – with others, things, institutions and different facets of culture – for the constitution of the mind; d) the importance of the temporal dimension at different scales, including the evolution of the species and the history of society, development across the life course, and even moment-to-moment interactions; and e) the fact that our psychological life and action in and on the world are mediated by the use of cultural resources, such as signs and tools, and this mediation creates a space for living outside the immediacy of the here and now. This is not meant to be an exhaustive list of assumptions and propositions but one that already highlights the profound implications sociocultural psychology has for our understanding of imagination. Within this view, imagination is a process as well as an experience, it is highly contextual, develops over time, mediates action and is, at once, mediated both by culture and its various social, material, and symbolic resources. This view diverges from contemporary cognitive or neuroscientific accounts and finds its origin in different psychological and philosophical orientations.

A Foundational Cultural Understanding of Imagination: Lev S. Vygotsky

One of the main inspirations for current explorations of imagination in sociocultural psychology can be found in the influential work of Russian psychologist Lev Vygotsky, living and writing in the Russian empire and the former Soviet Union between 1896 and 1934. Deeply interested in the historic and cultural shaping of the human mind and consciousness, as well as in the role of art in experience and development, he outlined important insights about imagination that can be summarized as follows.

First, Vygotsky was very aware of the classical division in the theorization of imagination at the turn of the nineteenth century. For him, imagination can indeed be the process by which we complete our perception of reality (as in Chapter 1 of this handbook, and Pelaprat and Cole, 2011). But the specificity of imagination is that it is a creative, higher mental function, processual, not limited to images, and a deeply cultural form of thinking; yet, it can also be more or less rational and emotional, depending on the distance taken from the objects at stake.

The argument supporting this claim is that imagination develops alongside the person's progressive mastery of a linguistic system, as well as of various culturally mediated conceptual systems. This reorganizes people's thinking, and gives them the means to regulate and organize it. "Higher psychological functions," like imagination, are thus culturally constructed, and help us achieve distance from the immediate stimulations and constraints of the environment. On this basis, Vygotsky saw imagination as intentional or "oriented" (Vygotsky, 2011: 173). It develops in the course of childhood and yet it is only during adolescence that a person can start to distinguish and separate more objective or subjective modes of imagining, and more or less concrete or abstract modes (Vygotsky, 1931/1994). Hence, with development, imagination becomes more differentiated and can be combined in various ways: daydreaming, inventing, planning, all of them variations of imagining, leaving more or less space to emotions (Vygotsky, 2011: 176).

Through these variations, a core characteristic remains: "the essential feature of imagination is that consciousness departs from reality. Imagination is a comparatively autonomous activity of consciousness in which there is a departure from any immediate cognition of reality" (Vygotsky, 1987: 349). We take this intuition as central: in effect, if imagination is characterized by a departure from the immediate situation, it is what gives us a degree of freedom from the constraints of an immediate situation.

Nevertheless, for Vygotsky, imagination is also deeply connected to social reality in four ways (Vygotsky, 1930/2004). First, it is nourished by one's experience of the social and cultural world; the richer the experience, the more complex and nuanced the imagination:

> The creative activity of the imagination depends directly on the richness and variety of a person's previous experience because this experience provides the material from which the products of fantasy are constructed. The richer a person's experience, the richer is the material his imagination has access to. This is why a child has a less rich imagination than an adult, because his experience has not been as rich. (Vygotsky, 1930/2004: 14–15)

Hence, a child can imagine a house on the basis of houses she has seen, stories she has heard, and her unique new synthesis of these; an architect, who has access to more encounters with houses and masters various conceptual systems, can, through his unique creative synthesis, imagine much more complex houses.

Second, imagination is a way to know the world: through books, pictures, narratives, we can build our knowledge of places to which we have never been, or of events we have not directly experienced. In this sense, it allows an expansion of experience via the experiences of others. Third, it is linked to our real, world-related emotional life; if we are touched by a novel, we engage emotions in resonance with experiences we actually had, as if it was a real-life occurrence. And fourth, imagination enables actual creation in the world: "finally, once they were given material form, they returned to reality, but returned as a new active force with the potential to alter that reality" (Vygotsky, 1930/2004: 21). It is the combination of these four elements that brings Vygotsky to this strong statement:

> It is precisely human creative activity that makes the human being a creature oriented toward the future, creating the future and thus altering his own present. This creative activity, based on the ability of our brain to combine elements, is called imagination or fantasy in psychology ... But in actuality, imagination, as the basis of all creative activity, is an important component of absolutely all aspects of cultural life, enabling artistic, scientific, and technical creation alike. (Vygotsky, 1930/2004: 9–10)

As part of his cultural-historical psychology, Vygotsky thus sketched an understanding of imagination as essentially cultural. We will now see how these intuitions have been pursued in contemporary research.

Four Fields of Study for Imagination as Sociocultural Dynamic Categories

In this section, we present current studies of imagination in sociocultural psychology, all working with assumptions inspired by Vygotsky. The section is organized in four parts, following the structure proposed by Abraham (Figure 1.3) in Chapter 1; the studies we mention use a variety of methodologies, both qualitative and quantitative (for recent methodological overviews, see Tanggaard and Brinkman, 2018; Zittoun, 2016a).

The relation between imagination and perception has been of key significance for philosophers and scientists working in both areas (Nanay, 2016; Pendlebury, 1996). While this concern has deep historical roots, going back to the old debates regarding the formation, role, and status of mental images, it has received considerable attention since Kant argued that "imagination is a necessary ingredient of perception itself" (*Critique of Pure Reason* A1 20, [Kant, 1787/1999: 269]). In an often-cited footnote, Kant argues that this contribution often escaped psychologists because they assumed that perception is limited to reproduction alone and failed to recognize that the "material" it supplies is combined or synthesized (functions that he associated with the imagination). In contrast, more recent accounts of "active perception" (see Thomas, 1999), give perception a major role in imagination itself. Instead of having imagination contributing to perception, we also have proponents of imagination emerging from perception. This itself is an old conception that goes back to Hume and his idea that imagined material is basically a paler version of perception (see Nanay, 2016). Adding to the similarity between the two, contemporary neurological research points to commonalities in brain activity when perceiving, remembering, and imagining, and their association to areas such as the anterior hippocampus (Zeidman and Maguire, 2016). While reviewing the philosophical debates concerning the direction of the relationship between perception and imagination is beyond the scope of this chapter, two main observations can be derived from these discussions. One is that perception and imagination "collaborate" in various ways and, while focusing on which brain areas engage both, as neuroscientific accounts sometimes do, might not differentiate them enough; it is the contribution each process makes to the other that needs to be recognized. Second, we need to notice that this relationship is premised on the importance of images and imagery (even if not only visual but, nonetheless, sensorial) for both perception and imagination.

The sociocultural approach, as described above, does not reduce imagination to imagery. From a Vygotskian perspective, imagination builds on and produces experience, and while this experience does integrate sensorial and perceptual content, it should not be equated with it. For instance, it has been proposed recently, drawing on Merleau-Ponty's notion of the imaginary texture of the real, that imagination doesn't only reveal the perceived world but gives it an affective logic (see Lennon, 2010). Indeed, experience is infused with emotion just as much (or perhaps more, depending on context), than with pure images and cognitions. Under these circumstances, it is imperative to develop a more nuanced account of the relationship between perception and imagination by placing it within the developmental history of the species and of the person. This is what Pelaprat and Cole (2011) attempted to do by proposing a gap-filling model of imagination. Basing their argument also on perception research (in particular rapid eye movements and fixed image experiments), the two authors assumed that what imagination does is resolve the gaps and contradictions that arise from both biological and cultural-historical constraints placed on our psychological functioning and, in doing so, it enables a better coordination between thought and action. In their words, "imagination *is* present in a primitive, yet clear, form even when an object is present to the senses" (Pelaprat and Cole, 2011: 339). This is an important conclusion that comes to address one of the biggest divides challenged by sociocultural research – that between what is imagined and what is real (see arguments against their separation in Vygotsky, 1930/2004). However, in building this account, Pelaprat and Cole still conceive of imagination primarily in terms of mental imagery. For them, "human beings are *by nature* always engaged in a process of image formation, of imagination" (Pelaprat and Cole, 2011: 402). While this account does give imagination a key role in constructing images of objects directly available to our senses, it remains largely silent about subjective experience. The issue of imagination as experience is perhaps best captured by considering phenomenological accounts, a topic briefly reviewed as follows.

Phenomenology of Art Experience

Among other phenomena, sociocultural psychologists have tried to understand the nature of cultural experiences, such as reading fiction or poetry (Lehmann et al., 2017; Vygotsky, 1971), watching a movie (Kuhn, 2013b), listening to music (Klempe, 2018), being absorbed by a painting or engulfed in an art installation (Benson, 1993, 2001; Zittoun and Gillespie, 2014), or being a member of a theater audience (Zittoun and Rosenstein, 2018). They also emphasized the transformative effects of these experiences.

A cultural experience can usually be described as an experience of guided imagination thanks to a specific cultural or artistic artifact. Various studies converge in considering that artistic or cultural experience demands a threshold – a ritual, a *mise en scène* – that signals, for the person, that she will leave the here-and-now world of experience. At the theater or the cinema, these are very clear: One typically sits in a room with red velvet upholstery, turns off one's mobile phone, and waits for the lights to change. Entering an art exhibition, one needs to find space in the wide silence to create a specific state of receptivity. Similarly, specific thresholds mark the end of the experience – lights come back on, phones ring, the souvenir shop is near. In between, the actual artistic or cultural experience that demands the work of imagination takes place. People have to leave the shores of the known and be taken by the hand, so to speak, into the unknown and strange world offered by the art piece – the liminal experience (Stenner, 2018). All along the way, the person "knows" that this is untrue, yet it is *as-if* it were (e.g. Hviid and Villadsen, 2018). The person engages actively in imagining: Only this imagination is guided, shaped, "scaffolded" by the specificities of the artifact's semiotic guidance. The art piece is not imposed upon the person; she actually has to draw on her personal experience, biographic trajectories, past knowledge of other cultural experiences; she responds with her embodied reactions – to sounds, space – and her own affects, so as to recreate the proposed piece. Different viewers, with different knowledge of art forms, different life trajectories, and different general systems of values, will have different imaginary experiences in relation to one and the same art piece.

People also often remember, mention or consider these imaginary guided experiences as important, and these can later be used as symbolic resources (Zittoun, 2006). Hence a person may feel happy and suddenly a song long forgotten comes to her mind, or, more deliberately, upon migrating to a new country, may use a song to imagine life in the homeland (Kadianaki, 2010); in such cases, people draw on the memory of the imaginary sphere of experience made possible once by the artifact. In turn, these symbolic resources now become further material for imagining and creating, as we will see.

Intentionality and Imagination

Each of the operations of imagination categorized as intentionality-based – mental state reasoning, moral decision-making, mental time travel and autobiographical memory – are commonly hailed as landmarks of *sui generis* human cognition that qualitatively differentiate our engagement with the world from that of nonhuman animals. Intentionality represents the connecting feature of these operations because they can be exercised intentionally, in specific situations and for diverse purposes. They also enable complex forms of intentionality such as shared intentionality and collaboration, planning an action on the basis of past experience and with regard to its potential future outcomes, and considering how those actions could affect others.

The significant contribution of imagination to social understanding is implicitly acknowledged throughout Theory of Mind literature; however, imagination has only recently become a direct object of study (Trevarthen and Delafield-Butt, 2017). Glăveanu et al., (2017) have proposed a perspectival model of imagination that positions perspective taking as the fundamental process in the operation of imagination. They investigated how people create perspectives of refugees – distant others that they have never personally met (Glăveanu and de Saint-Laurent, 2015; Glăveanu, de Saint-Laurent, and Literat, 2018). They showed how imagination is used to make sense of the other and how diverse sources of information are used as resources for constructing both positive and negative imaginings.

Imagination is not only used to understand absent others, but also facilitates collaboration and the sharing of unfamiliar ideas. A growing number of studies examine the role of imagination in task-solving, in quasi-experimental situations (Pelaprat and Cole, 2011; Zittoun and Cerchia, 2013), in classroom discussions or generally in learning (Akkerman, 2018). Hawlina, Gillespie, and Zittoun (2017) studied the processes of perspective taking in dyads who were asked to imagine an improbable scenario. They found that dyads who were more adept at perspective taking produced twice as many ideas. Hilppö et al. (2016) analyzed the discussion between children in a science class after one of them asked where stones came from. To answer that question, drawing on stories they heard or images they had seen, they imagined fireballs falling from the sky or sand being glued, before refuting these propositions and finding a more plausible explanation.

The processing of intentionality-based operations of imagination is seen as primarily recollective because they draw on a lifetime of experience and are thus at no point achieved or complete, but flexibly developing and transforming throughout life. The most obviously recollective is the process of mental time travel, in which imagination has been shown to be closely tied to memory operations (Schacter and Addis, 2007; Tulving and Kim, 2007), which allow us to travel into the personal or collective past (autobiographical, episodic, and collective memory) as well as into personal and collective futures (de Saint-Laurent, 2018; Jovchelovitch and Hawlina, 2018).

In development throughout the life course, imagination plays an important role in dealing with ruptures, life bifurcations and transitions (Zittoun and Valsiner, 2016), in reflecting on one's biographical past or collective past (de Saint-Laurent and Zittoun, 2018), maintaining continuity in the representation of self across time and contexts (Gillespie, Corti, and Heasman, 2018) and, importantly, in exploring one's alternatives and possible futures (Zittoun and de Saint-Laurent, 2015; Zittoun and Gillespie, 2015). Zittoun and Sato (2018) studied the case of an older woman (Ms. S)'s development after the Fukushima disaster that showed how trauma can constrain imagination and trap people in a foreclosed past, without connection to the present and the future. The restoration of the village graveyard made it possible for Ms. S to acknowledge the reality of the tsunami, connect to the personal and collective past, and start imagining new possibilities for the future. Here we see that imagination is crucial for the development of people and communities, and how it is facilitated by social recognition and material resources that have cultural meaning. This section has shown that even though recollection provides material for imagining, these processes are not merely reproductive but creative in their own right and it is not certain that a specific situation will produce a single most plausible imagining, but can produce many diverse reimaginings that help us find new ways forward.

Imagination as Generative

Last but not least, imagination is recognized by sociocultural accounts as *generative*. Since Kant's famous distinction between productive and reproductive imagination, the productive or creative dimension of imagination has received considerable attention, to the point of recognizing the generative nature of what was previously considered reproductive imagination (Glăveanu et al., 2017). It is most commonly assumed that imagination is creative because its dynamic is fundamentally associative or combinatorial. This point has been clearly made by Vygotsky himself, building on previous work by Ribot (2007).

For Vygotsky (2004), all human activity that "results not in the reproduction of previously experienced impressions or actions but in the creation of new images or actions is an example of this (. . .) combinatorial behavior" and "this creative activity, based on the ability of our brain to combine elements, is called imagination or fantasy in psychology" (Vygotsky, 1930/2004: 9). This strong assertion is made, in part, in order to support the broader argument that imagination is deeply connected with reality. Indeed, it uses components of what is real to generate more or less unusual combinations that, when externalized, constituted the basis of creative action (see Glăveanu, 2014). As we have seen above, Vygotsky considers that the richer human experience is, the richer the material for imagining. It is undeniable that both creativity and imagination proceed by transforming existing content acquired through perception, stored in memory, and infused by both cognition and affect. What imagination does is open this experience to the future and to the possible by combining it in ways that respond to both present and anticipated constraints. However, the processes of imagination cannot be reduced to simple dissociations and associations between existing elements in one's mind. Freud (1900/2001) added interesting dimensions to this discussion by focusing on the role played by displacement and condensation in the way dreams operate (see Pile, 2000). The elements of experience can also be augmented or simplified, broken into smaller parts and reassembled in a new manner. Reorganizing experience and trying to approximate the lived experience of others (for instance through perspective taking, Gillespie and Martin, 2014; Glăveanu et al., 2017), formulating hypotheses (Harris, 2000) and engaging in "as if" and "what if" explorations (Hviid and Villadsen, 2018) are also key imaginative processes.

In summary, combinations are one of the most basic and most widespread ways in which imagination operates, including in the sociocultural tradition, but this should not exclude other processes (e.g. perspective taking, divergent ideation) that build on, contribute to, or at times even come to replace combinatorial work.

An Integrative Model: The Imagination Loop

In our brief overview of the diverse operations of the imagination, it becomes clear that they are not functionally independent, but in fact highly interrelated and co-constructive. For example, in appreciating a conceptual artwork, mental imagery fills in the perceptual gaps and plays with ambiguities. We also experience aesthetic engagement, make inferences about the author's intent, and creatively construct our own interpretation and personal meaning of the work. Central operational features of the imagination can thus be seen as different aspects of one overarching process of imagining that is simultaneously perceptual, emotional, recollective, and generative. Furthermore, we can observe great similarity in the operation of imagination belonging to different categories; all of them begin with the perceptual engagement with the world, from where the movement of thought proceeds through internal landscapes using past experience and semiotic resources to construct a new perspective and transform ongoing activity. Imagination can thus be seen as a highly flexible general process that develops throughout the lifespan and can be employed in different contexts and for different aims. We recently proposed a synthetic model – the imagination loop, "mid-range" between concrete cases and abstract theorization, enabling us to see these various occurrences as variations of the same phenomena (Zittoun and Gillespie, 2016) (Figure 10.1).

The basic idea, as formulated in Vygotsky, is that imagination is a temporary decoupling from the here-and-now of socially shared experience. Imagination is usually triggered by an event – thresholds, as in the case of art experience; boredom, as when students "escape" from a long math class by daydreaming; or when we face an obstacle in the course of action. From this trigger, imagination can be represented as a loop, or rather, imagining deploys as a looping experience – an *as-if* experience, in which time can be undone, and the usual physical and logical rules do not have to be respected. Last but not least, imagination is nourished by various resources on which the person draws – personal experience, symbolic resources, social representations and discourses, discussions with others, etc.

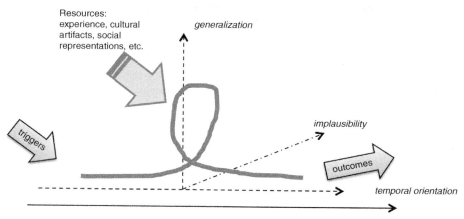

Figure 10.1 *The imagination loop. After Zittoun and Gillespie (2016),* Imagination in Human and Cultural Development, *London: Routledge.*

To account for the diversity of imagination, this loop can be described as varying along three dimensions. The first one is temporal: the loop can be oriented toward the past – in the sense that remembering can be seen as imagining about the past – the future, or alternative presents. The second dimension concerns the distance from material or embodied experience vs. the more abstract or general nature of the imagination. Hence, one can imagine the concrete taste of a strawberry, or imagine world peace, a very abstract value. The third dimension represents the degree to which the actual content or outcome of imagination is socially validated in a given sociocultural context and time: Imagining that the Earth was round was not socially validated in Galileo's time, but it is now.

Eventually, the person's loop closes and the flow of consciousness is recoupled to the here and now flow of experience. This looping, however, always has some outcomes: the slight relief of having let one's mind wander in a pleasant daydream, a new understanding of one's past, or the actual solution for a building problem. We believe that, with the help of this basic model, we can account for most individual and also collective forms of imagination (Zittoun and Gillespie, 2018; Zittoun and Glăveanu, 2018). We turn our attention to the latter in the final section.

New Directions: Imagination and Cultural Change

As proposed so far, sociocultural psychology invites us to conceive imagination as a social and cultural activity. This also means that the process of imagining can be done collectively, and that the outcomes of imagination can affect the social world. A paradigmatic example in the development of such ability of social imagining is pretend play, in which children collectively share their imaginings to construct elaborate scenarios, distribute roles, negotiate the parameters of invented reality, and give new meanings to material artifacts that they use in play (Harris, 2000). Through pretend play, children engage in embodied exploration of how the society functions, practice social roles and hierarchies, set their own laws, act out the operation of institutions such as a hospital or a prison, and rehearse economic participation (e.g. by using marbles as money) (Gillespie and Martin, 2014). As we grow up, we often forget or fail to notice that societies themselves are a sophisticated form of pretend play; they are an intricate, ever-evolving configuration of collective imagination that is intersubjectively shared and materialized in institutions and cultural artifacts such as constitutions, flags, history books, newspapers, monuments, national anthems, and so on. Maurice Bloch (2008) called this form of human social organizing "the transcendental social" because through imagination, essentialized roles, hierarchies, prescribed behavioral patterns, abstract rules, and institutional procedures persist in time and transcend moment-to-moment interactions. Cultural and semiotic artifacts are pivotal, themselves a product of imagination that anchors subsequent imaginings in material reality and provides common referents that enable the dissemination of relatively uniform and coherent images in the minds of millions (Anderson, 1991; Jovchelovitch, 2014; McBride, 2005). And each of these minds sustains an image of millions of others and the collective they form, be it a local community, nation, racial group or the entire human population. Based on such symbolic experience of the collective life and corresponding representations of the other and otherness, people make political decisions such as how to treat refugees (Glăveanu, de Saint-Laurent, and Literat, 2018) or how deserving welfare recipients are (Petersen and Aarøe, 2013). Glăveanu and de Saint-Laurent (2015) termed the process of intentionally seeking to construct a certain imagining of the society as "political imagination."

Their imagined construction can make societies and cultures seem fragile, insubstantial, and impermanent, and, in times of political crises, financial breakdowns, social unrest, or revolutions, they indeed prove to be less stable and enduring than we would perhaps like them to be. However, it is precisely their imagined nature (Castoriadis, 1997) that enables societies to innovate themselves and gives cultures a forward-oriented function. Appadurai (2013) recognizes the future as a cultural fact and emphasizes that while cultures are commonly defined by looking backward (at artifacts, traditions, historical narratives), it is the cultural capacity to aspire that enables, nurtures, and provides resources for visions of the future. Within sociocultural psychology, researchers have explored how the future is imagined collectively and how imaginings of the collective future are mobilized in the present to steer sociogenesis (see de Saint-Laurent, Obradović, and Carriere, 2018; Zittoun and Gillespie, 2016). In contrast, when communities lack the cultural capacity to aspire and create positive narratives for the future they can experience deprivation (Jovchelovitch and Priego-Hernández, 2013), or a collective rupture such as a financial crisis (Triliva, Varvantakis, and Dafermos, 2015). In such pessimistic conditions of being stuck in a miserable present, it is crucial to nourish imagination with the aid of meaningful cultural artifacts so that communities are able to construct new imaginings, rephrase the narratives of despair into ones of hope, make new meanings, and build a positive identity, because through symbolic transformation of how community is imagined, people have the vision and the courage to instantiate real social change (Bloch, 1995; Daiute, 2017).

This brings us back to the epigraph by Vygotsky and perhaps the most pervasive division in the conceptualization of imagination – the false separation between the real and the imagined, when in fact "the entire world of human culture ... is the product of human imagination" (Vygotsky, 1930/2004: 9–10), without this making it less real – quite the contrary: since imagination is afforded by and develops through our cultural experience and engagement with cultural artifacts, it is necessarily cultural. And, in turn, the whole of our sociocultural reality is at least partially imagined. It is thus imperative to study imagination and culture not as independent factors that may influence one another, but as completely intermeshed and recursively co-constructive facets of human experience.

Conclusion

In sociocultural psychology, imagination is not only an individual process. Even when daydreaming in solitude, one draws on culturally available resources as material for imagining, as well as memories of past social interactions and ideas voiced by others. Many times, the person is even "accompanied" in the daydream by imagined others. Furthermore, the operation of imagining itself has much in common with social processes such as perspective taking or movements between internalized positions and the dialogic interactions between them (Bakhtin, 1981; Glăveanu et al., 2017; Zittoun and Gillespie, 2016). Finally, the unfolding of the daydream often follows culturally transmitted narrative templates. Imagination is thus always both social and cultural, yet the complex human sociality and culture are also, in turn, enabled by imagination. Imagination is not always a solitary activity – people have the ability to create intersubjective worlds of imagination, to build them collaboratively in interaction with others, and to collectively participate in imagined scenarios. Moreover, individual and collective acts of imagination build new personal and societal resources for imagining and can, through social action, shape the society and culture they draw from.

Hence, sociocultural psychology proposes the reconceptualization of imagination as a process of temporary disengaging from the socially shared reality of the present. It also proposes the integration of various streams of research into imagination, and thus, to come back to the streams identified in Abraham (see Chapter 1), it considers imagination as including mental imagery, but also other modes of experiencing; it takes into account the phenomenological experience of engaging with art, but also considers it to be socially guided; it admits that it is partly intentional, and can take shape in specific interactions as well as through the course of a life; and it is highly generative, not only for the person, but also for society. As a whole, sociocultural psychology considers imagination to be much more than a fancy or a flight out of the real: On the contrary, as it demands that a person or a group of persons draw on available knowledge, experience, cultural artifacts, and complex skills, it is the fundamental process by which we can explore and share our past – individual and collective; define and visit alternative and possible worlds; and imagine the future – our own, and that of the world – and set us in motion toward it.

References

Akkerman, S. (2018). Imagination in and Beyond Education. In T. Zittoun and V. P. Glăveanu (eds.), *Handbook of Imagination and Culture*. Oxford, UK: Oxford University Press, 211–221.

Anderson, B. (1991). *Imagined Communities: Reflections on the Origin and Spread of Nationalism*. London, UK: Verso Books.

Appadurai, A. (2013). The Future as Cultural Fact. In *Essays on the Global Condition*. London, UK; New York, NY: Verso Books.

Bakhtin, M. M. (1981). *The Dialogic Imagination: Four Essays*. Austin, TX: University of Texas Press.

Bartlett, F. C. (1916). An Experimental Study of Some Problems of Perceiving and Imagining. *British Journal of Psychology, 8,* 222–266.

(1928). Types of Imagination. *Journal of Philosophical Studies, 3*(9), 78–85.

Benson, C. (1993). *The Absorbed Self*. Hemel Hempstead, UK: Harvester Wheatsheaf.

(2001). *The Cultural Psychology of Self: Place, Morality and Art in Human Worlds*. London, UK: Routledge.

Bloch, E. (1995). *The Principle of Hope*. Translated by N. Plaice. Cambridge, MA: MIT Press.

Bloch, M. (2008). Why Religion Is Nothing Special but Is Central. *Philosophical Transactions of the Royal Society of London B: Biological Sciences, 363*(1499), 2055–2061. doi.org/10.1098/rstb.2008.0007.

Bruner, J. S. (1990). *Acts of Meaning*. Cambridge, MA: Harvard University Press.

Byrne, R. M. J. (2005). *The Rational Imagination: How People Create Alternatives to Reality*. Cambridge, MA: MIT Press.

Castoriadis, C. (1997). Anthropology, Philosophy, Politics. *Thesis Eleven, 49*(1), 99–116.

Cerchia, F. (2009). Young Children's Use of Symbolic Resources in an Experimental Setting Testing Metaphor Comprehension. *Psychology & Society, 2*(2), 200–211.

Cole, M. (1996). *Cultural Psychology: A Once and Future Discipline*. Cambridge, MA; London, UK: The Belknap Press of Harvard University Press.

Cornejo, C. (2017). From Fantasy to Imagination: A Cultural History and a Moral for Cultural Psychology. In B. Wagoner, I. Brescó de Luna, and S. H. Awad (eds.), *The Psychology of Imagination: History, Theory, and New Research Horizons*. Charlotte, NC: Information Age Publishing, 3–44. www.ccp.aau.dk/digitalAssets/98/98719_from-20fantasy-20to-20imagination.pdf.

Daiute, C. (2017). *Imagination in Community Engagement*. Oxford, UK: Oxford University Press. www.oxfordscholarship.com/view/10.1093/oso/9780190468712.001.0001/oso-9780190468712-chapter-13.

de Saint-Laurent, C. (2018). Thinking Through Time: From Collective Memories to Collective Futures. In C. de Saint Laurent, S. Obradović, and K. R. Carriere (eds.), *Imagining Collective Futures*. Place of publication not identified: Palgrave MacMillan, 59–81.

de Saint-Laurent, C., Obradović, S., and Carriere, K. R. (2018). *Imagining Collective Futures: Perspectives from Social, Cultural and Political Psychology*. London: Palgrave MacMillan.

de Saint-Laurent, C., and Zittoun, T. (2018). Memory in Life Transitions. In B. Wagoner (ed.), *Oxford Handbook of Culture and Memory*. Oxford, UK; New York, NY: Oxford University Press, 209–236.

Descartes, R. (1641). *Meditationes de prima philosophia, in qua Dei existentia et animae immortalitas demonstrantur*. Paris, France: Michel Soly. gallica.bnf.fr/ark:/12148/btv1b86002964.r=.langEN.

Diriwächter, R., and Valsiner, J. (eds.) (2008). *Striving for the Whole: Creating Theoretical Syntheses*. New Brunswick, NJ: Transaction Publishers.

Freud, S. (1959). Creative Writers and Day-Dreaming. In J. Strachey (ed.), *The Standard Edition of the Complete Psychological Works of Sigmund Freud*. Original German publication 1907. Volume 9. London, UK: The Hogarth Press and the Institute of Psychoanalysis, 141–154.

(1963). *Jokes and their Relation to the Unconscious*. New York, NY: Norton.

(2001). *The Interpretation of Dreams*. Original publication 1900 (Volumes 4–5). London, UK: Vintage.

Gillespie, A., Corti, K., and Heasman, B. (2018). Imagining the Self through Cultural Technologies. In T. Zittoun and V. P. Glăveanu (eds.), *Handbook of Imagination and Culture*. Oxford, UK: Oxford University Press, 301–318.

Gillespie, A., and Martin, J. (2014). Position Exchange Theory: A Socio-Material Basis for Discursive and Psychological Positioning. *New Ideas in Psychology, 32*, 73–79. doi.org/10.1016/j.newideapsych.2013.05.001.

Glăveanu, V. P. (2014). *Distributed Creativity: Thinking Outside the Box of the Creative Individual*. New York, NY: Springer Science + Business Media.

Glăveanu, V. P., and de Saint-Laurent, C. (2015). Political Imagination, Otherness and the European Crisis. *Europe's Journal of Psychology, 11*(4), 557–564. doi.org/10.5964/ejop.v11i4.1085.

Glăveanu, V. P., de Saint-Laurent, C., and Literat, I. (2018). Making Sense of Refugees Online: Perspective Taking, Political Imagination, and Internet Memes. *American Behavioral Scientist, 62*(4), 440–457. doi.org/10.1177/0002764218765060.

Glăveanu, V. P., Karwowski, M., Jankowska, D. M., and de Saint-Laurent, C. (2018). Creative Imagination. In T. Zittoun and V. P. Glăveanu (eds.), *Handbook of Imagination and Culture*. Oxford, UK: Oxford University Press, 61–86.

Hargreaves, D. J., Miell, D., and MacDonald, R. A. R. (eds.). (2012). *Musical Imaginations: Multidisciplinary Perspectives on Creativity, Performance, and Perception*. Oxford, UK: Oxford University Press.

Harris, P. L. (2000). *The Work of the Imagination*. 1st edition. Oxford, UK/Malden, MA: Wiley-Blackwell.

Hawlina, H., Gillespie, A., and Zittoun, T. (2017). Difficult Differences: A Socio-Cultural Analysis of how Diversity can Enable and Inhibit Creativity. *The Journal of Creative Behavior, 0/online first, 0*, 1–12. doi.org/10.1002/jocb.182.

Heath, S. B. (1983). *Ways With Words: Language, Life, and Work in Communities and Classrooms*. Cambridge, UK: Cambridge University Press.

Hedegaard, M., Fleer, M., Bang, J., and Hviid, P. (2008). *Studying Children: A Cultural-Historical Approach*. Maidenhead, UK: Open University Press.

Hilppö, J. A., Rajala, A., Zittoun, T., Kumpulainen, K., and Lipponen, L. (2016). Interactive Dynamics of Imagination in a Science Classroom. *Frontline Learning Research, 4* (4), 20–29. doi.org/10.14786/flr.v4i4.213.

Hviid, P., and Villadsen, J. W. (2018). Playing and Being – Imagination in the Life Course. In T. Zittoun and V. P. Glăveanu (eds.), *Handbook of Imagination and Culture*. Oxford, UK: Oxford University Press, 137–166.

Jovchelovitch, S. (2014). The Creativity of the Social: Imagination, Development and Social Change in Rio de Janeiro's Favelas. In V. P. Glăveanu, A. Gillespie, and J. Valsiner (eds.), *Rethinking Creativity: Contributions from Cultural Psychology*. New York, NY: Routledge, 76–92.

Jovchelovitch, S., and Hawlina, H. (2018). Utopias and World-Making. In C. de Saint-Laurent, S. Obradovic, and K. Carriere (eds.), *Imagining Collective Futures: Perspectives from Social, Cultural and Political Psychology*. Basingstoke, UK: Palgrave Macmillan, 129–151.

Jovchelovitch, S., and Priego-Hernández, J. (2013). *Underground Sociabilities: Identity, Culture and Resistance in Rio de Janeiro's Favelas*. Brasilia: UNESCO. www.unesco.org/new/en/brasilia/.

Kadianaki, I. (2010). *Negotiating Immigration Through Symbolic Resources: The Case of Immigrants Living in Greece*. PhD Dissertation. Cambridge, UK: University of Cambridge.

Kant, I. (1787/1999). *Critique of Pure Reason*. Edited by P. Guyer and A. Wood. Cambridge, UK: Cambridge University Press.

Klempe, H. (2018). Music and Imagination. In T. Zittoun and V. P. Glăveanu (eds.), *Handbook of Imagination and Culture*. Oxford, UK: Oxford University Press, 243–269.

Kuhn, A. (2013a). Cultural Experience and the Gallery Film. In A. Kuhn (ed.), *Little Madnesses: Winnicott, Transitional Phenomena and Cultural Experience*. London, UK: Tauris, 159–172.

Kuhn, A. (ed.). (2013b). *Little Madnesses: Winnicott, Transitional Phenomena and Cultural Experience*. London, UK: Tauris.

Lehmann, O. V., Chaudhary, N., Bastos, A. C., and Abbey, E. (eds.). (2017). *Poetry and Imagined Worlds*. London, UK: Palgrave.

Lennon, K. (2010). Re-Enchanting the World: The Role of Imagination in Perception. *Philosophy, 85*(3), 375–389. doi.org/10.1017/S0031819110000239.

Marková, I. (2016). *The Dialogical Mind: Common Sense and Ethics*. Cambridge, UK: Cambridge University Press.

McBride, K. D. (2005). *Collective Dreams: Political Imagination and Community*. Pennsylvania, PA: Pennsylvania State University Press. www.jstor.org/stable/10.5325/j.ctt7v537.

Nanay, B. (2016). Imagination and Perception. In A. Kind (ed.), *The Routledge Handbook of Philosophy of Imagination*. London, UK; New York, NY: Routledge, 124–134.

Nelson, K. (2007). *Young Minds in Social Worlds. Experience, Meaning, and Memory*. Cambridge, MA/London, UK: Harvard University Press.

Pelaprat, E., and Cole, M. (2011). "Minding the Gap": Imagination, Creativity and Human Cognition. *Integrative Psychological and Behavioral Science, 45*, 397–418. doi.org/10.1007/s12124-011-9176-5.

Pendlebury, M. J. (1996). The Role of Imagination in Perception. *South African Journal of Philosophy, 15*(4), 133–138.

Petersen, M. B., and Aarøe, L. (2013). Politics in the Mind's Eye: Imagination as a Link between Social and Political Cognition. *American Political Science Review, 107*(2), 275–293. doi.org/10.1017/S0003055413000026.

Piaget, J. (1945/1992). *La formation du symbole chez l'enfant: Imitation, jeu et rêve, image et representation.* 8th edition. Neuchâtel, Switzerland; Paris, France: Delachaux et Niestlé.

Pile, S. (2000). Sleepwalking in the Modern City: Walter Benjamin and Sigmund Freud in the World of Dreams. In G. Bridge and S. Watson (eds.), *A Companion to the City.* Oxford, UK: Blackwell, 75–86.

Ratner, C. (2012). *Macro Cultural Psychology. A Political Philosophy of Mind.* New York, NY: Oxford University Press.

Ribot, T. (2007). *Essai sur l'imagination créatrice (1900).* Paris, France: L'Harmattan.

Rogoff, B. (2003). *The Cultural Nature of Human Development.* New York, NY: Oxford University Press.

Rosa, A., and Valsiner, J. (eds.) (2018). *The Cambridge Handbook of Sociocultural Psychology.* 2nd edition. Cambridge, UK: Cambridge University Press. doi.org/10 .1017/9781316662229.

Schacter, D. L., and Addis, D. R. (2007). The Cognitive Neuroscience of Constructive Memory: Remembering the Past and Imagining the Future. *Philosophical Transactions of the Royal Society of London B: Biological Sciences, 362*(1481), 773–786. doi.org/10.1098/rstb.2007.2087.

Stenner, P. (2018). *Liminality and Experience. A Transdisciplinary Approach to the Psychosocial.* London, UK: Palgrave Macmillan.

Tanggaard, L., and Brinkmann, S. (2018). Imagination – Methodological Implications. In T. Zittoun and V. P. Glăveanu (eds.), *Oxford Handbook of Imagination and Culture.* Oxford, UK: Oxford University Press, 87–105.

Thomas, N. J. (1999). Are Theories of Imagery Theories of Imagination?: An Active Perception Approach to Conscious Mental Content. *Cognitive Science, 23*(2), 207–245. doi.org/10.1016/S0364-0213(99)00004-X.

Trevarthen, C., and Delafield-Butt, J. (2017). Intersubjectivity in the Imagination and Feelings of the Infant: Implications for Education in the Early Years. In E. White and C. Dalli (eds.), *Under-Three Year Olds in Policy and Practice.* London, UK: Springer, 17–39.

Triliva, S., Varvantakis, C., and Dafermos, M. (2015). YouTube, Young People, and the Socioeconomic Crises in Greece. *Information, Communication & Society, 18*(4), 407–423. doi.org/10.1080/1369118X.2014.953564.

Tulving, E., and Kim, A. (2007). The Medium and the Message of Mental Time Travel. *Behavioral and Brain Sciences, 30*(03), 334–335. doi.org/10.1017/S0140525X070 02208.

Valsiner, J. (1997). *Culture and the Development of Children's Action.* 2nd edition. New York, NY: John Wiley & Sons.

(1998). *The Guided Mind: A Sociogenetic Approach to Personality.* Cambridge, MA: Harvard University Press.

(2012). *A Guided Science: History of Psychology in the Mirror of its Making.* New Brunswick, NJ: Transaction Publishers.

Valsiner, J., and van der Veer, R. (2000). *The Social Mind: Construction of the Idea.* Cambridge, UK: Cambridge University Press.

Vico, G. (1725/1993a). *La Science nouvelle.* Translated by C. Trivulzio. Paris, France: Gallimard.

(1710/1993b). *L'Antique sagesse de l'Italie.* Edited by B. Pinchard. Translated by J. Michelet. Paris, France: Flammarion.

(1728/2004). *Vie de Giambattista Vico écrite par lui-même.* Edited by D. Luglio. Translated by J. Michelet. Paris, France: Allia.

Vygotsky, L. S. (1971). *The Psychology of Art.* Cambridge, MA: MIT Press.

(1987). *The Collected Works of L. S. Vygotsky.* Edited by R. W. Rieber and A. S. Carton. Volume 1. New York, NY: Springer.

(1931/1994). Imagination and Creativity of the Adolescent. In R. van der Veer and J. Valsiner (eds.), *The Vygotsky Reader.* Original publication 1931. Oxford, UK: Blackwell Publishing, 266–288.

(1930/2004). Imagination and Creativity in Childhood. *Journal of Russian and East European Psychology, 42*(1), 7–97.

(2011). L'imagination et son développement chez l'enfant. In *Leçons de psychologie.* Paris: La Dispute, 155–180.

Wertsch, J. V. (1998). *Mind as Action.* New York, NY; Oxford, UK: Oxford University Press.

Zavereshneva, E., and van der Veer, R. (2018). *Vygotsky's Notebooks. A Selection.* New York, NY: Springer.

Zeidman, P., and Maguire, E. A. (2016). Anterior Hippocampus: The Anatomy of Perception, Imagination and Episodic Memory. *Nature Reviews. Neuroscience, 17*(3), 173–182. doi.org/10.1038/nrn.2015.24.

Zittoun, T. (2006). *Transitions. Development Through Symbolic Resources.* Greenwich, CT: Information Age Publishing.

(2016a). Studying "Higher Mental Functions": The Example of Imagination. In J. Valsiner et al. (eds.), *Psychology as a Science of Human Being: The Yokohama Manifesto.* Volume 13. Dordrecht, Netherlands: Springer, 129–147.

(2016b). The Sound of Music. In H. Klempe (ed.), *Cultural Psychology of Musical Experience.* Charlotte, NC: Information Age Publishing, 21–39.

Zittoun, T., and Cerchia, F. (2013). Imagination as Expansion of Experience. *Integrative Psychological and Behavioral Science, 47*(3), 305–324. doi.org/10.1007/s12124-013-9234-2.

Zittoun, T., and de Saint-Laurent, C. (2015). Life-Creativity : Imagining One's Life. In V. P. Glăveanu, A. Gillespie, and J. Valsiner (eds.), *Rethinking Creativity: Contributions from Cultural Psychology.* Hove, UK; New York, NY: Routledge, 58–75.

Zittoun, T., and Gillespie, A. (2014). Sculpture and Art Installations: Towards a Cultural Psychological Analysis. In B. Wagoner, N. Chaudhary, and P. Hviid (eds.), *Cultural Psychology and Its Future: Complementarity in a New Key.* Charlotte, NC: Information Age Publishing, 167–177.

(2015). Integrating Experiences: Body and Mind Moving between Contexts. In B. Wagoner, N. Chaudhary, and P. Hviid (eds.), *Integrating Experiences: Body and Mind Moving between Contexts.* Charlotte, NC: Information Age Publishing, 3–49.

(2016). *Imagination in Human and Cultural Development.* London, UK: Routledge.

(2018). Imagining the Collective Future: A Sociocultural Perspective. In C. de Saint-Laurent, S. Obradovic, and K. Carrière (eds.), *Imagining Collective Futures: Perspectives from Social, Cultural and Political Psychology*. London, UK: Palgrave, 15–37.

Zittoun, T., and Glăveanu, V. P. (2018). Imagination at the Frontiers of Cultural Psychology. In T. Zittoun and V. P. Glăveanu (eds.), *Handbook of Imagination and Culture*. Oxford, UK: Oxford University Press, 1–15.

Zittoun, T., and Rosenstein, A. (2018). Theatre and Imagination to (Re)Discover Reality. In T. Zittoun and V. P. Glăveanu (eds.), *Handbook of Imagination and Culture*. Oxford, UK: Oxford University Press, 223–242.

Zittoun, T., and Sato, T. (2018). Imagination in Adults and the Aging Person: Possible Futures and Actual Past. In T. Zittoun and V. P. Glăveanu (eds.), *Handbook of Imagination and Culture*. Oxford, UK: Oxford University Press, 187–208.

Zittoun, T., and Valsiner, J. (2016). Imagining the Past and Remembering the Future: How the Unreal Defines the Real. In T. Sato, N. Mori, and J. Valsiner (eds.), *Making of the Future: The Trajectory Equifinality Approach in Cultural Psychology*. Charlotte, NC: Information Age Publishing, 3–19.

11 Artificial Intelligence and Imagination

Jim Davies

In English, the term "imagination" tends to be used in three general ways (for a thorough discussion, see Chapter 1). First, it is often synonymous with "creativity." Second, it is used to mean sensory imagery. Third, it is used to indicate hypothetical thinking, that might or might not have a sensory or pseudo-sensory component.

All of these meanings of imagination have been implemented by computer scientists, cognitive scientists, and psychologists as artificial intelligence programs. There is creative software, software that models imagery, and software that generates hypothetical situations for consideration. This chapter reviews artificial intelligence programs (AIs) that generate situations in the mind and generate images of various modalities (e.g. music, pictures), as well as AIs designed to model human imagination.

Artificial Intelligence that Does Imagination

The prototypical act of imagination is to generate, in the mind, a rich visual scene that, though created from parts of memories, does not represent any particular episode in memory. For example, I might ask you to imagine a living room, but not one that you have seen before. Traditionally, computer graphics are designed by human beings, working more or less by hand. But there are many systems that create visual scenes automatically. Many computer scientists have done work to automate these kinds of imaginative abilities in AIs (Ebert et al., 2003; Hendrikx and Meijer, 2011). In computer science, this work goes by many names, including synthesis, dynamic generation, procedural generation, procedural modeling, generative art, evolutionary art, process-based art, electronic art, computational art, telematics, and visualization. It is also important to note that there are many examples of generative art that are not implemented in software, but rather are analog machines or instructions for humans.

There are practical reasons for getting software to be imaginative: When developing graphics-heavy products such as video games, computer training simulations, and computer-generated visual effects and animated films, a great deal of the cost, in terms of both time and money, goes to artists. A familiar example is the creation of the giant battle scenes in *The Lord of the Rings* film trilogy, where the virtual camera flies over huge, computer-generated battlefields, depicting hordes of fighting creatures. A piece of software called MASSIVE was used to generate these thousands of similar, but not identical, creatures and patterns of fighting motion to generate a realistic landscape of battle that would have been prohibitively expensive for artists to design (Aitken et al., 2004). To take another example, the producers of the popular video game *World of Warcraft* release expansions to allow players to enjoy new adventures. The "Cataclysm" expansion took two years to make, but many players consumed all of that content in just two weeks (Morris, 2011). Films show an even more striking time of effort to time of consumption mismatch: A multimillion dollar Hollywood film might take hundreds of people years to make, yet be consumed by audiences in an hour and a half. We simply don't have enough hands, or money to pay them, to keep up with consumer demand for artistic content.

The domains of interest for automated visual imagination are vast. There are, for example, AIs that create plants (Cohen, 1995; de la Re et al., 2009), faces, planets, mountains, hotels, or cities (Kelly and McCabe, 2006).

Arguably, the first software to have a visual imagination was a system created by George Nees's *Generative Computergraphik* in 1965 (described in Boden and Edmonds, 2009). Historically, procedural generation of graphic content is done using one of a few methods: grammars, cellular automata, fractals, and explicit knowledge. These methods are representations of the "model" used by the AI to generate novel but realistic content. Grammars (see, for example, Mueller et al., 2006) are typically used for architectural interiors, and fractal generation is typically used for natural environments such as landscapes and trees (e.g. Hammes, 2001). Cellular automata (and artificial life) create patterns that are often beautiful (e.g. the work of Paul Brown, described in Whitelaw, 2004).

Finally, procedural modeling can be done with explicitly encoded knowledge (e.g. Cohen, 1995; Parish and Mueller, 2001). For example, to describe a building the knowledge base might have representations indicating that all rooms must have doors, and that ceilings need to be higher than 6 feet (1.8 meters) tall. The system can then generate new buildings that satisfy the constraints in the knowledge base. The downside of this is that the knowledge takes a great deal of time and effort to put into the system and large knowledge bases are prone to contradiction. A project called "Uncharted Atlas" creates fantasy maps of the kind found in the front of fantasy novels, complete with location names that all sound like they are from the same language. It uses randomization, tempered with constraints from the domain (a bot regularly posts these maps to Twitter; see @unchartedatlas).

The Wordseye system takes a scene description in natural language as input and generates a scene in 3D graphics (Coyne and Sproat, 2001). It draws on a large database of 3D models as its memory. Cleverly, if it does not have a 3D model for something described in the input, it adds the word to the 3D scene. An input might look like this "*John uses the crossbow. He rides the horse by the store. The store is under the large willow. The small allosaurus is in front of the horse. The dinosaur faces John. A gigantic teacup is in front of the store. The dinosaur is in front of the horse. The gigantic mushroom is in the teacup. The castle is to the right of the store.*" By using natural language understanding, along with functional tags for the 3D models, Wordseye effectively acts as an illustrator for a given text.

Harold Cohen, who was a successful painter, turned to generative art because he thought that working with software could help him understand his own artistic mind (Boden and Edmonds, 2009). His software, *Aaron*, is one of the most successful artificial artists ever created.

Unfortunately, *Aaron*'s code is proprietary, and what *Aaron* could do and how was rarely published in journals (see a rare exception in Cohen, 1995). Some insight into how *Aaron* works comes from a book written about the project (McCorduck, 1991). *Aaron*'s capabilities evolved over the many years that Cohen worked on it: evocative shapes from 1973 to 1978, more complicated shapes with limited perspective from 1979 to 1984, figurative drawings in a more complex visual space from 1985 to 1988, and finally color theory and figure drawing of people and plants after that. *Aaron* never backtracks, working from objects close to the viewer to objects in the background. Its knowledge of composition keeps it from doing things like placing a large tree in a place that would block other things in picture. It uses heuristics to constrain the image, such as having a mixture of large and small things, some detailed and some simple, some objects clustered and others farther away, and not having human heads occluded by other objects.

Importantly, not all procedural generation is visual. Many video games use procedurally generated quests, giving players endless missions to accomplish without human authorship (Veale, 2017). There are also systems that dynamically create music (for a review, see Bernardes and Cocharro, 2019), kinetic sculpture, stories, and performance art (Boden and Edmonds, 2009).

Artistic generation by software provides a good opportunity to distinguish creativity involving varying degrees of imagination. If we assume that imagination has something to do with the generation of representations of things in the mind, then certain kinds of creativity are less imaginative, strictly speaking, than others. For example, creating an entire orchestral piece of music in one's head before ever putting any notes to paper, as Mozart was said to do, is a tremendous feat of imagination and creativity. But we might contrast that with improvisational jazz, which, though highly creative, requires intense coupling with the external environment and reactivity to the music being made in the moment, with less use of the imagination. In fact, having too many plans made ahead of time is said to be a *detriment* to effective improvisation because one can be fixated on something that is unlikely to be appropriate in a rapidly changing environment, and because holding the plan in mind uses working memory resources that could be put to better use (Johnstone, 1979). In certain situations, imagination impairs creativity.

Similarly, some AIs create music by generating an internal representation and modifying it before ever creating sound or a score. These AIs plan an entire piece before generating any output for an audience (de Mantaras and Arcos, 2002). Some systems, for example, use Markov chains to create music start to finish, but when constraints cannot be satisfied, the system backtracks and overwrites previous composition (e.g. the first computer-generated music, Hiller, Jr., and Isaacson, 1958). Others use heuristic, non-probabilistic techniques. These systems modify the composition in the AI's imagination/memory. In an improvisation, one cannot backtrack, because the music has already been output and heard by the audience.

This was done by the Band-out-of-a-box system (Thorn, 2001), which did real-time improvisation with a human music companion.

Some systems combine imagination on many fronts for an integrated experience. To date, two examples of procedural generation that are (arguably) the most impressive are video games: *Dwarf Fortress* and *No Man's Sky*. These, like many examples of software imagination, are software products, not scientific projects. As such, we do not have access to their code, and they don't typically publish scientific articles about how they work. What we can do is see the results, and glean how the algorithms work from interviews.

Dwarf Fortress is a game in which you control a group of dwarves trying to survive in a world. Every time you play, a new environment is created by the software. The algorithms are staggeringly complex, creating an entire world, including 16,000 square miles (around 40,000 square kilometers) of land, 250 miles (400 kilometers) thick, simulating geological changes over time, including soil erosion and rain shadows from mountains. It creates everything from gods, watersheds of the geography, economic patterns, the world political history, all the way down to fish and the personality traits of individual dwarves. One aerospace engineer familiar with the project said that the simulations in it are more complex than jet wing aerodynamic simulations (Weiner, 2011). As an interesting example of imagination without imagery, the game is experienced in ASCII characters. That is, it uses graphics no more complicated than colored letters, numbers, and punctuation on the screen. Comparing it to human imagination, we would consider this AI to be using a kind of suppositional or hypothetical imagination, in contrast with mental imagery.

No Man's Sky also does world creation, but creates entire planets for players to explore. When a player goes to a new planet, the software generates the land, ecosystems, and all of the alien flora and fauna, in a generally realistic way. In contrast to *Dwarf Fortress*, it is rendered during gameplay as 3D graphics, and even generates the sounds that the creatures make (Gaisbauer and Hlavacs, 2017). These are only two examples – there are dozens of impressive feats of procedural generation. Even if the worlds they create are not better than those created by the most creative humans, they do much more of it much faster. The worlds that *Dwarf Fortress* or *No Man's Sky* create in minutes would take days or years for a person to create by hand. These systems, like most of those used for entertainment purposes, were not made to do imagination in the same way as human beings. *Dwarf Fortress*, for example, uses mathematically complex geological simulation algorithms. Although humans use what they know of how the world works to create fictional worlds, people will use simulations of this complexity by running them on computers, rather than doing the math in their heads.

Machine-Learning Approaches

Contemporary approaches to computational imagination tend to use machine learning of various kinds. For example, the BoVW (Bag of Visual Words) system is designed to take as input a description of an image, and generates a static image that the description would describe (Kato and Harada, 2014). BoVW uses a large database of photographs to find visual "words" that can later be rearranged like a jigsaw puzzle to match the constraints of the words in the input. This task resembles the kind of imagining humans might do when picturing a scene while reading a description in a novel.

Other efforts have used probabilities based on learning from examples. In Fisher et al. (2012), for example, users input a few 3D scenes of the kind they wish the system to generate more examples of. The system uses this input and a database of other models, such as scenes of furniture and other objects placed in an office environment, to create new offices different from those in its memory.

Although artificial neural networks and connectionism have been around for decades, in the early 2010s a new approach brought about a revolution that changed the face of almost all aspects of AI, imagination included. In fact, one of the early successes of deep learning was Google's *DeepDream*, which created surreal images that seemed to have faces and animals seamlessly woven into images of landscapes. Deep learning (as well as other neural network techniques) have two elements that distinguish them from many other approaches used: They do what they do by learning from existing data, and they do not use explicit, human-generated rules or constraints.

The company DeepMind Technologies has an explicit goal of creating AIs with imagination capabilities. They have created software that can reconstruct 3D scenes from a small number of 2D images (the GQN; see Eslami et al., 2018), and planning systems that create imagined future scenarios, which are then evaluated to aid in decision-making (Pascanu et al., 2017).

Generative Adversarial Network techniques (GANs; see Goodfellow et al., 2014) are employed to train a network to form visual scenes depicting multiple objects. GANs work through interactions of generator and discriminator networks, the former to generate images and the latter to attempt to discriminate whether the input image is from the generator or from training data. Both networks learn over time, resulting in better and better output. GANs have been used to imagine novel but realistic faces and other images.

Cognitive Models of Imagination and Imagery

In cognitive science, a few researchers have created models of human imagination and imagery.

Kosslyn and Shwartz's (1977) simulation was the first cognitive model of human mental imagery. Although the system was only capable of imagining a chair or a car, the system successfully modeled some psychological findings of mental imagery such as taking longer to generate more complex images, and incremental increase in detail according to attentional shifting. This model can be included in a range of implemented "array theories" that eventuate in pixel placement, some explicitly symbolic and some that use artificial neural networks. These models do not speak to how elements are *selected* for inclusion in the scene, but provide a more realistic model of the final stage of imagination – creating a visible image in the mind's eye.

More recently, several projects have attempted to implement human cognition in software with cognitive modeling. Generally, these models attempt to replicate human imagination at a competency level, rather than by quantitatively fitting participant data. That is, they try to work by doing what humans can do, constrained by what we know about how they do it. The SOILIE project (Breault et al., 2013) uses a database of labeled photographs to know what objects tend to co-occur, and what their spatial relationships to one another are. It uses this information to construct novel, yet realistic visual scenes. The Integrative Computational Model of Visual Mentation models dreams, perception, and imagery based on high-level brain simulations (Bogart, Pasquier, and Barnes, 2013). The Associative Conceptual Imagination (ACI) Framework (Heath, Dennis, and Ventura, 2015) uses associative memory and vector space models to build new and interesting artifact plans.

Is it Really Imagination?

Acts of imagination, and products of imagination, are not classes that can be defined with necessary and sufficient conditions. This makes it difficult to determine whether a given piece of software is really doing imagination or not. The issue is also complicated by the vast variance in what software actually does.

For example, when your phone plays a song for you, is it engaging in auditory imagination? There are some reasons to think the answer is no. The phone is not composing the music, it is merely playing it exactly the way it is in memory. But note that although human memory retrieval is not perfect, attempts to accurately picture events from the past are considered imagination – though not a prototypical example of it, in that it does not involve an attempt at creating anything new (it is not "novel combinatorial," as described in Chapter 1). Similarly, bringing up a Paul Klee painting on your web browser isn't a great example of computer art because the software isn't designing anything. It is "computer-generated" only in a trivial sense ("recollective" as described in Chapter 1).

Then we have borderline cases of AI-assisted graphics generation. For example, in non-photorealistic rendering, the software takes a 3D model or a photo and renders it with some kind of style – that of an oil painting, or a pencil sketch, for example (some phone apps do this kind of thing to a user's photographs). Here the referent is (re) imagined by the software in a different style. There is an element of design to it, and the software is holding in memory a version of the created image, so this appears to be more like imagination.

We also have simulations that aid movies in generating computer graphics. When we watch a contemporary computer-generated animated film, and many digital effects in otherwise live-action films, often the waves in the ocean, the movement of crowds, and the folding of clothing as a character moves are created through computer simulation. When the computer generates what will be seen, this appears to be a mild form of computer creativity and imagination.

At the extreme we have software like *Aaron* and music composition software that is explicitly designed to make design and artistic decisions. These seem to be the best examples of software doing what we would consider imagination (and creativity) if a human were to do something similar.

Also problematic are cases of generation that at first glance seem to have nothing to with imagination, but might count anyway. Take, for example, chess-playing programs, which analyze thousands of possible moves per second. More recently, DeepMind created several programs that learned to play Go at levels of performance higher than grandmasters. *AlphaGo* (Silver et al., 2016) used deep learning in two networks: one to evaluate board positions (the value network), and the other to choose moves (the policy network). One of the novel contributions of the *AlphaGo* method was that it learned not only from previously played human games, but also from playing itself. Where the former is more like traditional machine learning from data, the latter is more like computer imagination – imagining games that might be, and seeing how they turn out, simulating all of it in the mind of the AI. The intellectual descendants of *AlphaGo*, *AlphaGo Zero* and *AlphaZero*, learn to play *only* using games played against themselves, not taking advantage of human games or expertise at all (Silver et al., 2018). They bested the original *AlphaGo* in every one of 100 test games. *AlphaZero*, requiring no world knowledge other than the rules of a game to get very good, also achieved chess grandmaster status (Silver et al., 2018). It is particularly remarkable that a single program can get so good at completely different games. For our purposes, it is noteworthy that the program does so through mental simulation—imagination. Interestingly, these various *Alpha-* systems do not look ahead when playing. They use imagination only when they learn. When actually playing, they simply select moves using a neural network – an "intuitive" method of choosing that does not explicitly evaluate consequences of actions taken.

The software is representing these possible board configurations in its memory for evaluation – dare we say that it is "imagining" them? When software searches though a space of possible designs to create a new computer chip design, are each of the designs it considers instances of imagination?

If your computer has images (from photos) on its hard drive, are those representations imaginings? We might say that they are not until they are accessed by software – merely being on the hard drive is not enough. This resonates with our intuition that an image or image description stored in some way in human memory is not an *imagined* image until it is retrieved, and perhaps "rendered" in visual or spatial imagery.

If we believe that visual and spatial imagery are necessarily conscious, then we might say that we would need to believe that a piece of software was capable of consciousness to accept that it engages in (visual) imagery. It is generally accepted that humans cannot have unconscious sensory-like imagery (evidence of this is that those with low imagery abilities perform poorly on imagery tasks), but imagination also includes hypothetical situations without a sensory component as well as ima-gery. If we are talking about the broader category of imagination, the issue of consciousness is not so clear. If human minds generate possible states of the world, but are only conscious of a few of them, then we are in a position to say that human imagination (though perhaps not imagery) can be unconscious. If this is the case, then there appears to be software that genuinely has imaginative abilities.

Unsurprisingly, answers to questions regarding whether software can have imagination depend on which aspects of imagination one is focusing on.

The Future

If one considers imagination as something that potentially could be done by many kinds of cognitive systems, including humans, some animals, and machines, then computational imagination is inherently interesting. But even if one is only interested in human cognition, there is value in paying attention to imaginative software.

Implemented software provides an existence proof. That is, it shows that whatever method the software uses *actually can* produce the output it did. This might not sound like much, but many theories in psychology have no such existence proof— the mechanism described in words might not even work.

Software models of human thought also provide value in that they force researchers to ask questions, and clarify assumptions, that would not be raised until one tries to build one's theory in software. For example, cognitive psychology studies mental imagery, but mostly in terms of vividness, detail, and how people can manipulate it (rotations, zooming, etc.). When one tries to implement imagination and imagery in software one runs into fundamental questions, such as: how does a mind choose what elements to put in a scene? Where do they go? How does the mind determine the imagined object's sizes, colors, orientations, and support? How does imagination interact with world knowledge to produce mental simulations?

The broad range of AI imagination provides inspiring ideas and possible existence tests of theories of imagination in both machines and humans.

References

de la Re, A., Abad, F., Camahort, E., and Juan, M. C. (2009). Tools for Procedural Generation of Plants in Virtual Scenes. In *International Conference on Computational Science*. Berlin, Germany: Springer, 801–810.

Aitken, M., Butler, G., Lemmon, D., Saindon, E., Peters, D., and Williams, G. (2004). *The Lord of the Rings*: The Visual Effects that Brought Middle Earth to the Screen. *Proceedings of the Conference on SIGGRAPH 2004 Course Notes – GRAPH '04*, 11-es. doi.org/10.1145/1103900.1103911.

Bernardes, G., and Cocharro, D. (2019). Dynamic Music Generation, Audio Analysis-Synthesis Methods. In N. Lee (ed.), *Encyclopedia of Computer Graphics and Games*, Berlin, Germany: Springer.

Boden, M. A., and Edmonds, E. A. (2009). What is Generative Art? *Digital Creativity, 20* (1–2), 21–46.

Bogart, B. D., Pasquier, P., and Barnes, S. J. (2013). An Integrative Theory of Visual Mentation and Spontaneous Creativity. Proceedings of the 9th ACM Conference on Creativity & Cognition – C&C '13, 264. doi.org/10.1145/2466627.2466639.

Breault, V., Ouellet, S., Somers, S., and Davies, J. (2013). SOILIE: A Computational Model of 2D Imagination. In R. West and T. Stewart (eds.), *Proceedings of the 12th International Conference on Cognitive Modeling*, Ottawa, Canada: Carleton University, 95–100.

Cohen, H. (1995). The Further Exploits of AARON, Painter. *Stanford Humanities Review, 4* (2), 141–158.

Coyne, B., and Sproat, R. (2001). WordsEye: An Automatic Text-to-Scene Conversion System. In *Proceedings of the 28th Annual Conference on Computer Graphics and Interactive Techniques*. Sydney, Australia: Association for Computing Machinery, 487–496.

Davies, J., and Francis, A. G. (2013). The Role of Artificial Intelligence Research Methods in Cognitive Science. In R. West and T. Stewart (eds.), *Proceedings of the 12th International Conference on Cognitive Modeling*, Ottawa, Canada: Carleton University, 439–444.

De Mantaras, R. L., and Arcos, J. L. (2002). AI and Music: From Composition to Expressive Performance. *AI Magazine, 23*(3), 43–43.

Ebert, D. S., Musgrave, F. K., Peachey, D., Perline, K., and Worey, S. (2003). *Texturing & Modeling: A Procedural Approach*. 3rd edition. New York, NY: Morgan Kaufmann.

Eslami, S. A., Rezende, D. J., Besse, F., et al. (2018). Neural Scene Representation and Rendering. *Science, 360* (6394), 1204–1210.

Fisher, M., Ritchie, D., Savva, M., Funkhouser, T., and Hanrahan, P. (2012). Example-Based Synthesis of 3D Object Arrangements. *ACM Transactions on Graphics – Proceedings of ACM SIGGRAPH Asia 2012. 31*(6), article 135.

Gaisbauer, W., and Hlavacs, H. (2017). Procedural Attack! Procedural Generation for Populated Virtual Cities: A Survey. *International Journal of Serious Games, 4*(2).

Goodfellow, I., Pouget-Abadie, J., Mirza, M., et al. (2014). Generative Adversarial Nets. In *Advances in Neural Information Processing Systems. 27*, 2672–2680.

Hammes, J. (2001). Modeling of Ecosystems as a Data Source for Real-Time Terrain Rendering. In *Digital Earth Moving*. Berlin, Germany: Springer, 98–111.

Heath, D., Dennis, A. W., and Ventura, D. (2015). Imagining Imagination: A Computational Framework Using Associative Memory Models and Vector Space Models. In *Proceedings of the Sixth International Conference on Computational Creativity*, 244–251.

Hendrikx, M., and Meijer, S (2011). Procedural Content Generation for Games: A Survey. *ACM Trans.Multimedia Comput. Commun. Appl.*, 1, February, 1–24.

Hiller, Jr., L. A., and Isaacson, L. M. (1958). Musical Composition with a High-Speed Digital Computer. *Journal of the Audio Engineering Society, 6*(3), 154–160.

Johnstone, K. (1979). *Impro: Improvisation and the Theatre*. London, UK: Faber and Faber.

Kato, H., and Harada, T. (2014). Image Reconstruction from Bag-of-Visual-Words. In *Proceedings of the IEEE Conference on Computer Vision and Pattern Recognition*. Washington, DC: IEEE Computer Society, 955–962.

Kelly, G., and McCabe, H. (2006). A Survey of Procedural Techniques for City Generation. *The ITB Journal, 7*(2), 5.

Kosslyn, S. M., and Shwartz, S. P. (1977). A Simulation of Visual Imagery. *Cognitive Science 1*, 265–295.

Liang, X., Zhuo, B., Li, P., and He, L. (2016). CNN Based Texture Synthesize with Semantic Segment. arxiv.org/abs/1605.04731.

McCorduck, P. (1991). *Aaron's Code: Meta-Art, Artificial Intelligence, and the Work of Harold Cohen*. New York, NY: Macmillan.

Meuller, P., Wonka, P., Haegler, S., Ulmer, A., and van Gul, L. (2006). Procedural Generation of Buildings. *ACM Transactions on Graphics*, 25(3), 614–623.

Morris, C. (2011). *World of Warcraft Maker Turns 20, Looks Ahead*. Plugged In. games.yahoo.com/blogs/plugged-in/world-warcraft-maker-turns-20-looks-ahead-450.html.

Parish, Y. I. H., and Mueller, P. (2001). Procedural Modeling of Cities. In *Proceedings of ACM SIGGRAPH 2001*. New York, NY: ACM Press/ ACM SIGGRAPH, 301–308.

Pascanu, R., Li, Y., Vinyals, O., et al. (2017). Learning Model-Based Planning from Scratch. arxiv.org/abs/1707.06170.

Silver, D., Huang, A., Maddison, C. J., et al. (2016). Mastering the Game of Go with Deep Neural Networks and Tree Search. *Nature*, 529(7587), 484.

Silver, D., Hubert, T., Schrittwieser, J., et al. (2018). A General Reinforcement Learning Algorithm that Masters Chess, Shogi, and Go Through Self-Play. *Science, 362* (6419), 1140–1144.

Thorn, B. (2001). *BoB: An Improvisational Music Companion*. PhD Dissertation, Computer Science Department. Pittsburgh, PA: Carnegie Mellon University, 281.

Veale, T. (2017). Déjà Vu All Over Again: On the Creative Value of Familiar Elements in the Telling of Original Tales. In *Proceedings of ICCC 2017, the 8th International Conference on Computational Creativity, Atlanta, Georgia*.

Weiner, J. (2011). "Where do Dwarf-Eating Carp Come From?" *The New York Times Magazine*. July 21.

Whitelaw, M. (2004). *Metacreation: Art and Artificial Life*. London: MIT Press.

PART II

Imagery-Based Forms of the Imagination

12 The Visual Imagination

Joel Pearson

Visual imagery typically refers to the voluntary creation of the conscious visual experience of an object or scene in its absence (e.g. solely in the mind). Commonly referred to as seeing with the mind's eye, visual imagery can be thought of as a cognitive tool (for those who have it), used to aid many everyday cognitive processes, such as spatial navigation, memory, reading comprehension and planning. Recently it has come to light that many individuals have no experience of imagery at all – their minds are completely blind: aphantasia. In contrast to this, imagery can play a core role in many anxiety disorders, depression, schizophrenia and Parkinson's disease, and is increasingly harnessed as a uniquely powerful tool for psychological treatment (Pearson et al., 2015). Mapping imagery's seemingly contradictory contributions to human cognition, whereby imagery can be advantageous, clinically disruptive, or even unnecessary (aphantasia), offers exciting and novel insights into an important dimension of the human mind.

Research into visual imagery perhaps officially began with Francis Galton's now famous paper from the 1800s (Galton, 1880). However, what could be referred to as modern-day research really began in force during the 1970s. Prior to this, mental imagery research went through a major disruption due to strong criticism from behavioral psychologists. The behaviorist revolution in psychological research around the 1950s directly denied the existence of internal representations like visual mental images. This extreme stance of psychological science detrimentally impacted visual imagery research and left lingering doubt about the viability of imagery research for decades after (Pearson, 2014). However, the 1970s saw a strong resurgence in visual imagery research centered on what is now referred to as the "imagery debate" (Pearson and Kosslyn, 2015), which lasted four decades and revolved around the representational format of a visual image (Kosslyn, 2005; Pearson and Kosslyn, 2015; Pylyshyn, 2001). One side of the debate proposed that visual images could only be represented in the brain with one format – propositional/symbolic. In such a representation symbols like words, letters or other things represent the content of imagery.

The other side of the debate argued that visual images could be represented in a number of different formats, including depictive representations. A depictive representation is one in which the spatial characteristics of the represented object are maintained in its representation (Pearson and Kosslyn, 2015). An easy way to envision this is an XY coordinate system or graphing space, in which the spatial properties, while perhaps warped, are maintained in a 2D plane. Depictive representations are often referred to as pictorial, as a shorthand, as pictures are typically represented depictively on a two-dimensional plane. The debate lasted several decades, with each side providing empirical data for their case, only to be followed by a counter from the opposing viewpoint showing that the data could be explained with an alternative hypothesis. It was not until the advent of functional brain imaging in the 1990s that cognitive neuroscience began to provide a new source of evidence that visual images could be depictive. More recently behavioral research has provided strong evidence that visual images can indeed be depictive (for examples, see Bergmann et al., 2016; Pearson, Clifford, and Tong, 2008). Further evidence has come from the new wave of decoding-based functional magnetic resonance imaging work such as (Naselaris et al., 2015). In 2015 we published a paper making the strong claim that the imagery debate was over and visual images could indeed take on a number of different representational formats (Pearson and Kosslyn, 2015).

How to Measure Imagery: Overcoming Methodological Challenges

One of the key limitations to studying visual imagery has been its internal private and subjective nature. Historically, these characteristics have made the objective and scientific investigation of visual imagery difficult. Self-report questionnaires have been the gold-standard tool used to measure imagery abilities, both because of their ease and scalability. The most commonly used questionnaire is the vividness of visual imagery questionnaire (VVIQ), which asks an individual first to imagine a scene (e.g. a sunrise) and then report the vividness of the imagined scene. Other methods of assessing imagery probe an interaction between imagery and visual perception (Perky, 1910). This effect generally refers to the decrement in perceptual performance due to concurrent imagery. However, subsequent research into visual attention has highlighted how strong an effect visual attention can have on concurrent perception (Carrasco, Ling, and Read, 2004), making it difficult to differentiate the effects of visual attention and imagery on concurrent perception.

Other methods used to measure visual imagery include mental rotation tasks, which typically involve getting an individual to mentally rotate an object and then compare it to different orientations of that same or different object and deduce which object is the same rotated version of the object and which ones are not (Shepard and Metzler, 1971).

Another line of research showed that mentally scanning across a mental image provided an interesting way to measure one's internal image (Kosslyn, 1973). This task would typically ask individuals to imagine an object – maybe a map with landmarks on it; the individual would answer questions about where on the map different landmarks are. Researchers found that it can take longer to answer questions about landmarks that are further apart than those that are closer together on the map – suggesting that individuals would scan across their mental imagery in order to answer the questions.

Later work showed that imagery and perception could interact in facilitative ways; in other words, the content of what someone imagines could boost elements of perception. This work showed that when stimuli were imagined next to an actual perceptual stimulus the imagery could have a facilitative effect on perceptual detection tasks – it might make perception better (Ishai and Sagi, 1995).

Other work showed that prior imagery could have time-dependent facilitative effects on subsequent perception in the form of binocular rivalry dominance (Pearson, Clifford, and Tong, 2008), and this could be dissociated from the effects of prior visual attention. This paradigm utilized a well-known visual illusion called binocular rivalry as a measurement tool to assess the sensory strength of imagery. What people imagine can literally change is the way they see the illusion, which in itself is interesting, but also provides a nice imagery measurement technique. For more information on how to use binocular rivalry like this see Pearson (2014). More recent work has taken this paradigm further by measuring rivalry dominance with an embedded probe task; this is interesting and useful because it allows researchers to use the binocular rivalry method to measure imagery without any subjective reports on imagery (Chang and Pearson, 2018). In other words, an individual performing this experiment does not need to subjectively report anything about her imagery; this version of the task is performance-based – researchers can indirectly infer which rivalry pattern was dominant via the accuracy for detecting the probe, and in turn from the rivalry dominance data measure imagery strength. This is one of the research goals of cognitive neuroscience, to develop measurement methods that are more objective and hence less susceptible to self-report bias and other things that can influence interview or questionnaire methodology.

Cross-Disciplinary Imagery Research

One of the other main difficulties in writing about or doing imagery research is that different fields refer to visual imagery differently and a clear definition across multiple fields of research is lacking. For example, mental imagery is studied and utilized in much clinical research and many treatments, but the way imagery is modeled and discussed clinically often differs to how cognitive neuroscientists or vision scientists think about imagery and its brain mechanisms. For example, cognitive neuroscientists will often operationalize visual imagery using an indirect or objective task in the lab, like the binocular rivalry method described above. Such a task or measure of imagery will be very specific (e.g. imagine red), and controlled (e.g. only image it for five seconds); other variables, like memory or emotion will have typically been removed. Measures of clinically relevant imagery might, in contrast, include subjective descriptions of traumatic imagery flashbacks, described as involuntary. It can be hard to mesh these different methodologies and imagery content. More cross-disciplinary work and conferences would help to overcome such misalignments and enable clinicians to capitalize on advances in fundamental brain science for clinical treatments.

Likewise, neurophysiology experiments using animals often indirectly investigate types of phantom vision (perhaps a type of imagery) that can directly inform human researchers about mental imagery (Albright, 2012; Pearson and Westbrook, 2015). In one example, monkeys learned to associate stationary arrow stimuli with different directions of visual motion (Schlack and Albright, 2007). Neurons in area MT (the motion selective area of the cortex) are known to be highly direction-selective for moving visual stimuli and typically do not respond to stationary stimuli such as arrows. Many of the MT neurons displayed directional selectivity to the stationary arrows post-training, almost as if the animal was viewing moving stimuli, but not before training. Did the arrow stimulus induce a type of imagery experience in the animal? This is as yet an open question.

There is a rich history of utilizing mental imagery as a form of rehearsing sports performances (Morris, Spittle, and Watt, 2005). However, research on imagery in sports rarely crosses over with that of the fundamental brain mechanisms of imagery in cognitive neuroscience and, like in much clinical research, it is often multimodal in nature (imaging both the visual scene and the movements that one will undertake). Just as in this handbook, taking a cross-disciplinary approach makes it possible for different perspectives on mental imagery research to learn from one another about assessment and measurement techniques, the underlying brain mechanisms and even how to use imagery as an applied tool in clinical and sports settings.

Applied imagery work with sports people, with artists and in clinical psychology likewise informs empirical researchers as to the practical utility of imagery in everyday life. This in turn speaks to the question of how and why people use imagery and informs the full repertoire of human cognition.

Visual Imagery as a Weak Form of Visual Perception

An easy way to sum up the functional effects of visual imagery is that it largely behaves like a weak version of visual perception – and to some it feels like this as well. Both imagining and perceiving oriented lines can produce an orientation or tilt aftereffect (Mohr et al., 2011). Mental images can undergo different types of learning, both visual perceptual learning (Tartaglia et al., 2009) and associative learning with an emotional stimulus (Lewis et al., 2013). The brightness of imagined stimuli corresponds to predictable changes in pupil diameter, without concurrent sensory stimulation (Laeng and Sulutvedt, 2014).

There is now substantive evidence that visual imagery can have a facilitative effect on visual perception (Ishai and Sagi, 1995; Pearson, 2014; Pearson, Clifford, and Tong, 2008; Pearson, Rademaker, and Tong, 2011). In other words, imagining something can literally change or boost the way we see the world. Indeed, even when imagery and perception are separated in time by another demanding cognitive task, these facilitatory effects remain (Pearson, Clifford, and Tong, 2008). Weak perceptual stimuli (low contrast or luminance) also show this same facilitatory priming effect on subsequent perception (Brascamp et al., 2007; Pearson, Clifford, and Tong, 2008; Tanaka and Sagi, 1998). The energy (strength or duration) of a prior stimulus seems to dictate whether it has a facilitatory (priming – weak images) or suppressive (adaptation – strong images) effect on subsequent perception (Brascamp et al., 2007). Likewise, longer durations or epochs of imagery have a stronger priming effect on subsequent perception (Koenig-Robert and Pearson, 2019; Pearson, Clifford, and Tong, 2008). In sum, visual mental images have a similar functional effect on subsequent perception as prior weak perceptual stimuli.

Brain imaging work also provides evidence that imagery can be thought of as a form of top-down weak perception. Multiple fMRI studies have used perceptual fMRI patterns to later decode the contents of mental images (Naselaris et al., 2015; Slotnick, Thompson, and Kosslyn, 2005; Thirion et al., 2006), suggesting an overlap in neural representation. However, despite this behavioral and brain imaging evidence of commonalities between weak perception and imagery, the two are clearly very different experiences and future work should aim to map out why imagery is not experienced with the full qualia of afferent perception.

The Neural Basis of Visual Imagery

Visual imagery involves activity across a large neural network spanning frontal areas to the primary visual cortex and maybe even earlier in the processing hierarchy (Pearson et al., 2015). Much work has been done investigating imagery responses in the primary visual cortex, for reasons relating to the imagery debate. In general, the data supports the hypothesis that visual imagery is based on information retrieved from memory in a reverse hierarchy process: beginning in the frontal cortex and ending with the visual representation in primary visual cortex and a conscious imagery experience (see Figure 12.1). Forming or manipulating a mental image involves activity in the frontal areas (Ishai, Ungerleider, and Haxby, 2000; Ranganath and D'Esposito, 2005; Schlegel et al., 2013; Yomogida, 2004). However, the activity in frontal areas seems largely independent of the precise content of the imagery (Goebel et al., 1998; Ishai, Ungerleider, and Haxby, 2000; Yomogida, 2004). This suggests that frontal areas play more of a general organizational or executive role in coordinating spatial and sensory areas, rather than holding

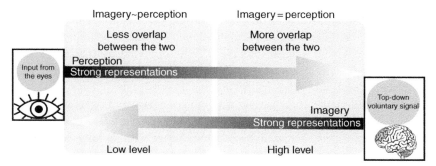

Figure 12.1 *A graphical depiction showing the two streams, bottom-up perception and top-down imagery. Visual imagery and perception have a greater overlap in high-level areas of the visual cortex than in lower-level areas.*

any imagery representations or content per se. Questions about the role of early visual areas, in particular the primary visual cortex or V1, in mental imagery have dominated brain imaging work on mental imagery for the last twenty-five years. From the early 1990s to the late 2000s more than twenty studies investigated the role of the primary visual cortex in imagery (Pearson et al., 2015). Most of these studies were motivated by the imagery debate, now generally considered to be over (Pearson and Kosslyn, 2015). Despite some controversy with the early brain imaging work, more recent studies using the pattern of fMRI response, a type of decoding approach, as opposed to the amplitude of blood flow, have provided strong evidence that if one has imagery, a representation of the image is evident in the primary visual cortex (Naselaris et al., 2015; Pearson et al., 2015; Stokes, et al., 2009).

Voluntary and Involuntary Visual Imagery

Hallucinations, synaesthesia, perceptual filling-in and many illusions are conscious visual experiences without corresponding retinal stimuli – just like mental imagery. We have previously mapped out an overarching framework for these two types of visual experience, one voluntary (e.g. mental imagery), the other involuntary (e.g. visual hallucinations, illusions, synaesthesia), both of which sit under the banner of "phantom visual experiences" (Pearson and Westbrook, 2015). This framework is analogous to the subtypes of visual attention: endogenous and exogenous (Egeth and Yantis, 1997). We can voluntarily attend to something at will; for example, I can pay attention to a piece of paper on my desk, or while still looking directly at the paper I can shift my attention to the door on my right. This is a form of voluntary or endogenous attention, because I want to pay attention to the door and voluntarily shift my attention to it. However, while looking at that piece of paper and paying attention to it, if someone knocks at my door, immediately my attention shifts to the door automatically and therefore does not entail wilful action. This form of attention is called exogenous or involuntary attention, which is typically captured by external things in the environment. It seems that phantom visual experiences can be split along these same endogenous and exogenous lines.

Indeed, intrusive mental images that occur as core symptoms of mental disorders such as post-traumatic stress disorder (PTSD) are described as being involuntary. Further evidence linking voluntary and involuntary forms of phantom vision come from empirical data that suggests that the strength or vividness of visual imagery is related to organic hallucinations in both Parkinson's disease (Shine et al., 2014), schizophrenia (Maróthi and Kéri, 2018) and synaesthesia (Chiou et al., 2018). Additionally, individuals with strong involuntary imagery as part of PTSD also report more vivid voluntary imagery (Morina, Leibold, and Ehring, 2013).

Many visual illusions also involve visual experience with no related retinal stimulation. Such experiences can also be classified as phantom vision (Meng, Remus, and Tong, 2005; Pearson and Westbrook, 2015; Sasaki and Watanabe, 2004) – the brain is filling in to create a visual phantom experience that does not directly correspond to the stimulation from the outside world. It will be interesting to follow future research that directly compares voluntary and involuntary forms of phantom vision, to see how related the mechanisms of voluntary and involuntary phantom vision are. For example, could using such visual illusions be the key to understanding the relationship between voluntary and involuntary phantom vision? Are the brain mechanisms in the visual cortex the same across these two very different experiences?

A range of psychological and neurological disorders are associated with elevated voluntary imagery and episodes of involuntary phantom experience, from involuntary imagery flashbacks in PTSD to strong visual hallucinations in Parkinson's disease. Like voluntary imagery these involuntary forms are also extremely difficult to study, as their timing is often unpredictable, and content typically differs from experience to experience. Because of these inherent difficulties, understanding the mechanisms behind such episodes of pathological phantom vision is difficult. The interesting and exciting hypothesis is that using forms of controlled phantom visuals in the laboratory as a model system for understanding organic pathological phantom vision episodes will shed new light on the mechanistic understanding and hence divulge new treatment avenues.

Aphantasia and Hyperphantasia: Life with the Extremes of Imagery

Despite the fact that we have known about the existence of individuals who claim to have no visual mental imagery at all since Francis Galton's nineteenth-century paper (Galton, 1880), this finding was largely ignored until recently. In 2015 the word aphantasia was coined to describe someone who is completely "blind" in his or her visual imagination. Since then, research has shown that this phenomenon is relatively common, with individuals often being genuinely surprised to discover that others have rich visual imagery.

Recent research has gone beyond self-report methods and shown that along with floor scores on imagery questionnaires, self-proclaimed aphantasics measure significantly lower on the sensory binocular rivalry measure of visual imagery discussed and described earlier (Keogh and Pearson, 2018), suggesting that aphantasia is more than poor metacognition of visual imagery and is lacking at a sensory level – most probably in the visual cortex.

Interestingly, while aphantasics scored lower than controls on all imagery vividness or content measures, they actually scored slightly higher than controls on spatial imagery questionnaires (Keogh and Pearson, 2018). This is interesting because it suggests that imagery, often discussed as a unitary phenomenon, is separable into what could be called object imagery (imagery about how things look) and spatial locations (where something is in space or 3D transformations). This new data suggests that aphantasia might involve more than spatial imagery. However, emerging data also suggests that there might be multiple types or subtypes of aphantasia, and that we should not overgeneralize a lack of imagery experience into one singular category.

While the popular media has shown a fascination with aphantasia,[1] it is still early days in terms of scientific research. Perhaps the most poignant question surrounds the idea that aphantasia could either be just one end of a spectrum of imagery abilities or a category all of its own, different from people with very weak imagery. We have known for over a century that some people report strong and vivid imagery, others report medium and some describe a complete lack of any sensory experience at all (Galton, 1880). Is very weak imagery completely different to no imagery at all? What are the subcategories of aphantasia – only visual or multisensory? Further research is needed to shed light on these possibilities and there are many more exciting questions that will arise with more research (see also Chapter 42).

The fact that aphantasic individuals can still perform many daily tasks for which non-aphantasics use mental imagery, such as visual working memory (Jacobs, Schwarzkopf, and Silvanto, 2018; Keogh and Pearson, 2011, 2014), suggests they use a different strategy and brain mechanisms. It is worth thinking about the possible implications of this: If one were to go simply by performance on a compound task like visual working memory, it would be very difficult to differentiate an aphantasic and non-aphantasic. However, it is safe to say the underlying neural mechanism used by these two individuals to perform a so-called visual working memory task would be quite different. Such a scenario underlines the importance of testing imagery ability when investigating cognitive processes like visual working memory or episodic memory (Pearson and Keogh, 2019). Further, this suggests that imagery as a cognitive tool is not fundamental to performing other cognitive functions – which in turn raises the interesting question of what is the role of imagery in human cognition? It seems useful if you have it, but based on the aphantasia research it does not seem to be necessary – and there are clinical examples in which imagery is pathological and disruptive. Not many cognitive tools show this diversity of use, which really puts imagery into a category of its own.

Hyperphantasia, or what has previously been called eidetic imagery, is at the other end of the imagery spectrum: strong and often photo-like imagery. Early in the twentieth century the topic of eidetic imagery attracted much attention: This phenomenon is commonly described as a highly detailed almost photo-realistic image experienced directly after seeing the object, but also days or weeks later (Allport, 1924; Gray and Gummerman, 1975; Haber, 1979; Stromeyer and Psotka, 1970). Eidetic imagery, like aphantasia, is only observed in a small percentage of the population, mainly in children, with frequency estimates of 0–11 percent in children (Gray and Gummerman, 1975). Because modern-day psychophysics, fMRI or TMS methods have not been used to investigate eidetic imagery we do not have much data to suggest a possible mechanism or why it seems more prevalent in children.

---

1 Media references: Grinnell, D. (2016) "My Mind's Eye is Blind – So What's Going on in my Brain?" *New Scientist*, April 20. www.newscientist.com/article/2083706-my-minds-eye-is-blind-so-whats-going-on-in-my-brain/. Clemens, A. (2018). When the Mind's Eye is Blind. *Scientific American*, August 1. www.scientificamerican.com/article/when-the-minds-eye-is-blind1/.

Hopefully, as imagery research gains popularity researchers will rei[
hyperphantasic imagery research.

Important Questions for Future Research

The current data supports the idea that visual imagery is a sensory cog....
tool that can be used at will to create sensory simulations of events or objects in their
absence. For those who have strong imagery, it is used ubiquitously, and could be
considered to be indispensable. At the same time, for some people imagery can
become strong and uncontrollable and contribute to or even be a mechanistic driving
factor in mental disorders. At the other end of the spectrum, however, aphantasic
individuals can perform very well on many of the tasks that would otherwise involve
imagery – suggesting that normal functioning in the world does not necessitate visual
imagery. What are we to make of this seemingly contradictory role of imagery in
daily life? Imagery is at once indispensable for some and not necessary – or even
clinically disruptive – in others. It is up to future research to figure out why mental
imagery may be indispensable, not necessary or clinically disruptive for any given
individual. There currently seems to be something of a resurgence in imagery
research, given the range of new objective measurement techniques now available
to researchers (Pearson, 2014).

Why do some people (aphantasics) not have mental imagery? We know that some
people are born without any imagery and others lose it, but we do not know why.
What is different in an aphantasic's brain when compared to someone with imagery?
Answering these questions would shed light not only on the brain mechanisms of
mental imagery but also on the causes of aphantasia – and whether it is reversible.

Can we train/improve mental imagery? Again, this question relates to aphantasia. Can
someone with medium imagery strength increase it via training? Can someone with no
imagery at all learn to have it through a training regime? Answering these questions
would not only inform us about the underlying mechanisms of mental imagery but also
lead to a practical method of self-training in imagery abilities. Some with aphantasia
have said they would like to have it; hence the understanding and development of such
a training protocol would have great impact for such individuals.

What is a mental image? Why are mental images generally weaker than
normal everyday perception? For example, imagining an apple is less clear
and vivid than seeing an apple. This question relates to the underlying brain
mechanisms of imagery. How are perceptual images and mental images
represented in the brain? What is the difference? Answering this question
would inform us as to why some have stronger imagery than others, and what
limits imagery from becoming realistic and indistinguishable from perception.

What is the relationship between voluntary and involuntary phantom vision?
Answering this question has important implications for mental and neurological
disorders. It might inform us as to how we control our imagery, which in turn would
be valuable information for developing new treatment options for those with
uncontrollable traumatic imagery.

References

Albright, T. D. (2012). On the Perception of Probable Things: Neural Substrates of Associative Memory, Imagery, and Perception. *Neuron, 74*(2), 227–245.

Allport, G. W. (1924). Eidetic Imagery. *British Journal of Psychology, 15*, 99–120.

Bergmann, J., Genc, E., Kohler, A., Singer, W., and Pearson, J. (2016). Smaller Primary Visual Cortex Is Associated with Stronger, but Less Precise Mental Imagery. *Cerebral Cortex, 26*(9), 3838–3850.

Brascamp, J. W., Knapen, T. H. J., Kanai, R., van Ee, R., and van den Berg, A. V. (2007). Flash Suppression and Flash Facilitation in Binocular Rivalry. *Journal of Vision, 7*(12), 12–12.

Carrasco, M., Ling, S., and Read, S. (2004). Attention Alters Appearance. *Nature Neuroscience, 7*(3), 308–313.

Chang, S., and Pearson, J. (2018). The Functional Effects of Prior Motion Imagery and Motion Perception. *Cortex, 105*, 83–96.

Chiou, R., Rich, A. N., Rogers, S., and Pearson, J. (2018). Exploring the Functional Nature of Synaesthetic Colour – Dissociations from Colour Perception and Imagery. *Cognition, 177*, 107–121.

Egeth, H. E., and Yantis, S. (1997). Visual Attention: Control, Representation, and Time Course. *Annual Review of Psychology, 48*(1), 269–297.

Galton, F. (1880). I.—Statistics of Mental Imagery. *Mind, 19*, 301–318.

Goebel, R., Khorram-Sefat, D., Muckli, L., Hacker, H., and Singer, W. (1998). The Constructive Nature of Vision: Direct Evidence from Functional Magnetic Resonance Imaging Studies of Apparent Motion and Motion Imagery. *The European Journal of Neuroscience, 10*(5), 1563–1573.

Gray, C. R., and Gummerman, K. (1975). The Enigmatic Eidetic Image: A Critical Examination of Methods, Data, and Theories. *Psychological Bulletin, 82*(3), 383–407.

Haber, R. N. (1979). Twenty Years of Haunting Eidetic Imagery: Where's the Ghost? *Behavioral and Brain Sciences, 2*(4), 583–594.

Ishai, A., and Sagi, D. (1995). Common Mechanisms of Visual Imagery and Perception. *Science, 268*(5218), 1772–1774.

Ishai, A., Ungerleider, L. G., and Haxby, J. V. (2000). Distributed Neural Systems for the Generation of Visual Images. *Neuron, 28*(3), 979–990.

Jacobs, C., Schwarzkopf, D. S., and Silvanto, J. (2018). Visual Working Memory Performance in Aphantasia. *Cortex, 105*, 61–73.

Keogh, R., and Pearson, J. (2011). Mental Imagery and Visual Working Memory. *PLoS ONE, 6*(12), e29221.

(2014). The Sensory Strength of Voluntary Visual Imagery Predicts Visual Working Memory Capacity. *Journal of Vision, 14*(12), 7–7.

Keogh, R., and Pearson, J. (2018). The Blind Mind: No Sensory Visual Imagery in Aphantasia. *Cortex, 105*, 53–60.

Koenig-Robert, R., and Pearson, J. (2019). Decoding the Contents and Strength of Imagery before Volitional Engagement. *Scientific Reports, 9*(1), 3504.

Kosslyn, S. M. (1973). Scanning Visual Images: Some Structural Implications. *Perception & Psychophysics, 14*(1), 90–94.

(2005). Mental Images and the Brain. *Cognitive Neuropsychology, 22*(3), 333–347.

Laeng, B., and Sulutvedt, U. (2014). The Eye Pupil Adjusts to Imaginary Light. *Psychological Science: a Journal of the American Psychological Society / APS*, *25*(1), 188–197.

Lewis, D. E., O'Reilly, M. J., Khuu, S. K., and Pearson, J. (2013). Conditioning the Mind's Eye: Associative Learning with Voluntary Mental Imagery. *Clinical Psychological Science*, *1*(4), 390–400.

Maróthi, R., and Kéri, S. (2018). Enhanced Mental Imagery and Intact Perceptual Organization in Schizotypal Personality Disorder. *Psychiatry Research*, *259*, 433–438.

Meng, M., Remus, D. A., and Tong, F. (2005). Filling-in of Visual Phantoms in the Human Brain. *Nature Neuroscience*, *8*(9), 1248–1254.

Mohr, H. M., Linder, N. S., Dennis, H., and Sireteanu, R. (2011). Orientation-Specific Aftereffects to Mentally Generated Lines. *Perception*, *40*(3), 272–290.

Morina, N., Leibold, E., and Ehring, T. (2013). Vividness of General Mental Imagery Is Associated with the Occurrence of Intrusive Memories. *Journal of Behavior Therapy and Experimental Psychiatry*, *44*(2), 221–226.

Morris, T., Spittle, M., and Watt, A. P. (2005). *Imagery in Sport*. Champaign, IL: Human Kinetics Books.

Naselaris, T., Olman, C. A., Stansbury, D. E., Ugurbil, K., and Gallant, J. L. (2015). A Voxel-Wise Encoding Model for Early Visual Areas Decodes Mental Images of Remembered Scenes. *NeuroImage*, *105*, 215–228.

Pearson, J. (2014). New Directions in Mental-Imagery Research: The Binocular-Rivalry Technique and Decoding fMRI Patterns. *Current Directions in Psychological Science*, *23*(3), 178–183.

Pearson, J., Clifford, C. W. G., and Tong, F. (2008). The Functional Impact of Mental Imagery on Conscious Perception. *Current Biology: CB*, *18*(13), 982–986.

Pearson, J., and Keogh, R. (2019). Redefining Visual Working Memory: A Cognitive-Strategy, Brain-Region Approach. *Current Directions in Psychological Science*, *28*(3), 266–273.

Pearson, J., and Kosslyn, S. M. (2015). The Heterogeneity of Mental Representation: Ending the Imagery Debate. *Proceedings of the National Academy of Sciences*, *112*(33), 10089–10092.

Pearson, J., Naselaris, T., Holmes, E. A., and Kosslyn, S. M. (2015). Mental Imagery: Functional Mechanisms and Clinical Applications. *Trends in Cognitive Sciences*, *19*(10), 590–602.

Pearson, J., Rademaker, R. L., and Tong, F. (2011). Evaluating the Mind's Eye: The Metacognition of Visual Imagery. *Psychological Science*, *22*(12), 1535–1542.

Pearson, J., and Westbrook, F. (2015). Phantom Perception: Voluntary and Involuntary Non-Retinal Vision. *Trends in Cognitive Sciences*, *19*(5), 278–284.

Perky, C. W. (1910). An Experimental Study of Imagination. *The American Journal of Psychology*, *21*(3), 422–452.

Pylyshyn, Z. (2001). Is the Imagery Debate Over? If So, What Was It About? In E. Depoux (ed.), *Language, Brain, and Cognitive Development: Essays in Honor of Jacques Mehler*. Cambridge, MA: MIT Press, 59–83.

Ranganath, C., and D'Esposito, M. (2005). Directing the Mind's Eye: Prefrontal, Inferior and Medial Temporal Mechanisms for Visual Working Memory. *Current Opinion in Neurobiology*, *15*(2), 175–182.

Sasaki, Y., and Watanabe, T. (2004). The Primary Visual Cortex Fills in Color. *Proceedings of the National Academy of Sciences of the United States of America*, *101*(52), 18251–18256.

Schlack, A., and Albright, T. D. (2007). Remembering Visual Motion: Neural Correlates of Associative Plasticity and Motion Recall in Cortical Area MT. *Neuron*, *53*(6), 881–890.

Schlegel, A., Kohler, P. J., Fogelson, S. V., et al. (2013). Network Structure and Dynamics of the Mental Workspace. *Proceedings of the National Academy of Sciences*, *110*(40), 16277–16282.

Shepard, R. N., and Metzler, J. (1971). Mental Rotation of Three-Dimensional Objects. *Science*, *171*(3972), 701–703.

Shine, J. M., Keogh, R., O'Callaghan, C., et al. (2014). Imagine That: Elevated Sensory Strength of Mental Imagery in Individuals with Parkinson's Disease and Visual Hallucinations. *Proceedings of the Royal Society B: Biological Sciences*, *282* (1798), 20142047.

Slotnick, S. D., Thompson, W. L., and Kosslyn, S. M. (2005). Visual Mental Imagery Induces Retinotopically Organized Activation of Early Visual Areas. *Cerebral Cortex*, *15* (10), 1570–1583.

Stokes, M., Thompson, R., Cusack, R., and Duncan, J. (2009). Top-Down Activation of Shape-Specific Population Codes in Visual Cortex During Mental Imagery. *Journal of Neuroscience*, *29*(5), 1565–1572.

Stromeyer, C. F., and Psotka, J. (1970). The Detailed Texture of Eidetic Images. *Nature*, *225* (5230), 346–349.

Tanaka, Y., and Sagi, D. (1998). A Perceptual Memory for Low-Contrast Visual Signals. *Proceedings of the National Academy of Sciences of the United States of America*, *95*(21), 12729–12733.

Tartaglia, E. M., Bamert, L., Mast, F. W., and Herzog, M. H. (2009). Human Perceptual Learning by Mental Imagery. *Current Biology: CB*, *19*(24), 2081–2085.

Thirion, B., Duchesnay, E., Hubbard, E., et al. (2006). Inverse Retinotopy: Inferring the Visual Content of Images from Brain Activation Patterns. *NeuroImage*, *33*(4), 1104–1116.

Yomogida, Y. (2004). Mental Visual Synthesis Is Originated in the Fronto-temporal Network of the Left Hemisphere. *Cerebral Cortex*, *14*(12), 1376–1383.

13 Musical Imagery

Kelly Jakubowski

Humans have a seemingly innate and universal capacity to engage with music (Fitch, 2015; McDermott and Hauser, 2005), which is underpinned by the emotional rewards (Blood and Zatorre, 2001; Koelsch, 2014), social benefits (Dunbar, 2012; Hallam, 2010), and cognitive stimulation (Chamorro-Premuzic and Furnham, 2007; Hyde et al., 2009) afforded by music. In addition to the vast quantities of time we often spend listening to music (North, Hargreaves, and Hargreaves, 2004; Sloboda, O'Neill, and Ivaldi, 2001), music is also a regular feature of our inner mental worlds. Having a tune "stuck" in one's head is a common everyday phenomenon, while it is also quite easy for most people to intentionally bring a piece of music to mind (e.g. "think of the first phrase of the song 'Happy Birthday'"). In addition, musicians regularly rely on more specialist usages of musical imagery, from mentally running through a piece during a practice session to anticipating the upcoming notes during the course of a performance. This chapter begins with an overview of the general features of musical imagery, before describing research on musical imagery in everyday life and outlining the ways in which imagery is used to facilitate aspects of musical performance. The concluding section offers some suggestions for bringing together several disparate aspects of previous research on this topic. Although the range of human experiences of musical imagery is quite diverse – from the simple replaying of a tune in a listener's head after hearing it on the radio to a composer conjuring up the next notes of a new symphony – it appears such experiences rely on similar underlying mechanisms that can be refined for expert purposes through practice.

Features of Musical Imagery

Musical imagery comprises the mental experience of music, which can be instigated even in the absence of a direct sensory experience (Intons-Peterson, 1992). Musical imagery has sometimes been classified as a type of auditory imagery; however, it is now clear that musical imagery also often comprises components of motor and visual imagery (Keller, 2012; Reybrouck, 2001). Many early studies on musical imagery focused on testing the extent to which particular perceptual properties of music (e.g. pitch, tempo, timbre, loudness) could be mentally represented, while some work has also investigated higher-level features (e.g. perceived emotions). One main challenge across this literature has been in creating behavioral paradigms that ensure the generation of a musical image (i.e. that the task at hand cannot be achieved using another, non-imagery-based strategy). This is an obstacle that will be familiar to researchers of any aspect of imagery or imagination, due to the fact that it can be difficult to confirm the intangible and ephemeral contents of the imagination, which may not be accompanied by overt behaviors. This issue has been dealt with in various ways; for instance, many studies have focused on investigating similarities between music perception and musical imagery, with the underlying assumption that similar behavioral responses across perception and imagery tasks indicate that the imagery task is evoking the generation of a mental image that is similar to a perceptual experience. In addition, the use of cognitive neuroscience methods has allowed for the confirmation that similar neural resources are being recruited during both music perception and imagery tasks.

Pitch

Early psychophysical research focused on imagery for single pitches, and demonstrated that imagining a pitch could either facilitate or interfere with subsequent detection of the same pitch played aloud, depending on the exact parameters of the task (Farah and Smith, 1983; Okada and Matsuoka, 1992). Janata and Paroo (2006) examined the acuity of pitch imagery in a more musical context, in which participants judged the intonation of the final note of an ascending major scale. Comparisons between a perceived (in which all pitches of the scale were heard) and imagined pitch task (in which three to five pitches of the scale were imagined) indicated equivalent performance on these tasks. Interestingly, performance on an analogous timing task (where the timing of the final note of the scale was judged) revealed that participants performed better on the perception than the imagery task, suggesting that temporal aspects of musical imagery may be more susceptible to distortion than the pitch content. Similar results, in which performance on pitch-related musical imagery tasks was superior to timing-related tasks, have been reported by Bailes (2002) and Weir, Williamson, and Müllensiefen (2015). In addition, participants with more musical training performed more accurately in several of the imagery tasks (pitch and timing tasks of Janata and Paroo, 2006; pitch task of Weir, Williamson, and Müllensiefen, 2015), suggesting these abilities can be refined with practice.

Halpern (1989) investigated the consistency of pitch imagery by asking participants to imagine and then produce (via singing, or a piano keyboard with the keys obstructed from view) the starting pitch to traditional songs such as "Twinkle, Twinkle Little Star" and found that the absolute pitch level of an individual's musical imagery for a specific song was quite stable over time. Pitch productions were also quite stable across sessions separated by forty-eight hours, although more so for musicians than nonmusicians. Finally, Gelding, Thompson, and Johnson (2015) have investigated the manipulation of pitch imagery using a novel paradigm called the Pitch Imagery Arrow Task (PIAT). This task requires participants to imagine a sequences of tones (following an initial presentation of the tonal context and pitch sequence played aloud) in correspondence with a series of upward and downward arrows presented on a screen. It was found that performance on this task substantially improved when participants employed an imagery-based strategy (confirming the task's validity), and was also positively related to musical training and self-reported auditory imagery vividness and control (measured using the Bucknell Auditory Imagery Scale; Halpern, 2015).

Tempo

Several studies have investigated the similarity between perceived and imagined musical tempo. Weber and Brown (1986) asked participants to track the contour of melodies as quickly as possible by tracing the ups and downs of each melody with a pencil; this was done both while singing each melody out loud (perception task) and while imagining each melody (imagery task). No significant difference was found in the amount of time taken to complete these two tasks, suggesting that participants were utilizing a common mental representation. Halpern (1988) compared perceived and imagined[1] tempo judgments for familiar songs, such as "Happy Birthday," and found a high correlation ($r = .63$) across all trials between perceived and imagined tempi for the same song.

Research on accuracy of tempo recall has revealed that the tempi of familiar pop songs (e.g. "Hotel California") were recalled more accurately in a perceived music condition than in two musical imagery tasks involving (1) tapping to the imagined beat and (2) adjusting a metronome to the imagined beat (Jakubowski, Farrugia, and Stewart, 2016). Tempo recall was also more accurate in the imagery task involving tapping to the beat than the imagery task involving adjusting a metronome, suggesting that motor engagement with imagery may increase the temporal fidelity of the mental image. This work extends the findings of Janata and Paroo (2006), Bailes (2002), and Weir, Williamson, and Müllensiefen (2015) noted in the previous section by revealing a disparity between perception and imagery in terms of *accuracy* of tempo recall, which is also partially influenced by the task via which imagined tempo is measured.

Finally, consistency of imagined tempo has been investigated by Clynes and Walker (1982), who asked musicians to imagine and tap along to a Mozart piano concerto on two consecutive days. Tapping speed when imagining this music was significantly more consistent than tapping to a verbally imagined phrase or tapping without any mental image. In a similar study, participants tapped to imagined versions of the same song across multiple trials within the same session and different sessions separated by two to five days (Halpern, 1992). Both musician and non-musician participants were highly consistent in their tapped tempo for the same song within the same session, whereas musicians showed greater consistency across sessions on different days than nonmusicians.

Timbre

Timbre, sometimes described as "sound quality," is a multidimensional, perceptual parameter of sound that is affected by acoustic features such as attack rate, spectral

---

1 Imagined tempo was measured by asking participants to set a metronome to match the beat of the imagined music.

centroid, and spectral variation (McAdams et al., 1995). Crowder (1989) highlighted the similarity between perceived and imagined musical timbre by showing that imagining a tone in a particular instrumental timbre (e.g. trumpet) can facilitate a pitch judgment of a subsequent perceived tone if the imagined and perceived tones are matching in timbre.[2] Pitt and Crowder (1992) built on this work using a more controlled stimulus set that varied timbre in either spectral (i.e. harmonic content) or dynamic (i.e. attack rate) properties only. Results suggested that spectral features were represented within imagery, but no evidence was found that participants were able to mentally represent the different attack rates used in this study. Halpern et al. (2004) found that participants performed similarly in a task in which they were asked to rate the similarity between pairs of perceived timbres and an analogous task of rating pairs of imagined timbres, while also displaying some commonalities in brain activation patterns between the perceived and imagined timbre tasks. Finally, Bailes (2007a) provided further evidence that timbre can be represented within musical imagery, but also revealed that participants did not always report timbre to be a conscious dimension of their imagery, suggesting that timbre is "optionally present in imagery for music" (Bailes, 2007a: 21).

Loudness

Evidence for the similarity between perceived and imagined loudness was revealed by Intons-Peterson (1980), who asked participants to imagine environmental sounds and found that as the difference between loudness ratings of the two imagined sounds increased, the time taken to identify the louder (or softer) of the two sounds decreased. Similar to results on timbre, however, Intons-Peterson also concluded that loudness is optionally represented within auditory imagery. The investigation of imagined loudness in a more musical context has been pursued by Bishop, Bailes, and Dean (2013a). In this study, participants listened to familiar classical music while continuously adjusting a slider to indicate perceived loudness; all participants also completed an analogous task of imagining and indicating the imagined loudness for the same music. Similarities between rating profiles in the perceived and imagined tasks suggest that the ability to represent loudness within musical imagery is widespread, although musical expertise did increase the fidelity with which loudness was represented in imagery. Bailes et al. (2012) have also provided evidence that imagined loudness within musical sequences relies on a motor representation, as imagined changes in loudness were significantly disrupted when participants were asked to concurrently remember movement sequences, but not when they were asked to remember tone or letter sequences.

Expressive Features

In addition to the lower-level perceptual features outlined above, some work has also investigated the similarity of emotion perception between perceived and imagined

2 Such a facilitation effect was also shown in a purely perceptual task in a separate experiment.

music (Lucas, Schubert, and Halpern, 2010). In this study, musician participants continuously rated the emotions expressed by familiar classical music (in terms of valence and arousal, and general "emotionality" in a second experiment) in both perceived and imagined conditions. Similar response profiles were found across the perception and imagery tasks. This ability to detect emotional expression in imagined music is likely underpinned by the mental representation of lower-level features such as tempo and loudness as outlined above, as a variety of previous research on perceived music has shown that such features play a key role in influencing judgments of emotional expression (e.g, Eerola, Friberg, and Bresin, 2013; Gabrielsson and Lindström, 2010).

The Neuroscience of Musical Imagery

Neuroscientific research using functional Magnetic Resonance Imaging (fMRI) has revealed several parallels, as well as some inherent differences, between the brain regions recruited in perceiving and imagining music (see Zatorre and Halpern, 2005, for an overview). Similar activation patterns of the secondary auditory cortex have been found in both music perception and imagery (Kleber et al., 2007; Kraemer et al., 2005; Zatorre and Halpern, 2005). Primary auditory cortex activation has been found during musical imagery only under certain conditions, such as when participants imagined familiar songs with no lyrics (Kraemer et al., 2005), despite the key role this area plays in music perception. Bilateral frontal cortical activations found during musical imagery tasks may relate to the memory retrieval component inherent in imagery (Herholz, Halpern, and Zatorre, 2012; Zatorre, Halpern, and Bouffard, 2010; Zatorre et al., 1996), while activation of the supplementary motor area (SMA) (Halpern et al., 2004; Herholz, Halpern, and Zatorre, 2012; Zatorre et al., 1996) indicates the potential involvement of a motor or sequencing component, which may be related to the rehearsal or maintenance of the image within working memory. Electroencephalography (EEG) studies have also confirmed the presence of similar activation patterns in musical imagery and perception, even across musical stimuli of varying complexity (Schaefer, Desain, and Farquhar, 2013), which may also be modulated by expertise (Herholz et al., 2008).

Summary

A variety of perceptual properties of music (e.g. pitch, tempo, timbre, loudness) can be represented within imagery, although not all features are necessarily present in all musical imagery experiences. It appears the representation of musical features within imagery can be refined with practice, as musicians' imagery experiences more closely replicated the perceptual experience of music than less musically trained participants in several studies. It is also clear that musical imagery is a multifaceted experience that not only involves auditory imagery but can also invoke aspects of motor representation; this point will be discussed further in section 3: Imagery Uses in Musicians in relation to how musicians use imagery to facilitate action planning in performance.

Everyday Experiences of Musical Imagery

Beyond the laboratory-based studies described in the previous section, a complementary body of literature has examined the experience of musical imagery in natural, everyday settings (e.g. Bailes, 2006, 2007b, 2015; Beaman and Williams, 2010; Beaty et al., 2013; Floridou and Müllensiefen, 2015; Halpern and Bartlett, 2011; Jakubowski et al., 2018; Jakubowski et al., 2015). This research has highlighted that imagining music is a common everyday occurrence for many people. For instance, Bailes (2015) contacted forty-seven participants (from a range of musical backgrounds) six times per day for one week and found that participants were hearing music 35 percent of the time and imagining music 17 percent of the time.[3] Perhaps the most widely recognized everyday manifestation of musical imagery is the *earworm* – the spontaneous mental recall and repetition of a tune on a loop. This phenomenon has been referred to by various terms in the literature – most commonly as *involuntary musical imagery (INMI)* – although there is some debate over whether this term is too broad (Williams, 2015), as *involuntary musical imagery* could also plausibly be used to describe other experiences such as musical obsessions (Taylor et al., 2014) and musical hallucinations (Stewart et al., 2006). Thus, the term *earworm* will be used here to describe the everyday (nonclinical) experience of having a tune come to mind and "play" on repeat, in which both the initial recall and the replay of the tune are involuntary processes. In one survey of more than 12,000 participants, around 90 percent reported experiencing earworms at least once per week, with around 33 percent reporting earworms at least once per day (Liikkanen, 2012a). Reports of earworms have also been collected from many countries through the world (Liikkanen, Jakubowski, and Toivanen, 2015).

Most studies of everyday musical imagery have focused specifically on the earworm phenomenon, although a few diary studies have explored musical imagery more broadly, including instances of both spontaneous and deliberate imagery (e.g. Bailes, 2006, 2007b, 2015; Beaty et al., 2013; Cotter, Christensen, and Silvia, 2018), while only a handful of studies have made more explicit comparisons between voluntary and involuntary musical imagery processes (Jakubowski et al., 2018; Weir et al., 2015). Thus, the majority of the following section will focus on the earworm experience, concluding with some discussion of the relationship between involuntary and voluntary musical imagery.

Methods for Investigating Everyday Musical Imagery

Several studies have examined musical imagery experiences using participant-led diary methods, in which participants are responsible for recording all musical imagery experiences over a certain time period in a paper or electronic diary, or the Experience Sampling Method (ESM), in which participants record information

---

3 Interestingly, an earlier study (Bailes, 2006) of 11 musicians using the same methodology revealed that participants were hearing music 44 percent of the time and imagining music 32 percent of the time, suggesting that musicians not only listen more but also imagine more music than participants with less musical experience.

about their musical imagery experiences when prompted by an experimenter (e.g. via experimenter prompts sent to their mobile phones throughout the day). These *in situ* methods are beneficial for capturing the transient experience of musical imagery as it is actually occurring, which can minimize memory biases and forgetting that might otherwise occur in retrospective reporting. However, retrospective methods have also proved useful in various contexts. For instance, the Involuntary Musical Imagery Scale (IMIS; Floridou et al., 2015) is a questionnaire developed for measuring multiple facets of earworms (e.g. frequency, length, appraisal, embodied responses), which has been used to reveal differences in brain structure related to the earworm experience (Farrugia et al., 2015) and has also been shown to correlate with some responses collected via ESM, at least in terms of estimations of earworm frequency, duration and appraisal (Cotter and Silvia, 2017). Efforts to investigate causal predictors of earworms under controlled conditions have also led to the development of experimental paradigms for inducing earworms (Floridou, Williamson, and Stewart, 2017; Hyman et al., 2013; Liikkanen, 2012b). The triangulation of results across these diverse methodologies has allowed researchers to begin to develop a comprehensive picture of the features and phenomenology, situational predictors, individual differences, and affective responses to earworms.

Features and Phenomenology of Earworms

Earworms most commonly comprise the repetition of a fragment/phrase of music, rather than an entire piece (Brown, 2006; Hyman et al., 2013; Liikkanen, 2012a). In two diary studies, the average reported durations of earworm episodes were 27.25 minutes (Beaman and Williams, 2010) and 36 minutes (Halpern and Bartlett, 2011), although the range of durations can vary widely (e.g. 2 minutes to an entire day, Halpern and Bartlett, 2011).[4] The music that appears as an earworm is typically familiar and liked by the experiencer (Byron and Fowles, 2015; Halpern and Bartlett, 2011; Hyman et al., 2013), which relates to the fact that most earworms are triggered by recent music listening (Williamson et al., 2012). Reports of earworms for entirely novel music are rare, and more typically reported by musicians (Floridou, 2016; Liikkanen, 2012a). It appears music from virtually any genre can become an earworm (Beaman and Williams, 2010; Halpern and Bartlett, 2011; see in particular Lancashire, 2017, in which earworms were experienced for atonal twentieth-century classical music). In many cases earworm experiences are quite idiosyncratic, as the vast majority of songs reported as earworms in previous studies were named by only one participant (e.g. Beaman and Williams, 2010; Jakubowski et al., 2017). However, despite this diversity, some common melodic features of tunes that are likely to be named as earworms have been revealed, including faster tempi, more generic melodic contours and small pitch intervals (Jakubowski et al., 2017; Williamson and Müllensiefen, 2012). It has been suggested that such features facilitate the ability

---

4 One challenge of attempting to measure earworm duration lies in defining an objective start and end point, as earworms often tend to fade in and out of consciousness.

to sing along to the music (Williamson and Müllensiefen, 2012), which might also facilitate "mental singing" of a tune as an earworm.

In a similar vein to previous laboratory studies on voluntarily generated musical imagery, several studies have offered evidence that *involuntary* musical imagery preserves many features of perceived music. Brown (2006) reported a detailed case study of his own near-constant musical imagery and highlighted that the pitch, loudness, rhythm, tempo and timbre of his imagery often closely replicated the original, perceptual version of the music. Similar qualitative evidence on this topic was provided in an interview study by Williamson and Jilka (2013). In a first attempt to provide objective evidence of the fidelity of earworms, Jakubowski et al. (2015) asked participants to tap to the beat of their earworms during their daily lives using a wrist-worn accelerometer. Most earworms were remembered within 10 percent of the tempo of the original recording of the musical piece, suggesting involuntary recall of musical tempo is typically quite accurate. Further evidence for the fidelity of both the pitch and tempo of earworms was provided by McNally-Gagnon (2016), who asked participants to sing their earworms into a recording device.

Various studies have focused on individual differences and revealed that several demographic and personality variables are positively related to the propensity to experience earworms, including musicianship/musical engagement,[5] openness to experience, neuroticism, transliminality and subclinical obsessive-compulsive traits (Baruss and Wammes, 2009; Beaman and Williams, 2013; Floridou, Williamson, and Müllensiefen, 2012; Liikkanen, 2012a; Müllensiefen et al., 2014). In addition, several such factors (neuroticism, obsessive-compulsive traits, thought suppression, schizotypy) can also explain individual differences in the appraisal of the earworm experience, in particular finding it bothersome or disruptive (Beaman and Williams, 2013; Floridou, Williamson, and Müllensiefen, 2012; Müllensiefen et al., 2014).

Situational Predictors of Earworms

The most commonly reported trigger of earworms in a large survey was recent and/or repeated exposure to music, although earworms can also be cued by other means, such as memory associations (e.g. seeing a word that reminds one of a piece of music) or affective states (e.g. association between one's current mood and the earworm music) (Williamson et al., 2012). In terms of the situations in which earworms are most likely to occur, Hyman et al. (2013) used multiple methods (survey, diary, experiment) to conclude that earworms occur more often during periods of low cognitive load (e.g. daily chores, walking) and high cognitive load (more earworms were experienced during challenging Sudoku puzzles and anagrams than easier puzzles). However, Floridou, Williamson, and Stewart (2017) examined the occurrence of earworms under conditions of varying cognitive load and found that earworm frequency and duration decreased as cognitive load increased; they

---

5 In some studies, active engagement with music (e.g. listening behavior and singing) has been shown to be a more significant predictor of earworm experiences than formal training/practice on an instrument (Müllensiefen et al., 2014; Williamson and Müllensiefen, 2012).

suggest that Hyman et al. (2013)'s findings may have been due to participants losing focus while attempting to solve the difficult puzzles, thereby inadvertently causing such tasks to also become low cognitive load tasks. This result shows parallels to other types of spontaneous cognition and task-unrelated thoughts, which also occur more frequently during conditions of low cognitive load, when there is greater cognitive capacity to spare (e.g. Forster and Lavie, 2009; Teasdale et al., 1995). There also appears to be a link between the earworm experience and physical movement: Participants often report that the beat/rhythm of earworms matches their movements (Floridou et al., 2015), 25 percent of earworms reported in a diary study occurred during repetitive movements (Jakubowski et al., 2015), and participants in one experiment were more likely to experience earworms for a song that they had moved or sung along to (McCullough Campbell and Margulis, 2015). Thus, the initiation and/or maintenance of involuntary instances of musical imagery may also draw on the close coupling between the auditory and motor systems.

Emotional Responses to Earworms

In one diary study, 67 percent of earworm episodes were rated as pleasant or neutral in valence (Beaman and Williams, 2010), while 89 percent of respondents to a questionnaire rated their earworms as typically pleasant or neutral (Halpern and Bartlett, 2011). These findings are in contrast to the commonly held conception that having an earworm is a negative or bothersome experience, which may be due to a recollection bias to more vividly recall episodes that are particularly troublesome (Beaman and Williams, 2010). Hyman et al. (2015) investigated factors that might contribute to such feelings of intrusiveness and revealed disliking a song and interference with concurrent tasks as two key predictors. Finally, two studies have revealed that earworms (Jakubowski et al., 2015) and everyday musical imagery more broadly (Bailes, 2015) show a similar relationship with the experiencer's current mood to perceived music, suggesting that musical imagery could serve analogous mood regulatory functions to perceived music.

Voluntary and Involuntary Musical Imagery

The research on earworms outlined above has evolved somewhat independently to that on voluntary musical imagery, which is partially due to the different methodologies employed (i.e. voluntary imagery is more suited to study under laboratory conditions than the ephemeral experience of earworms). However, several parallels have been revealed, including that both voluntary and involuntary occurrences of musical imagery tend to reproduce a perceptual experience with high fidelity, and that both types of imagery show links with sensorimotor processes, musical expertise and emotional responses. One study has compared voluntary and involuntary musical imagery for the same music within the same paradigm, and revealed that involuntary recall of music as an earworm is no less accurate than deliberate recall, at least in terms of musical tempo (Jakubowski et al., 2018). However, earworms had a more systematic effect on the mood of participants than voluntary imagery, suggesting that unplanned retrieval may heighten the emotional impact of imagined music.

Imagery Uses in Musicians

Beyond the everyday experience of having a tune playing in one's mind, musicians exhibit several specialist usages of musical imagery. Strategies such as mental practice and *audiation* (Gordon, 1999, 2003), or mentally hearing and comprehending a piece of music, have long been taught and employed by expert musicians. Musicians also rely on imagery during the course of live performances and when composing new music. The diversity, functions, and efficacy of such imagery experiences are now beginning to be understood in a psychological context.

Music Practice

Musicians rely on a variety of imagery-based strategies within their daily practice. *Mental practice* is a broadly defined and common technique used by musicians, which can also encompass non-imagery-based strategies, such as thinking about a piece or analyzing a score; however, the majority of activities typically described as mental practice fall under the category of imagery (Fine et al., 2015). This imagery is often multimodal in nature, as it may include auditory imagery for the notes to be played, as well as imagination of the movements needed to execute the notes, visual imagery of the score, audience, and performance venue, and so on. Such imagery may be used to aid in learning a piece (e.g. memorization of note sequences or motor commands) or preparing for a performance (e.g. visualization of the anticipated performance conditions). The practice of mentally simulating a performance situation has parallels to other domains requiring a high degree of cognitive and motor expertise, such as sports and surgery (Arora et al., 2011; Gould et al., 2014). One potential benefit of mental practice for musicians is being able to concentrate on aspects of the music without becoming physically tired, which is especially relevant for injury prevention (Holmes, 2005). In addition, qualitative reports from musicians indicate that imagery-based strategies can aid in many aspects of practice, from memorization and overcoming technical difficulties to gaining confidence and fluidity of movement, and connecting with an audience (Connolly and Williamon, 2004; Davidson-Kelly et al., 2015; Trusheim, 1991).

In terms of the efficacy of mental practice, there are mixed results in the literature. Most studies suggest that a combination of mental and physical practice can be as effective as physical practice alone, although mental practice alone is not as effective as physical practice (Coffman, 1990; Driskell, Copper, and Moran, 1994; Highben and Palmer, 2004; Ross, 1985). In a meta-analysis, Driskell, Copper, and Moran (1994) also reported that mental practice more substantially improved results on cognitive than physical tasks. One limitation of making generalizations in relation to efficacy is that the diversity of approaches to mental practice and range of previous experience in using mental practice techniques has often not been taken into account. Thus, future research is needed to more systematically probe the efficacy of specific facets of mental practice and how mental practice abilities develop over longer time periods.

Music Performance

In performance, musicians frequently rely on mental imagery of upcoming notes or actions (often referred to as "anticipatory" or "online" musical imagery), which can be multimodal in nature (e.g. auditory, motor, visual) and can involve both deliberate (e.g. planning the sound of the next note) and involuntary (e.g. expectancies automatically triggered by previous perceptual input) imagery (Keller, 2012). Anticipatory musical imagery may facilitate performance by aiding action planning and enhancing predictions of co-performers' actions (Keller, 2012). For instance, Pecenka and Keller (2009) and Keller and Appel (2010) have reported a correlation between auditory imagery abilities and sensorimotor synchronization in musicians, suggesting a link between anticipation of a sound and being able to synchronize with it. Anticipatory auditory imagery generated during musical performances has also been found to facilitate the accurate timing of movements (Keller and Koch, 2006) and can aid in controlling the speed and force of movements (Keller, Dalla Bella, and Koch, 2010; Keller and Koch, 2008), thus helping to optimize the precision and efficiency of motor aspects of a performance. In addition, auditory imagery can aid the planning of expressive elements of a performance, such as articulation and dynamics (Bishop, Bailes, and Dean, 2013b). These close relationships between auditory imagery and motor planning are likely underpinned by the increased interactions between the auditory and motor systems that are evidenced with greater musical expertise (Bangert et al., 2006; Chen, Penhune, and Zatorre, 2008).

Music Composition

One relatively under-researched area in relation to musical imagery usage is music composition. There are various historical reports indicating that famous composers have made extensive use of musical imagery when writing music (Agnew, 1922; Mountain, 2001). One commonly cited example is Ludwig van Beethoven, who composed many of what are now regarded as his greatest works (including Symphony No. 9) after having gone deaf,[6] suggesting an unusual ability to compose *entirely* using musical imagery. A mixture of deliberate and involuntary imagery processes appear to be implicated when composing, and such imagery can also be multimodal in nature (Aranosian, 1981; Mountain, 2001). Floridou (2016) interviewed six composers about the experience of "novel earworms" (i.e. earworms for music that has never been heard before, which may provide material for new

---

6 See also reports of musical hallucinations in cases of acquired deafness (e.g. Griffiths, 2000), which indicate the capacity for spontaneous (and persistent) musical imagery even in the absence of normal music perceptual functions.

compositions) and found these imagery experiences were more likely to occur during low attention states, periods of focus on inner experiences, and repetitive movements, which bears parallels to other research on earworms and the creative process more generally (e.g. Baird et al., 2012; Williamson et al., 2012). Future research could more closely investigate the balance between the use of strategic and involuntary musical imagery in both written composition and online improvisation (see Limb and Braun, 2008, for some neuroscientific evidence on the spontaneous, non-volitional cognitive processes underlying musical improvisation).

Key Themes and Future Directions

The literature reviewed above highlights the diversity of experiences that fall under the categorization of "musical imagery." Although having a tune stuck in one's head and anticipating the next notes to be played in a piano recital may seem at first distantly related concepts, these processes rely on similar underlying mechanisms that can be refined for specialist purposes. There are several key themes that emerge across these different streams of research on musical imagery that contribute to our wider understanding of the imagination.

The first theme is **expertise**. It is clear that the capacity to experience vivid and veridical musical imagery is widespread, as even non-experts can mentally replicate the pitch, tempo, timbre, and loudness of familiar music and spend a surprisingly large proportion of their everyday lives engaged in musical imagery. However, many studies have revealed expertise effects, demonstrating that musicians exhibit a more diverse range of imagery experiences and are often able to produce mental images that more closely replicate a perceptual experience. This suggests that imaginative processes related to music can be developed and diversified through experience. Although imagery-related processes such as audiation have been stressed for many years as a fundamental skill by music educators (e.g. Gordon, 1999, 2003), there is still much more interdisciplinary cross-talk needed to understand the psychological processes underlying imagery use in expert musicians, in particular in terms of how such abilities can be most efficaciously developed through long-term training.

A second theme is the **fidelity** of musical imagery. A large amount of research has investigated the degree to which imagery experiences replicate aspects of the perceptual experience and has revealed that both voluntary and involuntary experiences of musical imagery often exhibit a high degree of fidelity. This precise mental replication ability can serve important functions, for instance, in facilitating performance by enabling musicians to form vivid and accurate predictions via anticipatory images before producing a sound (Keller, 2012). The fidelity of musical imagery may also play a role in creative processes, such as composition, by allowing a composer to mentally simulate and vividly imagine new combinations of sounds before committing them to paper. Being able to mentally recreate a wide variety of sounds and features of music (e.g. timbre, dynamics) may thereby enhance the creative process, providing a more diverse "palette" of sounds for the musical artist to work with.

A third key theme is **intentionality**. Most previous research has focused specifically on either voluntary *or* involuntary musical imagery, although it is clear that both everyday and expert usages of musical imagery typically comprise a mixture of both types of imagery. Although there are parallels between findings on voluntary and involuntary imagery, some differences have been highlighted as well (Jakubowski et al., 2018), suggesting that the two types of imagery could play somewhat different roles in our everyday lives. In addition, there is a dearth of research examining the different functions that voluntary vs. involuntary imagery might play in musical practice and performance. Other possible directions for future research include the examination of fluctuations between spontaneous and deliberate imagery, as well as how intentionality of imagery might relate to other concepts such as creativity. One difficulty here is that the boundary between deliberate and spontaneous recall is often blurry, and may require methodological advances beyond self-report measures to fully capture the range of experiences in terms of intentionality.

A final theme is the **multimodality** of musical imagery. Musical imagery presents an ideal case for studying the intersection of auditory, motor, and visual imagery. Of particular note are the close links that have been highlighted throughout this chapter between the auditory and motor systems. For instance, it is clear that aspects of auditory imagery are affected by, or can affect,[7] motor processes both in everyday instances of imagery (e.g. earworms) and in expert usages (e.g. music performances). Thus, musical imagery research provides a diverse range of contexts in which to explore questions of how imagery in one modality can affect overt behaviors in another modality.

To conclude, there are many questions yet to be investigated in terms of how musical imagery research can inform our understanding of the imagination. A few of these are highlighted below.

1. What is the function of musical imagery in everyday life?
   Although the purposes for which musicians use imagery in practice and performance are fairly well defined, a less well understood question is why many people, regardless of expertise, spend a large proportion of their daily lives imagining music. The cognitive and emotional role these mental soundtracks may play in our lives is only beginning to be understood.
2. What is the relationship between musical imagery and creativity?
   Potential sub-questions here include whether and how the development of musical imagery abilities can facilitate creativity, and what reconstructive and recombinant imagery processes are at play when creating new music (e.g. via composition or improvisation).
3. How can we best integrate psychological research on musical imagery and creative musical practice?

As in any interdisciplinary undertaking, the definitions and goals outlined by researchers and practitioners of music may not always align. In particular, the typically slow and offline nature of psychological research and the instantaneous

---

7 In some cases a direction of causality has not yet been ascertained.

nature of music-making may be at odds in some cases. However, the questions of interest to musicians may facilitate the development of new methodological approaches and a more practical understanding of the nature of musical imagery in real-world performance contexts.

References

Agnew, M. (1922). The Auditory Imagery of Great Composers. *Psychological Monographs*, *31*(1), 279.

Aranosian, C. M. (1981). Musical Creativity: The Stream of Consciousness in Composition, Improvisation, and Education. *Imagination, Cognition and Personality*, *1*(1), 67–88.

Arora, S., Aggarwal, R., Sirimanna, P., et al. (2011). Mental Practice Enhances Surgical Technical Skills: A Randomized Controlled Study. *Annals of Surgery*, *253*(2), 265–270.

Bailes, F. A. (2002). *Musical Imagery: Hearing and Imagining Music*. Sheffield, UK: University of Sheffield, PhD thesis.

(2006). The Use of Experience-Sampling Methods to Monitor Musical Imagery in everyday life. *Musicae Scientiae*, *10*, 173–190.

(2007a). Timbre as an Elusive Component of Imagery for Music. *Empirical Musicology Review*, *2*, 21–34.

(2007b). The Prevalence and Nature of Imagined Music in the Everyday Lives of Music Students. *Psychology of Music*, *35*, 555–570.

(2015). Music in Mind? An Experience Sampling Study of What and When, Towards an Understanding of Why. *Psychomusicology: Music, Mind and Brain*, *25*(1), 58–68.

Bailes, F., Bishop, L., Stevens, C. J., and Dean, R. T. (2012). Mental Imagery for Musical Changes in Loudness. *Frontiers in Psychology*, *3* (Dec).

Baird, B., Smallwood, J., Mrazek, M. D., et al. (2012). Inspired by Distraction: Mind-Wandering Facilitates Creative Incubation. *Psychological Science*, *23*, 1117–1122.

Bangert, M., Peschel, T., Schlaug, G., et al. (2006). Shared Networks for Auditory and Motor Processing in Professional Pianists: Evidence from fMRI Conjunction. *NeuroImage*, *30*(3), 917–926.

Baruss, I., and Wammes, M. (2009). Characteristics of Spontaneous Musical Imagery. *Journal Of Consciousness Studies*, *16*(1), 37–61.

Beaman, C. P., and Williams, T. I. (2010). Earworms (Stuck Song Syndrome): Towards a Natural History of Intrusive Thoughts. *British Journal of Psychology*, *101*, 637–653.

(2013). Individual Differences in Mental Control Predict Involuntary Musical Imagery. *Musicae Scientiae*, *17*, 398–409.

Beaty, R. E., Burgin, C. J., Nusbaum, E. C., et al. (2013). Music to the Inner Ears: Exploring Individual Differences in Musical Imagery. *Consciousness and Cognition*, *22*(4), 1163–1173.

Bishop, L., Bailes, F., and Dean, R. T. (2013a). Musical Expertise and the Ability to Imagine Loudness. *PLoS ONE*, *8*(2).

(2013b). Musical Imagery and the Planning of Dynamics and Articulation During Performance. *Music Perception: An Interdisciplinary Journal*, *31*(2), 97–117.

Blood, A. J., and Zatorre, R. J. (2001). Intensely Pleasurable Responses to Music Correlate with Activity in Brain Regions Implicated in Reward and Emotion. *Proceedings of the National Academy of Sciences, 98*(20), 11818–11823.

Brown, S. (2006). The Perpetual Music Track: The Phenomenon of Constant Musical Imagery. *Journal of Consciousness Studies, 13*(6), 43–62.

Byron, T. P., and Fowles, L. C. (2015). Repetition and Recency Increases Involuntary Musical Imagery of Previously Unfamiliar Songs. *Psychology of Music, 43*(3), 375–389.

Chamorro-Premuzic, T., and Furnham, A. (2007). Personality and Music: Can Traits Explain How People Use Music in Everyday Life? *British Journal of Psychology, 98*(2), 175–185.

Chen, J. L., Penhune, V. B., and Zatorre, R. J. (2008). Moving on Time: Brain Network for Auditory-Motor Synchronization Is Modulated by Rhythm Complexity and Musical Training. *Journal of Cognitive Neuroscience, 20*(2), 226–239.

Clynes, M., and Walker, J. (1982). Neurobiologic Functions of Rhythm, Time, and Pulse in Music. In M. Clynes (ed.), *Music, Mind, and Brain: The Neuropsychology of Music*. New York: Plenum, 171–216.

Coffman, D. D. (1990). Effects of Mental Practice, Physical Practice, and Knowledge of Results on Piano Performance. *Journal of Research in Music Education, 38*(3), 187.

Connolly, C., and Williamon, A. (2004). Mental Skills Training. In A. Williamon (ed.), *Music Excellence: Strategies and Techniques to Enhance Performance*. Oxford, UK: Oxford University Press, 221–242.

Cotter, K. N., Christensen, A. P., and Silvia, P. J. (2018). Understanding Inner Music: A Dimensional Approach to Musical Imagery. *Psychology of Aesthetics, Creativity, and the Arts*. dx.doi.org/10.1037/aca0000195.

Cotter, K. N., and Silvia, P. J. (2017). Measuring Mental Music: Comparing Retrospective and Experience Sampling Methods for Assessing Musical Imagery. *Psychology of Aesthetics, Creativity, and the Arts, 11*(3), 335–343.

Crowder, R. G. (1989). Imagery for Musical Timbre. *Journal of Experimental Psychology: Human Perception and Performance, 15*(3), 472.

Davidson-Kelly, K., Schaefer, R. S., Moran, N., and Overy, K. (2015). "Total Inner Memory": Deliberate Uses of Multimodal Musical Imagery During Performance Preparation. *Psychomusicology: Music, Mind, and Brain, 25*(1), 83.

Driskell, J. E., Copper, C., and Moran, A. (1994). Does Mental Practice Enhance Performance? *Journal of Applied Psychology, 79*(4), 481–492.

Dunbar, R. (2012). On the Evolutionary Function of Song and Dance. In N. Bannan (ed.), *Music, Language and Human Evolution*. Oxford, UK: Oxford University Press, 201–214.

Eerola, T., Friberg, A., and Bresin, R. (2013). Emotional Expression in Music: Contribution, Linearity, and Additivity of Primary Musical Cues. *Frontiers in Psychology, 4*, 487.

Farah, M. J., and Smith, A. F. (1983). Perceptual Interference and Facilitation with Auditory Imagery. *Perception & Psychophysics, 33*(5), 475–478.

Farrugia, N., Jakubowski, K., Cusack, R., and Stewart, L. (2015). Tunes Stuck in Your Brain: The Frequency and Affective Evaluation of Involuntary Musical Imagery Correlate with Cortical Structure. *Consciousness and Cognition, 35*, 66–77.

Fine, P. A., Wise, K. J., Goldemberg, R., and Bravo, A. (2015). Performing Musicians' Understanding of the Terms "Mental Practice" and "Score Analysis". *Psychomusicology: Music, Mind, and Brain, 25*(1), 69–82.

Fitch, W. T. (2015). Four Principles of Bio-Musicology. *Philosophical Transactions of the Royal Society of London. Series B, Biological Sciences, 370*(1664), 20140091.

Floridou, G. A. (2016). *Investigating the Relationship between Involuntary Musical Imagery and Other Forms of Spontaneous Cognition*. London, UK: Goldsmiths, University of London, PhD thesis.

Floridou, G. A., and Müllensiefen, D. (2015). Environmental and Mental Conditions Predicting the Experience of Involuntary Musical Imagery: An Experience Sampling Method Study. *Consciousness and Cognition, 33*, 472–486.

Floridou, G., Williamson, V. J., and Müllensiefen, D. (2012). Contracting Earworms: The Roles of Personality and Musicality. In E. Cambouropoulos, C. Tsougras, K. Mavromatis, and K. Pastiadis, (eds.), *Proceedings of ICMPC-ESCOM 12, Thessaloniki, Greece,* 302–310.

Floridou, G. A., Williamson, V. J., and Stewart, L. (2017). A Novel Indirect Method for Capturing Involuntary Musical Imagery under Varying Cognitive Load. *Quarterly Journal of Experimental Psychology, 70*(11), 2189–2199.

Floridou, G. A., Williamson, V. J., Stewart, L., and Müllensiefen, D. (2015). The Involuntary Musical Imagery Scale (IMIS). *Psychomusicology: Music, Mind and Brain, 25*(1), 28–36.

Forster, S., and Lavie, N. (2009). Harnessing the Wandering Mind: The Role of Perceptual Load. *Cognition, 111*(3), 345–355.

Gabrielsson, A., and Lindström, E. (2010). The Role of Structure in the Musical Expression of Emotions. In P. N. Juslin and J. A. Sloboda (eds.), *Handbook of Music and Emotion: Theory, Research, and Applications*. Oxford, UK: Oxford University Press, 367–400.

Gelding, R. W., Thompson, W. F., and Johnson, B. W. (2015). The Pitch Imagery Arrow Task: Effects of Musical Training, Vividness, and Mental Control. *PLoS ONE, 10*(3), e0121809.

Gordon, E. E. (1999). All About Audiation and Music Aptitudes. *Music Educators Journal, 86*(2), 41–44.

   (2003). *Learning Sequences in Music: Skill, Content, and Patterns*. Chicago, IL: GIA Publications.

Gould, D., Voelker, D. F., Damarjian, N., and Greenleaf, C. (2014). Imagery Training for Peak Performance. In J. L. van Raalte and B. W. Brewer (eds.), *Exploring Sport and Exercise Psychology*. 3rd edition. Washington, DC: American Psychological Association, 55–82.

Griffiths, T. D. (2000). Musical Hallucinosis in Acquired Deafness: Phenomenology and Brain Substrate. *Brain, 123*(10), 2065–2076.

Hallam, S. (2010). The Power of Music: Its Impact on the Intellectual, Social and Personal Development of Children and Young People. *International Journal of Music Education, 28*(3), 269–289.

Halpern, A. R. (1988). Perceived and Imagined Tempos of Familiar Songs. *Music Perception, 6*(2), 193–202.

   (1989). Memory for the Absolute Pitch of Familiar Songs. *Memory & Cognition, 17*(5), 572–581.

   (1992). Musical Aspects of Auditory Imagery. In D. Reisberg (ed.), *Auditory Imagery*. Hillsdale, NJ: Erlbaum, 1–27.

   (2015). Differences in Auditory Imagery Self-Report Predict Neural and Behavioral Outcomes. *Psychomusicology: Music, Mind, and Brain, 25*(1), 37–47.

Halpern, A. R., and Bartlett, J. C. (2011). The Persistence of Musical Memories: A Descriptive Study of Earworms. *Music Perception*, *28*(4), 425–432.

Halpern, A. R., Zatorre, R. J., Bouffard, M., and Johnson, J. A. (2004). Behavioral and Neural Correlates of Perceived and Imagined Musical Timbre. *Neuropsychologia*, *42*(9), 1281–1292.

Herholz, S. C., Halpern, A. R., and Zatorre, R. J. (2012). Neuronal Correlates of Perception, Imagery, and Memory for Familiar Tunes. *Journal of Cognitive Neuroscience*, *24*(6), 1382–1397.

Herholz, S. C., Lappe, C., Knief, A., and Pantev, C. (2008). Neural Basis of Music Imagery and the Effect of Musical Expertise. *The European Journal of Neuroscience*, *28*(11), 2352–2360.

Highben, Z., and Palmer, C. (2004). Effects of Auditory and Motor Mental Practice in Memorized Piano Performance. *Bulletin of the Council for Research in Music Education*, *159*, 58–65.

Holmes, P. (2005). Imagination in Practice: A Study of the Integrated Roles of Interpretation, Imagery and Technique in the Learning and Memorisation Processes of Two Experienced Solo Performers. *British Journal of Music Education*, *22*(3), 217–235.

Hyde, K. L., Lerch, J., Norton, A., et al. (2009). The Effects of Musical Training on Structural Brain Development: A Longitudinal Study. *Annals of the New York Academy of Sciences*, *1169*(1), 182–186.

Hyman, I. E., Burland, N. K., Duskin, H. M., et al. (2013). Going Gaga: Investigating, Creating, and Manipulating the Song Stuck in My Head. *Applied Cognitive Psychology*, *27*, 204–215.

Hyman, I. E., Cutshaw, K. I., Hall, C. M., et al. (2015). Involuntary to Intrusive: Using Involuntary Musical Imagery to Explore Individual Differences and the Nature of Intrusive Thoughts. *Psychomusicology: Music, Mind and Brain*, *25*(1), 14–27.

Intons-Peterson, M. J. (1980). The Role of Loudness in Auditory Imagery. *Memory & Cognition*, *8*(5), 385–393. dx.doi.org/10.3758/BF03211134.

   (1992). Components of Auditory Imagery. In D. Reisberg (ed.), *Auditory Imagery*. Hillsdale, NJ: Lawrence Erlbaum Associates, 45–72.

Jakubowski, K., Bashir, Z., Farrugia, N., and Stewart, L. (2018). Involuntary and Voluntary Recall of Musical Memories: A Comparison of Temporal Accuracy and Emotional Responses. *Memory and Cognition*, *46*(5), 741–756.

Jakubowski, K., Farrugia, N., Halpern, A. R., Sankarpandi, S. K., and Stewart, L. (2015). The Speed of Our Mental Soundtracks: Tracking the Tempo of Involuntary Musical Imagery in Everyday Life. *Memory and Cognition*, *43*(8), 1229–1242.

Jakubowski, K., Farrugia, N., and Stewart, L. (2016). Probing Imagined Tempo for Music: Effects of Motor Engagement and Musical Experience. *Psychology of Music*, *44*(6), 1274–1288.

Jakubowski, K., Finkel, S., Stewart, L., and Müllensiefen, D. (2017). Dissecting an Earworm: Melodic Features and Song Popularity Predict Involuntary Musical Imagery. *Psychology of Aesthetics, Creativity, and the Arts*, *11*(2), 122–135.

Janata, P., and Paroo, K. (2006). Acuity of Auditory Images in Pitch and Time. *Perception & Psychophysics*, *68*(5), 829–844.

Keller, P. E. (2012). Mental Imagery in Music Performance: Underlying Mechanisms and Potential Benefits. *Annals of the New York Academy of Sciences*, *1252*, 206–213.

Keller, P. E., and Appel, M. (2010). Individual Differences, Auditory Imagery, and the Coordination of Body Movements and Sounds in Musical Ensembles. *Music Perception*, *28*(1), 27–46.

Keller, P. E., Dalla Bella, S., and Koch, I. (2010). Auditory Imagery Shapes Movement Timing and Kinematics: Evidence from a Musical Task. *Journal of Experimental Psychology: Human Perception and Performance*, *36*(2), 508–513.

Keller, P. E., and Koch, I. (2006). The Planning and Execution of Short Auditory Sequences. *Psychonomic Bulletin & Review*, *13*(4), 711–716.

(2008). Action Planning in Sequential Skills: Relations to Music Performance. *Quarterly Journal of Experimental Psychology*, *61*(2), 275–291.

Kleber, B., Birbaumer, N., Veit, R., Trevorrow, T., and Lotze, M. (2007). Overt and Imagined Singing of an Italian Aria. *NeuroImage*, *36*(3), 889–900.

Koelsch, S. (2014). Brain Correlates of Music-Evoked Emotions. *Nature Reviews Neuroscience*, *15*, 170–180.

Kraemer, D. J. M., Macrae, C. N., Green, A. E., and Kelley, W. M. (2005). Musical Imagery: Sound of Silence Activates Auditory Cortex. *Nature*, *434*(7030), 158.

Lancashire, R. (2017). An Experience-Sampling Study to Investigate the Role of Familiarity in Involuntary Musical Imagery Induction. In P. M. C. Harrison (ed.), *Proceedings of the 10th International Conference of Students of Systematic Musicology (SysMus17), London, UK.*

Liikkanen, L. A. (2012a). Musical Activities Predispose to Involuntary Musical Imagery. *Psychology of Music*, *40*, 236–256.

(2012b). Inducing Involuntary Musical Imagery: An Experimental Study. *Musicae Scientiae*, *16*(2), 217–234.

Liikkanen, L. A., Jakubowski, K., and Toivanen, J. M. (2015). Catching Earworms on Twitter: Using Big Data to Study Involuntary Musical Imagery. *Music Perception*, *33*(2), 199–216.

Limb, C. J., and Braun, A. R. (2008). Neural Substrates of Spontaneous Musical Performance: An fMRI Study of Jazz Improvisation. *PLoS one*, *3*(2), e1679.

Lucas, B. J., Schubert, E., and Halpern, A. R. (2010). Perception of Emotion in Sounded and Imagined Music. *Music Perception*, *27*(5), 399–412.

McAdams, S., Winsberg, S., Donnadieu, S., de Soete, G., and Krimphoff, J. (1995). Perceptual Scaling of Synthesized Musical Timbres: Common Dimensions, Specificities, and Latent Subject Classes. *Psychological Research*, *58*(3), 177–192.

McCullough Campbell, S., and Margulis, E. H. (2015). Catching an Earworm Through Movement. *Journal of New Music Research*, *44*(4), 347–358.

McDermott, J., and Hauser, M. (2005). The Origins of Music: Innateness, Uniqueness, and Evolution. *Music Perception*, *23*(1), 29–59.

McNally-Gagnon, A. (2016). *Imagerie musicale involontaire: caractéristiques phénoménologiques et mnésiques*. Montreal, Canada: University of Montreal, PhD thesis.

Mountain, R. (2001). Composers and Imagery: Myths and Realities. In R. I. Godøy and H. Jörgensen (eds.), *Musical Imagery*. New York, NY: Taylor & Francis, 271–288.

Müllensiefen, D., Jones, R., Jilka, S., Stewart, L., and Williamson, V. J. (2014). Individual Differences Predict Patterns in Spontaneous Involuntary Musical Imagery. *Music Perception*, *31*(4), 323–338.

North, A. C., Hargreaves, D. J., and Hargreaves, J. J. (2004). Uses of Music in Everyday Life. *Music Perception: An Interdisciplinary Journal, 22*(1), 41–77.

Okada, H., and Matsuoka, K. (1992). Effects of Auditory Imagery on the Detection of a Pure Tone in White Noise: Experimental Evidence of the Auditory Perky Effect. *Perceptual and Motor Skills, 74*(2), 443–448.

Pecenka, N., and Keller, P. E. (2009). Auditory Pitch Imagery and Its Relationship to Musical Synchronization. *Annals of the New York Academy of Sciences, 1169*, 282–286.

Pitt, M. A., and Crowder, R. G. (1992). The Role of Spectral and Dynamic Cues in Imagery for Musical Timbre. *Journal of Experimental Psychology. Human Perception and Performance, 18*(3), 728–738.

Reybrouck, M. (2001). Musical Imagery between Sensory Processing and Ideomotor Simulation. In R. I. Godøy and H. Jörgensen (eds.), *Musical imagery.* New York: Taylor & Francis, 117–136.

Ross, S. L. (1985). The Effectiveness of Mental Practice in Improving the Performance of College Trombonists. *Journal of Research in Music Education, 33*(4), 221.

Schaefer, R. S., Desain, P., and Farquhar, J. (2013). Shared Processing of Perception and Imagery of Music in Decomposed EEG. *NeuroImage, 70*, 317–326. dx.doi.org/10.1016/j.neuroimage.2012.12.064.

Sloboda, J. A., O'Neill, S. A., and Ivaldi, A. (2001). Functions of Music in Everyday Life: An Exploratory Study Using the Experience Sampling Method. *Musicae Scientiae, 5* (1), 9–32.

Stewart, L., von Kriegstein, K., Warren, J. D., and Griffiths, T. D. (2006). Music and the Brain: Disorders of Musical Listening. *Brain, 129*(10), 2533–2553.

Taylor, S., McKay, D., Miguel, E. C., et al. (2014). Musical Obsessions: A Comprehensive Review of Neglected Clinical Phenomena. *Journal of Anxiety Disorders, 28*(6), 580–589.

Teasdale, J. D., Dritschel, B. H., Taylor, M. J., et al. (1995). Stimulus-Independent Thought Depends on Central Executive Resources. *Memory & Cognition, 23* (5), 551–559.

Trusheim, W. H. (1991). Audiation and Mental Imagery: Implications for Artistic Performance. *Quarterly Journal of Music Teaching and Learning, 2*, 138–147.

Weber, R. J., and Brown, S. (1986). Musical Imagery. *Music Perception, 3*(4), 411–426.

Weir, G., Williamson, V. J., and Müllensiefen, D. (2015). Increased Involuntary Musical Mental Activity Is Not Associated with More Accurate Voluntary Musical Imagery. *Psychomusicology: Music, Mind, and Brain, 25*(1), 48–57.

Williams, T. I. (2015). The Classification of Involuntary Musical Imagery: The Case for Earworms. *Psychomusicology: Music, Mind and Brain, 25*(1), 5–13.

Williamson, V. J., and Jilka, S. R. (2013). Experiencing Earworms: An Interview Study of Involuntary Musical Imagery. *Psychology of Music, 42* (5), 653–670.

Williamson, V. J., Jilka, S. R., Fry, J., et al. (2012). How Do Earworms Start? Classifying the Everyday Circumstances of Involuntary Musical Imagery. *Psychology of Music, 40* (3), 259–284.

Williamson, V. J., and Müllensiefen, D. (2012). Earworms from Three Angles. In E. Cambouropoulos, C. Tsougras, K. Mavromatis, and K. Pastiadis, (eds.), *Proceedings of ICMPC-ESCOM 12, Thessaloniki, Greece,* 1124–1133.

Zatorre, R. J., and Halpern, A. R. (2005). Mental Concerts: Musical Imagery and Auditory Cortex. *Neuron 47*(1), 9–12.

Zatorre, R. J., Halpern, A. R., and Bouffard, M. (2010). Mental Reversal of Imagined Melodies: A Role for the Posterior Parietal Cortex. *Journal of Cognitive Neuroscience, 22*(4), 775–789.

Zatorre, R. J., Halpern, A. R., Perry, D. W., Meyer, E., and Evans, A. C. (1996). Hearing in the Mind's Ear: A PET Investigation of Musical Imagery and Perception. *Journal of Cognitive Neuroscience, 8*(1), 29–46.

14 Neurophysiological Foundations and Practical Applications of Motor Imagery

Aymeric Guillot

Introduction to the Multifaceted Nature of Motor Imagery

Among the many capacities of the human mind, one of the most remarkable is certainly the ability to mentally simulate sensations, actions, and other types of sensory and motor experiences (Moran et al., 2012). Such cognitive simulation process can be achieved in the absence of appropriate sensory input (Munzert, Lorey, and Zentgraf, 2009). Typically, mentally simulating a movement is referred to as motor imagery (MI), which is defined as a dynamic mental state during which the representation of a movement is rehearsed in working memory without engaging in the corresponding actual motoric execution. Early on, the seminal *motor simulation theory* of Jeannerod (1994, 2001) offered a relevant explanation for how action-related cognitive states such as MI are linked to motor execution states (O'Shea and Moran, 2017). In this vein, MI should be seen as an emulation of an internal state of action preparation. Jeannerod (2006) later considered the concept of motor cognition, in which the motor system draws on stored information to plan, mentally simulate and produce our own actions, as well as to anticipate, predict, and interpret the actions of others.

Imagining an action is certainly more complex than it appears at first glance. There has been a great deal of research on imagery processes for well over a century, and there is now compelling evidence that it is a multisensory construct based on different sensory modalities. While tactile MI (Schmidt et al., 2014) and auditory MI (Halpern, 2012) received some consideration, the vast majority of experimental investigations dealing with the MI experience primarily focused on visual and kinesthetic MI. Visual MI refers to the visualization of an action. Internal visual imagery is a form of visual imagery in which a person imagines herself performing an action from a first-person perspective, as would happen in the real-life situation, while in external visual imagery she sees herself performing the movement from a third-person perspective, as a spectator. The latter case involves imagining the action that one's self or someone else is performing, regardless of the agency of the movement. Kinesthetic imagery, on the other hand, involves the sensations of how it feels to perform an action, including the force and effort perceived during movement and balance (Callow and Waters, 2005), hence considering the body as a generator of forces (Jeannerod, 1994). Overall, research done on MI generally demonstrated that all imagery types and perspectives might serve different purposes, and that their respective effectiveness may depend on the nature of the motor task being imagined.

Apart from the type of MI that can be predominantly performed, the accuracy and quality of the imagery content is of critical importance. A first intrinsic characteristic of the imagery experience is its degree of *vividness*, which corresponds to the clarity and richness of the mental representation. Vivid MI therefore requires the recall of detailed sensory cues, i.e. colored and dynamic images of the movement, significant feeling and sensations of muscle contractions, and accurate movement-related auditory information or defined tactile sensations, which are similar to the actual experience of the corresponding movement. Vividness is probably the imagery dimension that has been most extensively examined by researchers, and it should be distinguished from the *exactness* of the imagery experience, which instead reflects the degree of similarity with the actual movement, including the corresponding spatio-temporal features. The *controllability* of MI refers to the manipulation and transformation of the image content, as well as its maintenance over time. This dimension is particularly important during mental rotation paradigms. As mental images can be easily inadequately transformed, they may alter the exactness of the imagery experience.

It is now well established that the temporal features of MI, reflecting the ease/difficulty that individuals encounter in preserving the temporal characteristics of the motor performance, must be considered and controlled (Guillot and Collet, 2005; Guillot et al., 2012b), as it may have considerable impact on subsequent motor performance duration (Louis et al., 2008). A handful of experimental studies have now examined the similarities and differences between MI duration and the time needed to physically execute the same action. While performing slow or fast imagery can have selective benefits (O and Hall, 2009; Shirazipour et al., 2016), achieving temporal congruence is a critical key-component of fruitful imagery interventions (Guillot and Collet, 2005; Guillot et al., 2012b). Note, however, that the importance of controlling imagery speed further depends on the MI outcome, as it is critical in the field of motor learning but not within MI interventions in clinical settings.

MI has multiple applications in sport sciences and clinical settings, and there is now converging evidence that MI positively contributes to promote motor learning and improves motor recovery. Motor learning is classically defined as a change in motor behavior resulting from practice. In the sport domain, MI is very popular among athletes and coaches, and has been described as a *"centre pillar of applied sport psychology"* (Morris, Spittle, and Perry, 2004: 344). MI has extensively been shown to positively affect the kinematic characteristics of movements, as well as movement accuracy, movement speed, movement efficacy, and strength (by facilitating strength gains or limitation of strength loss). Interestingly, MI has been shown to enhance motor performance both through *online* learning processes, which occur as a *direct* consequence of practice, and offline learning processes (delayed performance gains) *indirectly* resulting from practice (Di Rienzo et al., 2016). An important number of relevant reviews and meta-analyses focusing on such benefits of MI have been published in the scientific literature (Driskell, Copper, and Moran, 1994; Feltz and Landers, 1983; Schuster et al., 2011). From a more conjectural viewpoint, several theoretical models and MI frameworks were designed to support efficient MI interventions and cover the key components that need to be carefully controlled to achieve peak performance (e.g. Guillot and Collet, 2008; Holmes and Collins, 2001; Munroe et al., 2000). All provide a relevant contribution to the understanding of MI use, and the structuration of effective MI training programs. Fundamentally, due to the great overlap of active brain regions during both MI and motor performance of the same movement, these two kinds of practice are functionally equivalent and share behavioral matching, which may explain why mental practice based on MI improves motor performance (Lotze and Halsband, 2006).

After elaborating in this chapter on the progress of our understanding of the neural underpinnings of the MI process and its relations to corresponding actual practice, we outline how MI should ideally be performed to achieve peak performance by considering the main guidelines and rules of practice that must be controlled. We then discuss the new directions offered by the scientific literature to determine the optimal conditions of MI practice, depending upon the targeted imagery outcomes.

Neurophysiological Underpinning of Motor Imagery Processes

As outlined by Borst (2013), the neurophysiological foundations of MI are probably more closely defined than those of any other higher cognitive functions. MI and motor performance have been extensively shown to share parallel characteristics, both at the neural, physiological and behavioral levels.

Brain Activations

Understanding the neural correlates of goal-directed actions, whether executed or imagined, as well as the functional neuroanatomical networks associated with expertise in MI, has been an important purpose of cognitive brain research since the advent of neuroimaging techniques. Considerable experimental evidence has accumulated to suggest that movement execution and MI share substantial overlap of active brain regions. Such apparent (neuro)functional equivalence supports the hypothesis that the neural networks mediating MI and motor performance are, at least partially, similar (Hardwick et al., 2018; Hétu et al., 2013; Jeannerod, 1994). Although there are some differences, the motor systems including the premotor cortex, the supplementary motor area, the putamen and the cerebellum, as well as the inferior and superior parietal lobules, are substantially activated during MI (Decety et al., 1994; Guillot et al., 2009; Lotze et al., 1999). Even if there are some discrepancies, as MI activates only a subset of areas required for movement execution (Macuga and Frey, 2012), the primary motor cortex also seems to be, albeit more weakly, activated during MI (for reviews, see Lotze and Halsband 2006; Sharma et al., 2008). Interestingly, Ehrsson, Geyer, and Naito (2003) and Hétu et al. (2013) added that the content of MI was reflected in the pattern of motor cortical activations, as MI of specific body part movements selectively activated the corresponding body part sections of the contralateral primary motor cortex. Other researchers provided evidence that the cerebral plasticity that occurs following physical practice was also reflected during MI (Jackson et al., 2003; Lafleur et al., 2002), such preservation of the functional equivalence between MI and actual practice being later replicated in several experiments (Di Rienzo et al., 2016; Lacourse et al., 2004).

Despite strong evidence of the (neuro)functional equivalence between MI and motor performance, the neural networks underlying these behaviors are not strictly identical. First, one should keep in mind that when performing MI, participants are aware that movement will not be performed, and therefore that motor commands are inhibited (for a review focusing on motor inhibition during MI, see Guillot et al., 2012a). Second, there are several variables of influence that have been found to modulate the patterns of brain activations underlying MI, including imagery type, imagery speed, imagery intensity, imagery ability, and expertise level.

Although they share similar neuronal substrates (Filgueiras, Quintas Conde, and Hall, 2017), there is now clear evidence that the different types of MI are partially mediated through separate neural systems, and may therefore contribute differently during the process of motor learning and neurological rehabilitation. A first set of studies investigating the neural networks underlying first- vs. third-person imagery perspectives (Jackson, Meltzoff and Decety, 2006; Jiang et al., 2015; Lorey et al., 2009; Ruby and Decety, 2001; Seiler et al., 2015) revealed that the first-person perspective was more tightly coupled to the sensory-motor system than the third-person perspective, which required additional visuospatial transformations. Other researchers compared the neural networks activated during visual vs. kinesthetic imagery (Guillot et al., 2009; Jiang et al., 2015; Seiler, Monsma, and Newman-Norlund, 2015; Solodkin et al., 2004). Visual imagery predominantly activated the visual pathways including the temporal areas, the occipital regions, and the precuneus, whereas the pattern of kinesthetic imagery involved mainly motor-associated structures and the inferior parietal lobule. Kinesthetic imagery thus included motor simulation processes related to the form and timing of actual movements to a greater extent.

Brain areas involved in the control of speed were also found to be selectively different. Sauvage et al. (2013) nicely demonstrated that slow movements are predominantly monitored by a motor cortico-striato-cortical loop and cortical associative areas, while fast movements mainly activate (pre-)motor cortico-cerebellar regions. These findings provide neuroanatomical evidence of how/why modulating imagery speed is likely to harmfully affect actual movement speed (Louis et al., 2008), suggesting that different brain regions are involved in the patterning and sequencing of imagined movements. Using a similar approach, Mizuguchi, Nakata, and Kanosue (2014) examined the relationship between brain activity and imagined force level by comparing the neural networks activated during MI of muscular contractions performed at 10 percent, 30 percent, and 60 percent of the maximal voluntary contraction. Their original findings revealed that the pattern of activations in the frontoparietal regions increased along with the intensity of MI contractions, hence suggesting that the intended contractile force level of imagined movements might be decoded. The authors argued that monitoring activity in this region may be of particular interest when using MI to design brain–computer interfaces.

Finally, researchers examined the patterns of cerebral activity related to the degree of expertise of the participants with both the motor and imagery tasks (for extensive reviews, see Debarnot et al., 2014; Di Rienzo et al., 2016). Data strongly supports distinct neural mechanisms of expertise in MI, as a function of the individual skill level (Chang et al., 2011; Lotze et al., 2003; Milton, et al., 2007; Wei and Luo, 2010), with a more refined and circumscribed pattern of activity in experts compared to novices (Debarnot et al., 2014). By providing new and original insight about the time course of neural oscillations during MI in both an Olympic world-class athlete and a novice, Di Rienzo et al. (2016) recently confirmed these results and nicely illustrated the "expert brain" resulting from the neuroplasticity of successive online and offline learning processes. Regarding the expertise with the MI task per se, the functional neuroanatomical correlates of imagery ability revealed that both good and poor imagers recruited a network of similar brain activations, however with either greater or lower activity in different regions of interest according to the experimental studies (Guillot et al., 2009; Lorey et al., 2009; van der Meulen et al., 2014). As mentioned by Debarnot et al. (2014), differences in the experimental designs as well as the criteria for determining the individual imagery ability may explain such discrepancies. Interestingly, poor imagers were found to show greater activations of the cerebellum, thus suggesting that they do not only need to recruit the cortico-striatal system, but also to compensate by activating the cortico-cerebellar system during MI (Doyon and Benali, 2005). Some researchers also questioned the fidelity of motor intentions to the actual execution of the corresponding movement, by exploring differences in the neural bases of motor simulation of viewed, performed, and performable but not performed acts (e.g. Calvo-Merino et al., 2005). Their data underlined the selective influence of both the level of expertise and the motor repertoire during the motor simulation process.

Taken together, both the great overlap of active brain regions during actual practice and MI on the one hand and the selective neural patterns mediating the different forms and the content of the MI experience on the other extend our current understanding of the neurophysiological underpinnings of the individual predispositions to benefit from MI practice, as well as of MI effectiveness.

Autonomic Nervous System and Somatic Responses

Since the pioneering work by Decety et al. (1991), who monitored cardiac and respiratory activities during actual and mental locomotion as a function of increasing speeds, an important number of experimental studies provided evidence that MI and motor performance elicit very similar autonomic responses (Beyer et al., 1990; Deschaumes-Molinaro, Dittmar, and Vernet-Maury, 1992; Wang and Morgan, 1992; for a comprehensive overview, see Collet et al., 2013). Among the most frequently monitored autonomic parameters, cardiovascular responses and electro-dermal activity are of particular interest, and may even allow control and evaluation of the qualitative aspects of MI quality (Guillot and Collet, 2005; Guillot et al., 2009;

Roure et al., 1999). Accordingly, autonomic nervous system response patterns were found to thoroughly differentiate good and poor imagers, prompting researchers to advocate their monitoring to assess MI ability (Collet et al., 2011; Guillot et al., 2009). By providing critical information about both arousal and more qualitative processes such as the ability to adequately focus attention during MI, monitoring autonomic activity allows the ambulatory assessment of the multidimensional construct of MI, which can be directly compared to the physiological responses recorded during actual practice of the corresponding movement.

Muscular Activity and Postural Adjustments during MI

The lack/existence of a subliminal muscle activity during MI has been a subject of debate and confusion over years in the MI literature. While muscle quiescence during MI was reported in many experimental studies (Lotze et al., 1999; Mulder, de Vries, and Zijlstra, 2005), similar patterns of electromyographic activity have been observed during overt motor execution and MI, with a reduced magnitude in the simulated action (for an extensive review, see Guillot, Lebon, and Collet, 2010). Such muscle activity was observed not only in agonistic but also in antagonistic muscles, as a function of both the weight to be lifted and the muscle contraction type. Subliminal electromyographic activity was interpreted as incomplete inhibition of the motor command generated for simulation (Guillot et al., 2012a; see also Lebon et al., 2018, for in-depth consideration of motor inhibition during MI). Inconsistencies in the reports of concomitant electromyographic activity in muscles participating in the movement might be explained by differences in the experimental designs, as well as by the nature of the electromyographic recordings (Guillot et al., 2012a), muscle activity being not systematically discernible due to such confounding factors (Dickstein et al., 2005). Nonetheless, there is as yet no direct evidence that muscle activation during MI is associated with improved motor performance and/or imagery ability. Furthermore, the pattern of muscle activation has never been found to match the usual triphasic sequence generated during actual motor performance (Murphy, Nordin, and Cumming, 2008). Although the modulation of the electromyographic activity is certainly more than an epiphenomenon, these confounding factors prevent us from drawing firm conclusions and preclude clear interpretation of muscle activation/absence of activation during MI.

Likewise, whether different forms of MI are likely to influence the postural control has been questioned. Specifically, looking at whether MI is likely to increase/decrease body sway, which reflects whether a standing posture is maintained by slight backward and forward oscillations at a very low frequency, revealed inconsistent findings. Data suggest that anticipatory postural adjustments are not suppressed during MI (Boulton and Mitra, 2013; Grangeon, Guillot, and Collet, 2011), and that MI both influences body sway dynamics in a task-dependent manner, and relies on individual imagery ability (Lemos et al., 2014). Kinesthetic imagery might lead to subliminal and unintentional postural adjustments, and therefore affect balance (Stins et al., 2015), compared to visual imagery. Despite these promising findings, however, research in this area is sparse and further studies are necessary to understand the MI effect on postural adjustment in greater detail.

Modalities of Motor Imagery Practice

Determining the conceptual and theoretical issues that influence optimal MI use in sport remains a critical preoccupation for practitioners. Supporting evidence for some recommendations will here be discussed in light of the nature/content of the MI experience (MI modalities) and the major findings that have emerged from recent research on imagery processes.

Major Rules and Guidelines Structuring MI Interventions in Sport

Over the last three decades, an important number of MI models and guidelines have been developed with the aim of depicting why, when, where, and how athletes should use MI, as well as what they imagine. Overall, they provide a comprehensive explanation of imagery, including the major concepts that need to be considered with regard to the specific targeted imagery outcome. While no single set of procedures or guideline models have achieved universal approbation among practitioners and coaches, they must be seen as global guiding frameworks designed to develop more effective imagery interventions. Based on the Motor Imagery Integrative Model in Sport developed by Guillot and Collet (2008), we here distinguish four main MI outcomes, namely (i) Motor learning and Performance, (ii) Motivation, Self-confidence and Anxiety, (iii) Strategies and Problem-solving (including tactical skills), and (iv) Injury Rehabilitation (Figure 14.1). We endeavored to primarily consider both theoretical and applied suggestions of MI practice resulting from the existing scientific and sport literature, and further incorporated the main factors considered in other MI models. Without claiming to be exhaustive, we tried to cover the major key-components of MI training regarding the specific imagery outcomes that may be achieved by athletes, and their respective expected importance in each case.

Determining the Optimal Conditions of Motor Practice

As outlined in the previous section, determining the optimal conditions of MI practice directly depends on the targeted outcome. Basically, the content and the four Ws (*What, Where, When and Why*, Munroe et al., 2000) of the imagery experience can be very different if the aim is either to achieve peak performance and impact motor learning, or improve self-confidence and reduce anxiety (see Figure 14.2A for an illustration). Here, we will primarily consider the optimal conditions of MI practice when imagery interventions are designed to improve motor learning and performance (the cognitive specific imagery dimension, according to Paivio, 1985), i.e. promoting memorization and automatization, or facilitating the correction of a motor skill (Figure 14.2B).

Rules / Aim	Motor learning and Performance	Strategies and Problem-solving	Motivation, Self-confidence and Anxiety	Injury Rehabilitation		
				Psychological effects	Sport effects	Physiological effects
Spatio-temporal features of the motor skill	+++	++	-	-	+++	+++
Concurrent actual practice	+++	++	+	+	+++	+++
Combining imagery modalities/perspectives	+++	++	++	++	+++	+++
Environmental context	++	+	+	+	++	++
Physiological arousal	++	+	+	+	+	+
Positive imagery	+++	+++	+++	+++	+++	+++
Temporal congruence	+++	++	-	-	+++	+++
Varying consigns and guidelines	+++	+++	+++	+++	+++	+++
Individual characteristics	+++	+++	-	+++	++	+
Features of the motor skill	+	-	-	+	+	+
Duration and number of trials – Dose delivery	+++	++	+	+	++	++
MI accuracy/quality evaluation	+++	++	++	+	++	++

Figure 14.1 *Rules of motor imagery practice.*

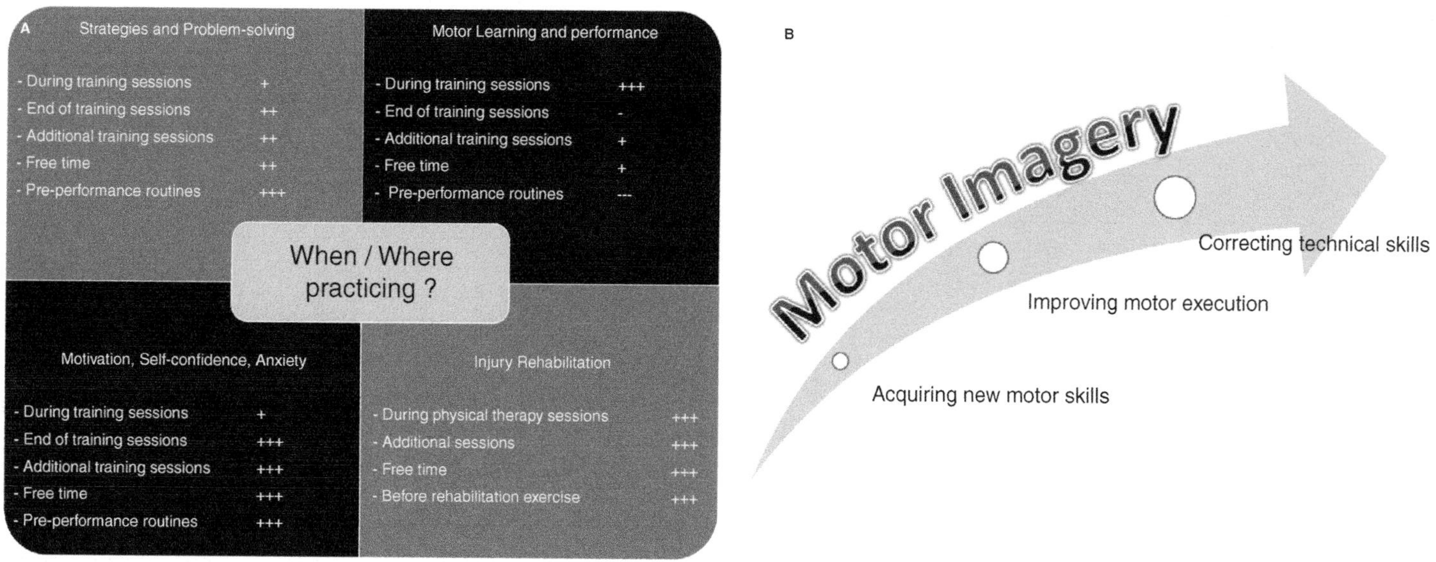

Figure 14.2 (A) Conditions of motor imagery practice and (B) Motor learning and performance outcomes.

A first variable to consider is the environmental constraints where MI is likely to be performed. Overall, there is now abundant evidence that MI should be performed in an environment that is very close to that experienced during actual practice (Guillot, Collet, and Dittmar, 2005; Holmes and Collins, 2001), in order to facilitate the ability to form an accurate and vivid mental representation of the corresponding movement. Typically, it is recommended that MI exercises should be performed while wearing adequate clothes, holding the corresponding equipment, and adopting the same position/posture as during actual practice. Wearing correct clothes and holding a piece of equipment might increase imagery vividness by enabling athletes to more easily recall appropriate kinesthetic sensations (Cumming and Williams, 2012). The environment has indeed a wider influence on cognition (MacIntyre et al., 2018), and the interaction between what persons wear and their cognition ("*enclothed cognition*") should be considered (Adam and Galinsky, 2012). Interestingly, neuroimaging evidence indicates that holding the corresponding object while imagining a movement enhances the activity of the frontoparietal network, which is likely to play a critical role in the simulation of feeling (Mizuguchi et al., 2013). In addition, performing MI in a congruent and compatible position/posture with that of actual practice is strongly recommended to facilitate the formation of adequate mental images (Lorey et al., 2009). In this vein, embedded MI is certainly the most adequate and fruitful form of MI practice to improve motor learning and performance (Guillot and Collet, 2008). If using MI in a similar environment is not possible, photographs of the venue, audio-tapes of crowd noise, or even videotapes, might be used to recreate the context of actual practice, as suggested by Wright and Smith (2009).

A second aspect that is held to influence the quality of MI is the physiological arousal reached by athletes while imagining the movement. As outlined in some early studies and contrary to popular thinking (e.g. Miller, 1994), athletes should reach a level of arousal close to that of the actual performance while imagining their movements (Guillot and Collet, 2008). While we agree with Janssen and Sheikh (1994), who reported that dynamic relaxation may be a starting point for the generation of vivid mental images and/or to reduce interferences from distractions and somatic tensions, it should certainly not be maintained during the entire MI session. Louis, Collet, and Guillot (2011) nicely demonstrated that while imagery vividness did not differ in aroused and relaxed conditions of practice, relaxation substantially altered the ability to reach temporal equivalence between imagined and actual practice, which can be very harmful for subsequent motor performance (Louis et al., 2008). The authors concluded that accuracy, speed, and vividness of the mental images are affected differently depending on the level of arousal experienced before imagery, and that extreme caution should be exercised when combining MI and relaxation to directly impact technical skills and motor performance (note that relaxing before imagery is, in contrast, important when using imagery to improve self-confidence and reduce anxiety).

Considering that most training frameworks recommend embedding MI into actual training sessions to maximize its benefits on performance (Guillot and Collet, 2008; Holmes and Collins, 2001), questioning the specific effect of physical fatigue appears critical when designing efficient MI training interventions. This variable of influence, however, has surprisingly been largely neglected in the imagery literature. Despite early challenging data (Guillot, Collet, and Ditmar, 2005), physical fatigue has been found to selectively affect MI, and more particularly its temporal congruence with physical practice (Demougeot and Papaxanthis, 2011; Di Rienzo et al., 2012). Based on these experimental studies, it still remains unclear whether the harmful effects of physical fatigue might predominantly result from a local muscular or a general physical fatigue. Di Rienzo et al. (2012) reported that physical fatigue was likely to primarily affect internal visual MI, i.e. while simulating the action as an actor of the movement. A more recent study by Kanthack et al. (2019) aimed at disentangling whether physical fatigue affected MI selectively with reference to the somatic effectors involved in the mental representation (i.e. fatigued or non-fatigued by the preceding exercise). Unexpectedly, their data supported that MI was positively influenced by a local physical fatigue elicited by resistance training exercises, and that both congruent and incongruent fatigues contributed to improve MI ability. Current knowledge of inconsistent findings outline the importance of conducting further research to understand in greater detail the relationships between fatigue states elicited by exercise and MI, in particular for complex and attention-demanding movements. Another interesting avenue that some researchers recently started to question as well is the fatigue elicited by MI practice (Rozand et al., 2014). Their results suggest that repetitive MI trials are likely to induce mental fatigue and negatively affect both mental simulation and actual execution processes of the movement.

The positive effects of coupling movements with imagery, also called dynamic imagery, have also been examined. Di Rienzo et al. (2016: 5) defined dynamic imagery as *"A form of MI where athletes adopt an adequate position of the body and move while imagining the movement, without fully performing the action, but sufficiently to embody some invariants of the motor program."* As underlined by Lorey et al. (2009), everyone is familiar with pictures of athletes moving while imagining their subsequent performance during pre-performance routines. Enhancing imagery effectiveness by performing dynamic imagery has been promoted early on by practitioners. Callow, Roberts, and Fawkes (2006) and Smith et al. (2007) nicely demonstrated that moving while imagining resulted in more vivid imagery, greater confidence to perform the task, and higher performance gains compared to MI while remaining motionless. Guillot, Moschberger, and Collet (2013) later showed that dynamic imagery enhanced both MI quality and temporal congruence between MI and motor performance, and further improved the technical efficacy of the movement. Athletes also reported more vivid representation while performing dynamic imagery. These findings sketched fruitful new directions for MI practice. Despite the substantial benefits offered by this form of practice, dynamic imagery should, however, not be systematically performed. This is in order to avoid dependence upon movement and remain able to purely simulate actions without moving. Interestingly, Kanthack et al. (2016) recently found that dynamic MI improved motor performance, except when athletes were physically exhausted, and that the current physical state affected the body representation. Under fatigue, static imagery would thus remain more effective than dynamic imagery.

Another promising avenue for MI practice is its combination with action observation (for reviews, see Eaves et al., 2016; Vogt et al., 2013). A handful of neuroimaging and electrophysiological studies have effectively demonstrated that combining MI and action observation contributed to enhance brain activations relative to each form of practice alone (Eaves et al., 2016; Macuga and Frey, 2012; Nedelko et al., 2012). A substantial overlap was also reported when comparing combined action observation/MI with action execution, hence supporting their functional equivalence (Taube et al., 2015). Practically, caution must once again be exercised as there is a spectrum ranging from congruent to conflicting action observation and MI coupling (Vogt et al., 2013), which is likely to directly influence the effectiveness of the mental training. Although research dealing with MI during action observation is still in its infancy, there is a growing body of experimental evidence supporting the contention that combining these two approaches is more effective in motor learning and rehabilitation settings than the more traditional application of MI or action observation independently (for an extensive review, see Eaves et al., 2016), thereby offering new perspectives for mental training.

A final variable of interest is related to the effects of sleep. While the contribution of sleep to motor memory consolidation is well known, research examining its effects following MI practice remains sparse. Interestingly, Debarnot et al. (2009, 2011) provided the first pieces of evidence that either a night of sleep or a daytime nap following MI is likely to elicit substantial delayed performance gains. The same authors further reported that delayed performance gains for imagined movements partially depend on motor skill complexity, with higher overnight performance improvement for complex movements (Debarnot, Castellani, and Guillot, 2012). In another original study, Debarnot et al. (2010) showed that performing a motor interference task, which is known to prevent delayed performance gains after physical training, did not alter the motor consolidation process when practicing the first motor learning through MI. These findings support that MI, and most especially variable MI (interleaved practice of different MI tasks), results in a durable and flexible abstract representation of task requirements that does not involve specific effectors, and might occasionally appear as a better alternative to consolidate motor skills than actual practice. Taken together, these data support the promising sleep contribution to motor (re)consolidation in both motor learning and (neuro)rehabilitation domains, hence suggesting that offline learning processes should be considered in greater detail in conceptual MI frameworks. Figure 14.3 illustrates the main variables of interest likely to impact MI as well as their primarily interrelationships.

Periodization and Dose Delivery of Imagery Sessions

This practical aspect of imagery interventions is certainly one of the most important to have in mind when devising effective training programs. Unfortunately, highly divergent patterns of findings emerge when summarizing data revealed by both fundamental and applied research as well as practice. Although detailed descriptions of MI training sessions and temporal parameters are usually lacking, hence preventing the drawing of firm conclusions, Schuster et al. (2011) made a systematic

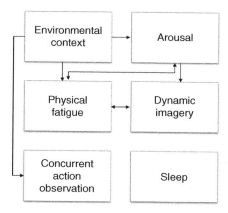

Figure 14.3 *Variables facilitating motor imagery practice.*

literature review and gathered information in five disciplines (Education, Medicine, Music, Psychology, and Sport) to determine the main characteristics of successful MI interventions. Based on this data, as well as more recent experimental evidence, short imagery intervention sessions are recommended depending upon the imagery outcome and the mental load constraints. Combining imagery and physical practice should be promoted when possible (when the aim is to improve motor learning and performance), especially using embedded imagery, but MI is a good alternative when physical practice is not available. The periodization (number of sessions per week) might vary according to the time athletes are likely to dedicate to mental training, to the nature of the motor skill or sport, as well as to the number of imagery outcomes that might be targeted simultaneously. Also, the number of imagery trials might depend on the mental fatigue perceived by the athletes and/or the time spent to practice mental training, and we postulate that it should be determined according to the duration and the complexity of the imagined movement (Figure 14.4).

Conclusion

The primary aim of this chapter was to provide an overview of the neurophysiological foundations of MI as well as to summarize how to implement and deliver effective imagery interventions. Accordingly, we examined the main influencing variables that are likely to facilitate MI and promote its beneficial effects. Readers should keep in mind that we predominantly focused on the use of imagery to impact motor learning and performance. Some of the guidelines recommended in this chapter should therefore be differently considered for other targeted imagery outcomes (see Figure 14.1 for a specific illustration of the importance of each rule of practice in the four main predetermined imagery outcomes). Spurred by these findings, examining and understanding in greater detail the most appropriate guidelines of MI practice for each specific imagery outcome and different athletes' levels of expertise will be an exciting focus of research in the coming years. Among them, the benefits and the optimal way to combine

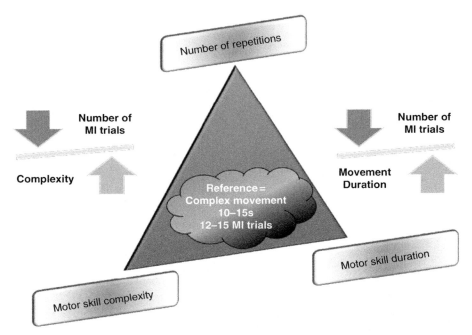

Figure 14.4 *Appropriate dosage of imagery interventions.*

action observation and MI appears a promising avenue. In addition, how MI can be considered and/or combined with other forms of practice in altered states of imagination (see Part VI: Altered States of Imagination) is of great interest. Finally, a detailed examination of the beliefs individuals have about the nature and regulation of their own imagery skills within a meta-imagery process definitely requires further experimental investigation.

References

Adam, H., and Galinsky, A. D. (2012). Enclothed Cognition. *Journal of Experimental Social Psychology*, *48*(4), 918–925.

Beyer, L., Weiss, T., Hansen, E., Wolf, A., and Seidel, A. (1990). Dynamics of Central Nervous Activation during Motor Imagination. *International Journal of Psychophysiology*, *9*, 75–80.

Borst, G. (2013). Neural Underpinning of Object Mental Imagery, Spatial Imagery, and Motor Imagery. In K. N. Oschner and S. Kosslyn (eds.), *The Oxford Handbook of Cognitive Neuroscience, Vol 2: The Cutting Edges*. Oxford, UK: Oxford University Press, 74–87.

Boulton, H., and Mitra, S. (2013). Body Posture Modulates Imagined Arm Movements and Responds to Them. *Journal of Neurophysiology*, *110*, 2617–2626.

Callow, N., Hardy, L., and Hall, C. (2001). The Effect of a Motivational General-Mastery Imagery Intervention on the Sport Confidence of High-Level Badminton Players. *Research Quarterly for Exercise and Sport*, *72*, 389–400.

Callow, N., Roberts, R., and Fawkes, J. Z. (2006). Effects of Dynamic and Static Imagery on Vividness of Imagery, Skiing Performance, and Confidence. *Journal of Imagery Research in Sport and Physical Activity, 1,* 1–15.

Callow, N., and Waters, A. (2005). The Effect of Kinesthetic Imagery on the Sport Confidence of Flat-Race Horse Jockeys. *Psychology of Sport and Exercise, 6,* 443–459.

Calvo-Merino Glaser, D. E., Grèzes, J., Passingham, R. E., and Haggard, P. (2005). Action Observation and Acquired Motor Skills: An fMRI Study with Expert Dancers. *Cerebral Cortex, 15,* 1243–1249.

Chang, Y., Lee, J. J., Seo, J. H., et al. (2011). Neural Correlates of Motor Imagery for Elite Archers. *NMR Biomedicine, 24,* 366–372.

Collet, C., Di Rienzo, F., El Hoyek, N., and Guillot, A. (2013). Autonomic Nervous System Correlates in Movement Observation and Motor Imagery. *Frontiers in Human Neuroscience, 7,* 415.

Collet, C., Guillot, A., Lebon, F., MacIntyre, T., and Moran, A. (2011). Measuring Motor Imagery Using Psychometric, Behavioural, and Psychophysiological Tools. *Exercise and Sport Sciences Reviews, 39,* 85–92.

Cumming, J., and Williams, S. E. (2012). Imagery: The Role of Imagery in Performance. In S. Murphy (ed.), *Handbook of Sport and Performance Psychology.* New York, NY: Oxford University Press, 213–232.

Debarnot, U., Castellani, E., and Guillot, A. (2012). Selective Delayed Gains Following Motor Imagery of Complex Movements. *Archives Italiennes de Biologie, 150,* 238–250.

Debarnot, U., Castellani, E., Valenza, G., Sebastiani, L., and Guillot, A. (2011). Daytime Naps Improve Motor Imagery Learning. *Cognitive and Affective Behavioral Neuroscience, 11,* 541–550.

Debarnot, U., Creveaux, T., Collet, C., Doyon, J., and Guillot, A. (2009). Sleep Contribution to Motor Memory Consolidation: A Motor Imagery Study. *Sleep, 32,* 1559–1565.

Debarnot, U., Maley, L., Rossi, D. D., and Guillot, A. (2010). Motor Interference Does Not Impair the Memory Consolidation of Imagined Movements. *Brain and Cognition, 74,* 52–57.

Debarnot, U., Sperduti, M., Di Rienzo, F., and Guillot, A. (2014). Experts' Bodies, Experts' Minds: How Physical and Mental Training Shape the Brain. *Frontiers in Human Neuroscience, 8,* 280.

Decety, J., Jeannerod, M., Germain, M., and Pastene, J. (1991). Vegetative Response during Imagined Movement Is Proportional to Mental Effort. *Behavioural Brain Research, 42,* 1–5.

Decety, J., Perani, D., Jeannerod, M., et al. (1994). Mapping Motor Representations with Positron Emission Tomography. *Nature, 371,* 600–602.

Demougeot, L., and Papaxanthis, C. (2011). Muscle Fatigue Affects Mental Simulation of Action. *Journal of Neuroscience, 31,* 10712–10720.

Deschaumes-Molinaro, C., Dittmar, A., and Vernet-Maury, E. (1992). Autonomic Nervous System Response Patterns Correlate with Mental Imagery. *Physiology and Behavior, 51,* 1021–1027.

Di Rienzo, F., Collet, C., Hoyek, N., and Guillot, A. (2012). Selective Effects of Physical Fatigue on Motor Imagery Accuracy. *PLoS One, 7,* e47207, 1–11.

Di Rienzo, F., Collet, C., Hoyek, N., and Guillot, A. (2014). Impact of Neurologic Deficits on Motor Imagery: A Systematic Review of Clinical Evaluations. *Neuropsychology Review, 24,* 116–147.

Di Rienzo, F., Debarnot, U., Daligault, D., et al. (2016). Online and Offline Performance Gains Following Motor Imagery: A Comprehensive Review of Behavioral and Neuroimaging Studies. *Frontiers in Human Neuroscience, 10,* article 315, 1–15.

Dickstein, R., Gazit-Grunwald, M., Plax, M., Dunsky, A., and Marcovitz, E. (2005). EMG Activity in Selected Target Muscles during Imagery Rising on Tiptoes in Healthy Adults and Poststroke Hemiparetic Patients. *Journal of Motor Behavior, 37,* 475–483.

Doyon, J., and Benali, H. (2005). Reorganization and Plasticity in the Adult Brain during Learning of Motor Skills. *Current Opinion in Neurobiology, 15,* 161–167.

Driskell, J. E., Copper, C., and Moran, A. (1994). Does Mental Practice Enhance Performance? *Journal of Applied Psychology, 79,* 481–492.

Eaves, D. L., Riach, M., Holmes, P. S., and Wright, D. J. (2016). Motor Imagery during Action Observation: A Brief Review of Evidence, Theory and Future Research Opportunities. *Frontiers in Neuroscience, 10,* 514.

Ehrsson, H. H., Geyer, S., and Naito, E. (2003). Imagery of Voluntary Movement of Fingers, Toes and Tongue Activates Corresponding Body-Part-Specific Motor Representations. *Journal of Neurophysiology, 90,* 3304–3316.

Feltz, D. L., and Landers, D. M. (1983). The Effects of Mental Practice on Motor Skill Learning and Performance: A Meta-Analysis. *Journal of Sport and Exercise Psychology, 5,* 25–57.

Filgueiras, A., Quintas Conde, E. F., and Hall, C. R. (2017). The Neural Basis of Kinesthetic and Visual Imagery in Sports: An ALE Meta-Analysis. *Brain Imaging Behaviour, 12,* 1513–1523.

Grangeon, M., Guillot, A., and Collet, C. (2011). Postural Control during Visual and Kinesthetic Motor Imagery. *Applied Psychophysiology and Biofeedback, 36,* 47–56.

Guillot, A., and Collet, C. (2005). Contribution from Neurophysiological and Psychological Methods to the Study of Motor Imagery. *Brain Research Review, 50,* 387–397.

(2008). Construction of the Motor Imagery Integrative Model in Sport: A Review and Theoretical Investigation of Motor Imagery Use. *International Review of Sport and Exercise Psychology, 1,* 31–44.

Guillot, A., Collet, C., and Dittmar, A. (2005). Influence of Environmental Context on Motor Imagery Quality. *Biology of Sport, 22,* 215–226.

Guillot, A., Collet, C., Nguyen, V.A., et al. (2009). Brain Activity during Visual versus Kinesthetic Imagery: An fMRI Study. *Human Brain Mapping, 30,* 2157–2172.

Guillot, A., Di Rienzo, F., Macintyre, T., Moran, A., and Collet, C. (2012a). Imagining Is Not Doing but Involves Specific Motor Commands: A Review of Experimental Data Related to Motor Inhibition. *Frontiers in Human Neuroscience, 6,* 1–22.

Guillot, A., Haguenauer, M., Dittmar, A., and Collet, C. (2005). Effect of a Fatiguing Protocol on Motor Imagery Accuracy. *European Journal of Applied Physiology, 95*(2–3), 186–190.

Guillot, A., Hoyek, N., Louis, M., and Collet, C. (2012b). Understanding the Timing of Motor Imagery: Recent Findings and Future Directions. *International Review of Sport and Exercise Psychology, 5,* 3–22.

Guillot, A., Lebon, F., and Collet, C. (2010). Electromyographic Activity during Motor Imagery. In A. Guillot and C. Collet (eds.), *The Neurophysiological Foundations of Mental and Motor Imagery.* New York, NY: Oxford University Press, 83–93.

Guillot, A., Moschberger, K., and Collet, C. (2013). Coupling Movement with Imagery as a New Perspective for Motor Imagery Practice. *Behavioural Brain Functions 9,* 8.

Halpern, A. R. (2012). Dynamic Aspects of Musical Imagery. *Annals of New York Academy of Science*, *1252*, 200–205.

Hardwick, R. M., Caspers, S., Eickhoff, S. B., and Swinnen, S. P. (2018). Neural Correlates of Action: Comparing Meta-Analyses of Imagery, Observation, and Execution. *Neuroscience and Biobehavioral Reviews*, *94*, 31–44.

Hétu, S., Grégoire, M., Saimpont, A., et al. (2013). The Neural Network of Motor Imagery: An ALE Meta-Analysis. *Neuroscience and Biobehavioral Reviews*, *37*(5), 930–949.

Holmes, P. S., and Collins, D. J. (2001). The PETTLEP Approach to Motor Imagery: A Functional Equivalence Model for Sport Psychologists. *Journal of Applied Sport Psychology*, *13*, 60–83.

Jackson, P. L., Lafleur, M. F., Malouin, F., Richards, C. L., and Doyon, J. (2003). Functional Cerebral Reorganization Following Motor Sequence Learning through Mental Practice with Motor Imagery. *NeuroImage*, *20*, 1171–1180.

Jackson, P. L., Meltzoff, A. L., and Decety, J. (2006). Neural Circuits Involved in Imitation and Perspective-Taking. *NeuroImage*, *31*, 429–439.

Janssen, J. J., and Sheikh, A. A. (1994). Enhancing Athletic Performance through Imagery: An Overview. In: A. A. Sheikh and E. R. Korn (eds.), *Imagery and Sports Physical Performance*. Amityville, NY: Bayood Publishing, 175–181.

Jeannerod, M. (1994). The Representing Brain: Neural Correlates of Motor Intention and Imagery. *Behavioural Brain Sciences*, *17*, 187–202.

(2001). Neural Simulation of Action: A Unifying Mechanism for Motor Cognition. *NeuroImage*, *14*, S103–109.

(2006). *Motor Cognition: What Actions Tell to the Self*. New York, NY: Oxford University Press.

Jiang, D., Edwards, M. G., Mullins, P., and Callow, N. (2015). The Neural Substrates for the Different Modalities of Movement Imagery. *Brain and Cognition*, *97*, 22–31.

Kanthack, T. F. D., Guillot, A., Altimari, L. R., et al. (2016). Selective Efficacy of Static and Dynamic Imagery in Different States of Physical Fatigue. *PLoS One*, *11*, e0149654.

Kanthack, T. F. D., Guillot, A., Clémençon, M., and Di Rienzo, F. (2019). Effect of Physical Fatigue Elicited by Continuous and Intermittent Exercise on Motor Imagery Ability. *Submitted for publication*.

Lacourse, M. G., Turner, J. A., Randolph-Orr, E., Schandler, S. L., and Cohen, M. J. (2004). Cerebral and Cerebellar Sensorimotor Plasticity Following Motor Imagery-Based Mental Practice of a Sequential Movement. *Journal of Rehabilitation Research and Development*, *41*, 505–524.

Lafleur, M. F., Jackson, P. L., Malouin, F., et al. (2002). Motor Learning Produces Parallel Dynamic Functional Changes during the Execution and Imagination of Sequential Foot Movements. *NeuroImage*, *16*, 142–157.

Lebon, F., Horn, U., Domin, M., and Lotze, M. (2018). Motor Imagery Training: Kinesthetic Imagery Strategy and Inferior Parietal fMRI Activation. *Human Brain Mapping*, *39*, 1805–1813.

Lemos, T., Souza, N. S., Horsczaruk, C. H., et al. (2014). Motor Imagery Modulation of Body Sway Is Task-Dependent and Relies on Imagery Ability. *Frontiers in Human Neuroscience*, *8*, 290.

Lorey, B., Bischoff, M., Pilgramm, S., et al. (2009). The Embodied Nature of Motor Imagery: The Influence of Posture and Perspective. *Experimental Brain Research*, *194*, 233–243.

Lotze, M., and Halsband, U. (2006). Motor Imagery. *Journal of Physiology (Paris)*, *99*, 386–395.

Lotze, M., Montoya, P., Erb, M., et al. (1999). Activation of Cortical and Cerebellar Motor Areas during Executed and Imagined Hand Movements: An fMRI Study. *Journal of Cognitive Neuroscience*, *11*, 491–501.

Lotze, M., Scheler, G., Tan, H. R., Braun, C., and Birbaumer, N. (2003). The Musician's Brain: Functional Imaging of Amateurs and Professionals during Performance and Imagery. *NeuroImage*, *20*, 1817–1829.

Louis, C., Collet, C., and Guillot, A. (2011). Differences in Motor Imagery Times during Aroused and Relaxed Conditions. *Journal of Cognitive Psychology*, *23*, 374–382.

Louis, M., Guillot, A., Maton, S., Doyon, J., and Collet, C. (2008). Effect of Imagined Movement Speed on Subsequent Motor Performance. *Journal of Motor Behavior*, *40*, 117–132.

MacIntyre, T. E., Madan, C. R., Moran, A. P., Collet, C., and Guillot, A. (2018). Motor Imagery, Performance and Motor Rehabilitation. *Progress in Brain Research*, *240*, 141–159.

Macuga, K. L., and Frey, S. H. (2012). Neural Representations Involved in Observed, Imagined, and Imitated Actions Are Dissociable and Hierarchically Organized. *NeuroImage*, *59*, 2798–2807.

Miller, E. (1994). Optimal Sports Performance Imagery. In A. A. Sheikh and E. R. Korn (eds.), *Imagery and Sports Physical Performance*. Amityville, NY: Bayood Publishing, 175–181.

Milton, J., Solodkin, A., Hlustik, P., and Small, S. L. (2007). The Mind of Expert Motor Performance Is Cool and Focused. *NeuroImage*, *35*, 804–813.

Mizuguchi, N., Nakata, H., Hayashi, T., et al. (2013). Brain Activity during Motor Imagery of an Action with an Object: A Functional Magnetic Resonance Imaging Study. *Neuroscience Research*, *76*(3), 150–155.

Mizuguchi, N., Nakata, H., and Kanosue, K. (2014). Activity of Right Premotor-Parietal Regions Dependent upon Imagined Force Level: An fMRI Study. *Frontiers in Human Neuroscience*, *8*, 810.

Moran, A., Guillot, A., MacIntyre, T., and Collet, C. (2012). Re-imagining Mental Imagery: Building Bridges Between Cognitive and Sport Psychology. *British Journal of Psychology*, *103*, 224–247.

Morris, T., Spittle, M., and Perry, C. (2004). Imagery in Sport. In T. Morris and J. Summers (eds.), *Sport Psychology: Theory, Applications and Issues*. 2nd edition. Brisbane, Australia: Wiley, 344–383.

Mulder, T., de Vries, S., and Zijlstra, S. (2005). Observation, Imagination and Execution of an Effortful Movement: More Evidence for a Central Explanation of Motor Imagery. *Experimental Brain Research*, *163*, 344–351.

Munroe, K. J., Giacobbi, P. R., Hall, C., and Weinberg, R. (2000). The Four Ws of Imagery Use: Where, When, Why and What. *The Sport Psychologist*, *14*, 119–137.

Munzert, J., Lorey, B., and Zentgraf, K. (2009). Cognitive Motor Processes: The Role of Motor Imagery in the Study of Motor Representations. *Brain Research Reviews*, *60*, 306–326.

Murphy, S., Nordin, S. M., and Cumming, J. (2008). Imagery in Sport, Exercise and Dance. In T. Horn (ed.), *Advances in Sport Psychology*. Champaign, IL: Human Kinetics, 306–315.

Nedelko, V., Hassa, T., Hamzei, F., Schoenfeld, M. A., and Dettmers, C. (2012). Action Imagery Combined with Action Observation Activates more Corticomotor Regions than Action Observation Alone. *Journal of Neurology and Physical Therapy*, *36*(4), 182–188.

O, J., and Hall, C. (2009). A Quantitative Analysis of Athletes' Voluntary Use of Slow Motion, Real Time, and Fast Motion Images. *Journal of Applied Sport Psychology*, *21*, 15–30.

O'Shea, H., and Moran, A. (2017). Does Motor Simulation Theory Explain the Cognitive Mechanisms Underlying Motor Imagery? A Critical Review. *Frontiers in Human Neuroscience*, *11*, 72.

Paivio, A. (1985). Cognitive and Motivational Functions of Imagery in Human Performance. *Canadian Journal of Applied Sport Science*, *10*(4), 22S–28S.

Roure, R., Collet, C., Deschaumes-Molinaro, C., et al. (1999). Imagery Quality Estimated by Autonomic Response Is Correlated to Sporting Performance Enhancement. *Physiology and Behavior*, *66*, 63–72.

Rozand, V., Lebon, F., Papaxanthis, C., and Lepers, R. (2014). Does a Mental Training Session Induce Neuromuscular Fatigue? *Medicine Science in Sports and Exercise*, *46*, 1981–1989.

Ruby, P., and Decety, J. (2001). Effect of Subjective Perspective Taking during Simulation of Action: A PET Investigation of Agency. *Nature Neuroscience*, *4*, 546–550.

Sauvage, C., Jissendi, P., Seignan, S., Manto, M., and Habas, C. (2013). Brain Areas Involved in the Control of Speed during a Motor Sequence of the Foot: Real Movement versus Mental Imagery. *Journal of Neuroradiology*, *40*, 267–280.

Schmidt, T. T., Ostwald, D., and Blankenburg, F. (2014). Imaging Tactile Imagery: Changes in Brain Connectivity Support Perceptual Grounding of Mental Images in Primary Sensory Cortices. *NeuroImage*, *98*, 216–224.

Schuster, C., Hilfiker, R., Amft, O., et al. (2011). Best Practice for Motor Imagery: A Systematic Literature Review on Motor Imagery Training Elements in Five Different Disciplines. *BMC Medicine*, *9*, 75.

Seiler, B. D., Monsma, E. V., and Newman-Norlund, R. D. (2015). Biological Evidence of Imagery Abilities: Intraindividual Differences. *Journal of Sport and Exercise Psychology*, *37*, 421–435.

Sharma, N., Jones, P. S., Carpenter, T. A., and Baron, J. C. (2008). Mapping the Involvement of BA 4a and 4p during Motor Imagery. *NeuroImage*, *41*, 92–99.

Shirazipour, C. H., Munroe-Chandler, K. J., Loughead, T. M., and Vander Laan, A. G. (2016). The Effect of Image Speed on Novice Golfers' Performance in a Putting Task. *Journal of Imagery Research in Sport and Physical Activity*, *11*, 1–12.

Smith, D., Wright, C., Allsopp, A., and Westhead, H. (2007). It's All in the Mind: PETTLEP-Based Imagery and Sport Performance. *Journal of Applied Sport Psychology*, *19*, 80–92.

Solodkin, A., Hlustik, P., Chen, E. E., and Small, S. L. (2004). Fine Modulation in Network Activation during Motor Execution and Motor Imagery. *Cerebral Cortex*, *14*, 1246–1255.

Stins, J. F., Schneider, I. K., Koole, S. L., and Beek, P. J. (2015). The Influence of Motor Imagery on Postural Sway: Differential Effects of Type of Body Movement and Person Perspective. *Advances in Cognitive Psychology*, *11*(3): 77–83.

Taube, W., Mouthon, M., Leukel, C., et al. (2015). Brain Activity during Observation and Motor Imagery of Different Balance Tasks: An fMRI Study. *Cortex*, *64*, 102–114.

van der Meulen, M., Allali, G., Rieger, S. W., Assal, F., and Vuilleumier, P. (2014). The Influence of Individual Motor Imagery Ability on Cerebral Recruitment during Gait Imagery. *Human Brain Mapping*, *35*, 455–470.

Vogt, S., Di Rienzo, F., Collet, C., Collins, A., and Guillot, A. (2013). Multiple Roles of Motor Imagery during Action Observation. *Frontiers in Human Neuroscience*, *7*.

Wang, Y., and Morgan, W. P. (1992). The Effect of Imagery Perspectives on the Psychophysiological Responses to Imagined Exercise. *Behavioural Brain Research*, *52*(2), 167–174.

Wei, G., and Luo, J. (2010). Sport Expert's Motor Imagery: Functional Imaging of Professional Motor Skills and Simple Motor Skills. *Brain Research*, *1341*, 52–62.

Wright, C. J., and Smith, D. (2009). The Effect of PETTLEP Imagery on Strength Performance. *International Journal of Sport and Exercise Psychology*, *7*, 18–31.

15 Temporal Mental Imagery

Gerardo Viera and Bence Nanay

Mental Imagery

The definition of mental imagery as perceptual processing that is not triggered by corresponding sensory stimulation in the relevant sense modality is a fair summary of the way the concept of mental imagery is used in psychology and neuroscience (Nanay, 2018a; Nanay, forthcoming; Pearson et al., 2015). In a recent review article on mental imagery, for example, the authors say: "We use the term 'mental imagery' to refer to representations ... of sensory information without a direct external stimulus" (Pearson et al., 2015: 590). And in a much older paper written by Kosslyn, Behrmann, and Jeannerod, the authors characterize the concept of visual mental imagery as "'seeing' in the absence of the appropriate immediate sensory input" (Kosslyn, Behrmann, and Jeannerod, 1995a: 1335).

But it is also easy to see that many everyday examples of mental imagery will also fit this definition. When you close your eyes and visualize an apple, there is no sensory input at all – your eyes are closed. But there is early cortical perceptual processing (sometimes as early as in the primary visual cortex – see Kosslyn et al., 1995b; Page, Duhamel, and Crognale, 2011; Slotnick, Thompson, and Kosslyn, 2005). You have early cortical perceptual processing that is not triggered by corresponding sensory stimulation in the relevant sense modality.

A lot more needs to be said about how to cash out this definition of mental imagery in general and temporal mental imagery in particular. Take vision as an example (see Bullier, 2004; Grill-Spector and Mallach, 2004). The light hits your retina. Then this sensory stimulation is processed via the primary visual pathway that connects neural networks in the retina to the primary visual cortex (V1) via the lateral geniculate nucleus (LGN) in the thalamus. Outputs from V1 activate other parts of the visual cortex and are also fed forward to a range of extrastriate areas (V2, V3, V4/V8, V3a, V5/MT).

Given that the early visual cortices are retinotopic, we can identify direction-sensitive neurons in, say, the primary visual cortex, that are sensitive to the retinal activation of a certain part of the retina. If there is retinal activation of a certain shape, then these direction-sensitive neurons will fire reliably. If, for example, the sensory stimulation is the visual input of a straight horizontal line in the middle of the visual field, then those direction-sensitive neurons in the middle of the field of the retinotopic primary visual cortex that are sensitive to horizontal input will fire.

This counts as corresponding sensory input. But a part of the primary visual cortex can be active even though there is no corresponding sensory input. When this happens, we talk of mental imagery.

In the visual case, it is easy enough to check whether there is (spatial) correspondence between the early cortices and the retina, given the retinotopy of the early visual cortices. Simply put, if there is a triangle in the middle of the retina and there is also an isomorphic triangle in the primary visual cortex, we have a match: The perceptual processing in V1 is triggered by corresponding sensory stimulation in the relevant sense modality.

But if there is no triangle in the middle of the retina but there is still a triangle in the V1, then we have no match: The perceptual processing in the primary visual cortex is not triggered by corresponding sensory stimulation in the relevant sense modality. In other words, we have an instance of mental imagery.

Such correspondences are relatively easy and straightforward enough to check in the case of V1. But it is neither easy nor straightforward if we go a bit further up in the visual processing hierarchy or if we focus on the non-visual sense modalities. Or if we focus on temporal and not spatial correspondence.

So instead of only relying on retinotopy, which is a convenient but not usually feasible way of assessing correspondence between sensory input and perceptual processing, we need a more general method of telling cases of correspondence from cases of non-correspondence (that is, mental imagery).

Suppose that a certain sensory stimulation-type, S1, reliably causes the perceptual processing of a type, P1, in a specific agent, A1. Each time A1 gets S1 as sensory input, A1's perceptual system engages in P1 processing. However, if we get P1 in this agent, but P1 is not triggered by S1 but rather by S2, which does not reliably cause P1 in A1, then we have a case of mental imagery. Indexing to an agent is required here, since for any given stimulation-type, different people may exhibit different subsequent sensory processing as a result of a range of individual differences.

Some clarifications are needed. S1 is a sensory stimulation-type, so it is a type of event that happens to our sense organs. P1 is perceptual processing, by which we mean processing in early cortical areas, from V1 to MT. There is an ongoing debate about how to delineate perception from cognition (or from post-perceptual processing, see Beck, 2018; Nanay, 2012; Phillips, 2019), but we do not need to take sides in this debate here (on tricky issues such as whether face perception is genuine perception). Even those who would want to restrict perceptual processing to the bare minimum would count the areas V1 to MT as perceptual areas.

Mental imagery may or may not be voluntary or conscious. Remember that it is defined in terms of early cortical activation with a certain kind of etiology (namely early cortical activation that is not triggered by corresponding sensory stimulation). So no necessary reference to consciousness or volition is built into this definition.

Amodal completion will count as mental imagery in the sense just described (Nanay, 2010, 2018b). When you see a cat behind a picket fence, you amodally complete the occluded parts of this perceived cat. There is early cortical perceptual processing of the occluded outlines of the hidden parts of the cat, but this processing does not correspond to any outline on the retina (see Bakin, Nakayama, and Gilbert, 2000; Ban, Yamamoto, and Hanakawa, 2013; Bushnell et al., 2011; Emmanuoil and Ro, 2014; Hazenberg et al., 2014; Hedgé et al., 2008; Komatsu, 2006; Kovacs et al., 1995; Lee and Nguyen, 2001; Lee et al., 2012; Pan et al., 2012; Scherzer and Ekroll, 2015; Shibata et al., 2011; Smith and Muckli, 2010; Sugita, 1999). The part of the retina that would correspond to the amodally completed outline is the homogenous monochrome white of the picket.

The amodal completion example is important for a number of reasons. First, it highlights that the concept of correspondence should be understood as local correspondence. In some (most) cases of amodal completion, the completion can be fully explained in a bottom-up manner: The entire retinal stimulation does reliably cause the amodally completed outlines in the entire V1. But the local input of the missing (because occluded) outline does not reliably cause the activation of this outline in the V1. So while there is global correspondence between the entire state of retinal activation and the subsequent spatiotopic sensory processes, there is no local correspondence and hence the amodal completion of this occluded outline (in V1) is not triggered by (locally) corresponding sensory stimulation in the relevant sense modality. Amodal completion amounts to mental imagery.

Amodal completion is also important because it highlights that mental imagery can be bottom-up but it may also be top-down influenced. The amodal completion of the hidden parts of the cat often depends on our prior knowledge of the anatomy of cats. Mental imagery can be bottom-up or top-down as can amodal completion. And the same is true of temporal mental imagery.

The Case for Temporal Mental Imagery

A helpful aspect of this way of thinking about mental imagery is that this could be applied to the temporal case very easily. Visual sensory stimulation reliably leads to V1 activation in 30 milliseconds (see Rauschenberger et al., 2006; Rolls and Tovee, 1994; Thorpe et al., 1996, for summaries). If we have V1 activation but no visual sensory stimulation that would have preceded this V1 activation by 30 milliseconds, then there is no temporal correspondence. The perceptual processing (in V1) is not triggered by temporally corresponding sensory stimulation. We have an instance of temporal mental imagery. As with mental imagery in general, temporal correspondence is also relative to the individual – some of us are slower than others. Temporal mental imagery is perceptual processing that is triggered by spatially corresponding sensory stimulation in the appropriate sense modality, but where this perceptual processing does not temporally correspond with the incoming stimulation.

There is a certain ambiguity in the definition of temporal mental imagery as early perceptual processing that is not triggered by temporally corresponding sensory stimulation. In cases in which there is no local correspondence of any sort between perceptual processes and sensory stimulation, there will by default also be no temporal correspondence (this would include cases in which you close your eyes and imagine an apple). Mental imagery of this sort would automatically count as temporal mental imagery. However, for our purposes in this chapter, we mean something narrower by temporal mental imagery. The cases on which we will focus are ones in which there is local sensory stimulation that corresponds, along some dimension with the perceptual processes, yet fails to temporally correspond with early perceptual processes. For instance, in the visual case, we have in mind cases such as predictive and postdictive perception in which there are perceptual processes that retinotopically correspond with the sensory stimulation but fail to correspond with the timing of the sensory stimulation.

Temporal correspondence can fail in two directions: The perceptual processing may come earlier than it should – this is a case of "predictive temporal mental imagery." Alternatively, it may come later than it should – this would amount to "postdictive temporal mental imagery."

One important advantage of this way of thinking about temporal mental imagery is that it can help us to explain a recurring theme in thinking about the experience of time. This was summarized memorably by William James, who writes that:

> . . . the practically cognized present is no knife-edge, but a saddle-back, with a certain breadth of its own. (James, 1890: 609)

In other words, our experiences have a certain temporal thickness. But what does this mean exactly? Here is a more contemporary philosophical spin on what James had in mind:

> The dynamic content of our experience at short timescales is metaphysically dependent on the content of experience over longer timescales (Phillips, 2011: 3).

So when we have an experience of, say, watching a football fly through the air and bounce off the goalpost, our experience should not be characterized as the sequence of dimensionless point-like experiences. Rather, my experience of the ball right now somehow represents the ball a split second ago and also represents where the ball would be in a split second. This phenomenon is often described, following James, as the "specious present."

Here is the saddle-back (Figure 15.1). The middle of the saddle would be the present. But we somehow represent the two flanks of this bell-shape, as well. The question is: how?

This raises some deep issues about the nature of perception. How is it possible to perceive something that is not present? The ball a split second ago is no longer

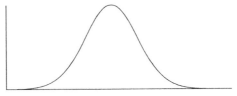

Figure 15.1 *A pictorial representation of the specious present. The peak of the saddle back would be the present moment, and our overall experience extends to a lesser degree to the past and future.*

present, and the ball in a split second is not present yet. According to an influential line of thought in philosophy, we can only perceive what is there to be perceived (e.g. Grice, 1961). But when it comes to time, only the present is present (sic!). So the past, let alone the future can't be perceptually represented.

There are various sophisticated ways of dealing with this problem – for example, extending the temporal dimension of not just the content, but also the vehicle of perceptual representations (see Phillips, 2010). But if we take the concept of temporal mental imagery seriously, then there is no need to complicate things unnecessarily.

We represent the flanks of the bell-shape by means of temporal mental imagery. We know that the early cortical processing of a temporal event has a much wider temporal profile then the retinal event. So some of this perceptual processing will be triggered by corresponding sensory stimulation (the middle), but most of it will not be. It will count as temporal mental imagery in which the early cortical processing is not triggered by temporally corresponding sensory stimulation. It is triggered by sensory stimulation that is either too early or too late.

The further away we veer from the sensory stimulation-driven perceptual processing (the middle of the saddle-shape), the bigger the role temporal mental imagery will play.

Amodal Completion and the Specious Present

To understand the role of mental imagery in an account of the specious present, it is useful to revisit the amodal completion case. When we see the cat hiding behind the picket fence, our sensory systems are only in causal contact with the unoccluded parts of the cat and the slats of the fence. Yet we do not take ourselves to only perceive undetached cat slices, but instead we take ourselves to see a complete cat partly hidden by the fence. This alone, however, does not establish that mental imagery is at play. Our sense of seeing an entire but partly occluded cat could be the result of a post-sensory belief about the world. It was an empirical discovery, not introspection, that showed that our early perceptual processes do not merely represent a cat-picket-cat pattern that corresponds with sensory stimulation, but instead these early perceptual processes (as early as V1 and V2) represent the entire partly occluded shape of the cat. In this way, amodal completion (in at least some central cases) employs perceptual processes that represent cat contours but that are retinotopically associated with regions of the retina that are receiving picket-stimulation. As a result, we have empirical evidence for the role of mental imagery in amodal completion.

Now, turn to the case of the specious present. When we see a football ricochet off of a goalpost, our current sensory stimulation is driven by the current state of the world (taking into account the time it takes the light to travel from the ball to the retina). Yet, just as in the amodal completion case, we do not have the sense that we are only perceiving the static snapshot of the world that is causally impinging on our retinas, but instead, we perceive a complete dynamic temporal interval. Following

James's characterization of the specious present, we seem to not only perceive the current location of the ball, but we are also perceptually aware of where the ball was a split second ago, of the ball's impact with the goalpost, and where the ball will likely be in a split second from now. In this way, the specious present is a temporal analog of the amodal completion case. While in the amodal completion case perception fills in spatial details of the perceived scene, the specious present fills in temporal details of the perceived scenario (i.e. the temporal structure of how events unfold over a period of time). What is left to establish is whether this sense of being aware of a temporally extended interval, the specious present, involves mental imagery or not.

On one philosophical account of temporal perception, *extensionalism*,[1] accounts of the specious present need not employ any appeal to mental imagery. According to extensionalism, the experience of a sequence of events in the world, say B as following A, requires that the overall experience can be decomposed into an experience of A and an experience of B, and that the experience of A, understood as a mental/neural event, precedes the experience of B. In the case of seeing the ball ricochet off the goalpost, our overall experience must decompose into distinct experiences of the ball at various locations on its trajectory, including an experience of the impact, and that these experiences must stand in the appropriate temporal relations to one another. In cases of straightforward veridical perception, the sequence of sensory stimulations will lead to a sequence of perceptual processes that underpin these distinct experiences. If, as the extensionalist would suggest, this suffices for an account of the specious present, then no temporal mental imagery would be needed. Every step of the processing sequence would appropriately correspond to the temporal structure of the incoming sequence of sensory stimulation.

However, a mere sequence of experiences cannot by itself account for the perception of temporal order. In order to perceive the ball *as ricocheting* off the goalpost, it is not enough that we recently perceived the ball approaching the goalpost, then impacting the goalpost, and that now we are perceiving the ball as having some distance from the goalpost. Instead, for us to currently be perceiving the ball as ricocheting off of the goalpost, we must somehow retain information about earlier perceptual states that represented the ball's approach and impact with the goalpost. As Geoffrey Lee (2014b) put it, our prior sensory responses to the world must leave behind traces in the current state of the perceptual system that can be usefully integrated with the current incoming sensory signals. To use another example, when we perceive a crash of thunder as following a flash of lightning, we can only perceive this temporal relation once the thunder influences our sensory receptors. But by that time we will have already processed the signal from the flash of lightning. If the prior perceptual processes representing the lightning left no trace in the current state of the brain, then we would be unable to perceive the thunder as following the lightning. The thunder would simply appear to occur in temporal isolation.

---

1 Terminology in the literature has not been settled. In calling the view extensionalism we are following usage in (Lee, 2014a); however, the view has also been called molecularism (Hoerl, 2009), the process-view (Lee, 2014b), and the naïve-theory of temporal perception (Phillips, 2010; 2014).

There must be some means, then, by which prior perceptual states leave a trace in the current workings of the perceptual/cognitive system. The question, then, is whether temporal mental imagery has a role to play in how these traces are retained. That is, is this information retained in perceptual processes that do not temporally correspond with the current sensory stimulation? This is not something that any armchair philosophical analysis can determine. Instead, just as in the case of amodal completion, we must turn to the sciences to see whether the relevant representational mechanisms amount to mental imagery.

Since the research on temporal perception is still very much in its infancy our claims here will be circumscribed. We cannot make general claims to the end that in all cases the specious present requires temporal mental imagery. In fact, given the variety of means by which perceptual systems keep track of the temporal structure of our world, it may very well turn out that the speciousness of the present will have several distinct accounts that apply in different contexts. However, what will follow are cases in which the empirical evidence clearly points to the role of temporal mental imagery in accounting for the specious present.[2]

Prediction and Mental Imagery

As James noticed, the breadth of the specious present extends into the past as well as the future. It involves predictive elements that provide us with expectations about what is to come. When we listen to a familiar song, for instance, we notice immediately if the musician misses a note. Or when we see two cyclists approaching an intersection from different directions, we grimace in expectation of the coming collision. Why do we react in these ways? A natural explanation is that we form predictions or expectations of what is going to occur. Any representation of these expectations would seem to precede the relevant sensory stimulation that would lead to perceptual processing of these expected scenarios. The question is, once again, whether these expectations are based in temporal mental imagery – that is, perceptual processes that do not temporally correspond to sensory stimulation (see Zatorre and Halpern, 2005), or whether these expectations are due to non-perceptual capacities that represent the expected scenarios.

While some violations of expectation might be the result of non-perceptual processes, in a recent study by Ekman, Kok, and de Lange (2017), they show that in at least some cases expectations about object trajectories employ temporal mental imagery. In their study they familiarized subjects with a particular dot sequence (a dot moving from the top-left of a monitor to the top-right) and using high speed fMRI they were able to

---

2 The examples discussed in this chapter are primarily visual ones. The general point that Geoffrey Lee describes, however, applies to all modalities. To experience succession in any non-visual modality, for instance hearing a tone increase in pitch over a temporal interval, requires the retention of information over time. More specifically, however, postdictive phenomena similar to those described below in vision can be found in touch (e.g. the cutaneous rabbit illusion [Geldard and Sherrick, 1972; Grush 2005, 2007]) and in audition (e.g. the auditory flash-lag effect (Alais and Burr, 2003)). However, in both cases the required imaging studies have not been conducted to see whether or not there is the appropriate temporal non-correspondence between the timing of sensory stimulation in these other modalities and the relevant perceptual processes.

successfully measure BOLD responses in V1 for retinotopic locations corresponding with the incoming sensory stimulation. In this way, they were able to map out the trajectory of the dot sequence in V1. They then ran subjects in two distinct conditions. In the control sequence they presented subjects with an initial display in which the dot was located at the end-location of the familiarization sequence (i.e. the dot was shown in the top-right). The corresponding BOLD response only showed activity in V1 areas with receptive fields for the location of the presented stimulus. In the *preplay* condition, subjects were presented with an initial display in which the dot was located at the start location of the familiarization sequence (i.e. the dot was shown in top-left). Interestingly, in this condition subjects showed BOLD responses that corresponded to a time-compressed trajectory of the entire familiarization sequence. That is, they showed BOLD responses for a dot moving from the top-left to the top-right of the display. The response was time-compressed in that the cortical processes traced out the expected trajectory of the dot quicker that they would if they were responding to the actual dot sequence. Furthermore, it was shown that when this cortical preplay was elicited by the initial dot display, subsequent detection performance for the location of the dot along that trajectory was enhanced.

In this case, we have predictive (or anticipatory) temporal mental imagery in that we have early cortical perceptual processes that do not temporally correspond with the relevant sensory stimulation. The V1 activity occurs *prior to* the relevant sensory stimulation.[3]

Postdiction, Apparent Motion, and Mental Imagery

Postdictive perception picks out a range of perceptual phenomena in which the perception of an earlier stimulus is modulated by the perception of a later stimulus. A classic example of postdiction is apparent motion. A standard setup for eliciting apparent motion is the following: A flash of light is presented at T_1 at location L_1, then a second light is presented at T_3 at location L_3. When presented with this sequence, subjects do not perceive the display as consisting of two spatiotemporally separated flashes of light, but instead, they perceive the display as consisting of a single light that smoothly travels from L_1 to L_3 while passing through the intermediary location of L_2 at T_2.

Researchers have found that in early perceptual cortices (as early as V1) (Larsen et al., 2006; Muckli et al., 2005) there is retinotopic activity that corresponds with the apparent trajectory and not just with the presentation of the two spatially separate flashes of light. In this way, the perceptual processes that are associated with activity of retinal regions encoding for the location L_2 are active despite not corresponding to the retinal activity at that retinal location. However, this finding only shows that there is a spatial form of mental imagery that underpins the perception of apparent motion.

---

3 The authors of this study deny that mental imagery plays a role in preplay. However, they are assuming that mental imagery must be driven through the deliberate top-down process of recreating a visual percept. Since we needn't build the idea of deliberate control into our notion of mental imagery, we needn't accept their conclusion that this is not a form of mental imagery.

Furthermore, since apparent motion may be entirely driven by bottom-up feedforward mechanisms (see Shimoji [2014] for a discussion), it is possible that the sensory stimulation does not require any temporal mental imagery in which there is temporal non-correspondence between perceptual processes and sensory stimulation.

However, in follow-up studies, it was found that area hMT+/V5 mediates the activation of V1 processes corresponding to the apparent motion trajectory (Larsen et al., 2006; Muckli et al., 2005; Sterzer, Haynes, and Rees, 2006). Given that there is a feedback mechanism at work in apparent motion, it shows that there must be a temporal non-correspondence between perceptual activity and the timing of sensory stimulation. In order for this feedback to influence the perception of the light as being at location L_2 at T_2, the perceptual system must first receive the modulatory sensory stimulation of the light being at location L_3 at T_3. Since the activation of V1 areas representing location L_2 is mediated by hMT+/V5 activity, then this activation must occur after the initial activation of V1 to the stimulus at location L_3. Since the activation of L_3 initially corresponded with the sensory stimulation, then it must be the case that any subsequent activation of V1 in response to the apparent motion display must no longer correspond to the temporal pattern of sensory stimulation. That is, in addition to spatial mental imagery, postdictive apparent motion employs temporal mental imagery in order to integrate the traces of past perceptual processes with the current incoming sensory stimulation. Our experience of the light as moving from L_1 to L_3, including the speciousness of the light having just been at locations L_1 and L_2, relies on temporal mental imagery.

Multimodal Temporal Mental Imagery

Apparent motion and perceptual preplay phenomena show that within individual sensory modalities temporal mental imagery plays a role in how the perceptual system fills in the details about the temporally extended world in a way that goes beyond a mere reflection of sensory stimulation. Temporal mental imagery also plays a role in the production of a coherent multisensory world.

It has been widely established that activity in sensory cortices can be entrained to rhythmic patterns in sensory stimulation (Rees, Green, and Kay, 1986; Regan, 1966). A rhythmic flashing of light will cause activity in the visual cortices to oscillate in phase with the flashing light. Similar entrainment can be found in the other sensory systems. In the unimodal cases, perceptual processes will naturally temporally correspond with the timing of sensory stimulation.

It has also been widely established, as a perceptual phenomenon, that when a rhythmic visual stimulus and a rhythmic auditory stimulus are shown to an individual, and the rhythms share a common frequency but are slightly out of phase with one another, the perceptual system will quickly adapt to the discrepancy in the stimuli and will come to perceive the auditory and visual stimuli as being in phase (for classic papers see Fujisaki et al., 2004; Vroomen et al., 2004; and see Vroomens and Keetels, 2010, for a review). There is a perceptual shift in the timing of the events in the world. Just as in the cases of apparent motion and amodal completion, the appearance of the auditory and visual stimuli as being in phase with one another could be accounted for without appealing to any temporal mental imagery. The perceptual recalibration could simply reflect the operation of a post- (or late) perceptual mechanism.

In recent series of experiments, Kösem, Gramfort, and van Wassenhove (2014) showed that this sort of temporal recalibration involved a shift in the timing of initial sensory processes. By using MEG imaging techniques, they were able to isolate the auditory and visual perceptual responses and show that individually the modality specific processes were entrained by their relevant stimuli. Then, after perceptual recalibration occurred, they found that there was a corresponding shift in the timing of the modality specific sensory processes. The timing of the perceptual processes no longer corresponded with the temporal pattern of sensory stimulation, but instead was shifted as the perceptual system tried to produce a coherent representation of the world in which a single audiovisual rhythm was impinging on the sensory receptors. Once again, we find a role for temporal mental imagery in our perception of the temporal structure of the world around.

Limits of Temporal Mental Imagery

At this point, a word of caution is needed. While temporal mental imagery seems to play a role in how we perceive the temporally structured world around us, it leaves certain important aspects of the perception of time unanswered. In order to see what gets left out, we can make a three-layer distinction between different aspects of our perceptual engagement with the world around us.

Let's begin with the case of visual space. First, (1) there is the spatial structure of our sensory stimulation. That is, the spatial distribution of activity on our retinas. Second, (2) there is the spatial structure of early cortical processes – i.e. the retinotopic structure of these early visual cortices. Third, (3) there is the spatial content of early vision. As it has been defined, cases of spatial mental imagery have been characterized as cases in which there is a failure of correspondence between (1) and (2) – that is, a failure of correspondence between the retinopically structured perceptual activity in early visual cortices and the spatial distribution of retinal activity. Given how spatial content of early vision is encoded via the retinotopic structure of the early cortical maps, a non-correspondence between (1) and (2), i.e. the existence of mental imagery, implies a non-correspondence between (1) and (3). Mental imagery in this case provides us with a straightforward account of the spatial content of visual mental imagery.

However, when we translate this three-layer distinction to the temporal case, the same transition does not hold. First, (1) there is the temporal structure of our sensory stimulation – i.e. the temporal sequence of activity on the sensory receptors. Second, (2) there is the temporal structure of early cortical processes. Third, (3) there is the temporal content of perception – e.g. the durations and temporal relations attributed to perceived events. While the existence of retinotopic structure, and its role in spatial representation, allowed for a non-correspondence between (1) and (2) to imply a non-correspondence between (1) and (3), the same cannot be said in the case of time. The timing of perceptual processes can be divorced from their temporal contents (Viera, 2019).

To see how this might be so, consider cases of visuomotor temporal recalibration. In a study by Stetson et al. (2006), subjects were asked to press a button and then after a 35-millisecond delay a flash of light would appear on the screen in front of them. After subjects did this for a while, the experimenters then inserted an extended delay of 135 milliseconds between the button press and the flash of light. It was determined that subjects would quickly adapt to the inserted delay and as a result the perceived interval between the button press and the flash of light would be misperceived as being shorter than it in fact was. However, the interesting part comes when experiments removed the extended delay and returned to the 35-millisecond delay condition. Subjects would report seeing the flash of light as coming before the button press even though the stimuli were identical to those used in the initial portion of the study. Somehow the perceptual system had recalibrated its perception of temporal order.

One possibility for what might have occurred here was that through recalibration there was a shift in the timing of the early sensory processes. Either there was a replaying of the button press after the flash of light (a type of filling in) or both the processing of the flash of light and button press were delayed and played out in an order that fit the perceived order of events. However, neither of these options were borne out by the imaging data. Instead, the initial perceptual processes had the same timecourse prior to and post recalibration.[4] In both cases, the timing of the perceptual processes corresponded with the timing of sensory stimulation. As a result, no temporal mental imagery was at play.[5]

What is posited as making the difference in the perceived order is a late perceptual mechanism that takes the events represented by earlier cortical processes and puts them into temporal relations with one another. The take home message, however, for this study is that unlike the representation of visual space in early visual processes, there is no straightforward way of moving from claims about the temporal structure of perceptual processes to their temporal contents. Temporal mental imagery might provide us with a form of representational access to events that are not currently stimulating our sensory receptors, but an explanation of how those events are perceived as occurring in time may need to appeal to further resources.

Finally, it is important to stress that we have been focusing on temporal mental imagery in the visual sense modality. Given that we know a lot about the neural correlates of mental imagery in other sense modalities, one important new research direction would be to examine the similarities and differences between temporal mental imagery in the different sense modalities. Auditory temporal mental imagery is an especially important subject of research given the importance of temporality in audition. And given the deep multimodality of our perceptual system, another important question is how the temporal mental imagery in all these different sense modalities interact.

4 For evidence see Cai et al. (2012) and Stekelenburg, Sugano, and Vroomen (2011).
5 The possible difference between the mechanism for recalibration in this case and the mechanism for recalibration for the rhythmic audiovisual stimuli might have to do with the fact that in this case the stimuli were non-rhythmic.

References

Alais, D., and Burr, D. (2003). The "Flash-Lag" Effect Occurs in Audition and Cross-Modally, *Current Biology*, *13*(1), 59–63.

Bakin, J., Nakayama, K., and Gilbert, C. (2000). Visual Responses in Monkey Areas V1 and V2 to Three-Dimensional Surface Configurations. *Journal of Neuroscience*, *20*, 8188–8198.

Ban, H., Yamamoto, H., Hanakawa, T., et al. (2013). Topographic Representation of an Occluded Object and the Effects of Spatiotemporal Context in Human Early Visual Areas. *Journal of Neuroscience*, *33*, 16992–17007.

Beck, J. (2018). Marking the Perception-Cognition Boundary. *Australasian Journal of Philosophy*, *96*, 319–334.

Bullier, J. (2004). Communications between Cortical Areas of the Visual System. In L. M. Chalupa and J. S. Werner (eds.), *The Visual Neurosciences*. Cambridge, MA: MIT Press, 522–540.

Bushnell, B. N., Harding, P. J., Kosai, Y., and Pasupathy, A. (2011). Partial Occlusion Modulates Contour-Based Shape Encoding in Primate Area V4. *Journal of Neuroscience*, *31*, 4012–4024.

Cai, M., Stetson, C., Eagleman, D. M. (2012). A Neural Model for Temporal Order Judgments and their Active Recalibration: A Common Mechanism for Space and Time? *Frontiers in Psychology*, *3*, 470.

Ekman, M., Kok, P., and de Lange, F. (2017). Time-Compressed Preplay of Anticipated Events in Human Primary Visual Cortex. *Nature Communications*, *8*.

Emmanouil, T., and Ro, T. (2014). Amodal Completion of Unconsciously Presented Objects. *Psychonomic Bulletin & Review*, *21*(5), 1188–1194.

Esterman, M., and Yantis, S. (2010). Perceptual Expectation Modulates Category-Selective Cortical Activity. *Cerebral Cortex*, *20*, 1245–1253.

Fujisaki, W., Shimojo, S., Kashino, M., and Nishida, S. (2004). Recalibration of Audiovisual Simultaneity. *Nature Neuroscience*, *7*, 773–778.

Geldard, F. A., and Sherrick, C. E. (1972). The Cutaneous "Rabbit": A Perceptual Illusion. *Science*, *178*, 178–179.

Grice, H. P. (1961). The Causal Theory of Perception. *Proceedings of the Aristotelian Society, Supplementary Volume*, *35*, 121–153.

Grill-Spector, K., and Malach, R. (2004). The Human Visual Cortex. *Annual Review of Neuroscience*, *27*, 649–677.

Grush, R. (2007). Time and Experience. In T. Muller (ed.), *Philosophie der Zeit: Neue Analytische Ansatze*. Frankfurt, Germany: Verlag Vittorio Klostermann.

(2005). Internal Models and the Construction of Time: Generalizing from State Estimation to Trajectory Estimation to Address Temporal Features of Perception, including Temporal Illusions. *Journal of Neural Engineering*, *2*(3), S209–218.

Hazenberg, S. J., Jongsma, M. L. A., Koning, A., and van Lier, R. (2014). Differential Familiarity Effects in Amodal Completion: Support from Behavioral and Electrophysiological Measurements. *Journal of Experimental Psychology: Human Perception and Performance*, *40*(2), 669–684.

Hedgé, J., Fang, F., Murray, S. O., and Kersten, D. (2008). Preferential Responses to Occluded Objects in the Human Visual Cortex. *Journal of Vision*, *8*, 16–35.

Hoerl, C. (2009). Time and Tense in Perceptual Experience. *Philosopher's Imprint*, *9*(12).

James, W. (1890). *The Principles of Psychology*. In 2 volumes. New York, NY: Henry Holt and Company.

Komatsu, H. (2006). The Neural Mechanisms of Perceptual Filling-in. *Nature Review Neuroscience*, *7*, 220–231.

Kosslyn, S. M., Behrmann, M., and Jeannerod, M. (1995a). The Cognitive Neuroscience of Mental Imagery. *Neuropsychologia*, *33*, 1335–1344.

Kosslyn, S. M., Thompson, W. L., Kim, I. J., and Alpert, N. M. (1995b). Topographical Representations of Mental Images in Primary Visual Cortex. *Nature*, *378*: 496–498.

Kösem, A., Gramfort, A., and van Wassenhove, V. (2014). Encoding of Event Timing in the Phase of Neural Oscillations. *NeuroImage*, *92*, 274–284.

Kovacs, G., Vogels, R., and Orban, G. A. (1995). Selectivity of Macaque Inferior Temporal Neurons for Partially Occluded Shapes. *Journal of Neuroscience*, *15*, 1984–1997.

Larsen, A., Madsen, K. H., Lund, T. E., and Bundesen, C. (2006). Images of Illusory Motion in Primary Visual Cortex. *Journal of Cognitive Neuroscience*, *18*(7), 1174–1180.

Leaver, A. M., van Lare, J., Zielinski, B., Halpern, A. R., and Rauschecker, J. P. (2009). Brain Activation during Anticipation of Sound Sequences. *Journal of Neuroscience*, *29* (8), 2477–2485.

Lee, G. (2014a). Extensionalism, Atomism, and Continuity. In N. Oaklander (ed.), *Debates in the Metaphysics of Time*. London: Bloomsbury.

  (2014b). Temporal Experience and the Temporal Structure of Experience. *Philosopher's Imprint 14*(3).

Lee, S. H., Kwan, A. C., Zhang, S., et al. (2012). Activation of Specific Interneurons Improves V1 Feature Selectivity and Visual Perception. *Nature*, *488*, 379–383.

Lee, T. S., and Nguyen, M. (2001). Dynamics of Subjective Contour Formation in the Early Visual Cortex. *Proceedings of the National Academy of Sciences*, *98*(4), 1907–1911.

Lerner, Y., Harel, M., and Malach, R. (2004). Rapid Completion Effects in Human High-Order Visual Areas. *NeuroImage*, *21*, 516–526.

Muckli, L., Kohler, A., Kriegeskorte, N., and Singer, W. (2005). Primary Visual Cortex Activity Along the Apparent-Motion Trace Reflects Illusory Perception. *PLoS Biology*, *3*(8), 1501–1510.

Nanay, B. (2010). Perception and Imagination: Amodal Perception as Mental Imagery. *Philosophical Studies*, *150*, 239–254.

  (2012). Perceptual Phenomenology. *Philosophical Perspectives*, *26*, 235–246.

  (2018a). Multimodal Mental Imagery. *Cortex*, *105*, 125–134.

  (2018b). The Importance of Amodal Completion in Everyday Perception. *I-Perception*. https://doi.org/10.1177/2041669518788887

  (Forthcoming). *Seeing Things You Don't See*. Oxford, UK: Oxford University Press.

Page, J. W., Duhamel, P., and Crognale, M. A. (2011). ERP Evidence of Visualization at Early Stages of Visual Processing. *Brain and Cognition*, *75*(2), 141–146.

Pan, Y., Chen, M., Yin, J., et al. (2012). Equivalent Representation of Real and Illusory Contours in Macaque V4. *Journal of Neuroscience*, *32*, 6760–6770.

Pearson, J., and Westbrook, F. (2015). Phantom Perception: Voluntary and Involuntary Nonretinal Vision. *Trends in Cognitive Sciences*, *19*, 278–284.

Pearson, J., Naselaris, T., Holmes, E. A., and Kosslyn, S. M. (2015). Mental Imagery: Functional Mechanisms and Clinical Applications. *Trends in Cognitive Sciences*, *19*, 590–602.

Phillips, B. (2019). The Shifting Boundary between Perception and Cognition. *Noûs*, *53*, 316–346.

Phillips, I. (2010). Perceiving Temporal Properties. *European Journal of Philosophy*, *18*(2), 176–202.

(2011). Perception and Iconic Memory: What Sperling Doesn't Show. *Mind & Language*, 281–311. doi.org/10.1111/j.1468-0017.2011.01422.x.

(2014). Experience of and in Time. *Philosophy Compass*, *9*, 131–144.

Rauschenberger, R., Liu, T., Slotnick, S. D., and Yantis, S. (2006). Temporally Unfolding Neural Representation of Pictorial Occlusion. *Psychological Science*, *17*, 358–364.

Rees, A., Green, G., and Kay, R. H. (1986). Steady-State Evoked Responses to Sinusoidally Amplitude-Modulated Sounds Recorded in Man. *Hearing Research*, *23*(2). 123–133.

Regan, D. (1966). Some Characteristics of Average Steady-State and Transient Responses Evoked by Modulated Light. *Electroencephalography and Clinical Neurophysiology*, *20*(3), 238–248.

Rolls, E. T., and Tovee, M. J. (1994). Processing Speed in the Cerebral Cortex and the Neurophysiology of Visual Masking. *Proceedings of the Royal Society: Biological Sciences*, *257*, 9–15.

Scherzer, T. R., and Ekroll, V. (2015). Partial Modal Completion under Occlusion: What do Modal and Amodal Percepts Represent? *Journal of Vision*, *15*, 1–20.

Shepard, R. N. (1978). Mental Images. *American Psychologist*, *33*, 125–137.

Shibata, K., Watanabe, T., Sasaki, Y., and Kawato, M. (2011). Perceptual Learning Incepted by Decoded fMRI Neurofeedback without Stimulus Presentation. *Science*, *334*, 1413–1415.

Shimoji, S. (2014). Postdiction: Its Implications on Visual Awareness, Hindsight, and Sense of Agency. *Frontiers in Psychology*, *5*, 196.

Slotnick, S. D., Thompson, W. L., and Kosslyn, S. M. (2005). Visual Mental Imagery Induces Retinotopically Organized Activation of Early Visual Areas. *Cerebral Cortex*, *15*, 1570–1583.

Smith, F. W., and Muckli, L. (2010). Nonstimulated Early Visual Areas Carry Information About Surrounding Context. *PNAS*, *107*, 20099–20103.

Stekelenburg, J., Sugano, Y., and Vroomen, J. (2011). Neural Correlates of Motor-Sensory Temporal Recalibration. *Brain Research*, *1397*, 46–54.

Sterzer, P., Haynes, J. D., and Rees, G. (2006). Primary Visual Cortex Activation on the Path of Apparent Motion is Mediated by Feedback from hTM + V5. *NeuroImage*, *32*, 1308–1316.

Stetson, C., Cui, X., Montague, P. R., and Eagleman, D. M. (2006). Motor-Sensory Recalibration Leads to an Illusory Reversal of Action and Sensation. *Neuron*, *51*(5), 651–659.

Sugita, Y. (1999). Grouping of Image Fragments in Primary Visual Cortex. *Nature*, *401*, 269–272.

Thorpe, S., Fize, D., and Marlot, C. (1996). Speed of Processing in the Human Visual System. *Nature*, *381*, 520–522.

Viera, G. (2019). The Fragmentary Model of Temporal Experience and the Mirroring Constraint. *Philosophical Studies*, 176, 21.

Vroomen, J., Keetels, M., de Gelder, B., and Bertelson, P. (2004). Recalibration of Temporal Order Perception by Exposure to Audio–Visual Asynchrony. *Cognitive Brain Research*, *22*, 32–35.

Vroomen, J., and Keetels, M. (2010). Perception of Intersensory Synchrony: A Tutorial Review. *Attention, Perception, and Psychophysics*, *72*, 871–884.

Zatorre, R. J., and Halpern, A. R. (2005). Mental Concert: Musical Imagery and Auditory Cortex. *Neuron*, *47*, 9–12.

16 Emotional Mental Imagery

Simon E. Blackwell

If you were to ask someone to describe the thoughts that went through their mind over the course of a typical day, and specifically those that took the form of mental images, you would discover that many of these had some kind of emotional tone. For example, someone might describe daydreaming about an upcoming holiday and enjoying the anticipated pleasure as they do so, replaying an argument with a friend and imagining how they wished they had responded, or being haunted by an image they saw on the television the previous evening. The idea that mental imagery, which can be defined as "representations and the accompanying experience of sensory information without a direct external stimulus" (Pearson, Naselaris, Holmes, and Kosslyn, 2015: 590), can have a powerful emotional impact will seem intuitive to many people: For most, the experience of emotional mental imagery will be a ubiquitous part of everyday life, and many emotional thoughts include the experience of mental imagery.

This chapter considers scientific research into the emotional nature of mental imagery, and why mental imagery can evoke emotion so strongly. It then considers the possible functions of such emotional mental imagery in daily life, before addressing how dysfunctions in emotional mental imagery may become problematic, for example in the context of depression and anxiety disorders. The ways in which we can make use of emotional mental imagery, for example in psychological therapy, are then discussed.

The chapter ends by returning to the broader topic of imagination. First, the question of what the scientific study of emotional mental imagery means for our understanding of the imagination is addressed, followed by a reflection on how considerations of emotional mental imagery can inform interdisciplinary research into the imagination. Finally, the chapter concludes by considering some of the major challenges for the current field of emotional mental imagery research.

Mental Imagery and Emotion

Although not all mental imagery is emotional, mental imagery is a form of thought that can have a particularly strong impact on emotion (Holmes and Mathews, 2005). The relationship between mental imagery and emotions has long both been the subject of scientific investigation (e.g. Golla, Hutton, and Walter, 1943), and been capitalized on in psychological therapies (e.g. to reduce fear responses via imaginal exposure; Wolpe, 1961). However, it is only more recently that the assumption of a "special relationship" between mental imagery and emotion has been systematically investigated (Holmes and Mathews, 2005). In an initial experimental study, Holmes and Mathews compared the impact on emotion of imagery-based processing of negative emotional stimuli (brief descriptions of situations that started ambiguously and ended negatively) to verbal processing of the same emotional stimuli. Imagery-based processing of the negative stimuli led to greater increases in state anxiety compared to verbal-based processing of the same stimuli, supporting the hypothesis that imagery has a greater impact on emotion than non-imagery-based (in this case verbal) thought (Holmes and Mathews, 2005). This basic effect has since been replicated for both negative and positive emotional material and using several different experimental paradigms (e.g. Görgen, Joormann, Hiller, and Witthöft, 2015; Holmes, Lang, and Shah, 2009; Mathews, Ridgeway, and Holmes, 2013).

Why might mental imagery have the capacity to evoke emotions so strongly? A plausible explanation for this phenomenon comes from considering the cognitive and neural operations involved in the generation or retrieval of a mental image (Pearson et al., 2015). Image generation or retrieval can occur deliberately, for example if we want to mentally rehearse an upcoming job interview, or involuntarily, for example if a song playing on the radio evokes a special memory. Generation of mental imagery (for example, picturing an interview room with a panel sitting across the table from you) involves the retrieval of the relevant sensory representations from memory, which may be simply re-experienced (e.g. when retrieving a memory of a specific instance), or re-combined with other representations and knowledge to produce an image of a scene or object that has never been experienced. In the case of preparing for a job interview, picturing the interview room with a panel sitting across the table from you may involve retrieving visual representations of specific faces, rooms, and furniture, to create a scene of a room with a panel of people whom one has never in fact seen or met. The sensory representations in the image may also involve senses other than vision, for example "hearing" the panel posing a question and your own answer, "feeling" the chair underneath you, and perhaps experiencing some of the bodily sensations associated with anxiety, such as tensed muscles. Other aspects of the scene in your imagination may include your inferences of the panel's reactions to your answers, and your own subsequent emotional responses.

Interestingly, imagining this scene and experiencing the sights, sounds, and other sensations in imagination will involve very similar patterns of neural activation as if the scene was being perceived and experienced in reality. The neural representation of mental imagery has been shown to be very similar to that of actual perception, even in relatively low-level areas of the visual cortex (Pearson et al., 2015; see also Chapter 12). Evidence from both neuroimaging and behavioral experiments indicating the similarity of imagery and perception representations has led to the idea that mental imagery can be thought of as like a "weak" form of perception (Pearson et al., 2015).

This overlap of representation is likely to account for one of the particular characteristics of mental imagery, that it can feel "real" and even be confused with reality (Mathews, Ridgeway, and Holmes, 2013); thus when imagining an emotional scene, the same emotions may be evoked (albeit generally with weaker intensity) as if the scene was actually being experienced. The "realness" of mental imagery is elaborated in Lang's bio-informational theory of emotional mental imagery (Ji et al., 2016; Lang, 1979), according to which the experience of a mental image activates an associative network of information as if the actual object or scene was being experienced. This information, which is automatically retrieved and activated, can include not only perceptual information (e.g. sights, sounds, smells), but also semantic information (e.g. factual knowledge), emotional responses (e.g. anxiety, with accompanying bodily reactions such as sweating or raised heart rate), and even preparatory motor responses (e.g. tensed muscles characteristic of the "fight or flight" response). Emotional mental imagery can therefore be thought of as a simulation of reality (Ji et al., 2016). From this perspective, the idea that mental imagery has a special relationship with emotion could be seen as self-evident: Mental imagery of emotional events often contains representations of emotional states, resulting in an experiencing of these states as part of the experience of emotional imagery. However, it is also possible to imagine emotional events without representing or experiencing any of the relevant emotional states.

Functions of Emotional Mental Imagery in Everyday Life

The idea that mental imagery allows us to simulate events in our imagination, and the properties of imagery-based thought, is key to understanding the functional roles that emotional mental imagery plays in everyday life (Blackwell, 2019). Mental imagery is often a core part of what is termed "mental time travel," the process by which we replay in our minds events from the past, or play out possible events in the future. Such mental time travel, and simulation of the past and future more broadly, is thought to play an important role in everyday functioning, for example in planning and decision-making (e.g. MacLeod, 2017), and the processes of projecting oneself into the past or future appear to share many common neural processes (e.g. Schacter, Addis, and Buckner, 2008; see also Chapter 8 and Chapter 26). The "as-if reality" nature of mental imagery (cf. Ji et al., 2016) and its tendency to evoke emotions means that we can not only re-experience events from the past when we recall them, including our mental state and emotional response at the time, but also "pre-experience" possible events in the future. That is, by simulating a potential event via mental imagery, we can "test out" in our mind the potential emotional consequences, for example how rewarding or anxiety-inducing it may be. This "preview" can then inform our decision-making, and also contribute to our motivation to work toward ensuring the event occurs. For example, when thinking about different holiday options we might imagine ourselves already on holiday in the different locations; how enjoyable each holiday "feels" in our imagination may influence our eventual decision. Similarly, if when we imagine an upcoming social event it feels enjoyable in our imagination, we may be more likely to make the effort required to attend. How easy or how difficult it is to imagine a specific event occurring, and the qualities of the image such as vividness or detail, may also influence our judgment about how likely the event is to occur (cf. Kahneman and Tversky, 1982); if we struggle to imagine something happening and the image we produce is only vague and dim, we may find it less plausible that the event will actually take place.

Recall and re-experiencing of past events may not only play important roles in guiding future behavior (for example, by reminding us how enjoyable or unpleasant a particular activity was), but may also provide broader functions such as contributing to and reinforcing our sense of identity as a person (e.g. Conway, Singer, and Tagini, 2004; Stopa, 2009). Given the link between imagery and emotion, re-experiencing past events or generating imagery of future events or other scenes can also be used to regulate mood and motivation. For example, recalling a positive memory can help improve someone's mood when feeling low, or imagining a soothing scene might help reduce anxiety.

Observational studies find that such "mental time travel" is indeed common in everyday life, and often involves the experience of mental imagery (e.g. Berntsen and Jacobsen, 2008; D'Argembeau, Renaud, and van der Linden, 2011). For example, one study investigating future-oriented thoughts found that participants on average experienced fifty-nine future-oriented thoughts in one day (D'Argembeau, Renaud, and van der Linden, 2011). A similar study specifically investigating emotional future-oriented thoughts found that participants recorded on average twenty-eight emotional future-oriented thoughts over a three-day period (Barsics, van der Linden, and D'Argembeau, 2016). Although in both these studies the thoughts recorded were not exclusively image-based, on average they tended to have a substantial imagery component. Mental time travel can occur both deliberately – for example, one can deliberately try to recall a conversation and replay it in one's mind – and involuntarily, as in the example of experiencing a memory triggered by hearing an old song on the radio (Berntsen and Jacobsen, 2008). Consistent with theoretical accounts of the functions of emotional mental imagery in daily life, people report perceiving emotional future-oriented thoughts as serving a purpose, such as helping to plan actions, set goals, regulate emotion, and make decisions (Barsics, van der Linden, and D'Argembeau, 2016). Further, the emotions associated with future projections may have an important functional impact; for example, some studies have found the emotions experienced when anticipating an action to be related to the subjective probability that the action will indeed be performed (Barsics, van der Linden, and D'Argembeau, 2016; Carrera, Caballero, and Muñoz, 2012).

In addition to these observational data, there is also evidence from experimental data for a functional role of imagery in relation to goal-directed behavior. This evidence comes from a range of areas including social psychology (e.g. Libby et al., 2007) and health psychology (Conroy and Hagger, 2018), and indicates that imagining engaging in a course of action can increase someone's intention to perform that course of action and even the likelihood that they do in fact later carry it out (e.g. Gregory, Cialdini, and Carpenter, 1982). Taken together, both the observational and experimental data support theoretical accounts that posit important roles for emotional mental imagery in goal-directed behavior (e.g. Conway, Meares, and Standart, 2004; Kavanagh, Andrade, and May, 2005).

Dysfunctions in Emotion Mental Imagery

Given that mental imagery can have a strong impact on emotion, and emotional mental imagery appears to play an important role in daily life, it is perhaps unsurprising that dysfunctions in the experience of emotional mental imagery are often associated with severe emotional problems and functional impairment.

One way in which dysfunctional mental imagery often occurs is in the experience of intrusive distressing mental images, and such intrusions characterize a number of mental disorders. For example, people who have experienced a traumatic event may go on to develop post-traumatic stress disorder (PTSD), a hallmark symptom of which is the experience of recurrent intrusive memories of the traumatic event. These memories tend to be image-based and rich in sensory detail, and in their extreme form as "flashbacks" are associated with the experience that the trauma is happening right now in the present moment. Intrusive memories of trauma are not only distressing in their own right, but can also contribute to other aspects of PTSD such as avoidance (for example, of situations that may trigger intrusive memories) and dysfunctional coping strategies (such as excessive use of alcohol or other substances to regulate negative emotions). Intrusive memories of past events are also common in depression, and are typically memories that bring a sense of shame or humiliation (Reynolds and Brewin, 1998). Such memories can have a profound impact on the person's mood, and also reinforce a negative sense of self, for example as worthless.

Intrusive negative imagery can also be of the future, for example "seeing" a negative event happening to oneself or loved ones. Perhaps due to the "as-if reality" nature of mental imagery, such future-oriented images (or "flashforwards") can feel like a premonition, increasing anxiety and leading to (potentially maladaptive) behavior designed to prevent the event from occurring (see e.g. Hales et al., 2014). The occurrence of such future-oriented intrusive imagery has been associated with higher levels of anxiety and lower levels of functioning across a range of mental disorders including anxiety disorders, depression, and bipolar disorder (e.g. Di Simplicio et al., 2016).

One particularly concerning kind of future-oriented imagery has been described in the context of depressed mood, and involves imagining the act of suicide or self-harm (e.g. Hales et al., 2011; Weßlau et al., 2015). While on the surface the content of such imagery is negative, the imagery may be experienced by the individual in a positive way, for example as comforting or as presenting a solution to a problem, and participants in the research studies often report that the images feel particularly compelling. However, although the individual may experience a rewarding emotional response in the short term, continued engagement in and elaboration of such imagery could potentially have harmful consequences. Particularly given the literature indicating that imagining an act can increase the likelihood of carrying it out, it is possible that repeatedly engaging in imagery of suicide could increase the risk of carrying out a suicidal act; consistent with this, suicidal "flashforwards" appear to be especially common in the context of bipolar disorder, which is associated with a relatively high rate of suicide (Hales et al., 2011).

Other kinds of dysfunctional emotional mental imagery include the experience of distorted mental imagery that can feel real and be interpreted as a reflection of reality, and such imagery appears across a range of anxiety disorders. One example is in the context of social phobia, which is characterized by extreme anxiety in social situations and the fear that others are judging one negatively. While engaged in conversation, people with social phobia may see in their mind's eye an image of themselves as they fear other people see them, perhaps shaking, blushing, and sweating. Such images not only increase anxiety and likely feed the individual's negative evaluation of how the interaction is going, but can also have negative impact on the quality of the social interaction (e.g. Hirsch et al., 2005). People with phobias of specific objects or situations may also experience distorted imagery; for example, people with spider phobia may see in their mind's eye a spider as being much larger than in reality and even having sharp teeth (Pratt, Cooper, and Hackmann, 2004). Such distorted emotional imagery will increase the sense that the phobic object or situation is dangerous, increasing anxiety and further driving avoidance and escape behavior.

While the above paragraphs have considered dysfunctional negative emotional mental imagery, dysfunction in positive imagery can also occur. Depression is associated with deficits in the quality of positive mental imagery (Holmes et al., 2016). For example, people who are depressed may tend to experience imagery from what is called the "observer perspective," seeing themselves in the image from the outside, which appears to be associated with a reduced emotional quality of the image or memory. When people who are depressed or suffering from low mood imagine possible positive events in the future, the images they generate tend to be less vivid than those generated by people who are not depressed (Holmes et al., 2016). If emotional mental imagery makes an important contribution to how we evaluate the future, for example in trying to predict the outcome of a situation, or whether engaging in an activity will be enjoyable or not, a selective inability or difficulty in generating vivid positive mental images could contribute to pessimism and hopelessness about the future, and reduce motivation to engage in potentially enjoyable activities – all of which are characteristic of depression (Holmes et al., 2016).

The *presence* of "positive" mental imagery can also be problematic in certain circumstances, for example in the case of an imagined positive or otherwise attractive outcome that may drive maladaptive behavior. For example, when people with bipolar disorder experience elevated positive mood, this can be associated with particularly attractive imagery of achieving desired goals (Ivins et al., 2014), which can further drive goal-directed behavior that may contribute to mood escalation into hypomania or mania. In substance abuse disorders, imagery of the desired substance (e.g. tobacco, alcohol, or another drug) can also feel attractive and compelling, and thus may also drive craving and attempts to seek out the substance (Kavanagh, Andrade, and May, 2005).

Individual Differences in Emotional Mental Imagery

Just as there is a large variation in how vividly people can imagine nonemotional scenes or objects, or how often such imagery comes to mind, there is also large inter-individual variation in terms of the tendency to experience emotional mental imagery and the quality of such imagery. Interestingly, individual differences in the experience of emotional mental imagery can be specific to imagery of a particular valence. As indicated in the previous section, depression and depressed mood are associated with reduced vividness of positive future-oriented imagery, but this does not appear to be a general deficit in imagery vividness, as negative imagery may be equally vivid or even more vivid than that experienced by people whose mood is not depressed (Holmes et al., 2016). Conversely, people who are particularly optimistic about the future tend to generate particularly vivid positive future-oriented imagery, but optimism does not show such a clear relationship with vividness for negative imagery or general experience of nonemotional imagery (e.g. Ji, Holmes, and Blackwell, 2017). Individual differences in imagery perspective can also be observed, for example with low mood being associated with a greater tendency to use observer perspective imagery (Nelis et al., 2013). It is not currently clear whether individual differences in the experience of emotional mental imagery are simply reflections of, for instance, depressed mood, or whether they do in fact represent risk factors for development of certain disorders (Holmes et al., 2016). However, given the roles of emotional mental imagery in everyday life, it seems plausible that individual differences in the extent to which someone can vividly imagine positive or negative events, or their tendency to experience such imagery in daily life, could have an impact on factors contributing to risk or resilience, such as optimism.

Making Use of the Properties of Emotional Mental Imagery

While much of the emotional mental imagery we experience occurs involuntarily, we can also use such imagery deliberately for a number of purposes. In fact, many people do deliberately use emotional mental imagery in daily life, for example reliving positive memories to improve their mood, or "pre-living" events to which they are looking forward to enjoy the anticipatory pleasure. Within the clinical field, emotional imagery has been used in a number of ways across a range of psychological therapeutic approaches (Edwards, 2007). For example, within a cognitive-behavioral tradition, imaginal exposure to feared events or objects has long been used to reduce fear responses (e.g. Wolpe, 1961). Imaginal exposure can also be applied to memories, for example via reliving of trauma memories in the context of PTSD to reduce their emotional impact and change maladaptive appraisals of the event (e.g. Ehlers et al., 2005). Imaginal exposure makes use of the "as-if reality" quality of imagery, and can lead to fear responses in much the same way as actual exposure would. Other imagery-based approaches make use of our ability to recombine information from memory and novel information to create images of events that have never taken place. For example in "imagery rescripting" the dysfunctional meaning and emotion of a distressing event are modified via reimagining the event from different perspectives or with alternative endings (Arntz, 2012).

Approaching the problem of distressing negative mental imagery from another angle, it may be possible to reduce the occurrence of distress caused by such imagery by capitalizing on the sensory representation of such imagery in memory. Due to the primarily visual nature of recurrent distressing images (such as those that characterize PTSD), interventions to reduce the occurrence of such memories can make use of the modality-specific limited processing capacity of our memory systems (Baddeley and Andrade, 2000). Thus, employing an activity that engages visuospatial working memory, such as directed eye movements, while recalling a distressing memory can reduce the vividness and emotional impact of that memory (e.g. Leer, Engelhard, and van den Hout, 2014). This is thought to be a working mechanism of one effective psychological intervention for PTSD, Eye Movement Desensitization and Reprocessing. Because memories of an event take a few hours to be "consolidated," engaging in a visuospatial task, such as the computer game *Tetris*, shortly after witnessing distressing scenes can reduce the occurrence of intrusive memories of those scenes in the subsequent week (e.g. Holmes et al., 2010). There are preliminary indications that an intervention including playing *Tetris* may be able to reduce intrusive memories of a traumatic event, such as a road traffic accident (Iyadurai, Blackwell, and Meiser-Stedman, 2017), and that benefits may even be experienced by patients with long-standing PTSD (Kessler et al., 2018). While this may seem surprising, these clinical applications represent a logical extension of theoretical ideas concerning mental imagery and corresponding experimental work. However, they are currently still in the early stages of development and evaluation.

Several recently developed approaches use systematic practice in imagery generation or retrieval to change maladaptive biases in information processing (Hitchcock et al., 2017). For example, a number of different approaches have been developed that involve repeated rehearsal of specific kinds of memories to increase the ease with which helpful memories can be retrieved (e.g. autobiographical memory flexibility training – Hitchcock et al., 2016; competitive memory training – Korrelboom et al., 2009; memory specificity training – Raes, Williams, and Hermans, 2009). From a future-oriented perspective, repeated rehearsal of a positive vision of oneself in the future has been investigated as a means to increase general optimism about the future (e.g. Meevissen, Peters, and Alberts, 2011). Furthermore, computer-guided repetitive practice in imagining positive outcomes for ambiguous situations has been investigated as a method to train a more positive cognitive bias in the context of depression (e.g. Blackwell and Holmes, 2010) or dysphoria (e.g. Pictet, Jermann, and Ceschi, 2016). Such methods are under development, but appear promising in terms of the potential to develop simple low-cost treatments, or treatment modules to be added to existing interventions, that capitalize on the properties of emotional mental imagery (Hitchcock et al., 2017).

Emotional mental imagery may also deliberately be used to enhance motivation or help support changes in behavior. The use of imagery to enhance healthy behavior has been explored across a range of areas, for example in relation to healthy eating (e.g. Knäuper et al., 2011) or physical activity (Chan and Cameron, 2012). Repeated practice in imagining rewarding outcomes from everyday activities may also help overcome the lack of motivation and behavioral inactivity that characterizes depression (e.g. Linke and Wessa, 2017; Renner et al., 2017). Such imagery-based techniques, which often include an emotional component such as imagining the rewarding outcome of the behavior, appear promising, but the factors that influence whether they are effective or not require much further investigation (Conroy and Hagger, 2018). For example, simply imagining the rewarding outcomes of a course of action may in fact act as a substitute for the actual achievement and reduce motivation, and thus it may be useful to simulate via imagery not only desired goals but also obstacles to reaching them and how they may be overcome (e.g. Fritzsche et al., 2016). Theories of imagery from sports psychology differentiate different types of imaginal rehearsal (e.g. imagining achieving the desired goal vs. detailed imaginal rehearsal of a specific movement), which may have different functions and impacts on factors such as motivation and actual performance (e.g. Cumming and Williams, 2012). Similarly, many professional dancers report using different kinds of mental imagery for a wide variety of purposes in both training and performance (Hanrahan and Vergeer, 2001). Given the complexity of the cognitive operations involved in generating mental imagery, and the range of different kinds of responses – from emotional to behavioral and physiological – that emotional mental imagery may elicit, it seems likely that different applications of emotional mental imagery will benefit from specific tailoring, and this may vary greatly across different areas of health or types of everyday behavior.

Implications for our Understanding of the Imagination

Consideration of emotional mental imagery has a number of implications for our understanding of the imagination. While the idea of the imagination as something that may be a vehicle for highly charged emotions has a long history outside of psychological research and treatment (e.g. in literature), the scientific study of emotional mental imagery provides a framework for understanding this phenomenon. Both theoretical accounts of emotional mental imagery and scientific investigations support the idea of mental imagery and emotion being tightly linked, and of emotional mental imagery providing a powerful route to experiencing and changing emotions. The scientific literature indicates that the experience of emotional mental imagery will automatically activate representations of linked memories and emotional states, and even behavioral responses. Further, the "as-if real" nature of mental imagery and its neural representation help to explain the potential impact of events that have only ever existed in the imagination. Indeed, experimental studies have shown that people can have intrusive memories of traumatic events that have never been actually experienced, only imagined (Krans et al., 2009), and intrusive images of feared future events (e.g. oneself or a loved one having a serious accident) can have a dramatic influence on behavior (e.g. taking steps to reduce the risk, including superstitious behavior).

It would therefore be helpful for studies of the imagination to consider whether the content or process studied is likely to involve the generation or retrieval of mental imagery, particularly when the content of the imagination is emotional. The potential impact of basic individual differences in the capacity to generate imagery of different valences or in the qualities of emotional imagery could also be considered, as these may have a broader impact on the imagination. For example, people differ in their capacity to generate vivid images of positive or negative events (e.g. Di Simplicio et al., 2016; Ji, Holmes, and Blackwell, 2017), and this basic individual difference may then have a widespread impact in determining the content of their imagination and its emotional tone. The literature showing the effects of visuospatial tasks on emotional memory also has interesting broader implications (particularly given that people are often engaged in multiple concurrent tasks in daily life), as it could be the case that tasks engaging visuospatial working memory have a broader impact on dampening certain aspects of the imagination. Interestingly, there are lines of research that have drawn on broader links between emotional mental imagery and other aspects of imagination, for example the extent to which reading fictional texts elicits automatic retrieval of episodic memories and accompanying emotion (Oatley, 2011), but there is clearly much more such interdisciplinary research to be done.

Implications for Interdisciplinary Research

From the perspective of the emotional mental imagery literature, a key implication for interdisciplinary research in imagery and imagination is the importance of considering whether the specific imagery under investigation is emotional or not. An extensive body of research into mental imagery, from a variety of disciplines including neuroscience, cognitive psychology and clinical psychology, has investigated the sensory experience of mental imagery or procedural aspects of its generation or manipulation, but much of this has either focused on nonemotional imagery or has not differentiated between imagery that may be neutral, emotionally positive, or emotionally negative. However, there appear to be many important individual differences relating to the generation or experience of mental imagery of specific emotional valence (e.g. positive imagery among individuals with depression or low mood). Not differentiating between mental imagery of different emotional valences and intensity misses a key facet of the experience of such imagery, and risks drawing erroneous conclusions. For example, it may be concluded that there is a lack of influence of mental imagery ability on the subject of investigation when in fact the influence is valence-specific. Similarly, not attending to the potential valence characteristics of the questions in mental imagery questionnaires or other measures may result in conclusions being drawn about mental imagery in general that are in fact driven by emotional items in the measures.

A second key implication is that when asking research participants about their thought processes or contents (e.g. in a questionnaire or interview), it is important to specify or enquire about the form that the thoughts take, for example whether they involve mental imagery or not. People may not spontaneously report mental imagery, particularly if the content is emotional (cf. Blackwell, 2019; Hales et al., 2014), or may not indicate that a thought took the form of an image, unless they are specifically asked to do so. Differentiating between imagery-based and non-imagery-based thoughts is necessary to avoid missing out on a potentially important individual difference with relevance for emotional experience.

A third and final implication to be drawn here concerns the observation that much of the mental imagery experienced in daily life occurs involuntarily, and that involuntary emotional imagery is common across many mental disorders such as PTSD, depression, and bipolar disorder. Thus, although much research into imagery, across scientific disciplines, is conducted via asking people to deliberately generate mental images, consideration of imagery in imagination also needs to include imagery that comes to mind spontaneously, and to differentiate between deliberately generated and spontaneous emotional imagery.

Major Challenges in the Investigation of Emotional Mental Imagery

A long-recognized challenge in investigating emotional mental imagery is demonstrating that any effects found are specific to the image-based representation of the thought or memory under investigation, rather than generic effects of emotional thoughts or stimuli. While there are experimental studies that through careful construction of stimuli and instructions have tried to differentiate between imagery and non-imagery processing of the same stimuli (e.g. Görgen et al., 2015; Holmes and Mathews, 2005), many studies do not do this satisfactorily. This is in part because it can often be difficult to find a non-imagery equivalent processing mode for participants to use, and also because if another comparison (e.g. emotional valence) is of primary interest, adding in non-imagery versions of each manipulation doubles the number of experimental conditions and participants required. Further, even when instructed to engage in non-imagery (e.g. verbal) processing of experimental stimuli many participants will automatically experience some (albeit reduced) amount of imagery (e.g. Holmes, Lang, and Shah, 2009), which makes a "pure" imagery vs. non-imagery manipulation difficult to achieve. However, researchers always need to ask themselves whether a set of results can really be interpreted in terms of a specific effect of mental imagery, and, if not, how such a specific effect could in fact be demonstrated.

A second long-recognized challenge in mental imagery research is the desire to go beyond subjective reports in assessing the quality of imagery generated or experienced. The development of neuroimaging methods has provided one means of doing this (e.g. Pearson et al., 2015), and if one is specifically interested in the emotional impact of imagery, then physiological measurement has long been used to this end (e.g. Golla, Hutton, and Walter, 1943; Mathews, 1971). However, simple behavioral measures are also desirable, and although objective behavioral indices of the vividness of emotionally neutral mental imagery have been developed (Pearson, 2014), similar objective performance-based measures isolating specific valences of imagery, or the emotional impact of imagery, would be extremely useful. Furthermore, such a measure should ideally be able to differentiate between imagery of different valences, and between imagery and non-imagery processing.

A third challenge concerns the investigation of involuntary mental imagery. While much of the mental imagery experienced in daily life is involuntary, studies investigating mental imagery and its effects often use measures or procedures relying on deliberate generation of imagery. Some lines of research have focused on the experience of involuntary mental imagery (generally in the context of autobiographical memories) in both laboratory and everyday life settings. These may be of personal events (e.g. Berntsen and Jacobsen, 2008; Cole, Staugaard, and Berntsen, 2016) or standardized experimental stimuli (e.g. Holmes et al., 2010). However, these methods as currently implemented do not necessarily allow strict experimental control over whether the involuntary thought experienced at a specific moment is imagery-based or non-imagery-based. Causal inferences are thus harder to draw than in studies investigating deliberately generated imagery, in which someone can be instructed to use an imagery or non-imagery processing style in a particular moment. Developing methods to induce and elicit involuntary images and non-image-based thoughts derived from standardized stimuli and then observe their effects on relevant emotional and behavioral outcomes would be extremely helpful in this regard.

A final challenge to be mentioned here is reconciling theoretical predictions and statements about the important role of emotional mental imagery in everyday life, and the fact that the experience of mental imagery lies on a continuum, with some people experiencing little imagery in everyday life, or none at all. A simplistic interpretation of the emotional imagery literature might lead to the conclusion that a lack of mental imagery would lead to a life devoid of emotion, particularly past- or future-oriented; however, instances of people who are "aphantasic" and experience no mental imagery at all show that this is not the case (e.g. Zeman, Dewar, and Della Sala, 2015; see also Chapter 42). Further, although some studies find associations between general use or vividness of imagery and specific aspects of psychopathology (e.g. in relation to psychotic-like experiences; Aynsworth et al., 2017), it is often the case that measures of the use or experience of nonemotional imagery show no relationship with aspects of psychopathology such as depression or anxiety (e.g. Di Simplicio et al., 2016). It may be that the relevance of emotional mental imagery for individuals is dependent on the extent to which they experience mental imagery at all, or that it is the relative accessibility and experience of positive or negative imagery (or perhaps functional vs. dysfunctional) that is important for psychological health. Exploring the function and impact of emotional mental imagery across the range of individual differences in the general tendency to experience mental imagery in daily life could provide valuable insights.

Conclusions

For most of us, imagery is a frequent aspect of our mental experience in daily life, and much of this mental imagery is emotional. Emotional mental imagery appears to play a role in a number of important aspects of daily life, such as anticipating the future, decision-making, and planning. Conversely, dysfunctional experience of emotional mental imagery is associated with a range of problems from depression to anxiety. The properties of emotional mental imagery can be used for beneficial purposes both in everyday life, and in treatment of disorders such as PTSD and depression. Despite the explosion of research into emotional mental imagery in the last decade or so, there is a huge amount of work to be done in tying together a number of disparate research lines and overcoming some of the challenges in studying emotional mental imagery. However, emotional mental imagery is a fundamental aspect of imagination and this research can shed light on some of the richest aspects of human experience.

References

Arntz, A. (2012). Imagery Rescripting as a Therapeutic Technique: Review of Clinical Trials, Basic Studies, and Research Agenda. *Journal of Experimental Psychopathology, 3,* 121–126.

Aynsworth, C., Nemat, N., Collerton, D., Smailes, D., and Dudley, R. (2017). Reality Monitoring Performance and the Role of Visual Imagery in Visual Hallucinations. *Behaviour Research and Therapy, 97,* 115–122.

Baddeley, A. D., and Andrade, J. (2000). Working Memory and the Vividness of Imagery. *Journal of Experimental Psychology-General, 129,* 126–145.

Barsics, C., van der Linden, M., and D'Argembeau, A. (2016). Frequency, Characteristics, and Perceived Functions of Emotional Future Thinking in Daily Life. *The Quarterly Journal of Experimental Psychology, 69,* 217–233.

Berntsen, D., and Jacobsen, A. S. (2008). Involuntary (Spontaneous) Mental Time Travel into the Past and Future. *Consciousness and Cognition, 17,* 1093–1104.

Blackwell, S. E. (2019). Mental Imagery: From Basic Research to Clinical Practice. *Journal of Psychotherapy Integration, 29*(3), 235–247.

Blackwell, S. E., and Holmes, E. A. (2010). Modifying Interpretation and Imagination in Clinical Depression: A Single-Case Series Using Cognitive Bias Modification. *Applied Cognitive Psychology, 24,* 338–350.

Carrera, P., Caballero, A., and Muñoz, D. (2012). Future-Oriented Emotions in the Prediction of Binge-Drinking Intention and Expectation: The Role of Anticipated and Anticipatory Emotions. *Scandinavian Journal of Psychology, 53,* 273–279.

Chan, C. K. Y., and Cameron, L. D. (2012). Promoting Physical Activity with Goal-Oriented Mental Imagery: A Randomized Controlled Trial. *Journal of Behavioral Medicine, 35,* 347–363.

Cole, S. N., Staugaard, S. R., and Berntsen, D. (2016). Inducing Involuntary and Voluntary Mental Time Travel using a Laboratory Paradigm. *Memory & Cognition, 44,* 376–389.

Conroy, D., and Hagger, M. S. (2018). Imagery Interventions in Health Behavior: A Meta-Analysis. *Health Psychology, 37,* 668–679.

Conway, M. A., Meares, K., and Standart, S. (2004). Images and Goals. *Memory, 12,* 525–531.

Conway, M. A., Singer, J. A., and Tagini, A. (2004). The Self and Autobiographical Memory: Correspondence and Coherence. *Social Cognition, 22,* 491–529.

Cumming, J., and Williams, S. E. (2012). The Role of Imagery in Performance. In S. M. Murphy (ed.), *Handbook of Sport and Performance Psychology*. Oxford, UK: Oxford University Press, 213–232.

D'Argembeau, A., Renaud, O., and van der Linden, M. (2011). Frequency, Characteristics and Functions of Future-Oriented Thoughts in Daily Life. *Applied Cognitive Psychology, 25,* 96–103.

Di Simplicio, M., Renner, F., Blackwell, S. E., et al. (2016). An Investigation of Mental Imagery in Bipolar Disorder: Exploring "the Mind's Eye". *Bipolar Disorders, 18,* 669–683.

Edwards, D. (2007). Restructuring Implicational Meaning through Memory-Based Imagery: Some Historical Notes. *Journal of Behavior Therapy and Experimental Psychiatry, 38,* 306–316.

Ehlers, A., Clark, D. M., Hackmann, A., McManus, F., and Fennell, M. (2005). Cognitive Therapy for Post-Traumatic Stress Disorder: Development and Evaluation. *Behaviour Research and Therapy, 43,* 413–431.

Fritzsche, A., Schlier, B., Oettingen, G., and Lincoln, T. M. (2016). Mental Contrasting with Implementation Intentions Increases Goal-Attainment in Individuals with Mild to Moderate Depression. *Cognitive Therapy and Research, 40,* 557–564.

Golla, F., Hutton, E. L., and Walter, W. G. (1943). The Objective Study of Mental Imagery. *Journal of Mental Science, 89,* 216–223.

Görgen, S. M., Joormann, J., Hiller, W., and Witthöft, M. (2015). Implicit Affect after Mental Imagery: Introduction of a Novel Measure and Relations to Depressive Symptoms in a Non-Clinical Sample. *Journal of Experimental Psychopathology, 6,* 1–23.

Gregory, W. L., Cialdini, R. B., and Carpenter, K. M. (1982). Self-Relevant Scenarios as Mediators of Likelihood Estimates and Compliance – Does Imagining Make it So? *Journal of Personality and Social Psychology, 43,* 89–99.

Hales, S. A., Blackwell, S. E., Di Simplicio, M., et al. (2014). Imagery-Based Cognitive Behavioral Assessment. In G. P. Brown and D. A. Clark (eds.), *Assessment in Cognitive Therapy*. New York, NY: Guilford Press.

Hales, S. A., Deeprose, C., Goodwin, G. M., and Holmes, E. A. (2011). Cognitions in Bipolar Disorder versus Unipolar Depression: Imagining Suicide. *Bipolar Disorders, 13,* 651–661.

Hanrahan, C., and Vergeer, I. (2001). Multiple Uses of Mental Imagery by Professional Modern Dancers. *Imagination, Cognition and Personality, 20,* 231–255.

Hirsch, C. R., Mathews, A., Clark, D. M., Williams, R., and Morrison, J. (2005). The Causal Role of Negative Imagery in Social Anxiety: A Test in Confident Public Speakers. *Journal of Behavior Therapy and Experimental Psychiatry, 37,* 159–170.

Hitchcock, C., Mueller, V., Hammond, E., et al. (2016). The Effects of Autobiographical Memory Flexibility (MemFlex) Training: An Uncontrolled Trial in Individuals in Remission from Depression. *Journal of Behavior Therapy and Experimental Psychiatry, 52,* 92–98.

Hitchcock, C., Werner-Seidler, A., Blackwell, S. E., and Dalgleish, T. (2017). Autobiographical Episodic Memory-Based Training for the Treatment of Mood, Anxiety and Stress-Related Disorders: A Systematic Review and Meta-Analysis. *Clinical Psychology Review, 52,* 92–107.

Holmes, E. A., Blackwell, S. E., Burnett Heyes, S., Renner, F., and Raes, F. (2016). Mental Imagery in Depression: Phenomenology, Potential Mechanisms, and Treatment

Implications. *Annual Review of Clinical Psychology, 12.* doi:10.1146/annurev-clinpsy-021815-092925.

Holmes, E. A., James, E. L., Kilford, E. J., and Deeprose, C. (2010). Key Steps in Developing a Cognitive Vaccine against Traumatic Flashbacks: Visuospatial Tetris versus Verbal Pub Quiz. *PloS One, 5,* e13706.

Holmes, E. A., Lang, T. J., and Shah, D. M. (2009). Developing Interpretation Bias Modification as a "Cognitive Vaccine" for Depressed Mood – Imagining Positive Events Makes you Feel Better than Thinking about them Verbally. *Journal of Abnormal Psychology, 118,* 76–88.

Holmes, E. A., and Mathews, A. (2005). Mental Imagery and Emotion: A Special Relationship? *Emotion, 5,* 489–497.

Ivins, A., Di Simplicio, M., Close, H., Goodwin, G. M., and Holmes, E. A. (2014). Mental Imagery in Bipolar Affective Disorder versus Unipolar Depression: Investigating Cognitions at times of "Positive" Mood. *Journal of Affective Disorders, 166,* 234–242.

Iyadurai, L., Blackwell, S. E., Meiser-Stedman, et al. (2017). Preventing Intrusive Memories after Trauma via a Brief Intervention Involving Tetris Computer Game Play in the Emergency Department: A Proof-of-Concept Randomized Controlled Trial. *Molecular Psychiatry, 23*(3), 674–682. doi:10.1038/mp.2017.23.

Ji, J. L., Burnett Heyes, S., MacLeod, C., and Holmes, E. A. (2016). Emotional Mental Imagery as Simulation of Reality: Fear and Beyond. A Tribute to Peter Lang. *Behavior Therapy, 47,* 702–719.

Ji, J. L., Holmes, E. A., and Blackwell, S. E. (2017). Seeing Light at the End of the Tunnel: Positive Prospective Mental Imagery and Optimism in Depression. *Psychiatry Research, 247,* 155–162.

Kahneman, D., and Tversky, A. (1982). The Simulation Heuristic. In D. Kahneman, P. Slovic, and A. Tversky (eds.), *Judgement Under Uncertainty: Heuristics and Biases.* Cambridge, UK: Cambridge University Press, 201–208.

Kavanagh, D. J., Andrade, J., and May, J. (2005). Imaginary Relish and Exquisite Torture: The Elaborated Intrusion Theory of Desire. *Psychological Review, 112,* 446–467.

Kessler, H., Holmes, E. A., Blackwell, S. E., et al. (2018). Reducing Intrusive Memories of Trauma using a Visuospatial Interference Intervention with Inpatients with Post-Traumatic Stress Disorder (PTSD). *Journal of Consulting and Clinical Psychology, 86*(12), 1076–1090.

Knäuper, B., McCollam, A., Rosen-Brown, A., et al. (2011). Fruitful Plans: Adding Targeted Mental Imagery to Implementation Intentions Increases Fruit Consumption. *Psychology & Health, 26,* 601–617.

Korrelboom, K., de Jong, M., Huijbrechts, I., and Daansen, P. (2009). Competitive Memory Training (COMET) for Treating Low Self-Esteem in Patients with Eating Disorders: A Randomized Clinical Trial. *Journal of Consulting and Clinical Psychology, 77,* 974–980.

Krans, J., Näring, G., Holmes, E. A., and Becker, E. S. (2009). "I See What You Are Saying": Intrusive Images from Listening to a Traumatic Verbal Report. *Journal of Anxiety Disorders, 24,* 134–140.

Lang, P. J. (1979). A Bio-Informational Theory of Emotional Imagery. *Psychophysiology, 16,* 495–512.

Leer, A., Engelhard, I. M., and van den Hout, M. A. (2014). How Eye Movements in EMDR Work: Changes in Memory Vividness and Emotionality. *Journal of Behavior Therapy and Experimental Psychiatry, 45,* 396–401.

Libby, L. K., Shaeffer, E. M., Eibach, R. P., and Slemmer, J. A. (2007). Picture Yourself at the Polls – Visual Perspective in Mental Imagery Affects Self-Perception and Behavior. *Psychological Science*, *18*, 199–203.

Linke, J., and Wessa, M. (2017). Mental Imagery Training Increases Wanting of Rewards and Reward Sensitivity and Reduces Depressive Symptoms. *Behavior Therapy*, *48*, 695–706.

MacLeod, A. (2017). *Prospection, Well-Being, and Mental Health*. Oxford, UK: Oxford University Press.

Mathews, A. (1971). Psychophysiological Approaches to the Investigation of Desensitisation and Related Processes. *Psychological Bulletin*, *76*, 73–91.

Mathews, A., Ridgeway, V., and Holmes, E. A. (2013). Feels like the Real Thing: Imagery is both More Realistic and Emotional than Verbal Thought. *Cognition & Emotion*, *27*, 217–229.

Meevissen, Y. M. C., Peters, M. L., and Alberts, H. J. E. M. (2011). Become more Optimistic by Imagining a Best Possible Self: Effects of a Two-Week Intervention. *Journal of Behavior Therapy and Experimental Psychiatry*, *42*, 371–378.

Nelis, S., Debeer, E., Holmes, E. A., and Raes, F. (2013). Dysphoric Students Show Higher use of the Observer Perspective in their Retrieval of Positive versus Negative Autobiographical Memories. *Memory*, *21*, 423–430.

Oatley, K. (2011). *Such Stuff as Dreams: The Psychology of Fiction*. Oxford, UK: Wiley-Blackwell.

Pearson, J. (2014). New Directions in Mental-Imagery Research: The Binocular-Rivalry Technique and Decoding fMRI Patterns. *Current Directions in Psychological Science*, *23*, 178–183.

Pearson, J., Naselaris, T., Holmes, E. A., and Kosslyn, S. M. (2015). Mental Imagery: Functional Mechanisms and Clinical Applications. *Trends in Cognitive Sciences*, *19*, 590–602.

Pictet, A., Jermann, F., and Ceschi, G. (2016). When Less Could Be More: Investigating the Effects of a Brief Internet-Based Imagery Cognitive Bias Modification Intervention in Depression. *Behaviour Research and Therapy*, *84*, 45–51.

Pratt, D., Cooper, M. J., and Hackmann, A. (2004). Imagery and Its Characteristics in People Who Are Anxious about Spiders. *Behavioural & Cognitive Psychotherapy*, *32*, 165–176.

Raes, F., Williams, J. G., and Hermans, D. (2009). Reducing Cognitive Vulnerability to Depression: A Preliminary Investigation of Memory Specificity Training (MEST) in Inpatients with Depressive Symptomatology. *Journal of Behavior Therapy and Experimental Psychiatry*, *40*, 24–38.

Renner, F., Ji, J. L., Pictet, A., Holmes, E. A., and Blackwell, S. E. (2017). Effects of Engaging in Repeated Mental Imagery of Future Positive Events on Behavioural Activation in Individuals with Major Depressive Disorder. *Cognitive Therapy and Research*, *41*, 369–380.

Reynolds, M., and Brewin, C. R. (1998). Intrusive Cognitions, Coping Strategies and Emotional Responses in Depression, Post-Traumatic Stress Disorder and a Non-Clinical Population. *Behaviour Research and Therapy*, *36*, 135–147.

Schacter, D. L., Addis, D. R., and Buckner, R. L. (2008). Episodic Simulation of Future Events: Concepts, Data, and Applications. *New York Academy of Sciences*, *1124*, 39–60.

Stopa, L. (2009). *Imagery and the Threatened Self: Perspectives on Mental Imagery and the Self in Cognitive Therapy*. London, UK: Routledge.

Weßlau, C., Cloos, M., Höfling, V., and Steil, R. (2015). Visual Mental Imagery and Symptoms of Depression: Results from a Large-Scale Web-Based Study. *BMC Psychiatry, 15*, 308.

Wolpe, J. (1961). The Systematic Desensitization Treatment of Neurosis. *Journal of Nervous and Mental Disease, 132*, 189–203.

Zeman, A., Dewar, M., and Della Sala, S. (2015). Lives without Imagery – Congenital Aphantasia. *Cortex, 73*, 378–380.

17 Multisensory Perception and Mental Imagery

Christopher C. Berger

Most of us have the uncanny ability to recreate sensations we have experienced in the world around us in our mind. If you are unsure of how many red stripes are on the American flag, for example, you can conjure in your "mind's eye" a vivid "image" of the flag in your mind to figure it out. Similarly, if you were asked whether the word "bad" is in the first verse of the classic Beatles song, "Hey Jude," you can clearly "hear" Paul McCartney's voice sing the first line of the first verse, "Hey Jude, don't make it bad" to check. The ability to conjure these basic sensory experiences at will has been termed "mental imagery," and is arguably the most fundamental aspect of the imagination. What exactly are these mental images we create in our minds, and how similar to real sensations are they? Can what we imagine affect how we perceive the real world around us? In this chapter, we aim to address this topic from a multisensory perspective.

For almost half a century, mental imagery has been the topic of a lively debate in the field of psychology over whether the internally generated images we conjure in our mind's eye are "picture-like" (i.e. analog) copies of sensory impressions that maintain essential features of the physical world (Halpern, 1988; Kosslyn, 1973, 1994), or whether they are the product of more basic propositional representations of thought, which are the result of accessing and combining discrete symbols that form an abstract (rather than analog) impression of the thing in mind (Pylyshyn, 1973, 2002). While researchers on both sides of the debate have provided empirical evidence to support their case, ultimately the bulk of the findings in psychology and cognitive neuroscience seem to suggest that mental imagery preserves at least some parts of its veridical counterpart (Halpern, 1988; Kosslyn, Ball, and Reiser, 1978). This chapter will examine the leading hypothesis that mental imagery is a quasi-perceptual phenomenon that relies on at least partially overlapping representations in the brain, by focusing on psychophysical and neuroimaging evidence of interactions between mental imagery and veridical perception *across* sensory modalities. We will also describe recent data from psychophysics experiments that suggests that mental imagery can also lead to crossmodal plasticity and change future perception (Berger and Ehrsson, 2018). In doing so, we aim to provide a multisensory account for the perception-based theories of mental imagery, and to develop a more comprehensive understanding of the imagination. We will mainly focus this chapter on the visual and auditory modalities in light of the fact that these modalities feature most prominently in the literature on multisensory perception and mental imagery (Kosslyn, Ganis, and Thompson, 2001; Stein and Stanford, 2008).

Perception is a Product of Multisensory Integration

As you walk the streets of a busy city during the day, you will see buildings, streets, cars, bicyclists, and fellow pedestrians. You will hear the cacophony of passing cars, bells of bicyclists, and the indistinct chatter of people around you. You will feel the wind, the sun, or the rain on your face, and perhaps the bump of a passing stranger. How is all of this information put together into a coherent perception of the world? How do we know which sights go with which sounds, or whether the bump we just felt was from a passing pedestrian, bicyclist, or car? Without some form of integration of these pieces of information, we would not be able to determine which sounds go with which objects we see, which touches go with which sounds or objects we see, etc. The proposed mechanism for how the brain solves this information-processing problem is referred to as "multisensory integration."

Multisensory integration is generally defined as the effect that sensory stimuli from different sensory modalities have on an organism when they are combined rather than independent (Stein and Stanford, 2008). In the case of human perception, this can take the form of an enhancement or hindrance of perception in one or more sensory modalities, as is the case in multisensory interactions (i.e. when one sensory modality affects the processing of another sensory modality). Multisensory integration is, in fact, so critical to our conscious perception of the world around us that in a review article assessing the operations of the brain essential for multisensory processing Ghazanfar and Schroeder (2006) were compelled to pose the question: "Is [the] neocortex essentially multisensory?" in the title. When it comes to multisensory processing and the imagination, however, despite the abundance of behavioral, psychophysical, and neuroimaging data suggesting that mental imagery and perception involve overlapping representations, until recently, the possibility of multisensory interactions from real and imagined sensory stimuli across sensory modalities had never been considered. In the section that follows, we will first describe key findings from neuroscience highlighting the importance of multisensory integration for our perception of the world around us, and will then present recent work, which suggests that the imagery-perception relationship extends beyond a within-modality framework.

Multisensory Illusions

Some of the most dramatic examples of the perceptual consequences of multisensory integration can be readily observed in multisensory illusions. These are perceptual illusions that arise through the integration of two or more sensory stimuli. One such illusion is the cross-bounce illusion in which two moving visual objects that are normally perceived as passing one another by are perceived as colliding and bouncing off one another when an auditory stimulus is presented at the moment they meet (Sekuler, Sekuler, and Lau, 1997). In this case, the heard sound integrates with the seen moving objects to change how one perceives their movement.

The cross-bounce illusion nicely demonstrates the influence sounds can have over visual perception, but the McGurk illusion is an example of the opposite: the influence of visual perception over auditory perception. The McGurk illusion is an audiovisual speech illusion in which an auditory stimulus (e.g. /ba/) dubbed over videos of people silently articulating an incongruent speech stimulus (e.g. /ga/) leads to an illusory fused auditory percept (e.g. /da/). This illusory fused percept is the result of the compromise between the seen articulation in the video and the heard sound (McGurk and MacDonald, 1976). Neuroimaging experiments have found that the superior temporal sulcus (STS) is critically involved in the illusion, and that creating a temporary virtual lesion to this region using transcranial magnetic stimulation (TMS) severely disrupts the illusion (Beauchamp, Nath, and Pasalar, 2010). The involvement of the STS in the McGurk illusion is also consistent with other studies implicating the STS as a key region involved in integrating both speech and non-speech audiovisual stimuli (Beauchamp et al., 2004a; Calvert, Campbell, and Brammer, 2000; Marchant, Ruff, and Driver, 2012; Noppeney et al., 2008; Perrodin et al., 2014; Stevenson and James, 2009; Szycik et al., 2012; Werner and Noppeney, 2010a).

Another well-studied multisensory illusion is the ventriloquist effect. This illusion gets its name from the classic act of stagecraft in which a puppeteer moves the mouth of a puppet while keeping his or her own mouth still, thereby shifting the perceived location of the puppeteer's voice to the mouth of the puppet. In the study of multisensory integration, however, the ventriloquist effect refers to the translocation of auditory stimuli (usually simple tones) toward the perceived location of visual stimuli (usually simple flashes of light or briefly presented shapes) (Howard and Templeton, 1966; Wallace et al., 2004). Psychophysical behavioral experiments have revealed that the ventriloquism effect is the result of near optimal binding of audiovisual stimuli (Alais and Burr, 2004). Studies investigating the neural substrates of the ventriloquism effect in humans have revealed the involvement of the STS in the ventriloquist effect (Bischoff et al., 2007), as well as dynamic changes in activity in the auditory cortex (Bonath et al., 2007); findings that correspond nicely with electrophysiology studies on nonhuman primates (Bruce, Desimone, and Gross, 1981; Kayser and Logothetis, 2009; Seltzer and Pandya, 1994). Even more intriguing, researchers have found that repeated exposure to spatially disparate audiovisual stimuli can lead to plasticity of the auditory perceptual system, causing observers to misperceive auditory stimuli in the direction of the previously related visual stimulus – a so-called ventriloquism aftereffect (Frissen, Vroomen, and de Gelder, 2012; Frissen et al., 2005; Recanzone, 1998; Woods and Recanzone, 2004; Wozny and Shams, 2011). Thus, the ventriloquism illusion has been a very powerful tool for investigating multisensory integration.

Together, multisensory illusions such as these demonstrate the profound influence that incoming sensory information from one sensory modality can have on another, and our perception of the world around us. What about our internal representations of sensory information we generate in our mind? While it is well understood that mental imagery can influence ongoing perception within a sensory modality (Farah, 1985, 1989a; Hubbard, 2010; Mast, Berthoz, and Kosslyn, 2001; Pearson, Clifford, and Tong,

2008; Segal and Fusella, 1970), until recently, it was unknown whether mental imagery could influence sensory perception across sensory modalities. In the section that follows, we will examine the hypothesis that mental imagery in one modality can, through the process of multisensory integration, change perception in a different sensory modality.

Mental Imagery and Multisensory Integration

Multisensory illusions such as the cross-bounce illusion, the ventriloquism effect, and the McGurk effect have played an important role in furthering our understanding of how sensory information from different sensory modalities are integrated. However, research on mental imagery suggests that due to at least partially overlapping representations (Cichy, Heinzle, and Haynes, 2011; Farah, 1989b; Kosslyn, Ganis, and Thompson, 2001; O'Craven and Kanwisher, 2000), mental imagery can actually change how we perceive the world around us (Craver-Lemley and Reeves, 1987; Farah, 1985, 1989a; Mast, Berthoz, and Kosslyn, 2001; Perky, 1910; Segal and Fusella, 1970). How far do these similarities between mental imagery and perception extend? Is it possible for what one imagines in one sensory modality to not only affect ongoing perception in that same modality but also to integrate with incoming sensory information from other sensory modalities to change what one perceives in those as well? Multisensory illusions such as those described above provide an ideal testing ground for such questions.

Mental Imagery-Induced Cross-Bounce Illusion

One of the first sets of experiments examining the potential crossmodal influence of mental imagery on perception made use of the cross-bounce illusion. Rather than examining whether a real auditory stimulus can influence the perceived motion of two passing objects (Sekuler, Sekuler, and Lau, 1997), we examined whether mental imagery of a sound can influence the perceived motion of two passing objects (Berger and Ehrsson, 2013). In one experiment, participants were instructed to imagine hearing a "beep-like" auditory stimulus at one of three time-points while they were viewing two discs move diagonally at a 45°: 500 milliseconds before the discs met in the center of the screen, at the moment they met, and 500 milliseconds after they met at the center of the screen. The results showed that the participants perceived the discs to bounce significantly more when they imagined the sound at the moment the discs met than when they imagined the sound before or after they met, or when they did not imagine the sound at all (Berger and Ehrsson, 2013). This constituted the first evidence that imagining a sound can influence visual perception. Moreover, this result suggests that it is not enough to simply have the sound in mind when viewing the visual stimulus, but rather that it is important that the sound is imagined at the critical moment (i.e. when the disks meet) for the illusion to occur.

This is consistent with the original veridical demonstration of the illusion (Sekuler, Sekuler, and Lau, 1997), and also suggests that crossmodal interactions between mental imagery and perception follow the temporal rule of multisensory integration (i.e. that the crossmodal stimuli must be close in time for them to be integrated; Stein and Stanford, 2008). This is evidenced by the fact that the auditory stimuli that were imagined closest to the moment of coincidence of the discs led to the largest change in visual perception. Additionally, subsequent controls revealed that if a tapping movement (with the right index finger on the desk in front of the participants) was imagined at the moment the discs met this could also elicit the illusion that the discs bounced rather than crossed; however, imagining the same movement without the tapping sensation (by having participants imagine the same movement but with the hand rotated 180° so that the palm was facing upward) did not elicit the illusion. This finding was consistent with previous research demonstrating that tactile sensations can also elicit the illusion (Shimojo and Shams, 2001), and revealed that tactile-motor imagery can also influence crossmodal sensory perception. Additionally, the absence of the illusion when the tactile component of the imagined movement was not included (with the hand rotated) suggests that the imagery-induced version of the illusion cannot be explained by changes in executive attention. If the effect were merely due to changes in executive attention when the disks met in the center of the screen, then one would expect the effect to be present for both of the motor imagery conditions, as changes in executive attention are equivalent in these two conditions.

The question of whether the cross-bounce illusion can be explained by changes in attention or response bias (i.e. that the participants responded in accordance to what they thought the experimenter wanted) has also been posed for the veridical version of the cross-bounce illusion (Grassi and Casco, 2009). Experiments conducted specifically to address this concern revealed that the cross-bounce illusion cannot be accounted for by attentional mechanisms or response bias (Grassi and Casco, 2009, 2012). Similarly, further experiments on the imagery-induced cross-bounce illusion were conducted to examine whether the content of the imagined auditory stimulus would change the illusory perception of bounce, and to rule out alternative explanations for the increase illusion.

Following the methodology of Grassi and Casco (2009), we examined whether imagining a damped auditory stimulus (artificially simulating the acoustics of a collision) at the moment the discs met significantly increased susceptibility to the illusory perception compared to imagining a ramped auditory stimulus (the damped sound played backward and not indicative of a collision) or not imagining an auditory stimulus at all (Berger and Ehrsson, 2017). Additionally, we manipulated the extent to which the discs overlapped in order to make the discs appear more bounce-like. Therefore, the discs overlapped 100 percent (least bounce-like), over-lapped by 80 percent (more bounce-like), or overlapped only by 60 percent (most bounce-like) in the center of the screen as they were passing. The rationale for this additional visual manipulation was as follows: If participants were responding on the basis of tacit knowledge or response bias, they would essentially disregard the subtle visual cues, and we would see uniform responses (of bounce or cross) for a given imagined sound across all three overlap conditions; however, if participants were reporting their genuine perception, then the probability of a bounce percept should scale according to the extent that the discs overlap. The results from this experiment revealed that only mental imagery of the damped sound at the moment the discs met significantly facilitated the illusory bounce percept compared to mental imagery of the ramped sound or no mental imagery. Moreover, consistent with the notion of a genuine perceptual phenomenon, the results indicated that this illusory perception of bounce scaled according to the extent that the discs overlapped (i.e. the less the discs overlapped, the more they were perceived as bouncing) (Berger and Ehrsson, 2017). These results dovetailed nicely with the results obtained using real ramped and damped auditory stimuli in a subsequent second experiment conducted in the same group of participants.

Following the experiment, the participants were also asked to rate how vividly they were able to imagine the auditory stimuli during the experiment. In examining whether there was a relationship between the strength of the participants' mental imagery and the strength of the cross-bounce illusion when imagining a damped auditory stimulus, we observed a significant positive relationship. That is, the more vividly the participants were able to imagine the auditory stimulus at the moment the discs met, the more likely they were to see them bounce off rather than cross by one another.

An additional third experiment using the same conditions as above was conducted to directly address the possibility that mental imagery of the damped or ramped sounds differentially affected visuospatial attention in a manner that could account for the significant differences in the reported perception of the bounce percept. Using the same visual stimuli (i.e. with different percentages of overlap at the center) as in the above experiment, the participants were again asked to imagine either the ramped, damped, or no sound at the moment the discs met; however, rather than reporting whether they perceived the discs to cross or bounce after every trial, they were asked to report whether they perceived the discs to fully overlap or not. A signal detection analysis (Macmillan and Kaplan, 1985) was then conducted to determine whether there were significant differences in participants' performance (i.e. as indicated by the sensitivity index = d') when imagining the damped vs. imagining ramped sounds. This analysis revealed that there was no difference between performances in the damped and ramped sound conditions, suggesting that there were no significant differences in visuospatial attention between the two tasks. Additional analyses revealed there were also no significant differences in participants' response strategy (i.e. as indicated by the response bias index = c) between these two conditions (Berger and Ehrsson, 2017). The results from this study show that imagined sounds are integrated with real visual stimuli to change visual perception in a content-specific manner that mirrors the integration of real auditory and visual stimuli, and that the mental imagery-induced cross-bounce illusion cannot be explained away by changes in executive attention or response bias.

Mental Imagery-Induced McGurk Illusion

In the above studies, we found that auditory mental imagery can change the perceived motion of visual objects. What about "higher-level" processes? Could auditory imagery affect visual speech perception? To test this, we devised a novel experimental paradigm that took advantage of the McGurk illusion (Berger and Ehrsson, 2013). However, whereas the McGurk illusion usually refers to the visual influence over auditory perception, we devised an experiment to examine whether auditory imagery can alter the perception of visual speech stimuli (McGurk and MacDonald, 1976). That is, can speech sounds one imagines hearing affect what we see people saying?

To examine whether auditory imagery of speech stimuli can influence visual speech perception, we examined whether imagining hearing /ba/ (as opposed to actually hearing the sound in the classic McGurk effect) at the moment participants saw someone in a silent video recording articulating /ga/ would lead to the illusory misperception that the person in the video was articulating /da/. This was compared to one control condition in which the participants imagined hearing /ka/ and another control condition when they did not imagine an auditory stimulus and simply viewed the silent video. In light of previous research demonstrating marked individual differences in the susceptibility of the classic McGurk illusion (Magnotti et al., 2015), the participants were also tested for whether they experienced the classic version of the illusion at the conclusion of the experiment.

The results from this experiment showed that imagining hearing /ba/ while viewing silent videos of someone articulating /ga/ significantly promoted the illusory perception that the person in the video was articulating /da/ compared to when participants were imagining /ka/ or were simply viewing the videos. Moreover, we found that this effect was specific to individuals who perceived the classic McGurk illusion in a post-experiment free-response test for the effect (Berger and Ehrsson, 2013). That is, the participants who did not experience the classic McGurk illusion also did not experience the imagery-induced McGurk effect. These findings are consistent with recent evidence of a reverse-McGurk effect (Spence and Deroy, 2012; Sweeny et al., 2012) for real speech stimuli, and suggest that auditory speech imagery can alter visual speech perception.

Mental Imagery-Induced Ventriloquism Illusion

So far, the above studies describe the crossmodal influence that the integration of imagined auditory and real visual stimuli could have on visual perception. However, it is also possible for visual stimuli to influence auditory perception. This is the case in the ventriloquist illusion, whereby simultaneously presented auditory and visual stimuli in spatially disparate locations leads to the illusory mislocalization of the auditory stimulus toward the location of the visual stimulus. We sought to examine whether visual mental imagery could also elicit this mislocalization of auditory stimuli toward the location of the imagined visual stimulus.

In one study, while keeping their eyes focused straight ahead of them at a fixation cross in the center of the screen, the participants were instructed to imagine seeing a brief flash of a small white disk on the screen in front of them at the end of a countdown. A visual cue just before the countdown instructed them where to imagine the brief visual stimulus in one of four possible locations on the screen. At the same time that they imagined the visual stimulus, an auditory stimulus was presented at the same location in which they imagined the light, at a slight angular offset of 15°, or at a greater angular offset of 30°. Additionally, on some of the trials, the participants were instructed not to imagine the visual stimulus, and only the auditory stimulus was presented. The participants were then asked to point (using a mouse linked to an overhead projector) where they perceived the source of the auditory stimulus.

The results from this experiment revealed that imagined visual stimuli altered the perceived location of auditory stimuli (Berger and Ehrsson, 2013). Specifically, we calculated a percentage visual bias – the mean localization error when the participants heard an auditory stimulus and did not imagine a visual stimulus minus the mean localization error when they imagined a visual stimulus at the same time as an auditory stimulus, then divided by the actual spatial disparity between the imagined visual and the real auditory stimulus and multiplied by 100 – for conditions in which the imagined visual and real auditory stimulus came from different locations. This analysis showed that imagining a visual stimulus at the same time but in a different location as an auditory stimulus led to an illusory translocation of the auditory stimulus towards the imagined visual stimulus. We also found a larger percentage visual bias when the disparity between the visual and auditory stimulus was greater (i.e. 15° vs. 30°) (Berger and Ehrsson, 2013).

Furthermore, we calculated a multisensory enhancement index (MEI) – the mean localization error when the auditory stimulus was presented alone minus the mean localization error when the participants imagined a visual stimulus at the same time as an auditory stimulus, divided by the mean localization error when the auditory stimulus was presented alone – and found that imagining a visual stimulus at the same time and same location as an auditory stimulus significantly enhanced auditory localization ability. That is, the participants were better at localizing an auditory stimulus when they imagined an auditory stimulus in the same location compared to when they heard the auditory stimulus alone. Both the percentage visual bias and MEI results from this experiment were also in line with the results from a "real-stimulus" version of the experiment (in which visual stimuli were actually presented rather than imagined) conducted with the same participants at the conclusion of the imagery version of the experiment.

One possible concern with the above results is that the effect could be explained not by a genuine shift in auditory perception resulting from multisensory integration, but rather by a bias to respond in the direction of the imagined visual stimulus. To address this concern, an additional experiment that made use of a psychophysical staircasing procedure was conducted. In this procedure, participants made binary (left or right) judgments about the location of sounds presented one at a time from the left or the right. The sounds began at the far left and right extreme edges of the visual display and moved gradually toward the center as participants made correct responses. When participants made a wrong response, the sound location moved back one step (i.e. away from fixation) in the staircase. Using this technique, a region of uncertainty for the location of auditory stimuli can be calculated by averaging the distance between the left and right staircases for the first eight response reversals the participants made. A response reversal is simply defined as a response that was different than a previous response. We found that the region of uncertainty significantly increased when participants imagined seeing a visual stimulus in the center of the screen at the same time as they heard the auditory stimuli compared to when they were localizing the auditory stimuli alone. This result is consistent with the hypothesis that auditory stimuli were translocated toward the imagined visual stimuli, causing response reversals earlier on than when no visual stimulus was imagined. This result was also consistent with a multisensory integration interpretation of the influence of the simultaneously imagined visual stimuli over the perceived location of the auditory stimuli.

Neuroimaging Evidence for an Imagery-Induced Ventriloquist Illusion

The above behavioral evidence suggests that imagined visual stimuli can integrate with simultaneously presented auditory stimuli to change the perceived location of auditory stimuli in our environment. We made use of functional magnetic resonance imaging (fMRI) to examine whether this imagery-induced ventriloquism effect was associated with activity in multisensory regions known to be involved in the integration of veridical audiovisual stimuli (Berger and Ehrsson, 2014). Specifically, we examined whether synchronous but spatially disparate imagined visual but real auditory stimuli led to increased activation in the superior temporal sulcus (STS). To accommodate the fMRI scanning protocol and environment, the ventriloquism experimental paradigm was modified so that the participants imagined seeing a white disk appear either to the left or to the right of the central fixation at the same time as a monophonic auditory stimulus (perceived as spatially centered). In this simplified version, the participants simply reported whether they perceived the auditory stimulus to be located in the center, to the left, or to the right. Consistent with the above imagery-induced ventriloquism studies, the behavioral results obtained during fMRI confirmed a significant ventriloquism effect for synchronously imagined visual stimuli. Imagining a visual stimulus at the same time but at a different location than an auditory stimulus led to a significant translocation of auditory stimuli toward the imagined visual stimuli's location compared to when the visual stimuli was imagined at a different time and location than auditory stimuli (i.e. asynchronous).

Analysis of the fMRI data compared the blood-oxygen level dependent (BOLD) signal for synchronously and asynchronously imagined visual and real auditory stimuli and showed significant activation within the left superior temporal sulcus (L. STS). This region was identified as a key region for the integration of real audiovisual stimuli from fMRI scans of the veridical version of the experiment run on the same group of participants that used real visual stimuli (rather than imagined visual stimuli), as well as previous studies (Barraclough et al., 2005; Ghazanfar, Chandrasekaran, and Logothetis, 2008; Marchant, Ruff, and Driver, 2012). Thus, these findings suggest that the imagery-induced ventriloquism effect is the product of the successful integration of imagined visual stimuli and real auditory stimuli in the STS. We also calculated the strength of the imagery ventriloquism effect for each participant and examined whether there was any brain activity that was related to the strength of the imagery-induced ventriloquism effect. This analysis revealed that activity in the STS could be predicted by the strength of the mental imagery-induced ventriloquist effect, further strengthening our conclusion that visual mental imagery and real auditory stimuli are integrated by the STS to elicit the ventriloquism illusion

(Berger and Ehrsson, 2014). The fMRI analyses also revealed increased connectivity between the STS and auditory cortex during the synchronous compared to the asynchronous condition. Furthermore, in assessing the relationship between the strength of the mental imagery-induced ventriloquism effect and the effective connectivity between the STS and the auditory cortex across participants, we found that a stronger imagery-induced ventriloquism effect was associated with stronger effective connectivity between the STS and the auditory cortex.

Together, the findings from this neuroimaging study suggest the integration of real and imagined audiovisual stimuli involves the same neural mechanisms as the integration of real audiovisual stimuli. These findings nicely converge with previous neuroimaging studies on the classic version of the ventriloquist effect (Bischoff et al., 2007; Bonath et al., 2007), and the involvement of the STS is consistent with previous neuroimaging studies that have implicated the STS in the integration of audiovisual stimuli across a range of stimulus types (Beauchamp, Nath, and Pasalar, 2010; Beauchamp et al., 2004b; Bischoff et al., 2007; Driver and Noesselt, 2008; Nath and Beauchamp, 2011; Noesselt et al., 2007; Werner and Noppeney, 2010b).

Crossmodal Plasticity from Mental Imagery

In a recent study we extended the above findings to investigate whether repeated exposure to the imagery-induced ventriloquist illusion could lead to plasticity of the auditory system (Berger and Ehrsson, 2018). Research on the classic ventriloquist effect has found that repeated exposure to synchronously presented spatially disparate audiovisual stimuli leads to a recalibration of the auditory system in the direction of the visual stimulus even when the visual stimulus is no longer present—i.e. a ventriloquism aftereffect (Lewald, 2002; Recanzone, 1998; Wozny and Shams, 2011). Thus, we took advantage of the imagery-induced ventriloquist effect to examine whether it, too, can lead to changes in *future* auditory perception. In this experiment participants imagined the visual stimulus for 100 milliseconds, once per second, in the center of the screen for 30 seconds. In separate blocks, a white-noise auditory stimulus was either presented in the same location as the imagined visual stimulus, 8° to the left of the imagined visual stimulus (i.e. rightward adaptation), or 8° to the right (i.e. leftward adaptation) of the imagined visual stimulus. Following this exposure phase, the participants heard white-noise stimuli come from five different locations (i.e. ±16°, ±8°, or 0°) and indicated whether they heard the sound come from the left or the right. From these data each participant's point of subjective equivalence (PSE) – the point at which the participant could no longer perceive an auditory stimulus from the left or the right – was calculated for each condition and then compared across participants.

The results from this experiment revealed a significant leftward shift in the PSEs for sounds localized following rightward adaptation compared to sounds localized following same-location adaptation. In the same vein, a significant leftward shift in the PSEs was observed for sounds localized following leftward adaptation, compared to same-location adaptation. These results were also consistent with a "real-stimulus" version of the experiment conducted on a separate group of subjects (Berger and Ehrsson, 2018).

Additional studies have examined whether this imagery-induced ventriloquism aftereffect was selective to the specific type of sound being played. This would strengthen the conclusion that the same neural mechanisms involved in the plasticity of the auditory system were engaged as with real stimuli in the classic ventriloquism aftereffect, which has been shown to be specific to the type of sounds being presented during adaptation (Recanzone, 1998; Woods and Recanzone, 2004). Furthermore, these experiments also served to rule out the possibility that the effect was merely the result of being presented with auditory stimuli in a spatial location to the left or right repeatedly (although this is highly unlikely given that this would mean that the participants responded counter to the location in which the auditory stimulus was presented, during the adaptation periods when making their responses in the test phases).

In line with previous studies on the ventriloquist aftereffect that have demonstrated that the ventriloquism aftereffect does not transfer across sounds with different frequencies (Recanzone, 1998; Woods and Recanzone, 2004), we found no transference of adaptation from the imagined visual stimulus and sine-wave auditory stimulus to a white noise stimulus presented in the test phase (a finding that was consistent with a real-visual-stimulus version of the experiment) (Berger and Ehrsson, 2018). Additional experiments also confirmed that a significant ventriloquism aftereffect was present when sine-wave auditory stimuli were used in both the adaptation and test phases of both visual imagery and real visual stimulus versions of the experiment. Together, the results from these experiments suggest that a systematic spatial discrepancy between visual mental imagery and a real auditory stimulus can lead to multisensory recalibration and plasticity in our auditory perceptual system. Moreover, these findings suggest that when we imagine something it not only has an effect on our current perception of the world around us, but also can lead to plastic changes in how we perceive the world in the future.

Unresolved Issues and Areas for Future Work

Here we have discussed the similarities between mental imagery and perception; however, there are also marked differences. For instance, under normal circumstances we are aware of when we are imagining and when we are perceiving, and we can manipulate and change what we are imagining at will, whereas there is usually little we can do to change how we perceive something (at least without appealing to imagination). Further research on mental imagery-induced multisensory illusions may be useful in examining exactly how it is that we are capable of distinguishing between real and imagined sensory stimuli during everyday perception. Perhaps, for example, the difference we experience between our perception of real and imagined stimuli relies on fine-grain patterns of activity within sensory and association cortices. Alternatively, it may also be the case that mental imagery and perception rely on the same fine-grain patterns of activity in these regions, and that the differences instead lie with connectivity of the prefrontal cortex to sensory and association cortices. Such a finding would be in line with the proposed mechanism for failures to distinguish between endogenous and exogenous sensory percepts during hallucinations in schizophrenic patients, for example (Johns et al., 2001; Plaze et al., 2011). Future neuroimaging experiments that make use of additional analysis techniques such as Multivariate Pattern Analysis (MVPA) might be useful in examining these questions.

What are the limitations of mental imagery-perception interactions? Although we have been able to establish a place for mental imagery in multisensory perception, there are also certain limitations to crossmodal interactions from imagined sensory stimuli. For instance, in pilot experiments that made use of the sound-induced flash illusion (Shams, Kamitani, and Shimojo, 2000) – an auditory-to-visual multisensory illusion whereby presentation of two or more beeps presented at the same time as a single visual stimulus produces the illusory perception that there was more than one visual stimulus presented – we were unable to elicit the illusion using auditory imagery. One possible explanation as to why imagined auditory stimuli were unable to produce this illusion is that mental imagery requires more processing time than its bottom-up counterpart. This is consistent with behavioral evidence suggesting that it can take 400–500 milliseconds for participants to successfully generate a clear mental image from cue (Weber and Castleman, 1970). In the sound-induced flash illusion the auditory stimuli that produce the illusion are presented for only 7 milliseconds and are only 57 milliseconds apart (Andersen, Tiippana, and Sams, 2004; Shams, Kamitanai, and Shimojo, 2000). Thus, these rapid stimulus presentations may very well lie outside the scope of what it is possible to simulate in our minds. Furthermore, matching the timing of the imagined auditory stimulus in this illusion is extremely difficult as the visual stimuli are only presented very briefly (< 20 milliseconds), and the sound-induced flash illusion is much less forgiving about temporal disparities between the audiovisual stimuli than the other multisensory illusions for which we have found crossmodal effects of imagery (Andersen, Tiippana, and Sams, 2004). For example, the sound-induced flash illusion is abolished with temporal disparities between the auditory and visual stimulus as small as 100 milliseconds (Shams, Kamitani, and Kimojo, 2000), whereas the McGurk illusion persists for temporal disparities between the auditory and visual stimuli of up to 200 milliseconds (van Wassenhove, Grant, and Poeppel, 2007). This point further highlights the differences between mental imagery and perception described above. Future work will be useful in determining the limits of mental imagery when it comes to simulating perception in our mind, as well as to explore more thoroughly what sets mental imagery apart from perception.

Most of what we know about the neural foundations of mental imagery comes from behavioral and neuroimaging techniques in humans. However, this is contrary to how research is conducted on the neural underpinnings of sensory perception, where much of our understanding of the neural mechanisms of sensory perception has been gleaned from models derived from experiments on nonhuman animals. Of course, this is a built-in limitation in the study of mental imagery because of its very nature: Generating mental images is a conscious (albeit seemingly low-level) cognitive process, and we cannot instruct monkeys, cats, mice, hamsters, or zebrafish to imagine things. However, it has been argued that mental imagery can be evoked clearly and vividly without the conscious intention to do so (Albright, 2012; Allen et al., 2013) – an implicitly elicited imagination, if you will. Conceptually, this is nicely demonstrated by Wegner's studies on ironic processing – one cannot help but imagine a white bear, even when explicitly instructed not to do so (Wegner, 1994). In Wegner's example, whether the result is a mental image or conceptual was not of particular interest; however, if I ask you *not* to imagine a spider, you likely do so, and if spiders bother you, I would wager that it is not the "idea" of the spider but your quasi-perceptual experience (i.e. your mental image) of it that you find disturbing.

One clear example of the automatic elicitation of visual mental images comes from experiments that have found that motion language (e.g. words and phrases describing motion in a particular direction) can produce a visual motion aftereffect (i.e. an aftereffect of visual perception in which static objects are perceived as moving in the opposite direction to previously moving visual stimuli), suggesting that the linguistic descriptions of visual motion produce sufficiently vivid mental images that a visual motion aftereffect could be induced as a result even without the participants' conscious intention to imagine the visual stimuli (Dils and Boroditsky, 2010; Winawer, Huk, and Boroditsky, 2010). Following this same logic, Schlack and Albright (2007) trained monkeys to associate visual motion of specific directions with specific static objects and then examined whether visual motion-sensitive neurons in the medial temporal cortex (i.e. visual area MT) demonstrated motion selectivity for the previously paired static objects. They found that MT neurons now displayed direction selectivity for the static objects compared to pre-training presentations of those same static objects, suggesting that following training, the static object automatically elicited a visual mental image of the moving stimulus (Albright, 2012; Schlack and Albright, 2007). This work provides a model of mental imagery that allows for the implicit involuntary triggering of specific mental images. The possibility of triggering specific and vivid mental images involuntarily may enable researchers to bypass the temporal limitations (and limitations in content specificity, etc.) of voluntary mental imagery, allowing for the exploration of more rapid and dynamic interactions with ongoing crossmodal sensory perception. While future work may examine this, this line of work will also serve to determine whether voluntary and involuntary mental imagery are fundamentally the same or represent distinct cognitive and/or perceptual processes.

Conclusions

Mental imagery enables us to do the impossible: It allows us to "see" what we do not see, "hear" what we do not hear, and "feel" what we do not feel. In this sense it is inherent to the imagination. In this chapter we have shown that mental imagery is a quasi-perceptual phenomenon with many overlapping features with veridical perception. Moreover, we have shown that mental imagery can interact and integrate with ongoing perception, not only within but also between the senses. We have also shown that this interaction between mental imagery and perception even has the potential to lead to brain plasticity and shape how we perceive the world in the future. Future work in this area should continue to explore the neural basis for the integration of mental imagery and crossmodal perception, and mental imagery-induced crossmodal plasticity. Such investigations will also help us to understand the neural basis for what sets mental imagery apart from sensory perception, and how we can know that what we are imagining is not real, yet it can still have such a profound effect on how we perceive reality itself.

References

Alais, D., and Burr, D. (2004). The Ventriloquist Effect Results from Near-Optimal Bimodal Integration. *Current Biology: CB, 14*(3), 257–262.

Albright, T. D. (2012). On the Perception of Probable Things: Neural Substrates of Associative Memory, Imagery, and Perception. *Neuron, 74*(2), 227–245.

Allen, A. K., Wilkins, K., Gazzaley, A., and Morsella, E. (2013). Conscious Thoughts from Reflex-Like Processes: A New Experimental Paradigm for Consciousness Research. *Consciousness and Cognition, 22*(4), 1318–1331.

Andersen, T. S., Tiippana, K., and Sams, M. (2004). Factors Influencing Audiovisual Fission and Fusion Illusions. *Cognitive Brain Research, 21*(3), 301–308.

Barraclough, N. E., Xiao, D., Baker, C. I., Oram, M. W., and Perrett, D. I. (2005). Integration of Visual and Auditory Information by Superior Temporal Sulcus Neurons Responsive to the Sight of Actions. *Journal of Cognitive Neuroscience, 17*(3), 377–391.

Beauchamp, M. S., Argall, B. D., Bodurka, J., Duyn, J. H., and Martin, A. (2004a). Unraveling Multisensory Integration: Patchy Organization within Human STS Multisensory Cortex. *Nature Neuroscience, 7*(11), 1190–1192.

Beauchamp, M. S., Lee, K. E., Argall, B. D., and Martin, A. (2004b). Integration of Auditory and Visual Information about Objects in Superior Temporal Sulcus. *Neuron, 41*(5), 809–823. www.ncbi.nlm.nih.gov/pubmed/15813999.

Beauchamp, M. S., Nath, A. R., and Pasalar, S. (2010). fMRI-Guided Transcranial Magnetic Stimulation Reveals that the Superior Temporal Sulcus is a Cortical Locus of the McGurk Effect. *Journal of Neuroscience, 30*(7), 2414–2417.

Berger, C. C., and Ehrsson, H. H. (2013). Mental Imagery Changes Multisensory Perception. *Current Biology, 23*, 1367–1372.

(2014). The Fusion of Mental Imagery and Sensation in the Temporal Association Cortex. *Journal of Neuroscience, 34*(41), 13684–13692.

(2017). The Content of Imagined Sounds Changes Visual Motion Perception in the Cross-Bounce Illusion. *Scientific Reports, 7*, 40123.

(2018). Mental Imagery Induces Crossmodal Sensory Plasticity and Changes Future Auditory Perception. *Psychological Science, 29*(6), 926–935.

Bischoff, M., Walter, B., Blecker, C. R., et al. (2007). Utilizing the Ventriloquism-Effect to Investigate Audiovisual Binding. *Neuropsychologia, 45*(3), 578–586.

Bonath, B., Noesselt, T., Martinez, A., et al. (2007). Neural Basis of the Ventriloquist Illusion. *Current Biology: CB, 17*(19), 1697–1703.

Bruce, C., Desimone, R., and Gross, C. G. (1981). Visual Properties of Neurons in a Polysensory Area in Superior Temporal Sulcus of the Macaque. *Journal of Neurophysiology, 46*(2), 369–384. www.ncbi.nlm.nih.gov/pubmed/6267219.

Calvert, G. A., Campbell, R., and Brammer, M. J. (2000). Evidence from Functional Magnetic Resonance Imaging of Crossmodal Binding in the Human Heteromodal Cortex. *Current Biology: CB*, *10*(11), 649–657. www.ncbi.nlm.nih.gov/pubmed/10837246.

Cichy, R. M., Heinzle, J., and Haynes, J.-D. (2011). Imagery and Perception Share Cortical Representations of Content and Location. *Cerebral Cortex*, *22*(2), 372–380.

Craver-Lemley, C., and Reeves, A. (1987). Visual Imagery Selectively Reduces Vernier Acuity. *Perception*, *16*(5), 599–614.

Dils, A. T., and Boroditsky, L. (2010). Visual Motion Aftereffect from Understanding Motion Language. *Proceedings of the National Academy of Sciences of the United States of America*, *107*, 16396–16400.

Driver, J., and Noesselt, T. (2008). Multisensory Interplay Reveals Crossmodal Influences on "Sensory-Specific" Brain Regions, Neural Responses, and Judgments. *Neuron*, *57*(1), 11–23.

Farah, M. J. (1985). Psychophysical Evidence for a Shared Representational Medium for Mental Images and Percepts. *Journal of Experimental Psychology. General*, *114*(1), 91–103. www.ncbi.nlm.nih.gov/pubmed/3156947.

(1989a). Mechanisms of Imagery-Perception Interaction. *Journal of Experimental Psychology. Human Perception and Performance*, *15*(2), 203–211. www.ncbi.nlm.nih.gov/pubmed/2525596.

(1989b). The Neural Basis of Mental Imagery. *Trends in Neurosciences*, *12*(10), 395–399. www.ncbi.nlm.nih.gov/pubmed/8137002.

Frissen, I., Vroomen, J., and de Gelder, B. (2012). The Aftereffects of Ventriloquism: The Time Course of the Visual Recalibration of Auditory Localization. *Seeing and Perceiving*, *25*(1), 1–14.

Frissen, I., Vroomen, J., de Gelder, B., and Bertelson, P. (2005). The Aftereffects of Ventriloquism: Generalization Across Sound-Frequencies. *Acta Psychologica*, *118* (1–2), 93–100.

Ghazanfar, A. A., Chandrasekaran, C., and Logothetis, N. K. (2008). Interactions Between the Superior Temporal Sulcus and Auditory Cortex Mediate Dynamic Face/Voice Integration in Rhesus Monkeys. *Journal of Neuroscience*, *28*(17), 4457–4469.

Ghazanfar, A. A., and Schroeder, C. E. (2006). Is Neocortex Essentially Multisensory? *Trends in Cognitive Sciences*, *10*(6), 278–285.

Grassi, M., and Casco, C. (2009). Audiovisual Bounce-Inducing Effect: Attention Alone Does Not Explain Why the Discs Are Bouncing. *Journal of Experimental Psychology. Human Perception and Performance*, *35*(1), 235–243.

(2012). Revealing the Origin of the Audiovisual Bounce-Inducing Effect. *Seeing and Perceiving*, *25*(2), 223–233.

Halpern, A. R. (1988). Mental Scanning in Auditory Imagery for Songs. *Journal of Experimental Psychology. Learning, Memory, and Cognition*, *14*(3), 434–443. www.ncbi.nlm.nih.gov/pubmed/2969942.

Howard, I. P., and Templeton, W. B. (1966). *Human Spatial Orientation*. London, UK: Wiley.

Hubbard, T. L. (2010). Auditory Imagery: Empirical Findings. *Psychological Bulletin*, *136* (2), 302–329.

Johns, L. C., Rossell, S., Frith, C., et al. (2001). Verbal Self-Monitoring and Auditory Verbal Hallucinations in Patients with Schizophrenia. *Psychological Medicine*, *31*, 705–715.

Kayser, C., and Logothetis, N. K. (2009). Directed Interactions between Auditory and Superior Temporal Cortices and their Role in Sensory Integration. *Frontiers in Integrative Neuroscience*, *3*(May), 1–11.

Kosslyn, S. M. (1973). Scanning Visual Images: Some Structural Implications. *Perception & Psychophysics*, *14*(1), 90–94.

(1994). *Image and Brain: The Resolution of the Imagery Debate*. Cambridge, MA: MIT Press.

Kosslyn, S. M., Ball, T. M., and Reiser, B. J. (1978). Visual Images Preserve Metric Spatial Information: Evidence from Studies of Image Scanning. *Journal of Experimental Psychology. Human Perception and Performance*, *4*(1), 47–60. www .ncbi.nlm.nih.gov/pubmed/627850.

Kosslyn, S. M., Ganis, G., and Thompson, W. L. (2001). Neural Foundations of Imagery. *Nature Reviews. Neuroscience*, *2*(9), 635–642.

Lewald, J. (2002). Rapid Adaptation to Auditory-Visual Spatial Disparity. *Learning & Memory*, *9*(5), 268–278.

Macmillan, N. A., and Kaplan, H. L. (1985). Detection Theory Analysis of Group Data: Estimating Sensitivity from Average Hit and False-Alarm Rates. *Psychological Bulletin*, *98*(1), 185–199.

Magnotti, J. F., Basu Mallick, D., Feng, G., et al. (2015). Similar Frequency of the McGurk Effect in Large Samples of Native Mandarin Chinese and American English Speakers. *Experimental Brain Research*, *233*(9), 2581–2586.

Marchant, J. L., Ruff, C. C., and Driver, J. (2012). Audiovisual Synchrony Enhances BOLD Responses in a Brain Network Including ultisensory STS While Also Enhancing Target-Detection Performance for Both Modalities. *Human Brain Mapping*, *33*(5), 1212–1224.

Mast, F. W., Berthoz, A., and Kosslyn, S. M. (2001). Mental Imagery of Visual Motion Modifies the Perception of Roll-Vection Stimulation. *Perception*, *30*(8), 945–957.

McGurk, H., and MacDonald, J. (1976). Hearing Lips and Seeing Voices. *Nature*, *264*(23), 746–748. www.nature.com/nature/journal/v264/n5588/abs/264746a0.html.

Nath, A. R., and Beauchamp, M. S. (2011). Dynamic Changes in Superior Temporal Sulcus Connectivity during Perception of Noisy Audiovisual Speech. *Journal of Neuroscience*, *31*(5), 1704–1714.

Noesselt, T., Rieger, J. W., Schoenfeld, M. A., et al. (2007). Audiovisual Temporal Correspondence Modulates Human Multisensory Superior Temporal Sulcus plus Primary Sensory Cortices. *Journal of Neuroscience*, *27*(42), 11431–11441.

Noppeney, U., Josephs, O., Hocking, J., Price, C. J., and Friston, K. J. (2008). The Effect of Prior Visual Information on Recognition of Speech and Sounds. *Cerebral Cortex*, *18*(3), 598–609.

O'Craven, K. M., and Kanwisher, N. (2000). Mental Imagery of Faces and Places Activates Corresponding Stimulus-Specific Brain Regions. *Journal of Cognitive Neuroscience*, *12*(6), 1013–1023. www.ncbi.nlm.nih.gov/pubmed/11177421.

Pearson, J., Clifford, C. W. G., and Tong, F. (2008). The Functional Impact of Mental Imagery on Conscious Perception. *Current Biology*, *18*(13), 982–986.

Perky, C. W. (1910). An Experimental Study of Imagination. *American Journal of Psychology*, *21*(3), 422–452.

Perrodin, C., Kayser, C., Logothetis, N. K., and Petkov, C. I. (2014). Auditory and Visual Modulation of Temporal Lobe Neurons in Voice-Sensitive and Association Cortices. *Journal of Neuroscience*, *34*(7), 2524–2537.

Plaze, M., Paillère-Martinot, M.-L., Penttilä, J., et al. (2011). "Where do Auditory Hallucinations Come From?"A Brain Morphometry Study of Schizophrenia

Patients with Inner or Outer Space Hallucinations. *Schizophrenia Bulletin*, *37*(1), 212–221.

Pylyshyn, Z. W. (1973). What the Mind's Eye Tells the Mind's Brain: A Critique of Mental Imagery. *Psychological Bulletin*, *80*(1), 1–12.

(2002). Mental Imagery: In Search of a Theory. *The Behavioral and Brain Sciences*, *25*, 157–182.

Recanzone, G. H. (1998). Rapidly Induced Auditory Plasticity: The Ventriloquism Aftereffect. *Proceedings of the National Academy of Sciences of the United States of America*, *95*(February), 869–875.

Schlack, A., and Albright, T. D. (2007). Remembering Visual Motion: Neural Correlates of Associative Plasticity and Motion Recall in Cortical Area MT. *Neuron*, *53*(6), 881–890.

Segal, S. J., and Fusella, V. (1970). Influence of Imaged Pictures and Sounds on Detection of Visual and Auditory Signals. *Journal of Experimental Psychology*, *83*(3), 458–464. www.ncbi.nlm.nih.gov/pubmed/5480913.

Sekuler, R., Sekuler, A. B., and Lau, R. (1997). Sound Alters Visual Motion Perception. *Nature*, *385*(6614), 308. www.ncbi.nlm.nih.gov/pubmed/9002513.

Seltzer, B., and Pandya, D. N. (1994). Parietal, Temporal, and Occipital Projections to Cortex of the Superior Temporal Sulcus in the Rhesus Monkey: A Retrograde Tracer Study. *The Journal of Comparative Neurology*, *343*(3), 445–463.

Shams, L., Kamitani, Y., and Shimojo, S. (2000). What You See Is What You Hear. *Nature*, *408*(6814), 788. doi:10.1038/35048669.

Shimojo, S., and Shams, L. (2001). Sensory Modalities Are Not Separate Modalities: Plasticity and Interactions. *Current Opinion in Neurobiology*, *11*(4), 505–509.

Spence, C., and Deroy, O. (2012). Hearing Mouth Shapes: Sound Symbolism and the Reverse McGurk Effect. *I-Perception*, *3*(8), 550–552.

Stein, B. E., and Stanford, T. R. (2008). Multisensory Integration: Current Issues from the Perspective of the Single Neuron. *Nature Reviews. Neuroscience*, *9*(4), 255–266.

Stevenson, R. A., and James, T. W. (2009). Audiovisual Integration in Human Superior Temporal Sulcus: Inverse Effectiveness and the Neural Processing of Speech and Object Recognition. *NeuroImage*, *44*(3), 1210–1223.

Sweeny, T. D., Guzman-Martinez, E., Ortega, L., Grabowecky, M., and Suzuki, S. (2012). Sounds Exaggerate Visual Shape. *Cognition*, *124*(2), 194–200.

Szycik, G. R., Stadler, J., Tempelmann, C., and Münte, T. F. (2012). Examining the McGurk Illusion Using High-Field 7 Tesla Functional MRI. *Frontiers in Human Neuroscience*, *6*(April), 95.

van Wassenhove, V., Grant, K. W., and Poeppel, D. (2007). Temporal Window of Integration in Auditory-Visual Speech Perception. *Neuropsychologia*, *45*(3), 598–607.

Wallace, M. T., Roberson, G. E., Hairston, W. D., et al. (2004). Unifying Multisensory Signals Across Time and Space. *Experimental Brain Research. Experimentelle Hirnforschung. Expérimentation Cérébrale*, *158*(2), 252–258.

Weber, R. J., and Castleman, J. (1970). The Time It Takes to Imagine. *Perception & Psychophysics*, *8*(3), 165–168.

Wegner, D. M. (1994). Ironic Processes of Mental Control. *Psychological Review*, *101*(1), 34–52.

Werner, S., and Noppeney, U. (2010a). Distinct Functional Contributions of Primary Sensory and Association Areas to Audiovisual Integration in Object Categorization. *Journal of Neuroscience*, *30*(7), 2662–2675.

Werner, S., and Noppeney, U. (2010b). Superadditive Responses in Superior Temporal Sulcus Predict Audiovisual Benefits in Object Categorization. *Cerebral Cortex*, *20*(8), 1829–1842.

Winawer, J., Huk, A. C., and Boroditsky, L. (2010). A Motion Aftereffect from Visual Imagery of Motion. *Cognition*, *114*(2), 276–284.

Woods, T. M., and Recanzone, G. H. (2004). Visually Induced Plasticity of Auditory Spatial Perception in Macaques. *Current Biology*, *14*, 1559–1564.

Wozny, D. R., and Shams, L. (2011). Recalibration of Auditory Space Following Milliseconds of Cross-Modal Discrepancy. *Journal of Neuroscience*, *31*(12), 4607–4612.

18 Evocation: How Mental Imagery Spans Across the Senses

Ophelia Deroy

Introduction

Closing one's eyes when listening to music seems to liberate a specific form of imagining. Certain pieces may even transport us into imaginary sensory universes – which are, however, hard to describe. Trying to capture his own experience, the psychologist MacDougal noted that "As [he] sat with closed eyes listening to the music, a succession of visual images appeared, in almost unbroken series, sometimes unrelated, here and there broken for a moment, but at other times developing continuously, into each other for the space of a minute or two, or even more" (MacDougal, 1898: 467). Although music seems a privileged place in which such visual imagining is reported, other sensory experiences, such as smelling a perfume, are sometimes granted a similar evocative power.

But, what does this evocation consist of ? How can we make sense of this rather poetic term in theoretical and scientific terms? It seems here that the idea of "evocation" is equivocal between two quite different interpretations: one that stresses the causal power of the music itself and the other that highlights the freedom and the engagement of the perceiver in the imaginary episode. According to the first interpretation, one should think that pieces of music or perfumes evoke images if and only if the music or smells are the *cause* of the elicitation of visual images, and/or if they somehow determine or constrain the contents of the imagining. According to the second interpretation, music and perfumes do not directly cause the images to appear, or to unfold in a certain way, but simply offer an *opportunity* for the perceiver to engage in a series of mental associations, which therefore are only loosely connected to the music or smell.

Of these two interpretations, the idea of a direct causal link between music and visual images is probably the one that has less popular support. This may be due in part to philosophers after Kant thinking of the exercise of the imagination as "free," but mostly this has come from the difficulty in making sense of a direct induction of visual imagery by sounds in our models of the mind. This is the difficulty tackled in the present chapter.

Musical imagery is probably here too complex an example of imagery to look at, given the many individual differences that the phenomenon offers. It might also be a mixed phenomenon, with multiple etiologies. Making the case for a direct induction of imagery across sensory modalities is more easily done by looking at simpler cases, in which being presented with one object in one sensory modality leads to imagining something in a second, non-stimulated sensory modality. Think, for instance, of how hearing the voice of a friend on the telephone may make you imagine his face; how watching television with the sound turned off makes you almost hear the sounds or speech in your head, or how watching someone being stroked with a feather may lead to you almost feeling a soft touch on our own hand. As with musical imagery, these phenomena correspond to cases in which a given sensory experience evokes another, in the imagination. As with musical imagery, they may vary in strength or frequency from person to person, but their content is more easily specified and it is more likely that people can relate to at least one of them.

These phenomena come as a challenge to the dominant idea that imagination can only be triggered in two ways: either from the inside, by our own process of thoughts; or from the outside, in which case it is supposed to follow a single sensory path. The idea that exogenous mental imagery was elicited on a modality by modality basis came naturally out of the claim that mental imagery operated like a form of simulated perception. This model runs deep in psychology, as illustrated by Shepard (1978), who insisted that "the relation of a mental image to its corresponding object is in some ways analogous to the relation of a lock to a key . . . the lock can be externally operated only by its corresponding key" (Shepard, 1978: 130).

The restriction to a single sensory path for externally triggered mental imagery is also reinforced by the quasi-exclusive focus on visual stimuli and tasks in the study of imagery. The classic mental rotation task, central to the debate about mental images, is here the perfect illustration: Mental imagery is measured and studied within a single modality, anchored at both ends by visual stimuli. In this task the participant is presented with an original three-dimensional shape, and asked to choose which of four other shapes corresponds to the same shape, after it has been rotated. The cue and the stimuli are both in the same visual format, and the mental rotation of the shape, which is seen as necessary to solve the task, is then said to also occur visually (e.g. Shepard and Metzler, 1971).

Could it not be the case, however, that the intermediate mental imagery episode draws on the tactile feel of turning these shapes in one's hands? Or couldn't a visual rotation be used to solve the same task, but starting with 3D objects that one would feel rather than see? The conceptual possibility here falls short of showing beyond doubt that these cases of imagery really occur. Phenomenological descriptions of everyday experiences cannot do much better. Hearing a friend's voice might be followed by a visual imagining, but it is difficult to tell for sure, from introspection alone, whether the visual imagery episode has been "unlocked" by the initial auditory stimulation rather than internally generated from the thoughts we happen to form about our friend as we listen to her voice. To go back to the other previous cases, we need to be able to show that the music or the silent images displayed on TV *caused* us to imagine a visual scene or a voice, not that it caused us to think about a landscape or a speech, which we then visually imagined.

To establish a causal connection requires the satisfaction of two requirements. First, can we show that the mental image is triggered by a given sensory stimulation rather than by any other thought process that we happen to have at the time? We can call this the *causal elicitation requirement* for a case of mental imagery occurring in a sensory modality (S1) to count as crossmodal imagery, a sensory stimulus presented in another sensory modality (S2) is causally necessary for the mental image in S1 to occur in that given moment.

The second requirement is a content requirement, which can be formulated in the following way: the content of the imagining in the sensory modality (S1) needs to be, if not determined, at least constrained by the initial sensory stimulation in the sensory modality (S2).

This second requirement is more flexible but no less necessary, as we will see, to avoid crossmodal imagery being extended to cases in which the external stimulus does explain the occurrence of the mental image but not in a crossmodal way.

It is necessary to establish that both the occurrence (section 3: The Causal Criterion) and the contents (section 4: The Content Criterion) of a mental image are constrained by sensory stimulation in another modality before we can see what crossmodal mental imagery brings to the debate about unconscious imagery (section 5: Justifying the Consciousness Requirement) and the questions it opens for future research (section 6: Implications and Open Questions).

Canonical Cases of Crossmodal Imagery

Imagine watching an interview with a famous person on television with the sound turned off: Perhaps you would report almost hearing the character speak. In this "silent speech" phenomenon, a stimulus presented in one modality is sufficient to elicit a mental image in another modality. When seeing someone's lip movements, you may form an auditory image of her voice, intonation, or eventually her specific utterances. As there is no auditory stimulus present, these auditory objects only exist in your head and imagination.

This case seems to satisfy both the causal and the content requirement: The auditory imagery seems to be elicited by the presence of a visual stimulus, as you start imagining it when you start watching the silent lip movement, and it may stop if you close your eyes. The presence of the visual stimulus seems necessary here to the occurrence of the mental imagery episode. The auditory imagery seems also to be guided by the visual stimulus that is presented, as the voice or features that are imagined are congruent – at least in some respects – with the person or speech that is being watched. If the person on the screen is a woman, for instance, it is more likely that the imagined voice will be a female one, or a high-pitched one, rather than a male or low-pitched one. How fine-grained the content of auditory imagery might be here remains difficult to establish, but certain principles of congruence seem to hold. Going from "seem" to "is," however, is what remains problematic. Phenomenological reports might be plausible, but one needs more evidence before concluding they correspond to a case of crossmodal imagery.

As indicated earlier, this involves showing that both the causal elicitation and the content of the mental image criteria are satisfied in the case of silent speech. A first reason to be *a priori* confident that those conditions hold come from the relation between crossmodal imagery and normal perception: Imagery seems to operate along the paths usually covered by speech perception. Mental imagery would here be filling in the gaps left by an incomplete causal structure (the missing auditory part of a speech event) as well as the incomplete content (the missing voice and spoken words of the speech event). The function of crossmodal imagery here, we can expect, is to complete a unisensory percept in order to re-establish a multisensory experience.

A second reason to grant that crossmodal imagery occurs comes from neural evidence: When one watches lip movements in the absence of the corresponding speech sounds, activation is still observed in the non-stimulated auditory cortex, suggesting it is spreading from one stimulated sensory area, to another, non-stimulated one. Neuroimaging studies (e.g. Calvert et al., 1997; Hertrich, Dietrich, and Akermann, 2011; Pekkola et al., 2005) show that the neural activation thus induced is similar, though less pronounced, than the one observed when participants listen to normal speech sounds (either on their own, or along with lip movements). The evidence demonstrates that stimuli presented in vision are sufficient to induce neural activation in the auditory cortex, but not that the activation underpins a conscious experience of any sort. The evidence also does not speak to the relation of correspondence between the relative strength of the activation and the extent to which the experience during silent speech resembles the one enjoyed during normal speech. In this respect, one can use the neural evidence to add to the plausibility of the subjective reports, but not *vice-versa*.

A third reason comes from behavioral studies. A key assumption in most of these studies is that the occurrence of a mental image in a certain modality interferes or facilitates the perception of a real stimulus presented in that very same modality. For silent speech, so far the closest evidence draws not on dynamic lip movements, but written speech. When reading the exact lyrics of a familiar song – for instance, "Regrets, I've had a few" – people are usually much slower than when reading the same sentence, organized differently – for instance, "I've had a few regrets." This suggests that as a reader you hear the first sentence, but not the second, sung or played in your head – that is, you do not read them like some unknown sentence, "pronounced" (so to say) neutrally (e.g. see Halpern, 1992; Hubbard, 2010; see also Abramson and Goldinger, 1997). Tactile imagery offers here another promising avenue, because it is, at least for many people, spatially felt on one's skin rather than simply in one's head. The occurrence of tactile imagery can then lead to a spatial interference with a real stimulus. When one sees someone being stroked on the left cheek with a brush and as a result experiences a tactile image of being stroked on one's own left cheek, it will be either easier or more difficult to localize a real touch at the same time. If the experimenter applies a small push on one cheek of the viewer, on the same side as the imagined one, it will be easier to identify its location than if it occurs on a different side – something that will be reflected by different response times (Banissy and Ward, 2007; see de Vignemont, 2016 for a review). However, the inference from behavioral interference to the occurrence of a conscious mental image rests on the assumption that the interference can only be introduced at the level of consciousness. This assumption needs to be checked by testing if a similar interference is not also observed in people who do not report conscious imagery in similar cases, as for instance, in the tactile case, by people who do not report any strong tactile imagery when seeing someone else being touched. Serino, Pizzoferrato, and Ladavas (2008) demonstrated, for instance, that the activation of the somatosensory system in participants who did not report consciously experiencing mirror-touch images was sufficient to lower the threshold for detection of real touch on one's own face, suggesting that not all behavioral effects should be attributed to the occurrence of mental imagery.

Both neural and behavioral evidence are then compatible with the idea that mental imagery can be induced across the senses. But does this evidence fit both the causal and content requirement expressed above?

The Causal Criterion

Immediate and Mediated Causal Routes

A good depiction of cases of crossmodal imagery is that they correspond to the elicitation of a mental image in a certain sensory modality, upon the presentation of a stimulus in a distinct sensory modality. The definition depends on accepting a distinction between sensory modalities – which in this case can be drawn by proper objects (e.g. color for visions, sounds for audition), typical stimulus (e.g. light waves for vision; sound waves for audition), and non-overlapping neural bases (e.g. Keeley, 2002). Independently of the definition of sensory modalities that one accepts, this characterization is meant to capture the crossmodal induction – from one modality where the stimulus is presented, to another one, where no stimulation occurs.

This direct induction can be contrasted with a case of crossmodal spread of imagery, where the crossmodal induction is mediated by another episode of imagery. Crossmodal spread of imagery can involve motor imagery: In silent speech, for instance, the sight of lip movements may first induce speech motor imagery, which in turn elicits an episode of auditory imagery. Another example would be what happens when one sees someone engaged in a certain action, for instance balancing on a tightrope: Vision may indirectly generate a certain imagined feeling of losing balance (vestibular imagery) mediated by the imagery of balancing one's legs on a rope (motor imagery, see Figure 18.1). Other cases of spread of imagery can occur, for instance if the smell of a lemon elicits the visual image of a lemon, and in turn a certain gustatory image.

In several cases, the two types of phenomena described above might co-occur, with a mental image in a sensory modality being caused both directly by the stimulation of another, and indirectly by the induction of a motor image, or another kind of mental image. Disentangling these two causal routes remains delicate. In the absence of a clear empirical distinction, crossmodal imagery, broadly speaking, can include cases in which a mental image occurs in one sensory modality as a result of

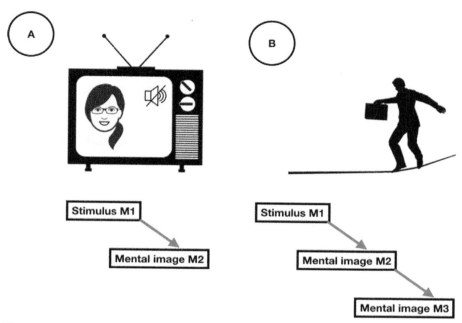

Figure 18.1 *Crossmodal imagery can occur directly or indirectly, notably via the elicitation of motor imagery when seeing a certain action being performed. (A) Silent speech occurs when visual stimuli elicit auditory imagery, which can feel "almost like hearing" the voice of the muted character. (B) Watching someone perform an action can lead to corresponding vestibular imagery.*

the presentation of a physical stimulus in another modality, either directly or indirectly, via the elicitation of another mental image (e.g. a motor image).

Other Causes for Neural Activation and Imagery

The occurrence of a crossmodal mental imagery episode, if it is backed up by evidence of neural activation upon the presentation of a stimulus in another modality, can only be ascertained once alternative explanations are ruled out. In the case of the activation of the auditory cortex by visual stimuli, for instance, thalamic connections can be sufficient to cause activation in the auditory cortex upon presentation of visual stimuli. In this case, the activation observed in the auditory cortex is due to connections from the part of the thalamus that receives visual input going both to the visual cortex and the auditory cortex – something that is likely to be occurring for many visual stimuli. There is growing evidence of such generic activation from visual stimuli to auditory cortex via thalamico-cortical connections in mice (Cappe, Rouiller, and Barone, 2009; Tyll, Budinger, and Noesselt, 2011), and reasons to think that they may occur in humans as well (e.g. van den Brink et al., 2013; but see Caron-Desrochers et al., 2018).

Why rule out that this causal route, from stimulus to activation in another modality, is a legitimate underpinning for crossmodal imagery? The main reason should certainly not be that only cortical routes count. For the moment, the main argument comes from the constant contribution of these connections. If the activation due to thalamic connections from, say, visual stimuli to auditory cortex is generic, and occurs for all sorts of stimuli, it will occur whether there is an auditory stimulus present or not. This causal route then does not depend on there being <u>no</u> corresponding auditory stimulus – which is key to the phenomenon of crossmodal imagery.

The occurrence of mental imagery, and the accompanying neural activation, upon the presentation of a stimulus in another modality may also be triggered in a top-down fashion, by beliefs or conceptual representations (see Hubbard, 2010, for a discussion). After all, there could be a chain of induction whereby a stimulus in one modality is interpreted conceptually and thereby induces an imagery episode in a second modality. Why exclude those from counting as a form of indirect crossmodal imagery? The reasoning against this chain induction argument is the following: Though it is true that sensory information can trigger concepts, it is also granted that the presence of a sensory stimulus is not necessary to trigger these concepts. In other words, the abstract conceptual representation that induces the mental imagery episode is not necessarily linked to the sensory presentation. It could have induced the same mental imagery episode if it had not been activated by the sensory stimulus, and for instance, been voluntarily entertained by the participant in a context in which the related sensory stimulus was absent. To remain valid, the concept of crossmodal imagery should exclude cases in which the crossmodal induction does not necessarily play any role, and in which the presence of a stimulus in a given modality is only an opportunity for conceptual thought.

What Are the Rules of Crossmodal Induction?

If crossmodal imagery is not mediated either by subcortical connections or by abstract concepts, how is it then induced? The challenge raised by crossmodal imagery is here partly empirical, but the conditions can be articulated in a more *a priori* way: To count as a crossmodal induction, the causal route must be such that it is necessary that stimulation occurs in one modality and that the activation and imagery observed in a second modality occurs through routes that are non-conceptual, or at least, necessarily linked to the occurrence of the first stimulation. (Not all conceptual representations need to be such that they can be triggered independently of a sensory stimulus. This may be the case for strong embodied views of concepts, but the focus here is on abstract concepts.)

Examples of non-conceptual mediations can be found in so-called "crossmodal correspondences": similarity relations holding across distinct sensory dimensions, across modalities. Growing out of the pioneering work on audiovisual correspondences by Lawrence Marks and Robert Melara (e.g. Spence, 2011; Spence and Deroy, 2013b; Parise, 2016 for reviews), crossmodal correspondences have been documented between most sensory dimensions, and across all combinations of sensory modalities. People consistently and reliably pair certain musical timbres with particular smells, shapes, and colors; they consider changes in pitch to match difference in height, and consider pitch to correspond to visual brightness or size; visual shapes are matched to tactile hardness, brightness, and pitch, tastes, smells and flavors while colors are matched to temperatures, odors, or tastes (see Deroy and Spence, 2016, for an overview).

Lakoff and Johnson (1980) first proposed that our tendency to cross domains was an instance of metaphorical transfer but of a more fundamental kind than transfers occurring in conceptual thought and language. In their influential book, *Metaphors We Live By*, their argument was that certain mappings had a special status over the making of our cognitive life, as they were constitutively involved in shaping it. Their key example was the fact that "up" is positive and "down" negative in almost all cultures, and that this mapping crops up in a range of practices, from linguistic expressions to gestures, and from dance to music. Sounds increasing in pitch also tend to be considered as going up, and eventually inherit those affective connotations. Both of these preconceptual mappings might be at stake when we mentally visualize the movement of a musical piece. In this respect, hearing a piece of music as "moving in space" is a key example of crossmodal imagery (Deroy et al., 2018) or metaphorical hearing (Peacocke, 2009; see Budd, 2012 for a discussion) rather than a conceptual interpretation.

What matters here in the correspondences or special kinds of metaphorical transfers is that the relation between the two dimensions is not captured or justified at the level of judgment: The two dimensions can indeed be labeled by a concept, but the *relation* between these two conceptualized elements is itself not conceptualized. It is only given as a mere "feeling of matching." For instance, we tend to consider that high-pitch sounds go together with bright visual stimuli rather than dark ones, but we can't explain conceptually what this relation amounts to. The results of a neuroimaging study by Sadaghiani, Maier, and Noppeney (2009) provides additional evidence that crossmodal correspondences of this type do not amount to conceptual relations, at least those captured linguistically. These neuroscientists investigated the different neural bases of the effects induced by pitch and linguistic labels. The motivation for the study was to investigate whether the biases on visual motion perception that can equally be induced by a rising or descending pitch, spatial words such as "left" or "up," or sounds actually moving from left to right, shared the same neural underpinnings. The study not only revealed that the three kinds of effects (pitch, words, and motion) operate at different levels of the cortical hierarchy, but also that the influence of linguistic signals emerged primarily in the right intraparietal sulcus while the effects of pitch could be seen both in these higher-level convergence regions and in the audiovisual motion areas (hMT+/V5+), in which the effects of actual auditory motion were shown.

Though crossmodal correspondences might prove successful in explaining some aspects of more complex cases of mental imagery, such as musical imagery (Deroy et al., 2018), they will probably not be sufficient to explain all cases, or all aspects, of crossmodal imagery, including a canonical case such as the auditory imagery induced by silent lip movements.

Another causal route from one modality to another may come from mere associations that are not reflected in concepts. For instance, it is possible to think that the associations between visual and auditory properties of phonemes are complex associations between sensory and motor representations, encoded in a way that is best captured as probability distributions, and not such that we have a conceptual knowledge of what they are (e.g. Hickock, 2014 for a review).

The Content Criterion

As we have seen above, the main evidence for the occurrence of crossmodal imagery stems from subjective reports. For silent speech, the strength of the evidence comes partly from the examples being of a specific speech phenomenology, where the voice is gender- or age-congruent with the speaker silently observed, or even sometimes congruent with a known individual speaker.

This content requirement can also be tested at the neural level, by testing whether similar brain activation patterns occur for different types of visual stimulation, matched as much as possible in terms of low-level properties but differing in their informational content. The documentation of auditory cortex activation by silent speech counts as evidence for the occurrence of a crossmodal imagery episode exactly because it shows a high degree of specificity. The authors can indeed infer that "silent speech" occurred both because of the specificity of the inducer (lips mouthing numbers and not still lips, or "gurning" or pseudo-speech) and because of the specificity of the corresponding auditory activation (similar to heard speech).

Note that functional neuroimaging is not the only source of evidence here: Other techniques can also provide neural evidence, as well as evidence for the specificity of the crossmodal activation such as the specific facilitation of silent speech recognition by transcranial direct current stimulation tDCS of the auditory cortex (Riedel et al., 2015) or specific interference in behavior, which can only be explained if a certain content occurs. For instance, if a tactile image is elicited by seeing someone touched, it will only interfere with an actual touch if it is imagined in the same location as this real touch.

The specificity of the consciously experienced content needs then to be supported by the specificity of the activation or interference. In other words, the reports of a conscious sensory experience in a given unstimulated modality, upon the presentation of a stimulus in another modality, or the activation of the cortical areas typically associated to this unstimulated modality, should only count as evidence of crossmodal mental imagery if their content can be related to the specific stimulus presented in the other modality.

Justifying the Consciousness Requirement

Is the occurrence of a conscious episode, rather than the mere presence of neural activation, necessary for a crossmodal imagery episode to occur? Several authors advocate giving up on this requirement, on the grounds that phenomenological reports constitute weak evidence at best (e.g. Nanay, 2017). Others, such as Schwitzgebel (2016), are willing to lower the requirement by accepting that the triggering of imagery is *typically* – if not necessarily – the triggering of a conscious episode:

Maybe there's unconscious imagery, but if there is, it's doubtful that you will be able to reflect upon an instance of it at will. Try to conjure a visual image – of the Eiffel Tower, say. Try to conjure an auditory image – of the tune of "Happy Birthday", for example. Imagine it sung in your head. Try to conjure a motor image. Imagine how it would feel to stretch your arms back and wiggle your fingers. You might not succeed in all of these imagery tasks, but hopefully you succeeded in at least one, which you can now think of as another example of phenomenal consciousness (Schwitzgebel, 2016: 14).

Giving up or relaxing the requirement of conscious awareness, however, runs into the risk of making the category of crossmodal imagery overinclusive, and much less useful. Let's go back to the silent speech example. Evidence suggests that visual information from lip movement is rich enough to be interpreted as speech, and it is specifically processed in the temporal visual speech area (TVSA), in the posterior temporal cortex, ventral and posterior to the multisensory posterior superior temporal sulcus (pSTS) (Berstein et al., 2011). This shows that crossmodal imagery is not necessarily involved in reconstituting spoken speech: If lipreading can occur through crossmodal imagery, it may also occur directly, from the visual lip movement only, providing then the linguistic content but not other properties such as the tone of voice with which it is delivered.

Take the case of Miss Sloane, in the eponymous 2016 movie, who is asked to wait outside a glass-walled office. She can see two male colleagues having an animated conversation. Though she can observe their faces and their body language, no sound is escaping from the closed office. As the meeting ends, one of the two men walks out, announcing they are happy to stand as her lawyers. Miss Sloane smiles and explains that despite the glass wall, it was easy to grasp what her colleagues said. Here, we may be curious to know whether Miss Sloane "almost heard" her colleagues, or whether she performed a form of direct lipreading. Giving up on the consciousness requirement means that the two cases would collapse into a single undifferentiated one, where our curiosity would be meaningless. Maintaining the distinction is not only a matter of curiosity: it is crucial (Figure 18.2) to avoid considering that every case of lipreading by, say, severely hearing-impaired individuals is a case of crossmodal imagery. Early-deaf individuals might have lost the capacity for conscious auditory imagery and still be able to lipread.

It is true that phenomenological reports are not necessarily reliable or systematically reported. It is also important to stress that, because of individual differences in the vividness of mental imagery, not all individuals may be able or ready to report, "almost hearing" a character on a silent screen, or behind a glass wall. For some individuals, the phenomenology can be very specific (which is different from being an accurate duplicate of the real voice or speech), whereas it is highly generic for others. Conscious imagery may not be reported because it is near threshold for consciousness, and participants are not confident that it occurred (via a report of confidence bias). This is not the only option: If one accepts that phenomenal consciousness overflows access consciousness (Block, 2011), then it is also possible that conscious episodes of imagery go unreported.

These cautionary remarks, however, do not provide reasons to give up on the requirement that a case of crossmodal imagery needs to have a conscious occurrence. They encourage us to be much more flexible on the requirement that they should be

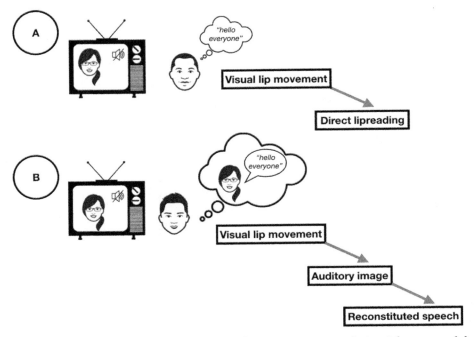

Figure 18.2 *The conscious imagery episode is necessary to distinguish crossmodal imagery from direct lipreading, in the silent speech example.*

easily, or spontaneously, reported. Some experimental corrective actions can be taken as, for instance, by asking people to report how vivid their crossmodal imagery experience was, or how confident they were that they had a conscious experience, rather than provide a mere "yes/no" answer to say whether they were consciously experiencing a mental imagery episode.

Implications and Open Questions

Some Imagining We Consider as Internally Triggered Might Be Externally Triggered

Accepting that crossmodal imagery occurs obliges us to widen the range of externally triggered mental images: A visual imagery episode can be triggered, to go back to Shepard's quote, by a sensory lock within the visual modality, but also by a variety of other stimuli, presented in audition, touch, olfaction, etc. We may label cases as "internally generated" mental imagery because of a lack of a corresponding modal trigger, when in fact the mental image has been crossmodally triggered by an external crossmodal trigger, which went unnoticed. This revision has consequences when it comes to the etiology of daydreaming, for instance. Many note that daydreaming occurs in the presence of stable sensory stimulation, for instance, while watching the landscape from a train window, or listening to music (e.g. Fox and Christoff, 2018, for overview). If that's the case, these sensory stimuli might play a role in inducing a sequence of mental images, including in other modalities, and explain some of the phenomenology and neural signature associated with daydreaming. Here, an open question is to consider how competent we are in telling whether a mental image has been internally or externally generated – a question that relates to the sense of agency we have when it comes to mental actions. Mental imagery, even if externally induced, certainly represents a delicate case here: It should feel passive, but it also requires some active contribution from the agent to be maintained, meaning that agents might still report some feeling of agency over their episodes of crossmodal imagery – such as silent speech or musically induced visual imagery.

Non-Visual Mental Imagery May Be More Frequent than We Think

Cases of crossmodal imagery also lead us to revise the common hypothesis that conscious visual imagery is more frequent than other kinds of conscious mental imagery such as auditory, tactile, or olfactory imagery. Although it is true that most people report visual imagery (except those with aphantasia, see Chapter 42), few report certain forms of mental imagery, such as olfactory, when tested as if they could be directly triggered. It might be easier for someone to imagine a smell starting with a visual image, than with another smell or simply instructions, for instance. While studies show that olfactory mental imagery arises from neural activity in early olfactory cortices, i.e. the piriform cortex (e.g. Bensafi and Rouby, 2007) large individual differences in the capacity to reproduce olfactory conscious images attribute this difficulty to the fact that olfactory mental imagery relies on the activity of high-level representations such as attention, expectation, and memory (Royet et al., 1999). The diminished capacity to entertain olfactory conscious images could, however, be separate from the difficulty in remembering olfactory information, and could be less variable across individuals if crossmodal induction was tested more widely.

Conclusion

Altogether, the concept of crossmodal imagery is of relatively recent history (see Spence and Deroy, 2013a) but relates to well-known phenomena such as musical imagery and silent speech. Crossmodal imagery revises our concepts of mental imagery, by adding a new causal route and series of relations between perception and imagination. More importantly, it dramatically changes the extension of our concept of mental imagery, shifting what we are ready to count as imagination, or lack thereof, and showing that the connections between inner imagery and the world might be more frequent, once we recognize that they go across sensory channels.

References

Abramson, M., and Goldinger, S. D. (1997). What the Reader's Eye Tells the Mind's Ear: Silent Reading Activates Inner Speech. *Perception and Psychophysics*, *59*, 1059–1068.

Banissy, M. J., and Ward, J. (2007). Mirror-Touch Synesthesia Is Linked with Empathy. *Nature Neuroscience*, *10*, 815–816.

Bensafi, M., and Rouby, C. (2007). Individual Differences in Odor Imaging Ability Reflected Differences in Olfactory and Emotional Perception. *Chemical Senses*, *32*, 237–244.

Bernstein, L. E., Jiang, J., Pantazis, D., Lu, Z. L., and Joshi, A. (2011). Visual Phonetic Processing Localized Using Speech and Nonspeech Face Gestures in Video and Point-Light Displays. *Human Brain Mapping*, *32*, 1660–1676.

Bernstein, L. E., and Liebenthal, E. (2014). Neural Pathways for Visual Speech Perception. *Frontiers in Neuroscience*, *8*, 386.

Block, N. (2011). Perceptual Consciousness Overflows Cognitive Access. *Trends in Cognitive Sciences*, *15*, 567–575.

Budd, M. (2012). The Musical Expression of Emotion: Metaphorical-as versus Imaginative-as Perception. *Estetika: The Central European Journal of Aesthetics*, *49*(2), 131–148.

Calvert, G. A., Bullmore, E. T., Brammer, M. J., et al. (1997). Activation of Auditory Cortex during Silent Lipreading. *Science*, *276*(5312), 593–596.

Cappe, C., Rouiller, E. M., and Barone, P. (2009). Multisensory Anatomical Pathways. *Hearing Research*, *258*(1–2), 28–36.

Caron-Desrochers, L., Schönwiesner, M., Focke, K., and Lehmann, A. (2018). Assessing Visual Modulation along the Human Subcortical Auditory Pathway. *Neuroscience Letters*, *685*, 12–17.

Deroy, O., Fernandez-Prieto, I., Navarra, J., and Spence, C. (2018). Unravelling the Paradox of Spatial Pitch. In T. L. Hubbard (ed.), *Spatial Biases in Perception and Cognition*. Cambridge, UK: Cambridge University Press.

Deroy, O., and Spence, C. (2016). Crossmodal Correspondences: Four Challenges. *Multisensory Research*, *29*(1–3), 29–48.

De Vignemont, F. (2016). Mirror-Touch Synaesthesia. In O. Deroy (ed.), *Sensory Blending: On Synaesthesia and Related Phenomena*. Oxford, UK: Oxford University Press, 275–292.

Fox, K. C., and Christoff, K. (eds.), (2018). *The Oxford Handbook of Spontaneous Thought: Mind Wandering, Creativity, and Dreaming*. Oxford, UK: Oxford University Press.

Halpern, A. R. (1992). Musical Aspects of Auditory Imagery. In D. Reisberg (ed.), *Auditory Imagery*. Hillsdale, NJ: Erlbaum.

Hertrich, I., Dietrich, S., and Ackermann, H. (2011). Cross-Modal Interactions during Perception of Audiovisual Speech and Nonspeech Signals: An fMRI Study. *Journal of Cognitive Neuroscience*, *23*(1), 221–237.

Hickok, G. (2014). The Architecture of Speech Production and the Role of the Phoneme in Speech Processing. *Language, Cognition and Neuroscience*, *29*(1), 2–20.

Hubbard, T. L. (2010). Auditory Imagery: Empirical Findings. *Psychological Bulletin*, *136*(2), 302.

Keeley, B. L. (2002). Making Sense of the Senses: Individuating Modalities in Humans and Other Animals. *The Journal of Philosophy*, *99*(1), 5–28.

Lakoff, G., and Johnson, M. (1980). *Metaphors We Live By*. Chicago, IL: University of Chicago Press.

MacDougal, R. (1898). Music Imagery: A Confession of Experience. *Psychological Review, 5* (5), 463.

Nanay, B. (2017). Multimodal Mental Imagery. *Cortex, 105*, 125–134.

Parise, C. V. (2016). Crossmodal Correspondences: Standing Issues and Experimental Guidelines. *Multisensory Research, 29*(1–3), 7–28.

Peacocke, C. (2009). Experiencing Metaphorically-as in Music Perception: Clarifications and Commitments. *The British Journal of Aesthetics, 49*(3), 299–306.

Pekkola, J., Ojanen, V., Autti, T., et al. (2005). Primary Auditory Cortex Activation by Visual Speech: An fMRI Study at 3 T. *Neuroreport, 16*(2), 125–128.

Riedel, P., Ragert, P., Schelinski, S., Kiebel, S. J., and von Kriegstein, K. (2015). Visual Face-Movement Sensitive Cortex Is Relevant for Auditory-only Speech Recognition. *Cortex, 68*, 86–99.

Royet, J. P., Koenig, O., Gregoire, M. C., et al. (1999). Functional Anatomy of Perceptual and Semantic Processing for Odors. *Journal of Cognitive Neuroscience, 11*(1), 94–109. PubMed PMID: 9950717.

Sadaghiani, S., Maier, J. X., and Noppeney, U. (2009). Natural, Metaphoric, and Linguistic Auditory Direction Signals Have Distinct Influences on Visual Motion Processing. *Journal of Neuroscience, 29*(20), 6490–6499.

Schwitzgebel, E. (2016). Phenomenal Consciousness, Defined and Defended as Innocently as I Can Manage. *Journal of Consciousness Studies, 23*(11–12), 224–235.

Serino, A., Pizzoferrato, F., and Ladavas, E. (2008). Viewing a Face (Especially One's Own Face) Being Touched Enhances Tactile Perception on the Face. *Psychological Science, 19*(5), 434–438.

Shepard, R. N. (1978). The Mental Image. *American Psychologist, 33*(2), 125–137.

Shepard, R. N., and Cooper L. A. (1982). *Mental Images and their Transformations*. Cambridge, MA: MIT Press.

Shepard, R. N., and Metzler, J. (1971). Mental Rotation of Three-Dimensional Objects. *Science, 171*, 701–703.

Spence, C. (2011). Crossmodal Correspondences: A Tutorial Review. *Attention, Perception, and Psychophysics, 73*(4), 971–995.

Spence, C., and Deroy, O. (2013a). Crossmodal Mental Imagery. In S. Lacey and R. Lawson (eds.), *Multisensory Imagery*. New York, NY: Springer, 157–183.

(2013b). How Automatic are Crossmodal Correspondences? *Consciousness and Cognition, 22*(1), 245–260.

Tyll, S., Budinger, E., and Noesselt, T. (2011). Thalamic Influences on Multisensory Integration. *Communicative & Integrative Biology, 4*, 378–381.

van den Brink, R. L., Cohen, M. X., van der Burg, E., et al. (2013). Subcortical, Modality-Specific Pathways Contribute to Multisensory Processing in Humans. *Cerebral Cortex, 24*, 2169–2177.

PART III

Intentionality-Based Forms
of the Imagination

19 Continuities and Discontinuities Between Imagination and Memory: The View from Philosophy

Kourken Michaelian, Denis Perrin,
and André Sant'Anna

Episodic Imagination and Episodic Memory: The Continuism-Discontinuism Debate

This chapter surveys the debate between continuists and discontinuists about the relationship between episodic memory and episodic imagination. *Episodic memory* can most easily be characterized by contrasting it with semantic memory: Whereas semantic memory is the capacity at work when one remembers that such-and-such is the case (e.g. that Ottawa is the capital of Canada), episodic memory involves mentally reconstructing an experienced episode (e.g. visiting Ottawa last year). *Episodic imagination* can similarly be characterized by contrasting it with semantic imagination:[1] Whereas semantic imagination is the capacity at work when one imagines that such-and-such is the case (e.g. that Toronto is the capital of Canada), episodic imagination involves mentally simulating a possible episode (e.g. visiting Toronto next year). Inasmuch as they both centrally involve mental imagery – quasi-sensory experience in the absence of corresponding sensory stimulation (Nanay, 2015) – episodic memory and episodic imagination would seem, on the face of it, to be intimately related. Beyond the involvement of mental imagery, however, it is not obvious just how much overlap there is between them, and philosophers of memory, in particular, have traditionally assumed that there is in fact very little (see Bernecker and Michaelian, 2017); indeed, they have traditionally taken as one of their primary goals the demarcation of memory from imagination.

This has, however, begun to change under the influence of impressive psychological research demonstrating that the existence of a deep difference between episodic memory and episodic imagination cannot simply be taken for granted. When Tulving (1972) first introduced the term, he defined episodic memory[2] as a specialized store devoted to information about the "what," the "when," and the

---

1 The terminology in this area is not settled, and episodic and semantic imagination are sometimes described, for example, as sensory and suppositional imagination.

2 Philosophers had traditionally referred to episodic memory as "recollective," "experiential," or "personal" (Brewer, 1996) memory but have, as we do here, increasingly adopted the psychological terminology.

"where" of experienced past events. As empirical findings indicating the existence of a tight relationship between remembering past events and imagining future events accumulated, however, Tulving (1985), along with most of his colleagues in psychology, came to adopt a definition of episodic memory as a form of *mental time travel* (MTT) in which the subject "re-experiences" past events and thus to see it as being cut from the same cloth as episodic future thought, in which the subject "pre-experiences" future events (see Michaelian, Klein, and Szpunar, 2016; Suddendorf and Corballis, 2007). By emphasizing the relationship between our ability to remember the past and our ability to imagine the future, research on MTT has suggested that the difference between episodic memory and episodic imagination may not be as deep as philosophers of memory have traditionally taken it to be.

Both "continuists" and "discontinuists" (our terminology) acknowledge similarities and differences between episodic memory and episodic future thought. Continuists maintain that although these two forms of MTT differ *in degree* they do not differ *in kind*, while discontinuists maintain that although they may be similar in degree they do differ in kind. Thus a discontinuist, on the one hand, might grant that the processes of remembering the past and imagining the future are executed by the same cognitive system but argue that, because remembering necessarily involves a causal connection with the relevant event whereas imagining does not, there is nevertheless a qualitative difference between them. Discontinuism, in fact, aligns naturally with the *causal theory of memory,* according to which the difference between remembering an event and imagining it consists precisely in the presence or absence of an "appropriate" causal connection between the subject's present representation of the event and his or her earlier experience of it. Martin and Deutscher's (1966) *classical* version of the causal theory of memory understands appropriate causation in terms of the transmission of content from experience to representation via a memory trace. More recent versions, such as Perrin's (2018) *procedural* causal theory, attempt to understand it without reference to contentful traces. The classical and procedural causal theories are discussed in section 2: Metaphysical (Dis)continuism.

A continuist, on the other hand, might grant that imagining the future is less reliable than remembering the past but argue that this amounts to a merely quantitative difference within a single cognitive process, carried out by a single cognitive system. If discontinuism aligns with causal theories, continuism aligns with noncausal theories, such as Michaelian's (2016c) simulation theory. According to the simulation theory, episodic memory no more presupposes the presence of a causal connection between the subject's representation of an event and his experience of it than does episodic future thought and therefore ultimately reduces to one kind of episodic imagination among others: Remembering is a matter of reliably imagining the past. The simulation theory is discussed further in section 2: Metaphysical (Dis)continuism.

Perrin and Michaelian (2017) have argued that the available empirical evidence does not by itself suffice to decide between continuism and discontinuism, and our focus here will accordingly be on philosophical arguments for these positions.[3] We

---

3 For additional discussion, see Gérardin-Laverge (2017) and Sant'Anna (2018a).

write as philosophers of memory, but both philosophers of memory and philosophers of imagination (who have been somewhat more receptive to the idea of an intimate relationship between episodic memory and episodic imagination; see Macpherson and Dorsch, 2018) have a stake in the continuism-discontinuism debate, for the appropriate relationship between their respective fields depends on how it is eventually resolved. If discontinuists are right, then philosophers of memory and philosophers of imagination may have little to learn from each other. If continuists are right, in contrast, then they likely have much to learn from each other. Accounts of the relationship between episodic memory and semantic memory (Werning and Cheng, 2017), for example, might be enriched by drawing on accounts of the relationship between episodic and semantic imagination (Arcangeli, 2018), while recent treatments of imagination as a source of knowledge (Kind and Kung, 2016), for example, might be clarified by looking to older treatments of the epistemology of memory (Frise, 2015).

This chapter is structured around a distinction between metaphysical and epistemological varieties of continuism and discontinuism, where *metaphysical* (dis)continuism rejects (accepts) the existence of fundamental differences between episodic memory and episodic future thought, understood as cognitive processes or mental states, and *epistemological* (dis)continuism rejects (accepts) the existence of fundamental differences between the knowledge of past events and the knowledge of future events that is provided by those processes or states. Beginning with metaphysical (dis)continuism, the following section considers two potential differences, one pertaining to the objects of memories and future thoughts, the other pertaining to their reference. Epistemological (dis)continuism is discussed in section 3: Epistemological (Dis)continuism.

Metaphysical (Dis)continuism

The Objects of Mental Time Travel

The question of *the objects of MTT* is a generalization of the traditional question of *the objects of memory* (Fernández, 2017), which concerns the nature of the entities to which we are related, in the first instance, when we remember. The two traditional answers to this question go back to the early modern period, with *direct realists,* the ancestors of current *relationalists,* arguing that, when one remembers, one is directly related to a past event itself (Reid, 1764/2000) and *indirect realists,* the ancestors of *representationalists,* arguing that, when one remembers, one is directly related to a mental representation of a past event and thus only indirectly related to the event (Locke, 1689/1975; Hume, 1738/2011). An understanding of memory as a form of MTT leads naturally to the more general question of the nature of the entities to which we are related, in the first instance, when we mentally travel in time. And this more general question is naturally approached via an attempt to generalize the traditional answers to the traditional question. Thus one might adopt a relationalist approach and argue that, when one engages in MTT, the immediate object of one's memory or future thought is a past or future event itself, or one might adopt a representationalist approach and argue that, when one engages in MTT, the immediate object of one's memory or future thought is a representation of a past or future event.

Relationalism has a good deal of intuitive plausibility, especially with respect to memory – we ordinarily say, after all, that we remember *events,* not *representations* of events. But relationalism also faces daunting problems, especially with respect to future thought. It is difficult to see how one might, when one engages in remembering, be in direct contact with a past event. It is far more difficult to see how one might, when one engages in future thinking, be in direct contact with a future event. Past events are past, and their temporal distance from the remembering subject is a serious difficulty for the relationalist approach, but at least they once existed. Future events, in contrast, are merely possible: They do not exist at the time at which they are imagined, and they might never exist. Thus, unless relationalists are willing to commit to the extremely strong ontological claim that events exist regardless not only of their temporal location (past/future) but also of their modal location (actual/possible),[4] they will need to explain not only how memory can put the subject in direct contact with no-longer-existent past events but also how future thought can put the subject in direct contact with not-yet-existent future events.

Relationalists, such as Debus (2008), have responded to this problem by combining the causal theory of memory with a form of *disjunctivism* about the objects of MTT inspired by disjunctivism about perception (see Byrne and Logue, 2009). The core idea of Debus's strategy is to argue, first, that the causal connection that, according to the causal theory, necessarily links a memory of an event to the remembered event enables the latter to serve as the direct object of the former; second, that, because no such causal connection exists in the case of future thought, the imagined event cannot be the direct object of a thought of an event; and third, that there is therefore a difference in kind, within the category of MTT, between memories and future thoughts. This emphatically discontinuist strategy, in short, consists in endorsing relationalism with respect to memory but rejecting it with respect to future thought.

While committed relationalists may find Debus's strategy appealing, Sant'Anna and Michaelian (2019) have argued that disjunctivism raises new problems for relationalism by making memory into an atypical member of the broader category of MTT, thereby implying that the centrality normally assigned to memory in investigations of MTT is unjustified. There are two points to note here. First, in cases of unsuccessful memory, such as confabulation (in which one "makes up" a past event that did not occur; see Schnider, 2018), no past event is available to serve as the object of the memory. Second, the category of MTT includes not only episodic future thought but also episodic counterfactual thought (in which one imagines an event that might have but did not occur; see De Brigard, 2014a), and, in episodic counterfactual thought as well, no event is available to serve as the object of the

---

4 See Bernecker (2008) for an argument for eternalism, the view that past events continue to exist; Bernecker does not discuss future events.

thought.[5] Given these two points, the "not memory" disjunct would need to include not only future thought but also counterfactual thought and various forms of unsuccessful memory and would therefore end up dwarfing the "memory" disjunct. From a disjunctivist point of view, in other words, episodic memory ends up looking like an exception, rather than the rule.

Relationalism has been relatively unpopular among philosophers of memory, and representationalism can fairly be said to be the standard approach to the objects of memory and, by extension, to the objects of MTT.[6] The key virtue of representationalism is that, simply because the existence of a mental representation of an event does not require the existence of the represented event, it allows us to say that all forms of MTT – memory, both successful and unsuccessful, and future and counterfactual thought – have objects of the same kind: Regardless of whether one remembers an actual past event, imagines a counterfactual past event, or imagines a future event, one is related, in the first instance, to a representation, not to an event. Since we are, given standard views in the philosophy of mind, required to posit mental representations for independent reasons, moreover, representationalism, unlike relationalism, comes at no significant ontological cost.

Representationalism rules out one potential metaphysical difference between memory and future thought and is thus compatible with continuism (since, as we will see in the following section, it does not rule out other potential differences, it does not *entail* continuism). But representationalism, like relationalism, faces important problems. Building on an analogous argument in the philosophy of perception (Travis, 2004), Sant'Anna and Michaelian (2019) have argued that one problem is that the representations produced by MTT are "silent" in the sense that they do not establish their own accuracy conditions. Suppose, for example, that one entertains a thought of a visit to Ottawa. The suggestion is that there is nothing internal to the thought that establishes whether it pertains to an actual past visit or, say, to a possible future visit. Accuracy conditions for an episodic thought, Sant'Anna and Michaelian argue, are established only when the thought is conjoined with further dispositions; a tendency to plan for the visit, for example, might locate the event in the future. And if episodic thoughts do not establish their own accuracy conditions, it is unclear whether they qualify as genuine representations.

Another problem for representationalism is simply that it has difficulty accommodating the intuition cited at the beginning of this section, namely, that, when we remember, we remember events, not representations. Sant'Anna (2018b) has argued that, in light of this problem, we should consider the prospects for a hybrid view that combines aspects of representationalism with aspects of relationalism. *Hybridism* about memory, modeled on a similar view of perception (Schellenberg, 2010), is the view that the objects of memory are representations of events but that those

---

5 Episodic counterfactual thought is a distinct form of MTT, but we will largely refrain from discussing it here; a fuller treatment of the continuism-discontinuism debate would take it into account. We briefly discuss confabulation in section 4 (The Future of the Continuism-Discontinuism Debate: Future-oriented Confabulation?).

6 Because it is the standard approach, it is often simply taken for granted; see Michaelian (2016c) for one recent explicit argument for the approach.

representations are themselves constitutively determined by their causal connection to the events that they represent; this is a compromise view that asks us to reconceive the nature of memory representations by taking them to be inherently relational. Applied to MTT, hybridism supports a form of continuism that may be sufficiently moderate to appeal to discontinuists, since it implies that the objects of both memory and future thought are representations of events but that only in the case of memory are those representations determined by causal connections to events. It remains to be seen whether this moderate form of continuism constitutes a stable middle ground between more standard continuist and discontinuist positions.

The Reference of Episodic Thought

While hybridism is a promising view, representationalism remains the standard approach. Representationalism, however, raises the difficult question of the mechanism by virtue of which a memory image refers to a particular past event. This question raises another: Might the mechanism by virtue of which an image refers to a particular event be at work not only in episodic memory but also in episodic future thought? The relationship that a memory bears to the event to which it refers is roughly the same as that borne by a name to the individual to which it refers. Philosophers have developed a variety of theories of the reference of proper names (see Devitt and Sterelny, 1999), and Lopes (1996) has argued that these can be extended from *names* to *images*. If they can be extended to physical images, there would seem to be no obvious barrier to extending them further in order to provide an account of the reference of the *mental* images at issue in MTT.

Consider the description theory of reference (DTR), according to which reference is determined by *content:* Names are associated with definite descriptions and refer to the entities that are singled out by the descriptions with which they are associated (Frege, 1892/1948; Russell, 1910). An utterance of "Toronto," for example, might refer to Toronto because the speaker associates the description "the city in which the CN Tower is located" with it and because Toronto is the city in which the CN Tower is located. Since it does not invoke causal history in order to explain reference, DTR is most naturally combined with the simulation theory of memory (STM), which does not invoke causal connection in order to explain remembering. On a combined DTR/STM account, remembering would be understood as being a matter of imagining events and the memory images it produces as having contents capable in principle of singling out events from the subject's personal past; the account would then treat a given memory image as referring to the event singled out by its content (if there is such an event), just as a name refers to the entity that is singled out by the associated description (if there is such an entity). A memory of a visit to Toronto, for example, might refer to a particular visit to Toronto because it includes a representation of the CN Tower and because one saw the CN Tower on that visit and no other.

The DTR/STM account is compatible with continuism: Because it treats reference as being underwritten by content (independent of causal history), the account implies that not only the mental images produced by remembering but also those produced by future thinking may sometimes refer to particular events. This does not entail that no other qualitative differences between these two forms of MTT will be identified, but it does rule out one important potential difference. The DTR/STM account, however, inherits a well-known problem from the theory of reference on which it is based. Being associated with an accurate description seems to be neither necessary nor sufficient for a name to refer to an entity: A speaker who mistakenly believes of Toronto that it is the capital of Canada may, under many conditions, nevertheless refer to Toronto (and not Ottawa) when she utters "Toronto." Similarly, being accurate with respect to an event seems to be neither necessary nor sufficient for a memory to refer to that event: A memory of a certain visit to Toronto can arguably get virtually everything about the visit wrong and still count as a memory of that visit, rather than another to which it happens to correspond more closely.

This problem has led many philosophers of language to turn to the causal theory of reference (CTR), according to which reference is determined by *causal history:* In the simplest case, a name is introduced via an initial "baptism," and subsequent uses of the name refer to the thing baptized because they are appropriately causally connected to this initial use of the name (Kripke, 1980). A typical current utterance of "Toronto," for example, might refer to Toronto regardless of the details of the description associated with it because the town then known as "York" was baptized in 1834 with the name "Toronto" and because there is an appropriate causal connection between the utterance and the baptism. Since it does not invoke content in order to explain reference, CTR is most naturally combined with the procedural causal theory of memory (PTM). The distinguishing feature of PTM is in fact its denial – motivated in part by a desire to reconcile the core of the causal theory of memory with recent contentless conceptions of memory traces (see, e.g. De Brigard, 2014b; Hutto and Peeters, 2018) – of the claim made by the classical causal theory that the causal connection constitutive of remembering involves the transmission of content from experience to retrieved memory. According to PTM, the causal connection in question links not the *content* of the experience to the *content* of the retrieved memory but rather the constructive *process* that produces the experience to the reconstructive *process* that produces the retrieved memory: In virtue of certain brain-level similarities between the two processes (see Perrin, 2018, for details), the former may affect the fluency of the latter, thus securing a causal connection between the two despite the fact that no content is transmitted from one to the other. On a combined CTR/PTM account, a memory would be understood as referring to a given event just in case it causally derives, in this "procedural" manner, from an experience of that event. A memory of a visit to Toronto, for example, might refer to a certain visit because the reconstructive process that generates the memory is facilitated by the earlier constructive process of experiencing that visit.

The CTR/PTM account supports discontinuism: Because it treats reference as being underwritten by causal history (independent of content), and because future thoughts are not caused by the events that they are about, the account implies that future thought, unlike memory, never involves reference to particular events (cf. Debus, 2014). And if memories sometimes refer to particular events and future thoughts do not, this would seem to amount to a fundamental metaphysical difference between them. Like the DTR/STM account, however, the CTR/PTM account inherits a well-known problem from the theory of reference on which it is based. Suppose that the baptism in 1834 assigned the name "Toronto" to Lake Ontario but, due to miscommunication, was taken by subsequent speakers to have assigned it instead to the neighboring city; because a typical current utterance of "Toronto" is causally connected to the baptism, CTR implies that it refers to Lake Ontario, despite the fact that Toronto is the dominant causal source of the information associated by the speaker with the name. One might suspect that, because PTM denies that content is transmitted from experiences of events to memories of them, an analogous problem cannot arise for the CTR/PTM account, but the account does in fact face a version of the problem: The fluency of the reconstructive process that generates a memory of a certain visit to Toronto, for example, might be affected not only by the earlier constructive process of experiencing that visit but also – and possibly primarily – by the processes of experiencing other, similar visits.

This problem motivates the hybrid theory of reference (HTR), according to which a name refers to the *dominant causal source* of the content associated with it (Evans, 1982): In the scenario described above, a typical utterance of "Toronto" would, if HTR is right, refer to Toronto, rather than Lake Ontario, because the content that the speaker associates with it derives primarily from the city, not the lake. HTR is a hybrid theory in the sense that it invokes both causation and content and is thus combined most naturally with CTM, which requires that the causal connection between a present memory image and a past event involve the transmission of content from the experience of the event to the image; if HTR is right, this causal connection is precisely of the right sort to secure reference to the event that gave rise to the experience from which content is transmitted. On a combined HTR/CTM account, then, memories refer to events because they are causally connected to experiences of those events and because the relevant causal connection involves the transmission of content from the experiences in question.

The HTR/CTM account, like the CTR/PTM account, supports discontinuism: Because it treats reference as being underwritten by the transmission of content, the account implies – given that future thoughts are never thus connected to the events that they are about – that future thought, unlike memory, never involves reference to particular events. The account, however, inherits a pair of problems from the theory of memory on which it is based. First, procedural causal theorists will object that it is straightforwardly incompatible with arguments for the contentless conception of memory traces. Second, simulation theorists will object that it cannot in fact explain why a given memory refers to a given event: Assuming that we grant that remembering involves the transmission of content, research on the reconstructive character of remembering will force us to acknowledge that content may be transmitted not only from the experience of the event that a memory is about but also from experiences of other events as well and indeed that, in some cases, the event that a memory is about may not be the dominant source of the content of the memory.

Of the three accounts of the reference of memory that we have discussed, one (the DTR/STM account) favors continuism and two (the CTR/PTM and HTR/CTM accounts) favor discontinuism. None of these accounts is fully satisfactory: The

DTR/STM and CTR/PTM accounts inherit problems from the relevant theories of reference, while the HTR/CTM account inherits problems from the relevant theory of memory. Some of these problems may eventually be solved, but it is unclear at present what implications an adequate account of the reference of memory will ultimately have for the continuism-discontinuism debate. It is, however, clear that the debate between metaphysical continuists and discontinuists tends to boil down to a disagreement over the necessity, for the occurrence of remembering, of a causal connection with the remembered event, with discontinuists endorsing one or another version of the causal theory and continuists rejecting it.

Epistemological (Dis)continuism

Whereas metaphysical (dis)continuism rejects (accepts) the existence of fundamental differences between episodic memory and episodic future thought, understood as cognitive processes or mental states, epistemological (dis)continuism rejects (accepts) the existence of fundamental differences between the knowledge of past events and the knowledge of future events that is provided by those processes or states. Given that the normative (including the epistemic) supervenes on the descriptive, adopting epistemological discontinuism commits one to the adoption of some form of metaphysical discontinuism. We will not discuss the relationship between particular forms of epistemological discontinuism and particular forms of metaphysical discontinuism in any detail here, but we will show that the debate between epistemological discontinuism and continuism, like that between metaphysical discontinuism and continuism, tends to boil down to a disagreement over causation. This section considers three potential epistemic discontinuities, one concerning the epistemic openness of the future, another concerning the directness of our knowledge of the past, and a third concerning immunity to error through misidentification in episodic memory and episodic future thought.

The Epistemic Openness of the Future

One motivation for epistemological discontinuism is the natural thought that, even if future thought can provide us with knowledge of future events, that knowledge is bound to be far less secure than is the knowledge of past events with which we are provided by memory, for, if there is controversy over whether the future is *metaphysically* open (Borghini and Torrengo, 2013), there is no controversy over whether it is *epistemically* open: Even if there is a fact of the matter about what will happen in the future, we cannot be *certain* about what will happen. Indeed, even if there is a fact of the matter about what will happen, we cannot be certain that *anything at all* will happen. It may be improbable, but it is perfectly consistent with the evidence available to us that the entire world will blink out of existence five minutes from now. The past, in contrast, is not epistemically open to nearly the same degree. We may be able to doubt the details of many of our memories, but we can at least be certain that the world did not blink into existence five minutes ago. There would thus seem to be a qualitative difference between the knowledge provided by memory and the knowledge provided by future thought.

Natural though this thought may be, it is mistaken. As Russell (1921/2005) pointed out, it is in fact perfectly consistent with the evidence available to us that the world blinked into existence five minutes ago, complete with our memories, no matter how detailed or subjectively convincing these might be. This is just a particular instance of a general skeptical point in epistemology: If we set the standards for knowledge sufficiently high, requiring not just reliability but certainty, we thereby deprive ourselves of virtually all knowledge, including knowledge of the very existence of the external world – if certainty is a prerequisite for knowledge, we can have knowledge neither of future events, nor of past events, nor even of present events. Thus, if we are to avoid skepticism, the standards for knowledge should be set well below the level of certainty. And if knowledge presupposes only some lower level of reliability, the openness of the future need no longer give us any reason to suppose that there is a qualitative epistemological difference between memory and future thought, for the past is to some extent open as well: Michaelian (2016a) thus argues that, though our beliefs about future events are likely to be significantly less reliable than our beliefs about past events, this may nevertheless amount to a merely quantitative difference – a difference of degree, rather than a difference in kind – between our knowledge of future events and our knowledge of past events.

The Directness of our Knowledge of the Past

Another motivation for epistemological discontinuism is the thought that, though memory may be on a par with future thought with respect to *indirect* or inferential knowledge, there is a qualitative difference between them with respect to their capacity to provide us with *direct* or noninferential knowledge. Kneale (1971), for example, while granting that both memory and future thought are imperfectly reliable, nevertheless argues that it is part of the very concept of memory that a memory "should have as a part-cause the occurrence of the event recollected" (Kneale, 1971: 2). This is, in effect, to invoke the causal theory of memory. But while the claim that memory but not future thought requires a causal connection with the event in question entails a metaphysical difference between the two, it does not entail an epistemological difference between them unless conjoined with the further claim that knowledge of an event (as opposed to mere true belief about it) requires a causal connection with it. Thus Kneale's view presupposes a *causal theory of knowledge* (Goldman, 1967).

Causal theories of knowledge rule out not only knowledge of future events but also a variety of other kinds of knowledge (e.g. of mathematical facts). They thus have few adherents and have largely been supplanted by *reliabilist theories of knowledge*, according to which knowledge requires reliability but not necessarily a causal connection (Goldman, 2012). Given reliabilism, a representation produced by a process that involves a causal connection to the represented event might well qualify as knowledge, but, if it so qualifies, it does so in virtue of the reliability of the process that produced it. A reliable process that does not involve a causal connection to the events of which it produces representations is just as capable of producing representations that qualify as knowledge. Michaelian (2016a) thus argues that the "directness" of memory knowledge (in Kneale's causal sense) is irrelevant: If reliabilism is right, then, if memory and future thought are both sufficiently reliable, they are both capable of providing us with knowledge of events.

Immunity to Error Through Misidentification in Episodic Memory and Episodic Future Thought

Neither the epistemic openness of the future nor the directness of our knowledge of the past, then, seems to give us good reason to endorse epistemological discontinuism. A third and final potential epistemological discontinuity between episodic memory and episodic future thought pertains to their *immunity to error through misidentification* (IEM) or lack thereof. There are two senses in which memory might be thought to be immune to error through misidentification. First, it might be *factually* IEM.[7] If it is, then, given the way memory actually works, if, for example, I have a memory on the basis of which I believe that I took a walk in Ottawa last year, then I might be wrong *that* a walk was taken, but, if I am not wrong about that, I cannot be wrong in thinking that it was *I* who took the walk. Second, it might be *logically* IEM. If it is, then, *no matter how memory might work,* if I have a memory on the basis of which I believe that I took a walk in Ottawa last year, then, if I am not wrong about whether a walk was taken, I cannot be wrong in thinking that it was I who took the walk (Hamilton, 2007; McDowell, 1997). It is plausible that memory is factually IEM, but factual IEM does not imply logical IEM,[8] and Perrin (2016) has argued that this points to a fundamental difference between memory and future thought: Memory may be factually IEM, but only future thought is logically IEM.

Perrin's argument appeals, first, to the claim that the sort of causal connection invoked by the causal theory of memory plays a role in determining the identities of the subjects – other than the subject whose experience is remembered – who figure in the memory. Consider, for example, a scenario in which I have a memory on the basis of which I believe that I took a walk with Paul but in which, unbeknownst to me, I in fact took a walk with Peter, Paul's identical twin brother. In this scenario, in virtue of the causal connection between the memory of the walk and the experience of it, I remember Peter but misidentify him as Paul. Memory, in other words, is not even factually IEM with respect to the identities of subjects other than the subject whose experience is remembered. His argument appeals, second, to the claim that the same causal connection determines the identity of the subject whose experience is remembered. Given the way memory actually works, this causal connection only ever links the subject at the time of remembering to the very same subject at the time of experiencing. Hence *memory is factually IEM* with respect to the identity of the

---

7 We will use "IEM" as an abbreviation for both *"immune* to error through misidentification" and *"immunity* to error through misidentification."

8 Note that, given how we have defined factual IEM, logical IEM implies factual IEM. If we were instead to define factual IEM as *mere* factual IEM, then factual IEM and logical IEM would be mutually exclusive.

subject whose experience is remembered. But if memory were to work differently, the causal connection might link the subject at the time of remembering to a different subject at the time of experiencing. Suppose, for instance, that a "memory transplant" technology were to be invented.[9] It could then turn out that, when I have a memory on the basis of which I believe that I took a walk, I am not wrong in thinking that a walk was taken but am wrong in thinking that it was me who took the walk, for it might be that I have retrieved a transplanted memory. In this case, I might misidentify another subject as myself: *Memory is not logically IEM* with respect to the identity of the subject whose experience is remembered (see Coliva, 2006). Perrin's argument appeals, finally, to the claim that, in contrast to memory, *future thought is logically IEM.* Consider a scenario in which I imagine taking a walk next year with Paul. Since no causal connection is available to determine the identity either of the subject with whom the walk will be taken or the identity of the subject who will take the walk, both identities are in effect stipulated by the imagining subject – that is, they are determined by his or her intentions (see Recanati, 2007). Thus, regardless of whether I intend to imagine myself taking the walk or to imagine another subject taking the walk, there is no possibility of error with respect to whose experience I am imagining.

A difference between memory and future thought with respect to logical IEM would mean that there is an important kind of false belief to which we are susceptible in one form of MTT but not the other and would thus amount to a fundamental epistemological discontinuity between them. But alternative continuist treatments of the question of IEM in episodic memory and episodic future thought are available. Michaelian (2016a) defends a view on which both memory and future thought are sometimes logically and therefore factually IEM and sometimes factually but not logically IEM. The basic thought behind the view is that, once we admit that memory is a form of MTT, then we have to admit that any mechanism capable of determining identity in future thought might sometimes also be at work in memory, and vice versa. Thus, while Perrin maintains that identity is determined by causation in future thought and by stipulation in memory, Michaelian argues, first, that identity is *sometimes* determined by stipulation not only in future thought but also in memory (and hence that memory, like future thought, is sometimes logically – and therefore factually – IEM) and, second, that identity is *sometimes* determined by causation not only in memory but also in future thought (and hence that future thought, like memory, is sometimes factually but not logically IEM).

On the one hand, the suggestion that future thoughts are sometimes logically IEM derives its plausibility from the fact that there is no causal connection between future events and present representations thereof, leaving the subject's intentions to determine identity, but, if memory is just as much a form of MTT as is future thought, then there is no guarantee that, when a subject remembers, there will inevitably be a causal connection between the past event and his present representation thereof, in which case it is just as plausible that identity is determined by the subject's intentions. If it is, then the memory is logically and hence factually IEM. On the

9 See Shoemaker (1970) and Parfit (1984) on "quasi-memory."

other hand, because the contents of simulations of both past and future events derive in part from the subject's experiences of past events, the identity of the subject whose experience is represented can be inherited via a causal connection between the present representation and a past experience not only in memory but also in future thought. Consider a simple case in which I, in a first step, remember taking a walk in Ottawa last year and, in a second step, imagine taking a walk in Ottawa next year by mentally projecting that experience forward in time. If one claims that the causal connection confers factual IEM on the memory, there would seem to be little reason to deny that it confers factual IEM on the future thought. By the same token, if one takes the in-principle possibility of memory transplants to rule out logical IEM with respect to the memory, one should likewise take it to rule out logical IEM with respect to the future thought: If a memory transplant were to lead to error due to misidentification at the first step, that error would presumably be inherited at the second step – I would be imagining not my own future walk but rather that of the subject whose memory has been transplanted.

If these arguments are right, then there will be cases of both future thought and memory that are logically and therefore factually IEM, and there will be cases of both memory and future thought that are factually but not logically IEM. Discontinuist replies to the arguments are, of course, available. Regarding the second part of the argument, the discontinuist might insist that memory is involved in the process of imagining and that, if the subject instead imagines himself taking a walk next year without drawing on a memory of himself taking a walk last year, the identity of the relevant subject will be determined entirely by his intentions. Regarding the first part of the argument, the discontinuist might insist that, if there is no causal connection to the "remembered" event, then the subject is not really remembering but rather imagining. If these replies are successful, then we are back to discontinuism: Future thought is logically and therefore factually IEM, and memory is factually but not logically IEM.

Another continuist alternative is suggested by Fernández's (2014) argument for the claim that memory is logically IEM. Fernández points out that the phenomenology of episodic memories is perspectival. The perspectival character of memories arguably derives from that of the past perceptual experiences on which they are based. In Fernández's view, the perspectival character of perception is due to the fact that it represents relations between the perceiving subject and objects in the external world. For example, as I see the CN Tower in the distance, I represent myself as occupying a certain position relative to it. Consequently, when I later remember having seen the CN Tower, I represent a determinate subject, myself, as having occupied that position. I thus necessarily represent *myself* as having had the experience. To be sure, I can be mistaken about whether I actually had *the experience,* but I cannot be mistaken about whether I am *the subject* represented as having had the experience. Crucially, this is so regardless of what happened in the past and, in particular, regardless of whether my current memory results from a memory transplant.

If Fernández's argument is successful, then memory is logically IEM. If this argument were to be combined with Perrin's argument for the claim that future thought is logically IEM, we would in effect have an argument for a combined view on which *both* memory and future thought are logically IEM. This combined view, however, sees entirely different mechanisms as being responsible for IEM in memory and in future thought and is thus of doubtful coherence. Moreover, a discontinuist might argue, first, that the perspectival character of memory does not fix the identity of the subject whose experience is being remembered but only the fact that the experience involved perception from a certain perspective. Memory representations would thus be silent with respect to identity, in which case the possibility of memory transplants would again entail the logical possibility of error due to misidentification. The discontinuist might argue, second, that Fernández assumes that, when one remembers, one represents the experience and the experiencing subject, whereas it is more parsimonious to assume that only the relevant event is explicitly represented (Zahavi, 2003). If the experiencing subject does not figure in the representation of the event, we arrive, again, at the possibility of memory transplants, entailing the logical possibility of error due to misidentification.

The continuist might be able to successfully defend a variety of epistemological continuism based on Fernández's claim that memory is logically IEM, but a variety that sees both memory and future thought as sometimes logically and therefore factually IEM and sometimes factually but not logically IEM is more likely to be coherent. An advocate of a continuist position of this sort might argue that the presence of an appropriate causal connection in cases of memory and the absence of such a connection in cases of imagination has, in the discontinuist objections to the position outlined above, the status of a dogma: If appropriate causation is indeed the dividing line between remembering and imagining, then there will, indeed, be a fundamental metaphysical difference between those two processes, in which case we should not be surprised to find fundamental epistemic differences between them as well, but, since the continuism-discontinuism debate was triggered in the first place by the fact that MTT research calls the role of appropriate causation in distinguishing between memory and imagination into question, the discontinuist is hardly entitled to take this role for granted. How, then, are we to settle the matter of the role of appropriate causation in distinguishing between memory and imagination? We noted at the outset that the available empirical evidence does not suffice to decide between continuism and discontinuism. It may, however, favour either the causal theory or the simulation theory. Since the former tends to support discontinuism and the latter to support continuism, the resolution of the continuism-discontinuism debate may ultimately be decided by the resolution of the causalist-simulationist debate.

The Future of the Continuism-Discontinuism Debate: Future-Oriented Confabulation?

The continuism-discontinuism debate is multifaceted, and there are a number of other issues that this chapter might have broached (see Perrin and Michaelian, 2017; Sant'Anna, 2018a; for a recent review from a psychological perspective, see Addis, 2018). Before concluding, we briefly explore just one of these – the implications of continuism and discontinuism for the possibility of future-oriented confabulation. *Confabulation* is, very roughly, a form of unsuccessful memory in which subjects unable to remember "make up" more or less plausible past events by, for example, combining aspects of different experienced events or radically displacing events in time (see Schnider, 2018). In the present context, it is natural to inquire into the utility of the concept of *future-oriented* confabulation analogous to this familiar concept of (past-oriented) confabulation. Whether we can make sense of the concept of future-oriented confabulation depends, once again, on our stance with respect to the necessity of a causal connection for the occurrence of memory.

There are accounts of the relationship between confabulation and remembering based both on the causal theory and on the simulation theory. *Causalist* accounts (Bernecker, 2017; Robins, 2016, 2018, 2019) treat the existence of an appropriate causal connection with the apparently remembered event as making the difference between remembering and confabulating. *Simulationist* accounts (Michaelian 2016b, forthcoming), in contrast, see the difference as being a matter of reliability, in effect characterizing confabulation as unreliable imagination. If what is distinctive of past-oriented confabulation is, as the causal theorist would have it, lack of causal connection, then the notion of future-oriented confabulation will make little sense, simply because future thought never involves a causal connection to the represented event. If what is distinctive of past-oriented confabulation is, instead, as the simulation theorist would have it, lack of reliability, then the notion of future-oriented confabulation may well make sense.

It is, of course, one thing for the concept to make sense and quite another for it to correspond to an empirical phenomenon, and one might maintain that, since successful future thoughts, unlike successful memories, need not correspond to actual events, there is simply no need for a concept of future-oriented confabulation. There is, however, considerable work showing that confabulators display not only defective remembering but also defective future thinking, in the sense that they produce representations of future events that fail to correspond to events that they are likely to experience (see, e.g. Dalla Barba et al., 1997; Schnider, 2018), suggesting that there is indeed a need for a concept of future-oriented confabulation. Whether the concept of future-oriented confabulation is viable will ultimately depend on whether a notion of reliability applicable to episodic future thinking (and potentially to episodic imagining more broadly) can be worked out, and this remains to be done.

Conclusions

Our aim in this chapter has been to review arguments for and against continuism and discontinuism; we have taken a stand in favor of neither view. The primary message of the chapter is thus that it is likely that the resolution of the continuism-discontinuism debate will depend on a resolution of the question of the necessity of a causal connection for the occurrence of memory. The causal theory of memory has been enormously influential among philosophers of memory (Michaelian and Robins, 2018), and, from the perspective of the philosophy of memory, the burden of proof tends to fall on those who would endorse the simulation theory. Things may, however, look very different from the perspective of the philosophy of imagination. We therefore close by inviting philosophers of imagination to consider what implications their accounts of the nature of episodic imagination might have for the continuism-discontinuism debate.

Acknowledgments

Thanks to Anna Abraham for detailed comments on an earlier draft of this chapter. The chapter is based in part on work done during a fellowship awarded to Kourken Michaelian by the Fondation Maison des sciences de l'homme. This work is supported by the French National Research Agency in the framework of the "Investissements d'avenir" program (ANR-15-IDEX-02).

References

Addis, D. R. (2018). Are Episodic Memories Special? On the Sameness of Remembered and Imagined Event Simulation. *Journal of the Royal Society of New Zealand*, *48*(2–3), 64–88.

Arcangeli, M. (2018). *Supposition and the Imaginative Realm: A Philosophical Inquiry.* New York, NY: Routledge.

Bernecker, S. (2008). *The Metaphysics of Memory*. New York, NY: Springer.

(2017). A Causal Theory of Mnemonic Confabulation. *Frontiers in Psychology*, *8*, 1207.

Bernecker, S., and Michaelian, K. (eds.) (2017). *The Routledge Handbook of Philosophy of Memory*. London, UK: Routledge.

Borghini, A., and Torrengo, G. (2013). The Metaphysics of the Thin Red Line. In F. Correia and A. Iacona (eds.), *Around the Tree*. Berlin, Germany: Springer, 105–125.

Brewer, W. F. (1996). What is Recollective Memory? In D. C. Rubin (ed.), *Remembering Our Past: Studies in Autobiographical Memory*. Cambridge, UK: Cambridge University Press, 19–66.

Byrne, A., and Logue, H. (eds.) (2009). *Disjunctivism: Contemporary Readings*. Cambridge, MA: MIT Press.

Coliva, A. (2006). Error Through Misidentification: Some Varieties. *The Journal of Philosophy*, *103*(8), 403–425.

Dalla Barba, G., Cappelletti, J. Y., Signorini, M., and Denes, G. (1997). Confabulation: Remembering "Another" Past, Planning "Another" Future. *Neurocase*, *3*(6), 425–436.

Debus, D. (2008). Experiencing the Past: A Relational Account of Recollective Memory. *Dialectica*, *62*(4), 405–432.

(2014). "Mental Time Travel": Remembering the Past, Imagining the Future, and the Particularity of Events. *Review of Philosophy and Psychology*, *5*, 333–350.

De Brigard, F. (2014a). Is Memory for Remembering? Recollection as a Form of Episodic Hypothetical Thinking. *Synthese*, *191*(2), 155–185.

(2014b). The Nature of Memory Traces. *Philosophy Compass*, *9*(6), 402–414.

Devitt, M., and Sterelny, K. (1999). *Language and Reality: An Introduction to the Philosophy of Language*. Cambridge, MA: MIT Press.

Evans, J. (1982). *The Varieties of Reference*. Oxford, UK: Clarendon Press.

Fernández, J. (2014). Memory and Immunity to Error through Misidentification. *Review of Philosophy and Psychology*, 5(3), 373–390.

Fernández, J. (2017). The Intentional Objects of Memory. In S. Bernecker and K. Michaelian (eds.), *The Routledge Handbook of Philosophy of Memory*. London, UK: Routledge, 88–99.

Frege, G. (1892/1948). Sense and Reference. *The Philosophical Review*, 57(3), 209–230.

Frise, M. (2015). Epistemology of Memory. In J. Fieser and B. Dowden (eds.), *Internet Encyclopedia of Philosophy*. www.iep.utm.edu/epis-mem/.

Gérardin-Laverge, L. (2017). Mémoire constructive, imagination et voyage mental dans le temps. *Cahiers philosophiques*, 2, 23–40.

Goldman, A. I. (1967). A Causal Theory of Knowing. *The Journal of Philosophy*, 64(12), 357–372.

(2012). *Reliabilism and Contemporary Epistemology: Essays*. Oxford, UK: Oxford University Press.

Hamilton, A. (2007). Memory and Self-Consciousness: Immunity to Error through Misidentification. *Synthese*, 171, 409–417.

Hume, D. (1738/2011). *A Treatise of Human Nature*. Oxford, UK: Clarendon Press.

Hutto, D. D., and Peeters, A. (2018). The Roots of Remembering: Radically Enactive Recollecting. In K. Michaelian, D. Debus, and D. Perrin (eds.), *New Directions in the Philosophy of Memory*. London, UK: Routledge, 97–118.

Kind, A., and Kung, P. (eds.) (2016). *Knowledge Through Imagination*. Oxford, UK: Oxford University Press.

Kneale, M. (1971). Our Knowledge of the Past and of the Future. *Proceedings of the Aristotelian Society*, 72:1–12.

Kripke, S. (1980). *Naming and Necessity*. Cambridge, MA: Harvard University Press.

Locke, J. (1689/1975). An Essay Concerning Human Understanding. In P. Nidditch (ed.), *The Clarendon Edition of the Works of John Locke: An Essay Concerning Human Understanding*. Oxford, UK: Oxford University Press.

Lopes, D. (1996). *Understanding Pictures*. Oxford, UK: Clarendon Press.

Martin, C. B., and Deutscher, M. (1966). Remembering. *The Philosophical Review*, 75(2), 161–196.

McDowell, J. (1997). Reductionism and the First Person. In J. Dancy (ed.), *Reading Parfit*. Oxford, UK: Blackwell, 230–250.

Macpherson, F., and Dorsch, F. (eds.) (2018). *Perceptual Imagination and Perceptual Memory*. Oxford, UK: Oxford University Press.

Michaelian, K. (2016a). Against Discontinuism: Mental Time Travel and Our Knowledge of Past and Future Events. In K. Michaelian, S. B. Klein, and K. K. Szpunar (eds.), *Seeing the Future: Theoretical Perspectives on Future-Oriented Mental Time Travel*. Oxford, UK: Oxford University Press, 69–92.

(2016b). Confabulating, Misremembering, Relearning: The Simulation Theory of Memory and Unsuccessful Remembering. *Frontiers in Psychology*, 7, 1857.

(2016c). *Mental Time Travel: Episodic Memory and Our Knowledge of the Personal Past*. Cambridge, MA: MIT Press.

(Forthcoming). Confabulating as Unreliable Imagining: In Defence of the Simulationist Account of Unsuccessful Remembering. *Topoi*.

Michaelian, K., Klein, S. B., and Szpunar, K. K. (eds.) (2016). *Seeing the Future: Theoretical Perspectives on Future-Oriented Mental Time Travel*. Oxford, UK: Oxford University Press.

Michaelian, K., and Robins, S. (2018). Beyond the Causal Theory? Fifty Years after Martin and Deutscher. In K. Michaelian, D. Debus, and D. Perrin (eds.), *New Directions in the Philosophy of Memory*. London, UK: Routledge, 12–32.

Nanay, B. (2015). Perceptual Content and the Content of Mental Imagery. *Philosophical Studies*, *172*(7), 1723–1736.

Parfit, D. (1984). *Reasons and Persons*. Oxford, UK: Oxford University Press.

Perrin, D. (2016). Asymmetries in Subjective Time. In K. Michaelian, S. B. Klein, and K. K. Szpunar (eds.), *Seeing the Future: Theoretical Perspectives on Future-Oriented Mental Time Travel*. Oxford, UK: Oxford University Press, 39–61.

(2018). A Case for Procedural Causality in Episodic Recollection. In K. Michaelian, D. Debus, and D. Perrin (eds.), *New Directions in the Philosophy of Memory*. London, UK: Routledge, 33–51.

Perrin, D., and Michaelian, K. (2017). Memory as Mental Time Travel. In S. Bernecker and K. Michaelian (eds.), *The Routledge Handbook of Philosophy of Memory*. London, UK: Routledge, 228–239.

Recanati, F. (2007). *Perspectival Thought: A Plea for (Moderate) Relativism*. Oxford, UK: Oxford University Press.

Reid, T. (1764/2000). *An Inquiry into the Human Mind on the Principles of Common Sense*. Pennsylvania, PA: Pennsylvania State University Press.

Robins, S. K. (2016). Misremembering. *Philosophical Psychology*, *29*(3), 432–447.

(2018). Mnemonic Confabulation. *Topoi*. doi.org/10.1007/s11245-018-9613-x.

(2019). Confabulation and Constructive Memory. *Synthese*, *196*(6), 2135–2151.

Russell, B. (1910). Knowledge by Acquaintance and Knowledge by Description. *Proceedings of the Aristotelian Society*, *11*, 108–128.

(1921/2005). *Analysis of Mind*. London, UK: Routledge.

Sant'Anna, A. (2018a). Mental Time Travel and the Philosophy of Memory. *Unisinos Journal of Philosophy*, *19*(1), 52–62.

(2018b). The Hybrid Contents of Memory. *Synthese*, March. doi:10.1007/s11229-018-1753-4.

Sant'Anna, A., and Michaelian, K. (2019). Thinking about Events: A Pragmatic Account of the Objects of Episodic Hypothetical Thought. *Review of Philosophy and Psychology*, *10*(1), 187–217.

Schellenberg, S. (2010). The Particularity and Phenomenology of Perceptual Experience. *Philosophical Studies*, *149*(1), 19–48.

Schnider, A. (2018). *The Confabulating Mind: How the Brain Creates Reality*. Oxford, UK: Oxford University Press.

Shoemaker, S. (1970). Persons and Their Pasts. *American Philosophical Quarterly*, *7*(4), 269–285.

Suddendorf, T., and Corballis, M. C. (2007). The Evolution of Foresight: What Is Mental Time Travel, and Is It Unique to Humans? *Behavioral and Brain Sciences*, *30*(3), 299–313.

Travis, C. (2004). The Silence of the Senses. *Mind*, *113*(449), 57–94.

Tulving, E. (1972). Episodic and Semantic Memory. In E. Tulving and W. Donaldson (eds.), *Organization of Memory*. New York NY: Academic Press, 381–402.

(1985). *Elements of Episodic Memory*. Oxford, UK: Oxford University Press.

Werning, M., and Cheng, S. (2017). Taxonomy and Unity of Memory. In S. Bernecker and K. Michaelian (eds.), *The Routledge Handbook of Philosophy of Memory*. London, UK: Routledge, 7–20.

Zahavi, D. (2003). *Husserl's Phenomenology*. Stanford, CA: Stanford University Press.

20 Imagining and Experiencing the Self on Cognitive Maps

Shahar Arzy and Amnon Dafni-Merom

Introduction

The imagination is that faculty which retains impressions of things perceptible to the mind, after they have ceased to affect directly, the senses which conceived them. This faculty, combining some of these impressions and separating others from one another, thus constructs out of originally perceived ideas some of which it has never received any impression, and which it could not possibly have perceived. For instance, one may imagine an iron ship floating in the air, or a man whose head reaches the heaven and whose feet rest on the earth, or an animal with a thousand eyes, and many other similar impossibilities which the imagination may construct and endow with an existence that is fanciful.

Maimonides (1135–1204 AD), translated and quoted in *The Eight Chapters of Maimonides on Ethics (Shemonah Perakim): A Psychological and Ethical Treatise* (1912), page 41, by Joseph Isaac Gorfinkle, Columbia University Press.

Once upon a time, I, Chuang Chou, dreamt I was a butterfly, fluttering hither and thither, a veritable butterfly, enjoying itself to the full of its bent, and not knowing it was Chuang Chou. Suddenly I awoke, and came to myself, the veritable Chuang Chou. *Now* I do not know whether it was then I dreamt I was a butterfly, or whether I am now a butterfly dreaming I am a man. Between me and the butterfly there must be a difference. This is an instance of transformation.

Chuang Chou (370–287 BC), translated by James Legge, and quoted in *The Three Religions of China: Lectures Delivered at Oxford* (1913), page 75, by William Edward Soothill, Oxford University Press.

The immediate intuitive response to reject a solipsist conception of the world such as "I am the only mind that surely exists" should not detract from the close examination the argument merits. Epistemological solipsism maintains that only the directly accessible mental contents of the self can be assured. While no serious philosophical theory embraced solipsism, the epistemological distinction between self-generated beliefs and information perceived from the external world is prominent in cognition. The confusion in the famous proposition of Chuang Chu derives from the fact that the perceived world is actually imagined. In recent years, such ideas have been translated to a wave of research aimed at comparing future simulations and imaginations to past experiences (e.g., Addis, Wong, and Schacter, 2007; Arzy, Molnar-Szakacs, and Blanke, 2008; Schacter et al., 2012; Szpunar, Watson, and McDermott, 2007). Following this, researchers have further argued that even the remembered past is actually imagined, similarly to the imagined future, which is partially based on experience and memory (St. Jacques et al., 2018). In other words, our memory is influenced by experience that occurs long after the remembered events. Remembering the past and imagining the future may be regarded as remembering the future and imagining the past. Our social perception also involves imagining the people around us (Uddin et al., 2007). We construct our social network according to beliefs we hold regarding the people in our life, assembling a web of images around each of them. Mostly, these beliefs hold, but sometimes they prove false. Our cognitive system is able to identify faces and postures effectively, yet our perception of the people in our lives relies heavily on the image we have of them rather than their objective characteristics. Following Chuang Chou's argument, this chapter examines the interplay between our prior beliefs about the world around us, the cognitive representations we create of this world, and the way the human self can imagine, remember, and simulate in these mental constructs of the world.

Cognitive Maps

A major theme in the study of how the external world is represented in the neurocognitive system is that of "cognitive maps" (Behrens et al., 2018; O'Keefe and Nadel, 1978; for a discussion on mental models in general see Tversky, 1993). While these maps supposedly provide the link between the world and the experiencing subject, here we claim that there is a crucial missing component, that is the imagination of the self in these maps (Arzy and Schacter, 2019).

The concept and mechanisms of cognitive maps have been brought to the forefront of neuroscience in recent years. While this review does not aim to cover this important topic (which is still evolving), some basic concepts and latest developments are worth mentioning. Cognitive maps were originally hypothesized by Craik (Craik, 1943) and Tolman (Tolman, 1948). Following his many experiments in freely moving rats Tolman hypothesized that there exists a "central office" in the brain that acts more like a map control room than an old-fashioned telephone exchange. The stimuli allowed in are not simply connected by one-to-one switches to the outgoing responses. Rather, the incoming impulses are usually worked over and elaborated in the "central control room" into a cognitive-like map of the environment. It is this tentative map, indicating routes, paths, and environmental relationships, that finally determines "what responses, if any, the animal will finally release" (Tolman, 1948).

Decades after Tolman's original hypothesis, John O'Keefe and colleagues revealed that specific hippocampal neurons fire whenever an animal arrives at a specific place in the environment ("place cells"; O'Keefe and Nadel, 1978). Later on, another cell-type was discovered in the entorhinal cortex, firing periodically at multiple locations to form a sixfold rotationally symmetrical grid-like pattern across space ("grid cells"; Hafting et al., 2005). Over the years the pieces of the puzzle have begun to fall into place, as several other cell-types have been discovered. For instance, "head-direction cells" code for an animal's movement direction, which is crucial for self-location-based navigation (Taube, Muller, and Ranck, 1990).

"Border cells" and "boundary vector cells" code for the boundaries of the environment, firing when the animal is close to the edge and enabling the animal to tune its navigation according to a specific arena's size (Solstad et al., 2008). Alongside these are cells that encode the vector relationships to borders (Lever et al., 2009), goals (Sarel et al., 2017), objects (Høydal et al., 2018), and rewards (Gauthier and Tank, 2018). Moreover, "time cells" are the equivalent of place cells in the temporal domain, coding for a specific time-epoch (MacDonald et al., 2011).

The mutual activity of these different types of cells makes up a "cognitive map," which is a maplike representation of the environment (Figure 20.1). Path integration is the process of identifying one's self-location using information about speed of movement, travel time, and directional change whenever visible landmarks are unavailable (Wallace and Whishaw, 2003). Specifically, path integration is a body-centered egocentric strategy of combining direction and velocity into an aggregate of routes that in turn give rise to the cognitive-map representation. Such a "bird's-eye view" map supports a world-centered allocentric representation of the world, which then enables further processing, such as calculations of routes and "short-cuts" (Epstein et al., 2017).

Interestingly, cognitive maps and their egocentric and allocentric subprocesses are applied not only to spatial navigation but also to other modalities. For example, in the time domain, a temporal cognitive map would represent the relationships between temporally noncontiguous events on which the self "navigates" her way in between memories, potential pasts, and differently simulated futures (Schmajuk and Buhusi, 1997). In the social domain one "navigates" across her social network, managing relations with people on this network and their characteristics (Parkinson, Kleinbaum, and Wheatley, 2017; Tavares et al., 2015). Cognitive maps may also combine domains, as seen in a spatial-social network coding for the localization of other animals in space (Danjo, Toyoizumi, and Fujisawa, 2018; Omer et al., 2018). Finally, traces were found for even more abstract cognitive maps, such as a map of potential decisions to be made (Wilson et al., 2014) or objects' characteristics (Constantinescu, O'Reilly, and Behrens, 2016).

While most of these studies have been carried out on rodents, a simple trigonometric manipulation enabled the identification of sixfold rotationally symmetrical grid cell-like activity in humans using functional neuroimaging (Doeller, Barry, and Burgess, 2010; Garvert, Dolan, and Behrens, 2017). Analysis of the brain response as a function of the participant's movement direction in a virtual reality-based arena revealed a sixfold rotational dependency of entorhinal activity to correlate with participants' ability to find "cues" hidden within the arena (Doeller, Barry, and Burgess, 2010). Interestingly, when an artificial agent based on deep multilayered networks was trained to navigate, armed with only basic features of head-direction and velocity, it spontaneously formed artificial units with properties similar to grid, border, and head-direction cells (Banino et al., 2018). Formation of these artificial grid cells therefore enabled the network to solve spatial tasks and generate shortcuts, as seen in animals.

"Map-anchoring" is another concept worth mentioning here. How is the cognitive map anchored to the environment around the behaving self? Visual cues such as landmarks in the environment or boundaries of the environment determine the relation of the map to the world it represents (Julian et al., 2018; Krupic et al., 2018). Notably, objects at the extremities of the environment have a major influence

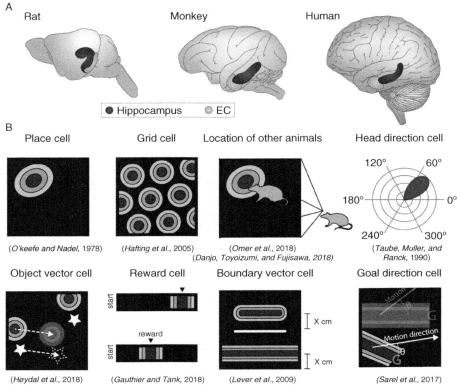

Figure 20.1 *The hippocampal zoo. (A) Anatomical location of the hippocampus and entorhinal cortex in different species. (B) A variety of cells in the hippocampal formation represent different spatial variables. Place cells (O'Keefe and Nadel, 1978) are active when an animal is in a single (sometimes multiple) location. Grid cells (Hafting et al., 2005) are active when an animal is in one of multiple locations on a triangular lattice. Social place cells (Danjo, Toyoizumi, and Fujisawa, 2018; Omer et al., 2018) are active in one animal when it observes that another animal is in a particular location. Head-direction cells (Taube, Muller, and Ranck, 1990) are active when an animal's head is facing a particular direction. Object-vector cells (Høydal et al., 2018) are active when an animal is in a particular direction and distance from any object. Reward cells (Gauthier and Tank, 2018) are active when an animal is in the vicinity of reward. Boundary vector cells (Lever et al., 2009) are active at a given distance away from a boundary in a particular allocentric orientation. Goal-direction cells (Sarel et al., 2017) are active when the goal of an animal is in a particular direction relative to its current movement direction. The "G" indicates the goal location.*

PANEL A: Reprinted from Neuron, *100(2): Behrens et al., What is a Cognitive Map? Organizing Knowledge for Flexible Behavior, 490–509. Copyright 2018, with permission from Elsevier.*

PANEL B: Reprinted by permission from Springer Nature, Nature Reviews Neuroscience *15(10): Strange et al., Functional Organization of the Hippocampal Longitudinal Axis, 655–669. Copyright 2014.*

on the map and help correct errors in path integration (Epstein et al., 2017). In addition, recent work suggests that environmental geometry may also influence the cognitive map (e.g. distortions applied on the edge of a non-rectangular shape) (Krupic et al., 2015; Nau et al., 2018). Taken together, this line of work shows that the changing environment has a role in shaping cognitive maps.

Locating the Self on Mental Lines and Cognitive Maps

While the aforementioned neurons create the representation of the world in the subject's brain, there is still a missing link with respect to how a person imagines herself within this representation. For instance, a unidimensional cognitive map of time (or "mental line") will similarly represent a past event or an imagined future event (Arzy, Adi-Japha, and Blanke, 2009a; Arzy, Molnar-Szakacs, and Blanke, 2008; Schacter et al., 2012). How may the brain further distinguish between the two? Theories like reality-monitoring (Simons, Garrison, and Johnson, 2017) claim that this information may be extracted out of the map itself, since future events will be more vague and less detailed as compared to past events, cuing the brain about their respective location in past or future. However, such a strategy seems limited and inefficient, since such an important character of the map must be extracted again and again a posteriori for each experience. Moreover, a recent study (Schurr et al., 2018) has shown that a decision about the past/future character of the event significantly precedes processing of the event itself. Thus, a more plausible strategy may rely on the dialogue between the experiencing self and the information as represented on the cognitive map (Arzy and Schacter, 2019). In this section we delineate different cognitive phenomena that rely on such a dialogue – namely those of mental lines, self-projection, self-reference, cognitive distance, and orientation. Furthermore, we detail the neuroanatomical basis of these phenomena, claiming that these two interlocutors rely on different brain networks: The cognitive maps are processed by the medial temporal lobe where the hippocampus and entorhinal and perirhinal cortices house different cellular substructures of the maps, while the experiential self relies on a cortical network including mostly frontal and parietal midline structures, as well as the temporoparietal junction.

Mental Lines

The concept of mental lines began with research on the mental number line (MNL; Banks and Hill, 1974; Dehaene, Bossini, and Giraux, 1993). The MNL depicts the way in which numbers are represented by humans (and perhaps other species as well; Rugani et al., 2015) on a horizontal spatial axis running from left to right, as is also expressed by some human cultures in written material (Dehaene et al., 1999). Interestingly, a natural logarithmic scaling was observed when performing numerical calculations. Specifically, experiments on mental number scaling in archaic cultures or children revealed the mapping of numbers along a logarithmic scale rather than a continuous, discrete and linear (monotonic) line (Dehaene and Cohen, 1995;

Dehaene et al., 2008; Siegler and Booth, 2004). An interesting phenomenon demonstrating spatial influence on the MNL is the Spatial-Numerical Association of Response Codes (SNARC) effect, which represents the finding that responses are faster for relatively small numbers while given with the left-hand side and faster for relatively large numbers while given with the right-hand side (Dehaene, Bossini, and Giraux, 1993). Furthermore, studies have described the presence of mental lines in other domains, such as time (from past to future: Arzy, Adi-Japha, and Blanke, 2009a) and emotion (from negative to positive: Holmes and Lourenco, 2011). Interestingly, this effect was found to be influenced by cultural factors and modes of operation (Anelli et al., 2018b; Göbel, Shaki, and Fischer, 2011; Shaki and Fischer, 2014).

Self-Projection of the Imagining Self and Self-Reference to the Imagined Events

While the original depiction of mental lines refers to the characteristics of the line itself, such as its logarithmic arrangement or proneness to cultural effect, mental lines also invite localization of the human self-representation along such a line. The ability to project oneself to a specific "self-location" along the mental line is termed "self-projection." In the time domain, for instance, one might "project" herself to different time-points in the past in order to re-experience an event, an ability referred to as "mental time travel" (Addis, Wong, and Schacter, 2007; Arzy et al., 2009c; Arzy, Molnar-Szakacs, and Blanke, 2008; Schacter et al., 2012). In the emotion domain, one might imagine herself in different emotional states (Holmes and Lourenco, 2011), and in the spatial domain – at different places (Gauthier and van Wassenhove, 2016). In the social domain, one might project herself to be "in the shoes" of other people, a crucial ability for social cognition labeled as "theory of mind" (Buckner and Carroll, 2007; Frith and Frith, 2003). This capacity to mentally "project" oneself to another imaginary point on a mental line and to dynamically refer the projected self to imagined and experienced points on this line (e.g. life-events, places, other people, different emotions) has led to the definition of two separate functions: self-projection and self-reference. Self-projection refers to one's ability to travel along the mental line and localize herself at different imaginary points. Taking the example of the mental time line, in a mental time travel (MTT) task participants are asked to "project" themselves to different locations in time, that may be the present time (now), several years ago (past), or several years ahead (future). Self-reference is the ability to refer to other events, places, people, or emotions from the newly imagined (or habitual) self-location. In the MTT task, for example, participants are first asked to project themselves to a specific self-location in time and are then presented with different life events (either personal life events or global public events) (Rappaport, Enrich, and Wilson, 1985). They are then asked to indicate if these events took place before (relative-past) or could take place after (relative-future) the imagined self-location in time (Arzy, Adi-Japha, and Blanke, 2009a; Figure 20.2). In several studies (Anelli et al., 2016a; Arzy, Adi-Japha, and Blanke, 2009a; Arzy, Molnar-Szakacs, and Blanke, 2008; Gauthier and van Wassenhove, 2016) we and others reported that reaction times (RTs) and success

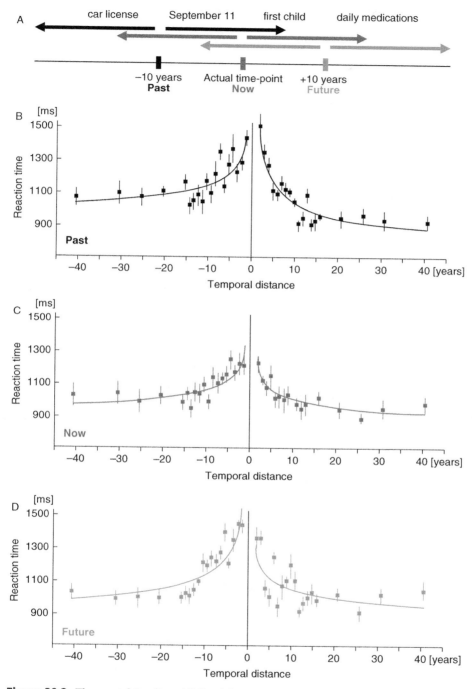

Figure 20.2 *The mental timeline. (A) Participants were presented with different events that could either happen in the past (obtaining car license, September 11) or are previewed to happen in the future (probable use of daily medications, birth of first child). From the present time as well as from the past and the future self-location in time, they had to judge if*

rates (SRs) were similar in the past and future conditions but slower and less accurate than in the present or "now" condition ("self-projection effect"). These studies have also revealed a "self-reference effect": A scenario may be considered as "relative-future" in the now condition and "relative-past" in the future condition, causing participants to respond differently for the same stimulus depending on their imagined self-location in time. Surprisingly, young adult participants were always faster and more accurate for relative-future than for relative-past in each self-location (Anelli et al., 2016b; Arzy, Molnar-Szakacs, and Blanke, 2008). These findings suggest that a mere act of imagination may change the way the cognitive system processes events. Moreover, the experiential self seems to have an important contribution to the way in which the events, represented on a temporal cognitive map, are formed and interpreted. Notably, these effects are not limited to the mental timeline, as similar effects were found on a mental space line (Gauthier and van Wassenhove, 2016). Presumably, similar self-projection and self-reference effects as well as logarithmic organization of distances may also be found over other mental lines.

Self-Reference and the Contiguity Effect

Cognitive distance (Liberman and Trope, 2008) refers to the principal spatial component of an individual's cognitive representation of her imagined self-location and the imagined elements in the environment (events, places, people, emotions, etc.). Considerations of cognitive distance therefore highlight the role of imagination in self-processing as well as its importance to the dialogue with the cognitive map, which is indifferent to the self-projection process despite its significant influence on its processing. Cognitive distance should be appreciated in conjunction with two effects in cognitive psychology that should be highlighted: the recency effect and the contiguity effect.

The recency effect is a well-established phenomenon in the cognitive science of memory, reflecting the finding that items that are more recently processed are better recalled than previous ones. This effect arises on account of "short-term memory buffers" (Atkinson and Shiffrin, 1968; Davelaar et al., 2005), the contents of which are continuously replaced by new information, leaving only the last pieces in the buffer for easy retrieval. Buffer models also account for another effect: the contiguity effect, which denotes the formation of an association between items that are

---

Caption for Figure 20.2   *(cont.)*

these events had already happened or not. (B–D) Reaction times are plotted here as function of the temporal distance between the presented event and the imagined self-location in time (error bars show the standard error of the mean). This analysis shows a logarithmic decreasing dependence of reaction times on temporal distance. This pattern was independent of the imagined time-point showing similar patterns for past and future events. Reprinted Consciousness and Cognition, *18(3): Arzy, Adi-Japha, and Blanke, The Mental Time Line: An Analogue of the Mental Number Line in the Mapping of Life Events, 781–785. Copyright 2009, with permission from Elsevier.*

presented close together in time (Howard, 2014). Like the recency effect, the contiguity effect was first described in the context of free recall (subjects recall a list in whatever order the listed items come to mind). The contiguity effect manifests in free recall as a difficulty in distinguishing words presented close together on the list (Kahana, 1996; Figure 20.3). Buffer models predict contiguity effects if connections in long-term memory are built up between items that are simultaneously active in the short-term memory buffer (Kahana, 1996; Raaijmakers and Shiffrin, 1980; Sirotin, Kimball, and Kahana, 2005). More recently, and in line with long-term memory connections, contiguity effects were also found in relation to episodic memory and mental time travel (Arzy, Adi-Japha, and Blanke, 2009a; see also Gershman and Daw, 2017). The examination of responses to imagined or remembered events according to their temporal distance from one's imagined self-location in time showed similar RTs to items that transpired close together in time. When an episodic memory is retrieved, the state of the original context is recovered, in relation to the experiencing self. Notably, Folkerts and colleagues recorded single-unit activity in the MTL of human patients and showed that the recovery of an episodic memory in humans is associated with retrieval of a gradually changing state of temporal context (Folkerts, Rutishauser, and Howard, 2018). These findings support the existence of a temporal-context-based contiguity effect in episodic memory, which is dependent on the self-location of the imagining self and the temporal distance to the imagined events.

Cognitive Distance and Inter-Subject Analyses

Classically in experimental psychology, data is averaged across trials within an individual subject and statistical analyses are applied on the data averaged across groups of subjects. The mental timeline is conceptually "drawn" as response to the question of how the response variables (e.g. RTs) vary as a function of the temporal distance between the imagined self-location in time (the present time or a certain time point in the past or future) and the imagined or experienced event (when a certain event is supposed to happen or already happened; Figure 20.2, B–D). The relations between the RTs and the temporal distances to the events were not linear (a linear regression model was not found to represent the participants' RTs (Arzy, Adi-Japha, and Blanke, 2009a). Rather, in all conditions, regardless of one's imagined self-location in time (past, now, or future) the relations between the RTs measured and the temporal distance were found to be logarithmically related (that is, a regression equation of the participants' RTs as a function of the log-transformed absolute value of temporal distance showed a negative coefficient, and RT distributions were positively skewed; Figure 20.2, B–D). To reiterate, the same pattern was found for all different self-projections, regardless of their location in past, present, or future. Statistical pairwise comparison of RT distributions in between different conditions of the imagined self-location in the past, now or the future did not show any significant difference, suggesting similar distributions of the log-transformed RTs over conditions. It is worth noting that such methods of inter-subject analysis have recently been adopted for functional neuroimaging studies, comparing brain recordings (time-courses) not across experimental conditions but across different

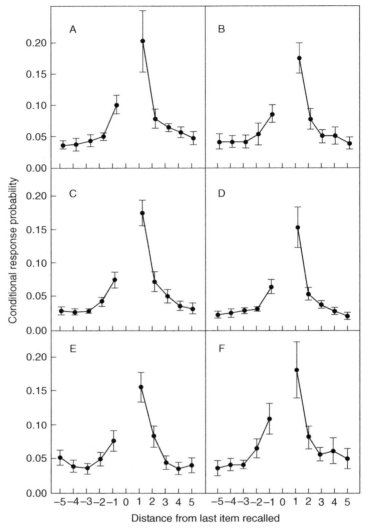

Figure 20.3 *The contiguity effect: conditional response probability curves for six studies of single-trial free recall. Panels A–D are based on data from Murdock (1962). Panel E is based on data from Murdock and Okada (1970). Panel F is based on data from Murdock and Metcalfe (1978). (A) List length = 20, auditory, 2 sec/item. (B) List length = 20, auditory, 1 sec/item. (C) List length = 30, auditory, 1 sec/item. (D) List length = 40, auditory, 1 sec/item. (E) List length = 20, visual, 1 sec/item and 0.5 sec/item combined. (F) List length = 20, visual, 5 sec/item. Error bars reflect 95 percent confidence intervals around each mean. Reprinted by permission from Springer Nature,* Memory & Cognition, *24(1): Kahana, Associative Retrieval Processes in Free Recall, 103–109. Copyright 1996.*

subjects over the course of the natural stimulation (e.g. listening to a story or watching a movie: Ben-Yakov et al., 2012; Simony et al., 2016). This method is further used to predict brain responses within other subjects.

Self-Reference Proneness to be Influenced by External Factors

The SNARC effect (Dehaene et al., 1993) demonstrated how judgment of numbers is influenced by spatial factors. Accordingly, the SNARC effect was affected by education, as seen in studies in an archaic tribe, children, and even newborn animals (Dehaene, Bossini, and Giraux, 2008; Rugani et al., 2015). These results were corroborated not only with respect to numbers but also with respect to time. A Spatial Temporal Association of Response Codes (STEARC) effect was found, similarly to the SNARC effect. Specifically, short temporal durations facilitated left-hand responses while long temporal durations facilitated right-hand responses (Ishihara et al., 2008; Vallesi, Binns, and Shallice, 2008). A similar effect has also been identified with temporal concepts: Faster responses were found when words with meanings referring to the past were presented on the left and words with meanings referring to the future on the right (Santiago et al., 2007; Torralbo, Santiago, and Lupiáñez, 2006). Like the SNARC effect, the STEARC effect is prompted by left-to-right reading and writing direction (left/past and right/future), while a reversed pattern (i.e. left/future and right/past facilitation effect) has been found in right-to-left readers/writers (Anelli et al., 2018b; Fuhrman and Boroditsky, 2010).

In a series of works, Anelli and colleagues have shown that self-reference of different events to the experiencing self is influenced by several external, spatial, and temporal factors. Mode of response (bimanually by left and right hands vs. vocal response without lateralization) was found to affect self-reference as in the STEARC effect, highlighting the role of spatialization in self-reference judgments. Cultural influence (whether people write from left to right or right to left) was found to significantly affect self-reference even when stimuli were presented in an auditive manner and responses were collected vocally, thus excluding spatial involvement (Anelli et al., 2018b). Several other spatial factors were found to influence self-reference including hemispatial neglect (Anelli et al., 2018a: patients with reduced attention to half-part of the world, usually the left and/or increased attention to the right side) as well as hemispatial-like behavior induced by a spatial attention manipulation known as "prismatic adaptation" (Anelli et al., 2016a). Finally, participants' age had a significant effect on one's self-reference in time, as younger people showed future facilitation while older people showed past facilitation (Anelli et al., 2016b). Taken together, self-reference was found to be affected by several factors including direct and indirect spatial and temporal factors. The way in which such external factors affect important aspects of our daily life is an open and important landscape that merits further investigation.

Orientation

The effect of self-reference is intimately related to the cognitive function of mental-orientation and its underlying system. Orientation is defined as the tuning between the behaving self and its internal representation of the surrounding environment, such as places visited, people one meets, or events experienced/imagined (Berrios, 1982; Peer et al., 2015). As such, it constitutes a complete system that includes both the representation of the external world (i.e. cognitive map) and its relations to the experiencing narrative self, thereby capturing a coherent image of the world. Orientation can be investigated through the combination of self-reference and cognitive distance factors, as seen in a designated orientation task. In this task participants are presented with pairs of stimuli consisting of the names of either two locations, two events, or two people, and are asked to determine which of these two stimuli are closer to themselves: spatially closer to their current location, chronologically closer to the present time, or personally closer to themselves (Peer et al., 2015). This procedure requires the subject not only to draw up a cognitive map of the relevant environment but also to imagine herself with respect to elements in this mental space in order to make a judgment.

It is worth mentioning that orientation takes a major role in the clinical setting. Patients undergoing neurological or psychiatric evaluation are first examined in terms of how they orient in time and space. Unfortunately, this is mostly translated in clinical practice to semantic knowledge of one's name, geographical location, and current date (Folstein, Folstein, and McHugh, 1975). Following this, it has been suggested that an evaluation of orientation should regard the way the patient imagines herself within the environment of people around her (Rapoport and Rapoport, 2015) as well as places and events rather than this mere knowledge of basic facts (Peer, Lyon, and Arzy, 2014). Several scholars have claimed that it is orientation that is disturbed in Alzheimer's disease (Coughlan et al., 2018), and indeed, such an evaluation has already proven efficient for clinical diagnosis in early stages of the disease (Dafni-Merom et al., 2019; Kunz et al., 2015; Peters-Founshtein et al., 2018). These efforts may be translated to clinical diagnostic criteria and neurocognitive biomarkers in the future.

Neuroanatomical Correlates

Imagination of oneself in the environment relies on an interplay between brain regions referred to as "the core network" or "the orientation system" (Benoit and Schacter, 2015; Peer et al., 2015) (Figure 20.4). The core network includes the medial prefrontal, posterior cingulate and retrosplenial cortices, the precuneus, several parts of the medial temporal lobes (MTL), as well as lateral temporal and parietal regions (Benoit and Schacter, 2015; Hassabis and Maguire, 2007; Schacter, Addis, and Buckner, 2007; Schacter et al., 2012). These regions have been implicated in self-related aspects of space (navigation) (Buckner and Carroll, 2007), time (autobiographical memory) (Cabeza and St. Jacques, 2007), and person (representation of self and others) (Saxe and Kanwisher, 2003). In addition, these regions are involved in specifying relations between landmarks in each domain: cognitive mapping of the spatial environment, recency judgments of life-events, and social proximity and hierarchy judgments (Epstein, Parker, and Feiler, 2007; Maguire et al., 1998; Mason, Magee, and Fiske, 2014; St. Jacques, Rubin, LaBar, and Cabeza, 2008). A neuroimaging study of the orientation system has revealed activations in several brain regions including the medial prefrontal cortex, the precuneus/retrosplenial cortex, and the temporoparietal junction (Peer et al., 2015). These regions, which are discussed below, highly overlap

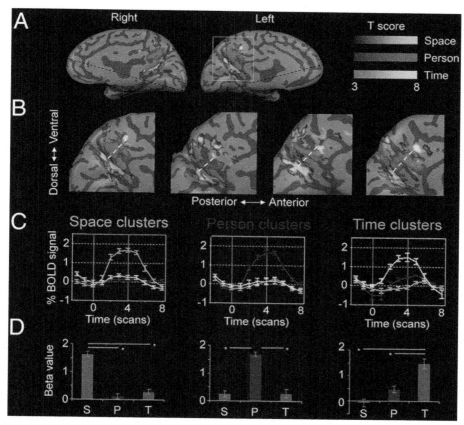

Figure 20.4 *Midsagittal cortical activity during orientation in space, time, and person. (A) Domain-specific activity in a representative subject, identified by contrasting activity between each orientation domain and the other two domains. The precuneus region is active in all three orientation domains, and the medial prefrontal cortex only in person and time orientation (P < 0.05, FDR-corrected, cluster size >20 voxels). Dashed black lines represent the limit of the scanned region in this subject. (B) Precuneus activity in four subjects, demonstrating a highly consistent posterior–anterior organization (white dashed line); all other subjects showed the same activity pattern. (C) Group average (n = 16) of event-related activity in independent experimental runs demonstrates the specificity of each cluster to one orientation domain. Lines represent activity in response to space, time, and person conditions. Error bars represent SEM between subjects. (D) Group average of beta plots from volume-of-interest GLM analysis, showing highly significant domain-specific activity. Error bars represent SEM between subjects. P, person; S, space; T, time. Reprinted from* Proceedings of the National Academy of Sciences, *112(35): Peer et al., Brain System for Mental Orientation in Space, Time, and Person, 11072–11077. Copyright 2015.*

the "core network" of episodic memory and future simulation (Buckner, Andrews-Hanna, and Schacter, 2008; Schacter et al., 2007), as well as the default mode network (DMN), a network dedicated to self-referenced internal thinking, including mind-wandering, theory of mind, and autobiographical memory (Buckner et al., 2008; Raichle et al., 2001). Notably, a subnetwork of the DMN termed DN-B (Buckner and DiNicola, 2019), identified using high-resolution fMRI in the single-subject level, overlapped mostly orientation in the person domain (Peer et al., 2015). Interestingly, brain activations for orientation in the space, time, and person domains were found to form a highly consistent posterior-anterior "gradient" with space at the most posterior, followed by person and then time in almost all subjects (Figure 20.5). This internal organization with distinct and adjacent domain-specific regions for space, time, and person supports the idea that orientation in these domains is processed by related cognitive systems working in concert. Further research is necessary to illustrate how different aspects of orientation are related to one another and how information is transformed between the general representations of the cognitive maps (carried out by a different system) and self-processing (carried out within the system). It is hypothesized that bidirectional information streaming is crucial for updating the cognitive maps and informing the self.

As previously noted, the orientation system significantly overlaps with brain regions within the core network and the DMN (Benoit and Schacter, 2015; Peer et al., 2015). While the DMN is mostly extracted in a data-based manner from the ongoing activity in

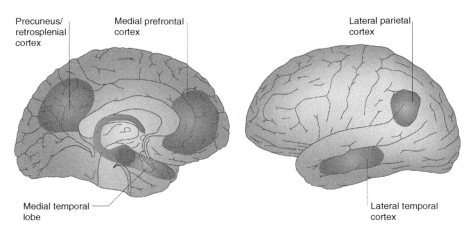

Precuneus/retrosplenial cortex   Medial prefrontal cortex   Lateral parietal cortex

Medial temporal lobe   Lateral temporal cortex

Figure 20.5 *The core brain system that mediates past and future thinking. The core brain system that is consistently activated while remembering the past, envisioning the future and during related forms of mental simulation is illustrated schematically. Prominent components of this network include medial prefrontal regions, posterior regions in the medial and lateral parietal cortex (extending into the precuneus and the retrosplenial cortex), the lateral temporal cortex, and the medial temporal lobe. Moreover, regions within this core brain system are functionally correlated with each other and, prominently, with the hippocampal formation. It has been suggested that this core brain system functions adaptively to integrate information about relationships and association from past experiences in order to construct mental simulations about possible future events. Reprinted by permission from Springer Nature,* Nature Reviews Neuroscience *8(9): Schacter, Addis, and Buckner, Remembering the Past to Imagine the Future: The Prospective Brain, 657–661. Copyright 2007.*

the resting brain, the core network is implicated in cognitive operations such as scene-construction (Hassabis and Maguire, 2007), episodic simulation of future or fictitious episodes (Benoit and Schacter, 2015), and the retrieval of autobiographical memories (Spreng and Grady, 2009). The relations between MTL structures (especially the hippocampal formation and the entorhinal cortex) and the cortical structures of the DMN are of much interest. Although the hippocampus is frequently considered as part of the DMN it is a distinguished region both with respect to gross structural and functional anatomy (Buckner aand DiNicola, 2019). The coupling of the hippocampus with other parts of the DMN is flexible and can depend on the behavioral context. For example, the hippocampus and the DMN are coupled during memory retrieval, but are dissociated during memory encoding (Huijbers et al., 2011). Disorders like anti-NMDAR encephalitis can cause a disruption of the coupling between the hippocampus and the rest of the DMN (Peer et al., 2017), leading to disturbances in autobiographical memory and future imagination (Arzy, Bick, and Blanke, 2009b; Hassabis and Maguire, 2007).

With respect to the MTL structures themselves, the hippocampal formation has been shown to be involved in MTT and autonoetic consciousness in a unique neurological model of a patient population with specific lesions in the CA1 region of the hippocampal formation (Bartsch et al., 2011). This involvement may relate to the place cells and head-direction cells located in this region. The hippocampus also contains time cells, which are active at specific time epochs (MacDonald et al., 2011). Interestingly, accumulating experimental evidence, mostly in rodents but also in humans, suggests that the hippocampus plays a central role in the temporal organization of memories (DeVito and Eichenbaum, 2011; for a review, see Eichenbaum, 2014), similar to the encoding of one's location in space (Kraus et al., 2015). Grid cells are located at the entorhinal cortex, adjacent to the hippocampus. Together, these two regions in the MTL contain the key elements that serve as the basis for the cognitive map. Remarkably, in an MTT study the MTL reflected self-projection of the subject to the past, the now, and the future, as well as self-reference on single events in relation to the subject's current self-location, while all other implicated brain regions reflected only one of these effects (Arzy et al., 2009c). Investigations using intracranial recordings from epilepsy patients undergoing presurgical evaluation for epilepsy showed that self-projection activated cortical regions in the lateral temporal lobe while self-reference activated the hippocampal formation in a later stage (Schurr et al., 2018), suggesting a division of labor between these brain regions for these two aspects of mental time travel and autonoetic consciousness.

Conclusion

As humans we constantly recall past memories and imagine future plans, two highly associated mental capacities in which we transcend ourselves outside the here and now. This is made possible partially by our ability to organize knowledge in map-like representations, encoding the relationships between entities in the world. While the novel ideas proposed by Craik, Tolman, Johnson-Laird and Tversky of cognitive maps and mental models materialized into truly remarkable findings illustrating the neural machinery spawning these maps, the way in which the self refers to these maps has been overlooked. Here we claim that reference and feedback loops of such representations to the experiencing self, who is the one imagining the world, is crucial for our understanding the world, its representation, and in an infinite regress manner, also the imagining self. What are the dynamics between the neural networks dedicated to the formation of cognitive maps and self-processing? Do mental representations of ourselves on these maps extend beyond the spatial, temporal, and social domains? What happens when these abilities are disturbed? Such a line of questions, if answered, may help us characterize human cognition and the way we imagine ourselves in the world.

Acknowledgments

The authors are grateful to Professor Daniel L. Schacter and Dr. Nimrod Shaham (Harvard University) for helpful discussions of the topics discussed. The work was supported by the Israeli Science Foundation (grant no. 2598/16) and the Orion Foundation.

References

Addis, D. R., Wong, A. T., and Schacter, D. L. (2007). Remembering the Past and Imagining the Future: Common and Distinct Neural Substrates During Event Construction and Elaboration. *Neuropsychologia*, *45*(7), 1363–1377.

Anelli, F., Avanzi, S., Arzy, S., Mancuso, M., and Frassinetti, F. (2018a). Effects of Spatial Attention on Mental Time Travel in Patients with Neglect. *CORTEX*, *101*, 192–205.

Anelli, F., Ciaramelli, E., Arzy, S., and Frassinetti, F. (2016a). Prisms to Travel in Time: Investigation of Time-Space Association through Prismatic Adaptation Effect on Mental Time Travel. *Cognition*, *156*, 1–5.

(2016b). Age-Related Effects on Future Mental Time Travel, *Neural Plasticity*, *1*(8), 1–25.

Anelli, F., Peters-Founshtein, G., Shreibman, Y., et al. (2018b). Nature and Nurture Effects on the Spatiality of the Mental Time Line. *Scientific Reports*, *8*(1), 11710.

Arzy, S., Adi-Japha, E., and Blanke, O. (2009a). The Mental Time Line: An Analogue of the Mental Number Line in the Mapping of Life Events. *Consciousness and Cognition*, *18*(3), 781–785.

Arzy, S., Bick, A., and Blanke, O. (2009b). Mental Time in Amnesia: Evidence from Bilateral Medial Temporal Damage Before and After Recovery. *Cognitive Neuropsychology*, *26*(6), 503–510.

Arzy, S., Collette, S., Ionta, S., Fornari, E., and Blanke, O. (2009c). Subjective Mental Time: The Functional Architecture of Projecting the Self to Past and Future. *The European Journal of Neuroscience*, *30*(10), 2009–2017.

Arzy, S., Molnar-Szakacs, I., and Blanke, O. (2008). Self in Time: Imagined Self-Location Influences Neural Activity Related to Mental Time Travel. *Journal of Neuroscience*, *28*(25), 6502–6507.

Arzy, S., and Schacter, D. L. (2019). Self-Agency and Self-Ownership in Cognitive Mapping. *Trends in Cognitive Sciences*, *23*(6), 476–487.

Atkinson, R. C., and Shiffrin, R. M. (1968). Human Memory: A Proposed System and its Control Processes. In K. W. Spence and J. T. Spence (eds.), *Psychology of Learning* and *Motivation: Advances in Research and Theory*. Volume 2. New York, NY: Academic Press, 89–195.

Banino, A., Barry, C., Uria, B., et al. (2018). Vector-Based Navigation Using Grid-Like Representations in Artificial Agents. *Nature*, *557*(7705), 429–433.

Banks, W. P., and Hill, D. K. (1974). The Apparent Magnitude of Number Scaled by Random Production. *Journal of Experimental Psychology*, *102*(2), 353–376.

Bartsch, T., Dohring, J., Rohr, A., Jansen, O., and Deuschl, G. (2011). CA1 Neurons in the Human Hippocampus Are Critical for Autobiographical Memory, Mental Time Travel, and Autonoetic Consciousness. *Proceedings of the National Academy of Sciences*, *108*(42), 17562–17567.

Behrens, T. E. J., Muller, T. H., Whittington, J. C. R., et al. (2018). What is a Cognitive Map? Organizing Knowledge for Flexible Behavior. *Neuron*, *100*(2), 490–509.

Ben-Yakov, A., Honey, C. J., Lerner, Y., and Hasson, U. (2012). Loss of Reliable Temporal Structure in Event-Related Averaging of Naturalistic Stimuli. *NeuroImage*, *63*(1), 501–506.

Benoit, R. G., and Schacter, D. L. (2015). Specifying the Core Network Supporting Episodic Simulation and Episodic Memory by Activation Likelihood Estimation. *Neuropsychologia*, *75*, 450–457.

Berrios, G. E. (1982). Disorientation States and Psychiatry. *Comprehensive Psychiatry*, *23*(5), 479–491.

Buckner, R. L., Andrews-Hanna, J. R., and Schacter, D. L. (2008). The Brain's Default Network: Anatomy, Function, and Relevance to Disease. *Annals of the New York Academy of Sciences*, *1124*, 1–38.

Buckner, R. L., and Carroll, D. C. (2007). Self-Projection and the Brain. *Trends in Cognitive Sciences*, *11*(2), 49–57.

Buckner, R. L., and DiNicola, L. M. (2019). The Brain's Default Network: Updated Anatomy, Physiology and Evolving Insights. *Nature Reviews Neuroscience*, *20*(10), 593–608.

Cabeza, R., and St Jacques, P. (2007). Functional Neuroimaging of Autobiographical Memory. *Trends in Cognitive Sciences*, *11*(5), 219–227.

Constantinescu, A. O., O'Reilly, J. X., and Behrens, T. E. (2016). Organizing Conceptual Knowledge in Humans with a Gridlike Code. *Science*, *1*(6292), 1–9.

Coughlan, G., Laczó, J., Hort, J., Minihane, A. M., and Hornberger, M. (2018). Spatial Navigation Deficits – Overlooked Cognitive Marker for Preclinical Alzheimer Disease? *Nature Reviews Neurology*, *14*(8), 1–11.

Craik, K. J. W. (1943). *The nature of explanation*. Cambridge University Press, Cambridge, UK.

Dafni-Merom, A., Peters-Founshtein, G., Kahana-Merhavi, S., & Arzy, S. (2019). A Unified Brain System of Orientation and Its Disruption in Alzheimer's Disease. *Annals of Clinical and Translational Neurology*, *6*(12), 2468–2478.

Danjo, T., Toyoizumi, T., and Fujisawa, S. (2018). Spatial Representations of Self and Other in the Hippocampus. *Science*, *218*(January), 213–218.

Davelaar, E. J., Goshen-Gottstein, Y., Ashkenazi, A., Haarmann, H. J., and Usher, M. (2005). The Demise of Short-Term Memory Revisited: Empirical and Computational Investigations of Recency Effects. *Psychological Review*, *112*(1), 3–42.

Dehaene, S., Bossini, S., and Giraux, P. (1993). The Mental Representation of Parity and Number Magnitude. *Journal of Experimental Psychology*, *122*(3), 371–396.

Dehaene, S., and Cohen, L. (1995). Towards an Anatomical and Functional Model of Number Processing. *Mathematical Cognition*, *1*(1), 83–120.

Dehaene, S., Spelke, E., Izard, V., and Pica, P. (2008). Log or Linear? Distinct Intuitions of the Number Scale in Western and Amazonian Indigene Cultures. *Science*, *1217*(May), 1217–1220.

Dehaene, S., Spelke, E., Pinel, P., Stanescu, R., and Tsivkin, S. (1999). Sources of Mathematical Thinking. *Science*, *284*(May), 970–974.

DeVito, L. M., and Eichenbaum, H. (2011). Memory for the Order of Events in Specific Sequences: Contributions of the Hippocampus and Medial Prefrontal Cortex. *Journal of Neuroscience*, *31*(9), 3169–3175.

Doeller, C. F., Barry, C., and Burgess, N. (2010). Evidence for Grid Cells in a Human Memory Network. *Nature*, *463*(7281), 657–661.

Eichenbaum, H. (2014). Time Cells in the Hippocampus: A New Dimension for Mapping Memories. *Nature Reviews Neuroscience*, *15*(11), 732–744.

Epstein, R. A., Parker, W. E., and Feiler, A. M. (2007). Where Am I Now? Distinct Roles for Parahippocampal and Retrosplenial Cortices in Place Recognition. *Journal of Neuroscience*, *27*(23), 6141–6149.

Epstein, R. A., Patai, E. Z., Julian, J. B., and Spiers, H. J. (2017). The Cognitive Map in Humans: Spatial Navigation and Beyond. *Nature Neuroscience*, *20*(11), 1504–1513.

Folkerts, S., Rutishauser, U., and Howard, M. W. (2018). Human Episodic Memory Retrieval Is Accompanied by a Neural Contiguity Effect. *Journal of Neuroscience*, *38*(17), 4200–4211.

Folstein, M., Folstein, S., and McHugh, P. (1975). "Mini-Mental State": A Practical Method for Grading the Cognitive State of Patients for the Clinician. *Journal of Psychiatric Research*, *12*(3), 189–198.

Frith, U., and Frith, C. D. (2003). Development and Neurophysiology of Mentalizing. *Philosophical Transactions of the Royal Society B: Biological Sciences*, *358*(1431), 459–473.

Fuhrman, O., and Boroditsky, L. (2010). Cross-Cultural Differences in Mental Representations of Time: Evidence From an Implicit Nonlinguistic Task. *Cognitive Science*, *34*(8), 1430–1451.

Garvert, M. M., Dolan, R. J., and Behrens, T. E. J. (2017). A Map of Abstract Relational Knowledge in the Human Hippocampal–Entorhinal Cortex. *Elife*, *6*, 1–20.

Gauthier, B., and van Wassenhove, V. (2016). Cognitive Mapping in Mental Time Travel and Mental Space Navigation. *Cognition*, *154*, 55–68.

Gauthier, J. L., and Tank, D. W. (2018). A Dedicated Population for Reward Coding in the Hippocampus. *Neuron*, *99*(1), 179–193.e7.

Gershman, S. J., and Daw, N. D. (2017). Reinforcement Learning and Episodic Memory in Humans and Animals: An Integrative Framework. *Annual Review of Psychology*, *68*, 101–128.

Göbel, S. M., Shaki, S., and Fischer, M. H. (2011). The Cultural Number Line: A Review of Cultural and Linguistic Influences on the Development of Number Processing. *Journal of Cross-Cultural Psychology*, *42*(4), 543–565.

Hafting, T., Fyhn, M., Molden, S., Moser, M. B., and Moser, E. I. (2005). Microstructure of a Spatial Map in the Entorhinal Cortex. *Nature*, *436*(7052), 801–806.

Hassabis, D., and Maguire, E. A. (2007). Deconstructing Episodic Memory with Construction. *Trends in Cognitive Sciences*, *11*(7), 299–306.

Holmes, K. J., and Lourenco, S. F. (2011). Common Spatial Organization of Number and Emotional Expression: A Mental Magnitude Line. *Brain and Cognition*, *77*(2), 315–323.

Howard, M. W. (2014). Mathematical Learning Theory through Time. *Journal of Mathematical Psychology*, *59*(1), 18–29.

Høydal, Ø. A., Skytøen, E. R., Moser, M., and Moser, E. I. (2018). Object-Vector Coding in the Medial Entorhinal Cortex. *Nature*, *568*, 400–404.

Huijbers, W., Pennartz, C. M. A., Cabeza, R., and Daselaar, S. M. (2011). The Hippocampus Is Coupled with the Default Network during Memory Retrieval but Not during Memory Encoding. *PloS ONE*, *6*(4).

Ishihara, M., Keller, P. E., Rossetti, Y., and Prinz, W. (2008). Horizontal Spatial Representations of Time: Evidence for the STEARC Effect. *Cortex*, *44*, 454–461.

Johnson-Laird, P. N. (1980). Mental Models in Cognitive Science. *Cognitive Science*, *4*(1), 71–115.

Julian, J. B., Keinath, A. T., Frazzetta, G., and Epstein, R. A. (2018). Human Entorhinal Cortex Represents Visual Space using a Boundary-Anchored Grid. *Nature Neuroscience*, *21*(2), 191–194.

Kahana, M. J. (1996). Associative Retrieval Processes in Free Recall. *Memory & Cognition*, *24*(1), 103–109.

Kraus, B. J., Brandon, M. P., Robinson, R. J., et al. (2015). During Running in Place, Grid Cells Integrate Elapsed Time and Distance Run. *Neuron*, *88*(3), 578–589.

Krupic, J., Bauza, M., Burton, S., Barry, C., and O'Keefe, J. (2015). Grid Cell Symmetry Is Shaped by Environmental Geometry. *Nature*, *518*(7538), 232–235.

Krupic, J., Bauza, M., Burton, S., and O'Keefe, J. (2018). Local Transformations of the Hippocampal Cognitive Map. *Science*, *359*(6380), 1143–1146.

Kunz, L., Schroder, T. N., Lee, H., et al. (2015). Reduced Grid-Cell-Like Representations in Adults at Genetic Risk for Alzheimer's Disease. *Science*, *350*(6259), 430–433.

Lever, C., Burton, S., Jeewajee, A., O'Keefe, J., and Burgess, N. (2009). Boundary Vector Cells in the Subiculum of the Hippocampal Formation. *Journal of Neuroscience*, *29*(31), 9771–9777.

Liberman, N., and Trope, Y. (2008). The Psychology of Transcending the Here and Now. *Science*, *322*(5905), 1201–1205.

MacDonald, C. J., Lepage, K. Q., Eden, U. T., and Eichenbaum, H. (2011). Hippocampal "Time Cells" Bridge the Gap in Memory for Discontiguous Events. *Neuron*, *71*(4), 737–749.

Maguire, E. A., Burgess, N., Donnett, J. G., et al. (1998). Knowing Where and Getting There : A Human Navigation Network. *Science*, *280*(May), 921–924.

Mason, M., Magee, J. C., and Fiske, S. T. (2014). Neural Substrates of Social Status Inference: Roles of Medial Prefrontal Cortex and Superior Temporal Sulcus. *Journal Of Cognitive Neuroscience*, *26*(5), 1131–1140.

Murdock, B. B., Jr. (1962). The Serial Position Effect of Free Recall. *Journal of Experimental Psychology*, *64*, 482–488.

Murdock, B. B., and Metcalfe, J. (1978). Controlled Rehearsal in Single-Trial Free Recall. *Journal of Verbal Learning and Verbal Behavior*, *17*, 309–324.

Murdock, B. B., and Okada, R. (1970). Interresponse Times in Single-Trial Free Recall. *Journal of Experimental Psychology*, *86*, 263–267.

Nau, M., Navarro Schröder, T., Bellmund, J. L. S., and Doeller, C. F. (2018). Hexadirectional Coding of Visual Space in Human Entorhinal Cortex. *Nature Neuroscience*, *21*(2), 188–190.

O'Keefe, J., and Nadel, L. (1978). *The Hippocampus as a Cognitive Map*. Oxford, UK: Clarendon Press.

Omer, D. B., Maimon, S. R., Las, L., and Ulanovsky, N. (2018). Social Place-Cells in the Bat Hippocampus. *Science*, *224*(January), 218–224.

Parkinson, C., Kleinbaum, A. M., and Wheatley, T. (2017). Spontaneous Neural Encoding of Social Network Position. *Nature Human Behaviour*, *1*(5), 1–7.

Peer, M., Lyon, R., and Arzy, S. (2014). Orientation and Disorientation: Lessons from Patients with Epilepsy. *Epilepsy and Behavior*, *41*, 149–157.

Peer, M., Prüss, H., Ben-Dayan, I., et al. (2017). Functional Connectivity of Large-Scale Brain Networks in Patients with Anti-NMDA Receptor Encephalitis : An Observational Study. *Lancet Psychiatry*, *4*(10), 768–774.

Peer, M., Salomon, R., Goldberg, I., Blanke, O., and Arzy, S. (2015). Brain System for Mental Orientation in Space, Time, and Person. *Proceedings of the National Academy of Sciences*, *112*(35), 11072–11077.

Peters-Founshtein, G., Peer, M., Rein, Y., et al. (2018). Mental-Orientation: A New Approach to Assessing Patients Across the Alzheimer's Disease Spectrum. *Neuropsychology*, *32*(6), 690–699.

Raaijmakers, J. G., and Shiffrin, R. M. (1980). SAM: A Theory of Probabilistic Search of Associative Memory. In G. Bower (ed.), *The Psychology of Learning and Motivation*. Volume 14. New York, NY: Academic Press, 207–262.

Raichle, M. E., Macleod, A. M., Snyder, A. Z., et al. (2001). A Default Mode of Brain Function. *Proceedings of the National Academy of Sciences*, *98*(2), 676–682.

Rapoport, B. I., and Rapoport, S. (2015). Orientation to Person, Orientation to Self. *Neurology*, *85*(23), 2072–2074.

Rappaport, H., Enrich, K., and Wilson, A. (1985). Relation between Ego Identity and Temporal Perspective. *Journal of Personality and Social Psychology*, *48*(6), 1609–1620.

Rugani, R., Vallortigara, G., Priftis, K., and Regolin, L. (2015). Number-Space Mapping in the Newborn Chick Resembles Humans' Mental Number Line. *Science*, *347*(6221), 534–537.

Santiago, J., Lupáñez, J., Pérez, E., and Funes, M. J. (2007). Time (Also) Flies from Left to Right. *Psychonomic Bulletin & Review*, *14*(3), 512–516.

Sarel, A., Finkelstein, A., Las, L., and Ulanovsky, N. (2017). Vectorial Representation of Spatial Goals in the Hippocampus of Bats. *Science*, *355*(6321), 176–180.

Saxe, R., and Kanwisher, N. G. (2003). People Thinking about Thinking People: The Role of the Temporo-Parietal Junction in "Theory of Mind". *NeuroImage*, *19*, 1835–1842.

Schacter, D. L., Addis, D. R., and Buckner, R. L. (2007). Remembering the Past to Imagine the Future: The Prospective Brain. *Nature Neuroscience*, *8*(9), 657–661.

Schacter, D. L., Addis, D. R., Hassabis, D., et al. (2012). The Future of Memory: Remembering, Imagining, and the Brain. *Neuron*, *76*(4), 677–694.

Schmajuk, N. A., and Buhusi, C. V. (1997). Spatial and Temporal Cognitive Mapping: A Neural Network Approach. *Trends in Cognitive Sciences*, *1*(3), 109–114.

Schurr, R., Nitzan, M., Eliahou, R., et al. (2018). Temporal Dissociation of Neocortical and Hippocampal Contributions to Mental Time Travel Using Intracranial Recordings in Humans. *Frontiers in Computational Neuroscience*, *12*(February), 1–12.

Shaki, S., and Fischer, M. H. (2014). Random Walks on the Mental Number Line. *Experimental Brain Research*, *232*(1), 43–49.

Siegler, R. S., and Booth, J. L. (2004). Development of Numerical Estimation in Young Children. *Child Development*, *75*(2), 428–444.

Simons, J. S., Garrison, J. R., and Johnson, M. K. (2017). Brain Mechanisms of Reality Monitoring. *Trends in Cognitive Sciences*, *21*(6), 462–473.

Simony, E., Honey, C. J., Chen, J., et al. (2016). Dynamical Reconfiguration of the Default Mode Network during Narrative Comprehension. *Nature Communications*, *7*, 12141. doi:10.1038/ncomms12141.

Sirotin, Y. B., Kimball, D. R., and Kahana, M. J. (2005). Going Beyond a Single List: Modeling the Effects of Prior Experience on Episodic Free Recall. *Psychonomic Bulletin and Review*, *12*(5), 787–805.

Solstad, T., Boccara, C. N., Kropff, E., Moser, M., and Moser, E. I. (2008). Representation of Geometric Borders in the Entorhinal Cortex. *Science*, *322*(5909), 1865–1868.

Spreng, R. N., and Grady, C. L. (2009). Patterns of Brain Activity Supporting Autobiographical Memory, Prospection, and Theory of Mind, and Their Relationship to the Default Mode Network. *Journal of Cognitive Neuroscience*, *22*(6), 1112–1123.

St. Jacques, P. L., Carpenter, A. C., Szpunar, K. K., and Schacter, D. L. (2018). Remembering and Imagining Alternative Versions of the Personal Past. *Neuropsychologia*, *110*, 170–179.

St. Jacques, P., Rubin, D. C., LaBar, K. S., and Cabeza, R. (2008). The Short and Long of it: Neural Correlates of Temporal-Order Memory for Autobiographical Events. *Journal of Cognitive Neuroscience*, *20*(7), 1327–1341.

Strange, B. A., Witter, M. P., Lein, E.S., and Moser, E. I. (2014). Functional Organization of the Hippocampal Longitudinal Axis. *Nature Reviews Neuroscience*, *15*(10), 655–669.

Szpunar, K. K., Watson, J. M., and McDermott, K. B. (2007). Neural Substrates of Envisioning the Future. *Proceedings of the National Academy of Sciences*, *104*(2), 642–647.

Taube, J. S., Muller, R. U., and Ranck, J. B. (1990). Head-Direction Cells Recorded from the Postsubiculum in Freely Moving Rats. I. Description and Quantitative Analysis. *Journal of Neuroscience*, *10*(2), 420–435.

Tavares, R. M., Mendelsohn, A., Grossman, Y., et al. (2015). A Map for Social Navigation in the Human Brain. *Neuron*, *87*(1), 231–243.

Tolman, E. C. (1948). Cognitive Maps in Rats and Men. *The Psychological Review*, *55*(4), 189–208.

Torralbo, A., Santiago, J., and Lupiáñez, J. (2006). Flexible Conceptual Projection of Time onto Spatial Frames of Reference. *Cognitive Science*, *30*(4), 745–757.

Tversky, B. (1993). Cognitive Maps, Cognitive Collages, and Spatial Mental Models. In *European Conference on Spatial Information Theory* (pp. 14–24). Springer, Berlin, Heidelberg.

Uddin, L. Q., Iacoboni, M., Lange, C., and Keenan, J. P. (2007). The Self and Social Cognition: The Role of Cortical Midline Structures and Mirror Neurons. *Trends in Cognitive Sciences*, *11*(4), 153–157.

Vallesi, A., Binns, M. A., and Shallice, T. (2008). An Effect of Spatial-Temporal Association of Response Codes: Understanding the Cognitive Representations of Time. *Cognition*, *107*(2), 501–527.

Wallace, D. G., and Whishaw, I. Q. (2003). NMDA Lesions of Ammon's Horn and the Dentate Gyrus Disrupt the Direct and Temporally Paced Homing Displayed by Rats Exploring a Novel Environment: Evidence for a Role of the Hippocampus in Dead Reckoning. *The European Journal of Neuroscience*, *18*(3), 513–523.

Wilson, R. C., Takahashi, Y. K., Schoenbaum, G., and Niv, Y. (2014). Orbitofrontal Cortex as a Cognitive Map of Task Space. *Neuron*, *81*(2), 267–278.

21 The Neuroscience of Imaginative Thought: An Integrative Framework

Quentin Raffaelli, Ramsey Wilcox, and Jessica Andrews-Hanna

Introduction: The Psychological Ingredients of Imaginative Thought

Human minds are undoubtedly wonders. Through millions of years of evolution, nature crafted complex beings capable of divorcing their attention from the present moment to create a personal mental universe in which an infinite number of possibilities may be realized. The contents of this mental universe can take many forms. They may be stories and other fantasies we make up to entertain ourselves when we daydream. They may be the re-experiencing of a past event or simulation of how a future event may unfold. They may be pondering and weighing different criteria while deciding where to go to university. They may be an act of creation, a mental conception of what does not yet exist. They may be surmising the reason a stranger is looking perplexed, the motivation behind a partner's actions, or the way a friend would react to a gift one has in mind for her birthday. All of these examples have one thing in common: They rely on the ability to generate mental content that is not currently available to the senses. In other words, in our view, they rely on what we operationalize as *imagination*.

In this chapter, we tackle the topic of imagination from a psychological and neuroscientific perspective. We first highlight some of the different forms and characteristics of imagination from studies assessing imaginative thoughts in the laboratory and everyday life. We next review the neuroimaging literature to highlight the role of a large-scale brain system called the default network (DN) in imaginative thought, and further consider the network's functional heterogeneity. Finally, we integrate these two lines of research to propose a neurocognitive model differentiating between *contextually detailed* forms of imagination – involving detailed imagery-based reconstruction of mental scenes (as in episodic memory and episodic future thinking) – and *conceptually abstract* forms of imagination – where imagination involves predominantly verbal or symbolic forms of thinking about high-level concepts, including mental states. When discussing these topics, we will consider different ways in which these forms of imaginative thought may arise, either in the presence or absence of constraints on cognition. Our hope is that this framework offers a conceptualization of imaginative thought guided by principles of brain organization. Thus armed, future research may unravel novel findings about the inner life of mentally typical and atypical populations.

Throughout the chapter, we adopt the broad definition of "imagination"[1] put forth by the Oxford English Dictionary as "The power or capacity to form internal images or ideas of objects and situations not actually present to the senses" (see also Chapter 1). Our review focuses on the intersection between imagination and *internal mentation*; that is, when mental images or ideas form the basis of thought (Buckner, Andrews-Hanna, and Schacter, 2008; Andrews-Hanna, 2012). Phrases such as *self-generated thought, internally guided thought, perceptually decoupled thought*, and *stimulus-independent thought* are all largely synonymous with internal mentation. To highlight these phrases' collective link with imagination, we often refer to them together as *imaginative thought*.

The many different musings highlighted in the introduction have in common a defining feature of imaginative thought – that is, they all pertain to mental content that is not currently available to the senses. Yet, within our seemingly infinite mental universe, our imaginative thoughts also have an incredible degree of heterogeneity. They may feel phenomenologically different from each other, and may pertain to different topics, or evoke different emotions. They may arise in different ways, unfold with different dynamics, take on different forms, and have different causes and consequences. We review some of these different ways to carve up imaginative thoughts below.

Where Is the Mind? Task-Related and Task-Unrelated Thought

One way to characterize imaginative thoughts is by whether they are related or unrelated to the "task at hand" (Smallwood and Schooler, 2015). When assessed in laboratory settings, the proportion of all sampled experiences that are both predominantly task-unrelated *and* imaginative (as opposed to perceptually coupled) have been estimated to be about 22 percent (Stawarczyk et al., 2011). Although task-unrelated thoughts (TUTs) often have negative consequences on task performance (Smallwood and Schooler, 2015), there is growing evidence suggesting they may serve important functions. One key theory is that imaginative TUTs function to remind us of our personal concerns, including our unresolved problems and future goals (Klinger, 2009). In line with this view, the phrase "task-unrelated thought" could be considered a misnomer of sorts as TUTs often concern a different "task" positioned higher in one's personal hierarchy of task goals (e.g. thoughts about an upcoming exam during an easy laboratory task). Until such tasks are completed or resolved, TUTs may continually supply value to these long-term goals/concerns, perhaps aiding in their resolution or completion. Other proposed functions of TUTs include alleviating boredom (Mooneyham and Schooler, 2013; Raffaelli, Mills, and Christoff, 2017) or mental exploration (Sripada, 2018). The benefits and costs of off-task, imaginative thoughts mark an area of active research (Smallwood and Andrews-Hanna, 2013; Mooneyham and Schooler, 2013).

---

1 "imagination, n." OED Online, Oxford University Press, March 2018, www.oed.com/view/Entry/91643.

What's In the Mind? Varieties of Imaginative Content

Temporally Oriented Imagination

One of the main characteristics of the imaginative minds of humans is that they often travel backward and forward in time. When adults are probed to describe naturally occurring thoughts, many such thoughts appear to have a prospective, as opposed to retrospective, bias (e.g. Andrews-Hanna et al., 2013; Baird, Smallwood, and Schooler, 2011). This future-oriented tendency is rather unsurprising considering it has long been considered that the human mind is wired to predict and prepare for the future (von Helmholtz, 1925), and that memory likely did not evolve to keep us constrained to the past, but rather propelled forward in time (Suddendorf and Corballis, 2007; Tulving, 1985).

Although the predictive capacities of animals is being increasingly appreciated (Pfeiffer, 2020; Suddendorf and Corballis, 2007), many researchers acknowledge that humans have a comparative advantage in this regard, in that humans can prospect in more complex ways about more distant and more hypothetical futures (Seligman et al., 2016).

It has been recently proposed that the mechanisms underlying memory and prospection are very similar (reviewed in Schacter et al., 2012). Some phenomenological differences have been noticed, however. For example, the past tends to be remembered with more perceptual detail and be associated with a stronger subjective feeling of being there (D'Argembeau and van der Linden, 2006; Ernst and D'Argembeau, 2017), called *autonoetic consciousness* (Tulving, 1985). In contrast, prospective thoughts are more likely to concern personal goals, and to be rated as more positive and personally significant (Andrews-Hanna et al., 2013; Ruby et al., 2013).

Social Imagination

Another important element of imaginative thoughts regards the nature of their social orientation, as well as the socio-cognitive and affective processes that may accompany thoughts concerning other people. In the course of evolution, an increased pressure to be efficient at navigating the social environment is thought to have selected for the most social individuals (Hare, 2017). Consequently, social imagination is highly developed in humans (Saxe, 2009). Humans have a remarkable ability to navigate the social environment by going beyond perceptual social cues to infer more complex hidden mental states of others, including their thoughts, beliefs, feelings, desires, and intentions – a faculty referred to as *theory of mind,* or *mentalizing* (Frith and Frith, 2006).

Given the evolutionary pressures for social cognition, it is no surprise that a large portion of what people naturally think about is related to other people. As social beings, we derive a good deal of our self-identity (Leary, Tipsord, and Tate, 2008) and our mental and physical health (Holt-Lunstad, Smith, and Layton, 2010) from our relationships, and people who daydream to a greater degree about close others are less lonely and more satisfied with life (Mar, Mason, and Litvack, 2012). A social bias to our imaginative thoughts can sometimes have detrimental correlates and consequences, however, particularly when TUTs primarily concern strangers or acquaintances (Mar, Mason, and Litvack, 2012), or when social thoughts are accompanied by a retrospective focus (Ruby et al., 2013).

Self-Focused Imagination

Even more pronounced than social content, adults think about topics they deem to be self-relevant (Andrews-Hanna et al., 2013). This is especially true for TUTs, where the mind frequently turns to personal goals, unresolved problems, items of personal value, and other self-related matters (Smallwood and Andrews-Hanna, 2013), consistent with Klinger's current concern hypothesis (Klinger, 2009). This relationship is also true in the other direction, as probing participants to think about personal goals can elevate the frequency of TUT (Stawarczyk et al., 2011).

The self-related nature of imaginative thought is especially apparent when it comes to memory (Prebble, Addis, and Tippett, 2013), and the self represents a defining feature of autobiographical memories in particular (Conway and Pleydell-Pearce, 2000). Episodic autobiographical memories – detailed memories of personal past events – are thought to involve a subjective sense of reliving the event in time, called *autonoetic consciousness,* or *mental time travel* (Tulving, 1985). These memories are thought to contribute to one's sense of self-identity over time when details of past events are integrated into one's "autobiographical knowledge base" – a conceptual storage system of one's personal history organized along different levels of temporal abstraction, from singular detailed events, to abstract summaries pertaining to longer life periods (Conway and Pleydell-Pearce, 2000; Grilli and Ryan, forthcoming; Prebble, Addis, and Tippett, 2013).

Some autobiographical episodic memories pertain to highly important personal concerns or goals reflecting enduring themes in an individual's life. These "self-defining memories" are thought to receive heightened priority in the autobiographical knowledge base, and are triggered more frequently given their association with numerous other memories related to a particular theme (Lardi et al., 2010). Self-defining memories evoke stronger emotions than other memories, and are recalled more vividly (Lardi et al., 2010).

Autobiographical memories and other imaginative thoughts are often accompanied by autobiographical reasoning processes, in which individuals reflect on the personal meaning of particular experiences (Lardi et al., 2010). Such reasoning processes are thought to strengthen the connection between one's past and the present, leading to a sense of temporal continuity in our sense of self. Reasoning processes can also be applied to our mental experiences in the moment, such as our current beliefs, desires, and emotions. This self-directed mentalizing process may help us make meaning out of our experiences, further cementing our sense of identity and contributing to the development of self-schemas, stable traits that form the basis of our personality (D'Argembeau, Lardi, and Van der Linden, 2012; see also Chapter 22).

How the Mind Thinks: Representational Format of Imaginative Thought

An intriguing aspect of imaginative thoughts is the representational format in which they are experienced. Two common ways in which thoughts are represented are as *mental images* and *words* (Amit et al., 2009; Paivio, 1986). When thoughts are experienced in the form of mental images, individuals see sequences of images or events unfold in their mind's eye. In contrast to picture-like representations, verbal representations are mainly mediated via language, in the form of inner speech. Though images and words have been found to be negatively correlated during laboratory tasks investigating TUTs (Stawarczyk, Cassol, and D'Argembeau, 2013), studies assessing such thoughts in daily life have observed no relationships between these variables (e.g. Klinger and Cox, 1987). Further, these two forms of representation were shown to frequently co-occur in a study in which participants were prompted to generate a thought in one or the other format (Amit et al., 2017). These findings suggest that inner speech and mental images are not mutually exclusive.

Individual differences have been reported with respect to the representational format of imaginative thought (Cui et al., 2007). For example, individuals scoring higher on visual imagery questionnaires self-report a greater level of perceptual detail when engaging in autobiographical memory and prospection (D'Argembeau and van der Linden, 2006; see also Sheldon et al., 2016). Though some individuals may rely more on one mode of representation than the other (Delamillieure et al., 2010), for a rare few the dominance may fall at the extremes. Individuals with *aphantasia* lack the ability to conjure up vivid images (Keogh and Pearson, 2018; Chapter 12). Instead, their thinking relies more heavily on verbal thinking, as suggested by this account: "I have never visualized anything in my entire life . . . If you tell me to imagine a beach, I ruminate on the 'concept' of beach. I know there's sand. I know there's water . . . I know facts about beaches" (Ross, 2016). Conversely, some individuals think solely in images, as illustrated by the renowned professor and autism spokesperson Temple Grandin in her book *Thinking in Pictures: My Life with Autism* (Grandin, 2006): "I think in pictures. Words are like a second language to me. I translate both spoken and written words into full-color movies, complete with sound, which run like a VCR tape in my head." In the next section, we discuss how representational format often interacts with a different element of imaginative thought: level of construal.

How the Mind Thinks: Level of Construal

A different yet related aspect of imaginative thoughts is the level of detail vs. abstraction with which they are imagined – that is their "level of construal" (Amit et al., 2009; Trope and Liberman, 2010). A thought experienced with a low level of construal is concrete and specific, representing a specific entity with clear unique features, often in a specific context. Alternatively, a thought experienced with a high level of construal is abstract and general, a more schematic and decontextualized representation of the entity it symbolizes.

One variable that has been repeatedly found to influence the degree of construal of a thought is psychological distance. Construal level theory proposes that mental representations that are psychologically distant from the self in the here and now are more likely to be abstract and schematic (Trope and Liberman, 2010). Psychological distance can take many forms, including social distance (i.e. thinking of Americans as opposed to Uzbeks) and temporal distance (thinking about the remote as opposed to the near past). Psychologically distant representations are more likely to be abstract as they strip down details to focus on the stable features, those that are most likely to be present across different situations.

Another variable found to relate to the degree of construal is the representational format of imaginative thought. Amit and colleagues (2009) argue that images are inherently more concrete because they represent a specific object, whereas words represent a multitude of the objects they symbolize. For instance, whereas picturing a dog restricts the level of representation (as what is being perceived in the mind's eye determines features such as the color and breed), the word "dog" itself is unconstrained and can thus represent any breed and any color. Supporting this idea, Rim and colleagues (2015) found evidence that participants are more likely to categorize stimuli more inclusively (i.e. more broadly) when stimuli are presented as words as opposed to pictures. Furthermore, the authors observed that the association runs in the other direction, as well. Participants primed to think abstractly were more likely to report thinking in words than images during a subsequent categorization test; conversely, those primed to think concretely were more likely to report the opposite. Relatedly, thoughts characterized as more detailed and specific are also more likely to be experienced using vivid image-based representations (Andrews-Hanna et al., 2013; Klinger and Cox, 1987).

How the Mind Flows: Emergence and Dynamics of Imaginative Thought

Novel efforts are being expended to consider the ways in which thoughts unfold over time – that is, their *dynamics* (e.g. Christoff et al., 2016; Mills et al., 2018). According to a recent theoretical model, the dynamics of thought are influenced by the absence or presence of different constraints imposed on cognition (Christoff et al., 2016). For instance, revisions of a manuscript for which the deadline is fast approaching will likely constrain thought towards the manuscript during one's commute to work. Conversely, going on a hike during a vacation is more likely to lead to a state of mind in which thoughts feel more spontaneous, as there may be little that constrains the mind toward a specific topic. Although the model is agnostic as to whether such experiences are imaginative as opposed to perceptually focused, here we hypothesize how the model might play out for imaginative thoughts.

When one willfully directs mental resources toward a specific train of thought, as when planning the itinerary of an upcoming trip or organizing the outline of a chapter, *deliberate constraints* are at play. During deliberately constrained thinking (encompassing goal-directed thoughts), the individual feels in control of the mental experience. According to the model, deliberate constraints serve to stabilize attention over time (Christoff et al., 2016).

A different kind of constraint could be at play when an individual is experiencing intrusive or highly salient imaginative thoughts, such as a flashback related to a past trauma or a current concern about a fast-approaching deadline. Like deliberate constraints, automatic constraints also serve to limit and stabilize the content of thoughts over time (Christoff et al., 2016). Automatically constrained thoughts are characterized by highly personally or emotionally salient content, perceived difficulty to control, and little variability in content over time. Anxious, ruminative, or obsessive thoughts – all under the category of negative repetitive thinking – are types of automatically constrained or habitual styles of thinking (Andrews-Hanna, Christoff, and O'Connor, in press).

Finally, when both deliberate and automatic constraints are low, unconstrained spontaneous thoughts are likely to emerge. In this case, since no constraints are imposed to stabilize attention over time, thoughts will be experienced as fleeting and varying in content over time, going seamlessly from one topic to the next (Christoff et al., 2016).

An important characteristic of this model is that deliberate and automatic constraints are conceptualized as continuums, such that imaginative thoughts can be characterized somewhere on each dimension, from none to extreme. Night dreaming represents a class of highly spontaneous imaginative thoughts in which deliberate and automatic constraints may be nearly completely relaxed (Fox et al., 2013). Relatedly, mind-wandering[2] is a class of cognition in which deliberate and automatic constraints are mostly relaxed, and thoughts *wander* from topic to topic, flowing with ease over time (Christoff et al., 2016). Creative thoughts are characterized by their hybrid nature, including phases of relatively flexible thinking (e.g. when brainstorming or generating ideas), as well as phases of more deliberately constrained thinking (e.g. when evaluating or fine-tuning one's ideas) (Ellamil et al., 2012).

Interim Summary

Although we have described these different elements of imaginative content separately, a single thought is characterized by the intersecting expressions of multiple co-occurring characteristics. For example, recalling breaking your sibling's toy when you were eight may be characterized as a concrete, visual, past-oriented, and social (yet self-relevant) memory. The memory may also be intentionally retrieved, highly imageable and detailed. Although a remarkable feature of the imaginative mind is that it is theoretically possible to string together any combination of the content characteristics described above, important patterns regarding relationships between content variables have begun to emerge across individuals and contexts. Before delving into a discussion of these patterns, however, we next discuss emerging literature regarding the neural underpinnings of imaginative thought.

Neuroscientific Underpinnings of Imaginative Thought

Growing consensus among brain imaging studies is that a large-scale brain system called the *default network* (DN) plays an important role in many aspects of imaginative thought (for reviews, see Buckner, Andrews-Hanna, and Schacter, 2008;

2 Note that this definition of mind-wandering diverges from more traditional definitions, which characterize mind-wandering by its task-unrelated and/or stimulus-independent content (reviewed in Smallwood and Schooler, 2015).

Andrews-Hanna, Smallwood, and Spreng, 2014). The DN includes distributed regions across association cortices that increase their activity when participants mentally project themselves away from the perceptual constraints of the present moment, to a different time, place, or perspective (Buckner and Carroll, 2007). This is the case both when participants are instructed to deliberately turn their attention inward in the context of an experimental paradigm (e.g. Spreng, Mar, and Kim, 2009), as well as when participants experience elements of imaginative thought without external prompting, such as during the "resting state" (Andrews-Hanna, Saxe, and Yarkoni, 2014), or during task-unrelated or spontaneously emerging thoughts (Fox et al., 2015). Activity in the DN has been demonstrated during all of the flavors of imaginative thought discussed in the previous section, spanning remembering past or imagining future events (e.g. Schacter, Addis and Buckner, 2007), self-referential thinking (Denny et al., 2012), theory of mind (Spreng and Andrews-Hanna, 2015), and more.

Despite the role of the DN in these processes, a closer look points to more fine-grained functional specificity within the network (Andrews-Hanna, Saxe, and Yarkoni, 2014). In this section, we review evidence that distinct components within the DN may preferentially support different elements of imaginative thought. These components are thought to form anatomically connected "subsystems," each of which is functionally coherent at rest and during imaginative tasks but can also interact with the others and with other large-scale brain systems in context-dependent ways. In the subsequent section, we integrate these neural findings with the psychological findings summarized above to propose an overarching neurocognitive framework for which researchers from multiple disciplines can conceptually organize the broad construct of imaginative thought.

Contextually Detailed Forms of Imagination and the Medial Temporal Lobe (MTL) Subsystem

One collection of regions within the DN, often called the *Medial Temporal Lobe (MTL) subsystem*, is centered around an important set of structures for episodic memory and related functions: the medial temporal lobe (Figure 21.1). The subsystem spans the hippocampus and parahippocampal cortex, as well as cortical regions connected to the MTL, including the bilateral angular gyrus and retrosplenial cortex (Andrews-Hanna et al., 2010). The MTL subsystem has most readily been discussed with respect to its role in episodic and autobiographical episodic memory (e.g. Cabeza and St. Jacques, 2007). More recently, however, the MTL subsystem has been appreciated for its contribution to a different type of temporally oriented thought: prospective thinking. Prospective tasks, spanning imagining future hypothetical events, formulating autobiographical plans, and entertaining one's personal goals, all robustly activate the MTL subsystem (Schacter et al., 2012; Stawarczyk and D'Argembeau, 2015). The neural convergence between autobiographical memory and autobiographical prospection is strong, lending support to the *constructive episodic simulation hypothesis*, in which the hippocampus contributes to past and prospective thinking by retrieving and binding different elements from memory together when constructing or reconstructing a mental scene (Schacter and Addis, 2007; Chapter 8).

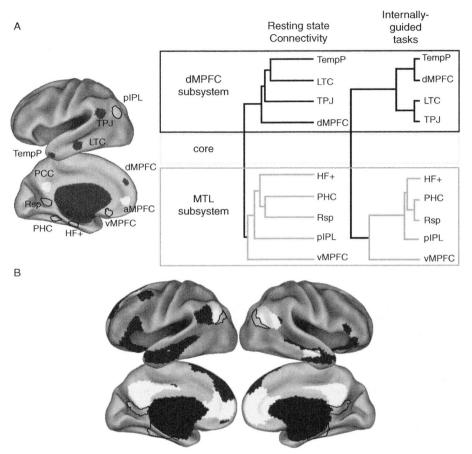

Figure 21.1 *Subdivisions of the default network. (A) At rest, and during a variety of imaginative tasks, the DN clusters into two subsystems, the MTL subsystem (black outline) and dMPFC subsystem (dark gray areas), converging on the DN-CORE regions, the posterior cingulate and anterior medial prefrontal cortex (white areas). amPFC, anterior medial prefrontal cortex; dMPFC, dorsal medial prefrontal cortex; HF, hippocampal formation; LTC, lateral temporal cortex; MTL, medial temporal lobe; PCC, posterior cingulate cortex; PHC, parahippocampal cortex; pIPL, posterior inferior parietal lobule; RSC, retrosplenial cortex; TempP, temporal pole; TPJ, temporoparietal junction; vmPFC, ventral medial prefrontal cortex. Data from Andrews-Hanna, Saxe, and Yarkoni (2014), Contributions of Episodic Retrieval and Mentalizing to Autobiographical Thought: Evidence from Functional Neuroimaging, Resting-State Connectivity, and fMRI Meta-Analyses, Neuroimage, 91, 324–335. (B) More recent whole-brain RSFC parcellations (color scheme same as A) are more extensive, yet broadly consistent with panel A (Yeo et al., 2011). Figure adapted from Andrews-Hanna, Smallwood, and Spreng (2014), The Default Network and Self-Generated Thought: Component Processes, Dynamic Control, and Clinical Relevance, Annals of the New York Academy of Sciences, 1316(1), 29–52.*

Critically, within the realm of memory and prospectively oriented thoughts, the level of perceptual vividness and contextual detail are important predictors of activity within the MTL subsystem (Andrews-Hanna et al., 2010; Sheldon et al., 2016). This finding extends both to laboratory-based memory tasks (in which the MTL subsystem becomes engaged when individuals re-experience the context in which an item was encoded [Kim, 2010]), as well as to retrieval of real-world autobiographical memories (in which episodic autobiographical memories engage the MTL subsystem to a greater degree than memories that lack contextual detail) (e.g. Brown et al., 2018). Episodic forms of counterfactual thinking – the process of imagining alternative scenarios to what has previously happened – also engage the MTL subsystem (e.g. Parikh et al., 2018), as do prospective simulations characterized as more detailed and specific (e.g. Andrews-Hanna et al., 2010; Spreng et al., 2015). Relatedly, atrophy or damage to the hippocampus and other structures within the MTL subsystem impairs the capacity for elaboration of memories and prospective thought with perceptually rich contextual detail (reviewed in Irish and Piolino, 2016; Mullally and Maguire, 2014).

The role of the MTL subsystem in imagining episodes with spatio-contextual detail invites the question of whether temporally oriented content is necessary and/or sufficient to evoke activity within the MTL subsystem. This question is a difficult one to tackle given the various control conditions used in the neuroimaging literature, but there is some suggestion that time, *per se*, may not be as critical a feature of MTL subsystem activity as previously anticipated. For example, it appears that contextually constructive aspects of imaginative thought might be sufficient to elicit MTL subsystem activity, even if an imaginative scene lacks a retrospective or prospective orientation. The MTL subsystem becomes engaged when individuals mentally construct novel, atemporal mental scenes (e.g. imagining lying on a white sandy beach, void of a temporal orientation) (Hassabis, Kumaran, and Maguire, 2007), and individuals with lesions to the hippocampus score particularly low in measures of spatial coherence when engaging in such mental simulations (Hassabis, Kumaran, Vann, and Maguire, 2007). Furthermore, the simple act of viewing individual objects commonly associated with a specific context (i.e. an oven) activates regions throughout the MTL subsystem to a greater degree than viewing items without a typical context (e.g. a cherry), as if individuals are imagining items in context (Bar et al., 2007). Integrating these findings, we suggest that the MTL subsystem may support the emergence of a particular kind of imaginative thought, characterized as being contextually specific, perceptually vivid and imageable, and often (but not always) oriented toward the past or future.

Interestingly, the MTL subsystem has been implicated in the spontaneous emergence of memories, as well as other types of imaginative thoughts characterized by their dynamic nature, including mind-wandering, dreams, and generative phases of creativity (reviewed in Christoff et al., 2016). Conversely, when imaginative thoughts emerge via deliberate constraints, the DN is thought to couple with the frontoparietal control network (FPCN) – a brain network supporting top-down control (e.g. Spreng et al., 2010). By providing constraints that guide cognition toward a particular goal, the FPCN is thought to contribute to the stability of imaginative thought over time (Christoff et al., 2016).

Conceptually Abstract Forms of Imagination and the Dorsomedial Prefrontal Cortex (dMPFC) Subsystem

In contrast to the perceptual/contextual forms of imagination that appear to be supported by the MTL subsystem, a second subdivision of the DN, often referred to as the dorsomedial prefrontal cortex subsystem (dMPFC subsystem), has been discussed most readily with respect to its role in social aspects of imaginative thought (reviewed in Spreng and Andrews-Hanna, 2015). This subsystem includes regions spanning the dorsal medial prefrontal cortex (dMPFC), temporoparietal junction (TPJ), lateral frontal and temporal cortices, and temporal pole (Andrews-Hanna, Saxe, and Yarkoni, 2014) (Figure 21.1). Regions corresponding to the dMPFC subsystem overlap with the *mentalizing network* (Andrews-Hanna, Saxe, and Yarkoni, 2014), a functional term that highlights their engagement during social cognitive tasks in which individuals cognitively infer the hidden mental states of other people, and reflect on their own mental states (Frith and Frith, 2006).

As with temporal orientation when it comes to the MTL subsystem, a debated question is whether social content *per se* is necessary and sufficient to engage the dMPFC subsystem. Tasks requiring participants to make primarily perceptual judgments about social stimuli often do not recruit the dMPFC subsystem (Spunt, Meyer, and Lieberman, 2015), nor do those in which individuals observe or imitate actions (Caspers et al., 2010), recognize pictures of oneself or others (van Veluw and Chance, 2014), or reflexively share the affective experiences of others in pain (so-called "experience sharing," "emotional contagion," or "affective empathy") (e.g. Zaki and Ochsner, 2012). Rather, the dMPFC subsystem appears to be sensitive to social processes requiring participants to mentally shift away from the *perceptual* features of the present environment, in order to imagine a different *cognitive* perspective (Lieberman, 2007).

Mental states are both internal and abstract, and arguably cannot be imagined using image-based representations. Rather, imagining others' mental states necessitates adopting symbolic, often verbally mediated forms of imagination. Indeed, mentalizing and language are deeply intertwined. From an evolutionary perspective, language is considered to serve a critical social function – as a means for individuals to communicate their mental states (e.g. thoughts, beliefs, intentions, feelings) with others (Seyfarth and Cheney, 2014). Numerous parallels also exist between the development of language and theory of mind across childhood (Milligan, Astington, and Dack, 2007). Supporting this link, functional MRI meta-analyses of language comprehension and semantic processing highlight the role of the dMPFC subsystem (e.g. Binder et al., 2009; Mar, 2011). Relatedly, a large-scale meta-analytic decoding of the dMPFC subsystem using the Neurosynth database revealed strong associations between the dMPFC subsystem and social cognitive terms such as "social," "mentalizing," "knowledge," and "person," as well as linguistic terms such as "comprehension," "sentence," "story," "semantic," "language," "word," and "syntactic" (Andrews-Hanna, Saxe, and Yarkoni, 2014).

Whether the role of the dMFPC subsystem extends beyond socially related content is a somewhat open question. On the one hand, the dMPFC subsystem appears to be preferentially recruited by socioemotional compared to nonsocial concepts such as landmarks and places (e.g. Binder and Desai, 2011; Huth et al., 2016). Social

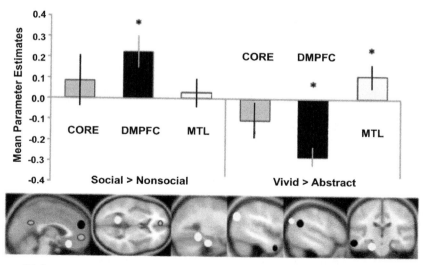

Figure 21.2 *Involvement of default network subdivisions when reading different types of literary passage. Whole-brain and ROI analyses showing that the dMPFC subsystem (black bars and dots) responds more robustly to reading social and/or abstract physical descriptions, whereas the MTL subsystem (white bars and dots) responds more robustly to vivid physical descriptions. Figure from Tamir, Bricker, Dodell-Feder, and Mitchell (2015), Reading Fiction and Reading Minds: The Role of Simulation in the Default Network,* Social Cognitive and Affective Neuroscience, *2015, 11(2), 215–224. By permission of Oxford University Press.*

narratives also recruit the dMPFC subsystem to a greater degree than nonsocial narratives, and the degree of dMPFC subsystem activity for this contrast mediates individual difference relationships between frequency of fiction reading and improved performance on a theory of mind task (Tamir et al., 2015). However, there is also evidence demonstrating that regions within the dMPFC subsystem – particularly the dMPFC and inferior frontal cortex – are recruited during nonsocial stimuli, particularly when such stimuli are processed in an abstract, high construal manner. For example, this is the case when making judgments about categories vs. items on verbal and visual stimuli (Baetens et al., 2014), when entertaining answers to abstract questions (Spunt, Kemmerer, and Adolphs, 2015), when reasoning about the broader meaning and significance of autobiographical memories (D'Argembeau et al., 2013), when evaluating coherent vs. unrelated sentence pairs related to inanimate objects (Ferstl and von Cramon, 2002), and when reading abstract vs. vivid narratives, irrespective of their social nature (Tamir et al., 2015) (Figure 21.2).

The reviewed evidence thus suggests an important link within the dMPFC between verbally mediated forms of imagination and imaginative thoughts construed at a higher, more abstract level of construal, such as mentalizing and reasoning.

Convergence of Imaginative Thought in the DN-CORE

When the MTL and/or dMPFC subsystems become recruited during the different types of imaginative thought summarized above, a core cluster of DN regions making up the third subdivision of the DN, anatomically positioned between the two subsystems (Andrews-Hanna, Saxe, and Yarkoni, 2010), also commonly increases its activity. Through its widespread connectivity patterns, the DN-CORE is recruited across a wide variety of imaginative tasks. These tasks range from the most basic – such as retrieving individual concepts (Binder et al., 2009) or engaging in executive function tasks in which decisions involve retrieving information from working or long-term memory (e.g. Konishi et al., 2015; Spreng et al., 2014) – to the most complex, including evaluating outputs of creativity (Ellamil et al., 2012) or engaging in autobiographical prospection (Schacter et al., 2012). Further, it demonstrates frequent engagement during periods of wakeful rest (e.g. Wang et al., 2018) and task-unrelated thought (Fox et al., 2015). Thus, the DN-CORE seems to play a fundamental role in imaginative thought, broadly construed.

Numerous studies suggest that on top of the basic imaginative properties of the DN-CORE, the anterior medial portion of the DN-CORE (aMPFC), and in some cases the posterior cingulate cortex (PCC), may track the personal or motivational significance of external stimuli and internal representations (Andrews-Hanna, Saxe, and Yarkoni, 2014). Indeed, the aMPFC has long been appreciated for its role in self-related processes, both in the context of explicit self-referential tasks (Abraham, 2013; Denny et al., 2012), as well as when one intrinsically devotes attentional resources to self-relevant material, such as one's own name (Moran, Heatherton, and Kelley, 2009). The role of the aMPFC in self-related processes also intersects with its related role in value computation, particularly because self-relevant stimuli are naturally deemed more important. Individuals also place high value on people with whom they hold close relationships; consequently, stimuli and/or decisions involving close others engage the aMPFC to a greater degree than strangers and others for whom we care to a lesser degree (D'Argembeau, 2013; Krienen, Tu, and Buckner, 2010).

The DN-CORE is appropriately wired to estimate the personal significance of incoming internal or external information by integrating such information with existing self-schemas and allowing that information to be referenced with respect to one's immediate and long-term goals. Once an estimate of personal significance is computed, this signal can be used to allocate an ideal amount of attentional resources toward such information, thus serving as an automatic constraint to stabilize attention on that deemed personally relevant (Christoff et al., 2016).

An Integrative Framework for Imagination

In this chapter, we approach the concept of imaginative thought as an umbrella term encompassing mental operations that require participants to decouple from current sensory input. We argue that neuroscience research lends support for this broad definition of imaginative thought because diverse tasks that involve various internal processes tend to recruit common and distinct elements of the DN (Buckner, Andrews-Hanna, and Schacter, 2008; Andrews-Hanna, Saxe, and Yarkoni, 2014). But on top of the fundamental similarities among the seemingly endless mental repertoire of our imagination, how can we organize these phenomenologically unique experiences? In this final section, we synthesize neurocognitive research to propose an organizational framework of imaginative thought with the aim of helping understand its many varieties and facilitate cross-disciplinary collaboration and discovery.

Our framework suggests we can broadly organize such varieties of mental experience into two broad classes of imaginative thought that preferentially recruit distinct subsystems within the DN. One class of imaginative thought is rooted in contextually specific and perceptually detailed mental imagery. This associative type of imagination accommodates theoretical views that focus on imagination as mental simulation of novel or old, fictional or real, temporal or atemporal processes. However, the framework emphasizes the importance of construing this content in a low-level fashion – that is, by accompanying mental simulations with abundant perceptual details, bound in a particular spatial and/or temporal context (Hassabis and Maguire, 2007). Indeed, the MTL subsystem – the key DN component we propose supports such imaginative processes – becomes engaged during a variety of tasks involving mental simulation of objects and their associative contexts, including episodic memory and episodic future thinking, constructing imaginative scenes, retrieving concrete/perceptual and contextually associated concepts, mental navigation, and reading narratives evoking vivid mental imagery (Binder et al., 2009; Spreng, Mar, and Kim, 2009; Tamir et al., 2015). These low-level, contextually specific forms of imagination tend to take on the form of internal mental images (Amit et al., 2017), presumably supported by medial temporal and cortical brain regions with strong connectivity to the ventral and dorsal visual streams (Lavenex and Amaral, 2000). This form of imaginative thought often activates spontaneously, void of external prompt, intentional control, or sometimes conscious awareness (Christoff et al., 2016). Spontaneously emerging thought manifests as a wandering imaginative mind, constantly consolidating past experience, predicting what may happen next, and generating new material.

Another broad class of imaginative thought encapsulates internal mental processes construed at a much higher level of association. Such conceptually abstract forms of imagination likely take on a verbal or symbolic representational format, often manifesting as an internal monologue (Amit et al., 2009). These abstract verbal processes are used across many varieties of imaginative thought, including those spanning social domains (e.g. mentalizing about self and other, reasoning about moral dilemmas, attributing traits, comprehending written and spoken narratives) and nonsocial domains (e.g. retrieving abstract concepts, metacognitively reflecting or reasoning about the broader meaning of prior experiences, and ruminating on the causes and consequences of one's emotional states). We propose that these abstract, predominantly verbally mediated processes rely heavily on the dMPFC subsystem.

Importantly, anterior medial elements of the DN-CORE appear to be additionally sensitive to the personal and motivational significance of stimuli and internal representations, perhaps through integration with regions that play an important role in the storage of autobiographical knowledge and the experience of affective responses. This heightened activity to personally relevant information could serve as a critical mechanism with which to guide and stabilize attention toward personally salient stimuli or internal representations, and away from information deemed unimportant or irrelevant. Altogether, the multiple DN components are ideally situated within the brain to allow imaginative

	Medial temporal lobe subsystem	Dorsal medial prefrontal cortex subsystem	DN-CORE
Imaginative content supported (Temporal, social, self, emotional, etc.)	Supports many different types of content, although most often studied with respect to the past and future content	Supports many different types of content, although most often studied with respect to social content	Supports many different types of content, although appears most sensitive to personally significant content
Construal level	Low (detailed and specific)	High (general and abstract)	Both
Representational format	Perceptual/image-based	Verbal/word	Both
Emergence and dynamics	MTL subsystem activity on its own: dynamic, spontaneously emerging thoughts. MTL subsystem coupled with frontoparietal control network: stable, deliberately constrained thoughts. MTL subsystem coupled with DN-CORE: stable, personally/motivationally salient thoughts	Unclear	Stable, automatically constrained thought
Hypothetical example	Recalling that one's wedding occurred on a hot April day in Ireland in which no one was ready for the heat, so attendees looked disheveled	Recalling that one's wedding felt like a natural step in life at the time and how much it meant that so many people came	Both examples hypothesized to engage the DN-CORE, but example in the second column may be recruited to a greater degree if more personally salient

Figure 21.3 *Integrative neurocognitive model of imaginative thought.*

thoughts to: (1) emerge across a variety of situational contexts (i.e. related or unrelated to the immediate task, evoked by either deliberate constraints, automatic constraints, or spontaneously), (2) be construed in a variety of different ways (on a continuum from highly abstract to highly specific and detailed), (3) be accompanied by a variety of different representational formats (as mental images, words, or other symbols), and (4) to concern a variety of different content (i.e. spanning variations in temporal content, social content, emotional content, and so on) (Figure 21.3).

It is important to note that aspects of conceptual content characterizing these two broad classes of imaginative thought (e.g. temporal orientation, self-focus, social orientation, emotional valence, etc.) can be quite similar. Rather, we propose that what distinguishes such thoughts are the level of detail and specificity by which they are construed. Consider the following answer to the prompt "How did your wedding go?": "*It went pretty well. Our wedding was the last weekend of April and it was a surprisingly very hot day. Nobody was ready for the heat so everyone ended up looking disheveled and casual when they arrived. Thankfully the reception was in a small Irish castle built on thick stones, so it felt pretty cool inside. Julia looked stunning in her satin wedding dress against the backdrop of the old stones.*" Now compare with an alternative answer: "*It went pretty well. The wedding felt like a natural step considering where we were in our lives at the time. The heat was so unexpected, though – I can just imagine what our guests must have been thinking! Overall, it meant so much to Julia and I that so many people whom we care about were there.*" Although both responses concern a past event and have social elements, the first account is a concrete, detailed description about what the scene was like. In contrast, the second account provides a reflection about the meaning and significance of the event, a more abstract reasoning-based style of thought offering minimal concrete details. We suggest the level of contextual detail with which the thought is conceptualized will relate to both its mode of representation (with the former example more likely to manifest as mental images than the latter), as well as its underlying neural substrates (engaging the MTL subsystem for the former example, the dMPFC subsystem for the latter, and the DN-CORE for both).

On a final note, we want to caution that we do not intend to suggest that the two classes of imaginative thought are mutually exclusive. For one, both classes of imaginative thought can be employed during a single train of thought, as when alternating between retrieving mnemonic details and reflecting on their broader meaning. Additionally, as reviewed earlier, there is evidence that different representational formats can co-occur (Amit et al., 2017, Klinger and Cox, 1987). Our inner monologue may be complemented with images, just as we can use our monologue to comment on picture-based thinking content. The neural underpinnings of this relationship remain speculative.

Conclusions and Future Directions

The breadth of imaginative thought in humans is very large. On the one hand, the capacity for imagination allows individuals to conjure up a multitude of perceptual scenes full of concrete details. On the other hand, it allows individuals to infer others' intentions and mental states, or to reflect on their own. These imaginative thoughts may take the form of images or words, or a mix of both. They may arise via deliberate constraints, automatic constraints, or spontaneously (i.e. unconstrained), and may be fleeting or persistent. Here we propose a neuroscience-guided framework in which the MTL subsystem is preferentially active when one generates mental representations that are contextually specific and perceptually vivid, a feature prevalent in recollection and episodic thinking, and the dMPFC subsystem is preferentially active when mental representations are conceptually abstract, as is the case for verbally mediated reflections.

On top of many important findings uncovered over the last decade, novel exciting avenues for future research are emerging. Of note, the bulk of the neural findings we summarized above are drawn from studies in which functional and structural data from individual participants are statistically aggregated across the sample, reflecting group-averaged findings. An exciting area of recent research hints that the functional network organization of the DN when assessed in individual participants may be more complex than previously anticipated (Braga and Buckner, 2017). When the resting state architecture is assessed in individuals, the DN often fractionates into parallel interdigitated subnetworks that vary in precise location from participant to participant, and that lack an obvious DN-CORE. How compatible this complex architecture is with the neurocognitive framework highlighted here remains an important avenue for future studies.

On the front of methodology, there is also an eagerness to develop more objective measures to overcome the limitations of introspection and self-report assessments. Smallwood and Schooler (2015) have proposed a triangulation procedure combining self-report measures with behavioral, physiological, and neural measures that can increase confidence in classifying the imaginative mind (see also Wang et al., 2018).

As mentioned previously, there is a growing interest in understanding the dynamics with which imaginative thoughts unfold. A recent study used the concept of freely moving thought as a novel index related to mind-wandering (Mills et al., 2018). Aberrations in dynamics may be particularly relevant to various mental disorders characterized by an overly flexible or overly sticky mind (Christoff et al., 2016; Andrews-Hanna et al., in press). After millennia of work, humans' imagination is currently facing one of its greatest challenges: understanding itself. The progress made since the fall of behaviorism and the rise of neuroimaging techniques is monumental, and the next chapter in research on imagination is sure to bring new and exciting insights about this undoubtedly wondrous capacity.

References

Abraham, A. (2013). The World According to Me: Personal Relevance and the Medial Prefrontal Cortex. *Frontiers in Human Neuroscience*, *7*, 341.

Amit, E., Algom, D., Trope, Y., and Liberman, N. (2009). "Thou Shalt not Make Unto Thee Any Graven Image": The Distance-Dependence of Representation. In K. D. Markman, W. M. Klein, and J. A. Suhr (eds.), *Handbook of Imagination and Mental Simulation*. New York, NY: Psychology Press, 53–68.

Amit, E., Hoeflin, C., Hamzah, N., and Fedorenko, E. (2017). An Asymmetrical Relationship between Verbal and Visual Thinking: Converging Evidence from Behavior and fMRI. *NeuroImage*, *152*, 619–627.

Andrews-Hanna, J. R. (2012). The Brain's Default Network and Its Adaptive Role in Internal Mentation. *The Neuroscientist*, *18*(3), 251–270.

Andrews-Hanna, J. R., Christoff, K., and O'Connor, M. F. (in press). Dynamic Regulation of Internal Experience. In R. Lane, L. Ryan, and L. Nadel (eds.), *The Neuroscience of Enduring Change: The Neural Basis of Talk Therapies*. New York, NY: Oxford University Press.

Andrews-Hanna, J. R., Kaiser, R. H., Turner, A. E., et al. (2013). A Penny for Your Thoughts: Dimensions of Self-Generated Thought Content and Relationships with Individual Differences in Emotional Wellbeing. *Frontiers in Psychology*, *4*, 900.

Andrews-Hanna, J. R., Reidler, J. S., Sepulcre, J., Poulin, R., and Buckner, R. L. (2010). Functional-Anatomic Fractionation of the Brain's Default Network. *Neuron, 65*(4), 550–562.

Andrews-Hanna, J. R., Saxe, R., and Yarkoni, T. (2014). Contributions of Episodic Retrieval and Mentalizing to Autobiographical Thought: Evidence from Functional Neuroimaging, Resting-State Connectivity, and fMRI Meta-Analyses. *Neuroimage, 91*, 324–335.

Andrews-Hanna, J. R., Smallwood, J., and Spreng, R. N. (2014). The Default Network and Self-Generated Thought: Component Processes, Dynamic Control, and Clinical Relevance. *Annals of the New York Academy of Sciences, 1316*(1), 29–52.

Baetens, K., Ma, N., Steen, J., and van Overwalle, F. (2014). Involvement of the Mentalizing Network in Social and Non-Social High Construal. *Social Cognitive and Affective Neuroscience, 9*, 817–824.

Baird, B., Smallwood, J., and Schooler, J. W. (2011). Back to the Future: Autobiographical Planning and the Functionality of Mind-Wandering. *Consciousness and Cognition, 20*(4), 1604–1611.

Bar. M., Aminoff, E., Mason, M., and Fenske, M. (2007). The Units of Thought. *Hippocampus, 17*(6), 420–428.

Binder, J. R., and Desai, R. H. (2011). The Neurobiology of Semantic Memory. *Trends in Cognitive Sciences, 15*(11), 527–536.

Binder, J. R., Desai, R. H., Graves, W. W., and Conant, L. L. (2009). Where is the Semantic System? A Critical Review and Meta-Analysis of 120 Functional Neuroimaging Studies. *Cerebral Cortex, 19*(12), 2767–2796.

Braga, R. M., and Buckner, R. L. (2017). Parallel Interdigitated Distributed Networks within the Individual Estimated by Intrinsic Functional Connectivity. *Neuron, 95*(2), 457–471.e5.

Braga, R. M., van Dijk, K. R., Polimeni, J. R., Eldaief, M. C., and Buckner, R. L. (2018). Parallel Distributed Networks Resolved at High Resolution Reveal Close Juxtaposition of Distinct Regions. *Journal of Neurophysiology, 121*(4), 1513–1534.

Brown, T. I., Rissman, J., Chow, T. E., Uncapher, M. R., and Wagner, A. D. (2018). Differential Medial Temporal Lobe and Parietal Cortical Contributions to Real-world Autobiographical Episodic and Autobiographical Semantic Memory. *Scientific Reports, 8*(1), 6190.

Buckner, R. L., and Carroll, D. C. (2007). Self-Projection and the Brain. *Trends in Cognitive Sciences, 11*(2), 49–57.

Buckner, R. L., Andrews-Hanna, J. R., and Schacter, D. L. (2008). The Brain's Default Network: Anatomy, Function, and Relevance to Disease. *Annals of the New York Academy of Sciences, 1124*(1), 1–38.

Cabeza, R., and St. Jacques, P. (2007). Functional Neuroimaging of Autobiographical Memory. *Trends in Cognitive Sciences, 11*(5), 219–227.

Caspers, S., Zilles, K., Laird, A. R., and Eickhoff, S. B. (2010). ALE Meta-Analysis of Action Observation and Imitation in the Human Brain. *Neuroimage, 50*(3), 1148–1167.

Christoff, K., Irving, Z. C., Fox, K. C., Spreng, R. N., and Andrews-Hanna, J. R. (2016). Mind-Wandering as Spontaneous Thought: A Dynamic Framework. *Nature Reviews Neuroscience, 17*(11), 718.

Conway, M. A., and Pleydell-Pearce, C. W. (2000). The Construction of Autobiographical Memories in the Self-Memory System. *Psychological Review, 107*(2), 261.

Cui, X., Jeter, C. B., Yang, D., Montague, P. R., and Eagleman, D. M. (2007). Vividness of Mental Imagery: Individual Variability Can Be Measured Objectively. *Vision Research, 47*(4), 474–478.

D'Argembeau, A. (2013). On the Role of the Ventromedial Prefrontal Cortex in Self-Processing: The Valuation Hypothesis. *Frontiers in Human Neuroscience*, 7, 372.

D'Argembeau, A., Cassol, H., Phillips, C., et al. (2013). Brains Creating Stories of Selves: The Neural Basis of Autobiographical Reasoning. *Social Cognitive and Affective Neuroscience*, 9(5), 646–652.

D'Argembeau, A., Lardi, C., and van der Linden, M. (2012). Self-Defining Future Projections: Exploring the Identity Function of Thinking about the Future. *Memory*, 20(2), 110–120.

D'Argembeau, A., and van der Linden, M. (2006). Individual Differences in the Phenomenology of Mental Time Travel: The Effect of Vivid Visual Imagery and Emotion Regulation Strategies. *Consciousness and Cognition*, 15(2), 342–350.

Delamillieure, P., Doucet, G., Mazoyer, B., et al. (2010). The Resting State Questionnaire: An Introspective Questionnaire for Evaluation of Inner Experience during the Conscious Resting State. *Brain Research Bulletin*, 81(6), 565–573.

Denny, B. T., Kober, H., Wager, T. D., and Ochsner, K. N. (2012). A Meta-Analysis of Functional Neuroimaging Studies of Self- and Other Judgments Reveals a Spatial Gradient for Mentalizing in Medial Prefrontal Cortex. *Journal of Cognitive Neuroscience*, 24(8), 1742–1752.

Ellamil, M., Dobson, C., Beeman, M., and Christoff, K. (2012). Evaluative and Generative Modes of Thought during the Creative Process. *Neuroimage*, 59(2), 1783–1794.

Ernst, A., and D'Argembeau, A. (2017). Make it Real: Belief in Occurrence within Episodic Future Thought. *Memory and Cognition*, 45(6), 1045–1061.

Ferstl, E. C., and von Cramon, D. Y. (2002). What Does the Frontomedian Cortex Contribute to Language Processing: Coherence or Theory of Mind? *Neuroimage*, 17(3), 1599–1612.

Fox, K. C., Nijeboer, S., Solomonova, E., Domhoff, G. W., and Christoff, K. (2013). Dreaming as Mind Wandering: Evidence from Functional Neuroimaging and First-Person Content Reports. *Frontiers in Human Neuroscience*, 7, 412.

Fox, K. C., Spreng, R. N., Ellamil, M., Andrews-Hanna, J. R., and Christoff, K. (2015). The Wandering Brain: Meta-Analysis of Functional Neuroimaging Studies of Mind-Wandering and Related Spontaneous Thought Processes. *Neuroimage*, 111, 611–621.

Frith, C. D., and Frith, U. (2006). The Neural Basis of Mentalizing. *Neuron*, 50(4), 531–534.

Grandin, T. (2006). *Thinking in Pictures: And Other Reports from my Life with Autism*. London, UK: Vintage.

Grilli, M. D., and Ryan, L. (Forthcoming). Autobiographical Memory and the Self-Concept. In R. Lane, L. Ryan, and L. Nadel (eds.), *The Neuroscience of Enduring Change: The Neural Basis of Talk Therapies*. New York, NY: Oxford University Press.

Hare, B. (2017). Survival of the Friendliest: Homo Sapiens Evolved via Selection for Prosociality. *Annual Review of Psychology*, 68, 155–186.

Hassabis, D., Kumaran, D., and Maguire, E.A. (2007). Using Imagination to Understand the Neural Basis of Episodic Memory. *Journal of Neuroscience*, 27(52), 14365–14374.

Hassabis, D., Kumaran, D., Vann, S. D., and Maguire, E. A. (2007). Patients with Hippocampal Amnesia Cannot Imagine New Experiences. *Proceedings of the National Academy of Sciences*, 104(5), 1726–1731.

Hassabis, D., and Maguire, E. A. (2007). Deconstructing Episodic Memory with Construction. *Trends in Cognitive Sciences*, 11, 299–306.

Holt-Lunstad, J., Smith, T. B., and Layton, J. B. (2010). Social Relationships and Mortality Risk: A Meta-Analytic Review. *PloS Medicine*, 7(7), e1000316.

Huth, A. G., de Heer, W. A., Griffiths, T. L., Theunissen, F. E., and Gallant, J. L. (2016). Natural Speech Reveals the Semantic Maps that Tile Human Cerebral Cortex. *Nature, 532*(7600), 453.

Irish, M., and Piolino, P. (2016). Impaired Capacity for Prospection in the Dementias – Theoretical and Clinical Implications. *British Journal of Clinical Psychology, 55*(1), 49–68.

Keogh, R., and Pearson, J. (2018). The Blind Mind: No Sensory Visual Imagery in Aphantasia. *Cortex, 105*, 53–60.

Kim, H. (2010). Dissociating the Roles of the Default-Mode, Dorsal and Ventral Networks in Episodic Memory Retrieval. *Neuroimage, 50*(4), 1648–1657.

Klinger, E., (2009). Daydreaming and Fantasizing: Thought Flow and Motivation. In K. D. Markman, W. M. P. Klein, and J. A. Suhr (eds.), *Handbook of Imagination and Mental Simulation*. New York, NY: Psychology Press, 225–240.

Klinger, E., and Cox, W. M. (1987). Dimensions of Thought Flow in Everyday Life. *Imagination, Cognition and Personality, 7*(2), 105–128.

Konishi, M., McLaren, D. G., Engen, H., and Smallwood, J. (2015). Shaped by the Past: The Default Network Supports Cognition that is Independent of Immediate Perceptual Input. *PloS one, 10*(6), e0132209.

Krienen, F. M., Tu, P. C., and Buckner, R. L. (2010). Clan Mentality: Evidence That the Medial Prefrontal Cortex Responds to Close Others. *Journal of Neuroscience, 30* (41), 13906–13915.

Lardi, C., D'Argembeau, A., Chanal, J., Ghisletta, P., and van der Linden, M. (2010). Further Characterisation of Self-Defining Memories in Young Adults: A Study of a Swiss Sample. *Memory, 18*(3), 293–309.

Lavenex, P., and Amaral, D. G. (2000). Hippocampal-Neocortical Interaction: A Hierarchy of Associativity. *Hippocampus, 10*(4), 420–430.

Leary, M. R., Tipsord, J. M., and Tate, E. B. (2008). Allo-Inclusive Identity: Incorporating the Social and Natural Worlds into One's Sense of Self. In H. A. Wayment and J. J. Bauer (eds.), *Decade of Behavior Transcending Self-interest: Psychological Explorations of the Quiet Ego*. Washington, DC: American Psychological Association, 137–147.

Lieberman, M. D. (2007). Social Cognitive Neuroscience: A Review of Core Processes. *Annual Review of Psychology, 58*, 259–289.

Mar, R. A. (2011). The Neural Bases of Social Cognition and Story Comprehension. *Annual Review of Psychology, 62*, 103–134.

Mar, R. A., Mason, M. F., and Litvack, A. (2012). How Daydreaming Relates to Life Satisfaction, Loneliness, and Social Support: The Importance of Gender and Daydream Content. *Consciousness and Cognition, 21*(1), 401–407.

Milligan, K., Astington, J. W., and Dack, L. A. (2007). Language and Theory of Mind: Meta-Analysis of the Relation between Language Ability and False-Belief Understanding. *Child Development, 78*(2), 622–646.

Mills, C., Raffaelli, Q., Irving, Z. C., Stan, D., and Christoff, K. (2018). Is an Off-Task Mind a Freely-Moving Mind? Examining the Relationship between Different Dimensions of Thought. *Consciousness and Cognition, 58*, 20–33.

Mooneyham, B. W., and Schooler, J. W. (2013). The Costs and Benefits of Mind-Wandering: A Review. *Canadian Journal of Experimental Psychology/Revue canadienne de psychologie expérimentale, 67*(1), 11.

Moran, J. M., Heatherton, T. F., and Kelley, W. M. (2009). Modulation of Cortical Midline Structures by Implicit and Explicit Self-Relevance Evaluation. *Social Neuroscience, 4*(3), 197–211.

Mullally, S. L., and Maguire, E. A. (2014). Memory, Imagination, and Predicting the Future: A Common Brain Mechanism? *The Neuroscientist*, *20*(3), 220–234.

Paivio, A. (1986). *Mental Representations: A Dual Coding Approach*. New York, NY: Oxford University Press.

Parikh, N., Ruzic, L., Stewart, G. W., Spreng, R. N., and De Brigard, F. (2018). What if? Neural Activity Underlying Semantic and Episodic Counterfactual Thinking. *Neuroimage*, *178*, 332–345.

Pfeiffer, B. E. (2020). The Content of Hippocampal "Replay". *Hippocampus*, *30*(1), 6–18.

Prebble, S. C., Addis, D. R., and Tippett, L. J. (2013). Autobiographical Memory and Sense of Self. *Psychological Bulletin*, *139*(4), 815.

Raffaelli, Q., Mills, C., and Christoff, K. (2017). The Knowns and Unknowns of Boredom: A Review of the Literature. *Experimental Brain Research*, *236*(9), 2451–2462.

Rim, S., Amit, E., Fujita, K., et al. (2015). How Words Transcend and Pictures Immerse: On the Association between Medium and Level of Construal. *Social Psychological and Personality Science*, *6*(2), 123–130.

Ross, B. (2016). Imagine a Dog. Got it? I Don't. Here's What it's Like to be Unable to Visualize Anything. *Vox*. May 19. www.vox.com/2016/5/19/11683274/aphantasia.

Ruby, F. J. M., Smallwood, J., Engen, H., and Singer, T. (2013). How Self-Generated Thought Shapes Mood – The Relation between Mind-Wandering and Mood Depends on the Socio-Temporal Content of Thoughts. *PloS ONE*, *8*, e77554.

Saxe, R. (2009). The Happiness of the Fish: Evidence for a Common Theory of One's Own and Others' Actions. In K. D. Markman, W. M. Klein, and J. A. Suhr, (eds.), *Handbook of Imagination and Mental Simulation*. New York, NY: Psychology Press, 257–266.

Schacter, D. L., and Addis, D. R. (2007). The Cognitive Neuroscience of Constructive Memory: Remembering the Past and Imagining the Future. *Philosophical Transactions of the Royal Society B: Biological Sciences*, *362*(1481), 773–786.

Schacter D. L., Addis D. R., and Buckner R. L. (2007). Remembering the Past to Imagine the Future: The Prospective Brain. *Nature Reviews Neuroscience*, *8*(9), 657.

Schacter, D. L., Addis, D. R., Hassabis, D., et al. (2012). The Future of Memory: Remembering, Imagining, and the Brain. *Neuron*, *76*(4), 677–694.

Seligman, M. E., Railton, P., Baumeister, R. F., and Sripada, C. (2016). *Homo Prospectus*. Oxford, UK: Oxford University Press.

Seyfarth, R. M., and Cheney, D. L. (2014). The Evolution of Language from Social Cognition. *Current Opinion in Neurobiology*, *28*, 5–9.

Sheldon, S., Farb, N., Palombo, D. J., and Levine, B. (2016). Intrinsic Medial Temporal Lobe Connectivity Relates to Individual Differences in Episodic Autobiographical Remembering. *Cortex*, *74*, 206–216.

Smallwood, J., and Andrews-Hanna, J. (2013). Not All Minds That Wander Are Lost: The Importance of a Balanced Perspective on the Mind-Wandering State. *Frontiers in Psychology*, *4*, 441.

Smallwood, J., and Schooler, J. W. (2015). The Science of Mind Wandering: Empirically Navigating the Stream of Consciousness. *Annual Review of Psychology*, *66*, 487–518.

Spreng, R. N., and Andrews-Hanna, J. R. (2015). The Default Network and Social Cognition. *Brain Mapping: An Encyclopedic Reference*, *1316*, 165–169.

Spreng, R. N., DuPre, E., Selarka, D., et al. (2014). Goal-Congruent Default Network Activity Facilitates Cognitive Control. *Journal of Neuroscience*, *34*, 14108–14114.

Spreng, R. N., Gerlach, K. D., Turner, G. R., and Schacter, D. L. (2015). Autobiographical Planning and the Brain: Activation and its Modulation by Qualitative Features. *Journal of Cognitive Neuroscience, 27*(11), 2147–2157.

Spreng, R. N., Mar, R. A., and Kim, A. S. (2009). The Common Neural Basis of Autobiographical Memory, Prospection, Navigation, Theory of Mind, and the Default Mode: A Quantitative Meta-Analysis. *Journal of Cognitive Neuroscience, 21*(3), 489–510.

Spreng, R. N., Stevens, W. D., Chamberlain, J. P., Gilmore, A. W., and Schacter, D. L. (2010). Default Network Activity, Coupled with the Frontoparietal Control Network, Supports Goal-Directed Cognition. *NeuroImage, 53*, 303–317.

Spunt, R. P., Kemmerer, D., and Adolphs, R. (2015). The Neural Basis of Conceptualizing the Same Action at Different Levels of Abstraction. *Social Cognitive and Affective Neuroscience, 11*(7), 1141–1151.

Spunt, R. P., Meyer, M. L., and Lieberman, M. D. (2015). The Default Mode of Human Brain Function Primes the Intentional Stance. *Journal of Cognitive Neuroscience, 27*(6), 1116–1124.

Sripada, C. S. (2018). An Exploration/Exploitation Trade-off Between Mind-Wandering and Goal-Directed Thinking. In K. C. Fox and K. Christoff (eds.), *The Oxford Handbook of Spontaneous Thought: Mind-Wandering, Creativity, and Dreaming.* Oxford, UK: Oxford University Press, 23–34.

Stawarczyk, D., and D'Argembeau, A. (2015). Neural Correlates of Personal Goal Processing during Episodic Future Thinking and Mind-Wandering: An ALE Meta-Analysis. *Human Brain Mapping, 36*(8), 2928–2947.

Stawarczyk, D., Cassol, H., and D'Argembeau, A. (2013). Phenomenology of Future-Oriented Mind-Wandering Episodes. *Frontiers in Psychology, 4*, 425.

Stawarczyk, D., Majerus, S., Maj, M., van der Linden, M., and D'Argembeau, A. (2011). Mind-Wandering: Phenomenology and Function as Assessed with a Novel Experience Sampling Method. *Acta Psychologica, 136*(3), 370–381.

Suddendorf, T., and Corballis, M. C. (2007). The Evolution of Foresight: What Is Mental Time Travel, and Is It Unique to Humans? *Behavioral and Brain Sciences, 30*(3), 299–313.

Tamir, D. I., Bricker, A. B., Dodell-Feder, D., and Mitchell, J. P. (2015). Reading Fiction and Reading Minds: The Role of Simulation in the Default Network. *Social Cognitive and Affective Neuroscience, 11*(2), 215–224.

Trope, Y., and Liberman, N. (2010). Construal-Level Theory of Psychological Distance. *Psychological Review, 117*(2), 440.

Tulving, E. (1985). Memory and Consciousness. *Canadian Psychology/Psychologie canadienne, 26*(1), 1.

van Veluw, S. J., and Chance, S. A. (2014). Differentiating between Self and Others: An ALE Meta-Analysis of fMRI Studies of Self-Recognition and Theory of Mind. *Brain Imaging and Behavior, 8*(1), 24–38.

von Helmholtz, H. (1925). *Treatise on Physiological Optics.* Translated from the 3rd German edition and edited by J. Southall. Volume 3: The Perceptions of Vision. Ithaca, NY: Secretary, Optical Society of America, Rockefeller Hall.

Wang, H. T., Poerio, G., Murphy, C., et al. (2018). Dimensions of Experience: Exploring the Heterogeneity of the Wandering Mind. *Psychological Science, 29*(1), 56–71.

Yeo, B. T. T., Krienen, F. M., Sepulcre, J., et al. (2011). The Organization of the Human Cerebral Cortex Estimated by Intrinsic Functional Connectivity. *Journal of Neurophysiology, 106*(3), 1125–1165.

Zaki, J., and Ochsner, K. N. (2012). The Neuroscience of Empathy: Progress, Pitfalls and Promise. *Nature Neuroscience, 15*(5), 675.

22 Imagination and Self-Referential Thinking

Arnaud D'Argembeau

Imagination is a fundamental aspect of human mental life. It enables us to transcend present circumstances, to think beyond perception and memory, and to construct alternative versions of reality. The self is often a central character in our imagined worlds: When musing about the future, for example, we think about the person we could become and envision events that might happen in our personal life. The aim of this chapter is to examine how these imagined aspects of the self are constructed and organized in the human mind, with a particular focus on the future-oriented dimension of self-referential thinking.[1] In brief, research suggests that imagined future selves rely on multiple representational systems that are used to imagine personal attributes, goals, and life events with more or less specificity.

To provide the necessary background for examining imagined aspects of the self, I first give an outline of the general structure of self-knowledge. With this background in place, a cognitive architecture of imagined selves is proposed and the role of its constituent knowledge structures is discussed in relation to personal goals, self-conceptions, and the imagination of future events.

Structure of Self-Knowledge

Self-knowledge can be broadly defined as all that we know or believe about ourselves and our life, which includes our personal characteristics (e.g. our physical attributes, personality traits, goals, abilities, values, likes and dislikes), memories of our past experiences, and knowledge of facts about our life (Conway, 2005; Klein and Gangi, 2010; Markus and Wurf, 1987; McAdams, 2013; Renoult et al., 2012). This set of mental representations about the self provides the foundation for the conception of ourselves as distinct entities with unique personal histories (Prebble, Addis, and Tippett, 2013).

---

1 While the present chapter focuses on imagined future selves, it should be noted that imagination is also frequently used to consider alternative versions of one's personal past (i.e. counterfactual thinking; Roese, 1997). Recent research has revealed important similarities in the cognitive and neural mechanisms of future-oriented and counterfactual thoughts (e.g. De Brigard et al., 2016; van Hoeck et al., 2013). However, differences between these two forms of thoughts have also been observed, notably because they are differentially constrained by reality (i.e. counterfactual thoughts are constrained by the context of past episodes, whereas future events are more open and controllable; Ferrante et al., 2013). A detailed account of these similarities and differences is beyond the scope of this chapter (but see Schacter et al., 2015).

Over the past fifty years, extensive research in psychology, and more recently in neuroscience, has been conducted with the aim of characterizing the representational systems that support self-knowledge (Conway and Pleydell-Pearce, 2000; Klein and Lax, 2010; Markus and Wurf, 1987; Wagner, Haxby, and Heatherton, 2012). This research has revealed that self-representations rely on multiple knowledge structures. A particularly influential model – the self-memory system (SMS) – distinguishes three main knowledge structures that vary in their level of abstraction (Conway, 2005; Conway, Singer, and Tagini, 2004). The first knowledge structure – referred to as the conceptual self – includes general representations of one's personal characteristics, such as one's traits, abilities, and preferences (Markus, 1977). These are abstract, summary representations of self-attributes that have been constructed from multiple experiences, behaviors, and feedback from others. The second knowledge structure – referred to as the autobiographical knowledge base – includes information about the broad periods (e.g. "when I was in elementary school") and general events (e.g. "our vacation in Italy last summer") of one's life. It provides summary representations of these autobiographical periods, including information about associated persons, places, objects, and activities (Thomsen, 2015). Memories for specific, unique events of one's life are represented in a third representational structure: the episodic memory system (Conway, 2009). This system retains records of specific happenings (e.g. the day I broke my leg when playing football), including the sensory-perceptual, contextual, cognitive, and emotional details of past experiences – what we perceived, felt, and thought during a particular event. These episodic details allow us to mentally re-experience events of our personal past.

According to the SMS, autobiographical knowledge and episodic memories are organized in partonomic hierarchies, in which specific events are part of general events, which in turn are part of lifetime periods (Conway and Pleydell-Pearce, 2000). A specific autobiographical memory is conceived of as a pattern of activation over these representational structures and, therefore, typically contains knowledge at different levels of specificity: Episodic details are contextualized within higher-order autobiographical knowledge, which locates specific events in the individual's life story (Conway, 2005). Thus, although represented separately, the SMS knowledge domains closely interact with each other.

Different lines of research support this organization of self-knowledge. First, there is evidence that knowledge of personal attributes – conceived as part of the conceptual self – is represented independently of memories for specific past experiences (for review, see Klein and Lax, 2010). For example, several studies have shown that to judge whether a given trait (e.g. stubbornness) is self-descriptive, people do not need to recall specific behavioral incidents in which they manifested that trait (e.g. Klein and Loftus, 1993). Furthermore, when asked to reflect on their personal characteristics (e.g. "what makes you say that you are a shy person?"), people only rarely rely on specific memories and instead describe personal semantic contents (Grilli, 2017). Other studies have shown that patients suffering episodic amnesia possess coherent and stable knowledge of their personal attributes despite being unable to recall the particular experiences from which that knowledge was derived (e.g. Klein, Loftus, and Kihlstrom, 1996; Rathbone, Moulin, and Conway, 2009).

Together, these findings indicate that knowledge of self-attributes does not require the retrieval of specific episodes from one's past and instead relies on abstract, semantic representations.

There is also evidence that general autobiographical knowledge and episodic memories are represented separately. This is for example illustrated in studies that investigated autobiographical memory retrieval processes (Conway and Pleydell-Pearce, 2000). In a typical experiment, participants are asked to remember specific events (i.e. unique events that occurred at a particular time and place) in response to cue words. To investigate the types of representations that are activated during the retrieval process, Haque and Conway (2001) included a series of thought probes: After different delays, participants were interrupted and asked what they just had in mind. It was found that in the initial stage of retrieval, participants most frequently reported general autobiographical knowledge (a general event or lifetime period), whereas specific events were typically reported later in the retrieval process. This suggests that autobiographical memory retrieval is a protracted process in which general knowledge about one's past (general events and lifetime periods) is used to access specific memories. For example, when attempting to retrieve a specific event in response to the cue "beach," someone might first recall that she used to go to the beach on weekends with her grandparents when she was a child (autobiographical knowledge) and then might remember a specific episode that happened during one of these weekends: She spent hours making a sand castle that was then destroyed in a few seconds when the tide came in. Importantly, however, autobiographical knowledge can be accessed without remembering a specific event[2] and, conversely, specific events are sometimes recalled without accessing autobiographical knowledge first (Uzer, Lee, and Brown, 2012), suggesting that they are represented independently in memory.

Neuroimaging studies provide further support for the distinction between the three kinds of self-knowledge. Indeed, different forms of self-representations have partly distinct neural substrates. Trait self-judgments (involving the conceptual self) are associated with activations in the medial prefrontal cortex, as well as regions supporting semantic processing such as the lateral temporal cortex (Araujo, Kaplan, and Damasio, 2013; Murray, Schaer, and Debbane, 2012; van der Meer et al., 2010). On the other hand, the retrieval of specific memories activates a more extended brain network that includes the medial prefrontal cortex, medial and lateral temporal areas, the posterior cingulate/retrosplenial cortex, and inferior parietal lobes (Cabeza and St Jacques, 2007; Kim, 2012; Spreng, Mar, and Kim, 2009; Svoboda, McKinnon, and Levine, 2006). Of particular interest, a meta-analysis compared the neural correlates of representations of personal characteristics, knowledge of personal facts, and memories for specific events (Martinelli, Sperduti, and Piolino, 2013). The results showed that each type of self-knowledge was associated with unique brain activations, with a shift from posterior to anterior regions with

---

2 On some retrieval attempts autobiographical knowledge is accessed but the retrieval process is aborted prematurely, resulting in a failure to retrieve a specific event. This is frequently observed in patients with emotional disorders (e.g. depression) who tend to report "overgeneral memories" when attempting to retrieve specific events (Williams et al., 2007).

increasing abstraction of representations. The medial prefrontal cortex was the only brain region that was consistently activated when thinking about one's traits, retrieving specific experiences from one's past, and accessing knowledge of facts about one's life, with both common and distinct activations across these three kinds of self-representations. While these results indicate that different types of self-knowledge are dissociable, it should be noted that the brain regions that have been associated with different forms of self-representations are highly interconnected and form a coherent network (which largely corresponds to the "default network"; Buckner, Andrews-Hanna, and Schacter, 2008): This supports the view that the SMS knowledge domains closely interact with each other (Conway, 2005).

Self-Knowledge and Imagined Selves

Self-knowledge not only includes representations of manifest (present or past) traits and experiences, but also imagined selves. Indeed, an important part of self-referential thinking involves the imagination of what our personal future might be like. Markus and Nurius (1986) introduced the concept of *possible selves* to refer to representations of what we might become, would like to become, and are afraid of becoming in the future. Possible selves are closely related to personal goals and function as incentives for behavior (i.e. they are selves to be approached or avoided). For example, one's sense of self in a desired end-state (e.g. me with a happy family) organizes and energizes actions in the pursuit of this state.

Possible selves vary in their scope and degree of abstraction: Some involve general representations of the self in the future (e.g. future traits, social roles, and occupations), while others include details that specify how and when an imagined future state could be attained (Oyserman and James, 2009; Packard and Conway, 2006). The latter kind of possible selves involves the mental simulation of specific events – referred to as episodic future thinking (see below) – and may provide an experiential understanding of what it would be like to be in imagined future states.

The cognitive architecture of the SMS has recently been extended to account for these future-oriented aspects of self-referential thinking (Conway, Justice, and D'Argembeau, 2019). According to this model, imagined future selves are supported by three main representational systems (Figure 22.1). Abstract representations of future selves are part of the conceptual self, along with representations of present and past selves. This portion of the conceptual self includes semantic knowledge about personal goals and anticipated self-attributes, such as one's future traits (e.g. being self-assured), physical features (e.g. being in good shape), general abilities (e.g. speak well publicly), occupations (e.g. owner of a business), social roles (e.g. being a parent), and life styles (e.g. travel widely).

The goals and self-images that constitute the conceptual self are represented independently from knowledge structures that support the formation of future event representations: the autobiographical knowledge base and episodic memory system. People possess general representations of what their future life might be like, along with general knowledge about their personal past. This future-oriented

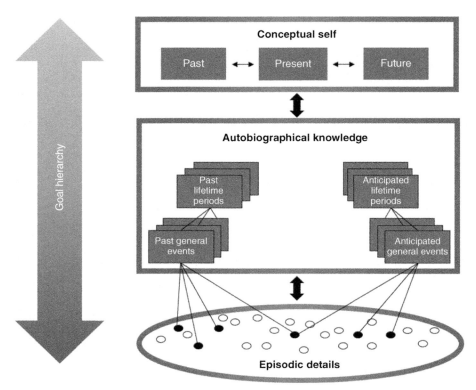

Figure 22.1 *Knowledge structures supporting self-representations according to the self-memory system (SMS).*

autobiographical knowledge is organized in a series of anticipated life periods (e.g. "when I'll have moved to X," "when I'll own my own business") that include knowledge about the people, places, activities, and objects associated with each period (Thomsen, 2015; Thomsen, Steiner, and Pillemer, 2016), and also contains representations of general events that one anticipates as occurring in the future, including summary representations of repeated events (e.g. "taking children to school") and events extended in time (e.g. "going on vacation in France next summer") (Anderson and Dewhurst, 2009; D'Argembeau, Renaud, and van der Linden, 2011). As with autobiographical knowledge of the past, future-oriented autobiographical knowledge is organized in partonomic hierarchies, with representations of general events being part of anticipated lifetime periods. These future periods and events are partly derived from cultural life scripts (i.e. shared knowledge about events that represent a prototypical life course in a given culture, such as graduation, marriage, and having children; Berntsen and Bohn, 2010), but also include more personalized representations (i.e. based on personal experiences, interests, and goals).

Finally, this extended version of the SMS conceives the episodic memory system as containing a pool of details that can be used not only to mentally reconstruct past events, but also to imagine specific events that might happen in the future (Schacter and Addis, 2007; Suddendorf and Corballis, 2007). These episodic details may consist of components of prior experience (i.e. sensory-perceptual-conceptual-affective details; Conway, 2009) that serve as the constitutive elements (e.g. places, objects, persons, actions, and so on) of remembered and imagined events. Most of these details derive from first-hand personal experiences but some may come from other sources of information, such as experiences shared by others or information gleaned from the media (Anderson, 2012). In addition, the construction of specific event representations also draws on semantic knowledge (e.g. event schemas) that is used to create coherent event models, given what one knows about the world and the typical unfolding of events (Irish and Piguet, 2013; Radvansky and Zacks, 2011; note that this type of semantic knowledge is not shown on Figure 22.1).

The idea that remembering and future thinking draw on the same pool of episodic details implies that the exact same element (e.g. a given place) can be used to reconstruct the memory of a past event and to generate the representation of a possible future event; it can even be used to construct a mental scene that is not located in time (Hassabis et al., 2007). On this view, episodic elements are "atemporal" in themselves and an event representation may only acquire a temporal dimension when it is linked to autobiographical knowledge structures that locate remembered or imagined events in the individual's life story. Supporting this view, there is growing evidence that the imagination of events that might happen in one's personal future not only involves episodic simulations but also higher-order autobiographical knowledge, which contextualizes imagined events in the individual's personal life. This evidence is reviewed in the next section.

Episodic Future Thinking in a Personal Context

The ability to imagine specific events and scenarios that might happen in one's personal future – referred to as *episodic future thinking* (Atance and O'Neill, 2001) – has attracted much attention in the past few years (Schacter, Benoit, and Szpunar, 2017; Suddendorf and Corballis, 2007; Szpunar, 2010). Episodic future thinking allows us to mentally explore what a future event might be like – a kind of "pre-experience" of our personal future (D'Argembeau and van der Linden, 2004, 2006). When thinking about a specific event that might happen next weekend, for example, we can easily imagine the place where we would be and picture ourselves moving around that place, grabbing objects, interacting with people, and even feel emotions. Such a "preview" of possible future states may then be used to guide decisions and actions (Boyer, 2008; O'Donnell, Oluyomi Daniel, and Epstein, 2017; Peters and Buchel, 2010; Taylor et al., 1998).

Substantial evidence indicates that episodic future thinking involves the mental simulation of events based on the retrieval and integration of relevant informational components in long-term memory (e.g. representations of locations, objects, people, actions, and emotions; Schacter, Benoit, and Szpunar, 2017). The pieces of information that are used to compose future event representations likely come from various sources, with some of them being extracted from single past experiences stored in episodic memory (Schacter and Addis, 2007; Suddendorf and Corballis, 2007), whereas others are based on semantic knowledge and event schemas that have been formed over multiple past experiences (Anderson, 2012; Klein, 2013; Szpunar, 2010). The role of episodic and semantic memory in episodic future thinking is indeed supported by extensive empirical data (for review, see Irish and Piguet, 2013; Schacter et al., 2012). For example, there is evidence that patients with episodic or semantic memory deficits present with difficulties in imagining specific events that might happen in their personal future (Addis et al., 2009; D'Argembeau, Raffard, and van der Linden, 2008; Irish et al., 2012; Klein, Loftus, and Kihlstrom, 2002; Tulving, 1985) and neuroimaging studies in healthy individuals have shown that episodic future thinking activates brain areas that have been traditionally associated with episodic and semantic memory (for meta-analyses, see Benoit and Schacter, 2015; Stawarczyk and D'Argembeau, 2015).

Other recent studies have shown that besides the mental simulation of specific events, episodic future thinking relies on higher-order self-knowledge (i.e. the conceptual self and autobiographical knowledge), which serves to relate imagined events to the individual's personal life. Autobiographical knowledge and self-images may indeed contribute to multiple facets of episodic future thinking. First, it has been shown that autobiographical knowledge plays a role in the construction of episodic future thoughts: The imagination of future events is not random and disorganized but is guided and constrained by personal goals, beliefs, and expectations for the future. Supporting this idea, D'Argembeau and Mathy (2011) found that when attempting to imagine specific events that might happen in their personal future, people frequently access abstract representations of themselves and their life (e.g. personal characteristics and/or general events) before producing a specific event (but see Jeunehomme and D'Argembeau, 2016, for evidence that episodic future thoughts can also be accessed more directly, especially when they refer to future events that have already been thought about on a previous occasion). This suggests that episodic future thinking is supported by autobiographical knowledge, which may provide a framework for imagining events that are coherent with one's self and life story.

Further evidence for the contribution of autobiographical knowledge in episodic future thinking has come from the finding that many imagined events are not represented in isolation but are part of higher-order themes and sequences. To investigate the organizational structure of episodic future thought, D'Argembeau and Demblon (2012) used an event-cueing paradigm in which participants imagined a series of future events and each of these events (which were called the cueing events) was then used to cue the imagination of another related future event (called the cued event). For example, when asked to imagine a specific future event in response to the cue "vacation" a person might imagine visiting the tower of Pisa; then, when asked to imagine another future event in relation to the first imagined event, this person might imagine eating a spaghetti frutti di mare on the seaside. When examining the nature of the relations that characterized imagined events, D'Argembeau and Demblon found that the cueing and cued events were frequently embedded in an event cluster, meaning that they were causally and/or thematically related to each other (rather than being related simply because they share surface features, such as the place or persons involved). In the above example, the two imagined events are related to each other because they are part of the general event "a vacation planned in Italy next summer," which organizes a sequence of specific events that might happen during this vacation. This organization of imagined events in clusters has also been observed when participants freely generate episodic future thoughts (i.e. without the explicit instruction to produce related events; Demblon and D'Argembeau, 2014). These findings suggest that future-oriented autobiographical knowledge links and organizes imagined events in broader themes and causal sequences.

Autobiographical knowledge also contributes to the temporal location of imagined events. Research on memory for the times of past events has shown that temporal information often is not an intrinsic property of memories but instead is inferred or reconstructed using various processes (Friedman, 1993). Notably, people frequently use general knowledge about personal life periods (e.g. the final part of a semester, a vacation in Europe) to determine when past events occurred (Thompson, Skowronski, and Betz, 1993). In a recent study, Ben Malek, Berna, and D'Argembeau (2017) compared the strategies used to locate past and future events in time. Participants were asked to generate a series of past and future events and, for each event, they described everything that came to their minds while attempting to determine when this event occurred or will likely occur. It was found that participants most frequently used references to lifetime periods and/or factual knowledge (about the self, others, and the world) to estimate the temporal location of both past and future events. Knowledge about anticipated life periods (e.g. my trip in France next summer) and circumstances (e.g. I know I'll be busy next month) may help people to form a personal timeline that can be used to locate imagined events in future times.

Role of Personal Goals in Future-Oriented Thought

The studies reviewed in the previous section indicate that autobiographical knowledge plays a key role in the construction and organization of prospective thought. Additional evidence suggests that future-oriented representations are structured around personal goals. Generally speaking, goals are cognitive representations of desired states or outcomes (Austin and Vancouver, 1996), and personal goals may be defined as personally salient objectives that people pursue in their lives (Emmons, 1986; Klinger, 2013; Little, 1983). Goal-related knowledge is represented at different levels of specificity, from very abstract and general aspirations (e.g. being a successful person) to concrete and specific objectives (e.g. striving to arrive at a particular meeting on time) (Austin and Vancouver, 1996). These different goal representations are organized in a hierarchy – in which higher-order goals (e.g. becoming an artist) determine the content of lower-order goals (e.g. taking painting lessons) – that may correspond to the knowledge structures of the SMS (Figure 22.1). Within this framework, episodic future thinking allows the detailed representation of specific events, plans, and outcomes that are related to higher-order personal goals, which are represented at the level of the autobiographical knowledge base and conceptual self. Thus, an important function of episodic future thinking may be to provide a detailed (quasi-experiential) representation or simulation of what it would be like to be in a desired end-state, and to mentally try out various steps and envisage potential obstacles in achieving this state. According to this view, personal goals drive and constrain future event representations, which in turn motivate and guide goal pursuit.

A growing number of studies support this idea that personal goals structure episodic future thinking (D'Argembeau, 2016). For example, there is evidence that personal goals facilitate the construction of episodic future thoughts (D'Argembeau and Mathy, 2011) and shape the content of imagined events (Christian et al., 2013; Cole and Berntsen, 2016; Stawarczyk, Cassol, and D'Argembeau, 2013). The phenomenology of imagined events is also sensitive to goal-related knowledge. Most notably, autonoetic experience (i.e. the subjective sense of "pre-experiencing" imagined events), which is considered as the hallmark of episodic future thinking (Klein, 2016; Suddendorf and Corballis, 2007; Tulving, 2005), is modulated by the goal-relevance of imagined events. For example, D'Argembeau and van der Linden (2012) found that variations in the intensity of autonoetic experience across a set of imagined events were not only predicted by the vividness of mental representations but also by their importance for personal goals – participants reported a higher sense of pre-experiencing for future events that were more important for their goals. Furthermore, the experimental manipulation of goal-relevance modulates the intensity of autonoetic experience in a similar way (Lehner and D'Argembeau, 2016). Another recent study showed that the belief that imagined events will actually materialize in the future increases with the importance of events for personal goals (Ernst and D'Argembeau, 2017). Taken together, these findings suggest that the subjective sense that an imagined event belongs to our personal future (rather than being a mere fantasy) depends on the extent to which it is placed in an autobiographical context. Future events that are in line with our goals, expectations, and knowledge about ourselves and our life feel more "real." This phenomenological experience might in turn play important roles in guiding and motivating actions to bring about desired future states.

The role of personal goals in episodic future thinking is also highlighted by studies that have examined the neural correlates of prospection. Neuroimaging studies have shown that the imagination of future events relies on a distributed brain network (comprising cortical midline structures, medial and lateral temporal regions, inferior parietal cortices, and parts of the lateral prefrontal cortex) that includes multiple systems and processes contributing to episodic future thought (for a meta-analysis, see Benoit and Schacter, 2015). If goal processing is an integral part of episodic future thinking, it should be associated with specific regions within this brain network. Stawarczyk and D'Argembeau (2015) tested this hypothesis by performing meta-analyses of neuroimaging studies of episodic future thinking, on the one hand, and of personal goal processing, on the other hand. A conjunction analysis indicated that the two sets of studies were associated with overlapping activation in several brain regions and most notably in the medial prefrontal cortex. Another study showed that the medial prefrontal cortex and other midline regions were more activated when people were asked to imagine future events that were related to their personal goals, compared to future events that were plausible but unrelated to their goals (D'Argembeau et al., 2010). These findings suggest that the medial prefrontal cortex may contribute to the processing of personal goals when imagining future events.

Although the medial prefrontal cortex is consistently involved in episodic future thinking, and more generally in self-referential thinking, its exact function remains unclear.[3] One possibility is that it plays a role in appraising or representing the subjective value or significance of self-related information (D'Argembeau, 2013; Roy, Shohamy, and Wager, 2012). This account is supported, for example, by the finding that medial prefrontal activity increases linearly with the personal importance of self-referential contents (Andrews-Hanna et al., 2010; D'Argembeau, et al., 2012). Another (not necessarily mutually exclusive but somewhat broader) view is that the medial prefrontal cortex mediates the integration of multiple representational levels during self-referential thought (see Brod, Werkle-Bergner, and Shing, 2013; Gilboa and Marlatte, 2017; van Kesteren et al., 2012, for evidence that the medial prefrontal cortex is involved in the integration of information to pre-existing knowledge structures). For example, when people engage in episodic future thinking, the medial prefrontal cortex may integrate imagined events with higher-order autobiographical knowledge, and may organize specific events in broader themes and causal sequences. Supporting this view, a recent study showed that the processing of event clusters (i.e. events that are part of higher-order themes and sequences) is associated with increased activation in the medial prefrontal cortex and with greater functional connectivity between the medial prefrontal cortex and posterior regions supporting episodic and semantic representations (Demblon, Bahri, and D'Argembeau, 2016).

Grounding the Self in Imagined Events

As detailed above, there is evidence that abstract knowledge of personal characteristics (the conceptual self) is represented separately from knowledge structures that support the (re)construction of past and future events (the autobiographical knowledge base and episodic memory system). Most of the time, however, these knowledge domains interact and constrain each other, such that episodic simulations exemplify, contextualize, and ground abstract self-views. In particular, the future-oriented aspects of the conceptual self may be nourished by the imagination of specific events that incarnate personal traits and social roles. For example, someone who envisions her future self as a mother may nourish this self-image by imagining herself at the maternity hospital, taking the children to school, playing with them in

---

3 The medial prefrontal cortex is a large brain region and it is likely that distinct medial prefrontal subregions support different aspects of self-referential thinking. For example, there is evidence that dorsal, anterior, and ventral medial prefrontal subregions are part of different subsystems within the default network that may support different functions (Andrews-Hanna et al., 2010).

the backyard, and so on. A number of studies have indeed shown that the conceptual self is in part grounded in the imagination of future events.

Rathbone, Conway, and Moulin (2011) investigated the temporal organization of imagined future events in relation to self-images. Participants were instructed to generate three "I will be" statements describing new selves that they might become in the future (e.g. I will be a mother). For each future self-image, participants were then asked to imagine five specific events that are linked to this future self. Finally, participants dated all future events, and estimated when each future self-image might become a stable part of their identity. A similar task was also administered for past events and self-images. The results showed that the temporal distribution of imagined future events clustered around the time of development of future self-images in a way that was highly similar to the clustering of memories around past self-images (see also Chessell et al., 2014). These findings suggest that some imagined events are temporally anchored to future self-images, which may contribute to creating a coherent sense of self in the future.

The role of imagined future events in grounding the self has also been investigated in a series of studies on *self-defining future projections*. Previous research has shown that self-images are supported and illustrated by self-defining memories – a set of vivid and emotionally intense memories that represent the dominant themes and concerns in a person's life (Blagov and Singer, 2004; Singer et al., 2013). D'Argembeau, Lardi, and van der Linden (2012) introduced the construct of self-defining future projections to refer to the future counterpart of self-defining memories: mental representations of highly significant future events that incarnate future self-images. These authors showed that people readily identify significant future events that they frequently think about and that convey core information about the person they wish or expect to become in the future. When thinking about these events, people not only imagine the concrete aspects of the situation, but sometimes also consider the broader meaning of imagined events and their potential implications for the self. This reflective process – referred to as autobiographical reasoning or meaning making – is important because it helps to link discrete events with each other and with more abstract self-views, thereby contributing to the construction of a coherent life story (Habermas and Bluck, 2000).

A recent study suggests that self-defining memories and future thoughts are organized in networks that play important roles in sustaining personal identity (Demblon and D'Argembeau, 2017). Participants were asked to generate a self-defining memory and a self-defining future projection, and then to report all other events (past or future) that spontaneously came to their mind when thinking about these self-defining events. Thus, the two self-defining events were each associated with a network of related events and these were compared to other sets of events that were produced in response to non-self-defining memories and future projections (i.e. past and future events that were marginal for personal identity). For each event network, participants rated the characteristics of each constituent event (e.g. its centrality for identity; the extent to which it served identity motives) and determined the nature of the relations linking events within networks (e.g. causal relations). The results showed that compared to networks of mundane events, networks of self-defining events were more extended (included more events), were more frequently organized in meaningful themes and sequences (i.e. event clusters), and satisfied identity motives (such as the sense of meaning and continuity in one's life) to a greater extent. Furthermore, identity motives were pivotal dimensions that linked events into networks and contributed to their perceived centrality to identity. These findings suggest that personally significant events are organized in coherent networks that include both memories and prospective thoughts, which together capture important aspects of self-understanding.

Finally, another characteristic of self-referential thinking is that most people hold flattering views of themselves and process self-related information in ways that maintain or increase the positivity of their self-concept (Leary, 2007; Sedikides and Gregg, 2008), and this positivity bias is also manifested in the way people imagine their personal future (Taylor and Brown, 1988). For example, positive future events are more easily constructed than negative events (i.e. people are faster in generating positive events; MacLeod and Byrne, 1996; Newby-Clark and Ross, 2003), and mental representations of positive events are subjectively more vivid and are associated with a more intense autonoetic experience (D'Argembeau and van der Linden, 2004; Rasmussen and Berntsen, 2013). Furthermore, prospective thinking in daily life most frequently involves positive events (Barsics, van der Linden, and D'Argembeau, 2016; Berntsen and Jacobsen, 2008; D'Argembeau, Renaud, and van der Linden, 2011). This positivity bias in future-oriented thought may be particularly pronounced when imagining self-defining events (Demblon and D'Argembeau, 2017), and may contribute to sustain the positivity of self-conceptions (D'Argembeau, Lardi, and van der Linden, 2012).

Conclusion

Extensive research over the past fifty years has shed important light on the nature and structure of self-knowledge. While most studies emphasized present and past selves, there is growing evidence that imagined future selves are an integral part of self-representation that play important roles in human behavior. Future-oriented selves rely on multiple knowledge structures that are used to represent personal attributes, goals, and life events at different levels of specificity – from abstract self-views to the mental simulation of specific experiences. These different knowledge structures interact and constrain each other, such that the imagination of specific events is structured by personal goals and autobiographical knowledge and, in turn, imagined events ground and exemplify higher-order self-knowledge.

An important question for future research is to determine how different forms of self-related future thoughts impact decisions, motivation, and ultimately behavior. Research has shown that episodic future thoughts and imagined future selves can promote adaptive decisions and self-regulation (e.g. Bulley, Henry, and Suddendorf, 2016; Oyserman and James, 2009), but when and in which situations different forms of future-oriented thoughts motivate people to take action towards their goals remain to be investigated in detail. Another related question is how different forms of future thought enable one to achieve balance between stability and change in one's sense of self. Future goals and identities involve change, and yet people tend to believe that they would change relatively little in the future (Quoidbach, Gilbert, and Wilson, 2013). The flexible use of different forms of future thoughts may enable one to grow and develop one's potential while at the same time ensuring coherence and stability in one's life.

Acknowledgments

Arnaud D'Argembeau is supported by the Fund for Scientific Research (F. R.S.-FNRS), Belgium.

References

Addis, D. R., Sacchetti, D. C., Ally, B. A., Budson, A. E., and Schacter, D. L. (2009). Episodic Simulation of Future Events Is Impaired in Mild Alzheimer's Disease. *Neuropsychologia, 47*, 2660–2671.

Anderson, R. J. (2012). Imagining Novel Futures: The Roles of Event Plausibility and Familiarity. *Memory, 20*, 443–451.

Anderson, R. J., and Dewhurst, S. A. (2009). Remembering the Past and Imagining the Future: Differences in Event Specificity of Spontaneously Generated Thought. *Memory, 17*, 367–373.

Andrews-Hanna, J. R., Reidler, J. S., Sepulcre, J., Poulin, R., and Buckner, R. L. (2010). Functional-Anatomic Fractionation of the Brain's Default Network. *Neuron, 65*, 550–562.

Araujo, H. F., Kaplan, J., and Damasio, A. (2013). Cortical Midline Structures and Autobiographical-Self Processes: An Activation-Likelihood Estimation Meta-Analysis. *Frontiers in Human Neuroscience, 7*, 548.

Atance, C. M., and O'Neill, D. K. (2001). Episodic Future Thinking. *Trends in Cognitive Sciences, 5*(12), 533–539.

Austin, J. T., and Vancouver, J. B. (1996). Goal Constructs in Psychology: Structure, Process, and Content. *Psychological Bulletin, 120*, 338–375.

Barsics, C., van der Linden, M., and D'Argembeau, A. (2016). Frequency, Characteristics, and Perceived Functions of Emotional Future Thinking in Daily Life. *The Quarterly Journal of Experimental Psychology, 69*, 217–233. Doi/10.1080/ 17470218.2015.1051560.

Ben Malek, H., Berna, F., and D'Argembeau, A. (2017). Reconstructing the Times of Past and Future Personal Events. *Memory, 25*, 1402–1411.

Benoit, R. G., and Schacter, D. L. (2015). Specifying the Core Network Supporting Episodic Simulation and Episodic Memory by Activation Likelihood Estimation. *Neuropsychologia, 75*, 450–457.

Berntsen, D., and Bohn, A. (2010). Remembering and Forecasting: The Relation between Autobiographical Memory and Episodic Future Thinking. *Memory & Cognition, 38*, 265–278.

Berntsen, D., and Jacobsen, A. S. (2008). Involuntary (Spontaneous) Mental Time Travel into the Past and Future. *Consciousnes and Cognition, 17*, 1093–1104.

Blagov, P. S., and Singer, J. A. (2004). Four Dimensions of Self-Defining Memories (Specificity, Meaning, Content, and Affect) and Their Relationships to Self-Restraint, Distress, and Repressive Defensiveness. *Journal of Personality*, 72, 481–511.

Boyer, P. (2008). Evolutionary Economics of Mental Time Travel? *Trends in Cognitive Sciences*, 12, 219–224.

Brod, G., Werkle-Bergner, M., and Shing, Y. L. (2013). The Influence of Prior Knowledge on Memory: A Developmental Cognitive Neuroscience Perspective. *Frontiers in Behavioral Neuroscience*, 7, 139.

Buckner, R. L., Andrews-Hanna, J. R., and Schacter, D. L. (2008). The Brain's Default Network – Anatomy, Function, and Relevance to Disease. *Annals of the New York Academy of Sciences*, 1124, 1–38.

Bulley, A., Henry, J., and Suddendorf, T. (2016). Prospection and the Present Moment: The Role of Episodic Foresight in Intertemporal Choices between Immediate and Delayed Rewards. *Review of General Psychology*, 20, 29–47.

Cabeza, R., and St Jacques, P. (2007). Functional Neuroimaging of Autobiographical Memory. *Trends in Cognitive Sciences*, 11, 219–227.

Chessell, Z. J., Rathbone, C. J., Souchay, C., Charlesworth, L., and Moulin, C. J. A. (2014). Autobiographical Memory, Past and Future Events, and Self-images in Younger and Older Adults. *Self and Identity*, 13, 380–397.

Christian, B. M., Miles, L. K., Fung, F. H. K., Best, S., and Macrae, C. N. (2013). The Shape of Things to Come: Exploring Goal-Directed Prospection. *Consciousness and Cognition*, 22, 471–478.

Cole, S. N., and Berntsen, D. (2016). Do Future Thoughts Reflect Personal Goals? Current Concerns and Mental Time Travel into the Past and Future. *The Quarterly Journal of Experimental Psychology*, 69, 273–284.

Conway, M. A. (2005). Memory and the Self. *Journal of Memory and Language*, 53, 594–628.

(2009). Episodic Memories. *Neuropsychologia*, 47, 2305–2313.

Conway, M. A., Justice, L., and D'Argembeau, A. (2019). The Self-Memory System Revisited: Past, Present, and Future. In J. H. Mace (ed.), *The Organization and Structure of Autobiographical Memory*. New York, NY: Oxford University Press, 28–51.

Conway, M. A., and Pleydell-Pearce, C. W. (2000). The Construction of Autobiographical Memories in the Self-Memory System. *Psychological Review 107*, 261–288.

Conway, M. A., Singer, J. A., and Tagini, A. (2004). The Self and Autobiographical Memory: Correspondence and Coherence. *Social Cognition*, 22, 495–537.

D'Argembeau, A. (2013). On the Role of the Ventromedial Prefrontal Cortex in Self-Processing: The Valuation Hypothesis. *Frontiers in Human Neuroscience*, 7, 372.

(2016). The Role of Personal Goals in Future-Oriented Mental Time Travel. In K. Michaelian, S. B. Klein, and K. K. Szpunar (eds.), *Seeing the Future: Theoretical Perspectives on Future-Oriented Mental Time Travel*. New York, NY: Oxford University Press, 199–214.

D'Argembeau, A., and Demblon, J. (2012). On the Representational Systems Underlying Prospection: Evidence from the Event-Cueing Paradigm. *Cognition*, 125, 160–167.

D'Argembeau, A., Jedidi, H., Balteau, E., et al. (2012). Valuing One's Self: Medial Prefrontal Involvement in Epistemic and Emotive Investments in Self-Views. *Cerebral Cortex*, 22, 659–667.

D'Argembeau, A., Lardi, C., and van der Linden, M. (2012). Self-Defining Future Projections: Exploring the Identity Function of Thinking about the Future. *Memory*, *20*, 110–120.

D'Argembeau, A., and Mathy, A. (2011). Tracking the Construction of Episodic Future Thoughts. *Journal of Experimental Psychology: General*, *140*, 258–271.

D'Argembeau, A., Raffard, S., and van der Linden, M. (2008). Remembering the Past and Imagining the Future in Schizophrenia. *Journal of Abnormal Psychology*, *117*, 247–251.

D'Argembeau, A., Renaud, O., and van der Linden, M. (2011). Frequency, Characteristics, and Functions of Future-Oriented Thoughts in Daily Life. *Applied Cognitive Psychology*, *25*, 96–103.

D'Argembeau, A., Stawarczyk, D., Majerus, S., et al. (2010). The Neural Basis of Personal Goal Processing when Envisioning Future Events. *Journal of Cognitive Neuroscience*, *22*, 1701–1713.

D'Argembeau, A., and van der Linden, M. (2004). Phenomenal Characteristics Associated with Projecting Oneself Back into the Past and Forward into the Future: Influence of Valence and Temporal Distance. *Consciousness and Cognition*, *13*, 844–858.

(2006). Individual Differences in the Phenomenology of Mental Time Travel: The Effect of Vivid Visual Imagery and Emotion Regulation Strategies. *Consciousness and Cognition*, *15*, 342–350.

(2012). Predicting the Phenomenology of Episodic Future Thoughts. *Consciousness and Cognition*, *21*, 1198–1206.

De Brigard, F., Giovanello, K. S., Stewart, G. W., et al. (2016). Characterizing the Subjective Experience of Episodic Past, Future, and Counterfactual Thinking in Healthy Younger and Older Adults. *Quarterly Journal of Experimental Psychology*, *69*, 2358–2375.

Demblon, J., Bahri, M. A., and D'Argembeau, A. (2016). Neural Correlates of Event Clusters in Past and Future Thoughts: How the Brain Integrates Specific Episodes with Autobiographical Knowledge. *NeuroImage*, *127*, 257–266.

Demblon, J., and D'Argembeau, A. (2014). The Organization of Prospective Thinking: Evidence of Event Clusters in Freely Generated Future Thoughts. *Consciousness and Cognition*, *24*, 75–83.

(2017). Contribution of Past and Future Self-Defining Event Networks to Personal Identity. *Memory*, *25*, 656–665.

Emmons, R. A. (1986). Personal Strivings: An Approach to Personality and Subjective Well-Being. *Journal of Personality and Social Psychology*, *51*, 1058–1068.

Ernst, A., and D'Argembeau, A. (2017). Make It Real: Belief in Occurrence within Episodic Future Thought. *Memory & Cognition*, *45*(6), 1045–1061.

Ferrante, D., Girotto, V., Straga, M., and Walsh, C. (2013). Improving the Past and the Future: A Temporal Asymmetry in Hypothetical Thinking. *Journal of Experimental Psychology: General*, *142*, 23–27.

Friedman, W. J. (1993). Memory for the Time of Past Events. *Psychological Bulletin*, *113*, 44–66.

Gilboa, A., and Marlatte, H. (2017). Neurobiology of Schemas and Schema-Mediated Memory. *Trends in Cognitive Sciences*, *21*, 618–631.

Grilli, M. D. (2017). The Association of Personal Semantic Memory to Identity Representations: Insight into Higher-Order Networks of Autobiographical Contents. *Memory*, *25*, 1435–1443.

Habermas, T., and Bluck, S. (2000). Getting a Life: The Emergence of the Life Story in Adolescence. *Psychological Bulletin, 126,* 748–769.

Haque, S., and Conway, M. A. (2001). Sampling the Process of Autobiographical Memory Construction. *European Journal of Cognitive Psychology, 13,* 529–547.

Hassabis, D., Kumaran, D., Vann, S. D., and Maguire, E. A. (2007). Patients with Hippocampal Amnesia Cannot Imagine New Experiences. *Proceedings of the National Academy of Sciences of the United States of America, 104,* 1726–1731.

Irish, M., Addis, D. R., Hodges, J. R., and Piguet, O. (2012). Considering the Role of Semantic Memory in Episodic Future Thinking: Evidence from Semantic Dementia. *Brain, 135*(Pt 7), 2178–2191.

Irish, M., and Piguet, O. (2013). The Pivotal Role of Semantic Memory in Remembering the Past and Imagining the Future. *Frontiers in Behavioral Neuroscience, 7,* 27.

Jeunehomme, O., and D'Argembeau, A. (2016). Prevalence and Determinants of Direct and Generative Modes of Production of Episodic Future Thoughts in the Word Cueing Paradigm. *Quarterly Journal of Experimental Psychology, 69,* 254–272.

Kim, H. (2012). A Dual-Subsystem Model of the Brain's Default Network: Self-Referential Processing, Memory Retrieval Processes, and Autobiographical Memory Retrieval. *Neuroimage, 61,* 966–977.

Klein, S. B. (2013). The Complex Act of Projecting Oneself into the Future. *Wiley Interdisciplinary Reviews: Cognitive Science, 4,* 63–79.

(2016). Autonoetic Consciousness: Reconsidering the Role of Episodic Memory in Future-Oriented Self-Projection. *Quarterly Journal of Experimental Psychology, 69,* 381–401.

Klein, S. B., and Gangi, C. E. (2010). The Multiplicity of Self: Neuropsychological Evidence and its Implications for the Self as a Construct in Psychological Research. *Annals of the New York Academy of Sciences, 1191,* 1–15.

Klein, S. B., and Lax, M. L. (2010). The Unanticipated Resilience of Trait Self-Knowledge in the Face of Neural Damage. *Memory, 18,* 918–948.

Klein, S. B., and Loftus, J. (1993). The Mental Representation of Trait and Autobiographical Knowledge about the Self. In T. K. Srull and R. S. Wyer (eds.), *Advances in Social Cognition.* Volume 5. Hillsdale, NJ: Erlbaum, 1–49.

Klein, S. B., Loftus, J., and Kihlstrom, J. F. (1996). Self-Knowledge of an Amnesic Patient: Toward a Neuropsychology of Personality and Social Psychology. *Journal of Experimental Psychology: General, 125,* 250–260.

(2002). Memory and Temporal Experience: The Effects of Episodic Memory Loss on an Amnesic Patient's Ability to Remember the Past and Imagine the Future. *Social Cognition, 20,* 353–379.

Klinger, E. (2013). Goal Commitments and the Content of Thoughts and Dreams: Basic Principles. *Frontiers in Psychology, 4,* 415.

Leary, M. R. (2007). Motivational and Emotional Aspects of the Self. *Annual Review of Psychology, 58,* 317–344.

Lehner, E., and D'Argembeau, A. (2016). The Role of Personal Goals in Autonoetic Experience when Imagining Future Events. *Consciousness and Cognition, 42,* 267–276.

Little, B. R. (1983). Personal Projects: A Rationale and Method for Investigation. *Environment and Behavior, 15,* 273–309.

MacLeod, A. K., and Byrne, A. (1996). Anxiety, Depression, and the Anticipation of Future Positive and Negative Experiences. *Journal of Abnormal Psychology, 105,* 286–289.

Markus, H. (1977). Self-Schemata and Processing Information about the Self. *Journal of Personality and Social Psychology*, *35*, 63–78.

Markus, H., and Nurius, P. (1986). Possible Selves. *American Psychologist*, *41*, 954–969.

Markus, H., and Wurf, E. (1987). The Dynamic Self-Concept: A Social Psychological Perspective. *Annual Review of Psychology*, *38*, 299–337.

Martinelli, P., Sperduti, M., and Piolino, P. (2013). Neural Substrates of the Self-Memory System: New Insights from a Meta-Analysis. *Human Brain Mapping*, *34*, 1515–1529.

McAdams, D. P. (2013). The Psychological Self as Actor, Agent, and Author. *Perspectives on Psychological Science*, *8*(3), 272–295.

Murray, R. J., Schaer, M., and Debbane, M. (2012). Degrees of Separation: A Quantitative Neuroimaging Meta-Analysis Investigating Self-Specificity and Shared Neural Activation between Self- and Other-Reflection. *Neuroscience & Biobehavioral Reviews*, *36*, 1043–1059.

Newby-Clark, I. R., and Ross, M. (2003). Conceiving the Past and Future. *Personality and Social Psychology Bulletin*, *29*, 807–818.

O'Donnell, S., Oluyomi Daniel, T., and Epstein, L. H. (2017). Does Goal Relevant Episodic Future Thinking Amplify the Effect on Delay Discounting? *Consciousness and Cognition*, *51*, 10–16.

Oyserman, D., and James, L. (2009). Possible Selves: From Content to Process. In K. D. Markman, M. P. Klein, and J. A. Suhr (eds.), *Handbook of Imagination and Mental Simulation*. New York, NY: Psychology Press, 373–394.

Packard, B. W.-L., and Conway, P. F. (2006). Methodological Choice and its Consequences for Possible Selves Research. *Identity: An International Journal of Theory and Research*, *6*, 251–271.

Peters, J., and Buchel, C. (2010). Episodic Future Thinking Reduces Reward Delay Discounting through an Enhancement of Prefrontal-Mediotemporal Interactions. *Neuron*, *66*, 138–148.

Prebble, S. C., Addis, D. R., and Tippett, L. J. (2013). Autobiographical Memory and Sense of Self. *Psychological Bulletin*, *139*, 815–840.

Quoidbach, J., Gilbert, D. T., and Wilson, T. D. (2013). The End of History Illusion. *Science*, *339*, 96–98.

Radvansky, G. A., and Zacks, J. M. (2011). Event Perception. *Wiley Interdisciplinary Reviews: Cognitive Science*, *2*(6), 608–620.

Rasmussen, A. S., and Berntsen, D. (2013). The Reality of the Past versus the Ideality of the Future: Emotional Valence and Functional Differences between Past and Future Mental Time Travel. *Memory & Cognition*, *41*, 187–200.

Rathbone, C. J., Conway, M. A., and Moulin, C. J. (2011). Remembering and Imagining: The Role of the Self. *Consciousness and Cognition*, *20*, 1175–1182.

Rathbone, C. J., Moulin, C. J., and Conway, M. A. (2009). Autobiographical Memory and Amnesia: Using Conceptual Knowledge to Ground the Self. *Neurocase*, *15*, 405–418.

Renoult, L., Davidson, P. S., Palombo, D. J., Moscovitch, M., and Levine, B. (2012). Personal Semantics: At the Crossroads of Semantic and Episodic Memory. *Trends in Cognitive Sciences*, *16*, 550–558.

Roese, N. J. (1997). Counterfactual Thinking. *Psychological Bulletin*, *121*(1), 133–148.

Roy, M., Shohamy, D., and Wager, T. D. (2012). Ventromedial Prefrontal-Subcortical Systems and the Generation of Affective Meaning. *Trends in Cognitive Sciences*, *16*, 147–156.

Schacter, D. L., and Addis, D. R. (2007). The Cognitive Neuroscience of Constructive Memory: Remembering the Past and Imagining the Future. *Philosophical Transactions of the Royal Society B: Biological Sciences, 362*, 773–786.

Schacter, D. L., Addis, D. R., Hassabis, D., et al. (2012). The Future of Memory: Remembering, Imagining, and the Brain. *Neuron, 76*, 677–694.

Schacter, D. L., Benoit, R. G., De Brigard, F., and Szpunar, K. K. (2015). Episodic Future Thinking and Episodic Counterfactual Thinking: Intersections between Memory and Decisions. *Neurobiology of Learning and Memory, 117*, 14–21.

Schacter, D. L., Benoit, R. G., and Szpunar, K. K. (2017). Episodic Future Thinking: Mechanisms and Functions. *Current Opinion in Behavioral Sciences, 17*, 41–50.

Sedikides, C., and Gregg, A. P. (2008). Self-Enhancement: Food for Thought. *Perspectives on Psychological Science, 3*, 102–116.

Singer, J. A., Blagov, P., Berry, M., and Oost, K. M. (2013). Self-Defining Memories, Scripts, and the Life Story: Narrative Identity in Personality and Psychotherapy. *Journal of Personality, 81*, 569–582.

Spreng, R. N., Mar, R. A., and Kim, A. S. (2009). The Common Neural Basis of Autobiographical Memory, Prospection, Navigation, Theory of Mind, and the Default Mode: A Quantitative Meta-Analysis. *Journal of Cognitive Neuroscience, 21*, 489–510.

Stawarczyk, D., Cassol, H., and D'Argembeau, A. (2013). Phenomenology of Future-Oriented Mind-Wandering Episodes. *Frontiers in Psychology, 4*, 425.

Stawarczyk, D., and D'Argembeau, A. (2015). Neural Correlates of Personal Goal Processing during Episodic Future Thinking and Mind-Wandering: An ALE Meta-Analysis. *Human Brain Mapping, 36*(8), 2928–2947.

Suddendorf, T., and Corballis, M. C. (2007). The Evolution of Foresight: What is Mental Time Travel and is it Unique to Humans? *Behavioral and Brain Sciences, 30*, 299–351.

Svoboda, E., McKinnon, M. C., and Levine, B. (2006). The Functional Neuroanatomy of Autobiographical Memory: A Meta-Analysis. *Neuropsychologia, 44*, 2189–2208.

Szpunar, K. K. (2010). Episodic Future Thought: An Emerging Concept. *Perspectives on Psychological Science, 5*, 142–162.

Taylor, S. E., and Brown, J. D. (1988). Illusion and Well-Being: A Social Psychological Perspective on Mental Health. *Psychological Bulletin, 103*, 193–210.

Taylor, S. E., Pham, L. B., Rivkin, I. D., and Armor, D. A. (1998). Harnessing the Imagination: Mental Simulation, Self-Regulation, and Coping. *American Psychologist, 53*, 429–439.

Thompson, C. P., Skowronski, J. J., and Betz, A. L. (1993). The Use of Partial Temporal Information in Dating Personal Events. *Memory & Cognition, 21*, 352–360.

Thomsen, D. K. (2015). Autobiographical Periods: A Review and Central Components of a Theory. *Review of General Psychology, 19*, 294–310.

Thomsen, D. K., Steiner, K. L., and Pillemer, D. B. (2016). Life Story Chapters: Past and Future, You and Me. *Journal of Applied Research in Memory and Cognition, 5*, 143–149.

Tulving, E. (1985). Memory and Consciousness. *Canadian Psychologist, 26*, 1–12.

(2005). Episodic Memory and Autonoesis: Uniquely Human? In H. S. Terrace and J. Metcalfe (eds.), *The Missing Link in Cognition: Origins of Self-Reflective Consciousness*. Oxford, UK: Oxford University Press, 3–56.

Uzer, T., Lee, P. J., and Brown, N. R. (2012). On the Prevalence of Directly Retrieved Autobiographical Memories. *Journal of Experimental Psychology: Learning, Memory, and Cognition, 38*, 1296–1308.

van der Meer, L., Costafreda, S., Aleman, A., and David, A. S. (2010). Self-Reflection and the Brain: A Theoretical Review and Meta-Analysis of Neuroimaging Studies with Implications for Schizophrenia. *Neuroscience & Biobehavioral Reviews, 34,* 935–946.

van Hoeck, N., Ma, N., Ampe, L., et al. (2013). Counterfactual Thinking: An fMRI Study on Changing the Past for a Better Future. *Social Cognitive and Affective Neuroscience, 8,* 556–564.

van Kesteren, M. T. R., Ruiter, D. J., Fernández, G., and Henson, R. N. (2012). How Schema and Novelty Augment Memory Formation. *Trends in Neurosciences, 35,* 211–219.

Wagner, D. D., Haxby, J. V., and Heatherton, T. F. (2012). The Representation of Self and Person Knowledge in the Medial Prefrontal Cortex. *Wiley Interdisciplinary Reviews: Cognitive Science, 3*(4), 451–470.

Williams, J. M. G., Barnhofer, T., Crane, C., et al. (2007). Autobiographical Memory Specificity and Emotional Disorder. *Psychological Bulletin, 133,* 122–148.

23 Imaginary Friends: How Imaginary Minds Mimic Real Life

Paige E. Davis

Mental State Reasoning

Two young children are playing with blocks. The first child says, "pretend this block is a monster and it's coming to get you!" Her playmate takes another block; while he moves it away he screams, "Ahhh, I'm running away."

This is a typical imaginative play scenario that could be acted out in households across the world. However, these simple imaginative play interactions actually take much more mental complexity than one might expect. These play episodes are influencing the development of mental state reasoning.

Mental state reasoning encompasses skills that help children begin to analyze and communicate about what they, or other people, may be thinking or feeling. This type of reasoning enables children to develop an understanding of the mind's processes, make predictions about how people may behave, and form explanations for people's past and future behavior. Mental state reasoning is integral to the everyday navigation of a social landscape. Without this ability, humans would be unable to fully understand the actions of themselves and other people.

Children develop mental state reasoning between the ages of 3 and 5 years (Wellman, Cross, and Watson, 2001; Wellman and Liu, 2004), a time in which play and imagination is used extensively (Singer and Singer, 1990). During this time, children experience drastic changes in these reasoning skills across the board. They have a newfound understanding that others can have different mental representations of the world (Harris, 2000). For example, during this period they begin to understand that people can have false beliefs, which translates to many higher order abilities such as deception (Wimmer and Perner, 1983). This development is accompanied by the appreciation that there can be a difference between how something appears and how it really is (Flavell, Flavell, and Green, 1983, 1987), as well as between fantasy and reality (Golomb and Galasso, 1995; Woolley and Ma, 2009; Woolley and van Reet, 2006), and even between different fantasy worlds (Skolnick and Bloom, 2006).

Theory of mind (ToM), (a term that encompasses many components of mental state reasoning) reaches maturity in most children by the age of 5 years (Lewis and Mitchell, 1994; Wellman, Cross, and Watson, 2001; Wellman and Liu, 2004). ToM is the ability to put yourself in someone else's shoes and see the world from his or her perspective in order to infer what he or she may be thinking or feeling. Part of this is the ability to recognize that other individuals may have thoughts and feelings that differ from one's own. That is, having a ToM entails imputing mental states to oneself and others (Premack and Woodruff, 1978).

Considering the breadth of mental state reasoning skills, scientists have come up with many different ways to measure this construct. Repacholi and Gopnik (1997) created a task in which a child sits at a table with two food options placed in front of her: broccoli and crackers. The experimenter takes the broccoli and acts as if she is very happy to eat it, then she takes the cracker and makes a face indicating that it's disgusting. The child is then asked to give the experimenter the snack she prefers. This task attempts to measure whether children understand that another person can have desires that differ from their own.

To investigate whether children have an appreciation that things may look like something but not actually be the same in reality, researchers have devised a task in which a child is given an object that resembles one thing, but is really something else (e.g. an eraser that looks like a biscuit; Flavell, Flavell, and Green, 1983). The child is asked what the object (in this case the eraser) looks like, what it feels like, and what it really is. Children who answer these questions correctly should communicate that even though the object looks like a biscuit, it's actually an eraser, i.e. that appearance can differ from reality.

ToM was classically measured using false belief paradigms where a child is told a story about a character's false belief (Wellman, Cross, and Watson, 2001); however, more recently, researchers have argued that children's developing ToM should include the understanding of multiple concepts (e.g. emotions, intentions, desires, and knowledge) (Cutting and Dunn, 1999; Ketelaars et al., 2010; Wellman and Liu, 2004). These concepts can be measured through different vignettes as well. There have also been suggestions to scale ToM tasks to measure on the gradient of ToM ability at which a child is functioning, as children will be more likely to understand and pass different ToM tasks at different ages (Hughes et al., 2008; Wellman and Liu, 2004). In this way, ToM assessment has changed drastically since the 1970s when the concept was first examined by Premack and Woodruff (1978) in chimpanzees to be far more nuanced in tapping different aspects of mental state reasoning.

In terms of mental state reasoning in the imaginative block play scenario, the children are not only using their imaginations to occupy themselves and have fun but also learning about each others' perspectives. The child who asks her to pretend that the block is a monster is developing an understanding of her friend's mind. For example, the second playmate cannot know that the block is going to represent a monster unless he is told. He understands that taking his block and making it scream at the monster in fear is an appropriate response that communicates to his partner that both are representing the make-believe world similarly. All the while, both are engaging in a shared transaction of thinking about how the imaginary block figures would think or feel, and acting on these imagined thoughts and emotions. Thus, mental state understanding is facilitated through this type of play as the children learn about each other's minds and representing a third party's mind.

Some theorists argue that pretend play may help children to, "appreciate that pretend actions are guided not by reality itself, but rather by the make-believe reality that is represented in the mind of the person engaged in the pretence" (Harris, 2000: 39). Imagination itself is integral to developing an understanding of others' minds as one must be able to imagine that person's mind. Although there is evidence that imaginative play helps children learn about mental states (Harris, 2000; Singer and Singer, 1990; Taylor, 1999), there are also other factors in a child's life that influence these developments.

For instance, the capacity for mental state reasoning has been shown to be related to the type of language a child is exposed to during early development (Astington and Baird, 2005; Ruffman, Slade, and Crowe, 2002). Maternal mental state language and its relationship to later mentalizing ability has been investigated by asking mothers to describe pictures to their children. The descriptions were then categorized by whether their mothers referred to a mental state such as a desire or emotion. Researchers found that the number of mental state descriptions correlated with later ToM in the children (Ruffman, Slade, and Crowe, 2002).

Mental state talk at home has also been investigated, and is held to be related to later mental state understanding (Dunn, Brown, and Beardsall, 1991; Jenkins et al., 2003; Youngblade and Dunn, 1995). Furthermore, there is evidence that language ability and ToM are inexorably intertwined. As children become more and more competent with their language ability their ToM improves (Astington and Jenkins, 1999). This is thought to be because language gives children the ability to represent information using syntax complementation and thus provides the mental format needed in order to represent false beliefs (Astington and Jenkins, 1999). Language lets children explore others' minds more thoroughly than previous means of exploration and inquiry used in infancy such as taste or touch. Because language is linked to ToM, socioeconomic status is also a factor in ToM ability as the sheer number of words spoken to a child positively correlates with socioeconomic status (Cutting and Dunn, 2003; Shatz et al., 2003).

Language and imagination are both important in the development of mental state reasoning; however, other environmental factors also play into this development of mentalizing ability. Mind-mindedness, or the tendency to treat a child as if he or she has a mind of his/her own rather than being just an organism with needs to be met, has also been shown to be related to later mental state understanding (Meins, 1997; Meins et al., 2002; Kirk et al., 2015). This is because parents who are more attuned to their children's mental states and the behavior representing what their children might be thinking or feeling may be inadvertently teaching children about the mind (Meins, 1997; Meins et al., 2012). Siblings have also been shown to improve mental state reasoning in children (Perner, Ruffman, and Leekam, 1994). Researchers have found that larger families with more siblings relate to better mental state understanding; however, the composition of siblings (older, younger, twin) has also been shown to influence ToM (Cassidy et al., 2005; Jenkins, et al., 2003; Leblanc, Bernier, and Howe, 2017; McAlister and Peterson, 2007; Perner, Ruffman, and Leekam, 1994). For example, while having an older (but not younger) sibling has been found to give a ToM advantage, this effect is only seen in younger siblings aged less than 12 years

(Ruffman et al., 1998). When examining research on twins, the ToM benefit seen in siblings disappears (Cassidy et al., 2005). This is thought to be because more developed or older siblings provide an avenue for practicing mental state understanding. Children with siblings have more opportunity to consider the feelings of others, as the sibling relationship is one of intensity. This creates more chances to talk about mental states, have conflicts, and engage together in pretend play (Hughes et al., 2006; Jenkins et al., 2003; Youngblade and Dunn, 1995). In fact, children are more likely to talk about mental states with their siblings than with their peers (Leach, Howe, and Dehart, 2016). However, the outcomes of better mental state reasoning relate to more positive peer interactions as well as peer acceptance (Slaughter, Dennis, and Pritchard, 2002; Suway et al., 2012), because children with better mentalizing ability would be more sensitive to what a friend might be thinking, feeling, or to how they might be behaving.

It's clear that the development of mental state reasoning is enhanced by interactions with other human beings, particularly sibling playmates (Hughes et al., 2006). However, what happens when the interaction occurs in the absence of a real stimulus and the interacting partner is imagined? This type of interaction happens whenever a child plays with an imaginary companion (IC).

A Short History of Imaginary Friend Play

Childhood IC play is thought to have evolved around the nineteenth century, a time when the concept of childhood as a sensitive period for development was first coming into fashion, and parents were giving children time to play alone (Klausen and Passman, 2007). Before this time period, children were not routinely given opportunities for solitary play, which is the integral ingredient for a child to create an IC (Taylor, 1999). The fact that a child needs to be alone to create an IC may seem counterintuitive, as IC play has been shown to aid children's social development (Davis, Meins, and Fernyhough, 2011; Giménez-Dasí, Pons, and Bender, 2016; Taylor and Carlson, 1997). Klausen and Passman (2007) have also suggested that before the nineteenth century, parents may have interpreted their children's ICs as spiritual beings or ghosts, so as the phenomenon began to be studied ICs were often given a "bad rap" as indicators of pathology (Gleason, 2004; Taylor, 1999; Vostrovsky, 1895). Now that researchers know more about ICs, it is becoming clear that instead of discouraging this type of play, parents should be embracing it. Not only is it normative, with researchers finding that between 20 percent and more than 50 percent of typically developing children create ICs (Carlson and Taylor, 2005; Gleason, 2005; Gleason and Hohmann, 2006), it is also a common occurrence across cultures (e.g. Davis, Meins, and Fernyhough, 2011; Fernyhough et al., 2007; Motoshima et al., 2014; Taylor, 1999; Wigger, 2017) and children who have ICs have been found to be significantly better at ToM tasks (Taylor and Carlson, 1997).

In terms of scientific inquiry into ICs, early work was anecdotal and based on case studies, so tended to be more theoretical (e.g. Vostrovsky, 1895). It was not until 1934 that ICs were first scientifically defined as "an invisible character named and referred to in conversation with other persons or played with directly for a period of time, at least several months, having an air of reality for the child, but no apparent objective basis. This excludes the type of imaginary play where an object is personified or in which the child takes on the role of a character" (Svendsen, 1934: 988). This definition is still used today in the scientific literature; however, many studies now incorporate personified object (PO) play as a type of IC interaction.[1] This is because, in terms of fantasy predisposition, children do not differ in these two types of play (Taylor, 1999). For both these forms of imaginary play, the child creates another mind and interacts with that material or immaterial being's personality (Carlson and Taylor, 2005). The interaction could be especially important to children's mental state reasoning and may impact children similarly in childhood, but may not lead to other differences in developmental outcomes seen in adulthood.[2] For example, some studies suggest that adults who report having a PO in childhood are more likely to use different types of self-talk than those reporting playing with an invisible IC as a child (Davis et al., in preparation).

Types and Functions of Imaginary Companions

Although in many studies POs and ICs are combined, the definition for inclusion of POs is still debated. Experimenters have used different justifications for why they choose to examine POs separately from ICs. For example, Bouldin (2006) asked children to describe their ICs in detail, and thus included only the classic invisible ICs. Gleason, Sebanc, and Hartup (2000) argued that it is important to distinguish ICs and POs based on parental reports of their children's invisible and personified friends' stability, ubiquity, or relationship qualities. They later added to this argument by showing that relationship characteristics (hierarchical vs. egalitarian) differ between children who create ICs and those who create POs (Gleason, 2002). Other researchers, particularly those looking at development relating to understanding one's own and others' minds, have argued that the same underlying mechanisms are used to create personalities for invisible ICs as well as POs, so researchers should treat these entities as equivalent and continue to combine the two, as both types of play enable a child to practice creating, conceptualizing, and interacting with another's mind (Carlson and Taylor, 2005; Davis, Meins, and Fernyhough, 2014; Fernyhough et al., 2007; McInnis, Pierucci, and Gilpin, 2013; Taylor et al., 2004). The combination of the two types of IC certainly depends upon what the researcher is trying to examine, especially when looking at different areas of cognition and behavior across the lifespan. Having an IC may initially relate to the development of mental state reasoning among other abilities, but its influence may change as the child grows into an adult.

---

1 Children who maintain that they speak with God or a higher religious power would not be classified as having an IC, as this behavior would not incorporate creating another mind, or interacting with a self-made being.

2 Davis, P. E., Webster, L., Kola-Palmer, S., and Stain, H. (In preparation). Adult Report of Childhood Imaginary Companions or Personified Objects to Current Self-Talk.

There are many other types of play that involve the imagination that may look like IC play; for example, when children create other worlds also known as paracosms, or when they impersonate other (usually more competent) individuals such as Batman or Elsa. These forms of play are not classified as IC play because they are qualitatively different from IC play in the sense that (1) they do not involve the child's solo creation of a social agent with a mind, especially in the case of role play as the character already has a set mind, and (2) there is a lack of imagined social experience and exchange in the absence of a real social partner (Singer and Singer, 1990; Taylor, 1999). Therefore, IC play is only considered play with an invisible IC or a PO, rather than any other type of imaginary play that could encompass people or objects.

Children differ in how they play with their ICs as well as what type of IC they create, and there's no single characteristic that runs through all children's ICs; rather each one is as unique as their child creator (Taylor and Carlson, 2002). Furthermore, when looking at the type of IC created, ICs and POs differ not just in the physical description made by the child, but also in the function they play for the child (Hoff, 2004). These functions can range from having a scapegoat to blame for mischief, to a friend whom the child communicates through (Hoff, 2004). Functions differ between visible and invisible friends as well, as POs are more likely to be used for comfort purposes and represent unilateral relationships, while invisible companions tend to function in more reciprocal relationships (Gleason and Hohmann, 2006; Gleason and Kalpidou, 2014). Examples of IC descriptions can be found in Figure 23.1.

Factors in the Creation of Imaginary Companions

There are some factors that influence whether a child is more or less likely to create an IC. One of the most important of these factors is age, as ICs generally begin to emerge when children are aged between 3 and 6 years (Singer and Singer, 1990), just 18 months after children begin to show imaginary play behavior (Lillard, 2017). When this age window of IC creation closes, it is less likely to see one appear; however, some researchers have found examples of ICs in older pre-teens and adolescents through looking at their diary writing (Seiffge-Krenke, 1997, 2001), and even adults (Gupta and Desai, 2006). Adult writers of fiction have been a topic of debate as to whether the characters they create can be classified as a construct akin to ICs. Authors' behavior may differ in that they do not physically play with the character, but once created, characters in novels have personalities and minds of their own, and many authors report their characters' antics being out of their control (Taylor, Hodges, and Kohanyi, 2003). Although the IC can be seen after this time period, the heyday of IC creation has been shown to be from 3 to 6 years old (Singer and Singer, 1990).

Gender also plays a part in determining which children will be more prone to interact and play with an IC. Girls are more likely to play with an IC than boys (Pearson et al., 2001; Carlson and Taylor, 2005; Gleason and Hohmann, 2006). In an examination of sex differences in play, Boone et al. (1999) found that 17.6 percent more girls than boys reported playing with ICs in their sample of participants. While

Type	Name	Description	From
IC	Andrew	An invisible boy who drives a rainbow coloured Lincoln and sleeps on a bunk bed	Davis et al. (2018)
IC	Simoney	Alligator with pink and green scales who is a wise instructor, lives in a tiny green house, likes to ride on shoulders, or in pockets	Taylor et al. (2013)
IC	Jack	A ghost who could grow, had the power to make himself 20 or 10, and was sometimes mean	Tahiroglu et al. (2011)
IC	Dogue	10 year old white dog, with holey black eyes and white teeth. He drives monster trucks and Ferraris. The child cannot make Dogue be nice, Dogue 'just decides' to	McInnis et al. (2013)
PO	Pinkie	Coloured blanket; misses the child when separated and stays in room to keep things safe	Gleason & Kalpidou (2014)
PO	Kumachan	A male bear who was big and played with the child anytime	Moriguchi & Shinohara (2012)
PO	Leppy	A stuffed leopard, who is only friends with other cats and speaks Leppy language	Gleason (2017)
PO	Fudge	A rabbit who has long, white and grey ears and a plaster on his foot, and who likes to go into the child's room and move things around	Davis et al. (2013)

Figure 23.1 *Descriptions of children's invisible imaginary companions (IC) and personified objects (PO) from the literature. The descriptions are directly quoted from the papers cited in the table.*

examining differences in fantasy play between genders, Carlson and Taylor (2005) suggested that parents may respond differently to girls' IC play than to boys', making it more acceptable for girls to have and report ICs than boys. Other studies have supported this theory by reporting gender differences in play, where boys were more likely to role play super-competent individuals, whereas girls were more likely to report invisible friends (Bauer and Dettore, 1997; Taylor et al., 2013).

While age and gender are key factors influencing IC creation, birth order can also be predictive. Being the first-born child relates positively to IC creation (Bouldin and Pratt, 1999; Manosevitz, Prentice, and Wilson, 1973). Bouldin and Pratt (1999) theorize that this is because ICs are often used in place of a real friend or sibling to alleviate loneliness. First-born children usually have fewer social outlets than subsequent children, and could create an IC in compensation for the lack of social opportunities available with peers. Hoff (2004) added to this by suggesting that a child may initially use the IC as a tool to fight loneliness; however, as other children are born into the family, the IC could have two possible fates, (1) either become obsolete and disappear, or (2) continue serving other functions for the child. These fates are also cohesive with the knowledge of the intensity of sibling relationship and that the IC may be acting to fill that gap and potentially providing insight into others' minds simultaneously.

Mental State Reasoning in Children with Imaginary Companions

Taylor and Carlson (1997) were the first researchers to make the connection between a child's invention of an imaginary personality via an IC and improved mental state understanding. Taylor and Carlson found that children with ICs scored significantly higher than their peers without ICs (NIC) on representational change, interpretive diversity, and false belief ToM tasks. Since this flagship research, Giménez-Dasí, Pons, and Bender (2016) have replicated Taylor and Carlson's ToM results; however, other studies have reported null findings for this relationship (Davis, Meins, and Fernyhough, 2011; Fernyhough et al., 2007). This incongruity may be a consequence of researchers using different ToM measures that target areas of ToM at which children with ICs are prone to excel. For example, the experimenters finding significant ToM results both used tests incorporating appearance and reality knowledge, such as the eraser that looks like a biscuit task; Taylor and Carlson also added interpretive diversity tasks to their ToM battery, while Giménez-Dasí instead used understanding of jokes and lies. Alternatively, the researchers who found null results used scaled theory of mind tasks that did not incorporate any of the measures above (Wellman and Liu, 2004), and a stream of consciousness task that is not a classic ToM task (Flavell, Green, and Flavell, 1993). Hence, collectively the research suggests that children creating ICs may be precocious in certain areas of ToM, but not others.

ToM is not the only domain of mental state reasoning and social competence in which children with ICs tend to outperform their NIC peers. Children who have created ICs have been found to better take into account the listener's perspective during a referential communication task (Roby and Kidd, 2008). They have also been found to produce more sophisticated private self-directed speech in a play session (Davis, Meins, and Fernyhough, 2013) and had the ability to form richer narratives than their NIC peers when engaging in a paradigm in which they were asked to retell a past event in their life as well as retell a story they had just heard (Trionfi and Reese, 2009). They are more likely than NIC children to describe their real best friend in terms of their internal and mental characteristics rather than in terms of the real friend's behaviors or physical appearance (Davis, Meins, and Fernyhough, 2014). Children with ICs have also been found to have better emotional understanding than their NIC counterparts (Giménez-Dasí, Pons, and Bender, 2016), and are better able to generate pretend conversations (Taylor, et al., 2013). Furthermore, IC children are reported to be less shy by their parents (Taylor et al., 2013), and are more likely to know that their thoughts, feelings, and ideas cannot leak out of their heads and that their mind is opaque (Davis, Meins, and Fernyhough,

2011). Taken together, this research suggests that IC creation is related to gains in certain mental state reasoning skills.

Although the literature supports the notion that children with ICs are more adept at mental state reasoning, the direction of causality for this relationship has still not been established. So, does creating an IC improve these skills, or are children who have been better at mental state reasoning from the start more likely to create an IC (see Taylor and Carlson, 1997)? There is some longitudinal research supporting the notion that mental state ability precedes IC creation, finding that attribution of psychological properties to inanimate objects before the age of 12 months is predictive of IC creation at 48 months (Moriguchi et al., 2016). However there are various methodological issues with this research including a small sample size. There is also research supporting the converse relationship, in which Lillard and Kavanaugh (2014) found that IC status contributed uniquely to the prediction of a child's symbolic ToM ability. Although these longitudinal studies make predictions, it is important to note that there has not been research using experimental methods to investigate whether children who have not previously created an IC can be encouraged to make one, and whether that will improve mental state reasoning, which would elucidate researchers to possible trends relating to IC creation and understanding of mind. A recent study has shown that after a three-month intervention in which the creation of an IC is endorsed, children who have never had an IC are able to generate ICs resembling those created spontaneously.[3] These are the first steps toward being able to look at direction of causality between mental state reasoning and spontaneous IC creation in childhood; however, only nine children participated in this exploratory study. More research needs to be done to understand how similar these endorsed ICs look. Future IC interventions should then incorporate longitudinal ToM, narrative, or private speech measures to determine whether children who have had endorsed ICs improve on these measures.

The Creation of Another Mind

The dominant theory attempting to explain why children with ICs fare better at mental state reasoning propounds the idea that pretend play develops a child's "understanding that mental representations may not constitute an accurate reflection of the external world" (Taylor and Carlson, 1997: 452) and that the creation of an IC affords the child the opportunities to think about internal states, making them more salient to the child. Thus, the child concentrates more on her own and others' internal states (Davis, Meins, and Fernyhough, 2011; Taylor and Carlson, 1997). In other words, creating a mind and interacting with imaginary personalities may aid children in the same way that interaction with real friends or siblings improves their knowledge about internal states (Astington and Baird, 2005; Hughes et al., 2006; Jenkins et al., 2003).

---

3 Davis, P. E., Meins, E., and Fernyhough, C. (In preparation). Children Can Be Taught to Play with Imaginary Friends: An Exploratory Study of Causal Direction.

In fact, when looking at real friends and comparing them to a child's ICs, there are many similarities between the two types of agents. Early on in IC research, Bouldin and Pratt (1999) found that children give their ICs the same status as their real friends. Other research has supported these findings by showing that no sharp distinctions are drawn by children between ICs and real best friends when it comes to conflict, power, instrumental help, and nurturance (Gleason, 2002). Children do not distinguish between imaginary and real reciprocal friendships in terms of the social provisions; companionship, intimacy, affection, enhancement of worth, and having a dependable/lasting bond (Gleason and Hohmann, 2006). In other words, when taking into account behavioral and emotional conceptions as well as characteristics of relationships, whether the agent is invisible does not seem to matter to children, because IC relationships tend to mirror real friendships and build on the children's real experiences (Bouldin and Pratt, 1999; Gleason, 2002; Gleason and Hohmann, 2006; Harris, 2000).

Children's ICs, in this sense, seem to be better defined in comparison to real friends rather than simply existing as fantasy play with no purpose. More recent studies support the similarities between real and imagined friendships suggesting that children with ICs envision their ICs to possess not just psychological states, but also biological properties, and that they experience realistic agency in their interactions with their IC (Moriguchi and Shinohara, 2012). Other research looking at the valence in IC relationships has found that, just like real friends, these imaginary relationships can be both positive and negative according to the child, and that even though they have created the IC themselves, children claim they are not in control of their ICs (McInnis, Pierucci, and Gilpin, 2013; Taylor, Carlson, and Shawber, 2007), much like how adult authors sometimes report not being in control of their fictional characters (Taylor, Hodges, and Kohanyi, 2003). In these ways, ICs can really take on a life of their own. They are viewed as autonomous agents with personalities and minds of their own, even though the child has created them.

There are some ways that the IC quasi-relationship does not resemble a real-life friendship. Some forms of ICs are nonhuman, however imbued with human characteristics (Taylor, 1999; Taylor, et al., 2013). Other human ICs are super-competent and have nonhuman abilities and powers (Harter and Chao, 1992). Obviously, these physical impossibilities make interactions with the IC different than those with a real friend, though the skills gained from the interaction and the characteristics of the relationship on the whole are congruent with real-life relationships (Gleason, 2017; Gleason and Hohmann, 2006; McInnis, Pierucci, and Gilpin, 2013; Moriguchi and Shinohara, 2012). There is some research on perspective taking that has found that 5- to 8-year-olds attribute more knowledge to an IC than a peer; however, there are methodological issues that are problematic here, as trials were not randomized, there was no analysis of the perceived competence of the children's ICs (whether they were seen as super competent or not), and the groups analyzed were small (Wigger, Paxson, and Ryan, 2013). Even with these methodological concerns, research into how children conceptualize what ICs know should nonetheless be further addressed. This could help to gain an understanding of how IC thought itself is conceptualized – especially when taking into account that practicing meta-representation with another being and engaging with the IC as if it had a mind of its own should be even more taxing on the representational imagination than pretend play with a real partner. It might be valuable to understand exactly how that mind is imagined.

Considering the evidence that invisible and real friends seem to be interchangeable in many ways to children who have ICs, the issue of whether these children understand the reality status of their own ICs has come into question (Woolley, 2003). It has been established that ICs are most likely to be created by typically developing children (Pearson et al., 2001), and that typically developing children acquire the ability to distinguish whether something is fantastic or real in their preschool years (e.g. Golomb and Galasso, 1995). This ability has been shown to be stronger in children with high fantasy orientation, where one of the measures of fantasy orientation included a child's creation of an IC (Sharon and Woolley, 2004). Researchers concluded that fantasy-oriented children were more likely to accrue knowledge about imagination that in turn increased their ability to distinguish imaginary from real beings. It has also been noted that children often want to make sure the experimenter knows that their IC is just in their imagination (Davis, 2011; Taylor, 1999). Thus, even though IC relationships are, for the most part, congruent with real-life relationships, this has nothing to do with a child's ability to distinguish real from imaginary friendships.

Theoretical Viewpoints: Mental State Reasoning and Imaginary Companions

The phenomenon of the IC is still an emerging research area, and one that experimenters know relatively little about in comparison to other forms of play (Klausen and Passman, 2007; Taylor, 1999). Current research points to a bigger question to be answered when looking into IC play: Why do children play with ICs at all? Lillard (2017) posits that because play is universal and has a developmentally predictable sequence, this suggests that it is an evolved behavior, which might, in turn, increase the fitness of human children. ICs could be an offshoot of this evolved play behavior, as this type of play is unique to humans and has been found to improve "social fitness." However, this does not account for the 40–70 percent of children who do not play with ICs. It is also important to remember that IC play is a fairly recent development in human history. Much more research would need to be done in order to ascertain whether this type of play could be classified as an evolutionary adaptation.

Other researchers may argue that IC creation has to do with personality-based factors. For example, Manosevitz, Prentice, and Wilson (1973) posit that children create ICs because they have a predisposition for self-initiated play, reporting that 97 percent of children who had created ICs were described as having play behavior that was self-initiated in comparison to the 86 percent of NIC children in their sample. However, looking at the phenomena through a developmental lens rather than as a personality trait, it is clear that the explanation is more complicated and transactional in nature. Engaging with an IC creates greater opportunities to pretend, making it difficult to parse apart cause and effect between a child's creation of an IC and his/her active engagement in fantasy play. As Vygotsky (1931/1993: 161) stated, "The very idea of practical application of play would be impossible if the development of personality were a passive unfolding of innate primary abilities." Hence, the transactions that children have with their ICs may be an example of intentional play in which the child is involved in the active use of her imagination to create a tool for honing higher cognitive functions, which she may be unknowingly seeking out.

Another way to view why children may play with ICs is to consider them self-scaffolds. Wood, Bruner, and Rose (1976) first coined the term "scaffold" to explain the act of an individual who has already mastered a task helping a learner to complete that task, which would otherwise be too difficult for the second learner to do alone. In this scenario, one would consider the IC as a scaffold made by the child, hence self-scaffold. Taking into account the variability in the forms and functions of ICs, and the breadth of the positive outcomes for children in the social domain, it would seem that different ICs could be acting as a means for mastering varying social skills without the child being aware (Davis, 2011; Gleason, 2017). In looking at IC play from a Vygotskian (1931/1998) perspective, "ICs can be seen as examples of play as a zone of proximal development, foreshadowing what cognitive functions and social tools the child will be utilising in later development" (Davis, 2011: 20). For example, this could be seen in a scenario in which a child has a fear of the dark: Interacting with an IC to conquer that fear while using cognitive strategies to learn about his own thoughts and feelings could be immensely helpful to the way that he faces and deals with other fears, not only at that time but also later in life.

If ICs are indeed self-tailored learning tools, this suggests that they could possibly be used in interventions in the future to help children gain skills they do not already possess, especially when it comes to children who lack mental state understanding. Interventions in which ICs are endorsed could be particularly useful for children with Autism Spectrum Disorder (ASD). Recent findings indicate that children diagnosed with ASD create ICs (Davis et al., 2018), even though they exhibit quantitatively less imagination play (Jarrold, 2003). If children diagnosed with ASD have the same profile as IC creators in typically developing populations, interventions could potentially improve this population's social cognitive skills. Hence, interventions could be organized to encourage children to create an IC themselves, thus self-tailoring their own IC to their own needs. These IC interventions could potentially be very useful for a broad range of children with differing skill sets and could be used in the future as a completely new form of play therapy. These possibilities suggest that the future is looking bright for ICs.

Acknowledgments

Katie-Anderson-Morrison should be thanked for her help with preliminary edits to the original manuscript.

References

Astington, J. W., and Baird, J. A. (eds.) (2005). *Why Language Matters for Theory of Mind*. New York, NY: Oxford University Press.

Astington, J. W., and Jenkins, J. M. (1999). A Longitudinal Study of the Relation between Language and Theory-of-Mind Development. *Developmental Psychology, 35*(5), 1311–1320.

Bauer, K. L., and Dettore, E. (1997). Superhero Play: What's a Teacher to Do? *Early Childhood Education Journal, 25*(1), 17–21.

Boone, O., Canetti, L., Bachar, E., De-Nour, A. K., and Shaley, A. (1999). Childhood Imaginary Companionship and Mental Health in Adolescence. *Child Psychiatry and Human Development, 29*(4), 277–286.

Bouldin, P. (2006). An Investigation of the Fantasy Predisposition and Fantasy Style of Children with Imaginary Companions. *The Journal of Genetic Psychology, 167*(1), 17–29.

Bouldin, P., and Pratt, C. (1999). Characteristics of Preschool and School-Age Children with Imaginary Companions. *Journal of Genetic Psychology, 160*(4), 397–410.

Carlson, S. M., and Taylor, M. (2005). Imaginary Companions and Impersonated Characters: Sex Differences in Children's Fantasy Play. *Merrill-Palmer Quarterly Journal of Developmental Psychology, 51*(1), 93–118.

Cassidy, K. W., Fineberg, D. S., Brown, K., Perkins, A. (2005). Theory of Mind May Be Contagious, but You Don't Catch It from Your Twin. *Child Development, 76*(1), 97–106.

Cutting, A. L., and Dunn, J. (1999). Theory of Mind, Emotion Understanding, Language, and Family Background; Individual Differences and Interrelations. *Child Development, 70*(4), 853–865.

Davis, P. E. (2011). *Does Having an Imaginary Companion Relate to Children's Understanding of Self and Others?* (Unpublished doctoral dissertation). Durham, UK: Durham University.

Davis, P.E., Meins, E., and Fernyhough, C. (2011). Self-Knowledge in Childhood: Relations with Children's Imaginary Companions and Understanding of Mind. *British Journal of Developmental Psychology, 29*, 680–686.

(2013). Individual Differences in Children's Private Speech: The Role of Imaginary Companions. *Journal of Experimental Child Psychology, 116*, 561–571.

(2014). Children with Imaginary Companions Focus on Mental Characteristics when Describing Their Real-Life Friends. *Journal of Infant and Child Development, 23*(3), 622–633.

Davis, P. E., Simon, H., Robins, D., and Meins, E. (2018). Imaginary Companions in Children with Autism Spectrum Disorder. *Journal of Autism and Developmental Disorders, 48*(8), 2790–2799.

Dunn, J., Brown, J., and Beardsall, L. (1991). Family Talk about Feeling States and Children's Later Understanding of Others' Emotions. *Developmental Psychology, 27*(3), 448–455.

Fernyhough, C., Bland, K. A., Meins, E., and Coltheart, M. (2007). Imaginary Companions and Young Children's Responses to Ambiguous Auditory Stimuli: Implications for Typical and Atypical Development. *Journal of Child Psychology and Psychiatry, 48*(11), 1094–1101.

Flavell, J. H., Flavell, E. R., and Green, F. L. (1983). Development of the Appearance-Reality Distinction. *Cognitive Psychology*, *15*, 95–120.

(1987). Young Children's Knowledge about the Apparent-Real and Pretend-Real Distinctions. *Developmental Psychology*, *23*, 816–822.

Flavell, J. H., Green, F. L., and Flavell, E. R. (1993). Children's Understanding of the Stream of Consciousness. *Child Development*, *64*, 387–398.

Giménez-Dasí, M., Pons, F., and Bender, P. (2016). Imaginary Companions, Theory of Mind and Emotion Understanding in Young Children. *European Early Childhood Education Research Journal*, *24*(2), 186–197.

Gleason, T. R. (2002). Social Provisions of Real and Imaginary Relationships in Early Childhood. *Developmental Psychology*, *38*(6), 979–992.

(2004). Imaginary Companions: An Evaluation of Parents as Reporters. *Journal of Infant and Child Development*, *13*(3), 199–215.

(2005). Mothers' and Fathers' Attitudes Regarding Pretend Play in the Context of Imaginary Companions and of Child Gender. *Merrill-Palmer Quarterly Journal of Developmental Psychology*, *51*(4), 412–436.

(2017). The Psychological Significance of Play with Imaginary Companions in Early Childhood. *Learning Behaviour*, *45*, 432–440.

Gleason, T. R., and Hohmann, L. M. (2006). Concepts of Real and Imaginary Friendships in Early Childhood. *Social Development*, *15*(1), 128–144.

Gleason, T. R., and Kalpidou, M. (2014). Imaginary Companions and Young Children's Coping and Competence. *Social Development*, *23*(4), 820–839.

Gleason, T. R., Sebanc, A. M., and Hartup, W. W. (2000). Imaginary Companions of Preschool Children. *Developmental Psychology*, *36*(4), 419–428.

Golomb, C., and Galasso, L. (1995). Make Believe and Reality: Explorations of the Imaginary Realm. *Developmental Psychology*, *31*(5), 800–810.

Gupta, A., and Desai, N. G. (2006). Pathological Fantasy Friend Phenomenon. *International Journal of Psychiatry in Clinical Practice*, *10*(2), 149–151.

Harris, P. L. (2000). *The Work of the Imagination*. Malden, MA: Blackwell.

Harter, S., and Chao, C. (1992). Role of Competence in Children's Creation of Imaginary Friends. *Merrill-Palmer Quarterly*, *38*(3), 350–363.

Hoff, E. V. (2004). A Friend Living Inside Me – The Forms and Functions of Imaginary Companions. *Imagination, Cognition and Personality*, *24*(2), 151–189.

Hughes, C., Adlam, A., Happé, F., et al. (2008). Good Test-Retest Reliability for Standard and Advanced False Belief Tasks Across a Wide Range of Abilities. *Journal of Child Psychology and Psychiatry*, *41*(4), 483–490.

Hughes, C., Fujisawa, K. K., Ensor, R., Lecce, S., and Marfleet, R. (2006). Cooperation and Conversations about the Mind: A Study of Individual Differences in 2-Year-Olds and Their Siblings. *British Journal of Developmental Psychology*, *24*, 53–72.

Jarrold, C. (2003). A Review of Research into Pretend Play in Autism. *Autism*, *7*(4), 379–390.

Jenkins, J. M., Turrell, S. L., Kogushi, Y., Lollis, S., and Ross, H. S. (2003). A Longitudinal Investigation of the Dynamics of Mental State Talk in Families. *Child Development*, *74*(3), 905–920.

Ketelaars, M. P., van Weerdenburg, M., Verhoeven, L., Cuperus, J. M., and Jansonius, K. (2010). Dynamics of the Theory of Mind Construct: A Developmental Perspective. *European Journal of Developmental Psychology*, *7*(1), 85–103.

Kirk, E., Pine, K., Wheatley, L., et al. (2015). A Longitudinal Investigation of the Relationship between Maternal Mind-Mindedness and Theory of Mind. *British Journal of Developmental Psychology, 33*(4), 434–445.

Klausen, E., and Passman, R. H. (2007). Pretend Companions (Imaginary Playmates): The Emergence of a Field. *Journal of Genetic Psychology, 167*(4), 349–364.

Leach, J., Howe, N., and DeHart, G. (2016). "I Wish My People Can Be like the Ducks": Children's References to Internal States with Siblings and Friends from Early to Middle Childhood. *Infant and Child Development, 26e.*

Leblanc, É., Bernier, A., and Howe, N. (2017). The More the Merrier? Sibling Composition and Early Manifestations of Theory of Mind in Toddlers. *Journal of Cognition and Development, 18*(3), 375–391.

Lewis, C., and Mitchell, P. (eds.). (1994). *Children's Early Understanding of Mind: Origins and Development.* Hillsdale, NJ: Erlbaum.

Lillard, A. S. (2017). Why Do the Children (Pretend) Play? *Trends in Cognitive Sciences, 21* (11), 826–834.

Lillard, A. S., and Kavanaugh, R. D. (2014). The Contribution of Symbolic Skills to the Development of an Explicit Theory of Mind. *Child Development. 85*(4), 1535–1551.

Manosevitz, M., Prentice, N. M., and Wilson, F. (1973). Individual and Family Correlates of Imaginary Companions in Preschool Children. *Developmental Psychology, 8*(1), 72–79.

McAlister, A., and Peterson, C. (2007). A Longitudinal Study of Child Siblings and Theory of Mind Development. *Cognitive Development, 22*(2), 258–270.

McInnis, M. A., Pierucci, J. M., and Gilpin, A. T. (2013). Investigating Valence and Autonomy in Children's Relationships with Imaginary Companions. *International Journal of Developmental Science, 7,* 151–159.

Meins, E. (1997). *Security of Attachment and the Social Development of Cognition.* Hove, UK: Psychology Press.

Meins, E., Fernyhough, C., de Rosnay, et al. (2012). Mind-Mindedness as a Multidimensional Construct: Appropriate and Nonattuned Mind-Related Comments Independently Predict Infant-Mother Attachment in a Socially Diverse Sample. *Infancy, 17*(4), 393–415.

Meins, E., Fernyhough, C., Johnson, F., and Lidstone, J. (2006). Mind-Mindedness in Children: Individual Differences in Internal-State Talk in Middle Childhood. *British Journal of Developmental Psychology, 24,* 181–196.

Meins, E., Fernyhough, C., Wainwright, R., et al. (2002). Maternal Mind-Mindedness and Attachment Security as Predictors of Theory of Mind Understanding. *Child Development, 73*(6), 1715–1726.

Moriguchi, Y., Kanakogi, Y., Todo, N., et al. (2016). Goal Attribution toward Non-Human Objects during Infancy Predicts Imaginary Companion Status during Preschool Years. *Frontiers in Psychology, 7,* 221.

Moriguchi, Y., and Shinohara, I. (2012). My Neighbor: Children's Perception of Agency in Interactions with an Imaginary Agent. *PLoS One, 7*(9), e44463.

Motoshima, Y., Shinohara, I., Todo, N., and Moriguchi, Y. (2014). Parental Behavior and Children's Creation of Imaginary Companions: A Longitudinal Study. *European Journal of Developmental Psychology, 11*(6), 716–727.

Pearson, D., Rouse, H., Doswell, S., et al. (2001). Prevalence of Imaginary Companions in a Normal Child Population. *Child Care, Health and Development, 27*(1), 13–22.

Perner, J., Ruffman, T., and Leekam, S. R. (1994). Theory of Mind Is Contagious: You Catch It from Your Sibs. *Child Development, 65*, 1228–1238.

Premack, D., and Woodruff, G. (1978). Does the Chimpanzee Have a Theory of Mind? *Behavioral and Brain Sciences, 1*(4), 515–526.

Repacholi, B. M., and Gopnik, A. (1997). Early Reasoning about Desires: Evidence from 14- and 18-Month-Olds. *Developmental Psychology, 33*(1), 12–21.

Roby, A. C., and Kidd, E. (2008). The Referential Communication Skills of Children with Imaginary Companions. *Developmental Science, 11*(4), 531–540.

Ruffman, T., Perner, J., Naito, M., Parkin, L., and Clements, W. A. (1998). Older (But Not Younger) Siblings Facilitate False-Belief Understanding. *Developmental Psychology, 34*(1), 161–174.

Ruffman, T., Slade, L., and Crowe, E. (2002). The Relation Between Children's and Mothers' Mental State Language and Theory-of-Mind Understanding. *Child Development, 73*(3), 734–751.

Seiffge-Krenke, I. (1997). Imaginary Companions in Adolescence: Sign of a Deficit or Positive Development? *Journal of Adolescence, 20*, 137–154.

(2001). "Dear Kitty, You Asked Me …": Imaginary Companions and Real Friends in Adolescence. *Praxis der Kinderpsychologie und kinderpsychiatrie, 50*(1), 1–15.

Sharon, T., and Woolley, D. (2004). Do Monsters Dream? Young Children's Understanding of the Fantasy/Reality Distinction. *British Journal of Developmental Psychology, 22*, 293–310.

Shatz, M., Diesendruck, G., Martinez-Beck, I., and Akar, D. (2003). The Influence of Language and Socioeconomic Status on Children's Understanding of False Belief. *Developmental Psychology, 39*(4), 717–729.

Singer, D. G., and Singer, J. L. (1990). *The House of Make-Believe: Children's Play and the Developing Imagination*. Cambridge, MA: Harvard University Press.

Skolnick, D., and Bloom, P. (2006). What Does Batman Think about SpongeBob? Children's Understanding of the Fantasy/Fantasy Distinction. *Cognition 101, 1*, B9–B18.

Slaughter, V., Dennis, M. J., and Pritchard, M. (2002). Theory of Mind and Peer Acceptance in Preschool Children. *British Journal of Developmental Psychology, 20*, 545–564.

Suway, J. G., Degan, K. A., Sussman, A. L., and Fox, N. A. (2012).The Relations Among Theory of Mind, Behavioural Inhibition, and Peer Interactions in Early Childhood. *Social Development, 21*(2), 331–342.

Svendsen, M. (1934). Children's Imaginary Companions. *Archives of Neurology and Psychiatry, 2*, 985–999.

Tahiroglu, D., Mannering, A. M., and Taylor, M. (2011). Visual and Auditory Imagery Associated with Children's Imaginary Companions. *Imagination, Cognition, and Personality, 31*(1–2), 99–112.

Taylor, M. (1999). *Imaginary Companions and the Children Who Create Them*. Oxford, UK: Oxford University Press.

Taylor, M., and Carlson, S. (1997). The Relation between Individual Differences in Fantasy and Theory of Mind. *Child Development, 68*(3), 436–455.

(2002). Imaginary Companions and Elaborate Fantasy in Childhood: Discontinuity with Non-Human Animals. In R. Mitchell (ed.), *Pretending and Imagination in Animals and Children*. Cambridge, UK: Cambridge University Press, 67–180.

Taylor, M., Carlson, S. M., Maring, B. L., Gerow, L., and Charley, C. M. (2004). The Characteristics and Correlates of Fantasy in School-Age Children: Imaginary

Companions, Impersonation, and Social Understanding. *Developmental Psychology, 40*(6), 1173–1187.

Taylor, M., Carlson, S. M., and Shawber, A. B. (2007). Autonomy and Control in Children's Interactions with Imaginary Companions. In I. Roth (ed.), *Imaginative Minds*. Oxford, UK: British Academy and Oxford University Press.

Taylor, M., Hodges, S. D., and Kohanyi, A. (2003). The Characters Created by Adult Novelists and the Imaginary Companions Created by Children. *Imagination, Cognition and Personality, 22*, 361–380.

Taylor, M., Sachet, A. B., Maring, B. L., and Mannering, A. M. (2013). The Assessment of Elaborated Role-Play in Young Children: Invisible Friends, Personified Objects, and Pretend Identities. *Social Development, 22*(1), 75–93.

Trionfi, G., and Reese, E. (2009). A Good Story: Children with Imaginary Companions Create Richer Narratives. *Child Development, 80*(4), 1301–1313.

Vostrovsky, C. (1895). A Study of Imaginary Companions. *Education, 15*, 383–398.

Vygotsky, L. S. (1931/1993). *The Collected Works of L. S. Vygotsky. Volume 2: The Fundamentals of Defectology*. Edited by R.W. Reiber and A. S. Carton. Translated by J. E. Knox and C. B. Stevens. New York, NY: Plenum.

(1931/1998). *The Collected Works of L. S. Vygotsky. Volume 5: Child Psychology*. Edited by R. W. Reiber. Translated by M. J. Hall. New York, NY: Plenum.

Wellman, H. M., Cross, D., and Watson, J. (2001). Meta-Analysis of Theory-of-Mind Development: The Truth about False Belief. *Child Development, 72*(3), 655–684.

Wellman, H. M., and Liu, D. (2004). Scaling of Theory-of-Mind Tasks. *Child Development, 75*(2), 523–541.

Wigger, J. B. (2017). Invisible Friends Across Four Countries: Kenya, Malawi, Nepal, and the Dominican Republic. *International Journal of Psychology, 53*(1), 46–52.

Wigger, J. B., Paxson, K., and Ryan, L. (2013). What Do Invisible Friends Know? Imaginary Companions, God, and Theory of Mind. *The International Journal for the Psychology of Religion. 23*, 2–14.

Wimmer, H., and Perner, J. (1983). Beliefs about Beliefs: Representation and Constraining Function of Wrong Beliefs in Young Children's Understanding of Deception. *Cognition, 13*, 103–128.

Wood, D., Bruner, J., and Ross, G. (1976). The Role of Tutoring in Problem Solving. *Journal of Child Psychology and Child Psychiatry, 17*, 89–100.

Woolley, J. D. (2003). The Fantasy/Reality Distinction Revisited: The Case of Imaginary Companions. *Social Development, 12*(4), 622–625.

Woolley, J. D., and Ma, L. (2009). Children's Use of Conversational Cues to Infer Reality Status. In A. Gopnick (chair), *The Role of Testimony and Domain Knowledge in Children's Navigation of the Reality/Fantasy Distinction. Symposium conducted at the Society for Research in Child Development Biennial meeting, May, Denver, Colorado, USA*.

Woolley, J. D., and van Reet, J. (2006). Effects of Context on Judgements Concerning Reality Status of Novel Entities. *Child Development, 77*(6), 1778–1793.

Youngblade, L. M., and Dunn, J. (1995). Individual Differences in Young Children's Pretend Play with Mother and Sibling: Links to Relationships and Understandings of Other People's Feelings and Beliefs. *Child Development, 66*, 1472–1492.

24 Imagination and Moral Cognition

Giorgio Ganis

Imagination is pervasive in our daily lives as we often engage in a variety of mental simulations, ranging from solving immediate and practical tasks such as packing our suitcase to envisaging the details of long-term plans such as whether to move to a different country. Given the social nature of much of our lives, many of these mental simulations take place within the social domain and specifically they involve judging the ethicality of our own actions and plans, as well as those of other people. The aim of this chapter is to provide a selective and critical review of the current evidence about the role of imagination on key aspects of moral cognition.

Moral Cognition

Just by glancing at the literature of the last two decades, it is clear that the empirical study of moral cognition has encompassed a broad range of research topics, going from the psychology of prosocial decisions and behavior (Civai et al., 2010; Gaesser, Dodds, and Schacter, 2017; Gaesser and Schacter, 2014; Lim and DeSteno, 2016; Schmidt, Rakoczy, and Tomasello, 2012) to the psychology and neuroscience of moral dilemmas (FeldmanHall et al., 2012; Greene, 2013; Greene et al., 2001), from the psychology and neuroscience of moral responsibility (Leloup et al., 2016; Young and Phillips, 2011), to that of moral luck (Cushman, 2008; Young, Nichols, and Saxe, 2010; Young and Saxe, 2011) and of the precursors of moral action (Francis et al., 2016, 2017, 2018). Furthermore, these topics have been investigated with a broad array of paradigms and methodologies (Greene, 2015).

Moral Cognition or "Just" Cognition?

In fact, it has been noted that the range of phenomena under the umbrella of moral cognition is so disparate that it seems unlikely that a common set of cognitive and neural processes, reflecting a unitary "moral sense," will be able to account for all of them. Using an analogy put forward by Greene (2014), these phenomena are likely to be unified at the functional rather than at the mechanistic level, in the same way that what different vehicles such as a sailboat, an airplane, and a bike have in common is a certain function (to move from one location to another) more than specific mechanisms such as wheels or sails. In other words, it is unlikely that we will find a set of cognitive processes or brain networks that selectively and exclusively support what we classify as moral cognitive phenomena. The exact function of morality is still controversial, but an intriguing possibility is that it has to do with fostering within-group cooperation (Greene, 2013).

Indeed, research in psychology and cognitive neuroscience seems to indicate that moral cognition relies on a broad set of general-purpose processes that are not specialized for the moral cognitive domain per se (Greene, 2015). That is, as far as we can tell, there is no "moral brain network" that only supports moral decision-making (see also Chapter 25). Indeed, the brain regions that are engaged during moral cognitive tasks, such as parts of the medial prefrontal cortex, are also engaged by other tasks that we would not consider as having to do with moral cognition per se (Sevinc, Gurvit, and Spreng, 2017). Imaginative processes may be one such type of general-purpose process that interacts with and supports moral cognition. Figuring out the details of these interactions is made more difficult by the variety of processes and phenomena that fall under the "imagination" tent illustrated in this voluminous book, and summarized in Chapter 1. Similar observations have been made in other areas of psychology and cognitive neuroscience, such as the study of imagination itself, or the study of creative cognition (Abraham, 2013), where a seemingly disparate set of phenomena may be unified only at the functional level.

Dual Processing Approaches and Moral Dilemmas

All this said, a substantial part of the field of moral cognition can be broadly defined, to a first approximation, as the study of how people carry out judgments about what is right and what is wrong. For example, using a classic scenario from moral psychology known as the "Heinz dilemma," how do we judge the actions of Heinz, a man who breaks into a pharmacist's laboratory and steals an expensive drug that may save the life of his sick wife (Kohlberg, 1981)? Since the cognitive revolution of the 1960s, and until relatively recently, the study of moral cognition had placed an emphasis on moral reasoning (Kohlberg, 1971). According to this view, when faced with these kinds of moral dilemmas, people act like methodical scientists and go through a conscious, language- and rule-based thinking process in order to make moral judgments. In the last two decades or so, however, there has been a growing recognition that moral intuitions play a key role in moral cognition and in the way people make moral judgments (e.g. Greene, 2013; Greene and Haidt, 2002; Haidt, 2001). According to this view, reminiscent of David Hume's emotivist views on ethics (Haidt, 2001), in most situations moral judgments are effortless and they appear in people's mind automatically because of moral intuitions. Acknowledging both views, much recent thought and research on moral cognition has adopted variants of a general dual processing framework (for an alternative view, see for example Mikhail, 2007) like the one proposed by Kahneman (2011), trying to understand the relative contribution of "slow" controlled processes (such as reasoning and self-control) and "fast" automatic processes (such as emotional "gut reactions") in the way people make moral judgments (Chaiken and Trope, 1999; Haidt, 2001; Helion and Pizarro, 2015). Importantly, although dual processing frameworks focus on the polarity and differences between the processes they postulate, there is evidence that such processes interact in substantial ways (Helion and Pizarro, 2015).

In order to understand these two kinds of processes in moral cognition, a large body of behavioral and neuroscientific research has focused on how people and their brains respond to variants of moral dilemmas that pit these processes against each other, such as the so-called Trolley and the Footbridge dilemmas (e.g. Christensen and Gomila, 2012; Christensen et al., 2014; FeldmanHall et al., 2012; Foot, 1967; Garrigan, Adlam, and Langdon, 2016; Greene, 2013; Greene et al., 2001; Thomson, 1985). In the classic Trolley dilemma, five people will be killed by an out-of-control trolley unless a switch is hit to turn the course of the trolley to a different track, where it will kill a single person instead. When asked whether they ought to hit the switch in order to save five people at the expense of one, the majority of people say yes (Greene et al., 2001). This kind of choice is referred to as a "utilitarian" or "con-sequentialist" moral choice, because it agrees with the utilitarian moral principle that one ought to favor the greater good: Killing one person is preferable to killing five. The Trolley dilemma is an example of an impersonal moral dilemma because hitting a switch does not require interacting directly with a person (Greene et al., 2001).

The classic Footbridge dilemma is structurally similar to the Trolley dilemma, but in this scenario the only way to prevent a train from killing the five people is to push a large stranger off a footbridge onto the tracks below. Doing so would result in his death, but his body would stop the train before it can run over the five people. When people are asked whether they ought to push the large stranger off the footbridge, most people say no (Greene et al., 2001). This kind of choice is referred to as a "deontological" moral choice, because it agrees with the deontological moral rule in favor of the rights of the individual: Killing someone is wrong under any circumstances, even if the goal would be to save five other individuals. The Footbridge dilemma is an example of a personal moral dilemma because pushing someone off the bridge requires a direct interaction with a person (Greene et al., 2001).

One prominent explanation for why people react differently to moral dilemmas that are identical at an abstract level (in both cases the problem is to decide whether to sacrifice one person in order to save five other people) relies on the idea that dilemmas such as the Footbridge one trigger stronger negative emotional responses in people than dilemmas such as the Trolley one. According to this idea, such negative emotional responses are due to the personal and direct nature of the interaction in the Footbridge dilemma, compared to the impersonal and indirect nature of the interaction in the Trolley dilemma (Greene, 2014). Neuroimaging evidence has generally supported this idea, by showing increased activation in cognitive control brain regions such the dorsolateral prefrontal cortex (DLPFC) for utilitarian judgments, and increased activation in brain regions involved in emotional processing such as the amygdala for personal dilemmas (e.g. Greene, 2014; Greene et al., 2004).

Note that dual processing theories vary in the details of the processes they postulate. For example, a recent proposal has suggested that consequentialist and deontological ethics may map roughly onto model-based and model-free learning systems (Crockett, 2013; Cushman, 2013). The model-based system selects actions using inferences about their consequences, whereas the model-free system does so based on reinforcement history (Crockett, 2013). Imagination may have different effects on these two systems. For example, it may make certain inferential paths more or less salient than others in one case, and amplify or inhibit emotional responses in the other (Ochsner and Gross, 2005).

Imagination and Moral Cognition

The most basic question one can ask is whether and to what extent imagination affects our moral judgments. Some indirect effects of imagination on our moral judgments are well known. For example, lawyers have known for a long time that the vividness of the testimony offered by a witness can have an effect on the judgments made by a jury (Bell and Loftus, 1985) at least in part because "the jury is more likely to perceive, store in memory and retrieve for use in decision-making, that evidence which is portrayed in vivid form" (Gold, 1987: 569); but is there evidence for a more direct and consistent effect of imagination on our moral judgments? The literature on imagination and moral cognition is sparse and rather varied, but it has provided evidence that imagination can affect our moral judgments in a number of different ways, from amplifying or suppressing our emotions, to enabling counterfactual simulations. A representative sample of this literature is reviewed below.

Closing One's Eyes and Mental Simulations

One of the simplest manipulations that has provided some evidence of imagination effects on moral cognition involves merely asking people to close their eyes while they perform moral judgments (Caruso and Gino, 2011). A series of studies using this manipulation has shown that people make more ethical judgments and choices when they keep their eyes closed. The first study in this series established the basic phenomenon that participants with eyes closed rated immoral actions (e.g. inflating the number of hours spent at work in order to receive more money) to be less ethical, and moral actions to be more ethical, than participants with eyes open. An effect in the same direction was found when participants rated the likelihood that they would behave in the way described by the scenarios: Participants with eyes closed indicated that they would be more likely to carry out moral actions and less likely that they would engage in immoral actions (Caruso and Gino, 2011). The second study showed that this effect extended to actual behavior, as participants were more altruistic in a one-shot dictator game (Forsythe et al., 1994) involving giving away some of the money received from the experimenter to a stranger when they had their eyes closed than open (Caruso and Gino, 2011). The third study showed directly that participants engaged more frequently in mental simulations when they closed their eyes. Furthermore, the results showed that mental simulations actually mediated the effect of closing one's eyes on unethicality ratings (Caruso and Gino, 2011).

Finally, in the last study of this series, participants were divided into four groups and they listened to, and rated the ethicality of, a scenario in which a company employer decided to hire the least qualified of two candidates because of a financial conflict of interest. The four groups resulted from the two-by-two combination of whether people kept their eyes closed or open when carrying out the ethicality ratings, and whether they were explicitly instructed or not to do their best to mentally simulate the experimental scenario. Participants also rated the extent to which listening to the scenario elicited negative emotions in them (feeling guilty, at fault, and sinful), and reported the extent to which they had engaged in mental simulations. The results showed that participants rated the scenario as more unethical in the closed than in the open-eyes condition, and in the simulation than in no-simulation condition. Interestingly, the instructions to mentally simulate only had an effect in the eyes-open condition because people automatically engaged in mental simulation when they closed their eyes. Importantly, the negative emotion ratings predicted the unethicality ratings (i.e. the more negative the participants felt while reading the scenario, the more they rated the scenario as being unethical) and actually mediated the effect of simulation on the unethicality ratings (Caruso and Gino, 2011). Overall, these studies provide evidence that when people close their eyes they engage in mental simulations that result in stronger negative emotions about unethical scenarios, and these negative emotions lead to higher ratings of unethicality. These results, as most results in the field, are based on mentally simulating scenarios with unfamiliar agents, raising the interesting question of whether they may be affected by the identity of the agents during the simulation, and by our relationship with these agents. Although there is no direct evidence on this specific question, hints that this may be the case, come from a study that used moral decisions in dilemmas involving helping others and in which the agent could be a friend, an acquaintance, or a stranger. Even though mental simulations were not manipulated in the study, results showed that friends elicited the highest proportion of altruistic choices, followed by acquaintances and then strangers (Zhan et al., 2018). This pattern may be more pronounced when we explicitly use mental simulation, as imagining the making of a utilitarian choice in which we don't help our friend may elicit stronger negative emotions and be judged as more unethical. The opposite may occur if the agent is a person we dislike. More generally, it would be interesting to know the extent to which simulating others who are more or less similar to us affects our moral choices.

Although these results already provide intriguing evidence that mental simulations can affect the way we perform moral judgments by modulating negative emotions, the manipulation used in the study resulted in unconstrained mental simulations. Furthermore, the study did not measure specific features of the mental simulations generated by participants, such as their content, vividness, or modality. For example, although mental simulations resulted in participants experiencing the emotional consequences of the simulated scenario more strongly, it is difficult to know what exact type of mental simulation participants were engaged in: Were they focusing on perceptual features of the scenarios? What perceptual features? Were they engaging in theory of mind simulations? And so on. Some of the subsequent research in the field has attempted to measure the effect of mental simulations on moral judgments in more detail.

The Effect of Visual Mental Imagery on Moral Dilemmas

A series of studies (Amit and Greene, 2012) tested the hypothesis that one type of mental simulation, visual mental imagery, affects moral judgments, and examined whether it does so by enhancing the saliency of certain judgments more than others. In the first study, participants' cognitive style was measured with an objective task, by using similarity judgments on visual or verbal sets of items to determine if there was any relationship with their moral judgments on a set of personal moral dilemmas (Crying Baby, Sophie's Choice, Lifeboat, Safari, Plane Crash, Sacrifice, and Footbridge). Results showed the participants who scored higher on the visual cognitive style task (relative to the verbal cognitive style task) tended to give more deontological responses to the moral dilemmas than participants who scored lower, tending not to sacrifice a single person for the benefit of others. A second study aimed at disrupting specific kinds of mental simulations by using an interference paradigm that employed either a visual or verbal working memory task at the same time the moral judgments were carried out. Results showed that participants in the visual interference condition made more utilitarian judgments than participants in both the verbal interference and a control, no-interference condition. Verbal interference, in contrast, did not differ from the no-interference condition (Amit and Greene, 2012). Finally, a third study asked participants whether they had pictured events in the dilemma in their "mind's eye," and then examined self-reports of the content of participants' visual imagery in the Footbridge and Trolley dilemmas to determine whether there was an asymmetry in the imagery vividness of the harm that is done to the pushed person compared to the potential harm to the five people that is avoided. Results indicated that participants generated more vivid images of the single person than of the five individuals in the Footbridge dilemma, but not in the Trolley dilemma. Furthermore, imagery vividness of the single person (relative to the five people) also predicted more deontological judgments. Overall, the results of these studies show that visual imagery vividness can affect our moral judgments, and that we tend to visualize more vividly the harmful means than the beneficial ends (Amit and Greene, 2012).

Thus, visual imagery does not seem to enhance the saliency of moral judgments uniformly, but it favors certain types over others. Specifically, visual imagery increases the frequency of deontological moral judgments over utilitarian ones. There are at least two potential explanations for these effects. The first explanation is that visual images are more emotionally salient than words. This is consistent with evidence that, for example, when asked to integrate word-picture pairs (e.g. a picture of a window and the word "fall" or "look"), people report stronger emotional responses (both negative and positive, in the corresponding scenarios) when they do so using visual mental imagery than descriptive sentences (Holmes et al., 2008). The second potential reason is that visual mental images are more concrete than words, in the sense that by their nature they specify and represent lower-level details of a situation than words do. Thus, by their concreteness, visual mental images may depict the details of a harmful action performed on an immediate person in more detail than the potential benefits to remote others, and thus favor deontological responses, whereas words may represent the "greater good" ends of the action and therefore favor utilitarian responses (Amit and Greene, 2012). Note that theory of mind ratings were not collected in these studies, and so it is not possible to know for sure if theory of mind simulations had a role in the pattern of results.

The Effect of Image Vividness and Perspective Taking

Further evidence that mental simulations can affect our moral judgments and decisions comes from a number of studies by Gaesser and collaborators that explored the effect of imagination on prosocial judgments (Gaesser, Dodds, and Schacter, 2017; Gaesser and Schacter, 2014). The first study established the basic effect by showing that people rated themselves as more willing to help the person in need described in a story (e.g. recovering from an illness) after they imagined a vivid scenario of helping the person in need, compared to a neutral (no help) math condition (Gaesser and Schacter, 2014). This finding is consistent with studies showing that imagined events are generally judged as more likely to occur (Crisp and Turner, 2009). A second study used a more stringent control condition in which participants were asked to visualize the website from which the story came and the comments people would post there as to how the person in need could be helped. This control condition was designed to activate the same semantic knowledge as the main condition. In addition to rating their willingness to help the person in need, participants also rated on a trial-by-trial basis the extent to which they considered the thoughts and feelings of the person in need (theory of mind/perspective taking), their own emotional responses, and the vividness and coherence of their mental images. Results replicated the initial helping effect, and also showed that the increase in helping willingness ratings was due to imagery of the specific episode, not just to thinking about how the person could be helped in the abstract. A linear mixed analysis also showed that the effect was due to the ratings of imagery coherence and vividness, not to the emotional ratings or perspective taking (Gaesser and Schacter, 2014). A third study showed that remembering a real helping episode from the past was also effective at promoting willingness to help, but not as much as imagining it. The reason for this advantage of imagery over memory was attributed to the lower availability of past helping episodes that were close enough in content to the current helping story (Gaesser and Schacter, 2014). Overall, these studies show that the vividness of episodic simulations of events may directly affect our moral judgments in prosocial scenarios.

In these studies, imagery vividness was not manipulated, but it varied naturally from trial to trial. A recent series of studies went one step further and actually manipulated imagery vividness to establish a causal role on willingness to help (Gaesser, Keeler, and Young, 2018). The key experimental manipulation in these studies was to vary the strength of the spatial context by asking participants to imagine the helping event to occur either in a familiar or in an unfamiliar location.

The rationale was that a stronger spatial context would enable participants to generate more vivid images of the helping episode (Maguire and Mullally, 2013). Results indicated that imagery vividness was reliably higher in the strong than weak spatial context condition and that spatial context strength and imagery vividness predicted one's willingness to help. A subsequent online study with a larger sample replicated these findings and found that part of the effect of spatial context on the willingness to help was via changes in theory of mind and perspective taking (measured with questions asking participants whether they had considered the person's thoughts and feelings when imagining helping). In other words, a familiar spatial context made it easier not only to create vivid visual images, but also (to a lesser extent) to mentally simulate the thoughts and feelings of the person in need, and both factors contributed to the willingness to help (Gaesser, Keeler, and Young, 2018). Finally, another online study using the same spatial context manipulation tested the idea that the imagery vividness may predict actual prosocial behavior in a dictator game in which participants could decide whether to donate a proportion of their payment to the person in need of help. Results showed that participants donated more in the strong spatial context condition, and this effect was mediated by imagery vividness and by theory of mind (Gaesser, Keeler, and Young, 2018). In sum, these results indicate that episodic simulations can affect our moral judgments and behavior in prosocial situations by means of creating vivid visual representations of these situations and by enabling perspective taking.

Visual Mental Imagery and the Foreign Language Effect on Moral Dilemmas

Imagination may also be one of the causes of some well-known phenomena in moral cognition. For example, several studies have shown that people tend to make more utilitarian moral judgments in a foreign than in their native language (Cipolletti, McFarlane, and Weissglass, 2016; Corey et al., 2017; Costa et al., 2014; Geipel, Hadjichristidis, and Surian, 2015, 2016). A recent series of studies indicated that at least part of this effect of foreign language may be accounted for by a reduction in mental imagery abilities in a foreign language (Hayakawa and Keysar, 2018). In the first study, vividness ratings on a shortened version of Bett's Questionnaire Upon Imagery (Sheeham, 1967) were shown to be lower when the questionnaire was in a foreign tongue, compared to the participants' native language. In a second study, an objective measure of visual imagery abilities was used. In the main condition of this study, participants had to visualize the objects named by triplets of words and decide which one was the odd one in terms of shape (for instance, if the triplet was "mushroom," "pen," and "carrot," the odd object would be "mushroom"). A control condition included the same stimuli but participants had to identify the object from the odd category. Further control conditions (no-imagery conditions) included pictures of the stimuli instead of words. Results showed that using a foreign language was more disruptive for shape judgments than category judgments, but only for words, when visual imagery was required. Finally, the last study used the Footbridge dilemma to determine if people would make more utilitarian choices in their second language rather than native language. As expected, participants reported higher imagery vividness ratings for the single man on the footbridge than for the five men on the tracks, and vividness ratings were higher when the scenario was in the participant's native tongue. Importantly, the imagery vividness ratings for the single man inversely predicted utilitarian moral choices and mediated the effect of using a foreign language (Hayakawa and Keysar, 2018). Although the effect in this study was small, explaining only 7 percent of the effect that foreign language had on moral judgments, the results show that using a foreign language affects moral judgments in part by reducing the vividness with which the potential victim is visualized (Hayakawa and Keysar, 2018).

Counterfactual Thought and Moral Cognition

Another type of mental simulation that can affect moral cognition, either indirectly by modulating emotions, or more directly, involves counterfactual thought (Byrne, 2016). Counterfactuals are a specific type of mental simulation in which people imagine how things could have turned out differently than they did (Byrne, 2016) (also see Chapter 32). Counterfactuals can modulate both positive and negative emotions. For example, tourists exposed to natural disasters such as the 2014 "Boxing Day tsunamis" in Southeast Asia tended to see themselves as lucky survivors (rather than unlucky victims) by spontaneously generating counterfactuals about how things could have been worse, and had been in fact worse for many other people (Teigen and Jensen, 2011).

Counterfactuals can also strongly influence moral judgments directly. For example, the behavior of an attacker is judged more negatively if any changes to the actual victim's behavior are seen as something that could not have changed the outcome. Conversely, the attacker is judged less negatively (and the victim more negatively) if the victim's behavior is seen as something that could have changed the outcome (Branscombe et al., 1996). In other words, the specifics of the moral judgment can be modulated by the type of counterfactuals one generates and by how easily such counterfactuals can be imagined (Goldinger et al., 2003; Macrae, Milne, and Griffiths, 1993).

Considerations from Neuroimaging

The imagination effects found in behavioral studies are consistent with the considerable overlap seen between the brain networks usually engaged during moral cognitive tasks and the default mode network (Shulman et al., 1997; Spreng, Mar, and Kim, 2009) thought to be involved in generating at least some types of mental simulations (Sevinc et al., 2017). Indeed, a meta-analysis of moral cognition (which included studies about moral violations or dilemmas) and unconstrained cognition tasks (Schilbach et al., 2012) found an overlap between these two domains in the ventromedial prefrontal cortex (VMPFC), the dorsomedial prefrontal cortex (DMPFC), the precuneus, and the bilateral temporo-parietal junction (TPJ). Even though this overlap per se does not demonstrate causality, and the precise roles of these regions in moral cognition and mental simulations is still under debate, this evidence is consistent with a role for imagination in moral cognition (Bzdok, Groß, and Eickhoff, 2015).

Importantly, there is robust evidence that people can down- or up-regulate their emotions, and corresponding activation in brain networks that support them (e.g., including brain structures such as the amygdala), by various means, including mental simulations (e.g. Ochsner and Gross, 2005). For example, it is possible to up-regulate emotions in response to a negative picture (e.g. a car accident) by actively imagining a close friend or a family member in the situation depicted in the picture (Morawetz et al., 2017). Similarly, it is possible to down-regulate emotions by imagining the situation from a detached, third-person perspective (e.g. Ochsner and Gross, 2005). At the neural level, these effects usually are associated with effective connectivity changes between cognitive control structures such as the ventral (VLPFC) and dorsolateral prefrontal cortex (DLPFC) and affective processing structures such as the amygdala (Morawetz et al., 2017; Sripada et al., 2014; Urry et al., 2009). Thus, an important route by which mental simulations may affect moral cognition may be by modulating the interactions between cognitive control and affective processing networks.

Summary and Future Directions

The overall picture painted by the evidence reviewed in this chapter is that imagination processes can affect moral cognition in a number of ways. On the one hand, the perceptual details constructed by visual mental simulations can enhance our emotional responses to moral scenarios and affect our moral judgments. For example, in unethical scenarios (Caruso and Gino, 2011) and in personal moral dilemmas (Amit and Greene, 2012) they can amplify negative emotions, which in turn tend to increase people's unethicality ratings of the situation at hand. On the other hand, they can also facilitate theory of mind, perspective taking, and counter-factual simulations that can in turn alter our moral judgments and behaviors (Byrne, 2016; Gaesser, Keeler, and Young, 2018).

This final section outlines a few ideas for future research directions. First, as in other fields of psychology and neuroscience, theoretical progress in understanding the cognitive and neural mechanisms of moral phenomena and how they interact with other cognitive processes will require more extensive use of computational models (Crockett, 2013; Cushman, 2013; Hackel and Amodio, 2018). For example, what are the exact mechanisms that explain why visual mental imagery seems to emphasize certain aspects of moral dilemmas rather than others?

Second, given the potential role of imagination discussed in this chapter, one would expect that any situations that affect our ability to visualize events and situations may affect the details of our moral judgments. For example, individuals with mental visual imagery deficits such as in aphantasia (Fulford et al., 2018; Zeman, Dewar, and Della Sala, 2015, 2016) should show a different pattern of judgments relative to individuals with normal mental imagery. The prediction, given the literature we reviewed, is that aphantasic individuals would tend to show lower prosocial choices in response to helping scenarios and a tendency to make utilitarian choices in personal moral dilemmas like the Footbridge one. Conversely, hyperphantasic individuals at the opposite visual imagery extreme should exhibit the opposite pattern (Zeman, Dewar, and Della Sala, 2015, 2016). Similarly, patients with amnesia who exhibit deficits in generating episodic simulations (Race, Keane, and Verfaellie, 2011) would also be expected to show some changes in moral cognition.

Third, so far there have not been systematic studies on the role of imagination on actual moral action, although the study by Gaesser, Keeler, and Young (2018) used small donations as a measure of prosocial behavior. An important future goal is to determine whether the pattern of effects of imagination on moral judgments found with simplified scenarios extends to more ecologically valid situations. It is possible that some of the documented effects of mental simulation on moral cognition are an artifact of essentially probing participants to generate mental simulations of the experimental scripts, rather than dealing with real situations. Virtual reality may be a promising direction towards achieving this goal (Francis et al., 2016, 2017, 2018).

Fourth, it seems important to determine if the results of research on imagination and moral cognition can be used for applied purposes. For example, recent applied research in the field of health and well-being has shown that specialized imagery training methods work extremely well in certain situations such as body weight management (Andrade et al., 2016; Parham et al., 2018; Solbrig et al., 2018) and they do so by training positive goal imagery. With these methods, multimodal episodic imagery of proximal personal goals is elicited and practiced to sustain motivation and to compete with less functional mental images. Similar training methods may be devised to help people make more prosocial choices, for example by using vivid mental simulations to make certain ethical choices more concrete than unethical ones and to facilitate perspective taking.

Clearly, given the breadth and complexity of both fields of imagination and moral cognition, much work remains to be done to adequately understand the multifaceted relationship between them.

References

Abraham, A. (2013). The Promises and Perils of the Neuroscience of Creativity. *Frontiers in Human Neuroscience*, *7*, 246. doi:10.3389/fnhum.2013.00246.

Amit, E., and Greene, J. D. (2012). You See, the Ends Don't Justify the Means: Visual Imagery and Moral Judgment. *Psychological Science*, *23*(8), 861–868. doi:10.1177/0956797611434965.

Andrade, J., Khalil, M., Dickson, J., May, J., and Kavanagh, D. J. (2016). Functional Imagery Training to Reduce Snacking: Testing a Novel Motivational Intervention Based on Elaborated Intrusion Theory. *Appetite*, *100*, 256–262. doi:10.1016/j.appet.2016.02.015.

Bell, B. E., and Loftus, E. F. (1985). Vivid Persuasion in the Courtroom. *Psychological Journal of Personality Assessment*, 49(6), 659–664. doi:10.1207/s15327752jpa4906_16.

Branscombe, N. R., Owen, S., Garstka, T. A., and Coleman, J. (1996). Rape and Accident Counterfactuals: Who Might Have Done Otherwise and Would It Have Changed the Outcome? *Journal of Applied Social Psychology*, 26(12), 1042–1067.

Byrne, R. M. (2016). Counterfactual Thought. *Annual Review of Psychology*, 67, 135–157. doi:10.1146/annurev-psych-122414-033249.

Bzdok, D., Groß, D., and Eickhoff, S. B. (2015). The Neurobiology of Moral Cognition: Relation to Theory of Mind, Empathy, and Mind-Wandering. In J. O. Clausen and N. Levy (eds.), *Handbook of Neuroethics*. Dordrecht, Netherlands: Springer, 127–148.

Caruso, E. M., and Gino, F. (2011). Blind Ethics: Closing One's Eyes Polarizes Moral Judgments and Discourages Dishonest Behavior. *Cognition*, 118(2), 280–285. doi:10.1016/j.cognition.2010.11.008.

Chaiken, S., and Trope, Y. (1999). *Dual Process Theories in Social Psychology*. New York, NY: Guildford Press.

Christensen, J. F., Flexas, A., Calabrese, M., Gut, N. K., and Gomila, A. (2014). Moral Judgment Reloaded: A Moral Dilemma Validation Study. *Frontiers in Psychology*, 5, 607. doi:10.3389/fpsyg.2014.00607.

Christensen, J. F., and Gomila, A. (2012). Moral Dilemmas in Cognitive Neuroscience of Moral Decision-Making: A Principled Review. *Neuroscience & Biobehavioral Reviews*, 36(4), 1249–1264. doi:10.1016/j.neubiorev.2012.02.008.

Cipolletti, H., McFarlane, S., and Weissglass, C. (2016). The Moral Foreign-Language Effect. *Review of Philosophy and Psychology*, 29(1), 23–40.

Civai, C., Corradi-Dell'Acqua, C., Gamer, M., and Rumiati, R. I. (2010). Are Irrational Reactions to Unfairness Truly Emotionally-Driven? Dissociated Behavioural and Emotional Responses in the Ultimatum Game Task. *Cognition*, 114(1), 89–95. doi:10.1016/j.cognition.2009.09.001.

Corey, J. D., Hayakawa, S., Foucart, A., et al. (2017). Our Moral Choices Are Foreign to Us. *Journal of Experimental Psychology: Learning, Memory, and Cognition*, 43(7), 1109–1128. doi:10.1037/xlm0000356.

Costa, A., Foucart, A., Hayakawa, S., et al. (2014). Your Morals Depend on Language. *PLoS One*, 9(4), e94842. doi:10.1371/journal.pone.0094842.

Crisp, R. J., and Turner, R. N. (2009). Can Imagined Interactions Produce Positive Perceptions? Reducing Prejudice Through Simulated Social Contact. *American Psychologist*, 64(4), 231–240. doi:10.1037/a0014718.

Crockett, M. J. (2013). Models of Morality. *Trends in Cognitive Sciences*, 17(8), 363–366. doi:10.1016/j.tics.2013.06.005.

Cushman, F. (2008). Crime and Punishment: Distinguishing the Roles of Causal and Intentional Analyses in Moral Judgment. *Cognition*, 108(2), 353–380. doi:10.1016/j.cognition.2008.03.006.

   (2013). Action, Outcome, and Value: A Dual-System Framework for Morality. *Personality and Social Psychology Review*, 17(3), 273–292. doi:10.1177/1088868313495594.

FeldmanHall, O., Dalgleish, T., Thompson, R., et al. (2012). Differential Neural Circuitry and Self-Interest in Real vs Hypothetical Moral Decisions. *Social Cognitive and Affective Neuroscience*, 7(7), 743–751. doi:10.1093/scan/nss069.

Foot, P. (1967). The Problem of Abortion and the Doctrine of the Double Effect. *Oxford Review*, 5, 1–7.

Forsythe, R., Horowitz, J. L., Savin, N. E., and Sefton, M. (1994). Fairness in Simple Bargaining Experiments. *Games and Economic Behavior*, *6*, 347–369.

Francis, K. B., Gummerum, M., Ganis, G., Howard, I. S., and Terbeck, S. (2018). Virtual Morality in the Helping Professions: Simulated Action and Resilience. *British Journal of Psychology*, *109*(3), 442–465. doi:10.1111/bjop.12276.

Francis, K. B., Howard, C., Howard, I. S., et al. (2016). Virtual Morality: Transitioning from Moral Judgment to Moral Action? *PLoS One*, *11*(10), e0164374. doi:10.1371/journal.pone.0164374.

Francis, K. B., Terbeck, S., Briazu, R. A., et al. (2017). Simulating Moral Actions: An Investigation of Personal Force in Virtual Moral Dilemmas. *Scientific Reports*, *7*(1), 13954. doi:10.1038/s41598-017-13909-9.

Fulford, J., Milton, F., Salas, D., et al. (2018). The Neural Correlates of Visual Imagery Vividness – An fMRI Study and Literature Review. *Cortex*, *105*, 26–40. doi:10.1016/j.cortex.2017.09.014.

Gaesser, B., Dodds, H., and Schacter, D. L. (2017). Effects of Aging on the Relation Between Episodic Simulation and Prosocial Intentions. *Memory*, *25*(9), 1272–1278. doi:10.1080/09658211.2017.1288746.

Gaesser, B., Keeler, K., and Young, L. (2018). Moral Imagination: Facilitating Prosocial Decision-Making Through Scene Imagery and Theory of Mind. *Cognition*, *171*, 180–193. doi:10.1016/j.cognition.2017.11.004.

Gaesser, B., and Schacter, D. L. (2014). Episodic Simulation and Episodic Memory Can Increase Intentions to Help Others. *Proceedings of the National Academy of Sciences of the United States of America*, *111*(12), 4415–4420. doi:10.1073/pnas.1402461111.

Garrigan, B., Adlam, A. L., and Langdon, P. E. (2016). The Neural Correlates of Moral Decision-Making: A Systematic Review and Meta-Analysis of Moral Evaluations and Response Decision Judgements. *Brain and Cognition*, *108*, 88–97. doi:10.1016/j.bandc.2016.07.007.

Geipel, J., Hadjichristidis, C., and Surian, L. (2015). The Foreign Language Effect on Moral Judgment: The Role of Emotions and Norms. *PLoS One*, *10*(7), e0131529. doi:10.1371/journal.pone.0131529.

(2016). Foreign Language Affects the Contribution of Intentions and Outcomes to Moral Judgment. *Cognition*, *154*, 34–39. doi:10.1016/j.cognition.2016.05.010.

Gold, V. (1987). Psychological Manipulation in the Courtroom. *Nebraska Law Review*, *66*(3), 562–583.

Goldinger, S. D., Kleider, H. M., Azuma, T., and Beike, D. R. (2003). "Blaming the Victim" Under Memory Load. *Psychological Science*, *14*(1), 81–85. doi:10.1111/1467-9280.01423.

Greene, J. D. (2013). *Moral Tribes: Emotion, Reason, and the Gap Between Us and Them*: New York, NY: The Penguin Press.

(2014). The Cognitive Neuroscience of Moral Judgment and Decision-Making. In M. S. Gazzaniga (ed.), *The Cognitive Neurosciences V*. Cambridge, MA: MIT Press.

(2015). The Rise of Moral Cognition. *Cognition*, *135*, 39–42. doi:10.1016/j.cognition.2014.11.018.

Greene, J. D., and Haidt, J. (2002). How (and Where) Does Moral Judgment Work? *Trends in Cognitive Sciences*, *6*(12), 517–523.

Greene, J. D., Nystrom, L. E., Engell, A. D., Darley, J. M., and Cohen, J. D. (2004). The Neural Bases of Cognitive Conflict and Control in Moral Judgment. *Neuron*, *44*(2), 389–400. doi:10.1016/j.neuron.2004.09.027.

Greene, J. D., Sommerville, R. B., Nystrom, L. E., Darley, J. M., and Cohen, J. D. (2001). An fMRI Investigation of Emotional Engagement in Moral Judgment. *Science, 293* (5537), 2105–2108. doi:10.1126/science.1062872.

Hackel, L. M., and Amodio, D. M. (2018). Computational Neuroscience Approaches to Social Cognition. *Current Opinion in Psychology, 24*, 92–97. doi:10.1016/j.copsyc.2018.09.001.

Haidt, J. (2001). The Emotional Dog and its Rational Tail: A Social Intuitionist Approach to Moral Judgment. *Psychological Review, 108*(4), 814–834.

Hayakawa, S., and Keysar, B. (2018). Using a Foreign Language Reduces Mental Imagery. *Cognition, 173*, 8–15. doi:10.1016/j.cognition.2017.12.010.

Helion, C., and Pizarro, D. A. (2015). Beyond Dual-Processes: The Interplay of Reason and Emotion in Moral Judgment. In J. O. Clausen and N. Levy (eds.), *Handbook of Neuroethics*. Dordrecht, Netherlands: Springer, 109–126.

Holmes, E. A., Mathews, A., Mackintosh, B., and Dalgleish, T. (2008). The Causal Effect of Mental Imagery on Emotion Assessed Using Picture-Word Cues. *Emotion, 8*(3), 395–409. doi:10.1037/1528-3542.8.3.395.

Kanheman, D. (2011). *Thinking, Fast and Slow*. New York, NY: Farrar, Strauss and Giroux.

Kohlberg, L. (1971). From Is to Ought: How to Commit the Naturalistic Fallacy and Get Away with It in the Study of Moral Development. In T. Mischel (ed.), *Cognitive Development and Epistemology*. New York, NY: Academic Press, 151–235.

(1981). *Essays on Moral Development, Vol. I: The Philosophy of Moral Development*. San Francisco, CA: Harper & Row.

Leloup, L., Miletich, D. D., Andriet, G., Vandermeeren, Y., and Samson, D. (2016). Cathodal Transcranial Direct Current Stimulation on the Right Temporo-Parietal Junction Modulates the Use of Mitigating Circumstances during Moral Judgments. *Frontiers in Human Neuroscience, 10*, 355. doi:10.3389/fnhum.2016.00355.

Lim, D., and DeSteno, D. (2016). Suffering and Compassion: The Links among Adverse Life Experiences, Empathy, Compassion, and Prosocial Behavior. *Emotion, 16*(2), 175–182. doi:10.1037/emo0000144.

Macrae, C. N., Milne, A. B., and Griffiths, R. J. (1993). Counterfactual Thinking and the Perception of Criminal Behaviour. *British Journal of Psychology, 84*(2), 221–226.

Maguire, E. A., and Mullally, S. L. (2013). The Hippocampus: A Manifesto for Change. *Journal of Experimental Psychology: General, 142*(4), 1180–1189. doi:10.1037/a0033650.

Mikhail, J. (2007). Universal Moral Grammar: Theory, Evidence and the Future. *Trends in Cognitive Sciences, 11*(4), 143–152. doi:10.1016/j.tics.2006.12.007.

Morawetz, C., Bode, S., Baudewig, J., and Heekeren, H. R. (2017). Effective Amygdala-Prefrontal Connectivity Predicts Individual Differences in Successful Emotion Regulation. *Social Cognitive and Affective Neuroscience, 12*(4), 569–585. doi:10.1093/scan/nsw169.

Ochsner, K. N., and Gross, J. J. (2005). The Cognitive Control of Emotion. *Trends in Cognitive Sciences, 9*(5), 242–249. doi:10.1016/j.tics.2005.03.010.

Parham, S. C., Kavanagh, D. J., Shimada, M., May, J., and Andrade, J. (2018). Qualitative Analysis of Feedback on Functional Imagery Training: A Novel Motivational Intervention for Type 2 Diabetes. *Journal of Health Psychology, 33*(3), 416–429. doi:10.1080/08870446.2017.1360493.

Race, E., Keane, M. M., and Verfaellie, M. (2011). Medial Temporal Lobe Damage Causes Deficits in Episodic Memory and Episodic Future Thinking not Attributable to

Deficits in Narrative Construction. *Journal of Neuroscience*, *31*(28), 10262–10269. doi:10.1523/JNEUROSCI.1145-11.2011.

Schilbach, L., Bzdok, D., Timmermans, B., et al. (2012). Introspective Minds: Using ALE Meta-Analyses to Study Commonalities in the Neural Correlates of Emotional Processing, Social and Unconstrained Cognition. *PLoS One*, *7*(2), e30920. doi:10.1371/journal.pone.0030920.

Schmidt, M. F., Rakoczy, H., and Tomasello, M. (2012). Young Children Enforce Social Norms Selectively Depending on the Violator's Group Affiliation. *Cognition*, *124*(3), 325–333. doi:10.1016/j.cognition.2012.06.004.

Sevinc, G., Gurvit, H., and Spreng, R. N. (2017). Salience Network Engagement with the Detection of Morally Laden Information. *Social Cognitive and Affective Neuroscience*, *12*(7), 1118–1127. doi:10.1093/scan/nsx035.

Sheeham, P. W. (1967). A Shortened Form of Betts' Questionnaire upon Mental Imagery. *Journal of Clinical Psychology*, *23*(3), 386–389.

Shulman, G. L., Fiez, J. A., Corbetta, M., et al. (1997). Common Blood Flow Changes across Visual Tasks: II. Decreases in Cerebral Cortex. *Journal of Cognitive Neuroscience*, *9*(5), 648–663. doi:10.1162/jocn.1997.9.5.648.

Solbrig, L., Whalley, B., Kavanagh, D. J., et al. (2018). Functional Imagery Training versus Motivational Interviewing for Weight Loss: A Randomised Controlled Trial of Brief Individual Interventions for Overweight and Obesity. *International Journal of Obesity*. doi:10.1038/s41366-018-0122-1.

Spreng, R. N., Mar, R. A., and Kim, A. S. (2009). The Common Neural Basis of Autobiographical Memory, Prospection, Navigation, Theory of Mind, and the Default Mode: A Quantitative Meta-Analysis. *Journal of Cognitive Neuroscience*, *21*(3), 489–510. doi:10.1162/jocn.2008.21029.

Sripada, C., Angstadt, M., Kessler, D., et al. (2014). Volitional Regulation of Emotions Produces Distributed Alterations in Connectivity between Visual, Attention Control, and Default Networks. *Neuroimage*, *89*, 110–121. doi:10.1016/j.neuroimage.2013.11.006.

Teigen, K. H., and Jensen, T. K. (2011). Unlucky Victims or Lucky Survivors?: Spontaneous Counterfactual Thinking by Families Exposed to the Tsunami Disaster. *European Psychologist*, *16*(1), 48–57.

Thomson, J. J. (1985). The Trolley Problem. *Yale Law Journal*, *94*, 1395–1415.

Urry, H. L., van Reekum, C. M., Johnstone, T., and Davidson, R. J. (2009). Individual Differences in Some (But Not All) Medial Prefrontal Regions Reflect Cognitive Demand While Regulating Unpleasant Emotion. *Neuroimage*, *47*(3), 852–863. doi:10.1016/j.neuroimage.2009.05.069.

Young, L., Nichols, S., and Saxe, R. (2010). Investigating the Neural and Cognitive Basis of Moral Luck: It's Not What You Do but What You Know. *Review of Philosophy and Psychology*, *1*(3), 333–349. doi:10.1007/s13164-010-0027-y.

Young, L., and Phillips, J. (2011). The Paradox of Moral Focus. *Cognition*, *119*(2), 166–178. doi:10.1016/j.cognition.2011.01.004.

Young, L., and Saxe, R. (2011). When Ignorance Is no Excuse: Different Roles for Intent across Moral Domains. *Cognition*, *120*(2), 202–214. doi:10.1016/j.cognition.2011.04.005.

Zeman, A., Dewar, M., and Della Sala, S. (2015). Lives without Imagery – Congenital Aphantasia. *Cortex*, *73*, 378–380. doi:10.1016/j.cortex.2015.05.019.

(2016). Reflections on Aphantasia. *Cortex, 74*, 336–337. doi:10.1016/j.cortex.2015.08.015.

Zhan, Y., Xiao, X., Li, J., et al. (2018). Interpersonal Relationship Modulates the Behavioral and Neural Responses during Moral Decision-Making. *Neuroscience Letters, 672*, 15–21. doi:10.1016/j.neulet.2018.02.039.

25 Moral Reasoning: A Network Neuroscience Perspective

Evan D. Anderson and Aron K. Barbey

Introduction

Humans are moral creatures – uniquely capable of drawing on beliefs about morality in order to distinguish between actions that are right or wrong. Neuroscience research has investigated the neural substrates that underlie this reasoning process, identifying multiple regions of the brain that are recruited to facilitate performance on moral reasoning tasks. Current evidence indicates that reasoning about morality recruits a distributed collection of brain areas functioning variously in conflict or agreement (Pascual, Rodrigues, and Gallardo-Pujol, 2013).

Recently, dual-process frameworks have been employed to operationalize moral reasoning in terms of two distinct cognitive systems (Crockett, 2013; Cushman, 2013; Greene, 2017; Greene et al., 2001). This dual-process framework posits that, when faced with a moral dilemma, individuals will predominantly rely on one of two reasoning systems (heuristic, or model-based) to produce deontological or conse-quentialist moral judgments. Fundamental questions remain, however, as to whether these two reasoning processes depend on distinct neurobiological substrates, and to what extent moral cognitions may result from dynamic interactions between these two cognitive systems. To expand our understanding of how judgments about morality might depend on the brain's systems and organization, this chapter con-siders moral reasoning in terms of the topology and dynamics of brain networks.

The emerging field of network neuroscience uses tools and methods from the network sciences to characterize the topology and dynamics of brain networks (see Barbey, 2018; Bassett and Sporns, 2017; Bressler and Menon, 2010). Regions of neural tissue are defined as topological elements (nodes) in a network, and physio-logical signatures are measured and used to infer their relationships (edges). Evidence from this literature suggests that the brain is a complex, self-organized structure constructed to be at once highly efficient, flexible, and specialized.

Network neuroscience's set of conceptual and empirical tools affords the oppor-tunity to investigate neural circuits for moral reasoning at a new level of resolution – that of communication and interactions occurring within and between large-scale functional brain networks (see Chiong et al., 2013; Young and Saxe, 2008). Current neuroscience accounts recognize that moral reasoning depends on relationships between a number of regions and circuits in the brain, but have yet to address the relevance of these functional interrelationships to the integration of reasoning systems within the dual-process framework. A network neuroscience perspective affords the opportunity to theorize about the underlying topology and dynamics of network interactions that mediate either heuristic or model-focused processing. In turn, better characterizing the neurobiological mechanisms of these systems provides guidance for future research into how individuals reason when they need to deploy elements of both processing systems.

In this chapter, we review evidence for dual-process accounts of moral reasoning from a network neuroscience perspective. Neuroscientific evidence suggests that moral reasoning (consequentialist, and deontological ethics) depends on activity in distinct, functionally interacting brain networks (frontoparietal and limbic; Chiong et al., 2013, Jeurissen et al., 2014; Moll et al., 2008). Evidence also suggests that the ability to combine processing from these two systems is specifically dependent on activity in a particular anatomical region (ventromedial prefrontal cortex; Ciaramelli et al., 2007; Shenhav and Greene, 2014). This process of integration involves simulating (imagining) a hypothetical model of the world, and is mediated by activity in a third brain network, the default-mode (Chiong et al., 2013; Greene et al., 2001). All three of these functional networks share a single network hub (ventromedial prefrontal cortex), and research suggests that interactions between that hub and those networks serve to influence the ultimate form of reasoning (consequentialist or deontological) we tend to rely on when forming a moral judgment (e.g. Cima, Tonnaer, and Hauser, 2010; Friesdorf, Conway, and Gawronski, 2015; Koenigs et al., 2007). We begin by discussing moral reasoning itself, and then review the literature on dual-process theories, and on the neuroscience of moral reasoning. We then review network neuroscientific evidence that bears on a dual-process theory of moral reasoning and discuss implications for future research into its cognitive and neural foundations.

The Trolley Problem

Imagine a train leaving the station at thirty-two miles an hour, headed along a straight path. You meet it in the middle of its journey and find it barreling down a track toward five people, who are tied to the rails and in imminent peril. Situated nearby is a switch box with a lever on top and pulling the lever will divert the train onto a second track, where only one person is tied. In the absence of any intervention, the train will continue toward the five, flipping the switch will effectively save four lives in net. Would you intervene, and pull the lever, or not? *What course of action would you take?*

When presented with this problem (see also Chapter 24), people often decide to pull the lever, choosing to save the greatest number of lives (Greene et al., 2001; Thomson, 1985). Concrete problems of this sort assess moral reasoning – they ask participants to reason logically about what practical decision they would pursue, based on what they think should be done, or ought to be done, according to their definition of morally acceptable behavior. The moral decision to sacrifice one life and save five, for example, reflects reasoning through a consequentialist model of ethics. In this model, a utilitarian value is assigned to each outcome (i.e. saving one vs. five lives) and the morally preferable choice is selected on the basis of their relative utility (i.e. choosing the action that saves the greatest number of lives). Consequentialism values the morality of our actions in terms of the outcomes those actions will produce, and thus, electing to save four lives in net is a utilitarian response. Alternate versions of the Trolley problem, however, reveal that our moral reasoning is influenced by the way in which the problem is framed.

In a formally equivalent variant of the Trolley problem, a "fat man" stands on a bridge as a train barrels toward five people below (Greene et al., 2001; Thomson, 1985). The man can be pushed onto the rails from above, presenting a significant obstacle for the train that is capable of halting it in its tracks. Thus, instead of pulling a lever to divert a train onto a second track and therefore causing one person to die, the participant is confronted with the decision to actively push a fat man off a bridge and onto the tracks to block the train from killing five people. Critically, the net utilitarian outcome of this decision is identical to the original problem: One person is sacrificed to save five. Participants will now judge this choice to be an immoral action. In contrast to a utilitarian approach, this decision reflects a deontological model of ethics, which values choices in terms of moral beliefs about the actions themselves. Pushing a person off a bridge is an inherently harmful act – as opposed to pulling a lever – and is therefore judged to be an immoral action.

The two versions of this problem illustrate an interesting feature of moral reasoning: When presented with equivalent choices under different framings, people will employ different normative ethical standards and arrive at different decisions. Moral reasoning, then, is the set of cognitive processes that lead to the retrieval of a relevant model in the face of a particular moral problem and the use of that model to weight and select between actions on the basis of their moral value. These processes depend critically then on the ability to represent and manipulate valid *representations* of the external world – that is, to recollect and imagine the moral value of individual actions, or of those actions' causal consequences.

Dual-Process Theories of Moral Reasoning

Dual-process theories of human inference (see Evans, 2008) propose that there is a distinction between automatic and deliberate processing streams during reasoning tasks, and have been argued to be one framework that supports the pattern of responses observed across variants of the Trolley problem. From a dual-process perspective, human inference depends on dissociable cognitive systems for intuition (e.g. based on an emotional response) and deliberation (e.g. based on critical thought and evaluation). Evidence suggests this dual-process system is engaged during tasks of moral reasoning. Cohen (2005) reviews evidence establishing the interactive role of deliberative and emotional systems in moral reasoning, demonstrating that controlled processing during reasoning tasks can be easily overridden by more salient emotional cognition. That is – intuitive, emotional, intuition-based processing will override deliberative, considered processing during moral reasoning tasks, consistent with many dual-process theories.

Research in the psychological sciences has specifically considered moral reasoning (and the Trolley problem) through the lens of a dual-process theory of human inference (e.g. Cushman, 2013). The dual-process theory proposes that moral reasoning engages two distinct sets of information-processing systems: one heuristic system that operates through mechanisms that are fast and automatic, and another system that is rule-based and reflects slow, deliberative mechanisms. According to this framework, utilitarian and deontological ethics reflect the respective engagement of two distinct deliberative and heuristic systems. More recently, these two processing systems have been suggested to reflect specific computational approaches to decision-making: model-based (deliberative) and model-free (heuristic) systems (see Daw et al., 2011; Dayan and Berridge, 2014; Gläscher et al., 2010).

Model-Based and Model-Free Learners

Model-based and model-free systems acquire representations of the world through learning; however, they differ in the way they represent and process that information. Model-based learning involves encoding schemas and causal relationships from prior experience, which allow the respondents to construct causal models of possible actions and to reason about the moral value of their consequences. This is precisely how consequentialist ethics operates: The ultimate consequences of actions are determined and valued, and the choice that maximizes utility is selected. In contrast, model-free systems do not employ a causal model of action and consequence. Instead, model-free systems employ a sparse and heuristic approach that retrieves the values of possible actions and chooses between them on the basis of that information alone. This is the operation that defines deontological ethics, as well: The moral value of actions is considered, and the consequences of those actions are not.

Together, these two systems provide a framework for understanding the cognitive differences between consequentialist (model-based) vs. deontological (model-free) ethics in moral reasoning – one reflects slow, effortful, goal-directed deliberation, the other reflects fast, automatic, heuristic processing. Participants value the actions of flipping a switch and pushing a man to his death differently; the dual-process framework suggests the aversion to pushing people in front of trolleys and affecting their demise to be an automatic, heuristic tendency. Participants are driven to recollect or imagine the morality of an action in that particular situation, engaging a cognitive system that overrides the judgments of causal models about the consequences of actions. Critically, this process suggests that moral reasoning requires interactions between model-based and model-free systems during moral reasoning: In order to evaluate model-free representations of actions that have (presumably) never been directly performed (e.g. pushing a man to his death, committing incest with a sibling), model-based representations would first be required to construct or imagine such a simulation of that scenario (Crockett, 2013) to then serve as input to a model-free system. In particular, better understanding how properties of brain networks support this interaction between model-based and model-free systems will further our understanding of how neural systems converge on a particular decision-making strategy.

The Neuroscience of Moral Reasoning

Research in neuroscience has investigated the neurobiological foundations of reasoning – specifically, the brain regions and networks responsible for implementing model-based and model-free systems (Dayan, 2012; Wunderlich, Dayan, and Dolan, 2012). Across several species, this research variously identifies model-based reasoning within prefrontal, striatal, parietal, and default-mode structures, and identifies model-free reasoning within striatal and other subcortical structures. In general, neuroscience research suggests that model-based reasoning recruits brain areas involved in reasoning and cognitive control, and that model-free reasoning recruits brain areas involved in emotional processing.

Further neuroscience research has specifically investigated the neural correlates of moral reasoning in humans. In their review of the cognitive neuroscience literature, Pascual, Rodrigues, and Gallardo-Pujol (2013) conclude that moral reasoning depends on several overlapping networks and processes, suggesting that moral reasoning does not depend on the activity of a single neural substrate or system. Many of the neurobiological structures identified in this meta-review (Figure 25.1) overlap with regions associated with model-based or model-free systems as components of the limbic, frontoparietal, and default-mode networks.

Pascual et al. (2013) suggest that moral reasoning is implemented within a broadly distributed network of regions that are functionally integrated across the brain. The breadth and number of brain regions known to be engaged during moral reasoning suggests that neural mechanisms governing the coordination and integration of large-scale brain networks play a role in cognition during moral reasoning tasks. A central question remains: What neural and cognitive mechanisms are engaged in cases in which individuals rely on a mixture of model-based and model-free systems?

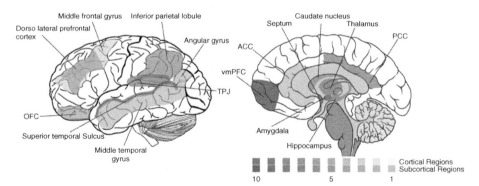

Figure 25.1 *Brain regions associated with tasks of moral reasoning. Darker colors indicate more frequent citation. ACC: Anterior Cingulate Cortex, PCC: Posterior Cingulate Cortex, vmPFC: Ventromedial Prefrontal Cortex, OFC: Orbitofrontal Cortex, TPJ: Temporoparietal Junction. Reproduced from Pascual, Rodrigues, and Gallardo-Pujol (2013), How Does Morality Work in the Brain? A Functional and Structural Perspective of Moral Behavior,* Frontiers in Integrative Neuroscience, *7, 65. CC BY 2.0.*

The diversity of neurobiological regions involved in moral reasoning, and the putative network interactions required to coordinate them, resist explanations that appeal to single regions or mechanistic circuits (for additional reviews, see Garrigan, Adlam, and Langdon, 2016, and Young and Dungan, 2012). A network neuroscience framework provides an integrative path forward by allowing us to conceptualize moral reasoning in terms of emergent interactions at the level of brain networks.

Functional Brain Networks in Moral Reasoning

Network neuroscience examines information processing in the brain in terms of neurobiological principles that govern the structure and communication of brain networks. Evidence from the field suggests that the brain is organized according to an interactive *hierarchy* of components (Meunier, Lambiotte, and Bullmore, 2010), with network attributes at one scale constraining attributes at another. For example, the organization of structural brain networks (properties of how the brain is physically wired) will support dynamic patterns of connectivity and organization that are present in functional brain networks (properties of how the brain is connected) (Sporns, Tononi, and Edelman, 2000).

Neuroscientific evidence suggests that model-free and model-based systems depend on activity in three distinct functional brain networks, the frontoparietal, limbic, and default-mode. Research indicates that the brain is organized according to several such intrinsic connectivity networks (e.g. Power et al., 2011; Yeo et al., 2011), in which intrinsic connectivity reflects the default, resting state organization of functional brain regions across the cortex. At rest, activity in these networks will fluctuate in an anticorrelated manner. During a task, however, brain networks modify their activity to produce patterns of functional connectivity that dynamically respond to task demands. This emergent connectivity is constrained by the brain's underlying neural architecture, and in this way, the structural (and functional) connectivity of brain networks at rest informs the set of possible task-based configurations networks can achieve. That is, the ease of any required network reconfigurations during task-based activity depends on a network's specific topological properties (see Cole et al. 2014, 2016). The extent to which model-based and model-free systems can integrate their processing together, or operate in isolation, therefore depends in part on the underlying properties of brain networks.

Two prominent intrinsic connectivity networks have been widely implicated in moral reasoning – the frontoparietal control network (Spreng et al., 2010; Vincent et al., 2008) and the limbic network (Carmichael and Price, 1995; Morgane, Galler, and Mokler, 2005). Network neuroscience also identifies a third network, the default-mode (Chiong et al., 2013; Spreng et al., 2010), that is specifically recruited during situations in which model-based and model-free systems must integrate their activity to imagine and simulate hypothetical events.

The frontoparietal control network is responsible for orchestrating cognitive control and supporting goal-directed behavior (Barbey et al., 2014; Cole et al.,

2012). Collectively, frontoparietal control systems are engaged during general tasks of value-based decision-making – assessing the utilitarian value of possible actions and making a choice between them (Domenech et al., 2018; Gläscher et al., 2012; Polanía et al., 2015). During moral reasoning, multiple components of the frontoparietal network, including portions of the dorsolateral prefrontal (dlPFC) and ventromedial prefrontal (vmPFC) cortices, are engaged to facilitate cognitive control and valuation during decision-making (Harenski et al., 2010; Jeurissen et al., 2014; Kédia et al. 2008; see Figure 25.1). Cognitively, these operations entail the same processes ascribed to consequentialist, model-based reasoning: consciously deliberating about causal models and evaluating actions based on their consequences. Moral reasoning has been specifically associated with activity in the frontoparietal control network during model-based processing of consequentialist decisions (i.e. flipping a lever to save four lives in net; Chiong et al., 2013).

A second intrinsic connectivity network recruited during moral reasoning is the limbic network, a system comprised of orbitofrontal cortex, insular cortex, ventral striatum, and deep-brain nuclei. This network is primarily engaged during the representation and processing of emotion (Power et al., 2011; Rajmohan and Mohandas, 2007; Schneider et al., 2013) and is responsible for processing associations between stimuli and their immediate rewards (Everitt et al., 1991) – all processes engaged during model-free moral reasoning. During moral reasoning, orbitofrontal and subcortical components of the limbic network demonstrate functional integration, facilitating representations of moral value for individual actions and enabling assessments of their respective utility (Greene et al., 2001; Moll et al., 2008; Pascual, Rodrigues, and Gallardo-Pujol, 2013).

One difficulty for dual-process theories arises from considering when and how the two (nominally distinct) processing systems they posit would need to coordinate activity, for example to produce complex deontological reasoning. The model-free system, for example, would need to engage with the model-based system in order to evaluate hypothetical events not encoded by previous experience (see Crockett, 2013). In this situation, model-based representations would first be required to construct or imagine a simulation of that scenario, to then serve as input to model-free systems (also see Cushman, 2013). Neuroscientific evidence provides support for such a process, mediated by a specific anatomical region: the ventromedial prefrontal cortex, whose activity is associated with deontological judgments of personal harms (electing to push the fat man off the bridge; Greene et al., 2001). To represent this hypothetical model of the world, the brain must maintain a description of agents and their interactions for manipulation outside of the normal frontoparietal mechanisms that mediate learned, model-based systems. Network neuroscience identifies this process with activity in a third brain network, the default-mode (Chiong et al., 2013). One cognitive process associated with this form of task-based, default-mode activity is imagination – accessing or envisioning imagery and knowledge through internal simulation of models (e.g. Østby et al., 2012). Thus, in addition to the model-free and model-based systems employed during moral reasoning, activity in the default-mode network also mediates a third system for *model-simulation*, possibly distinguishing moral reasoning from other (more domain-general) systems for assessing value.

Functional Connectivity of the Ventromedial Prefrontal Cortex

How do these three networks coordinate their activity during moral reasoning? Neuroscientific evidence suggests that interactions between model-based and model-free systems during moral reasoning may be mediated by a central network hub, the ventromedial prefrontal cortex (Figure 25.2). The orbitofrontal component of the limbic network overlaps anatomically with the vmPFC, a region with structural projections to the dlPFC and other prefrontal regions. The vmPFC is also considered a part of the default-mode network. The vmPFC has been previously identified as an important functional hub for the integration of representations between limbic and frontocortical structures (e.g. Benoit et al., 2014; Roy et al., 2012), involved in propagating information between the limbic system and regions of the frontoparietal control network. Several studies indicate the vmPFC/OFC serves a critical role in several decision-making processes that involve determining the values of potential choices (Hare et al., 2009; Rangel and Hare, 2012; Levy and Glimcher 2012; Sescousse et al., 2013). The vmPFC has also been more specifically associated with moral reasoning abilities (Raine and Yang, 2006), and with encoding value during both model-based (Ballenie and O'Doherty, 2010) and model-free (Daw et al., 2011)

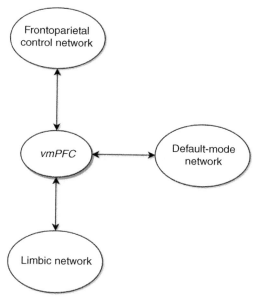

Figure 25.2 *Interactions between vmPFC and functional ICNs figure prominently during moral reasoning. Emotional, model-free appraisals depend on limbic network activity, and rational, model-based appraisals depend on frontoparietal control network activity. The integration of model-based and model-free processes during complex deontological judgments depends on a third intrinsic connectivity network, the default mode.*

learning and reasoning. That is, evidence suggests the vmPFC may be an important hub region between the networks involved in moral reasoning, capable of transferring information between a processing intensive, model-based system mediated by prefrontal areas, and a more heuristic, model-free system dependent on limbic areas. Granger causality analyses indicate that the vmPFC also indirectly mediates the recruitment of default-mode processing during moral reasoning, facilitating the imagination of events through an interaction between model-based and model-free systems (Chiong et al., 2013).

The ultimate reliance on either a consequentialist or deontological mode of judgment during moral reasoning may depend on the relative network connectivity of the vmPFC to frontoparietal vs. limbic structures. This hypothesis would align with previous research on the role of vmPFC connectivity in impaired moral reasoning (e.g. Koenigs et al., 2007), and explain contradictory patterns of results previously reported in the field (e.g. Chiong et al., 2013). Through its network-level connectivity, the vmPFC is positioned to act as an influential node in coordinating or routing activity between prefrontal and limbic regions of the brain. One topological function of the vmPFC may be to direct processing during moral reasoning toward brain networks that implement model-based and model-free systems, determining what sort of cognitive processing (effortful, or heuristic) is engaged during moral reasoning tasks (also see Pessoa, 2008). How readily individuals can deploy model-based or model-free reasoning may therefore depend on how readily the underlying topology and connectivity of vmPFC supports communication with these brain networks. Relative differences in the connectivity of vmPFC to other brain networks (thought to index the ability of vmPFC/OFC to send and receive information) may produce different patterns of dynamic connectivity during moral reasoning tasks – for example, by altering the energy cost of routing communications through different network topologies, serving to index the relative susceptibility to model-free vs model-based reasoning.

Activation in the vmPFC is known to conflict with prefrontal activity – interfering with ongoing utilitarian (model-based) reasoning and instead facilitating the emotional processing thought to mediate model-free reasoning (Shenhav and Greene., 2014). Activation of vmPFC appears to be associated with transferring information between brain networks, allowing information from previously *segregated* model-based and model-free systems to propagate through to other areas. This phenomenon has been studied in the context of moral reasoning in patients with focal brain lesions to the vmPFC, who sit at one (clinical) extreme of network disconnectivity. In patients with a focal vmPFC lesion, impaired moral reasoning is often observed, such that the absence of a connecting network hub leads subjects to resist employing model-free reasoning during moral dilemmas (Koenigs et al., 2007). That is, vmPFC patients perform consequentialist, model-based reasoning in the same manner as healthy controls, and also apply model-based reasoning in situations in which healthy controls would employ model-free reasoning (Ciaramelli et al., 2007), utilizing a utilitarian judgment system and always electing to push the fat man off the bridge.

This selective deficit in model-free reasoning observed with vmPFC lesions (and limbic/frontoparietal disconnectivity) can be further contrasted with other network connectivity profiles that alter the moral reasoning process. An interesting pattern of findings has emerged from comparisons between vmPFC lesion patients and psychopaths – individuals who share the same behavioral deficits in everyday life (blunted emotions, antisocial behavior), but who possess an intact, if dysfunctional, vmPFC (see Koenigs, 2012; Motzkin et al., 2011). Individuals with psychopathic personalities have been observed to display reduced emotional responses during both model-based and model-free moral reasoning. These individuals simultaneously experience a similar amount of disconnectivity between the vmPFC and areas of the frontoparietal, default-mode, and limbic networks (Motzkin et al., 2011). Critically however, an intact vmPFC still allows for communication between these networks for model-based and model-free systems, such that psychopaths present identical patterns of model-based and model-free reasoning to healthy individuals when considering moral dilemmas in a laboratory setting (Cima, Tonnaer, and Hauser, 2010; but see Koenigs et al., 2012). Though dysfunctional in emotional processing and more weakly connected to all other relevant structures, an intact vmPFC is still capable of serving as a hub for communication, such that psychopaths present with patterns of utilitarian and deontological judgment that match those of normal controls – despite their dysregulated application of these same judgments to everyday life. Intact network hubs in healthy controls, and connectivity-reduced, dysfunctional hubs in psychopathic individuals both facilitate equivalent amounts of connectivity between limbic and prefrontal structures; both produce identical patterns of consequentialist and deontological reasoning during moral reasoning tasks. A lesioned vmPFC prevents the integration of model-based and model-free systems; consequently, vmPFC patients are more reliant on model-free, deontological processing.

Research into neurodegenerative disorders further elucidates the relationship between vmPFC connectivity and utilitarian judgments, suggesting that employing model-free systems is specifically sensitive to relative differences in the connectivity of vmPFC with limbic structures. Behavioral Variant Frontotemporal Dementia (bvFTD) and Alzheimer's disease (AD) selectively display tropism for distinct brain networks, with AD producing damage to the posterior default-mode network, and bvFTD producing damage to vmPFC and limbic structures (Mendez and Shapira, 2009). In both cases, frontoparietal structures are largely spared, and individuals present with normal rates of utilitarian judgment on moral reasoning tasks. Individuals with AD will experience default-mode degeneration, impairing their ability to simulate models during personal moral dilemmas (i.e. when pushing a fat man from a bridge). Strikingly, AD patients still respond to these sorts of moral dilemmas in the same way as healthy controls. bvFTD patients, experiencing degeneration of the vmPFC, striatum, and paralimbic structures, do present with impaired moral reasoning, behaving identically to patients with vmPFC lesions (Chiong et al., 2013). This evidence suggests that neurodegeneration in the default-mode network still preserves healthy patterns of moral reasoning – instead, losing the ability to integrate model-based and model-free systems results from damage to medial prefrontal structures that connect all three networks.

Evidence for sex differences in healthy individuals also suggests that variation in the underlying connectivity of vmPFC to the frontoparietal and limbic networks index the relative reliance on consequentialist and deontological reasoning. Sex differences exist in the prefrontal cortex, such that males exhibit greater connectivity within prefrontal cortex regions (Chuang and Sun, 2014), increasing the density of connections between vmPFC and other portions of the frontoparietal control network. Sex differences in emotional processing have also been observed, such that females possess a larger vmPFC (Welborn et al., 2009), overall greater density of gray matter connectivity (Tomasi and Volkow, 2012), and higher evoked, task-based connectivity between orbitofrontal cortex and limbic structures (Koch et al., 2007). This suggests that males may experience greater connectivity between vmPFC and prefrontal structures, and females may experience greater connectivity between vmPFC and limbic structures. Selective differences in healthy vmPFC connectivity may be associated with a relative reliance on model-based or model-free systems – in contrast with psychopathic individuals, who experience universally decreased vmPFC connectivity and no differences in utilization of model-free reasoning. Gender differences in vmPFC connectivity may therefore explain the robust finding that females are less likely to employ model-based, utilitarian moral reasoning than males, and are instead more likely to employ deontological, model-free reasoning (Friesdorf, Conway, and Gawronski, 2015).

Dynamic Network Connectivity during Moral Reasoning

Research in network neuroscience suggests that neural activity is an adaptive and *dynamic* phenomenon, reflecting the capacity of brain regions to create new information-processing networks by altering their connectivity in a task-dependent manner (Braun et al., 2015; Shine et al., 2016). Frontoparietal regions of the brain, for example, are either specialized or flexible in their task-based engagement. Specialized regions generally serve a fixed set of specific information-processing functions. More flexible regions are instead capable of functionally modifying their network membership through task-based coupling with other regions, altering network connectivity in response to task demands (Yeo et al., 2015).

These same organizational properties can be used to describe many "real-world" networks – subway systems, commercial airline traffic, social groups – in which multiple entities are communicating with some cost. The biological cost of building and maintaining a neural architecture imposes pressure to optimize the brain across all scales, resulting in efficient organization that respects the physiological and metabolic costs inherent in assembling, maintaining, and operating neural tissue (Bullmore and Sporns, 2012). Models of cortical function constructed to respect these biological constraints (across multiple brain imaging modalities) have arrived at modular, hierarchical organizations of both structural and functional dynamics as a highly efficient way to optimize the brain's architecture (e.g. Gray and Robinson 2013). The network properties facilitated by this hierarchical structure provide an optimal balance between communication at a local and global scale, enabling more efficient transitions between functional brain networks (see Gallos, Makse, and Sigman, 2012).

One mechanism through which the relative network connectivity of vmPFC to frontal, limbic, and default-mode structures could produce individual differences in rates of consequentialist and deontological reasoning is through relative differences in the underlying topology of structural connections that affect the difficulty of network transitions required to coordinate activity between model-based and model-free systems. The dynamic brain-network reconfigurations evoked during moral reasoning (imagining pushing a man from a bridge through modal-based systems and communicating that information to model-free systems) are necessarily constrained by the underlying structural anatomy and topology of relevant brain regions. Approaches that model this underlying structure, such as network control theory (Gu et al., 2015), analyze structural connections between brain regions and characterize how well-connected nodes (hubs) exert influence on the functional trajectory of brain states (Figure 25.3). As one such hub node, the vmPFC asymmetrically affects network controllability to exert influence over the set of functional brain state transitions possible from moment to moment (Kerr et al., 2012; also see Betzel et al., 2016). In this way, differences in the network connectivity of vmPFC to limbic and prefrontal areas may influence the ability of the vmPFC to control the trajectories of task-based networks, affecting the relative ease of deploying consequentialist or deontological reasoning when faced with a moral dilemma.

Network control theory offers insight into the types of network operations required to assemble model-based and model-free representations. Model-based reasoning requires slow, effortful processing to assemble and manipulate mental models. This process is cognitively demanding and sensitive to additional sources of cognitive load. When placed under cognitive load (for example during stress, or while required to perform additional cognitively demanding tasks), subjects will forego model-based reasoning and rely instead on a less demanding, heuristic system for model-free reasoning (Economides et al., 2015). The effortful construction of causal models for moral reasoning may therefore require a more demanding series of network operations and transitions. That is, model-based systems may depend on a series of dynamic shifts in connectivity that transition the brain away from a less demanding, more baseline processing system (model-free) to a more demanding, difficult-to-reach network state (model-based). Critically, determining whether to pursue model-based processing or to engage a model-free system would depend on the relative ability to inhibit activity in the vmPFC, facilitating persistence in model-based reasoning by maintaining an effortful, difficult-to-reach network state.

Network transitions that drive the brain into difficult-to-reach states are in general associated with activity within the frontoparietal control network (Dosenbach et al., 2008; Gu et al., 2015), and the ability of frontoparietal regions to control network state transitions is specifically indexed by regional measures of global connectivity (Cole et al., 2012; van den Heuvel et al., 2009). The increased cognitive demands associated with model-based reasoning suggest that the energy costs, topological requirements, and processing time required to engage in model-based reasoning are higher than model-free reasoning, and that increased frontoparietal connectivity should better facilitate the maintenance of these difficult-to-reach brain states. Conversely, enhanced connectivity between vmPFC and limbic structures should lower the difficulty of

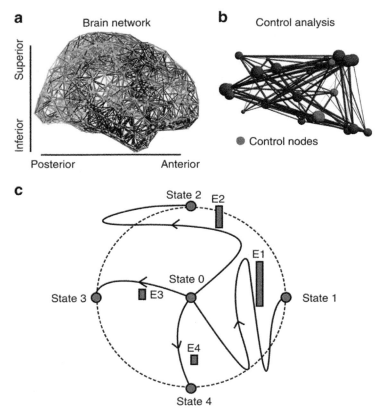

Figure 25.3 *Structural network controllability. The capacity of a brain region to influence the trajectory of functional connectivity depends on how centrally it is positioned in paths between other regions. (a) Structural connectivity is analyzed (b) to identify anatomical regions that can exert an outsized influence on brain-state transitions. (c) Transitions from state 0 to equidistant states 1–4 require traversing paths with different lengths and energy expenditures (E1–E4), as a function of structural brain topology. Reproduced from* Nature Communications, *6, 8414. Gu et al., 2015. CC BY 4.0.*

network-state transitions that facilitate model-free reasoning, which should depend on easier-to-reach network states. Dynamic integration between these two brain networks (the operations required to imagine pushing a man in front of a train, and then heuristically judge that action to be a moral wrong) should depend critically on the joint connectivity of vmPFC to limbic and prefrontal regions.

Future Directions and Conclusions

The current neuroscience literature supports eight conclusions about the nature of moral reasoning. (1) Dual-process reasoning is implemented within multiple functional brain networks. (2) Model-based reasoning is implemented by the frontoparietal control network. (3) Model-free reasoning is implemented by the limbic network. (4) Model-simulating interactions are implemented by the default-mode network. (5) The vmPFC is a hub node involved in mediating responses across these three networks. (6) The relative connectivity strength of the vmPFC to fronto-parietal and limbic networks indexes susceptibility to model-based or model-free reasoning. (7) Neurobiological changes that alter the connectivity of vmPFC to limbic network will alter rates of utilitarian moral reasoning. (8) Neurobiological changes that do not affect the relative connectivity of vmPFC to limbic regions will not alter rates of utilitarian reasoning.

The neurobiological account provided above offers an explanation of how model-based and model-free systems interact. We suggest that systems which support moral reasoning are mediated by activity within specific brain networks, and that the rate of consequentialist and deontological judgments during moral reasoning is influenced by the underlying topological relationships between those networks.

This model motivates two novel predictions for future research. Neuroscientific evidence indicates that structural and resting-state functional connectivity constrain the network transitions and states the brain can manifest during any task. Neuroscience research has yet to directly investigate how the topology of prefrontal and limbic networks might influence rates of utilitarian response to moral dilemmas. Reliance on a particular form of moral reasoning should reflect the availability of existing cognitive models and the ability of brain networks to support their manipulation. For example, individuals who engage in more utilitarian, model-based valuations during real-world decision-making may be more resistant to model-free reasoning when reasoning about moral dilemmas and should display greater connectivity within the prefrontal cortex. A second prediction addresses the inferential strength of moral reasoning – for example, how confidently a moral judgment can be drawn. A network neuroscience framework predicts that the speed with which moral judgments can be drawn will depend on the ease of network transitions and functional integration between requisite prefrontal, default-mode, and limbic structures. Processes that underlie moral reasoning depend in part on modifying networks in response to the environment to derive a task-based network – so, the strength and speed of moral inferences should depend on the degree to which topological properties of the vmPFC and related networks lead to easy or difficult transitions into relevant brain states.

Resolving moral dilemmas involves imagining novel or hypothetical scenarios, a cognitive process that depends on constructing, representing, and manipulating causal models as part of the reasoning process. Greene et al. (2001) identified unique contributions to this process made by rational and emotional systems and suggested that their interactions play an important role in producing moral judgments. Today, network neuroscience is interested in studying a similar phenomenon – how networks in the brain interact to produce emergent behavior. To the extent that models for moral reasoning posit multiple areas, networks, or systems for generating judgments and inferences, network neuroscience has an important role to play in studying how the dynamic and topological properties of distributed brain networks enable them to interact and collectively facilitate cognition. By representing neural activity as a distributed and dynamic system, network neuroscience can advance our understanding of the mechanisms that govern moral judgments, helping elucidating the relationship between moral reasoning and the neurobiological mechanisms that facilitate it.

References

Barbey, A. K. (2018). Network Neuroscience Theory of Human Intelligence. *Trends in Cognitive Sciences, 22,* 8–20.

Barbey, A. K., Colom, R., Paul, E. J., and Grafman, J. (2014). Architecture of Fluid Intelligence and Working Memory Revealed by Lesion Mapping. *Brain Structure & Function, 219*(2), 485–494.

Bassett, D. S., and Sporns, O. (2017). Network Neuroscience. *Nature Neuroscience, 20*(3), 353–364.

Benoit, R. G., Szpunar, K. K., and Schacter, D. L. (2014). Ventromedial Prefrontal Cortex Supports Affective Future Simulation by Integrating Distributed Knowledge. *Proceedings of the National Academy of Sciences, 111*(46), 16550–16555.

Betzel, R. F., Gu, S., Medaglia, J. D., Pasqualetti, F., and Bassett, D. S. (2016). Optimally Controlling the Human Connectome: The Role of Network Topology. *Scientific Reports, 6,* 30770.

Braun, U., Schäfer, A., Walter, H., et al. (2015). Dynamic Reconfiguration of Frontal Brain Networks during Executive Cognition in Humans. *Proceedings of the National Academy of Sciences of the United States of America, 112*(37), 11678–11683.

Bressler, S. L., and Menon, V. (2010). Large-Scale Brain Networks in Cognition: Emerging Methods and Principles. *Trends in Cognitive Sciences, 14*(6), 277–290.

Bullmore, E., and Sporns, O. (2012). The Economy of Brain Network Organization. *Nature Reviews Neuroscience, 13,* 336–349.

Carmichael, S. T., and Price, J. L. (1995). Limbic Connections of the Orbital and Medial Prefrontal Cortex in Macaque Monkeys. *The Journal of Comparative Neurology, 363*(4), 615–641.

Chiong, W., Wilson, S. M., D'Esposito, M., et al. (2013). The Salience Network Causally Influences Default Mode Network Activity during Moral Reasoning. *Brain, 136*(6), 1929–1941.

Chuang, C.-C., and Sun, C.-W. (2014). Gender-Related Effects of Prefrontal Cortex Connectivity: A Resting-State Functional Optical Tomography Study. *Biomedical Optics Express, 5*(8), 2503–2516.

Ciaramelli, E., Muccioli, M., Làdavas, E., and di Pellegrino, G. (2007). Selective Deficit in Personal Moral Judgment Following Damage to Ventromedial Prefrontal Cortex. *Social Cognitive and Affective Neuroscience, 2*(2), 84–92.

Cima, M., Tonnaer, F., and Hauser, M. D. (2010). Psychopaths Know Right from Wrong but Don't Care. *Social Cognitive and Affective Neuroscience, 5*(1), 59–67.

Cohen, Jonathan, D. (2005). The Vulcanization of the Human Brain: A Neural Perspective on Interactions between Cognition and Emotion. *Journal of Economic Perspectives, 19* (4), 3–24.

Cole, M. W., Bassett, D. S., Power, J. D., Braver, T. S., and Petersen, S. E. (2014). Intrinsic and Task-Evoked Network Architectures of the Human Brain. *Neuron, 83*(1), 238–251.

Cole, M. W., Ito, T., Bassett, D. S., and Schultz, D. H. (2016). Activity Flow over Resting-State Networks Shapes Cognitive Task Activations. *Nature Neuroscience*, *19*(12), 1718–1726.

Cole, M. W., Yarkoni, T., Repovs, G., Anticevic, A., and Braver, T. S. (2012). Global Connectivity of Prefrontal Cortex Predicts Cognitive Control and Intelligence. *Journal of Neuroscience*, *32*(26), 8988–8999.

Crockett, M. J. (2013). Models of Morality. *Trends in Cognitive Sciences*, *17*(8), 363–366.

Cushman, F. (2013). Action, Outcome, and Value: A Dual-System Framework for Morality. *Personality and Social Psychology Review: An Official Journal of the Society for Personality and Social Psychology, Inc*, *17*(3), 273–292.

Daw, N. D., Gershman, S. J., Seymour, B., Dayan, P., and Dolan, R. J. (2011). Model-Based Influences on Humans' Choices and Striatal Prediction Errors. *Neuron*, *69*(6), 1204–1215.

Dayan, P. (2012). How to Set the Switches on this Thing. *Current Opinion in Neurobiology*, *22*(6), 1068–1074.

Dayan, P., and Berridge, K. C. (2014). Model-Based and Model-Free Pavlovian Reward Learning: Revaluation, Revision and Revelation. *Cognitive, Affective and Behavioral Neuroscience*, *14*(2), 473–492.

Domenech, P., Redouté, J., Koechlin, E., and Dreher, J.-C. (2018). The Neuro-Computational Architecture of Value-Based Selection in the Human Brain. *Cerebral Cortex*, *28*(2), 585–601.

Dosenbach, N. U. F., Fair, D. A., Cohen, A. L., Schlaggar, B. L., and Petersen, S. E. (2008). A Dual-Networks Architecture of Top-Down Control. *Trends in Cognitive Sciences*, *12*(3), 99–105.

Economides, M., Kurth-Nelson, Z., Lübbert, A., Guitart-Masip, M., and Dolan, R. J. (2015). Model-Based Reasoning in Humans Becomes Automatic with Training. *PLOS Computational Biology*, *11*(9), e1004463.

Evans, J. S., (2008). Dual-Processing Accounts of Reasoning, Judgment, and Social Cognition. *The Annual Review of Psychology*, *59*, 255–278.

Everitt, B. J., Morris, K. A., O'Brien, A., and Robbins, T. W. (1991). The Basolateral Amygdala-Ventral Striatal System and Conditioned Place Preference: Further Evidence of Limbic-Striatal Interactions Underlying Reward-Related Processes. *Neuroscience*, *42*(1), 1–18.

Friesdorf, R., Conway, P., and Gawronski, B. (2015). Gender Differences in Responses to Moral Dilemmas: A Process Dissociation Analysis. *Personality & Social Psychology Bulletin*, *41*(5), 696–713.

Gallos, L. K., Makse, H. A., and Sigman, M. (2012). A Small World of Weak Ties Provides Optimal Global Integration of Self-Similar Modules in Functional Brain Networks. *Proceedings of the National Academy of Sciences of the United States of America*, *109*(8), 2825–2830.

Garrigan, B., Adlam, A. L. R., and Langdon, P. E. (2016). The Neural Correlates of Moral Decision-Making: A Systematic Review and Meta-Analysis of Moral Evaluations and Response Decision Judgements. *Brain and Cognition*, *108*, 88–97.

Gläscher, J., Adolphs, R., Damasio, H., et al. (2012). Lesion Mapping of Cognitive Control and Value-Based Decision Making in the Prefrontal Cortex. *Proceedings of the National Academy of Sciences*, *109*(36), 14681–14686.

Gläscher, J., Daw, N., Dayan, P., and O'Doherty, J. P. (2010). States versus Rewards: Dissociable Neural Prediction Error Signals Underlying Model-Based and Model-Free Reinforcement Learning. *Neuron, 66*(4), 585–595.

Gray, R. T., and Robinson, P. A. (2013). Stability Constraints on Large-Scale Structural Brain Networks. *Frontiers in Computational Neuroscience, 7.*

Greene, J. D. (2017). The Rat-a-Gorical Imperative: Moral Intuition and the Limits of Affective Learning. *Cognition, 167*, 66–77.

Greene, J. D., Sommerville, R. B., Nystrom, L. E., Darley, J. M., and Cohen, J. D. (2001). An fMRI Investigation of Emotional Engagement in Moral Judgment. *Science, 293* (5537), 2105–2108.

Gu, S., Pasqualetti, F., Cieslak, M., et al. (2015). Controllability of Structural Brain Networks. *Nature Communications, 6*(1), 1–10.

Hare, T. A., Camerer, C. F., and Rangel, A. (2009). Self-Control in Decision-Making Involves Modulation of the vmPFC Valuation System. *Science (New York, N.Y.), 324*(5927), 646–648.

Harenski, C. L., Antonenko, O., Shane, M. S., and Kiehl, K. A. (2010). A Functional Imaging Investigation of Moral Deliberation and Moral Intuition. *NeuroImage, 49*(3), 2707–2716.

Jeurissen, D., Sack, A. T., Roebroeck, A., Russ, B. E., and Pascual-Leone, A. (2014). TMS Affects Moral Judgment, Showing the Role of DLPFC and TPJ in Cognitive and Emotional Processing. *Frontiers in Neuroscience, 8.*

Kédia, G., Berthoz, S., Wessa, M., Hilton, D., and Martinot, J.-L. (2008). An Agent Harms a Victim: A Functional Magnetic Resonance Imaging Study on Specific Moral Emotions. *Journal of Cognitive Neuroscience, 20*(10), 1788–1798.

Kerr, D. L., McLaren, D. G., Mathy, R. M., and Nitschke, J. B. (2012). Controllability Modulates the Anticipatory Response in the Human Ventromedial Prefrontal Cortex. *Frontiers in Psychology, 3*, 557.

Koch, K., Pauly, K., Kellermann, T., et al. (2007). Gender Differences in the Cognitive Control of Emotion: An fMRI Study. *Neuropsychologia, 45*(12), 2744–2754.

Koenigs, M. (2012). The Role of Prefrontal Cortex in Psychopathy. *Reviews in the Neurosciences, 23*(3), 253.

Koenigs, M., Kruepke, M., Zeier, J., and Newman, J. P. (2012). Utilitarian Moral Judgment in Psychopathy. *Social Cognitive and Affective Neuroscience, 7*(6), 708–714.

Koenigs, M., Young, L., Adolphs, R., et al. (2007). Damage to the Prefrontal Cortex Increases Utilitarian Moral Judgements. *Nature, 446*(7138), 908–911.

Kogler, L., Müller, V. I., Seidel, E.-M., et al. (2016). Sex Differences in the Functional Connectivity of the Amygdalae in Association with Cortisol. *NeuroImage, 134*, 410–423.

Levy, D. J., and Glimcher, P. W. (2012). The Root of All Value: A Neural Common Currency for Choice. *Current Opinion in Neurobiology, 22*(6), 1027–1038.

Medaglia, J. D., Satterthwaite, T. D., Kelkar, A., et al. (2018). Brain State Expression and Transitions Are Related to Complex Executive Cognition in Normative Neurodevelopment. *NeuroImage, 166*, 293–306.

Mendez, M. F., and Shapira, J. S. (2009). Altered Emotional Morality in Frontotemporal Dementia. *Cognitive Neuropsychiatry, 14*(3), 165–179.

Meunier, D., Lambiotte, R., and Bullmore, E. T. (2010). Modular and Hierarchically Modular Organization of Brain Networks. *Frontiers in Neuroscience, 4*, 200.

Moll, J., de Oliveira-Souza, R., Zahn, R., and Grafman, J. (2008). The Cognitive Neuroscience of Moral Emotions. In W. Sinnott-Armstrong (ed.), *Moral Psychology, Vol 3. The Neuroscience of Morality: Emotion, Brain Disorders, and Development*. Cambridge, MA: MIT Press, 1–17.

Morgane, P. J., Galler, J. R., and Mokler, D. J. (2005). A Review of Systems and Networks of the Limbic Forebrain/Limbic Midbrain. *Progress in Neurobiology*, *75*(2), 143–160.

Motzkin, J. C., Newman, J. P., Kiehl, K. A., and Koenigs, M. (2011). Reduced Prefrontal Connectivity in Psychopathy. *Journal of Neuroscience*, *31*(48), 17348–17357.

Østby, Y., Walhovd, K., Tamnes, C., et al. (2012). Mental Time Travel and Default-Mode Network Functional Connectivity in the Developing Brain. *Proceedings of the National Academy of Sciences of the United States of America*, *109*, 16800–16804.

Pascual, L., Rodrigues, P., and Gallardo-Pujol, D. (2013). How Does Morality Work in the Brain? A Functional and Structural Perspective of Moral Behavior. *Frontiers in Integrative Neuroscience*, *7*, 65.

Pessoa, L. (2008). On the Relationship between Emotion and Cognition. *Nature Reviews Neuroscience*, *9*(2), 148–158.

Polanía, R., Moisa, M., Opitz, A., Grueschow, M., and Ruff, C. C. (2015). The Precision of Value-Based Choices Depends Causally on Fronto-Parietal Phase Coupling. *Nature Communications*, *6*, 8090.

Power, J. D., Cohen, A. L., Nelson, S. M., et al. (2011). Functional Network Organization of the Human Brain. *Neuron*, *72*(4), 665–678.

Raine, A., and Yang, Y. (2006). Neural Foundations to Moral Reasoning and Antisocial Behavior. *Social Cognitive and Affective Neuroscience*, *1*(3), 203–213.

Rajmohan, V., and Mohandas, E. (2007). The Limbic System. *Indian Journal of Psychiatry*, *49*(2), 132–139.

Rangel, A., and Hare, T. (2010). Neural Computations Associated with Goal-Directed Choice. *Current Opinion in Neurobiology*, *20*(2), 262–270.

Roy, M., Shohamy, D., and Wager, T. (2012). Ventromedial Prefrontal-Subcortical Systems and the Generation of Affective Meaning. *Trends in Cognitive Sciences*, *16*(3), 147–156.

Schneider, K., Pauly, K. D., Gossen, A., et al. (2013). Neural Correlates of Moral Reasoning in Autism Spectrum Disorder. *Social Cognitive and Affective Neuroscience*, *8*(6), 702–710.

Sescousse, G., Caldú, X., Segura, B., and Dreher, J.-C. (2013). Processing of Primary and Secondary Rewards: A Quantitative Meta-Analysis and Review of Human Functional Neuroimaging Studies. *Neuroscience and Biobehavioral Reviews*, *37* (4).

Shenhav, A., and Greene, J. D. (2014). Integrative Moral Judgment: Dissociating the Roles of the Amygdala and Ventromedial Prefrontal Cortex. *Journal of Neuroscience*, *34* (13), 4741–4749.

Shine, J. M., Bissett, P. G., Bell, P.T., et al. (2016). The Dynamics of Functional Brain Networks: Integrated Network States during Cognitive Task Performance. *Neuron*, *92*(2), 544–554.

Sporns, O., Tononi, G., and Edelman, G. M. (2000). Theoretical Neuroanatomy: Relating Anatomical and Functional Connectivity in Graphs and Cortical Connection Matrices. *Cerebral Cortex*, *10*(2), 127–141.

Spreng, R. N., Stevens, W. D., Chamberlain, J. P., Gilmore, A. W., and Schacter, D. L. (2010). Default Network Activity, Coupled with the Frontoparietal Control Network, Supports Goal-Directed Cognition. *NeuroImage*, *53*(1), 303–317.

Thomson, J. J. (1985). The Trolley Problem. *The Yale Law Journal*, *94*(6), 1395–1415.

Tomasi, D., and Volkow, N. D. (2012). Gender Differences in Brain Functional Connectivity Density. *Human Brain Mapping*, *33*(4), 849–860.

van den Heuvel, M. P., Stam, C. J., Kahn, R. S., and Hulshoff Pol, H. E. (2009). Efficiency of Functional Brain Networks and Intellectual Performance. *Journal of Neuroscience*, *29*(23), 7619–7624.

Vincent, J. L., Kahn, I., Snyder, A. Z., Raichle, M. E., and Buckner, R. L. (2008). Evidence for a Frontoparietal Control System Revealed by Intrinsic Functional Connectivity. *Journal of Neurophysiology*, *100*(6), 3328–3342.

Welborn, B. L., Papademetris, X., Reis, D. L., et al. (2009). Variation in Orbitofrontal Cortex Volume: Relation to Sex, Emotion Regulation and Affect. *Social Cognitive and Affective Neuroscience*, *4*(4), 328–339.

Wunderlich, K., Dayan, P., and Dolan, R. J. (2012). Mapping Value Based Planning and Extensively Trained Choice in the Human Brain. *Nature Neuroscience*, *15*(5), 786–791.

Yeo, B. T. T., Krienen, F. M., Eickhoff, S. B., et al. (2015). Functional Specialization and Flexibility in Human Association Cortex. *Cerebral Cortex (New York, NY)*, *25*(10), 3654–3672.

Yeo, B. T. T., Krienen, F. M., Sepulcre, J., et al. (2011). The Organization of the Human Cerebral Cortex Estimated by Intrinsic Functional Connectivity. *Journal of Neurophysiology*, *106*(3), 1125–1165.

Young, L., and Dungan, J. (2012). Where in the Brain is Morality? Everywhere and Maybe Nowhere. *Social Neuroscience*, *7*(1), 1–10.

Young, L., and Saxe, R. (2008). The Neural Basis of Belief Encoding and Integration in Moral Judgment. *NeuroImage*, *40*(4), 1912–1920.

26 The Future-Directed Functions of the Imagination: From Prediction to Metaforesight

Adam Bulley, Jonathan Redshaw, and
Thomas Suddendorf

"Man alone is able to manipulate time into past and future, transpose objects or abstract ideas in a similar fashion, and make a kind of reality which is not present, or which exists only as potential in the real world. From this gift comes his social structure and traditions and even the tools with which he modifies his surroundings. They exist in the dark confines of the cranium before the instructed hand creates the reality."

Loren Eiseley (1970, p. 145)

Where does our imagination come from, and what is it for? Here we argue that one of the primary roles of the imagination as an evolved system is to facilitate the acquisition of future benefits and the avoidance of future harms. To support this claim, we survey some of the most critical abilities enabled by the future-oriented imagination: anticipating future emotions, setting and pursuing goals, preparing for threats, making flexible decisions, acquiring masterful skills, and building powerful tools.

The idea that the capacity to imagine the future has adaptive behavioral consequences has a long history. The ancient Greeks believed that Prometheus (which translates to '*foresight*') stole fire from heaven and gave it to human beings – the lowly animal left unequipped for the battleground of nature when capacities like teeth, claws, and thick hides were doled out (Suddendorf, 1994). The ability to harness fire is indeed a prime example of the future-oriented power of imagination. Controlled fires demand not only a stockpile of combustible materials, but also knowledge of techniques to start, maintain, and contain the flames. Mastery in this domain thus requires a suite of cognitive capacities that draw heavily on the imagination, such as deliberate practice and planning. But the benefits are numerous and profound: light, warmth, protection, and cooking – to name a few. Human control of fire therefore illustrates the more general principle that imagining the future can be decidedly useful. Despite whatever costs it may entail, foresight has been a driving force in the evolutionary success of our species.

Surveying the Future-Oriented Functions of Imagination

Among the first modern thinkers to identify the significant adaptive future-oriented benefits of the imagination were the cyberneticists of the 1940s and 1950s. In an oft-quoted passage, Craik (1943: 59–61) noted:

> If the organism carries a "small-scale model" of external reality and of its own possible actions within its head, it is able to try out various alternatives, conclude which is the best of them, react to future situations before they arise, utilise the knowledge of past events in dealing with the present and the future, and in every way to react in a much fuller, safe, and more competent manner to the emergencies which face it.

Many authors have built on this concept of future-oriented "mental models," and the resulting intellectual tradition is too rich for a full discussion here (see Bulley, 2018, for a review). In short, many prominent theories suggest we should consider the imagination as a kind of *simulation* – often *predictive* – of interactions with the environment (e.g. Barsalou, 2009; Clark, 2015; Hesslow, 2012; Pezzulo, 2008; Schacter, Addis, and Buckner, 2008).[1] Seen through this lens, the experiences that people have throughout their lives form the raw material for the predictions they make about the future (Hassabis and Maguire, 2009; Irish and Piguet, 2013; Klein, 2013; Schacter et al., 2012; Suddendorf and Corballis, 1997; Szpunar, 2010). This does not mean, however, that people are inflexibly bound to anticipate only that which has come before. On the contrary, human imagination enables people to foresee situations they have never previously experienced by combining basic elements from memory into novel constellations. The scenarios people build in their imaginations transform and branch in real time as different paths of future action are considered and compared in terms of their likelihood and desirability.

Humans often *deliberately* imagine the future, for instance when hatching a plan or pondering what goals to pursue. However, at times people seem just to daydream and inadvertently stumble upon future possibilities. Thus, some researchers have suggested a distinction between voluntary and involuntary mental time travel into the future (Finnbogadóttir and Berntsen, 2013), and others have suggested that people tend to move back and forth between these modes when their minds wander (e.g. Seli et al., 2018). The key point to recognize is that imagining the future is a decidedly common human activity, even to the extent that people cannot help but occupy themselves with it when they have nothing much else to focus on (Corballis, 2013). In this section, we consider why this tendency is so quintessentially human, by highlighting some of the powerful abilities that imagining the future enables. We then explore how even more powerful benefits are unlocked by our capacity to reflect on and critically appraise our simulations of the future – through what we call *metaforesight*.

Affective Forecasting and Goals

Imagining the future enables people to *evaluate* alternate possible paths forward, and to therefore choose which to pursue. A common way to evaluate outcomes is to anticipate how we would *feel* if they happened, and this has been called *affective forecasting* (Gilbert and Wilson, 2007). Simulating an interaction with the environment allows people to respond emotionally "as-if" the event were really occurring

---

1 For a discussion of simulations about atemporal or fictitious events and the past, as well as the relationship between mental time travel into the past and future, see Chapters 8 and 19 in this handbook, as well as Suddendorf (2010).

(Damasio, 1994; Pezzulo, 2008). However, the relationship between emotion and foresight is complex. Aside from *anticipated* emotions (those predicted to occur in response to a future event), humans also have *anticipatory* emotions felt in the present about an upcoming event, such as excitement or dread (Berns et al., 2006; Loewenstein and Lerner, 2003). The very act of anticipation can be strongly emotive – as the German vernacular recognizes: *Vorfreude ist die schönste Freude* ("anticipated joy is the greatest joy").

Goals are desired possible future states, which implies an emotional assessment of potential scenarios. However, a goal is more than an "affective forecast" or a basic evaluation of a possible situation – it is a *motivator* (Pezzulo and Rigoli, 2011). Once emotions have been forecast, they can rally cognitive and behavioral resources toward or away from different possible future scenarios. Indeed, mental simulations of the future tend to cluster around personal objectives (D'Argembeau, 2016). People can even anticipate drive states and physiological needs they do not currently possess – an ability perhaps out of reach for other animals (Bischof-Köhler, 1985; Köhler, 1925; Suddendorf and Corballis, 2007). Humans alone build fires before they are cold and stuck in the dark.

Preparation for Threats

This same ability to anticipate future emotions and organize current behavior accordingly underlies flexible and advanced preparation for future dangers (Miloyan, Bulley, and Suddendorf, 2016, 2019). Of course, many different species exhibit a capacity for defence in the face of *immediate* danger. Indeed, some animals even have sophisticated responses to indicators of their own vulnerability (Bateson, Brilot, and Nettle, 2011). For example, starlings spend more time glancing around when they are foraging further apart from their flock neighbors – and thus are more succeptible to attacks (Devereux et al., 2006). But humans can prop open the window of time for defense still farther. With the imagination, anxiety can be evoked regardless of what is currently perceived. Humans were therefore motivated to craft spears that would only later pierce the heart of their predators (Bulley, Henry, and Suddendorf, 2017).

In addition to extending the preparatory window, it is the *flexibility* afforded by foresight that makes human defense so uniquely powerful. Consider the burrows that many animals create, into which they can scurry when they sense a nearby predator. Although burrows can be very complex, they are nevertheless built according to fixed rules and offer only a limited set of hiding places. Humans, however, can anticipate the failure of their hiding place and therefore place a trap at the entrance, cause a distraction, or create a hidden escape route, and rapidly adjust these strategies when they learn about new threats and possibilities. Consider, for instance, the ingenious ways in which human cities have subsisted during prolonged periods of siege warfare, by employing walls, tunnels, moats, traps and all sorts of sophisticated battle plans, distractions, and deceit.

Flexible Decision-Making

It should be clear that imagining the future allows humans to fine-tune their behavior to optimize long-term outcomes. Often, however, present-moment behavior is pitted *in opposition* to future outcomes – for example when capitalizing on some opportunity *now* cuts off paths to a possibly greater but *delayed* reward. Humans, like other animals, face a variety of "intertemporal" trade-offs as a result (Loewenstein, Read, and Baumeister, 2003; Stevens and Stephens, 2008). To eat the fruit now, or wait for the added taste and nutrition afforded by its ripening?

The capacity to subordinate immediate pleasure to more long-term aims has long been emphasized as a strategy for personal success and as a powerful tool in the arsenal of human cognition (Ainslie, 1975; Baumeister and Tierney, 2011). Mischel's seminal marshmallow tests with young children are prominent examples of early psychological work on the topic (Mischel, Shoda, and Rodriguez, 1989). However, the question of how humans deal with such trade-offs has been studied since antiquity; for instance as Plato's concept of *akrasia* (e.g. Rorty, 1980). Akratic behaviors are those in opposition to one's own better judgment, with the word *akrasia* literally translating to "without strength" or "lacking command." Akrasia is also core to many world religious traditions: One must wait patiently and act prudently in the now for the promise of reward in the afterlife. Thus, there is often a struggle between immediate gratification and higher ideals or goals (which is in many cases to simply say imagined future payoffs).

Human adults' intertemporal trade-offs are studied in many ways, but perhaps most commonly with so-called *intertemporal choice tasks*. In such tasks, participants make choices between immediate and delayed rewards, such as between $25 today and $60 in 14 days (Kirby, Petry, and Bickel, 1999). The extent to which someone discounts future rewards can be calculated based on their answers to multiple intertemporal questions with different values and delays. Recent evidence suggests that imagining future events when making intertemporal choices can shift preferences toward future outcomes, reducing delay discounting. For example, in a study by Peters and Büchel (2010), participants chose between monetary rewards such as €20 now, or €35 in forty-five days – while sometimes being cued to imagine an actual event they had planned around the same time as the delayed option. When they were cued in this way, participants more often said they would be willing to wait for the extra euros, and the more vividly they reported imagining the event, the stronger the shift in their preferences (for reviews see Bulley, Henry, and Suddendorf, 2016; Schacter, Benoit, and Szpunar, 2017). This work dovetails with numerous theoretical perspectives on the role of the imagination in intertemporal preferences. Boyer (2008), for instance, suggested that one evolutionary function of imagining the future is to act as a motivational brake on shorter-term impulses such as the temptation to take advantage of another person for selfish gains.

It is important to note, however, that prudent reflection may not always encourage choices for delayed over immediate rewards. Sometimes it is most beneficial to pursue instantly available rewards. As the saying goes: A bird in the hand is worth two in the bush. In nature, and in human cultural systems, delaying gratification fundamentally relies on trust that the anticipated or promised outcome will manifest. There are thus many circumstances where it is smart to take the immediate but smaller reward, such as when the future outcome is particularly uncertain or remote (Fawcett, McNamara, and Houston, 2012; Stevens and Stephens, 2008). When put to the extreme, too much patience can result in decision-makers dying "of starvation waiting for the windfall" (Santos and Rosati, 2015: 337). The challenge is to know when to pursue immediate gratification and when to work toward longer-term payoffs.

Many critical human systems (including, but not limited to banks) fundamentally rely on the capability of establishing long-term trust in the name of collaboration. The same is true even of rudimentary trading relationships in which goods and services are exchanged after a delay. A growing body of evidence suggests that foresight can encourage prosocial behavior, implicating future-oriented imagination in establishing and solidifying interpersonal trust (e.g. Gaesser and Schacter, 2014). Conversely, violations of trust undermine the reasons for delaying gratification (Mischel, 2014). Even young children are less willing to wait for a delayed reward if the experimenter has broken a promise (Kidd, Palmeri, and Aslin, 2013).

Deliberate Practice

To build a sustained fire, craft and use a sturdy weapon, or play an instrument, one must attain mastery of a skill. Practicing is the way to achieve such mastery. It requires thinking about one's future self as alterable. Once an upgraded future self can be envisioned, say with improved abilities and knowledge, people can become motivated to pursue steps towards making this a reality (Davis, Cullen, and Suddendorf, 2016; Suddendorf, Brinums, and Imuta, 2016). Through many hours of practice humans pursue a seemingly endless variety of skills. And while deliberate practice usually involves repetition of physical actions, it is also the case that humans can improve their skills by merely *imagining* the relevant actions (e.g. Coffman, 1990).

Some of the earliest material evidence for deliberate practice in our lineage comes in the form of Acheulean handaxes and cleavers associated with *Homo erectus* (Suddendorf, Brinums, and Imuta, 2016). The oldest surviving examples of the symmetrical handaxes – which potentially had many different uses, including cutting meat from carcasses, digging for tubers, and woodworking – are more than 1.76 million years old (Lepre et al. 2011). There are some archaeological sites where a bounty of bifacial handaxes lies discarded, for example at Olorgesailie in Kenya. This apparent abundance of intricately crafted tools suggests that their makers were *practicing* the manufacturing skill. After all, if they needed a handaxe, they could have just picked up one of the ones lying around. Instead, new ones were made again and again, and their makers would have carried with them not just a tool, but the capacity to craft a new one whenever needed (Suddendorf, Brinums, and Imuta, 2016). The tools themselves exhibit signs of effortful and detailed production, such as an aesthetic bidirectional symmetry that would have required mastery of the relevant knapping skills (Mithen, 1996; Shipton and Nielsen, 2015). The tools are complex and uniform enough that they must also have emerged through iterative social learning, and perhaps teaching (Legare and Nielsen, 2015; Whiten and Erdal, 2012).

Another hypothesis about the apparent overabundance of Acheulean handaxes is that they represent a form of sexual signaling of desirable qualities such as the competence of the creator (Kohn and Mithen, 1999). However, this possibility is clearly complementary with the deliberate practice account. Even as a sexual signal,

Figure 26.1 *The West Tofts handaxe. A shell of the Cretaceous bivalve mollusc* Spondylus spinosus *is embedded at the center of the tool. This image is copyrighted. Reproduced by permission of the University of Cambridge Museum of Archaeology and Anthropology (accession number 1916.82).*

the creation of a bifacial handaxe requires deliberate practice of flint knapping. Consider the West Tofts handaxe, which has a shell embedded at its center (Figure 26.1). The creator of this object appears to have selected the flint and knapped it so that the shell stayed in the middle – demonstrating not only competence but perhaps also a sense of beauty (Oakley, 1981)[2]

Compensating for Anticipated Limits: Introducing "Metaforesight"

Humans, perhaps uniquely, are capable of meta-representational insight into the relationship between their imagination and reality. In other words, people can evaluate how imagined scenarios link in with the external world, and thus assess

2 It is also possible that the shell placement is a complete coincidence. The interpretation of handaxes in general, and especially with regards to what they tell us about ancient cognition, is contentious within archaeology (for example see Machin, 2008).

whether what is imagined is likely to actually occur in the future, and whether it is biased, pessimistic, or hopeful and so forth. In the broad sense, meta-representation involves representing the relation between (1) a representation and (2) what that representation is *about* (Pylyshyn, 1978). The development of such a capacity in childhood is widely considered as critical to the emergence of an understanding of *other people's* minds (e.g. Perner, 1991). In the domain of foresight, this form of metacognition has long been given a central role (Suddendorf, 1999). Once one appreciates that one's thoughts about the future are *just* representations, one is in a position to evaluate them, to modify them, to discount them, to discuss them, and to try to compensate for their shortcomings (Redshaw, 2014; Redshaw and Bulley, 2018). Indeed, this capacity may be crucial to children acquiring a mature sense of future time itself – as a series of possible chains of events of which only one will actually happen (see Hoerl and McCormack, 2018).

In this section, we will discuss a number of ways that metacognition and foresight interact to unlock a new suite of adaptive benefits for future-oriented imagination in each of the domains surveyed above. Our primary argument is that metacognition enables people to evaluate the strengths and limitations of their own predictions and the future operation of other cognitive systems. These insights can then drive compensatory action in preparation for possible cognitive failures, such as contingency planning and the use of external reminders (Redshaw and Bulley, 2018; Risko and Gilbert, 2016). We propose that together these processes be called *metaforesight*. Given the established links between memory and foresight, this name offers a fitting parallel to *metamemory*. Metamemory processes are those that enable people to monitor and control their memory capacities, and this has long been a subject of intense research (Bjork, 1994; Dunlosky and Tauber, 2016; Flavell and Wellman, 1977; Nelson and Narens, 1990).

We have recently begun to examine how aspects of metaforesight develop in childhood, and whether certain fundamentals are shared with other animals. In one study, children and great apes were given the opportunity to catch a desirable target dropped into an inverted "Y" shaped tube. Childen aged 2 years old and apes typically covered only a single exit from the tube, and thus missed the reward on approximately half of the trials. By the age of 4 years, however, most children consistently covered both exits from the first trial onward, ensuring they would always catch the reward (Redshaw and Suddendorf, 2016). One interpretation is that the older children understood that their prediction of the future target location *could be wrong*, and that therefore it was worth "covering both bases" (Redshaw et al., 2019; Suddendorf, Crimston, and Redshaw, 2017).

In another recent study, we tested young children's metacognitive compensation for their anticipated memory failures (Redshaw et al., 2018). Children aged 7 to 13 were given a computerized task that required them to remember to carry out future intentions after a delay – analogous to a prospective memory situation such as needing to remember to bring home a book from school (Brandimonte, Einstein, and McDaniel, 2014). We then gave participants the opportunity to *set themselves reminders* of the future intentions if they wished to do so. Children of all ages demonstrated appropriate knowledge about their potential memory failures – recognizing that it would be harder to perform the task when there were more intentions to remember. However, we found that only children aged about 9 years and upwards set themselves more reminders in conditions in which they anticipated their future memory performance would be worse.

Children's age-related improvements on these specific tasks may be driven by more general developments in both *metacognitive insight* and *metacognitive control*. Metacognitive insight refers to beliefs about the capacities and limitations of our own minds (Nelson and Narens, 1990), and typically develops during the preschool years. Even 3.5-year-olds, for instance, seem to understand when they are uncertain about the location of a hidden object (Neldner, Collier-Baker, and Nielsen, 2015) or if they have previously learned an item from a memory list (Balcomb and Gerken, 2008). Metacognitive control, on the other hand, refers to the use of metacognitive insight to flexibly adopt behavioral strategies in varied situations, and typically develops during the primary school years. For example, although 6- and 7-year-olds know the difference between easy and hard items to learn for a memory test, only around age 9 do children dedicate proportionately more time to studying hard items than easy items (Dufresne and Kobasigawa, 1989). Such fundamentals of metaforesight may underlie a range of powerful abilities that we will now explore in more detail (Figure 26.2).

The Power of Metaforesight

Appreciating that the future may not pan out according to their best-laid plans, people frequently establish diverse contingencies and "if-then" conditionals – much to their benefit (and to the profit of insurance salespeople). Counterfactual thinking about how things *might have been* is a boon to this kind of flexible planning because it lets people simulate how their mistakes might have cost them – and how to avoid repeating errors (Beck et al., 2006; Byrne, 2016; Rafetseder, Cristi-Vargas, and Perner, 2010; Schacter et al., 2015). People also frequently set up choices that are changeable – for instance by keeping receipts so that clothing can be returned if one no longer likes how it looks once one gets it home. In setting out on a clear morning, with fine weather predicted all day, people might nonetheless decide to bring a coat because they realize that their initial sunny outlook (or that of the weather forecaster) could be mistaken.

In the domain of deliberate practice, humans frequently face the problem of deciding *what* skills to try and master given that there is only so much time in a day. *Should I try and master the piano, or pick an easier but perhaps less impressive instrument?* Notably, this can also take the form of "second-order volitions" – attempting to determine *what we should want,* and, indeed, *wanting to want other things* (Frankfurt, 1988). Together, these processes enable people to become knowledgable and proficient in vastly disparate areas of mastery. The fact that individuals make such different choices goes some way to explaining why humans are so diverse in their expertise. Indeed, when wired together in reciprocal networks, this range of expertise has accelerated human innovation and potent cooperation, and has played a critical role in our dominance on the planet (Legare and Nielsen, 2015; Suddendorf, 2013).

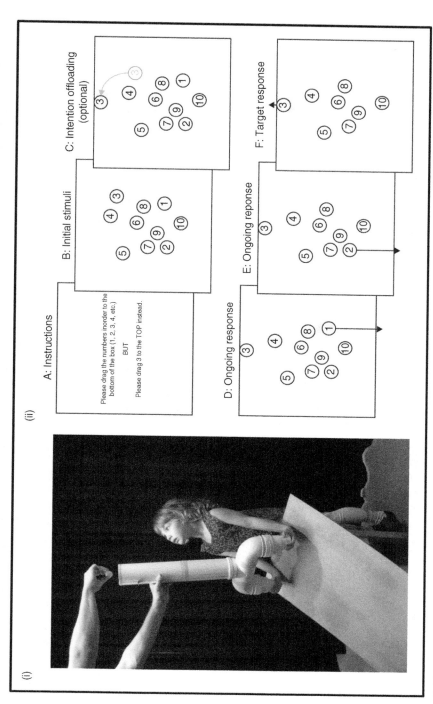

Figure 26.2 *Recent studies into the fundamentals of metaforesight in development. (i) Catching the ball dropped into the tube is guaranteed only by covering both exits simultaneously – a rudiment of contingency planning. Reprinted from Current Biology, 26(13): Redshaw and Suddendorf; Children and Apes' Preparatory Responses to Two Mutually Exclusive Possibilities, 1758–1762. Copyright 2016 with permission from Elsevier. (ii) In a reminder-setting task, participants drag numbered circles in ascending order to the bottom of the box. They must also remember to carry out either one or three alternative actions for specific numbers (dragging them to a particular edge) (A–B). In some conditions, participants have the option of dragging the target circles to the relevant edge of the box at the beginning of the trial – a reminder-setting strategy (C). If participants do pursue this option, then – after dragging non-target circles to the bottom of the box (D–E) – the new location of the target circles will remind them of the required action (F). Reprinted from Child Development, 89(6): Redshaw et al., Development of Children's Use of External Reminders for Hard-to-Remember Intentions, 2099–2108. Copyright 2018 with permission from John Wiley & Sons. Child Development © 2018 Society for Research in Child Development, Inc. All rights reserved. 009–3920/ 2018/8906–0015.*

Most research on the role of metacognition in future-oriented mental time travel comes from the domain of flexible decision-making and willpower. This reflects the practical importance of this question for understanding a vast swathe of unhealthy behavior in so-called "impulse-related disorders," including drug use and overeating (Koffarnus et al., 2013): Why, exactly, do people often fail to control their behavior even when they are fully aware of the prospective costs? However, even everyday drug use such as drinking coffee involves, often implicitly, some strategic compensation for one's own future cognitive limitations. One might hope for a perfectly chipper morning meeting, but also realize that without some caffeine this is likely to be little more than wishful thinking. The vast majority of human drug use is not clinically problematic and does not reach the threshold for diagnosis, leading some authors to argue that most drugs are instead used strategically as tools to modify and enhance cognition in various domains (Müller and Schumann, 2011).

On the other hand, people often employ metaforesight to align their anticipated future behavior with their "better judgment" – as in the *akrasia* examples discussed earlier. Odysseus, in the archetypal display, has himself lashed to the mast of his ship to prevent an anticipated failure of willpower when he hears the sirens calling (Ainslie, 1975; Boyer, 2008; Elster, 2000). Here, Odysseus realized that an imagined future in which he successfully avoided the sirens was just one way things could turn out, and a dangerous alternative was likely unless he took steps in the present to guard against his future temptations. To do it, he offloaded his cognition – relying on other people in the environment as mechanisms for situational self-control (Duckworth, Gendler, and Gross, 2016). The dieter who, in a cool moment of insight, tells his spouse to hide the cookies is applying the same strategy.

Humans implement such strategies in a form of negotiation with their own future self (Parfit, 1971; Rachlin, 2016; Schelling, 1960; Thaler and Shefrin, 1981). There are apps one can download, for example, that once activated simply block access to various social media, news, and entertainment websites. It is common practice in trying to quit biting one's nails to apply a clear nasty-tasting liquid so that future failures are punished and corrected by one's own past compensatory behavior. A clinical treatment, "Antabuse" (*disulfiram*) produces the effects of a hangover immediately after consuming alcohol, and not after the typical delay (Rachlin, 1995; Shelling, 1984). In all of the above cases the common thread is that a future is imagined wherein the person recognizes that their future self will have particular limits – with precursory compensating action a downstream effect of this insight.

Finally, we note that metaforesight may play a particularly crucial role in solving one of the most archetypal future-oriented problems that humans face: How to anticipate and act to satisfy future desires that we currently do not experience (Suddendorf and Corballis, 1997). Indeed, anticipation of future desire states need not necessarily be based on pre-*experiencing* these desire states. Rather, we may often project our *current* drive states and physiological needs into our future selves – and then metacognitively recognize that these imagined states are misleading and alter our behavior accordingly (Redshaw and Bulley, 2018). Thus a fully sated shopper does not necessarily need to imagine being hungry in order to buy next week's groceries; she merely needs to *know* that she (and the rest of her family) will not be sated in the future.

Tools that Metaforesight Helps to Build

As discussed earlier, bifacial hand axes from the Acheulean represent perhaps the earliest hard evidence for complex prospective cognition in any *Homo* species (Hallos, 2005). However, metaforesight allows humans to create still more complex tools – or *cognitive artifacts* – that extend and buttress the mind (Clark, 2008, 2015; Clark and Chalmers, 1998; Donald, 1991; Dror and Harnad, 2008; Heersmink, 2013; Hutchins, 1999; Jones, 2007; Sterelny, 2010; Sutton, 2006). There is some Palaeolithic evidence for representations of landscape features for use in navigation or planning that might fairly be called "maps" (Clarke, 2013; Smith, 1987), including a recently discovered set of engraved stone blocks from Abauntz Cave in Navarra, Spain dating back approximately 13,000 years (Utrilla et al., 2009). The tablets may have been portable, weighing less than the average modern laptop (Clarke, 2013), and thus built in advance to compensate and extend for known limitations in unaided navigation. Interpretations of these engravings and other similar artifacts, such as an 8,200-year-old Neolithic "settlement plan map" in Çatalhöyük, Anatolia (Mellaart, 1967), are contentious (Meece, 2006; Woodward and Harley, 1987). We must also consider that maps are most useful if they can be created and used "on-the-go," and are thus likely to have been produced for thousands of years with transient materials prior to the earliest remaining evidence (Dawkins, 1998). Lines drawn in the sand, however, are famously ephemeral.

Indications of metaforesight in tool use are non-contentious by the time of Babylonian Mesopotamia around 5,000 years ago, where evidence for expert cartography abounds, as does cuneiform script (Clarke, 2013; Fischer, 2001; Woodward and Harley, 1987). Maps and writing are of course both excellent evidence that future-directed metacognitive insight and control had emerged because they enable the user to outsource various cognitive processes including memory, mathematics, and even trust. Consider also that early recordings of trade and debt took the form of a single marked wooden block called a tally that could be split into two halves – the 'foil' and the 'stock' (Baxter, 1989). Putting both halves back together again in the future to read the inscription would expose any tampering, negating the need for perfect mental accounting of what was sold or owed.

Numerous artifacts abound from diverse cultures that served similar roles, for example the intricate knotted string "khipu" used by the Inka and other Andean cultures to store complex records including census and tax information (for multiple other examples, see Kelly, 2017). By the rise of ancient Greece, complex water clocks had been developed to keep track of time during political speeches (Dohrn-van Rossum, 1996). All subsequent alarm clocks and external reminders employ the same underlying logic – recognition of, and compensation for, an expected failure of prospective memory.

Once these kinds of complex tools are invented, it becomes fruitful to assess their ability to perform cognitive work in a similar way to how one might evaluate one's own abilities (Risko and Gilbert, 2016). Thus, although one might use Google to help plan the location of a first date, it is inadvisable to use Google *during* the date to help plan the next topic of conversation. Science, as a "thinking tool" takes this to its extreme: A hypothesis is generated alongside an explicit assessment of its possible incorrectness, and, furthermore, a test that could falsify it (Popper, 1934). Indeed, it is now customary to report metacognitive assessments such as confidence intervals, statistical power, and the standard errors of estimates in empirical articles. Scientific instruments are often themselves extensions of sensory apparatuses (like telescopes) as well as tools for the enhancement of cognitive labor (like computers) – but their capacities and uses must be assessed accurately for offloading to be productive (Heersmink, 2016).

People may likewise selectively offload cognitive tasks into other people's minds, for instance when trusting an elder with the details of a creation myth, an experienced tracker to navigate through treacherous terrain, or a spouse with remembering a family appointment (Kelly, 2015; see also Michaelian and Sutton, 2013; Nestojko, Finley, and Roediger, 2013; Palermos, 2016).[3] There is, however, limited research on how and when people perform prospective cognitive offloading into the minds of other people ("distributed cognition"), or its development in children (though see, for example, Barnier et al., 2008; Hirst and Echterhoff, 2012). In further studying social cognitive offloading, it may prove fruitful to borrow from the growing body of work on the role of metacognition in social learning strategies – that is, how people come to "know who knows" desired information and use that information to learn selectively from others (Heyes, 2016).

Future Directions and Concluding Remarks

The human imagination facilitates a large array of future-oriented faculties. These include anticipating future emotions, complex planning, preparation for threats, flexible decision-making, and deliberate practice, all of which are immensely powerful in their own right. However, we have also identified how a capacity for metacognition bolsters these capacities even further. We have proposed *"metaforesight"* – the processes involved in monitoring, controlling, and ultimately augmenting foresight – as an important and understudied parallel of metamemory. The study of this set of processes is in its infancy. There are numerous open questions, such as how metaforesight develops in childhood, what aspects of it are shared with other animals, when and where it emerges in the archaeological record, its underlying cognitive and neural mechanisms, and its deterioration in aging and disease. When is it optimal to "offload" cognition on the basis of our anticipated limits, and does frequent offloading have any negative

3 Andy Clark has gone one step further still, and argues that language itself evolved because it enables people to offload their thoughts into the external environment as perceptible "objects" that they and other people can then "use" in further cognition (Clark, 2006).

consequences? Do nonhuman animals ever place objects strategically to remind themselves of things in the future? Can metaforesight degrade in clinical disorders while foresight remains intact? With the capacity to recognize and reflect on the natural limits of foresight comes the creation of mental, cultural, and technological means to compensate for these limits. The human imagination is a tool – and like all tools it is wielded more effectively when you know where its limits lie.

References

Ainslie, G. (1975). Specious Reward: A Behavioral Theory of Impulsiveness and Impulse Control. *Psychological Bulletin, 82*, 463–496.

Balcomb, F. K., and Gerken, L. A. (2008). Three-Year-Old Children Can Access Their Own Memory to Guide Responses on a Visual Matching Task. *Developmental Science, 11*, 750–760.

Barnier, A. J., Sutton, J., Harris, C. B., and Wilson, R. A. (2008). A Conceptual and Empirical Framework for the Social Distribution of Cognition: The Case of Memory. *Cognitive Systems Research, 9*, 33–51.

Barsalou, L. W. (2009). Simulation, Situated Conceptualization, and Prediction. *Philosophical Transactions of the Royal Society B: Biological Sciences, 364*, 1281–1289.

Bateson, M., Brilot, B., and Nettle, D. (2011). Anxiety: An Evolutionary Approach. *The Canadian Journal of Psychiatry, 56*, 707–715.

Baumeister, R. F., and Tierney, J. (2011). *Willpower: Rediscovering the Greatest Human Strength.* New York, NY: Penguin Press.

Baxter, W. T. (1989). Early Accounting: The Tally and the Checkerboard. *The Accounting Historians Journal, 16*, 43–83.

Beck, S. R., Robinson, E. J., Carroll, D. J., and Apperly, I. A. (2006). Children's Thinking about Counterfactuals and Future Hypotheticals as Possibilities. *Child Development, 77*, 413–426.

Berns, G. S., Chappelow, J., Cekic, M., et al. (2006). Neurobiological Substrates of Dread. *Science, 312*, 754–758.

Bischof-Köhler, D. (1985). Zur Phylogenese menschlicher Motivation. In L. H. Eckensberger, M. M. Baltes (eds.), *Emotion und Reflexivität.* Munich, Germany: Urban & Schwarzenberg, 3–47.

Bjork, R. A. (1994). Memory and Metamemory Considerations in the Training of Human Beings. In J. Metcalfe and A. Shimamura (eds.), *Metacognition: Knowing about Knowing.* Cambridge, MA: MIT Press, 185–205.

Boyer, P. (2008). Evolutionary Economics of Mental Time Travel? *Trends in Cognitive Sciences, 12*, 219–224.

Brandimonte, M. A., Einstein, G. O., and McDaniel, M. A. (2014). *Prospective Memory: Theory and Applications.* New York, NY: Psychology Press.

Bulley, A. (2018). The History and Future of Human Prospection. *Evolutionary Studies in Imaginative Culture, 1*, 75–93.

Bulley, A., Henry, J., and Suddendorf, T. (2016). Prospection and the Present Moment: The Role of Episodic Foresight in Intertemporal Choices between Immediate and Delayed Rewards. *Review of General Psychology, 20*, 29–47.

(2017). Thinking about Threats: Memory and Prospection in Human Threat Management. *Consciousness and Cognition*, *49*, 53–69.

Byrne, R. M. J. (2016). Counterfactual Thought. *Annual Review of Psychology*, *67*, 135–157.

Clark, A. (2006). Language, Embodiment, and the Cognitive Niche. *Trends in Cognitive Sciences*, *10*, 370–374.

(2008). *Supersizing the Mind: Embodiment, Action, and Cognitive Extension.* Oxford University Press. doi:10.1093/acprof:oso/9780195333213.001.0001.

(2015). *Surfing Uncertainty: Prediction, Action, and the Embodied Mind.* Oxford, UK: Oxford University Press.

Clark, A., and Chalmers, D. (1998). The Extended Mind. *Analysis*, *58*, 7–19.

Clarke, K. C. (2013). What is the World's Oldest Map? *The Cartographic Journal*, *50*, 136–143.

Coffman, D. D. (1990). Effects of Mental Practice, Physical Practice, and Knowledge of Results on Piano Performance. *Journal of Research in Music Education*, *38*(3), 187–196.

Corballis, M. C. (2013). Wandering Tales: Evolutionary Origins of Mental Time Travel and Language. *Frontiers in Psychology*, *4*, 485.

Craik, K. J. W. (1943). *The Nature of Explanation.* Cambridge, UK: Cambridge University Press.

D'Argembeau, A. (2016). The Role of Personal Goals in Future-Oriented Mental Time Travel. In K. Michaelian, S. B. Klein, and K. K. Szpunar (eds.), *Seeing the Future: Theoretical Perspectives on Future-Oriented Mental Time Travel.* New York, NY: Oxford University Press. doi:10.1093/acprof:oso/9780190241537.003.0010.

Damasio, A. R. (1994). *Descartes' Error: Emotion, Reason, and the Human Brain.* New York, NY: Putnam Publishing.

Davis, J. T. M., Cullen, E., and Suddendorf, T. (2016). Understanding Deliberate Practice in Preschool Aged Children. *The Quarterly Journal of Experimental Psychology*, *69* (2), 361–380.

Dawkins, R. (1998). *Unweaving the Rainbow: Science, Delusion and the Appetite for Wonder.* Boston, MA: Houghton Mifflin Harcourt.

Devereux, C. L., Whittingham, M. J., Fernández-Juricic, E., Vickery, J. A., and Krebs, J. R. (2006). Predator Detection and Avoidance by Starlings under Differing Scenarios of Predation Risk. *Behavioral Ecology*, *17*, 303–309.

Dohrn-van Rossum, G. (1996). *History of the Hour: Clocks and Modern Temporal Orders.* Chicago, IL: University of Chicago Press.

Donald, M. (1991). *Origins of the Modern Mind: Three Stages in the Evolution of Culture and Cognition.* Cambridge, MA: Harvard University Press.

Dror, I., and Harnad, S. (2008). Offloading *Cognition* onto *Cognitive Technology*. Amsterdam, Netherlands: JohnBenjamins Publishing.

Duckworth, A. L., Gendler, T. S., and Gross, J. J. (2016). Situational Strategies for Self-Control. *Perspectives on Psychological Science*, *11*, 35–55.

Dufresne, A., and Kobasigawa, A. (1989). Children's Spontaneous Allocation of Study Time: Differential and Sufficient Aspects. *Journal of Experimental Child Psychology*, *47*, 274–296.

Dunlosky, J., and Tauber, S. K. (2016). *The Oxford Handbook of Metamemory.* Oxford, UK: Oxford University Press.

Eiseley, L. C. (1970). *The Invisible Pyramid.* Lincoln, NE: University of Nebraska Press.

Elster, J. (2000). *Ulysses Unbound: Studies in Rationality, Precommitment, and Constraints.* Cambridge, UK: Cambridge University Press.

Fawcett, T. W., McNamara, J. M., and Houston, A. I. (2012). When Is it Adaptive to Be Patient? A General Framework for Evaluating Delayed Rewards. *Behavioural Processes*, 89, 128–136.

Finnbogadóttir, H., and Berntsen, D. (2013). Involuntary Future Projections Are as Frequent as Involuntary Memories, but More Positive. *Consciousness and Cognition*, 22, 272–280.

Fischer, S. R. (2001). *A History of Writing.* London, UK: Reaktion Books.

Flavell, J. H., and Wellman, H. M. (1977). Metamemory. In R. V. Kail, Jr., and J. Hagen (eds.), *Perspectives on the Development of Memory and Cognition.* Hillsdale, NJ: Erlbaum, 3–33.

Frankfurt, H. G. (1988). Freedom of the Will and the Concept of a Person. In M. F. Goodman (ed.), *What Is a Person?* Clifton, NJ: Humana Press: 127–144.

Gaesser, B., and Schacter, D. L. (2014). Episodic Simulation and Episodic Memory Can Increase Intentions to Help Others. *Proceedings of the National Academy of Sciences*, 111, 4415–4420.

Gilbert, D. T., and Wilson, T. D. (2007). Prospection: Experiencing the Future. *Science*, 317, 1351–1354.

Gullo, M. J., Dawe, S., Kambouropoulos, N., Staiger, P. K., and Jackson, C. J. (2010). Alcohol Expectancies and Drinking Refusal Self-Efficacy Mediate the Association of Impulsivity with Alcohol Misuse. *Alcoholism: Clinical and Experimental Research*, 34, 1386–1399.

Hallos, J. (2005). "15 Minutes Of Fame": Exploring the Temporal Dimension of Middle Pleistocene Lithic Technology. *Journal of Human Evolution*, 49(2), 155–179.

Hassabis, D., and Maguire, E. A. (2009). The Construction System of the Brain. *Philosophical Transactions: Biological Sciences*, 364, 1263–1271.

Heersmink, R. (2013). A Taxonomy of Cognitive Artifacts: Function, Information, and Categories. *Review of Philosophy and Psychology*, 4, 465–481.

(2016). The Cognitive Integration of Scientific Instruments: Information, Situated Cognition, and Scientific Practice. *Phenomenology and the Cognitive Sciences*, 15, 517–537.

Hesslow, G. (2012). The Current Status of the Simulation Theory of Cognition. *Brain Research*, 1428, 71–79.

Heyes, C. (2016). Who Knows? Metacognitive Social Learning Strategies. *Trends in Cognitive Sciences*, xx, 1–10.

Hirst, W., and Echterhoff, G. (2012). Remembering in Conversations: The Social Sharing and Reshaping of Memories. *Annual Review of Psychology*, 63, 55–79.

Hoerl, C., and McCormack, T. (2018). Thinking in and About Time: A Dual Systems Perspective on Temporal Cognition. *Behavioral and Brain Sciences*, 1–77. doi:10.1017/S0140525X18002157.

Hutchins, E. (1999). Cognitive Artifacts. *The MIT Encyclopedia of the Cognitive Sciences*, 126, 127.

Irish, M., and Piguet, O. (2013). The Pivotal Role of Semantic Memory in Remembering the Past and Imagining the Future. *Frontiers in Behavioral Neuroscience*, 7, 27.

Jones, A. (2007). *Memory and Material Culture.* Cambridge, UK: Cambridge University Press.

Kelly, L. (2015). *Knowledge and Power in Prehistoric Societies: Orality, Memory, and the Transmission of Culture.* Cambridge, UK: Cambridge University Press.

(2017). *The Memory Code: The Secrets of Stonehenge, Easter Island and Other Ancient Monuments.* New York, NY: Pegasus Books. books.google.com.au/books?id=dfa8DAEACAAJ.

Kidd, C., Palmeri, H., and Aslin, R. N. (2013). Rational Snacking: Young Children's Decision-Making on the Marshmallow Task Is Moderated by Beliefs about Environmental Reliability. *Cognition, 126*, 109–114.

Kirby, K. N., Petry, N. M., and Bickel, W. K. (1999). Heroin Addicts Have Higher Discount Rates for Delayed Rewards than Non-Drug-Using Controls. *Journal of Experimental Psychology: General, 128*, 78–87.

Klein, S. B. (2013). The Temporal Orientation of Memory: It's Time for a Change of Direction. *Journal of Applied Research in Memory and Cognition, 2*, 222–234.

Koffarnus, M. N., Jarmolowicz, D. P., Mueller, E. T., and Bickel, W. K. (2013). Changing Delay Discounting in the Light of the Competing Neurobehavioral Decision Systems Theory: A Review. *Journal of the Experimental Analysis of Behavior, 99*, 32–57.

Köhler, W. (1925). *The Mentality of Apes.* New York, NY: Read Books Ltd.

Kohn, M., and Mithen, S. (1999). Handaxes: Products of Sexual Selection? *Antiquity, 73*, 518–526.

Legare, C. H., and Nielsen, M. (2015). Imitation and Innovation: The Dual Engines of Cultural Learning. *Trends in Cognitive Sciences, 19*, 688–699.

Lepre, C. J., Roche, H., Kent, D. V., et al. (2011). An Earlier Origin for the Acheulian. *Nature, 477*(7362), 82–85.

Loewenstein, G. F., and Lerner, J. (2003). The Role of Affect in Decision-Making. In R. Davidson, H. Goldsmith, and K. Scherer (ed.), *Handbook of Affective Science.* Oxford, UK: Oxford University Press, 619–642.

Loewenstein, G. F., Read, D., and Baumeister, R. F. (2003). *Time and Decision: Economic and Psychological Perspectives of Intertemporal Choice.* New York, NY: Russell Sage Foundation. books.google.com.au/books?id=iHJcQJcg3BICx.

Machin, A. J. (2008). Why Handaxes Just Aren't That Sexy: A Response to Kohn & Mithen (1999). *Antiquity, 82*(317), 761–766.

Meece, S. (2006). A Bird's Eye View – of a Leopard's Spots: The Çatalhöyük "Map" and the Development of Cartographic Representation in Prehistory. *Anatolian Studies, 56*, 1–16.

Mellaart, J. (1967). *Çatal Hüyük: a Neolithic Town in Anatolia.* New York, NY: McGraw-Hill.

Michaelian, K., and Sutton, J. (2013). Distributed Cognition and Memory Research: History and Current Directions. *Review of Philosophy and Psychology, 4*, 1–24.

Miloyan, B., Bulley, A., and Suddendorf, T. (2016). Episodic Foresight and Anxiety: Proximate and Ultimate Perspectives. *British Journal of Clinical Psychology, 55*(1), 4–22.

(2019). Anxiety: Here and Beyond. *Emotion Review, 11*(1), 39–49.

Mischel, W. (2014). *The Marshmallow Test: Understanding Self-Control and How to Master it.* New York, NY: Random House.

Mischel, W., Shoda, Y., and Rodriguez, M. I. (1989). Delay of Gratification in Children. *Science, 244*, 933–938.

Mithen, S. J. (1996). *The Prehistory of the Mind: a Search for the Origins of Art, Religion and Science.* London, UK: Weidenfeld & Nicholson.

Müller, C. P., and Schumann, G. (2011). Drugs as Instruments: A New Framework for Non-Addictive Psychoactive Drug Use. *Behavioral and Brain Sciences, 34,* 293–310.

Neldner, K., Collier-Baker, E., and Nielsen, M. (2015). Chimpanzees (Pan Troglodytes) and Human Children (Homo Sapiens) Know When They Are Ignorant about the Location of Food. *Animal Cognition, 18,* 683–699.

Nelson, T., and Narens, L. (1990). Metamemory: A Theoretical Framework and New Findings. *Psychology of Learning and Motivation, 26,* 125–173.

Nestojko, J. F., Finley, J. R., and Roediger, H. L. (2013). Extending Cognition to External Agents. *Psychological Inquiry, 24,* 321–325.

Oakley, K. P. (1981). Emergence of Higher Thought 3.0-0.2 Ma B.P. *Philosophical Transactions of the Royal Society B: Biological Sciences, 292,* 205–211.

Palermos, S. O. (2016). The Dynamics of Group Cognition. *Minds and Machines, 26,* 409–440.

Parfit, D. (1971). Personal Identity. *The Philosophical Review, 80,* 3–27.

Perner, J. (1991). *Learning, Development, and Conceptual Change. Understanding the Representational Mind.* Cambridge, MA: MIT Press.

Peters, J., and Büchel, C. (2010). Episodic Future Thinking Reduces Reward Delay Discounting through an Enhancement of Prefrontal-Mediotemporal Interactions. *Neuron, 66,* 138–148.

Pezzulo, G. (2008). Coordinating with the Future: The Anticipatory Nature of Representation. *Minds and Machines, 18,* 179–225.

Pezzulo, G., and Rigoli, F. (2011). The Value of Foresight: How Prospection Affects Decision-Making. *Frontiers in Neuroscience, 5,* 79.

Popper, K. (1934). *The Logic of Scientific Discovery.* London, UK: Routledge.

Pylyshyn, Z. W. (1978). When Is Attribution of Beliefs Justified? *Behavioral and Brain Sciences, 1*(4), 592–593.

Rachlin, H. (1995). Self-Control: Beyond Commitment. *Behavioral and Brain Sciences, 18* (1), 109–121.

(2016). Self-Control Based on Soft Commitment. *Behavior Analyst, 39,* 259–268.

Rafetseder, E., Cristi-Vargas, R., and Perner, J. (2010). Counterfactual Reasoning: Developing a Sense of "Nearest Possible World". *Child Development, 81,* 376–389.

Redshaw, J. (2014). Does Metarepresentation Make Human Mental Time Travel Unique? *Wiley Interdisciplinary Reviews: Cognitive Science, 5*(5), 519–531.

Redshaw, J., and Bulley, A. (2018). Future-Thinking in Animals Capacities and Limits. In G. Oettingen, A. T. Sevincer, and P. Gollwitzer (eds.), *The Psychology of Thinking about the Future.* New York, NY: Guilford Press, 31–51.

Redshaw, J., and Suddendorf, T. (2016). Children's and Apes' Preparatory Responses to Two Mutually Exclusive Possibilities. *Current Biology, 26*(13), 1758–1762.

Redshaw, J., Suddendorf, T., Neldner, K., et al. (2019). Young Children From Three Diverse Cultures Spontaneously and Consistently Prepare for Alternative Future Possibilities. *Child Development, 90*(1), 51–61.

Redshaw, J., Vandersee, J., Bulley, A., and Gilbert, S. J. (2018). Development of Children's Use of External Reminders for Hard-to-Remember Intentions. *Child Development, 89*(6), 2099–2118.

Risko, E. F., and Gilbert, S. J. (2016). Cognitive Offloading. *Trends in Cognitive Sciences, 20,* 676–688.

Rorty, A. O. (1980). Where Does the Akratic Break Take Place? *Australasian Journal of Philosophy, 58,* 333–346.

Santos, L. R., and Rosati, A. G. (2015). The Evolutionary Roots of Human Decision-Making. *Annual Review of Psychology*, *66*, 321–347.

Schacter, D. L., Addis, D. R., and Buckner, R. L. (2008). Episodic Simulation of Future Events: Concepts, Data, and Applications. *Annals of the New York Academy of Sciences*, *1124*, 39–60.

Schacter, D. L., Addis, D. R., Hassabis, D., et al. (2012). The Future of Memory: Remembering, Imagining, and the Brain. *Neuron*, *76*, 677–694.

Schacter, D. L., Benoit, R. G., De Brigard, F., and Szpunar, K. K. (2015). Episodic Future Thinking and Episodic Counterfactual Thinking: Intersections between Memory and Decisions. *Neurobiology of Learning and Memory*, *117*, 14–21.

Schacter, D. L., Benoit, R. G., and Szpunar, K. K. (2017). Episodic Future Thinking: Mechanisms and Functions. *Current Opinion in Behavioral Sciences*, *17*, 41–50.

Schelling, T. C. (1960). The *Strategy* of *Conflict*. Cambridge, MA: Harvard University Press.
  (1984). Self-Command in Practice, in Policy, and in a Theory of Rational Choice. *The American Economic Review*, *74*(2), 1–11.

Seli, P., Kane, M. J., Smallwood, J., et al. (2018). Mind-Wandering as a Natural Kind: A Family-Resemblances View. *Trends in Cognitive Sciences*, *22*, 479–490.

Shipton, C., and Nielsen, M. (2015). Before Cumulative Culture: The Evolutionary Origins of Overimitation and Shared Intentionality. *Human Nature*, *26*, 331–345.

Smith, C. D. (1987). Cartography in the Prehistoric Period in the Old World: Europe, the Middle East, and North Africa. *The History of Cartography*, *1*, 54–102.

Sterelny, K. (2010). Minds: Extended or Scaffolded? *Phenomenology and the Cognitive Sciences*, *9*, 465–481.

Stevens, J. R., and Stephens, D. (2008). Patience. *Current Biology: CB*, *18*, R11–2.

Suddendorf, T. (1994). Discovery of the Fourth Dimension: Mental Time Travel and Human Evolution. Waikato, New Zealand: University of Waikato, PhD thesis. cogprints.org /729/1/THESIS.txt.
  (1999). The Rise of the Metamind. In M. Corballis and S. Lee (eds.), *The Descent of Mind: Psychological Perspectives on Hominid Evolution*. Oxford, UK: Oxford University Press, 218–260.
  (2010). Episodic Memory versus Episodic Foresight: Similarities and Differences. *Wiley Interdisciplinary Reviews: Cognitive Science*, *1*, 99–107.
  (2013). *The Gap: The Science of What Separates us from Other Animals*. New York, NY: Basic Books.

Suddendorf, T., Brinums, M., and Imuta, K. (2016). Shaping One's Future Self – The Development of Deliberate Practice. In K. Michaelian, S. B. Klein, and K. K. Szpunar (eds.), *Seeing the Future: Theoretical Perspectives on Future-Oriented Mental Time Travel*. New York, NY: Oxford University Press, 343–366.

Suddendorf, T., and Corballis, M. C. (1997). Mental Time Travel and the Evolution of the Human Mind. *Genetic Social and General Psychology Monographs*, *123*, 133–167.
  (2007). The Evolution of Foresight: What Is Mental Time Travel, and Is it Unique to Humans? *Behavioral and Brain Sciences*, *30*, 299–351.

Suddendorf, T., Crimston, J., and Redshaw, J. (2017). Preparatory Responses to Socially Determined, Mutually Exclusive Possibilities in Chimpanzees and Children. *Biology Letters*, *13*.

Sutton, J. (2006). Exaograms and Interdisciplinarity: History, the Extended Mind, and the Civilizing Process. In R. Menary (ed.), *The Extended Mind*. Cambridge, MA: MIT Press, 189–225.

Szpunar, K. K. (2010). Episodic Future Thought: An Emerging Concept. *Perspectives on Psychological Science, 5,* 142–162.

Thaler, R. H., and Shefrin, H. (1981). An Economic Theory of Self-Control. *Journal of Political Economy, 89*(2), 392–406.

Utrilla, P., Mazo, C., Sopena, M. C., Martínez-Bea, M., and Domingo, R. (2009). A Palaeolithic Map from 13,660 calBP: Engraved Stone Blocks from the Late Magdalenian in Abauntz Cave (Navarra, Spain). *Journal of Human Evolution, 57,* 99–111.

Whiten, A., and Erdal, D. (2012). The Human Socio-Cognitive Niche and its Evolutionary Origins. *Philosophical Transactions of the Royal Society B: Biological Sciences, 367,* 2119–2129.

Woodward, D., and Harley, J. B. (1987). *The History of Cartography, Volume 1: Cartography in Prehistoric, Ancient, and Medieval Europe and the Mediterranean.* Chicago, IL: University of Chicago Press.

PART IV

Novel Combinatorial Forms of the Imagination

27 On the Interaction Between Episodic and Semantic Representations – Constructing a Unified Account of Imagination

Muireann Irish

Episodic memory, namely the capacity to recollect past experiences, has long been heralded as a constructive endeavor (Bartlett, 1932; Schacter, Norman, and Koutstaal, 1998), and one that appears particularly well suited to supporting acts of imagination. The discovery of striking similarities in the cognitive and neural processes that support past and future thinking has led to a significant paradigm shift in the field, prompting reconsideration of the ways by which episodic memory might not only facilitate, but be *essential*, for imagination (Schacter and Addis, 2007). Since then, episodic memory research has undergone a dramatic revival, with hundreds of papers seeking to explicate the neurocognitive machinery by which humans flexibly (re)construct past, future, and atemporal representations. Guided by the centrality of the hippocampus in retrieving the past, a foundational role for episodic memory in event construction has been specified (reviewed by Schacter et al., 2012) leading to the somewhat privileged status of episodic memory in the domain of imaginative capacity.

While there is little dispute that episodic memory for the past and the capacity to envisage the future are inextricably linked, conceptualizing imagination as exclusively underwritten by the episodic memory system precludes a thorough understanding of its many manifestations (e.g. Klein, 2013). Imagination is inherently multifaceted, and its products rely upon a diverse range of capacities. The tendency to couch imagination in terms of episodic memory function, to the neglect of other core processes, therefore results in an incomplete theoretical account. In this chapter, I put forward the idea that imagination cannot be understood independently of semantic memory. This thesis stems from a large corpus of research implicating conceptual processing across myriad internally driven forms of cognition including remembering, imagining, planning, and reasoning (Binder and Desai, 2011) and the proposal that semantic memories are "the basic material from which complex and detailed episodic memories are constructed" (Greenberg and Verfaellie, 2010: 750). Building on these observations, I will synthesize evidence from neuropsychological studies of clinical populations harboring differential damage to the episodic and semantic memory systems to illustrate the necessary *confluence* of episodic and semantic elements in the service of imagination. Accordingly, I will demonstrate that the output from imagination varies in terms of its episodic and semantic constituents, the relative weighting of which depends upon a host of factors including task-driven variations in content, invocation of prior knowledge and experience, and the accessibility of that information. As such, the aim of this chapter is to demonstrate that the outcome of imagination is best conceptualized as the convergence of episodic and semantic elements, moving toward an all-encompassing and unified theory of imagination.

Imagination as a Multimodal Constructive Process

Despite the tendency to view imagination as a unitary mental faculty, it is clear that humans engage in an array of imaginative endeavors that differ based on temporal context and representational content. For example, imagination can be temporally bound toward the future, a process commonly referred to as "future thinking" (Atance and O'Neill, 2001), whereby we mentally project ourselves forward in subjective time to envisage or simulate a possible future event. Similarly, imagination can be oriented toward the past, enabling us to envisage alternate outcomes to events that have already occurred, as is the case with counterfactual thinking. Further, we can harness our imagination in an atemporal manner enabling us to mentally construct fictitious scenes or scenarios free from past or future temporal constraints (e.g. scene construction). While the preceding examples can be thought of as task-mediated or deliberate instantiations of imagination, the products of our imagination may also occur unbidden, as is the case with mind-wandering. Irrespective of the output of imagination, however, a number of core component processes have been consistently implicated, including the retrieval of sensory-perceptual details from episodic memory, the harnessing of general conceptual knowledge from semantic memory, as well as executive function, fluency, and introspective processes (e.g. D'Argembeau, Ortoleva, Jumentier, and van der Linden, 2010).

Limitations of a Sharp Episodic-Semantic Distinction

Semantic memory represents an individual's repository of acquired knowledge of the world, comprising constructs that are "conceptual" in nature and largely divorced from any specific experience or temporal signature. For example, we possess the semantic knowledge that "Paris is the capital of France" vs. the episodic recollection of "My holiday last year in Paris." Conceptual knowledge can be likened to an atemporal, multimodal semantic database that imparts meaning to all stimuli and experiences encountered in daily life. These conceptual representations play a central role in promoting knowledge generalization across items and contexts, and can be used, manipulated, and generalized to support a variety of verbal and non-verbal behaviors (Lambon Ralph, 2014) as well as cognitive capacities (Binder and Desai, 2011). The proposal that semantic knowledge may underpin many, if not all, everyday behaviors and cognitive capacities represents a nascent topic in the literature. Accordingly, the field of semantic cognition has undergone a shift in emphasis, moving away from traditional studies of object knowledge to becoming a topic of formal investigation in its own right (Binder et al., 2009). Throughout this chapter, these theoretical refinements will be considered with respect to mental construction, with a view to repositioning semantic memory as central in the imagination debate.

The tendency to conceptualize semantic memory as orthogonal to episodic memory can be dated back to Tulving's influential theory of declarative memory, which positioned episodic memory as "temporally dated episodes or events, and the temporal-spatial relations" between these events (Tulving, 1972: 385). In contrast, semantic memory was regarded as conceptual knowledge experienced independently from the original source of acquisition (Tulving, 1972, 1985). The episodic-semantic heuristic was then extended to the temporal phenomenology and self-referential quality experienced by the individual during memory retrieval (reviewed by Klein, 2016). Whereas episodic memory was ascribed a unique temporal stamp (e.g. past or future), the temporal signature of semantic memory was confined to the "here and now" and considered to be devoid of a feeling of re-experiencing the original act of acquisition (Klein, 2016). Moreover, episodic memory was posited as imbued with an autonoetic (self-knowing) consciousness, whereas semantic memory was seen to lack this self-referential quality. By this view, only episodic memory would be hypothesized to play a substantive role in mediating the construction of temporally constrained and self-referential events.

This strict delineation between episodic and semantic memory, and the emphasis on their accompanying temporal experience, thus served to relegate semantic memory to a system that lacks the temporal resources that are fundamental for past and future-oriented thinking (Suddendorf and Corballis, 2007). Although originally proposed more than forty years ago, this dichotomy has persisted to the present day, resulting in widespread underappreciation of the dynamic interplay between the episodic and semantic memory systems (e.g. Lane et al., 2015). This distinction, however, is far from ubiquitously accepted and as recently noted, "the dividing line between semantic and episodic memory is getting harder to see" (Lane et al., 2015: 48). From a conceptual standpoint, the constituent elements of episodic memory, namely the "what," "where," and "when," can also be found within semantic memory in that we can know specific events, spatial and temporal information without necessarily retrieving the original source of acquisition of such information (Grilli and Verfaellie, 2014). Similarly, semantic memory comprises self-referential information, as in the case of personal semantics (e.g. "my birthday is in February"; Renoult et al., 2012). Functional neuro-imaging studies further demonstrate striking overlap between the autobiographical (episodic) memory network and the semantic memory system (e.g. Binder et al., 2009; Maguire, 2001), corroborating the proposal that autobiographical memories invariably contain semantic concepts (Greenberg and Verfaellie, 2010; Irish and Piguet, 2013). Converging evidence from clinical populations further underscores the unclear boundaries that exist between these two memory systems (Irish et al., 2011a; Irish et al., 2014; McKinnon et al., 2006) and suggest that, rather than viewing episodic and semantic memory as diametrically opposed, we should instead view these systems as intricately intertwined (see also Renoult, Irish, Moscovitch, and Rugg, 2019).

When applied to the realm of imagination, the distinction between episodic and semantic memory is equally problematic. Functional neuroimaging studies of past and future thinking across personal (episodic) and non-personal (semantic) settings reveal significant activation of semantic processing regions (e.g. inferior temporal gyrus, temporal poles), irrespective of temporal context or self-referential condition (Abraham, Schubotz, and von Cramon, 2008). A consistent finding across the neuro-imaging literature is the recruitment of lateral temporal regions crucial for semantic processing when healthy individuals envision future plans or scenarios (reviewed by Abraham and Bubić, 2015). Indeed, studies suggest that more than half of future-oriented thoughts in daily life are fundamentally conceptual in nature (D'Argembeau and Mathy, 2011), in keeping with the proposal that semantic memory perfuses all aspects of inner mentation (Binder and Desai, 2011). More tellingly, and as will be discussed in more detail below, neuropsychological studies reveal that damage to either the episodic or semantic memory systems impairs the capacity for imagination (reviewed by Irish and Piolino, 2016). Collectively, these findings resonate with a recent push toward an episodic-semantic continuum during autobiographical retrieval (Renoult et al., 2012; Strikwerda-Brown et al., 2018) with calls for a similar framework to be applied in the context of imagination (e.g. Irish, 2016).

The "Episodic Bottleneck" vs. a Flexible Semantic Conduit

Episodic memory is typically conceived of as providing the raw material from which future events can be generated. If we cast a critical lens on the episodic memory system, however, a number of computational challenges arise. By its nature, an episodic memory is bound to a specific time and place. While these elements are essential for event construction, our imaginative capacity may also be limited by these features. If imagination is largely underwritten by the episodic memory store, we are, in principle, constrained by those events that we have previously experienced, resulting in a "computational bottleneck" (Hegdé, 2007: 324). Although perceptual details from unique episodes can be called up in isolation and flexibly reconfigured in new and novel ways (Schacter et al., 2012), it has been argued that, "what one can predict about the future will be limited by one's episodic memory" (Hegdé, 2007: 324). Recent commentaries have argued that the imagination of future events should rely upon semantic as opposed to episodic contributions (Mahr and Csibra, 2018). This proposal is not new, however, as Ingvar (1985) made the prescient observation that episodic memory "pertains to actual sensory and cognitive percepts in the past and present" (Ingvar, 1985: 29), representing time-locked events that are largely immutable. A memory system that is unconstrained and divorced from any specific experience, by contrast, can provide the organizational framework from which a detailed and novel event can be constructed (Irish, 2016). Therein lies the foundational role of semantic memory.

As a general conceptual knowledge store, semantic memory benefits from a number of attributes that render it particularly well suited to organize, guide, and support the construction of event representations. Notably, semantic memory is free from the temporal constraints that befall episodic memory. Ironically, a lack of temporal phenomenology has contributed to semantic memory being largely dismissed from the mental time travel literature, the argument being that some form of temporal phenomenology must be present to experience events in the past or future (reviewed by Klein, 2016). Rather, this lack of temporal signature ensures that semantic memory can be efficiently deployed across past, future, and atemporal contexts, resonating with Ingvar's proposal that semantic memory is "mainly involved in the cognitive or future consequences and meaning of events" (Ingvar, 1985: 129). Moreover, semantic memory is derived from the accumulation of myriad experiences, resulting in abstracted organizational constructs that can be generalized from one experience or exemplar to another (Binder and Desai, 2011). The resultant constructs are therefore free from the spatial constraints of episodic memory and can be deployed flexibly across a range of diverse contexts and spatial settings.

Semantic Scaffolding, Schemas, and the Constructive Endeavor

Recent theoretical refinements on constructive simulation have attempted to bring semantic knowledge back into the fray (e.g. Addis, 2018), drawing upon the consistent finding of semantic brain network activation during event simulation and the deleterious effect of semantic memory disruption on constructive simulation. These findings lend compelling support for the *semantic scaffolding hypothesis* (Irish, 2016; Irish and Piguet, 2013), which emphasizes the pivotal role of semantic memory in all aspects of constructive simulation. By this view, semantic knowledge provides the organizational framework that guides (re)construction of the past, simulation of the future, and the realization of spatially contiguous atemporal scenes. For event construction to be successful, abstract semantic representations (i.e. schemas) must be set in place *prior* to harnessing event-specific details via episodic memory. Once this framework has been set in place, sensory-perceptual details can be co-opted into the simulation, creating a unique and novel mental representation. Consistent with this proposal, functional neuroimaging studies reveal that conceptual knowledge is harnessed prior to the invocation of sensory-perceptual episodic details during event simulation in healthy adults (D'Argembeau and Mathy, 2011). Notably, similar arguments have been made in relation to acts of conceptual expansion, whereby existing semantic concepts are broadened to include additional features and attributes (Rutter et al., 2012), thus facilitating the creative endeavor.

Semantic scaffolding relies upon the deployment of schemas – "superordinate knowledge structures that reflect abstracted commonalities across multiple experiences" (Gilboa and Marlatte, 2017: 618). In essence, schemas distil the similarities of multiple episodes into "ready-made" heuristics that can be rolled out depending on task demands and situational constraints (Robin and Moscovitch, 2017). As such, we carry around a store of abstract representations which impart the central elements of how an event typically unfolds (e.g. trip to the doctor, going to the supermarket), with the ventromedial prefrontal cortex posited as a putative schema storage hub (Sheldon and Levine, 2016). Schemas thus serve as general reference templates against which new experiences can be compared and updated (Gilboa and Marlatte, 2017) and occupy a crucial role in the construction of event representations. As will be discussed, however, a host of factors invariably influence the degree to which the imagined representation is biased toward episodic or semantic content, and the degree to which prior knowledge is invoked during construction.

Event-Based Forms of Construction

Open-Ended vs. Well-Defined Tasks

Considering first the specificity of the task itself, the distinction between open-ended and closed cueing approaches becomes particularly salient (Sheldon and Levine, 2016), studies that require participants to mentally envisage and describe future events have typically used the Adapted Autobiographical Interview (e.g. Addis, Wong, and Schacter, 2008), whereby a future event is constructed in response to a single cue word (e.g. "apple," "baby"; see Figure 27.1). Few other constraints are imposed on the constructive endeavor other than situating the event within a specific temporal window (e.g. within the next twelve months) and requiring the event to be in line with the participant's current goals and plans. This task is ostensibly open-ended in that it does not have a prescribed definitive answer and there are multiple ways in which one could accomplish the task (see Sheldon and Levine, 2016). The ambiguity imposed by such open-ended tasks disproportionately taxes the semantic memory system in that a semantic scaffold must first be put in place to guide the constructive endeavor (reviewed by Irish and Piolino, 2016). On open-ended future thinking paradigms, therefore, it is not surprising that mental construction should come undone in the face of semantic memory deficits (e.g. semantic dementia, see below); the requisite semantic framework cannot be harnessed to impart meaning and structure to the simulation.

In contrast, well-defined tasks are characterized by closed-cueing methods in which a single outcome is anticipated if a set path is traversed (Sheldon et al., 2015). Such paradigms may serve to bypass the requirement to search for the appropriate semantic scaffold as, inherent in the task instructions, is the schema itself. Atemporal scene construction represents an apposite example of a well-defined mental construction task, in that participants are required to generate descriptions of commonly experienced scenes in response to detailed probes (Hassabis et al., 2007). In essence, the provision of a detailed closed cue (e.g. "Imagine you are lying on a deserted white sandy beach in the middle of a beautiful tropical bay"), articulates the requisite semantic framework to guide the constructive endeavor (see Figure 27.1). With such well-defined scene cues for commonly experienced events, we can readily invoke the appropriate schema that captures similarities across our multiple experiences of lying on a beach. This abstracted "beach" representation represents a general fit-for purpose framework that can be deployed as is, and serves as

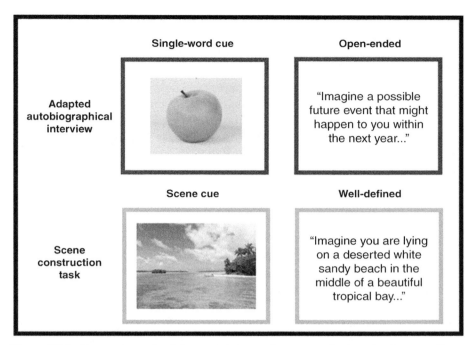

Figure 27.1 *Comparison of task demands inherent in two popular imagination paradigms. The Adapted Autobiographical Interview (top row: Addis, Wong, and Schacter, 2008) represents an open-ended task in that participants are required to envisage an unspecified event that will likely occur at some point in the future, typically in the next twelve months. The task stipulates that constructed events should be spatiotemporally specific; however, this framework is not explicitly embedded within the task instructions. Instead, participants must generate the requisite semantic scaffold as part of the constructive endeavor. By contrast, the Scene Construction Task (bottom row: Hassabis et al., 2007) represents a well-defined task in that the specificity of the scene cue circumvents the need to generate an appropriate semantic framework from which to construct the scene. See Sheldon and Levine (2016) for a similar discussion.*

a particularly efficient strategy to reduce the generative demands inherent in open-ended tasks. With the overarching framework in place, episodic and semantic information can be harnessed to populate the scene representation. Evidence from clinical populations supports this view in that, under certain conditions, mental construction mediated by intact semantic memory can be achieved. For example, amnesic patients can construct spatially contiguous scenes despite marked episodic memory impairments due to hippocampal dysfunction (e.g. Mullally, Vargha-Khadem, and Maguire, 2014). Similarly, patients who have undergone hippocampal resection for temporal lobe epilepsy (TLE) demonstrate intact script generation for familiar activities such as washing the dishes, or eating at a restaurant, in the context of marked autobiographical memory impairments (St-Laurent et al., 2009). As such, the well-defined nature of the task merely calls for the invocation of an appropriate schema, which can then be populated with episodic or semantic elements, as necessary.

Loss of the Semantic Knowledge Base

What, then, arises in the face of profound semantic impairment on such well-defined tasks? The syndrome of semantic dementia provides important insights in this regard. Semantic dementia is a younger-onset neurodegenerative disorder characterized by progressive deterioration of the conceptual knowledge base due to pathological insult of the anterior temporal lobes. This syndrome has illuminated our understanding of the neurocognitive architecture of the brain in the context of the systematic and coordinated degeneration of the semantic memory system (Irish, Piguet, and Hodges, 2012). One of the most striking features of semantic dementia is that the loss of world knowledge occurs irrespective of modality and is suggested to reflect the collapse of a central amodal semantic hub (Patterson, Nestor, and Rogers, 2007). Despite far-reaching semantic impairments, patients with semantic dementia display a wide range of relatively intact cognitive functions, most notably that of episodic memory retrieval – particularly when non-verbal tasks are employed (e.g. Bozeat et al., 2000; Irish et al., 2016a).

This unique neuropsychological profile of relatively circumscribed conceptual knowledge loss has served to clarify the contribution of the semantic memory system to a range of complex cognitive endeavors including autobiographical memory (e.g. Irish et al., 2011a; Maguire et al., 2010), and more recently, episodic future thinking (reviewed by Irish and Piolino, 2016). A consistent finding in the future thinking literature is of striking impairments in the generation of self-representations at a future timepoint (Duval et al., 2012; Hsiao et al., 2013) and the constructive simulation of future events (Irish et al., 2012a, 2012b). Critically, these impairments arise despite the spared ability to retrieve contextually rich episodic memories from the recent past, and are mediated exclusively by semantic processing impairments. This relationship is borne out at the neuroanatomical level with future thinking deficits attributable to gray matter intensity decrease in the left anterior temporal gyrus and the bilateral temporal poles (Irish et al., 2012a). Despite retaining an intact store of contextually rich episodic details, which remain available during the process of future simulation, the constructive endeavor fails in the absence of an appropriate semantic scaffold (Figure 27.2). These studies thus provide the first definitive evidence that imagining future events depends crucially upon semantic knowledge.

A recent study investigating the capacity for scene construction in a case study of semantic dementia provides further important insights in this regard (Irish et al., 2017). Despite widespread loss of conceptual knowledge, patient G.C. demonstrated a relatively intact capacity to construct spatially coherent scenes. The resultant constructions, however, appeared to draw heavily upon his relatively preserved store of recent episodic memories. The well-defined nature of the scene probe circumvents the requirement for G.C. to generate the organizational framework for the scene, enabling him to continue the constructive act largely unimpeded (Figure 27.2). With the appropriate semantic framework already in place, G.C. deferred to his episodic memories to populate his constructions, a compensatory strategy that resulted in mental (re)constructions of previously experienced events (Irish et al., 2017). Interestingly, the provision of an appropriate semantic framework via predetermined and detailed event cues has been

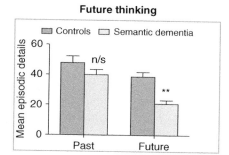

Figure 27.2 *Task demands modulate the capacity for imagination in semantic dementia. On open-ended tasks (e.g. Adapted Autobiographical Interview, left panel: Irish and Piguet, 2013), patients with semantic dementia display striking impairments, producing impoverished descriptions of events that are largely recapitulated from the past. In contrast, a recent case study of semantic dementia patient G.C. reveals a relatively intact capacity to generate and describe spatially contiguous events on a well-defined task (i.e. Scene Construction, right panel: Irish et al., 2017). Future thinking data adapted from: Irish and Piguet (2013), The Pivotal Role of Semantic Memory in Remembering the Past and Imagining the Future,* Frontiers in Behavioural Neuroscience, 7, 27.

shown to bolster episodic future thinking in semantic dementia (Viard et al., 2014). Relatives of participants were asked to provide plausible event cues for future events likely to be experienced by the individual, and these predetermined events were presented as descriptor sentences to participants. The provision of well-defined event cues likely alleviates some of the demands placed on semantic and generative processes inherent in open-ended paradigms such as the Autobiographical Interview, enabling semantic dementia patients to draw upon sensory-perceptual processes that remain relatively preserved (reviewed by Irish and Piolino, 2016). These examples suggest that far from residing exclusively within an episodic or semantic domain, mental construction is built on a semantic foundation that anchors episodic contributions.

The Other Side of the Coin – Semantic Forms of Imagination

Up to this point, I have predominantly considered episodic or event-based expressions of imagination whereby we place ourselves at the centre of the mental construction. However, it is clear that humans can engage in non-personal or semantic manifestations of imagination, extrapolating from our rich store of conceptual knowledge to understand the present and predict how the future may unfold. Semantic prospection, taken to its extreme, represents our capacity to imagine multiple contingencies, future alternatives, and outcomes solely within the public or non-personal domain. For example, we can reflect upon past world events to make informed inferences regarding potential non-personal occurrences in the future (Klein, 2013). Such "semantic" forms of imagination are best exemplified by our propensity to envisage future issues facing society (e.g. politics, healthcare, the environment) without recourse to any personal experience of such occurrences. From an evolutionary standpoint, it would seem highly prudent to draw upon abstracted representations of past events to construct future alternatives, enabling humans to prepare for multiple contingencies and to actively pursue one path over another (Suddendorf and Redshaw, 2013).

In this vein, the decontextualized nature of semantic memory represents a highly efficient conduit for semantic prospection. By preserving the most important elements from past experiences, semantic memory is arguably less malleable and error-prone than its episodic counterpart and provides a veridical record from which the future can be inferred (Hayes, Ramanan, and Irish, 2018). Mounting evidence suggests that amnesic patients with marked episodic memory impairments can achieve certain forms of future-oriented mental time travel mediated by intact semantic memory (Craver et al., 2014). For example, the densely amnesic patient D.B. demonstrated a remarkably preserved capacity to retrieve non-personal events (e.g. important political issues over the previous ten years), and could harness his semantic knowledge to anticipate issues likely to occur in the public domain (e.g. issues facing the country in the coming ten years). This spared ability to engage in exclusively semantic forms of imagination occurred in the context of profound impairments in retrieving previously experienced events from the past or in generating events that might reasonably occur in his personal future (Klein, Loftus, and Kihlstrom, 2002). The case study of patient D. B. elegantly demonstrates that, under certain conditions, episodic memory is not required for imagination. Rather, the semantic memory system can be exclusively engaged to achieve non-personal forms of prospection.

Episodic-Semantic Interactions during "Semantic" Prospection

Tulving's original model of declarative memory positioned episodic and semantic memory as largely independent systems (Tulving, 1983, 1985); however, it is important to note that in his subsequent treatise, Tulving presented a novel refinement (Tulving, 2002). By this updated view, episodic and semantic memory were considered as interactive and complementary systems, both of which capture the regularities and irregularities of the world (reviewed by Lane et al., 2015). Just as episodic future thinking relies upon the interdependence between episodic and semantic elements (Irish and Piguet, 2013), so, too, might semantic prospection. When healthy individuals were asked to envisage personal (episodic) and non-personal (semantic) future scenarios, Abraham, Schubotz and von Cramon (2008) revealed significant medial temporal lobe recruitment, irrespective of condition, suggesting a common underlying process subserved by the hippocampus. The potential interplay between episodic memory processes and semantic forms of prospection is further highlighted by a study of hippocampal amnesics, who displayed an intact capacity to generate semantic facts about the future, yet could not elaborate in detail when probed about these facts (Race, Keane, and Verfaellie, 2013). This impoverished description of the non-personal future arose independently of general conceptual knowledge, as patients displayed intact semantic processing on neuropsychological tests. A similar pattern of findings was recently reported in Alzheimer's disease and frontotemporal dementia, dementia syndromes characterized by marked episodic memory impairments in the context of variable semantic performance. Semantic prospection was grossly impoverished in both patient groups and could not be explained in terms of overall semantic memory proficiency. Moreover, voxel-based morphometry analyses revealed significant associations between hippocampal integrity and semantic prospection across the patient groups (Irish, Eyre, et al., 2016b).

Collectively these findings suggest a domain-general role for the hippocampus in supporting future forms of imagination across personal and non-personal contexts, and intimate that the interplay between episodic and semantic memory extends to non-personal future simulation. That semantic future thinking should hinge upon the integrity of both the semantic and episodic memory systems makes intuitive sense if we consider the nuances of a semantic prospection task. In anticipating non-personal issues that are temporally distal from the present day, we generate and select from an assortment of permutations, the undifferentiated nature of which renders semantic prospection a relatively open-ended task (Abraham, Schubotz, and von Cramon, 2008). It is possible therefore that semantic prospection recruits many of the essential mechanisms implicated in the episodic domain, but with additional demands placed upon generativity and recombinational processes. The inherent interdependency between the two systems confers remarkable flexibility in that we can, on the one hand, distil experiences into concepts and categories but at the same time extract the time and place when one pertinent combination of such entities was, or might be, experienced (Lane et al., 2015).

Temporal Distance as a Determinant of Semantic Contributions to Construction

As has been demonstrated, whether we are engaging in predominantly episodic or semantic forms of prospection, we oscillate between drawing upon schematized representations and invoking prior personal experiences as further support for such representations. The temporal constraints imposed by the task become important in this regard, in that the further one is required to project into the future, the more likely semantic constructs will be invoked (Arnold, McDermott, and Szpunar, 2011). This disproportionate recruitment of conceptual knowledge forms the basis for many of the tasks used to assess semantic prospection, as participants are instructed to consider time periods that are temporally distal from the present moment (e.g. ten years from now; Klein, Loftus, and Kihlstrom, 2002). Indeed, when healthy individuals imagine events in the far future, the settings tend to be derived from semantic knowledge (Arnold, McDermott, and Szpunar, 2011), suggesting that far future simulation becomes less reliant upon episodic contributions and imposes greater demands on semantic generativity. Interestingly, the increasing remoteness of future events is associated with bilateral hippocampal activation, potentially reflecting the intensive relational processing demands required to reconfigure disparate details into a meaningful whole (Addis and Schacter, 2008). Differential right hippocampal engagement has further been observed during autobiographical planning of distal goals, which in turn may reflect the abstract nature and high novelty of such goal states (Spreng et al., 2015). It is therefore critical to consider event plausibility as a core factor in modulating the resultant contents of an imagined scenario.

Novelty of Scenarios

While the majority of imagination tasks stipulate that the to-be-constructed event should be plausible, it is clear that humans possess a unique capacity to generate novel and irregular mental representations, for which we have no prior episodic experience. For example, it is not necessary for us to walk on the moon to provide a plausible and perceptually rich account of what this experience might entail. This form of imagination represents an open-ended task taken to the extreme. In this context, the undifferentiated nature of semantic memory is crucial in that we can draw upon the appropriate conceptual framework for the moon without having to invoke a detailed episodic memory of ever having been there (see also Devitt and Addis, 2016). In this light, some have suggested that the reconstructive nature of episodic memory could be considered a "design flaw" (Lane et al., 2015), limiting us to that pool of experiences that have already transpired. In contrast, semantic memory emerges as a highly flexible system that facilitates extrapolation across contexts without recourse to any specific experience (Hegdé, 2007).

The generalizability of the semantic structure appears particularly well-suited for the construction of new and novel events. Taking our previous example of imagining a trip to the moon, we can invoke our conceptual knowledge of "space travel" to infer our means of transport, equipment needed, as well as details pertaining to the moon's rocky surface and the absence of gravity. Given the novelty of this occurrence, however, the semantic framework that is called upon via established schemas may not be sufficiently detailed, and it may be necessary to leverage the episodic memory system to provide additional perceptual details. Novel event construction thus represents a unique class of imagination whereby conceptual representation converges with the configuring of sensory-perceptual details to ensure that the resultant representation is sufficiently detailed (Sheldon and Levine, 2016). As previously discussed, the dynamic nature of schemas ensures that they can be updated with new information depending on task requirements and situational constraints (Gilboa and Marlatte, 2017). In the case of novel event simulation, we can co-opt multimodal sensory-perceptual details from episodic memory, overlaid on the semantic framework of "moon," to ensure the resultant representation is vivid, richly detailed, and unique. The blending of episodic and semantic elements thus elevates a rudimentary conceptual outline to an evocative and novel representation embedded within a specific spatiotemporal setting.

Loss of Novelty due to Semantic Memory Dysfunction

What befalls novelty then in the case of semantic dementia? If the coordinated activity of episodic and semantic memory is pivotal for novel event generation, we would expect to see marked difficulties in the construction of events that deviate in any way from previously experienced episodes. Loss of semantic memory, therefore, should translate into a cognitively rigid thinking style that precludes the ability to engage in flexible forms of imagination. This point is illustrated by our finding that 80 percent of future events generated by semantic dementia patients encompass previously experienced events recapitulated from the past into the future (Irish et al., 2012a). Patients defaulted to recounting previous experiences from episodic memory at the expense of diverse and novel event generation. This marked propensity to "recast" the past in semantic dementia reflects their severely deficient capacity for flexible thought and a rigid cognitive style that is centered on previous experiences. Interestingly this inflexible form of thinking has been shown to manifest on the behavioral level (Kamminga et al., 2014), with patients clinging to recent experiences and stereotypical routines, potentially as a way of grounding the self (Strikwerda-Brown, Grilli, Andrews-Hanna and Irish, 2019). As such, patients with semantic dementia can imagine well-defined, prescribed events (Irish et al., 2017; Viard et al., 2014), if they have an appropriate episode to draw upon. Event construction, however, inevitably fails once the imagined scenario is required to be novel.

Fluctuations in Representational Content of Imagination

As has been alluded to throughout this chapter, a host of factors impinge upon the constructive endeavor, and necessarily influence the weighting of episodic and semantic elements within the resultant simulation. The mechanisms underwriting the representational contents of imagination can thus be conceptualized as operating akin to a pendulum, the relative loadings of which can be differentiated to the extent that perceptual (episodic) or conceptual (semantic) elements are required (see also Addis, 2018). In healthy participants, the pendulum maintains a delicate and dynamic balance between the episodic and semantic memory systems, with fluctuations in the representational contents of imagined scenarios contingent largely on task demands (Figure 27.3A). In the face of changing task demands, the pendulum may swing intermittently between episodic and semantic loadings. For example, where an imagination task requires a plausible personally relevant event to be simulated in a familiar spatiotemporal setting, perceptual details from our repository of episodic experiences will be invoked. On the other hand, in circumstances in which the task stipulates that we should construct temporally distant or highly implausible events *de novo*, the pendulum will invariably swing toward semantic elements, harnessing the appropriate schema and conceptual knowledge to build the required representation.

Taking this argument one step further, in the case of clinical populations with differential damage to the episodic or semantic memory systems, we see the pendulum shift toward the side of least damage, biasing the contents of the resultant

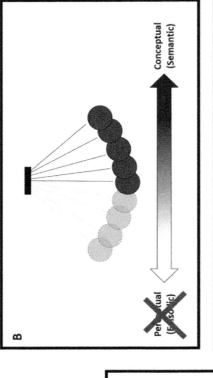

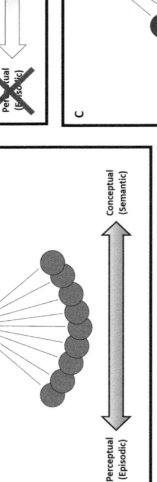

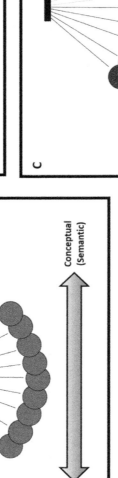

Figure 27.3 *Rethinking construction as a dynamic, content-agnostic system. The representational content of imagination is depicted as oscillating between either end of an episodic-semantic continuum, with the pendulum leaning to one side over the other, contingent on task demands (A). The balance between perceptually (episodic) vs. conceptually (semantic) driven output is compromised when the integrity of the underlying memory systems is disrupted. In the case of episodic memory dysfunction (B), the pendulum is thrust toward the relatively intact semantic memory system, resulting in a mental construction that is largely schematic and devoid of perceptually rich contextual details. By contrast, damage to the semantic memory system (C) biases the pendulum to sample previously experienced events in their entirety from intact episodic memory, compromising the novelty of the construction.*

construction. For example, patients with episodic memory dysfunction due to Alzheimer's disease (AD) would be predicted to rely upon semantic (conceptual) elements to supplement event constructions in the absence of perceptual details from episodic memory (Figure 27.3B). This has been demonstrated where mental reconstruction of the past is concerned, with AD patients defaulting to overgeneral, schematic accounts of formerly evocative autobiographical memories (e.g. Irish et al., 2011b). When envisaging the future, AD patients similarly rely disproportionately upon schemas to provide a general framework for how an event typically unfolds in the absence of perceptually rich contextual details from episodic memory (e.g. Addis et al., 2009; Irish, Hodges, and Piguet, 2013). This is further evident when imagination occurs in atemporal contexts; AD patients provide overgeneral script-like accounts of each setting, yet appear deficient in populating such schematics with sensory-perceptual details (Irish et al., 2015; Ramanan et al., 2018). As has been discussed, the pendulum swings toward episodic content in patients with semantic dementia (Figure 27.3C), who appear adept at completing well-defined construction tasks, if and only if they can recapitulate a previously experienced event in its entirety from recent episodic memory (Irish et al., 2012a). This phenomenon of "recasting" illustrates the extreme weighting of the simulation toward perceptual elements, which for the most part enables patients to predict and anticipate events if they fall along a well-worn path. When events deviate from the norm, or novelty is called for, the imaginative endeavor comes unstuck.

Toward a Unified Theory of Imagination

The objective of this chapter is to encourage a shift in perspective to consider the representational content of imagination as reflecting the intersection of episodic and semantic elements, the relative weighting of which fluctuates according to task demands, prior experience, and integrity of the underlying memory systems. In keeping with prior suggestions that imagination might be best conceptualized in episodic-semantic neutral terms (Stocker, 2012), a recent theoretical refinement posits that the process of constructive simulation is held constant across diverse expressions of memory and imagination (Addis, 2018) (see also Chapter 8). If we accept that a central constructive mechanism represents the core underlying process of imagination, the effectiveness of this system will be vastly enhanced if the central mechanism is agnostic to content. A temporally unconstrained system that accords equal importance to episodic and semantic elements represents the most efficient means to co-opt suitable perceptual details and conceptual knowledge and to reconfigure this information against the appropriate semantic backdrop. The relative weighting of the reinstated perceptual and conceptual details, however, is flexible and likely to vary across experimental conditions and clinical populations.

Imagination takes many different forms, which in turn are supported by distinct cognitive and neural mechanisms. To arrive at a comprehensive understanding of imagination in its many guises, we as a field need to move away from the episodic dominance to consider dynamic fluctuations in conceptual vs. perceptual weightings of constructed representations. Moreover, how such episodic/semantic interactions play out in the unconstrained arena of mind-wandering remains an open question and one which will be crucial to address in the years to come. Addressing such questions will enable us to reconcile conflicting theoretical views on the interplay between episodic and semantic memory in the service of imagination, moving toward a unified perspective in which representational content is key.

Acknowledgments

This work was supported in part by the Australian Research Council (ARC) Centre of Excellence in Cognition and its Disorders (CE110001021). MI is supported by an ARC Future Fellowship (FT160100096) and an ARC Discovery Project (DP180101548). MI is grateful to Matt D. Grilli for providing helpful comments on an earlier draft of this manuscript.

References

Abraham, A., and Bubić, A. (2015). Semantic Memory as the Root of Imagination. *Frontiers in Psychology, 6*, 325.

Abraham, A., Schubotz, R. I., and von Cramon, D. Y. (2008). Thinking About the Future versus the Past in Personal and Non-Personal Contexts. *Brain Research, 1233*, 106–119.

Addis, D. R. (2018). Are Episodic Memories Special? On the Sameness of Remembered and Imagined Event Simulation. *Journal of the Royal Society of New Zealand, 48*(2–3), 1–25.

Addis, D. R., Sacchetti, D. C., Ally, B. A., Budson, A. E., and Schacter, D. L. (2009). Episodic Simulation of Future Events Is Impaired in Mild Alzheimer's Disease. *Neuropsychologia, 47*(12), 2660–2671.

Addis, D. R., and Schacter, D. L. (2008). Constructive Episodic Simulation: Temporal Distance and Detail of Past and Future Events Modulate Hippocampal Engagement. *Hippocampus, 18*(2), 227–237.

Addis, D. R., Wong, A. T., and Schacter, D. L. (2008). Age-Related Changes in the Episodic Simulation of Future Events. *Psychological Science, 19*(1), 33–41.

Arnold, K. M., McDermott, K. B., and Szpunar, K. K. (2011). Imagining the Near and Far Future: The Role of Location Familiarity. *Memory and Cognition, 39*(6), 954–967.

Atance, C. M., and O'Neill, D. K. (2001). Episodic Future Thinking. *Trends in Cognitive Sciences, 5*(12), 533–539.

Bartlett, F. C. (1932). *Remembering*. Cambridge, UK: Cambridge University Press.

Binder, J. R., and Desai, R. H. (2011). The Neurobiology of Semantic Memory. *Trends in Cognitive Sciences, 15*(11), 527–536.

Binder, J. R., Desai, R. H., Graves, W. W., and Conant, L. L. (2009). Where Is the Semantic System? A Critical Review and Meta-Analysis of 120 Functional Neuroimaging Studies. *Cerebral Cortex, 19*(12), 2767–2796.

Bozeat, S., Lambon Ralph, M. A., Patterson, K., Garrard, P., and Hodges, J. R. (2000). Non-Verbal Semantic Impairment in Semantic Dementia. *Neuropsychologia, 38*(9), 1207–1215.

Craver, C. F., Kwan, D., Steindam, C., and Rosenbaum, R. S. (2014). Individuals with Episodic Amnesia Are Not Stuck in Time. *Neuropsychologia, 57*, 191–195.

D'Argembeau, A., and Mathy, A. (2011). Tracking the Construction of Episodic Future Thoughts. *Journal of Experimental Psychology-General, 140*(2), 258–271.

D'Argembeau, A., Ortoleva, C., Jumentier, S., and van der Linden, M. (2010). Component Processes Underlying Future Thinking. *Memory and Cognition, 38*(6), 809–819.

Devitt, A. L., and Addis, D. R. (2016). Bidirectional Interactions between Memory and Imagination. In K. Michaelian, S. B. Klein, and K. Szpunar (eds.), *Seeing the Future: Theoretical Perspectives on Future-Oriented Mental Time Travel.* New York, NY: Oxford University Press, 93–115.

Duval, C., Desgranges, B., de La Sayette, V., et al. (2012). What Happens to Personal Identity when Semantic Knowledge Degrades? A Study of the Self and Autobiographical Memory in Semantic Dementia. *Neuropsychologia, 50*(2), 254–265.

Gilboa, A., and Marlatte, H. (2017). Neurobiology of Schemas and Schema-Mediated Memory. *Trends in Cognitive Sciences, 21*(8), 628–631.

Greenberg, D. L., and Verfaellie, M. (2010). Interdependence of Episodic and Semantic Memory: Evidence from Neuropsychology. *Journal of the International Neuropsychological Society, 16*(5), 748–753.

Grilli, M. D., and Verfaellie, M. (2014). Personal Semantic Memory: Insights from Neuropsychological Research on Amnesia. *Neuropsychologia, 61*, 56–64.

Hassabis, D., Kumaran, D., Vann, S. D., and Maguire, E. A. (2007). Patients with Hippocampal Amnesia Cannot Imagine New Experiences. *Proceedings of the National Academy of Sciences U S A, 104*(5), 1726–1731.

Hayes, B. K., Ramanan, S., and Irish, M. (2018). "Truth Be Told" – Semantic Memory as the Scaffold for Veridical Communication. *Behavioral and Brain Sciences, 41*, 27–28.

Hegdé, J. (2007). Mental Time Travel Sickness and a Bayesian Remedy. *Brain and Behavioral Sciences, 30*, 323–324.

Hsiao, J. J., Kaiser, N., Fong, S. S., and Mendez, M. F. (2013). Suicidal Behavior and Loss of the Future Self in Semantic Dementia. *Cognitive and Behavioral Neurology, 26*(2), 85–92.

Ingvar, D. H. (1985). "Memory of the Future": An Essay on the Temporal Organization of Conscious Awareness. *Human Neurobiology, 4*(3), 127–136.

Irish, M. (2016). Semantic Memory as the Essential Scaffold for Future Oriented Mental Time Travel. In K. Michaelian, S. B. Klein, and K. Szpunar (eds.), *Seeing the Future: Theoretical Perspectives on Future-Oriented Mental Time Travel.* New York, NY: Oxford University Press, 388–408.

Irish, M., Addis, D. R., Hodges, J. R., and Piguet, O. (2012a). Considering the Role of Semantic Memory in Episodic Future Thinking: Evidence from Semantic Dementia. *Brain, 135*(Pt 7), 2178–2191.

(2012b). Exploring the Content and Quality of Episodic Future Simulations in Semantic Dementia. *Neuropsychologia, 50*(14), 3488–3495.

Irish, M., Bunk, S., Tu, S., et al. (2016a). Preservation of Episodic Memory in Semantic Dementia: The Importance of Regions beyond the Medial Temporal Lobes. *Neuropsychologia, 81*, 50–60.

Irish, M., Eyre, N., Dermody, N., et al. (2016b). Neural Substrates of Semantic Prospection – Evidence from the Dementias. *Frontiers in Behavioral Neuroscience, 10*, 96.

Irish, M., Halena, S., Kamminga, J., et al. (2015). Scene Construction Impairments in Alzheimer's Disease – A Unique Role for the Posterior Cingulate Cortex. *Cortex, 73*, 10–23.

Irish, M., Hodges, J. R., and Piguet, O. (2013). Episodic Future Thinking Is Impaired in the Behavioural Variant of Frontotemporal Dementia. *Cortex, 49*(9), 2377–2388.

Irish, M., Hornberger, M., El Wahsh, S., et al. (2014). Grey and White Matter Correlates of Recent and Remote Autobiographical Memory Retrieval – Insights from the Dementias. *PLoS One, 9*(11), e113081.

Irish, M., Hornberger, M., Lah, S., et al. (2011a). Profiles of Recent Autobiographical Memory Retrieval in Semantic Dementia, Behavioural-Variant Frontotemporal Dementia, and Alzheimer's Disease. *Neuropsychologia*, *49*(9), 2694–2702.

Irish, M., Lawlor, B. A., O'Mara, S. M., and Coen, R. F. (2011b). Impaired Capacity for Autonoetic Reliving during Autobiographical Event Recall in Mild Alzheimer's Disease. *Cortex*, *47*(2), 236–249.

Irish, M., Mothakunnel, A., Dermody, N., et al. (2017). Damage to Right Medial Temporal Structures Disrupts the Capacity for Scene Construction – A Case Study. *Hippocampus*, *27*(6), 635–641.

Irish, M., and Piguet, O. (2013). The Pivotal Role of Semantic Memory in Remembering the Past and Imagining the Future. *Frontiers in Behavioral Neuroscience*, *7*, 27.

Irish, M., Piguet, O., and Hodges, J. R. (2012). Self-Projection and the Default Network in Frontotemporal Dementia. *Nature Reviews Neurology*, *8*(3), 152–161.

Irish, M., and Piolino, P. (2016). Impaired Capacity for Prospection in the Dementias – Theoretical and Clinical Implications. *British Journal of Clinical Psychology*, *55*(1), 49–68.

Kamminga, J., O'Callaghan, C., Hodges, J. R., and Irish, M. (2014). Differential Prospective Memory Profiles in Frontotemporal Dementia Syndromes. *Journal of Alzheimer's Disease*, *38*(3), 669–679.

Klein, S. B. (2013). The Complex Act of Projecting Oneself into the Future. *WIREs Cognitive Science*, *4*, 63–79.

(2016). Autonoetic Consciousness: Reconsidering the Role of Episodic Memory in Future-Oriented Self-Projection. *Quarterly Journal of Experimental Psychology (Hove)*, *69*(2), 381–401.

Klein, S. B., Loftus, J., and Kihlstrom, J. F. (2002). Memory and Temporal Experience: The Effects of Episodic Memory Loss on an Amnesic Patient's Ability to Remember the Past and Imagine the Future. *Social Cognition*, *20*(5), 353–379.

Lambon Ralph, M. A. (2014). Neurocognitive Insights on Conceptual Knowledge and Its Breakdown. *Philosophical Transactions of the Royal Society B*, *369*(1634), 20120392.

Lane, R. D., Ryan, L., Nadel, L., and Greenberg, L. (2015). Memory Reconsolidation, Emotional Arousal, and the Process of Change in Psychotherapy: New Insights from Brain Science. *Behavioral and Brain Sciences*, *38*, e1.

Maguire, E. A. (2001). Neuroimaging Studies of Autobiographical Event Memory. *Philosophical Transactions of the Royal Society of London. Series B: Biological Sciences*, *356*(1413), 1441–1451.

Maguire, E. A., Kumaran, D., Hassabis, D., and Kopelman, M. D. (2010). Autobiographical Memory in Semantic Dementia: A Longitudinal fMRI Study. *Neuropsychologia*, *48*(1), 123–136.

Mahr, J., and Csibra, G. (2018). Why Do We Remember? The Communicative Function of Episodic Memory. *Behavioral and Brain Sciences*, *41*, 1–93.

McKinnon, M., Black, S., Miller, B., Moscovitch, M., and Levine, B. (2006). Autobiographical Memory in Semantic Dementia: Implications for Theories of Limbic-Neocortical Interaction in Remote Memory. *Neuropsychologia*, *44*(12), 2421–2429.

Mullally, S. L., Vargha-Khadem, F., and Maguire, E. A. (2014). Scene Construction in Developmental Amnesia: An fMRI Study. *Neuropsychologia*, *52*, 1–10.

Patterson, K., Nestor, P., and Rogers, T. (2007). Where Do You Know What You Know? The Representation of Semantic Knowledge in the Human Brain. *Nature Reviews Neuroscience*, *8*(12), 976–987.

Race, E., Keane, M. M., and Verfaellie, M. (2013). Losing Sight of the Future: Impaired Semantic Prospection Following Medial Temporal Lobe Lesions. *Hippocampus*, *23*(4), 268–277.

Ramanan, S., Alaeddin, S., Goldberg, Z. L., et al. (2018). Exploring the Contribution of Visual Imagery to Scene Construction – Evidence from Posterior Cortical Atrophy. *Cortex, 106,* 261–274.

Renoult, L., Davidson, P. S., Palombo, D. J., Moscovitch, M., and Levine, B. (2012). Personal Semantics: At the Crossroads of Semantic and Episodic Memory. *Trends in Cognitive Sciences, 16*(11), 550–558.

Renoult, R., Irish, M., Moscovitch, M., & Rugg, M.D. (2019). From Knowing to Remembering: The Semantic-Episodic Distinction. *Trends in Cognitive Sciences, 23*(12), 1041–1057.

Robin, J., and Moscovitch, M. (2017). Details, Gist and Schema: Hippocampal–Neocortical Interactions Underlying Recent and Remote Episodic and Spatial Memory. *Current Opinion in Behavioral Sciences, 17,* 114–123.

Rutter, B., Kroger, S., Stark, R., et al. (2012). Can Clouds Dance? Neural Correlates of Passive Conceptual Expansion Using a Metaphor Processing Task: Implications for Creative Cognition. *Brain and Cognition, 78*(2), 114–122.

Schacter, D. L., and Addis, D. R. (2007). On the Constructive Episodic Simulation of Past and Future Events. *Behavioral and Brain Sciences, 30*(3), 331–332.

Schacter, D. L., Addis, D. R., Hassabis, D., et al. (2012). The Future of Memory: Remembering, Imagining, and the Brain. *Neuron, 76*(4), 677–694.

Schacter, D. L., Norman, K. A., and Koutstaal, W. (1998). The Cognitive Neuroscience of Constructive Memory. *Annual Review of Psychology, 49,* 289–318.

Sheldon, S., and Levine, B. (2016). The Role of the Hippocampus in Memory and Mental Construction. *Annals of the New York Academy of Sciences, 1369*(1), 76–92.

Sheldon, S., Vandermorris, S., Al-Haj, M., et al. (2015). Ill-Defined Problem Solving in Amnestic Mild Cognitive Impairment: Linking Episodic Memory to Effective Solution Generation. *Neuropsychologia, 68,* 168–175.

Spreng, R. N., Gerlach, K. D., Turner, G. R., and Schacter, D. L. (2015). Autobiographical Planning and the Brain: Activation and Its Modulation by Qualitative Features. *Journal of Cognitive Neuroscience, 27*(11), 2147–2157.

St-Laurent, M., Moscovitch, M., Levine, B., and McAndrews, M. P. (2009). Determinants of Autobiographical Memory in Patients with Unilateral Temporal Lobe Epilepsy or Excisions. *Neuropsychologia, 47*(11), 2211–2221.

Stocker, K. (2012). The Time Machine in our Mind. *Cognitive Science, 36*(3), 385–420.

Strikwerda-Brown, C., Grilli, M.D., Andrews-Hanna, J. R., & Irish, M. (2019). All Is Not Lost: Rethinking the Nature of Memory and The Self in Dementia. *Ageing Research Reviews, 54,* 100932.

Strikwerda-Brown, C., Mothakunnel, A., Hodges, J. R., Piguet, O., and Irish, M. (2018). External Details Revisited – A New Taxonomy for Coding "Non-Episodic" Content during Autobiographical Memory Retrieval. *Journal of Neuropsychology, 13*(3), 371–397.

Suddendorf, T., and Corballis, M. C. (2007). The Evolution of Foresight: What Is Mental Time Travel, and Is It Unique to Humans? *Behavioral and Brain Sciences, 30*(03), 299–313.

Suddendorf, T., and Redshaw, J. (2013). The Development of Mental Scenario Building and Episodic Foresight. *Annals of the New York Academy of Sciences, 1296*(1), 135–153.

Tulving, E. (1972). Episodic and Semantic Memory. In E. Tulving and W. Donaldson (eds.), *Organization of Memory.* New York, NY: Academic Press, 381–403.

(1983). *Elements of Episodic Memory.* New York, NY: Oxford University Press.

(1985). Memory and Consciousness. *Canadian Psychology, 26,* 1–12.

(2002). Episodic Memory: From Mind to Brain. *Annual Review of Psychology, 53,* 1–25.

Viard, A., Piolino, P., Belliard, S., et al. (2014). Episodic Future Thinking in Semantic Dementia: A Cognitive and FMRI Study. *PLoS One, 9*(10), e111046.

28 How Imagination Supports Narrative Experiences for Textual, Audiovisual, and Interactive Narratives

Joshua A. Quinlan and Raymond A. Mar

Our imagination is the faculty through which we contemplate anything that is not currently being directly sensed (Abraham, 2016), and one of the ways in which imagination supports our daily life is in helping us to comprehend fictional stories (Harris, 2000). Narrative fiction is central to many of our leisure-time activities, with reading books, watching television and film, and even playing certain kinds of videogames all constituting important encounters with narrative. These stories are defined by the portrayal of a central protagonist who experiences an inciting incident or central conflict, motivating the pursuit of goals that structure a series of causally related events extending over time, with the success and failure of these goals adding to an increase in dramatic tension until an inevitable resolution occurs at the climax, followed by a brief denouement (Rumelhart, 1975; Stein and Glenn, 1975; Trabasso and van den Broek, 1985). Comprehending these stories relies heavily on the imagination, with several different aspects of narrative comprehension resting on our imaginative capacities. Moreover, the imagination appears to act in a uniquely dynamic fashion in this context, bridging the perception of narrative cues (e.g. words in a book) with the imagining of the experiences being represented by these cues, in a rapid and free-flowing manner. In other words, the imagination in the service of narrative comprehension appears to occupy a unique space that is separate from pure unconstrained imagination and the direct perception of events. We directly perceive aspects of a narrative, such as words on a page or even the events on a screen, and these perceptions serve to cue our imagination, which then helps us to comprehend the story by building complex representations, elaborating on and enriching these representations, making them feel more real, and even extending these stories in ways that are totally unique to each audience member. In this chapter, we briefly touch on the various ways in which imagination supports story comprehension, focusing first on the comprehension of concrete elements of the story, followed by more elaborative processes that help audiences to "co-create" the story with the author, and finally delving into the more complicated instance of interactive multimedia storytelling as it appears within videogames.

Imagination and Narrative Comprehension

In order to simplify our discussion of how imagination supports story comprehension we will begin with literary texts, before explaining how these same ideas relate to audiovisual narratives like television and film, and finally the interactive narratives found in videogames. One of the greatest developments in the study of discourse comprehension (i.e. the comprehension of connected sentences) was the realization that text comprehension is not merely the sequential decoding of words, but rather the construction and maintenance of what these words represent as a whole, across words and across sentences. In order to comprehend complex discourse, such as stories, we construct mental models (Johnson-Laird, 1983) or situation models (van Dijk and Kintsch, 1983) that represent at a larger scale what is being represented by the text (Bower and Morrow, 1990; Zwaan, 1999, 2004; Zwaan and Radvansky, 1998). We construct models of the characters in a story, including their traits and mental states (Gernsbacher, Hallada, and Robertson, 1998; Rapp, Gerrig, and Prentice, 2001), models of the setting or world in which the story takes place, and models of the events portrayed and how they relate to one another (causally, temporally, and spatially). Moreover, these rich models of the characters and situations being described are constantly being built and updated as the narrative is processed and new information is presented (Gernsbacher, 1997; Kurby and Zacks, 2012). Empirical demonstrations that the construction and maintenance of these models are what supports the comprehension of narratives, rather than simply decoding the text itself, were absolutely groundbreaking. We learned from these studies that the mental accessibility of a concept mentioned in a text depends on the nature of its representation within a mental model, as opposed to its mere presence, absence, or even position within a text (e.g. Bower and Morrow, 1990; MacDonald and Just, 1989; Morrow, Greenspan, and Bower, 1987). Imagination supports the construction and updating of these mental models, and in doing so is absolutely central to the comprehension of stories. Without being able to imagine characters, settings, objects, and situations, as well as the complex relationships among all these elements, we would not be able to understand stories at all.

Creating and maintaining these mental models, for characters and situations, can be considered to be a minimum requirement for the understanding of stories. There are, however, several additional aspects of story comprehension that also rely on our imagination. Consider the broad category of transportation, also known as narrative engagement, a construct based on the idea that narratives transport us to a new world of experiences from which we return somewhat changed (Gerrig, 1993). Transportation includes several different facets, including an attentional focus on the narrative resulting in a loss of access to the outside world, emotional reactions consistent with the narrative events, mental imagery of the events described, and feeling like you are actually a part of the story or physically present within the narrative (Braun and Cupchik, 2001; Busselle and Bilandzic, 2009; Gerrig, 1993; Green and Brock, 2000). Many of these elements of transportation are heavily supported by our imaginative capacities. In the case of literary texts, engaging in visual imagery to see in our mind's eye what a "slight young girl with straight brown hair" looks like, helps us to not only understand the text, but also to perceive it in more detail and therefore experience it as more "real" (Busselle and Bilandzic, 2008) as well as more enjoyable (Green, Brock, and Kaufman, 2004). Another aspect of story processing that is highly related to transportation is the degree to which we identify with the characters portrayed (Tal-Or and Cohen, 2010). Being able to understand characters, and imagine the world from their perspective, helps us to better understand their goals, around which narrative events are inevitably structured (Cohen, 2001).

Although the above discussion should make obvious the impressive degree to which imagination permeates many aspects of story comprehension for literary texts, it might not be so obvious how the same holds for audiovisual narratives. After all, in a film, one does not need to imagine what a "slight young girl with straight brown hair" looks like because we can now directly perceive her appearance on screen. This salient contrast between the need for visual imagery in literary texts and its seeming absence in audiovisual narratives should not distract us from the many other aspects of narrative comprehension that imagination supports, and which remain relevant for audiovisual narratives. In television and film, for example, we must still build our mental models of the situations being represented and the relationships between them (Zacks, Speer, and Reynolds, 2009), along with our mental models of the characters, their personalities, and their motivations (Rapp, Gerrig, and Prentice, 2001); we are still transported into the world of the narrative (Busselle and Bilandzic, 2009), feeling present in that world and losing access to the world around us; we still identify with the characters being portrayed (Cohen, 2001); and we might even engage in visual imagery for events described but not portrayed onscreen. Imagination, then, plays an absolutely central role for the comprehension of both textual and audiovisual narratives. In addition, by imagining the characters, situations, and events in a story, these elements of a narrative come to seem more real to us and thereby become more impactful.

The Role of Imagination in the Co-Creation of Narratives

Although we certainly use the imagination to mentally simulate what is depicted in a story, our experiences with narrative are not constituted solely of what is presented by the author in text or video. Rather, our experiences with stories are constructed from both the story object and the audience's interpretation of that object. No fictional narrative contains a concrete depiction of every aspect of its characters, plot, and world. In all stories, many details are omitted, ranging from the appearance of local flora to the laws governing a unique fictional world. With these details not explicitly represented or defined, many are instead created by each individual's imagination (Cupchik, 2002). In this way, each audience member colors within the lines provided by the fiction, allowing each individual to co-construct a unique interpretation of a narrative (Martínez, 2014). Other gaps in a narrative are created not by omission but through ambiguity: Figurative language and symbolism require effortful interpretation from the audience that may differ from person to person (Miall and Kuiken, 1994). Stories are therefore a co-production orchestrated between the author, who has created a necessarily partial glimpse into a fictional world, and the audience, who expands it into a complete vision by filling in gaps in the plot, interpreting ambiguities in language or presentation, and drawing connections to personal knowledge and memories. In this way, the fiction is "somewhat like a play script that the reader uses like a theater director to construct in imagination a full stage production" (Bower and Morrow, 1990: 44).

A large number of empirical studies have affirmed this idea that imagination does more than represent what is explicitly described by a narrative text, but rather goes beyond what is said to represent what might only be implied. For example, in one study, one set of participants read the phrase "After standing through the 3-hr debate, the tired speaker walked over to his chair." Another set of participants in the same study read a highly similar sentence, with the key inclusion of the speaker taking the action to sit down: "After standing through the 3-hr debate, the tired speaker walked over to his chair and sat down" (Keefe and McDaniel, 1993). What the researchers found was that both sets of participants were equally quick at recognizing the word "sat," regardless of whether this word was present in the text or not. This demonstrates how readers spontaneously represent actions of a character that are only implied, rather than explicitly stated in the text.[1] Moreover, this imagining of implied story features goes far beyond this rather basic example. Audiences also make inferences about other aspects of fictional characters, such as their emotional states, their personal history, their relationships with other characters, or (in the case of text- and audio-based media) their physical appearance. This is well-illustrated by a recent study, which found that readers have vivid auditory "hallucinations" of characters' voices when reading literary fiction (Alderson-Day, Bernini and Fernyhough, 2017). In other words, we imagine all manner of story content, going far beyond what is prompted by explicit mention in a story. By filling in these gaps, we give fictional characters and fictional worlds a richness of detail that would not be possible using the medium alone, making stories seem both real and familiar. Moreover, by making these inferences about fictional characters' internal states, we become more engaged with these characters, identifying more strongly with them characters (Kotovych et al., 2011), and becoming more engaged in their experiences within the story.

As should be obvious, however, the level and type of imaginative inference both required and prompted by stories likely differs for separate forms of narrative media. Although television and film provide audiences with audiovisual information about the fictional world and characters that thus no longer needs to be imagined, these presentations often fail to represent directly the mental and emotional states of characters (voiceovers and other less commonly used techniques aside). This is in contrast to written texts, which often represent the mental states of characters quite explicitly. Text-based and audiovisual narratives thus *both* provide some information while typically omitting other information, a fact that is frequently overlooked.

---

1 Whether this is achieved by inferring the mental states of a character or through some more basic form of coherence-processing remains unclear (Ferstl and von Cramon, 2002; Mar, 2011).

Audiences of the *Harry Potter* films need not conjure their own mental image of Harry's appearance, but they may have to exert more effort in inferring his emotional state compared to readers of the *Harry Potter* novels.

It is also the case that even within a particular medium, the amount of imaginative inference required may vary widely across individual stories. In the case of literature, this variability has been described as the distinction between: (1) readerly texts, which entertain readers without requiring much contribution by way of imagination and inference; and (2) writerly texts, which "make the reader no longer a consumer, but a producer of the text" (Barthes, 1974: 4). When reading a writerly text, the reader would contribute to the narrative experience by interpreting ambiguous or unusual language (Miall and Kuiken, 1994), inferring the thoughts and emotions of characters (Zunshine, 2006), or elaborating on the details of the narrative world. A readerly text would instead provide these elements of the narrative unambiguously. The amount and type of inference demanded by a story likely also differs based on genre. Readers of a romance novel, for example, are unlikely to exert much effort making inferences about the history of the fictional world, but would instead focus on the emotions, relationships, and backgrounds of characters. Other genres, in contrast, might demand more of our imagination when it comes to inferring how the fictional world operates, and direct less imaginative resources to inferring things related to a character's mental state. Confirming this intuition, Gavaler and Johnson (2017) found that readers who thought they were reading a science fiction story expended more effort making inferences about the fictional world and less effort in understanding the cognitive or emotional state of characters, compared to readers who thought they were reading contemporary fiction. Genre will also likely constrain the types of inferences an audience will make. One is more likely to attribute a mysterious noise in a horror movie to a ghost, for example, than if one was watching a drama. All this is to say that every narrative requires an imaginative contribution from its audience, often going beyond what is explicitly described or represented, with the amount and form of that contribution varying widely across media, genres, and even individual stories.

The imaginative contribution that each person brings to a narrative will also differ depending on the individual, as one's values, interests, beliefs, and memories all influence how one interprets and imagines a given story. Incorporating personal experiences in support of imaginative processes serves to personalize and enrich our narrative experience, giving flesh to the skeleton provided by the author. Studies have found that readers spontaneously report the evocation of autobiographical memories during reading (Seilman and Larsen, 1989). Just as a reader uses semantic knowledge to understand the words in a novel, readers may also use personal experiences to better comprehend a story and imagine the experiences of characters. Accordingly, readers who have personal experience with the theme of a story report feeling more transported into that narrative (Green, 2004), and also evaluate it more positively (Larsen and Laszlo, 1990). These likely result from past experience facilitating the imagination: We are better able to mentally simulate experiences when we can draw from our own related past experiences. For example, when watching a character in a film learn that his spouse was unfaithful, a person who can draw upon a personal experience of being betrayed will likely be more engaged with the story and imagine the experience of the character in greater depth. This personal memory might provide detail that goes beyond what is represented or portrayed by the story, such as how it feels to be betrayed, how one is likely to respond after betrayal, and how one's view of the betrayer changes. In this way, personal experience deepens comprehension of both plot and character in a way that might not otherwise be possible. Moreover, the role of past experience in narrative comprehension can be observed through neuroimaging. In a functional magnetic resonance imaging (fMRI) study, readers who had more personal experience with the events described in a story also exhibited greater connectivity between typical language networks in the brain and modality-specific regions linked to embodied processes (e.g. sensorimotor areas; Chow et al., 2015).

Co-creating the experience of a story goes beyond incorporating our past experiences, however; we also use our current selves to help imagine the experience of characters. Readers participate in stories, by responding to the events portrayed (Bezdek, Foy, and Gerrig, 2013; Polichak and Gerrig, 2002) and imagining how they would behave in a similar position. In doing so, we develop an understanding of the plot and characters that is more personal and concrete, informed by our own perspective, beliefs, and attitudes. Finally, we also co-create our narrative experiences by selectively directing our attention to the features of a story that are most personally appealing. One person reading a sci-fi novel may focus her attention and imaginative efforts on the intergalactic political structures of the fictional universe. Another reader of the same novel may instead concentrate on the histories, emotions, and relationships of the characters. In this way, we collaborate with the author to produce the narrative that we want to experience. Beyond increased interest, the practice of injecting one's self into a narrative may have other benefits, such as helping underrepresented people (such as people of color and members of the LGBTQ community) feel more represented in fiction. In one such case, *The Adventure Zone* podcast did not specify the ethnicities of its main protagonists, and many fans took this as an opportunity to imagine these characters as people of color, thereby feeling better represented in the narrative.[2] This one example helps to illustrate how any ambiguities in a narrative, be they unusual uses of language in the form of foregrounding (Miall and Kuiken, 1994) or various forms of symbolism, serve as spaces for imagination to blossom in personally rewarding ways.

It is also possible that both the kind and degree of co-creation that occurs for narratives might vary as a function of genre. Reality television, for example, which often portrays relatively banal yet relatable daily interactions between individuals, might be particularly successful in leveraging past personal experiences. This genre

2 The inferred ethnicities of these characters became the root of dissatisfaction when *The Adventure Zone* was adapted into a new medium: a graphic novel. Because the art now clearly depicted the ethnic backgrounds of each character, there was considerable backlash when this was at odds with what fans had imagined (The Adventure Zone Tumblr, 2017). Similar examples abound when novels are adapted to films. These examples illustrate how the aspects of a narrative that audiences imagine are often deeply meaningful at a personal level. What audiences provide in the co-creation of a story experience is just as valuable, to the audience, as what the author provides.

also presents itself as less "fictional" than other genres, perhaps further encouraging identification and relatability. What is important to keep in mind is that all of these factors – genre, past experiences, current selves, etc. – are likely to interact and combine in complex ways to influence the role of imagination for narrative comprehension.

The Role of Imagination in Interactive Media

We have discussed how both textual and audiovisual narratives rely on imagination, albeit in slightly different ways, but what about interactive forms of narrative? The most common form of interactive narrative, videogames, have rocketed in popularity over recent years, with an estimated 160 million players in the United States (Newzoo, 2017) and a market value that exceeds that of movies or music (Nath, 2016). Just as with novels and films, videogames provide both entertainment and the opportunity for personal insight and growth (Oliver et al., 2016). Modern games vary widely in the degree to which they incorporate narrative, however. Some games, such as *Super Mario Bros.*, ask the player to complete dexterity-based challenges but present only very small and simple scripted plots. Other games, such as the long-running *Final Fantasy* series, present players with dense and complex stories, with dozens of characters and thousands of lines of dialogue.[3] Finally, online competitive games, such as the multiplayer game *Fortnite*, offer players no scripted story. That said, almost every game will ask its players to engage the imagination to some degree along the lines discussed above: making inferences about the internal states of characters, imagining aspects of the world not explicitly depicted, and drawing connections between plot events. However, videogames are unique among narrative media in the level of interactivity and agency that they afford: Players *control* characters (they do not just identify with them) and, to varying degrees based on the game, control the direction of the plot. This ability to interact directly with fictional characters, plots, and worlds in videogames demands some new thinking with respect to how imagination supports narrative experiences.

Many videogames do contain highly scripted linear narratives, very much akin to what is found in novels and films. These games ask the player to take on the role of a character who has a predetermined personality, and the player has little influence on how the plot evolves or how characters develop. Although players are still responsible for advancing the story, each player will be exposed to very similar narratives. For such games, imagination is likely to work in ways quite similar to what we have discussed for audiovisual narratives. In contrast, other games allow players to determine the personality of their character and influence the progression of the plot. The *Mass Effect* trilogy, for example, gives players an impressive amount of control over the narrative. Players determine the background and personality of the protagonist and the relationships s/he will have with other characters, in addition to

---

3 The English-language version of *Final Fantasy VII*, for example, presents approximately 344,000 words.

dozens of crucial plot decisions. Each of these plot choices has distinct consequences that carry over across all three games: In essence, the player determines how the story unfolds. Moreover, each of these decisions evokes the imagination, as players infer how each action will affect their own character, the other characters, and the story. Players also see the consequences of their choices, providing feedback that confirms or contradicts their anticipatory inferences. In part, their ability to succeed in the game is based on their ability to accurately imagine how their actions will affect other characters and the fictional world at large. This role for the imagination in a narrative is unique to videogames. The plot of *Harry Potter* will continue unchanged regardless of the reader's ability to accurately imagine the perspectives of other characters, for example. In contrast, when playing *Mass Effect*, the shape of the narrative is largely based on this ability. As a result, comprehension of the narrative within videogames might be deeper because behaviors and decisions have a direct impact on the narrative. Moreover, in allowing for detailed character customization, players are able to create a protagonist that appeals most to them, which is likely to encourage strong identification with the character and deeper transportation into the narrative. It is not at all uncommon for players to customize the main protagonist in a videogame to resemble themselves, or an ideal version of themselves. In fact, when left to their own devices with no specific instructions, people spontaneously customize the appearance of videogame characters in such a way as to accurately communicate some aspects of their actual personality (Fong and Mar, 2015). By putting more of ourselves into a story, into how we customize a character or in deciding what direction the story should go, interactive videogames give players unique opportunities for imaginative thinking, which may in turn enrich both comprehension of and engagement with the narrative.

Not all videogame narratives are driven by scripted plots, however. Many videogames instead give players the opportunity to create their own narratives, which were not prepared (or sometimes even anticipated) by the game's developers. This is achieved by designing basic mechanics that can be combined in novel ways, resulting in "emergent gameplay" that provides players with the freedom to create their own stories. Players get to decide who they want to be, what their motivations and goals are, and how they relate to other characters. Emergent gameplay first appeared in "immersive simulation" games (e.g. *Deus Ex* or *Thief*), but now appears more often in "open-world sandbox" games (e.g. *Grand Theft Auto* or *The Legend of Zelda: Breath of the Wild*). Open-world sandbox games give players a large and unrestricted world, along with the freedom to interact with that world however they want. *Breath of the Wild*, for example, gives players the ability to climb on to or glide off of any surface in its massive world. This enables an unparalleled ability to explore and create nonlinear narratives that can take place anywhere with events occurring in any order. Beyond this freedom to explore, *Breath of the Wild* also provides the player with several basic abilities, such as the power to move metal objects or to temporarily freeze objects in time. Combining these basic mechanics can result in a nearly infinite number of personalized scenarios – creating totally unique adventures within the main story. A player might, for example, line metal crates up from the top of a hill to a patch of tall grass and wait for a storm. Once lightning strikes the metal crates on the top of the hill, the current traveling through the crates would light a fire in the tall grass at the other end. The player could then jump off the hill, release a paraglider, and use the heat from the fire to ride high into the air, using this height as a tactical advantage for an assault on an enemy encampment. Complex scenarios like these were not scripted by the game's developers, but, rather, are enabled by the basic mechanics of the game and its world. In this way, videogames can offer audiences the ability to produce totally unique narratives all on their own, using only the basic tools that the game provides. As another example, it is possible to play *Grand Theft Auto* as a pizza delivery person, or as an ambulance driver that helps people: Players get to choose the content of story and how they experience the narrative. Imagination continues to play an inferential role in these open-world sandbox games, however: Players must still infer how the narrative world will change as a result of actions or how characters might treat them in response to different decisions. What is unique about these games is the degree to which these aspects of a story engage the imagination. Instead of asking players to infer the outcomes of a handful of different possibilities (e.g. "Do you want to save your comrade or protect the bunker?"), as one sees in narrative videogames like *Mass Effect*, open-world sandbox games have players invent the possibilities themselves. So, in addition to inferring the outcomes of their actions, players can creatively combine different systems to produce an incredible range of possible actions or choices. In this way, players become even more active in co-creating the narrative compared to noninteractive narrative media, and so lean more heavily on the imagination relative to these other forms of narrative. In a sense, narrative-heavy games such as *Mass Effect* provide stories in the form of a question with a multiple-choice response format (e.g. akin to a choose-your-own-adventure book), whereas sandbox games have players create both the question and the possible answers. For multiplayer online games with open-world aspects, the collaborative creativity afforded by this environment can result in an even more diverse and wide-ranging realm of narrative possibilities.

That said, it is worth keeping in mind that even when provided with great opportunities for imagination, on the whole there are limits to how exploratory we as humans tend to be. In general, exploring the unknown produces anxiety (Hirsh, Mar, and Peterson, 2012), and so even when given ample freedom our imagination tends not to stray exceedingly far into unknown realms of thought and behavior. Furthermore, some videogame fans are categorically uninterested in the open-ended and self-driven experiences offered by open-world sandbox games. Although these games have the potential to engage one's imagination and creativity beyond what is offered by traditional linear narrative experiences, they may also lack certain other opportunities for imaginative engagement. For example, although a traditional linear narrative may offer a carefully written and paced plot, these are much more difficult to achieve when the player has total freedom in the game world. To borrow a metaphor from videogame commentariats Ashly and Anthony Burch, some players are interested in a buffet with the freedom to eat whatever they want in whatever order and quantities, while other players would prefer a curated prix fixe meal that sacrifices choice for quality (Burch and Burch, 2012).

Conclusion

In this brief chapter we have outlined myriad ways in which imagination supports and enriches our interactions with stories. Our imagination underlies several aspects of narrative comprehension including visual imagery for textual narratives, but also the construction of the mental models – for characters and for situations – that are absolutely essential for the understanding of stories. Imagination does more than help us to represent what a story describes, however; it also permits us to elaborate upon what is presented in individually unique ways, by drawing upon our personal memories and past experiences. Doing so fills stories with detail and nuance, making them feel more real to us. Audiences use the imagination to co-create narrative experiences in collaboration with authors, for all sorts of narrative media, including those that involve interactive audiovisual presentations. This is still a nascent area of research, however, and there remain several pressing questions for investigators interested in this topic. What is the nature of imagination in this context, and how does the flexible transition between perceiving external narrative cues and imagining narrative experiences take place? What factors moderate the level of imagination brought to bear on different types of stories, for different people, in different media modalities? How might we leverage the role of the imagination in narrative comprehension for prosocial aims, helping us to experience in a compelling way the lives of others quite different from us?

Although we use our own experiences to help understand stories, it should not be ignored that we also use stories to help understand our own experiences: to understand ourselves. By drawing upon our personal history to imagine the experiences of a character, we draw explicit parallels between the experiences being depicted in a story and our own past experiences. In doing so, we can come to gain insight into complicated or difficult aspects of our past. If we draw a parallel between a character's struggle and view it as symbolic of our own journey, or identify with a character who overcomes adversity and persecution, this can change how we view our own self and situation, as well as our potential. Stories are also a launching point to imagine how our lives might be different if we made different decisions, or how we might react in the face of adversity. The idea that stories shape us harkens back to the very foundations of the concept of transportation, with Gerrig (1993) noting that we are not only transported into a narrative world by imagining the experiences depicted, we also return from that world somewhat changed as a result of those experiences. Koopman (2015, 2016) has studied extensively the potential for narrative fiction to elicit reflection and contemplation, particularly in regard to difficult emotional situations. Moreover, entire fields have emerged around the potential impact of stories on our attitudes and beliefs (Green, Strange, and Brock, 2002; Marsh, Meade, and Roediger, 2003; Rapp, 2016) and perhaps even how we think about others (Mar, 2018). There is even evidence that the mere presence of a fictional character can affect us in the same way as a real person, provided that we care deeply about that character, which makes us view them as more real (Gardner and Knowles, 2008). Importantly, it is our ability to imagine that drives the power of stories to shape and influence us. By employing elements of our self to richly imagine the details of a story, we make that story more real to us and these imagined experiences thereby become more likely to have an impact on us. In this way, imagination not only aids our comprehension and our appreciation of stories, but also its influence. Our lives not only inform how we perceive narratives, but narratives also inform how we perceive our lives.

References

Abraham, A. (2016). The Imaginative Mind. *Human Brain Mapping*, *37*(11), 4197–4211.

Alderson-Day, B., Bernini, M., and Fernyhough, C. (2017). Uncharted Features and Dynamics of Reading: Voices, Characters, and Crossing of Experiences. *Consciousness and Cognition: An International Journal*, *49*, 98–109.

Appel, M., and Richter, T. (2010). Transportation and Need for Affect in Narrative Persuasion: A Mediated Moderation Model. *Media Psychology*, *13*(2), 101–135.

Barthes, R. (1974). *S/Z*. English edition. Translated by Richard Miller. New York, NY: Hill and Wang.

Bezdek, M. A., Foy, J. E., and Gerrig, R. J. (2013). "Run for It!": Viewers' Participatory Responses to Film Narratives. *Psychology of Aesthetics, Creativity, and the Arts*, *7*(4), 409.

Bower, G. H., and Morrow, D. G. (1990). Mental Models in Narrative Comprehension. *Science*, *247*(4938), 44–48.

Braun, I. K., and Cupchik, G. C. (2001). Phenomenological and Quantitative Analyses of Absorption in Literary Passages. *Empirical Studies of the Arts*, *19*(1), 85–109.

Burch, A., and Burch, A. [HAWPOfficial]. (2012, November 13). *Dinner Metaphors – Hey Ash Whatcha Playin'?* [Video file]. youtube.com/watch?v=SCjp7T6xVnU.

Busselle, R., and Bilandzic, H. (2008). Fictionality and Perceived Realism in Experiencing Stories: A Model of Narrative Comprehension and Engagement. *Communication Theory*, *18*(2), 255–280.

(2009). Measuring Narrative Engagement. *Media Psychology*, *12*(4), 321–347.

Chow, H. M., Mar, R. A., Xu, Y., et al. (2015). Personal Experience with Narrated Events Modulates Functional Connectivity within Visual and Motor Systems during Story Comprehension. *Human Brain Mapping*, *36*, 1494–1505.

Cohen, J. (2001). Defining Identification: A Theoretical Look at the Identification of Audiences with Media Characters. *Mass Communication & Society*, *4*(3), 245–264.

Cupchik, G. C. (2002). The Evolution of Psychical Distance as an Aesthetic Concept. *Culture & Psychology*, *8*(2), 155–187.

Ferstl, E. C., and von Cramon, D. Y. (2002). What Does the Frontomedian Cortex Contribute to Language Processing: Coherence or Theory of Mind? *NeuroImage*, *17*, 1599–1612.

Fong, K., and Mar, R. A. (2015). What Does My Avatar Say about Me?: Inferring Personality from Avatars. *Personality and Social Psychology Bulletin*, *41*, 237–249.

Gardner, W. L., and Knowles, M. L. (2008). Love Makes You Real: Favorite Television Characters Are Perceived as "Real" in a Social Facilitation Paradigm. *Social Cognition 26*(2): 156–168.

Gavaler, C., and Johnson, D. (2017). The Genre Effect: A Science Fiction (vs. Realism) Manipulation Decreases Inference Effort, Reading Comprehension, and Perceptions of Literary Merit. *Scientific Study of Literature*, *7*(1), 79–108.

Gernsbacher, M. A. (1997). Two Decades of Structure Building. *Discourse Processes, 23*(3), 265–304.

Gernsbacher, M. A., Hallada, B. M., and Robertson, R. R. W. (1998). How Automatically Do Readers Infer Fictional Characters' Emotional States? *Scientific Studies of Reading, 2,* 271–300.

Gerrig, R. J. (1993). *Experiencing Narrative Worlds: On the Psychological Activities of Reading.* New Haven, CT: Yale University Press.

Green, M. C. (2004). Transportation into Narrative Worlds: The Role of Prior Knowledge and Perceived Realism. *Discourse Processes, 38*(2), 247–266.

Green, M. C., and Brock, T. C. (2000). The Role of Transportation in the Persuasiveness of Public Narratives. *Journal of Personality and Social Psychology, 79*(5), 701.

Green, M. C., Brock, T. C., and Kaufman, G. F. (2004). Understanding Media Enjoyment: The Role of Transportation into Narrative Worlds. *Communication Theory, 14*(4), 311–327.

Green, M. C., Strange, J. J., and Brock, T. C. (eds.). (2002). *Narrative Impact: Social and Cognitive Foundations.* New York, NY: Psychology Press/Taylor & Francis.

Harris, P. L. (2000). *The Work of the Imagination.* Oxford, UK: Blackwell.

Hirsh, J. B., Mar, R. A., and Peterson, J. B. (2012). Psychological Entropy: A Framework for Understanding Uncertainty-Related Anxiety. *Psychological Review, 119,* 304–320.

Johnson-Laird, P. N. (1983). *Mental Models: Towards a Cognitive Science of Language, Inference, and Consciousness.* Cambridge, MA: Harvard University Press.

Keefe, D. E., and McDaniel, M. A. (1993). The Time Course and Durability of Predictive Inferences. *Journal of Memory and Language, 32*(4), 446–463.

Koopman, E. M. E. (2015). How Texts About Suffering Trigger Reflection: Genre, Personal Factors, and Affective Responses. *Psychology of Aesthetics, Creativity, and the Arts, 9*(4), 430–441.

(2016). Effects of "Literariness" on Emotions and on Empathy and Reflection After Reading. *Psychology of Aesthetics, Creativity, and the Arts, 10*(1), 82–98.

Kotovych, M., Dixon, P., Bortolussi, M., and Holden, M. (2011). Textual Determinants of a Component of Literary Identification. *Scientific Study of Literature, 1*(2), 260–291.

Kurby, C. A., and Zacks, J. M. (2012). Starting from Scratch and Building Brick by Brick in Comprehension. *Memory & Cognition, 40*(5), 812–826.

Larsen, S. F., and Laszlo, J. (1990). Cultural-Historical Knowledge and Personal Experience in Appreciation of Literature. *European Journal of Social Psychology, 20*(5), 425–440.

MacDonald, M. C., and Just, M. A. (1989). Changes in Activation Levels with Negation. *Journal of Experimental Psychology: Learning, Memory, and Cognition, 15*(4), 633.

Mar, R. A. (2011). The Neural Bases of Social Cognition and Story Comprehension. *Annual Review of Psychology, 62,* 103–134.

(2018). Evaluating Whether Stories Can Promote Social Cognition: Introducing the Social Processes and Content Entrained by Narrative (SPaCEN) Framework. *Discourse Processes, 5*(6), 454–479.

Marsh, E. J., Meade, M. L., and Roediger, H. L. (2003). Learning Facts from Fiction. *Journal of Memory and Language, 49*(4), 519–536.

Martínez, M. A. (2014). Storyworld Possible Selves and the Phenomenon of Narrative Immersion: Testing a New Theoretical Construct. *Narrative, 22*(1), 110–131.

Miall, D. S., and Kuiken, D. (1994). Beyond Text Theory: Understanding Literary Response. *Discourse Processes*, *17*, 337–352.

Morrow, D. G., Greenspan, S. L., and Bower, G. H. (1987). Accessibility and Situation Models in Narrative Comprehension. *Journal of Memory and Language*, *26*(2), 165–187.

Nath, T. (2016). *Investing in Video Games: This Industry Pulls in More Revenue than Movies*. Nasdaq, June 13. *Music*. nasdaq.com/article/investing-in-video-games-this-industry-pulls-in-more-revenue-than-movies-music-cm634585.

Newzoo. (2017). *The American Gamer | 2017*. June 14. newzoo.com/insights/infographics/the-american-gamer-2017/.

Oliver, M. B., Bowman, N. D., Woolley, J. K., et al. (2016). Video Games as Meaningful Entertainment Experiences. *Psychology of Popular Media Culture*, *5*(4), 390–405.

Polichak, J. W., and Gerrig, R. J. (2002). "Get Up and Win!": Participatory Responses to Narrative. In M. C. Green, J. J. Strange, and T. C. Brock (eds.), *Narrative Impact*. Mahwah, NJ: Lawrence Erlbaum Associates, 71–95.

Rapp, D. N. (2016). The Consequences of Reading Inaccurate Information. *Current Directions in Psychological Science*, *25*(4), 281–285.

Rapp, D. N., Gerrig, R. J., and Prentice, D. A. (2001). Readers' Trait-Based Models of Characters in Narrative Comprehension. *Journal of Memory and Language*, *45*, 737–750.

Rumelhart, D. E. (1975). Notes on a Schema for Stories. In D. G. Bobrow and A. Collins (eds.), *Representation and Understanding: Studies in Cognitive Science*. New York, NY: Academic Press, 2–34.

Seilman, U., and Larsen, S. F. (1989). Personal Resonance to Literature: A Study of Remindings While Reading. *Poetics*, *18*(1–2), 165–177.

Stein, N. L., and Glenn, C. G. (1975). An Analysis of Story Comprehension in Elementary School Children: A Test of a Schema. ERIC Document Reproduction Service. ED *121* (474), 53–120.

Sun, L. (2014). *What EA Must Do to Make "Mass Effect 4" a Blockbuster*. The Motley Fool, July 5. fool.com/investing/general/2014/07/05/what-ea-must-do-to-make-mass-effect-4-a-blockbuste.aspx.

Tal-Or, N., and Cohen, J. (2010). Understanding Audience Involvement: Conceptualizing and Manipulating Identification and Transportation. *Poetics*, *38*(4), 402–418.

The Adventure Zone Tumblr. (2017). On The Adventure Zone Graphic Novel, Blue Taako, and Representation. The Adventure Zone, June 2. theadventurezone.tumblr.com /post/161367685782/on-the-adventure-zone-graphic-novel-blue-taako.

Trabasso, T., and van den Broek, P.W. (1985). Causal Thinking and the Representation of Narrative Events. *Journal of Memory and Language*, *24*(5), 612–630.

van Dijk, T. A., and Kintsch, W. (1983). *Strategies of Discourse Comprehension*. New York, NY: Academic Press.

Zacks, J. M., Speer, N. K., and Reynolds, J. R. (2009). Segmentation in Reading and Film Comprehension. *Journal of Experimental Psychology: General*, *138*(2), 307.

Zunshine, L. (2006). *Why We Read Fiction: Theory of Mind and the Novel*. Columbus, OH: Ohio State University Press.

Zwaan, R. A. (1999). Situation Models: The Mental Leap into Imagined Worlds. *Current Directions in Psychological Science*, *8*(1), 15–18.

(2004). The Immersed Experiencer: Toward an Embodied Theory of Language Comprehension. *Psychology of Learning and Motivation*, *44*, 35–62.

Zwaan, R. A., and Radvansky, G. A. (1998). Situation Models in Language Comprehension and Memory. *Psychological Bulletin*, *123*(2), 162.

29 Development of the Fantasy-Reality Distinction

Jacqueline D. Woolley and Jenny Nissel

In this chapter, we explore a subset of human imaginative abilities: our ability to imagine the impossible. First, we ask how do humans decide what to accept as true or real in our world? As with many questions, we can shed light on this by addressing the origins and development of the ability to differentiate fantasy from reality. Second, we ask why is it important to make the distinction between fantasy and reality? The ability to make this distinction is a hallmark of functional adult cognition. Those who lack it have difficulty interacting with others, holding a job, and simply functioning in society. But are there more specific benefits of making this distinction? What role does fantasy play in our lives, and must we be able to distinguish fantasy from reality to reap these benefits?

Of course there is nothing uniquely childlike about making the fantasy-reality distinction – as adults we do it frequently, when we read fiction, consider the future, and differentiate fabricated from real news on the Internet. Children, however, are required to do so just as often if not more. Daily, children are required to distinguish between fantasy and reality in a range of situations, from deciphering their play-mate's pretense to encountering mythical characters in storybooks. Making the distinction between possible and impossible, or real and imaginary, is a critical achievement for young children, as basic beliefs about what kinds of entities exist and what sorts of events are possible form the foundation for their naïve theories about how the world works.

However, adults often make it difficult for children to keep fantasy and reality distinct. Through books, television, and the Internet, children frequently encounter a mixture of real and fictional characters performing possible and impossible actions. Elmo, a monster, teaches children science, while Dora, a human girl, has a talking backpack. Parents often encourage children to believe in various counterintuitive beings, such as God and Santa Claus. From this, one might expect children to be quite confused.

Reflecting these myriad fantasy-reality distinctions, literature on children's fantasy-reality distinction is multifaceted. Research topics range from pretense to beliefs in Santa Claus to understanding television. We present this diverse literature in two sections: (1) self-generated fantasy, and (2) culture-generated fantasy. We hope this organizational schema will enable us to consider the distinct implications of each type of fantasy on children's ability to differentiate them from reality (Taylor, 1997). In a nutshell, when children create their own fantasies, they generally understand that they are distinct from reality. For culture-generated fantasies, however, the line between what's real and what's not may be muddier. In each section, we explore developmental and individual differences in making the fantasy-reality distinction. After reviewing this literature, most of which focuses on *when* children make these distinctions, we turn to the question of *how* children do it. Here we highlight a series of studies from our own lab, in which we explore the tools children use when reasoning about this distinction. At the end of the chapter we address possible outcomes of imagining the impossible, and potential benefits of making the fantasy-reality distinction.

Self-Generated Fantasy

Pretense

Perhaps the earliest forum in which children are faced with the fantasy-reality distinction is pretend play. Lillard and Witherington (2004: 111) suggest that, "Pretending in childhood is a major point of entry into dealing in hypothetical worlds." Most children begin pretending during their second year of life, and by age 2 or 3 spend a significant amount of time engaged in pretend activities (e.g. Haight and Miller, 1993). However, even prior to this, adults may try to engage children in pretense (Haight and Miller, 1993). What do children make of this potentially puzzling behavior?

Lillard and Witherington (2004) showed that 18-month-olds recognize when their mother is pretending vs. really engaging in a behavior, by attending to cues such as looking and smiling. Subsequent research by Ma and Lillard (2006; see also Richert and Lillard, 2004) revealed that children as young as 2½ could distinguish between real and pretend acts on the basis of behavioral cues alone (see also Ma and Lillard, 2017). Moreover, although 5-year-old children differentiate pretend from real acts, they rely on different cues than do adults (Ma and Lillard, 2013). Children place greater weight on content, noting when it is different from reality, whereas adults rely more heavily on behavioral cues (e.g. movement) when content information is not available.

Other evidence that children differentiate pretend worlds from the real world comes from the examination of their ability to transition from one to the other. In a study by DiLalla and Watson (1988), experimenters interfered in a pretend game, changing elements like roles and prop identity. Based on how children dealt with these interruptions, they concluded that 2½- to 3-year-old children lack a boundary between fantasy and reality, and that by age 5–6 they have a solid, yet flexible, boundary. One concern with these conclusions is that responding appropriately to interruptions to pretense might require more than just understanding the boundary. Golomb and Keursten (1996) used interruptions that they argued better address children's ability to make the distinction, and showed that even 3- to 5-year-olds dealt well with them. They therefore contend that children are adept at switching back and forth from pretense to reality, demonstrating a solid grasp of the boundary.

Finally, Woolley and Wellman (1990) used children's everyday conversations as evidence for their understanding of the distinction between pretense and reality. Examining 1- to 6-year-olds' use of the words "real" and "really" recorded in the CHILDES database, they concluded that children first begin to differentiate reality from nonreality around age 3, when referencing pretend actions and also toys and pictures. The ability to make these distinctions can be considered precursors to making the fantasy-reality distinction.

Imagined Representations

Imaginary Companions. In Bill Watterson's comic strip *Calvin and Hobbes*, it's only reasonable that Calvin's mother might suspect that her son confuses fantasy and reality when she observes him conversing with his stuffed tiger. Indeed, in anecdotal reports, children with imaginary companions appear to fully believe that their imaginary friends are real (Taylor, 1999). Taylor relays a story of one child's family having to reserve larger tables at restaurants to accommodate the child's imaginary friends. However, experimental work shows that children understand that their imaginary companions are just pretend from the start (e.g. Taylor, 1999; Taylor, Cartwright, and Carlson, 1993). Furthermore, children with and without imaginary companions do not seem to differ in their ability to differentiate fantasy from reality, though children with imaginary companions are more likely to engage in fantasy and to show a more mature level of pretense (Taylor, Cartwright, and Carlson, 1993). For more information on imaginary companions, please refer to Chapter 13 in this handbook).

Other imagined entities. Imaginary companions are a specific case, however, occurring in an estimated 28 percent of preschool-age children (Taylor, 1999). What about more universally occurring imagined representations? One might expect children to have difficulty differentiating imagined from real objects, for example. Investigating this, Wellman and Estes (1986) demonstrated the contrary: By age 3, children understood that one can touch and eat a real cookie but one cannot touch and eat an imagined cookie. Children of the same age also understand how dreams differ from reality, and are aware of their fictional nature (Woolley and Wellman, 1992). Continuing this line of work, Woolley and Wellman (1993) found that, between the age of 3 and 4, children begin to understand the origins of imagination, realizing that they can imagine entities that they have never seen and do not believe exist (e.g. a purple frog). This work also showed that children are aware that to know something (e.g. the contents of a closed box) they must have a visual experience, whereas one can imagine without perceptual access. Understanding that imagination has different origins from knowledge might help children maintain the distinction between imagination and reality. These studies show that even preschool-age children distinguish between the contents of their imagination and the real world.

Harris et al. (1991), noting that children often seem fearful of entities like monsters and witches, wondered if they might be confused about whether imagined entities can become real. They had 4- to 6-year-old children imagine a monster or a bunny inside a box. Children often acted as if they believed the entities were really in the boxes and admitted wondering about it. Harris et al. (1991) suggest that the process of imagining something makes that entity more available, and thus increases the likelihood in the child's mind that it might exist. However, it is not clear whether findings using this method inform us about whether children really believe the products of their imagination can become real. Children's apparent fear of the monster might also be akin to adults being hesitant to take a shower after watching the movie *Psycho*. Certainly adults are not confused about whether the movie was real; instead, emotion, rather than ontological knowledge drives their behavior (Harris, 2000). Furthermore, children's behavior toward the boxes may have been governed by other factors, for example, wanting to continue the pretense (Golomb and Galasso, 1995).

To investigate whether children actually attributed reality status to their imagined objects beyond the pretense scenario, Woolley and Phelps (1994) gave 3- to 5-year-olds an opportunity to imagine everyday items in boxes. When these objects were requested by someone in need, children demonstrated a clear understanding that they had not materialized. The type of item children imagine – in this case, practical and commonplace, not fantastical like a monster – might also affect their understanding of its real vs. fantastical nature. Using a similar design to Harris et al. (1991), Johnson and Harris (1994) uncovered evidence that children might master the imagination-reality distinction first for everyday objects. For example, children seemed to understand early on that imagined ice cream was not real. Only later did they begin to be able to apply the distinction to supernatural entities, as evidenced by their difficulty determining that an imagined entity like a fairy was also not real. Individual differences emerged as well: "Credulous" children (those who explicitly entertained the belief that the imaginary objects were actually in the boxes) behaved as if the entities were really inside the boxes, while "skeptical" children did not.

Bourchier and Davis (2000) explored two additional factors that might affect children's fantasy-reality distinction in this box scenario: (1) the emotional valence of the imagined entity, and (2) the accessibility of empirical evidence regarding the content of the boxes. Although they found no effect of the latter, they did find effects of emotional valence, with children responding in ways that would either appear to increase positive affect (e.g. open a box with an imagined fairy inside) or decrease negative affect (e.g. avoid a box with an imagined monster). Like Johnson and Harris (1994), they suggest that there are two types of children, some who are skeptical by nature, and some who are credulous. For skeptical children, these response patterns reflect their continuation of the pretense game rather than a fantasy-reality confusion. For credulous children, though, who might be more apt to overestimate the probability of something being real just by virtue of being able to imagine it, these response patterns might be seen as legitimate confusions. This contrast is a provocative demonstration of individual differences in children's fantasy-reality differentiation.

Overall, the studies reviewed here show evidence of fantasy-reality differentiation in children as young as 3, but some confusion in children as old as 6 with regard to whether products of the imagination can become real. Individual and situational differences appear to play a greater role than age in children's understanding.

Culture-Generated Fantasy

Fantastical Beings

As discussed by Taylor (1997), the developmental story regarding children's understanding of self-generated imaginings may be very different from that regarding their understanding of beings presented to them by their culture. This, she argues, is due to the degree of control children have over these two sorts of beings – essentially full control over self-generated imaginary representations but little control over cultural beings. Cultural beings range widely; they may be generic (e.g. fairies) or specific and event-related (e.g. Santa Claus). They may have positive or negative emotional valence (e.g. monsters vs. fairies). Finally, children learn about these entities in a variety of ways. Some are encountered primarily through testimony, whereas others are introduced via storybooks and television. We begin this section by discussing studies that include a range of entities, generic and specific, positive and negative. We then focus on specific beings introduced primarily through testimony, before discussing beings also encountered through storybooks and television.

Children's General Beliefs About Fantastical Beings. Morison and Gardner (1978) assessed children's understanding of the reality status of various entities and found that even kindergarteners were able to correctly categorize most as real or pretend, but that this ability developed through grade 6 (age 11–12). Interestingly, children seemed more skeptical than credulous: They often judged real entities that are removed from their daily lives (e.g. a knight) as fantastical. Rosengren and Hickling (1994) investigated children's credulity further, interviewing parents about children's beliefs in different entities. They found that belief varied by entity type: Parents reported greater belief in event-related beings like Santa Claus vs. generic beings like fairies. Parental encouragement of belief was strongly related to their children's beliefs. Martarelli and Mast (2013) also had children aged 3–8 judge a range of real and fantastical entities, and found that accuracy increased with age. In this case, children appeared more credulous than skeptical, judging fantastical entities as real more often than the reverse. Confirming Rosengren et al.'s (1994) previous findings, they found that children were more accurate in their judgments of generic beings than of specific ones. Following up on this work, Martarelli, et al. (2015) assessed the role of individual differences and found that theory of mind predicted fantasy understanding.

Suspecting that children's performance on sorting tasks might not fully reflect their ability to distinguish real from fantastical entities, Sharon and Woolley (2004) asked children about the properties these entities possess (e.g. whether they dream or get hurt). Indeed, they found that older children differentiated fantastical and real entities in terms of their properties before being able to explicitly identify their reality status. Additionally, researchers found that children with higher fantasy orientation (those who engaged in more fantastical imaginative play) categorized more entities correctly than did other children, perhaps because these children had more practice navigating the boundary between fantasy and reality.

Harris et al. (2006) moved beyond properties of the entity itself, highlighting the role that testimony and cultural endorsement play in the formation of children's beliefs. They presented 4- to 8-year-olds with real everyday entities (e.g. cats), scientific entities (e.g. germs), culturally endorsed fantastical beings (e.g. Santa), fantastical beings that are not endorsed (e.g. monsters), and impossible beings (e.g. flying pigs). They found that, although children were most certain of the existence of everyday and scientific entities, they also affirmed the existence of fantastical but culturally endorsed entities. By contrast, they denied the existence of unendorsed and impossible beings. Thus cultural testimony alone serves as an additional and powerful mechanism driving children's fantasy-reality differentiation.

Boerger (2011) explored the role of another potential underlying mechanism, causal understanding. Though children possess a strong understanding of possible vs. impossible events, they still believe in cultural fantasy figures like Santa Claus beyond the preschool years. Boerger proposed that this incongruity exists because, although causal violations are central to adults' conceptions of these characters (e.g. Santa traveling around the world in one night), the same properties may not yet be salient to children, who might focus on more peripheral properties (e.g. eating cookies or bringing presents). To address this, she probed 3- to 9-year-old children's beliefs about the properties held by humans vs. fantasy figures. She found that, with age, children demonstrated increasing understanding that impossible abilities are uniquely associated with fantastical characters. This work suggests that the ability to think about how fantasy figures violate causal regularities might play a role in children's understanding of their nonreality. This insight receives empirical support from studies discussed later by Shtulman and Yoo (2015) on children's judgments about Santa Claus, by Bunce and Harris (2013) on children's judgments about television characters, and by Corriveau et al. (2009) on children's judgments about story characters.

The studies reviewed here show increased understanding with age of the nature of both real and fantastical entities. They also identify various individual difference factors, such as fantasy orientation and theory of mind, as well as characteristics of the entities (e.g. event-related or generic) that affect understanding. The studies also explore potential mechanisms, such as use of testimony and conceptual development, that contribute to the ability to make the fantasy-reality distinction.

Beliefs in Specific Beings. Western culture encourages widespread belief in Santa Claus: Children may sit on his lap at the mall, send him letters through the mail or via email, listen to songs about him, and receive presents from him on Christmas morning. Belief in cultural beings like Santa and the Easter Bunny peaks around age 4 or 5, and declines significantly by age 8 (Blair, McKee, and Jernigan, 1980). Parental support has been shown to be more important than other factors, such as fantasy orientation, in driving belief in these sorts of fantasy figures (Prentice, Manosevitz, and Hubbs 1978).

To isolate the effects of cultural and parental support, Prentice and Gordon (1987) turned their attention to 3- to 10-year-old Jewish children's belief in Santa and the Tooth Fairy. They expected that Jewish children would believe less in Santa Claus than in the Tooth Fairy, and less in Santa than Christian children, but that both groups would believe equally in the Tooth Fairy. As expected, Jewish children did express a lower level of belief in Santa than did Christian children. Contrary to expectations, however, Jewish children also expressed a lower level of belief in the Tooth Fairy than did their Christian counterparts. In fact, Jewish children believed equally in Santa Claus and the Tooth Fairy, regardless of both parental encouragement and the child's participation in the myth. Prentice and Gordon suggest that children's first experience with a fantasy figure might affect their beliefs in later ones: Children tend to learn about Santa Claus before the Tooth Fairy. That Santa Claus is presented as unreal to Jewish children makes them less likely to believe in the Tooth Fairy once they are introduced to her.

Woolley, Boerger, and Markman (2004) explored children's initial encounter with a fantastical being by introducing 3- to 5-year-old preschool children to a made-up novel entity called the Candy Witch, who visits children on Halloween night and leaves them a new toy in exchange for their candy. A subset of parents agreed to simulate her presence in their household by switching candy for toys during the night. Thus some of the children were "visited" at home by the Candy Witch, whereas others only heard about her at school. Among older preschoolers, children who were visited believed more strongly than did children who were not. Among children who were visited, older children had stronger beliefs than younger children. There was no effect of the visit condition on younger children, suggesting that older children were better able to use the events they experienced as evidence in favor of the Candy Witch's existence (see the discussion later about how children make the fantasy-reality distinction). Children who believed in more fantastical beings in general also believed more strongly. Additionally, among children who only heard about the Candy Witch at school, children with a high fantasy orientation believed more strongly than did children with a low fantasy orientation.

Boerger, Tullos, and Woolley (2009) also explored belief in the Candy Witch in a sample of 5- to 7-year-old elementary school children. The most surprising finding was that these children believed just as strongly as the preschool children had in the Woolley, Boerger, and Markman (2004) study. Factors that increased belief in the Candy Witch were existing beliefs in fantastical beings and whether the child was visited. Being visited reflected parental support of the Candy Witch's existence but also entailed the provision of evidence of her existence. Either or both of these factors may have been critical to belief.

Finally, Shtulman and Yoo (2015) probed the role of children's understanding of possibility in their conceptions of Santa. Children aged 3–9 wrote a letter asking Santa some questions. Children with greater understanding of what is possible in the real world were more likely to ask questions about Santa's extraordinary abilities (e.g. how he could travel the world in one night), whereas children with less understanding asked more superficial questions (e.g. about what Mrs. Claus looked like). This suggests that children's developing understanding of possibility may play an important role in leading them to eventually question the existence of magical beings.

Overall, the studies in this section show that, with regard to familiar fantastical beings, belief level decreases linearly with age, which may be a result of increasing understanding of possibility. When first introduced to fantastical beings, certain basic cognitive abilities may be necessary for a child to form an initial belief, and individual differences, such as the number of beings in which a child already believes, may also influence how they conceive of the being.

Fictional Beings in Media: Story Contexts. Children are often exposed to new information through stories. Many children's books contain information about the natural world and about historical events and people. Others offer accounts of religious characters and events. Storybooks of all types can present fantasy-reality challenges, as they often interweave possible and impossible events, and realistic and fantastical characters.

To assess children's ability to gauge the reality of characters appearing in various genres, Woolley and Cox (2007) presented preschool-age children with realistic, fantastical, and religious storybooks and asked them to judge whether the characters were real or pretend. Overall, preschoolers exhibited a tendency to doubt the reality of characters in books across genre. However, 5-year-olds judged characters in religious stories as more likely to be real than characters in realistic books, suggesting an influence of cultural learning. To further explore children's beliefs about religious characters in stories, Vaden and Woolley (2011) told 4- to 6-year-olds about impossible events either in a religious (using Bible stories) or nonreligious (using Bible stories with religious references removed) context. Children who heard religious stories demonstrated higher levels of belief in the reality of the characters, and this effect increased with age. In addition, children with higher family religiosity believed more strongly than did children with lower family religiosity. Vaden and Woolley (2011) conclude that children use God's involvement in a story to assess the reality of its characters.

To further examine the role of context in children's beliefs about character reality, Corriveau et al. (2009) presented children with novel figures embedded in either realistic or fantastical story contexts. Results showed that 5- to 7-year-olds used the plausibility of story events to assess the character's reality status. In a second study, they found that, when given training, certain preschoolers could use story plausibility to judge reality status. In contrast to Woolley and Cox (2007), children did not exhibit a bias to reject the reality status of the characters. This may have been because, in this case, the characters were presented less like storybook characters and more like real characters: Children were told a story without an accompanying storybook, and children saw photographs in place of storybook illustrations.

Corriveau, Chen, and Harris (2015) went on to study individual difference factors that might affect children's use of story cues in determining character reality status. Using a design similar to Vaden and Woolley (2011), they asked 5- and 6-year-olds to judge the reality of characters in realistic, religious, and fantastical stories. All children judged that protagonists in realistic stories were real. In stories with religious (i.e. impossible) events, children with exposure to religious teachings judged the protagonists to be real, whereas secular children judged them to be fictional. Strikingly, children with religious exposure were also more likely to judge characters in fantastical stories to be real.

Davoodi, Corriveau, and Harris (2016) examined this issue in a country where children are regularly exposed to religious narratives – Iran. Like the religious children in Corriveau, Chen, and Harris (2015), not only did Iranian 5- and 6-year-olds conceive of protagonists in religious stories as real, they also believed characters in the fantastical stories to be real. Davoodi, Corriveau, and Harris (2016) conclude that exposure to religious narratives affects children's understanding of the fantasy-reality distinction, expanding their conception of what is possible. They also explored two potential sources of individual differences: (1) Theory of Mind (ToM), and (2) Executive Function (EF). They found that children with poor EF were just as likely to incorrectly judge reality status whether they had a high or a low ToM, whereas children with high EF performed better if they had a high ToM. Thus, as shown in previous work (Corriveau, Chen, and Harris, 2015), ToM can help children understand that stories can represent both fiction and reality, but EF may influence how much it can help.

The extent to which children transfer information from fictional vs. realistic stories to another situation reveals their understanding of the fiction-reality distinction. Richert and Smith (2011) found that preschoolers were less likely to transfer analogical problem solutions to a novel problem from stories about fantastical characters than from stories about real people. They also assessed the effects of fantasy orientation on transfer, and found that children with higher fantasy orientation were less likely to transfer information from the fantastical story. They concluded that children who are more involved in fantastical pursuits maintain a stronger boundary between real and fantastical worlds.

Summarizing, with age, children become better at using various cues to judge the reality status of characters in storybooks. However, individual differences, such as family religiosity, theory of mind, executive function, and fantasy orientation might play a more critical role than age in children's ability to make the fantasy-reality distinction.

Fantastical Beings in Media: Television. One might expect children to exhibit greater confusion about the reality status of television characters than storybook characters, as they are actively represented, whether by live persons or animated figures. Bunce and Harris (2013) explored 3- to 5-year-old children's understanding of the reality status of animated television characters like Bob the Builder. Interestingly, children tended to judge these characters as real. Children's understanding of the fictional nature of animated television characters increased with age, and their performance improved when they compared two characters of divergent reality status instead of judging them in isolation. Mares and Sivakumar (2014) similarly found that younger preschoolers tended to believe that novel TV characters were real, while older children tended to believe that novel TV content was real. A related study by Goldstein and Bloom (2015) explored whether children understand that real actors are separate from the character they play on TV by investigating whether they grasp that actors do not actually feel the emotions of the characters they represent. Results showed that 3- and 4-year-old children thought that actors really experienced the emotions they acted out, but 5-year-olds performed in an adult-like manner, distinguishing actor emotion from character emotion. Overall, there is significant development between the age of 3 and 5 in children's understanding of fantasy and reality regarding TV characters.

Fantastical Events

Possibility. Young children understand that events that violate their naïve physical, biological, and psychological theories about the world are impossible. For example, they know that one solid object cannot pass through another (Johnson and Harris, 1994), and that animals cannot shrink in size (Rosengren et al., 1994). Yet work by Shtulman and Carey (2007) indicates that, although children can differentiate possible from impossible events, they struggle with events that are possible but unusual or extraordinary (e.g. a boy finding an alligator under his bed), and often claim that these sorts of events cannot occur. The understanding that improbable events are possible develops significantly between the ages of 4 and 8.

Weisberg and Sobel (2012) reasoned that, because thinking about fictional worlds activates children's concept of possibility, assessing their understanding of improbable events implicitly within a story context might provide early evidence of understanding. They asked 4-year-olds to choose endings for stories containing primarily either improbable or impossible events. They found that, when hearing stories containing improbable events, children chose to continue them with other improbable events rather than with impossible events, thus exhibiting an implicit understanding of the distinction between improbable and impossible.

Lane et al. (2016) asked children to imagine improbable events, suspecting that children's ability to picture these events might lead them to understand that they are possible. Indeed, results showed that children who claimed to have successfully imagined improbable events were more likely to judge that the phenomena could actually occur. The authors proposed that, as children develop, they gain facility in using their imagination to evaluate the possibility of an event. This, in combination with increasing knowledge about the world, enables children to be able to imagine ways that improbable events could take place. Thus the earliest understanding of improbability might occur when children are mentally engaging with these phenomena, whether through being transported into a story or when inspired to use their imagination.

Magic. As young children's understanding of possibility matures, many parents introduce them to the concept of magic, hence suggesting to them that impossible events could happen with the aid of magical forces. Various studies indicate that children accept magic as a way to make impossible events happen. Johnson and Harris (1994), for example, found that children age 3–5 claim that outcomes brought about by normal physical processes (e.g. someone drawing a picture) are not magical, whereas outcomes that violate physical principles (e.g. a picture appearing to draw itself) are. Rosengren, Kalish, Hickling, and Gelman (1994) showed that 4- and 5-year-olds claim that impossible transformations concerning animals could be performed by a magician. Also, after seeing seemingly impossible events happen, children appealed to magic to explain them. These studies show that children may blur the line between fantasy and reality when they can turn to magic as a possible explanation.

Phelps and Woolley (1994) explored when 4- to 8-year-old children would use magic to explain events. They found that, although children of all ages referred to magic to explain seemingly impossible events, the extent to which children did so depended on whether they had access to a natural explanation for the events. They suggest that magic is used as an explanatory tool by children when they encounter events that violate their expectations and when they lack a natural way to explain such events. But to what extent do children believe magic is real? Overall, these studies tend to show that, whereas 4-year-olds view magic as real, slightly older children (5- to 7-year-olds) view it as trickery, indicating a clear understanding of its fantastical nature.

The most extensive research on children's beliefs in magic comes from the lab of Eugene Subbotsky (e.g. 1993; 2004). In a seminal study, Subbotsky (1994) showed 4- to 6-year-olds a "magic" box and told them that it could transform pictures into real objects. After the experimenter left the room, children tried various incantations and hand gestures aimed at producing this transformation, and expressed disappointment when these efforts did not produce the expected outcome. Subbotsky proposes that the fact that a reputable adult suggested the magical possibility played a significant role in children's behavior. He argues that this apparent confusion about the reality of magic is not simply a product of childish immaturity, and he supports this with demonstrations that adults will also engage in magical behavior given similar circumstances (Subbotsky, 1993). He argues that the fantasy-reality boundary is permeable throughout development, and that various conditions can result in increases or decreases in magical thinking.

Lastly, Kim and Harris (2014) investigated potential consequences of believing in magic. They found that children who were credulous toward magic were more likely to accept information from someone who had produced magical outcomes than from someone who had produced ordinary ones. Thus children's beliefs in magic affected their trust of sources and subsequent learning from testimony. Summarizing across the studies, children of all ages, and even adults, will appeal to magic to explain impossible events. However, their conception of where magic falls on the fantasy-reality spectrum shifts with age, as younger children are more apt to categorize it as real, while older children and adults acknowledge its fantastical status. Various situational factors, such as endorsement by a credible other and availability of a natural explanation, influence how likely both children and adults are to appeal to magic in explaining events.

Fantastical Events in Media. Children's books and television shows consistently interweave fantastical and realistic events. In a fictional world, a girl may fly away on the back of a swan. A child reader might have seen swans, and so might understand that they are real, but not have thought about whether a girl could sit on one's back or order it to carry her away. A girl is real, a swan is real, and flying is real, but an event intertwining these may not be. As they must with fictional characters, children must come to understand which sorts of media events are simply fantastical and which could actually occur in reality.

Taylor and Howell (1973) presented children with pictures of fantastical events (e.g. rabbits baking a cake) and realistic events (e.g. a mother bird feeding a baby bird), and asked them to judge whether the events could happen. They found that children did not consistently differentiate between real and fantastical events until age 5. Using similar stimuli, Samuels and Taylor (1994) explored the role of emotion in differentiating fantastical from real storybook events. Across both real and fantastical events, children claimed that negatively valenced events could not happen. Thus children did not differentiate the events on the basis of their fantastical or realistic nature; rather, they did so on the basis of the emotions they elicited.

Carrick and Quas (2006) investigated this phenomenon with a wider range of emotions. Children reported that happy fantastical and real events could happen more often than both frightening and angry fantastical and real events. Such responses were elevated in children who experienced stronger emotions about the events, suggesting that emotions affect this ability (see also Metlicar, 2014). Carrick and Quas suggest that these responses might mirror children's desires, in that they presumably want positive, but not negative, events to happen. This may also contribute to higher levels of belief in positive vs. negative fantastical beings, as discussed earlier. In essence, children might be expressing their wishes – or even attempting to protect themselves from bad things by asserting that they can't happen – rather than making ontological judgments.

However, the patterns may have resulted from children not having experienced the negative events. Carrick, Quas, and Lyon (2010) explored this by including maltreated children in another sample. Indeed, they found maltreated children correctly stated that negative real events could occur, but also incorrectly stated that negative fantastical events could occur, supporting the idea that experience is driving judgments to some extent. Carrick and Ramirez (2012) also tested the idea that children's wishes were guiding their judgments. They found that when emphasis was put on responding correctly, accuracy improved for fantastical but not real events. The authors suggest that most children may lack the knowledge that frightening real events can occur. They also propose that children's understanding of the fantastical nature of fantastical events may be better than their understanding of the real nature of real events.

Televised events present unique challenges, requiring children not only to reason about whether the events really happened or are happening, but also whether the events are representative of what could happen in the real world. In addition, children must differentiate between a wide range of television genres, from cartoons to documentaries to the news. In Downs (1990), 4- to 6-year-olds differentiated between cartoon and realistic events, claiming that cartoon events were pretend whereas realistic events were real. However, Wright et al. (1994) proposed that 5-year-old children have a bias to think that everything on TV is fictional. Confirming this, Li, Boguszewski, and Lillard (2015) showed 4- to 6-year-olds video clips of real and fantastical TV events, using both cartoons and real people in videos. Overall, children understood that the fantastical events were not real, but underestimated the reality of the real events. The latter pattern was found for both cartoons and real people. However, when videos showed real people performing fantastical events, 4-year-olds tended to judge the fantastical events as real.

In summary, children's understanding of the reality status of events they encounter in storybooks and television develops with age and can be dependent on the emotional valence of the content. As with their understanding of storybook characters, children increasingly use context and their existing beliefs to make judgments about the reality status of storybook events. Children are at times credulous, judging that fantastical events are real, and at times skeptical, judging that real events are fantastical.

How Do Children Make the Fantasy-Reality Distinction?

The work presented thus far indicates that even preschool children are often quite good at making the fantasy-reality distinction, yet there is also significant development during the preschool and elementary school years. To date, we have considerable information on *when* children make various fantasy-reality distinctions. One goal of work in my lab is to determine *how* children make the fantasy-reality distinction, particularly when they encounter novel entities. We have found that children use a variety of tools in assessing reality status. These fall into two broad categories: (1) gathering and evaluating cues in their immediate environment, and (2) using existing beliefs about reality. Within each of these broader categories children display a number of more specific abilities.

Regarding the former class of tools, Tullos and Woolley (2009) demonstrated that the ability to use evidential cues to determine the identity of a novel entity developed significantly between the ages of 4 and 8 years, and that children's ability to make accurate reality status judgments depended on their ability to use material evidence to determine identity. Children also use verbal cues, paying special attention to the way people talk about reality. Woolley, Ma, and Lopez-Mobilia (2011) found that even 3-year-olds picked up on some conversational cues – if someone denied the existence of an entity in a conversation with another person, children were less likely to believe in it. By age 7, children were able to use statements that only implied a novel entity's existence (e.g. "I saw a baby dugong") to conclude that those entities were real. With age, children believed more strongly when people used these implicit statements than when they used explicit claims about reality. In contrast, however, Dore, Jaswal, and Lillard (2015) found that 9-year-olds were more likely to believe in entities introduced by explicit statements of belief, as long as those statements included additional information about the novel entity. Thus children are able to use material evidence as well as implicit, explicit, and informative verbal evidence to inform their beliefs about a novel entity's reality status.

Another cue children use is the context in which a novel entity is encountered. Woolley and van Reet (2006) introduced preschoolers to a novel entity described in one of three contexts: scientific (referring to scientists), fantastical (referring to dragons), or everyday (referring to other children). Though 3-year-olds did not yet use the contextual cues, 4-year-olds did: Those in the scientific condition were more likely to believe in the novel entities than those in the fantastical condition. By age 5, children also attributed positive reality status to those entities introduced in an everyday context significantly more frequently than to those introduced in a fantastical context. In a like manner, Corriveau et al. (2009) demonstrated that children use the realistic or fantastical context of story events to judge the reality status of a protagonist.

The second set of tools children use to judge the reality of novel entities is their own existing beliefs and knowledge. Within the context of religious beliefs, children often use their own bank of culturally imparted knowledge to evaluate the reality status of novel information. Vaden and Woolley (2011) showed that with age children increasingly used the presence of God in a story to affirm the reality of seemingly impossible story events (see also Corriveau, Chen, and Harris, 2015). Thus, an existing belief in God led them to conclude that events in which God took part were also real. Children also evaluate the fit between new information and their own knowledge when judging reality status within natural contexts. Lopez-Mobilia and Woolley (2016) presented 4- to 8-year-olds with novel entities with characteristics that were possible and typical (e.g. a bird that eats bugs), possible and atypical (e.g. a bird that has a blue beak), or impossible (e.g. a bird that can become invisible). They let children choose whether to determine reality immediately or ask for help from an informant. If the properties of an entity conflicted with children's knowledge about the world, they immediately and independently considered it to be impossible. Existing knowledge guided their decision to seek advice as well: Children sought and utilized testimony most when novel entities were possible but atypical, that is, when they were unusual but not inconsistent with their existing knowledge.

Implications: Outcomes and Benefits of Making the Distinction

Lillard and Witherington (2004: 111) argue that "dealing in hypothetical worlds" is "a skill that crucially underpins much of human culture and progress." Many researchers have argued that fantastical thinking plays an important role in children's cognitive development (e.g. Harris, 2000; Lillard, 2001; Taylor, 1999; Weisberg and Gopnik, 2013). When evaluating this argument, two primary questions arise: (1) does simply thinking about fantasy have some cognitive benefit? and (2) does being able to successfully make the distinction result in specific cognitive outcomes? Regarding the former, research has shown that children can perform certain reasoning tasks within a fantasy context that they have difficulty performing otherwise (e.g. Dias and Harris, 1988; Lillard and Sobel, 1999). Thus engaging in fantastical thinking might aid conceptual development and benefit logical reasoning skills. Weisberg and Gopnik (2013) argue that thinking about fantastical scenarios allows children to practice counterfactual reasoning, an ability that is critical to future thinking, moral reasoning, and scientific discovery. Alternatively, some studies suggest that engaging with fantastical content may have negative effects, particularly on children's inhibitory control (e.g. Lillard and Peterson, 2011).

Regarding the second question – whether being able to actually make the distinction yields particular benefits – it certainly seems that children's ability to differentiate possible from impossible events must play a critical role in the development of their theories about the world. First, rejection of the possibility of unusual, yet still possible, events would clearly limit young children's causal understanding of how the world works (Schultz, Bonawitz, and Griffiths, 2007; Weisberg and Sobel, 2012). A fully developed understanding of possibility is especially important for children's learning from fictional media. In order to learn from fictional worlds, children must master the "reader's dilemma" (e.g. Gerrig and Prentice, 1991): That is, they must determine whether new information is true only in the fictional world or is also true in reality. Beliefs about what can and cannot take place in the real world govern our use of fiction in learning about the world. Research shows that children with a better understanding of the fantasy-reality distinction are more receptive to learning new information from television (Bonus and Mares, 2015; Mares and Sivakumar, 2014). Richert and Smith (2011) suggest that greater involvement with fantasy helps children determine what elements to apply to the real world from a mix of fantasy and reality within storybooks, enabling them to solve the reader's dilemma. For an excellent review of children's learning from fiction, see Hopkins and Weisberg (2017).

Making the fantasy-reality distinction has other potential effects on cognition. Principe and Smith (2008) argue that children's naive fantastical beliefs might bias their memories of events that could potentially be explained by magical processes. For example, they found that children who believed more strongly in the Tooth Fairy misremembered events surrounding their tooth losses, often claiming to have seen or heard the Tooth Fairy. A mature ability to make the fantasy-reality distinction could also help children interpret the testimony of others. Kim and Harris (2014) showed that children who understood that magic is not real were less susceptible to others' misleading claims about events. Similarly, Lee et al. (2002) showed that children who understood that ghosts were fantastical were more likely to reject false claims about the actions of a ghost in reality. Thus, making the fantasy-reality distinction can both: (1) help children search for and obtain accurate explanations for events, and (2) determine whether someone should be trusted.

Unanswered Questions and Directions for Future Research

Although there are many unanswered questions about the development of the fantasy-reality distinction, two stand out: (1) what is the role of individual differences? and (2) what cognitive processes and brain structures are involved in making decisions about reality status? Regarding the first, a number of studies reveal significant individual differences in children's reality status judgments about novel entities; some children seem compelled to consistently reject the existence of novel entities, whereas others seem to find it quite easy to believe in them, in many cases without much effort or thought. Still others seem more responsive to or dependent on cues or evidence. Some researchers have proposed that some children are inherently credulous and some inherently skeptical (e.g. Bourchier and Davies, 2000; Johnson and Harris, 1994); might certain personality variables, like openness to experience, underlie these differences? A range of individual difference factors have been shown to affect fantasy-reality differentiation, including fantasy orientation, executive function, and emotional reactivity. Since findings regarding some of these, such as fantasy orientation, are mixed, researchers might engage in more fine-grained analyses of the phenomena, for example, exploring which aspects of fantasy orientation matter and which do not. Research on the effects of parental encouragement are also mixed. A more fine-grained analysis would also be helpful here: What kinds of behaviors and attitudes do parents transmit, and which among these matter most? Studies increasingly point toward a role for children's understanding of mental states in their ability to make the fantasy-reality distinction (e.g. Corriveau, Chen, and Harris, 2015; Martarelli, et al., 2015); future work should probe the role of children's metacognitive understanding more generally.

To shed light on the second question – which cognitive processes and brain structures underlie reality status decisions – we need to increase our understanding of the differences between children's and adults' reasoning in making these decisions. Various studies suggest that children rely more heavily than adults do on personal experiences – their explanations for their judgments often reference either their lack of experience with an entity (e.g. Harris et al., 2006, Tullos and Woolley, 2009) or their imagined experiences with them (Principe and Smith, 2008). Research should explore the processes by which developing children come to rely less on personal experience and more on real world causal principles when determining reality status. Some studies also suggest that children and adults recruit different brain regions to make these distinctions (Han, Jiang, and Humphreys, 2007; Li, Liu, Woolley, and Zhang, 2019). Finally, adults appear to use different brain regions to judge fictional and real entities. Abraham and colleagues (Abraham and von Cramon, 2009; Abraham, von Cramon, and Schubotz, 2008) suggest that, rather than thinking about fantasy and reality as a dichotomy, adults reason about it as a spectrum, driven by personal relevance. Entities with greater personal relevance are conceptualized as more "real," while those with less are considered to be more "fantastical." It remains to be explored whether this is also true of children.

Conclusion

In summary, the fantasy-reality distinction is multifaceted and tells numerous developmental stories. Overall, the findings reviewed here are consistent with the idea that children are not inherently credulous. At the same time, they are not inherently skeptical. Many factors influence children's ability to make the fantasy-reality distinction. These factors can be grouped into three types: (1) child attributes and characteristics, such as age or fantasy orientation, (2) entity or event characteristics, such as whether it is self-generated or a product of culture, and (3) environmental features, such as the context in which the entity or event is encountered. Future research should clarify the roles of each of these factors, in isolation and in concert. In doing this, we will achieve a greater depth of understanding of imagination and make further progress toward charting its importance in the lives of both children and adults.

References

Abraham, A., and von Cramon, D. Y. (2009). Reality=Relevance? Insights from Spontaneous Modulations of the Brain's Default Network When Telling Apart Reality from Fiction. *PLoS One*, *4*(3), 1–9.

Abraham, A., von Cramon, D. Y., and Schubotz, R. I. (2008). Meeting George Bush versus Meeting Cinderella: The Neural Response When Telling Apart What Is Real from What Is Fictional in the Context of Our Reality. *Journal of Cognitive Neuroscience*, *20*(6), 965–976.

Blair, J. R., McKee, J. S., and Jernigan, L. F. (1980). Children's Belief in Santa Claus, Easter Bunny and Tooth Fairy. *Psychological Reports*, *46*(3), 691–694.

Boerger, E. A. (2011). "In Fairy Tales Fairies Can Disappear": Children's Reasoning About the Characteristics of Humans and Fantasy Figures. *British Journal of Developmental Psychology*, *29*(3), 635–655.

Boerger, E. A., Tullos, A., and Woolley, J. D. (2009). Return of the Candy Witch: Individual Differences in Acceptance and Stability of Belief in a Novel Fantastical Being. *British Journal of Developmental Psychology*, *27*(4), 953–970.

Bonus, J. A., and Mares, M. L. (2015). Learned and Remembered but Rejected: Preschoolers' Reality Judgments and Transfer from Sesame Street. *Communication Research*, *46* (3), 375–400.

Bourchier, A., and Davis, A. (2000). Individual and Developmental Differences in Children's Understanding of the Fantasy-Reality Distinction. *British Journal of Developmental Psychology*, *18*(3), 353–368.

Bunce, L., and Harris, M. (2013). "He Hasn't Got the Real Toolkit!" Young Children's Reasoning About Real/Not-Real Status. *Developmental Psychology*, *49*(8), 1494–1504.

Carrick, N., and Quas, J. A. (2006). Effects of Discrete Emotions on Young Children's Ability to Discern Fantasy and Reality. *Developmental Psychology*, *42*(6), 1278–1288.

Carrick, N., Quas, J. A., and Lyon, T. (2010). Maltreated and Non-Maltreated Children's Evaluations of Emotional Fantasy. *Child Abuse and Neglect*, *34*(2), 129.

Carrick, N., and Ramirez, M. (2012). Preschoolers' Fantasy-Reality Distinctions of Emotional Events. *Journal of Experimental Child Psychology*, *112*(4), 467–483.

Corriveau, K. H., Chen, E. E., and Harris, P. L. (2015). Judgments about Fact and Fiction by Children from Religious and Nonreligious Backgrounds. *Cognitive Science*, *39*(2), 353–382.

Corriveau, K. H., Kim, A. L., Schwalen, C. E., and Harris, P. L. (2009). Abraham Lincoln and Harry Potter: Children's Differentiation between Historical and Fantasy Characters. *Cognition*, *113*(2), 213–225.

Davoodi, T., Corriveau, K. H., and Harris, P. L. (2016). Distinguishing between Realistic and Fantastical Figures in Iran. *Developmental Psychology, 52*(2), 221.

Dias, M. G., and Harris, P. L. (1988). The Effect of Make-Believe Play on Deductive Reasoning. *British Journal of Developmental Psychology, 6*(3), 207–221.

DiLalla, L. F., and Watson, M. W. (1988). Differentiation of Fantasy and Reality: Preschoolers' Reactions to Interruptions in Their Play. *Developmental Psychology, 24*(2), 286–291.

Dore, R. A., Jaswal, V. K., and Lillard, A. S. (2015). Real or Not? Informativeness Influences Children's Reality Status Judgments. *Cognitive Development, 33*, 28–39.

Downs, A. C. (1990). Children's Judgments of Televised Events: The Real versus Pretend Distinction. *Perceptual and Motor Skills, 70*(3), 779–782.

Gerrig, R. J., and Prentice, D. A. (1991). The Representation of Fictional Information. *Psychological Science, 2*(5), 336–340.

Goldstein, T. R., and Bloom, P. (2015). Characterizing Characters: How Children Make Sense of Realistic Acting. *Cognitive Development, 34*, 39–50.

Golomb, C., and Galasso, L. (1995). Make Believe and Reality: Explorations of the Imaginary Realm. *Developmental Psychology, 31*(5), 800–810.

Golomb, C., and Kuersten, R. (1996). On the Transition from Pretence Play to Reality: What Are the Rules of the Game? *British Journal of Developmental Psychology, 14*(2), 203–217.

Haight, W. L., and Miller, P. J. (1993). *Pretending at Home: Early Development in a Sociocultural Context*. Albany, NY: SUNY Press.

Han, S., Jiang, Y., and Humphreys, G. W. (2007). Watching Cartoons Activates the Medial Prefrontal Cortex in Children. *Chinese Science Bulletin, 52*(24), 3371–3375.

Harris, P. L. (2000). *The Work of the Imagination*. Hoboken, NJ: Blackwell Publishing.

Harris, P. L., Brown, E., Marriott, C., Whittall, S., and Harmer, S. (1991). Monsters, Ghosts and Witches: Testing the Limits of the Fantasy-Reality Distinction in Young Children. *British Journal of Developmental Psychology, 9*(1), 105–123.

Harris, P. L., Pasquini, E. S., Duke, S., Asscher, J. J., and Pons, F. (2006). Germs and Angels: The Role of Testimony in Young Children's Ontology. *Developmental Science, 9*(1), 76–96.

Hopkins, E. J., and Weisberg, D. S. (2017). The Youngest Readers' Dilemma: A Review of Children's Learning from Fictional Sources. *Developmental Review, 43*, 48–70.

Johnson, C. N., and Harris, P. L. (1994). Magic: Special but Not Excluded. *British Journal of Developmental Psychology, 12*(1), 35–51.

Kim, S., and Harris, P. L. (2014). Belief in Magic Predicts Children's Selective Trust in Informants. *Journal of Cognition and Development, 15*(2), 181–196.

Lane, J. D., Ronfard, S., Francioli, S. P., and Harris, P. L. (2016). Children's Imagination and Belief: Prone to Flights of Fancy or Grounded in Reality? *Cognition, 152*, 127–140.

Lee, K., Cameron, C. A., Doucette, J., and Talwar, V. (2002). Phantoms and Fabrications: Young Children's Detection of Implausible Lies. *Child Development, 73*(6), 1688–1702.

Li, H., Boguszewski, K., and Lillard, A. S. (2015). Can That Really Happen? Children's Knowledge about the Reality Status of Fantastical Events in Television. *Journal of Experimental Child Psychology, 139*, 99–114.

Li, H., Liu, T. Woolley, J., & Zhang, P. (2019). Reality Status Judgments of Real and Fantastical Events in Children's Prefrontal Cortex: An fNIRS Study. *Frontiers in Human Neuroscience, 13*:444.

Lillard, A. (2001). Pretend Play as Twin Earth: A Social-Cognitive Analysis. *Developmental Review, 21*(4), 495–531.

Lillard, A. S., and Peterson, J. (2011). The Immediate Impact of Different Types of Television on Young Children's Executive Function. *Pediatrics, 128*(4), 644–649.

Lillard, A. S., and Sobel, D. (1999). Lion Kings or Puppies: The Influence of Fantasy on Children's Understanding of Pretense. *Developmental Science, 2*(1), 75–80.

Lillard, A. S., and Witherington, D. C. (2004). Mothers' Behavior Modifications during Pretense and Their Possible Signal Value for Toddlers. *Developmental Psychology, 40*(1), 95–113.

Lopez-Mobilia, G., and Woolley, J. D. (2016). Interactions between Knowledge and Testimony in Children's Reality-Status Judgments. *Journal of Cognition and Development, 17*(3), 486–504.

Ma, L., and Lillard, A. S. (2006). Where Is the Real Cheese? Young Children's Ability to Discriminate between Real and Pretend Acts. *Child Development, 77*(6), 1762–1777.

(2013). What Makes an Act a Pretense One? Young Children's Pretend-Real Judgments and Explanations. *Child Development Research, 2013*, 1–9.

(2017). The Evolutionary Significance of Pretend Play: Two-Year-Olds' Interpretation of Behavioral Cues. *Learning & Behavior, 45*(4), 441–448.

Mares, M. L., and Sivakumar, G. (2014). "Vámonos Means Go, but That's Made up for the Show": Reality Confusions and Learning from Educational TV. *Developmental Psychology, 50*(11), 2498–2511.

Martarelli, C. S., and Mast, F. W. (2013). Is It Real or Is It Fiction? Children's Bias toward Reality. *Journal of Cognition and Development, 14*(1), 141–153.

Martarelli, C. S., Mast, F. W., Läge, D., and Roebers, C. M. (2015). The Distinction between Real and Fictional Worlds: Investigating Individual Differences in Fantasy Understanding. *Cognitive Development, 36*, 111–126.

Metlicar, S. (2014). Happy Dragon Is Real, Frightening Dragon Is Not: Children's Fantasy-Reality Distinction of Emotional Stimuli. *Studia Psychologica, 56*(2), 155–168.

Morison, P., and Gardner, H. (1978). Dragons and Dinosaurs: The Child's Capacity to Differentiate Fantasy from Reality. *Child Development, 49*(3), 642–648.

Phelps, K. E., and Woolley, J. D. (1994). The Form and Function of Young Children's Magical Beliefs. *Developmental Psychology, 30*(3), 385–394.

Prentice, N. M., and Gordon, D. (1987). Santa Claus and the Tooth Fairy for the Jewish Child and Parent. *Journal of Genetic Psychology, 148*(2), 139–151.

Prentice, N. M., Manosevitz, M., and Hubbs, L. (1978). Imaginary Figures of Early Childhood: Santa Claus, Easter Bunny, and the Tooth Fairy. *American Journal of Orthopsychiatry, 48*(4), 618–628.

Principe, G. F., and Smith, E. (2008). Seeing Things Unseen: Fantasy Beliefs and False Reports. *Journal of Cognition and Development, 9*(1), 89–111.

Richert, R. A., and Lillard, A. S. (2004). Observers' Proficiency at Identifying Pretense Acts Based on Behavioral Cues. *Cognitive Development, 19*(2), 223–240.

Richert, R. A., and Smith, E. I. (2011). Preschoolers' Quarantining of Fantasy Stories. *Child Development, 82*(4), 1106–1119.

Rosengren, K. S., and Hickling, A. K. (1994). Seeing Is Believing: Children's Explanations of Commonplace, Magical, and Extraordinary Transformations. *Child Development, 65*(6), 1605–1626.

Rosengren, K. S., Kalish, C. W., Hickling, A. K., and Gelman, S. A. (1994). Exploring the Relation between Preschool Children's Magical Beliefs and Causal Thinking. *British Journal of Developmental Psychology*, *12*(1), 69–82.

Samuels, A., and Taylor, M. (1994). Children's Ability to Distinguish Fantasy Events from Real-Life Events. *British Journal of Developmental Psychology*, *12*(4), 417–427.

Schulz, L. E., Bonawitz, E. B., and Griffiths, T. L. (2007). Can Being Scared Cause Tummy Aches? Naive Theories, Ambiguous Evidence, and Preschoolers' Causal Inferences. *Developmental Psychology*, *43*(5), 1124–1139.

Sharon, T., and Woolley, J. D. (2004). Do Monsters Dream? Young Children's Understanding of the Fantasy/Reality Distinction. *British Journal of Developmental Psychology*, *22*(2), 293–310.

Shtulman, A., and Carey, S. (2007). Improbable or Impossible? How Children Reason about the Possibility of Extraordinary Events. *Child Development*, *78*(3), 1015–1032.

Shtulman, A., and Yoo, R. I. (2015). Children's Understanding of Physical Possibility Constrains their Belief in Santa Claus. *Cognitive Development*, *34*, 51–62.

Subbotsky, E. V. (1993). *Foundations of the Mind: Children's Understanding of Reality.* Cambridge, MA: Harvard University Press.

(1994). Early Rationality and Magical Thinking in Preschoolers: Space and Time. *British Journal of Developmental Psychology*, *12*(1), 97–108.

(2004). Magical Thinking in Judgments of Causation: Can Anomalous Phenomena Affect Ontological Causal Beliefs in Children and Adults? *British Journal of Developmental Psychology*, *22*(1), 123–152.

Taylor, B. J., and Howell, R. J. (1973). The Ability of Three-, Four-, and Five-Year-Old Children to Distinguish Fantasy from Reality. *Journal of Genetic Psychology*, *122*, 315–318.

Taylor, M. (1997). The Role of Creative Control and Culture in Children's Fantasy-Reality Judgments. *Child Development*, *68*(6), 1015–1017.

(1999). *Imaginary Companions and the Children Who Create Them.* Oxford, UK: Oxford University Press.

Taylor, M., Cartwright, B. S., and Carlson, S. M. (1993). A Developmental Investigation of Children's Imaginary Companions. *Developmental Psychology*, *29*, 276–285.

Tullos, A., and Woolley, J. D. (2009). The Development of Children's Ability to Use Evidence to Infer Reality Status. *Child Development*, *80*(1), 101–114.

Vaden, V. C., and Woolley, J. D. (2011). Does God Make It Real? Children's Belief in Religious Stories from the Judeo-Christian Tradition. *Child Development*, *82*(4), 1120–1135.

Weisberg, D. S., and Gopnik, A. (2013). Pretense, Counterfactuals, and Bayesian Causal Models: Why What Is Not Real Really Matters. *Cognitive Science*, *37*(7), 1368–1381.

Weisberg, D. S., and Sobel, D. M. (2012). Young Children Discriminate Improbable from Impossible Events in Fiction. *Cognitive Development*, *27*(1), 90–98.

Wellman, H. M., and Estes, D. (1986). Early Understanding of Mental Entities: A Reexamination of Childhood Realism. *Child Development*, *57*(4), 910–923.

Woolley, J. D., Boerger, E. A., and Markman, A. B. (2004). A Visit from the Candy Witch: Factors Influencing Young Children's Belief in a Novel Fantastical Being. *Developmental Science*, *7*(4), 456–468.

Woolley, J. D., and Cox, V. (2007). Development of Beliefs about Storybook Reality. *Developmental Science*, *10*(5), 681–693.

Woolley, J. D., Ma, L., and Lopez-Mobilia, G. (2011). Development of the Use of Conversational Cues to Assess Reality Status. *Journal of Cognition and Development*, *12*(4), 537–555.

Woolley, J. D., and Phelps, K. E. (1994). Young Children's Practical Reasoning about Imagination. *British Journal of Developmental Psychology*, *12*(1), 53–67.

Woolley, J. D., and van Reet, J. (2006). Effects of Context on Judgments Concerning the Reality Status of Novel Entities. *Child Development*, *77*(6), 1778–1793.

Woolley, J. D., and Wellman, H. M. (1990). Young Children's Understanding of Realities, Nonrealities, and Appearances. *Child Development*, *61*(4), 946–961.

(1992). Children's Conceptions of Dreams. *Cognitive Development*, *7*(3), 365–380.

(1993). Origin and Truth: Young Children's Understanding of Imaginary Mental Representations. *Child Development*, *64*(1), 1–17.

Wright, J. C., Huston, A. C., Reitz, A. L., and Piemyat, S. (1994). Young Children's Perceptions of Television Reality: Determinants and Developmental Differences. *Developmental Psychology*, *30*(2), 229–239.

30 Imagining the Real: Buddhist Paths to Wholeness in Tibet

Anne Carolyn Klein (Rigzin Drolma)

In the ocean of reality, here of its own accord and free of frills,

Swim the golden fish, no sign of thingness in them.[1]

In many Buddhist traditions, confusion is intrinsic to ordinary experience. This confusion, or ignorance, consists either of imagining as existent something is that isn't, like an inviolable self, or denying into no-existence something that does exist, like cause and effect. Buddhist practitioners seek freedom from all such mesmerizing imaginals. And yet the path to freedom itself involves intentional imagining. How can this be?

In making the multifaceted role of the imagination in Buddhist thought and contemplative practice our focus here, we note how such imagining differs from thinking, especially through its integration of the cognitive emotional and somatic or embodied experience. And we take particular interest in how this works in the most revered system of practice among the Ancient (Nyingma) Tibetan Buddhist paths known as Dzogchen, which translates as "Great Completeness." The path is so-called because it understands itself to include all paths, and to provide the most subtle descriptions and realizations of reality (Klein, 2011: 265–278). Most especially we consider Dzogchen's way of handling the apparent conundrum that imagination's ability to bring freedom from itself is key to Dzogchen's inclusive vision. We introduce the stages of such training by referring to an especially succinct distillation of them in the eighteenth-century Jigme Lingpa's reflections (see Dahl, 2016) on a short work by the fourteenth-century Longchen Rabjam (also referred to as Longchenpa) architect and preserver whose work remains at the core of Dzogchen traditions today. We'll begin with an overview, then introduce Jigme Lingpa's brief vignettes illustrating the entire path and, for the bulk of our discussion, note how the imagination figures in such practices as a basis for showing how this relationship goes to the heart of Buddhist phenomenologies of consciousness.

Imagination: An Overview

"Imagination" here encompasses both confused elements of conceptual and sensory experience and the intentionally cultivated imaginaire that removes such confusion. The "imaginaire" is what one is left with as a result of intentionally

---

1 Longchenpa (2009). For an excellent and different translation see Barron (2001: 58).

engaging the imagination. In particular, in the Tibetan context, it refers to the mental state or image one has conjured through a training that explicitly employs acts of the imagination, Any experience short of fully realized direct perception – what Buddhists call awakening *(bodhi)* – is to some degree imaginal. In so many ways, for better and for worse, the imagination is what we call home.

Intentional imagining is used to dissolve the lens of confusion. Dissolving isn't always easy or welcome, however. For one thing, we feel our perception is correct. We feel beauty is objectively present, not in the eye of the beholder, or that steady-state solidity and separateness are simply out there, not imagined at all. Buddhist analysis, like Western science, shows they are not. For Buddhists this is an inborn ignorance. Buddhist philosophy, starting with the great Indian logicians Dignaga and Dharmakirti, and later Tibetan Middle Way teachings that incorporated their perspectives, carefully categorizes what sorts of minds are associated with what sorts of errors, and what is needed to remedy them. Practitioners continually dance between imaginal confusion and the rectifying imaginaire. From the earliest to the very advanced stages of practice, artful and intentional imagining is a core strategy for getting free from such confusion. This confusion is partly learned and partly intrinsic to everyday cognitive and sensory experience.

Imagination is flexible, multipurpose, and infinitely creative. Imagining that you can succeed. Imagining what release from anger will feel like, or boundless love. Or even using imagination to magnify your own confusion so you can recognize it, dissolve the confusion, and experience authentic reality, how things really are. For Dzogchen, imagination shares with that reality an unstoppable creativity. Even confused imagination is not outside the domain:

> Awakened mind, source of all that is, creates everything –
> However these appear, they are my essence.
> However they arise, they are my magical displays . . .[2]

Already, as we read this, we are imagining *something*. Reality in this view is, is an unceasing and unstoppable process and thus by definition can never be fully imagined. Even so, the family resemblance imagination bears to reality means that even as it participates in confusion, it can also help usher one out of confusion. In this way, imagination is bilateral. A vibrant imagination can exacerbate error – I am the worst person in the world, I am the most special – while intentional imagining furthers a felt sense of loosening up such fabrications.

Buddhists ask: You want to train on a path? You want to meditate? In that case your imagination is indispensable. Paths to freedom require cognitive, sensory, and embodied somatic knowing. Imagination participates in all of these, either as part of the confusion being addressed or as the means of its transformation. Therefore, thinking and imagining intertwine on the path, as we see in Jigme Lingpa's essentialized sequencing, which will be our focus here, and in his Heart Essence

---

2 Longchenpa (2009) *Chos dbyings rin po che'i mdzod kyi 'grel pa lung gter mdzod,* citing *The Majestic Creator of Everything (Kun byed rgyal po)*: 75.14 BDRC W1KG4884-I1KG4901-65–412. For published English translation see Barron (2001: 47). See also Neumaier-Dargyay (1992).

foundational practices, which are closely related to this.[3] First, however, let's consider some of the wrongful impressions that Jigme Lingpa's deployments of a rectifying imagination will address.

Error starts with the sensory experience. By and large, things look pretty stable and we regard them as such. In fact there is no stability at all except what I imagine. At some level we know this, but this knowing doesn't impact our felt sense of stability. We don't feel "I imagine this"; we feel we see what is there.

To overcome this blindness, practitioners reflect on causality, interdependence, and the impermanence that is key to both. Reflection includes imagining flickering momentariness. But mind-pictures are not enough; there is resistance to overcome. Not everyone wants to hear about impermanence. It is not the intellect but the psycho-emotional self that rejects this. The young and healthy can hardly bring attention to it. And they are not the only ones. We all want and imagine an impossible stability within imagining. We don't want to feel impermanence applies to us. At least not now.[4] Such resistance is part of the confusion practice addresses. But our confusion isn't asking to be addressed!

Still, with practice and good will the rectifying imagination can undermine confused imaginations. In some ways Buddhism teaches what life teaches. Even without meditation, as we grow older, as impermanence becomes more and more apparent in our own bodies and minds, we notice. We recognize that this flux is what my confused imagination has long obscured from my ordinary experience. We likely digest this more readily if we have already imagined it coming.

Confusion regarding stability or permanence is a function of the imagination – we are taking as an object something that isn't there, like seeing water where there is only a mirage. Imagination errs either on the side of overreach *('gro dog)*, imagining what isn't there, or underestimation *('gur 'debs)*, denying what does exist. These errors combine to corroborate the most egregious imagined object of all – the overwrought, underanalyzed sense of self. Practice that can undo this confusion engages visual, emotional, and embodied imaginations, often coalescing these with a culturally grounded aesthetic.

In order to shift what Buddhists understand as confusion, a rectifying imaginaire must extend to the depth and source of perception itself. Much as exercise engages different muscle groups in varied ways, release from confusion requires retraining and relaxing a wide spectrum of habits. Governing our mind, emotions, embodied experience, and even the play of our senses. The bidirectional and multifaceted functioning of the imagination, as well as its intimate connection with the body is core to Buddhist scholarship and practice.

---

3 For Jigme Lingpa's foundational practices see Klein (2009). For a classic discussion of these see Rinpoche (1994). Patrul Rinpoche died in 1887. My colleague Elizabath Napper and I are currently translating and annotating the commentary on these verses by his renowned student Adzom Rinpoche (d. 1924), *Lamp Lighting the Path (Thar lam gsal sgron)*.

4 For the psychological benefits of reckoning with impermanence and death, see the classic *Existential Psychotherapy* by Irvin D. Yalom (1980).

Imagination And Its Discontents: The Seven Trainings

We are such stuff as dreams are made of .

Prospero, The Tempest

Dreams are fleeting, nothing but mind-light. But while we are in them, they feel compellingly real. We suffer when things go wrong. The root problem, though, is not what happens in the dream, but our confused sense that the dream is real. Similarly, in waking life we think pleasant and painful experiences are far more real than they are. One vector of this error, already noted, is our unaware assent to the stability that seems baked into things. Our furniture, our bodies, our friends, all seem to have the heft of durability. But this exists only in our imagination. Recognizing that everything changes is a big step toward being in sync with what is real, and not erroneously imagined. And an understanding of impermanence "will ultimately release you into the clear light of your own mind" (Sangpo, 1982: 62).

Impermanence is the first of Longchenpa's seven trainings for Dzogchen. How do we learn to see and feel the world differently? Notice seasonal changes, he suggests, which is an outer form of impermanence. Discern inner impermanence through changes in your body. Most intimately, impermanence is the loss of friends and family or the flux of our own thoughts.[5] Seeing thusly can rectify our passive assent to apparent stability, unmasking its total fabrication. How do we know when this training is successful? Success, says Longchenpa, is when we immediately recognize everything we see – trees, animals, our own mind-wanderings – as instances of impermanence.

Longchenpa's eighteenth-century spiritual heir, Jigme Lingpa, expands on this training. By way of preface he notes that although long-time learned practitioners make progress through studying scripture, many of us find insight comes more easily with story (Dahl, 2016: 29).[6] Jigme Lingpa therefore steps in, offering a dramatic vignette with you at the center, revving up a psycho-emotional imaginaire in which you find yourself face to face with death. The progression of the story proper and its aftermath form stages, analogues to the classic ninefold path of Nyingma, which is subdivided into three main categories of outer, inner, and secret, or *sutra, tantra,* and *dzogchen.* Each phase has its own distinct relationship with the practitioner's imagination.

At the vignette opens, you are alone in an unknown place, with no sign of human habitation whatever. You are desolate. Two strangers, a man and a woman, approach and precipitously invite you to journey with them to an island of immense wealth. You agree. You join them in a rickety boat that is soon careening on sky-high waves, then plunging into cavernous depths, all in this fragile vessel whose oars now crack into total uselessness. What will you do? With rising despair, you cry out for help

---

5 This last commentary is a personal communication from Adzom Paylo Rinpoche, winter, 2007–2008.

6 Jigme Lingpa here instructs teachers as well as students: "Individuals who already have some comprehension of the Dharma will be able to invoke a sense of weariness [in samsara] by examining scripture. This is the best approach for impacting the minds of such individuals. The mind of the novice practitioner, on the other hand, will be more intractable, so it must be enticed with examples, stories, and more accessible methods." Lightly tweaked from Dahl (2016).

and, as the boat grows ever shakier, you see a luminous figure dancing in the sky before you, clothing swaying gently in the breeze. You recognize him as your teacher in the form of the legendary and iconic Padmasambhava (also known as Guru Rinpoche) who established tantric Buddhist practices in Tibet.[7] He speaks, reminding you of life's precariousness, noting that you have given this no attention at all until now. As the boat splits apart, ready to topple you into the sea, Guru's luminous rays pour down, wash you into light, and draw you up until you unite with Padmasambhava's awakened mind. Now fully awakened, you immediately act to awaken and free others from their own painful circumstances, extending light to them as had been given to you. This part of the sequence, beginning with your recognition of your teacher in Guru Rinpoche, distills the essential tantric practice of guru yoga. The drama seems resolved.

However, there is one more instruction:

> Once you have imagined all this, relax and leave your thoughts of the three times to themselves, without support. Then, whether your mind is active or at rest, simply maintain a state of mindful vigilance (Dahl, 2009: 31).

Now all imagining is released. You attend only to your mind, inevitably either active or at rest, in harmony with the naked "mind-minding" that is a core Dzogchen practice.

Thus in a single session of meditation you moved through sutra, tantric and dzogchen modalities, the entire spectrum of the path, including the different deployments of imagination in each. Imagination remains in play until it facilitates its own dissolution, a fearless intimacy with sheer and naked knowing. Longchenpa advises repeating the steps of this process in subsequent meditation sessions for three or twenty-one days.[8] Likewise we now look at these steps more closely.

***

In his debut sermon at the Sarnath Deer Park, the recently awakened Gautama taught that imagining the impermanent and evanescent to be permanent and stable is a key source of suffering. Understanding – really *digesting* – the fact of impermanence and insubstantiality is key. That Longchenpa makes it his first training indicates he means to include the entirety of the path in preparing practitioners for Dzogchen.

One challenge here is that we don't *feel* like we are imagining permanence or substance. Yet our surprise at inevitable change suggests otherwise. If we hadn't been assuming steadfast continuity, why when we or a friend suddenly become ill, do we feel surprise and shock? Partly because this was not what we had imagined, not really. Hence the need for reconstructive imagining.

Repurposing the imagination on the path cultivated is rooted in Buddhist philosophies of mind that distinguish image-making from sensory perception, or somatic experience. For Dzogchen, imagining is rooted in the mind's natural creativity and

---

7 On how legends associated with Padmasambhava became central to the Tibetan cultural imaginaire, see Hirshberg (2016).
8 On the significance of repetition in ritual practice, see Klein (2016). Also on Anne Carolyn Klein page, academia.edu.

responsiveness. Creativity and responsiveness are sourced in mind's very nature *(sems nyid)*, which is free from all imagining *and* the freedom to imagine anything at all. For Dzogchen practitioners, the richness and ontic status of tantric imagery can bridge the imaginary synapse between ordinary experience and mind's real nature.[9] In Jigme Lingpa's sequencing, and in tantra generally, imagination moves right to the cusp of that nature before dissolving into wisdom-space, undisturbed by imagery.

The reader-practitioner is invited to slow down and notice hitherto overlooked evidence of impermanence in everything we see, touch, taste, or long for, and thus to gradually weaken wrongheaded overreach of imagination that has prevented us from noticing the actual flux of things. We digest the import of seasonal change, recognize our own and dear ones' mortality; even, sometimes with surprise, note the fleeting nature of our own turbulent emotions. Finally we detect that we have been deceived by our own imaginal force field. Intentional imagining has facilitated this shift.

Tantric Imagining

The luminous lama dancing in space who appears at the nadir of the seafaring journey marks a shift to tantric perspective in Jigme Lingpa's sequencing.

A practitioner's relationship with iconic enlightened beings, such as Guru Rinpoche, and with a human teacher as the essence of that being, is the core of tantric practice. As the traveler, you encounter and recognize a connection with Guru Rinpoche. This recognition has an emotional dimension; it is an *affective* imagination, heightening the sense of affection and closeness: The iconic figure is someone we know well, and who knows us well. Formal guru yoga practices involve chanting and a precisely articulated series of images, including one's own body imagined as light culminating, as here, in unification. One's ordinary flesh-and-bone body becomes, to one's own mind and experience, a body of light. Such imagining has a distinct kinesthetic quality, it is an embodied imaginaire, melded with a uniquely expanded mind-feeling sensibility. In all these ways the tantric imagination in particular is different from *thinking*.

This imagining is not just pictures, it is a full-being process that integrates the felt dynamics of attention, emotions, and bodily presence. It requires and fosters attention that is relaxed and clear. These qualities allow it to facilitate an emotional state fluidly open to the deep feelings that contemplation of death and impermanence can elicit, and yet not caught in anxiety or despair. Such imagination is in intimate conversation with cognitive, somatic, and emotional dimensions of actual lived experience. Integration of the imaginal, cognitive, and somatic conduce to a fulsome state of wholeness, a resolving of the alienation from parts of oneself, others, or aspects of one's culture that, from Buddhist and psychological perspectives, is a key source of suffering.

---

9 This nature is also called primordial wisdom, the way things are, the ultimate, basic space, open awareness, awakened mind, union of primordial purity or spontaneous presence, or respectively, in Tibetan: *ye shes; gnas tshul, don dam pa, dbyings, dharma-dhātu, rig pa, byang chub sems, ka dag lhun grub bzung 'jug.*

The significance of the embodied imagination cannot be overestimated. Dissolving into light is a key element of tantric practice; it trains subtle kinesthetic awareness tracing moving streams, both imagined and palpable, through the body's deep interior. In such practices, which accord with Tibetan and other Asian mappings of the living body, it is neither feasible, necessary, nor desirable to separate the imaginal from palpable energetic sensibility. The streams have color, sometimes imagined, sometimes seen directly, and they are also felt somatically. The point is, these dimensions are interconnected, not alienated like a fish tossed to shore or lost in unfamiliar waters. Indeed, in the seventh and final training, your body is light, your mind is space, your energy optimally flowing through both. Through the transmodal interfusion of these – no longer locked into any one sensory dimension, sometimes feeling sound and hearing color – a fuller measure of wholeness, or completeness, can occur.[10]

Although partly the fruit of imagination, such integration is deeply felt. The kinesthetic imaginaire is not a realm apart from felt experience. Whereas imagination, in the sense of rumination or anticipation takes us away from the present, felt experience is *always* in the present moment. When the trained imagining described here brings one to this fresh sense of the present moment, the imaginal melts away, with the resulting integration felt throughout one's organism. This is the heart of *Guru Yoga*. Within this state of integration, one looks directly at the mind-states of activity and rest (which have been occurring throughout) and as the knower aware of those states, the unmoving source of all imagining:

> awareness is clean when it comes to [sense] objects, there being no interruption between thoughts' arising and being freed [i.e. action and rest].[11]

All that preceded has set the scene for the letting go of the imagination and resting in the invisible arena from which it emerged. No longer simply imagaic, reactively emotional, or intellectual, the horizon of experience feels expanded, all-encompassing. Practice is simple, if not easy. Rest in this wholeness.

What Imagination Is Not

This sense of wholeness is not an idea, it is a felt sense, to use Gendlin (1982)'s term, or a lived experience, to use a term common in the emerging field of micro-phenomenology.[12] In Indian-based exoteric Tibetan Buddhist philosophies of mind, your mind is a knower that is either conceptual or nonconceptual. The conceptual mind always involves images, however abstract. Compared with direct experience, thinking and the images that accompany it are generic, not precise. They function not to represent the object of thought, but simply to eliminate everything *not*

10 For descriptions of the importance of engaging cognitive and somatic learning together, see Fosha, Siegel, and Solomon (2009). Much of Buddhist practice, but especially tantra, interweaves the cognitive and somatic throughout its many otherwise different practices, and adds a third element, as well, the richly endowed imaginaire. On transmodal element of lived experience, see Petitmengin (2007).

11 Adapted from Barron (2001: 58). Tibetan text, 83.15.   12 See for example Petitmengin (2007).

that object. But it does allow direct experience to more fully ascertain what appears to it. Thinking about or imagining impermanence can facilitate full-on direct knowing of impermanence that is both emotionally and somatically impactful.

Again, imagining is bilateral. The confused imagination takes one away from the real world by imagining, for example, that we are permanent. Or the center of the universe. Or unequivocally irrelevant. None of this bears scrutiny, yet part of us is impossibly persuaded. Skillfully deployed imagination becomes part of an intentional process of gaining access to what unintentional imagining has invented and obscured.

What is this imagination? There is no exact Tibetan word for it though several terms describe it partially. The imagination described here overlaps with but is different from thought (*rtog pa, kalpanā*). In particular, I want to note how it differs from thought as detailed in the sixth-century Indian works of Dignāga and Dharmakīrti and Tibetan commentaries on them, for these are the basis for exoteric Tibetan understandings of the mind. Most significantly, their descriptions do not identify emotional, psychological, or physiological elements intrinsically related with imagining on the path.

Also distinguishing thinking from imagining is that any image appearing to thought, for example when you think "mother," is generic, and possibly so abstract that it has no representational value at all; it functions simply to isolate any other image that is not linked with "mother." This description, too,[13] takes no account of the emotions, kinesthetic impression, or overall impact of the image on your felt sense in the moment of recollection. Whatever their representational properties, these images are not *felt* abstractly.

Yet "objective distance" is not the point, either. Thought consistently conflates the image appearing to it with the actual object that image references. This error is intrinsic to thought. When you bring to mind your mother's face, however abstract the image, you seem to see your mother herself. Thus there is an implicit intimacy with whatever appears to our minds. This is especially important with guru or deity yoga. One does not feel "I have this image," but "I am" or, finally, simply an *am-ness* that is utterly conflated with, in this case, with the essential being of Guru Rinpoche and one's own teacher. Thought's tendency to conflate object with image, while in one sense an error, yields an intimacy quite beyond that of ordinary thought, yet made possible by it.[14] "Imagination" in the context of these practices captures this intimacy; to my knowledge this is never mentioned in classic Buddhist discourse on thought. It may in fact be that sense of focused intimacy that partly distinguishes thought from imagination.[15]

---

13 Thought is contrasted with direct perception in Klein (1978/1999) chapters 2 and 3 for thought and direct perception and chapters 5–7 on the functioning of thought by its eliminating all that is not its focal object *(apoha, gzhan gsel)*. Available also on Anne Carolyn Klein academia.edu.

14 Neurological research on the effect of visual practices is relatively scarce. See Kozhevnikov et al. (2009: 645). Recent studies of experienced deity yoga practitioners suggest brain plasticity allows skill enhancement in visuospatial tasks and increased ability in image maintenance.

15 Even when we imagine something not so emotionally salient or impinging on our sense of self as mortality and death, there is an intimacy that is not there in simply by bringing that thing to mind. Conversely, one could think about death without imagining in the way described here. The difference

This is tricky, because thought easily becomes entangled in, or at least flavored by imagination. Still, distinguishing "imagination" from "thought" clarifies the felt richness of practices such as Longchenpa and Jigme Lingpa describe. And there is another reason to distinguish these. The Tibetan word often, unfortunately, translated as "visualize" as in "visualize a deity" *(dmigs byed)* really simply means "take as your object." This goes beyond seeing, or visualizing; and leaves space for sensing emotional, somatic, or other shifts in one's experience as one takes this object in. Imagining, or taking on, an object again, is here an inclusive, full-bodied term, engaging all the creative, sensory, and emotional aspects associated with an actual felt sense of being in the world. In particular, in tantra, the somatic is crucial. Longchenpa explains, for the body gives access to wisdom:

> Supreme primordial wisdom, is there of its own accord
> In the precious unbounded mansion of your heart center.[16]

There are many, virtually infinite, variations of using imaginative light in connection with the body, and this, too, is not only a visual endeavor. In the course of daily meditation rituals, Buddhas – that is, images vividly imagined with deep conviction – dissolve into you; or, you may dissolve into them. In either case, the dissolving doesn't end there, for the unified luminosity melts into its own center and into space. Sometimes the body's interior lights up, highlighting and making kinesthetically knowable constellations of subtle channels and the energies they carry. Sometimes light shines out and fills the universe, showing that universe to be intimately part of one's own mind, and the universe of experience the mind's own playing field. Eventually, alienation can fall away. Nothing abrogates connection and integration. One never leaves the mind behind, a point very significant for the gnostic orientation to wholeness, a great completeness from which nothing is excluded. To dissolve into light, to imagine or feel open-hearted connection to one who imaginatively *is* the fruit of wisdom-learning, engages our entire human being, not just the light of the mind, but the correlative felt senses of a body dissembling its solidity, a mind resolving its alienated solitude.[17]

Imagination is powerfully useful. Yet, dissolving imagination is imperative. Though differently inflected, this is true in the earliest Indian Buddhist traditions and Dzogchen. In the *Bāhiya Sutta*, from the early Indian Pāli tradition, Buddha advises a student thus:

> In reference to the seen, there will be only the seen. In reference to the heard, only the heard. In reference to the sensed, only the sensed. In reference to the cognized, only the cognized. That is how you should train yourself.[18]

has to do with a felt vitality in the process itself, a keenness of attention, and a receptivity to being impacted by what is imagined. Otherwise, there is no imaginaire. (Thanks to this volune's editor, Anna Abraham, for her interesting questions on this and other matters.)

16 For an alternative translation of this line see Barron (2001: 341). BDRC Tibetan text, *Grub mtha' mdzod*: 1183.1

17 See Kapstein (2004), especially preface and chapter X.

18 Translated from the Pāli by Thanissaro Bhikkhu at accesstoinsight.org/tipitaka/kn/ud. See also discussion in Anālayo (2003: 243ff).

Stop imagining. Stay with what is. Imagination is discouraged. In popular modern iterations of Theravada such as Goenka's *Insight Meditation*, one focuses on bare experience in the present moment. Theravada's final goal or *nibbana*[19] is the cessation of all cognitive and sensory overlays.

In Mahayana, ultimate freedom is not mere cessation, it is suffused with equanimity, love, compassion, and joy; qualities that are also part of Theravada but cease with one's final nirvana. For Mahayana, Buddhas model these qualities before and after awakening without, however, imagining any action, agent, or recipient of such compassion. Historically and in practice, these harbinger Dzogchen's orientation to mindnature.

Imagination and Wholeness

Dzogchen practitioners seek to recognize the radical inclusivity of their own nature. Separateness, the perceived distance between subject and object, self and other, or even layers of oneself, is a product of confused imagination. Longchenpa often cites ancient tantras that voice this all-inclusive reality; for example, The *Six Expanses:*

> I manifest as undivided and indivisible
> Since my objects, actions, and conduct
> cannot be differentiated from me . . .
> I am not an object and am free of any concept or underlying bias.[20]

The wisdom-ground[21] is not an object. Practitioners don't try to imagine it, which is impossible, but to recognize it as the source and ultimate nature of images, concepts, and everything else one experiences. Nothing is excluded from the unbounded horizon of wholeness *(thig le nyag cig).*

Attending to mind-images, their absence, or to mindlight itself – to a mind active or at rest – eventually points to the source from whence minding comes. Longchenpa and Jigme Lingpa express wonder, delight, and amazement at their naked recognition of this intimate reality, a state deliciously indescribable, yet about which there is much to say, and which is infinitely various. Wholeness doesn't preclude variety, but no amount of even unharmonious variety can actually broach completeness as understood in this tradition. At the emotional level, this means that one can feel whole even while present to experiences that, in theory, would cancel each other out. When relaxed and expansive, it is possible to realize that, for example, you are very happy about one thing, and devastated about another. Not identifying either as a reified "me," these two very different responses can be recognized as simultaneously present. At the ontological level, Dzogchen says that the reality they describe is equally present everywhere and in everything. Reality in this sense of whole, and always complete.

---

19 More recent scholarship questions this description of Theravada. See Crosby (2013).
20 Barron (2001: 39). Tibetan text, p. 68.16.
21 Dzogchen discussions of this ground (*gzhi*) is a relevant issue here, but beyond the scope of what can be covered in this space.

A crucial event in the life of a Dzogchen practitioner is recognizing that this source, ineffable and all-suffusing, is a wholeness encompassing all the infinite varieties of life. Variety remains. Alienation does not. This topic is vast, but our point here is simple: There is nothing outside or alienated from this wisdom-nature that is also the most intimate part of lived experience and its source. How might this inclusive ubiquity relate to contemporary phenomenological and scientific reflections on consciousness?

What scientists have called the "problem of consciousness" is for Dzogchen a secret to freedom and wholeness. Dzogchen distinguishes itself from the Middle Way Mahayana schools in that while they take "a sheer emptiness which is like space" as the basic matrix for its understanding of reality, Dzogchen takes an unconfused awareness *(rig pa)*, "pure and simple – originally pure in all its nakedness and unceasing, though it has never existed as anything."[22] Ineffable wisdom is the actual nature of everything *as it is experienced*. Longchenpa is not saying that if you take apart a mountain you will find wisdom as its nature. He says that you cannot separate the mountain from your experience of it, and that the final nature of your all-inclusive field of knowing is this wisdom-presence.[23] This ubiquity is not a problem for Dzogchen, it is essential to their world view.

This knowingness is not the consciousness defined as "that which is clear and knowing" *(gsal shing rig pa)*[24] in classic Indian and Indian-based Tibetan exoteric texts. It does not have the subject-object structure apparent in ordinary knowing. It is not identical with the consciousness that science calls a problem either. However, like that problematic consciousness, it is part of all experience. There is no encountering any sensory or mental object free of it, and thus it can't be subjected to scientifically objective investigation. But for Dzogchen such objectivity is itself confused imagination.

Some modern Western philosophers of mind also doubt that this ubiquity is a problem. For neuroscientist Francisco Varela, "Lived experience is where we start from and where all must link back to, like a guiding thread." For Adam Zeman, consciousness "might be described more accurately as the fundamental fact of our human lives."[25] Bitbol further observes that for Husserl consciousness is inextricably present in all experience because "any ascription of existence *presupposes* the existence of conscious experience" (Bitbol, 2008: 5).

The intrinsically occurring wisdom *(rang byung ye shes)* Longchenpa describes has properties that distinguish it from the consciousness that Bitbol and the others discern, but shares with it the key quality of ubiquity. *Nothing occurs outside it.*[26] For scientists seeking (imagining!) pure objectivity, this is a problem. In Bitbol's reading of Husserl, it is not. Bitbol writes:

---

22 Also translated in Barron (2001: 163). Tibetan text, p. 162.2–7.
23 Thanks to Lama Tenzin Samphel for clarifying this crucial point.
24 See Rinbochay (1981: 45–47).
25 For these citations see Bitbol (2008: 4). For original French on this matter, see Bitbol (2014).
26 Space permitting, it would be appropriate to consider how Husserl takes consciousness to be absolute insofar as experience cannot be second guessed (Bitbol, 2008: 5).

Consciousness is not an object. Not a phenomenon either. Why? Because phenomenon is part of a field of consciousness. But consciousness is more than that . . . It is not a phenomenon.[27]

For Longchenpa and Jigme Lingpa, the very possibility of imagination arises from its intimate connection with this ubiquitous presence, which is not a subjective state separate from objects, but the unimpeded *(zang thal)* nature of everything, knower and known alike.[28] We cannot do justice to it here, or to the evocative, shimmering poetry that gives voice to it. Still, simply identifying this general point of agreement, that nothing exists outside the field of our own experience,[29] means that when imagination emerges from and dissolves back into that field, it models what is also true for every other kind of experience. The mind is always full of ideas, images, to-do lists, worries, excitations, intentions. These images can mask a consciousness masquerading as unconfused, or they can lead to its source, for the masks are themselves included in this completeness beyond all imagining.

What else can a practitioner do but see more clearly? Thinking won't get one there. One's natural completeness can only be intuited until, somehow, it spontaneously is known. Intuition is also a type of *imaginaire*, and its family resemblance with Dzogchen practice helps us understand both.

Claire Petitmengin, a leading figure in microphenomenology who works closely with Michel Bitbol, has extensively studied intuition. Her research finds that a similar cluster of qualities attend most first-person reports of intuition. Freedom from tension, spatial constraint, and efforting toward a goal appear to play an essential role in the arising of intuition and is, perhaps, at the source of all thinking:

> Mindnature is the ground of arising *('char gzhi)*
> from which things arise, comparable to a mirror[30]

Dzogchen, too, finds that ease, shift in one's sense of space, and giving up goal-orientation is crucial, and that all imagining arises from, leads to, hides, and discloses its source. Hence, in Jigme Lingpa's sequencing, the more thorough one's final dissolving into a panoramic spacious nature, the more capacity one has to rescue others from their imagined limitations. In this way, connection with one's wisdom-nature also brings responsive connection with others that is unimpeded by imagined greatness or lowliness, and is sensitive to both their confusion and potential for a richly variegated wholeness.

And as we saw, Jigme Lingpa's sequence did not end with the story, nor even with dissolving all confused imaginings, but with an orientation to the source awareness that lies beyond imagination, and ongoing responsiveness to others' pain. Only then comes the concluding instruction to set it all aside, relax, and observe your own mind, whether active or at rest.

27 My notes from his three-hour lecture, Fall 2016, Paris, as part of Claire Petitmengin's training seminar in microphenomenology.
28 Longchenpa, Discussion of iMadhyamaka and Dzogchen, Longchen Rabjam. See Barron (2007: 112, 312). Tibetan text, *Grub mtha' mdzod*: 799.2 and 1133.4–5.
29 Author/Buddhist teacher Ken McLeod reports Kalu Rinpoche often used this phrase in teaching.
30 Longchenpa. For alternate translation see Barron (2007: 312). Tibetan text, *Grub mtha' mdzod*: 1133.4–5. See also Klein (2018) and Petitmengin (2007, 1999).

And so we see that imagination is multivalent. It can bind or it can liberate, and sometimes might even need to bind in particular ways before it can liberate. And it can also simply dissolve. Working with the imagination in some of the ways described above, especially associated with creation-phase tantric essentials, easily produces the kind of transmodal experience that we knew as infants. All of which indicates there is more to mind than thinking, more to the senses than honing in on an object, more to somatic flows than a one-to-one ratio with particular sensations. Experience becomes much richer when we are not limited to thought alone, when we include the intimacy of somatic, cognitive, affective, emotional, and spatial knowings. Microphenomenology and focusing are modern ways of accessing the nuances of lived experiences. These refined sensibilities share with the contemplative arts a strategy of focusing not simply on the *what* but also, and sometimes exclusively, on the *how*. Not *what* you see, but *how* you do it, and how it affects you. In classic Buddhist practice, mindfulness is trained to move from *what* to *how,* and ultimately from reified certainty about some particular thing to an openness not just to anything, but to the similar fundamental *how* of everything. Awakening, as well as the symbols of awakening such as Padmasambhava, arise when the ordinary mind abates, leaving a different kind of space, clarity, and possibility. Similarly, intuition arises when mind and body is open, relaxed, spacious in psyche and soma. Imagination of all kinds, it seems, is furthered as it grows less inhibited by habit, weariness, self-doubt, or whatever else limits its spacious natural capaciousness.

A shift that makes a difference here is recognizing imagination as nothing more or less than the creativity intrinsic to mind's own nature. With this knowing comes the potential for any image, thought, or sensory experience to reveal the unquenchable, unbounded freshness of which it is part. An ocean as vast as space in which the golden fish finally feel at home, fully free, and definitely in wholeness. And perhaps you, kind intrepid reader, have already imagined just what that is like.

References

Anālayo. (2003). *Satipaṭṭāna*. Cambridge, UK: Windhorse Publications.

Barron, R., (tr.) (2001). *A Treasure Trove of Scriptural Transmission*. Translation of *Chos dbyings mdzod 'grel*. Junction City, CA: Padma Publishing.

Barron, R. (2007). *The Precious Treasury of Philosophical Systems: A Treatise Elucidating the Meaning of the Entire Range of Buddhist Teachings*. 1st edition. Junction City, CA: Padma Publishing.

Bhikkhu, T., (tr.) (2012). *Udana: Exclamations. Third book of the Khuddaka Nikaya*. acces stoinsight.org/tipitaka/kn/ud.

Bitbol, M. (2008). Is Consciousness Primary? Moving Beyond the "Hard Problem". NeuroQuantology, *6*(1), 53–72.

(2014). *La conscience a-t-elle une origine?* Paris, France: Flammarion.

Crosby, K. (2013). *Theravada Buddhism*. Oxford, UK: Wiley-Blackwell.

Dahl, C., (tr.) (2016). *Steps to the Great Perfection: The Mind-Training Tradition of the Dzogchen Masters*. Boulder, CO: Snow Lion.

Fosha, D., Siegel, D. J., Solomon, M. F. (2009). *The Healing Power of Emotion: Affective Neuroscience, Development and Clinical Practice*. New York, NY; London, UK: William Norton & Company.

Gendlin, E. (1982). *Focusing*. New York, NY: Bantam New Age.

Hirshberg, D. (2016). *Remembering the Lotus-Born: Padmasambhava in the History of Tibet's Golden Age*. Boston, MA: Wisdom.

Kapstein, M. (ed.) (2004). *The Presence of Light: Divine Radiance and Religious Experience*. Chicago, IL: University of Chicago Press.

Klein, A. (1978/1999). *Knowledge & Liberation: Buddhist Epistemology in Service of Transformative Religious Experience*. Ithaca, NY: Snow Lion.

(2009). *[Jigme Linpga's] Heart Essence of the Vast Expanse*. Boulder, CO: Snow Lion.

(2011). Dzogchen. In J. L. Garfield and W. Edgeglass (eds.), *Oxford Handbook of World Philosophy*. New York, NY: Oxford University Press, 265–278.

(2016). Revisiting Ritual. *Tricycle*, Fall. Or see Anne Carolyn Klein, academia.edu.

(2018). Feelings Bound and Freed: Wandering and Wonder on Buddhist Pathways. *Contemporary Buddhism*, *19*(1), 83–101.

Kozhevnikov, M., Louchakova, O., Josipovic, Z., and Motes, M. A. (2009). The Enhancement of Visuospatial Processing Efficiency through Buddhist Deity Meditation. *Psychological Science*, *20*(5), 645–653.

Longchen Rabjam, (Longchenpa). (2009). *Kun mkhyan klong chen rab 'byams kyi gsung 'bum: Chos dbyings mdzod 'grel*. n.p. 83.19–84.1. Buddhist Digital Resource Center.

Neumaier-Dargyay, E. (tr.) (1992). *The Sovereign All-Creating Mind: A Translation of the Kun byed rgyal po'i mdo'*. SUNY Series in Buddhist Studies. Albany, NY: State University of New York Press.

Petitmengin, C. (1999). The Intuitive Experience. *Journal of Consciousness Studies*, *6*(2–3), 43–77.

(2007). Towards the Source of Thoughts: The Gestural and Transmodal Dimensions of Lived Experience. *Journal of Consciousness Studies*, *14*(3), 54–82.

Rinbochay, L. (1981). *Mind in Tibetan Buddhism*. Translated by Elizabeth Napper. Ithaca, NY: Snow Lion.

Rinpoche, P. (1994). *Words of My Perfect Teacher* (*Kun bzang bla ma' zhal lung*). Translated by Padmakara. San Francisco, CA: HarperCollins.

Sangpo, K. (1982). *Tantric Practice in Nyingma*. Translated by J. Hopkins. Ithaca, NY: Snow Lion.

Yalom, I. D. (1980). *Existential Psychotherapy*. New York, NY: Basic Books.

31 Hypothetical Thinking

Linden J. Ball

Introduction

Hypothetical thinking involves imagining possibilities and exploring their consequences through a process of mental simulation. Such hypothetical thinking is very useful because it allows for an examination of the *cause-effect relationships* that may exist between putative actions and their resulting, downstream outcomes. This means that available options can be envisaged and evaluated prior to deciding on a course of action to pursue in the physical world, where actions have real consequences. In this way hypothetical thinking represents a "safe" way to think and reason about would-be options in the mind's eye, so that when decisions are played out in the real world the reasoner at least has some expectations about what should happen as a consequence.

Whether, of course, events that are consequent on one's actions actually unfold in the real world in precisely the way predicted in the imagination is another matter. Indeed, there are good reasons as to why there may be a disconnect between one's predictions based on hypothetical thinking and how choices lead to future outcomes in the physical world. We may, for example, have misrepresented the starting point of a situation in our imagination, as when we decide to cheer up a friend who is feeling despondent by making a joke but end up upsetting her even more because we didn't appreciate how deflated she was feeling. This shows how sometimes we can make poor decisions because we have an impoverished understanding of the current situation. This may arise because we don't have knowledge of all relevant facts or because we have a biased representation of the available information as a result of our tendency to attend selectively to some aspects of a situation and to fail to attend adequately to others. This latter issue of *biases* and *selectivity* in information processing underscores an important theme in this chapter, which relates to the way in which the inherent capacity limitations of our cognitive machinery often means that it is very difficult for us to make optimal decisions on the basis of hypothetical thinking.

In considering the issue of hypothetical thinking in the context of the human imagination my aim in this chapter is to show how contemporary theorizing is able to provide a coherent conceptual account of a range of phenomena that have been identified through decades of research on human reasoning, judgment, and decision-making. To do this

I will commence with theoretical considerations, progressing next to a consideration of some key empirical findings, then returning again to theory. More specifically, I will begin with an overview of a contemporary, conceptual account of hypothetical thinking, that is, Jonathan Evans's *hypothetical thinking theory* (e.g. Evans, 2006, 2007). This theory is situated within a "dual-process" view of cognition, which assumes that reasoning involves a complex interplay between two qualitatively distinct types of processes. A key attraction of this theory resides in its unique capacity to provide an integrated explanatory account of a diverse range of phenomena relating to hypothetical thinking. I will then move on to exemplify the strengths of this hypothetical thinking theory with specific reference to empirical work on *hypothesis testing*, which is a core aspect of hypothetical thinking whereby people have to generate and evaluate hypotheses in order to inform their understanding of given information.

Hypothesis testing is just one area of hypothetical thinking, which also encapsulates the thinking that underpins decision-making, forecasting, counterfactual reasoning, suppositional reasoning and deductive inference, among other areas of high-level cognition. Although I will be unable to consider all of these varied aspects of hypothetical thinking, I nevertheless contend that the more restricted analysis of hypothesis testing provides an exemplary range of evidence to illustrate the explanatory capacity of Evans's hypothetical thinking theory. Having demonstrated how findings relating to hypothesis testing can be explained by the hypothetical thinking theory, I will finally consider some limitations of this account. This will allow me to point to some future directions for studying hypothetical thinking, including areas for further empirical investigation and theoretical development.

A Theoretical Perspective on Hypothetical Thinking

In proposing his hypothetical thinking theory, Evans (2007) built upon extensive previous research exploring the nature of *cognitive biases* in human thinking, reasoning, and judgment. Such biases have traditionally been defined as being *systematic* errors (as opposed to random ones), as assessed against normative systems such as formal logic, probability theory, and decision theory. Nowadays, however, this conceptualization of bias is controversial, not least because of the challenges in determining the "right" normative system against which to judge performance. There are, for example, numerous normative systems of formal logic, such that behavior might be described as correct and unbiased if judged against one system but incorrect and biased if evaluated against a different system. Given this controversy and other concerns, Evans has recently subscribed to an approach whereby the study of human thinking and reasoning should avoid normative comparisons altogether, instead, focusing on *describing* observed behaviors (Elqayam and Evans, 2011; Evans and Elqayam, 2011; see also Stupple and Ball, 2014).

Notwithstanding the potential pitfalls associated with the application of normative standards when evaluating the effectiveness of thinking and reasoning, there is, as Evans (2007) explains, an alternative, more positive way to consider the nature of biases that is less burdened by normative considerations. This is to think about biases in terms of the inherent design limitations of the human brain. This approach emphasizes the notion of "bounded rationality" (Simon, 1982), according to which we are not inherently *irrational* but are simply cognitively constrained in how we reason because of the way in which our cognitive machinery has evolved to meet adaptive constraints in the real world. A case in point is our limited working-memory capacity, which presumably evolved to afford survival advantages in our evolutionary environment. Indeed, having a high working-memory capacity in our evolutionary prehistory could have left us dangerously "lost in thought," rendering us vulnerable to the negative consequences of *inaction* in a dynamically changing and high-risk world as we attempted to reason out optimal courses of action to every immediate problem. For example, when faced by the threat of a proverbial saber-toothed tiger, it would be far better to use limited-capacity working memory to consider a few options and act quickly rather than to use a high-capacity system to consider systematically a multiplicity of options, albeit with fatal consequences because only a fast decision could save our life.

From the perspective of bounded rationality, although it might not be possible to use our imaginations to compute an *optimal* choice of action in a complex situation, we can nevertheless apply our more limited cognitive apparatus to devise a solution that is *good enough* to allow us to make effective progress. An example of where bounded rationality often gives rise to good but nonoptimal decisions is in the game of chess, especially when nonexperts are playing. To determine an optimal response to an opponent's move would require considerable mental effort to imagine the detailed consequences that might arise from each of several possible move options. Instead, players are more likely to stick with the first move that they identify that should produce a reasonable outcome for their current attack or defence strategy (Simon, 1996).

Hypothetical Thinking and Dual Reasoning Processes

Whether cognitive biases are examined from a normative or a descriptive perspective they are, nevertheless, typically viewed as arising from the operation of two distinct types of processes, variously referred to in dual-process theories as being intuitive, heuristic, or associative on the one hand and deliberative, analytic, or controlled on the other (e.g. Evans, 2008; Sloman, 1996; Stanovich, 1999). Although many dual-process theories of thinking and reasoning have been developed, I will limit my discussion to the recent framework espoused by Evans and Stanovich (2013a, 2013b) given its core focus on encapsulating and clarifying the key tenets of dual-process theorizing. According to this framework, processes that are intuitive, heuristic, and associative are referred to as *Type 1* processes and have two defining features: (1) they are relatively undemanding of working-memory resources; and (2) they are autonomous, running to completion whenever a relevant cue triggers them. This latter feature means that Type 1 processes are obligatory and cannot be discontinued or altered at the behest of the reasoner (Thompson, 2013). Type 1 processes also tend to be fast, high-capacity, nonconscious and capable of running in parallel, but these are merely correlated features rather than defining features. In contrast, deliberative, analytic, controlled, *Type 2* processes are defined in terms of requiring working-memory resources and being focused on cognitive decoupling (i.e. imagining new or alternative possibilities), as well as mental simulation (e.g. envisaging cause-effect relationships), which are both critical for hypothetical thinking. Type 2 processes also tend to be slow, capacity-limited, conscious, and serial, but again, these are correlated features rather than defining features.

According to this dual-process framework, hypothetical thinking is a two-stage process in which Type 1 processes quickly deliver an answer based on prior beliefs, preconceptions, and pragmatic assumptions. This default answer may subsequently be intervened upon and analyzed in a more thorough way by slower Type 2 processes that serve to determine whether an initial, intuitive decision is justified or needs to be replaced. If, however, such Type 2 intervention is relatively cursory then it is possible for a Type 1 response to prevail, which is fine if prior beliefs and assumptions are sound, but problematic and can lead to error and bias if prior beliefs and assumptions are unfounded. This kind of sequential processing account, in which an initial Type 1 response may or may not be subjected to further in-depth scrutiny by Type 2 processes, is referred to as a *default–interventionist* model (Evans, 2018). In further explaining limitations in human hypothetical thinking in terms of default–interventionist concepts, it is also recognized that additional biases may arise at the Type 2 processing stage, for example, because of capacity limitations in evaluating default responses (and alternatives to them) or because of the application of faulty analytic processing, or what Stanovich (e.g. 2004, 2009) refers to as defective "mindware."

Evans's Hypothetical Thinking Theory

I now turn to a consideration of Evans's (2007) hypothetical thinking theory, which encapsulates the dual-process ideas described above. Before doing so, however, I first address a matter that attentive readers may have noticed and be curious about, which is that the dual-process framework I have just summarized predates Evans's (2007) hypothetical thinking theory by several years. This temporal disconnect, however, is unproblematic, given that the hypothetical thinking theory is consonant with the core processing assumptions of the later-developed dual-process framework. Indeed, as hinted at already, Evans and Stanovich's (2013a, 2013b) framework is the culmination of many years of research and primarily serves to integrate prior concepts and ideas while also advancing the ongoing debate regarding the appropriate way in which to theorize about dual processes in higher level cognition. In many ways, then, there is a very close alignment between the dual-process framework as espoused by Evans and Stanovich (2013a, 2013b) and the earlier hypothetical thinking theory forwarded by Evans (2007), with perhaps the one exception being the use of the Type 1 and Type 2 terminology in more recent theorizing as an alternative to the now-outmoded distinction between System 1 and System 2 processing in previous theorizing, where such systems were assumed to reflect evolutionary older vs. more recent brain mechanisms, respectively. This "systems" terminology has connotations that many dual-process theorists do not subscribe to (Evans, 2018) such that the Type 1 vs. Type 2 distinction is more broadly appealing.

Evans's (2007) hypothetical thinking theory can be viewed as involving the following components: (1) a set of three *principles* that describe the general characteristics of hypothetical thought; (2) a proposal that hypothetical thinking involves the manipulation of "epistemic mental models"; and (3) a processing model based on default-interventionist, dual-process assumptions as already described. The three principles of hypothetical thinking are referred to by Evans (2007) as the *singularity principle*, the *relevance principle*, and the *satisficing principle*. The singularity principle claims that when we think hypothetically we consider only one possibility (or epistemic mental model) at a time. This is because hypothetical thinking is based around Type 2 processing, which is inherently sequential in nature and constrained by working-memory limitations. As Evans (2007) notes, the singularity principle is supported by prior research showing that people are only able to consider one hypothesis at any particular moment (Mynatt, Doherty, and Dragan, 1993) and focus on just a single, explicit option when engaged in decision-making (Legrenzi, Girotto, and Johnson-Laird, 1993). Although people only seem to evaluate or simulate hypotheses or options singly, they may nevertheless consider alternatives sequentially, but to do so means that they need to store intermediate results in working memory to enable comparisons to be made so that a favored option can be chosen. In practice, the demands of such a process mean that people will rarely give full consideration to alternatives and may simply stick with the first option that comes to mind.

Evans's (2007) relevance principle captures the idea that mental models are generated by heuristic and pragmatic processes that function to maximize the relevance of mentally represented information given the reasoner's current goals. What is most relevant to a person is, by default, that which is most plausible, likely, salient or easily brought to mind (cf. Tversky and Kahneman's, 1973, "availability heuristic"). Evans's (2007) satisficing principle assumes that the *first* hypothesis a person considers will typically be evaluated and accepted by Type 2 analytic processes unless there is a good reason for it to be rejected, modified, or replaced. This analytic evaluation may be either cursory or more effortful, in the latter case involving active, deliberative reasoning and mental simulation. Only if the initial hypothesis is considered to be unsatisfactory will an alternative one be considered.

In relation to the second component of the hypothetical thinking model, it is worth examining what Evans (2007) has in mind with the proposal that hypothetical thinking involves the manipulation of *epistemic mental models*. The idea is that these mental models encode not just "possibilities" but also our beliefs about such possibilities and our attitudes toward them. For example, when we consider a possible action as part of a decision-making process we mentally simulate not only the downstream consequences of taking the action but also our belief about how probable these consequences are and how favorable it would be if they transpired. The third component of the hypothetical thinking model is the default-interventionist architecture of the dual-process framework, whereby Type 1, heuristic processes set up default responses that will occur unless Type 2, analytic processes intervene to alter them. Evans's (2007) view is that Type 2 processes will always have at least some minimal involvement during hypothetical thinking, even if this is merely to approve without much deliberation the default epistemic mental model suggested on the basis of initial, Type 1 processing. Furthermore, the factors that are likely to increase Type 2 intervention are primarily fourfold (Evans, 2018), and include: (1) the presence of a strong instructional set encouraging the application of analytic reasoning; (2) the reasoner's possession of a high working-memory capacity or IQ; (3) the reasoner's inherent disposition or motivation to reason effectively; and (4) the availability of sufficient time to allow for deliberative reasoning to unfold once triggered. These factors can interact and combine in important ways to increase or decrease the effortful Type 2 evaluation of a default mental model.

Returning to the issue of biases in hypothetical thinking, it should be readily apparent from Evans's (2007) theory how biases can arise from the operation of either Type 1 or Type 2 processes. First, Type 1 processes can bias hypothetical thinking via the relevance principle, which leads to the selective representation and contextualization of information that is preconsciously cued by linguistic, pragmatic, and attentional factors. Second, Type 2 processes can bias hypothetical thinking via the operation of the singularity and satisficing principles because only a single model (hypothesis, option, or possible action) will typically be considered, which will be accepted if there is no good reason to reject it. The Type 2 evaluation process may be deficient because of a lack of motivation, low cognitive capacity or impoverished cognitive mindware. Finally, and importantly, Evans (2007) emphasizes how these biases are only biases in the sense that they reflect a disposition of our cognitive systems to function in particular ways, rather than being biases in a pejorative sense of implying *irrationality* on the basis of deviations from normative standards.

Hypothetical Thinking Theory and Hypothesis Testing

In this section I explore the way in which Evans's (2007) hypothetical thinking theory has advanced a conceptual understanding of a specific aspect of hypothetical thinking, namely the way in which people go about *testing* hypotheses. Hypothesis testing relies only partly on the evaluation of *imagined* possibilities to simulate consequences as it also typically involves the reasoner observing the world and gathering evidence relevant to the hypothesis under consideration. Through this dynamic interaction between predictions in the hypothesis tester's imagination and observations in the world it is possible for hypotheses to be supported and retained or else refuted, revised, or abandoned (Evans, 2007). The critical issue that I consider here concerns the extent to which people's hypothesis-testing behavior conforms to the assumptions of Evans's hypothetical thinking theory. To examine this question I will draw on the extensive literature relating to the "2–4-6 task," a paradigm for exploring hypothesis testing that was developed in 1960 by the pioneering reasoning researcher Peter Wason.

The 2–4-6 Task: Key Findings and Conceptual Issues

Wason's interest in devising the 2–4-6 task (Wason, 1960) was to ascertain whether people could discover that a concept or rule is *necessary* rather than merely being *sufficient*. In the 2–4-6 task the experimenter explains to the participant that they have in mind a rule concerning number triples that are made up of three integers. The rule is that these integers must be in *ascending order of magnitude*, but, importantly, the participant does not know what this rule is and has to go about trying to discover it. To start with, the experimenter gives the participant an example triple "2–4-6," which they are told conforms to the rule. The participant is then asked to generate their own number triples and for each one feedback is given as to whether or not it conforms to the experimenter's rule. In Wason's (1960) study, participants could write down each triple together with reasons for their choice of numbers and the feedback received. The experimenter also reminded participants: (1) that their task was not simply to find numbers that conformed to the rule but to discover the rule itself; and (2) that they should only announce the rule when highly confident that they had discovered it. If a participant announced an incorrect rule they were invited to continue with more testing and announcements. The experiment ended at the point of correct rule announcement or if the session reached 45 minutes – or if the participant gave up!

Wason (1960) observed that of the twenty-nine participants attempting his task, just six announced the correct rule at the first attempt, ten at the second attempt, four at the third attempt and one after a fifth attempt. Wason viewed this poor performance as being a direct consequence of participants' pursuit of *enumerative* (i.e. positive) tests to check that a triple was compatible with a current hypothesis about the to-be-discovered rule. Recall that participants wrote down their reasons for triple choices, such as testing 8–10-12 on the grounds that the rule is "ascending with equal intervals." In contrast to abundant enumerative testing, Wason observed few *eliminative* (i.e. negative) tests aimed at determining if a triple was incompatible with a current hypothesis (e.g. testing 8–10-23 for the same hypothesis "ascending with equal intervals"). Eliminative tests are critical to enable the *disconfirmation* of an incorrect working hypothesis, as receiving feedback that 8–10-23 fits the experimenter's rule immediately indicates that the "ascending with equal intervals" hypothesis must be wrong. In support of an association between task success and eliminative testing, Wason (1960) showed that participants who announced the correct rule on their first or second attempts tended to be those who generated more eliminative tests. Wason also observed that many incorrect rule announcements were more restricted versions of the to-be-discovered rule (e.g. "numbers increasing with equal intervals"; "numbers increasing by two"), with repeated enumerative testing evidently reinforcing beliefs about the correctness of such overly restricted hypotheses.

Wason's (1960) paper is frequently cited as a seminal source of evidence for so-called *confirmation bias* in human reasoning (i.e. a disposition or attitude toward confirmatory testing). As Evans (2014) points out, however, the term confirmation bias did not appear in Wason's paper, nor did the synonymous term *verification bias* as subsequently used by Wason (Wason, 1966; Wason and Johnson-Laird, 1972). Evans (2014) also explains how research reported by Wetherick (1962) presented a persuasive challenge to the credibility of confirmation bias as a cause of failure on the 2–4-6 task. Wetherick's important insight was that an enumerative test is not necessarily a *confirmatory* test, as for some rules an enumerative test will readily lead to disconfirmation of a current hypothesis. For example, an enumerative test such as 10–12-14 on the assumption that the rule is "ascending with equal intervals" could disconfirm this hypothesis if the experimenter's rule is "numbers less than ten ascending with equal intervals." Wetherick's (1962) critique was formalized and corroborated by Klayman and Ha (1987, 1989), who proposed that the application of a "positive test strategy" will frequently be successful for eliminating hypotheses in the real world, such as in scientific enquiry. This strategy, however, causes significant difficulties in the 2–4-6 task because the extremely *general* nature of the to-be-discovered rule means that positive tests are unable to disconfirm the participant's working hypothesis. Nowadays it is almost universally accepted by reasoning theorists that people's application of a positive test strategy is an important aspect of their difficulties on the 2–4-6 task and that a confirmation bias account is untenable.

Can Hypothesis-Testing Performance Be Improved on the 2–4-6 Task?

Numerous attempts have been made to find manipulations to facilitate performance on the 2–4-6 task, particularly through efforts to increase eliminative testing via instructions and exposure to different types of test triples. Most studies have had little, if any, success (e.g. Gorman and Gorman, 1984; Kareev and Halberstadt, 1993; Kareev, Halberstadt, and Shafir, 1993). However, one powerful facilitatory manipulation involves the use of "dual-goal" instructions (Tweney et al., 1980), which ask participants to discover *two* complementary rules that the experimenter has in mind, one called DAX and the other called MED. Participants are given 2–4-6 as an example of DAX and are asked to generate triples that are classified as either conforming to DAX ("any ascending sequence") or to MED ("all triples that are not DAX"). Success rates for initial DAX rule announcements are typically greater than 60 percent (Gale and Ball, 2006; Vallée-Tourangeau, Austin, and Rankin, 1995; Wharton, Cheng, and Wickens, 1993). Subsequent studies have also shown that strict complementarity in relation to the DAX and MED rules is not critical for facilitated performance (Gale and Ball, 2009; Vallée-Tourangeau, Austin, and Rankin, 1995).

Several accounts of the dual-goal facilitation effect have emerged, yet it remains unclear how best to explain the phenomenon. Although we do not have space to review these competing accounts, it does seem that a key aspect of the facilitation derives from the way in which positive tests of the MED hypothesis are effectively negative tests of the DAX hypothesis; as such, they benefit participants' understanding of the overly restrictive nature of their current DAX hypotheses. This account draws on the primary involvement of a positive test strategy in hypothesis testing (Klayman and Ha, 1987, 1989), although recent research by Gale and Ball (2006, 2009) also emphasizes the critical role played by "descending" triples (e.g. "6–4-2") in driving the dual-goal facilitation effect, with descending-triple generation emerging as the main predictor of success. Gale and Ball suggest that descending triples provide useful "contrast-class cues" that make salient the way in which key DAX and MED triples fall along a descending/ascending dimension. Indeed, when Gale and Ball (2012) manipulated the availability of contrast-class cues within a dual-goal study they showed major benefits arising from the direct provision of an example MED triple with descending properties. The presentation of such a triple seems to emphasize the relevance of "descendingness" for the MED rule, and thereby the relevance of "ascendingness" for the DAX rule.

A few other manipulations also facilitate performance on versions of the 2–4-6 task, some of which implicate cognitive factors in failed task performance, while others speak to pragmatic effects relating to reasoners' goals. Vallée-Tourangeau and Payton (2008), for example, found facilitation when presenting participants with graphical representations of generated triples, suggesting that working-memory limitations contribute to task difficulty. More recently, Vallée-Tourangeau (2012) reported research addressing the pragmatics of the 2–4-6 task in terms of participants' goals and the *utilities* associated with particular triple tests. In his study, Vallée-Tourangeau manipulated the payoffs associated with testing critical, eliminative triples such "2–4-11" so as to increase their perceived utility for attaining task goals. In the presence of these pragmatic cues, participants were more likely to generate triples in which numbers ascended with *unequal* intervals, subsequently benefiting from the disconfirmatory evidence provided.

Hypothetical Thinking Theory as Applied to the 2–4–6 Task

How might observations from studies of the 2–4-6 task be explained by Evans's (2007) hypothetical thinking theory? First, the fact that people are highly influenced by the inherent properties of the example 2–4-6 triple speaks to the involvement of the relevance principle. Indeed, the experimenter's presentation of such a specific exemplar triple seems to *overemphasize* its relevance, conveying the message that the triple has *all* of the key properties relevant to discovering the overarching rule (Ball and Wade, 2017; van der Henst, Rossi, and Schroyens, 2002). Is it any surprise, then, that participants are drawn toward basing their initial hypotheses around the parameters established by the 2–4-6 exemplar such that they end up exploring a narrow range of hypotheses? Research by Cherubini, Castelvecchio, and Cherubini (2005) supports the supposition that participants ascribe a particularly high value to the example triple in terms of its information relevance. In their study, Cherubini et al. varied the types and number of *perceivable relationships* in example triples. For example, a triple such as 2–4-6 involves various relationships between numbers, including that they are all even, that they are ascending, and that they increase by twos. Using various exemplar triples, Cherubini et al. showed that participants derive initial hypotheses that maintain the maximum amount of information that is salient in the relational regularities within a given exemplar.

What about the role of the other principles of Evans's hypothetical thinking theory in explaining behavior on the 2–4-6 task? The fact that in the standard single-goal version of the task participants tend to stick with an initial hypothesis until it is disconfirmed is exactly what would be predicted by the involvement of the singularity principle, as testing multiple hypotheses is *not* consistent with this principle. Instead, people are assumed to form a single mental model and thence simulate the consequences that are likely to follow from this, for example, reasoning that a triple like 10–12–14 that conforms to the hypothesis "numbers ascending by two" will receive positive feedback. As Evans (2007) explains, we would not normally think about what would *not* be the case, as that would involve simulating a different possibility. As such, the generation of positive tests to the exclusion of negative ones is a manifestation of both the relevance principle and the singularity principle. The third principle of Evans's hypothetical thinking theory – the satisficing principle – also seems critical to understanding aspects of performance on the 2–4-6 task. The manner in which people maintain a current hypothesis with insufficient consideration and testing of alternative hypotheses, appears to be a clear case of satisficing. Having generated positive tests that are repeatedly confirmed, people develop a strong belief in their working hypothesis and fail to consider alternatives to it.

What about the facilitatory effects observed in the 2–4-6 task when dual-goal instructions inform reasoners of the existence of two rules, DAX and MED, with 2–4-6 being an example of DAX? How might the hypothetical thinking theory explain how this simple manipulation benefits rule discovery? In this case the principles of the theory still pertain but function to support rule discovery. The presence of two hypotheses (DAX and MED) means that positive tests of MED (a triple like 2–3-11) also act as negative tests of DAX. The resulting DAX feedback for a triple such as 2–3-11 immediately informs the reasoner that her working hypothesis for DAX is overly restrictive, thereby challenging a satisficing solution. In addition, the dual-goal paradigm increases the variety of all types of triples that participants generate (Gale and Ball, 2009, 2012), which presumably serves to weaken further the hold that the properties of the 2–4-6 exemplar have on participants because of the relevance principle.

Conclusions and Future Directions

In this chapter I have introduced the concept of hypothetical thinking and overviewed an integrative account of such thinking in the form of Evans's (2007) hypothetical thinking theory, which operates according to principles of relevance, singularity, and satisficing that are embedded in a two-stage, default-interventionist process model. This theory appears to provide a powerful framework for understanding many phenomena associated with hypothesis testing, including biases that arise during initial, default processing and subsequent, analytic processing. To illustrate the strengths of Evans's theory I reviewed a range of empirical evidence arising from studies of one aspect of hypothetical thinking, that of hypothesis testing, which involves people generating and evaluating hypotheses as they attempt to derive a more general understanding of given or observed information.

The key psychological paradigm deployed to study hypothesis testing is Wason's (1960) 2–4-6 task, which has generated a wealth of interesting findings for close to sixty years, with research on this task continuing to the present day, albeit at a reduced rate. In summarizing key findings from this task I showed how the principles of the hypothetical thinking theory can explain why it is that participants: (1) focus on the salient properties of the exemplar triple; (2) generate an initial hypothesis that captures these properties; (3) evaluate this initial hypothesis with positive tests; (4) form a strong belief about the correctness of the hypothesis based on repeated confirmatory feedback; (5) fail to discover the rule governing the nature of triples; and (6) show enhanced rule discovery in conditions where the testing of multiple rules is encouraged. Although the present chapter has applied the hypothetical thinking theory to just a single paradigm, it is important to stress that the theory has been invoked far more broadly as an explanation of key phenomena relating to judgment, decision-making, suppositional reasoning, and deductive inference (e.g. Evans, 2006, 2007, 2018).

A critic of the research summarized here might question whether the laboratory-based analysis of behavior on a contrived puzzle has much to tell us about hypothetical thinking in the real world. This is a fair point, although there is good evidence from studies of real-world hypothesis testing in domains such as scientific thinking and creative invention that the same biases that arise in the laboratory can play out in the real world (Gorman, 2018). For example, Tweney (2009) analyzed Michael Faraday's detailed notebooks and observed that Faraday would typically engage in extensive positive testing of ideas when conducting experimental investigations of a phenomenon. Gorman (1995) reported similar findings based on an analysis of Alexander Graham Bell's notebooks and correspondences pertaining to his experimental work during his efforts to invent the telephone.

The latter evidence in support of Evans's (2007) hypothetical thinking theory arises from studies of eminent scientists and inventors from the past. It is important to recognize, however, that nowadays scientific hypothesis testing almost always arises in conjunction with collaborating colleagues such that it is scrutinized and impacted by other scientists, including ones based in external research groups. Such individuals, whether colleagues or competitors, can act directly (e.g. as part of a collaborating team or via open debate) or indirectly (e.g. via published research) to challenge one's working hypothesis and offer alternative perspectives, thereby mitigating tendencies toward biased thinking that can arise at an individual level (e.g. see Dunbar, 1997, 2001). There is, therefore, a need for much more work to be done to address the topic of real-world hypothesis testing in collaborative contexts, including research beyond the domain of scientific thinking.

In this latter respect, one particularly interesting area for future research relates to contexts associated with criminal investigation, such as when assessing evidence of potentially fraudulent activity. Initial work on this topic has revealed that experienced fraud investigators may be able to hold in mind and test mutiple, alternative hypotheses, such as competing hypotheses about a suspect's guilt vs. their innocence (Morley, Ball, and Ormerod, 2006; Ormerod, Ball, and Morley, 2012; Walsh, Dando, and Ormerod, 2018). Further research is needed to generalize such findings to other investigative situations and to explore the role of possible moderating factors (e.g. investigative expertise).

Another major area for new research in relation to hypothetical thinking concerns the neuroscientific analysis of the brain systems underpinning such thinking as a way to inform theoretical development. To date, the majority of neuroimaging studies of human reasoning have focused on pinpointing the brain regions and neuronal connectivity associated with people drawing logical inferences when presented with *deductive* reasoning problems possessing different contents, such as items involving familiar vs. unfamiliar information or having believable vs. unbelievable conclusions (see Goel and Waechter, 2018, for a review). In contrast, research examining the neuroscience of *inductive* reasoning with problems involving rule discovery and hypothesis testing is extremely sparse.

The paucity of neuroscience research on hypothetical thinking may, in part, relate to the challenges of conducting neuroimaging investigations with tasks that are time-consuming for participants and that are associated with multiple processes (e.g. hypothesis formation, test selection, hypothesis revision, and the like). In addition, neuroimaging studies necessitate the use of multiple items to establish consistent results, whereas hypothesis-testing tasks are typically presented as "one-shot" problems. These issues represent challenges for researchers interested in studying the neuroscience of hypothetical thinking, although such challenges are not insurmountable if suitable tasks and paradigms can be developed. In this respect there are lessons to be learned from the neuroscientific study of creativity, where similar challenges have existed but have largely been overcome, with research in this area now burgeoning (Abraham, 2018; Jung and Vartanian, 2018).

Finally, and building on the latter point, it seems very likely that a strong association should exist between an individual's capacity to think creatively in terms of producing a multiplicity of novel and useful ideas in divergent thinking contexts and his ability to generate and explore multiple hypotheses in ways that are less constrained by the principles of singularity, relevance, and satisficing that seem to govern so much hypothetical thinking in everyday and professional activity. Systematic research to investigate this assumed link between heightened creative ability and enhanced hypothetical thinking seems long overdue, despite anecdotal evidence suggesting that many experts in domains involving hypothetical thinking – whether in science, business, design, innovation, the arts, or other areas of professional practice – also have unique capacities for creative idea generation. In sum, there is clearly much still to be discovered about the relationship between the creative imagination and hypothetical thinking and the way in which dispositional factors (e.g. relating to people's intrinsic motivation or their openness to ideas) might modulate any such association. Importantly, researchers are now starting at least to ask the kinds of questions that need to be answered (e.g. Abraham, 2016, 2018; Kaufman et al., 2016; Roberts and Addis, 2018; Silvia, Beaty, and Nusbaum, 2013).

References

Abraham, A. (2016). The Imaginative Mind. *Human Brain Mapping, 37*, 4197–4211.

   (2018). *The Neuroscience of Creativity.* Cambridge, UK: Cambridge University Press.

Ball, L. J., and Wade, C. N. (2017). Pragmatic Factors in Wason's 2–4-6 Task: Implications for Real-World Hypothesis Testing. In N. Galbraith, E. J. Lucas, and D. E. Over (eds.), *The Thinking Mind: A Festschrift for Ken Manktelow.* Abingdon, UK: Routledge, 29–39.

Cherubini, P., Castelvecchio, E., and Cherubini, A. M. (2005). Generation of Hypotheses in Wason's 2–4–6 Task: An Information Theory Approach. *Quarterly Journal of Experimental Psychology, 58A*, 309–332.

Dunbar, K. N. (1997). How Scientists Think: On-line Creativity and Conceptual Change in Science. In T. B. Ward, S. M. Smith, and J. Viad (eds.), *Creative Thought: An Investigation of Conceptual Structures and Processes.* Washington, DC: American Psychological Association, 461–493.

Dunbar, K. (2001). What Scientific Thinking Reveals about the Nature of Cognition. In K. Cowley, C. D. Schunn, and T. Okada (eds.), *Designing for Science: Implications from Everyday, Classroom, and Professional Settings.* Mahwah, NJ: Lawrence Erlbaum Associates, 115–140.

Elqayam, S., and Evans, J. St. B. T. (2011). Subtracting "Ought" from "Is": Descriptivism versus Normativism in the Study of Human Thinking. *Behavioral and Brain Sciences, 34*, 233–248.

Evans, J. St. B. T. (2006). The Heuristic-Analytic Theory of Reasoning: Extension and Evaluation. *Psychonomic Bulletin & Review, 13*, 378–395.

   (2007). *Hypothetical Thinking: Dual Processes in Reasoning and Judgement.* Hove, UK: Psychology Press.

   (2008). Dual-Processing Accounts of Reasoning, Judgment and Social Cognition. *Annual Review of Psychology, 59*, 255–278.

   (2010). *Thinking Twice: Two Minds in One Brain.* Oxford, UK: Oxford University Press.

   (2014). Reasoning, Biases and Dual Processes: The Lasting Impact of Wason (1960). *Quarterly Journal of Experimental Psychology, 69*, 2076–2092.

   (2018). Dual-Process Theories. In L. J. Ball and V. A. Thompson (eds.), *The Routledge International Handbook of Thinking and Reasoning.* Abingdon, UK: Routledge, 151–166.

Evans, J. St. B. T., and Elqayam, S. (2011). Towards a Descriptivist Psychology of Reasoning and Decision Making. *Behavioral and Brain Sciences, 34*, 275–290.

Evans, J. St. B. T., and Stanovich, K. E. (2013a). Dual-Process Theories of Higher Cognition: Advancing the Debate. *Perspectives on Psychological Science, 8*, 223–241.

   (2013b). Theory and Metatheory in the Study of Dual Processing: Reply to Comments. *Perspectives on Psychological Science, 8*, 263–271.

Gale, M., and Ball, L. J. (2006). Dual-Goal Facilitation in Wason's 2–4-6 Task: What Mediates Successful Rule Discovery? *Quarterly Journal of Experimental Psychology, 59*, 873–885.

   (2009). Exploring the Determinants of Dual Goal Facilitation in a Rule Discovery Task. *Thinking and Reasoning, 15*, 294–315.

   (2012). Contrast Class Cues and Performance Facilitation in a Hypothesis-Testing Task: Evidence for an Iterative Counterfactual Model. *Memory & Cognition, 40*, 408–419.

Goel, V., and Waechter, R. (2018). Inductive and Deductive Reasoning: Integrating Insights from Philosophy, Psychology, and Neuroscience. In L. J. Ball and V. A. Thompson (eds.), *The Routledge International Handbook of Thinking and Reasoning.* Abingdon, UK: Routledge, 218–247.

Gorman, M. E. (1995). Confirmation, Disconfirmation, and Invention: The Case of Alexander Graham Bell and the Telephone. *Thinking and Reasoning, 1,* 31–53.

(2018). Scientific Thinking. In L. J. Ball and V. A. Thompson (eds.), *The Routledge International Handbook of Thinking and Reasoning.* Abingdon, UK: Routledge, 248–267.

Gorman, M. E., and Gorman, M. E. (1984). Comparison of Disconfirmatory, Confirmatory and Control Strategies on Wason's 2-4-6 Task. *Quarterly Journal of Experimental Psychology, 36A,* 629–648.

Jung, R. E., and Vartanian, O. (eds.) (2018). *The Cambridge Handbook of the Neuroscience of Creativity.* Cambridge, UK: Cambridge University Press.

Kareev, Y., and Halberstadt, N. (1993). Evaluating Negative Tests and Refutations in a Rule Discovery Task. *Quarterly Journal of Experimental Psychology, 46A,* 715–727.

Kareev, Y., Halberstadt, K., and Shafir, D. (1993). Improving Performance and Increasing the Use of Non-Positive Testing in a Rule-Discovery Task. *Quarterly Journal of Experimental Psychology, 46A,* 729–742.

Kaufman, S. B., Quilty, L. C., Grazioplene, R. G., et al. (2016). Openness to Experience and Intellect Differentially Predict Creative Achievement in the Arts and Sciences. *Journal of Personality, 84,* 248–258.

Klayman, J., and Ha, Y.-W. (1987). Confirmation, Disconfirmation, and Information in Hypothesis Testing. *Psychological Review, 94,* 211–228.

(1989). Hypothesis Testing in Rule Discovery: Strategy, Structure and Content. *Journal of Experimental Psychology: Learning, Memory & Cognition, 15,* 596–604.

Legrenzi, P., Girotto, V., and Johnson-Laird, P. N. (1993). Focussing in Reasoning and Decision Making. *Cognition, 49,* 37–66.

Morley, N. J., Ball, L. J., and Ormerod, T. C. (2006). How the Detection of Insurance Fraud Succeeds and Fails. *Psychology, Crime & Law, 12,* 163–180.

Mynatt, C. R., Doherty, M. E., and Dragan, W. (1993). Information Relevance, Working Memory, and the Consideration of Alternatives. *The Quarterly Journal of Experimental Psychology, 46,* 759–778.

Ormerod, T. C., Ball, L. J., and Morley, N. J. (2012). Informing the Development of a Fraud Prevention Toolset through a Situated Analysis of Fraud Investigation Expertise. *Behaviour & Information Technology, 31,* 371–381.

Roberts, R. P., and Addis, D. R. (2018). A Common Mode of Processing Governing Divergent Thinking and Future Imagination. In R. E. Jung and O. Vartanian (eds.), *The Cambridge Handbook of the Neuroscience of Creativity.* Cambridge, UK: Cambridge University Press, 211–230.

Silvia, P. J., Beaty, R. E., and Nusbaum, E. C. (2013). Verbal Fluency and Creativity: General and Specific Contributions of Broad Retrieval Ability (Gr) Factors to Divergent Thinking. *Intelligence, 41,* 328–340.

Simon, H. A. (1982). *Models of Bounded Rationality.* Cambridge, MA: MIT Press.

(1996). *The Sciences of the Artificial.* 3rd edition. Cambridge, MA: MIT Press.

Sloman, S. A. (1996). The Empirical Case for Two Systems of Reasoning. *Psychological Bulletin, 119,* 3–22.

Stanovich, K. E. (1999). *Who is Rational? Studies of Individual Differences in Reasoning.* Mahwah, NJ: Erlbaum.

   (2004). *The Robot's Rebellion: Finding Meaning in the Age of Darwin.* Chicago, IL: University of Chicago Press.

   (2009). Distinguishing the Reflective, Algorithmic, and Autonomous Minds: Is It Time for a Tri-Process Theory? In J. St. B. T. Evans, and K. E. Frankish (eds.), *In Two Minds: Dual Processes and Beyond.* Oxford, UK: Oxford University Press, 55–88.

Stupple, E. J., and Ball, L. J. (2014). The Intersection between Descriptivism and Meliorism in Reasoning Research: Further Proposals in Support of "Soft Normativism". *Frontiers in Psychology, 5,* article no. 1269.

Thompson, V. A. (2013). Why it Matters: The Implications of Autonomous Processes for Dual Process Theories – Commentary on Evans & Stanovich (2013). *Perspectives on Psychological Science, 8,* 253–256. doi:10.1177/1745691613483476.

Tversky, A., and Kahneman, D. (1973). Availability: A Heuristic for Judging Frequency and Probability. *Cognitive Psychology, 5,* 207–232.

Tweney, R. D. (2009). Mathematical Representations in Science: A Cognitive–Historical Case History. *Topics in Cognitive Science, 1,* 758–776.

Tweney, R. D., Doherty, M. E., Warner, W. J., et al. (1980). Strategies of Rule Discovery in an Inference Task. *Quarterly Journal of Experimental Psychology, 32,* 109–123.

Vallée-Tourangeau, F. (2012). Utilities in the 2-4-6 Task. *Experimental Psychology, 59,* 265–271.

Vallée-Tourangeau, F., Austin, N. G., and Rankin, S. (1995). Inducing a Rule in Wason's 2–4–6 Task: A Test of the Information-Quantity and Goal-Complementarity Hypotheses. *Quarterly Journal of Experimental Psychology, 48A,* 895–914.

Vallée-Tourangeau, F. and Payton, T. (2008). Graphical Representation Fosters Discovery in the 2-4-6 Task. *Quarterly Journal of Experimental Psychology, 61*(4), 625–640.

van der Henst, J. B., Rossi, S., and Schroyens, W. (2002). When Participants Are Not Misled They Are Not so Bad after All: A Pragmatic Analysis of a Rule Discovery Task. In W. D. Gray and C. Schunn (eds.), *Proceedings of the 24th Annual Conference of the Cognitive Science Society.* Mahwah, NJ: Erlbaum, 902–907.

Walsh, D., Dando, C. J., and Ormerod, T. C. (2018). Triage Decision-Making by Welfare Fraud Investigators. *Journal of Applied Research in Memory & Cognition, 7,* 82–91.

Wason, P. C. (1960). On the Failure to Eliminate Hypotheses in a Conceptual Task. *Quarterly Journal of Experimental Psychology, 12,* 129–140.

   (1966). Reasoning. In B. M. Foss (ed.), *New Horizons in Psychology I.* Harmondsworth, UK: Penguin, 106–137.

Wason, P. C., and Johnson-Laird, P. N. (1972). *Psychology of Reasoning: Structure and Content.* London, UK: Batsford.

Wetherick, N. E. (1962). Eliminative and Enumerative Behaviour in a Conceptual Task. *Quarterly Journal of Experimental Psychology, 14,* 129–140.

Wharton, C. M., Cheng, P. W., and Wickens, T. D. (1993). Hypothesis-Testing Strategies: Why Two Goals Are Better Than One. *Quarterly Journal of Experimental Psychology, 46A,* 743–758.

32 The Counterfactual Imagination: The Impact of Alternatives to Reality on Morality

Ruth M. J. Byrne

People often imagine how things could have turned out differently, especially after a bad outcome (e.g. Kahneman and Tversky, 1982). Such "if only ..." and "what if ..." thoughts are a pervasive sort of everyday "mundane" imagination. To illustrate, consider the tragic case of the American Airlines flight that crashed in November 2001. It fell out of the sky into Queen's in New York just a few minutes after takeoff, killing all 260 people on board and five people on the ground. The subsequent investigation established that the crash happened because – shockingly – the airplane's tail fell off. The investigation pointed to the co-pilot's overuse of the rudder pedal in response to "wake" turbulence from another aircraft ahead of it. It concluded with a poignant and powerful imagined alternative to reality, "had the first officer stopped making inputs ... the natural stability of the aircraft would have returned ... and the accident would not have happened" (National Transportation Safety Board, 2004). Thoughts about what could have happened are often invoked to explain the past (see Byrne, 2016 for a review), sometimes to excuse and justify it, and other times to allocate fault, responsibility and blame (e.g. Markman, Mizoguchi, and McMullen, 2008; Parkinson and Byrne, 2017).

Imagined alternatives to reality also help in the formulation of intentions to improve in the future (e.g. Roese and Epstude, 2017; Smallman and McCulloch, 2012). Thoughts about how things could have turned out differently provide a roadmap for change. For example, the investigation of the American Airlines 2001 crash also identified as culpable the airlines' improper training of pilots in rudder use and Airbus's overly sensitive rudder design, and made recommendations for the future to improve pilot training and to modify rudder control designs (National Transportation Safety Board, 2004). But imagined alternatives make imperfect arguments and American Airlines and Airbus countered ascriptions of blame by appealing to other imagined alternatives: Airbus argued that the pilot used force "which would have resulted in full rudder reversals on any commercial aircraft anywhere in the world"; American Airlines suggested they and the pilot "had no way of knowing the design sensitivities of that airplane because Airbus, who did know, never told," and the co-pilot's father lamented the media condemnation of his dead son, saying "it's always the easiest thing to do, to blame the pilots" (e.g. Martinez, 2002; Wald, 2004). As these examples illustrate, the use of imagined alternatives to apportion blame and fault, and to construct rebuttals to moral judgments, is complex and nuanced. And strikingly, such imagined alternatives may underpin the experience of emotions such as guilt, remorse, and shame (e.g. Kahneman and Tversky, 1982).

In this chapter, I consider the cognitive processes that enable the everyday counterfactual imagination to have such widespread effects. I rely on the example of the effects of imagined alternatives on moral judgments to illustrate their profound impact. In the first section, I consider evidence that imagined alternatives have far-reaching effects in daily life because they assist in the identification of causes, and I illustrate these effects by considering their impact on moral judgments. In the second section, I consider evidence that imagined alternatives assist in the evaluation of mental states, beliefs, and desires, once again illustrating these effects for moral judgments. In the third section, I outline theoretical proposals about the cognitive processes that underlie the imagination of alternatives to reality. Such alternatives are often expressed as counterfactual conditionals, such as "if the pilot had stopped pressing the rudder pedal, the aircraft would have stabilized" and counterfactual conditionals are understood by constructing an enriched mental simulation that explicitly represents not only the conjectured alternative to reality but also the presupposed factual reality. In the fourth section, I turn from the consideration of the effects of imagined alternatives on moral judgments, to the converse – the evidence that moral thoughts affect the imagination, primarily because people often rely on their knowledge of moral norms to imagine alternatives to reality. In the final section I consider the wider implications of discoveries about the creation of alternatives, in particular for a key issue in understanding the human mind: whether the human imagination depends on processes that are distinct from other sorts of thinking and reasoning. I argue that discoveries about the role of imagined alternatives in moral judgment expands our understanding of how the rich diversity of thought may be rooted in a common pool of cognitive processes.

Imagined Alternatives Affect Inferences About Causes

The creation of alternatives to reality has widespread effects, in part because it enables the identification of possible causes of an outcome. This impact can be illustrated by a consideration of the effects of imagined alternatives on moral judgments, which occur in several ways, and one important way is in the allocation of causal responsibility among several candidate causes. Consider the following question as an illustration: Who is more to blame for killing 265 people in the American Airlines crash, the pilot who misused an instrument, the airline who failed to train him properly, or the manufacturer who failed to disclose design flaws?

A key discovery is that the perceived contribution of a candidate cause can be amplified or diminished by an imagined alternative (e.g. McCloy and Byrne, 2002). For example, when people hear that an athlete who took a painkiller for an ankle injury experienced known side effects such as fatigue and lost a big race by just a few seconds, they consider that the painkiller had a causal role in her losing the race.

Their causal judgments are *amplified* when they know about an imagined alternative that results in a different outcome, such as another painkiller taken by other competitors with no side effects. The available counterfactual enables people to think "if only she had taken the other painkiller, she wouldn't have lost the race." And their causal judgments are *diminished* when they know about a "semi-factual" alternative – that is, an imagined alternative that results in the same outcome as reality, such as another painkiller taken by other competitors that had the same side effects. The available semi-factual enables them to think, "even if she had taken the other painkiller, she would have lost the race" (e.g. McCloy and Byrne, 2002).

Similarly, imagined alternatives can amplify or diminish moral judgments. For example, when people listen to a lawyer who claims that changes to actions taken by the victim would have changed the outcome of an attack, they tend to blame the victim; when they hear that changes to the actions taken by the victim would not have changed the outcome, they tend to blame the attacker (e.g. Branscombe et al., 1996). The impact of imagined alternatives on moral judgments arises because people attempt to construct a mental simulation of events that explicitly captures the relations between an action and its outcome. They construct a model that represents an action and its outcome, such as "the policeman fired a shot and the thief died" and a model of a counterfactual alternative, such as "the policeman did not fire and the thief did not die," which provides a comparison that emphasizes the causal relation between the policeman's action and the outcome. In contrast, a model of a semi-factual alternative, such as "the policeman did not fire and the thief died anyway," provides a comparison that denies a causal relation (e.g. Cushman, 2013; Lagnado, Gerstenberg, and Zultan, 2013; McEleney and Byrne, 2006).

The impact of imagined alternatives on moral causal inferences leads to an important question about the implications of the nature of the human imagination on social interaction: Is the effect of the counterfactual imagination on moral judgments good or bad? In some instances people make better moral judgments when they create an alternative to reality. Consider the curious incident of "moral luck" as an example. Suppose Cynthia drives through a leaf pile at the side of the road and accidentally kills two children who were hiding there. It seems clear she should be punished for such a terrible outcome. Of course if she drives through a leaf pile in which there were no children hiding, there is nothing for which she should be punished. But it is a matter of luck whether there are children hiding in a leaf pile (e.g. Martin and Cushman, 2016a). The effects of "moral luck" on blame and punishment can seem unfair. The terrible outcome of killing children evokes an emotional reaction that may overshadow consideration of Cynthia's intentions. But it also leads people to reconsider whether Cynthia acted reasonably in the first place, and with moral hindsight, they may decide she did not (e.g. Byrne and Timmons, 2018; Fleischhut, Meder and Gigerenzer, 2017). Imagined alternatives can help rebalance this potentially flawed asymmetry in judgments. For example, consider Al and Bob who intentionally threw bricks over a high wall from an overpass bridge to harm drivers passing underneath. Al's brick hit the pavement and did no harm but Bob's brick hit a car and killed the driver. Al and Bob carried out the same action with the same intentions and knowledge, yet people blame Bob more and want to punish him more. But the condemnation of Al is amplified when people imagine an alternative to reality about how things could have turned out worse – for example, if Al had thrown his brick from another section of the bridge he would have hit a car (e.g. Lench et al., 2015). Moreover, this moral counterfactual amplification effect occurs when people believe the person had no reason to harm, but not when the person had a reason (e.g. Parkinson and Byrne, 2017). Imagined alternatives also affect moral judgments about whether a person should have carried out a self-sacrificial good action, such as running into traffic to save a child who has fallen in front of a truck (e.g. Byrne and Timmons, 2018; see also Timmons and Byrne, 2018; Timmons et al., 2019). These examples indicate that people can make better moral judgments when they imagine an alternative to reality.

However, in other instances people make worse moral judgments when they imagine how things could have been different. Iraqi prisoners at Abu Ghraib were abused and tortured by American soldiers. When people imagined how the prisoners would have been worse off under Saddam Hussein, they felt less morally outraged by the soldiers' treatment of them. Their judgments about the ethical standards by which the United States should treat prisoners of war in the future with respect to human rights were also lower compared to participants who imagined how the prisoners could have been better off (e.g. Markman, Mizoguchi, and McMullen, 2008). In such instances, people use counterfactuals not to explain the past, but to "explain away" events, to derogate and excuse immoral actions (e.g. McCrea, 2008). Such examples indicate that people sometimes make worse moral judgments when they imagine an alternative to reality. Overall, the evidence suggests that people rely on imagined alternatives to reality as a crucial point of comparison, which can anchor or distort their moral compass. Whether the effects of imagined alternatives differ depending on where one's moral compass points at the outset is as yet unknown.

Intriguingly, sometimes counterfactuals and moral judgments are not closely aligned at all. For example, suppose Joe does not pick up his son from school, his neighbor collects him instead, and on the way the boy is injured when a drunk driver crashes into them. People assign more fault – blame, responsibility, and causality – to the drunk driver than to Joe, but they imagine alternatives to reality in which the boy's injuries could have been avoided if Joe had collected him (e.g. N'gbala and Branscombe, 1995). And people sometimes blame themselves for events they know they did not cause. For example, the parents and spouses of the victims of car accidents are frequently haunted by thoughts about how they could have prevented the accident, "if only I hadn't let him take the car that evening . . ." and they blame themselves for not intervening (e.g. Davis et al., 1995). In these instances counterfactuals and moral judgments do not seem to be in step with each other. The dissociation of counterfactuals and moral judgments reflects a similar dissociation that sometimes occurs between counterfactuals and causal judgments. For example, suppose a drunk driver crashed into Mr. Jones when he was driving home by an unusual route. People identify the cause of the accident as the drunk driver, but they create counterfactuals in which the crash could have been avoided if Mr. Jones had driven home by his usual route (e.g. Mandel and Lehman, 1996). The dissociation of counterfactuals and causal thoughts arises because causal explanations focus on strong causes that covary with the outcome, such as the drunk driver, whereas imagined alternatives consider how to prevent an outcome by removing enabling causes that are necessary but not sufficient, such as Mr. Jones's route (Byrne, 2005; Frosch and Byrne, 2012). Likewise, the dissociation of counterfactuals and moral thoughts arises when moral thoughts focus on strong causes, such as the drunk driver in the story about Joe's son's injury, but imagined alternatives focus on enabling ones, the boy's injuries would not have happened if any one of several individuals – Joe, his neighbor, the drunk driver – had acted differently. People consider one individual to be causally and morally responsible more than others if they can more easily imagine how changes to his or her action would have changed the outcome (e.g. Cushman, 2013; Lagnado et al., 2013).

Of course, people do not always blame a person who was causally responsible for an event – a policeman who shoots a thief and causes his death may not be blamed at all, for example, if the thief fired a gun at the policeman first. In most cases, people make inferences not only about who caused the outcome, but also about the intentions, desires, and knowledge of the person who caused it (Alicke et al., 2008; Lagnado and Channon, 2008; Malle, Guglielmo, and Monroe, 2014), to which we now turn.

Imagined Alternatives Affect Inferences About Intentions

The widespread effects of the creation of alternatives to reality occur in part because thinking in this way facilitates inferences about intentions. For example, people blame someone who intentionally caused a bad outcome more than someone who accidentally caused a bad outcome. To illustrate the contrast, compare the blame to be allocated to the co-pilot of the American Airlines crash who killed 265 people by mistake, to the blame to be allocated to the co-pilot of the Germanwings crash in the French Alps in 2015. He deliberately locked the captain out of the cockpit and initiated a controlled descent into the mountainside to commit suicide (French Civil Aviation Safety Investigation Authority, 2016). He killed his five fellow crew members and the 144 passengers in his care – on purpose. Clearly the Germanwings pilot deserves more moral condemnation than the American Airlines pilot. And indeed, experiments show that people tend to blame someone who caused a bad outcome intentionally far more than one who caused it accidentally (e.g. Cushman, 2008; Parkinson and Byrne, 2018; Young and Saxe, 2011). In fact, when a person caused an outcome intentionally, people may not even try to imagine how the person could have prevented the outcome (e.g. Malle, Guglielmo, and Monroe, 2014).

Intriguingly, people tend to assume that a person will have the same intention in any imagined alternative to reality and that the individual will tend to pursue his or her intention despite obstacles – the relation between a person's intentions and an outcome can appear counterfactually robust (e.g. Murray and Lombrozo, 2016).

Hence, people create very different sorts of alternatives to reality when faced with cause-effect sequences compared to reason-action sequences. They focus on different aspects of an event when they think about the relation of a cause and a bad outcome, compared to when they think about the relation of a person's intentions and the bad outcome. For example, participants were directed to imagine a counterfactual alternative to a bad outcome such as someone failing an exam. When the bad outcome was the result of a cause-effect sequence, such as "a staff shortage caused the library to close early," they created counterfactuals that focused on what would have happened if the cause had not occurred, "if only there hadn't been a staff shortage ..." But when the bad outcome of failing the exam was the result of a reason-action sequence, "Paul wanted to meet some friends so he went to a party," they created counterfactuals that focused on what would have happened if the action had not occurred, "if only Paul did not go to the party ..." In the cause-effect sequence, they imagined alternatives to the cause, but in the reason-action sequence they did not imagine alternatives to the reason (e.g. Walsh and Byrne, 2007; see also Juhos, Quelhas, and Byrne, 2015). People tend to assume that a person will have the same intention in any imagined alternative.

In contrast, when a person caused an outcome accidentally, people tend to imagine how the person could have prevented the outcome (e.g. Malle, Guglielmo, and Monroe, 2014). As a result, even when a person did not intend an outcome, such as the pilot of the American Airlines crash, people sometimes blame him because they can imagine how things could have been different. People imagine alternatives to reality to think about whether the person *could* have done something differently – about whether the person had the knowledge, skill, or choice to do otherwise. To illustrate, suppose a doctor gives a drug to a patient who has an allergic reaction to it and dies. Even though the doctor did not intend for the patient to die, people tend to blame him anyway, when they can imagine that he *could* have done something differently, say, prescribe a different drug (e.g. Alicke et al., 2008). Their imagined alternatives help them to probe an individual's capacity to prevent the outcome. They also rely on imagined alternatives to think about whether a person *should* have done something differently – whether the person had an obligation to prevent the outcome. For example, they blame the doctor when they know he should have checked the patient's records for allergies (e.g. Alicke et al., 2008; Malle, Guglielmo, and Monroe, 2014). Hence, people blame a person who caused a bad outcome accidentally, such as the American Airlines pilot, when they can imagine an alternative to reality in which he prevented the outcome – the crux of their allocation of blame to him is whether they consider that he could have known that his use of the rudder would cause the tail to fall off.

People also imagine alternatives to reality to assess whether a person could reasonably foresee an outcome. An individual who has knowledge relevant to an outcome is considered to have caused it more than one who did not have such knowledge. For example, Josh is judged to be the cause of Sarah's car crash when he lends his car to Sarah knowing there is a fault with the brakes, because people imagine ways Josh could have prevented the outcome, such as by telling her about the fault. When he does in fact take the precaution of telling Sarah about the faulty brakes, he is not considered to be the cause as much (e.g. Gilbert et al., 2015). Likewise, people blame a person for an outcome when they believe the person expected the outcome – for example, they blame Anne who assembled a chair that broke and injured Jill, if Anne believed she did not assemble the chair properly and thought it was likely to break. In fact, they even blame a person when the person didn't expect the outcome provided it was objectively foreseeable, for example, they blame Anne when she did not assemble the chair properly and it was likely to break, regardless of her expectations (e.g. Lagnado and Channon, 2008). These experimental results show that people make a moral judgment to blame someone who caused a bad outcome accidentally if they can imagine an alternative to reality in which the person prevented the outcome. They construct a model that represents the relations between an action and an outcome, including not only causal information, but also mental state information about intentions, beliefs, and desires.

In general, people rely on their imagination to understand other people's beliefs and intentions – for example, to help them infer that another person's knowledge is different from their own. A dramatic illustration of this use of the counterfactual imagination is its role in helping children to understand that other people have beliefs and knowledge that are different to their own, including, sometimes, false beliefs. Children appear to begin to appreciate that there are alternatives to reality and to understand words such as "almost" as early as 2 years of age, but their true understanding of counterfactual alternatives continues to develop throughout middle childhood (Beck et al., 2006; Harris, 2000). And their ability to imagine alternatives to reality enables them to overcome many other cognitive challenges. For example, suppose John hears Anne say she is picking up toys from her bedroom floor because she wants to look for her ball. While he is away Anne's mother tells her to tidy her room. When John comes back he sees Anne picking up toys. What will John believe is the reason Anne is picking up toys? It is not until the age of 8 years that children begin to understand that John will have a false belief about Anne's reason for her action – that John will believe she is picking up toys to find her ball (e.g. Rasga, Quelhas, and Byrne, 2016). By this age they have become accomplished at imagining alternatives to reality about other people's intentions, and they can accurately answer counterfactual questions such as, if Anne's mother hadn't told her to tidy her room, what would have been the reason for her action? Their false belief reasoning depends on their counterfactual imagination, which emerges earlier (e.g. Rasga, Quelhas, and Byrne, 2016; 2017). The two sorts of inferences require similar sorts of comparisons of a representation of reality to an alternative to it, and they activate similar regions of the brain (Guajardo, Parker, and Turley-Ames, 2009; van Hoeck et al., 2014). How adults estimate children's capacities to imagine alternatives to reality remains an open question.

People imagine alternatives to reality not only to understand other people's intentions, but also to formulate their own, to learn from mistakes in the past about how to prevent the same bad outcome occurring in the future. A counterfactual thought such as "I would have won the game if only I had changed strategy earlier" provides a blueprint for an intention to change, a plan that can be readily implemented to transform the current situation to a better one (e.g. Rim and Summerville,

2014; Roese and Epstude, 2017). People think about how things could have turned out better more often when they believe they will confront the same situation again (e.g. Markman, McMullen, and Elizaga, 2008). Pre-factual thoughts – imagined alternatives about the future – such as "things would be better for me next time if I could concentrate" are especially important for the formation of intentions to improve (e.g. Byrne and Egan, 2004; Ferrante et al., 2013). And imagined alternatives affect the formulation of moral intentions, too. For example, participants identified a person as a likely criminal suspect, from a set of photographs that consisted of a white and a black person, or of two white people. Those who had the opportunity to demonstrate their moral integrity by showing they were not racist (they chose the white person as the likely suspect instead of the black person) subsequently made morally *worse* judgments – for example, they judged that a woman alone at night who crossed a street when she saw a black man coming toward her was not behaving in a racist manner (e.g. Effron, Miller, and Monin, 2012). The result indicates that a person may be affected by the availability of an imagined counterfactual about how their own behavior could have been worse, which appears to give them a "moral license" to act immorally.

Just as we asked whether the effect of imagined alternatives on moral causal inferences is good or bad, so, too, we can ask whether the effect of imagined alternatives on moral intention inferences is good or bad. The ready availability of an imagined alternative can distort moral judgments about other people's intentions. Consider a doctor who must choose between a treatment that has a high chance of a successful outcome for a patient, or an alternative treatment that has a much lower chance of success for the patient but is one from which the doctor could benefit – she can publish in a prestigious journal only if the treatment is unsuccessful. The doctor chooses the treatment with the highest chance of success, but unfortunately it is not successful. Curiously, the doctor is judged to deserve more punishment for the bad outcome compared to another doctor who had no choice – she was forced to give the best treatment because she did not have access to the alternative one. Even though the first doctor had good intentions, people can readily imagine an alternative to her action (Martin and Cushman, 2016b). Conversely, the absence of an available counterfactual can also distort moral judgments. Individuals with impairments to the prefrontal cortex experience difficulties in imagining alternatives to reality (e.g. Gomez Beldarrain et al., 2005). And individuals with such impairments also experience difficulty in allocating blame appropriately for intentional vs. accidental harm (e.g. Young and Tsoi, 2013).

Of course, people do not always morally condemn a person even when the person caused an outcome and even when he or she intended it, for example, a person is judged less morally responsible when the person's normal reasoning was bypassed by manipulation, as people consider what the individual would have done if he or she had not been manipulated (e.g. Murray and Lombrozo, 2016). Even when someone's actions are intentional and they desire and foresee the heinous outcome, such as the Germanwings pilot's decision to commit suicide and kill 149 individuals by flying into a mountain, people may imagine alternatives; for example, they may consider the nuances of his mental state and imagine, "if only he had received better psychiatric treatment during his documented depressive episodes ..." and the counterfactual may affect the degree of blame ascribed to him. The mere availability of a salient counterfactual alternative can affect the experience of sympathy (e.g. Macrae, Milne, and Griffiths, 1993), possibly even to shift the balance of sympathy for the Germanwings pilot to exceed that for the American Airlines one.

Imagined alternatives to reality have a remarkable everyday impact, as these examples of their role in moral judgments illustrate. The cognitive processes that enable the counterfactual imagination to have such widespread effects are operations that construct dynamic mental simulations, to which I now turn.

Cognitive Processes in the Counterfactual Imagination

At the heart of the counterfactual imagination are cognitive processes that include operations to construct a mental representation of reality – for example, a mental representation that the American Airlines pilot overused the rudder pedal and the airplane's tail fell off, and cognitive processes to select aspects of the mental representation of reality as candidates for mutation in the creation of an alternative. An alternative may be created by deleting information – for example, the pilot stops pressing the rudder pedal; or by adding new information – for example, an alarm warns the pilot that the tail is in danger (e.g. Kahneman and Tversky, 1982). A key discovery is that when people understand a counterfactual conditional, such as "if the pilot had stopped pressing the rudder pedal, the aircraft would have stabilized," they keep in mind two possibilities, the conjecture, "the pilot stopped pressing the rudder pedal and the aircraft stabilized," and the known or presupposed reality, "the pilot did not stop pressing the rudder pedal and the aircraft did not stabilize" (see Byrne, 2017 for a review). In contrast, for the corresponding factual conditional, "if the pilot stopped pressing the rudder pedal, the aircraft stabilized," they envisage just a single possibility at the outset, "the pilot stopped pressing the rudder pedal and the aircraft stabilized" (e.g. Johnson-Laird and Byrne, 2002).

Evidence that people keep in mind dual possibilities when they understand a counterfactual comes from many converging sources. For example, people judge that the situations that best fit the description in a counterfactual conditional such as "if the pilot had stopped pressing the rudder pedal, the aircraft would have stabilized," include "the pilot did not stop pressing the rudder pedal" and "the aircraft did not stabilize" (e.g. Byrne and Tasso, 1999). They consider that someone uttering the counterfactual meant to imply this situation (Thompson and Byrne, 2002). And they tend to misremember the counterfactual and believe they were told the factual situation (Fillenbaum, 1974).

People also make many more inferences from the counterfactual than the corresponding factual conditional. For example, they make the *modus tollens* inference, from "the aircraft did not stabilize" to "therefore the pilot did not stop pressing the rudder pedal" far more often from a counterfactual compared to a factual conditional (e.g. Byrne and Tasso, 1999; Thompson and Byrne, 2002). But they make the *modus ponens* inference, from "the pilot stopped pressing the rudder pedal" to "the aircraft stabilized" just as often from the counterfactual as they do from the factual conditional. This counterfactual inference effect provides strong evidence that people envisage dual possibilities for counterfactuals.

Strikingly, participants read a description of the situation corresponding to the presupposed facts such as "the pilot did not stop pressing the rudder pedal and the aircraft did not stabilize," more quickly when they are "primed" by first reading the counterfactual, compared to when they have first read the factual conditional (e.g. Santamaria, Espino, and Byrne, 2005). They read the situation, "the pilot stopped pressing the rudder pedal and the aircraft stabilized" equally quickly from both sorts of conditional. The consideration of such dual possibilities has been tested for the content that concerns causes, definitions, promises, threats, obligations, or everyday scenarios (e.g. Frosch and Byrne, 2012; Egan and Byrne, 2012).

Because people think about two possibilities at the outset when they understand a counterfactual, but only one possibility when they understand a factual conditional, counterfactuals can seem to mean something very different from factual conditionals. But people can flesh out their mental models for both sorts of conditionals to be more explicit – for example, to think about the possibility not only that "the pilot did not stop pressing the rudder pedal and the aircraft did not stabilize" but also that "the pilot pressed the rudder pedal and the aircraft stabilized," and even, on at least a conditional interpretation, "the pilot did not stop pressing the rudder pedal and the aircraft stabilized." Their underlying semantics is similar even though their initial mental representations appear to be quite different (e.g. Johnson-Laird and Byrne, 2002; Khemlani, Johnson-Laird, and Byrne, 2018; see also Lewis, 1973; Stalnaker, 1968).

The cognitive processes that underlie the counterfactual imagination also depend on various general executive functions, such as working memory resources that enable a representation of reality and a representation of an alternative to be held in mind at the same time, attentional resources that enable switching from one representation to the other, and inhibitory processes that enable the representation of reality to be temporarily suppressed so that an alternative to it can be entertained (e.g. Beck, Riggs, and Gorniak, 2009). The dual mental simulation of the conjecture and the factual reality enables the counterfactual imagination to have its widespread effects – for example, to facilitate the identification of causal or intentional factors. We turn now to consider the cognitive processes that mutate an aspect of a mental representation of reality to create an alternative to it.

The Creation of Counterfactual Alternatives

When people imagine how things could have turned out differently, they find some aspects of reality easier to change than others. Remarkably, most people tend to create the same sorts of counterfactuals, and the regularities arise because people focus on the same sorts of "fault lines" in their representation of reality (e.g. Kahneman and Tversky, 1982). People create plausible counterfactuals modulated by the knowledge they retrieve from memory, or by the information provided about the situation; for instance, they retrieve information from memory about what normally or usually happens, or the description of the situation provides such information (e.g. Kahneman and Miller, 1986).

One example is that people imagine an alternative to reality by recasting an exceptional event as normal. Suppose Mr. Jones was in a car crash after he left the office at his usual time but he drove home by an unusual route. Most people imagine the crash could have been avoided if he had gone home by his usual route (e.g. Dixon and Byrne, 2011; Kahneman and Tversky, 1982). Likewise people make the moral judgment that a perpetrator should be punished more when a victim was attacked on the way home by an unusual route rather than by his usual route, or shopping in a shop he rarely shops in rather than one he usually shops in (e.g. Macrae, Milne, and Griffiths, 1993). Their moral judgment is influenced by the ready availability of an imagined alternative, because the intrapersonal norm of what the individual usually does provides a ready made counterfactual. Hence, just as imagined alternatives to reality affect moral thoughts, so, too, moral thoughts affect the creation of alternatives to reality.

A moral violation leads people to access the corresponding moral norm, and so people readily imagine counterfactuals to the violation. Suppose in a storm a ship's captain throws his cargo overboard in order to lighten the load and so ensure that the ship does not sink. People judge that he was forced to throw his cargo overboard. But suppose that instead the ship's captain throws his wife overboard to lighten the load. People do not tend to judge that he was forced to throw his wife overboard (e.g. Phillips and Cushman, 2017). The moral violation of throwing his wife overboard brings to mind the corresponding moral norm of not harming her, which makes available the counterfactual that the ship's captain could have acted in accordance with the moral norm and not thrown his wife overboard. Because people can imagine this alternative to reality, they judge that he was not forced to do so. In contrast, the morally neutral action of throwing cargo overboard does not violate any moral regulation and does not bring to mind any corresponding norm of not throwing it overboard. However, when people are explicitly asked to think about the captain's alternatives to throwing his cargo overboard, they then judge that he was not forced to do so either (e.g. Phillips, Luguri, and Knobe, 2015; Young and Phillips, 2011). Importantly, people do not tend to blame someone for a morally bad action if they believe the person was coerced or forced to carry it out (e.g. Murray and Lombrozo, 2016). Similarly, suppose that in a philosophy department administrative assistants are allowed to take pens but professors are not, and an administrator and a professor each take the two last pens, which creates a problem when there are no more pens. People judge that the professor caused the problem. The violation of the regulation by the professor taking a pen brings to mind the norm created by the department's regulation, and so people can readily imagine that the professor could have or should have acted differently. When people are asked explicitly to think about the administrator's alternatives to taking one of the last pens, they then judge that the administrator caused the problem (e.g. Phillips,Luguri, and Knobe, 2015).

Another example of a "fault line" in the counterfactual imagination is that people tend to imagine an alternative by mentally undoing events within their own control. Suppose that Steven arrives home too late to save his dying wife because he was delayed by several events such as stopping for a beer at a bar and a traffic jam. People imagine the delay could have been avoided if Steven had not stopped at the bar, the event within his control, rather than if there had been no traffic jam, an event outside his control (e.g. Girotto, Legrenzi, and Rizzo, 1991; see also Pighin et al., 2011). Here, too, moral norms can impose limitations on the ready access to alternatives to reality. People do not tend to imagine alternatives to a controllable event that adheres to moral norms. For example, they do not tend to imagine that he should not have called to visit his elderly parents on the way home (e.g. McCloy and Byrne, 2000). Likewise, when Mark goes to a party the night before an important concert performance, which then goes badly, people do not tend to imagine he shouldn't have gone to the party if the reason he went adheres to moral norms, such as that he was obliged to go to help with fundraising; but they do tend to imagine he shouldn't have gone to the party if the reason was a personal goal, such as he wanted to meet another musician (e.g. Walsh and Byrne, 2007). Hence, moral norms can make some aspects of reality appear immutable. When someone violates a moral norm, people can readily access a counterfactual, retrieved from memory or constructed from information provided about the situation; but when someone adheres to the moral norm, people may not be as readily able to imagine how things could have turned out differently.

Yet moral judgments do not always follow the "fault lines" of counterfactual thoughts. For example, people imagine an alternative in which they change the most recent event rather than earlier events in a temporal sequence of independent events. Suppose two people toss a coin, and if they toss the same face coin they will both win $1,000. Alicia goes first and tosses heads, Laura goes second and tosses tails, and so they both lose. People imagine they could have won if Laura had tossed heads, the second event, more than they imagine they could have won if Alicia had tossed tails (e.g. Byrne et al., 2000; see also Segura, Fernandez-Berrocal, and Byrne, 2002). They also judge that the second player, Laura, will feel more guilt and be blamed more by the first one, Alicia. But the context can make a counterfactual alternative available to the first event. For example, suppose Alicia tossed heads, but there was a technical hitch and the game was restarted; this time, Alicia tossed tails and Laura tossed heads. Now people tend to imagine they would have won if Alicia had tossed heads, just as often as they imagine they would have won if Laura had tossed tails. But curiously, they continue to consider that Laura will be blamed more by Alicia (e.g. Byrne et al., 2000; Walsh and Byrne, 2004). The dissociation of moral judgments of blame from the "fault lines" of counterfactuals may arise because people think about whether the protagonists could have done anything differently.

Intriguingly, people sometimes make errors in their judgments of the relation between what is possible and what is permissible. They sometimes judge that an immoral event – say, sneaking onto public transport – is impossible when they make a fast judgment, more so than when they can take a longer time to think about it, that is, they seem to consider impermissible events to be impossible, at least initially (e.g. Phillips and

Cushman, 2017). They also sometimes judge impossible events to be obligatory. If someone should do something it implies they could do it, but people sometimes judge that a person should do something even when they are not able to (e.g. Chituc et al., 2016). For example, when Lisa cannot make it to meet Jenny for lunch as arranged at noon at a venue thirty minutes from her home because her car broke down, they do not judge that she ought to make it; but when she cannot make it there on time because she has intentionally stayed at home until 11.45, they judge that she ought to make it, even though she cannot. Their judgment may be a counterfactual moral one, that she *should* have been able to make it. Hence, the bidirectional relation between counterfactuals and moral judgments ensures that moral knowledge can affect people's understanding of causes and intentions.

Is the Counterfactual Imagination Special?

One view of the human imagination is that it is underpinned by special processes distinct from those that are implicated in any other sort of thinking; another view is that although the human imagination gives rise to extraordinary and unique thoughts, it is underpinned by the same common pool of cognitive processes that underlie other sorts of thinking, such as reasoning and decision-making (e.g. see the commentaries on Byrne, 2005, 2007). The effects of counterfactual thoughts on moral judgments, and of moral norms on counterfactual thoughts, may provide some support for the idea that the counterfactual imagination relies on the same sorts of processes that underlie other sorts of thinking.

The effects of counterfactual thoughts and moral judgments on each other may occur in various ways, through shared deliberative reasoning processes, intuitive processes, or emotional processes. For example, counterfactuals may affect moral judgments through the effortful, deliberative construction of alternatives to reality (e.g. Lench et al., 2015). In this case, the creation of alternatives to reality and moral judgments may both rely on the construction of dynamic mental simulations of events, such as iconic mental models with a structure that corresponds to the structure of what they represent (e.g. Byrne and Johnson-Laird 2009; Johnson-Laird and Byrne, 1995, 2002). Usually people tend to represent what is possible, not what is impossible, in line with a principle of truth, and they tend to represent few possibilities because of working memory constraints, in line with a principle of parsimony (Johnson-Laird and Byrne, 2002). Counterfactuals are notable in that people think about what was once possible but is so no longer, and they can envisage multiple possibilities from the outset, appearing to overcome working memory constraints, perhaps because they keep track of the epistemic status of the possibilities, as real or imagined (e.g. Espino and Byrne, 2013, 2018).

Counterfactuals may also affect moral judgments through the operation of intuitive processes. Intuitive processes are unconscious inferences to conscious conclusions (e.g. Bucciarelli, Khemlani, and Johnson-Laird, 2008). In this case counterfactuals may affect moral judgments through the invocation of a default implicit representation of what is possible (e.g. Phillips and Cushman, 2017). Moral judgments are often made quickly and in such instances deliberative counterfactual construction may not be implicated. One example is that people can readily imagine what an individual could have done differently in the situation in which he or she had to decide whether to hit a switch to divert a train that is about to kill five workmen, onto another track on which one workman will be killed. They take longer to imagine what the individual could have done differently in the situation in which he or she had to decide whether to push a man in front of the train to stop it instead (e.g. Migliore et al., 2014; see also Gubbins and Byrne, 2014).

And counterfactual thoughts may affect moral judgments through the experience of emotions, since counterfactuals amplify moral emotions such as regret, guilt, shame, and self-blame. Such counterfactual emotions can affect decisions, for example, the experience of regret on identifying that a better outcome would have followed from a different choice leads to a different choice next time (e.g. McCormack et al., 2016). Most people judge they would experience emotions such as guilt and shame after making the typical moral decision to hit the switch to divert the train, and the typical decision not to push a man from a footbridge in front of the train to stop it (e.g. Tasso, Sarlo, and Lotto, 2017). Their judgments of such emotions are even more intense when they imagine what would have happened if they had made the alternative choice to the one they made.

The spectacular effects of the counterfactual imagination in daily life can lead to the conclusion that it is special and unique. After all, when people think about how things could have turned out differently, their counterfactual thoughts provide a unique learning mechanism, helping them to avoid past mistakes and to work out how to prevent bad things from happening again in the future. Yet the creation of alternatives to reality is disciplined, and people show significant regularities in what they change in their mental representation of reality to create an alternative to it. The bidirectional effects of counterfactual thoughts on moral judgments provide some corroboration for the suggestion that the imagination of alternatives to reality, dramatic and powerful though it may be, relies on similar sorts of processes as other sorts of thinking.

Concluding Remarks

The imagination of alternatives to reality has profound and pervasive effects on daily mental life. One illustration of the impact of the counterfactual imagination is its effects on moral judgments. People have strong views on moral issues, such as whether refugees should be granted asylum in their country, or women should have the right to choose abortion, or gay couples should be allowed to marry. Imagining alternatives to reality enables them to make decisions on such important matters by identifying causes of outcomes and detecting intentions. Imagined alternatives are constrained by "fault lines" in the mental representation of reality, and moral norms form one such important fault line. Fruitful avenues for future research include closer examination of the nature of the counterfactuals that impact moral judgments, increased investigation of the sorts of moral norms that make counterfactual alternatives salient, and detailed scrutiny of the cognitive processes implicated in understanding and reasoning from counterfactual conditionals about moral events.

References

Alicke, M. D., Buckingham, J., Zell, E., and Davis, T. (2008). Culpable Control and Counterfactual Reasoning in the Psychology of Blame. *Personality and Social Psychology Bulletin, 34*, 1371–1381.

Beck, S. R., Riggs, K. J., and Gorniak, S. L. (2009). Relating Developments in Children's Counterfactual Thinking and Executive Functions. *Thinking and Reasoning, 15*, 337–354.

Beck, S. R., Robinson, E. J., Carroll, D. J., and Apperly, I. A. (2006). Children's Thinking about Counterfactuals and Future Hypotheticals as Possibilities. *Child Development, 77*, 413–426.

Branscombe, N. R., Owen, S., Garstka, T. A., and Coleman, J. (1996). Rape and Accident Counterfactuals: Who Might Have Done Otherwise and Would It Have Changed the Outcome? *Journal of Applied Social Psychology, 26*(12), 1042–1067.

Bucciarelli, M., Khemlani, S., and Johnson-Laird, P. N. (2008). The Psychology of Moral Reasoning. *Judgment and Decision Making, 3*(2), 121–139.

Byrne, R. M. J. (2005). *The Rational Imagination: How People Create Alternatives to Reality.* Cambridge, MA: MIT Press.

(2007). Précis of *The Rational Imagination*: How People Create Alternatives to Reality. *Behavioral and Brain Sciences, 30*(5–6), 439–453.

(2016). Counterfactual Thoughts. *Annual Review of Psychology, 67*, 135–157.

(2017). Counterfactual Thinking: From Logic to Morality. *Current Directions in Psychological Science, 26*(4), 314–322.

Byrne, R. M. J., and Egan, S. M. (2004). Counterfactual and Prefactual Conditionals. *Canadian Journal of Experimental Psychology, 58*(2), 113.

Byrne, R. M. J., and Johnson-Laird, P. N. (2009). "If" and the Problems of Conditional Reasoning. *Trends in Cognitive Sciences, 13*(7), 282–287.

Byrne, R. M. J., Segura, S., Culhane, R., Tasso, A., and Berrocal, P. (2000). The Temporality Effect in Counterfactual Thinking about What Might Have Been. *Memory & Cognition, 28*(2), 264–281.

Byrne, R. M. J., and Tasso, A. (1999). Deductive Reasoning with Factual, Possible, and Counterfactual Conditionals. *Memory & Cognition, 27*, 726–740.

Byrne, R. M. J., and Timmons, S. (2018). Moral Hindsight for Good Actions and the Effects of Imagined Alternatives to Reality. *Cognition, 178*, 82–91.

Chituc, V., Henne, P., Sinnott-Armstrong, W., and De Brigard, F. (2016). Blame, not Ability, Impacts Moral "Ought" Judgments for Impossible Actions: Toward an Empirical Refutation of "Ought" Implies "Can". *Cognition, 150*, 20–25.

Cushman, F. (2008). Crime and Punishment: Distinguishing the Roles of Causal and Intentional Analyses in Moral Judgment. *Cognition, 108*(2), 353–380.

(2013). Action, Outcome, and Value: A Dual-System Framework for Morality. *Personality and Social Psychology Review, 17*(3), 273–292.

Davis, C. G., Lehman, D. R., Wortman, C. B., Silver, R. C., and Thompson, S. C. (1995). The Undoing of Traumatic Life Events. *Personality and Social Psychology Bulletin, 21*, 109–124.

Dixon, J., and Byrne, R. M. J. (2011). "If Only" Counterfactual Thoughts about Exceptional Actions. *Memory & Cognition*, *39*(7), 1317–1331.

Effron, D. A., Miller, D. T., and Monin, B. (2012). Inventing Racist Roads Not Taken: The Licensing Effect of Immoral Counterfactual Behaviors. *Journal of Personality and Social Psychology*, *103*(6), 916–932.

Egan, S., and Byrne, R. M. J. (2012). Inferences from Counterfactual Threats and Promises. *Experimental Psychology*, *59*(4), 227–235.

Espino, O., and Byrne, R. M. J. (2013). The Compatibility Heuristic in Non Categorical Hypothetical Reasoning: Inferences Between Conditionals And Disjunctions. *Cognitive Psychology*, *67*(3), 98–129.

  (2018). Thinking about the Opposite of What Is Said: Counterfactual Conditionals and Symbolic or Alternate Simulations of Negation. *Cognitive Science*, *42*(8), 2459–2501.

Ferrante, D., Girotto, V., Straga, M., and Walsh, C. (2013). Improving the Past and the Future: A Temporal Asymmetry in Hypothetical Thinking. *Journal of Experimental Psychology: General*, *142*(1), 23–27.

Fillenbaum, S. (1974). Information Amplified: Memory for Counterfactual Conditionals. *Journal of Experimental Psychology*, *102*(1), 44.

Fleischhut, N., Meder, B., and Gigerenzer, G. (2017). Moral Hindsight. *Experimental Psychology*, *64*, 110–123.

French Civil Aviation Safety Investigation Authority (2016). *Final Report*. www.bea.aero /uploads/tx_elydbrapports/BEA2015-0125.en-LR.pdf.

Frosch, C., and Byrne, R. M. J. (2012). Causal Conditionals and Counterfactuals. *Acta Psychologica*, *141*(1), 54–66.

Gilbert, E. A., Tenney, E. R., Holland, C. R., and Spellman, B. A. (2015). Counterfactuals, Control, and Causation Why Knowledgeable People Get Blamed More. *Personality and Social Psychology Bulletin*, *41*(5), 643–658.

Girotto, V., Legrenzi, P., and Rizzo, A. (1991). Event Controllability in Counterfactual Thinking. *Acta Psychologica*, *78*, 111–133.

Gomez Beldarrain, M., Garcia-Monco, J. C., Astigarraga, E., Gonzalez, A., and Grafman, J. (2005). Only Spontaneous Counterfactual Thinking Is Impaired in Patients with Prefrontal Cortex Lesions. *Cognition and Brain Research*, *24*(3), 723–726.

Guajardo, N. R., Parker, J., and Turley-Ames, K. (2009). Associations among False Belief Understanding, Counterfactual Reasoning, and Executive Function. *British Journal of Developmental Psychology*, *27*(3), 681–702.

Gubbins, E., and Byrne, R. M. J. (2014). Dual Processes of Emotion and Reason in Judgments about Moral Dilemmas. *Thinking and Reasoning*, *20*(2), 245–268.

Harris, P. L. (2000). *The Work of the Imagination*. Oxford, UK: Blackwell.

Johnson-Laird, P. N., and Byrne, R. M. J. (1995). A Model Point of View. *Thinking and Reasoning*, *1*(4), 339–350.

  (2002) Conditionals: A Theory of Meaning, Pragmatics, and Inference. *Psychological Review*, *109*, 646–678.

Juhos, C., Quelhas, A. C., and Byrne, R. M. J. (2015). Reasoning about Intentions: Counterexamples to Reasons for Actions. *Journal of Experimental Psychology: Learning, Memory & Cognition*, *41*(1), 55–76.

Kahneman, D, and Miller, D. T. (1986). Norm Theory: Comparing Reality to its Alternatives. *Psychological Review*, *93*(2), 136–153.

Kahneman, D, and Tversky A. (1982). The Simulation Heuristic. In D. Kahneman, P. Slovic, and A. Tversky (eds.), *Judgment Under Uncertainty: Heuristics and Biases.* New York, NY: Cambridge University Press, 201–208.

Khemlani, S., Johnson-Laird, P. N., and Byrne, R. M. J. (2018). Facts and Possibilities: A Model-Based Theory of Sentential Reasoning. *Cognitive Science, 42*(6), 1887–1924.

Lagnado, D. A., and Channon, S. (2008). Judgments of Cause and Blame: The Effects of Intentionality and Foreseeability. *Cognition, 108,* 754–770.

Lagnado, D. A., Gerstenberg, T., and Zultan, R. I. (2013). Causal Responsibility and Counterfactuals. *Cognitive Science, 37*(6), 1036–1073.

Lench, H. C., Domsky, D., Smallman, R., and Darbor, K. E. (2015). Beliefs in Moral Luck: When and Why Blame Hinges on Luck. *British Journal of Psychology, 106* (2), 272–287.

Lewis, D. (1973). *Counterfactuals.* Oxford, UK: Basil Blackwell.

Macrae, C. N., Milne, A. B., and Griffiths, R. J. (1993). Counterfactual Thinking and the Perception of Criminal Behaviour. *British Journal of Psychology, 84*(2), 221–226.

Malle, B. F., Guglielmo, S., and Monroe, A. E. (2014). A Theory of Blame. *Psychological Inquiry, 25*(2), 147–186.

Mandel, D. R., and Lehman, D. R. (1996). Counterfactual Thinking and Ascriptions of Cause and Preventability. *Journal of Personality and Social Psychology, 71*(3), 450–463.

Markman, K. D., McMullen, M. N, and Elizaga, R. A. (2008). Counterfactual Thinking, Persistence, and Performance: A Test of the Reflection and Evaluation Model. *Journal of Experimental Social Psychology, 44*(2), 421–428.

Markman, K. D., Mizoguchi, N., and McMullen, M. N. (2008). "It Would Have Been Worse under Saddam": Implications of Counterfactual Thinking for Beliefs Regarding the Ethical Treatment of Prisoners of War. *Journal of Experimental Social Psychology, 44*(3), 650–654.

Martin, J. W., and Cushman, F. A. (2016a). The Adaptive Logic of Moral Luck. In J. Sytsma and W. Buckwalter (eds.), *The Blackwell Companion to Experimental Philosophy.* Oxford, UK: Wiley Blackwell, 190–202.

(2016b). Why We Forgive What Can't Be Controlled. *Cognition, 147,* 133–143.

Martinez, J. (2002) Flight 587's Last Moments. *New York Daily News.* October 30.

McCloy, R., and Byrne, R. M. J. (2002). Semifactual "Even If" Thinking. *Thinking and Reasoning, 8*(1), 41–67.

(2000). Counterfactual Thinking about Controllable Events. *Memory & Cognition, 28*(6), 1071–1078.

McCormack, T., O'Connor, E., Beck, S., and Feeney, A. (2016). The Development of Regret and Relief about the Outcomes of Risky Decisions. *Journal of Experimental Child Psychology, 148,* 1–19.

McCrea, S. M. (2008). Self-Handicapping, Excuse Making, and Counterfactual Thinking: Consequences for Self-Esteem and Future Motivation. *Journal of Personality and Social Psychology, 95,* 274–292.

McEleney, A., and Byrne, R. M. J. (2006). Spontaneous Causal and Counterfactual Thoughts. *Thinking and Reasoning, 12,* 235–255.

Migliore, S., Curcio, G., Mancini, F., and Cappa, S. F. (2014). Counterfactual Thinking in Moral Judgment: An Experimental Study. *Frontiers in Psychology, 5,* 451.

Murray, D., and Lombrozo, T. (2016). Effects of Manipulation on Attributions of Causation, Free Will, and Moral Responsibility. *Cognitive Science*, *41*(2), 447–481.

National Transportation Safety Board (2004). NTSB Says Pilots Excessive Rudder Pedal Inputs Led to Crash of American Flight 587. *Press Release.* www.ntsb.gov/news/press-releases/Pages/NTSB_Says_Pilots_Excessive_Rudder_Pedal_Inputs_Led_to_Crash_of_American_Flight_587;_Airbus_Rudder_System_Design_Amp;_Eleme.aspx.

N'gbala, A., and Branscombe, N. R. (1995). Mental Simulation and Causal Attribution: When Simulating an Event Does Not Affect Fault Assignment. *Journal of Experimental Social Psychology*, *31*, 139–162.

Parkinson, M., and Byrne, R. M. J. (2017). Counterfactual and Semifactual Thoughts in Moral Judgments about Failed Attempts to Harm. *Thinking and Reasoning*, *23*(4), 409–448.

(2018). Judgments of Moral Responsibility and Wrongness for Intentional and Accidental Harm and Purity Violations. *Quarterly Journal of Experimental Psychology*, *71*(3), 779–789.

Phillips, J., and Cushman, F. (2017). Morality constrains the default representation of what is possible. PNAS, *114*(18), 4649–4654.

Phillips, J., Luguri, J. B., and Knobe, J. (2015). Unifying Morality's Influence on Non-Moral Judgments: The Relevance of Alternative Possibilities. *Cognition*, *145*, 30–42.

Pighin S., Byrne R. M. J., Ferrante D., Gonzalez, M., and Girotto, V. (2011). Counterfactual Thoughts about Experienced, Observed, and Narrated Events. *Thinking and Reasoning*, *17*(2), 197–211.

Rasga, C., Quelhas, A. C., and Byrne, R. M. J. (2016). Children's Reasoning about Other's Intentions: False-Belief and Counterfactual Conditional Inferences. *Cognitive Development*, *40*, 46–59.

(2017). How Children with Autism Reason about Other's Intentions: False-Belief and Counterfactual Inferences. *Journal of Autism and Developmental Disorders*, *47*(6), 1806–1817.

Rim, S., and Summerville, A. (2014). How Far to the Road Not Taken? The Effect of Psychological Distance on Counterfactual Direction. *Personality and Social Psychology Bulletin*, *40*(3), 391–401.

Roese, N. J., and Epstude, K. (2017). The Functional Theory of Counterfactual Thinking: New Evidence, New Challenges, New Insights. In J. M. Olson (ed.), *Advances in Experimental Social Psychology: Vol. 56. Advances in Experimental Social Psychology.* San Diego, CA: Academic Press, 1–79.

Santamaría, C., Espino, O., and Byrne, R.M.J. (2005). Counterfactual and Semifactual Conditionals Prime Alternative Possibilities. *Journal of Experimental Psychology: Learning, Memory and Cognition*, *31*, 1149–1154.

Segura, S., Fernandez-Berrocal, P., and Byrne, R. M. J. (2002). Temporal and Causal Order Effects in Thinking about What Might Have Been. *The Quarterly Journal of Experimental Psychology: Section A*, *55*(4), 1295–1305.

Smallman, R., and McCulloch, K. C. (2012). Learning from Yesterday's Mistakes to Fix Tomorrow's Problems: When Functional Counterfactual Thinking and Psychological Distance Collide. *European Journal of Social Psychology*, *42*(3), 383–390.

Stalnaker, R. C. (1968). A Theory of Conditionals. In N. Rescher (ed.), *Studies in Logical Theory.* Oxford, UK: Basil Blackwell.

Tasso, A., Sarlo, M., and Lotto, L. (2017). Emotions Associated with Counterfactual Comparisons Drive Decision-Making in Footbridge-Type Moral Dilemmas. *Motivation and Emotion*, *41*(3), 410–418.

Thompson, V., and Byrne, R. M. J. (2002). Reasoning Counterfactually: Making Inferences about Things That Didn't Happen. *Journal of Experimental Psychology: Learning, Memory & Cognition*, *28*, 1154–1170.

Timmons, S., and Byrne, R. M. J. (2018). Moral Fatigue: The Effects of Cognitive Fatigue on Moral Reasoning. *Quarterly Journal of Experimental Psychology*, *72*(4), 943–954.

Timmons, S., Gubbins, E., Almeida, T. & Byrne, R.M.J. (2019). Imagined Alternatives to Episodic Memories of Morally Good Acts. *Journal of Positive Psychology*. DOI: 10.1080/17439760.2019.1689410

Wald, M. L (2004). Investigators Fault Co-Pilot's Actions in Crash That Killed 265. *New York Times*. October 26. www.nytimes.com/2004/10/26/nyregion/investigators-fault-copilots-actions-in-crash-that-killed-265.html?_r=0.

van Hoeck, N., Begtas, E., Steen, J., et al. (2014). False Belief and Counterfactual Reasoning in a Social Environment. *NeuroImage*, 90, 315–325.

Walsh, C. R., and Byrne, R. M. J. (2007). How People Think "If Only . . ." About Reasons for Actions. *Thinking and Reasoning*, *13*(4), 461–483.

  (2004). Counterfactual Thinking: The Temporal Order Effect. *Memory & Cognition*, *32*, 369–378.

Young, L., and Phillips, J. (2011). The Paradox of Moral Focus. *Cognition*, *119*(2), 166–178.

Young, L., and Saxe, R. (2011). When Ignorance Is No Excuse: Different Roles for Intent across Moral Domains. *Cognition*, *120*(2), 202–214.

Young, L., and Tsoi, L. (2013). When Mental States Matter, When They Don't, and What That Means for Morality. *Social and Personality Psychology Compass*, *7*(8), 585–604.

33 A Look Back at Pioneering Theories of the Creative Brain

Rex E. Jung

Imagination is funny
It makes a cloudy day sunny
Makes a bee think of honey
Just as I think of you

Imagination is crazy
Your whole perspective gets hazy
Starts you asking a daisy
"What to do, what to do?"

Have you ever felt
A gentle touch and then a kiss
And then and then and then and then
Find it's only your imagination again?
Oh, well

Imagination is silly
You go around willy-nilly
For example, I go around wanting you
And yet I can't imagine
That you want me, too

Written by Anka Wolbert/Ronnie Moerings
(although you might imagine it being sung by Ella Fitzgerald)

When I blundered into the field of creativity neuroscience in 2007, I had little idea what I was getting into. My area of research had been intelligence for well over a decade, extending to my graduate studies where we had been fortunate enough to be early in linking measures of neuroimaging – including magnetic resonance spectroscopy, voxel-based morphometry, and cortical thickness (Haier et al, 2004; Jung et al., 1999; Karama et al., 2011) – to that vexing construct (IQ) that no one seems to really like, but all acknowledge to be important, giving it pseudonyms such as "reasoning," "higher cognitive functioning" and the like, to placate funding sources and the public at large.

Definitions of intelligence run on for paragraphs at a time, reminiscent of a very bad dinner date, involving: "understand(ing) complex ideas, adapt(ing) effectively to the environment, learn(ing) from experience, engag(ing) in various forms of reasoning, and overcom(ing) obstacles by taking thought" (Neisser et al., 1996: 77). This definition seems vaguely unfalsifiable by its expansive inclusivity. Given my early focus on the white matter of the brain, I had come to think of intelligence in a rather simple, binary, framework: *rapid and accurate problem-solving*. Indeed, this framework could be applied across species from low to high, and across time from the Cambrian to last week: If you solve problems too slowly, you die; if you solve them inaccurately, you also die. It is the dynamic interplay of speed and accuracy (some psychologists call this "power") that constrains success, just as the white and gray matter are viewed to facilitate their implementation (respectively). It is a dynamic behavioral balance undertaken by the brain as it interacts with environmental challenges. This definition is testable and falsifiable.

We have had much success in the neuroscience of intelligence over the years, moving the field from the dark and disreputable practice of craniometry and eugenics to a more sober assessment of the role that brain structure and function plays in the manifestation of intelligent behavior in humans (Jung and Haier, 2007) and other higher animals (Emery and Clayton, 2004). I was unsatisfied, however. Take that last reference for example: "The Mentality of Crows." Those authors note in their abstract (Emery and Clayton, 2004: 1903) that "complex cognition depends on a 'tool kit' consisting of causal reasoning, flexibility, imagination, and prospection." Could it be that intelligence was not all that I had been told? Could things like flexibility, imagination, prospection, be providing some extra bang for the evolutionary buck? Where would I find this thing that looks like cognitive flexibility, imagination, and prospection, in human behavior?

There was this silly field of creativity, which had been rumbling along for some 50 plus years, with its uses for bricks, and connecting 9 dots with four lines, and thumbtacking candles to a wall. But they had that definition: "novel and useful problem solving" (Stein, 1953). It seems even the earliest measure of intelligence, invented by Alfred Binet, included measures of creativity, although these had been abandoned in subsequent adaptations (Binet, 1905). For example, "synthesis of three words in one sentence" is described as a "test in spontaneity, facility of invention and combination, aptitude to construct sentences" (Binet, 1905: 65). A subject is given three words – say, Paris, River, Fortune – and asked to combine these into a sentence of their choosing. Intelligence and creativity have been entangled with one another from the very beginning. So, from the world of "rapid and accurate" problem-solving, I ventured into the world of "novel and useful" problem-solving.

As I had hoped, there were few players in the field, with the usual cast of soothsayers, rogues, and zealots that characterizes a new discipline (or religion). Some very good work was also being done by a few brave souls. Roland Grabner and Andreas Fink were vigorously exploring the limits and reach of measures of divergent thinking using Electroencephalography (EEG) (Fink et al., 2006, 2007; Fink and Neubauer, 2006; Grabner, Fink, and Neubauer, 2007). Mark Beeman had established neural correlates of verbal insight and metaphor with EEG and functional Magnetic Resonance Imaging (fMRI) (Jung-Beeman et al., 2004; Mashal et al., 2007). And three brilliant, groundbreaking reviews existed, trying to assemble some coherence around the diaspora of efforts that characterized the field (Dietrich, 2004; Flaherty, 2005; Heilman, Nadeau, and Beversdorf, 2003). To my eye, it looked like there were only a half dozen labs doing consistent work in creativity, scattered across Russia (Razumnikova, Bekhtereva), Austria (Fink), and the United States (Heilman,

Jung-Beeman). No work had been done in structural correlates of creativity. No one appreciated the possible neural links between intelligence and creativity via fundamental reasoning processes. The time was ripe for the emergence of a neuroscience of creativity.

So what sort of reasoning ability would creativity comprise? It is not rapid, and it is often inaccurate (i.e. trial and error); thus, it can be distinguished from intelligence. It is slower and more meandering. It is contemplative, emergent, and communal where intelligence is certain, factual, and individual. It involves imagination – leading to novelty generation – resulting in a creative product found useful to the world. Creativity does not happen in the brain *per se*, but the processes that lead to its emergence can be understood through brain processes, particularly imagination, novelty generation, and selection of a useful path to pursue in the world. I have argued elsewhere that particular brain networks are central to the informed guesses that progress increasingly toward probable solutions in a back-and-forth neural network akin to the incubation and verification phases of creativity described by Helmholtz, Wallace, and Campbell (Jung et al., 2013). The Default Mode Network (DMN) has emerged as a major player in creative cognition, with its role being essential to the novelty generation central to the "Blind Variation" part of the "Blind Variation Selective Retention (BVSR)" theory put forth by Donald Campbell (Campbell, 1960).

There are those who will tell you that the field of creativity is hopeless, that we are lost in our delusions of localizing creativity in the brain, and that there is no mental phenomena about which we know so little. These cries from the wilderness are becoming increasingly implausible in light of the mounting – indeed overwhelming – evidence supporting a coherent neuroscience of creative cognition with testable theories. What once was a diaspora of disconnected laboratories, studying creative cognition with few tools, now represents dozens of labs keenly focused on studying various aspects of creativity, using techniques ranging from pharmacological interventions (Hecht et al., 2014), neuroimaging (Beaty et al., 2015), genetics (Liu et al., 2018), exogenous neural stimulation (Green et al., 2017), and computational modelling (Kenett et al., 2018). Let me tell you where we now stand some ten years after my haphazard entry into the fray.

There were three early theorists in the field of creativity, namely Ken Heilman (a neurologist), Arne Dietrich (a cognitive neuroscientist), and Alice Flaherty (a psychiatrist). These three came at the problem of how creative cognition was manifested in the brain from very different perspectives – Heilman was largely informed by brain structure and function, Flaherty by neurochemical perspectives, and Dietrich by cognitive constructs. The theories were very different from one another with very little overlap – reflective of the disparate perspectives from which they derived, but also reflecting the rather inchoate stage of research that had been undertaken to date. Indeed, in 2007, there were only some 200 or so research articles involving creativity and the brain to inform such theorizing (there are now more than 750, in 2018). For some perspective, only three studies at that time had utilized fMRI (Goel and Vartanian, 2005; Howard-Jones et al., 2005; Jung-Beeman et al., 2004). These theories are worth reviewing both for their differences in perspective as well as their sheer gumption in putting some skin in the game well before the data could support such notions. None of the three explicitly mention imagination.

Ken Heilman and Early Hints of Frontal Lobe Network Dynamics

Ken Heilman is a hero to most neuropsychologists, who regard him as one of the founders of our field (Heilman and Valenstein, 2012). In his review, he makes note of the many great innovators – such as Einstein and Picasso – who needed to prepare their minds before making a great advance, noting that the prepared mind is best able to perceive the importance of an observed anomaly. He acknowledges that preparation and verification are key components of the creative process, but that incubation and illumination "have received much criticism," (e.g. creativity does not require great leaps; creativity often involves the culmination of conscious as opposed to unconscious steps) choosing instead to convolve these into the term "creative innovation." He acknowledges the relationship between creativity and IQ (weak), and that there has been found a threshold (around 120) beyond which increased intelligence does not yield increased creativity – our group subsequently supported this notion with neuroimaging data (Jung et al., 2009).

Then he begins theorizing. First, he notes that a corollary to Hebb's hypothesis (i.e. neurons that fire together wire together) would imply "that the more neurons with which a person is endowed, the greater their ability to learn and store knowledge. Thus, a person with high levels of knowledge might have more neurons in the brain region that stores these representations and this could be reflected in the size of this region" (Heilman, Nadeau, and Beversdorf, 2003: 372). This happens to be a prescient hypothesis, which our work and the work of others helped direct towards the field of creative cognition in structural studies over subsequent years (Jung et al., 2013). Similarly, he notes that:

> ... the frontal lobes are important for disengagement and developing alternating strategies (divergent thinking) ... The frontal lobes have strong connections to the polymodal and supramodal regions of the temporal and parietal lobes (Pandya and Kuypers, 1969). Perhaps these connections are important for inhibiting the activated networks that store semantically similar information while exciting or activating the semantic conceptual networks that have been only weakly activated or not activated at all. Support for the postulate that the frontal lobe might be important in either activating of inhibiting semantic networks comes from a recent study, using positron emission tomography (PET), that suggested different roles for medial and lateral rostral prefrontal cortex (Brodmann's area 10), with the former involved in suppressing internally-generated thought and the latter in maintaining them (Burgess et al., 2003) (Heilman, Nadeau, and Beversdorf, 2003: 373).

How did Dr. Heilman do with respect to his theorizing regarding creative cognition? He is right to note that preparation and verification are more tractable to scientific inquiry, with incubation and illumination being much more difficult to discern reliably. Indeed, a recent meta-analysis appears to indicate that creative insight is task specific, with measures of compound remote associates being localized to the right parahippocampal, right superior frontal, and right inferior frontal gyrus, and other measures of insight (i.e. prototype heuristic, Chinese character chunk decomposition) being localized to completely different, non-overlapping regions of the brain (Shen et al., 2016). Other aspects of his notion of creative innovation appear to have, at least partially, been taken up within the neurosciences, with rather dramatic progress being made with respect to concepts of suppressing internally generated thought and/or maintaining these thoughts in service of creative cognition. This notion corresponds well to the downregulation of the Executive Control Network, first described in improvisational jazz musicians (Limb and Braun, 2008), then supported by structural neuroimaging studies (Jung et al., 2013), and finally confirmed in complex network dynamics (Beaty et al., 2015). Heilman was extremely prescient in his theorizing about creative cognition.

Arne Dietrich – Some Organizing Principles, and Specific Predictions

Dr. Dietrich comes at the problem of creativity from the perspective that it has been poorly researched (e.g. "little is known about the brain mechanisms that underlie creative thinking" – Dietrich, 2004: 1011), disconnected from modern brain research (e.g. "the findings of modern brain research have not been incorporated into research on creativity" Dietrich, 2004: 1011), and methodologically lacking (e.g. "due to the lack of communication between neuroscience and creativity research, none of these psychometric measures – divergent thinking, candle problem, remote associates test – has been used in combination with functional neuroimaging tools, optical imaging tools, transcranial magnetic stimulation, or EEG equipment" – Dietrich, 2004: 1022). These are strong statements, and a quick scan of the literature prior to this paper's publication in 2004 can refute all of them readily: (Carlsson, Wendt, and Risberg, 2000; Heilman, Nadeau, and Beversdorf, 2003; Jaušovec, 2000; Jones-Gotman and Milner, 1977; Martindale and Greenough, 1973; Martindale and Hasenfus, 1978; Miller et al., 1998; Mölle et al., 1996; Petsche, 1996). In spite of these quibbles, I found the rest of the article to be inspired.

The most important admonition offered is one that is true of most complex cognitive constructs, but especially so for creativity: "The capacity to identify the brain areas that are recruited during normative information processing, coupled with the data that suggest that creative thinking is the result of ordinary mental processes, forms the foundation for the framework of creativity proposed in this article" (Dietrich, 2004: 1011). Dietrich then goes on to give some much-needed structural organization to a field that was sorely lacking it, for want of some tractable cognitive boxes within which to work outward. He lays out the functional and structural organization of the prefrontal cortex, noting distinctions between the ventromedial prefrontal cortex (VMPFC) and dorsolateral prefrontal cortex (DLPFC) although his dichotomy emphasized emotional processing of the former (with its high connectivity to the limbic system) as opposed to more cognitive processing of the latter (with its connectivity to other cortical regions including temporal, occipital, and parietal lobes). "Creativity is the epitome of cognitive flexibility," therefore the prefrontal cortex must be critical to creative cognition; however, it should not be seen as the seat of creativity by any stretch of the imagination (no pun intended). "Rather, the prefrontal cortex contributes highly integrative computations to the conscious experience, which enables novel combinations of information to be recognized as such and then appropriately applied to works of art and science" (Dietrich, 2004: 1011–1012). So far so good.

Dietrich goes on to outline four basic types of creative cognition on two major axes: Processing modes can be either deliberate or spontaneous; knowledge domains are comprised of emotional and cognitive. Harkening back to Helmholtz, both anecdotal and experimental evidence has noted that creative ideas can emerge either deliberately, through trial and error and rational thought, or seemingly effortlessly – via flashes of insight – sometimes through dreams, reveries, under the influence of drugs, or even psychopathology. At one extreme is the obsessive trial and error of an Edison, while at the other is Kekule's (apocryphal) daydream of a snake swallowing its own tail, and the (purported) insight of the chemical structure of a benzene ring. On the other axis are emotional and cognitive knowledge domains, with the arts residing more on the emotional axis, and the sciences on the cognitive – however, Dietrich remarks that "creative works arise naturally from a mix of these four basic components" (Dietrich, 2004: 1018) and that no individual is stuck in a particular box.

Various predictions are made. For example, the deliberate-cognitive mode would imply that "frontal attentional network(s) (are) recruited to search for task-relevant information in the TOP" (temporal, occipital, parietal lobes) (Dietrich, 2004: 1018). Analogously, creativity within the deliberate-emotional zone would imply that attentional resources search affective memory for stored emotional structures. He mentions regions including the amygdala, cingulate, VMPFC, and DLPFC in relation to processing this type of information, with the amygdala interacting with the VMPFC in providing input of basic emotions, while the VMPFC, cingulate, and DLPFC process more complex social emotions. Spontaneous-cognitive modes of thought more clearly appear to be associated with downregulating frontal attentional systems via the DLPFC – a process most associated with incubation and the emergence of spontaneous insight. The spontaneous-emotional mode occurs "when the neural activity of structures that process emotional information is spontaneously represented in working memory" (Dietrich, 2004: 1019). In his future research section, he notes that many creativity tests – such as the Remote Associates Test (RAT), and candle problem, involve deliberate and innovative problem-solving. "The framework predicts these tests to be associated primarily with the activation of the DLPFC regions but not the VMPFC or TOP regions" (Dietrich, 2004: 1022). Torrance tests of divergent thinking on the other hand, being open ended, would be associated with "primarily the activation of the TOP regions more than the DLPFC regions" (Dietrich, 2004: 1022).

How did Dr. Dietrich do with respect to his theorizing regarding creative cognition? There is no disputing the central role of the prefrontal cortex in creative cognition, particularly in upregulating attentional functioning during more deliberate creative processing, and downregulating attentional functioning during more spontaneous processing in a manner consistent with "transient hypofrontality" (Dietrich, 2003). This has been borne out, in particular, by functional work by Limb and Braun (and others), showing transient downregulation of DLPFC during improvizational music production (and poetry composition), with corresponding increased activity within VMPFC, which could also correspond to heightened emotional processing (as predicted) (Limb and Braun, 2008; Liu et al., 2012, 2015).

With regard to his more specific hypotheses regarding activations associated with creativity tests, the record is mixed. In a large meta-analysis of insightful problem-solving, including four studies of compound remote associates (CRA) (Shen et al., 2016), activations were noted within right parahippocampal, right superior frontal, and right inferior frontal regions. These authors suggest (Shen et al., 2016: 87) that this network is associated with "a plan for top-down activation of semantic fields relevant to the problem at hand" (Binder and Desai, 2011) although significant parahippocampal activations would suggest "the formation of contextual associations compared to non-contextual associations." (Aminoff, Gronau, and Bar, 2007). So a lot of right DLPFC and a fair amount of "T" from TOP. With respect to divergent thinking, a recent meta-analysis (Wu et al., 2015) found more activation within bilateral DLPFC than TOP (BA 46), counter to predictions, with additional activations within anterior cingulate (BA 32), posterior parietal (BA 7 and 40), left frontal (BA 37), and middle temporal gyri (BA 39). Like anything in the brain, it is a more complex story than we could ever have imagined; however, Dietrich should be commended for putting hypotheses forward well before much of the neuroimaging data was available to populate such bold predictions.

Alice Flaherty – A Fully Formed, Testable Theory (Largely Ignored)

Finally, Flaherty notes that interest in creativity research is growing, the definition "captures the cultural relativity" spanning across both ancient and modern civilizations, and that behavioral tests now exist with good interrater reliability and predictability. She makes a unique contribution: noting that the last major theory of creativity regarded hemispheric lateralization (i.e. the so-called right-hemisphere locus – Bogen and Bogen, 1988), but that these notions failed to recognize the role of language-based innovations. Moreover, subsequent research utilizing EEG showed that both hemispheres were critical in producing creative cognition (Martindale, 1999). Her goal was to shift the focus away from the predominant left-right axis, to a fronto-temporal (and limbic) model. Her focus was on creative drive, with psychiatric and neurological syndromes providing case examples of either increased or decreased drive states leading to testable hypotheses. She succeeds magnificently.

Flaherty discusses numerous neurological and psychiatric syndromes within the context of creative drive. For example, hypergraphia (the compulsive drive to write), has been localized to abnormalities within the temporal lobe – usually epilepsy – (Waxman and Geschwind, 1974), with decreased right temporal activity hypothesized to disinhibit the left, language-dominant lobe in a manner usually under more symmetric (mutually inhibitory) control (Yamadori et al., 1986). Temporal lobe changes measured with EEG, fMRI, and PET have also been associated with increased behavioral output including hypomania, pressured speech, and pressured writing (see Table 1 in Flaherty, 2005: 149). Perhaps most interesting to creativity researchers is a subset of frontotemporal dementia patients who developed creative or artistic tendencies, even without pre-existing talent or interest (Miller et al., 1998). Flaherty asks rhetorically (Flaherty, 2005: 148): "Is the temporal lobe, then, the seat of creativity?" Not so fast.

Flaherty next notes that creative drive can vastly improve creative skill, with Darwinian theories of creativity reflecting a Gaussian distribution of quantity and quality of creative ideas (Simonton, 2003). The driver of this creative engine, according to Flaherty, could be mesolimbic dopaminergic activity. She notes that dopamine mediates reward seeking activity, triggers the drive to communicate, and can cause excessively focused, highly complex motor stereotypies (e.g. repeatedly disassembling and reassembling a motorcycle engine) (Fernandez and Friedman, 1999). Dopamine antagonists, used to suppress hallucinations in schizophrenia, also reduce free associations and neologisms known to be associated with creative cognition. She notes that "one possible mechanism for dopamine's role in focused reward-seeking behavior is a center-surround inhibition model . . . (in which) dopamine facilitates voluntary, goal-directed activity and inhibits competing behaviors" (Flaherty, 2005: 150) (Mink, 1996).

Finally, the frontal lobes make their inevitable entry to the hypothetical fray, but in a very interesting way. Flaherty conceptualizes the frontal and temporal lobes as "mutually inhibitory," and therefore in a rather delicate balance that, when disrupted, leads to disorders ranging from depression (frontal lesion), writer's block (frontal dysfunction), hypergraphia (temporal lobe lesion), and the like. This is an important concept for creativity researchers (and was for me when entering the field): Namely, that there will not likely be a locus or region *per se* associated with creative cognition, but rather that brain regions would be working in dynamic opposition in excitatory and inhibitory networks. Lesions within a network can unmask creativity in unusual ways (see frontotemporal dementia); however, the subtle increases and decreases of cortical neurons, white matter connectivity, and even neurotransmitter activity would be a much more interesting story than a locus of creative cognition. She had it just right – a network of mutually cooperative regions throughout the brain were working in tandem to inform creative cognition. Her regions were frontal, temporal, and limbic, which were good first approximations based on the neurological, pharmacological, and neuroanatomical correlates of creative cognition.

But then she says this: "Lesions of medial prefrontal cortex can produce amotivational, abulic states of decreased creative drive. Dorsolateral prefrontal cortex's importance for working memory and flexible problem-solving suggests a greater role in creative skill than in drive" (Flaherty, 2005: 151). Compare this to the most recent theorizing on how creative cognition is manifested in the brain (Beaty et al., 2016): "We suggest that the default network contributes to the generation of candidate ideas (potentially useful information derived from long-term memory) in light of its role in self-generated cognition (e.g. episodic memory). Yet, the control network is often required to evaluate the efficacy of candidate ideas and modify them to meet the constraints of task-specific goals." It is my opinion that Flaherty was precisely on the right track in her focus on the interplay between medial and dorsolateral prefrontal cortex in constraining creative drive and creative skill (respectively), and as dozens of subsequent studies supported. She acknowledges, in an appropriately humble aside that "these hypotheses are oversimplified," but that testing these theories "may prepare the way for the rigorous neuroscientific studies of creativity that are greatly needed" (Flaherty, 2005: 152). Indeed.

Looking Forward, Looking Back

We should not forget that a few brave souls were putting forth theories regarding how creative cognition was manifested in the brain well before much neuroscientific research had been done. They were using their raw thinking power to reason out how creative cognition *should* look based on the data at hand, be it from patients, neuroscientific research, or anecdote. They were pioneers in a field that sorely needed guidance. Now we have the benefit of hindsight to see how right (or wrong) they were, but that is not really the point. We now have new theories, steeped in research and the confidence of masses of data accumulated over time. The data is coalescing around a consensus that appears to implicate large-scale brain networks including (of course) the frontal lobes, but also regions within the parietal and temporal lobes, that were only hinted at in previous theories. This reminds me of the incredible confidence expressed by many prominent researchers regarding the primacy of the frontal lobes as the "seat" of intelligence in humans, before the Parieto-Frontal Integration Theory of Intelligence emerged (Jung and Haier, 2007).

Alas, no theories mentioned (but many hinted at) the importance of imagination in creativity, an oversight since ameliorated by Anna Abraham (Abraham, 2016). She notes that much work in the neurosciences work under the S-O-R model: *stimuli* are perceived by *organisms* who generate *responses*. What about internally generated thought – what my former mentor Leonard Giambra called Task Unrelated Thoughts (TUTs) (Giambra, 1995). These internal thoughts are of increasing interest to the neurosciences, as they appear to be relevant to a wide range of behaviors including (but not limited) to: mental rotation, moral decision-making, creativity, aesthetic response, meditative states, and delusions. There are a host of internal states that are worth pursuing, with mental imagery holding the lion's share of research within the neurosciences, and nearly nothing known about altered states of imagination. Abraham defines imagination as "representation of conceptual content in the absence of external input" (Abraham, 2016: 3), noting that this definition is somewhat imprecise given the ability to maintain rules in working memory in the absence of sensory perception.

There is a pronounced two-axis representation regarding imagination ability that has largely been missing from our discussion of creativity, namely medial (Default Mode Network – DMN) to lateral (Executive Control Network – ECN) and parietal to frontal lobes. Internal representations (i.e. imaginations) for which action or judgment is not required are represented in more medial brain structures and structures drawing from sensory and association cortices within temporal, occipital, and parietal (TOP) lobes. Imagination with action or judgment requires additional representation from the salience network (particularly the anterior insula), and lateral frontal lobes (ECN). Imagination could very well be the driver of the engine in the "novelty" part of the creativity definition, with increasing levels of action, judgment, and evaluation providing constraint mediated by executive control networks. Indeed, in our examination of the brain correlates of imagination, we note that imagination has been thought to be "a critical mediating linkage between acquired knowledge and creative insight, constraining the possible solutions through mental simulations or 'incubation.'" (Jung, Flores, and Hunter, 2016: 2). Our research found significant overlap between imagination ability and decreased volume within regions of the DMN associated with novelty generation, including the precuneus, posterior cingulate, and transverse temporal lobe, supporting interaction between imagination and novelty generation aspects of creative cognition.

There are five main domains within the imagination taxonomy (Abraham, 2016), each involving largely different but sometimes overlapping/interacting brain networks. For example, mental imagery-based imagination has a decidedly sensory/motor representation in the brain, with visual, auditory, and sensory modalities activating primary and secondary cortical structures (TOP), with a modality independent core residing within the DMN (Daselaar et al., 2010). Intentionally based imagination – more commonly known as reminiscing, daydreaming, or running mental simulations – clearly activates the DMN, with numerous researchers supporting this notion (Mak et al., 2017). Creative cognition involves a complex interplay of the DMN, semantic, and ECN as discussed previously, with generative modes (i.e. imagination) being more associated with DMN function and evaluation with ECN (Jung et al., 2013). Aesthetic engagement (phenomenology-based imagination) has consistently been found to engage the anterior insula (Vartanian and Skov, 2014). Altered states of imagination change connectivity between key nodes of the brain, particularly the DMN and ECN, although results vary depending upon whether subjects are dreaming, undergoing hypnosis, meditating, or taking psychedelics. Abraham concludes with cautionary remarks regarding the specificity of these five categories, noting that they work in dynamic interplay with one another, and that a hierarchical structure is likely (i.e. mental imagery accompanies all other imagination types). She notes that little research has been done in imagination proper, and that "it is time to bring it center stage" (Abraham, 2016: 4208). Her taxonomy also provides a nice path forward for researchers in creative cognition, who might suffer from delusions that the question of how creativity "works" in the brain has been largely solved.

Final Words

Creativity research has come far in the last ten years since I entered the field and read the theories of three pioneers in the field: Heilman, Dietrich, and Flaherty.

All of these researchers noted the importance of the frontal lobes to creative cognition. All lamented the rather limited neuroimaging research that had been directed toward creative cognition to date (2003–2005). Since 2005, at least 300 articles have been written specifically on creativity (in title) using neuroimaging techniques including EEG, fMRI, tDCS, and structural neuroimaging. The field has expanded dramatically from a handful of labs limited to Russia, North America, and Germany, to several dozen laboratories spread across all continents of the world (save Antarctica). The field has a coherent theory regarding the interaction of the DMN, ECN, and SN in the expression of novelty generation and evaluation of utility components of creative cognition (Beaty et al., 2015). And yet, something feels unfinished.

Creativity research spent nearly fifty years in the wilderness, following J. P. Guilford's call for a research program in the psychometrics of creativity to the American Psychological Association (Guilford, 1950). While scholars developed a psychometric test of divergent thinking, research appeared to languish once such measures were arrived upon. Creativity is not divergent thinking, nor is it insight, nor is it imagination. However, if there is one cognitive construct that might separate human progress from that of other higher mammals it very likely involves the singular capacity of imagination. What did humans do during the long winters once they had migrated far north, out of more temperate zones? Did they imagine how they might use a tool in a slightly different way so that there would be more food in the larder during the winter? Did they invent songs, and dance, and games to keep occupied when lack of light and heat required that they stay indoors? Did they tell stories of gods and heroes? What role did this imaginative ability play in the development of the written word to transmit information, memories, and accumulated knowledge with much higher fidelity, speed, and breadth? These questions remain unanswered in both evolutionary and creative circles. Understanding the "creative" in imagination could very likely be the key cognitive component allowing research to progress beyond our recent gains in the domain of creativity (Jung and Vartanian, 2018).

References

Abraham, A. (2016). The Imaginative Mind. *Human Brain Mapping*, *37*(11), 4197–4211. doi:10.1002/hbm.23300.

Aminoff, E., Gronau, N., and Bar, M. (2007). The Parahippocampal Cortex Mediates Spatial and Nonspatial Associations. *Cerebral Cortex*, *17*(7), 1493–1503. doi:10.1093/cercor/bhl078.

Beaty, R. E., Benedek, M., Kaufman, S. B., and Silvia, P. J. (2015). Default and Executive Network Coupling Supports Creative Idea Production. *Scientific Reports*, *5*, 10964. doi:10.1038/srep10964.

Beaty, R. E., Benedek, M., Silvia, P. J., and Schacter, D. L. (2016). Creative Cognition and Brain Network Dynamics. *Trends in Cognitive Sciences*, *20*(2), 87–95. doi:10.1016/j.tics.2015.10.004.

Binder, J. R., and Desai, R. H. (2011). The Neurobiology of Semantic Memory. *Trends in Cognitive Sciences*, *15*(11), 527–536. doi:10.1016/j.tics.2011.10.001.

Binet, A. (1905). New Methods for the Diagnosis of the Intellectual Level of Subnormals. *L'Année Psychologique*, *12*, 191–244.

Bogen, J. E., and Bogen, G. M. (1988). Creativity and the Corpus Callosum. *Psychiatric Clinics of North America*, *11*(3), 293–301.

Campbell, D. T. (1960). Blind Variation and Selective Retention in Creative Thought as in Other Knowledge Processes. *Psychological Review*, *67*(6), 380–400. doi:Doi 10.1037/H0040373.

Carlsson, I., Wendt, P. E., and Risberg, J. (2000). On the Neurobiology of Creativity: Differences in Frontal Activity between High and Low Creative Subjects. *Neuropsychologia*, *38*, 873–885.

Daselaar, S. M., Porat, Y., Huijbers, W., and Pennartz, C. M. (2010). Modality-Specific and Modality-Independent Components of the Human Imagery System. *Neuroimage*, *52*(2), 677–685. doi:10.1016/j.neuroimage.2010.04.239.

Dietrich, A. (2003). Functional Neuroanatomy of Altered States of Consciousness: The Transient Hypofrontality Hypothesis. *Consciousness and Cognition*, *12*, 231–256.

(2004). The Cognitive Neuroscience of Creativity. *Psychonomic Bulletin & Review*, *11*, 1011–1026.

Emery, N. J., and Clayton, N. S. (2004). The Mentality of Crows: Convergent Evolution of Intelligence in Corvids and Apes. *Science*, *306*(5703), 1903–1907. doi:10.1126/science.1098410.

Fernandez, H. H., and Friedman, J. H. (1999). Punding on L-dopa. *Movement Disorders*, *14*(5), 836–838.

Fink, A., Benedek, M., Grabner, R. H., Staudt, B., and Neubauer, A. C. (2007). Creativity Meets Neuroscience: Experimental Tasks for the Neuroscientific Study of Creative Thinking. *Methods*, *42*, 68–76.

Fink, A., Grabner, R. H., Benedek, M., and Neubauer, A. C. (2006). Divergent Thinking Training Is Related to Frontal Electroencephalogram Alpha Synchronization. *The European Journal of Neuroscience*, *23*, 2241–2246.

Fink, A., and Neubauer, A. C. (2006). EEG Alpha Oscillations during the Performance of Verbal Creativity Tasks: Differential Effects of Sex and Verbal Intelligence. *International Journal of Psychophysiology*, *62*, 46–53.

Flaherty, A. W. (2005). Frontotemporal and Dopaminergic Control of Idea Generation and Creative Drive. *Journal of Comparative Neurology*, *493*, 147–153.

Giambra, L. M. (1995). A Laboratory Method for Investigating Influences on Switching Attention to Task-Unrelated Imagery and Thought. *Consciousness and Cognition*, *4*(1), 1–21. doi:10.1006/ccog.1995.1001.

Goel, V., and Vartanian, O. (2005). Dissociating the Roles of Right Ventral Lateral and Dorsal Lateral Prefrontal Cortex in Generation and Maintenance of Hypotheses in Set-Shift Problems. *Cerebral Cortex*, *15*(8), 1170–1177. doi:10.1093/cercor/bhh217

Grabner, R. H., Fink, A., and Neubauer, A. C. (2007). Brain Correlates of Self-Rated Originality of Ideas: Evidence from Event-Related Power and Phase-Locking Changes in the EEG. *Behavioral Neuroscience*, *121*, 224.

Green, A. E., Spiegel, K. A., Giangrande, E. J., et al. (2017). Thinking Cap Plus Thinking Zap: tDCS of Frontopolar Cortex Improves Creative Analogical Reasoning and Facilitates Conscious Augmentation of State Creativity in Verb Generation. *Cerebral Cortex*, *27*(4), 2628–2639. doi:10.1093/cercor/bhw080.

Guilford, J. P. (1950). Creativity. *American Psychologist*, 5(9), 444–454.

Haier, R. J., Jung, R. E., Yeo, R. A., Head, K., and Alkire, M. T. (2004). Structural Brain Variation and General Intelligence. *Neuroimage*, 23(1), 425–433. doi:10.1016/J. Neuroimage.2004.04.025.

Hecht, P. M., Will, M. J., Schachtman, T. R., Welby, L. M., and Beversdorf, D. Q. (2014). Beta-Adrenergic Antagonist Effects on a Novel Cognitive Flexibility Task in Rodents. *Behavioral Brain Research*, 260, 148–154. doi:10.1016/j. bbr.2013.11.041.

Heilman, K. M., Nadeau, S. E., and Beversdorf, D. O. (2003). Creative Innovation: Possible Brain Mechanisms. *Neurocase*, 9(5), 369–379. doi:10.1076/neur.9.5.369.16553.

Heilman, K. M., and Valenstein, E. (2012). *Clinical Neuropsychology*. 5th edition. Oxford, UK: Oxford University Press.

Howard-Jones, P. A., Blakemore, S.-J., Samuel, E. A., Summers, I. R., and Claxton, G. (2005). Semantic Divergence and Creative Story Generation: An fMRI Investigation. *Cognitive Brain Research*, 25, 240–250.

Jaušovec, N. (2000). Differences in Cognitive Processes between Gifted, Intelligent, Creative, and Average Individuals while Solving Complex Problems: An EEG Study. *Intelligence*, 28, 213–237.

Jones-Gotman, M., and Milner, B. (1977). Design Fluency: The Invention of Nonsense Drawings after Focal Cortical Lesions. *Neuropsychologia*, 15(4–5), 653–674.

Jung, R. E., Brooks, W. M., Yeo, R. A., et al. (1999). Biochemical Markers of Intelligence: A Proton MR Spectroscopy Study of Normal Human Brain. *Proceedings of the Royal Society B-Biological Sciences*, 266(1426), 1375–1379.

Jung, R. E., Flores, R. A., and Hunter, D. (2016). A New Measure of Imagination Ability: Anatomical Brain Imaging Correlates. *Frontiers in Psychology*, 7, 496. doi:10.3389/fpsyg.2016.00496.

Jung, R. E., Gasparovic, C., Chavez, R. S., et al. (2009). Biochemical Support for the "Threshold" Theory of Creativity: A Magnetic Resonance Spectroscopy Study. *Journal of Neuroscience*, 29(16), 5319–5325. doi:10.1523/ Jneurosci.0588–09.2009.

Jung, R. E., and Haier, R. J. (2007). The Parieto-Frontal Integration Theory (P-FIT) of Intelligence: Converging Neuroimaging Evidence. *Behavioral and Brain Sciences*, 30(2), 135–154. doi:10.1017/S0140525x07001185.

Jung, R. E., Mead, B. S., Carrasco, J., and Flores, R. A. (2013). The Structure of Creative Cognition in the Human Brain. *Frontiers in Human Neuroscience*, 7. doi:Artn 330 Doi 10.3389/Fnhum.2013.00330.

Jung, R. E., and Vartanian, O. (2018). *The Cambridge Handbook of the Neuroscience of Creativity*: Cambridge, UK: Cambridge University Press.

Jung-Beeman, M., Bowden, E. M., Haberman, J., et al. (2004). Neural Activity When People Solve Verbal Problems with Insight. *PLoS Biology*, 2, e97.

Karama, S., Colom, R., Johnson, W., et al. (2011). Cortical Thickness Correlates of Specific Cognitive Performance Accounted for by the General Factor of Intelligence in Healthy Children Aged 6 to 18. *Neuroimage*, 55(4), 1443–1453. doi:10.1016/J. Neuroimage.2011.01.016.

Kenett, Y. N., Levy, O., Kenett, D. Y., et al. (2018). Flexibility of Thought in High Creative Individuals Represented by Percolation Analysis. *Proceedings of the National Academy of Sciences of the United States of America*, 115(5), 867–872. doi:10.1073/pnas.1717362115.

Limb, C. J., and Braun, A. R. (2008). Neural Substrates of Spontaneous Musical Performance: An FMRI Study of Jazz Improvisation. *PLoS One, 3*(2), e1679. doi:10.1371/journal. pone.0001679.

Liu, S., Chow, H. M., Xu, Y., et al. (2012). Neural Correlates of Lyrical Improvisation: An FMRI Study of Freestyle Rap. *Scientific Reports, 2*, 834. doi:10.1038/srep00834.

Liu, S., Erkkinen, M. G., Healey, M. L., et al. (2015). Brain Activity and Connectivity during Poetry Composition: Toward a Multidimensional Model of the Creative Process. *Human Brain Mapping.* doi:10.1002/hbm.22849.

Liu, Z., Zhang, J., Xie, X., et al. (2018). Neural and Genetic Determinants of Creativity. *Neuroimage, 174*, 164–176. doi:10.1016/j.neuroimage.2018.02.067.

Mak, L. E., Minuzzi, L., MacQueen, G., et al. (2017). The Default Mode Network in Healthy Individuals: A Systematic Review and Meta-Analysis. *Brain Connect, 7*(1), 25–33. doi:10.1089/brain.2016.0438.

Martindale, C. (1999). Biological Bases of Creativity. In R. J. Sternberg (ed.), *Handbook of Creativity.* New York, NY: Cambridge University Press, 137–152.

Martindale, C., and Greenough, J. (1973). The Differential Effect of Increased Arousal on Creative and Intellectual Performance. *The Journal of Genetic Psychology, 123*, 329–335.

Martindale, C., and Hasenfus, N. (1978). EEG Differences as a Function of Creativity, Stage of the Creative Process, and Effort to Be Original. *Biological Psychology, 6*, 157–167.

Mashal, N., Faust, M., Hendler, T., and Jung-Beeman, M. (2007). An fMRI Investigation of the Neural Correlates Underlying the Processing of Novel Metaphoric Expressions. *Brain and Language, 100*, 115–126.

Miller, B. L., Cummings, J., Mishkin, F., et al. (1998). Emergence of Artistic Talent in Frontotemporal Dementia. *Neurology, 51*, 978–982.

Mink, J. W. (1996). The Basal Ganglia: Focused Selection and Inhibition of Competing Motor Programs. *Progress in Neurobiology, 50*(4), 381–425.

Mölle, M., Marshall, L., Lutzenberger, W., et al. (1996). Enhanced Dynamic Complexity in the Human EEG during Creative Thinking. *Neuroscience Letters, 208*, 61–64.

Neisser, U., Boodoo, G., Bouchard Jr, T. J., et al. (1996). Intelligence: Knowns and Unknowns. *American Psychologist, 51*, 77.

Petsche, H. (1996). Approaches to Verbal, Visual and Musical Creativity by EEG Coherence Analysis. *International Journal of Psychophysiology, 24*, 145–159.

Shen, W., Yuan, Y., Liu, C., et al. (2016). Is Creative Insight Task-Specific? A Coordinate-Based Meta-Analysis of Neuroimaging Studies on Insightful Problem Solving. *International Journal of Psychophysiology, 110*, 81–90. doi:10.1016/j. ijpsycho.2016.10.001.

Simonton, D. K. (2003). Scientific Creativity as Constrained Stochastic Behavior: The Integration of Product, Person, and Process Perspectives. *Psychological Bulletin, 129*(4), 475–494.

Stein, M. I. (1953). Creativity and Culture. *Journal of Psychology, 36*, 311–322. doi:10.1080/ 00223980.1953.9712897.

Vartanian, O., and Skov, M. (2014). Neural Correlates of Viewing Paintings: Evidence from a Quantitative Meta-Analysis of Functional Magnetic Resonance Imaging Data. *Brain and Cognition, 87*, 52–56. doi:10.1016/j.bandc.2014.03.004

Waxman, S. G., and Geschwind, N. (1974). Hypergraphia in Temporal Lobe Epilepsy. *Neurology, 24*(7), 629–636.

Wu, X., Yang, W., Tong, D., et al. (2015). A Meta-Analysis of Neuroimaging Studies on Divergent Thinking Using Activation Likelihood Estimation. *Human Brain Mapping, 36*(7), 2703–2718.

Yamadori, A., Mori, E., Tabuchi, M., Kudo, Y., and Mitani, Y. (1986). Hypergraphia: A Right Hemisphere Syndrome. *Journal of Neurology, Neurosurgery, and Psychiatry, 49* (10), 1160–1164.

PART V

Phenomenology-Based Forms of the Imagination

34 Imagination in the Philosophy of Art

David Davies

Overview

What does it mean for something to be an artwork, or to be a particular kind of artwork? What is the nature of the creative processes by which artworks come into existence? What kinds of cognitive capacities and processes enter into the reception and appreciation of artworks? These are three central questions in the philosophy of art, and the imagination has been held to make a central contribution to answering each of them. However, as we shall see, contemporary writers have focused on the first and third of these questions and not, as in earlier philosophical reflections on art, on the second. In section 2: Imagination and the Creation of Artworks, I consider some ways in which philosophers of art have understood the nature and role of the imagination in artistic creation, and why the connection between imagination and creation is now viewed as more problematic. In section 3: Artistic Representation and Make-Believe, I outline Kendall Walton's highly influential analysis of the nature and appreciation of artistic representations in terms of a kind of imagining that he terms "make-believe." In section 4 Imagination, Fictionality, Simulation, and the Reception of Fictional Narratives, I consider Gregory Currie's analysis of the nature of literary and cinematic fictions in terms of prescriptions to imagine various things, and of the role of the imagination in our engagement with such fictions. In section 5: Criticisms of Imagination-Based Accounts of Fictionality, I address recent critical responses to the roles ascribed to the imagination by Walton and Currie. Finally, in section 6: The Puzzle of Imaginative Resistance, I look briefly at what has been termed the puzzle of "imaginative resistance," our reluctance or refusal to engage in some of the imaginings prescribed by literary and cinematic fictions.

Imagination and the Creation of Artworks

It is natural for us to think that the imagination plays a central role in the activities whereby artworks come into existence. One reason why this seems so natural is that our conception of art is still deeply inflected by nineteenth-century Romantic conceptions of the artistic genius and of art as a means whereby artists transcend our everyday concerns and achieve imaginative self-expression. The idea of an essential connection between artistic creativity and the imagination predates Romanticism. It was poetically expressed by Shakespeare, for example, in *A Midsummer Night's Dream*:

> And as imagination bodies forth
> The forms of things unknown, the poet's pen
> Turns them to shapes, and gives to airy nothing
> A local habitation, and a name
>
> (Act 5, Scene 1, 8–17: cited in Gaut, 2003, 148).

But it finds a fuller philosophical elaboration in the writings of Romantic poets and theorists such as Coleridge. In his later reflections on the cognitive basis for artistic creation, Coleridge distinguished between the "primary" and the "secondary" imagination. The former was taken to play a constitutive role in our ordinary perceptual experience of the world: The model here was the role played by the imagination in Kant's account of such experience in the *Critique of Pure Reason* (1787/1929). The "secondary" or "poetic" imagination was taken to be operative in the act of poetic creation. According to Coleridge, the poet begins with those elements furnished in perceptual experience and then reworks these elements through an imaginative process that "dissolves, diffuses, dissipates, in order to recreate" (Coleridge, 1817/1969: 202). This view is not only theoretically elucidated by Coleridge in the *Biographia Literaria* but also, according to at least one critic (Bernstein, 1981), exemplified in his early poem "The Nightingale," which represents the poet/narrator as going through the various stages of this process in arriving at poetic self-expression.

Berys Gaut (2003), in an extensive contemporary philosophical assessment of the claimed connection between creativity and imagination, notes that the nature of the link has seldom been spelled out in any detail and is difficult to assess because both of the notions in question – "creativity" and "imagination" – are themselves in need of further elucidation. Artistic creativity seems to require that something that is original and of value be generated by some deliberate and nonmechanical means. But the term "imagination" and its derivatives are more difficult to pin down, at least as employed in the relevant literature on artistic creativity. One problem is that the derived term "imaginative" is sometimes used as a synonym for "creative," rendering the connection trivial. A further problem is that many writers, including philosophical theorists, tend to identify the activity of imagination with the formation of mental imagery (e.g. Warnock, 1976), something that does not seem to be essentially involved in the kinds of activities comprised by Coleridge's "secondary imagination."

In attempting to impose some philosophical order on these issues, Gaut suggests that the central notion of imagination in this context should be that of entertaining something without any commitment to the truth or reality of what is being entertained. For convenience we may call this "imagination(e)." This conception of imagination most clearly applies to the entertaining of propositions. For example, I may imagine that there is an accident on the road I shall be taking to the airport without any commitment to this actually being the case. But it can also capture other kinds of imagining whose entertained objects are not propositions. We may, for example, entertain the idea of a mountain composed entirely of gold without any commitment to its actual existence, or imagine visually engaging with such an object, or imagine how it would feel were we to discover it. While imagination(e) may involve the having of mental imagery, it need not, since no such imagery need attend my entertaining, for example, the mere idea of solving the "enigma" posed by Elgar's *Enigma Variations*. And mental imagery frequently occurs without imagination(e), as when I recall a room in which I lived as a child.

Gaut maintains that while imagination(e) is an important *vehicle* that the artist can use in the creative process, it is questionable whether, as the Romantics claimed, it is the essential *source* of creative ideas and insights. Imagination(e), he argues, is neither necessary nor sufficient for artistic creativity. It is not necessary because the source of a creative idea may be the workings of the unconscious mind. It is not sufficient because many of the objects of our imagining(e) are unoriginal, as with much fantasizing. But, insofar as the creative process is a temporally extended one in which the artist, in working with the products of inspiration, needs to consider and compare various alternative courses of action, it is the imagination(e) that is naturally suited for this role. Unlike belief and intention, it permits the entertaining of such alternatives without commitment to a particular way of proceeding.

However, to the extent that such vehicular use of the imagination can obviously subserve many purposes other than artistic creation, we have here no special insight into *artistic* creativity. In trying to identify imaginative activity that can plausibly be taken to be distinctive of artworks, Gaut draws upon some fascinating but enigmatic remarks in Kant's *Critique of Judgement*. Kant ascribes to the "genius" who produces works of fine art both originality and the ability to exhibit what he terms *aesthetic ideas*, products of the imagination that occasion much thought without being subsumable under a concept as is the case with ordinary cognition (Kant, 1790/1951: 157–161). Gaut suggests that what Kant calls "aesthetic ideas" are metaphors, and that metaphor-making displays how creative imagining can work. But he also points to the role that imagination(e) plays in the *reception* of metaphors. A metaphor – for example, the much cited "Romeo is the sun," spoken by Juliet in Shakespeare's play – invites the receiver to think of one thing – here, Romeo – as something else – here, the sun. We are invited to imaginatively adopt a particular *perspective* on the focus of the metaphor – Romeo – and to think of him from that perspective.

Artistic Representation and Make-Believe

This idea ties in with a central theme in much recent work on imagination in the philosophy of art. The imagination, it is claimed, plays a central role in the *reception* of artworks because the latter require that we adopt a distinctive kind of *perspective* on the content of a work (e.g. Hamlyn, 1994: 362). This perspective – often characterized as one of "making believe" rather than believing that content – is central to recent work on artistic representation, the nature of fiction, and the nature of our engagement with fictions in literature and cinema. Two of the most significant figures here are Kendall Walton and Gregory Currie, but, as we shall see, recent theorists have challenged some of the roles they accord to the imagination.

Walton's work, *Mimesis as Make-Believe* (1990), has influenced not only work in the philosophy of art but also work in metaphysics on "fictionalism." Fictionalists hold that some apparently serious and truth-apt discourses – for example ethical or pure mathematical discourse – are properly viewed as "useful fictions" (see, for example, the papers collected in Kalderon, 2005). Walton's professed aim is to provide a general theory of the kinds of representations we encounter in the arts. Representational artworks usually employ visual or verbal media, or, as in theater, some combination thereof. Paintings, for example, use a visual medium to *depict* their subjects, while novels use language to *describe* the things they represent. As a basis for clarifying the distinction between depiction and description, Walton offers a general theory of representation that applies both to artworks and to more mundane things such as children's games. He describes a game in which two children walking in a wood play a game of pretending tree stumps are bears. In such a game, the stumps serve as "props." A prop in a game of make-believe is a generator of truths in that game: Facts about the props generate such truths. For example, that one stump is bigger than another makes it true in the game that one bear is bigger than another. Something acquires the status of prop in a game thanks to an explicit rule, or to an implicit understanding among its players, which Walton terms a "principle of generation." Given such a principle, whether something is true in the game is independent of whether anyone believes it to be true in the game or imagines that it is the case. In the "stumps are bears" game, for example, a stump, even if unnoticed, makes it true in the game that a bear is lurking nearby. Props, then, *prescribe* what is to be imagined. This provides the basis for a general theory of *fictional truth*: A proposition is true in a fiction just in case there is a prescription that, in engaging with that fiction, we are to imagine that proposition.

Artistic representations, Walton argues, are also props in games of make-believe. A representation prescribes that we imagine certain things. "Imagining" here is what we termed "imagination(e)" above – the entertaining of something without commitment to its truth, existence, accuracy, etc. The content of the prescribed imagining depends upon the relevant principles of generation, and the intended audience for an artistic representation understands what it prescribes because they understand these principles. Walton stresses the varied nature of the principles of generation operative in the arts. The occurrence of the name "London" in the opening line of *Bleak House*, for example, prescribes that we imagine the events narrated in the immediately following pages of the novel to be occurring in London. The title and painted surface of Piero della Francesca's *The Resurrection* prescribes that we imagine, in accordance with the way the subject is depicted, Christ rising from his tomb.

The difference between descriptive and depictive representations is to be explained in terms of a more general difference in the kind of imagining prescribed. In the case of novels, readers are prescribed to imagine that certain events take place or that certain circumstances hold and they further imagine that they are learning this from a narrator. In the case of paintings, on the other hand, what is prescribed is that the viewer imagines that her seeing of the painted surface is a *seeing* of what the picture depicts – for example, a seeing of Christ rising from his tomb in the case of Piero's painting. While what is true in the world of the work is determined by principles of generation, what is true in the world of the game *we play* with the work also includes facts about our relation to the world of the work as the confidants of narrators or as viewers of what is depicted. These imaginings about ourselves are *de se* imaginings "from the inside."

Walton argues (2002) that his account of depiction in terms of imagined seeing captures what is left unelucidated in Richard Wollheim's talk (1987) of the "twofoldness" of our perceptual engagement with visual artworks; our seeing the subject of a painting *in* the array of pigment on canvas. It also accounts, he argues (Walton, 1990), for a crucial difference between our appreciative engagement with artistic representations and our engagement in ordinary games of make-believe. In the former, we are interested not only in the content that we are prescribed to make-believe but also in how the work's creator has made these things fictional by manipulating the medium to produce a prop that articulates that content. A further significant difference, for Walton, is between what he terms "content-oriented" and "prop-oriented" make-believe. In the former, our aim, in determining what we are prescribed to imagine, is to engage in the very imaginings prescribed, as in the case of the children playing "stumps are bears." In the latter, our grasp of what imaginings are prescribed is in the interest of better understanding the nature of the thing that is functioning as a prop. Walton argues (1993) that many metaphors work through our engagement in prop-oriented make-believe. It is in reflecting upon what we are invited to imagine in a game in which facts about Romeo generate certain truths about the sun that we come to see Romeo (the prop) in a new way.

Imagination, Fictionality, Simulation, and the Reception of Fictional Narratives

Like Walton, Gregory Currie appeals to the imagination in providing an account of the reception rather than the creation of artworks. To this end, he distinguishes between what he terms the "*creative imagination*" and the "*recreative imagination*." The former, as its name suggests, is the kind of capacity central to Romantic conceptions of the ways in which artworks are created. It involves putting ideas or images together in a way that defies expectation or convention, where this is taken to be at least part of what is involved in artistic creativity. Recreative (pronounced "re-creative"!) imagination, on the other hand, is "the imaginative capacity, whatever it is, that underpins perspective-shifting" (Currie and Ravenscroft, 2002: 8–9). Perspective-shifting is the capacity to put ourselves in the place of another, or in the place of our own past, future, or counterfactual self: seeing, thinking about, and responding to the world as that other does. In their book on the nature of recreative imagination so construed, Currie and Ian Ravenscroft maintain that:

> imaginative projection involves the capacity to have, and in good measure to control the having of, states that are not perceptions or beliefs or decisions

or experiences of movements of one's body, but which are in various ways like those states – like them in ways that enable the states possessed through imagination to mimic and, relative to certain purposes, to substitute for perceptions, beliefs, decisions and experiences of movements. (Currie and Ravenscroft, 2002: 11)

Recreative imagination, they maintain, is what is involved in visual imagery, auditory imagery, and other "perception-like imaginings," and also in those "propositional imaginings" that have beliefs and desires as their counterparts. Currie, both in his own work (1995; see also Currie, 2003; Currie and Achino, 2013) and in his work with Ravenscroft, draws upon literature in contemporary cognitive science in offering an account of how such "perspective shifting" is accomplished. He subscribes to "the simulation programme" (see below) where perspective-shifting involves not so much conscious recourse to a psychological theory, but rather the ability to "simulate" the mental states of others. The central commitment here is to "a belief in the existence of states of recreative imagining, their role in our everyday understanding of minds, and their capacity to reduce the amount of psychological theorizing that we need to attribute to people in explaining their mentalizing capacity" (Currie and Ravenscroft, 2002: 51).

Recreative imagination is also central to Currie's account of our engagement with fictional narratives in literature and film. He seeks to provide a unified picture of such engagements that minimizes the differences between fictions articulated in a verbal and in a visual medium (Currie, 1995). One obvious *difference* is that, in accessing the narrative of a film, we draw upon certain more general perceptual skills. I use the same cognitive capacities in recognizing an x-picture as I use in recognizing an x. The capacities in question involve the operation of *feature-detectors* at the sub-personal level (Currie, 1995: 80–85). The claim, then, is that I recognize a horse-picture because spatial features of the design trigger a subset of the same feature-detectors as do horses. Currie further maintains that, in watching a film, we typically take ourselves to be watching a *representation*, and that it is the content of that representation that serves as the basis for our interpretation of the film. On the basis of my experience so construed, I form beliefs about what is true in the presented fiction by referring the representations to the agency of a maker. The viewer of a film, for example, asks, of each succeeding shot, why a shot with that appearance is inserted into the film at this point. The receiver's interpretation of the narrative content of the representation reflects the assumption, structuring her reception of the cinematic narrative, that someone has ordered these representations in a particular way to tell a particular story.

Recreative imagination plays two distinct roles in Currie's account. Most importantly, our engagement with a fictional cinematic or literary work is a matter of *imagining* that X is true – adopting the perspective of one who believes that X is true – for all X judged to be true in the story. This is what Currie terms "primary imagining." It ties in with Currie's view of what it is for something to be a fictional utterance in the first place. Imagining that X is true is the response the receiver takes to be prescribed by the author of a fiction, and it is in virtue of there being such a prescription that something qualifies as a fictional utterance, according to Currie.

Simplifying slightly, for Currie an utterance is fictional if its author intends that receivers make believe the content of what is uttered and do so through recognizing that this is the utterer's intention, with the additional proviso that if the content of the utterance is true, it is only accidentally true (Currie, 1990, chapter 1; for a related view, see Davies, 2007, chapter 3, and Davies, 2015). The input to imagination, here, is the output from our interrogation of the verbal or visual manifold.

Currie differs from Walton in holding that, with visual fictional narratives, our imaginative engagement with the narrative is *impersonal* rather than *personal*. Currie labels the idea that such engagement involves personal imagining the "Imagined Observer Hypothesis" (IOH). The IOH holds that, in engaging with a visual representation, I imagine, of myself, that I am *observing or witnessing* the events that I take to be represented. Personal imagining is thus a kind of "imagining seeing." This is supposed to explain the greater affective power of cinematic narratives. Currie rejects this view, however, partly on the grounds that it misrepresents the phenomenology of our cinematic experience (Currie, 1995: 167–179). If the IOH were true, we would have to imagine all sorts of things that we surely do not imagine when we watch a film, given that cinematic narratives are usually conveyed by shots of the narrated events taken from different perspectives, as in the shot/reverse shot convention used when two characters are talking to one another. To avoid the idea that we imagine ourselves moving about in the space of the fictional world in a manner corresponding to these changes of perspective, we must say that we somehow extract from the presented images an understanding of what is happening. But then, Currie argues, what we imagine is that the represented events take place, not that we see them taking place.

What really distinguishes our engagement with literary fictions from our engagement with filmic fictions, for Currie, is the manner in which the imagination is furnished with the material for its imaginings. He distinguishes (Currie, 1995: 181–191) between "perceptual beliefs about X" based on *seeing* X, and "symbolic beliefs about X" based on *reading about* X. For example, if I *see* two politicians debating, either in person or on TV, then I form perceptual beliefs that have the following features: (a) the content of my belief is counterfactually dependent on the content of the perceived content of the debate – for example, I will believe that A wagged her finger in a particularly way only if she did so, and (b) if I form beliefs about one visual aspect of the debate, I will have many different beliefs about that visual aspect – for example, if I form beliefs about the color of the tie B is wearing, I will also form beliefs about its shape, how it matches his suit, etc. But if I form beliefs about the debate by reading about it, my beliefs do not have either of these features. Currie then claims that our imaginative engagement with visual representations such as films mirrors our epistemic engagement with things we perceive – he terms this "perceptual imagining" – whereas in the case of our imaginative engagement with literary representations, this mirrors our epistemic engagement with things we read – he terms this "symbolic imagining." On the basis of this model of film experience, Currie maintains that there is no interesting respect in which film experience involves illusion. Some critics, however, while granting Currie's argument against personal imagining, have insisted that there is a distinctly *visual* quality to our imagining in response to films that is missed in his account. Allen (1995), for example, speaks of a "projective illusion" whereby we imagine portrayed events fully realized before us in a "virtual reality." Lopes (1998) speaks of a distinctly visual experience "as of" the thing portrayed. And Davies (2003) distinguishes three different senses in which we may be "medium-aware" in watching a film: (1) having a dispositional belief that one is engaging with a cinematic representation that can be cited in explanation of one's failure to respond actively to what is portrayed – by running away from a represented monster, for example; (2) occurrently thinking about what one is watching as a cinematic representation, and (3) being perceptually aware of something as an x-representation rather than as an x. We need the three notions to explain visual illusions such as the Mueller-Lyer illusion – where we are medium-aware in senses (1) and (2), but not (3) – and, Davies argues, to explain the phenomenology of film experience.

Currie also maintains that we employ what he terms "secondary imagining" (not to be confused with Coleridge's "secondary imagination"!), as *a way of determining some of the things that are true in the fiction*. For example, if we are shown or told that a particular character behaves in a certain way, we use our imagination in ascribing to that character various motivations and mental processes to which we are given no explicit access. The mental capacity that we draw on here is the same one that we call upon in making sense of the behaviors of other people in everyday life, and, as we saw, for Currie this is a capacity to "simulate" the behavior of the other person by imagining that we are behaving in the way that she is in the circumstances that confront her and ascribing to her the mental states that we would have in such circumstances. The same simulatory capacity allows us to *predict* the behaviors of others based on what we have independent grounds to believe are their mental states. The "mental simulation" theory that underlies Currie's claims about the role of secondary imagining in our understanding of visual and literary narratives is offered as an alternative to the "theory theory," which holds that, in interpreting and predicting the behaviors of others, either in real life or in our engagement with fictional narratives, we rely upon a "theory of mind" in inferring explanations or predictions, the input to that theory being, again, either an agent's observed behaviors or her presumed mental states.

Criticisms of Imagination-Based Accounts of Fictionality

A prominent criticism of imagination-based accounts of fictionality is that an author's prescription that we make believe certain elements in a work is not sufficient for its being a work of fiction, and that some works of fiction also prescribe belief (see for example Friend, 2008; Gibson, 2007, chapter 5; Matravers, 2014). Friend (2008), for example, argues that some canonical works of nonfiction – for example, scientific or philosophical works containing thought experiments, and classical histories containing imaginative reconstructions of the thoughts and conversations of historical agents – prescribe that we imagine rather than believe parts of those works. She also argues that authors of canonical works of fiction sometimes prescribe that we believe part of what is narrated in those works. For example, when Ian Fleming writes in Chapter 12 of his novel *Thunderball*, "New Providence, the island containing Nassau, the capital of the Bahamas, is a drab sandy slab of land fringed with some of the most beautiful beaches in the world," he intends that readers believe, and not merely make-believe, what these words affirm. Matravers (2014) also charges what he terms the "post-Waltonian consensus" with holding, incorrectly, that fictional works are made up of propositions that we are prescribed to make-believe. However, those supposedly making up this "consensus" might object that they have not in fact proposed that prescriptions to imagine various things distinguish fictional from nonfictional *works*. Currie (1990), for example, explicitly rejects the idea of defining fictionality for *works* and offers only an account of what makes something a fictional *utterance*. Davies (2015) offers an account of fictional *narratives* in terms of prescriptions to imagine a fictive content of a "real setting" while holding that such narratives appear in both works of fiction and works of nonfiction.

Matravers's more radical attack (2014) on any appeal to the imagination in an account of fictionality takes his opponents to be committed to the following claims: (1) what it is for a proposition to be fictional is for there to be a mandate to imagine it, and (2) the mental state of imagining can be given a functional definition that distinguishes it from belief – for example, Currie's "simulation" account of imagination in terms of running mental states "off line." Matravers argues that imagination, so conceived, cannot be distinctive of fictions because "what goes on in the reader's head" in reading nonfiction involves just as much simulation as what goes on in reading fiction. Citing Currie's "secondary imagining," which is a capacity supposedly manifest not only in our engagement with fictions but also in our interpretation of the behavior of other people both in real life and as described in nonfictional narratives, he claims that "it is difficult to see where Currie could locate any difference between what a reader does with a fiction and what a reader does with a non-fiction" (Matravers, 2014: 30). He proposes that, rather than think that fictional and nonfictional narratives are processed differently, we should "divide the problem into two tasks: first that of providing an account of engaging with representations that is neutral between nonfiction and fiction, and second that of providing an account of the relations between the propositions in the representations and our pre-existing structures of belief" (Matravers, 2014: 76). The first task, he suggests, can be cashed out in terms of the construction of "mental models" of the sort proposed by Johnson-Laird (1983) on narrative comprehension. For the second task, all we need is a difference in what we are prescribed to believe. Something's being fictional is just one reason why we might decline to believe something included in a narrative. There is therefore no role in an account of fiction for a distinctive mental capacity of "imagination."

Matravers's division of labor seems eminently sensible. In essence, the two questions that need to be addressed are: (1) What is involved in understanding a narrative? and (2) What kinds of things can we do with a narrative once we understand it? But it is unclear why this division of labor would be objectionable to those who appeal to the imagination in drawing a distinction between fictional and nonfictional narratives. Currie's "secondary imagining" is clearly supposed to be part of an answer to (1), applicable to both fictional and nonfictional narratives, while primary imagining is supposed to be an answer to (2) that distinguishes between fictional and nonfictional narratives. Matravers's suggestion that an answer to (2) need not traffic in a capacity to imagine seems unmotivated, unless we are going to eschew talk of imagination in other contexts such as the children's games to which Walton appeals. Matravers suggests that talk of "imagining" makes sense only when what is to be imagined depends upon some "transformation" of materials, as with Walton's props and principles of generation, but this seems a restricted conception of imagination. We can agree that there is no salient difference in *understanding* between fictional and nonfictional verbal narratives – in each case, to understand is to have a mental model (in some sense) that represents the content of the narrative. What seems distinctive about those narratives we tend to classify as fiction, however, is not that they alone require imagination for their *comprehension* but that they alone yield "fictional worlds" with which we are prescribed to engage in specific games of make-believe in virtue of principles of generation.

The Puzzle of Imaginative Resistance

David Hume held the view, endorsed by a number of present-day theorists, that moral blemishes in a work constitute artistic failings. He held that, where a work prescribes a response that is morally defective, this will deter the morally sensitive receiver from responding in the prescribed manner. But he also remarked on what he took to be the singular nature of this phenomenon:

> Whatever speculative errors may be found in the polite writings of any age or country, they detract but little from the value of those compositions. There needs but a certain turn of thought or imagination to make us enter into all the opinions, which then prevailed, and relish the sentiments or conclusions derived from them. But a very violent effort is requisite to change our judgment of manners, and excite sentiments of approbation or blame, love or hatred, different from those to which the mind from long custom has been familiarized. And where a man is confident of the rectitude of that moral standard, by which he judges, he is justly jealous of it, and will not pervert the sentiments of his heart for a moment, in complaisance to any writer whatsoever. (Hume, 1757/1993: 152)

The puzzle here, usually termed the puzzle of "imaginative resistance," concerns our imaginative responses to works of fiction. We are willing to make believe all sorts of things that we take to be false about the actual world, including even things that we take to be physically and metaphysically impossible (e.g. travel faster than the speed of light, and time travel, respectively). But we seem resistant to the invitation to imagine worlds in which moral truths obtain that are strikingly incompatible with our actual moral beliefs. Kendall Walton (1994) proposes, as an example, the one-line fiction: "In killing her baby, Giselda did the right thing, after all, it was a girl." Rather than take this to be true in the story, we tend to respond by attributing this belief to the narrator or the culture being described in the narrative, holding that it is also true in the story that the belief is false, and that the moral status of the described act in the world of the "Giselda" story is the same as it would be in the actual world.

Why, then, does "imaginative resistance" of this sort occur? A flourishing literature on this topic has sprung up since Walton's paper, much of it in response to a more recent paper by Tamar Gendler (2000). One question is whether the phenomenon is indeed as singular as it is made out to be, or whether there are other fictional invitations to which we manifest a similar resistance. For example, it has been suggested that there is a similar problem if we are asked to imagine that other kinds of normative predicates have very different conditions of application in a fiction – that, for example, things we would take to be grotesque are beautiful, or things we would take to be irrational are rational (Weatherson, 2004). Another suggestion that would broaden the scope of the puzzle is that imaginative resistance will arise whenever we are dealing with a predicate whose content is determined by our dispositions to respond in certain ways in the actual world. Stephen Yablo (2002) contrasts two kinds of predicates: (1) predicates like "ticklish," where something (e.g. a feather) is ticklish in a world (actual or possible) if it produces in us standard tickle-responses in *that* world – so different things might be ticklish in different possible worlds; (2) predicates like "oval," where something is oval in a world (actual or possible) if it has the physical properties that affect us in a certain way in the actual world. In the latter kind of case, we will resist any invitation to imagine that something lacking the relevant properties in some fictional world could nonetheless fall under the predicate.

One proposed explanation of "imaginative resistance" is that it arises when we are asked to imagine something that turns out to be conceptually impossible. Walton, for example, suggests that we take moral properties to "supervene" on certain kinds of non-moral properties, so that a given moral property can be instantiated only where the relevant kinds of non-moral properties are also exemplified. We are therefore unable to imagine a situation in which the moral properties are instantiated in the absence of the relevant kinds of nonmoral properties – for example, a situation in which an act having all of the nonmoral properties possessed by an act of torturing and killing a young child has a positive rather than a negative moral value. However, while this seems to cover some cases of imaginative resistance, it arguably does not cover others (see Gendler, 2000, for this response). An alternative proposal is that we refrain from imagining what is prescribed in the "Giselda" story because, given the lack of detail in the story, we do not yet understand *how* the moral predicate in question is supposed to apply (Stock, 2005). But this, it seems, cannot explain why imaginative resistance can still occur even if the detail is filled in, as it would be if we took the "Giselda" story to be one that is set in our contemporary world (Matravers, 2003). A third suggestion is that we generally acquiesce in the game of make-believe proposed by a fiction because we trust that the narrator, or "fictional author," of the story is a reliable authority on what is true. But, while the narrator is generally taken to occupy a privileged position in this respect, we do not extend this privilege to the knowledge of moral truths, and perhaps of normative claims more generally (Matravers, 2003).

It is not clear, however, why we should not take the narrator to be equally privileged as to normative facts in "worlds" distant from our own. Gendler's own solution to the puzzle addresses this question. She argues that our concern about entering imaginatively into certain morally and normatively deviant fictions is generated by our general practice of "exporting" certain things taken to be true in the story into our understanding of the actual world, if such exportation does not generate any contradiction (Gendler, 2000). In the case of prescriptions to imagine deviant moral worlds, she claims, we are concerned that, if we enter into the fiction imaginatively, this will involve "exporting" the morally deviant "truths" from the fiction to the real world.

Questions for Further Investigation

(1) Is there something ineliminably visual about the imagining prompted by cinematic narratives and visual artworks and, if so, how is this kind of imagining best understood?

(2) Does the imagination, under some description, play a central role in something's being, and being apprehended as, fictional and, if so, does this enable us to distinguish between works of fiction and works of nonfiction?

(3) To what extent can work on the imagination in cognitive psychology and cognitive neuroscience either illuminate or answer philosophical questions about the nature of artworks and our engagements with them? For a critical examination of possible answers to this kind of question, see Davies, (2013, 2014). For papers on the bearing of empirical work in psychology and neuroscience on issues in aesthetics, see Currie et al. (2014).

References

Allen, R. (1995). *Projecting Illusion: Film Spectatorship and the Impression of Reality.* New York, NY: Cambridge University Press.

Bernstein, G. M. (1981). The Recreating Secondary Imagination in Coleridge's "The Nightingale". *ELH, 48*(2), 339–350.

Coleridge, S. T. (1817/1969). *Biographia Literaria.* Volume 1. Edited by J. Shawcross. Oxford, UK: Oxford University Press.

Currie, G. (1990). *The Nature of Fiction.* Cambridge, UK: Cambridge University Press.
   (1995). *Image and Mind: Film, Philosophy, and Cognitive Science.* Cambridge, UK: Cambridge University Press.
   (2003). The Capacities that Enable Us to Produce and Consume Art. In M. Kieran and D. M. Lopes (eds.), *Imagination, Philosophy, and the Arts.* London, UK: Routledge, 293–304.

Currie, G., and Ravenscroft, I. (2002). *Recreative Minds.* Oxford, UK: Oxford University Press.

Currie, G., and Ichino, A. (2013). Imagination and Make-Believe. In B. Gaut and D. M. Lopes (eds.), *The Routledge Companion to Aesthetics.* 3rd edition. London, UK: Routledge, 320–330.

Currie, G., Kieran, M., Meskin, A., and Robson, J. (eds.) (2014). *Aesthetics and the Sciences of Mind.* Oxford, UK: Oxford University Press.

Davies, D. (2003). The Imaged, the Imagined, and the Imaginary. In M. Kieran and D. M. Lopes (eds.), *Imagination, Philosophy, and the Arts*. London, UK: Routledge, 225–244.

(2007). *Aesthetics and Literature*. London, UK: Continuum.

(2013). Dancing around the Issues: Prospects for an Empirically Grounded Philosophy of Dance. *Journal of Aesthetics and Art Criticism, 71*(2), 195–202.

(2014). "This is your Brain on Art": What Can Philosophy of Art Learn from Neuroscience? In G. Currie, M. Kieran, A. Meskin, and J. Robson (eds.), *Aesthetics and the Sciences of Mind*. Oxford, UK: Oxford University Press, 57–74.

(2015). Fictive Utterance and the Fictionality of Narratives and Works. *The British Journal of Aesthetics, 55*(1), 39–55.

Friend, S. (2008). Imagining Fact and Fiction. In K. Stock and K. Thompson-Jones (eds.), *New Waves in Aesthetics*. New York, NY: Palgrave Macmillan, 150–169.

Gaut, B. (2003). Creativity and Imagination. In B. Gaut and P. Livingston (eds.), *The Creation of Art*. Cambridge, UK: Cambridge University Press, 148–173.

Gendler, T. (2000). The Puzzle of Imaginative Resistance. *Journal of Philosophy, 97*, 55–81.

Gibson, J. (2007). *Fiction and the Weave of Life*. Oxford, UK: Oxford University Press.

Hamlyn, D. W. (1994). Imagination. In S. Guttenplan (ed.), *A Companion to the Philosophy of Mind*. Oxford, UK: Blackwell, 361–366.

Hume, D. (1757/1993). Of the Standard of Taste. In S. Copley and A. Edgar (eds.), *Selected Essays*. Oxford, UK: Oxford University Press, 133–154.

Johnson-Laird, P. (1983). *Mental Models*. Cambridge, MA: Harvard University Press.

Kalderon, M. (2005). *Fictionalism in Metaphysics*. Oxford, UK: Clarendon Press.

Kant, I. (1787/1929). *Critique of Pure Reason*. 2nd edition. Translated by Norman Kemp-Smith. London, UK: Macmillan.

(1790/1951). *Critique of Judgment*. Translated by J. H. Bernard. New York, NY: Haffner Press.

Lopes, D. M. (1998). Imagination, Illusion, and Experience in Film. *Philosophical Studies, 89*, 343–353.

Matravers, D. (2003). Fictional Assent and the (So-Called) "Puzzle of Imaginative Resistance". In M. Kieran and D. Lopes (eds.), *Imagination, Philosophy, and the Arts*. London, UK: Routledge, 91–106.

(2014). *Fiction and Narrative*. Oxford, UK: Oxford University Press.

Stock, K. (2005). Resisting Imaginative Resistance. *Philosophical Quarterly, 55*, 607–624.

Walton, K. (1990). *Mimesis as Make-Believe*. Cambridge, MA: Harvard University Press.

(1993). Metaphor and Prop-Oriented Make-Believe. *European Journal of Philosophy, 1*(1), 39–57.

(1994). Morals in Fiction and Fictional Morality. *Proceedings of the Aristotelian Society*, supplementary volume, *68*, 27–50.

(2002). Depiction, Perception, and Imagination: Responses to Richard Wollheim. *The Journal of Aesthetics and Art Criticism, 60*(1), 27–35.

Warnock, M. (1976). *Imagination*. London, UK: Faber and Faber.

Weatherson, B. (2004). Morality, Fiction, and Possibility. *Philosophers' Imprint 4*(3), 1–27.

Wollheim, R. (1987). *Painting as an Art*. London, UK: Thames and Hudson.

Yablo, S. (2002). Coulda, Woulda, Shoulda. In T. Gendler and J. Hawthorne (eds.), *Conceivability and Possibility*. Oxford, UK: Oxford University Press, 441–492.

35 Imagination in Aesthetic Experience

Oshin Vartanian

Imagination in the Creation and Appreciation of Art

Generally speaking, we tend to think of creative people as imaginative. Indeed, the creativity literature is replete with methods that use imagination as a way to measure a person's creativity. For example, in a well-known procedure developed by Ward and colleagues, participants are asked to imagine a planet somewhere in the universe that is very different from Earth, and to imagine and draw an animal that might live there (see Ward, Patterson, and Sifonis, 2004). The products of this exercise are in turn rated on various indices to assess their level of creativity, taking into consideration atypical use of sensory abilities (e.g. ability to hear up to thirty miles away), major sense organs (e.g. the presence of only one eye), and appendages (e.g. absorbing nutrients through the feet), among others. Other examples that have been used in more recent neuroscientific studies of creativity include instructing participants to "Imagine you are able to fly," as well as more elaborate creative story-generation paradigms such as "A man meets a woman and asks her out on a date. Make up a story about who the people are, how they met and what will happen. Use your imagination." (For review see Fink et al., 2007).

As these examples illustrate, we have no difficulty considering imagination as an engine for generating creative thoughts in scientific (i.e. problem-solving) and artistic (e.g. story-writing) domains of creativity. Indeed, major theories of creativity have either implicitly or explicitly acknowledged the contribution of imagination to the creative process. For example, according to the influential blind variation and selective retention (BVSR) theory of creativity (and other knowledge processes) first proposed by Campbell (1960), creative ideas emerge in accordance with a two-step process in which the first step involves generating many possible solutions or ideas in response to a problem, whereas the second step involves testing those solutions and ideas and selecting the best option(s) available (Simonton, 1999). As described by Simonton (2013), the first step of this process "requires that the person go beyond the information given, to take intellectual risks, to hazard guesses that may turn out to be no more than shots in the dark – in short, to dare to be wrong" (Simonton, 2013: 254). When Simonton (2007) applied the BVSR lens to study the evolution of Picasso's sketches of *Guernica* over time, he was able to show that the process was unsighted in that Picasso engaged in the production of blind monotonic variants rather than following a more systematic, expertise-driven process that converged predictably on the end product. In the course of his analysis Simonton (2007) reviewed the scientific literature on various personality traits and cognitive styles and abilities associated with creative persons to argue that "taken together, these traits would suggest that the creative imagination would be relatively unrestricted, the mind freely exploring possibilities as dictated by both internal associative networks and external stimuli, however rationally irrelevant" (Simonton, 2007: 330). Described as such, one can clearly see a role for imagination in the creative process.

However, for every artwork such as *Guernica* there is also an audience that engages in an interaction with it. As consumers of art, our interactions with artworks can result in aesthetic pleasure and the derivation of meaning, among other end-points. What are some of the psychological processes that support our aesthetic *experience* of art? Winner (2019) tackled this question in her recent book *How Art Works*. Early on, she discussed the work of philosopher Denis Dutton (2009), who has offered a list of twelve prototypical features that characterize *typical* works of art, some of which involve psychological responses to artworks. Dutton focused on typical art in order to allow us to understand "the center of art and its values," rather than listing a set of conditions that are necessary and jointly sufficient to categorize an object as art. Among those psychological responses he lists *imaginative experience*, which he believes might be the most important of all the features that characterize typical artworks. This, he argues, is because imaginative experience allows us to experience the artworks in a pretend world. This feature is also critical to our experience of emotions while interacting with artworks, because it enables us to imagine what it feels like to feel sorrow, anger, or joy in the absence of real-world events that might otherwise trigger those emotions in real life. Sheppard (1991) has echoed a similar argument regarding the importance of imagination in experiencing emotions during aesthetic experiences:

> By "imagining what it is like to feel sad" I did not mean that we feel some faint, shadowy kind of sadness but that we feel sad imaginatively, we feel *as if* we were reacting to some sad event. Such "as if" emotions do not move us to action, and we know they are not "for real." Even if a scene in a film makes us weep, we make no attempt to rescue the dying heroine. This kind of imagining is in some ways like daydreaming, but there is an important difference. In dreaming we can imagine what we please, but when we listen to the music or watch the film we are guided in our imagining by what we are presented with in the work of art. Mozart's cheerful Clarinet Concerto, for example, could not sensibly be described as "mournful" or "anguished" (Sheppard, 1991: 35).

In essence, what Dutton (2009) and Sheppard (1991) have argued for is that it is precisely the ability to imagine that enables us to experience emotions in the context of a pretend world during aesthetic experiences (see also Cupchik, 2016).

Given the important role given to imagination by philosophers (Dutton, 2009; Sheppard, 1991) and scientists (Winner, 2019; see the section on "Phenomenology-Based Imagination" in Abraham, 2016) alike, it would seem that the construct of imagination would be given a central role in contemporary theoretical accounts of aesthetic experience. Paradoxically, although the field of empirical (experimental) aesthetics is concerned with understanding the psychological and neurological processes and mechanisms that underlie our aesthetic experiences in the course of interacting with artworks, none of the mainstream theories have assigned an explicit role to imagination in the architecture of aesthetic experience. This is puzzling for a number of reasons. First, interestingly, the ability to be creative and the ability to engage with the world aesthetically are related to the same Big Five personality factor, namely *openness to experience* – defined as "the breadth, depth, originality, and complexity of an individual's experiential life" (John, Naumann, and Soto, 2008: 120). Indeed, openness to experience has been shown to be the best predictor of creativity regardless of whether one is focusing on creative self-beliefs, creative performance (e.g. divergent thinking), or creative achievement (Karwowski and Lebuda, 2016; Silvia et al., 2009). In addition, openness to experience is also the best predictor of aesthetic attitudes and participation in aesthetic activities (McManus and Furnham, 2006), as well as aesthetic preference for a broad range of art forms (Chamorro-Premuzic et al., 2009, 2010; Furnham and Walker, 2001; Rawlings, 2003; see also Fayn et al., 2015). Thus, in terms of personality structure, it seems that the ability to create art is related to the ability to appreciate art. This suggests that facets of openness to experience including imagination and fantasy (measured by items such as *have a vivid imagination* and *seldom daydream* [this latter item is reverse scored]) could form some of the *same* cognitive mechanisms and processes that contribute to both art-making as well as the aesthetic appreciation of aesthetic objects.

Second, phenomenologically, our interactions with artworks can frequently absorb us in the form of triggering our imagination. In their classic work, Tellegen and Atkinson (1974) defined absorption as "a disposition for having episodes of 'total' attention that fully engage one's representational (i.e. perceptual, enactive, imaginative, and ideational) resources" (Tellegen and Atkinson, 1974: 268). Defined as such, people who enjoy art can recollect and envision such episodes of deep immersion in art in the museum and beyond. Indeed, there is research to show that people who score high on absorption enjoy many forms of art (Wild, Kuiken, and Schopflocher, 1995), including complex music (Rhodes, David, and Combs, 1988). More recent work has shown that trait and state absorption exhibit different relationships with preference for music, with the former being more strongly associated with preference for music that involves negative emotions (Hall, Schubert, and Wilson, 2016). This might be because persons high in trait absorption are better able to disconnect from the unpleasant aspects of negative emotion, instead becoming immersed in the pleasurable aspects of the music such as its energizing properties, among others.

(Absence of) Imagination in Theories of Aesthetics

Although space limitations will not permit me to review all the mainstream theories of aesthetic experience in this chapter, I will briefly review three contemporary models of aesthetic experience to illustrate the absence of imagination – at least explicitly – in their structure. Importantly, I do not claim that these three models exhaust all contemporary models of aesthetic experience. Rather, they are sufficiently general in nature to give a flavor of the kinds of theoretical approaches that motivate research in empirical aesthetics at the moment.

First, in their well-known model of aesthetic appreciation, Leder and colleagues presented a descriptive information-processing account of aesthetic experience within which the aesthetic processing of artworks occurs in the course of five stages, each of which is devoted to analyzing specific aspects of the artwork (Leder et al., 2004; Leder and Nadal, 2014; see also Pelowski et al., 2017). Importantly, the entire information-processing sequence is preceded by a pre-classification step in which the object is categorized as an artwork so that it can be considered from an aesthetic perspective. The information-processing stages involve (1) perceptual analyses, (2) memory integration, (3) explicit classification, (4) cognitive mastering, and (5) evaluation. The first three stages are largely devoted to bottom-up processing of input (e.g. its perceptual aspects and automatic activation of memories), whereas the latter stages exert largely top-down effects on the process (e.g. imposing self-related interpretations on the artwork as well as deriving understanding from the work). The final outputs of this information-processing sequence involve aesthetic judgment and emotion. Although imagination has not been given an explicit role within this model, it would seem that it would exert its role most readily in the cognitive mastering and evaluation stages of information processing. This is because it is within those stages that the person would impose his/her personally relevant interpretation to derive meaning and value from the work. Indeed, if cognitive mastery (i.e. understanding) of an artwork is successful, then aesthetic pleasure might follow suit. Leder et al. (2004) cite Tyler (1999) and Zeki (1999) to argue that certain types of art such as modern art offer particularly good opportunities for cognitive mastery because in a sense they are open-ended, and can be interpreted in many ways:

> Modern art provides such a large number of varieties in styles, which require the perceiver to invest great effort to extract meaning, that the aesthetic experience can be understood as a challenging perceptual problem-solving process. Modern art allows a very differentiated search for meaning, linking perceptual-based analyses (by processing style and visual properties of a painting) with a search through concepts that a perceiver has adopted through previous experience and explicit knowledge (Zeki, 1999). Thus, modern art empowers loops of processing in which hypotheses concerning the meaning of an artwork are continuously altered and tested until a satisfactory result is achieved. The processing of these loops can be pleasing itself and essential for aesthetic experiences (Leder et al., 2004: 499–500).

My reading of this paragraph suggests that it is precisely imagination that to a large extent powers the generation of the aforementioned hypotheses, the resolution of which can result in aesthetic pleasure.

A second influential model has been Graf and Landwehr's (2015; see also 2017) dual-process approach to aesthetic experience, entitled the Pleasure-Interest Model of Aesthetic Liking (PIA). According to the PIA model there are two paths to aesthetic judgment. One path involves aesthetic preferences that arise due to rapid stimulus-driven processing of art objects, resulting in states of pleasure or displeasure. According to the PIA model such states of aesthetic pleasure and/or displeasure that arise rapidly are rooted in largely automatic (i.e. bottom-up) processes. However, should there be a motivation and cognitive ability on behalf of the viewer to proceed beyond this initial stage, then more top-down and perceiver-driven processing of the art object can occur. This, in turn, can give rise to evaluations of interest, boredom, or confusion. According to the PIA model, an important factor determining whether people feel inclined to pursue deeper processing of artworks is their epistemic motivation, such as a need for cognitive enrichment. Although this model does not explicitly stipulate a role for imagination in aesthetic experience, the authors' description of how the need for cognitive enrichment can support motivated processing of art suggests some clues. Specifically, Graf and Landwehr (2015) argue that:

> because stimulus knowledge formed by preexisting knowledge structures follows directly from automatic processing, we suggest that a need for cognitive enrichment will increase people's tendency not to "freeze" on this available knowledge but to engage in adapting and revising their knowledge structures to the demands of the stimulus. Because this is only feasible with controlled processing, a need for cognitive enrichment will trigger the motivation for controlled processing. (Graf and Landwehr, 2015: 402).

I believe that such engagement in adapting and revising knowledge structures to the demands of the stimulus is precisely where imagination would exert its influence on aesthetic experience most readily. In other words, assuming that the epistemic motivation is in place to engage with artworks beyond pleasure/displeasure, the consumer of art can flexibly manipulate his/her interactions with the artwork in multiple ways to derive deeper meaning and understanding that extend beyond strictly stimulus-driven features of the artwork.

Finally, within their model referred to as the aesthetic triad, Chatterjee and Vartanian (2014, 2016) have proposed that at the level of the brain, aesthetic experiences likely emerge from the interaction between emotion–valuation, sensory–motor, and meaning–knowledge neural systems. Within this model aesthetic judgments are viewed broadly to encompass much more than the arts alone – indeed, any evaluative appraisal of objects (see also Brown et al., 2011; Skov and Vartanian, 2009). In other words, one can be said to have engaged in aesthetic judgment whenever one generates an implicit or explicit assessment of any object along what Osgood (1962) termed the *evaluation* dimension (i.e. good-bad). An important aspect of this model is that aesthetic experiences are perceived to be born out of the interaction of various neural systems, rather than produced following a sequence of information-processing steps. In addition, there is acknowledgment that aesthetic experiences surface from the interaction of bottom-up and top-down processes arising within and between the three systems.

Although imagination has not been incorporated explicitly into this model, it is likely to exert its influence on aesthetic experiences within this framework, as well. For example, the knowledge-meaning system is primarily involved in the derivation of meaning from art, and is modulated by contextual, cultural, formal and personal knowledge that the viewer brings to bear in the aesthetic encounter. Historically, the influence of such top-down effects on aesthetic experience was downplayed by classical theories in the field. Specifically, beginning with Fechner's (1876) psycho-physical approach to experimental aesthetics, there had been a push by major thinkers in the field to discover a finite set of universal laws that explain people's aesthetic interactions with objects (see Martindale, 1990; McManus, 2013). Such models advocated strongly for an experimental aesthetics "from below," meaning that they emphasized the search for bottom-up processes that originate in sensation and perception as key drivers of aesthetic experiences. As noted by Berlyne (1971), one's aim was "to relate preferences to the properties of the works of art or other objects that are presented" (Berlyne, 1971: 12). However, we now know that the same works of art can trigger divergent reactions in viewers. For example, Vessel et al. (2018) found that compared to faces and landscapes, for which there is a high degree of shared preference, there is much less uniformity in preferences for cultural artifacts such as architecture and paintings. The authors argued that because artifacts of human culture "lack uniform behavioral relevance for most individuals, [they] require the use of more individual aesthetic sensibilities that reflect varying experiences and different sources of information" (Vessel et al., 2018: 121). I will argue below that imagination is an important mental capacity that such individual aesthetic sensibilities use to exert their influence on aesthetic evaluation because imagination enables perceptual and conceptual flexibility during engagement with art. As noted by Sheppard (1991), this capacity enables the viewer to consider multiple possibilities, including the experience of as-if emotions that may accompany those possibilities.

In summary, a brief review of some current models within empirical aesthetics (Chatterjee and Vartanian, 2014, 2016; Graf and Landwehr, 2015, 2017; Leder et al., 2004; Leder and Nadal, 2014; Pelowski et al., 2017) demonstrates that none of them has explicitly incorporated imagination within its framework. However, it is also clear that in all cases the involvement of imagination is implicitly assumed in the models. In the next section I will make the case that models of aesthetic experience will benefit by explicitly incorporating imagination into their frameworks by demonstrating the importance of imagination to specific aspects of the aesthetic experience.

Imagination and the Search for Meaning in Aesthetic Experience

I argue that imagination is an important component of aesthetic experience in at least two ways. First, imagination likely guides our search for meaning when interacting with artworks. The idea that deriving meaning is an important component of interacting with artworks emphasizes the role of top-down processing in aesthetic experience. For example, Kirk and colleagues presented their participants in the functional magnetic resonance imaging (fMRI) scanner with images of artworks that were labeled either as sourced from a museum (i.e. "GALLERY") or computer-generated (i.e. "COMPUTER") (Kirk et al., 2009). Importantly, the labeling was counterbalanced across participants, such that visual parameters were balanced across label conditions, thus ensuring that systematic differences in visual properties between the two conditions were controlled for. In turn, this enabled the experimenters to manipulate only the context within which each stimulus was viewed. They found that people were more likely to find paintings that were sourced from a museum to be beautiful than those that were computer-generated. In addition, this contextual modulation was associated with greater activation in the brain's reward system (i.e. orbitofrontal cortex), as well as in the prefrontal cortex. In another similar study, Silveira and colleagues presented participants with paintings from the Museum of Modern Art (MoMA) that were labeled as being either from the MoMA or from an adult education center (Silveira et al., 2015). The authors found greater neural activation in a set of regions including the left precuneus for the MoMA condition compared to the control condition. The involvement of the precuneus is interesting because of its sensitivity to a host of higher-cognitive functions including consciousness, autobiographical memory, and the experience of agency (Cavanna and Trimble, 2006). When the aesthetic preference for a painting was also taken into account, the MoMA condition elicited higher involvement of a set of regions including the right precuneus. The findings of Kirk et al. and Silveira et al. suggest that our aesthetic preferences are not governed exclusively by bottom-up perceptual inputs from the stimulus, but are also strongly influenced by top-down contextual factors that affect viewers' evaluations of those inputs, in this case provenance.

Along similar lines, we also have a similar preference for artworks that we believe are authentic rather than fake (Newman and Bloom, 2012). In a very interesting study on the neural correlates of authenticity perception, Huang and colleagues presented their participants with portraits that were labeled as authentic Rembrandts or fakes in the fMRI scanner (Huang, Bridge, Kemp, and Palmer, 2011). They found that authentic portraits evoked greater OFC activity, whereas fakes evoked neural responses in the frontopolar cortex and the right precuneus. In conjunction with the results of Silveira et al. (2015), this suggests that the precuneus might be sensitive to the way in which objects are labeled (i.e. framed), consistent with its involvement in consciousness-related processes (Cavanna, 2007; Cavanna and Trimble, 2006; Cunningham, Tomasi, and Volkow, 2017). Here, too, we see that our brains are sensitive to contextual variations when we view art.

The reason why we prefer art that is authentic and/or made by artists rather than fake and/or generated by nonartists is likely related to the value and meaning we assign to works of art. Within their psychohistorical framework, Bullot and Reber (2013) argue that "a science of art appreciation must investigate how appreciators process causal and historical information to classify and explain their psychological responses to art" (Bullot and Reber, 2013: 123). In other words, in what Bullot and Reber refer to as "artistic understanding of the work," our psychological responses to art include a sense-making component that involves broad consideration of the epistemic, causal (proximal and distal), and historical (developmental) factors that underlie and support the work. I believe that this meaning-making process requires imagination to support processes such as simulating the artist's mental states that led to the generation of the artwork or the labor that generated it.

Here, Tinio's (2013; see also Specker, Tinio, and van Elk, 2017) *Mirror Model of Art* is germane. According to this model, "aesthetic experiences *mirror* the art-making process such that the early stages of aesthetic processing correspond to the final stages of art-making; conversely, the late stages of aesthetic processing correspond to the initial stages of art-making" (Tinio, 2013: 265). Within this model the art-making process consists of three stages: initialization, expansion and adaptation, and finalizing. In the initialization stage the artist creates sketches that are meant to represent visually what was hitherto an idea or a concept in the artist's mind. In this sense the sketches represent the development of an idea in visual form. Two important elements that emerge from those early sketches in the initialization stage consist of the work's underwriting and structural skeleton. The underwriting is the visual representation of what will underlie the individual elements in the work, including their spatial relationships. In turn, the structural skeleton is – to use Arnheim's (1954/1974) words – "the configuration of visual forces that determines the character of the visual object" (Arnheim, 1954/1974: 93). In this sense the structural skeleton is the scaffolding (i.e. guiding image) that represents the core components of the work and their relationships in the artist's mind. Next, in the expansion and adaptation stage, the artist develops and fine-tunes the artwork following the initialization stage. Here one observes instances of additions and deletions of elements as well as the adjusting of the overall composition. Eventually, in the third and finalizing stage, the artist enhances and modifies the work toward completion. In this stage the artist deals less with the structure of the work and more with refinements such as color, texture, and other subtle manipulations that affect the surface layer of the work that the viewer is most likely to process initially when approaching the work of art.

In turn, according to Tinio's model, the consumer of art traverses the three stages *in reverse order*. Specifically, when encountering a work of art for the first time, one is likely to engage in the processing of its perceptual features involving colors and textures embedded in its surface, among others (see Leder et al., 2004). Much of this early processing is likely to be automatic, driven by bottom-up features of the stimulus. Next, in the second stage, one is likely to engage in intermediate, memory-based processing, such as identification of the work's content and determining the style of the artwork. Finally, if successful, the final stage involves meaning-making processes, including understanding the initial concepts, ideas, and intentions of the artist that motivated the work. As noted by Tinio (2013), "the viewer may be seen as not only trying to determine the visual characteristics of an artwork or attempting to understand its meaning, but also searching for ways to discover the many different processes that transpired when the work was created" (Tinio, 2013: 274). Described as such, the artwork can be seen as a medium through which the viewer can gain insights into the mental state of the artist. This is because at its core, the canvas is the developed visual representation of the concepts and ideas in the mind of the artist.

Aside from driving our search for the underlying concepts and causes that originated the artwork, imagination can also facilitate our search for meaning in the form of supporting deeper ways of interacting with art that draw on our internal thoughts and emotions. From a phenomenological perspective, many of us have had the experience of being deeply moved by art, both in the museum and beyond. Some researches in the field have begun to probe the neural and psychological correlates of such deep engagements with art. For example, Vessel, Starr, and Rubin (2012) have shown that the default-mode network (DMN) is engaged when participants explicitly focus on internal thoughts and emotions while viewing paintings. Specifically, in the fMRI scanner they presented their participants with a variety of paintings and asked "How strongly does this painting move you?", requiring a response on a four-point rating scale. The wording of the question was purposeful, meant to tap into deeper, internally oriented aesthetic experiences. They found that relatively speaking, DMN regions were more active when participants viewed paintings that they rated as most moving, including in the medial prefrontal cortex and the posterior cingulate cortex. The involvement of the DMN in association with the most moving artworks is consistent with the idea that deeper aesthetic moments are associated with an internal orientation. Indeed, a meta-analysis of the neural correlates of viewing paintings has shown the involvement of DMN regions (Vartanian and Skov, 2014).

However, we also have the sense that such deeper states of interaction with art do not occur rapidly, but rather take time to develop. There is now some empirical evidence in support of this notion, as well. For example, Cela-Conde and colleagues (2013) proposed that two different neural systems exert their effects within distinct time frames. Using magnetoencephalography (MEG), they probed the time course of aesthetic judgments of artworks. They found that an initial appraisal of an object as "beautiful" or "not beautiful" emerges rapidly within 250–750 milliseconds in structures including the orbitofrontal cortex. In turn, a more particular appraisal of the beauty of the object in terms of "the extent to which the stimulus is moving, whether it is interesting or original, how to rate it, and the reasons for considering it attractive" emerges later around 1,000–1,500 milliseconds in the DMN. Their findings suggest that the DMN comes online in the later stages of aesthetic judgment. In a recent fMRI study, Belfi and colleagues (2019) have demonstrated that DMN activity varies in the course of interacting with artworks, and that it tracks the internal dynamics of the observer during aesthetic experience – engaging and disengaging with pleasing and non-pleasing stimuli, respectively. These findings are consistent with various theoretical accounts according to which more deliberate and top-down effects exert an influence on aesthetic judgment, including those that underlie the application of personally relevant input into judgment, reflecting more processing time, effort, and motivation than rapid judgments of liking (e.g. Graf and Landwehr, 2015, 2017; Leder et al., 2004).

I argue that just as it did in our search for concepts and ideas that originate artworks (see Tinio, 2013), imagination likely also plays a role in deeper states of interaction with artworks that involve internally generated thoughts. In other words, imagination likely facilitates the type of absorption and mind-wandering that accompany deeply immersive, personally laden aesthetic experiences. There are a few lines of evidence that support this idea. First, we know that art can trigger mind-wandering, and that different types of art can do so to different extents. For example, unlike Western representational landscape paintings that are typically filled with various elements (e.g. mountains, rivers, trees, etc.), traditional Chinese landscape paintings purposefully include blank spaces within the canvas to prompt viewers to wander, imagine, and create images in their minds. It has recently been shown that, compared to Western representational landscape paintings, traditional Chinese landscape paintings elicit greater levels of mind-wandering in viewers (Wang et al., 2015). Second, the viewing orientation that we take when we enter an interaction with an artwork predisposes us to interact with it in ways that facilitate aesthetic engagement. For example, when we enter a museum with the explicit intention of viewing art, we likely have a greater propensity for deeper aesthetic experiences than if we were exposed to the same objects under different circumstances. Cupchik et al. (2009) looked into this possibility by instructing their participants to view paintings under two different conditions in the fMRI scanner. Under the *pragmatic orientation* participants were instructed to approach the images in an objective and detached manner to obtain information about the content of the painting and its visual narrative. This orientation is similar to how we typically process visual input in everyday life. In contrast, under the *aesthetic orientation* they were instructed to approach the paintings in a subjective and engaged manner, experiencing the mood of the work and the feelings it evokes, and to focus on its colours, tones, composition, and shapes. This orientation mimics what would occur in a museum setting when we are open to engage with art aesthetically. They found that the aesthetic orientation activated bilateral insula, which they attributed to the experience of emotion. Moreover, adopting the aesthetic orientation activated the left lateral prefrontal cortex, consistent with the involvement of this region not only in top-down control of cognition, but also in higher-order self-referential processing and the evaluation of internally generated information. In contrast, viewing paintings in the pragmatic orientation activated the fusiform gyrus, consistent with the role of that region in object recognition.

These findings suggest that the aesthetic orientation adopted while viewing art goes beyond mere object recognition, enabling the viewer to bring to bear their feelings and personal aspects of experience to the interaction (Cupchik et al., 2009). Indeed, depending on the specific artwork under consideration, this interaction could result in varying levels of mind-wandering as well (Wang et al., 2015). Within this setting imagination could be considered a potent capacity that enables the viewer to engage flexibly with the artwork in multiple ways, in the process deriving meaning from it from many perspectives.

Imagination and the Drive toward Uncertainty Reduction

Relatively recently, van de Cruys and Wagemans (2011) have proposed the *prediction error account* of processing (visual) art. According to this account, the brain actively anticipates incoming sensory input rather than passively receiving it. This involves actively generating predictions (based on priors), and testing them against the available data. They note that according to the predictive coding approach *all* perception is a form of expert perception, because people are always testing the data against their expectations built up through past experience and implicit statistical learning. Of course, predictions can be either accurate or inaccurate. When predictions are accurate, efficient processing of input occurs. This ease of processing is experienced as pleasant.

Conversely, when there is a difference between prediction and the actual state of affairs, a prediction error ensues. Prediction errors are therefore typically emotional and negative in valence. Van de Cruys and Wagemans proposed that artists habitually manipulate conditions that initially increase viewers' prediction error, which is subsequently resolved as the stimulus becomes predictable. This transition from unpredictability to predictability is experienced as particularly rewarding. In the context of indeterminate paintings that are made to be purposefully ambiguous and difficult to decode, it has been shown that there is a positive correlation between the time needed to understand a painting and the aesthetic value one assigns to it (Ishai, Fairhall, and Pepperell, 2007). This suggests that the transition from unpredictability to predictability might be experienced as particularly pleasant if it is preceded by greater effort.

Van de Cruys and Wagemans (2011) review many different types of art to demonstrate their point. For example, surrealistic art that typically depicts seemingly contradictory and unexpected juxtapositions against dreamlike backgrounds certainly represents an opportunity for transitioning from unpredictability to predictability. Prime examples include works by Salvador Dali, Max Ernst, and René Magritte, among others. The same can be said about indeterminate paintings, represented by the work of Robert Pepperell (see Ishai, Fairhall, and Pepperell, 2007). Such works activate one's imagination to simulate various possibilities embedded within them before a resolution is eventually achieved. Although imagination is likely not involved in all forms of prediction error as described by van de Cruys and Wagemans (2011), there are nevertheless certain classes of art within which imagination likely plays a role in the process to reach predictable states, due to its involvement in simulating various perceptual outcomes as the viewer hones in on a stable and predictable endpoint.

Conclusions

I have tried to argue that models of aesthetic experience would benefit by explicitly incorporating imagination into their frameworks. In support of this suggestion, I have reviewed some empirical evidence to demonstrate that imagination contributes to our aesthetic experiences by facilitating our search for meaning, and by facilitating transitioning from states of unpredictability to predictability. The explicit acknowledgment of the role of imagination in aesthetic experience would benefit models of aesthetic experience, and make the correspondence between our accounts of art-making and art appreciation stronger. It is also clear that there is a dearth of research regarding the role of imagination in aesthetic experience, and it is my hope that this chapter will contribute toward motivating a greater examination of this important question in empirical aesthetics.

Ideas for Further Investigation

I would like to close by highlighting a few important issues the investigation of which would likely move the field forward. First, consistent with the idea that creativity and imagination are related constructs, it has been shown that more creative people excel at imagination involving vivid distal simulations across temporal, spatial, social, and hypothetical domains (Meyer et al., 2019). Accordingly, given that art expertise is known to influence the breadth and depth of aesthetic appreciation (see Chatterjee and Vartanian, 2014, 2016), it would be interesting to study whether expertise (e.g. formal training in art) influences one's imaginative ability *specifically* while viewing artworks. If so, imagination could be one vehicle via which art expertise exerts its influence on aesthetic appreciation. Second, given that openness to experience is the personality factor most closely associated with both creative production and aesthetic appreciation, it would be useful to study more precisely the cognitive and emotional processes that underlie individual differences in this multifaceted personality construct. Doing so has the potential to reveal the specific processes that form bridges between production and appreciation – for which imagination could be a prime candidate.

References

Abraham, A. (2016). The Imaginative Mind. *Human Brain Mapping, 37,* 4197–4211.

Arnheim, R. (1954/1974). *Art and Visual Perception.* Berkeley, CA: University of California Press.

Belfi, A. M., Vessel, E. A., Brielmann, A., et al. (2019). Dynamics of Aesthetic Experience Are Reflected in the Default-Mode Network. *Neuroimage, 188,* 584–597.

Berlyne, D. E. (1971). *Aesthetics and Psychobiology.* New York, NY: Appleton-Century-Crofts.

Brown, S., Gao, X., Tisdelle, L., Eickhoff, S. B., and Liotti, M. (2011). Naturalizing Aesthetics: Brain Areas for Aesthetic Appraisal across Sensory Modalities. *Neuroimage, 58,* 250–258.

Bullot, N. J., and Reber, R. (2013). A Psycho-Historical Research Program for the Integrative Science of Art. *Behavioral and Brain Sciences, 36,* 163–180.

Campbell, D. T. (1960). Blind Variation and Selective Retentions in Creative Thought as in Other Knowledge Processes. *Psychological Review, 67,* 380–400.

Cavanna, A. E. (2007). The Precuneus and Consciousness. *CNS Spectrums, 12,* 545–552.

Cavanna, A. E., and Trimble, M. R. (2006). The Precuneus: A Review of its Functional Anatomy and Behavioural Correlates. *Brain, 129,* 564–583.

Cela-Conde, C. J., Garcia-Prieto, J., Ramasco, J., et al. (2013). Dynamics of Brain Networks in the Aesthetic Appreciation. *Proceedings of the National Academy of Sciences USA, 110 (Suppl. 2),* 10454–10461.

Chamorro-Premuzic, T., Burke, C., Hsu, A., and Swami, V. (2010). Personality Predictors of Artistic Preferences as a Function of the Emotional Valence and Perceived Complexity of Paintings. *Psychology of Aesthetics, Creativity, and the Arts, 4,* 196–204.

Chamorro-Premuzic, T., Reimers, S., Hsu, A., and Ahmetoglu, G. (2009). Who Art Thou? Personality Predictors of Artistic Preferences in a Large UK Sample: The Importance of Openness. *British Journal of Psychology, 100,* 501–516.

Chatterjee, A., and Vartanian, O. (2014). Neuroaesthetics. *Trends in Cognitive Sciences, 18,* 370–375.

(2016). Neuroscience of Aesthetics. *Annals in the New York Academy of Sciences*, *1369*, 172–194.

Cunningham, S. I., Tomasi, D., and Volkow, N. D. (2017). Structural and Functional Connectivity of the Precuneus and Thalamus to the Default Mode Network. *Human Brain Mapping*, *38*, 938–956.

Cupchik, G. C. (2016). *The Aesthetics of Emotion*. New York, NY: Cambridge University Press.

Cupchik, G. C., Vartanian, O., Crawley, A., and Mikulis, D. J. (2009). Viewing Artworks: Contributions of Cognitive Control and Perceptual Facilitation to Aesthetic Experience. *Brain and Cognition*, *70*, 84–91.

Dutton, D. (2009). *The Art Instinct*. New York, NY: Oxford University Press.

Fayn, K., MacCann, C., Tiliopoulos, N., and Silvia, P. J. (2015). Aesthetic Emotions and Aesthetic People: Openness Predicts Sensitivity to Novelty in the Experiences of Interest and Pleasure. *Frontiers in Psychology*, *6*, article 1877.

Fechner, G. T. (1876). *Vorschule der Aesthetik* [Experimental Aesthetics: *"Pre-School"* of *Aesthetics*]. Leipzig, Germany: Breitkopf & Härtel.

Fink, A., Benedek, M., Grabner, R. H., Staudt, B., and Neubauer, A. C. (2007). Creativity Meets Neuroscience: Experimental Tasks for the Neuroscientific Study of Creative Thinking. *Methods*, *42*, 68–76.

Furnham, A., and Walker, J. (2001). The Influence of Personality Traits, Previous Experience of Art, and Demographic Variables on Artistic Preference. *Personality and Individual Differences*, *31*, 997–1017.

Graf, L. K. M., and Landwehr, J. R. (2015). A Dual-Process Perspective on Fluency-Based Aesthetics: The Pleasure-Interest Model of Aesthetic Liking. *Personality and Social Psychology Review*, *19*, 395–410.

(2017). Aesthetic Pleasure versus Aesthetic Interest: The Two Routes to Aesthetic Liking. *Frontiers in Psychology*, *8*, article 15.

Hall, S. E., Schubert, E., and Wilson, S. J. (2016). The Role of Trait and State Absorption in the Enjoyment of Music. *PLoS One*, *11*, e0164029.

Huang, M., Bridge, H., Kemp, M. J., and Parker, A. J. (2011). Human Cortical Activity Evoked by the Assignment of Authenticity when Viewing Works of Art. *Frontiers in Human Neuroscience*, *5*, 134.

Ishai, A., Fairhall, S. L., and Pepperell, R. (2007). Perception, Memory and Aesthetics of Indeterminate Art. *Brain Research Bulletin*, *73*, 319–324.

John, O. P., Naumann, L. P., and Soto, C. J. (2008). Paradigm Shift to the Integrative Big Five Trait Taxonomy. In O. P. John, R. W. Robbins, and L. A. Pervin (eds.), *Handbook of Personality: Theory and Research*. New York, NY: Guilford Press, 114–158.

Karwowski, M., and Lebuda, I. (2016). The Big Five, the Huge Two, and Creative Self-Beliefs: A Meta-Analysis. *Psychology of Aesthetics, Creativity, and the Arts*, *10*, 214–232.

Kirk, U., Skov, M., Hulme, O., Christensen, M. S., and Zeki, S. (2009). Modulation of Aesthetic Value by Semantic Context: An fMRI Study. *Neuroimage*, *44*, 1125–1132.

Leder, H., Belke, B., Oeberst, A., and Augustin, D. (2004). A Model of Aesthetic Appreciation and Aesthetic Judgments. *British Journal of Psychology*, *95*, 489–508.

Leder, H., and Nadal, M. (2014). Ten Years of a Model of Aesthetic Appreciation and Aesthetic Judgments: The Aesthetic Episode – Developments and Challenges in Empirical Aesthetics. *British Journal of Psychology*, *105*, 443–464.

Martindale, C. (1990). *The Clockwork Muse: The Predictability of Artistic Change.* New York, NY: Basic Books.

McManus, I. C. (2013). "The Anti-Developmental, the Anti-Narrative, the Anti-Historical": Mondrian as a Paradigmatic Artist for Empirical Aesthetics. *Behavioral and Brain Sciences, 36*, 152–153.

McManus, I. C., and Furnham, A. (2006). Aesthetic Activities and Aesthetic Attitudes: Influences of Education, Background and Personality on Interest and Involvement in the Arts. *British Journal of Psychology, 97*, 555–587.

Meyer, M. L., Hershfield, H. E., Waytz, A. G., Mildner, J. N., and Tamir, D. I. (2019). Creative Expertise Is Associated with Transcending the Here and Now. *Journal of Personality and Social Psychology, 116*, 483–494.

Newman, G. E., and Bloom, P. (2012). Art and Authenticity: The Importance of Originals in Judgments of Value. *Journal of Experimental Psychology: General, 141*, 558–569.

Osgood, C. E. (1962). Studies on the Generality of Affective Meaning Systems. *American Psychologist, 17*, 10–28.

Pelowski, M., Markey, P. S., Forster, M., Gerger, G., and Leder, H. (2017). Move Me, Astonish Me . . . Delight my Eyes and Brain: The Vienna Integrated Model of Top-Down and Bottom-Up Processes in Art Perception (VIMAP) and Corresponding Affective, Evaluative, and Neurophysiological Correlates. *Physics of Life Reviews, 21*, 80–125.

Rawlings, D. (2003). Personality Correlates of Liking for "Unpleasant" Paintings and Photographs. *Personality and Individual Differences, 34*, 395–410.

Rhodes, L. A., David, D. C., and Combs, A. L. (1988). Absorption and Enjoyment of Music. *Perceptual and Motor Skills, 66*, 737–738.

Sheppard, A. (1991). The Role of Imagination in Aesthetic Experience. *The Journal of Aesthetic Education, 25*, 35–42.

Silveira, S., Fehse, K., Vedder, A., Elvers, K., and Hennig-Fast, K. (2015). Is It the Picture or Is It the Frame? An fMRI Study on the Neurobiology of Framing Effects. *Frontiers in Human Neuroscience, 9*, article 528.

Silvia, P. J., Nusbaum E. C., Berg C., Martin C., and O'Connor A. (2009). Openness to Experience, Plasticity, and Creativity: Exploring Lower-Order, High-Order, and Interactive Effects. *Journal of Research in Personality, 43*, 1087–1090.

Simonton, D. K. (1999). Creativity as Blind Variation and Selective Retention: Is the Creative Process Darwinian? *Psychological Inquiry, 10*, 309–328.

   (2007). The Creative Imagination in Picasso's Guernica Sketches: Monotonic Improvements or Nonmonotonic Variants? *Creativity Research Journal, 19*, 329–344.

   (2013). Creative Thought as Blind Variation and Selective Retention: Why Creativity Is Inversely Related to Sightedness. *Journal of Theoretical and Philosophical Psychology, 33*, 253–266.

Skov, M., and Vartanian, O. (eds.) (2009). *Neuroaesthetics.* Amityville, NY: Baywood Publishing Company.

Specker, E., Tinio, P. P. L., and van Elk, M. (2017). Do You See What I See? An Investigation of the Aesthetic Experience in the Laboratory and Museum. *Psychology of Aesthetics, Creativity, and the Arts, 11*(3), 265–275.

Tellegen, A., and Atkinson, G. (1974). Openness to Absorbing and Self-Altering Experiences ("Absorption"), a Trait Related to Hypnotic Susceptibility. *Journal of Abnormal Psychology, 83*, 268–277.

Tinio, P. P. L. (2013). From Artistic Creation to Aesthetic Reception: The Mirror Model of Art. *Psychology of Aesthetics, Creativity, and the Arts*, 7, 265–275.

Tyler, C. W. (1999). Is Art Lawful? *Journal of Consciousness Studies*, 6, 673–674.

van de Cruys, S., and Wagemans, J. (2011). Putting Reward in Art: A Tentative Prediction Error Account of Visual Art. *i-Perception*, 2, 1035–1062.

Vartanian, O., and Skov, M. (2014). Neural Correlates of Viewing Paintings: Evidence from a Quantitative Meta-Analysis of Functional Magnetic Resonance Imaging Data. *Brain and Cognition*, 87, 52–56.

Vessel, E. A., Maurer, N., Denker, A. H., and Starr, G. G. (2018). Stronger Shared Taste for Natural Aesthetic Domains than for Artifacts of Human Nature. *Cognition*, 179, 121–131.

Vessel, E. A., Starr, G. G., and Rubin, N. (2012). The Brain on Art: Intense Aesthetic Experience Activates the Default Mode Network. *Frontiers in Human Neuroscience*, 6, article 66.

Wang, T., Mo, L., Vartanian, O., Cant, J. S., and Cupchik, G. (2015). An Investigation of the Neural Substrates of Mind Wandering Induced by Viewing Traditional Chinese Landscape Paintings. *Frontiers in Human Neuroscience*, 8, article 1018.

Ward, T. B., Patterson, M. J., and Sifonis, C. M. (2004). The Role of Specificity and Abstraction in Creative Idea Generation. *Creativity Research Journal*, 16, 1–9.

Wild, T. C., Kuiken, D., and Schopflocher, D. (1995). The Role of Absorption in Experiential Involvement. *Journal of Personality and Social Psychology*, 69, 569–579.

Winner, E. (2019). *How Art Works*. New York, NY: Oxford University Press.

Zeki, S. (1999). *Inner Vision*. Oxford, UK: Oxford University Press.

36 The Arts and Human Symbolic Cognition: Art is for Social Communication

Dahlia W. Zaidel

An Interdisciplinary Approach to Art and the Brain

Art is currently expressed ubiquitously across human societies, and this attests to a basic human social need to communicate with others through art. The arts showcase the cultural rules, norms, values, and fashions of a society, as well as advertise cross-culturally the available collective artistic cognition, talent, and skills. Forms of art are even pervasive in societies with rigid restrictions on the types that can be displayed publicly. The very fact that there are restrictions on its contents, exemplifies art's recognized social communicative power. Art has become a valued practice in human cultures, so much so that it is now synonymous with what people commonly mean by high culture. It can be seen in paintings, drawings, sculptures, photography, theater, and music, as well as in architecture, clothes fashion, food trends, and in a myriad of ever growing and expanding combinations and extensions.

Effective social communication requires a signal to which a recipient resonates, overtly or covertly. The powerful effectiveness of the signal as it pertains to art can be seen in its cross-cultural influence. The classic example is how art from Africa, Oceania, and Japan influenced the works of European artists from the mid-1880s to the early 1900s; they had never visited those geographical parts of the world nor spoken the languages used there, nor did they know the history, motivation, or cultural context of that art. Works of well-known visual artists such as Picasso, Monet, Manet, Degas, Van Gogh, and Modigliani, to name but a few, illustrate the power of this influence. Some of their artworks show modification of their techniques, styles, and configurations to match those practiced in the distant exotic cultures (Le Fur and Martin, 2017; Wichmann, 1988). By comparison, language does not spontaneously communicate cross-culturally, and this attests to the nature of art itself, namely its fundamental social communication capacity.

Considering the fact that only humans create and practice art spontaneously raises obvious questions about how and why it became a rich and varied mode of social communication. Aspects of language have a long evolutionary history spanning many millions of years, yet language's functions have not provided the sole communication system for humans. Support for this idea comes from neuropsychological observations that when language and other sensory or perceptual abilities are compromised following brain injury in professional artists, their artistic abilities are preserved, or when linguistic communication is compromised in nonartists, some resort to communicating through *de novo* visual artworks. Clearly, then, language is not the only communicative channel available to humans, and not the sufficient one, although the underpinnings for both lie in symbolic and abstract cognition. Both this cognition and language-based communication have a long evolutionary trajectory. But whereas elements of language's antecedents are found in ancestral apes (Burling et al., 1993), and in species from whom the human line has diverged more than 400 million years ago (e.g. birds, whales), this is not so with art practice. The practice is a relative latecomer on the human scene. The eventual emergence of a supplementary system of communication embodied in art implies that it gained adaptive survival value for humans through social-cultural practice, while the very mechanisms of attraction to its display mode are linked to specific ancient biological strategies (Miller, 2000; Zahavi, 1978; Zaidel, 2015a).

Upon viewing or listening to art, we are conscious of our aesthetic reactions to it and assume that artists create art for aesthetic reasons, but in current debates on the early emergence of art in prehistory, only a fraction can be explained by aesthetics (Zaidel, 2018). Exploring art's origins, something that is linked with the *Homo sapiens* (HS), who arose some ~315,000 years ago in Africa (Hublin et al., 2017; Richter et al., 2017; Stringer and Galway-Witham, 2017), provides critical clues: The argument for the presence of brain substrates for symbolic and abstract cognition in early HS comes from assessing the archaeological evidence of their increasingly socially oriented group existence and the progressive nature of their stone tools (for food procurement and weaponry), as well as evidence for behaviors that bespeak of planning and long-distance mining (Brooks et al., 2018; McBrearty, 2007; McBrearty and Brooks, 2000; Potts et al., 2018; Wadley, Hodgskiss, and Grant, 2009; Wurz, 2013). In total, this suggests that forms of art could have emerged for social communication of symbols denoting group unity and cohesion, and that art's incorporation into cultural practice stemmed from evolutionarily advantageous needs for survival (Zaidel, 2017a, 2018, 2019). Although material art traces are not among the archaeological finds from the first 200,000 years of the HS, nonmaterial art forms such as communal group formation dance, chorus of singing voices, story telling and theater-like acting around the central camp fire hearth, could nevertheless have been practiced to enhance the group's success as a whole. What is proposed here is that art's emergence was gradual and tied to its collective usefulness in socially based human survival strategies.

Today's arts are practiced in myriad forms and formats worldwide, but it is unlikely that they originated in a single suite. Rather, it is likely that different expressions emerged gradually, building on natural biological attributes such as entrainment, motoric coupling, and rhythmical co-timing, and leading to the art forms of dance and music. It is reasonable to propose that initially these forms percolated individually into already existing nonartistic cultural practices consisting of hunting, foraging, stone toolmaking, and so on (Zaidel, 2018). The earliest arts harnessed biological attributes conserved in humans to symbolically communicate social unity and cooperation. The social aspect of the early HS was crucial for their survival; mutual understanding through language did not provide sufficient bonding power and had to be supplemented with messages conveyed in certain formats of art. The discussions developed here represent the intersection of several fields of inquiry, integrating clues to the communicative nature of art as gleaned from (1) the effects of brain injury in established (professional) artists, (2) *de novo* art following brain injury in nonartists, (3) earliest expressions of art in distant prehistorical times, and (4) the evolutionary adaptive purpose of art.

The Symbolic and Abstract Cognition Underlying Art and Language Communication

The human brain supports rich symbolic and abstract cognition (Deacon, 1998, 2011), which is harnessed in the attainment of meaning and understanding of arbitrary signals agreed upon by the culture. Both language and art communication build on the cognition, which itself co-evolved with other brain functions. There is evidence for presence of the cognition in apes, albeit minimally compared to humans (Fuentes, 2015; Stevens and Stevens, 2012; Whiten, 2011, 2017). However, major differences between art and language emanate from how far back in distant biological times the underlying neural mechanisms evolved. Human language depends on purposeful vocal emission of precisely crafted sounds, but humans are not the only ones in nature to communicate with each other through meaningful sounds. In the biological world, various animals utilize a repertoire of sounds and visual signals to communicate states of emotion, dangers, territoriality, and experiences. Communication through vocalizations and visual signals are observed in today's apes, humans' close biological cousins (Burling et al., 1993). Scholars argue that the neuroanatomical underpinnings for language-related properties, such as emotional expressions and explicit signifiers, vocal and visual, have been evolving for millions of years, before the HS arose (Arbib, 2005; Clark, 2013; Fitch, 2011; Seyfarth and Cheney, 2014), and this is exceptionally long prior to the earliest dated examples of material art.

Moreover, human language is heavily dependent on syntax, which contributes critically to its unique feature of conveying a seemingly infinite variety of meanings. Unlike the largely vocally dependent communication of nonhuman primates (they use gestures, too, but less so), humans can develop a language through nonvocalization, as in spontaneously created elaborate sign-language by deaf-mute people. The ability to do so is facilitated by an underlying symbolic cognition. The syntactic capability is thought by some scholars to have emerged with HS and to be explained by increased brain volume, and presumably rich neuronal connectivity (Clark, 2013; Luuk and Luuk, 2014), but its antecedents are argued by scholars to already be expressed by birds (e.g. Griesser et al., 2018). Important for the present discussion, language is controlled by highly specialized regions in the brain, localized mainly in the left cerebral hemisphere, and neuroanatomical evidence shows that some of these asymmetrical regions are present in nonhuman primates, albeit much smaller and with less connectivity between them compared to humans (see review in Fitch, 2011). In other words, vocal explicit communication, a principal mode of communication by humans (but not exclusively so) originated long ago in the biological ancestry (Beaudet, 2017; Burling et al., 1993), and co-evolved together with expansion of ear sensitivity to specific sounds and the corresponding neural mechanisms in the auditory cortex.

Art production, in sharp contrast, is a relative latecomer in human brain evolution and is used both to communicate with others when language alone fails (following brain injury to language brain areas) and to supplement language communication ("a picture is worth a thousand words"), and, so far, there do not appear to be specialized localized brain regions or pathways underlying art production, or its perception. The point emphasized is that because human language communication has roots that reach much further back in biological times than art, specialized regions for art have not yet evolved, or, alternatively, might not evolve at all. Currently, art appreciation appears to have diffuse functional representation in the brain. It may turn out that art's uniqueness lies in its human-specific social needs and as such engages multiple, widely distributed neural brain regions.

And what about the imagination? One could argue that such a diffuse system affords flexibility in the nature of the communicated artistic expression for a reason, namely for broadly tapping the cognitive symbolic and abstract substrates to convey a wide range of thoughts, ideas, and experiences. In order to be an effective communicator, art "has" to recruit such a broad range. Or, put differently, to facilitate the expression of the imagination. While language is explicit and detailed, art, by comparison, has looser semantic boundaries and thus affords the conjuring of expansive imaginary possibilities for its articulation. The latter system is useful not only for art but also for technological advances and innovations.

Lessons from Brain Injury in Professional Artists: Functional Localization for Art?

Unlike human language, with its vocabulary, syntax, and immeasurable combinatorial power, and the specialized brain regions supporting its expression, the bulk of the evidence from professional artists with brain injury suggests that there are no specific neural centers, pathways, or circuitry specializing in art-making (Zaidel, 2015b), or even in art perception, evaluation, and aesthetic assessment, as is revealed in functional neuroimaging studies (Boccia et al., 2016; Nadal, 2013). Rather, multiple and widely distributed brain regions seem to be involved in producing and viewing art. Several sensory and motor regions in the artist's brain are recruited during artistic cognition. For painting and drawing alone, eyes, hands, motor cortex, the occipital lobes, eye-hand coordination, and the pathways connecting them are essential. Artistic cognition, thinking, problem-solving, and understanding all contribute to the final product, and together reflect functional recruitment of diffuse, widely distributed brain areas.

The underlying brain circuitry of art production in professional artists can be investigated with the widely accepted method of functional localization following brain injury. The modern era of localization in the brain was launched more than 150 years ago when neurologist Paul Broca reported on his work with patients who had an injury to the brain region that controls language production (reviewed in Rutten,

2017). The region has come to be known as Broca's area in the left hemisphere; it is localized in the inferior portion of the third frontal convolution, that is, in the left posterior-inferior frontal lobe. The region encompasses Brodmann's areas 44 and 45. When damaged, Broca's aphasia results in slow, hesitant speech, mostly single words and short phrases, accompanied by agrammatism, which makes it difficult for the patient to comprehend sentences laden with conjunction words. Language comprehension, however, is relatively functional in this aphasia. A little over a decade after Broca's seminal publication, the neurologist Carl Wernicke published an equally important finding regarding functional localization in the brain, namely that the region in the left superior-posterior portion of the first temporal gyrus is critical for language comprehension. It is known as Wernicke's area, and fits within Brodmann's area 22, which is part of the auditory cortex. The language deficits known as Wernicke's aphasia consist of fluent speech accompanied by serious comprehension deficits. Broca's and Wernicke's conclusions followed observations of their patients with acquired brain injury. Countless other studies soon followed zeroing in on brain regions that when damaged lead to specific behavioral deficits in cognition, semantic knowledge (agnosia), motoric schemas (apraxia), emotions, and so on. Even currently, functional localization with the use of modern-day neuroimaging techniques measuring blood concentration and oxygenation is directed at detecting brain regions and pathways that specialize in specific behaviors.

To explore the effects of localized brain injury on art, the focus is on professional artists, those who have had a lifelong commitment to art-making, as distinguished from "hobbyists" or occasional artists. This is analogous to the approach used to study the breakdown of language, cognition, and actions following brain injury, namely in people who had normal language from a young age and onward, who have used language continuously, and who demonstrated normal landmarks in thinking and knowledge throughout their developmental years going into adulthood.

Numerous neurological cases of established artists have by now been reviewed (Bogousslavsky and Boller, 2005; Rose, 2004; Zaidel, 2015b). They cover etiologies originating in stroke, tumor, various dementias, Parkinson's disease, and other neurological conditions. More than fifty such cases have been reported. The most relevant to localization are those professional artists whose brain injury was not caused by widespread damage such as occurs with dementia. In reviewing about forty such published cases (Zaidel, 2015b), inspecting the published pictorial illustrations of their pre- and post-stroke art, it does not appear that there was loss of artistic skill, talent, creativity, or cognition. Moreover, there did not appear to be a shift in artistic genre compared to that practiced in the time period preceding the stroke, which supports the notion that artistic conceptualization, intention, and style of expression are not affected by a localized neural region (Fornazzari et al., 2013; Petcu et al., 2016; Zaidel, 2017b).

So far, these observations suggest that artistic cognition is flexible with regard to the recruitment and contribution of multiple brain regions. Functionally, either the symbolic and abstract semantic system tapped by artistic expression is highly malleable or, alternatively, the network of neural access routes to tap it is not only widely spread but also comprised of functionally noncommitted, multimodal, multifunctional pathways, or possibly both scenarios are true. Regardless, it is reasonable to suppose that they provide the basis for creativity, imagination, and flexibility in artistic expression. Art's appeal and cultural practice may lie in provoking thought and contemplation, rather than in depicting veridical reality.

Independently of the patient's profession, a cerebral injury in a circumscribed region within a cortical hemisphere can lead to specific deficits in sensory, perceptual, motoric, attentional, or cognitive functions. Both artists and nonartists share a commonality in that they are vulnerable in this regard. The key is to identify those that are unique to art, those that produce noticeable alterations in artworks, especially with respect to the cerebral laterality of the injury and the localized region within the hemisphere. Thus, the phenomenon of hemi-neglect where the patient ignores the left half of space, which is typically linked to right-hemisphere injury (Guariglia et al., 2005; Vallar and Calzolari, 2018), expresses itself in visual artists by way of leaving the left half of the canvas blank (e.g. Butter, 2004). The phenomenon is somewhat short-lived in the majority of cases. Nonartists and artists alike display the neglect symptoms, which means that it is not art-specific. Along the same lines, injury to the left motor cortex (precentral gyrus) typically results in paralysis, weakness, or motor difficulties in the right hand, and since most people are right-handed, in artists this would force a switch to the use of the left hand. Undeterred, they switch to produce their art, even for sculpting, which normally is executed bimanually (Zaidel, 2015b). Again, judging from the published illustrations accompanying the text, the quality of the works has not been compromised, and has not shown to result in loss of skill, talent, or creativity, not unexpectedly considering that multiple brain areas are recruited in the production.

One would have to identify specific elements in the art itself, visual or musical, to determine the specific components that could be altered or compromised by brain injury in artists. However, unlike language, art does not have precise and explicit vocabulary and syntax. In the visual arts, such components have not been fully identified and there has been little effort to explore their nature. In the musical arts, some have been identified, but no specific alterations have been observed in compositions of composers with brain injury with regards to these components (Foerch and Hennerici, 2015; Newmark, 2009; Zagvazdin, 2015). However, there are debates and discussions about a particular composer, namely Maurice Ravel, in this regard (Cavallera, Giuduci, and Tommasi, 2012; Kanat et al., 2010; Seeley et al., 2008). On the whole, compared to the number of professional visual artists, there are far fewer cases of composers with brain injury, which, in turn makes inferences about the underlying neural circuitry in the creation of musical composition speculative (Zaidel, 2015b).

De novo Art Following Brain Injury: The Communicative Nature of Art

A few unusual cases of individuals whose lifelong professions were not in the arts, have been reported to produce visual art for the first time following brain injury (Bergeron et al., 2016; Erkkinen et al., 2018; Miller and Hou, 2004; Miller and Miller, 2013; Miller et al., 1998; Pollak, Mulvenna, and Lythgoe, 2007; Simis et al., 2013; Thomas-Anterion et al., 2010). Their post-injury art is known as *de novo*. Prior to the injury, they reportedly did not engage in art-making. The etiology in the majority of these cases consists of cerebral vascular stroke or dementia (Alzheimer's disease, several variants of frontotemporal dementia), and the symptoms invariably include deficits in language functions. However, judging from the published illustrations in the reports, one would be hard pressed to conclude that the *de novo* works display artistic excellence. Whether or not this can be attributed to lack of lifelong practice of artistic skill, or to the erosion of neural access routes to symbolic cognition, particularly in the dementia cases in which there is diffuse brain damage and major neural connectivity disruption, cannot be determined with the available published information.

The *de novo* art is expressed mostly in the form of paintings. Musical compositions, or any other of the multiple available art forms are largely absent. The rate of production is characterized as obsessive/compulsive, and they themselves describe an almost irresistible need to satisfy a drive to make the art. They find it difficult to stop. Thomas-Anterion et al. (2010) calls it "hyperpainting." Nevertheless, such *de novo* phenomena raise several issues about art itself, its communicative nature, latent artistic talent, and its neuronal underpinnings.

What these special cases almost invariably share is the loss of language functions. Arguing that the phenomenon reflects right-hemisphere specialization in art-making does not hold up to scrutiny if we consider that many professional established artists with right-hemisphere injury do continue to produce their art, regardless of its format, as described above. Normally, art expression taps the neural underpinning of symbolic cognition. Semantic cognition, independently of language semantics, is functional in both hemispheres (Gainotti, 2014; Jefferies, 2013).

Similarly, to attribute *de novo* visual paintings and drawings to newly formed creativity, as some have suggested, "released and unbound" from the "shackles" of normal neural connectivity, is tenuous given robust contrary evidence (de Souza et al., 2014; Palmiero et al., 2012). One would have to wonder, again, why the phenomenon is so rare given the large numbers of cases with brain injury worldwide, affecting the left more than the right hemisphere. Furthermore, taken in perspective, the creative individuals judged to be so by human history did not suffer from extensive brain injury, of the type reported for the *de novo* cases.

Importantly, the *de novo* cases do not create anything that they have not already experienced through exposure in their culture. That is, they do not innovate extra-cultural forms of expression, nor does their art introduce new ideas, styles, techniques, or genres that encourage imitation by others. Their work does not seem to influence the artworks of professional artists.

Furthermore, it is both interesting and significant that paintings and drawings are the principal artistic expressions in *de novo*. In this regard, we do not know with certainty how much was copied compared to spontaneously expressed. Are pictorial representations easier to apply than other types? Looking to examples from behavior in children, the activity of drawing figurative representation is practiced spontaneously by young children before the age of 2 years and is encouraged in school educational activities. Even children who are congenitally blind or have visual impairments are capable of spontaneously drawing and painting figurative objects without much instruction (see review, Vinter, Bonin, and Morgan, 2018). This attests to a basic human capacity to represent reality pictorially. In the same vein, adult blind artists have also been able to paint and draw (reviewed in Zaidel, 2015b). Taken together, the *de novo* works can be interpreted to reflect inherent capacities that were laid down early in healthy brain development, but subsequently not practiced artistically in the life profession. It is noteworthy that upon retirement from the non-art jobs, a large number of healthy adults who do not suffer from dementia or cerebral vascular stroke, take up painting and drawing as a hobby (Davies, Knuiman, and Rosenberg, 2016; Jensen et al., 2017).

In addition, there are lessons from autism for this whole issue. Normally, children learn language earlier than picture drawing but their drawings also undergo characteristic age-related changes. Children diagnosed with autism spectrum disorder have communication problems in language and in social interactions; their pictorial drawings lack emotional or human interactions that are characteristics depicted by healthy children (Jolley et al., 2013; Ten Eycke and Müller, 2016). This supports the notion that the disorder consists of disruption in tapping symbolic semantic cognition for communication, or that the cognition itself is underdeveloped. The foregoing evidence is consistent with the notion that some forms of visual art represent a communicative system.

Interestingly, however, there is the published case of a Parkinson's patient who developed symptoms of the disease at age 40, but only upon being treated with dopamine agonist and levodopa began writing poetry for the first time (Schrag and Trimble, 2001). With this case, "one has to wonder the extent to which elements of poetry conceptualization expressed themselves in the patient's pre-morbid existence" (Zaidel, 2015b: 212), considering that one grandfather was a poet, thereby implying genetic inheritance of brain pathways. Obviously, we also need to wonder if the effects of dopaminergic and serotonergic pathways played a role in this particular patient. The relationship of the medication in Parkinson's patients to art has been raised and debated previously in several publications (e.g. Inzelberg, 2013; Zaidel, 2013). Similarly, the obsessive/compulsive feature in *de novo* cases has implications regarding the extent of the brain tissue injury itself, and the influence of imbalance in neurotransmitter pathways affected by the damage (the cerebral stroke, the different dementias) in conjunction with the medications used for treatment. The unique combination of such factors together with the intersection of genetic inheritance of artistic conceptual talent could help future understanding of this phenomenon, and its implications for artistic expression.

Notably missing from *de novo* works are forms such as theater, music composition, prose writing, dance, storytelling, and much more. What can such omissions reveal about the nature of those arts? Arts such as music composition, theater acting, dance choreography, and prose writing, all require recruitment of multiple brain networks to tap into semantic symbolic cognition. They represent multilayered, multimodal, multiregional expressions, and brain injury, regardless of its etiology, disrupts some of the neural connectivity between the regions. In other words, some art forms are particularly sensitive to brain injury, while others are relatively spared. This attests to the nonuniformity of art, particularly its underlying neural bases.

Beginnings Are Important: Possible Earliest Expressions of Art in Distant Prehistory

Insights into the communicative value of art in human society can be gleaned from exploring how and why art emerged in distant prehistorical time. Typically, the clearest evidence for art practice in the archaeological record consists of physical traces. The record does not indicate that material art was practiced when the hominin line emerged following the split from chimpanzees, nor are there signs that the subsequent homo lines such as *Homo habilis* or *Homo erectus* practiced art. Such physical signs are associated principally with HS, who first emerged in Africa some ~300, 000 years ago. Art-specific objects were uncovered a long time after this emergence, specifically in South Africa and dated to around ~77,000 years ago in the form of shell beads that were purposefully punctured and strung (see Henshilwood, d'Errico, and Watts, 2009). Ornaments are conjectured to have been used as signals of group identification.

As mentioned above, clues to complex modern human behavior have been dated to periods earlier than the beads, to ~350,000 years ago, and are associated with increased spatial mobility across the African landscape in search of animal hunting, food gathering, long-distance material mining, and symbolic cognition, and, importantly, to reflect adaptation to cycles of climate change and their effects on the environment (Brooks et al., 2018; Potts et al., 2018). The presence of symbolic cognition and such behaviors by early humans suggest that some forms of art, particularly those that do not fossilize or leave traces, could nevertheless have been practiced, as I explain below. The early bands of humans were relatively small and relied on cohesion for survival (Tooby and Cosmides, 2016). Language communication alone would not have served as a sufficient channel for achieving the unity. The impetus for the earliest art would have originated in nonlanguage expressions of social cohesion, namely artistic expression. In previous publications, I proposed that these included dance, music, and body painting (Zaidel, 2017a, 2018, 2019). The explanation for the first two is that they have biological attributes that were exploited symbolically, while the third grew from camouflage strategies in hunting and protection from predators (and one could argue that camouflage strategies arose from fundamental biological survival needs). Mental rehearsal of these needs and activities around the campsite would have included the expression of thoughts through art behavior. The argument is that the earliest arts arose because they served a social purpose usefully communicated through symbolic displays when members gathered together.

What percolated them into the culture in the first place? I propose that the initial arts were not selected from a list of possibilities, or chosen randomly, or purposefully. Rather, they stemmed naturally, under evolutionary pressures, from biological attributes with ancient precursors in the animal ancestry, namely in entrainment, the co-timing of motoric movements, which metamorphosed into group formation dances, as well as into rhythmical sound patterns through humming, whistling, and vocal singing. Rhythmical foot thumping and object percussion blended and complemented music-making.

The auditory system has been evolving for millions of years prior to HS emergence; rhythms of sounds emanating from many different animal species are pervasive in nature. The art of body painting is conjectured to have grown into an art form from sources such as camouflage strategy for hunting, predator protection (Zaidel, 2015a; Lombard, 2016). It would have consisted of mimicking animal sounds and, at minimum, use of plant-based body paints. The inclusiveness of all group members in chain dance formations accompanied by rhythmical vocal singing relays the symbolic message of oneness, unity, and cooperation; the same can be said about signals of identity and belonging through body paints. In the participatory application of these art forms lies their appeal to the social nature of the early culture. This would represent a biologically adaptive survival strategy.

Once the artistic expressions outlined above took hold as beneficial for the culture as a whole, which at that early time was based on stone tool technology, art took off as an acceptable, adaptive feature of cultural norms. Material art, by contrast, appears quite late after the emergence of the HS. The process of adding it was gradual time-wise but, as argued here, all the while socially based nonmaterial art forms are speculated to have been practiced. The gene-culture co-evolution theory explains how cultural practices affect human behavior (Feldman and Cavalli-Sforza, 1976; Feldman and Laland, 1996; Kolodny et al., 2018). The present argument supports gene-culture evolution as it pertains to the practice of art and the human brain. The prolonged practice, spanning hundreds of thousands of years, as outlined above, could have contributed to gains in progressive fine-tuning of intrasocial communication, cooperation, possibly even brain-size volume, neuronal connectivity, and abstract cognition (Zaidel, 2019).

The relative late arrival of material art in human cultures does not have to argue for a new type or enriched symbolic cognition supported by a newly evolving brain mutation, or that material art represents the absolute ultimate definition of art, more so than nonmaterial art. Rather, it is reasonable to speculate that the later addition of material art, as in decorated ostrich egg shells in Africa (Henshilwood et al., 2014; Hodgson, 2014), or the abundant production of ivory and stone carvings, statues, cave wall paintings, and the like, in the Upper Paleolithic in western Europe (Lewis-Williams, 2002), together reflect the recognition that such artistic endeavors have gains for society; they share symbols of group identity, unity, values, and precious talents, features that would have already proven much earlier to be adaptive for survival through the practice of nonmaterial arts.

Future Explorations into Brain Mechanisms of Imagination

In order to be an effective communicator of experiences, ideas, concepts, and emotions, artistic expressions tap a broad range of abstract cognition and the imagination. Unlike language, which is explicit and detailed, artistic expression taps into looser semantic boundaries, and future research into the imagination should investigate the distinction between tight semantic categories vs. those with malleable boundaries. Gaining a handle on this distinction can go a long way to explain the neural underpinning of imagination in all domains of human endeavor, including importantly in technological advances and innovations. Cognitive psychologists have laid the groundwork for understanding the cognitive semantic system. Applying their theoretical and empirical foundations, functional neuroimaging techniques such as fMRI are bound to yield important findings regarding areas of the brain that play an important role in imagination.

References

Arbib, M. (2005). From Monkey-Like Action Recognition to Human Language: An Evolutionary Framework for Neurolinguistics. *Behavioral and Brain Sciences*, *28*, 105–167.

Beaudet, A. (2017). The Emergence of Language in the Hominin Lineage: Perspectives from Fossil Endocasts. *Frontiers in Human Neuroscience*, *11*, 427.

Bergeron, D., Verret, L., Potvin, O., Duchesne, S., and Laforce, R., Jr. (2016). When the Left Brain's Away, the Right Will Play – Emergent Artistic Proficiency in Primary Progressive Apraxia of Speech. *Cortex*, *76*, 125–127.

Boccia, M., Barbetti, S., Piccardi, L., et al. (2016). Where Does Brain Neural Activation in Aesthetic Responses Occur? Meta-Analytic Evidence from Neuroimaging Studies. *Neuroscience and Biobehavioral Reviews*, *60*, 65–71.

Bogousslavsky, J., and Boller, F. (2005). *Neurological Disorders in Famous Artists (Part 1)*. Basel, Switzerland: Karger.

Brooks, A. S., Yellen, J. E., Potts, R., et al. (2018). Long-Distance Stone Transport and Pigment Use in the Earliest Middle Stone Age. *Science*, *360*(6384), 90–94.

Burling, R., Armstrong, D. F., Blount, B. G., et al. (1993). Primate Calls, Human Language, and Nonverbal Communication [and Comments and Reply]. *Current Anthropology*, *34*, 25–53.

Butter, C. M. (2004). Anton Raederscheidt's Distorted Self-Portraits and Their Significance for Understanding Balance in Art. *Journal of the History of the Neurosciences*, *13*, 66–78.

Cavallera, G. M., Giudici, S., and Tommasi, L. (2012). Shadows and Darkness in the Brain of a Genius: Aspects of the Neuropsychological Literature about the Final Illness of Maurice Ravel (1875–1937). *Medical Science Monitor*, *18*, 1–8.

Clark, B. (2013). Syntactic Theory and the Evolution of Syntax. *Biolinguistics*, *7*, 169–197.

Davies, C., Knuiman, M., and Rosenberg, M. (2016). The Art of Being Mentally Healthy: A Study to Quantify the Relationship between Recreational Arts Engagement and Mental Well-Being in the General Population. *BMC Public Health*, *16*, 15.

De Souza, L. C., Guimarães, H. C., Teixeira, A. L., et al. (2014). Frontal Lobe Neurology and the Creative Mind. *Frontiers in Psychology*, *5*, 761.

Deacon, T. W. (1998). *The Symbolic Species: The Co-Evolution of Language and the Brain*. New York, NY: W. W. Norton and Company.

(2011). The Symbol Concept. In M. Tallerman and K. Gibson (eds.), *The Oxford Handbook of Language Evolution*. Oxford, UK: Oxford University Press.

Erkkinen, M. G., Zúñiga, R., Pardo, C., Miller, B. L., and Miller, Z. A. (2018). Artistic Renaissance in Frontotemporal Dementia. *JAMA: The Journal of the American Medical Association, 319*, 1304–1306.

Feldman, M. W., and Cavalli-Sforza, L. L. (1976). Cultural and Biological Evolutionary Processes, Selection for a Trait under Complex Transmission. *Theoretical Population Biology, 9*, 238–259.

Feldman, M. W., and Laland, K. N. (1996). Gene-Culture Co-Evolutionary Theory. *Trends in Ecology and Evolution, 11*, 453–457.

Fitch, W. T. (2011). The Evolution of Syntax: An Exaptationist Perspective. *Frontiers in Evolutionary Neuroscience, 3*, 9.

Foerch, C., and Hennerici, M. G. (2015). Organists and Organ Music Composers. In E. Altenmüller, S. Finger, and F. Boller (eds.), *Progress in Brain Research Vol. 216*. Oxford, UK; New York, NY: Elsevier, 331–341.

Fornazzari, L. R., Ringer, T., Ringer, L., and Fischer, C. E. (2013). Preserved Drawing in a Sculptor with Dementia. *The Canadian Journal of Neurological Sciences, 40*, 736–737.

Fuentes, A. (2015). Integrative Anthropology and the Human Niche: Toward a Contemporary Approach to Human Evolution. *American Anthropologist, 117*, 302–315.

Gainotti, G. (2014). Why Are the Right and Left Hemisphere Conceptual Representations Different? *Behavioural Neurology, 2014*, 10.

Griesser, M., Wheatcroft, D., and Suzuki, T. N. (2018). From Bird Calls to Human Language: Exploring the Evolutionary Drivers of Compositional Syntax. *Current Opinion in Behavioral Sciences, 21*, 6–12.

Guariglia, C., Piccardi, L., Iaria, G., Nico, D., and Pizzamiglio, L. (2005). Representational Neglect and Navigation in Real Space. *Neuropsychologia, 43*, 1138–1143.

Henshilwood, C. S., d' Errico, F., and Watts, I. (2009). Engraved Ochres from the Middle Stone Age Levels at Blombos Cave, South Africa. *Journal of Human Evolution, 57*, 27–47.

Henshilwood, C. S., van Niekerk, K. L., Wurz, S., et al. (2014). Klipdrift Shelter, Southern Cape, South Africa: Preliminary Report on the Howiesons Poort Layers. *Journal of Archaeological Science, 45*, 284–303.

Hodgson, D. (2014). Decoding the Blombos Engravings, Shell Beads and Diepkloof Ostrich Eggshell Patterns. *Cambridge Archaeological Journal, 24*, 57–69.

Hublin, J.-J., Ben-Ncer, A., Bailey, S. E., et al. (2017). New Fossils from Jebel Irhoud, Morocco and the Pan-African Origin of Homo Sapiens. *Nature, 546*, 289–292.

Inzelberg, R. (2013). The Awakening of Artistic Creativity and Parkinson's Disease. *Behavioral Neuroscience, 127*, 256–261.

Jefferies, E. (2013). The Neural Basis of Semantic Cognition: Converging Evidence from Neuropsychology, Neuroimaging and TMS. *Cortex, 49*(3), 611–625.

Jensen, A., Stickley, T., Torrissen, W., and Stigmar, K. (2017). Arts on Prescription in Scandinavia: A Review of Current Practice and Future Possibilities. *Perspectives in Public Health, 137*, 268–274.

Jolley, R. P., O'Kelly, R., Barlow, C. M., and Jarrold, C. (2013). Expressive Drawing Ability in Children with Autism. *British Journal of Developmental Psychology, 31*, 143–149.

Kanat, A., Kayaci, S., Yazar, U., and Yilmaz, A. (2010). What Makes Maurice Ravel's Deadly Craniotomy Interesting? Concerns of One of the Most Famous Craniotomies in History. *Acta Neurochirurgica, 152*, 737–742.

Kolodny, O., Feldman, M. W., and Creanza, N. (2018). Integrative Studies of Cultural Evolution: Crossing Disciplinary Boundaries to Produce New Insights. *Philosophical Transactions of the Royal Society B: Biological Sciences, 373* (1743). doi:10.1098/rstb.2017.0048.

Le Fur, Y., and Martin, S. (2017). *Through the Eyes of Picasso: Face to Face with African and Oceanic Art*. Paris, France: Flammarion.

Lewis-Williams, D. (2002). *The Mind in the Cave: Consciousness and the Origins of Art*. London, UK: Thames and Hudson.

Lombard, L. (2016). Camouflage: The Hunting Origins of Worlding in Africa. *Journal of African Studies, 34*, 147–164.

Luuk, E., and Luuk, H. (2014). The Evolution of Syntax: Signs, Concatenation, and Embedding. *Cognitive Systems Research, 27*, 1–10.

McBrearty, S. (2007). Down with the Revolution. In P. Mellars, K. Boyle, O. Bar-Yosef, and C. Stringer (eds.), *Rethinking the Human Revolution*. Cambridge, UK: McDonald Institute for Archaeological Research, 133–152.

McBrearty, S., and Brooks, A. S. (2000). The Revolution That Wasn't: A New Interpretation of the Origin of Modern Human Behavior. *Journal of Human Evolution, 39*, 453–563.

Miller, B. L., Cummings, J., Mishkin, F., et al. (1998). Emergence of Artistic Talent in Frontotemporal Dementia. *Neurology, 51*, 978–982.

Miller, B. L., and Hou, C. E. (2004). Portraits of Artists: Emergence of Visual Creativity in Dementia. *Archives of Neurology, 61*, 842–844.

Miller, G. F. (2000). *The Mating Mind: How Sexual Choice Shaped the Evolution of Human Nature*. New York, NY: Doubleday.

Miller, Z. A., and Miller, B. L. (2013). Artistic Creativity and Dementia. *Progress in Brain Research, 204*, 99–112.

Nadal, M. (2013). The Experience of Art: Insights from Neuroimaging. *Progress in Brain Research, 204*, 135–158.

Newmark, J. (2009). Neurological Problems of Famous Musicians: The Classical Genre. *Journal of Child Neurology, 24*, 1043–1050.

Palmiero, M., Di Giacomo, D., and Passafiume, D. (2012). Creativity and Dementia: A Review. *Cognitive Processing, 13*, 193–209.

Petcu, E. B., Sherwood, K., Popa-Wagner, A., et al. (2016). Artistic Skills Recovery and Compensation in Visual Artists after Stroke. *Frontiers in Neurology, 7*, 76.

Pollak, T. A., Mulvenna, C. M., and Lythgoe, M. F. (2007). De Novo Artistic Behaviour Following Brain Injury. *Frontiers in Neurological Neuroscience, 22*, 75–88.

Potts, R., Behrensmeyer, A. K., Faith, J. T., et al. (2018). Environmental Dynamics during the Onset of the Middle Stone Age in Eastern Africa. *Science, 360*, 86–90.

Richter, D., Grün, R., Joannes-Boyau, R., et al. (2017). The Age of the Hominin Fossils from Jebel Irhoud, Morocco, and the Origins of the Middle Stone Age. *Nature, 546*, 293–296.

Rose, F. C. (ed.) (2004). *Neurology of the Arts: Painting, Music, Literature*. London, UK: Imperial College Press.

Rutten, G.-J. (2017). *The Broca-Wernicke: A Historical Clinical Perspective on Localization of Language Functions*. Cham, Switzerland: Springer.

Schrag, A., and Trimble, M. (2001). Poetic Talent Unmasked by Treatment of Parkinson's Disease. *Movement Disorders, 16*, 1175–1176.

Seeley, W. W., Matthews, B. R., Crawford, R. K., et al. (2008). Unravelling Boléro: Progressive Aphasia, Transmodal Creativity and the Right Posterior Neocortex. *Brain*, *131*, 39–49.

Seyfarth, R. M., and Cheney, D. L. (2014). The Evolution of Language from Social Cognition. *Current Opinion in Neurobiology*, *28*, 5–9.

Simis, M., Bravo, G. L., Boggio, P. S., et al. (2013). Transcranial Direct Current Stimulation in *de novo* Artistic Ability after Stroke. *Neuromodulation*, *17*, 497–501.

Stevens, A. N. P., and Stevens, J. R. (2012). Animal Cognition. *Nature Education Knowledge*, *3*, 1.

Stringer, C., and Galway-Witham, J. (2017). Palaeoanthropology: On the Origin of Our Species. *Nature*, *546*, 212–214.

Ten Eycke, K. D., and Müller, U. (2016). Drawing Links between the Autism Cognitive Profile and Imagination: Executive Function and Processing Bias in Imaginative Drawings by Children with and without Autism. *Autism*, *22*, 149–160.

Thomas-Anterion, C., Creac'h, C., Dionet, E., et al. (2010). De novo Artistic Activity Following Insular-SII Ischemia. *Pain*, *150*, 121–127.

Tooby, J., and Cosmides, L. (2016). Human Cooperation Shows the Distinctive Signatures of Adaptations to Small-Scale Social Life. *Behavioral Brain Science*, *39*, e54.

Vallar, G., and Calzolari, E. (2018). Unilateral Spatial Neglect after Posterior Parietal Damage. In G. Vallar and H. B. Coslett (eds.), *Handbook of Clinical Neurology Vol. 151*. Amsterdam, Netherlands: Elsevier, 287–312.

Vinter, A., Bonin, P., and Morgan, P. (2018). The Severity of the Visual Impairment and Practice Matter for Drawing Ability in Children. *Research in Developmental Disabilities*, *78*, 15–26.

Wadley, L., Hodgskiss, T., and Grant, M. (2009). Implications for Complex Cognition from the Hafting of Tools with Compound Adhesives in the Middle Stone Age, South Africa. *Proceedings of the National Academy of Science USA*, *106*, 9590–9594.

Whiten, A. (2011). The Scope of Culture in Chimpanzees, Humans and Ancestral Apes. *Philosophical Transactions of the Royal Society B*, *366*, 997–1007.

(2017). Culture Extends the Scope of Evolutionary Biology in the Great Apes. *Proceedings of the National Academy of Sciences USA*, *114*, 7790–7797.

Wichmann, S. (1988). *Japonisme: The Japanese Influence on Western Art in the 19th and 20th Centuries*. New York, NY: Random House.

Wurz, S. (2013). Technological Trends in the Middle Stone Age of South Africa between MIS 7 and MIS 3. *Current Anthropology*, *54*, S305–S319.

Zagvazdin, Y. (2015). Stroke, Music, and Creative Output: Alfred Schnittke and Other Composers. *Progress in Brain Research*, *216*, 149–165.

Zahavi, A. (1978). Decorative Patterns and the Evolution of Art. *New Scientist*, *19*, 182–184.

Zaidel, D. W. (2013). Biological and Neuronal Underpinnings of Creativity in the Arts. In O. Vartanian, A. S. Bristol, and J. C. Kaufman (eds.), *Neuroscience of Creativity*. Cambridge, MA: MIT Press, 133–148.

(2015a). Neuroesthetics Is Not Just about Art. *Frontiers in Human Neuroscience*, *9*, 80.

(2015b). *Neuropsychology of Art: Neurological, Biological and Evolutionary Perspectives*. 2nd edition. Hove, UK: Psychology Press.

(2017a). Art in Early Human Evolution: Socially Driven Art Forms versus Material Art. *Evolutionary Studies in Imaginative Culture*, *1*, 149–157.

(2017b). Braque and Kokoschka: Brain Tissue Injury and Preservation of Artistic Skill. *Behavioral Sciences*, *7*, E56.

(2018). Culture and Art: Importance of Art Practice, not Aesthetics, to Early Human Culture. *Progress in Brain Research*, *23*, 25–40.

(2019). Coevolution of Language and Symbolic Meaning: Co-opting Meaning Underlying the Initial Arts in Early Human Culture. *WIREs Cognitive Science*, e1520.

37 Aesthetic Engagement: Lessons from Art History, Neuroscience, and Society

Noah Hutton

To see something – to do what one might call "viewing" art – is also to express oneself; it is an act that exists on a continuum with the same faculties required for the imagining and making of things. To engage with art is to bring equal parts active expectation and passive sensory collection. One affects the outcome of an entanglement with art simply by the act of bringing one's own body to the task, an apparatus chock full of the personal interior and intimately linked to the political exterior. In quantum physics, there is the colloquial understanding of *indeterminacy*, the strange reality that things at the quantum scale seem to behave in ways unlike the easily measurable matter around us. But within the field, there is significant theoretical divergence about the precise causal mechanisms at play when a quantum phenomenon is measured. Neils Bohr's theory about the act of measurement could be helpful to us in our aesthetic journey in this chapter. For in Bohr's model, it's not the experimenter's willful gaze itself that affects the results of the experiment (this was Heisenberg's uncertainty principle); rather, it's the specific physical properties of the experimental apparatus itself, set to record the quantum phenomena, that governs the nature and possibility of the experimental results (Barad, 2007). Heisenberg and Bohr represent a significant fork in the quantum road: In the former's theory, the willful human gaze itself is alone enough to achieve causative force upon the object of the experiment; in the latter's, the willful gaze is not enough – it must be extended to include the apparatus of the engagement, which becomes treated as an equally significant mediator of experience, a thing that spells out the possible results through the arrangements of its physical structure. So, too, in aesthetic encounters: We may bring ourselves willfully, but the act of engagement relies upon the distributed apparati of culture, social context, a curated viewing context, personal memory, and what you ate for breakfast. In this sense, we might say that a Bohrian framing of aesthetic engagement reminds us that we meet the world halfway, and that we ought to interrogate the apparati of our engagements with the same fervor we bring to the pristine aesthetic objects themselves.

As a way of finding our bearings, let us first examine two potential traps in aesthetic engagement: first we will explore what is known as the *pathographic* approach, all too common in art historical discourse, wherein aesthetic objects are viewed as quasi-divine products of their creator's mind and ought to be seen in tight causal association with the creator's biography. Next, we'll examine *neuroaesthetics*, which takes seriously the fact that we all have brains, and tries to sidestep the causal power of biographical context and sociopolitical particularity by identifying universal neural principles of seeing, evaluating, and creating art.

The Pathographic Problem

In its emphasis on the feedback loops of top-down and bottom-up signal processing in the brain, and the exquisitely muddy area where they meet, the last century of psychology and neuroscience supports a Bohrian model of aesthetic engagement. But in the annals of art historical discourse, we ought to be keenly aware that there is a risk in bringing too much of one's expectation to the interpretive moment, of reading (and writing) too much biographical information on the gallery's wall labels. Excessive attention paid to the intent of the artist is an all-too-attractive trap, and can provoke an interpretive imagination run wild. In art historical discourse, one repeatedly runs up against the myth of the aesthetic object as interpretable first and foremost through the biography of its creator, leading to the inevitable portrait of the artist as an isolated, mythic figure in society. Indeed, Foucault (1979) pointed to the phenomenon of all art as somehow suggesting an author outside the work, the original creator. But once suggested, the biographical sketch of the artist can be imbued with too much causative force, which only pushes crucial webs of peer relations, social contexts, and political forces further into the background. Foucault calls for a historicization of the author function – an interpretive approach that foregrounds such contexts and demands that we treat personal, biographical details with the same weight as larger sociopolitical forces that shaped the society in which that artist grew up and began making his or her aesthetic contribution.

Kris et al. (1979) investigated the possible chain of logic behind the tendency to foreground biography: Once an artist is described as creating works that surpass nature in their emotive qualities, such as in exquisite landscape paintings that seem more beautiful than the view itself, the artist is thought to possess a certain divinity, elevating them to the realm of the superhuman. This tradition in art history, which has been called the *pathographic* approach, is perhaps no more evident than in interpretations of Vincent Van Gogh's art – insisting over and over again, according to Kris and Kurz, on seeing the man and his work as inseparable. For a demonstration of this line of art historical discourse, we can turn to H. P. Bremmer (1974), who discusses Van Gogh's "psychic force" as "determining" the sense of movement in Van Gogh's *The Potato Eaters*. Bremmer even directly refers to *Sunflowers* as an "emotionalized" work that came into being "spontaneously from the inner life of the artist." He also treats *Bedroom in Arles* as a "revelation" and ties it to what he believes to be Vincent's abnormal sensory perception. Aurier (1974) similarly equates Van Gogh's art directly to his idea of a man "always near the brink of the pathological." Similarly, Meier-Graefe (1974), in his discussion of Van Gogh's choice of subject matter, insists that the artist poured his own "fervor" into still life works, rendering them "personal outpourings." The pathographic approach presupposes that the artist had every-thing he needed inside him from the mythic biographic details of his own isolated life, a sea of imagination waiting to spontaneously flood the canvas. Instead of destabilizing this causative primacy of the individual by pointing to the wide range of influence and dialogue that Van Gogh drew upon and was drawn by, the ultimate emphasis becomes a one-to-one emotional connection between painting and painter, the "fervor" that singularly defines an image. There is no larger apparatus by which the art is situated or viewed: Its emotional resonance passes straight from a genius to you.

The Universal Aesthetic Object

It's no surprise, then, that in approaching questions of art and subjectivity, the discipline of neuroaesthetics – the scientific probing of how the brain views, evaluates, and creates art – has run in the opposite direction, leaving behind the psychology and biographical sketch of the creator in favor of an objectification of the art object itself, a return to a version of a Kantian ideal of beauty and universal meaning. But in the rush to seek out universals, to pull general principles out of the muck of chaotic difference, do we find in the corridors of neuroaesthetics an opposite but equally blinding trap?

Though it was German philosopher Alexander Baumgarten who coined the term "aesthetics" in 1750, it was with Immanuel Kant's 1790 treatise *Critique of Judgement* that the focus on beauty as a universal property of aesthetic objects was born. Other philosophers, like Leibniz, shifted the focus to the observer, but were equally interested in aesthetic universals. Leibniz treated aesthetic objects in relation to the emotional valence in their holder or perceiver, specifically interested in their relationship to pleasure:

> *Pleasure* is the feeling of a perfection or an excellence, whether in ourselves or in something else. For the perfection of other beings is also agreeable, such as understanding, courage, and especially beauty in another human being, or in an animal or even in a lifeless creation, a painting or a work of craftsmanship, as well (Leibniz and Loemker, 1976: 697).

There has been much refutation and complication of this kind of universal aesthetic idealism in the ensuing decades, the most potent of which decenters the program of universal cultural norms from a decidedly Eurocentric point-of-view. Yet the notion of beauty and pleasure as measurable aesthetic features across all brains persists in the field of neuroscience, egged on by the supposed universalism of the neural structures underpinning aesthetic engagement. In this sense, though the last century of art theory and criticism and the gradual development of the neuroscience of aesthetic experience have destabilized the notion of the lone artistic genius, neu-roaesthetics has perhaps overcorrected into its reductionist roots, gradually walking itself toward the attractive promise of genericized universalism, and in the process risking an erasure of cultural specificity and personal context. In its search to "crack the code" of how aesthetic meaning is shaped in "the brain," the desire is to place all humans in the same brain-bucket, but as yet the question remains as to how big of a bucket will be needed to fit the totality of aesthetic engagement into its scientific program.

Indeed, those who turn to neuroscience for an explanation of beauty display an optimism in their interdisciplinary pursuits that is anchored by two core beliefs. One is the general, unshakable logic of materialism: Everything we experience, think, or do is tethered to our nervous system, and thus illuminating that system naturally informs the study of things we see and create, like art (Livingstone and Hubel, 2014). The second looks to evolutionary science to inject the weight of history into the pursuit, for if evolution has shaped our brains its teachings might help explain why we all do what we do, even if that doing seems to take varying eventual forms, a "cheesecake" issue of cultural specificity that belies deep evolutionary similarities (Changizi, 2011). These beliefs are buoyed by the early promise of discoveries in neuroscience, which provided dazzling, albeit preliminary, accounts of how parts of the visual cortex organize and process information, and how certain instincts for attraction and revulsion to visual information may indeed be hardwired. Thus the optimism in the ability of neuroscience to explain the lofty questions bound up in seeing and making art is considered by the purveyors of neuroaesthetics to be a continuation of where the field is heading, rather than a blind leap with no hard evidence, as certain outspoken critics of neuroaesthetics would attest (Noë, 2011). So for those eager to set forth answers now, the question looms large: Are the returns from the present-day interdisciplinary dialogue of neuroaesthetics original and of use? And if so, in returning to our Bohrian model of engagement, are brains themselves not the ultimate apparati? For in their biases and their predictions, their squeezing of perception through narrow bands of sensory input, and their vast oceans of memory containing all the context of a person's life, what else – beyond the detailed account of this neurobiological instrument – must we seek out?

A Fateful Encounter

Ideally, interdisciplinarity is the act of two fields entwining to produce something new. This newness ought to happen in the space opened up by the encounter, inaccessible by either field left to its own devices. I first studied art history and neuroscience separately as an undergraduate and failed to figure out a way to relate those two interests to one another. I became interested in neuroaesthetics precisely because I saw it as an interdisciplinary field by definition: It had two things smashed together in its name, and it needed both to exist – the breathtaking science of the brain encountering the world of culture and aesthetics. Perhaps neuroscience could offer something that the humanities could not; perhaps the humanities could offer science something it desperately needed as it began probing the seat of subjective experience. I began blogging about the field, interviewing neuroaesthetics researchers, and though their insights and research are illuminating and worth longer discussions, I want to turn now to a description of one fateful encounter at one specific interdisciplinary event. I do this because I believe that too often in the annals of theoretical essays and critical nonfiction the actual real-world friction that occurs when disciplines rub up against one another is lost, replaced by long-winded arguments (as I've likely been doing so far, here). But for me, personally, it was only when I ran into some of the fiercest critics of my own interests that I began to widen my perspective on aesthetic engagement, so I offer this account as a snapshot of interdisciplinarity, a moment in time that reshaped my thinking.

We were at the 2013 Venice Biennale as part of a symposium organized by the Association for Neuroaesthetics to respond to the work of the performance artist Tino Seghal, who had been making sensational waves in the art world not only for the nature of his work but for the nature of his post-contractual art transactions, which famously avoid written documentation and insist on unconventional definitions.

In the Giardini, the main gallery space in the Biennale park, a group of us – philosophers, neuroscientists, art historians, and me – came upon Seghal's esoteric piece (which would go on to win the top prize at the Biennale) involving several performers who would rotate into sitting and laying positions in the center of a large hall throughout the day, voicing slowed-down versions of pop songs and other vaguely familiar incantations. Standing next to me in our group was Olaf Blanke, who investigates the mysterious fluidity of body perception, and Vittorio Gallese, one of the co-discoverers of mirror neurons and the leader of a subfield of cognitive science now known as "embodied simulation" (Gallese, 2017).

Standing across the room was the philosopher Alva Noë, Berkeley professor and author of *Out of Our Heads*, a manifesto of "embodied cognition" (not to be confused with Gallese's theory of *embodied simulation*, the process of empathically simulating the actions of others inside one's own motor system without necessarily acting externally – Noë's *embodied cognition,* on the other hand, argues for extending our concept of the boundaries of the human mind out of the brain and into the external environment, literally). Earlier that year, Noë had written an opinion piece for the *New York Times* entitled "Art and the Limits of Neuroscience" in which he railed against any neuroscientific approach to art and aesthetics, and even to understanding consciousness. I wrote what now appears to me to be a somewhat bitter paragraph-by-paragraph response to Noë's article, and though I still would contest the overreach of his statements, there is something that continues to ring true about one of the baseline critiques he offered in his piece:

> What is striking about neuroaesthetics is not so much the fact that it has failed to produce interesting or surprising results about art, but rather the fact that no one – not the scientists, and not the artists and art historians – seem to have minded, or even noticed. What stands in the way of success in this new field is, first, the fact that neuroscience has yet to frame anything like an adequate biological or "naturalistic" account of human experience – of thought, perception, or consciousness (Noë, 2011).

If someone asked me to quickly describe what neuroscience has produced that is of interest to art – what the true bumper crop of neuroaesthetics has been – I might unfurl a laundry list of findings, mostly from visual neuroscience, and plenty from Gallese's explorations into the empathic motor system. I would hope to convince you based on the sheer quantity of experiments that in one way or another neuroscience has offered something worthwhile about how we understand the creative, perceptual, or evaluative process. You might notice that this list would be made up of small and finite experimental examples, many tethered to the coarse explanatory weight of neuroimaging.

With the list spooled out, you might wonder whether there's an overarching theoretical framework that could tie all of this together, could connect the dots between the silos of the research community. If I were trying to summon an overarching theoretical framework in a book, as many have, I might present pieces of visual art, music, dance, or films along the way that would each dovetail with discussions of scientific studies on related aspects of perception, emotion, or memory, as I tell you how I think the brain works and why we make art and why these pieces of art I presented are how they are and why many people consider them to be great.

But what I would still be missing – and indeed what much of neuroscience seems to still be missing – is that overarching theory, what Noë calls a "naturalistic account of human experience." What can neuroscience really add to art theory, practice, and criticism that is of clear and present use – and vice versa? Do we need a neural theory of consciousness before any overarching theory of neuroaesthetics can bear full weight? And how do we avoid the omnipresent trap – prevalent in books on art and neuroscience as well as in sexy public-facing discussions between artists and scientists – of ascribing neuroscience a key interpretive role in engaging with art, where the former is treated as the ultimate Truth and the latter as the exotic, intuitive Other?

The next day, we sat around a table in front of a small audience gathered in the Peggy Guggenheim Library in Venice and discussed Seghal's work. Art historians described what the work reminded them of; neuroscientists described how the work might be experienced (a routine that can dance perilously close to suggestions of how it might be *explained*) by means of certain regions, connections, and processes of the brain.

When it was my turn to present, I first introduced the distinction between *descriptive* neuroaesthetics (science that correlates activity in brain regions to features in artworks that seem to depend on the functions of those regions), and *experimental* neuroaesthetics (a more mature line of work, where experiments are devised to study the perceptual process itself, rather than matching things up with the art after the fact).

But when it came to speaking specifically about Seghal's work, I fell into the same old trap of descriptive neuroaesthetics, of talking broadly about the brain and letting the specificity of the artwork slip away, just as Noë had warned it would. I wanted to respond to what Noë had said in his opening remarks, that talking about how "art activates us" is a mistake, and that art should be thought of as "providing us an activity to activate the work of art."[1] To me his insistence on keeping the

1 I rely here on an unpublished transcript of the event provided to me by the Association for Neuroaesthetics.

conversation outside the brain and never bringing in a thread of cognitive science into a symposium organized by the Association for Neuroaesthetics seemed particularly stubborn. So in my response to Seghal's piece I described how the knowledge of two seemingly opposing cognitive processes – top-down processing and bottom-up sensory perception – are themselves locked in an ongoing piece of interior performance art. Because of how long it took me to sink into the rhythms and vocabularies of Seghal's piece in the Giardini, the relationship between this interior dance of top-down and bottom-up – the expectations based on experiences of previous work mixing with the actual sensory information arriving in the moment – seemed appropriate to discuss at a neuroaesthetics symposium. But in doing so I slid down that perilous cliff of *explanation*, letting the art recede into a mirage of a neuroscientific catch-all.

As soon as I finished giving these opening remarks, my misstep was brought to the foreground by the art historian Sigrid Weigel, who immediately challenged my comments. "When you talked about top-down and bottom-up, not only the metaphor irritates me, but also the question of how one can bring neuroscience into art history and the other way around," she said. "When seeing and reflecting on Seghal's work, I would say, this – this is not enough." Weigel's issue was with the dominance of visual neuroscience, which she rightly sees as too often taking precedence over motor, auditory, or more complex emotional systems when infusing neuroscience into discussions of art.

After I added some assurances that my comments were not meant to explain anything, but rather to "add a layer that could enrich and expand the discussion as opposed to explaining or limiting," a full-fledged turf battle broke out. Art historian Michael Diers asked why I am so interested in art: "Is it to ennoble your neuroscience?"

Vittorio Gallese interjected on my behalf, responding to Diers:

> Why are you so puzzled? Let's look at the past and progress will ensue. When Warburg was in Florence he was heavily reading Charles Darwin, and I don't think he read Darwin to ennoble the history of art or the other way around. People are curious. So why should we prevent ourselves from an additional perspective just because we cross boundaries? Are we afraid of losing our specificity? I don't see why so many people are puzzled, afraid, angry, confronting themselves with these topics from people from other fields.

The art historians claimed that neuroscience always skews discussions of art toward the visual; the neuroscientists protested. Alva Noë returned to his entirely valid stump speech about art disappearing from neuroaesthetic discussions, that it "is never actually made the focus of attention, why? Because what we end up looking at is something as a stimulus, but of course everything is a stimulus, there is no human experience without the brain, there is also no human experience without the body and a situated animal interacting dynamically with the environment."

I left the symposium scratching my head: If the point was to find new approaches to art through the infusing of neuroscience (hence the Association for Neuroaesthetics), where were the new ideas?

I have come to agree with Noë that art disappears from many neuroaesthetic papers, books, and public discussions (Noë, 2011). In these cases, the art is treated as a mere stimulus, a rocket booster that can be discarded on the way to X, where X is inevitably a brain-based answer. But while Noë does point out the pitfalls of this rocket-booster approach, he does not integrate cognitive science in any meaningful way into his discussions, and thus I do not believe his approach offers a new way of approaching art. Noë's insistence on shifting the discussion out of the head and into the environment, thereby neglecting neuroscience altogether, may clear away the shaky causal foundation of early neuroaesthetics but eventually ends up feeling just as devoid of new ideas as that which he seeks to destabilize. His coldness toward neuroscience is just another way to draw battle lines in the dialogue between the humanities and the sciences, an all-too-easy territorialism that promotes more turf battles than it opens new questions.

My hunch is that there is a false appraisal of neuroscience that dead-ends interdisciplinary presentations, including my own spiel in Venice. In such situations, neuroscience is mistakenly (by scientists and philosophers alike) treated as an end-domain: a place we arrive at for an answer and in turn receive quixotic scientific visuals of the brain. From Legrenzi and Umiltà's (2011) *Neuromania* to Noë (2011), backlash in this context makes sense: The current answers to weighty questions about art and existence are weak placeholders that gain steam from the nebulous authority of anything *brain*, but in the end the paucity of the current understanding of the brain betrays any hopes at an appropriately complex view of cause and effect. It is in these shortcomings that the dead ends of current dialogues are sensed and the regressive backlash against future attempts sown. Whether it flows from genuine excitement over early indications from neuroscience research itself or comes in reaction to backlash from the humanities, the overhyping of neuro-truth as an end-domain has led those of us actively interested in interdisciplinary dialogues to the precipice of our own disappointment: the sinking feeling that neuroscience might not be able to land us on that moon where we'd hoped to one day plant our flags and write a universal guide to aesthetic engagement. Then we arrive at an event like the one in Venice to try to find new connections between the arts and sciences, but all too often interdisciplinarity resembles the now-withered concept of bipartisan political compromise, where, like a bill that is stripped of its most potent actions so that it can receive a majority vote, the attempt to bridge a divide ends up leaving behind the most virtuous elements of each field in the pursuit of a valorized middle ground. It's that strange feeling in the room after an interdisciplinary exchange, when it seems the artist and scientist have talked at and through one another, but not really *with* one another.

So in hopes to surmount the twin challenges of false end-domains and false niceties, in recent interdisciplinary exchanges I've been testing a new approach to engaging with the neuroscience of aesthetics, one that acknowledges the strong gravitational pull of a neural end-domain but offers a handpicked analogy from the space race era to replace the classic image of a flag-planting triumph. I argue that when the humanities, social sciences, or any other discipline engages with – or is engaged by – the neurosciences, the metaphor we ought to keep in mind is that of Apollo 13, for it was in that near-disaster that the human agents were able to transform their intended end-domain from the ominous site of an inevitable crash-landing to the engine for their slingshot back to Earth, and thus a source of renewed momentum.

In the same way, we might imagine aesthetic engagements from the perspective of the arts and art history that swing close to neuroscience for its new ideas, tuning into the undeniably attractive force of its material lessons about the seat of human subjectivity, but remaining acutely aware that they may never offer end-all answers to our individual questions about art and the imagination, let alone scale up to universals to touch all of aesthetic experience. The Apollo 13 approach is ultimately more curious about how the gravitational pull of neuroscience can help us get back to the personal and the political; how its transformational knowledge can reactivate and re-engage us as active aestheticians.

Toward Future Engagements

A new trend in neuroaesthetics suggests a way in which aesthetic engagement, infused with explanatory momentum from brain science, can ask new questions of the personal and the political. In an ironic twist, this insight arrives by means of a line of research that concerns the *unengaged* brain, at rest, and its lessons as to how meaning is formed during artistic engagements.

The Default Mode Network (DMN) is a distributed network of brain regions whose activity seems to reappear in the valleys between the peaks of outward-focused attention, when you are not necessarily *doing* anything. The spike in research interest about the DMN marks a fundamental paradigm shift in neuroscience, one that goes against the traditional modus operandi of brain scanning, wherein a researcher measures the effect on the brain of active engagement with a certain stimulus, usually coming from the external world. Indeed, "finding a network of brain areas frequently seen to decrease its activity during attention-demanding tasks was both surprising and challenging," notes Marcus Raichle of Washington University, "because initially it was unclear how to characterize their activity in a passive or resting condition" (Raichle, 2015: 416). In approaching the DMN, Raichle's work has pointed toward the need to reorient our binary notions of *active* vs. *inactive*, for with the DMN we find the omnipresent "baseline" brain, the parts that brain imaging studies always seek to cancel out so that the true point of "activation" can be seen. It turns out that the full apparatus of aesthetic engagement involves not just our active, willful gaze, but the "resting" brain itself – the stars in the sky, ever-present behind the bright beams of the day.

The DMN consumes most of the energy metabolized by the brain as a whole. It's an omnipresent, baseline state, but it is most active during the in-between moments when you're staring up at the ceiling, riding on the train, reflecting at the end of a long day – moments that seem to be tethered in study after study to activity in regions such as the angular gyrus, the posterior cingulate cortex, and the medial prefrontal cortex, which are regions that have been implicated in autobiographical thinking, and in the relation of the self to other people, events, and planning for the future (Buckner, Andrews-Hanna, and Schacter, 2008).

Though these are massive areas of the brain to be tossing around in any kind of ultimate explanatory way, it hasn't stopped some researchers from beginning to probe how the DMN may be involved in aesthetic engagement. Neuroscientist Ed Vessel devised an appraisal system for viewers to rate a wide range of artworks – from abstraction to portraiture and landscapes – while lying in an fMRI scanner (Vessel, Starr, and Rubin, 2013). The participants were shown the artwork for a brief interval, then given four seconds to submit a rating on a scale of 1-4 of how powerful, pleasing, and profound they found the image. Vessel's key finding is that for ratings of 1–3, the DMN showed fairly low activity, with subtle, linear increases as evaluations improved. But for the top rating of 4, there was a dramatic, steplike jump in activity, as if the DMN fully "came online" for the highest aesthetic appraisals. At these moments, the sensory areas involved in viewing the art stayed online as well – a rare co-activation of two networks that usually exhibit toggling behavior, depending on whether you are focusing attention outward or at "resting state," looking inward. Vessel described this steplike activation of the DMN during "4" ratings as a "signature" of peak aesthetic response, and argued that this activity supports the notion that the DMN is about self-referential processing, as in, "*I* love this painting."

We might rephrase the conclusion of this line of research as suggesting that "self-relevance is an integral part of aesthetic experience." For someone coming at this from the humanities, this big takeaway still ends up sounding like a self-evident, intuitive truth known to the arts and art historical practices for eons. The results may speak volumes for the neuroscience of the DMN and its relationship to aesthetic appraisal, and they may make significant progress from past studies, which is how much of science works; for art theory, though, these statements can continue to sound like counting to ten.

What if we paused for a moment to consider an interpretive use of the DMN that was not just about bringing personal taste to the act of engagement, but also social and political taste? What is the Default Mode Network of a larger unit than the individual; say, contemporary capitalism? And in asking such a question, how can we better orient ourselves with the aesthetic preferences of the world around us?

Columbia's Zuckerman Institute recently named Jeff Koons as its first artist-in-residence, centering that work above other possibilities (say, a local Harlem artist). Koons's work, like other mega-successful contemporary artists, is made for and sold to a global financial elite. What is the nature of a society governed by those whose peak aesthetic experience brings a DMN-associated brain network online that sees a piece of themselves in Jeff Koons's ironically disengaged, meta-upon-meta, wealth-signifying balloon-poodles?

If we buy into the adage often tossed around in the arts that "the personal is political," then in our moments of active engagement with aesthetic objects we must begin to treat not just artworks but also the full human apparatus – the brain, and all its contexts, active and passive – as a site of politics. In this way, aesthetics becomes a critical weapon, and neuroaesthetics the site of a forthcoming battle.

For in the gap between the sweet-nothings of neuroscience and the hallowed hall-ways of art history and criticism, brain-platitudes – like Koons-platitudes – would have us believe they are not intimately linked to the technocratic and ethically fraught world that continues to reproduce itself around them. In a world in which more than half of the U.S. BRAIN Initiative[2] was funded by the Defense Advanced Research Projects Agency (DARPA), where tech companies edge ever closer to creating their own brain-modeled, deeply learned algorithms to maximize revenue, what is the full range of what twenty-first century neuroscience will pursue and enable? And how can we paint a more complete picture of its aims, complicate its platitudes, so that we can engage with the world with a more complete awareness of the apparati in which we engage?

The neuroscientist would undoubtedly stand behind the ethical shield of disease prevention and treatment – an entirely valid stance. But as reductionistic methods probe deeper into the subjectivity of the human mind, and as pharmaceutical corporations pump their prices and pathologizations, this Valid and Good stance is no longer enough. This is what Yuval Noah Harari alludes to in *Homo Deus*, noting that "No clear line separates healing from upgrading. Medicine almost always begins by saving people from falling below the norm, but the same tools and know how can then be used to surpass the norm" (Harari, 2015: 51).

By omitting any such contextual discussion, valorizations of neuroscience thereby ignore the ethical and political embeddedness of the field, and thus risk distancing the general public from the crucial interrogations ahead of us. Over and over again we instead receive unfettered utopianism, as in Eric Kandel's closing lines to *Reductionism in Art and Brain Science*: "the new science of mind seems on the verge of bringing about a dialogue between brain science and art that could open up new dimensions in intellectual and cultural history" (Kandel, 2016: 189). I wish I was as optimistic, but the world I see around me suggests a more ethically complex picture of some of the places brain science may be employed, like DARPA gobbling up those BRAIN insights to help drone operators stop sweating their remote deeds and start forgetting them faster. One might protest that a chapter on aesthetic engagement is the last place to mount such a political critique. I would argue that the exact opposite is true. As neuroscience increasingly encroaches on the domain of human subjectivity – our sacred imaginative apparatus itself – the discussion of aesthetic engagement, of what happens in the brain when we view or create art, becomes merely a proxy conversation for the real change ahead: the reduction of subjectivities to their constituent parts so that they can then be put back together again in more sublime ways, if you can afford it.

References

Andrews-Hanna, J. R., Reidler, J. S., Sepulcre, J., Poulin, R., and Buckner, R. L. (2010). Functional-Anatomic Fractionation of the Brain's Default Network. *Neuron*, *65*(4), 550–562.

2 See www.braininitiative.org.

Aurier, Albert. (1974). Vincent, an Isolated Artist. In Welsh-Ovcharov, B. (ed.), *Van Gogh in Perspective*. Englewood Cliffs, NJ: Prentice Hall.

Barad, K. M. (2007). *Meeting the Universe Halfway: Quantum Physics and the Entanglement of Matter and Meaning*. Durham, NC: Duke University Press.

Bremmer, H. (1974). Introductory Appreciations. In Welsh-Ovcharov, B. (ed.), *Van Gogh in Perspective*. Englewood Cliffs, NJ: Prentice Hall.

Buckner, R. L., Andrews-Hanna, J. R., and Schacter, D. L. (2008). The Brain's Default Network: Anatomy, Function, and Relevance to Disease. *Annals of the New York Academy of Sciences*, *1124*, 1–38.

Changizi, M. (2011). *Harnessed: How Language and Music Mimicked Nature and Transformed Ape to Man*. Dallas, TX: BenBella Books.

Foucault, M. (1979). Authorship: What is an Author? *Screen*, *20*(1), 13–34. doi:10.1093/screen/20.1.13.

Gallese, V. (2017). The Empathic Body in Experimental Aesthetics – Embodied Simulation and Art. In V. Lux and S. Weigel (eds.), *Empathy: Palgrave Studies in the Theory and History of Psychology*. London, UK: Palgrave Macmillan, 181–199.

Harari, Y. N. (2015). *Homo Deus: A Brief History of Tomorrow*. Toronto, Canada: McClelland & Stewart.

Kandel, E. (2016). *Reductionism in Art and Brain Science: Bridging the Two Cultures*. New York, NY: Columbia University Press.

Kris, E., Kurz, O., Laing, A., and Newman, L. M. (1979). *Legend, Myth and Magic in the Image of the Artist: A Historical Experiment*. New Haven, CT: Yale University Press.

Legrenzi, P., and Umiltà, C. A. (2011). *Neuromania: On the Limits of Brain Science*. New York, NY: Oxford University Press.

Livingstone, M., and Hubel, D. (2014). *Vision and Art: The Biology of Seeing*. New York, NY: Abrams.

Leibniz. G. W., and Loemker, L. (1976). *Philosophical Papers and Letters*. 2nd edition. Dordrecht, Netherlands; Boston, MA: D. Reidel Publishing Company.

Meier-Graefe, Julius. (1974). Vincent and Socialism. In Welsh-Ovcharov, B. (ed.), *Van Gogh in Perspective*. Englewood Cliffs, NJ: Prentice Hall.

Noë, A. (2011). Art and the Limits of Neuroscience. The *New York Times*, December 4. opinionator.blogs.nytimes.com/2011/12/04/art-and-the-limits-of-neuroscience/.

Raichle, M. E. (2015). The Brain's Default Mode Network. *Annual Review of Neuroscience*, *38*(1), 433–447.

Vessel, E. A., Starr, G. G., and Rubin, N. (2013). Art Reaches Within: Aesthetic Experience, the Self and the Default Mode Network. *Frontiers in Neuroscience*, *7*.

38 Dance and the Imagination: Be a Butterfly!

Julia F. Christensen and Khatereh Borhani

"To dance is to dream with your feet."

– A saying from Finland

We confess that with this chapter, we are not only examining dance *imagination* through the lens of neuroscience. We are also hoping to convince the reader to turn to the practice of dance! It feels good to dance – and if we use our imagination while dancing, it gets even better.

"Let Your Imagination Dance!" – Kinesthetic and Visual Imagery as a Tool to Get the Move

JFC: *My first memories as a 5-year old ballet student involve my Russian ballet teacher telling me to hold my arms as if I was embracing the huge trunk of a tree and then opening them according to the tree "growing" and getting a bigger trunk. She didn't say, put your arms in first position, and now second; although that was exactly what my arms did. As a "side effect" of me imitating a growing tree, my arms hit a perfect "first" and "second" position of the ballet syllabus. My elbows and wrists automatically formed a soft curve, my shoulders dropped to a relaxed position and my body weight spontaneously shifted toward the balls of my feet (since I was leaning slightly forward to hug the tree of course). My performance was much better than if she had asked me to lift my arms 90° degrees away from the body axe, forming an oval shape with my arms, without the fingers touching, elbows pointing outwards, wrists curved slightly at 110°, weight towards the ball of the feet, rip cage closed, chest up, belly sucked in, etc. Especially as a child, all these instructions would have been a nightmare to remember and the result wouldn't have been great. The "growing tree" image in my mind did it all for me. Madame Razumova was clever.*

On a summer day in 2017, the authors of this chapter went to watch a rehearsal of a London-based ballet company. It was a Sunday matinee show open to the public "to help everybody understand more about the work of the ballet company of the city" – it said in the ad. At some point in the rehearsal, the choreographer stopped the music and told one of the dancers to make her last movement of the sequence more squared and tall, like a skyscraper. The dancer found this instruction perfectly reasonable, as did JFC. In the next attempt of the sequence, her final movement was awesome. But KB looked at JFC in bewilderment, "Like a skyscraper?!" she whispered. Her analytic neuroscientist mind was clearly making a twist here. She raised her eyebrows and asked "Later?" implying that she'd like to speak about this after the rehearsal.

JFC: *While I watched the remaining hour of the rehearsal, I understood that this was something that people just don't normally do. People that are not dancers don't regularly stand tall like skyscrapers, move their arms delicately like the wings of a butterfly, nor do they walk as if inhaling a beautiful perfume with their chest opening like a flower petal blooming . . .*

KB: *No – definitely not. I remember this summer day very well and how puzzled I was at the choreographer's instruction. In my culture, it is socially not very common to dance in public. Seeing this dance rehearsal, where each movement was practiced to perfection like a movement technique, was new to me. In Iran, if we dance, it is commonly just for joy and happiness. At the rehearsal matinee in London, however, I was watching a completely different way of conceiving dance, like a movement art, based on skilled hard work and using imagination-based techniques like imagery to improve movements.*

This was how we two neuroscientists embarked on the journey of researching for this chapter about dance and imagination together. There is plenty of neuroscientific evidence that indicates that if we use more of our imagination to guide our movements we would find even our everyday movements much improved as a result.

Let us start with an example from everyday life. How many times have we heard the instruction: "Sit straight"? The problem with this instruction is that our natural inclination when "sitting straight" is not ergonomic, and even bad for our back. We push back our shoulders with an unnatural exaggeration that makes our neck curve forwards like a duck's to provide counterweight for the sudden weight change of the trunk. Similarly, the natural S-curve of the lower back is shifted into a straight line because we tuck the basin under in this attempt to make a straight back. In other words, we put a lot of strain to our neck, shoulders, lower back and basin. Conversely, if you imagined someone pulling you gently upward by your hair, your back would automatically straighten, your shoulders would drop, you would align your neck with the soft S-curve of the spine and you would sit comfortably on both sit bones (instead of rolling around on them if you followed the other instruction). One way that imagery gives rise to efficient movement in dance is by helping achieve alignment of skeletal structure (Perica, 2010). The reason why this imagery-instruction works for a dancer (and for all of us), while the direct instruction does not, has got something to do with how our brain "makes" movement.

Many dancers think that their movements are made by their muscles and that it is a special kind of "muscle memory" that remembers the moments. Yet the truth is that movements are made by our brain and the broader "motor system" of our body ("motor" means "movement" in Latin). This motor system includes the brain (which provides the instructions to move, and how to move), the nerves of the peripheral nervous system (which transmit the electrical and biochemical signals from the brain to the muscles), and the muscles themselves, which execute the final movement. All these components of the motor system are interconnected and form feedback loops to ensure optimal movement. For example, the sensorimotor cortex in the brain (the strip of brain that is located at your temples and stretches over the top of your head, from ear to ear) is concerned with planning a movement. It controls the muscle contractions that are necessary for a particular movement to happen. At the same time, it is monitoring sensory feedback about the state of the body, including whether the movement is happening correctly, or whether adjustments need to be made. Further parts of the motor system in the brain include the primary motor cortex, the premotor area, the supplementary motor area, the cerebellum and frontal association cortices. None of these areas could produce movement by itself. Movements are the result of a careful interplay between all of these regions. One extraordinary aspect of the motor system is that it functions on the basis of loops, and not as some sort of chain reaction from the brain to the muscles, as one might suspect. The good thing about this is that these loops allow for continuous adjustments of ongoing movements as they happen (instead of having to wait for an entire chain reaction to happen). The motor system relies especially on two loops. Loop 1 controls *why* we move and receives feedback about whether or not the movement happened successfully, and enables us to repeat that movement if necessary. Loop 2 is essentially concerned with *how* we move and therefore especially coordinates multijoint movements. Hence, this second loop is also particularly important when we dance, and for imagery-based dance practice (Carlson, 2004; Karin, Haggard, and Christensen, 2016; Wolpert and Gharamani, 2000).

These two loops are highly sensitive to learning and they enable us to execute most movements in a very efficient way without consciously having to think about them. You pick up a pen and write something down without thinking about *how* to write, but about *what* to write; your motor system does it all for you so you can focus entirely on the letter that you are currently writing. Likewise, you pick up a piece of jewelry with a pincer grasp, which is a neural masterpiece in terms of fine motor control – and unique in the animal kingdom. Even our closest relatives, the chimpanzees, need a very long time to learn this grasp, and then will still be many times clumsier than the clumsiest of humans. Thus, the human motor system is very accurate and demonstrates excellent plasticity (i.e. ability to learn) throughout the lifespan. That is how it provides us with a capacity to learn the most complex of movements, like the pointe-shoe dance of a classical ballerina.

Each movement that we perform (be it writing a letter, picking up a piece of jewelry, or a dance on pointe shoes) is made up of a motor plan that consists of a selection of specific motor commands (signals communicated from neuron to neuron). They occur in a particular order, like a plan, and our muscles act accordingly – automatically and without our having to think about all the details. Your brain retrieves from memory the right motor plan for a specific movement that you want to do, and executes it by translating it into the required motor commands. Billions of neurons (Carlson, 2004) are involved in this complex task of making a single movement like lifting your arm in a particular way, for example, to do the "first position" of the ballet syllabus. So it is very helpful (and quite exciting!) that most of this happens without our conscious thought.

The disadvantage with this system is that we cannot access the motor plan to improve the movement. While we move, while we *dance*, our brain receives a great deal of sensory feedback from our senses and via the feedback loops it automatically adjusts and improves the ongoing movement, based on this information. For instance, if the surface we are dancing on is suddenly slightly inclined, proprioceptive feedback from our feet reaches the brain's motor planner at millisecond speed and makes it account for this change. And in fact at any given moment proprioceptive sensory feedback from muscles, skin, tendons, and joints is updating our brain about the ongoing movement and telling it whether it is successful or not. Conversely, information that we might receive via verbal instruction or via visual feedback about how a dance movement is supposed to look, is unable to access the motor planner because the information is simply too slow. It doesn't reach the motor planner in time to modify the motor commands.

The only way to have the right movement ready for our motor planner to translate it into motor commands, *in time*, is to have the right movement already stored in the memory systems of our brain, ready to be retrieved when we need it. Motor imagery can be performed either internally or externally (Mahoney and Avener, 1977). During internal imagery of a movement, we imagine being inside our body and we experience all the sensations that we would experience if actually doing the movement. External imagery is also effective. Here we view ourselves from another person's point of view. For instance, we might imagine what we might look like if we were moving our arms like a butterfly, in other people's eyes (Goldschmidt, 2002; Overby and Dunn, 2011). Dancers spontaneously use both these types of imagery simultaneously to prepare their motor planner for the right movement execution (Coker, McIsaac, and Nilsen, 2015; Giron, McIsaac, and Nilsen, 2012; Golomer et al., 2008; Pavlik and Nordin-Bates, 2016). The good news for hobby dancers and professional dancers who do not routinely use imagery in their practice is: The above studies show that even if we are not very good at imagining things at the beginning, a few weeks of practice will make us better at letting our mind imagine what we need (see also: Williams, Cooley, and Cumming, 2013).

Using our imagination while we dance is simply a way to access our motor planner directly. The most important features of *how* we want the movement to look are already stored in our memory systems. Our mental image of "inhaling our favorite perfume" contains the representation of the tactile, visual, olfactory, and auditory sensations and our brain automatically adopts the right motor plan. There are several different types of imagery that dancers use to inspire and improve their (dance) movements. *Mental imagery* is used extensively in the sports domain (see Chapter 14), and it is also used by dancers. It consists of imagining the movement in terms of how it would look if it were perfect, doing a type of mental rehearsal of the correct movement before actually performing it yourself. *Visual imagery* means using specific mental images of things in the physical world to guide our brain's motor planner toward the right type of movement, such as "move your arms in diagonal, as if you are shooting an arrow." When using *kinesthetic imagery*, we basically use physical sensations that we know from the physical world, for example, we can "walk as if we're inhaling our favorite perfume coming from somewhere." We use *metaphorical imagery* when we imagine something that doesn't really make direct sense like when we "move our arms like a butterfly's wings." We are humans and we have arms not wings, of course. But our brain has designated systems for processing and storing in memory motion of any kind (what the movement *looks like* and *what it might feel like* if we did it with our body). Besides, human imagination is unlimited, so that it can effortlessly juxtapose the movement-features of a butterfly's movements with those of our own arms. Because this mental image will access the motor planner of our brain for this arm movement, our arm movement may – with training – indeed acquire the delicate nature of the movement of a butterfly's wings.

The Australian ballet dancer and dance pedagogue Janet Karin, OAM, is a pioneer in the use of what she has coined Mental Training in dance teaching (Karin, 2016; Karin, Haggard, and Christensen, 2016). This technique involves using our imagination to improve movements in the context of dance education. During her classes the air is full of metaphors and images that guide the dancers' brains to bring their dance movements to perfection. However, importantly, for Karin the "perfection" of a movement is only a secondary objective of her teaching. In her words, "the process of transmitting ballet's complex technique to young dancers can interfere with the innate processes that give rise to efficient, expressive and harmonious movement" (Karin, 2016: 1). She wants dancers to focus on their internal sensations such as imagery to guide the body's movements. This avoids strain – as in the example above "imagine someone is gently pulling you upward by your hair" instead of "sit straight." She also advocates the use of other types of imagery that help with the authentic emotional expression in a dance, *subjective* and *somatic imagery*, which we will speak about in the third part of this chapter.

Thus, the answer to the question "why does imagination-based instruction work better than detailed movement instruction?" is that with our imagination we access the motor planner of our brain directly. Using imagery is the way to unlock the motor planner of our brain and to make our movement efficient and harmonious. If you still think that you cannot do motor imagery like a dancer (mental practice, visual imagery of movements, metaphorical or kinesthetic imagery), think about the word "plasticity." By just practicing a little bit every day, you're modifying your brain. As Ramón I Cajal put it: "Every man if he so desires becomes sculptor of his own brain."

What is more, choosing the right kind of imagery to motivate our dance practice might help us to develop a successful mastery of the movements. In the context of performing athletes, we generally differentiate five types of imagery: (1) imagery of skills (e.g. how to do a specific step), (2) imagery of strategies, routines, game plans (e.g., "first I'll do this, then that, then that . . . " etc.), (3) imagery of goal achievement (e.g. imagine yourself holding the trophy), (4) imagery of stress, anxiety, and arousal (e.g. heart beating rapidly), and (5) imagery of being self-confident, mentally tough, focused and positive (e.g. imagine being in complete control) (Murphy, Nordin, and Cumming, 2008; Nordin and Cumming, 2008a). In the dance domain, the Dance Imagery Questionnaire by Nordin and Cumming (2006) is often used to assess dance students' preferred type of imagery.

Which type of imagery do you think makes us more self-confident, less anxious, more creative and motivated to dance? Research has found that the answer is: the fifth type of imagery indicated above. And this is true for recreational and professional dancers, alike (Brampton, 2018; Fish, Hall, and Cumming, 2004; Nordin and Cumming, 2006, 2008b).

Imagery contributes to the successful mastery of a movement in the dance domain. This is because imagery acts directly on the motor planner of our brain, and because strategically used imagery can boost our confidence to succeed. Besides, one series of studies found that purposefully using imagery in dance practice increased the experience of flow (Jeong, 2012). "Flow" is that much sought after experience of connectedness with the here and now, where time and space disappear, often referred to as moments of "optimal experience" (Csikszentmihalyi, 2008).

"Let the Music Take Control!" – Auditory Imagery to Get into the Move

The second component of a dance is music – most of us cannot imagine a dance without music. The neural systems responsible for movement and those responsible for processing sounds from our environment are closely interrelated in the human brain – much more than, for instance, in the brains of our closest relatives, the nonhuman primates (Honing and Merchant, 2014; Merchant and Honing, 2013; Merchant et al., 2015). This interrelation between movement and sound processing is thought to be one of the main reasons why humans are the only species to have such a complex dance repertoire. Our brain *wants* to dance every time it hears a rhythm. We have all experienced that once music is in the air, we tap the beat with our foot or nod our head to the rhythm of the beat.

KB: *Since we are not really used to dance in Iran, when we are invited to a party, many of us feel very shy. It is not common to attend dance classes in my country, so we don't develop any particular dancing skills while we grow up. I was no exception to that rule. So when I'm invited to a party, where we're supposed to dance, I suffer a lot. Of course, I want to honor the host of the party, since she invited me. However, since I never learned to dance, this is usually a terrible experience for me. You are there in the middle of a big room, the music is playing and you are supposed to dance. Oh my.*

The good news for all shy dancers out there, is that neuroscience has provided some comforting evidence in the past few years. The human brain is preprogrammed to be able to dance. The ability for rhythmic entrainment is present in the brains of newborn babies and does not disappear throughout the entire life span. There is only a very small proportion of the population (about 1.5 percent) that suffers from a particular type of music blindness (*amusia*) (Omigie et al., 2013). To find out whether you suffer from this blindness, you simply need to ask yourself this question: Do I like music? If the answer is "yes," you do not suffer from *amusia*. People with *amusia* do not like music and perceive it as some sort of noise or random hammering. The rest of us *can* definitely dance "free" dance. Of course, if you want to learn choreographic dances, folk dances, or couple dances, you need to practice the steps like any other skill that needs practice! You would not expect to be able to drive a car without practicing before, either. For free dancing, the general rule is: let the music take control. There are many accounts of dancers saying, after a particularly good dance, that it was as if the music took command of their legs.

In a certain way, this is indeed the case. As mentioned above, motor and auditory systems are closely interrelated in the human brain. In fact, in some instances sounds are translated directly into electrical signals that are sent to our muscles and make them move (for landmark studies about this, see: Paltsev and Elner, 1967; Xenos, Rossignol, and Jones, 1976; but see also: Cesari et al., 2014; Kornysheva et al., 2010; Mainka, 2015; Molinari et al., 2003; Olshansky et al., 2015; Poikonen, Toiviainen, and Tervaniemi, 2016; Schmahmann and Pandya, 2009; Thaut, 2003; Thaut et al., 1999; Zatorre, Chen, and Penhune, 2007).

JFC: *In fact, as a dancer, it is impossible for me to listen to music when I'm trying to fall asleep. Music invariably triggers images of dance movements in my mind, or it gives me the feeling of what specific dance movements that would fit the music would feel like. It doesn't matter whether I know the music or not. I find myself composing entire dance choreographies with leaps and pirouettes all inclusive. It is a very nice pastime; however, it has the exact opposite effect of making me fall asleep. In fact, it makes me wide awake. Listening to music and doing "mental rehearsal" of a piece is another technique used in dance training to optimize movements of a choreography. You sort of practice the choreography "offline," without doing the movements, just while listening to the music and imagining how you would optimally dance the choreography. My (and all dancers') sleepless dancing nights with earplugs in our ears are one proof of how the practice of these mental imagery techniques stir the plasticity of our brain. We get so good at it that we can't stop doing it anymore. The moment we hear music, our brain composes the matching movements.*

Since the interrelatedness of motor and auditory processing is inherent to brain function, everybody can use music as a guide to optimal dance movement, and the plasticity of our brain will take care of strengthening this basic skill and making us better at it every time.

Musical imagery has been described as including many components, including imagery for auditory features (e.g. loudness), imagery for verbal sounds (words, dialogue, text, interior monologue), imagery of nonverbal sounds (e.g. musical melodies), etc. (see Chapter 13). Notably, imagined auditory events seem to engage the same brain regions as the actual perception – producing similar emotional input as the actual experience would (Hubbard, 2010). For example, daydreaming of movements and other sensory experiences is very easily elicited by means of music, which guides the mind (Juslin and Vastfjall, 2008). One study found that multisensory integration is sensitive to musical and movement cues. Participants were asked to listen to a piece of music in a minor or a major key. Meanwhile they watched short segments of dance movements that were either sad or happy. Although participants were blind to the actual categories of the musical pieces and the dance movements (and they were not dancers themselves), their rating of the clips in terms of emotional experience was more accurate when the music was minor key and the dance was sad and when the music was major key and the dance was happy. Moreover, participants' physiological responses (as measured by means of galvanic skin response electrodes attached to the tip of their fingers to record any subtle changes in their bodily response to the stimuli they saw and heard), were also sensitive to the coupling of "congruent" music and dance. This suggests that music elicits a certain universal understanding of what an accompanying movement might look like in spectators' minds (Christensen et al., 2014). Mental imagery in the form of mental motor practice is also a technique used in the music domain to train the musical movements, and has been related to improved performance (Keller, 2012) and to optimized motor performance on an instrument (Keller, Dalla Bella, and Koch, 2010). This suggests that musical training increases the ability for imagery by acting on the perception-action networks of the brain (Herholz et al., 2008) and musical training strengthens these links (Meister et al., 2004).

"Feel it!" – Emotional and Interoceptive Imagery to Get the Move

JFC: *While dancing, you are supposed to endow your movements with authentic emotions. I remember during dance education how we all cherished a famous sentence by Paris Étoile dancer Sylvie Guillem: "Technical perfection is insufficient. It is an orphan without the true soul of the dancer." Today there is even scientific evidence that shows that for an audience to really like a dance movement, it needs to have genuine emotional expression – pure perfection is not enough to move an audience. One of the techniques that we were taught to achieve this was the "letter from a friend" technique. You imagine that you receive a letter from a dear friend that you haven't seen for a long time. As you read through it, you realize that it contains many happy parts, but also sad and terrifying ones, and some parts even make you feel angry, hurt, and disgusted. As your reading progresses, you enter these different emotional experiences. Later, when you're supposed to dance a dance with a specific emotional quality, you use this technique to elicit the true feeling in yourself – and you dance it out.*

If you look at the word "emotion," it consists of the word "motion," which means "to move," and the prefix "e," which comes from the Latin prefix *ex* that means "out." Basically, the word "emotion" means "to move out." If we use our emotional imagination, our movements automatically follow the movement qualities of that emotion. We dance out the feeling that we have – with the movements of our body. This is because, in our brain, the motor commands for these emotional movements are stored safely in our brain already. We have all been sad, happy, hurt, angry, scared, and disgusted at some point in our lives, and we remember what our body feels like and how we would move if we were feeling one of these emotions right now. We do not even have to consciously think about it, having the emotion in our imagination is enough for the movement planner of our brain to execute the right motor commands. In acting practice, this "letter from a friend" technique is known as "Alexander Technique" and helps actors achieve the authentic expression in their practice. For dancers, the music can also help us to get a specific emotion elicited in our imagination. For instance, when dancing to music in a minor or major key, our dance moves automatically adopt the emotional movement qualities of the music. This is again due to the interrelation between motor and auditory systems in the brain, discussed in the previous section. When we *imagine* being sad, happy, fearful, or angry, and so on, this imaginative emotion becomes part of our movements while we dance. We can play with this tool as a way to cope with emotions that are difficult for us. Therefore, dance is used in the therapeutic domain (Hanna, 1995a; Jeong et al., 2005; Koch et al., 2014; Shafir, 2016; Shafir, Tsachor, and Welch, 2015; Shafir et al., 2013). Briefly explained: If we recall past events and their emotional "hue" in our imagination, we can "try out" these emotions in the safe space of the dance floor (which is not the real world), and then dance it out.

KB: *Actually, my strategy when having to dance in a party – even if it is just to please the host since she invited me – is to mirror the movement of the dancer that I'm currently dancing with. If she lifts her arm, I lift mine, too. If she takes a step to the right, I take a step to the left, following her in the same direction. This is real fun and usually everybody enjoys this mirror dance type of dance arrangement. And then there is of course the Persian snap. It is a specific type of movement that you do with both hands, a bit like clicking your thumbs during Flamenco dance, but different. It is very difficult and when I was 11 it took me three weeks of daily practice to learn it. The funny thing is that on the dance floor, if one person starts Persian snap, everybody joins in.*

Humans *love* to imitate. And luckily so. Imitation is the basic way how humans learn much about the complex motor actions that are part of the human movement repertoire – like the pincer grasps that we discussed in the beginning of the chapter, as well as the complex movement of a ballerina dancing on pointe shoes. This ability to learn via imitation is quite unusual in the animal kingdom. Comparative psychologists have spent considerable time trying to teach our closest relatives, the chimpanzees, to learn simple actions from imitation, such as nutcracking. These attempts have only met with very limited success. Imitation and the ability to *mentally simulate*, or imagine, actions that we are not yet able to perform, relies on the complex mirror neuron system of the human brain. This also gives us the ability to *simulate* and understand others' emotions from their movements (Freedberg and Gallese, 2007; Shafir et al., 2015; Sumanapala et al., 2017).

Try a small experiment with a friend, called "mirror game" (Noy, Dekel, and Alon, 2011). Sit face to face and place your hands in front of each other as if there was a transparent window between you. Your hands should be close (about 2–5 cm apart), but not touching. Then start to do movements together – up, down, to the sides, in circles, etc. You can choose one of you to be leader, while the other follows, and then switch after a while. However, with a little practice you will realize that there is no need for a designated leader; you can create new hand movements together without deciding who leads and who follows. Without speaking a word, you were able to follow your friend's hand, and she was able to follow yours.

This is because the human brain is an expert in simulating. This is the neural explanation for (1) why we are able to learn from others (i.e. our brain automatically simulates the action that we see – this enables us to execute the action by means of this simulation and sometimes aided by conscious imagination), (2) why we understand others' mental states (i.e. our brain simulates their point of view; for instance, if I see a car behind my friend, I understand that she can't see it because her back is turned in that direction, so I warn her – this is called the ability of "Theory of Mind" in psychology), (3) why we have empathy (i.e. our brain simulates others' emotional state), and (4) how we can evoke emotional experiences in our imagination, either by imagery alone, aided by music, or by eliciting the postures and bodily sensations of an emotion. We saw in the previous sections how movement imagery and music can aid the elicitation of specific movements and emotional states during a dance. Let us now have a look at how we can guide our imagination into emotional experiences via the postures and bodily sensations of emotions.

Our emotions have a good deal to do with bodily sensations. When we're scared, we get cold hands; when we're angry, our face burns; when we're excited, we feel butterflies in our belly; and so on. There is considerable agreement within and across cultures about where in the body different emotions are felt. For instance, in an interesting study by Nummenmaa and colleagues (2013), "body heat-maps" of emotions were created. The researchers asked a group of more than 700 Finnish and Taiwanese participants to look at pictures of emotional facial expressions and watch affective movies of different emotional expressions on a computer screen. While doing so, participants had pictures of human bodies on another screen and they colored different body regions based on the increasing or decreasing viscerosensory feeling that they experienced inside their own body. The drawings of all the participants were then superposed to create "body heat maps" of these drawings that showed where in the body people generally feel different emotions. The researchers found out that most basic emotions, namely happiness, fear, anger, sadness, and surprise caused sensations of stronger activity in the upper chest area and head, and, that they might manifest with elevated heartbeats, faster breathing, and a rise in perceived body temperature. Experiencing happiness caused a sensation of increased activity all over the body, while experiencing sadness was mostly associated with decreased sensation of limb activity.

Thus our body's response during an emotional episode is an important aspect of experiencing emotions and we can use visual imagery to produce the bodily responses of emotional experience. For instance, research has shown that reading (or listening to) emotional scripts evokes the same somatic and psychophysiological responses as genuine emotional experiences, including heart rate and galvanic skin response (Peasley-Miklus, Panayiotou, and Vrana, 2016). This means that people can come to experience full-blown emotions including subjective feelings and bodily reactions like accelerating heartbeat or sweating that happens when we feel emotions, via their imagination alone.

In a very nice series of studies, Israeli scientist Tal Shafir demonstrated how the mere imagery of emotional body postures (jumping with hands up to elicit happiness) can elicit strong emotional experiences in participants. She and her team propose that such emotion-imagery techniques hold great potential for the therapeutic context. Here the aim is to provide patients with a "safe space" to "try on" specific emotions and to learn to cope with them. Within the therapeutic context, emotions experienced during a dance have no implications for the real world and the dance context is therefore a safe space in whch emotions have no further consequences but can be experienced and explored to one's heart's content. Rena Kornblum, a dance therapist and a senior lecturer at the University of Wisconsin-Madison who is working with children who are dealing with physical and sexual abuse trauma or other forms of violence, uses dance practice to help these children express their suppressed emotions. Launching the dance therapy session with performing gross and intense movements and gradually moving toward slow and smooth movements is a way to facilitate emotion regulation that Rena Kornblum uses in her work with traumatized children[1].

"Just Dance!" – Discussion and Conclusion

In summary, it is a good idea to use kinesthetic, auditory, and interoceptive (somatic) imagery while dancing. Our imagination allows us to access the motor planning system of our brain and use the dance moves stored in our memory systems. Using imagination enables the dancer to rehearse a dance before perform- ing it in the real world, boosting skill, self-confidence, and creativity. Moreover, the imagination of music, an inseparable component of dance, activates brain areas responsible for auditory processing and even helps induce emotional signals that we can complement with emotion induction procedures via our imagination. Dancing in the real world and mentally imagining dance result in similar effects in the body and brain. Dance-imagination can scaffold difficulties with real dance moves, as well as help the shy to find "their" dance moves, and finally, help professional dancers with improving their movements according to external aes- thetic ideals.

Recent evidence has revealed that both dancers and musicians are particularly good at detecting their bodily states (Christensen, Gaigg, and Calvo-Merino, 2018; Schirmer-Mokwa et al., 2015). It might be that this heightened ability to detect bodily signals (interoception) (Garfinkel and Critchley, 2013; Garfinkel et al., 2015) is also at the basis of dance practice driven by imagery-tools. In the 1970s, a discipline called "somatics" emerged among dancers (Hanna, 1995b). It specifi- cally sets genuine expressivity center stage in dance practices, and is said to have "transformed [dance] pedagogy into a more 'active' and exploratory experience of the student, in which physical sensations are more important than the mirroring and reproduction of forms" (Ginot, Barlow, and Franko, 2010: 12). This is closely related to what dance pedagogue Janet Karin, OAM, has implemented in her practice as *subjective* and *somatic imagery*. The basic premise of these types of imagery is that we should focus on the inside of our body and the phenomena that we have in our mind while dancing, and on our sensations. We should stop worrying about what our movements "look like," and instead focus on what they "feel like." If we do this, we'll find the cathartic effects that emotional expression via dance can have. Karin warns that if we do not use this important imaginative capacity when we dance, to create our dance, we might become obsessed with the external aspects of our movements and the strive for aesthetic perfection in a way that is not necessarily healthy for our body.

1 For more information, visit "The Moving Child" Project: themovingchild.com/project/rena-kornblum/.

Future Directions

(1) For the professional dance domain: Future research may use neuroscientific methods to increase our understanding of the neurocognitive mechanisms by which imagery can be used to optimize dance movements and dancer creativity, and, at the same time, reduce anxiety and self-doubt in dancers.

(2) In the context of recreational dance: If we are not spontaneously using the imagination for dancing, how can we learn to use the imagination to make our movements healthier, more ergonomic and more successful? This goes for professional and recreational dancers.

(3) Basic research questions for the future: By which neurocognitive mechanisms can individuals gain expertise in the use of imagery in their dance practice? A possible neurocognitive mechanism that has been suggested to embrace several regulatory faculties of the human mind is interoception. Future research might explore in what way imagination, dance practice, and interoceptive awareness and accuracy relate to performance improvements.

Dance is born in our brain, and in the interplay between the brain, the music and our feelings. Dance is, in a certain way, imagination made visible.

Acknowledgments

The work was funded by a British Academy Mobility grant (PM160240) (JFC & KB).

References

Brampton, S. (2018). Cognitive Imagery Training in a Dancer's Deliberate Practice: Skills Development, Confidence and Creativity. Perth, Australia: Edith Cowan University, BA of Arts (Dance) thesis.

Carlson, N. R. (2004). *Physiology of Behavior*. 8th edition. New York, NY: Pearson.

Cesari, P., Camponogara, I., Papetti, S., Rocchesso, D., and Fontana, F. (2014). Might as Well Jump: Sound Affects Muscle Activation in Skateboarding. *PLoS One*, *9*(3), e90156.

Christensen, J. F., Gaigg, S. B., and Calvo-Merino, B. (2018). I Can Feel My Heartbeat: Dancers Have Increased Interoceptive Awareness. *Psychophysiology*, 55:e13008.

Christensen, J. F., Gaigg, S. B., Gomila, A., Oke, P., and Calvo-Merino, B. (2014). Enhancing Emotional Experiences to Dance through Music: The Role of Valence and Arousal in the Cross-Modal Bias. *Frontiers in Human Neuroscience*, *8*. doi:10.3389/fnhum.2014.00757.

Coker, E., McIsaac, T. L., and Nilsen, D. (2015). Motor Imagery Modality in Expert Dancers: An Investigation of Hip and Pelvis Kinematics in Demi-Plie and Saute. *Journal of Dance Medicine & Science*, *19*(2), 63–69.

Csikszentmihalyi, M. (2008). *Flow: The Psychology of Optimal Experience*. New York, NY: Harper Perennial Modern Classics.

Fish, L., Hall, C., and Cumming, J. (2004). Investigating the Use of Imagery by Elite Ballet Dancers. *AVANTE*, *10*(3), 26–39.

Freedberg, D., and Gallese, V. (2007). Motion, Emotion and Empathy in Esthetic Experience. *Trends in Cognitive Sciences*, *11*(5), 197–203.

Garfinkel, S. N., and Critchley, H. D. (2013). Interoception, Emotion and Brain: New Insights Link Internal Physiology to Social Behaviour. Commentary on: "Anterior Insular Cortex Mediates Bodily Sensibility and Social Anxiety" by Terasawa et al. (2012). *Social Cognitive and Affective Neuroscience*, *8*(3), 231–234.

Garfinkel, S. N., Seth, A. K., Barrett, A. B., Suzujum, J., and Critchley, H. (2015). Knowing Your Own Heart: Distinguishing Interoceptive Accuracy from Interoceptive Awareness. *Biological Psychology*, *104*, 65–74.

Ginot, I., Barlow, A., and Franko, M. (2010). Shusterman's Somaesthetics to a Radical Epistemology of Somatics. *Dance Research Journal*, *42*(1), 12–29.

Giron, E. C., McIsaac, T., and Nilsen, D. (2012). Effects of Kinesthetic versus Visual Imagery Practice on Two Technical Dance Movements: A Pilot Study. *Journal of Dance Medicine & Science*, *16*(1), 36–38.

Goldschmidt, H. (2002). Dancing with Your Head On: Mental Imagery Techniques for Dancers. *Journal of Dance Education*, *2*(1), 15–22.

Golomer, E., Bouillette, A., Mertz, C., and Keller, J. (2008). Effects of Mental Imagery Styles on Shoulder and Hip Rotations during Preparation of Pirouettes. *Journal of Motor Behavior*, *40*(4), 281–290.

Hanna, J. L. (1995a). The Power of Dance: Health and Healing. *The Journal of Alternative and Complementary Medicine*, *1*(4), 323–331.

Hanna, T. (1995b). What is Somatics? In D. H. Johnson (ed.), *Bone, Breath, and Gesture*. Berkeley, CA: North Atlantic Books, 339–359.

Herholz, S. C., Lappe, C., Knief, A., and Pantev, C. (2008). Neural Basis of Music Imagery and the Effect of Musical Expertise. *The European Journal of Neuroscience*, *28*(11), 2352–2360.

Honing, H., and Merchant, H. (2014). Differences in Auditory Timing between Human and Nonhuman Primates. *Behavioral and Brain Sciences*, *37*(6), 557–558; discussion 577–604.

Hubbard, T. L. (2010). Auditory Imagery: Empirical Findings. *Psychological Bulletin*, *136* (2), 302–329.

Jeong, E.-H. (2012). The Application of Imagery to Enhance "Flow State" in Dancers. Melbourne, Australia: Victoria University, PhD thesis.

Jeong, Y. J., Hong, S. C., Lee, M. S., et al. (2005). Dance Movement Therapy Improves Emotional Responses and Modulates Neurohormones in Adolescents with Mild Depression. *International Journal of Neuroscience*, *115*(12), 1711–1720.

Juslin, P. N., and Vastfjall, D. (2008). Emotional Responses to Music: The Need to Consider the Underlying Mechanisms. *Behavioral and Brain Sciences*, *31*(6), 559–575.

Karin, J. (2016). Recontextualizing Dance Skills: Overcoming Impediments to Motor Learning and Expressivity in Ballet Dancers. *Frontiers in Psychology*, 7, 431.

Karin, J., Haggard, P., and Christensen, J. F. (2016). Mental Training. In V. Wilmerding and D. Krasnow (eds.), *Dancer Wellness*. Champaign, Canada: Human Kinetics, 57–70.

Keller, P. E. (2012). Mental Imagery in Music Performance: Underlying Mechanisms and Potential Benefits. *Annals of the New York Academy of Sciences*, *1252*, 206–213.

Keller, P. E., Dalla Bella, S., and Koch, I. (2010). Auditory Imagery Shapes Movement Timing and Kinematics: Evidence from a Musical Task. *Journal of Experimental Psychology: Human Perception and Performance, 36*(2), 508–513.

Koch, S., Kunz, T., Lykou, S., and Cruz, R. (2014). Effects of Dance Movement Therapy and Dance on Health-Related Psychological Outcomes: A Meta-Analysis. *The Arts in Psychotherapy, 41*(1), 46–64.

Kornysheva, K., von Cramon, D. Y., Jacobsen, T., and Schubotz, R. I. (2010). Tuning-in to the Beat: Aesthetic Appreciation of Musical Rhythms Correlates with a Premotor Activity Boost. *Human Brain Mapping, 31*(1), 48–64.

Mahoney, M. J., and Avener, M. (1977). Psychology of the Elite Athlete: An Exploratory Study. *Cognitive Therapy and Research, 1*(2), 135–141.

Mainka, S. (2015). Music Stimulates Muscles, Mind, and Feelings in One Go. *Frontiers in Psychology, 6*, 1547–1547.

Meister, I. G., Krings, T., Foltys, H., et al. (2004). Playing Piano in the Mind – An fMRI Study on Music Imagery and Performance in Pianists. *Cognitive Brain Research, 19*(3), 219–228.

Merchant, H., Grahn, J., Trainor, L., Rohrmeier, M., and Fitch, W. T. (2015). Finding the Beat: A Neural Perspective across Humans and Non-Human Primates. *Philosophical Transactions of the Royal Society B: Biological Sciences, 370*(1664), 20140093.

Merchant, H., and Honing, H. (2013). Are Non-Human Primates Capable of Rhythmic Entrainment? Evidence for the Gradual Audiomotor Evolution Hypothesis. *Frontiers in Neuroscience, 7*, 274.

Molinari, M., Leggio, M. G., de Martin, M., Cerasa, A., and Thaut, M. (2003). Neurobiology of Rhythmic Motor Entrainment. *Annals of the New York Academy of Sciences, 999*, 313–321.

Murphy, S. M., Nordin, S. M., and Cumming, J. I. E. (2008). Imagery in Sport, Exercise and Dance. In T. Horn (ed.), *Advances in Sport Psychology*. 3rd edition. Champaign, IL: Human Kinetics, 297–324.

Nordin, S., and Cumming, J. (2006). Measuring the Content of Dancers' Images: Development of the Dance Imagery Questionnaire (DIQ). *Journal of Dance Medicine and Science, 10*(3).

(2008a). Types and Functions of Athletes' Imagery: Testing Predictions from the Applied Model of Imagery Use by Examining Effectiveness. *International Journal of Sport and Exercise Psychology, 6*(2), 189–206.

(2008b). Exploring Common Ground: Comparing the Imagery of Dancers and Aesthetic Sport Performers. *Journal of Applied Sport Psychology, 20*(4), 375–391.

Noy, L., Dekel, E., and Alon, U. (2011). The Mirror Game as a Paradigm for Studying the Dynamics of Two People Improvising Motion Together. *Proceedings of the National Academy of Sciences of the United States of America, 108*(52), 20947–20952.

Nummenmaa, L., Glerean, E., Hari, R., and Hietanen, J. K. (2014). Bodily Maps of Emotions. *Proceedings of the National Academy of Sciences, 111*(2), 646–651.

Olshansky, M. P., Bar, R. J., Fogarty, M., and DeSouza, J. F. (2015). Supplementary Motor Area and Primary Auditory Cortex Activation in an Expert Break-Dancer during the Kinesthetic Motor Imagery of Dance to Music. *Neurocase, 21*(5), 607–617.

Omigie, D., Pearce, M. T., Williamson, V. J., and Stewart, L. (2013). Electrophysiological Correlates of Melodic Processing in Congenital Amusia. *Neuropsychologia, 51*(9), 1749–1762.

Overby, L. Y., and Dunn, J. (2011). The History and Research of Dance Imagery: Implications for Teachers. *IADMS Bulletin for Teachers*, *2*, 9–11.

Paltsev, Y. I., and Elner, A. M. (1967). Change in Functional State of the Segmental Apparatus of the Spinal Cord under the Influence of Sound Stimuli and its Role in Voluntary Movement. *Biophysics*, *12*, 1219–1226.

Pavlik, K., and Nordin-Bates, S. (2016). Imagery in Dance: A Literature Review. *Journal of Dance Medicine and Science*, *20*(2), 21–53.

Peasley-Miklus, C. E., Panayiotou, G., and Vrana, S. R. (2016). Alexithymia Predicts Arousal-Based Processing Deficits and Discordance between Emotion Response Systems during Emotional Imagery. *Emotion*, *16*(2), 164.

Perica, R. (2010). The Dancing Imagination: How Does Imaginative Imagery Facilitate Movement Qualities in Dance Training and Performance? Perth, Australia, Edith Cowan University, BA (Hons) thesis. ro.ecu.edu.au/theses_hons/1407.

Poikonen, H., Toiviainen, P., and Tervaniemi, M. (2016). Early Auditory Processing in Musicians and Dancers during a Contemporary Dance Piece. *Scientific Reports*, *6*, 33056.

Schirmer-Mokwa, K. L., Fard, P. R., Zamorano, A. M., et al. (2015). Evidence for Enhanced Interoceptive Accuracy in Professional Musicians. *Frontiers in Behavioral Neuroscience*, *9*, 349.

Schmahmann, J. D., and Pandya, D. N. (2009). *Fiber Pathways of the Brain*. Oxford, UK: Oxford University Press.

Shafir, T. (2016). Using Movement to Regulate Emotion: Neurophysiological Findings and Their Application in Psychotherapy. *Frontiers in Psychology*, *7*, 1451.

Shafir, T., Taylor, S. F., Atkinson, A. P., Langenecker, S. A., and Zubieta, J. K. (2013). Emotion Regulation through Execution, Observation, and Imagery of Emotional Movements. *Brain and Cognition*, *82*(2), 219–227.

Shafir, T., Tsachor, R. P., and Welch, K. B. (2015). Emotion Regulation through Movement: Unique Sets of Movement Characteristics Are Associated with and Enhance Basic Emotions. *Frontiers in Psychology*, *6*, 2030.

Sumanapala, D. K., Fish, L. A., Jones, A. L., and Cross, E. S. (2017). Have I Grooved to This Before? Discriminating Practised and Observed Actions in a Novel Context. *Acta Psychologica*, *175*, 42–49.

Thaut, M. H. (2003). Neural Basis of Rhythmic Timing Networks in the Human Brain. *Annals of the New York Academy of Sciences*, *999*, 364–373.

Thaut, M. H., Kenyon, G. P., Schauer, M. L., and McIntosh, G. C. (1999). The Connection between Rhythmicity and Brain Function. *IEEE Engineering in Medicine and Biology Magazine*, *18*(2), 101–108.

Williams, S. E., Cooley, S. J., and Cumming, J. (2013). Layered Stimulus Response Training Improves Motor Imagery Ability and Movement Execution. *Journal of Sport and Exercise Psychology*, *35*(1), 60–71.

Wolpert, D. M., and Ghahramani, Z. (2000). Computational Principles of Movement Neuroscience. *Nature Reviews Neuroscience*, *3* (supplement 1212–1217).

Xenos, S., Rossignol, S., and Jones, G. M. (1976). Audio-Spinal Influence in Man Studied by the H-Reflex and its Possible Role on Rhythmic Movements Synchronized to Sound. *Electroencephalography of Clinical Neurophysiology*, *41*(1), 83–92.

Zatorre, R. J., Chen, J. L., and Penhune, V. B. (2007). When the Brain Plays Music: Auditory-Motor Interactions in Music Perception and Production. *Nature Reviews Neuroscience*, *8*(7), 547–558.

39 Imagination, Intersubjectivity, and a Musical Therapeutic Process: A Personal Narrative

Nigel Osborne

Although this volume is intended to celebrate the idea of imagination in what the editor beautifully describes as its "exuberance of disparate meanings," this chapter focuses, in the first instance, on a parallelogram of concerns within the wider conceptual space: that is to say, the relationship between communicative musicality and its neural substrates, phenomenology and intersubjectivity, imagination and creativity, and therapeutic process (Figure 39.1).

In terms of the OED dictionary definitions, this chapter is focused on descriptions of imagination 1(a), 3, and 5. It is concerned with the first of Stevenson's twelve conceptions (Stevenson, 2003) – "the ability to think of something that is not presently perceived but is, was or will be spatio-temporally real" – as well as the final four conceptions, all linked directly to creativity. In terms of Abraham's holistic framework (Abraham, 2016), the chapter moves systematically through the categories and beyond, with a specific worked example at the end.

This is in part a personal narrative of a journey from music into theories of creativity and imagination, the biological sciences, in particular neurophysiology, and therapeutic practice.

Communicative Musicality

The psychobiologist Colwyn Trevarthen has been both an inspiration and a mentor to me in the fields of psychobiology and child development. He is a New Zealander who worked at Caltech under the Nobel prizewinner Roger Sperry, pioneer of split-brain research, and at Harvard with Jerome Bruner, father of cognitive science, adviser to John F. Kennedy, and an important figure and colleague in my own life. It was during his time with Bruner that Colwyn began his work on infancy research. In the more than half century since, he has been based primarily in Edinburgh, and published a large body of work on neuropsychology, brain development, infant communication, and child learning and emotional health.

It was Peter Nelson, my colleague in the Music Faculty at Edinburgh University, who suggested I should contact Colwyn, so I began to attend his seminars in the Department of Psychology. It was the early 1990s – a time when Colwyn was beginning to take an interest in the connection between mother-infant communication and music, so I could

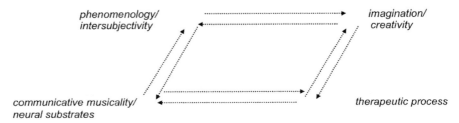

Figure 39.1 *The parallelogram of concerns explored within the chapter.*

make the occasional contribution. For example, I remember, at one seminar, pointing out that in a video of a baby moving its hand in time with the rhythm of its mother's voice, the baby was anticipating the beat – and in fact almost trying to "conduct" its mother. But most of the intellectual traffic was of course one-way.

Colwyn and I fell into a rhythm of meeting weekly at a restaurant called The Phoenicia, equidistant from Colwyn's office in George Square and mine in Nicolson Square. The Phoenicia conversations were my introduction to the world of psycho-biology (basically the threshold of connections between mind and body and how they influence one another) and to the sciences that had clustered around the study of mother-infant communication.

Colwyn's groundbreaking work had played an important role in a major shift in thinking in developmental science – for the purposes of this chapter, it is best described as the study of children's biological, psychological, and social development. This shift had begun in the 1970s and accelerated through the following decades. It was, in Colwyn's words, "a new theory of how human will and emotion are immediately shareable with others through gestures of the body and voice" (Malloch and Trevarthen, 2009: 1). Before this shift in developmental science, infants were not on the whole credited with complex skills or creative capacities, but rather seen as the object of a mother's protection and nourishment, and, of course, when the time eventually came, education. The new science revealed that babies may indeed be creative, be imaginative, have innate skills of communication, and be capable of both following and leading vocal and gestural conversations. It also demonstrated that through these conversations, babies were able to share sympathy, complex emotions, and rhythm and time. As the new theory unfolded, increasing attention was focused on infant and mother vocalizations.

Contributions were made by figures such as American psychiatrist Daniel Stern (Stern, 1974), who had established bridges between psychodynamic psychoanalysis and developmental science, and later by researchers such as Jesus Alegria and Éliane Noirot (Alegria and Noirot, 1978) and Sandra Trehub (Trehub, 1987). These vocalizations could no longer be dismissed as simply "baby talk."

They clearly had implications for, and an impact upon, the emotional growth and mental lives of children. They were also clearly highly "imaginative and creative."

A significant watershed came in 1979, when Colwyn invited a six-week-old Scottish girl called Laura and her mother into his laboratory in George Square, filmed them together, using a mirror to capture both Laura's and her mother's gestures, and made acoustic analyses of their interactions. The analysis revealed a sophisticated dialogue of emotionally modulated sound, where the mother invited and provoked the baby into a "musical" conversation, with expressive glides of the voice, sometimes with words, sometimes just with sounds, sharing through these sounds complex and joyful states of mind, body, and emotion (Trevarthen, Gratier, and Osborne, 2014). Of course, there is nothing new here. We are describing what is probably one of the most ancient and familiar behaviors of human beings. But Colwyn recognized its importance – a parcel of human knowledge, signed and sealed many scores of millennia ago, waiting to be unwrapped – and its relevance to emerging ways of thinking. These sorts of observations and findings were to inspire many gifted young researchers, psychologists, and music therapists to join Colwyn in mother-infant research during the years that followed. In the meantime, the work of developmental scientists like Anne Fernald (Fernald, 1985) and Patricia Kuhl (Kuhl et al., 1997) in Boston and Washington, DC, Nobuo Masataka (Masataka, 1993) in Kyoto, and Mechthild and Hanuš Papoušek in Munich (Papoušek, 1987), was helping reveal a wider picture – that Laura and her mother were not alone, that mother-infant communication was a universal human phenomenon and that the same sounds, glides, pulses, sympathy, and use of time were used by all mothers and infants in all human cultures. This was confirmed by a raft of evidence from countries and cultures as far apart as Germany, Nigeria, Sweden, and Japan.

One lunchtime in the Phoenicia, probably late in 1995, Colwyn asked me if I happened to know of some kind of automated graphic notation for music or sound that would go further than normal spectrograms could, and make visible the subtle changes and glides of pitch, sound quality, and volume of, say, a mother's or an infant's voice. By an extraordinary coincidence I had taken part in a seminar just the day before with some of our doctoral students in the Music Faculty. Stephen Malloch, one of Peter Nelson's students, had presented some acoustic analyses of works by the Hungarian composer György Ligeti. Ligeti was mostly known to a general public through Stanley Kubrick's use of his works *Atmosphères*, *Requiem*, and *Lux Aeterna* in *2001: A Space Odyssey* and *Lontano* in *The Shining*. Stephen, with support from the Physics Department, had created a timbral notation to capture Ligeti's sonoristic/cinematic magic, combining spectrograms with visual representations of qualities such as "roughness," or the beating between partials close together, dissonances detected initially in the brainstem; "width," or how wide the sound is heard to be; and "sharpness," or how high in a sound its center of loudness lies. It seemed to me it was more or less what Colwyn was looking for, so I put him in contact with Peter and Stephen.

By the following year, Stephen had become Colwyn's postdoctoral student developing and adapting his timbral notational system to the analysis of mother-infant communication, and contributing significantly to the evolution of the research. It was Stephen who moved the thinking a critical step forward by discovering that mother-infant communication could be analyzed in purely musical terms – that there was always a clear pulse, and even metrical divisions like musical bars; that the contours of pitch and time could be described like melodies; and that the narrative structures could be interpreted in terms of musical forms. One day Stephen was walking down the stairs from his window-less postdoc room to Colwyn's office, and the term "communicative musicality" came into his head.

One of Stephen's first tasks as a researcher was to revisit some of the key mother-infant communication research milestones, to see what further evidence his notations and analyses might yield. An early candidate was, of course, Laura and her mother (Trevarthen, Gratier, and Osborne, 2014) (Figure 39.2).

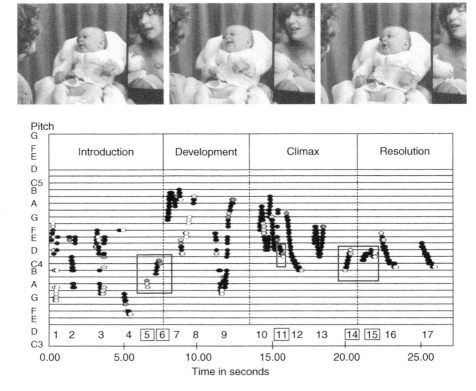

Introduction	Development	Climax	Resolution
1 Come on	7 Oh yes!	10 Tell me some	15 Ch ch
2 Again	8 Is that right?	more then	With INFANT
3 Come on then	9 Well tell me	11 INFANT	16 Ahgoo
4 That's clever	some more then	12 Ooorrh	17 Goo
5 INFANT		13 Come on	
6 INFANT		14 Ch ch ch ch	
		with infant	

Figure 39.2 *Indices of mother-infant early communication. With permission from Trevarthen and Aitken (2003), Regulation of Brain Development and Age-Related Changes in Infants' Motives: The Developmental Function of "Regressive" Periods, in M. Heimann (ed.),* Regression Periods in Human Infancy, *Mahwah, NJ: Erlbaum, 107–184.*

In Stephen's own words:

> The dramatic narrative structure of the exchange between Laura and her mother can be seen in the shape of the pitch contour of their exchange. From vocalisations centred on C4 at the start of the exchange, the mother takes her cue from Laura's upward moving vocalisation by abruptly moving her pitch to C5. This sudden upwards movement is "reprised" by the mother during the rising pitch "swoop" of utterance number 9. From here till the end, the pitch level slowly descends back to C4, reflected in the downwards pitch movement of Laura (utterance 11). In the figure it is also suggested that the narrative structure may be thought of in a "classical" four-part evolution of a story, through Introduction, Development, Climax, and Resolution. (Malloch and Trevarthen 2009: 4),

Here is a highly musical form of communication of moment-by-moment, evolving emotional expression of states of mind and body, shared together in sound by Laura and her mother in surprisingly "original" and sometimes unique ways. These moments of expression form a narrative in time, which I suggest is a point of origin of some significant aspects of human creativity, where "original" vocal expression from both mother and baby take place within a "received" structure fully understood by both participants. This could equally be an effective description of a jazz improvization or the *alap* of an Indian raga performance.

Studies of such comparisons became an important part of later stages of development of the theory of Communicative Musicality, for example in the work of Ben Schogler (Schogler and Trevarthen, 2007) linking communicative musicality to TAU theory (Lee, 2005), a neural mathematics relating to intrinsic and perceptual guidance of movement, and in my own studies of therapeutic uses of Indian music, e.g. in "The Human Nature of Culture and Education" (Trevarthen, Gratier, and Osborne, 2014: 177–178). At the same time, other disciplines, as described below, were influencing and at times directing the progression of the theory of Communicative Musicality. Evolutionary biology and Colwyn's own work in child development, dating back to his time with Bruner, had informed the work from the beginning and now, as the early 2000s unfolded, began to exert a strong renewed influence. The work in psychiatry of the late Daniel Stern had also influenced early phases of the evolution of theories of mother-infant communication. Now it provided a fresh and "pragmatic" perspective on the relationship between the phenomenology of the present moment, vitality affects, or vehicles for affective sharing, and what Stern calls the intersubjective matrix (Stern, 2004). Stern in some ways provided a "map" of the place and time in consciousness at which certain forms of creativity might take place. The late Jaak Panksepp, a pioneer of the neuroscience of the emotions, investigated the neural substrates of communicative musicality, ranging from the subcortical origins of musical "chills" to the circuits of neurotransmission and endocrine activity associated with the powerful emotions of separation cries (Panksepp and Trevarthen, 2009). Panksepp described a subcortical neurophysiology that was capable of explaining how and why people might share, and even imagine and "invent" new ways of experiencing emotion through sound, and how such sharing might form an important part of both the motivation for and realization of creative and therapeutic processes.

Child Development

In many ways as individual human beings we "relive" the evolution of our species in our personal development. In evolution, the reptilian brain grew into the mammalian brain and the mammalian brain into the human brain. When a child is born, the most developed part of its brain is the brain stem – the "reptilian" brain, connected to an evolving auditory cortex and largely mammalian limbic system. In the first three months the parietotemporal cortex (responsible for putting auditory, visual, and somatosensory information together) and the visual cortex develop, both located relatively low in the "mammalian" lobes. It is not until a child is twelve months old that elements of a more mature brain appear, such as specialized activity in dorsal and medial frontal lobes, and a few months later, Broca's area, associated with the acquisition of language. Although other mammals have similar structures, they do not operate in the same, human way (Figure 39.3). This is not to suggest that young babies are somehow not yet fully "human"; on the contrary, their personal development follows the collective development of all human beings, and, as the history of study of mother-infant communication and the theory of communicative musicality suggests, uniquely human capacities to interact in time, sympathy, gesture, and sound are present from birth and before. Colwyn refers to this development as the "Internal Motive Formation" (Trevarthen and Aitken, 2003).

I suggest that the Internal Motive Formation may be the location of origin of much human creativity and prosocial aspects of imagination.

The progress of brain development is of course reflected in increasing and changing capacities in babies, which are in turn reflected in changes in the nature of mother-infant communication and communicative musicality. But there is a chicken

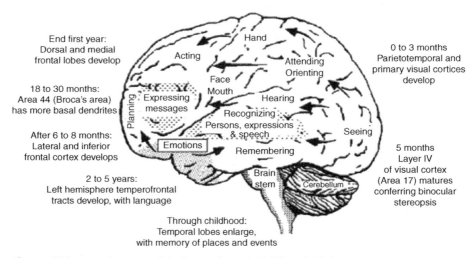

Figure 39.3 *Development of the brain through childhood. With permission, from Trevarthen (2004), Brain Development, in R. L. Gregory (ed.),* Oxford Companion to the Mind. *2nd edition, Oxford, UK; New York, NY: Oxford University Press, 116–127.*

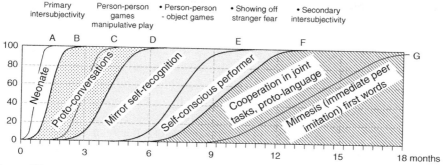

Figure 39.4 *The evolution of mother-infant communication. This graph describes precisely a timeline for the evolution of creativity and imagination through intersubjectivity – from spontaneous (and already creative) proto-conversations to mirroring and self-conscious performance. With permission, from Malloch and Trevarthen (2009),* Communicative Musicality: Exploring the Basis of Human Companionship, *Oxford, UK; New York, NY: Oxford University Press.*

and egg question here. Sometimes, in my experience of applying the principles of communicative musicality in work with children, it seems that musically communicative interactions are "activating," "attracting," and "exercising" capacities emerging in the child, rather than, in some way, issuing directly from them. A good example is gesturing with the impulse of a sound, or moving in time to rhythmic sound. Another is the sharing of sympathy, where communicative musicality appears to help build both a field of empathy and the capacity for emotional response. In other words it may be that it is through creative impulse and later creative play with sound, that capacities for sympathy and sharing states of mind and body are in part activated and formed.

The graph and table in Figure 39.4 chart respectively the evolution of interactions between mothers and babies in the first eighteen months of infancy, and cognitive and somatic developments related to communication during the same period.

Phenomenology and Intersubjectivity

The concepts of phenomenology and intersubjectivity are rooted in philosophy. It was of course Edmund Husserl who first introduced and popularized the terms (Husserl, 1913/2011) and described the link between them in a series of definitions subsequently modified by Heidegger (Heidegger, 1927/2005). For both, phenomenology was the philosophical background and intersubjectivity the functionality. But whereas Husserl based his ideas of intersubjectivity on empathy (*Einfühlung*), as in the empathetic recognition and understanding of, for example, pain in the other, Heidegger was more interested in ontology: "being-in-the-world" and entering intersubjectivity, or sharing knowledge and feelings with others, through experience.

During the course of the long march of ontologies and epistemologies in the twentieth century, the legacies of Husserl and Heidegger were inevitably the subject of both controversy and modification. Perhaps the most significant of these changes in outlook was linguistic philosophy, and the work of figures like Lacan and Habermas, who preferred to dismiss individual consciousness as potentially solipsistic and to examine intersubjectivity through the more objective and culturally processed medium of language (Habermas, 1979; Lacan, 1964/1977).

In *The Present Moment* Daniel Stern seemed to transcend these differences, and to provide a location in time for the concept of phenomenology, at a point where being and consciousness meet, and where intersubjectivity may operate within its own structure or "matrix." For Stern the present moment, the fleeting "now" of human experience, has an average duration of 3–4 seconds, but may range from 1 to 10 seconds. It is a "chunking" of meaningful subjective experience, particularly as it occurs when shared between people, and corresponds to a phrase in poetry, dance or music, and to cycles of breath. It is also reflected in Laura's communication with her mother (above), which may be parsed, according to Stern's principles, into four "present moments" roughly corresponding to Malloch's four formal divisions. Stern's theory advances beyond the realm of words – it is capable of embracing all forms of human expression and communication, and this is how it became an important step forward in the evolution of the theory of communicative musicality.

According to Stern, communication within the present moment may be achieved and intersubjectivity may take place through "vitality affects." These are gestures that may be physical and/or vocal, with or without the use of words, which normally display microsecond by microsecond fluctuations and shifts in arousal, energy, flow, feeling, and rhythm. As he writes, vitality affects are to emotional communication what words are to verbal communication, and are key to dyadic regulation of affective states.

Stephen Malloch's notations allowed fellow researchers to identify vitality affects in the flow of intersubjectivity within individual "present moments." Returning once again to Laura, it is clear that her mother's provocative descending vocal gestures (1-4) are a cluster of vitality affects, which Laura responds to with a gesture mirroring her intonation (5), before changing the emotional quality of the dialogue with a surge of upward-moving sound energy (6). This is immediately responded to by her mother with coupled vitality affects (7 and 8) – oh yes; is that right? – with a similar affirmative upward-surging energy. It is noticeable that Laura herself effects the key changes in the dialogue, for example toward the end (14 and 15), where in unison with her mother she redirects the sound energy downward in pitch.

All such exchanges between mothers and infants are unique, and essentially creative. But within the whole, moments of change (such as 7 and 8 above), initiated by vitality affects within and between present moments are especially and profoundly creative in terms of both disrupting and redirecting the flow of communication. This is where the process moves close to Stevenson's first conception of imagination – the ability to think of something not presently perceived, but that will be. It is something resembling a musical creativity, capable of operating within larger-scale received structures (like Stephen Malloch's introduction-development-climax-resolution structures – a "formal" linking of present moments) and of unfolding consistently within a shared repertoire of vitality affects, where unexpected gestures and changes may redirect the emotional experience, just as unexpected notes or musical gestures within musical phrases may redirect the flow of musical emotion.

All of this takes place within the intersubjective matrix, which is the intimate context for connectedness with others. Laura and her mother are a vital and necessary part of one another's matrices, and share an intersubjective consciousness in which repeated exchanges between two people may, as Stern argues, give rise to a single shared emergent experience – implicitly, a shared, emergent, creative, and imaginative experience.

Neural Substrates of Communicative Musicality

Jaak Panksepp, psychobiologist and inventor of the term "affective neuroscience," had a significant influence on the evolution of the theory of communicative musicality. A large part of his work was on rats, including examination of emotions such as joy and fear. This research led Panksepp to conclude that the substrates of such emotions are low in the rodent brain, and to speculate that aspects of human emotions may also be associated with subcortical systems.

Of particular relevance to communicative musicality is his work on the relationship between vocalizations and emotion, and how animal and human vocalizations (including musical expression) have related neural substrates, and neural "hotlines" to the sensation and experience of emotion. For example, according to Panksepp (Panksepp and Bernatzky, 2002) the mammalian separation-distress vocalization system (the descending "whimper" of the little lamb lost in the snow) resembles the subcortical circuitry that mediates human sadness, as suggested by PET imaging. One of the main neurochemical systems that reduce arousal of this circuitry, i.e. brain opioids that activate *mu* receptors, show lower levels of activity during human sadness. Panksepp found similar parallels with laughter-joy vocalizations of rats, manifest in 50kHz ultrasonic utterances, readily observed in juvenile rat rough-and-tumble play (Panksepp, 2007). Part of this vocal behavior appears to be prosocial – indicating readiness to play, but when it occurs in response to joyful stimulation, it appears to be related to the mesolimbic dopamine energized brain "reward" system. Panksepp suggests that similar systems may be at work in the neurodynamics of human social joy and laughter.

Panksepp's work is complemented by a raft of related observations. The acoustic startle reflex (the human physical reaction to sudden unexpected sound), for example, involves a pathway directly from the cochlea along cranial (auditory) nerve VIII by way of the lateral leminiscus to the caudate reticular nucleus, whence there are descending projections to spinal and limb motor neurons, thus provoking the "jump" or "blink" effect (Osborne, 2009a), the equivalent of a vitality affect that may occur in communication with babies (boo! whoops! gotcha!). Research with rats has suggested there is also an ascending pathway to the amygdala, where cholecystokinin B receptors potentiate the effect of acoustic startle (Frankland et al., 1997), and activate autonomic and endocrine systems for stress.

Closely related to acoustic startle response and its origins in human evolution are sounds that signal danger, have evolutionary/survival value, or are particularly indicative of the positioning and movement of the body in space and time. This may extend from the hissing of snakes (Erlich, Lipp, and Slaughter, 2013) to rapidly approaching sounds, glides, falling, fast crescendos, loud bursts of sound and the like – indeed to vocal gestures resembling many of the features of vitality affects of mother-infant communication. Evidence suggests that these sounds are recognized by innate systems early in auditory pathways (Erlich, Lipp, and Slaughter, 2013). The Inferior Colliculus (IC) appears to be an important collecting point for such information in the ascending sensory pathway for sound (Jorris, Schreiner, and Rees, 2004). The IC generates powerful neuronal responses to significant changes in sound intensity, regulated by neurotransmitter GABA A (Sivaramakrishnan et al., 2004). There is clear evidence of pathways ascending to emotional systems (Heldt and Falls, 2003), as well as a descending, emotional "feedback" pathway from the amygdala (Marsh et al., 2002).

These findings suggest that there may be something resembling an innate lexicon of vitality affects and their neural substrates present in communicative musicality. Such a lexicon may, in theory, extend from almost "hardwired" connections between vocal gestures and affective response in the brain, such as the acoustic startle response, separation cries, and laughter, through creative modifications, adaptations, and exaptations of such hardwired responses, through to creative play with gestures such as glides, crescendos, decrescendos, climbing, and falling, associated with the neurodynamics of changing emotional intensity, intentionality, and location in space.

It is almost certain that music evolved from early communicative musicality, and it is possible that it continues – after hundreds of millennia of evolution – to make use of similar neural substrates. For example, the "formal" structure of present moments that Malloch identifies in Laura and her mother's interaction may well be an ancient origin of musical forms. Vitality affects may be seen as the origin of notes and gestures within the musical phrase. Carmen's dark *L'Amour est un oiseau rebelle*, with its "melancholic" stepwise descending melodic gestures, may be seen, in theory at least, as a distant relative and adaptation of a separation vocalization; Stravinsky's *Danse Sacrale* may be seen, with the same caveats, as a sequence of acoustic startle reflexes; the ascending clusters of The Beatles' *A Day in the Life* as a surge of sound energy, generating powerful neuronal responses and an imaginary positioning of the body in space and time. Such ancient origins in communicative musicality and intersubjectivity may well help explain the power of music in therapeutic processes.

Communicative Musicality, Creativity, Imagination and Trauma Therapy

In the early 1990s, at the time when Colwyn and I started our Phoenicia conversations, I began to work with music to support children who are victims of war. The first pilots took place in Sarajevo during the siege of the city (1992–1995). I had been engaged in human rights work, and had witnessed the appalling conditions for children in a city under constant mortar and sniper fire, where there was no electricity or water supply, little food, daily terror, and no school.

I joined with local artists and musicians to provide support for the children through creative activities, primarily to try to distract them from the horror around them. The approach was very much based on the principles of communicative musicality as they were emerging at the time, fostering shared positive feelings through both group and dyadic intersubjectivity and using music and its affective power to take children on safe emotional journeys. The principal activities were singing, movement, and creative work. The objectives included building self-confidence, self-belief, and self-respect through creative activity, as well as developing focus, relaxation, joy, motivation, positivity, communication among individuals and groups, trust, and empathy (Osborne, 2009b, 2012, 2014, 2017a).

The most commonly used diagnostic criteria for PTSD are those described in the Diagnostic and Statistical Manual of Mental Disorders of the American Psychiatric Association (DSM/APA). The fifth edition (DSM-V), published in 2013, identifies four symptom clusters: re-experiencing; avoidance; negative cognitions and mood; and arousal. During the time of the Bosnian war, the principal reference was DSM-IV, with four related symptom clusters: traumatic experience; traumatic recall; hypervigilance; and avoidance. At that time we were unable to judge in any scientific way the extent of trauma among the children with whom we were working. But a longitudinal study carried out by the Harvard Medical School Department of Social Medicine (Goldstein, Wampler, Wise, 1997), among a similar population of children in the Sarajevo region, revealed that almost 94 percent of the children met DSM-IV criteria for posttraumatic stress disorder.

During the course of our work we observed improvements in the children's presentation. They appeared calmer, more socially at ease, more communicative – including emotionally communicative – and more joyful and motivated. At one point we were visited and assessed by the Ministry of Health, still functioning within the besieged city. They liked our program, described it as "therapeutic," and suggested we should if possible scale up.

We considered this as permission to describe our approach as "therapeutic." And as the program progressed, we saw the need to establish a more rigorous scientific base for the work, to inform our dialogues with the medical and psychosocial services, but also to complement a robust emerging methodology rooted in communicative musicality.

An area of interest for us was one not particularly highlighted in the psychiatric literature on PTSD: the neurophysiological symptoms of trauma. The research was a natural extension of the work of Panksepp and others on the neural substrates of communicative musicality. It was also work I was able to carry forward in research in music and the autonomic nervous system, and music and cardiology as part of the development of X-System, a musical-medical-streaming technology (www.x-system.co.uk/index.html).

There is a large raft of literature on the effects of music on the autonomic nervous system (e.g. Aragon, Farris, and Byers, 2002; Byers and Smyth, 1997; Cardigan et al., 2001; Gerra et al., 1998; Iwanaga, Kobayashi, and Kawasaki, 2005; Iwanaga and Trukamoto, 1997; Knight and Rickard. 2001; Lee et al., 2005; Mok and Wong, 2003; Updike and Charles, 1987). Our research showed that this relationship is particularly fine-tuned, with a direct and detailed influence on the behavior of the heart. In general, relaxing music may activate the parasympathetic nervous system, which releases acetylcholine by way of the vagus nerve into the sinoatrial node and slows down the heart. Exciting music may activate the sympathetic nervous system, which releases norepinephrine (noradrenaline) by way of the accelerans nerve to the sinoatrial node, which speeds up the heart.

But the system may generate extraordinarily subtle and powerful autonomic responses to music, navigating sympathetic and parasympathetic response in fluid ways. Figure 39.5 shows an example of the heart rate of someone listening to Gustav Holst's *Venus* from the The Planets Suite.

Examples like this demonstrate the therapeutic potential of music and communicative musicality. Children and adults with PTSD have autonomic systems on constant alert and an average heart rate locked 5 to 6 beats faster than non-traumatized individuals (Beckham et al., 2002; Buckley et al., 2001, 2004; Cohen et al., 1998, 2000; Forneris, Butterfield, and Bosworth, 2004; Kibler and Lyons, 2004). Music has the capacity both to exercise and to release this system in present moment by present moment fine-tuned interaction with the autonomic nervous system. Research for X-system[1] shows correlations (potentially useful for therapeutic practice) between heart rate variability and valence – in other words how positively or negatively aroused a listener may be (highly aroused and happily excited, or highly aroused and fearful or stressed). The next stage of investigation will also include respiratory sinus arrhythmias.

There is evidence that the experience of music may help to regulate the HPA axis and modulate cortisol levels. As in the evidence for the autonomic nervous system, the effect depends on the kind of music. For example, listening to techno music appears to raise cortisol levels (Gerra et al., 1998), and the music built into video games increases the cortisol/stress response during game playing (Hebert et al., 2005). As in the case of the heart, the more common effect of music is to lower or

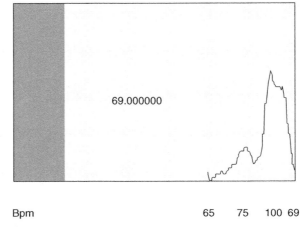

Bpm   65   75   100 69

Figure 39.5 *A "present moment" of 8-10 seconds. This is where a powerful "chill"-like vitality affect occurs in the music, exciting the listener's sympathetic nervous system, with dramatic neural arousal, before descending to parasympathetic frequencies.*

1 See Patel, H., Sice, P., Rauch, H., Osborne, N., and Bentley, M. (in preparation), Predicting the Psycho-Physiological Effects of Pre-Selected Music – A Feasibility Study.

stabilize levels of stress, and consequently levels of cortisol (e.g. Miluk-Kolasa et al., 1994; Nilsson, Unosson, and Rawal, 2005; Uedo et al., 2004). This endocrinal evidence is supported by evidence from electroencephalograms (EEG), functional magnetic resonance imaging (fMRI), and positron emission tomography (PET scans), which shows activity associated with music and emotional responses to music in key components of the HPA axis, in particular the amygdala and hippocampus (e.g. Baumgartner et al., 2006; Blood and Zatorre, 2001; Brown, Martinez, and Parsons, 2004; Koelsch et al., 2006; Wieser and Mazzola, 1986).

In PTSD there is usually dysregulation of the HPA axis. Normally cortisol levels rise dramatically directly after a traumatic experience, but in chronic trauma tend to fall to below normal (Goenjian et al., 1996; Yehuda, 2000). Music is a means for exercising and potentially helping to regulate the system (Miluk-Kolasa et al., 1994; Uedo et al., 2004).

PTSD is also associated with breathing difficulties (Donker et al., 2002; Nixon and Bryant, 2005; Sack, Hopper, and Lambrecht, 2004; Sahar, Shalev, and Porges, 2001), generally poorly reported in the trauma literature. These problems seem to be linked to vagal pathways for anxiety, leading to dysregulation of the flow of breath and speech. Music and singing may have a powerful regulatory effect, including exercise of full lung capacity through vocalization, breath control through phrasing, and regulation of related neural circuits in the medulla oblongata (Bernardi, 2006; Fried, 1990a, 1990b; Mccoy, 2004; Osborne, 2009b).

Finally, PTSD leads to the dysregulation of movement repertoires (Adler et al., 2004; Brent et al., 1995; Famularo et al., 1996; Yule, 1994), including on the one hand sluggishness and on the other behaviors comorbid with ADHD. Musical rhythm may have a powerful regulatory effect on movement; I have proposed a chronobiology of musical rhythm that may help to explain this effect (Osborne 2009a, 2017b). Rhythmic frequencies and the subconscious and emotional modulation of moving engage the emotional core of the brainstem, the limbic system, the basal ganglia, important for the inhibition and selection of premotor cortical areas to facilitate "smoothing" of voluntary movement, and the cerebellum, which integrates inputs from the spinal cord and other areas to fine tune motor activity (Panksepp, 1998; Sacks, 2007).

The primary access to these regulatory and therapeutic effects of music is through communicative musicality within dyadic and group intersubjectivity operating in the present moment. Usually this intersubjectivity involves individuals and groups occupying the same space and time. But there is an important exception for music. It is likely that musical intersubjectivity stretches further – to the performer and/or the composer who share an imagined intersubjectivity through and within the experience and vitality affects of the music itself, whether it be recorded or performed live.

The Intervention

As has been described, the intervention, which evolved from the early pilots in Bosnia, is based, on principles of communicative musicality and on a neurophysiological approach to the symptoms of trauma, and may be summarized in the following biopsychosocial model (Osborne, 2012) (Figures 39.6 and 39.7).

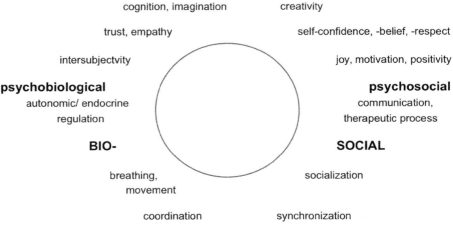

Figure 39.6 *The biopsychosocial model of communicative musicality. After (Osborne, 2012), Neuroscience and "Real World" Practice: Music as a Therapeutic Resource for Children in Zones of Conflict, Annals of the New York Academy of Sciences, 1252(1), 69–76.*

An Exuberance of Disparate Meanings

I am finishing writing this article as I travel home from Beirut in Lebanon. Yesterday (June 30, 2018), I took part in a performance in a community center in Bar Elias in the Bekaa Valley involving Syrian refugee children from the surrounding camps. After more than seven years of exile, the children and their families are still living in makeshift tents of tarpaulin, cardboard, matchwood, and plastic bags, with very little material support, and a high level of trauma.

For the last three years I have collaborated with SAWA for Development and Aid, a local Lebanese NGO, in a therapeutic and educational program for the children based on the principles of the intervention (Osborne 2009b, 2017b). Yesterday's performance was the culmination of a three-month cycle of work supported by the charity Penny Appeal. The idea was to take an imaginary journey by train from Beirut to Damascus, and then around the Syrian railway system. Sadly the system is now destroyed, but adults and some older children remember the trains. Most of the refugees come from cities along the former tracks, so in a sense it is an imaginary journey home, made vivid by songs and visual images from the towns – Hama, Homs, Aleppo, Raqaa, Deraa and so on – along the way. The children have participated in creative musical, visual and movement work, and have learned songs for each of the "stations." They have even built a lifelike, glittering, multi-colored miniature train, which winds its way across the stage, and three-dimensional images and acrobatic human reconstructions of well-known landmarks. We received

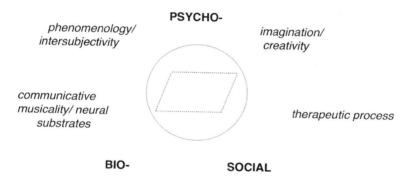

PSYCHO-

phenomenology/
intersubjectivity

imagination/
creativity

communicative
musicality/ neural
substrates

therapeutic process

BIO-   **SOCIAL**

Figure 39.7 *The location of the parallelogram of concerns within the biopsychosocial model of communicative musicality.*

the generous permission of Yusuf Islam (Cat Stevens) to adapt his song *Peace Train*, with a chorus translated into Arabic, to start us on the journey.

As the children perform on stage (Figure 39.8), it is possible to follow their progress through Abraham's imagination framework (Abraham, 2016). The

Figure 39.8 *Children performing at the Beqaa event in June 2018*

journey begins with perceptual and motor mental imagery, in this case, with visual, auditory, and musical imagery. Already this is a nested expression of imagination. It is not only how the visual arts work – the train, the water wheel of Hama, the amphora and grapes of Deraa – conjures up images of the "real thing"; it is how imagination was used to create the images themselves. There is an auditory equivalent. The children have created a soundscape of a train arriving in a station. They listened to recordings of trains and then created their own sound composition with claves, maracas, woodblocks, darabouka, and castanets. Once again, the soundscape invites us to imagine a real train, but the act of creating the composition has led to transformations and adaptations; it is now something different, and an experience – a composition – of its own, where the real thing informs the act of imagination, just as much as imagination conjures up the real thing.

The children's journey is full of emotion and aesthetic engagement and response. Once again the experience of imagination is nested. The music itself, through its communicative musicality, generates emotions in the children. But the children are also the performers and creators. They have aesthetic and personal satisfaction in performing and communicating the music and its emotions well, just as the visual artists derive aesthetic satisfaction from both making the objects and displaying them – a whole second raft of intersubjectivity.

The performance is replete with intentionality and recollection. This is a journey home in the imagination – a journey, for refugees, in the most emotionally charged domain of autobiographical, episodic memory. It is a therapeutic experience but also full of challenges. Bar Elias is only a few kilometers from the Syrian Border. The refugees can see their homeland from the flaps of their tents, but cannot go there; they can only imagine – and wonder about the might-have-beens in their lives, and imagine how their thoughts and their decisions may have been different.

And the performance is full of novel combinatorial and generative imagination, from the children's original creative work to their originality in interpretation of existing songs.

Then the children's journey moves further, into the space implicit beyond Abraham's framework. These experiences of imagination and creativity lead directly to therapeutic processes – to motivation and joy (the children's faces and body language tell the story – no need here for psychometrics or neurophysiological measures), to self-confidence, self-belief, and self-respect, and even pride in the beauty and emotional power of the performance. Then there is communication, motivation, trust, positivity, empowerment, a sense of identity ("No I am not from Dalhamiyeh camp, I am from Homs!").

And finally, the journey completes its course through fine and gross motor skills, concentration, memory, and cognition to the neurophysiological regulation of heart, breathing, movement, and bodily chemistry afforded by the effects of communicative musicality, intersubjectivity, imagination, and creativity in the present moment.

Several key areas of development remain for the intervention and related research. In terms of practice, the intervention is currently expanding to include work with young people, families, and communities. This forms part of a new, holistic approach to aid work, including health care, social care, shelter, food security, and education.

There is a strong evidence base validating the principles of the therapeutic work, in particular relating to music and the neurophysiological concerns described in this chapter. But there have been few standard clinical trials, and many obstacles to implementation of such trials. Control groups, randomized controls, and blind testing are problematic in the refugee camp environment, where there is a moral imperative to support as many people as possible, where populations are not stable, where "blind" objectivity may bring insufficient insight and have a paradoxical "non-scientific" effect, where there can be no question of invasive procedures, and where successful work comes from trust, reliability, and no fear that "men in white coats" have arrived to appropriate the details of people's personal lives and experience.

There are currently changes in outlook in the health and social care worlds that may favor more acceptable qualitative and hybrid approaches. And the X-System team has developed a platform whereby basic physiological measures may be taken noninvasively and in an enjoyable, participatory manner. As these new approaches evolve, there is hope that they may form a basis for viable clinical trials.

In the meantime, I continue background research in music and the autonomic nervous system, and in particular the use of Heart Rate Variability and possibly Respiratory Sinus Arrhythmias as measures of vagal power, and therefore as a means to predict valence and related emotional effects in music. And of course I continue to work with colleagues such as Colwyn Trevarthen, Dave Lee, and Ben Schogler, following the journey of the theory of communicative musicality and its implications for therapy, creativity, and imagination.

References

Abraham, A. (2016). The Imaginative Mind. *Human Brain Mapping, 37*, 4197–4211.

Adler, L. A., Kunz, M., Chua, H. C., Rotrosen, J., and Resnick, S. G. (2004). Attention-Deficit /Hyperactivity Disorder in Adult Patients with Posttraumatic Stress Disorder (PTSD): Is ADHD a Vulnerability Factor? *Journal of Attention Disorders, 8*(1), 11–16.

Alegria, J., and Noirot, E. (1978). Neonate Orientation Behaviour Towards the Human Voice. *Early Human Development, 1*, 291–312.

Aragon, D., Farris, C., and Byers, J. F. (2002). The Effects of Harp Music in Vascular and Thoracic Surgical Patients. *Alternative Therapies in Health and Medicine, 8*(5), 52–60.

Baumgartner, T., Lutz, K., Schmidt, C. F., and Jancke, L. (2006). The Emotional Power of Music: How Music Enhances the Feeling of Affective Pictures. *Brain Research, 1075*(1), 151–164.

Beckham, J. C., Vrana, S. R., Barefoot, J. C., et al. (2002). Magnitude and Duration of Cardiovascular Responses to Anger in Vietnam Veterans with and without Posttraumatic Stress Disorder. *Journal of Consulting and Clinical Psychology, 70*, 228–234.

Bernardi, L., Porta, C., and Sleight, P. (2006). Cardiovascular, Cerebrovascular, and Respiratory Changes Induced by Different Types of Music in Musicians and Non-Musicians: The Importance of Silence. *Heart (British Cardiac Society)*, *92* (4), 445–452.

Blood, A. J., and Zatorre, R. J. (2001). Intensely Pleasurable Responses to Music Correlate with Activity in Brain Regions Implicated in Reward and Emotion. *Proceedings of the National Academy of Sciences USA*, *98*(20), 11818–11823.

Brent, D. A., Perper, J. A., Moritz, G., et al. (1995). Posttraumatic Stress Disorder in Peers of Adolescent Suicide Victims: Predisposing Factors and Phenomenology. *Journal of the American Academy of Child and Adolescent Psychiatry*, *34*(2), 209–215.

Brown, S., Martinez, M. J., and Parsons, L. M. (2004). Passive Music Listening Spontaneously Engages Limbic and Paralimbic Systems. *Neuroreport*, *15*(13), 2033–2037.

Buckley, T. C., Holohan, D., Greif, J. L. et al. (2004). Twenty-Four-Hour Ambulatory Assessment of Heart Rate and Blood Pressure in Chronic PTSD and non-PTSD Veterans. *Journal of Traumatic Stress*, *17*, 163–171.

Buckley, T. C., and Kaloupek, D. G. (2001). A Meta-Analytic Examination of Basal Cardiovascular Activity in Posttraumatic Stress Disorder. *Psychosomatic Medicine*, *63*, 585–594.

Byers, J. F., and Smyth, K. A. (1997). Effect of a Musical Intervention on Noise Annoyance, Heart Rate, and Blood Pressure in Cardiac Surgery Patients. *American Journal of Critical Care*, *6*(3), 183–191.

Cardigan, M. E., Caruso, N. A., Haldeman, S. M., et al. (2001). The Effects of Music on Cardiac Patients on Bed Rest. *Progress in Cardiovascular Nursing*, *16*(1), 5–13.

Cohen, H., Benjamin, J., Geva, A. B., et al. (2000). Autonomic Dysregulation in Panic Disorder and in Post-Traumatic Stress Disorder: Application of Power Spectrum Analysis of Heart Rate Variability at Rest and in Response to Recollection of Trauma or Panic Attacks. *Psychiatry Research*, *96*, 1–13.

Cohen, H., Kotler, M., Matar, M. A. et al. (1998). Analysis of Heart Rate Variability in Posttraumatic Stress Disorder Patients in Response to a Trauma-Related Reminder. *Biological Psychiatry*, *44*, 1054–1059.

Donker, G. A., Yzermans, C. J., Spreeuwenberg, P., and van der Zee, J. (2002). Symptom Attribution after a Plane Crash: Comparison between Self-Reported Symptoms and GP Records. *British Journal of General Practice*, *52*(484), 917–922.

Erlich, N., Lipp, O. V., and Slaughter, V. (2013). Of Hissing Snakes and Angry Voices: Human Infants Are Differently Responsive to Evolutionary Fear-Relevant Sounds. *Developmental Science*, *16*(6), 894–904.

Famularo, R., Fenton, T., Kinscherff, R., and Augustyn, M. (1996). Psychiatric Comorbidity in Childhood Post Traumatic Stress Disorder. *Child Abuse and Neglect*, *20*(10), 953–961.

Fernald, A. (1985). Four-Month-Old Infants Prefer to Listen to Motherese. *Infant Behavior and Development*, *8*, 181–195.

Forneris, C. A., Butterfield, M. I., and Bosworth, H. B. (2004). Physiological Arousal among Women Veterans with and without Posttraumatic Stress Disorder. *Military Medicine*, *169*, 307–312.

Frankland, P. W., Josselyn, S. A., Bradweijn, J., Vaccarino, F. J., and Yeomans, J. S. (1997) Activation of Amygdala Cholecystokinin B Receptores Potentiates the Acoustic Startle Response in Rats. *Journal of Neuroscience*, *17*(5), 1838–1847.

Fried, R. (1990a). Integrating Music in Breathing Training and Relaxation: I. Background, Rationale and Relevant Elements. *Biofeedback and Self-Regulation, 15*(2), 161–169.

(1990b). Integrating Music in Breathing Training and Relaxation: II. Applications. *Biofeedback and Self-Regulation, 15*(2), 171–177.

Gerra, G., Zaimovic, A., Franchini, D., et al. (1998). Neuroendocrine Responses of Healthy Volunteers to "Techno-Music": Relationships with Personality Traits and Emotional State. *International Journal of Psychophysiology, 28*(1), 99–111.

Goenjian, A. K., Yehuda, R., Pynoos, R. S., et al. (1996). Basal Cortisol, Dexamethasone Suppression of Cortisol and MI-IPG in Adolescents after the 1988 Earthquake in Armenia. *American Journal of Psychiatry, 153*(7), 929–934.

Goldstein, R. D., Wampler, N. S., and Wise, P. H. (1997). War Experiences and Distress Symptoms of Bosnian Children. *Pediatrics, 100*(5), 873–878.

Habermas, J. (1979). *Communication and the Evolution of Society.* Translated by Thomas McCarthy. Boston, MA: Beacon Press.

Hebert, S., Beland, R., Dionne-Fournelle, O., Crete, M., and Lupien, S. J. (2005). Physiological Stress Response to Video-Game Playing: The Contribution of Built-In Music. *Life Sciences, 76*(20), 2371–2380.

Heidegger, M. (1927/2005). *Sein und zeit.* Tübingen, Germany: Niemeyer Verlag.

Heldt, S. A., and Falls, W. A. (2003). Destruction of the Inferior Colliculus Disrupts the Production and Inhibition of Fear Conditioned to an Acoustic Stimulus. *Behavioural Brain Research, 144*(1–2), 175–185.

Husserl, E. (1913/2011). *Ideen zu einer reinen Phänomenologie und phänomenologischen Philosophie.* New York, NY: Springer.

Iwanaga, M., Kobayashi, A., and Kawasaki, C. (2005). Heart Rate Variability with Repetitive Exposure to Music. *Biological Psychology, 70*(1), 61–62.

Iwanaga, M., and Tsukamoto, M. (1997). Effects of Excitative and Sedative Music on Subjective and Physiological Relaxation. *Perceptual and Motor Skills, 85*(1), 287–296.

Jorris, P. X., Schreiner, C. E., and Rees, A. (2004). Neural Processing of Amplitude-Modulated Sounds. *Physiological Reviews, 84,* 541–577.

Kibler, J. L., and Lyons, J. A. (2004). Perceived Coping Ability Mediates the Relationship between PTSD Severity and Heart Rate Recovery in Veterans. *Journal of Traumatic Stress, 17,* 23–29.

Knight, W. E. J., and Rickard, N. S. (2001). Relaxing Music Prevents Stress-Induced Increases in Subjective Anxiety, Systolic Blood Pressure and Heart Rate in Healthy Males and Females. *Journal of Music Therapy, 38*(4), 254–272.

Koelsch, S., Fritz, T. V., Cramon, D. Y., Muller, K., and Friederici, A. D. (2006). Investigating Emotion with Music: An fMRI Study. *Human Brain Mapping, 27*(3), 239–250.

Kuhl, P. K., Andruski, J. E., Chistovich, I. A., et al. (1997). Cross-Language Analysis of Phonetic Units in Language Addressed to Infants. *Science, 277,* 684–686.

Lacan, J. (1964/1977) *The Seminar of Jacques Lacan, Book XI: The Four Fundamental Concepts of Psychoanalysis.* Edited by J. A. Miller. Translated by A. Sheridan. New York, NY: Norton.

Lee, D. N., (2005). Tau in Action in Development. In J. J. Rieser, J. J. Lockman, and C. A. Nelson (eds.), *Action as an Organiser of Learning and Development.* Hillsdale, NJ: Erlbaum, 3–49.

Lee, O. K., Chung, Y. F., Chan, M. F., and Chan, W. M. (2005). Music and its Effect on the Physiological Responses and Anxiety Levels of Patients Receiving Mechanical Ventilation: A Pilot Study. *Journal of Clinical Nursing, 14*(5), 609–620.

Malloch, S., and Trevarthen, C. (eds.) (2009). *Communicative Musicality: Exploring the Basis of Human Companionship.* Oxford, UK; New York, NY: Oxford University Press.

Marsh, R. A., Fuzessery, Z. M., Grose, C. D., and Wenstrup, J. J. (2002). Projection to the Inferior Colliculus from the Basal Nucleus of the Amygdala. *Journal of Neuroscience, 22*(23), 10449–10460.

Masataka, N. (1993). Relation between Pitch Contour of Prelinguistic Vocalisations and Communicative Functions in Japanese Infants. *Infant Behavior and Development, 16*, 397–401.

Mccoy, S. J. (2004). *Your Voice, an Inside View: Multimedia Voice Science and Pedagogy.* Princeton, NJ: Inside View Press.

Miluk-Kolasa, B., Obminski, Z., Stupnicki, R., and Golec, L. (1994). Effects of Music Treatment on Salivary Cortisol in Patients Exposed to Pre-Surgical Stress. *Experimental and Clinical Endocrinology & Diabetes, 102*, 118–120.

Mok, E., and Wong, K. Y. (2003). Effects of Music on Patient Anxiety. *AORN Journal, 77*(2), 396–397, 401–406, 409–410.

Nilsson, U., Unosson, M., and Rawal, N. (2005). Stress Reduction and Analgesia in Patients Exposed to Calming Music Postoperatively: A Randomized Controlled Trial. *European Journal of Anaesthesiology, 22*(2), 96–102.

Nixon, R. D., and Bryant, R. A. (2005). Induced Arousal and Reexperiencing in Acute Stress Disorder. *Journal of Anxiety Disorders, 19*(5), 587–594.

Osborne, N. (2009a). Towards a Chronobiology of Musical Rhythm. In S. Malloch and C. Trevarthen (eds.), *Communicative Musicality: Exploring the Basis of Human Companionship.* Oxford, UK; New York, NY: Oxford University Press, 545–564.

(2009b). Music for Children in Zones of Conflict and Post-Conflict: A Psychobiological Approach. In S. Malloch and C. Trevarthen (eds.), *Communicative Musicality: Exploring the Basis of Human Companionship.* Oxford, UK; New York, NY: Oxford University Press, 331–356.

(2012). Neuroscience and "Real World" Practice: Music as a Therapeutic Resource for Children in Zones of Conflict. *Annals of the New York Academy of Sciences, 1252* (1), 69–76.

(2014). The Plenum Brain in Unbribable Bosnia and Herzegovina. In D. Arsenijević (ed,), *South East European Integration Perspectives.* Baden-Baden, Germany: Nomos Verlag, 174–185.

(2017a). The Identities of Sevda: From Graeco-Arabic Medicine to Music Therapy. In R. MacDonald, R. Hargreaves, and D. Miell (eds.), *Handbook of Musical Identities.* Oxford, UK; New York, NY: Oxford University Press.

(2017b). Love, Rhythm and Chronobiology. In S. Daniel and C. Trevarthen (eds.), *Rhythms of Relating in Children's Therapies: Connecting Creatively with Vulnerable Children.* London, UK; Philadelphia, PA: Jessica Kingsley Publishers.

Panksepp, J. (1998). The Periconscious Substrates of Consciousness: Affective States and Evolutionary Origins of the SELF. *Journal of Consciousness Studies, 5*(5–6), 566–582.

(2007). Neuroevolutionary Sources of Laughter and Social Joy: Modelling Primal Human Laughter in Laboratory Rats. *Behavioral Brain Research, 182*, 231–244.

Panksepp, J., and Bernatzky, G. (2002). Emotional Sounds and the Brain: The Neuro-Affective Foundations of Musical Appreciation. *Behavioral Processes, 60* (2), 133–155.

Panksepp, J., and Trevarthen, C. (2009). The Neuroscience of Emotion in Music. In S. Malloch and C. Trevarthen (eds.), *Communicative Musicality: Exploring the Basis of Human Companionship*. Oxford, UK; New York, NY: Oxford University Press, 105–146.

Papoušek, M. (1987). Models and Messages in the Melodies of Maternal Speech in Tonal and Non-Tonal Languages. *Society for Research in Child Development*, 6, 407.

Sack, M., Hopper, J. W., and Lamprecht, F. (2004). Low Respiratory Sinus Arrhythmia and Prolonged Psychophysiological Arousal in Posttraumatic Stress Disorder: Heart Rate Dynamics and Individual Differences in Arousal Regulation. *Biological Psychiatry*, *55*(3), 284–290.

Sacks, O. (2007). *Musicophilia: Tales of Music and the Brain*. New York, NY: Random House.

Sahar, T., Shalev, A. Y., and Porges, S. W. (2001). Vagal Modulation of Responses to Mental Challenge in Posttraumatic Stress Disorder. *Biological Psychiatry*, *49*, 637–643.

Schogler, B., and Trevarthen, C. (2007). To Sing and Dance Together – From Infants to Jazz. In Braten, S. (ed.), *On Being Moved: From Mirror Neurons to Empathy*. Amsterdam, Netherlands; Philadelphia, PA: John Benjamins Publishing Company.

Sivaramakrishnan, S., Sterbino-D'Angelo, S. J., Filipovic, B., et al. (2004). GABA (A) Synapses Shape Neuronal Responses to Sound Intensity in the Inferior Colliculus. *Journal of Neuroscience*, *24*(21), 5031–5043.

Stern, D. N. (1974). Mother and Infant at Play: The Dyadic Interaction Involving Facial, Vocal and Gaze Behaviours. In M. Lewis and L. A. Rosenblum (eds.), *The Effect of the Infant on its Caregiver*. New York, NY: Wiley, 187–213.

   (2004). *The Present Moment in Psychotherapy and Everyday Life*. New York, NY; London, UK: Norton.

Stevenson, L. (2003). Twelve Conceptions of Imagination. *The British Journal of Aesthetics*, *43*(3), 238–259.

Trehub, S. E. (1987). Infants' Perception of Musical Patterns. *Perception and Psychophysics*, *41*(6), 635–641.

Trevarthen, C. (2004). Brain Development. In R. L. Gregory (ed.), *Oxford Companion to the Mind*. 2nd edition. Oxford, UK; New York, NY: Oxford University Press, 116–127.

Trevarthen, C., and Aitken, K. (2003). Regulation of Brain Development and Age-Related Changes in Infants' Motives: The Developmental Function of Regressive Periods. In M. Heimann, (ed.), *Regression Periods in Human Infancy*. Mahwah, NJ: Erlbaum, 107–184.

Trevarthen, C., Gratier, M., and Osborne, N. (2014). The Human Nature of Culture and Education. *Wiley Interdisciplinary Reviews: Cognitive Science*, *5*(2), 173–192. doi:10.1002/wcs.1276. ISSN 1939–5078.

Uedo, N., Ishikawa, H., Morimoto, K., et al. (2004). Reduction in Salivary Cortisol Level by Music Therapy During Colonoscopic Examination. *Hepato-Gastroenterology*, *51* (56), 451–453.

Updike, P. A., and Charles, D. M. (1987). Music Rx: Physiological and Emotional Responses to Taped Music Programs of Preoperative Patients Awaiting Plastic Surgery. *Annals of Plastic Surgery*, *19*(1), 29–33.

Wieser, H. G., and Mazzola, G. (1986). Musical Consonances and Dissonances: Are They Distinguished Independently by the Right and Left Hippocampi? *Neuropsychologia*, *24*(6), 805–812.

Yehuda, R. (2000). Neuroendocrinology. In D. Nutt, J. Davidson, and J. Zohar, (eds.), *Posttraumatic Stress Disorder: Diagnosis, Management and Treatment*. London, UK: Martin Dunitz, 53–67.

Yule, W. (1994). *Posttraumatic Stress Disorder*. New York, NY: Plenum.

PART VI

Altered States of the Imagination

40 Dreaming: Beyond Imagination and Perception

Jennifer M. Windt

Philosophical discussions of dreaming often raise big ontological questions. When we see something in a dream, do we undergo the same kind of experience as when we see something in wakefulness? That is, when we dream of exploring a strange and labyrinthine building, are we undergoing visual hallucinations or merely lost in the figments of our imagination?

How one answers these questions has consequences beyond the philosophy of dreaming, reaching into scientific dream research, psychology, and even psychiatry. If to dream is to imagine, dream research is part of a broader field of research on daydreams and waking fantasy. But if to dream is to hallucinate, dream research might help understand wake-state psychosis or delusions (Hobson, 1999).

Even where ontological questions about dreaming are not in the foreground, the adoption of one position or another is often implied. Take as an example the most famous philosophical question about dreaming of all: How can I be certain that I am awake and not dreaming? Descartes' argument in the *Meditations* that dreaming undermines the trustworthiness of all our sensory-based beliefs stems from his assumption that dream imagery perfectly mimics waking perception. By contrast, if dreams, including the beliefs we entertain in dreams, are imaginings, Descartes' epistemological nightmare might be averted. Even the most vivid dream could not truly deceive us because, when dreaming, we would not really believe ourselves to be awake (for discussion and further references, see Ichikawa 2016).

So far, only the most basic questions about dreaming have been resolved. Dreams are now commonly accepted to be conscious experiences in sleep and the study of dreaming has been established as an important contributor to interdisciplinary consciousness science.[1] But agreement tends to end here, and what exactly to say about the ontology of dreaming remains controversial. Whether dreams are experience at all was a live question for just a few decades, but questions about what kinds of experiences we undergo when dreaming have been debated for centuries, dating back to Aristotle's treatises *On Sleep* and *On Dreams*.

---

1 Whether dreams are experiences at all was at the center of the philosophy of dreaming for much of the twentieth century. For two of the most prominent arguments against saying that dreams are experiences, see Dennett (1976) and Malcolm (1959). For an overview of the discussion, see Windt (2015a).

In this chapter, I try to take a fresh look at the perceptual vs. imaginative character of dreaming. But instead of maximizing points of disagreement between the two opposing views, I begin by introducing a view both sides can agree on: the simulation view. I then revisit the debate on the imaginative vs. perceptual character of dreaming and sketch how the simulation view can help reconcile both sides. Describing dreams as immersive mental simulations helps tackle what I take to be the two main characteristics of dreaming, namely their *here* and *now* character and the spontaneity of dream imagery formation. The former establishes a deep similarity between dreaming and standard waking perception; the latter highlights the continuity between dreaming and spontaneous thoughts in waking, including mind-wandering, daydreams, and imagination. Yet dreams strike this balance in an utterly unique way, requiring a description of their own.

Dreams Are Immersive Mental Simulations

Simulation views focus on the *here* and *now* structure of dreaming. Dreams are immersive: They involve the feeling of presence in a world (Revonsuo, Tuominen, and Valli, 2015). And because the appearance of a world requires a self at its center, simulation views make self-experience central to the definition of dreaming. Their immersive character is also what distinguishes dreams from other mental simulations such as waking imagery or daydreams.

Simulation views are attractive for a number of reasons. They form a point of convergence within a field that was long plagued by lack of agreement about its target. Some researchers narrowly focused on narratively complex, multimodal, and emotional dreams, while others more broadly classified any conscious experience or thought occurring in sleep as dreaming (Nielsen, 2000; Pagel et al., 2001). Simulation views strike a happy medium between being overly restrictive about what counts as a dream and being completely permissive. Dreams, no matter how defined, are diverse, including a range of sensory experiences, emotions, and thoughts; they also vary in length, complexity, and bizarreness (Windt, 2015a).[2] Definitions that are too narrow risk introducing arbitrary distinctions. But when we consider the entire range of experiences in sleep, we also find important structural differences. Specifically, some sleep experiences seem to lack the immersive structure of dreaming (Windt, 2015b; Windt, Nielsen, and Thompson, 2016). Examples are repetitive thoughts, isolated imagery, residual sensory perceptions, and bodily sensations occurring independently of a larger context and lacking integration into a virtual scene. Given this diversity, a more differentiated framework in which some (but not all) sleep experiences count as dreams seems prudent.

Simulation views resolve this problem by using immersion as a criterion to distinguish between dreaming and experiences in sleep that count as dreamless. *Here* and *now* experience seems to have the right grain to draw this distinction:

---

2 Self-experience appears to be an exception, and the vast majority of dream reports describe the presence of a self (see for example Strauch and Meier, 1996).

Whether an experience is organized around a first-person perspective, giving rise to the experience of a self in a world, is not a mere difference in content (such as dreaming of one topic rather than another) or modality (e.g. visual vs. nonvisual dreams), but marks a large-scale transition in experience.

Another advantage of simulation views is that they define dreaming independently of sleep stages. Historically, disagreement about the definition of dreaming was paralleled by disagreement about its sleep-stage correlates. Early dream researchers believed that the contrast between REM (rapid eye movement) and NREM (or non-REM) sleep marked the presence vs. absence of consciousness (Dement and Kleitman, 1957). It soon became clear, however, that dreams occur in all stages of sleep (Nielsen, 2000). Serial awakening paradigms (Noreika, Valli, Lahtela, and Revonsuo, 2009; Siclari, LaRocque, Postle, and Tononi, 2013), in which participants are awakened multiple times throughout the night from different sleep stages and at short time intervals, suggest that the deep stages of NREM sleep are in fact phenomenologically rich. Reports from these stages describe roughly equal proportions of dreaming, unconscious sleep, and having had experiences but being unable to recall any details. High-density EEG recordings suggest that these phenomenological differences are paralleled by regional differences in brain activation. Dreaming as opposed to non-dreaming is associated with activity in a parieto-occipital hot zone, and this is true in both REM and NREM sleep (Siclari and Tononi, 2017).

Simulation views are also productive, leading to precise follow-up questions on different aspects of self- and world-simulation. What is the typical profile of self-simulation in dreams, and how does it compare to waking self-experience, for instance in terms of conscious thought and bodily experience (Revonsuo, 2005; Windt, 2018)? Can the analysis of dreams help identify the conditions for minimal phenomenal selfhood, or the simplest type of self-experience (Windt, 2010)?

Simulation views can also focus on various aspects of world-simulation. Threat simulation theory focuses on the occurrence of different kinds of threats and their relation to waking experience (Revonsuo, 2000; Valli and Revonsuo, 2009). Social simulation theory investigates social interactions between the dream self and non-self dream characters and relates them to social cognition (Revonsuo, Tuominen, and Valli, 2015). These two views lead to different claims about the evolutionary function of dreaming, but together also contribute to a rich, multilayered picture: Dream threats tend to be directed at the dream self and are often experienced as highly realistic; the same is true for social interactions, suggesting that dreams simulate not only a world but also a vibrant social environment. Simulation views are therefore also integrative, uniting research on different aspects of dreaming under a common framework.

This is also true for questions on the perceptual vs. imaginative character of dreaming. With their emphasis on *here* and *now* experience, simulation views identify a basic structural similarity between dreaming and waking perception. In dreams as in wakefulness, we have the experience of being present in and interacting with an external world. This line of thought seems to imply that dreams are hallucinatory: Dreaming *feels* like being awake because it simulates the relation we have to other people and objects in standard perceptual experience, where no such people and objects are actually being perceived. Yet this claim is ambiguous. A strong reading says that dreaming and waking are qualitatively equivalent: Dreaming mimics waking in all of its detail. This places dreams squarely in the category of quasi-perceptual phenomena, or phenomena that share the phenomenology of perception but lack its close link to an external stimulus source. A weak reading says that dreaming and waking do indeed feel the same in an important sense: Both involve the feeling of presence. This does not require, however, that dreaming exactly replicate waking experience, thus opening the door to saying dreams resemble perception in some respects and imagination in others. It also explains why the stronger view is intuitively attractive: The feeling of presence in dreams glosses over the subtler phenomenological differences between dreaming and waking perception, leading us to describe them as similar even where they are not.

Describing dreams as immersive mental simulations naturally leads us beyond comparisons with standard waking perception, placing dreams in the vicinity of other forms of mental simulation in wakefulness. These include imagination and daydreams, but also mental time travel, as in episodic memory and future planning (Suddendorf, Addis, and Corballis, 2009). Recent years have seen a virtual explosion of research on mind-wandering, or spontaneous thoughts that unfold dynamically and in an associative manner, largely independently of ongoing tasks and environmental demands (Christoff et al., 2016; Smallwood and Schooler, 2015, see also Chapter 21). Like dreams, waking mind-wandering draws from memories and self-related concerns and often contains strong emotions. Yet dreams are typically longer and more narratively complex as well as more bizarre than waking mind-wandering. They are also more immersive: Even in our most vivid daydreams, we don't quite lose touch with our actual environments and bodies and so don't quite feel present in the ones we are mentally simulating. This has led to the suggestion that dreams are an intensified form of waking mind-wandering (Fox et al., 2013).

By acknowledging the affinity of dreaming to both perception and mental simulation in wakefulness, categorizing dreams as immersive mental simulations promises novel perspectives on our mental lives. In a very general sense, we can describe perception and mental simulation as two sides of the same coin: Where perception is about grasping and interacting with the actual world, mental simulation allows us to take a step back to remember and reassess previous experiences, imagine alternative outcomes and actions, and decide between them. Whether and how dreams contribute to these dual modes of engaging with the world is unclear, and the functions of dreaming (if any) are controversial. But even from this superficial characterization we can see how dreaming seems to strike a perfect balance between these two modes: Its immersive character allows it to be both the fullest expression of our simulational capacity and deeply similar in structure to perception. It is tempting to speculate that to be able to simulate alternative realities, we need to be able to sometimes feel they are real (Windt, 2015a). If that were the case, the best way to do so would be in the comparative isolation and safety of sleep.

Resisting Classification: The Two Sides of Immersive Mental Simulation

The view that dreams are quasi-perceptual experiences – that is, experiences that feel like instances of perception but lack an appropriate external stimulus source – is often accepted on default. The imagination view is typically construed in opposition to this view, which is possibly why the arguments for and against tend to be spelled out more explicitly. Yet both views come in different strengths. In this section, I give an overview of both positions (for a more in-depth analysis see Windt, 2015a), with a focus on how to integrate their respective strengths. In particular, we can use arguments associated with one side or the other to identify questions for future research and work toward a more integrative view.

Dreaming as Quasi-Perceptual Experience

The most important difference within quasi-perceptual views is the familiar contrast between saying that dreams typically or even always replicate the phenomenology of waking perception and saying that they resemble perception in some ways but not others. The weaker claim better suits the variability of dreaming. For example, most but not all dreams are visual (Kerr, 1993; Solms, 2014); in most dreams we fail to realize we are dreaming, but lucid dreams are an exception (Voss and Hobson, 2015); and so on. Moreover, all-encompassing claims that dreams mimic waking perceptual experience are vague and leave unspecified which are the relevant points of similarity and difference.

A more constructive approach is to formulate narrower questions that can guide the theoretical and empirical comparison of dreams with waking perception. For example, we can ask whether the occurrence and distribution of multimodal imagery in dreams is similar to wakefulness. Studies from different historical periods show there are systematic differences in the occurrence of modality-specific imagery in dreams (Schwartz, 2000; Strauch and Meier, 1996). Visual imagery and movement sensations occur in the vast majority of dreams, followed by auditory sensations. By contrast, sensations of touch, taste, smell, pain, and thermal sensations are rare, suggesting they are underrepresented in dreams as compared to waking (Windt, 2015a, 2017). The next step would be to investigate the frequency of modality-specific imagery in reports from waking and dreaming from the same participants.

Another possibility is to investigate the quality of specific types of dream imagery. In some fascinating studies, participants were asked to compare their visual dream imagery to photographs with different degrees of color saturation, background detail, focus, and so on. Results suggest that dream imagery is overall realistic but marked by a loss of color saturation, background detail (Rechtschaffen and Buchignani, 1983) and focus (Antrobus et al., 1987). Perhaps visual dream imagery shares the greater indeterminacy and gappiness of imagination; but then again we shouldn't assume actual seeing has the same level of uniform detail as high-resolution photographs. Again, systematic comparisons with both dream and waking experience, including real and imagined seeing, are needed to move forward.

It is sometimes suggested that dreaming feels like perceiving because the same brain activity underlies dreaming and waking perception (e.g. Hobson, Pace-Schott, and Stickgold, 2000; Horikawa et al., 2013). Neuroimaging studies show, for instance, that the visual areas are even more active in REM sleep than in waking (Desseilles et al., 2011). However, without dream reports from the same period we cannot draw any strong conclusions about the phenomenology of associated dreams (see Windt, 2015a: 237 f). Claims about the similarity between the neural correlates of dreaming and waking perception are further complicated by the fact that there is also strong overlap in cortical activity associated with visual imagery and perception (Zeidman and Maguire, 2016; see also Chapter 12). Therefore, similarity between waking perception and dream imagery does not provide evidence against the imagination view, but rather suggests imagining, dreaming, and perceiving are all closely related.[3]

Another line of enquiry that is relevant to the quasi-perceptual view comes from external stimulus incorporation in dreams. A familiar example is dreaming of a loud sound, such as a siren, just to wake up and realize the alarm clock is ringing. In laboratory studies, a variety of stimuli ranging from sounds to flashing lights and sprays of water on the skin have been presented to participants during sleep, with very mixed results (for discussion and further references, see Windt, 2017). Some of the highest incorporation rates, reaching 40–80 percent, were achieved using a blood pressure cuff inflated on the leg (Nielsen, 1993; Sauvageau, Nielsen, and Montplaisir, 1998). Even here, incorporation was often indirect, meaning participants often did not dream of the blood pressure cuff itself but of wearing strange shoes, having difficulty walking, or even seeing another dream character have their leg run over.

---

3 Similar difficulties arise when investigating how the eye movements associated with REM sleep dreams compare to visual perception and waking imagery. It has long been thought that the characteristic rapid eye movements observed in REM sleep correspond to gaze shifts experienced within the dream. According to the so-called scanning hypothesis (Dement and Kleitman, 1957), a series of right–left gaze shifts in a dream – as in watching a tennis match – should lead to corresponding real-eye movements. Lucid dream experiments, in which participants can signal that they have just realized they are dreaming by performing a previously agreed upon pattern of gaze shifts, seem to confirm this. The eye movement signals can be read out on the electro-oculogram and are later confirmed by the dreamer's subjective report (Voss and Hobson, 2015). A recent study asked participants to track objects while having a lucid dream; results were compared to tracking real and imaginary objects (LaBerge, Baird, and Zimbardo, 2018). In both waking perception and lucid dreams, eye tracking was smooth, whereas eye movements for imagined objects were discontinuous.

Yet there is something strange about the implication that in REM sleep, eye movements are engaged in scanning the dream world. Unlike in waking perception, there is no mind-independent world to be scanned in dreams, and we should not think of dream persons and objects as having any kind of existence outside of the dream. A different way to make sense of dream-related eye movements is to say they are involved in the generation of dream imagery. The dream world would then be created in response to scanning-like visual activity – without presuming the existence of anything that could actually be scanned (Windt, 2017).

This idea of on-demand dream imagery generation driven by real-eye movements is consistent with the notorious discontinuity and instability (but see Rosen, 2019) of dreams. If dream imagery is indeed a dynamic (and often slapdash) attempt to make sense of eye movements, sudden changes in the dream environment or in the appearance of persons or objects, as well as indeterminacy, would be expected. This idea lends a nicely cognitive flavor to dream generation while at the same time acknowledging the similarity to eye tracking in actual seeing.

Instances of sensory incorporation in dreams lend partial support to the quasi-perceptual view because they seem to be smoothly integrated with dream imagery. If dreaming felt like imagining we would expect such instances of illusory incorporation – essentially distorted perception of actual stimuli – to stand out. Yet this doesn't necessarily speak against the imagination view. It is possible that in the process of incorporating external stimuli, dreams put their own gloss on them, rendering them more imagination-like after all.

The main lesson from sensory incorporation is that the conceptual repertoire for describing dream imagery should be extended. This is true even if we stay within the confines of the quasi-perceptual view. When a dream of hearing a siren is prompted by a beeping alarm clock, the auditory imagery fits the philosophical concept of illusion, where an object is perceived as having different properties from the ones it actually has. But in the contemporary literature, it has become so common to regard dreams as purely offline states that describing them as quasi-perceptual seems to imply they are hallucinatory.[4] Certainly, some dream imagery fits the bill. But this does not imply that it always does, and we should allow for the existence of a broad spectrum of cases. If dreaming of hearing a siren is prompted by an actual siren, this would bring us close to veridical perception; but this is consistent with other aspects being hallucinatory or illusory, and yet again others being imagination-like. We should remain open to all of these possibilities.

Dreaming as Imaginative Experience

The imagination view is possibly even more diverse than the quasi-perceptual view, and this diversity is flanked by diversity in accounts of the imagination (see also Chapter 1). A foundational question for the philosophy of imagination is whether these different strands can be integrated into a unified account. Ryle (2009) famously argued that there is no such thing as a special faculty of the imagination, and more recently Kind (2013) proposed that the heterogeneity of the imagination runs too deep to allow for the identification of a single target phenomenon.

As a first pass at a general definition, we can say that imagination is in the business of representing possibilities rather than actualities (Liao and Gendler, 2019). A wide range of representational activities are candidates for being described as imaginative. A basic distinction is between sensory (e.g. visual or auditory) imagery and propositional imagining. This quickly leads to questions about the relation of imagination to perception and hallucination on the one hand and belief and delusion on the other hand (Liao and Gendler, 2019), as well as to broader questions about the (pictorial vs. descriptive) format of mental representations (Thomas, 2018). All of this fits in well with the terminology of mental simulation. We can also see how these debates are mirrored in the imagination view of dreaming.

---

4 This was not always the case. The idea that illusory own-body perception plays an important role in dream formation was popular in the late nineteenth century (Schönhammer, 2004, 2005). It then fell out of favor when Freudian dream theory directed attention away from the somatic to the psychic sources of dreaming. Elsewhere, I have argued that bodily experiences in dreams often involve illusory misperception of one's sleeping body (Windt, 2017).

There, the most important distinction is between claiming that dream imagery is akin to sensory imagining – as contrasted with perceiving or hallucinating – and claiming that dream belief is a form of propositional imagination and make-believe (Ichikawa, 2016). The strongest version of the imagination view endorses both claims.

Versions of the imagination view focusing on dream beliefs owe an explanation of our cognitive stance in relation to dreaming. If while dreaming we don't falsely believe (but merely imagine) ourselves to be awake, then why do we so rarely realize we are dreaming and become lucid? I'll focus on the other strand here, which provides the clearest contrast to the quasi-perceptual view. That strand claims that if seeing in a dream is akin to imagined rather than actual seeing, maybe it also feels more like imagining or having a particularly vivid daydream (Ichikawa, 2009).

A major challenge for this strand of the imagination view is how to explain the relationship between dream imagery and deliberate control. The problem arises because our waking imaginings are thought to be under our control: Even when lost in a daydream, we retain some awareness of the fact that none of this is real; likewise, in failing to control our daydreams we have not lost the ability to do so, but are merely failing to exercise this ability. But while asleep and dreaming, the loss of control seems more radical in that we typically do not even realize that we could take control if we wanted. Proponents of the imagination view then have to explain why dreaming is a form of imagination despite the apparent lack of deliberate control.

To explain away the apparent difference between control over daydreams and sleep-dreams, proponents of the imagination view often raise the example of lucid dreams. Lucid dreamers realize they are now dreaming and often have some degree of control, allowing them to actively tamper with unfolding dream events (Baird, Mota-Rolim, and Dresler, 2019; Voss et al., 2013). Imagination theorists then argue that lucid dreams show that dreams in general, including nonlucid ones, are subject to the will and in some sense under our control (Ichikawa, 2009). Hence, they can be assimilated to waking imagination after all.

However, classifying dreams as imaginings on the grounds of control misconstrues the relation between control and spontaneous processes both in imagining and dreams. Appreciating this point leads us to a richer understanding of the relation between control and spontaneity and will pave the way from the imagination view of dreaming to recent mind-wandering research.

Research on mind-wandering suggests that we often do not notice that our minds have wandered until after the episode has ended (Smallwood and Schooler, 2015); the frequency and pervasiveness of mind-wandering even during attention-demanding tasks suggests that we are also often unable to control the focus of our conscious thoughts and attention. Yet the issue of awareness of and control over mind-wandering is far from resolved. Some theorists think that lack of deliberate guidance is a defining feature of mind-wandering (Irving, 2016). Others argue that intentional forms of mind-wandering exist, with intentional mind-wandering being more frequent in easy tasks and unintentional mind-wandering more frequent in difficult tasks, suggesting their occurrence is context-sensitive (Seli et al., 2016).

This leads to more complex questions about whether to classify mind-wandering as mental action or behavior.

Here, my point is that because certain types of mind-wandering, such as daydreams and spontaneous imagery, overlap closely with imagination – and because there are independent reasons for describing dreams as an intensified form of waking mind-wandering (Fox et al., 2013) – we should be careful not to model dreams on waking imaginings by claiming that the latter are deliberately scripted and controlled. Surely, we sometimes have control over our imaginings, just as we sometimes have control over our dreams. But if we recognize that at other times we do not, then the problem of how to assimilate seemingly uncontrolled dreams to seemingly controlled (or controllable) daydreams evaporates.

These considerations should also lead us to rethink basic assumptions about the relation between deliberate control and spontaneity. Implicit in the control argument for the imagination view is a dichotomy between control and spontaneity, between states that can be brought under our deliberate control and those that cannot. But these contrasts may be too starkly drawn. Spontaneity and control may in fact be consistent with each other, and states such as imagining, mind-wandering, and dreaming allow for different levels of insight and control. This means control cannot be used as a criterion to distinguish between different kinds of mental states.

Lucid dreams illustrate this point clearly. In a majority of cases, both control and awareness fluctuate considerably (Baird, Mota-Rolim, and Dresler, 2019; Windt and Voss, 2018). Dreamers may realize they are dreaming but believe other dream characters to be real or expect their dream actions to have real-world consequences. Attempts to exercise dream control often lead to unexpected results, and more often than not, lucid dreamers cannot remember their waking intentions to perform particular actions within their dream (Stumbrys et al., 2014). Lucid dreamers are not, in other words, virtual puppeteers, able to control and deliberately script all aspects of their ongoing dream; spontaneity lies at the heart even of lucid control dreams.

This fits in well with descriptions of lucid control dreams as involving a balancing act between belief and insight, control and spontaneity (Brooks and Vogelsong, 2000; LaBerge and Ornstein, 1985). For example, rather than just changing the scenery of their dream, dreamers may choose to travel by car or bicycle; and rather than just making these appear out of nowhere, they might go check in the garage of their dream house (Brooks and Vogelsong, 2000). None of these detours are strictly necessary, but they may help thicken the plot; we should think of them not so much as a limitation of control but as an effective strategy for its exercise. The challenge, after all, is to maintain insight and exercise control while also enjoying the ongoing flow of the dream – to feel present in a world one realizes is not real, and to exercise control in a way that enhances rather than disrupts the illusion. Even lucid control dreams are, in the end, distinctly dreamlike, both in their immersive structure and in the spontaneity underlying their generation (Windt and Voss, 2018).

"In the submitted manuscript, I had an empty line before this paragraph. I did not want to insert a separate section heading, but I am taking a step back here to reflect on the two views contrasted in this section. Please reinsert that empty line."

We can now begin to see how describing dreams as both perception-like and imagination-like is no contradiction. Like waking perception, dreams are immersive – they are the quintessential virtual realities (Metzinger, 2009; Revonsuo, 2006). Simulation views explain this through their *here* and *now* quality, giving rise to the experience of presence in a world. But dreams are also deeply imaginative. Even where dreams come closest to mimicking waking perception – for instance, by incorporating external stimuli – spontaneous processes still provide a distinctively dreamlike gloss, guiding the mode of incorporation. Dreams have even been suggested to be a purer form of imagination than waking fantasy, both in terms of phenomenology and their neural correlates (Nir and Tononi, 2010).

***

Importantly, the way in which dreams are both imaginative and perceptual is not contingent on specific contents or phenomenological characteristics of dreaming, all of which are variable both within and across dreams. Rather, these similarities run deeper, lying in the immersive structure of dreams on one hand and the spontaneous dynamics of imagery formation on the other hand.[5] This combination is unique, preventing dreams from being classified as either perceptual or imaginative.

Perhaps no one has expressed this dual nature of dreaming better than Leibniz:

> There is one very remarkable thing in dreams, for which I believe no one can give a reason. It is the formation of visions by a spontaneous organization carried out in a moment – a formation more elegant than any which we can attain by much thought while awake. To the sleeper there often occur visions of great buildings which he has never seen, while it would be difficult for me, while awake, to form an idea of even the smallest house different from those I have seen, without a great amount of thought ... Even such unnatural things as flying men and innumerable other monstrosities can be pictured more skillfully than a waking person can do, except with much thought. They are sought by the waker; they offer themselves to the sleeper. There must therefore necessarily be some architectural and harmonious principle, I know not what, in our mind, which, when freed from separating ideas by judgment, turns to compounding them. (Leibniz, 1956, Vol. 1: 177–178).

As Leibniz notes, the challenge is to capture both the uniqueness of dreams and their continuity with waking.

Reimagining Dreams, Past and Future

Conceptualizing dreams as immersive mental simulations can lead the way forward, carrying us beyond the debate on their perceptual vs. imaginative character. This allows us to integrate findings from research on sleep, dreaming, and mind-wandering research; it may also revive older ways of thinking about dreams and spontaneous thought from the history of philosophy. In this last section we'll take a brief tour of some of these areas, with a focus on how they can lead to new avenues of research.

---

5 Rosen (2018) recently suggested a pluralist view in which dream content should be compared to waking perception and dream thought to waking thought. I like this approach but think such comparisons between dreaming, waking perception, and imagination should be made even more fluidly, on a case-by-case basis.

Dream researchers have long emphasized the cognitive sources of dreaming. This includes continuity between dream content and waking experiences, thoughts, and concerns, as well as continuity between imagery skills in waking and the visuospatial characteristics of dreaming.[6] The former are supported by dream diaries (Domhoff, 2013; Schredl, 2006), the latter by evidence on changes in dreaming (such as the loss of visual dreaming) following brain lesions (Solms, 2014) and the development of dreaming in children, which coincides with the emergence of visuospatial skills (Foulkes, 2009).

How dreams feed off waking memory sources is a particularly fascinating question. On the one hand, the sources of dreams are clearly to be found in waking memories; on the other hand, dreams mold waking memories into their own thing, and only rarely do dreams simply replay episodic memories (Fosse, Stickgold, and Hobson, 2004; Nielsen and Stenstrom, 2005). The ways in which dreams select, alter, and recombine different memories from waking is incompletely understood. Complex temporal patterns seem to be at play, with thematically similar memories from different periods often being combined (Blagrove et al., 2011; Nielsen and Powell, 1989), especially if they are personally significant (van Rijn et al., 2015).

Connecting this work to mind-wandering research seems promising. Like dreams, waking mind-wandering often revolves around ongoing concerns, incorporating memories as well as future planning; both states also typically have the self and self-related concerns at their center and often include visual and auditory imagery (Fox et al., 2013). At sleep onset, the musings of a wandering mind can merge into more immersive dreams; and thoughts that were suppressed in waking often return with a vengeance as we drift off to sleep (Schmidt and Gendolla, 2008).

While dream and mind-wandering research remain largely separate, we can take inspiration on how to integrate these fields from the history of philosophy. Here I will briefly sketch Hobbes's (2006) analysis of dreaming as a single example of a historical view spanning many of the issues discussed throughout this chapter.

For Hobbes, dreams were imaginings in sleep, and imagination a decaying sense. At the same time, he adopted the Aristotelean view that dream imagery is the aftereffect of waking sensory impressions resulting from the continued motions of the sensory organs during sleep, long after the original stimulus (such as a sound) has ceased. In waking, the ongoing flow of new sensory impressions drowns out these comparatively subtler motions. But in the calm of sleep, they can lead to experiences whose vividness equals or even surpasses waking perception.

In addition, Hobbes believed other factors can influence our dreams, ranging from sensations before sleep to longer-term memories, ongoing concerns, and personality factors. He also allowed that sensations within sleep can play a role, such as sounds in the sleeper's environment and bodily sensations. For example, he claimed that sleeping in a room that is too hot could cause dreams of anger and thought this was the reverse of waking, where anger causes heat in the body.

We do not need to agree with the details of Hobbes's account. What matters is that here is a line of thought in which the imaginative and perceptual aspects of dreaming,

6 There have also been some promising findings linking the frequency of lucid dreams and nightmares to individual differences. But beyond this, the identification of trait-like differences in dream content and recall frequency has largely remained elusive (Blagrove and Pace-Schott, 2010).

as well as its immediate bodily and longer-term mnemonic sources, do not stand in opposition, but are jointly put to work to form a rich and multilayered account. Importantly, this account has the potential to link dreaming to spontaneous thought in waking, suggesting that similar factors could explain how seemingly disparate thoughts and images are stitched together to form a longer train of thought. This broader project of understanding the association of ideas provided the general context and motivation for Hobbes's discussion of dreaming.

A similar interest and openness about the sources of dreaming and waking thought was shared by other early modern philosophers (for an insightful tour of these theories, see Sutton, 2010). Dreams played an important role in these discourses and were often theorized, as was the case for Hobbes, as exemplars of our sponta- neous, restless minds. These authors very naturally linked dreams to conscious thought in wakefulness; at the same time, they resisted the temptation to view them as purely mental and exclusively internal phenomena, considering them as both imaginative and embodied (Sutton, 2010).

Nielsen's recent theory on the generation of sleep onset experience suggests how such an inclusive view might translate into an empirically informed theory. As we move from waking into sleep, there is a progression from simple, unimodal, and snapshot-like imagery to fully formed imagery involving visuospatial scenes and spanning longer episodes that tend to be dynamic and narratively organized (Nielsen, 2017; Windt, 2015a). Sleep onset imagery is often accompanied by changes in bodily experience (i.e. sensations from the body, the bedsheets, etc. are dampened), move- ment illusions (such as sensations of falling, floating, or separating from the physical body), and feelings of paralysis (Cheyne and Girard, 2007).

The later stages of sleep onset experience are often immersive and dreamlike; I like to think of them as oneiragogic experiences, or experiences leading into dreams (Windt, 2015a). Nielsen (2017) calls them microdreams and suggests that by disentangling the factors underlying their formation, we can gain insights about the formation of fully fledged dreams. To explain imagery formation during sleep onset, he proposes that bodily and movement sensations – for instance from muscular twitching, which is frequent at sleep onset – merge with short- and long- term memories to create novel images. These different sources pinballing off each other could explain the novelty and the dynamic, constantly changing quality of microdreams and maybe even of more complex dream imagery. Both the dream self and the dream world would then be attempts to make sense of the altered sensory information experienced in sleep, some of which is produced internally, some of which has external sources (Windt, 2017).[7] The most plausible account might be mixed, allowing that own-body experience sometimes triggers appro- priate dream imagery and guides the selection of memory sources whereas at other times ongoing concerns, pre-sleep thoughts, memories, and emotions might be the guiding factors. As suggested by Nielsen, these processes might already be at work during sleep onset. Moreover, analyzing changes in experience as we slip

7 This idea complements the possibility, sketched in footnote 3, that eye movements may be involved not so much in the scanning as in the generation of dream imagery.

from waking into sleep might not only provide a window into more complex dreams, but could also build a bridge for the joint investigation of dreaming and waking spontaneous thought.

Conclusions

Like a tapestry, the genealogy of a given dream is multilayered, spanning cognitive and mnemonic sources as well as emotions and bodily sensations; individual threads can span long distances, resurfacing at different points to weave seemingly disparate images into a complex and dynamic narrative stream. This does not rule out describing dreams, variously, as imaginative, hallucinatory, illusory, or even perceptual – rather, it highlights how dreams, in resembling different wake states, combine these in a novel way, occupying a unique position relative to different modes of waking experience.

Perhaps we should strive to move beyond these categories and develop an entirely new taxonomy, reflecting the uniqueness of dreaming. But while these familiar labels can be misleading if used unreflectively, they are also handy; and more importantly, they hold the promise of placing dreams within a broader context of related mental states. What I hope to have shown here is that perception and imagination are not mutually exclusive in their application to dreaming. In the possibility space for describing dreaming, there are more options than often assumed. In particular, the contrast between the claim that dreams are either imaginative or hallucinatory presents a false dichotomy. Ontological questions about dreaming should be expanded by considering illusions and own-body perception on the one hand, and mind-wandering and spontaneous thought on the other hand.

While we should allow for much variation within individual dreams, I have argued that we can identify two general characteristics: their immersive, *here* and *now* structure and the spontaneous processes underlying their generation, which dreams share with waking mind-wandering and daydreams. Both strands are related to opposing sides in the debate on the perceptual vs. imaginative character of dreaming; yet by exploring new trajectories through familiar conceptual territory, we can see how they complement each other and begin to make sense of both the uniqueness and the familiarity of dreaming.

Describing dreams as immersive mental simulations is a first step in this direction. It also holds the resources for tapping both contemporary theories and historical sources. Along the way, we'll have to overcome deeply engrained dichotomies between imagining and perceiving, but also between spontaneous and controlled, mental and bodily, internal and external sources and processes. This is challenging but can also lead us to a new and informative view of dreaming.

Acknowledgments

This research was funded by the Australian Government through the Australian Research Council Discovery Early Career Researcher Award.

Bibliography

Antrobus, J., Hartwig, P., Rosa, D., Reinsel, R., and Fein, G. (1987). Brightness and Clarity of REM and NREM Imagery: Photo Response Scale. *Sleep Research*, *16*(1958), 240.

Baird, B., Mota-Rolim, S. A., and Dresler, M. (2019). The Cognitive Neuroscience of Lucid Dreaming. *Neuroscience & Biobehavioral Reviews*, *100*, 305–323.

Blagrove, M., Henley-Einion, J., Barnett, A., Edwards, D., and Seage, C. H. (2011). A Replication of the 5–7 Day Dream-Lag Effect with Comparison of Dreams to Future Events as Control for Baseline Matching. *Consciousness and Cognition*, *20*(2), 384–391.

Blagrove, M., and Pace-Schott, E. F. (2010). Trait and Neurobiological Correlates of Individual Differences in Dream Recall and Dream Content. *International Review of Neurobiology*, *92*, 155–180.

Brooks, J. E., and Vogelsong, J. A. (2000). *The Conscious Exploration of Dreaming: Discovering How We Create and Control our Dreams*. Bloomington, IN: 1st Books Library.

Cheyne, J. A., and Girard, T. A. (2007). Paranoid Delusions and Threatening Hallucinations: A Prospective Study of Sleep Paralysis Experiences. *Consciousness and Cognition*, *16*(4), 959–974.

Christoff, K., Irving, Z. C., Fox, K. C. R., Spreng, R. N., and Andrews-Hanna, J. R. (2016). Mind-Wandering as Spontaneous Thought: A Dynamic Framework. *Nature Reviews Neuroscience*, *17*(11), 718–731.

Dement, W., and Kleitman, N. (1957). The Relation of Eye Movements during Sleep to Dream Activity: An Objective Method for the Study of Dreaming. *Journal of Experimental Psychology*, *53*(5), 339.

Dennett, D. C. (1976). Are Dreams Experiences? *The Philosophical Review*, *85*(2), 151–171.

Desseilles, M., Dang-Vu, T. T., Sterpenich, V., and Schwartz, S. (2011). Cognitive and Emotional Processes during Dreaming: A Neuroimaging View. *Consciousness and Cognition*, *20*(4), 998–1008.

Domhoff, G. W. (2013). *Finding Meaning in Dreams: A Quantitative Approach*. New York, NY: Springer Science & Business Media.

Fosse, R., Stickgold, R., and Hobson, J. A. (2004). Thinking and Hallucinating: Reciprocal Changes in Sleep. *Psychophysiology*, *41*(2), 298–305.

Foulkes, D. (2009). *Children's Dreaming and the Development of Consciousness*. Cambridge, MA: Harvard University Press.

Fox, K. C., Nijeboer, S., Solomonova, E., Domhoff, G. W., and Christoff, K. (2013). Dreaming as Mind Wandering: Evidence from Functional Neuroimaging and First-Person Content Reports. *Frontiers in Human Neuroscience*, *7*, 412.

Hobbes, T. (1651/2006). *Leviathan*. London, UK: A. & C. Black.

Hobson, J. A. (1999). *Dreaming as Delirium: How the Brain Goes out of Its Mind*. Cambridge, MA: MIT Press.

Hobson, J. A., Pace-Schott, E. F., and Stickgold, R. (2000). Dreaming and the Brain: Toward a Cognitive Neuroscience of Conscious States. *Behavioral and Brain Sciences*, *23*(6), 793–842.

Horikawa, T., Tamaki, M., Miyawaki, Y., and Kamitani, Y. (2013). Neural Decoding of Visual Imagery during Sleep. *Science*, *340*(6132), 639–642.

Ichikawa, J. (2009). Dreaming and Imagination. *Mind & Language*, *24*(1), 103–121.

(2016). Imagination, Dreaming, and Hallucination. In A. Kind (ed.), *The Routledge Handbook of Philosophy of Imagination*. London, UK; New York, NY: Routledge, 149–162.

Irving, Z. C. (2016). Mind-Wandering Is Unguided Attention: Accounting for the "Purposeful" Wanderer. *Philosophical Studies*, *173*(2), 547–571.

Kerr, N. H. (1993). Mental Imagery, Dreams, and Perception. In C. Cavallero and D. Foulkes (eds.), *Dreaming as Cognition*. New York, NY: Harvester Wheatsheaf, 18–37.

Kind, A. (2013). The Heterogeneity of the Imagination. *Erkenntnis*, *78*(1), 141–159.

LaBerge, S., Baird, B., and Zimbardo, P. G. (2018). Smooth Tracking of Visual Targets Distinguishes Lucid REM Sleep Dreaming and Waking Perception from Imagination. *Nature Communications*, *9*(1), 3298.

LaBerge, S., and Ornstein, S. (1985). *Lucid Dreaming*. Los Angeles, CA: J. P. Tarcher.

Leibniz, G. (1956). *Philosophical Papers and Letters*. Volumes 1 and 2. Edited and translated by L. E. Loemker. Chicago, IL: University of Chicago Press.

Liao, S., and Gendler, T. (2019). Imagination. In E. N. Zalta (ed.), *The Stanford Encyclopedia of Philosophy* (Spring). plato.stanford.edu/archives/spr2019/entries/imagination/.

Malcolm, N. (1959). *Dreaming*. London, UK: Routledge & Kegan Paul.

Metzinger, T. (2009). *The Ego Tunnel: The Science of the Mind and the Myth of the Self*. New York, NY: Basic Books (AZ).

Nielsen, T. A. (1993). Changes in the Kinesthetic Content of Dreams following Somatosensory Stimulation of Leg Muscles during REM Sleep. *Dreaming*, *3*(2), 99.

(2000). A Review of Mentation in REM and NREM Sleep: "Covert" REM Sleep as a Possible Reconciliation of Two Opposing Models. *Behavioral and Brain Sciences*, *23*(6), 851–866.

(2017). Microdream Neurophenomenology. *Neuroscience of Consciousness*, *2017*(1), nix001.

Nielsen, T. A., and Powell, R. A. (1989). The "Dream-Lag" Effect: A 6-Day Temporal Delay in Dream Content Incorporation. *Psychiatric Journal of the University of Ottawa*, *14*(4), 561–565.

Nielsen, T. A., and Stenstrom, P. (2005). What Are the Memory Sources of Dreaming? *Nature*, *437*(7063), 1286–1289.

Nir, Y., and Tononi, G. (2010). Dreaming and the Brain: From Phenomenology to Neurophysiology. *Trends in Cognitive Sciences*, *14*(2), 88–100.

Noreika, V., Valli, K., Lahtela, H., and Revonsuo, A. (2009). Early-Night Serial Awakenings as a New Paradigm for Studies on NREM Dreaming. *International Journal of Psychophysiology*, *74*(1), 14–18.

Pagel, J. F., Blagrove, M., Levin, R., Stickgold, B., and White, S. (2001). Definitions of Dream: A Paradigm for Comparing Field Descriptive Specific Studies of Dream. *Dreaming*, *11*(4), 195–202.

Rechtschaffen, A., and Buchignani, C. (1983). Visual Dimensions and Correlates of Dream Images. *Sleep Research*, *12*(189).

Revonsuo, A. (2000). The Reinterpretation of Dreams: An Evolutionary Hypothesis of the Function of Dreaming. *Behavioral and Brain Sciences*, *23*(6), 877–901.

(2005). The Self in Dreams. In T. E. Feinberg and J. P. Keenan (eds.), *The Lost Self: Pathologies of the Brain and Identity*. Oxford, UK: Oxford University Press, 206–219.

(2006). *Inner Presence: Consciousness as a Biological Phenomenon*. Cambridge, MA: MIT Press.

Revonsuo, A., Tuominen, J., and Valli, K. (2015). The Avatars in the Machine: Dreaming as a Simulation of Social Reality. In T. Metzinger and J. M. Windt (eds.), *Open MIND*. Frankfurt am Main, Germany: MIND Group.

Rosen, M. G. (2018). How Bizarre? A Pluralist Approach to Dream Content. *Consciousness and Cognition*, *62*, 148–162.

(2019). Dreaming of a Stable World: Vision and Action in Sleep. *Synthese*, 1–36. doi:10.1007/s11229-019-02149-1.

Ryle, G. (2009). *The Concept of Mind*. Abingdon, UK: Routledge.

Sauvageau, A., Nielsen, T. A., and Montplaisir, J. (1998). Effects of Somatosensory Stimulation on Dream Content in Gymnasts and Control Participants: Evidence of Vestibulomotor Adaptation in REM Sleep. *Dreaming*, *8*(2), 125.

Schmidt, R. E., and Gendolla, G. H. (2008). Dreaming of White Bears: The Return of the Suppressed at Sleep Onset. *Consciousness and Cognition*, *17*(3), 714–724.

Schönhammer, R. (2004). *Fliegen, fallen, flüchten: Psychologie intensiver Träume*. Tübingen, Germany: Dgvt-Verlag.

(2005). "Typical Dreams": Reflections of Arousal. *Journal of Consciousness Studies*, *12* (4–5), 18–37.

Schredl, M. (2006). Factors Affecting the Continuity between Waking and Dreaming: Emotional Intensity and Emotional Tone of the Waking-Life Event. *Sleep and Hypnosis*, *8*(1), 1.

Schwartz, S. (2000). A Historical Loop of One Hundred Years: Similarities between 19th Century and Contemporary Dream Research. *Dreaming*, *10*(1), 55.

Seli, P., Risko, E. F., Smilek, D., and Schacter, D. L. (2016). Mind-Wandering with and without Intention. *Trends in Cognitive Sciences*, *20*(8), 605–617.

Siclari, F., LaRocque, J. J., Postle, B. R., and Tononi, G. (2013). Assessing Sleep Consciousness within Subjects Using a Serial Awakening Paradigm. *Frontiers in Psychology*, *4*, 542.

Siclari, F., and Tononi, G. (2017). Local Aspects of Sleep and Wakefulness. *Current Opinion in Neurobiology*, *44*, 222–227.

Smallwood, J., and Schooler, J. W. (2015). The Science of Mind Wandering: Empirically Navigating the Stream of Consciousness. *Annual Review of Psychology*, *66*(1), 487–518.

Solms, M. (2014). *The Neuropsychology of Dreams: A Clinico-Anatomical Study*. New York, NY: Psychology Press.

Sosa, E. (2007). *A Virtue Epistemology: Apt Belief and Reflective Knowledge*. Volume 1. Oxford, UK: Oxford University Press.

Strauch, I., and Meier, B. (1996). *In Search of Dreams: Results of Experimental Dream Research*. Albany, NY: SUNY Press.

Stumbrys, T., Erlacher, D., Johnson, M., and Schredl, M. (2014). The Phenomenology of Lucid Dreaming: An Online Survey. *The American Journal of Psychology*, *127*(2), 191–204.

Suddendorf, T., Addis, D. R., and Corballis, M. C. (2009). Mental Time Travel and the Shaping of the Human Mind. *Philosophical Transactions of the Royal Society B: Biological Sciences*, *364*(1521), 1317–1324.

Sutton, J. (2010). Carelessness and Inattention: Mind-Wandering and the Physiology of Fantasy from Locke to Hume. In C. T. Wolfe and O. Gale (eds.), *The Body as Object and Instrument of Knowledge: Embodied Empiricism in Early Modern Science*. Dordrecht, Netherlands: Springer, 243–263.

Thomas, N. J. T. (2018). Mental Imagery. In E. N. Zalta (ed.), *The Stanford Encyclopedia of Philosophy* (Spring). plato.stanford.edu/archives/spr2018/entries/mental-imagery/.

Valli, K., and Revonsuo, A. (2009). The Threat Simulation Theory in Light of Recent Empirical Evidence: A Review. *The American Journal of Psychology*, 122(1), 17–38.

van Rijn, E., Eichenlaub, J.-B., Lewis, P. A., et al. (2015). The Dream-Lag Effect: Selective Processing of Personally Significant Events during Rapid Eye Movement Sleep, but Not during Slow Wave Sleep. *Neurobiology of Learning and Memory, 122*, 98–109.

Voss, U., and Hobson, A. (2015). What is the State-of-the-Art on Lucid Dreaming? Recent Advances and Questions for Future Research. In T. Metzinger and J. M. Windt (eds.), *Open MIND*. Frankfurt am Main, Germany: MIND Group.

Voss, U., Schermelleh-Engel, K., Windt, J. M., Frenzel, C., and Hobson, A. (2013). Measuring Consciousness in Dreams: The Lucidity and Consciousness in Dreams Scale. *Consciousness and Cognition, 22*(1), 8–21.

Windt, J. M. (2010). The Immersive Spatiotemporal Hallucination Model of Dreaming. *Phenomenology and the Cognitive Sciences, 9*(2), 295–316.

(2013). Reporting Dream Experience: Why (Not) to Be Skeptical about Dream Reports. *Frontiers in Human Neuroscience, 7*, 708.

(2015a). *Dreaming: A Conceptual Framework for Philosophy of Mind and Empirical Research*. Cambridge, MA: MIT Press.

(2015b). Just in Time – Dreamless Sleep Experience as Pure Subjective Temporality. In T. Metzinger and J. M. Windt (eds.), *Open MIND*. Frankfurt am Main, Germany: MIND Group.

(2017). Predictive Brains, Dreaming Selves, Sleeping Bodies: How the Analysis of Dream Movement Can Inform a Theory of Self- and World-Simulation in Dreams. *Synthese, 195*(6), 2577–2625.

(2018). Consciousness and Dreams: From Self-Simulation to the Simulation of a Social World. In R. J. Gennaro (ed.), *The Routledge Handbook of Consciousness*. New York, NY: Routledge, 420–435.

Windt, J. M., Nielsen, T., and Thompson, E. (2016). Does Consciousness Disappear in Dreamless Sleep? *Trends in Cognitive Sciences, 20*(12), 871–882.

Windt, J. M., and Voss, U. (2018). Spontaneous Thought, Insight, and Control in Lucid Dreams. In K. C. R. Fox and K. Christoff (eds.), *The Oxford Handbook of Spontaneous Thought: Mind-Wandering, Creativity, and Dreaming*. New York, NY: Oxford University Press, 385–410.

Zeidman, P., and Maguire, E. A. (2016). Anterior Hippocampus: The Anatomy of Perception, Imagination and Episodic Memory. *Nature Reviews. Neuroscience, 17*(3), 173–182.

41 Dreaming is Imagination Roaming Freely, Based On Embodied Simulation, and Subserved by an Unconstrained Default Network

G. William Domhoff

Dreaming is based on the cognitive process of simulation, which can be usefully defined for the purposes of this chapter as "a particular kind or subset of thinking that involves imaginatively placing oneself in a hypothetical scenario and exploring possible outcomes" (Schacter, Addis, and Buckner, 2008: 42). Moreover, dreaming often includes a vivid sensory environment, interpersonal interactions, and emotions. It is subjectively "felt" as the experienced body in action, and sometimes unfolds over a period of 15–30 minutes. Dreaming is therefore an exemplary example of "embodied simulation" in which there is not only some degree of imaginative narrative flow, but also an activation of secondary sensorimotor and visual areas of the cortex when imagining different actions or events. For example, somatosensory areas of the brain are more active when people are making aesthetic judgments of dance movements. (Domhoff, 2018: 3–4, 92; Gibbs, 2014: 27–29, for overviews and examples).

In terms of their content, most dreams can be understood as dramatized presentations of personal conceptions and concerns that are embedded within larger cognitive networks of scripts, schemas, and general knowledge. Dreams have several parallels with theatrical plays, which also contain settings and a cast of characters. The dreamer and the other characters are engaged in one or another activity (e.g. watching, swimming, running) or a social interaction (e.g. helping, arguing, kissing) in 86.7 percent of dream reports (another 6.7 percent involve the dreamer only observing or thinking about other people, 2.2 percent include only the dreamer and one or more animals, and 4.3 percent include only the dreamer) (Domhoff and Schneider, 2018). Dreaming is distinguished from other forms of thinking and imagining by the sense of being an actual, embodied participant in (or observer of) an event that seems upon awakening as if it had been "real" while it lasted.

Although dreaming most frequently occurs during REM sleep, it also can occur during NREM Stage 2 sleep, especially in the last two hours of the sleep period, when the brain is returning to a daytime level of activation (Cicogna et al., 1998; Pivik and Foulkes, 1968). Auditory waking thresholds and cerebral blood flow, which are indicators of levels of brain activation, are very similar in REM and NREM 2, and unlike those found in slow-wave sleep (Madsen et al., 1991; Zimmerman, 1970). Dreaming can also occur during the sleep-onset process, before there are any signs of the standard indicators of sleep (Foulkes and Vogel, 1965; Hori, Hayashi, and Morikawa, 1994). Moreover, brief episodes of dreaming are reported after about 20 percent of the probes during long periods of drifting waking thought when a participant is alone in a laboratory setting, with wakefulness monitored by the polysomnograph. One person, for example, dreamed she was back in her hometown, another was pressing on a vein to try to stop it from bleeding, and another was watching a judge who was wearing an old-fashioned powdered wig (Foulkes, 1985: 72). In another 20 percent of the probes the participants were mind-wandering, in 22 percent they were lost in deep thought, and in 38 percent they were fully aware of what they were doing and where they were (Foulkes and Fleisher, 1975: 72).

Based on these findings, dreaming is a unique mental state that is not dependent upon sleep. Contrary to clinical lore, neuroimaging and studies based on experiential reports show that dreaming has little in common with hallucinations, psychotic states, drug states, or hypnotic states (Abraham, 2016: 4206–4207; Pace-Schott, 2003; Sacks, 2013). Combining what is known from laboratory dream studies and neurocognitive studies, it seems likely that the neural substrate that subserves dreaming becomes operative when the following five conditions are met:

(1) There is a mature neural network for dreaming, a qualification that allows for its gradual development, which does not reach adultlike status in terms of dream content until ages 12–13;
(2) An adequate level of cortical activation is present, which is provided by subcortical ascending pathways and crucial regions in the hypothalamus;
(3) There is an occlusion of external stimuli, which likely involves the posterior thalamus and may include some neurochemical dampening in primary sensorimotor areas;
(4) There is a cognitively mature imagination system, a necessity indicated by the near absence of dreaming in preschoolers and its infrequency and lack of cognitive complexity until ages 9–11; and
(5) There is a loss of conscious self-control, which may be neurologically mediated, as the final step in a complex process, by the decoupling of the frontoparietal and dorsal attentional control networks from the two functional subsystems of the default network that remain activated during dreaming.

The Nature of Dream Content

Dreaming is seldom influenced by specific stimuli introduced shortly before going to bed or during dreaming in sleep-dream laboratories. On the few occasions when stimuli seem to be incorporated, "the narrative seems to determine the fate of the stimulus, rather than the stimulus determining the fate of the narrative" (Foulkes and Domhoff, 2014: 168). Nor do significant events of the previous day very often have an effect on dream content (e.g. Roussy et al., 1996, 2000). A study using ten-day dream diaries concluded that incorporation "is dependent on the salience or personal importance of waking life events" (van Rijn et al., 2015: 107).

The largest study of adult REM dream content in the sleep-dream laboratory, based on 635 dream reports collected "for a variety of experimental purposes" in several different investigations over a period of years, concluded that "dreaming consciousness" is a "remarkably faithful replica of waking life" (Snyder, 1970: 133). Nor are there many differences between dream reports collected in sleep-dream labs and those collected in non-lab settings from the same participants, except for aggression indicators (Domhoff and Schneider, 1999; Weisz and Foulkes, 1970). Emotions are absent from at least 25–30 percent of dream reports in both lab and non-lab settings (e.g. Domhoff, 2018: 61; Fosse, Stickgold, and Hobson, 2001; Strauch and Meier, 1996). There are virtually no episodic memories (Baylor and Cavallero, 2001; Fosse, Hobson, and Stickgold, 2003), and there are only rare indications of possible symbolism (Domhoff, 2003: 33–36, 128–133; 2015, 12–16, 21). Recurrent dreams, which many people claim they experience, are less than 2 percent of all dreams (Desjardins and Zadra, 2006). Typical dreams, which are dreams many people report they have experienced, are less than 1 percent of all dreams for any type of typical dream in both lab and non-lab studies (Domhoff, 1996; Snyder, 1970; Strauch and Meier, 1996). The appearance of everyday issues such as politics, economics, and religion is very infrequent (e.g. Hall, 1951).

Although dreams are often thought of as bizarre and disjointed, laboratory studies reveal they are far more coherent and faithful to waking life than is widely believed. In a detailed lab study of unusual and anomalous elements in dream reports, the researchers concluded their results "emphasize the rarity of the bizarre in dreams" (Dorus, Dorus, and Rechtschaffen, 1971: 367). Similar findings on the relative infrequency of bizarre elements in dreams were reported in other lab and non-lab studies (e.g. Revonsuo and Salmivalli, 1995; Snyder, 1970; Strauch and Meier, 1996).

A study comparing REM dream reports to streams of waking thought reported by individual participants alone in a darkened room found that there were more abrupt topic changes or scene changes ("discontinuities") in the waking sample than in REM reports. In addition, there were as many "improbable combinations," such as unusual juxtapositions of objects, in waking as in REM. The REM dream reports were higher only on "improbable identities," such as metamorphoses and blended characters (Reinsel, Antrobus, and Wollman, 1992: 169–170, 173). This study shows that discontinuities cannot be used to study alleged bizarreness in dreams, which is one of several problems with the few studies claiming frequent bizarreness in dreams (Domhoff, 2018: 220–223, for a detailed critique).

Systematic studies of adult dream content reveal that there is considerable psychological meaning in dream content in terms of correspondences with waking demographic variables, such as nationality, gender, and age, but there are more similarities than differences (Domhoff, 1996, 2003; Pesant and Zadra, 2006). There also have been numerous quantitative studies of individual dream series written in dream diaries by a small but diverse set of individuals for their own reasons, which never have to do with psychotherapy or an interest in dream theories, nor with any intention of later offering them to dream researchers.

Dream series have long-standing methodological legitimacy in psychology as a form of unobtrusive, nonreactive archival data, because the demand characteristics and expectancy effects that can arise as subtle confounds in experimental settings do not influence them (Rosenthal and Ambady, 1995; Webb et al., 1981). Comparison studies using approximate randomization, which requires no assumptions about the independence of observations, demonstrate that dream series can be analyzed with the same statistical tests used in studies that compare samples based on numerous individuals; in addition, the possibility of autocorrelation has been ruled out as a potential confound by a study of 125 runs in four different dream series using the Wald-Wolfowitz runs test for assessing independence with nominal data (Domhoff, 2003; Domhoff and Schneider, 2008, 2015). The findings from analyses of an individual dream series can be compared with replicated norms for American men and women (Hall et al., 1982; Hall and van de Castle, 1966; Tonay, 1990/1991).

Detailed blind quantitative analyses of about two dozen different dream series, which range in length from several hundred to several thousand dream reports, demonstrate there is great consistency in what adults dream about over months, years, and decades (Domhoff, 1996, Chapter 7; 2018, chapters 3–4). Then, too, similar blind content analyses of about a dozen dream series, which led to inferences that could be accepted or rejected by the dreamer and close friends, demonstrate that there is continuity between many of the conceptions and personal concerns expressed by individuals in dreaming and waking thought. In the process, these studies revealed that the frequency of the appearance of a person or activity is a reliable index of the intensity of a personal concern. These continuities most often involve the important people in a dreamer's life and the nature of the social interactions with them. There is also good evidence for continuity with many of the dreamer's main interests and activities (Bulkeley, 2014; Domhoff, 1996, Chapter 8; 2003, Chapter 5).

Based on these studies, as many as 70–75 percent of dreams have at least one element that is continuous with waking conceptions and concerns (Domhoff, 2018, chapters 2–3). The remaining 25–30 percent of dream reports often have the flavor of adventure stories, complete with dangers (Foulkes, 1999: 136). In a study of a sample of 1,000 dream reports, 500 from 100 college woman and 500 from 100 college men, the 26 percent of dreams that have *neither* familiar characters nor familiar settings have more animal characters, more acts of physical aggression, and more misfortunes than the 65 percent of the dreams that contain *both* familiar characters and familiar settings (Domhoff, 2018: 64–65).

The dream series that has been studied in the most detail consists of 4,254 dream reports written down over a forty-one-year period by a now-elderly woman. The pattern of friendly and aggressive interactions with the most frequently appearing characters in her dreams, along with the percentage of the time she initiated the friendly or aggressive interactions, provide an accurate portrait of how she regards and interacts with these people in waking life, as subsequently determined in lengthy interviews with the dreamer and four of her close women friends. For example, the elevated levels of aggressive interactions with her mother (as determined by a comparison with the frequency of aggressive interactions with all characters in a representative sample of 250 of her dreams), along with the fact that she and her mother were equally likely to initiate both their many aggressive and fewer friendly interactions, was consistent with her waking conception of her relationship with her mother. So, too, the dreamer's even higher levels of aggressive interactions with her middle daughter, the great majority of which the dreamer initiated, fit with how she conceived of that relationship. On the other hand, she had overwhelmingly friendly interactions with her favorite brother and her closest woman friend (Domhoff, 2003: 111–128; 2018: 100–111 for a summary of all past findings as well as new findings with this series).

The findings on consistency and continuity suggest there may be a degree of lawfulness in some aspects of dreaming. This hypothesis derives from pathbreaking work, based on five dream series, ranging in length from 208 to 423 dream reports. The researchers discovered that the social networks in dreams are similar to waking social networks in that they are both "small-world" networks. Such networks are characterized by several features, including short paths to other people via shared connections, a tendency for two people who are known by another person to know each other, a strong tendency for a few characters to be more central to the overall network than others, and for a large number of characters to be connected in a large general component (Han et al., 2015).

The findings with the first five dreamers were replicated and extended through a comparison of the waking social network and the network of dream characters in the series of 4,254 dream reports written down by the woman whose patterns of social interactions in her dreams with important people in her life were discussed two paragraphs ago. The results were compared with the findings from the dreamer's waking social network, which was constructed from a questionnaire in which she rated how well each possible pair of people actually knew each other in waking life and how emotionally close they were on a 1 (low) to 5 (high) scale (Han, 2014: 36). She also rated her own emotional closeness to each person on the same five-point scale.

The dream and waking social networks were similar in several ways, beginning with the "density" of the networks (Han, 2014: 47). Then, too, a measure of centrality, based on how connected a person is to other well-connected people, revealed a high correlation between the dream and waking-life networks. Suggesting once again that most dreams are about highly personal concerns, the dreamer's network of dream characters more often brought together immediate family members, other relatives, and friends than was the case in waking life (Han, 2014: 48–49). Similarly, the people who were emotionally close to the dreamer in waking life tended to appear in dreams together even though they were not in the same social networks in waking life (Han, 2014: 50).

Dreaming Is a Gradual Cognitive Achievement

A longitudinal laboratory study of several dozen participants ages 3 to 15, and a cross-sectional laboratory replication with children ages 5 through 8, both revealed that dreaming is a gradual cognitive achievement in terms of frequency, complexity, and content, as well as in the inclusion of emotions (Foulkes, 1982; Foulkes et al., 1990). Preschool and young elementary school children reported dreams after only 15–20 percent of REM awakenings, even though their verbal skills were excellent and there was every indication that they were comfortable in the laboratory setting. In addition, children's dream reports were not adultlike in frequency, length, and form until ages 9–11, and the content did not regularly include emotions, personal concerns, and avocations in an adultlike way until ages 12–13 (Foulkes, 1982, 1999; Foulkes et al., 1990). The results for children ages 9 to 15 were later replicated in a six-year longitudinal study in Switzerland, which also included new findings on friendship patterns (Strauch, 2005; Strauch and Lederbogen, 1999).

Overall, these results suggest that there are cognitive prerequisites for dreaming. Drawing on findings in developmental cognitive psychology, as well as the cognitive testing that was carried out as part of the longitudinal and cross-sectional dream studies of children, it seems likely there are four cognitive processes that are necessary for dreaming – mental imagery, narrative skills, imagination, and an autobiographical self.

The ability to produce mental imagery, which is a significant feature of dreaming, seems to be lacking in preschool children. This conclusion is derived from numerous different types of detailed studies of visual mental imagery that are too complex to be summarized within the confines of this chapter (Domhoff, 2018: 59–162 for a literature review). Nor did the mental imagery tests used in conjunction with the cross-sectional dream study of children 5 through 8 detect sufficient capacity to create mental imagery at age 5; the investigators concluded that "the possibility of kinematic imaging emerges somewhere between 5 and 8 years of age, rather than being generally well-developed in 5-year-olds" (Foulkes et al., 1989: 450).

These findings are supported by the absence of visual imagery in people who are born blind, or lose their sight before age 5, in contrast to the continuing presence of visual imagery in the dreams of people who become blind after age 7. Taken together, these findings suggested that visual mental imagery develops somewhere between ages 5 and 7 (Foulkes, 1999: 15; Hurovitz et al., 1999; Kerr, 1993). The continuing ability of those who became blind after age 7 to generate visual imagery includes the creation of visual dream images of people they met after they became blind. It therefore seems likely that they have retained a developmentally acquired system of visual imagery that is independent of their visual-perceptual capabilities (Kerr, 1993: 30–35).

Children do not have good narrative skills until they near preadolescence. Only half of young children's statements about an event are narratives by age 3, albeit limited ones, but by age 5 or 6 many children can tell a story that contains a beginning, middle, and end (Reese, 2013: 197–198). In a study of children age 7, it was found that they included only three of the eight basic elements that are part of a well-developed narrative, but by age 11 they included six of the eight. Similar insufficiencies in narrative skills were also found in the cross-sectional laboratory study of dreaming and its waking cognitive correlates. Participants aged 5–7 were able to produce only simple narrative scenes without chronology or sequence, but at age 8 they were able to generate a narrative with continuity in two temporal units, along with evidence of causality (Foulkes et al., 1990: 456, 461).

Nor do children have the ability to engage in "pretend dramatic play" until they are aged 4 or 5, even in stimulating preschool environments (Nelson, 2007: 170). Before that age they seem to lack the ability to simulate versions of past and future events, which is considered essential to imagination. Similarly, in the cross-sectional sleep-dream laboratory study of children 5 through 8, the ability to produce complex imaginative narratives in response to story prompts significantly correlated with the participants' overall rate of dream recall when age was held constant (Foulkes et al., 1990: 458).

Finally, personal (episodic, autobiographical, autonoetic) memories only gradually develop and become organized into an autobiographical self around age 6 (Bauer, 2013: 521–522; Gopnik, 2009, Chapter 5). Studies including specific questions about conscious thoughts found that preschool children do not seem to have much awareness of a spontaneous inner mental life, in contrast to those aged 6–7. Apparently due to this inability to consciously experience their own thinking, preschool children "don't experience their lives as a single timeline stretching back into the past and forward into the future," or "feel immersed in a constant stream of changing thoughts and feelings" (Gopnik, 2009: 153).

It therefore seems that children do not have "the basics of autobiographical memory," along with an inner mental life and "a roughly adult understanding of consciousness," until they are around the age of 6 (Gopnik, 2009: 156). This finding parallels the results for the longitudinal dream study of young children, which included seven boys and seven girls who were studied in the laboratory at ages 3–5, 5–7, and 7–9: "self involvement in dream scenarios reliably appeared only later (age 7+) than a first stage (age 5+) in which simple dream actions were performed by others" (Foulkes, 2017: 4).

If the gradual independent development of mental imagery, narrative skills, imagination, and an autobiographical self in young children are considered in combination, it may help to explain why preschool children seldom dream and why the dream reports of children aged 5–7 often lack a sense of sequence, complexity, visual imagery, and a central role for the dreamer.

The Neural Substrates That Support Dreaming

Neuroimaging, intracranial electrical brain stimulation, and lesion studies provide converging evidence suggesting that the neural substrate that enables the cognitive processes involved in dreaming is located within the default network. If future studies continue to support the evidence assembled to date for this hypothesis, then the gradual development of the default network between infancy and preadolescence may help to explain the infrequency and relative simplicity of children's dreaming. Two cross-sectional studies of many dozens of children, preadolescents, and adolescents, aged 7 to 15, one in the United States, one in Brazil, discovered that the default network does not approach adultlike complexity until ages 10–11 in terms of increased within-network connectivity and integration, strong connections among its major hubs, and increased segregation from other networks (Fair et al., 2008; Sato et al., 2014).

The results from the two cross-sectional studies were replicated and refined in a longitudinal study of both the default and frontoparietal control networks in forty-five participants (twenty-four girls, twenty-one boys) at ages 10 and 13. These investigators report that "by age 10, the basic functional architecture of the default mode network is in place," and more generally conclude that the "participants' functional networks resembled those found in mature adults in previous work" (Sherman et al., 2014: 151, 154). The fact that the default network becomes similar to the adult default network between ages 10 and 13 is consistent with the finding in lab studies that the frequency of dream recall and the content of dream reports become more adultlike during this time period.

There are two distinct, functionally connected subsystems within the waking adult default network that are relevant to dreaming, the dorsal medial prefrontal cortex system and the medial temporal lobe system (Andrews-Hanna et al., 2010). Both subsystems are also active during dreaming, as found in a meta-analysis comparing studies of mind-wandering with studies of REM sleep, which is a good proxy for the neural substrate that enables dreaming (Fox et al., 2013). The dorsal medial subsystem, which is differentially activated by instructions to think about the person's present situation or present mental state ("present self"), includes the dorsal medial prefrontal cortex, the temporoparietal junction, the lateral temporal cortex, and the temporal pole of the temporal lobe. The medial temporal lobe system, which is differentially activated by thinking about personal situations and decisions in the future ("future self"), includes the ventral medial prefrontal cortex, posterior inferior parietal lobule, retrosplenial cortex, parahippocampal cortex, and hippocampal formation (Andrews-Hanna et al., 2010: 554, 559; Andrews-Hanna, Smallwood, and Spreng, 2014; Fox et al., 2015).

The importance of the medial temporal lobe to dreaming according to neuroimaging studies is supported by an electrical brain stimulation study that had a large enough sample size to distinguish a sense of dreaming from the range of reminiscence states, such as déjà vu, vivid memories, and a feeling of dreaminess, reported in past intracranial brain stimulation studies (e.g. Vignal et al., 2007). This more focused analysis demonstrated that the "experiential phenomena" explicitly mentioning dreams are all evoked by electrical stimulation in regions in the temporal lobe, and most frequently in the medial temporal lobe (Curot et al., 2018: 9–10). The study is based on forty-two instances, seven from six patients in the authors' own extensive database, and thirty-five from the neurological case-study literature concerning electrical brain stimulation in general. These results are consistent with other electrical brain stimulation evidence suggesting that the medial temporal lobe is important in the initiation of spontaneous thought in general (Fox, 2018: 170, 175).

Returning to the neuroimaging studies, it is noteworthy that the prefrontal and posterior areas that support executive functions are less active or are deactivated during dreaming. They include the dorsolateral prefrontal cortex, the orbitofrontal cortex, the rostrolateral prefrontal cortex, the posterior cingulate cortex, and the precuneus (Fox et al., 2013). Based on these findings, dreaming can be considered an enhanced form of intense daydreaming that is not constrained by sensory input or the executive and attentional control networks, which provides the neurocognitive explanation for why dreaming is imagination roaming freely. However, as a result of these deactivations, it is also noteworthy that the neural network that underlies dreaming may not be sufficient to support the generation or comprehension of metaphors, which require a combination of regions within the frontoparietal and default networks (e.g. Beaty, Silvia, and Benedek, 2017). This finding may help explain the unexpectedly few instances of symbolism in systematic, nonclinical dream research.

The neural network that subserves dreaming, located primarily within the two functional subsystems within the default network mentioned above, is supplemented by the lingual gyrus, located in the medial occipital lobe, and the caudate nucleus, located in the basal ganglia, both of which are more active during dreaming than during mind-wandering (Fox et al., 2013). This discovery is significant because the lingual gyrus supports the generation of visual imagery and the caudate nucleus supports the initiation of movement, among other functions. The two functional subsystems of the default network that are highly active during dreaming include within them the mentalizing network, which subserves the ability to infer other people's thoughts and intensions, and also the network that supports social cognition in general. Moreover, the wide range of enactments related to the past, present, and future that can arise during dreaming may be possible because there is an overlap between the neural network that mediates associative thinking and the regions in the default network that are active during dreaming. In addition, the inclusion of language areas, located in regions in the temporal lobes, is consistent with the frequency, correctness, and specificity of language use in dreams (Domhoff, 2018: 171–175, for a synthesis of the large literature on the default network that can be related to dreaming). Perhaps most significant of all, there is a greater activation of the medial prefrontal cortex, which serves as a central hub in the widely distributed waking self-system (e.g. Abraham, 2013; Jenkins and Mitchell, 2011). This finding may help explain why preadolescent, teenage, and adult dreamers are usually at the center of their dream scenarios.

In addition to the brain regions that support the executive and attentional control networks, there is one other notable absence from the neural substrate that supports dreaming, the posterior cingulate cortex, which is a key connection between the default network and the dorsal attentional network. Its decoupling from the dorsal attentional network may be the final step in the complex neurocognitive process of losing conscious self-control, which begins with the gradual deactivation of the frontoparietal control network and the increasing activation of the default network (Domhoff, 2018: 194–196, for a discussion of the transition from focused thinking to mind-wandering to dreaming). Then, too, the absence of activity in the posterior cingulate cortex, which seems to be involved in retrieving past episodic memories, may help explain the rarity of episodic memories during dreaming. It is notable that the decoupling of the posterior cingulate cortex and the dorsal attentional network was also found in the largest and most detailed study of the sleep-onset process, which may be one reason why dreaming can occur during the transition to sleep (Sämann et al., 2011).

Finally, the amygdala is another prominent brain structure that is not implicated in the meta-analysis of REM sleep (Fox et al., 2013), nor in the meta-analyses of the waking default network and mind-wandering (Andrews-Hanna, Smallwood, and Spreng, 2014; Fox et al., 2015). This absence is surprising because the amygdala has long been associated primarily with fear, which is central to dreaming according to long-standing cultural beliefs (see LeDoux, 2019: 188–191, 364–367, for a refutation of this theory). This deactivation may help explain the absence of emotions from at least 25–30 percent of dream reports.

The neuroimaging findings on which areas remain activated or are deactivated during dreaming converge with and are supported by the results of lesion studies. Summarizing several studies, lesions *outside* the neural network that subserves dreaming, in regions such as the dorsolateral prefrontal cortex, the primary visual cortex, and primary sensorimotor cortices, have no impact upon dreaming (Domhoff, 2018: 187–194, for a synthesis of several studies; Solms, 1997: 82, 153, 219–223, 237 for original findings and a summary of past neurological cases). Conversely, injuries *inside* the neural network that subserves dreaming, in the ventral medial prefrontal cortex, or in the area of the temporoparietal junction, lead to a global loss of dreaming (Solms, 1997, chapters 4 and 16). In addition, injuries in regions of the secondary visual cortex lead to the loss of visual imagery in both dreaming and waking, as best shown in a study that included both waking cognitive testing and awakenings from REM sleep in a laboratory setting (Kerr, Foulkes, and Jurkovic, 1978). These experiential reports of continued dreaming, loss of dreaming, and the loss of visual imagery in dreaming provide the crucial subjective evidence that the neural network detected in neuroimaging studies is related to the cognitive process of dreaming.

The absence of amygdala activity during both mind-wandering and REM sleep in the earlier-cited meta-analytic study (Fox et al., 2013), and its consequent implications for dreaming, receives support from a study of the subjective reports of eight patients suffering from an atrophied basolateral amygdala, all of whom reported a continuance of dreaming (Blake et al., 2019). Just as in waking life, in which they experienced primarily positive emotions and a lack of fear, the content in the twenty-three dream reports they provided was "more pleasant and less unpleasant" than was the case for a control group (Blake et al., 2019: 11). This finding raises the possibility that the amygdala only becomes part of the neural network that supports dreaming when the neurocognitive system that manages anxiety breaks down (Pyszczynski and Taylor, 2016). Such a breakdown is most likely in the highly activated and agitated sleep that characterizes PTSD patients and others who suffer frequent nightmares (e.g. Germain, et al., 2013; Marquis et al., 2017).

Are Dreams Useful By-Products of Adaptive Selection for Imagination?

The many replicated lab and non-lab findings concerning the process of dreaming, such as the regularity of nightly dreaming, along with the lack of dreaming in young children and the consistency of adult dream content over decades, do not fit with any of the past conjectures about the possible adaptive function of dreaming (e.g. Blagrove, 2000; Domhoff, 2003, chapter 6; Foulkes, 1993, for critiques of past claims about the adaptive function of dreaming). Also, the fact that so few dreams are remembered by most people, that dreams rarely relate to recent events or to intellectual, political, or economic issues and rarely if ever contain solutions to problems, along with the replicated findings on the large percentage of dreams based on past personal failures and unsatisfactory personal relationships, contradict claims that dreams have any forward-looking, problem-solving function (Blagrove, 1992, 1996; Domhoff, 2003: 159–162). Social-rehearsal theories suffer from many of the same defects that plague problem-solving theories; they also make unsupported assumptions about the possibility of "implicit learning" during unrecalled dreams and the "transfer of learning" to waking-life situations, both of which are minor processes during waking life, and for which there is no evidence during dreaming. For example, implicit *sequence* learning, which is the most relevant type of implicit learning in terms of the sequential, quasi-narrative nature of most dreams, has not been convincingly demonstrated in waking studies. Similarly, transfer of learning is limited in its scope, and seems to require cognitive processes that are supported by the dorsolateral prefrontal cortex, which is deactivated during sleep (Domhoff, 2018: 258–275; Domhoff and Schneider, 2018: 14–19, for literature summaries and critiques of social-rehearsal theories).

However, the issue of adaptation may be approachable from a new angle if the default network has adaptive value due to the cognitive capacity it provides to rethink the past, plan imaginatively for the future, and think creatively, when working in conjunction with specific regions in the frontoparietal control network (e.g. Suddendorf and Dong, 2013). Any seeming effects of dreaming on post-awakening insight and creativity (e.g. Fiss, Ellman, and Klein, 1969; Stickgold et al., 1999) may be the result of the early-morning activation of the default network and the drifting waking thoughts that it supports. Viewed in this way, dreaming may be best understood as an accidental by-product of the selection pressures that led to a highly imaginative waking human brain. Dreaming is most likely the result of the coincidental intersection of periodic activation during sleep, which goes back to the earliest mammals, with augmented portions of the human default network after age 5.

Even though it is unlikely that dreaming has any adaptive function, the fact remains that dreams have been put to use by people in many different cultures. Dreams are occasionally so dramatic, overwhelming, and realistic, at least for some individuals, that they have often become crucial aspects of religious and healing ceremonies in many different societies. They thereby have an emergent cultural function that stands as another testimony to imaginative human inventiveness. If that is the case, the psychological meaning that can be found in many dream reports, and the cultural uses of dreams, have to be distinguished from each other and from the issue of adaptive function in order to develop an adequate understanding of dreaming and dream content.

At this juncture, the task confronting dream researchers is to grasp that dreaming is the form that the process of imagining takes under certain very specific conditions.

This realization would lead to the incorporation of dreaming into neurocognitive psychology, with a focus on self-generated and inner-directed thought, not on the rare stimulus-induced incorporations that command the attention of many dream researchers. The neural network that supports dreaming could then be studied in more detail through varying combinations of neuroimaging, electrical brain stimulation, and focal brain lesions. The development of dreaming in children and preadolescents between the ages of 7 and 13 could be studied longitudinally and cross-sectionally through studies that include both the development of the default network and the frequency, complexity, and content of dream reports. Perhaps such studies could be carried out in home settings using functional near-infrared spectroscopy (fNIRS), which is portable and tolerates motion well. In addition, the full range of dream content could be plumbed using the 25,000+ dream reports available to researchers through dreambank.net, including as yet unstudied dream series. Finally, the recall and content of dreams from middle childhood to old age could be studied anew with original data using simultaneous voice-recording and voice-to-text apps on smartphones, with both types of reports immediately relayed to a database center for proofreading and storage. Such studies could start with thousands of pre-selected participants, who would quickly access their smartphones upon awakening each morning to report their dream recall with an immediacy and accuracy never attained before outside a lab setting (Domhoff, 2018, Chapter 9).

References

Abraham, A. (2013). The World According to Me: Personal Relevance and the Medial Prefrontal Cortex. *Frontiers in Human Neuroscience, 7,* 341–344.

(2016). The Imaginative Mind. *Human Brain Mapping, 37,* 4197–4211.

Andrews-Hanna, J., Reidler, J., Sepulcre, J., Poulin, R., and Buckner, R. (2010). Functional-Anatomic Fractionation of the Brain's Default Network. *Neuron, 65,* 550–562.

Andrews-Hanna, J., Smallwood, J., and Spreng, R. (2014). The Default Network and Self-Generated Thought: Component Processes, Dynamic Control, and Clinical Relevance. *Annals of the New York Academy of Science, 1316,* 29–52.

Bauer, P. (2013). Memory. In P. Zelazo (ed.), *The Oxford Handbook of Developmental Psychology (Volume 1): Body and Mind.* New York, NY: Oxford University Press, 503–541.

Baylor, G., and Cavallero, C. (2001). Memory Sources Associated with REM and NREM Dream Reports throughout the Night: A New Look at the Data. *Sleep, 24,* 165–170.

Beaty, R. E., Silvia, P. J., and Benedek, M. (2017). Brain Networks Underlying Novel Metaphor Production. *Brain and Cognition, 111,* 163–170.

Blagrove, M. (1992). Dreams as a Reflection of Our Waking Concerns and Abilities: A Critique of the Problem-Solving Paradigm in Dream Research. *Dreaming, 2,* 205–220.

(1996). Problems with the Cognitive Psychological Modeling of Dreaming. *Journal of Mind and Behavior, 17,* 99–134.

(2000). Dreams Have Meaning but No Function. *Behavioral and Brain Sciences, 23,* 910.

Blake, Y., Terburg, D., Balchin, R., Morgan, B., van Honk, J., and Solms, M. (2019). The Role of the Basolateral Amygdala in Dreaming. *Cortex*, *113*, 169–183.

Bulkeley, K. (2014). Digital Dream Analysis: A Revised Method. *Consciousness and Cognition*, *29*, 159–170.

Cicogna, P., Natale, V., Occhionero, M., and Bosinelli, M. (1998). A Comparison of Mental Activity during Sleep Onset and Morning Awakening. *Sleep*, *21*(5), 462–470.

Curot, J., Valton, L., Denuelle, M., et al. (2018). Déjà-rêvé: Prior Dreams Induced by Direct Electrical Brain Stimulation. *Brain Stimulation*, *11*(4), 875–885.

Desjardins, S., and Zadra, A. (2006). Is the Threat Simulation Theory Threatened by Recurrent Dreams? *Consciouness and Cognition*, *15*, 470–474.

Domhoff, G. W. (1996). *Finding Meaning in Dreams: A Quantitative Approach*. New York, NY: Plenum.

(2003). *The Scientific Study of Dreams: Neural Networks, Cognitive Development, and Content Analysis*. Washington, DC: American Psychological Association.

(2015). Dreaming as Embodied Simulation: A Widower Dreams of his Deceased Wife. *Dreaming*, *25*, 232–256.

(2018). *The Emergence of Dreaming: Mind-Wandering, Embodied Simulation, and the Default Network*. New York, NY: Oxford University Press.

Domhoff, G. W., and Schneider, A. (1999). Much Ado about Very Little: The Small Effect Sizes When Home and Laboratory Collected Dreams Are Compared. *Dreaming*, *9*, 139–151.

(2008). Similarities and Differences in Dream Content at the Cross-Cultural, Gender, and Individual Levels. *Consciousness and Cognition*, *17*, 1257–1265.

(2015). Assessing Autocorrelation in Studies using the Hall and van de Castle Coding System to Study Individual Dream Series. *Dreaming*, *25*, 70–79.

(2018). Are Dreams Social Simulations? Or Are They Enactments of Conceptions and Personal Concerns? An Empirical and Theoretical Comparison of Two Dream Theories. *Dreaming*, *28*, 1–23.

Dorus, E., Dorus, W., and Rechtschaffen, A. (1971). The Incidence of Novelty in Dreams. *Archives of General Psychiatry*, *25*, 364–368.

Fair, D., Cohen, A. L., Dosenbach, N., et al. (2008). The Maturing Architecture of the Brain's Default Network. *Proceedings of the National Academy of Sciences*, *105*, 4028–4032.

Fiss, H., Ellman, S. J., and Klein, G. S. (1969). Waking Fantasies following Interrupted and Completed REM Periods. *Archives of General Psychiatry*, *21*(2), 230–239.

Fosse, R., Hobson, J. A., and Stickgold, R. (2003). Dreaming and Episodic Memory: A Functional Dissociation? *Journal of Cognitive Neuroscience*, *15*, 1–9.

Fosse, R., Stickgold, R., and Hobson, J. A. (2001). The Mind in REM Sleep: Reports of Emotional Experience. *Sleep*, *24*, 947–955.

Foulkes, D. (1982). *Children's Dreams: Longitudinal Studies*. New York, NY: Wiley.

(1985). *Dreaming: A Cognitive-Psychological Analysis*. Hillsdale, NJ: Erlbaum.

(1993). Data Constraints on Theorizing about Dream Function. In A. Moffitt, M. Kramer and R. Hoffmann (eds.), *The Functions of Dreaming*. Albany, NY: State University of New York Press, 11–20.

(1999). *Children's Dreaming and the Development of Consciousness*. Cambridge, MA: Harvard University Press.

(2017). Dreaming, Reflective Consciousness, and Feelings in the Preschool Child. *Dreaming*, *27*, 1–13.

Foulkes, D., and Domhoff, G. W. (2014). Bottom-Up or Top-Down in Dream Neuroscience? A Top-Down Critique of Two Bottom-Up Studies. *Consciousness and Cognition*, *27*, 168–171.

Foulkes, D., and Fleisher, S. (1975). Mental Activity in Relaxed Wakefulness. *Journal of Abnormal Psychology*, *84*, 66–75.

Foulkes, D., Hollifield, M., Sullivan, B., Bradley, L., and Terry, R. (1990). REM Dreaming and Cognitive Skills at Ages 5–8: A Cross-Sectional Study. *International Journal of Behavioral Development*, *13*, 447–465.

Foulkes, D., Sullivan, B., Hollifield, M., and Bradley, L. (1989). Mental Rotation, Age, and Conservation. *Journal of Genetic Psychology*, *150*, 449–451.

Foulkes, D., and Vogel, G. (1965). Mental Activity at Sleep Onset. *Journal of Abnormal Psychology*, *70*, 231–243.

Fox, K. (2018). Neural Origins of Self-Generated Thought: Insights from Intracranial Electrical Stimulations and Recordings in Humans. In K. Fox and K. Christoff (eds.), *Handbook of Spontaneous Thought: Mind-Wandering, Creativity, and Dreaming*. New York, NY: Oxford University Press, 165–179.

Fox, K., Nijeboer, S., Solomonova, E., Domhoff, G. W., and Christoff, K. (2013). Dreaming as Mind Wandering: Evidence from Functional Neuroimaging and First-Person Content Reports. *Frontiers in Human Neuroscience*, *7*, article 412, 1–18. doi:10.3389/fnhum.2013.00412. eCollection 02013.

Fox, K., Spreng, R., Ellamila, M., Andrews-Hanna, J., and Christoff, K. (2015). The Wandering Brain: Meta-Analysis of Functional Neuroimaging Studies of Mind-Wandering and Related Spontaneous Thought Processes. *NeuroImage*, *111*, 611–621.

Germain, A., Jeffrey, J., Salvatore, I., et al. (2013). A Window into the Invisible Wound of War: Functional Neuroimaging of REM Sleep in Returning Combat Veterans with PTSD. *Psychiatry Research: Neuroimaging*, *211*, 176–179.

Gibbs, R. (2014). Conceptual Metaphor in Thought and Social Action. In M. Landau, M. Robinson, and B. Meier (eds.), *The Power of Metaphor: Examining its Influence on Social Life*. Washington, DC: American Psychological Association, 17–40.

Gopnik, A. (2009). *The Philosophical Baby: What Children's Minds Tell us About Truth, Love, and the Meaning of Life*. New York, NY: Farrar, Straus, and Giroux.

Hall, C. (1951). What People Dream About. *Scientific American*, *184*, 60–63.

Hall, C., Domhoff, G. W., Blick, K., and Weesner, K. (1982). The Dreams of College Men and Women in 1950 and 1980: A Comparison of Dream Contents and Sex Differences. *Sleep*, *5*, 188–194.

Hall, C., and van de Castle, R. (1966). *The Content Analysis of Dreams*. New York, NY: Appleton-Century-Crofts.

Han, H. (2014). Structural and Longitudinal Analysis of Cognitive Social Networks in Dreams. West Lafayette, IN: Purdue University Unpublished PhD Dissertation.

Han, H., Schweickert, R., Xi, Z., and Viau-Quesnela, C. (2015). The Cognitive Social Network in Dreams: Transitivity, Assortativity, and Giant Component Proportion Are Monotonic. *Cognitive Science*, doi:10.1111/cogs.12244.

Hori, T., Hayashi, M., and Morikawa, T. (1994). Topographic EEG Changes and the Hypnagogic Experience. In R. Ogilvie and J. Harsh (eds.), *Sleep Onset: Normal and Abnormal Processes*. Washington, DC: American Psychological Association, 237–253.

Hurovitz, C., Dunn, S., Domhoff, G. W., and Fiss, H. (1999). The Dreams of Blind Men and Women: A Replication and Extension of Previous Findings. *Dreaming, 9*, 183–193.

Jenkins, A., and Mitchell, J. (2011). Medial Prefrontal Cortex Subserves Diverse Forms of Self-Reflection. *Social Neuroscience, 6*, 211–218.

Kerr, N. (1993). Mental Imagery, Dreams, and Perception. In D. Foulkes and C. Cavallero (eds.), *Dreaming as Cognition*. New York, NY: Harvester Wheatsheaf, 18–37.

Kerr, N., Foulkes, D., and Jurkovic, G. (1978). Reported Absence of Visual Dream Imagery in a Normally Sighted Subject with Turner's Syndrome. *Journal of Mental Imagery, 2*, 247–264.

LeDoux, J. (2019). *The Deep History of Ourselves: The Four-Billion Year Story of How We Got Conscious Brains*. New York, NY: Viking Press.

Madsen, P. L., Schmidt, F., Wildschidtz, G., et al. (1991). Cerebral O2 Metabolism and Cerebral Blood Flow in Humans during Sleep and Rapid-Eye-Movement Sleep. *Journal of Applied Physiology, 70*, 2597–2601.

Marquis, L.-P., Paquette, T., Blanchette-Carrière, C., Dumel, G., and Nielsen, T. (2017). REM Sleep Theta Changes in Frequent Nightmare Recallers. *Sleep, 40*, 1–12.

Nelson, K. (2007). *Young Minds in Social Worlds: Experience, Meaning, and Memory*. Cambridge, MA: Harvard University Press.

Pace-Schott, E. (2003). Postscript: Recent Findings on the Neurobiology of Sleep and Dreaming. In E. Pace-Schott, M. Solms, M. Blagrove, and S. Harnad (eds.), *Sleep and Dreaming: Scientific Advances and Reconsiderations*. New York, NY: Cambridge University Press, 335–350.

Pesant, N., and Zadra, A. (2006). Dream Content and Psychological Well-Being: A Longitudinal Study of the Continuity Hypothesis. *Journal of Clinical Psychology, 62*(1), 111–121.

Pivik, R. T., and Foulkes, D. (1968). NREM Mentation: Relation to Personality, Orientation Time, and Time of Night. *Journal of Consulting and Clinical Psychology, 32*, 144–151.

Pyszczynski, T., and Taylor, J. (2016). When The Buffer Breaks: Disrupted Terror Management in Posttrauamtic Stress Disorder. *Current Directions in Psychological Science, 25*, 286–290.

Reese, E. (2013). Culture, Narrative, and Imagination. In M. Taylor (ed.), *The Oxford Handbook of the Development of Imagination*. Oxford, UK; New York, NY: Oxford University Press, 196–211.

Reinsel, R., Antrobus, J., and Wollman, M. (1992). Bizarreness in Dreams and Waking Fantasy. In J. S. Antrobus and M. Bertini (eds.), *The Neuropsychology of Sleep and Dreaming*. Hillsdale, NJ: Erlbaum, 157–184.

Revonsuo, A., and Salmivalli, C. (1995). A Content Analysis of Bizarre Elements in Dreams. *Dreaming, 5*, 169–187.

Rosenthal, R., and Ambady, N. (1995). Experimenter Effects. In A. Manstead and M. Hewstone (eds.), *Encyclopedia of Social Psychology*. Oxford, UK: Blackwell, 230–235.

Roussy, F., Brunette, M., Mercier, P., et al. (2000). Daily Events and Dream Content: Unsuccessful Matching Attempts. *Dreaming, 10*, 77–83.

Roussy, F., Camirand, C., Foulkes, D., et al. (1996). Does Early-Night REM Dream Content Reliably Reflect Presleep State of Mind? *Dreaming, 6*, 121–130.

Sacks, O. (2013). *Hallucinations*. New York, NY: Knopf.

Sämann, P., Wehrle, R., Hoehn, D., et al. (2011). Development of the Brain's Default Mode Network from Wakefulness to Slow Wave Sleep. *Cerebral Cortex, 21*, 2082–2093.

Sato, J. R., Salum, G. A., Gadelha, A., et al. (2014). Age Effects on the Default Mode and Control Networks in Typically Developing Children. *Journal of Psychiatric Research, 58*, 89–95.

Schacter, D., Addis, D., and Buckner, R. (2008). Episodic Simulation of Future Events: Concepts, Data, and Applications. *Annals of the New York Academy of Sciences, 1124*, 39–60.

Sherman, L. E., Rudie, J. D., Pfeifer, J. H., et al. (2014). Development of the Default Mode and Central Executive Networks across Early Adolescence: A Longitudinal Study. *Developmental Cognitive Neuroscience, 10*, 148–159.

Snyder, F. (1970). The Phenomenology of Dreaming. In L. Madow and L. Snow (eds.), *The Psychodynamic Implications of the Physiological Studies on Dreams*. Springfield, IL: Thomas, 124–151.

Solms, M. (1997). *The Neuropsychology of Dreams: A Clinico-Anatomical Study*. Hillsdale, NJ: Erlbaum.

Stickgold, R., Scott, L., Rittenhouse, C., and Hobson, J. A. (1999). Sleep-Induced Changes in Associative Memory. *Journal of Cognitive Neuroscience, 11*, 182–193.

Strauch, I. (2005). REM Dreaming in the Transition from Late Childhood to Adolescence: A Longitudinal Study. *Dreaming, 15*, 155–169.

Strauch, I., and Lederbogen, S. (1999). The Home Dreams and Waking Fantasies of Boys and Girls Ages 9–15. *Dreaming, 9*, 153–161.

Strauch, I., and Meier, B. (1996). *In Search of Dreams: Results of Experimental Dream Research*. Albany, NY: State University of New York Press.

Suddendorf, T., and Dong, A. (2013). On the Evolution of Imagination and Design. In M. Taylor (ed.), *The Oxford Handbook of the Development of Imagination*. Oxford, UK; New York, NY: Oxford University Press, 453–467.

Tonay, V. (1990/1991). California Women and their Dreams: A Historical and Sub-Cultural Comparison of Dream Content. *Imagination, Cognition, and Personality, 10*, 83–97.

van Rijn, E., Eichenlaub, J. B., Lewis, P. A., et al. (2015). The Dream-Lag Effect: Selective Processing of Personally Significant Events during Rapid Eye Movement Sleep, but Not during Slow Wave Sleep. *Neurobiology of Learning and Memory, 122*, 98–109.

Vignal, J.-P., Maillard, L., McGonigal, A., and Chauvel, P. (2007). The Dreamy State: Hallucinations of Autobiographic Memory Evoked by Temporal Lobe Stimulations and Seizures. *Brain, 130*, 88–99.

Webb, E., Campbell, D., Schwartz, R., Sechrest, L., and Grove, J. (1981). *Nonreactive Measures in the Social Sciences*. Boston, MA: Houghton Mifflin.

Weisz, R., and Foulkes, D. (1970). Home and Laboratory Dreams Collected under Uniform Sampling Conditions. *Psychophysiology, 6*, 588–596.

Zimmerman, W. B. (1970). Sleep Mentation and Auditory Awakening Thresholds. *Psychophysiology, 6*, 540–549.

42 Aphantasia

Adam Zeman

Definition

We coined the term "aphantasia" in 2015 to refer to the absence of the mind's eye, the inability to visualize (Zeman, Dewar, and Della Sala, 2015). The term owes a debt to Aristotle, who described the capacity for visual imagery as "phantasia" (Aristotle, 1968): the "a" in aphantasia denotes its absence, by analogy with "aphasia," the absence of language, or "amnesia," the absence of memory. A convenient term was needed as the preceding literature had used unwieldy phrases for the same purpose such as "defective visualisation" (Botez, et al., 1985) and "visual irreminiscence" (Nielsen, 1946). We employed the word initially to describe a small group of individuals who had *never* been able to visualize, with lifelong or "congenital" aphantasia.

Although the term was new, the phenomenon was not. In this contribution I first describe the "prehistory" of aphantasia: the scanty literature on lifelong absence of the mind's eye, and the much richer literature on "acquired aphantasia," the loss of the mind's eye due to neurological or psychiatric disorder, preceding the creation of the term "aphantasia." In the next section, I report preliminary findings from the unexpectedly large and sustained public response to our description of congenital aphantasia, reporting some provisional associations and dissociations, and early attempts to find objective correlates for self-reported aphantasia. I next describe conceptual and neural models of visualization that may be useful in understanding the likely mechanism or mechanisms of aphantasia. These are relevant to the nature of aphantasia: Is it a variation of normal psychology, a symptom or a syndrome? The fifth section (Related Research on Variations in Imagery Vividness) places the variation of imagery vividness apparent in aphantasia, and its converse hyperphantasia, in the context of other work on vividness: in particular, the study of autobiographical memory, psychedelics, and hallucinations. I conclude by reflecting on why the naming of aphantasia evoked such a strong public response, on the vital distinction between *visualization* and *imagination*, and on some key questions for future research.

Throughout this chapter, the emphasis will be on visual imagery (see also Chapter 12), as this was the context in which the term aphantasia was coined. However, imagery can of course be more or less vivid in other sensory modalities – the mind's ear, for example, can be more or less keen – and I will refer from time to time to the other senses.

The Prehistory of Aphantasia

Congenital Aphantasia

Sir Francis Galton, the nineteenth-century British psychologist, is often credited with devising the first measure of imagery vividness (Galton, 1880). His "breakfast table questionnaire" invited participants to score the illumination, definition, and coloring of the recollected image of your "breakfast table as you sat down to it this morning" (Galton, 1880: 301). Galton noted that a small handful of those he surveyed claimed to have "no power of visualising" (Galton, 1880: 306). One such participant responded: "My powers are zero ... I recollect the breakfast table but do not see it" (Galton, 1880: 306). Galton himself was a weak visualizer, and believed that faint imagery was common among "men of science" (Galton, 1880: 302), though this was later challenged (Brewer and Schommer-Aikins, 2006). Interestingly, among the numerous exceptions to this rule was a certain Charles Darwin, Galton's cousin, whose image of the breakfast table included some objects "as distinct as if I had photos before me" (Brewer and Schommer-Aikins 2006: 140).

Curiously, although visual imagery attracted much interest from psychologists during the following century, the existence of otherwise normal individuals lacking the power to visualize received almost no scientific attention at all. There was one honorable exception: the American psychologist Bill Faw, himself a "wakeful non-imager," reported that 2.1–2.7 percent of a total of 2,500 participants lacked visual imagery, but Faw does not provide details of his study's methods or results (Faw, 2009). Subsequently, Greenberg and Knowlton, in a study of the role of visual imagery in autobiographical memory, reported two individuals with lifelong absence of imagery associated with a markedly reduced sense of "reliving" in autobiographical recall, an observation that anticipates other findings, discussed below, on the relationship between imagery vividness and memory (Greenberg and Knowlton, 2014).

Some independent lines of work have suggested that variations in imagery vividness, not usually as extreme as those seen in a- and hyperphantasia, can accompany other lifelong psychological traits. Thus research into individuals with lifelong prosopagnosia, the inability to recognize faces, indicates that this characteristic is associated with a reduction in the vividness of visual imagery (Gruter et al., 2009). Conversely, synaesthesia, the "merging of the senses" that can lead, for example, to the reliable perception of specific letters as evoking the associated perception of specific colors, is associated with increased imagery vividness (Barnett and Newell, 2008). These findings hint that congenital aphantasia may be related to other stable psychological characteristics affecting perception as well as imagery.

We all tend, of course, to regard our own experience as "normal," with the result that unusual variations of experience can easily "escape attention" – we and others may be unaware that our experience varies from the norm (Gruter and Carbon, 2010). Both extreme variations, such as those seen in a- and hyperphantasia, and more subtle variations in imagery vividness, may have exerted an unrecognized influence on the views of imagery researchers and previous generations of philosophers. Reisberg and colleagues (Reisberg, Pearson, and Kosslyn, 2003) provided evidence that individual scientists' imagery vividness influenced their views in the "imagery debate" of the late twentieth century regarding the depictive vs. propositional nature of imagery. While we can only speculate about the imagery experience of thinkers from the more distant past, it is plausible, for example, that Aristotle's view that "the soul never thinks without a phantasma" reflects the experience of someone with relatively vivid imagery, while Wittgenstein's utterance that "a verbal description ... can ... simply take the place of the image" expresses the introspection of someone for whom visual imagery is faint or absent (MacKisack et al., 2016: 5, 10).

A skeptic might reasonably question whether it is ever possible to be certain that the absence of the mind's eye is truly "congenital" or lifelong. At present this judgment relies entirely on the memory of those who describe the phenomenon: All that can be said with confidence is that such people cannot remember ever having been able to visualize. Whether this incapacity is strictly congenital awaits further investigation.

Neurogenic Aphantasia

While recent findings, discussed below, suggest that congenital aphantasia is more common than loss of visualization as a result of neurological disorders, the historical literature on acquired aphantasia is more extensive.

The "father of French neurology," Jean-Martin Charcot, described one of the earliest cases of what we might now call "acquired aphantasia" in 1883 – "On a Case of Sudden and Isolated Suppression of the Mental Vision of Signs and Objects" (Charcot, 1889). This description was written three years after Galton's work, cited above, on *Statistics of Mental Imagery,* of which Charcot was aware. Charcot's patient, Monsieur X, had abruptly developed aphantasia, prosopagnosia, topographical agnosia (difficulty recognizing familiar landmarks), a visual memory impairment and avisual dreams or "restriction of visual dream imagery" (Solms, 2009). While the sudden onset, neuropsychological associations and persistence of Monsieur X's symptoms make it likely, in my view, that his presentation was the result of a neurological event, some commentators have raised the possibility that it was in fact caused by a psychiatric illness, specifically depersonalization disorder (Zago et al., 2011). We will never know for sure the cause of Monsieur X's "sudden ... suppression of ... mental vision," but, as discussed below (see Psychogenic Aphantasia), there is no doubt that psychological state – as well as neurological condition – can markedly affect the vividness of visual imagery. A second classical case of imagery loss, was described four years later, by Willbrand: This included *global* cessation of dreaming and prosopagnosia, due to occipitotemporal infarction; the term "Charcot-Willbrand syndrome" is sometimes used to refer to the cessation of dreaming as a consequence of focal brain damage. As Solms has noted, this term blurs the distinction between avisual dreaming and total cessation of dreaming (Solms, 2009).

In 1984 Martha Farah summarized 37 cases of presumed "neurogenic" aphantasia published in English (Farah, 1984). She classified these in terms of an information processing model of imagery, based on Kosslyn's theoretical approach (see Figure 42.1). In ten cases insufficient detail was provided to be confident of the presence of an imagery deficit; in eight cases there was evidence for a *"generation deficit,"* leading to impairment of imagery in the absence of perceptual impairment; 13 cases displayed a *"long-term visual memory deficit"* affecting perception and visualization in parallel (in one case Farah was unable to decide between a generation and a visual memory deficit); five cases evinced a disorder of the *"inspection process"* required to "identify parts and relations within the image," whether perceptual or imaginary. Farah concluded that the existence of this distinctive, albeit diverse, group of neurogenic imagery disorders supported the hypothesis that visualization is a distinctive psychological process with separable components. She argued that Kosslyn's theoretical model helped to make sense of the diversity of these disorders, and that in turn the disorders supported his model. Specific findings from her review of these thirty-seven cases included the observations that posterior left-hemisphere lesions were primarily responsible for generation deficits, and that the neural processes involved in imagery, visual recognition and dreaming share at least some common ground. In particular, several cases indicated that deficits of perception and imagery often occur in parallel: For example, an impairment of face imagery might accompany impaired face recognition (prosopagnosia), an impairment of color imagery accompany impaired color perception (achromatopsia).

The substantial literature on neurogenic aphantasia since 1984 lacks a synthesis of clinical findings with a theoretical model of visualization as ambitious as Farah's review, though the time is ripe for one. While this literature is informative, and draws attention to the shortcomings of Farah's model, the reports unfortunately often fail to provide all the information required for a comprehensive analysis of the relationship between lesion and symptoms. This should include an account of the subject's subjective report of his or her visual experience of voluntary and involuntary wakeful and dreaming imagery, alongside the results of "imagery tests" – tasks

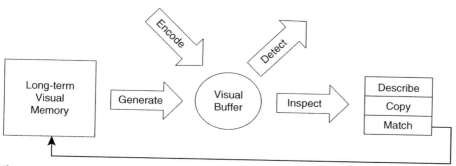

Figure 42.1 *Farah's 1984 model of neurogenic visual imagery impairments. Cases distinguished as arising from (1) loss of representations in long-term visual memory, (2) disorders of the "generate" step, and (3) disorders of the "inspect" step (see text for further details).*

assumed to require imagery, such as the Animals' Tails Test (Behrmann, Moscovitch, and Winocur, 1994) or "high imagery questions" (Eddy and Glass, 1981) – and other objective data required for the precise neuropsychological and anatomical definition of these complex cases. The subjective reports are crucial, as it appears that successful performance on "imagery tests" does not always require experience of imagery: For example, patient MX (see below, Aphantasia, Après la Lettre) "just knew" the answers to questions that most of us would answer with the aid of conscious imagery.

Several of the studies published since Farah's review have highlighted the ambiguity of the concept of the "visual buffer" in her model, adducing evidence that impairments of perception are not always accompanied by impairments of imagery and that substantial damage to parts of the visual cortices that might be expected to contribute to the "visual buffer" can occur with preservation of imagery. Many of these papers are discussed in Bartolomeo's thoughtful reappraisal of the topic (Bartolomeo, 2002). For example, Behrmann and colleagues (Behrmann, Winocur, and Moscovitch, 1992) describe a patient, CK, in whom performance on standard measures of imagery was preserved despite profound object agnosia following a closed head injury; Chatterjee and Southwood (1995) report three patients with extensive damage to visual cortices causing cortical blindness, two of whom nevertheless performed well on supposed tests of imagery; Servos and Goodale (1995) report that DF, a well-studied patient with object agnosia following carbon monoxide poisoning, nevertheless experienced "vivid and well-structured dreams" and performed normally on tests of imagery; Shuren and colleagues (Shuren et al., 1996) describe a patient with apparently preserved color imagery despite central achromatopsia following bilateral temporo-occipital strokes; Bartolomeo and colleagues (Bartolomeo et al., 1998) report a case of "multidomain dissociation" between impaired visual perception and preserved mental imagery in a patient with bilateral extrastriate lesions due to successive bilateral temporo-occipital strokes; Bridge and colleagues (Bridge et al., 2012) show that a patient with severely damaged primary visual cortex was nevertheless capable of vivid visual imagery associated with activation of extrastriate visual areas. Conversely, Moro and colleagues (Moro et al., 2008) describe two cases with selective impairment of imagery despite intact perception and intact primary visual cortex following closed head injury. In both patients there was evidence of damage to the left temporal lobe; the superior parietal lobes were damaged bilaterally in the second case.

Other relatively recent contributions to this literature include a case report of a patient with total loss of the experience of dreaming, despite preservation of REM sleep, following bilateral posterior cerebral artery stroke (Bischof and Bassetti, 2004); a report of the "visual variant" of Alzheimer's disease, posterior cortical atrophy, associated with visual imagery impairment (Gardini et al., 2011), and a series of papers on the relationship between representational and imaginal neglect: Patients with neglect of the left-hand side of space sometimes also neglect the left-hand side of visual images, as shown originally by Bisiach and colleagues (Bisiach and Luzzatti, 1978; Bisiach et al., 1981). However, just as perception and visualization are sometimes dissociated, so, too, can visual and imaginal neglect occur in isolation (e.g. Beschin, Basso, and Della Sala, 2000).

The large and somewhat confusing literature on neurogenic aphantasia allows a few confident conclusions and some tentative ones: First and most obviously, brain damage can undoubtedly impair the ability to visualize. Indeed, the opportunity to compare imagery experience pre- and post-event makes the testimony of such patients especially valuable. Brain damage can impair imagery selectively, but other capacities are often affected, sometimes including those, such as face recognition and visual dreaming, noted in Charcot's original report. Deficits of imagery and perception often occur in parallel. However, they can dissociate: patients with "imagery generation deficits" are unable to visualize despite intact perception, while some patients with marked central perceptual impairments, often associated with damage to visual cortices, may remain capable of imagery. A critical role for "the inferotemporal cortex, the mesio-temporo-limbic regions and perhaps the temporal pole" (Bartolomeo, 2002: 373) has been proposed. Future studies should seek to reconcile these findings with what we know now of the underlying neurobiology of imagery in the healthy brain. Researchers should ensure that the phenomenology of imagery – in wakefulness and dreams – are fully described in future cases, a striking omission in many previous reports, alongside appropriate behavioral and neural measures. There is still much to learn about how brain damage impacts imagery, dreaming, and perception in cases of acquired aphantasia.

Psychogenic Aphantasia

Remarkably, the occurrence of aphantasia as an outcome of *psychiatric* disorder was described in the same decade, the 1880s, that Galton recognized the phenomenon of the lifelong absence of the mind's eye and Charcot recorded its loss in Monsieur Z. Jules Cotard was a French psychiatrist who trained in part under Charcot. He is famed for his eponymous syndrome, Cotard's Syndrome, the *"delire des negations"* [roughly translated as "nihilistic delusions"], which leads the sufferer to declare that she herself, her organs or the entire world has died or no longer exists (Cotard, 1882). This syndrome most often occurs on a background of psychotic depression. In 1884 Cotard described two patients who complained of *"perte de la vision mentale"* ("loss of mental vision") in the context of *"melancolie anxieuse"* ("anxious depression") (Cotard, 1884). One of the patients also described the *delire des negations*. Indeed, Cotard speculated that his nihilistic delusions might be secondary to his "loss of mental vision."

Related cases have been described intermittently since then, particularly in France and Italy. Zago et al. tabulate twenty-five cases in which they believe imagery loss occurred on a "functional" basis, with the implication that a psychological or psychiatric explanation was more appropriate and revealing than a neurological account (Zago et al., 2011). The psychiatric context of these cases is typically one in which "depressive and anxious symptomatology coexist with depersonalisation and derealisation" (these have been defined respectively as "an alteration in the perception or experience of the self so that one feels detached from and as if one is an outside observer of one's mental processes or body" and "an alteration in the perception or experience of the external world so that it seems strange or unreal"). A separate study of twenty-eight patients with depersonalization disorder revealed a significant impairment of imagery vividness evident both in vividness of visual imagery and vividness of movement imagery questionnaires (Lambert et al., 2001).

Thus, just as brain damage can dim the mind's eye, so psychiatric conditions can lead to acquired aphantasia. However, everything that is functional is organic: psychological and psychiatric processes and disorders have neural correlates. This should be true of psychogenic aphantasia (de Vito and Bartolomeo, 2016; Zeman, Dewar, and Della Sala, 2016). While these correlates have not yet, to my knowledge, been studied specifically to date, it is interesting that a functional imaging study of depersonalization revealed altered activity in Area 19 of the left hemisphere (Phillips et al., 2001), a region in which brain activity correlates with imagery vividness in five of the six studies that have so far examined this relationship (Fulford et al., 2018 and see further discussion in the section entitled Models of Visualization : The Nature of Aphantasia, below).

Aphantasia, Après la Lettre

We coined the term "aphantasia" to describe a group of twenty-one individuals who had contacted us spontaneously via email after reading an article in the US popular Science journal, *Discover*, about our scientific report of a patient with acquired imagery loss (Zeman et al., 2010; Zimmer, 2010). MX had lost the ability to visualize following a cardiac procedure. An articulate and highly visual man, a retired surveyor, he had previously relished his visual imagery. Soon after this procedure he realized that he could no longer call images to mind; when he read novels, he did not enter a visual world; he continued to dream, but his dreams were now avisual. He performed normally on tests thought to be sensitive to visual imagery (e.g. which is darker, the green of grass or the green of a pine tree?), explaining that he "just knew" the answers, and could not call upon imagery to answer them. As this seemed plausible, we chose an alternative tack, adapting a functional imaging task to investigate whether there might be a neural correlate for MX's imagery loss. So it proved: When MX *looked* at faces, he activated visual regions, including the fusiform gyrus, entirely normally; but when he visualized faces he failed to activate a range of occipitotemporal regions, including part of the fusiform gyrus, with hyperactivation of part of the anterior cingulate gyrus (see Figure 42.2). We described him as a case of "blind imagination," by analogy with "blindsight": people with blindsight lack conscious vision in one half of visual space, yet can make accurate guesses about visual events occurring there – analogously, MX lacked any conscious experience of visual imagery but was able to answer questions that one might expect to require it. The American science journalist, Carl Zimmer, picked up MX's story from our technical account (Zimmer, 2010).

The twenty-one individuals who subsequently contacted us recognized themselves in Zimmer's description, but with one salient difference: Their minds' eyes had *always* been blind (Zeman, Dewar, and Della Sala, 2015). There were some notable similarities between their accounts. Their median score on the adapted Vividness of Visual Imagery Questionnaire (VVIQ) was 16/80, at floor, compared to a median score of 58/80 in our student control group, similar to control group

(a)

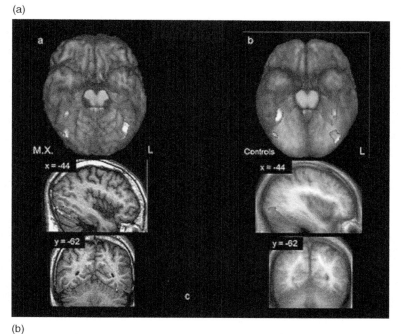

(b)

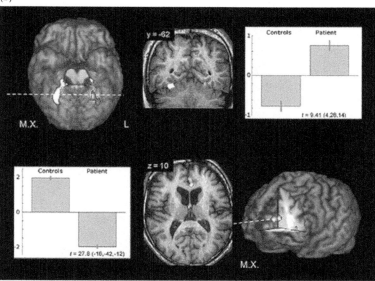

Figure 42.2 *Brain activity in a case of aphantasia. (a) Brain activation in participant MX and matched controls while viewing famous faces, adapted from Zeman et al. (2010), Loss of Imagery Phenomenology with Intact Visuo-Spatial Task Performance: A Case of "Blind Imagination,"* Neuropsychologia, *48(1), 145–155): These were not significantly different. (b) Brain activation in participant MX by comparison with matched controls while imagining famous faces (adapted from Zeman et al., 2010) where the upper images demonstrate hyperactivation in occipitotemporal regions, including left fusiform cortex (shown at far right) in MX, with hypoactivation of right anterior cingulate cortex in the lower images.*

scores reported by others (McKelvie, 1995). Most realized, at some point in their teens or twenties, that when others spoke of "visualizing" or "seeing in the mind's eye" they were speaking literally: They could enjoy something approaching visual experience in the absence of the visualized item. Until then our participants had assumed that such talk was purely metaphorical. This discovery usually had a modest emotional effect, exciting curiosity as much as regret, though some felt that they had been "cheated." The majority, intriguingly, had some understanding of what imagery was like, as they *dreamed* visually, pointing to a dissociation between waking and dreaming imagery. Two-thirds described a relative impoverishment of autobiographical memory. About half told us that *all* modalities of imagery were affected: They lacked a mind's ear just as they lacked a mind's eye; but for the others, visual imagery was selectively affected. The majority regarded themselves as being of superior ability in verbal, mathematical, and logical domains – but all, of course, were readers of *Discover*! We were intrigued by their descriptions of counting mentally the number of windows in their house or apartment. They could all accomplish this but used unusual strategies drawing on schematic "memory," "knowledge," and "subvisual" models. As one wrote: "I sort of fly through the house and inspect every room if the "idea" of a window is present and where. It's definitely not an image, it's more like understanding the idea of a window being there. I "know" it's there. In the absence of a convenient description for this neglected variation in human experience, we suggested the term "aphantasia."

This term, and the phenomenon it describes, attracted great public interest. *The New York Times*, *Le Monde*, the BBC, and other news outlets around the world carried the story of this intriguing variation in human experience, which had largely – and oddly – escaped attention over the 135 years since Galton's description. Since then we have been contacted by around 12,000 people, most of them reporting a form of "extreme imagery," either aphantasia or its converse, hyperphantasia, the experience of visual imagery "as vivid as real seeing." We have responded to this bonanza of interest by inviting those contacting us to complete the VVIQ and to complete a questionnaire probing aspects of the experience of aphantasia and hyperphantasia. This research could not have happened in the absence of the internet, and embodies a form of "citizen science." The resulting data are still undergoing analysis and description, and the findings are so far unpublished. I will give a brief, provisional, account of some key outcomes and findings here.[1]

The first, striking, feature of the response to the coinage of aphantasia and our research effort was its warmth. It was clear that a great many people had identified this quirk in their psychological nature, but had been frustrated by the lack of a term with which to describe it. The participant who told us that this was "the greatest mystery of my life explained" was particularly emphatic, but many spoke of their relief at discovering that they were not alone and of their curiosity to learn more about the implications of their aphantasia. We have yet to do justice to the eloquent descriptions that many participants have provided of alternative modes of a-visual, and even a-sensory, forms of representation: "the shape of an apple if you felt it in your hands in the dark"; "like painting with jet-black paint on a jet-black canvas, you

---

1 See medicine.exeter.ac.uk/research/neuroscience/theeyesmind/ for more information on the project.

can see it in the movement"; "thinking only in radio"; "being the object"; "I excel in mental rotation – I can't begin to describe how."

Our data point to an association between hyperphantasia and careers in "creative" industries, while aphantasia is overrepresented in professions linked to mathematics and computing. Interestingly, this bears out Galton's early observation, challenged by later work (Brewer and Schommer-Aikins, 2006). Two other associations with aphantasia emerge from our questionnaire data: around one-third of participants describe difficulty in recognizing faces that should be familiar, while a roughly similar proportion describe an impoverishment of autobiographical memory. Reports of autistic spectrum disorder have been a recurring theme – but we did not enquire about this systematically. We have not seen these three associations in participants with hyperphantasia: Their first-person testimony does, however, suggest an elevated frequency of synaesthesia.

The data suggests variability in two other respects. First, much as in our original, much smaller, sample, a slender majority of participants with aphantasia describe visual dreaming, again hinting at a dissociation between visual imagery in wakefulness and dreams. Many of those who do not dream visually report dreams with narrative, "conceptual," auditory and emotional content. By contrast, visual dreaming is almost universal among those with hyperphantasia. Second, another slender majority of participants with aphantasia report the absence of imagery in any modality: The remainder, however, experience imagery in at least one other modality, suggesting that there are both modality-general and modality-specific influences on imagery vividness.

The associations described so far relate to relatively discrete aspects of experience. It may be that imagery vividness is also associated with more pervasive features of our emotional lives and behavior, though these associations are especially tentative. Thus while many participants with aphantasia regret that they cannot visualize the faces of friends and loved ones, some describe a relative immunity to emotions such as nostalgia and disgust at recollected images and an enhanced ability to "live in the present." Conversely, while individuals with hyperphantasia frequently enjoy their vivid imagery, they can find that it distracts them from immediate concerns, and may experience difficulty in distinguishing imagined from real events.

Both participants with aphantasia and those with hyperphantasia have told us that close relatives share their imagery extreme more often than we would expect by chance. It is too early to conclude that this reflects a genetic influence, but this is clearly possible. A survey of more than 1,000 individuals in our local Biobank suggests a prevalence of extreme aphantasia (16/80 on VVIQ) of 0.7 percent, while extreme hyperphantasia (corresponding to a score of 80/80) is more common at 2.6 percent.

The results described just now derive from questionnaire data and first-person reports. We believe that these provide the appropriate point of departure, but we need to triangulate these results, obtained through introspection, with behavioral measures, using memory tests for example, and neural measures, using brain imaging. This work is now in hand in our laboratory, with early reports from some others (Jacobs, Schwarzkopf, and Silvanto, 2018; Keogh and Pearson, 2018; Watkins, 2017).

A pleasing surprise emerged from this line of research. We were contacted by a substantial number of aphantasic visual artists. All reported that they had realized in the course of their development that they differed from the majority of their artist peers in lacking a mind's eye. Some told us that they relied on having their subject in front of them as they worked; others described using their paper or canvas *as* their mind's eye, deploying a kind of imagination-in-action. Aphantasic novelists and architects also described their distinctive experience. These participants brought home to us the important difference, discussed more fully below, between visualization and imagination: Aphantasia does not imply a lack of imagination. We celebrated the creativity of artists at both extremes of the vividness spectrum in a 2019 exhibition, "Extreme Imagination – inside the Mind's Eye."[2]

This section has focused on the large majority of participants who have told us that they believe their aphantasia is lifelong. We have also heard from people whose imagery vividness has been affected, almost always reduced, by illness. Neurological causes have included head injury, stroke, near-drowning; psychological causes have included depression and psychosis. These cases have much to teach us about the anatomy and physiology of imagery, and should be a target for future research.

Models of Visualization: The Nature of Aphantasia

The neural basis of visual imagery has been studied for more than twenty-five years using noninvasive brain imaging techniques. These have revealed, as might be expected, a network of regions that play a role in visualization (Winlove et al., 2018). The phenomena and associations of extreme imagery vividness – aphantasia and hyperphantasia – demand an explanation in the light of our understanding of this network and its activity.

From first principles, one would expect an act of visualization to call on a number of psychological capacities (see Figure 42.3). Imagine an apple! If you do so, the process will have engaged your linguistic abilities (you must have understood the instruction), your decision-making and attentional abilities (you consented to follow the instruction and focused your mental energies briefly on doing so), your long term visual memory (reminding you of the appearance of an apple) and your visual brain (the experience was somewhat like seeing the apple). Informed by recent research, one might suspect that the task will also engage the brain's capacity for introspection, embodied in the "default mode network." Affect must also play an easily neglected, modulatory, role. Our meta-analysis of functional imaging studies of visualization broadly supports this model (Winlove et al., 2018). It revealed consistent activation across studies in areas linked to language, attention and working memory, vision, introspection, and, also, eye movements, a reminder that the brain system controlling eye movements probably contributes importantly to visualization (see Figure 42.4). Only the long-

2 See sites.exeter.ac.uk/eyesmind/extreme-imagination-exhibition-catalogue/.

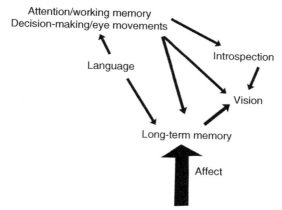

Figure 42.3 *Psychological capacities involved in visualization.*

term memory system – notably the hippocampus – was missing from these results, perhaps for technical reasons, including the tendency for the hippocampus to be engaged by "control" conditions.

A few studies have examined the neural correlates of imagery vividness specifically (Fulford et al., 2017). These are summarized in Figure 42.5. While this is a very crude analysis, there is a convergence of evidence from these studies on the key role of higher order visual regions (Brodmann areas 18, 19, 37) and memory/default mode related regions (Brodmann areas 7, 30, 31, and the medial temporal lobes).

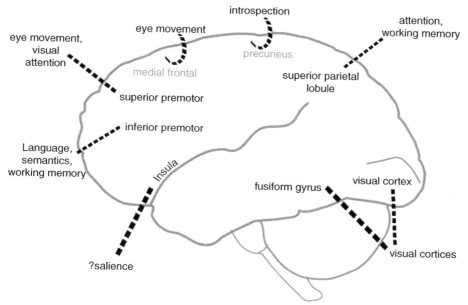

Figure 42.4 *Summary of brain regions engaged by visualization. Cf. Winlove et al. (2018).*

Study	|	Frontal						|	Cingulate					|	Temporal			M T L	|	Parietal			|	Occipital		
BA	|	10	9	8	6	45	46	| 32	24	31	29	30	| 21	22	37	MTL	| 7	40	39	| 17	18	19
(1)	|							|				>	|		~	~35 36	|			| >	>	<
(2)	|	~	<		~	~		| <	>	<		<	|				|	~		|	<	~
(3)	|	<	~	~	<			| <		>	>	>	|				|	~	~	~	|		~
(4)	|						>*	|					| > *		~ *	>	|			|		
(5)	|	<						|					|	~		< ~30	| >			| ~	~	~
(6)	|					<	<	|	>		<	<	| <	>	~	~36	| ~		~	|		~
N		3	2	1	2	2	2	2	1	3	2	5	2	1	4	4	3	2	2	2	3	5

Figure 42.5 *Brain regions showing positive correlations with imagery vividness in five comparable fMRI studies. Study references: (1) Amedi, Malach, and Pascual-Leone (2005), (2) Palmiero et al. (2009), (3) Daselaar et al. (2010), (4) Zvyagintsev et al. (2013), (5) De Araujo et al. (2012), (6) Fulford et al. (2018). Abbreviations – BA: Brodmann area, * BAs inferred from paper, > left-sided activation, < right-sided activation, ~bilateral activation, N = number of studies reporting activation in this Brodmann area, MTL-medial temporal lobe (Table reproduced with permission from Fulford, Milton, Salas, Smith, Simler, Winlove & Zeman, 2018,* Cortex, *105: 26–40).*

These findings provide a fertile basis for hypotheses about the genesis of extreme imagery vividness: It might result from focal alterations of brain function or anatomy in the key nodes of this network, or from alteration in the connections between them. I have not so far mentioned the dynamics of the network, but these have also been studied (de Borst et al., 2012): alterations in the time course of activation among regions of the visualization network could be relevant to vividness, as could variations in the parameters of neurotransmitter systems. Future comparisons of the visualization network with other imagery networks – for example, auditory or motor – should identify shared and distinctive features, which will help to explain the variable involvement of forms of imagery other than visual among people with aphantasia. Finally, fractionation of the visual imagery network may also be relevant, given the possibility that "object imagery" and "spatial imagery" dissociate both in brain and in behavior: Aphantasia appears likely primarily to reflect a variation in *object* imagery vividness (e.g. Blazhenkova, 2016).

In the light of our developing knowledge of the imagery network, how is aphantasia, in particular, best conceptualized? For the great majority of those describing an apparently lifelong lack of imagery, the most common form of aphantasia, it seems best conceptualized as an intriguing variation in normal experience, contrasting with but analogous to synaesthesia. There may well be a range of causative pathways, involving multiple genetic and environmental influences and neural instantiations, giving rise to the variety of associated features mentioned in the last section. In the less frequent cases in which it occurs as a result of brain damage or psychological upset, aphantasia is a symptom. It seems unlikely to be a single, unitary, "disorder" or "syndrome."

Related Research on Variations in Imagery Vividness

Several other lines of research that have shed light on the neural correlates of imagery vividness may be relevant to the understanding of aphantasia, in particular studies of autobiographical memory, psychedelic experience, and hallucinations. We have recently reviewed these (Fulford et al., 2017). I will provide a brief summary here.

Work on autobiographical recollection suggests that the strength of activation of visual cortices (cuneus, lingual, and fusiform gyri), the medial temporal lobes, and medial parietal regions (the precuneus and posterior cingulate) influences the richness and vividness of "autobiographical re-experiencing" (Addis et al., 2004; Cabeza and St, 2007; Daselaar et al., 2010; Gardini et al., 2006; Gilboa et al., 2004; Milton et al., 2011). The importance of visual imagery in re-experiencing is underlined by the existence of a syndrome of "visual-memory deficit amnesia" (Rubin and Greenberg, 1998).

Functional imaging studies of psychedelic experiences induced by Ayahuasca, psilocybin and LSD suggest that modulation of activity levels in and connectivity of visual cortices shape psychedelic experience (Carhart-Harris et al., 2016; de Araujo et al., 2012). The uncoupling of connections between hub regions within relevant networks may be a second key to the strength – and perhaps the autonomy – of psychedelic visions (Carhart-Harris et al., 2016; de Araujo et al., 2012).

The neural correlates of the vividness of psychotic hallucinations have not, so far, been explored, but their occurrence is related to activity in subsets of the regions discussed above, in particular sensory cortices and the medial temporal lobes (Allen et al., 2008; Zmigrod et al., 2016). Alterations in connectivity between anterior and posterior brain regions are likely to be relevant in this domain also (Allen et al., 2008; Zmigrod et al., 2016).

Vividness has not been studied extensively in modalities beyond the visual, but limited work on motor and auditory imagery suggests that in this context, also, mirroring findings in the visual domain, vivid imagery is associated with selective increases in activation within areas traditionally associated with motor control and audition respectively (Guillot et al., 2008; Lorey et al., 2011; Zatorre, Halpern, and Bouffard, 2010). Thus common themes and findings are emerging from research variously on imagery vividness, memory vividness, psychedelic experience, and hallucinations: Activity in sensory cortices, memory cortices and the default mode network, and connectivity within and between these networks are likely to codetermine variations in the vividness of imagery experience.

Finally, work using the paradigm of binocular rivalry has both provided a novel measure of imagery strength and suggested that it may have a structural correlate within the brain (Pearson, Clifford, and Tong, 2008). Pearson and colleagues have shown that preceding imagery biases the results of subsequent perception. Subjective estimates of imagery vividness predict the magnitude of this effect (Pearson, Rademaker, and Tong, 2011). There is evidence for a positive correlation between vividness and the volume of prefrontal cortex, while imagery strength is inversely related to the area of primary visual cortex (Bergmann et al., 2016). A recent study suggests that people with aphantasia do not show the usual biasing effect of imagery on binocular rivalry, in keeping with their subjective reports (Keogh and Pearson, 2018). Correlation with cortical volumes awaits further research.

The Charisma of Aphantasia – and What Lies Ahead

The discovery – or rediscovery – of aphantasia, and, importantly, its naming, has attracted much wider interest than we had anticipated: Most notably, interest from people outside the academy, intrigued by this unfamiliar variation in experience, but also from artists (see our exhibition above), novelists (Miller, 2017), philosophers (D'Aloisio-Montilla, 2017) and scientists (Clemens, 2018). I believe that this level of interest reflects the centrality of imagination to our everyday lives. As Robin Dunbar has written, "what sets us apart is a life in the mind, the ability to imagine" (Dunbar, 2004): Our capacity to detach ourselves from the here and now, to enter the virtual worlds of memory and prospection, the fictional world of a novel, the creative worlds of science – or just to daydream – defines our human existence. And for most of us visualization is a key facet of imagination: The discovery that some people get along fine in the absence of visualization, and indeed, apparently, without *any* sensory imagery, is striking.

It prompts two reflections in particular. While our ability to represent things in their absence – or "displaced reference" (Bickerton, 2014) – is crucial both to our inner experience and to our social exchanges, sensory imagery does not seem to be required: Aristotle was informatively wrong when he wrote that "the soul never thinks without a phantasm," perhaps seduced by the strength of his own imagery. Collectively we have access to many forms of representation, visual, a-visual, even a-sensory: language, after all, is, at least potentially, a powerful medium for a-sensory reference.

Second, relatedly, while visualization is, for most of us, an eye-catching ingredient of imagination, it is no more than that, and the concept of imagination is much richer and more extensive. It is possible to be aphantasic and yet highly imaginative, as evinced by the examples of the prolific neurologist, Oliver Sacks, who had a blind mind's eye, though could hear music in his mind's ear; Craig Venter, the first person to decode the human genome in its entirety, who attributes his scientific prowess at least partly to his aphantasia; and the Silicon Valley entrepreneur, Blake Ross, co-creator of Mozilla Firefox, who described his lack of all sensory imagery in a "viral" Facebook post that alerted many to the existence of aphantasia (Ross, 2016).

What does the future hold for aphantasia? The topic is fertile, teeming with topics for future study. I will, rather arbitrarily, highlight three broad questions:

(1) Does aphantasia exist? If you have read this contribution, you may be persuaded that it does, but there remains some scope for skepticism: How accurately can

people describe their imagery experience? Can we be sure that someone describing aphantasia really lacks imagery? We are, of course, unable to observe the imagery of others directly, and introspection can be unreliable. Edging toward an answer to these questions requires a gradual triangulation: If this distinctive variation in experience exists, we should expect it to have both behavioral and neural correlates. We and others are seeking to measure these.

(2) If it exists, can it be understood using the model of predictive coding that is being widely employed in models of both perception and action? Our capacity for visualization is a natural outcome of a predictive model of perception: Its absence in some individuals poses an interesting challenge for such models.

(3) Can we "cure" aphantasia? This question has been posed by many of our research participants. While it appears to be entirely possible to lead a normal, fulfilling and indeed creative life with aphantasia, many people with aphantasia would like to be able to experience visual imagery at will. This reasonable question deserves careful study: a recent report (Keogh, Bergmann, and Pearson, 2016), showing that it is possible to modulate imagery vividness in people with "average" imagery, using transcranial electrical stimulation, may point the way.

References

Addis, D. R., Moscovitch, M., Crawley, A. P., and McAndrews, M. P. (2004). Recollective Qualities Modulate Hippocampal Activation during Autobiographical Memory Retrieval. *Hippocampus, 14*(6), 752–762.

Allen, P., Laroi, F., McGuire, P. K., and Aleman, A. (2008). The Hallucinating Brain: A Review of Structural and Functional Neuroimaging Studies of Hallucinations. *Neuroscience & Biobehavioral Reviews, 32*(1), 175–191.

Amedi, A., Malach, R., and Pascual-Leone, A. (2005). Negative BOLD Differentiates Visual Imagery and Perception. *Neuron, 48*(5), 859–872.

Aristotle. (1968). *De Anima. Books II and III (with certain passages from Book I)*. Translated by D. W. Hamlyn. Oxford, UK: Clarendon Press.

Barnett, K. J., and Newell, F. N. (2008). Synaesthesia is Associated with Enhanced Self-Rated Visual Imagery. *Consciousness and Cognition, 17*(3), 1032–1039.

Bartolomeo, P. (2002). The Relationship between Visual Perception and Visual Mental Imagery: A Reappraisal of the Neuropsychological Evidence. *Cortex, 38*(3), 357–378.

Bartolomeo, P., Bachoud-Levi, A.-C., de Gelder, B., et al. (1998). Multiple-Domain Dissociation Between Impaired Visual Perception and Preserved Mental Imagery in a Patient with Bilateral Extrastriate Lesions. *Neuropsychologia, 36*, 239–249.

Behrmann, M., Moscovitch, M., and Winocur, G. (1994). Intact Visual Imagery and Impaired Visual Perception in a Patient with Visual Agnosia. *Journal of Experimental Psychology: Human Perception and Performance, 20*(5), 1068–1087.

Behrmann, M., Winocur, G., and Moscovitch, M. (1992). Dissociation Between Mental Imagery and Object Recognition in a Brain-Damaged Patient. *Nature, 359*(6396), 636–637.

Bergmann, J., Genc, E., Kohler, A., Singer, W., and Pearson, J. (2016). Smaller Primary Visual Cortex Is Associated with Stronger, but Less Precise Mental Imagery. *Cerebral Cortex, 26*(9), 3838–3850.

Beschin, N., Basso, A., and Della Sala, S. (2000). Perceiving Left and Imagining Right: Dissociation in Neglect. *Cortex, 36*(3), 401–414.

Bickerton, D. (2014). *More than Nature Needs: Language, Mind and Evolution*. Cambridge, MA.: Harvard University Press.

Bischof, M., and Bassetti, C. L. (2004). Total Dream Loss: A Distinct Neuropsychological Dysfunction after Bilateral PCA Stroke. *Annals of Neurology, 56*(4), 583–586.

Bisiach, E., Capitani, E., Luzzatti, C., and Perani, D. (1981). Brain and Conscious Representation of Outside Reality. *Neuropsychologia, 19*(4), 543–551.

Bisiach, E., and Luzzatti, C. (1978). Unilateral Neglect of Representational Space. *Cortex, 14*, 129–133.

Blazhenkova, O. (2016). Vividness of Object and Spatial Imagery. *Perceptual and Motor Skills, 122*(2), 490–508.

Botez, M. I., Olivier, M., Vezina, J. L., Botez, T., and Kaufman, B. (1985). Defective Revisualization: Dissociation between Cognitive and Imagistic Thought Case Report and Short Review of the Literature. *Cortex, 21*(3), 375–389.

Brewer, W. F., and Schommer-Aikins, M. (2006). Scientists Are Not Deficient in Visual Imagery: Galton Revisited. *Review of General Psychology, 10*(2), 130–146.

Bridge, H., Harrold, S., Holmes, E. A., Stokes, M., and Kennard, C. (2012). Vivid Visual Mental Imagery in the Absence of the Primary Visual Cortex. *Journal of Neurology, 259*(6), 1062–1070.

Cabeza, R., and St, J. P. (2007). Functional Neuroimaging of Autobiographical Memory. *Trends in Cognitive Sciences, 11*(5), 219–227.

Carhart-Harris, R. L., Muthukumaraswamy, S., Roseman, L., et al. (2016). Neural Correlates of the LSD Experience Revealed by Multimodal Neuroimaging. *Proceedings of the National Academy of Sciences of the United States of America, 113*(17), 4853–4858.

Charcot, J. M. (1889). *Clinical Lectures on Diseases of the Nervous System*. Volume 3. London, UK: The New Sydenham Society.

Chatterjee, A., and Southwood, M. H. (1995). Cortical Blindness and Visual Imagery. *Neurology, 45*(12), 2189–2195.

Clemens, A. (2018). When the Eye's Mind is Blind. *Scientific American*, August 1. www.scientificamerican.com/article/when-the-minds-eye-is-blind1/.

Cotard, J. (1882). Du delire des negations. *Archives de Neurologie, 4*, 152–170; 282–296.
    (1884). Perte de la vision mentale dans la melancolie anxieuse. *Archives de Neurologie, 7*, 289–295.

D'Aloisio-Montilla, N. (2017). Imagery and Overflow: We See More than We Report. *Philosophical Psychology, 30*(5), 545–570.

Daselaar, S. M., Porat, Y., Huijbers, W., and Pennartz, C. M. (2010). Modality-Specific and Modality-Independent Components of the Human Imagery System. *Neuroimage, 52*(2), 677–685.

de Araujo, D. B., Ribeiro, S., Cecchi, G. A., et al. (2012). Seeing with the Eyes Shut: Neural Basis of Enhanced Imagery following Ayahuasca Ingestion. *Human Brain Mapping, 33*(11), 2550–2560.

de Borst, A. W., Sack, A. T., Jansma, B. M., et al. (2012). Integration of "What" and "Where" in Frontal Cortex during Visual Imagery of Scenes. *Neuroimage, 60*(1), 47–58.

de Vito, S., and Bartolomeo, P. (2016). Refusing to Imagine? On the Possibility of Psychogenic Aphantasia. A Commentary on Zeman et al. (2015). *Cortex, 74*, 334–335.

Dunbar, R. (2004). *The Human Story: A New History of Mankind's Evolution*. London, UK: Faber and Faber.

Eddy, J. K., and Glass, A. L. (1981). Reading and Listening to High and Low Imagery Sentences. *Journal of Verbal Learning and Verbal Behavior, 20*(3), 333–345.

Farah, M. J. (1984). The Neurological Basis of Mental Imagery: A Componential Analysis. *Cognition, 18*, 245–272.

Faw, B. (2009). Conflicting Intuitions May Be Based on Differing Abilities – Evidence from Mental Imaging Research. *Journal of Consciousness Studies, 16*, 45–68.

Fulford, J., Milton, F., Salas, D., et al. (2018). The Neural Correlates of Visual Imagery Vividness – An fMRI Study and Literature Review. *Cortex, 105*, 26–40.

Galton, F. (1880). Statistics of Mental Imagery. *Mind, 5*, 301–318.

Gardini, S., Concari, L., Pagliara, S., et al. (2011). Visuo-Spatial Imagery Impairment in Posterior Cortical Atrophy: A Cognitive and SPECT Study. *Behavioural Neurology, 24*(2), 123–132.

Gardini, S., Cornoldi, C., De, B. R., and Venneri, A. (2006). Left Mediotemporal Structures Mediate the Retrieval of Episodic Autobiographical Mental Images. *Neuroimage, 30*(2), 645–655.

Gilboa, A., Winocur, G., Grady, C. L., Hevenor, S. J., and Moscovitch, M. (2004). Remembering our Past: Functional Neuroanatomy of Recollection of Recent and Very Remote Personal Events. *Cerebral Cortex, 14*(11), 1214–1225.

Greenberg, D. L., and Knowlton, B. J. (2014). The Role of Visual Imagery in Autobiographical Memory. *Memory and Cognition, 42*(6), 922–934.

Grüter, T., and Carbon, C. C. (2010). Escaping Attention. *Science, 328*(5977), 435–436.

Grüter, T., Grüter, M., Bell, V., and Carbon, C. C. (2009). Visual Mental Imagery in Congenital Prosopagnosia. *Neuroscience Letters, 453*(3), 135–140.

Guillot, A., Collet, C., Nguyen, V. A., et al. (2008). Functional Neuroanatomical Networks Associated with Expertise in Motor Imagery. *Neuroimage, 41*(4), 1471–1483.

Jacobs, C., Schwarzkopf, D. S., and Silvanto, J. (2018). Visual Working Memory Performance in Aphantasia. *Cortex, 105*, 61–73.

Keogh, R., Bergmann, J., and Pearson, J. (2016). Cortical Excitability Controls the Strength of Mental Imagery. *BioRxiv. org.* doi.org/10.1101/093690.

Keogh, R., and Pearson, J. (2018). The Blind Mind: No Sensory Visual Imagery in Aphantasia. *Cortex, 105*, 53–60.

Lambert, M. V., Senior, C., Phillips, M. L., et al. (2001). Visual Imagery and Depersonalisation. *Psychopathology, 34*(5), 259–264.

Lorey, B., Pilgramm, S., Bischoff, M., et al. (2011). Activation of the Parieto-Premotor Network Is Associated with Vivid Motor Imagery – A Parametric FMRI Study. *PLoS. One, 6*(5), e20368.

MacKisack, M., Aldworth, S., Macpherson, F., et al. (2016). On Picturing a Candle: The Prehistory of Imagery Science. *Frontiers in Psychology, 7*, 515.

McKelvie, S. (1995). The VVIQ as a Psychometric Test of Individual Differences in Visual Imagery Vividness: A Critical Quantitative Review and Plea for Direction. *Journal of Mental Imagery, 19*, 1–106.

Miller, L. (2017). *All Things New*. Los Angeles, CA: Three Saints Press.

Milton, F., Muhlert, N., Butler, C. R., Benattayallah, A., and Zeman, A. Z. (2011). The Neural Correlates of Everyday Recognition Memory. *Brain and Cognition, 76*(3), 369–381.

Moro, V., Berlucchi, G., Lerch, J., Tomaiuolo, F., and Aglioti, S. M. (2008). Selective Deficit of Mental Visual Imagery with Intact Primary Visual Cortex and Visual Perception. *Cortex, 44*(2), 109–118.

Nielsen, J. (1946). *Agnosia, Apraxia, Aphasia: Their Value in Cerebral Localisation*. 2nd edition. New York, NY: Hoeber.

Palmiero, M., Belardinelli, M. O., Nardo, D., et al. (2009). Mental Imagery Generation in Different Modalities Activates Sensory-Motor Areas. *Cognitive Processing, 10* (Suppl 2), S268–271.

Pearson, J., Clifford, C. W., and Tong, F. (2008). The Functional Impact of Mental Imagery on Conscious Perception. *Current Biology, 18*(13), 982–986.

Pearson, J., Rademaker, R. L., and Tong, F. (2011). Evaluating the Mind's Eye: The Metacognition of Visual Imagery. *Psychological Science, 22*(12), 1535–1542.

Phillips, M. L., Medford, N., Senior, C., et al. (2001). Depersonalization Disorder: Thinking without Feeling. *Psychiatry Research, 108*(3), 145–160.

Reisberg, D., Pearson, D. G., and Kosslyn, S. M. (2003). Intuitions and Introspections about Imagery: The Role of Imagery Experience in Shaping an Investigator's Theoretical Views. *Applied Cognitive Psychology, 17*, 147–160.

Ross, B. (2016). Aphantasia: How It Feels To Be Blind in your Mind. www.facebook.com/notes/blake-ross/aphantasia-how-it-feels-to-be-blind-in-your-mind/10156834777480504/.

Rubin, D. C., and Greenberg, D. L. (1998). Visual Memory-Deficit Amnesia: A Distinct Amnesic Presentation and Etiology. *Proceedings of the National Academy of Sciences of the United States of America, 95*(9), 5413–5416.

Servos, P., and Goodale, M. A. (1995). Preserved Visual Imagery in Visual Form Agnosia. *Neuropsychologia, 33*, 1383–1394.

Shuren, J. E., Brott, T. G., Schefft, B. K., and Houston, W. (1996). Preserved Colour Imagery in an Achromatopsic. *Neuropsychologia, 34*, 485–489.

Solms, M. (2009). *The Neuropsychology of Dreams*. New York, NY: Psychology Press.

Watkins, N. W. (2017). (A)phantasia and SDAM: Scientific and Personal Perspectives. psyarxiv.com/d7av9/.

Winlove, C. I. P., Milton, F., Ranson, J., et al. (2018). The Neural Correlates of Visual Imagery: A Co-ordinate-Based Meta-Analysis. *Cortex, 105*, 4–25.

Zago, S., Allegri, N., Cristoffanini, M., et al. (2011). Is the Charcot and Bernard Case (1883) of Loss of Visual Imagery Really Based on Neurological Impairment? *Cognitive Neuropsychiatry, 16*(6), 481–504.

Zatorre, R. J., Halpern, A. R., and Bouffard, M. (2010). Mental Reversal of Imagined Melodies: A Role for the Posterior Parietal Cortex. *Journal of Cognitive Neuroscience, 22*(4), 775–789.

Zeman, A., Dewar, M., and Della Sala, S. (2015). Lives without Imagery – Congenital Aphantasia. *Cortex, 73*, 378–380.

  (2016). Reflections on Aphantasia. *Cortex, 74*, 336–337.

Zeman, A. Z., Della Sala, S., Torrens, L. A., et al. (2010). Loss of Imagery Phenomenology with Intact Visuo-Spatial Task Performance: A Case of "Blind Imagination". *Neuropsychologia, 48*(1), 145–155.

Zimmer, C. (2010). The Brain. *Discover*, 28–29.

Zmigrod, L., Garrison, J. R., Carr, J., and Simons, J. S. (2016). The Neural Mechanisms of Hallucinations: A Quantitative Meta-Analysis of Neuroimaging Studies. *Neuroscience & Biobehavioral Reviews, 69*, 113–123.

Zvyagintsev, M., Clemens, B., Chechko, N., et al. (2013). Brain Networks Underlying Mental Imagery of Auditory and Visual Information. *The European Journal of Neuroscience, 37*(9), 1421–1434.

43 Hypnosis and Imagination

Devin B. Terhune and David A. Oakley

In the late eighteenth century, the French government commissioned an inquiry into *animal magnetism*, a historical precursor to hypnosis (Gauld, 1992). Animal magnetism consisted of a set of practices that purportedly enabled practitioners to heal individuals through the transmission of a universal magnetic fluid that would pass from a practitioner's body to the individual. The inquiry, directed by Benjamin Franklin, performed some of the first double-blind experiments in the modern era and observed that positive responses to treatment were associated with the *suggestion* that one had received the treatment, rather than whether one had actually received the treatment. It was concluded that the effects of animal magnetism were attributable to *imagination* (Franklin et al., 2002). Although in contemporary parlance the mechanism underlying such effects would be viewed as a confluence of suggestion, response expectancies, and/or demand characteristics (e.g. Lynn, Kirsch, and Hallquist, 2008), imagination continues to be closely associated with hypnosis and viewed as a germane phenomenon or one that may exert a mechanistic influence in hypnotic phenomena.

In this chapter we aim to synthesize contemporary knowledge of the relations between hypnosis and imagination. Following a brief overview of hypnosis and hypnotic suggestibility, we describe various lines of research pertaining to whether and how hypnosis may relate to imagination, understood as the process of forming images, or the ability to do so. In particular, we consider how imagery abilities may relate to hypnotic suggestibility, how imagery may spontaneously manifest in the context of hypnosis, and to what extent response to hypnotic suggestion recruits imagery-specific mechanisms. We also draw a distinction between voluntary and involuntary processes in imagery. Subsequently, we review research pertaining to whether hypnotic suggestion shares overlapping neurophysiological substrates with imagination and how imagery can be incorporated into clinical applications of hypnosis. We conclude by highlighting outstanding questions and specifying future directions for research in these domains. Our overarching conclusion is that hypnosis and imagination represent distinct phenomena.

Hypnosis and Hypnotic Suggestibility

Hypnosis is most parsimoniously conceptualized as a set of techniques involving the use of verbal suggestion to produce changes in behavior and awareness. A session typically begins with an induction; inductions vary considerably but most consist of instructions and suggestions for relaxation and reduced meta-awareness. The utility of an induction, in terms of its effect on suggestibility, differs based on the mode of assessment as well as the individual respondent, with the sources of this variability poorly understood (Terhune and Cardeña, 2016). However, there is broad agreement that the induction functions as a sociocultural ritual and capitalizes on perceptions of hypnosis as a method for modulating awareness. Following an induction, individuals frequently report spontaneous changes in different experiential dimensions including time perception, body image, and imagery (Pekala and Kumar, 2007). Although poorly understood, these effects seem to be driven by a confluence of beliefs, expectations, contextual factors, and suggestibility (Cardeña and Terhune, 2019).

Following the induction, an experimenter or clinician will administer one or more suggestions for alterations in awareness and concomitant changes in behavior (Kirsch and Lynn, 1995). *Suggestions* are communications for involuntary experiences (Kirsch, 1999): They are phrased as something that *happens* to an individual as opposed to something that they willfully *perform*, so as to augment the extra-volitional phenomenology of the suggested response (Spanos and Gorassini, 1984). Suggestions can be used to modulate a range of motor, cognitive, and perceptual functions and broadly fall into two classes: *Facilitative* suggestions are those for a motor response or positive cognitive or perceptual state whereas *inhibitory* suggestions are those for the disruption of such responses. Factor analyses of standardized scales indicate that response to suggestions is subserved by both a core latent trait of *hypnotic suggestibility* and ancillary componential traits related to responsiveness to specific suggestions (Woody and Barnier, 2008).

It has long been known that members of the general population exhibit marked variability in hypnotic suggestibility (Laurence, Beaulieu-Prévost, and du Chéné, 2008) and it is widely accepted that individual differences in hypnotic suggestibility represent the principal moderator of responsiveness to hypnotic interventions. Hypnotic suggestibility can be reliably measured using work-sample assessments in which an induction is followed by a set of suggestions and tests of responsiveness (Woody and Barnier, 2008). Approximately 10–15 percent of the population display low hypnotic suggestibility, another 10–15 percent display high hypnotic suggestibility, and the remaining 70–80 percent display a modest level of hypnotic suggestibility. Twin studies strongly suggest that hypnotic suggestibility is heritable (Morgan, 1973) although its genetic basis is poorly understood (Rominger et al., 2014). Evidence suggests that hypnotic suggestibility peaks in pre-adolescence, subsequently declines, and plateaus in late adolescence (Rhue, 2004) with high stability in adulthood (Piccione, Hilgard, and Zimbardo, 1989). The sources of developmental changes are unknown but may relate to changes in imagination and fantasizing (e.g. Rhue, 2004) or the development of the prefrontal cortex and corresponding (meta)cognitive functions (Terhune et al., 2017). Multiple lines of evidence point to heterogeneity among highly suggestible individuals, which may be accounted for by the presence of two subtypes (Carlson and Putnam, 1989): a *dissociative subtype*, characterized by increased involuntariness during response to suggestion and an *imagery* subtype, characterized by superior imagery (King and Council, 1998; Terhune, Cardeña, and Lindgren, 2011).

The principal phenomenological feature of response to hypnotic suggestion is an attenuation in the *sense of agency*, the cognitive attribution that one is the author of one's actions and experiences (Haggard, 2017). Distorted volition is so prominent during hypnotic responding that it has come to be referred to as the *classic suggestion effect* (Weitzenhoffer, 1974). In turn, the absence of involuntariness during response to suggestion is widely viewed as indicative of *compliance* and is not considered a hypnotic response (Bowers, Laurence, and Hart, 1988) – a positive response to a suggestion is only considered as reflective of a genuine response if it is accompanied by a reduction in the sense of agency. This attenuation covaries with hypnotic suggestibility such that highly suggestible individuals experience less agency when responding to suggestions (Polito et al., 2014). Although inherently subjective, these alterations have been corroborated with implicit perceptual measures of the sense of agency, such as *intentional binding*, the perceived temporal contraction of the duration between actions and their consequences (Moore and Obhi, 2012). In particular, recent research found that highly suggestible individuals exhibited *less* intentional binding during response to suggestion (Lush et al., 2017).

Despite significant advances in recent years, current understanding of the mechanisms underlying response to suggestion remains poor. One promising line of research is the proposal that responses to suggestion are implemented through normal cognitive control mechanisms but in the absence of awareness that control is being implemented (Dienes and Perner, 2007). For example, while top-down mechanisms may enable the suppression of pain in response to an analgesia suggestion, the individual remains unaware of this and experiences the concomitant analgesic response as extra-volitional. In support of this account, recent studies have demonstrated that highly suggestible individuals have *delayed* awareness of intentions and *impaired* metacognition pertaining to their sense of agency (Lush, Naish, and Dienes, 2016; Terhune and Hedman, 2017). An outstanding question, though, is how control is implemented in this account (Terhune, 2012): How are some highly suggestible individuals able to exercise such remarkable feats of top-down regulation such as complete analgesia? One possibility is that response to suggestion is facilitated by superior cognitive control. However, there is no robust evidence for superior control in this population at baseline (e.g. Varga, Nemeth, and Szekely, 2011), although some research hints at different brain activation patterns during selective attention in highly suggestible participants relative to controls (Cojan, Piguet, and Vuilleumier, 2015). Whether and to what extent such effects facilitate response to suggestion is unknown.

A perennial question is where hypnosis falls within the broader domain of suggestion and suggestibility, and whether the various phenomena linked under this term can be encapsulated within a broader category such as *direct verbal suggestibility* (Halligan and Oakley, 2014; Oakley and Halligan, 2017). Although it is conceptually appealing to consider hypnosis as a member of a broader class, the evidence that these different phenomena form a single homogeneous category is mixed. Hypnotic suggestibility covaries moderately to highly with non-hypnotic suggestibility when the measures are functionally equivalent and administered in the same context (Braffman and Kirsch, 1999). Other studies have revealed smaller, or nonsignificant, effects when the measures differ more considerably (Tasso and Perez, 2008). Similarly, there is mixed evidence regarding the relationship between hypnotic suggestibility and placebo responsiveness (e.g. Raz, 2007), which similarly depends in part on suggestion. These studies suggest a relationship between hypnotic suggestibility and non-hypnotic forms of suggestibility although the magnitude of such covariance is unclear and subject to moderators that have yet to be properly elucidated.

Imagination and Hypnotic Suggestibility

Response to suggestion involves the generation of representational states that can effect pronounced changes in behavior and thus it is plausible that imagination is used in the production of these representations. Here we take *imagery* to reflect a percept-like mental state in the absence of a corresponding sensory stimulus and *imagination* as the ability to voluntarily generate or manipulate imagery for task-specific goals. Hypnosis and suggestion-based phenomena are widely referred to as *imaginative* (e.g. Kihlstrom, 2008) and standardized behavioral measures of non-hypnotic suggestibility, which are otherwise identical to hypnotic suggestibility scales but without an induction, are often referred to as indices of *imaginative suggestibility* (Braffman and Kirsch, 1999). A corollary of the assumption that imagination is involved in hypnosis is that highly suggestible individuals should display superior imagery abilities.

There is broad evidence that highly suggestible individuals score higher on psychometric measures indexing the propensity for *spontaneous* imaginative experiences in one's daily life (for a review, see Cardeña and Terhune, 2014). For example, they reliably score higher on measures of *absorption*, the propensity for experiencing all-encompassing states in which one's attention is consumed by some type of activity (e.g. Roche and McConkey, 1990). They also often report greater vividness of mental imagery (e.g. Marucci and Meo, 2000), imaginative involvement (Glisky et al., 1991), fantasy-proneness (e.g. Braffman and Kirsch, 1999), and use of an imagic cognitive style (Sheehan and Robertson, 1996), although some studies report mixed or nonsignificant results (e.g. Kogon et al., 1998). Similarly, highly suggestible individuals reliably experience greater *spontaneous* imagery in response to an induction (Pekala and Kumar, 2007) and imaginative involvement and absorption during stimulus exposure (e.g. (Maxwell, Lynn, and Condon, 2015). Multiple studies also suggest an association between suggestibility and the capacity to become immersed in a dramatic role (Panero et al., 2016; Sarbin and Lim, 1963).

Despite these consistencies, these effects tend to be modest in size and are subject to interpretational debate. They could be artifactual owing to a context-based administration effect: Correlations between self-report measures are often higher when measured in the same context (Council, Kirsch, and Grant, 1996). Insofar as highly suggestible individuals may be more responsive to contextual cues (e.g. Marucci and

Meo, 2000), this criticism should be considered although there is as yet no consensus on what constitutes a *suitable* context (Barnier and McConkey, 1999). Similarly, these relationships may be inflated by the explicit invocation of imagination on certain suggestions on some suggestibility scales (Woody and Barnier, 2008). A further consideration is whether these effects reflect greater imaginative involvement or a generalized propensity for alterations in awareness (Cardeña and Terhune, 2014). For example, absorption covaries with the tendency to have anomalous perceptual states in a variety of contexts (e.g. Granqvist et al., 2005); possessing the foregoing constellation of characteristics may render one prone to liminal experiential states that are easily shaped by environmental cues and suggestions. Moreover, aside from a few studies (e.g. Sarbin and Lim, 1963), extant studies provide little information regarding the extent to which highly suggestible individuals possess the capacity to *control* imaginative episodes, a theoretical requirement for any account proposing a role for imagination in hypnotic responding.

The latter criticism can be addressed by the administration of cognitive tasks requiring the use of visual imagery. Research studies pursuing such an approach suggest a complex relationship between hypnotic suggestibility and imagery. Multiple studies have reported that highly suggestible individuals display superior performance on visual imagery tasks (Sheehan and Robertson, 1996). However, these effects are not reliably observed (e.g. Carli et al., 2007) and may be nonlinear. In particular, imagination might not be a strong correlate of hypnotic suggestibility but poor imagery may be a marker of *low* hypnotic suggestibility (Sheehan and Robertson, 1996). Moreover, multiple studies suggest the presence of an imagery subtype among highly suggestible individuals (Wallace, Allen, and Propper, 1996), which appears to be distinct from the dissociative subtype (Terhune, Cardeña, and Lindgren, 2011).

Research in this domain has traditionally focused on visual imagery but there is good reason to question this somewhat myopic orientation. The suggestions on hypnotic suggestibility measures mostly target motor and somatosensory systems, such as the perceptions that one's arm is paralyzed or incredibly heavy, respectively (Woody and Barnier, 2008), thereby warranting greater consideration of these domains. In recent years, a number of studies have pursued such an approach and indicate that highly suggestible individuals may have superior imagery pertaining to the body. An early study found that hypnotic suggestibility was associated with greater vividness of motor imagery (Glisky, Tataryn, and Kihlstrom, 1995) and multiple laboratory studies suggest that highly suggestible individuals have superior kinesthetic, tactile, and pain imagery than low suggestible controls (for a recent review, see Srzich et al., 2016). However, nearly all of these studies used an *extreme groups design*, in which low suggestible individuals (who are not representative of the general population) acted as controls (Lynn et al., 2007), and thus these apparent differences should be interpreted cautiously (discussed further below).

Further research on imagery abilities in highly suggestible individuals will benefit from using more rigorous measures of imagery and adhering to double-blind protocols. Many older studies used cognitive tasks for which the interpretation of performance is ambiguous (for a review, see Sheehan and Robertson, 1996). Many also relied solely on self-report measures that may be more easily influenced by demand characteristics and may also be poor indices of actual imagery ability (Srzich et al., 2016). Moreover, few studies have adhered to double-blind protocols. The use of double-blind experiments is nearly universally valuable and is essential with highly suggestible individuals who may display hypersensitivity to environmental cues that could function as suggestions (Marucci and Meo, 2000). This implies a strong potential for artifactually superior imagery performance among the highly suggestible individuals in unmasked experiments – it will be imperative for future research to more stringently control for these effects. A final concern with extant studies is an overreliance on extreme-groups designs contrasting high with low suggestible individuals (Lynn et al., 2007). This design is problematic because the latter represent an atypical subset (~10–15 percent) of the population. Any studies showing *superior* imagery among highly suggestible individuals may merely reflect *inferior* imagery among low suggestible individuals. Medium suggestible individuals, are a superior control group, especially if low suggestible individuals have poorer imagery (Sheehan and Robertson, 1996).

A more refined understanding of the relations between hypnotic suggestibility and imagination may be developed by considering this association through the lens of the phenomenology of hypnosis. Insofar as distorted volition represents the primary signature of hypnotic responding (Bowers, 1981), it is important to distinguish between *voluntary* and *involuntary* imagery, namely the generation and manipulation of imagery (imagination) vs. the experience of *intrusive* images. Response to suggestion may share more in common with the latter. Indeed, research has shown that the experience of involuntary goal-directed imagery is associated with response to suggestion whereas voluntary goal-directed imagery may impede responsiveness (Comey and Kirsch, 1999). By contrast, one might argue that elevated absorption among highly suggestible individuals reflects a learned capacity to voluntarily use fantasy for psychological protection during exposure to stressful life events (Wilson and Barber, 1983). However, absorption may reflect an automatic dissociative coping response to stress or a nonpathological form of perseveration (Jamieson and Woody, 2007) rather than a manifestation of the higher-order control of imagery. Preliminary evidence hints that highly suggestible individuals are more likely to experience intrusive thoughts (and potentially imagery) (Bryant and Idey, 2001) (see also Terhune and Cardeña, 2015). One parsimonious way to integrate these data is that the imagery subtype will display superior voluntary imagery (Terhune, Cardeña, and Lindgren, 2011; Wallace, Allen, and Propper, 1996), whereas the highly suggestible dissociative subtype will display more involuntary imagery, although we suspect that the relations among these variables will probably be far more complex. Nevertheless, future research may benefit from coupling cognitive tasks indexing imagination with recent methods for studying intrusive imagery in the laboratory (Lau-Zhu, Holmes, and Porcheret, 2018).

Imagination and Hypnotic Responding

Here we consider the question of whether – and, if so, how – imagination plays a role in response to hypnotic suggestions. Before doing so, it is important to distinguish two mechanistic paths through which imagination might influence hypnotic responding. On the one hand, response to suggestion could be considered to be fundamentally an imaginative phenomenon in which one explicitly uses imagery to facilitate response to suggestion. On the other hand, imagination may be recruited while responding to suggestion, or in response to specific suggestions as part of a broader mechanistic sequence, but not be a central driving mechanism that enables hypnotic responding. Here we examine whether imagery ability confers any benefits in responsiveness to hypnotic suggestions and whether imagery plays a causal role in hypnotic responding.

Little attention has been devoted to the specific question of whether imaginative ability is specifically linked to superior hypnotic responding and the available evidence is mixed. For example, when comparing imagery and dissociative subtypes of highly suggestible individuals (Terhune, Cardeña, and Lindgren, 2011), the former were *less* responsive than the latter to hallucination suggestions, even though these suggestions might be expected to involve the recruitment of imagery. Another study showed that participants who were responsive to a false memory suggestion displayed lower scores on a measure of imagic cognitive style than those who were less responsive, even though this style was positively and linearly related to hypnotic suggestibility (Sheehan and Robertson, 1996). By contrast, some studies have reported that imagery ability correlates with responsiveness to specific suggestions (Laurence, Beaulieu–Prévost, and du Chéné, 2008) and that responsiveness to hypnotic suggestions is associated with greater vividness of suggested imagery (Spanos, Stenstrom, and Johnston, 1988). On the whole, these studies hint at a possible role for imagery in hypnotic responding but this evidence is correlational.

Multiple studies that have examined the utilization of imagery strategies during hypnotic responding present a clearer picture and suggest that imagination does not play a causal role in facilitating response to suggestion. Perhaps the most damning evidence against a role for voluntary imagery in hypnotic responding is provided by a study on hypnotic analgesia in highly suggestible participants (Hargadon, Bowers, and Woody, 1995). Hargadon and colleagues contrasted two procedures involving the prescription or proscription of the use of counter-pain imagery during hypnotic analgesia and observed that the two were essentially equally effective in reducing pain relative to baseline. This strongly suggests that the *intentional* use of imagery does not augment hypnotic responding. These results are further corroborated by studies suggesting that goal-directed imagery during hypnotic responding does not facilitate response to suggestion and may even impede responsiveness (e.g. Comey and Kirsch, 1999). Moreover, mental representations associated with pain reduction in the aforementioned study (Hargadon, Bowers, and Woody, 1995) were actually associated with pain reduction to a greater extent when they were experienced as *involuntary* rather than as *active* strategies, again highlighting how imagination does not provide an added advantage in hypnotic responding.

There are multiple competing ways of reconciling the foregoing results with the research described above (see Imagination and Hypnotic Suggestibility) which seems to point to superior imagery among highly suggestible individuals. First, imagery may be correlated with hypnotic suggestibility but *epiphenomenal* in the context of hypnotic responding. That is, superior imagery may be part of the broader neurocognitive profile of high hypnotic suggestibility but not play a causal role in response to suggestion. Second, imagery may only be beneficial, and play a mechanistic role, in some individuals, which is broadly consistent with evidence for an imagery subtype and variability in strategy use among highly suggestible individuals (e.g. Terhune, Cardeña, and Lindgren, 2011). Although Hargadon and colleagues' (Hargadon, Bowers, and Woody, 1995) study considered variability in imagery during hypnotic responding, they did not investigate whether imagery in hypnotic responding was moderated by subtype. Third, insofar as response to different types of suggestions may represent partially distinct componential abilities (Woody and Barnier, 2008), it is possible that imagery is utilized in only certain types of suggestions. For example, motor imagery and motor suppression imagery may predict responsiveness to facilitative and inhibitory motor suggestions, respectively (Srzich et al., 2016). A final possibility, alluded to above, is that response to suggestion is facilitated by imagery, but its strategic use is implemented outside of awareness. According to this account, voluntary imagery during hypnotic responding is epiphenomenal or even counterproductive in effecting hypnotic responding but involuntary, suggestion-mediated, imagery plays a mechanistic role.

Neuroimaging of Imagination and Suggestion in Hypnosis

Perhaps the most robust assessment of the role of imagery in hypnosis is afforded through neuroimaging studies that address the last of the above possibilities, namely whether voluntary imagery (related to imagination) and involuntary imagery (related to suggestion) have overlapping neurophysiological substrates. In a study of pain, researchers used fMRI (functional Magnetic Resonance Imaging) to explore brain activity in three conditions in highly suggestible participants (all following a hypnotic induction) (Derbyshire et al., 2004). In two of the conditions participants were given the suggestion that, following a cue, a painful heat stimulus would be delivered to their right hand. In one, the heat stimulus was administered, creating an actual pain experience, whereas in the second the cue was not followed by the stimulus and acted as a suggestion to experience pain. In the third condition, the participants were told that there would be no pain stimulus following the cue but that they should "imagine the pain as clearly as possible." Pain ratings taken after each trial demonstrated that the participants experienced pain in the first two conditions (physically induced and suggestion-induced pain). In addition, they confirmed that they imagined pain clearly in the third condition. The fMRI data showed activation of pain-related areas in the first two conditions but not in the imagined condition. A similar study using PET (Positron Emission Tomography) compared patterns of brain activation during real, imagined, and suggested (hallucinated) auditory experiences in highly suggestible participants following a hypnotic induction and found activity in auditory cortex in the real and the suggested conditions but not in the imagined condition (Szechtman et al., 1998). Other studies have yielded similar results (for a review, see Oakley and Halligan, 2013).

These studies suggest that imagination and hypnotic suggestion engage different neurophysiological substrates, thereby providing further corroboration for the self-report and behavioral studies described in previous sections. That is, there seems to be a clear difference between simply imagining an experience and having what is essentially an "as-real" experience in response to a hypnotic suggestion. Indeed, the overlap between activation patterns of real perceptual states and suggested experiences strongly suggests that hypnotic experiences more closely resemble perceptual than imaginative states. Moreover, both studies demonstrate that brain changes corresponding to real, physical events can be generated by psychological processes, such as suggestion, and resulting experiences are not simply products of the individual's voluntary imagination (Oakley and Halligan, 2013). Nevertheless, one line of criticism of these studies is that imagination and suggestion conditions have not always been properly matched for wording, and participants' response expectancies (Braffman and Kirsch, 1999). Moreover, none of these studies have controlled for the possibility that highly suggestible individuals merely "held back" in the imagination conditions due to demand characteristics and the concomitant belief that they should be less responsive in the imagination conditions (Spanos, 1986). Nevertheless, these studies provide the most compelling demonstration yet that suggested responses are implemented through distinct mechanisms from those involved in imagination. These and other studies are also relevant to the long-standing question of whether clinical symptoms of functional neurological disorders (historically referred to as hysteria or conversion disorder) with no obvious clinical cause can be dismissed as *simply* imaginary or indicative of malingering (Oakley, 2012; Oakley et al., 2003). With the increasing accessibility of neuroimaging techniques to clinical and psychological research it became possible to explore brain changes that might accompany such symptoms.

Early single-case studies of medically unexplained (hysterical) and hypnotically suggested left-sided paralysis found that failure to move the leg when requested to do so was accompanied by brain activity typically associated with the inhibition of voluntary motor responding (Halligan et al., 2000). The remaining possibility that the failure to move was simulated was addressed in a subsequent PET study (Ward et al., 2003) involving a groups of participants who received instructions to move their leg following a left-sided paralysis suggestion or while simulating the same paralysis (both following a hypnotic induction). No leg movements were seen in either condition and an independent examination of participants revealed no differences between them. The participants, however, rated the involuntariness of their failure to move in the suggested paralysis condition as substantially higher than in the simulation condition. The PET data also showed a clear difference in brain activity between the two conditions, consistent with the view that participants *cannot*, rather than *will not*, move their leg. Overall, these results support the view that hypnotically suggested paralysis, in common with conversion disorder paralysis, is experienced as real rather than being imaginary and under voluntary control (see also Srzich et al., 2016; Vuilleumier, 2014).

More recent research has used fMRI to explore further the neural basis of suggested limb paralysis (Deeley et al., 2013) and other psychiatric and cultural experiences that are reported as occurring involuntarily such as spirit possession and alien control as well as automatic writing and thought insertion (Walsh et al., 2015). These studies have shown that these phenomena are accompanied by subjective reports and brain activity that are consistent with their status as involuntary experiences rather than voluntarily imagined events. Based on this evidence, hypnotic experiences have been characterized as socially driven role-plays or strategic enactments, orchestrated outside awareness in response to a direct verbal suggestion and involving the creation of neural activity consistent with the suggested change (Oakley and Halligan, 2009, 2013, 2017).

Clinical Applications of Imagery in Hypnosis

Voluntary imagery is commonly used to explore past and future events and situations in psychological therapies. Using hypnotic suggestion to create what we have labeled "involuntary imagery" in the form of "as real" experiences, however, raises the possibility of taking that process a step further by facilitating a virtual reality context within which to experience and to resolve psychological problems. Though the empirical evidence is not extensive (Moore and Tasso, 2008), an influential meta-analysis of eighteen studies that compared the outcome of Cognitive Behavioral Therapy (CBT) with and without hypnosis over a wide range of psychological symptoms concluded that the inclusion of hypnosis procedures enhanced outcomes for more than 70 percent of patients (Kirsch, Montgomery, and Sapirstein, 1995). Similarly, in a review of randomized controlled studies, the adjunctive use of hypnosis was found to produce better outcomes in the treatment of a range of pain conditions than other treatments (Patterson and Jensen, 2003). There is also good evidence from case studies (Walters and Oakley, 2006) and randomized control trials (Gonsalkorale et al., 2003; Whorwell, Prior, and Faragher, 1984) for the greater efficacy of behavioral therapy when combined with hypnotically suggested gut-directed imagery in treating irritable bowel syndrome.

As an example, patients can be taught techniques to control their pain using hypnotically suggested imagery that they can then use later for themselves with or without hypnosis. In an fMRI study addressing the efficacy of this procedure, fibromyalgia patients were shown, prior to the experimental session, a diagram of a pain dial that was used to represent their level of pain while receiving hypnotic suggestions to increase or decrease dial ratings to modulate their pain (Derbyshire, Whalley, and Oakley, 2009). During the scanning sessions, the patients were asked to bring the dial to mind and use it to increase or decrease their pain both with and without a hypnotic induction (the order of these conditions was counterbalanced across groups). The patients reported significant changes in their pain experience in both conditions though they reported a feeling of being more in control, with greater reduction in their pain in the hypnosis condition. In the two conditions the reported pain changes were reflected in appropriate reductions or increases in brain activity in areas associated with the pain *neuromatrix*. In actual clinical practice, patients are encouraged to rehearse and strengthen the pain dial effect by rehearsing it in self-hypnosis.

A number of effective psychological procedures for the treatment of phobias involve exposure to the feared object or situation while practicing anxiety reduction procedures. Ideally this is carried out *in vivo*, though this is often impractical – with live spiders, for example, or where the fear is associated with heights. Simply imagining the situation is only partially effective. In our own clnical experience, however, the virtual reality aspect of hypnotically suggested scenarios can quickly and flexibly create an *in vivo* experience in the clinic without the need for expensive equipment and individualized programming of real scenarios from a client's past, which is required by computerized alternatives (see below). Imagined spiders are typically perceived by clients to "not be real" and in practice real spiders are uncontrollable. In contrast, hypnotically suggested spiders are not only perceived as being real but with appropriate additional suggestions, including client-originated self-suggestions, can be rendered "obedient" and can change location, shape, size, or physical appearance as well as take on less threatening "personal" characteristics.

One of our own case studies combined progressive desensitization and hypnotic suggestion in a participant with an environmental phobia, which had affected all parts of her life at home and in her workplace whenever it was windy (Walters and Oakley, 2003). In particular, she reported that the musical sound of a familiar fountain she had re-experienced in hypnosis evoked calming and reassuring feelings and was subsequently able to use that association to control her fear of the wind. She lived on a houseboat and had a particular anxiety watching an elder tree with its branches moving dangerously in the wind. Re-experiencing the tree's movement in the context of hypnosis as one of "dancing to the trickling sound" of her fountain (which spontaneously transformed to the more robust sounds of a waterfall) was instrumental in her overcoming her phobia. A clear conclusion drawn from this and similar clinical experiences, underpinned by the neuroimaging evidence describe above, is that in using hypnotic interventions in clinical practice the word *imagine* should be replaced with *experience* – suggestions evoking perceptual states seem to be more effective than instructions for the use of imagination.

Summary and Outstanding Questions

Despite the widespread view that hypnosis and imagination engage overlapping processes, the present review suggests that they are dissimilar phenomena. Multiple lines of evidence imply that hypnotic suggestibility may be associated with imagery vividness, or perhaps even imagery ability, although these effects may be nonlinear (Sheehan and Robertson, 1996). There is only weak evidence that imagery ability translates to superior hypnotic responding but this question has not been systematically investigated (Laurence, Beaulieu-Prévost, and du Chéné, 2008). Moreover, empirical studies measuring imagery during hypnotic responding suggest that the voluntary use of imagery does not seem to play a causal role in response to suggestion (Hargadon, Bowers, and

Woody, 1995) but this research does not rule out the possibility that responses are facilitated by the recruitment of imagery outside of awareness (involuntary imagery). The view that mental representations that are produced by voluntary acts of imagination are different from those resulting from hypnotic suggestion is further corroborated by neuroimaging research, which indicates that suggested and imagined states are associated with differential brain activation patterns (Oakley and Halligan, 2013). A similar picture emerges in the clinical application of hypnotic suggestion, which appears to be more effective than the use of imagination alone. Cumulatively, the available evidence suggests that responses to hypnotic suggestions among highly suggestible individuals are independent of imagery and imagination.

Despite our tentative conclusion that imagination and hypnotic suggestion are dissimilar processes, there are numerous outstanding questions with considerable theoretical import. Although hypnotic suggestion does not seem to rely on, or benefit, from suggestion-congruent imagery (Hargadon, Bowers, and Woody, 1995), whether different subtypes of highly suggestible individuals differentially utilize imagery during hypnotic responding has not yet been explored and will be valuable in coming to grips with heterogeneity in strategy utilization more generally. Similarly, the possibility that imagery may facilitate response to suggestions in modality-specific ways has not been afforded sufficient attention and may help in understanding the componential mechanisms that underlie response to suggestion (Woody and Barnier, 2008). Although research implies that imagination and suggestion have dissimilar neural correlates, these studies have not harnessed state-of-the-art methods for decoding overlapping recruitment of neural assemblies, such as multivariate pattern and representational similarity analyses (Haxby, Connolly, and Guntupalli, 2014). These methods will significantly advance understanding of the extent to which suggestion and imagination activate shared and distinct neural representations. Pursuing these and other avenues of research will help to strengthen our understanding of the similarities and dissimilarities between suggested experiences and imagination.

Acknowledgments

DBT acknowledges the support of bursary 70/16 from the Bial Foundation.

References

Barnier, A. J., and McConkey, K. M. (1999). Absorption, Hypnotizability and Context: Non-Hypnotic Contexts Are Not All the Same. *Contemporary Hypnosis*, *16*(1), 1–8.

Bowers, K. S. (1981). Do the Stanford Scales Tap the "Classic Suggestion Effect"? *International Journal of Clinical and Experimental Hypnosis*, *29*(1), 42–53.

Bowers, P., Laurence, J. R., and Hart, D. (1988). The Experience of Hypnotic Suggestions. *International Journal of Clinical and Experimental Hypnosis*, *36*(4), 336–349.

Braffman, W., and Kirsch, I. (1999). Imaginative Suggestibility and Hypnotizability: An Empirical Analysis. *Journal of Personality and Social Psychology*, 77(3), 578–587.

Bryant, R. A., and Idey, A. (2001). Intrusive Thoughts and Hypnotizability. *Contemporary Hypnosis*, 18(1), 14–20.

Cardeña, E., and Terhune, D. B. (2014). Hypnotizability, Personality Traits and the Propensity to Experience Alterations of Consciousness. *Psychology of Consciousness: Theory, Research, and Practice*, 1, 292–307.

Cardeña, E., and Terhune, D. B. (2019). The Roles of Response Expectancies, Baseline Experiences, and Hypnotizability in Spontaneous Hypnotic Experiences. *International Journal of Clinical and Experimental Hypnosis*, 67(1), 1–27.

Carli, G., Cavallaro, F. I., Rendo, C. A., and Santarcangelo, E. L. (2007). Imagery of Different Sensory Modalities: Hypnotizability and Body Sway. *Experimental Brain Research*, 179(2), 147–154.

Carlson, E. B., and Putnam, F. W. (1989). Integrating Research on Dissociation and Hypnotizability: Are There Two Pathways to Hypnotizability? *Dissociation*, 2, 32–38.

Cojan, Y., Piguet, C., and Vuilleumier, P. (2015). What Makes Your Brain Suggestible? Hypnotizability Is Associated with Differential Brain Activity during Attention outside Hypnosis. *Neuroimage*, 117, 367–374.

Comey, G., and Kirsch, I. (1999). Intentional and Spontaneous Imagery in Hypnosis: The Phenomenology of Hypnotic Responding. *International Journal of Clinical and Experimental Hypnosis*, 47(1), 65–85.

Council, J. R., Kirsch, I., and Grant, D. L. (1996). Imagination, Expectancy, and Hypnotic Responding. In R. G. Kunzendorf, N. P. Spanos, and B. Wallace (eds.), *Hypnosis and Imagination*. Amityville, NY: Baywood, 41–66.

Deeley, Q., Oakley, D. A., Toone, B., et al. (2013). The Functional Anatomy of Suggested Limb Paralysis. *Cortex*, 49(2), 411–422.

Derbyshire, S. W., Whalley, M. G., and Oakley, D. A. (2009). Fibromyalgia Pain and Its Modulation by Hypnotic and Non-Hypnotic Suggestion: An fMRI Analysis. *European Journal of Pain*, 13(5), 542–550.

Derbyshire, S. W., Whalley, M. G., Stenger, V. A., and Oakley, D. A. (2004). Cerebral Activation during Hypnotically Induced and Imagined Pain. *Neuroimage*, 23(1), 392–401.

Dienes, Z., and Perner, J. (2007). Executive Control without Conscious Awareness: The Cold Control Theory of Hypnosis. In G. A. Jamieson (ed.), *Hypnosis and Conscious States: The Cognitive Neuroscience Perspective*. Oxford, UK: Oxford University Press, 293–314.

Franklin, B., Majault, Le, Sallin, R., et al.(2002). Report of the Commissioners Charged by the King with the Examination of Animal Magnetism. 1784. *International Journal of Clinical and Experimental Hypnosis*, 50(4), 332–363.

Gauld, A. (1992). *A History of Hypnotism*. Cambridge, UK: Cambridge University Press.

Glisky, M. L., Tataryn, D. J., and Kihlstrom, J. F. (1995). Hypnotizability and Mental Imagery. *International Journal of Clinical and Experimental Hypnosis*, 43(1), 34–54.

Glisky, M. L., Tataryn, D. J., Tobias, B. A., Kihlstrom, J. F., and McConkey, K. M. (1991). Absorption, Openness to Experience, and Hypnotizability. *Journal of Personality and Social Psychology*, 60(2), 263–272.

Gonsalkorale, W. M., Miller, V., Afzal, A., and Whorwell, P. J. (2003). Long Term Benefits of Hypnotherapy for Irritable Bowel Syndrome. *Gut*, 52(11), 1623–1629.

Granqvist, P., Fredrikson, M., Unge, P., et al. (2005). Sensed Presence and Mystical Experiences Are Predicted by Suggestibility, Not by the Application of Transcranial Weak Complex Magnetic Fields. *Neuroscience Letters*, *379*(1), 1–6.

Haggard, P. (2017). Sense of Agency in the Human Brain. *Nature Reviews Neuroscience*, *18* (4), 196–207.

Halligan, P. W., Athwal, B. S., Oakley, D. A., and Frackowiak, R. S. (2000). Imaging Hypnotic Paralysis: Implications for Conversion Hysteria. *Lancet*, *355*(9208), 986–987.

Halligan, P. W., and Oakley, D. A. (2014). Hypnosis and Beyond: Exploring the Broader Domain of Suggestion. *Psychology of Consciousness: Theory, Research, and Practice*, *1*, 105–122.

Hargadon, R., Bowers, K. S., and Woody, E. Z. (1995). Does Counterpain Imagery Mediate Hypnotic Analgesia? *Journal of Abnormal Psychology*, *104*(3), 508–516.

Haxby, J. V., Connolly, A. C., and Guntupalli, J. S. (2014). Decoding Neural Representational Spaces using Multivariate Pattern Analysis. *Annual Review of Neuroscience*, *37*, 435–456.

Jamieson, G. A., and Woody, E. (2007). Dissociated Control as a Paradigm for Cognitive Neuroscience Research and Theorising in Hypnosis. In G. A. Jamieson (ed.), *Hypnosis and Conscious States: The Cognitive Neuroscience Perspective*. Oxford, UK: Oxford University Press, 111–129.

Kihlstrom, J. F. (2008). The Domain of Hypnosis, Revisited. In M. R. Nash and A. J. Barnier (eds.), *The Oxford Handbook of Hypnosis: Theory, Research and Practice*. Oxford, UK: Oxford University Press, 21–52.

King, B. J., and Council, J. R. (1998). Intentionality during Hypnosis: An Ironic Process Analysis. *International Journal of Clinical and Experimental Hypnosis*, *46*(3), 295–313.

Kirsch, I. (1999). Clinical Hypnosis as a Nondeceptive Placebo. In I. Kirsch, A. Capafons, E. Cardeña-Buelna, and S. Amigó (eds.), *Clinical Hypnosis and Self-Regulation: Cognitive-Behavioural Perspectives*. Washington, DC: American Psychological Association, 211–225.

Kirsch, I., and Lynn, S. J. (1995). Altered State of Hypnosis: Changes in the Theoretical Landscape. *American Psychologist*, *50*(10), 846–858.

Kirsch, I., Montgomery, G., and Sapirstein, G. (1995). Hypnosis as an Adjunct to Cognitive-Behavioral Psychotherapy: A Meta-Analysis. *Journal of Consulting and Clinical Psychology*, *63*, 214.

Kogon, M. M., Jasiukaitis, P., Berardi, A., et al. (1998). Imagery and Hypnotizability Revisited. *International Journal of Clinical and Experimental Hypnosis*, *46*(4), 363–370.

Lau-Zhu, A., Holmes, E. A., and Porcheret, K. (2018). Intrusive Memories of Trauma in the Laboratory: Methodological Developments and Future Directions. *Current Behavioral Neuroscience Reports*, *5*(1), 61–71.

Laurence, J.-R., Beaulieu-Prévost, D., and du Chéné, T. (2008). Measuring and Understanding Individual Differences in Hypnotizability. In M. R. Nash and A. J. Barnier (eds.), *The Oxford Handbook of Hypnosis: Theory, Research and Practice*. Oxford, UK: Oxford University Press, 225–253.

Lush, P., Caspar, E. A., Cleeremans, A., et al. (2017). The Power of Suggestion: Posthypnotically Induced Changes in the Temporal Binding of Intentional Action Outcomes. *Psychological Science*, *28*(5), 661–669.

Lush, P., Naish, P., and Dienes, Z. (2016). Metacognition of Intentions in Mindfulness and Hypnosis. *Neuroscience of Consciousness*, 2016(1), niw007.

Lynn, S. J., Kirsch, I., and Hallquist, M. (2008). Social Cognitive Theories of Hypnosis. In M. R. Nash and A. J. Barnier (eds.), *The Oxford Handbook of Hypnosis: Theory, Research and Practice*. Oxford, UK: Oxford University Press, 111–140.

Lynn, S. J., Kirsch, I., Knox, J., Fassler, O., and Lilienfeld, S. O. (2007). Hypnosis and Neuroscience: Implications for the Altered State Debate. In G. A. Jamieson (ed.), *Hypnosis and Conscious States: The Cognitive Neuroscience Perspective*. Oxford, UK: Oxford University Press, 145–165.

Marucci, F. S., and Meo, M. (2000). Suggestibility and Imagery during Attribution of Meaning to Ambiguous Figures. In V. de Pascalis, V. A. Gheorghiu, P. W. Sheehan, and I. Kirsch (eds.), *Suggestion and Suggestibility: Theory and Research*. Munich, Germany: M.E.G.-Stiftung, 167–175.

Maxwell, R., Lynn, S. J., and Condon, L. (2015). Hypnosis, Hypnotic Suggestibility, Memory, and Involvement in Films. *Consciousness and Cognition*, 33, 170–184.

Moore, J. W., and Obhi, S. S. (2012). Intentional Binding and the Sense of Agency: A Review. *Consciousness and Cognition*, 21(1), 546–561.

Moore, M., and Tasso, A. F. (2008). Clinical Hypnosis: The Empirical Evidence. In M. R. Nash and A. J. Barnier (eds.), *The Oxford Handbook of Hypnosis: Theory, Research and Practice*. Oxford, UK: Oxford University Press, 697–725.

Morgan, A. H. (1973). The Heritability of Hypnotic Susceptibility in Twins. *Journal of Abnormal Psychology*, 82(1), 55–61.

Oakley, D. A. (2012). From Freud to Neuroimaging: Hypnosis as a Common Thread. In A. Fotopoulou, D. Pfaff, and M. A. Conway (eds.), *From the Couch to the Lab: Trends in Psychodynamic Neuroscience*. Oxford, UK: Oxford University Press, 356–372.

Oakley, D. A., and Halligan, P. W. (2009). Hypnotic Suggestion and Cognitive Neuroscience. *Trends in Cognitive Sciences*, 13(6), 264–270.

   (2013). Hypnotic Suggestion: Opportunities for Cognitive Neuroscience. *Nature Reviews Neuroscience*, 14(8), 565–576.

   (2017). Chasing the Rainbow: The Non-Conscious Nature of Being. *Frontiers in Psychology*, 8, 1924.

Oakley, D. A., Ward, N. S., Halligan, P. W., and Frackowiak, S. J. (2003). Differential Brain Activations for Malingered and Subjectively "Real" Paralysis. In P. W. Halligan, C. Bass, and D. A. Oakley (eds.), *Malingering and Illness Deception*. Oxford, UK: Oxford University Press, 267–284.

Panero, M. E., Goldstein, T. R., Rosenberg, R., Hughes, H., and Winner, E. (2016). Do Actors Possess Traits Associated with High Hypnotizability? *Psychology of Aesthetics, Creativity, and the Arts*, 10(2), 233–239.

Patterson, D. R., and Jensen, M. P. (2003). Hypnosis and Clinical Pain. *Psychological Bulletin*, 129(4), 495–521.

Pekala, R. J., and Kumar, V. K. (2007). An Empirical-Phenomenological Approach to Quantifying Consciousness and States of Consciousness: With Particular Reference to Understanding the Nature of Hypnosis. In G. A. Jamieson (ed.), *Hypnosis and Conscious States: The Cognitive Neuroscience Perspective*. Oxford, UK: Oxford University Press, 167–194.

Piccione, C., Hilgard, E. R., and Zimbardo, P. G. (1989). On the Degree of Stability of Measured Hypnotizability over a 25-year Period. *Journal of Personality and Social Psychology, 56*(2), 289–295.

Polito, V., Barnier, A. J., Woody, E. Z., and Connors, M. H. (2014). Measuring Agency Change across the Domain of Hypnosis. *Psychology of Consciousness: Theory, Research, and Practice, 1*(1), 3–19.

Raz, A. (2007). Hypnobo: Perspectives on Hypnosis and Placebo. *American Journal of Clinical Hypnosis, 50*(1), 29–36.

Rhue, J. (2004). Developmental Determinants of High Hypnotizability. In M. Heap, R. J. Brown, and D. A. Oakley (eds.), *The Highly Hypnotizable Person: Theoretical, Experimental and Clinical Issues.* New York, NY: Brunner-Routledge, 115–132.

Roche, S. M., and McConkey, K. M. (1990). Absorption: Nature, Assessment, and Correlates. *Journal of Personality and Social Psychology, 59*(1), 91–101.

Rominger, C., Weiss, E. M., Nagl, S., et al. (2014). Carriers of the COMT Met/Met Allele Have Higher Degrees of Hypnotizability, Provided That They Have Good Attentional Control: A Case of Gene-Trait Interaction. *International Journal of Clinical and Experimental Hypnosis, 62*(4), 455–482.

Sarbin, T. R., and Lim, D. T. (1963). Some Evidence in Support of the Roletaking Hypothesis in Hypnosis. *International Journal of Clinical and Experimental Hypnosis, 11*, 98–103.

Sheehan, P. W., and Robertson, R. (1996). Imagery and Hypnosis: Trends and Patternings in Effects. In R. G. Kunzendorf, N. P. Spanos, and B. Wallace (eds.), *Hypnosis and Imagination.* Amityville, NY: Baywood, 1–17.

Spanos, N. P. (1986). Hypnotic Behavior: A Social Psychological Interpretation of Amnesia, Analgesia and Trance Logic. *Behavioral and Brain Sciences, 9*(3), 449–467.

Spanos, N. P., and Gorassini, D. R. (1984). Structure of Hypnotic Test Suggestions and Attributions of Responding Involuntarily. *Journal of Personality and Social Psychology, 46*(3), 688–696.

Spanos, N. P., Stenstrom, R. J., and Johnston, J. C. (1988). Hypnosis, Placebo, and Suggestion in the Treatment of Warts. *Psychosomatic Medicine, 50*(3), 245–260.

Srzich, A. J., Byblow, W. D., Stinear, J. W., Cirillo, J., and Anson, J. G. (2016). Can Motor Imagery and Hypnotic Susceptibility Explain Conversion Disorder with Motor Symptoms? *Neuropsychologia, 89*, 287–298.

Szechtman, H., Woody, E., Bowers, K. S., and Nahmias, C. (1998). Where the Imaginal Appears Real: A Positron Emission Tomography Study of Auditory Hallucinations. *Proceedings of the National Academy of Sciences of the United States of America, 95*(4), 1956–1960.

Tasso, A. F., and Perez, N. (2008). Parsing Everyday Suggestibility: What Does It Tell Us about Hypnosis? In M. R. Nash and A. J. Barnier (eds.), *The Oxford Handbook of Hypnosis: Theory, Research and Practice.* Oxford, UK: Oxford University Press, 283–309.

Terhune, D. B. (2012). Metacognition, Cold Control and Hypnosis. *Journal of Mind-Body Regulation, 2*, 75–79.

Terhune, D. B., and Cardeña, E. (2015). Dissociative Subtypes in Posttraumatic Stress Disorders and Hypnosis: Neurocognitive Parallels and Clinical Implications. *Current Directions in Psychological Science, 24*, 452–457.

(2016). Nuances and Uncertainties Regarding Hypnotic Inductions: Toward a Theoretically Informed Praxis. *American Journal of Clinical Hypnosis*, 59(2), 155–174.

Terhune, D. B., Cardeña, E., and Lindgren, M. (2011). Dissociative Tendencies and Individual Differences in High Hypnotic Suggestibility. *Cognitive Neuropsychiatry*, 16(2), 113–135.

Terhune, D. B., Cleeremans, A., Raz, A., and Lynn, S. J. (2017). Hypnosis and Top-Down Regulation of Consciousness. *Neuroscience and Biobehavioral Reviews*, 81(Pt A), 59–74.

Terhune, D. B., and Hedman, L. R. A. (2017). Metacognition of Agency Is Reduced in High Hypnotic Suggestibility. *Cognition*, 168, 176–181.

Varga, K., Nemeth, Z., and Szekely, A. (2011). Lack of Correlation between Hypnotic Susceptibility and Various Components of Attention. *Consciousness and Cognition*, 20(4), 1872–1881.

Vuilleumier, P. (2014). Brain Circuits Implicated in Psychogenic Paralysis in Conversion Disorders and Hypnosis. *Neurophysiologie Clinique-Clinical Neurophysiology*, 44 (4), 323–337.

Wallace, B., Allen, P. A., and Propper, R. E. (1996). Hypnotic Susceptibility, Imaging Ability, and Anagram-Solving Activity. *International Journal of Clinical and Experimental Hypnosis*, 44(4), 324–337.

Walsh, E., Oakley, D. A., Halligan, P. W., Mehta, M. A., and Deeley, Q. (2015). The Functional Anatomy and Connectivity of Thought Insertion and Alien Control of Movement. *Cortex*, 64, 380–393.

Walters, V. J., and Oakley, D. A. (2003). Does Hypnosis Make in Vitro, in Vivo? Hypnosis as a Possible Virtual Reality Context in Cognitive Behavioural Therapy for an Environmental Phobia. *Clinical Case Studies*, 2(4), 295–305.

(2006). Hypnotic Imagery as an Adjunct to Therapy for Irritable Bowel Syndrome: An Experimental Case Report. *Contemporary Hypnosis*, 23(3), 141–149.

Ward, N. S., Oakley, D. A., Frackowiak, R. S., and Halligan, P. W. (2003). Differential Brain Activations during Intentionally Simulated and Subjectively Experienced Paralysis. *Cognitive Neuropsychiatry*, 8(4), 295–312.

Weitzenhoffer, A. M. (1974). When Is an "Instruction" an "Instruction"? *International Journal of Clinical and Experimental Hypnosis*, 22(3), 258–269.

Whorwell, P. J., Prior, A., and Faragher, E. B. (1984). Controlled Trial of Hypnotherapy in the Treatment of Severe Refractory Irritable-Bowel Syndrome. *Lancet*, 2(8414), 1232–1234.

Wilson, S. C., and Barber, T. X. (1983). The Fantasy-Prone Personality: Implications for Understanding Imagery, Hypnosis, and Parapsychological Phenomena. In A. A. Sheik (ed.), *Imagery: Current Theory, Research and Application*. New York, NY: Wiley, 340–390.

Woody, E. Z., and Barnier, A. J. (2008). Hypnosis Scales for the Twenty-First Century: What Do We Know and How Should We Use Them? In M. R. Nash and A. J. Barnier (eds.), *The Oxford Handbook of Hypnosis: Theory, Research and Practice*. Oxford, UK: Oxford University Press, 255–281.

44 Hallucinations and Imagination

Daniel Collerton, Elaine Perry,
and Alan Robert Bowman

In this chapter, we explore the relationships of one form of perception, the hallucinatory, to imagination in its many forms. We review the different types of hallucinations, their associations with both veridical and non-veridical perception, and the subtle, complex, and individual relationships that they have with differing aspects of imagination.

Why are hallucinations relevant to imagination, one might ask? One answer is that imagination is a fundamental component of creativity and there have been long-standing suggestions of a link between madness and creativity – the crazy genius is a staple of book and film (the portrayal of the mathematician John Forbes Nash in the 2001 film, *A Beautiful Mind*, illustrates a modern sympathetic treatment of the link between hallucinations, distress, and creativity) – and, in the popular imagination, hallucinations are one sign of madness; though in reality many hallucinations are not associated with clinical disorders.

What is a Hallucination?

Classically, hallucinations are defined as involuntary sensory percepts, occurring while awake, which do not relate to the current existence of things in the environment – to see, feel, hear, or otherwise experience something that is not there (Waters et al., 2014). Their involuntary nature distinguishes them from voluntary images or internal speech, and the specification "while awake" from dreams. They are further separated from illusions and misperceptions in which the percept is of something that is there, but which is perceived incorrectly in some meaningful manner (Blom, 2015).

Though these are nicely clear-cut boundaries in theory, in practice they can be difficult to establish. Communicating these subjective experiences is difficult and prone to the interpretation of the listener; people may have more than one type of disturbed perception; and there may be intermediate forms between, for example, illusions and hallucinations (see Figure 44.1 for an example from visual perception).

Though hallucinations are associated with mental ill-health in the popular mind, most people who hallucinate do not have a clinical disorder. Occasional hallucinations appear to be a feature of a normally functioning sensory system. Frequent and persisting hallucinations are, however, features of many types of disorders

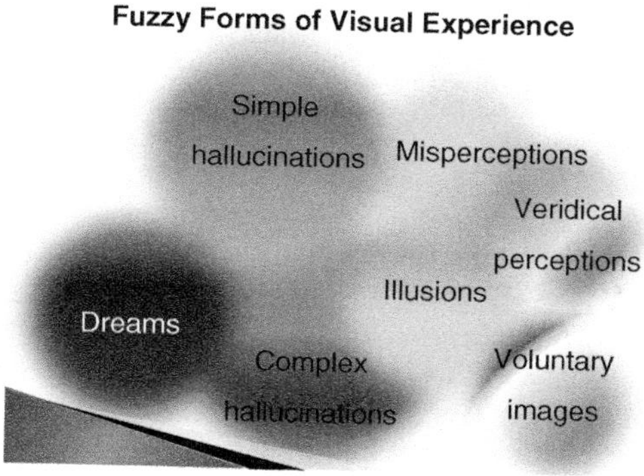

Fuzzy Forms of Visual Experience

Figure 44.1 *Fuzzy boundaries of visual perception.*

(Collerton, Perry, and McKeith, 2005): some *sensory*, such as the visual hallucinations of Charles Bonnet syndrome in eye disease or the musical hallucinations of deafness; some *neurological*, such as the visual and tactile hallucinations of Lewy body disorders; some *medical*, like the multisensory hallucinations of delirium; and some *psychological*, such as in the multimodal meaning-filled hallucinations of psychosis. Additionally, many temporary states can induce hallucinations even in well people – sensory deprivation, social isolation, stress and bereavement, and drug use.

Hallucinations come in many forms (for a review, see Aleman and Larøi, 2008) and across all modalities. Some are representations of things and are labeled as *complex* or formed – for example, a voice speaking, or a figure appearing. Others, called *simple* or unformed, are without shape – auditory noise, or visual dots and flashes, for instance. We will focus more on complex hallucinations since they have the closest relationships with imagination.

The Interplay between Hallucination and Imagination

In the introduction, Anna Abraham reviews twelve concepts of imagination. As we have illustrated in Figure 44.2, the relationship of these concepts to hallucinations varies considerably. The first nine concepts, those on the upper three lines, have a distinct overlap with the nature of hallucinations. Since a hallucination is an imagined perception in the sense of being nonveridical at the time it occurs, we can consider hallucinations to be a subset of imaginary phenomena; both exist only in the mind.

Both hallucinations and the effects that they have on people are highly variable. This variability maps on to the imagination of real and unreal things, with or without insight (the understanding that the perception is real or unreal), and with a whole range of subjective reactions from fear, to disgust, to comfort, to rhapsody (see Dudley et al., 2012; Thomson et al., 2017, for clinical examples in the visual sphere).

The ability to think of something that is not presently perceived but is, was, or will be spatiotemporally real. **Hallucinations of known things (e.g. visual hallucination of a relative).**	*The ability to think of whatever one acknowledges as possible in the spatiotemporal world.* **Hallucinations of unknown things. Strange and fantastical hallucinations (e.g. distorted figure of dwarves in an unreal landscape).**	The ability to think of something the subject believes to be real, but is not real. **Hallucinations without insight (e.g. believing that a hallucinated voice is truly that of a demon).**
The ability to think of things that one conceives of as fictional, as opposed to what one believes to be real, or conceives of as possibly real. **Hallucinations with insight (e.g. knowing that a touch is a hallucination, and not due to something brushing against you).**	The ability to entertain mental images. **Visual and other hallucinations (e.g. seeing a house that is not there, or hearing a voice that is not present).**	The ability to think of (conceive of, or represent) anything at all. **All hallucinations (e.g. sounds, visions, feelings, tastes, smells, or other perceptions).**
The nonrational operations of the mind, i.e. those kinds of mental functioning that are explicable in terms of causes rather than reasons. **Emotional components of hallucinations (e.g. the sense of wonder that may accompany a hallucination).**	The ability to form beliefs, on the basis of perception, about public objects in three-dimensional space that can exist unperceived, with spatial parts and temporal duration. **Attributions about hallucinations (e.g. that a voice is that of a malevolent entity who is going to harm you).**	The sensuous component in the appreciation of works of art or objects of natural beauty without classifying them under concepts or thinking of them as practically useful. **Subjective reactions to hallucinations (e.g. to become engrossed in the complex visual hallucinations created by drugs).**
The ability to create works of art that encourage such sensuous appreciation. **Hallucination-inspired art (e.g. Munch's *The Scream*).**	The ability to appreciate things that are expressive or revelatory about the meaning of human life. **Meaningful hallucinations (e.g. to believe that hallucinations create access to another, spiritual, world).**	The ability to create works of art that express something deep about the meaning of life, as opposed to the products of mere fantasy. **Meaningful art inspired by hallucinations. (e.g. Huxley's *The Doors of Perception*).**

Figure 44.2 *Concepts of imagination mapped on to hallucinatory phenomena.*

These latter, more indirect, creative aspects of imagination are also related to hallucinations in particular people, but the relationships are complex, often indirect, and highly individual. Thus, for those who have experienced hallucinations, the first nine aspects of imagination are generally present in their hallucinatory experiences, but the contributions of the latter three aspects are more variable across individuals.

Creative Relationships between Hallucinations and Imagination

Take the case of Edvard Munch, for example, as highlighted by Albert Rothenberg (Rothenberg, 2001; Howe, 2001). The relationship of hallucinatory experiences to his most famous work, *The Scream*, highlights many of the complexities and subjective interpretation needed to investigate this area. He described the initial impetus of his painting as:

> I was walking along the road with two of my friends. Then the sun set. The sky suddenly turned into blood, and I felt something akin to a touch of melancholy. I stood still, leaned against the railing, dead tired. Above the blue black fjord and city hung clouds of dripping, rippling blood. My friends went on and again I stood, frightened with an open wound in my breast. A great scream pierced through nature (Heller, 1972: 109).

On the face of it, these are visual hallucinations of blood, visual and tactile hallucinations of a wound, and an auditory hallucination of a scream, and are accepted as such by Rothenberg. But are they? Or are they a metaphorical artistic interpretation and report of how Munch was feeling? The red sunset sky reminds him of blood, the pain in his chest was like an open wound, the scream was an expression of his melancholy. The distinction between hallucinating – a very literal experience – and metaphor – as if the thing is as described – can be very difficult to judge, especially when one is unable to question the reporter. Disentangling the effects on imagination of hallucinations in people who are already imaginative and creative is not at all straightforward.

In any event, the transformation of these experiences into the final definitive artwork took a year and much revision. Munch's first representation was very different to his eventual image (Figure 44.3).

 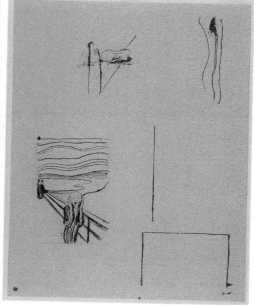

Figure 44.3 *Changes in Edvard Munch's artistic response to his hallucinatory experiences over twelve months as recorded in his sketchbooks. (a) Initial response to his experiences while walking (MunchMuseet, Oslo). (b) Final interpretation of his experiences (MunchMuseet, Oslo). Reproduced with permission of the MunchMuseet, Oslo, Norway, under the terms of Creative Commons Attribution 4.0 International (CC BY 4.0).*

Munch's initial experience on that walk, and the subsequent development of his ideas over the next year draw upon many of the different forms of imagination in Figure 44.2. Thus, they have familiar and unfamiliar content, they are representations of what is not there, they are loaded with meaning, and they come with a strong emotional response. It is not clear what understanding Munch had at the time, but an appreciation of the unreality of his experience is implied by his later actions. These multiple reactions to hallucinations are characteristics of just about all events in both clinical and mundane settings.

In Munch's case, it is the relationship of these experiences to his art that has attracted most attention. His life makes the argument that not only can imagination can be stimulated by hallucination, but that hallucinations may have an aspect of artistic imagination within them, and that the two have a complex relationship that is influenced by many other factors and that plays out over a long period of time.

For other visual artists, the link may be much more direct. Their art becomes a representation of their hallucinations, as in Figure 44.4 inspired by the visual hallucinations of an artist with Parkinson's disease. For others, hallucinations become the inspiration for the subject matter of their paintings.

Another instance comes from the hallucinations that can occur when someone is semi-awake and in a state of sleep paralysis. In earlier times, these phenomena were thought to be caused by the night demons called incubi. They became the inspiration for the 1781 painting *The Nightmare* by Henry Fuseli[1] among other works of art.

Figure 44.4 *Artistic response to the visual hallucinations of Parkinson's disease. Figure reprinted from: Frucht and Bernsohn (2002), Visual Hallucinations in PD,* Neurology, *59(12), 1965. n.neurology.org/content/59/12/1965.abstract Copyright © 2002, American Academy of Neurology. Reproduced by permission of Wolters Kluwer Health, Inc.*

---

[1] Detroit Institute of Arts: www.dia.org/art/collection/object/nightmare-45573

Similarly, many religious visions, some of which may have been hallucinatory, have become the inspiration for art from earliest times. Kennaway (2017), for example, has a good discussion on different interpretations of hallucinatory experiences and their relationship to music.

Similarly, hallucinations can become the focus of written work. Shakespeare provides an early example in Macbeth's dagger:

> Is this a dagger which I see before me,
> The handle toward my hand? Come, let me clutch thee: –
> I have thee not, and yet I see thee still.
> Art thou not, fatal vision, sensible
> To feeling as to sight? Or art thou but
> A dagger of the mind, a false creation

(Macbeth, II i 33–38)

This interplay highlights the complex, idiosyncratic relationship between hallucination, imagination, and creativity, and the subsequent role of involuntary and voluntary experience. Munch's initial hallucinations are involuntary, but his reaction to them is mostly, if not entirely, voluntary. His creative response, which produces something tangible, useful, and lasting from something subjective, intangible, and fleeting, illustrates not only how hallucinations may stimulate wider aspects of imagination, but that many individual factors come into play.

Dickens provides a good example of how imagination may influence, rather than be influenced by, auditory and visual hallucinations (if hallucinations are what he is truly reporting; as with Munch it is hard to know how literally to take his words). "Dickens . . . wrote to his friend John Forster: "when I sit down to my book, some beneficent power shows it all to me, and tempts me to be interested, and I don't invent it – really do not – but see it, and write it down." Mrs Gamp, the disreputable nurse from *Martin Chuzzlewit*, intruded repeatedly on Dickens when he was writing that novel, "whispering to him in the most inopportune places – sometimes even in church – that he was compelled to fight her off by force."[2]

In Dickens's case, his sensory experiences related directly and constructively to his imagination and creativity. Virginia Woolf shows the contrary, destructive, effect of experiencing hallucinations. Her auditory hallucinations interfered with her creativity. As she put it in her suicide note "I feel certain that I am going mad again. I begin to hear voices, and I can't concentrate" (Kenney, 1975: 265). Similarly, Chopin described how visual hallucinations of imps disturbed his playing during a concert:

> A strange adventure happened to me while I was playing my B flat Sonata for some English friends. I had played the Allegro and the Scherzo more or less correctly and I was about to play the March when, suddenly, I saw emerging from the half-open case of my piano those cursed creatures that had appeared to me on a lugubrious night at the Carthusian monastery [Majorca]. I had to leave for a while in order to recover myself, and after that I continued playing without saying a word. (Chopin to Solange Clésinger, George Sand's daughter, letter dated September 9, 1848, quoted in Caruncho and Fernández, 2011: 5)

---

[2] hearingvoicescymru.org/positive-voices/famous-voice-hearers/creative-people/

In a different sensory modality, Schuman heard a variety of auditory hallucinations over the years: initially a single note, then melodies, then an angelic choir, and finally, as he became more disturbed and distressed, demonic choral music (Ostwald, 1987).

In these three cases, the artist's hallucinations (if that is what they were) were involuntary. Others, though, have set out to directly cultivate abnormal sensory experiences in one way or another.

Dali, for example, induced "paranoiac critical" states in himself in order to foster his art, a process he described as a "spontaneous method of irrational knowledge based on the critical and systematic objectivity of the associations and interpretations of delirious phenomena" – or an induced hallucination (Finkelstein, 1975: 63). He used to hold a spoon between his fingers and doze until the spoon fell from his hand; waking him and giving him access to his hypnogogic hallucinations (Nielsen, 1992).

In the nineteenth century, Thomas De Quincey produced the drug-fueled, hallucination-filled *Confessions of an English Opium-Eater*. Compelled by debt, he turned his use of laudanum (and the hallucinations that it created in later days – "A theatre suddenly seemed opened and lighted up within my brain nightly spectacles of more than earthly splendour" [De Quincy, 1821: 3]) into a literary sensation that indirectly stimulated the imagination of other artistic figures. Berlioz, for example, based the Symphonie Fantastique on his book.

Later, Havelock Ellis consciously sought peyote-induced hallucinations as part of a creative endeavor:"I would see thick glorious fields of jewels ... they would spring up into flower-like shapes ... and then seem to turn into gorgeous butterfly forms" (Ellis, 1898: 132). In the subsequent century, Aldous Huxley (Huxley, 1954/2004) wrote of his hallucinatory experiences with mescaline under the title *The Doors of Perception*, drawing inspiration from William Blake (whose own visual hallucinations highly influenced his work) and his poem "The Marriage of Heaven and Hell," which contains the words, "If the doors of perception were cleansed everything would appear to man as it is, infinite." This shows again how hallucinations in one person can indirectly stimulate the imagination of another.

What these cases illustrate is the wide range of possible relationships between hallucinations and imagination – direct and indirect, positive and negative, constructive or destructive. However, they leave open the possibility that these relationships are a matter of chance; of unusual people reporting unusual experiences. To see if there are reliable links between imagination and hallucinations we need to turn to scientific studies.

Hallucinations, Imagination, and Cognitive Processes

As we have discussed, there is a close relationship between hallucinations and the internal representations separate from outside reality that imagination produces, according to some views. However, relationships with other concepts of imagination, especially those linked to creativity, may be more indirect and individual. In this section, we look at the overlap between veridical and imagined sensory representations and hallucinations for the light that this may cast upon shared mechanisms for imagination and hallucinations.

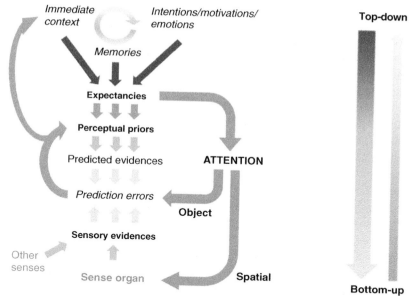

Figure 44.5 *Cognitive sensory processing.*

Figure 44.5 illustrates our current model of sensory perception. Perception is seen as an interaction between top-down, generated predictions and bottom-up data-driven processes. The central concept is that what is subjectively experienced (the *perception*) is an internal representation of the external sensory world. This representation is used to predict what sensory input would be consistent with that model (*predicted evidences*), which are then compared to the actual sensory input (*sensory evidences*), with the difference (*prediction errors*) modifying the *perception*. *Perception* is further influenced by the likelihood of particular perceptions (*expectancy*), given past experiences (*memories*), the current situation (*immediate context* – which is itself created from perceptions), and future guides to action (*intentions, motivations*, and *emotions*). *Expectations* also influence what sensory information is influential (*attention*).

Within this model, both hallucinations and imagined perceptions replace veridical representations, but imagined perceptions have more specific links with intentions and memories and none with sensory input, while hallucinations have a reduced relationship to sensory input but more links to immediate context (see Collerton et al., 2016, for an example from the visual sphere).

Cognitive models that suggest a commonality between imagined, veridical, and hallucinatory perceptions can be empirically tested. We have drawn from the visual literature below, but similar evidence is available in other modalities.

In a small number of studies that have examined both imagined and hallucinated perceptions, the findings suggest that the two are closely related. Using a binocular rivalry task to measure mental imagery strength, and a bistable perception task to measure frequency of hallucinatory experiences, Shine et al. (2015) examined the interplay between imagery and hallucinations in a sample of patients with

Parkinson's disease (both hallucinating and non-hallucinating). They showed that hallucinating participants had stronger mental imagery then the non-hallucinating groups. In addition, both Parkinson's groups exhibited a positive correlation between strength of mental imagery and rate of hallucinatory experiences during the bistable perception task. Put another way: the stronger their imagination, the more illusory experiences they had. This finding did not extend to the nonclinical control group. Frequency of misperceptions and strength of mental imagery both predicted increased connectivity in brain networks subserving attention and vision. The authors conclude that visual imagery and visual hallucinations may be different expressions of the same or similar underlying neurobiological mechanism.

Sireteanu et al. (2008) conducted a single-case experiment of a healthy female participant who underwent sensory deprivation for three weeks (via blindfolding) and began to experience simple visual hallucinations. The participant underwent functional magnetic resonance imaging (fMRI) while actively hallucinating and also provided detailed verbal and visual descriptions of what she saw. She was then asked to mentally picture the hallucinatory content and she was scanned again. During hallucinations, increased neural activity was observed in the extrastriate occipital cortex, posterior parietal cortex, and a number of frontal regions. During imagery of the same visual experiences, prefrontal activation was observed but posterior parietal and occipital activation was not. The authors suggest that in deprivation-induced visual hallucinations, the process of deprivation creates increased visual cortical excitability, and a concomitant increase in hallucination-proneness. In contrast, imagery is in this instance a volitional affair and this requires top-down control from frontal structures.

Bolstering the argument that imagination and hallucinations overlap at the brain level, there is some evidence that imagined and veridical perceptions and hallucinated and veridical perceptions all map to similar brain areas.

To test the argument that there is an overlap between the brain processes responsible for imagined and veridical perceptions, McNorgan (2012) examined imagery in visual, auditory, gustatory, olfactory, tactile, and motor domains in a meta-analytic review of sixty-five neuroimaging studies. He reported that in some, but not all cases, there was overlap in neural activity patterns between actual and imagined perception. More importantly, he also found that there is a core network of upstream brain regions that are recruited during mental imagery, independent of task. This network consists of bilateral dorsal parietal, left inferior frontal, and anterior insular regions.

O'Craven and Kanwisher (2000) more specifically examined neural activity for imagined and actual visual perception of faces and places. They demonstrated that the same brain regions that were recruited for visual perception were also recruited for visual imagery (the parahippocampal place area for place perception, and the fusiform face area for face perception). The magnitude of activation in these areas was greater for veridical stimuli than for imagined stimuli, suggesting that imagery might be a "weaker" form of perceptual experience. Notably, however, the patterns of neural activity were distinct enough that naive observers were able to determine accurately what a participant was imagining (a face or a place) simply by studying the raw MRI data.

Turning now to visual hallucinations and veridical perceptions, brain imaging has been employed to understand what happens in the brain during a hallucinatory event. Ffytche et al. (1998) asked participants with Charles Bonnet syndrome to indicate the onset and cessation of their visual hallucinations while undergoing functional imaging. There was a close correspondence between the visual properties of a hallucination and the functional specialization of the brain region activated during the hallucinatory event. For example, increased activity was observed in the area V4 of the fusiform gyrus when colored hallucinations occurred, and texture hallucinations were associated with increased activity in the collateral sulcus, a brain region that is implicated in texture perception.

More recently, Goetz et al. (2014) conducted a case study of a hallucinating individual with Parkinson's disease who reported sixteen visual hallucinations during a scan. During hallucinatory episodes, increased neural activation was observed in anterior brain regions typically associated with "top-down" high-level visual processing, while decreased activation was observed in posterior visual brain regions associated with low-level visual processing.

A complementary approach to understanding the neuroscience of hallucinations is to study analogous phenomena. One such phenomenon is pareidolia – the perceptual experience of seeing meaningful visual objects in meaningless or ambiguous visual noise (Uchiyama et al., 2012). Seeing "faces in objects" is a common, everyday example that all of us will have experienced at some point (Figure 44.6). The phenomenological content of pareidolia has been shown to be similar to that of visual hallucinations (Uchiyama et al., 2015). Pareidolia frequency correlates with hallucination severity in patients with dementia with Lewy bodies, and both pareidolia and visual hallucinations are affected by cholinesterase inhibitors (Yokoi et al., 2014).

In a pareidolia study by Liu et al. (2014), participants were presented with randomly generated visual noise and were asked to look for faces or letters in this noise. They were instructed that 50 percent of trials contained real visual objects to detect, when in fact the testing trials were 100 percent "pure noise" (i.e. there were no veridical stimuli to detect). Interestingly, in the face condition, participants saw illusory faces 34 percent of the time, and in the letter condition saw illusory letters 38 percent of the time. What is more, seeing illusory faces was associated with increased activity in the right fusiform face area, and the magnitude of this activation was correlated with the strength of the illusory experience. Whole brain analyses were also conducted, revealing a network specialized to the processing of face pareidolia extending from the ventral occipitotemporal cortex to the prefrontal cortex. The authors comment on the importance of upstream frontal regions in the processing of facial stimuli and suggest that these regions may send modulatory signals to influence low-level visual processes.

Thus, at the level of brain function, there is a distinct overlap between the areas associated with visual imagery (one aspect of imagination), veridical perception, and hallucinations.

Figure 44.6 *Examples of face pareidolia. Reproduced from: Takahashi and Watanabe (2013), Gaze Cueing by Pareidolia Faces,* i-Perception, *4, 490–492. By permission of Sage Publications under the terms of the Creative Commons Attribution 3.0 License.*

Drugs, Hallucinations, and Imagination

Drug effects provide an additional avenue for systematically exploring links between hallucinations and imagination. The effects of psychedelic drugs provide a rich source of relevant information and, as noted previously, have attracted attention because of their use by authors and visual artists. Figure 44.7 illustrates both representational and abstracted art influenced by different hallucinogens, both as a focus of content (a), and as an impact on process (b).

Sweat, Bates, and Hendricks (2016), surveying circumstances associated with mystical experiences in conjunction with a test of creative problem-solving ability, concluded that psychedelic use may increase creativity since imagination and hallucination both involve the making of new connections between previously unconnected brain areas and networks – facilitating pathways not normally active. Imagination as a function of the primarily "thinking" brain involves experiencing an idea, insight, or concept that has not previously been formulated. Hallucination as a function of the primarily sensing brain involves experiencing what is not there in reality. Neither experience, at the conscious or subconscious level, is usually under voluntary control. Both can be altered by chemicals acting on the brain. However, there are limits to the use of psychedelics to stimulate the imagination and creative cognition – unsupervised use, overdose, and addiction being the most obvious. Gallimore (2015: 14) comments that "whilst cognitive flexibility, creativity, and imagination are enhanced during the psychedelic state, this occurs at the expense of cause-effect information, as well as degrading the brain's ability to organize, categorize, and differentiate the constituents of conscious experience." Based on a study of the behavior of the pop icon Jim Morrison as an exemplary case, Holm-Hadulla and Bertolino (2014: 171) caution that "the abuse of LSD (lysergic acid diethylamide), mescaline and amphetamines damages the capacity to realize creative motivation."

Less potent but safer botanic agents that alter consciousness in a milder but still creative way are noted later, but are not in wide use (Perry and Perry, 2018).

Demonstrating a possible biological basis for some of the lasting consequences of psychedelic use, Martin and Nichols (2017: 143) have summarized what is currently known about molecular genetic responses to psychedelics within the brain and discuss how gene expression changes may contribute to chronic altered cellular physiology and behavior. They suggest that "acute molecular processes also influence gene expression changes, which likely influence synaptic plasticity and facilitate more long-term changes in brain neurochemistry." There are hundreds of studies in animal models (used to analyze changes in gene expression rather than behavior) that identify altered expression of target transmitter and receptor genes or genes controlling downstream molecular events, all affected by psychedelic drugs. Orsolini et al. (2017), reporting on hallucinogen-persisting perception disorder, found that psychedelics leave people with long-term visual, thought, and mood alterations. Effects of hallucinogenic experiences on imagination persisting long after the actual experience could account for reports of long-term stimulation

(a)

(b)

Figure 44.7 *Hallucinogen-inspired art. (a) Marijuana-inspired representational art. Pedro Lozano,* Fade into Darkness, *2015. Reproduced with kind permission of the artist. (b) Opiate-inspired nonrepresentational art. Stanisław Ignacy Witkiewicz,* Composition, *1922, oil and tempera on canvas, 91 x 115 cm., inv.no. MNK II-b-1566. Reproduced with kind permission of the National Museum in Krakow, Poland.*

of creativity related to original use of the psychedelic. Noted in passing, long-term epigenetic changes, some of which may even be passed to offspring (transgenerational epigenetics), provide food for thought for users of psyche-delics (for evidence on effects of paternal alcohol use on subsequent genera-tions, see Finergersh et al., 2015).

Hallucinogen Use to Enhance Imagination

We have already seen in De Quincey and Huxley how drug use can stimulate the imagination both in the narrow sense of creating imaginary (hallucinatory) percep-tions, and in the wider sense of a creative reaction to those experiences. Predating these by millennia, murals and rock paintings from prehistoric times indicate the use of psychedelic plants such as magic mushrooms and cannabis for ritualistic or mystical purposes (Figure 44.8). It has even been proposed that the effects of such mind-altering, hallucinogenic agents on the human brain contributed to the evolution of human consciousness. According to Terence McKenna (1999: 19) psilocybin brought us "out of the animal mind and into the world of articulated speech and imagination." In historic times, as noted later, hallucinogens were used to induce oracles, and access spirit worlds.

States of "intoxication" induced by such psychedelic plants or drugs were once viewed as being "possessed" or under the influence of an external agency. Artists who worked while taking LSD, mescaline, or psilocybin referred to feeling under external influences. More recently plant preparations such as ayahuasca, increas-ingly used by Westerners seeking insight into personal or existential issues, have led to claims that the user is contacting the "plant spirit" for guidance. Sessa (2008),

Figure 44.8 *Hallucinogen-inspired prehistoric art. Reprinted by permission from Springer Nature,* Economic Botany: *Akers et al., A Prehistoric Mural in Spain Depicting Neurotropic* Psilocybe *Mushrooms? 65(2), 121–128. C.A.P. Copyright 2011.*

noting similarities between the traits of creative people and the subjective effects of the psychedelic (including the hallucinogenic) drug experience, suggested that although this was studied in small trials and case studies in the 1960s with inconclusive results, it was time to revisit such studies.

Among innumerable agents known to induce hallucinations – plants and isolated or synthetic chemicals – some are reported not only anecdotally but also in scientific studies to alter imagination or creativity (artistic, musical, or literary). Many famous figures including artists, writers, and musicians have used such agents to stimulate their imagination and creativity, though there is the confounding factor that creative people may tend to use psychedelic agents more than other people.

Agents that induce hallucinations and also stimulate imagination are reviewed below and include: anticholinergic drugs and plants, ayahuasca, cannabis, divine sage, dimenthyltryptamine (DMT), dopaminergic drugs, LSD, mescaline, morphine and related drugs, opium, and psilocybin (magic mushrooms). However, there are also psychedelics associated with hallucinations but not noted for effects on creativity, which include: cocaine, amphetamine, ketamine, 3,4-methylenedioxy-methamphetamine (MDMA, ecstasy), designer or street drugs, and legal or illegal chemical highs, suggesting that there is not an invariable link between increased hallucinations and enhanced creativity.

In the next section, we briefly review the modes of action and effects of those classes of drugs that are commonly associated both with hallucinations and with effects on wider aspects of imagination.

Relative to other neurotransmitters, serotonin (5HT) is implicated in the action of the largest number of psychedelics (see Figure 44.9). Creative cognitive ability is correlated with 5HT1B receptor imaging in normal subjects (Varrone et al., 2015) and ayahuasca, which enhances serotonergic transmission, also enhances creative divergent thinking (Kuypers et al., 2016). Such observations are consistent with effects of other 5HT active hallucinogens including, DMT, LSD, psilocybin and mescaline. DMT, one of the most potent hallucinogens, induces an altered state of consciousness that has been described as "a complete replacement of normal subjective experience with a novel 'alternate universe' often densely populated with a variety of strange objects and other highly complex visual content, including what appear to be sentient 'beings'" (Gallimore and Strassman, 2016: 1). In the mid-1950s, intellectuals in Southern California considered LSD to be a psychedelic capable of producing mystical enlightenment, and by the late 1950s, psychiatrists and psychologists were administering it to cure neuroses and addiction as well as to enhance creativity (Novak, 1997). In the same period, artwork produced by artists taking LSD was judged objectively to be strikingly different to drug-free productions, and the artists themselves considered their LSD works to be more interesting and aesthetically superior (Janiker and Dobkin de Rios, 1989; Figure 44.8). For all of the serotonergic psychedelics, 5-HT2A/1A-receptors are implicated in hallucinations and by inference, though not yet established, also in creative cognition.

Plant or chemical	Active ingredient(s)	Hallucinatory effect: anecdotal and scientific studies	Effect on imagination / creativity: anecdotal and scientific studies	Relevant neurobiological mechanisms involving neuromodulatory systems
Mescaline from the peyote cactus (Lophophora williamsii).	Active alkaloid (3,4,5-trimethoxyphenethylamine).	No systematic studies but mescaline is included because of the impact of Huxley's book, The Doors of Perception (1953) in which he describes "animated stained glass illuminated from light coming through the eyelids" after taking mescaline. Others also report visual hallucinations of brilliant kaleidoscopic images.	Subjective effects include altered thinking processes, altered self-awareness. Ken Kasey wrote One Flew over the Cuckoo's Nest while on a peyote "trip." No published studies on imagination or creativity.	Binds to serotonin 5HT1A and 5HT2A subtypes; also facilitates release of dopamine.
Psilocybin / magic mushrooms or "shrooms"	Psilocybin ([3-(2-Dimethylaminoethyl)-1H-indol-4-yl] dihydrogen phosphate) in mushrooms such as P. azurescens, P. semilanceata, P. cyanescens. Converted to psilocin.	Visual hallucinations are most common (ranging from distortions at low doses to novel images at higher doses), but auditory, olfactory, and tactile hallucinations are also reported. One of few systematic studies mentions hallucinations altering perspectives (Riley and Blackman, 2008).	Feelings of "enlightenment" often reported and new artistic styles emerging are reported by users. Research restricted by illegality, in one early study linguistic function in creative performance and psilocybin-induced experience were noted to be similar (Landon and Fischer, 1970)	Psilocin is a partial agonist for serotonin 5HT1A and 5HT2 receptor subtypes but not for dopamine receptors though it increases dopamine release. Hallucinations involve 5HT2 receptors (Kometer et al., 2013).
LSD (lysergic acid diethyl Amide), also known as "acid."	Synthesized from ergotamine, one of the ergot family of alkaloids found in the ergot fungus (Claviceps purpurea). Chemically similar to the transmitters serotonin and dopamine.	Visual (often swirling colors) and auditory hallucinations, sense of self dissolving and synaesthesia are all reported by users. Few systematic studies: "illusions of color and sound" and only rarely complex hallucinations (Kulig, 1990); hallucinations, pseudohallucinations, and illusions (Leiken et al, 1989).	Enhanced creativity of artists under the influence of LSD (Janiker and Dobkin de Rios, 1989). Increased connectivity with LSD and music induced imagery (Kaelen et al., 2016). Systematic study (Leichti, 2017) lists bliss, audiovisual synesthesia, altered meaning of perceptions, derealization, depersonalization, and mystical experiences.	Serotonin receptor (mainly 5-HT 2A subtype) and dopamine D2 agonist.

Plant or chemical	Active ingredient(s)	Hallucinatory effect: anecdotal and scientific studies	Effect on imagination / creativity: anecdotal and scientific studies	Relevant neurobiological mechanisms involving neuromodulatory systems
Ayahuasca, a psychedelic brew of plants concocted by S American tribes	Combination of the vine *Banisteriopsis caapi*, which contains DMT, and another plant such as *Psychotria viridis* containing a MAO inhibitor to prevent the DMT breaking down.	Visual and auditory altered perception reported, including simple and complex hallucinations, mixing of sensory modalities. fMRI imaging detects activation of occipital and other cortical areas (de Araujo et al., 2012)	Anecdotally both creative and noncreative people report greatly enhanced creativity as a result of ingesting ayahuasca. Increased creative divergent thinking reported (Kuypers et al., 2016). fMRI indicates modulation of activity and connectivity of default mode network (Palhano-Fontes et al., 2015).	Serotonergic action via 5HT1A and 5HT2A receptor blockade; also increases levels of serotonin (transporters inhibition). Serotonin involved in mood and social behavior. Receptor or transporter genes implicated in creativity (e.g. Volf et al., 2009).
DMT or *N,N*-DMT (*N,N*-Dimethyltryptamine)	Tryptamine analogue of serotonin found in many plants (e.g. ayahuasca, above; can be extracted from plants or synthesised from tryptophan.	Hallucinations are primarily visual – intensely colored moving images. Both auditory and visual hallucinations assessed in an early survey of DMT-induced alterations in consciousness (Dittrich et al., 1976).	Induces mystical and profound life-altering experiences. Stimulates divergent thinking (see ayahuasca above).	Disrupts visual and auditory cortical activity via 5HT1A and 5HT2A receptors. DMT occurs in human brain, though whether endogenous or exogenous and whether at a functional level are not established.

Figure 44.9 *Imaginative effects of serotonin active hallucinogens.*

In terms of other neurotransmitters, though cholinergic systems are implicated in dreaming sleep and hallucinations, both potentially related to imagination, there are few, if any, relevant scientific studies (Figure 44.10). While muscarinic receptor blockade can induce hallucinations, numerous studies show that it impairs rather than enhances cognition (Iwaki & Nomoto, 2014).

Academic reports on the hallucinogenic properties of cannabis are confined to the 1970s or earlier; and these reports are not now readily accessible. Hallucinations are not a common acute effect, but may occur with prolonged heavy use (Figure 44.11). Associations with creative imagination are contested. The idea that cannabis stimulates creativity is only supported by a limited number of studies. The cannabinoid receptor implicated in cognition and vision, and therefore by implication in creativity, is the CB1 subtype. In one recent study of creativity, it was concluded that "while cannabis users appear to demonstrate enhanced creativity, these effects are an artefact of their heightened levels of openness to experience" (LaFrance and Cuttler, 2017: 74).

Kowal et al. (2015: 1132) had previously concluded from their study of regular cannabis users "that cannabis with low potency does not have any impact on creativity, while highly potent cannabis actually impairs divergent thinking." In addition, marijuana decreases visual imagery suggesting a further negative effect on imagination (Block and Wittenborn, 1984). Legalization of cannabis for medical use in many countries and states of the United States may prompt new studies on more positive aspects of the drug. Already there is evidence of cognitive enhancing effects of cannabidiol, a noneuphoric cannabinoid in the cannabis plant, which is being investigated in the therapy in psychiatric and neurological disorders (Osborne, Solowij, and Weston-Greek, 2017).

Reports on dopamine, hallucinations, and creativity are so far limited (Figure 44.12). The unexpected finding that there are more reports on creativity and dopaminergic drugs for Parkinson's disease than for any of the other psychedelics reflects intensive research on the symptoms of this major disease of the brain, rather than a core role for dopamine per se. It was originally unclear if changes in creativity in Parkinson's were a consequence of the disease or of dopaminergic drug treatment (Inzelberg, 2013). Drug treatment, which can also induce hallucinations (Wood, 2010), has recently been implicated. Faust-Socher et al. (2014) noted enhanced verbal and visual creativity in Parkinson's patients treated with dopaminergic drugs and speculated that the drugs reduced inhibition in associative networking, so promoting divergent thinking. Lhommée at al. (2014) reported that "hobbyism" decreased after surgery and consequent reduction of dopamine agonists (drugs relatively specific for mesolimbic D3 receptors), indicating that creativity (e.g. artistic ability) emerging in PD is drug-related. However, Canesi et al. (2016) suggest that the drugs increase the drive to create, not creativity itself.

As with cannabis, opiate research tends to focus on the adverse effects of natural or synthetic opiates, especially in view of addictive and potentially lethal effects of potent analgesics like fentanyl (Figure 44.13). Opioid-induced hallucinations are

Plant or chemical	Active ingredient(s)	Hallucinatory effect: anecdotal and scientific studies	Effect on imagination / creativity: anecdotal and scientific studies	Relevant neurobiological mechanisms involving neuromodulatory systems
Anticholinergic drugs used medically (e.g. bladder control, travel sickness, antipsychotics)	Atropine for pupil dilation, oxybutynin (bladder), scopolamine (travel) and atypical neuroleptics e.g. clozapine for psychosis.	Hallucinations, particularly visual associated with the medical use of each of these drugs and with the recreational use of scopolamine (Perry and Perry, 1995).	No reports of increased creativity but association with cognitive changes similar to those in disorders associated with hypocholinergic activity and dementia (Alzheimer's disease and dementia with Lewy bodies).	Preventing the action of acetylcholine, involved in conscious awareness and learning, through blockade of muscarinic receptors (subtypes M1-M4) variously implicated in delusions, visual hallucinations and alterations in consciousness, and in DLB (e.g. Teaktong et al., 2005).
Plants with anticholinergic activity	Mandrake, belladonna, datura, henbane, and scopolia, containing tropane alkaloids such as atropine, hyoscine or scopolamine and hysoscamine.	Used in witches' brews to induce visions of animals and people from the "spirit world." Recreational use of datura and other plants associated with visual hallucinations (Wiebe, Sigurdson and Katz, 2006).	Henbane used by the priestesses of the oracle of Delphi to prophesy. Datura given to American Indian youngsters to meet their lifetime "animal guide." Lack of scientific studies on imagination or creativity (plants are highly toxic).	As above.

Figure 44.10 *Imaginative effects of acetylcholine active hallucinogens.*

Plant or chemical	Active ingredient(s)	Hallucinatory effect(s): anecdotal and scientific studies	Effect on imagination / creativity: anecdotal and scientific studies	Relevant neurobiological mechanisms involving neuromodulatory systems
Cannabis or marijuana as dried flowers or (hashish), the resin from *Cannabis sativa*	Cannabinoid terpenoid chemicals, of which THC (tetra hydrocannabinol) has the most potent psychedelic activity.	Visual and auditory hallucinations often reported as a dreamlike state by users. Scientific reports on hallucinatory mechanisms predate reports on psychosis and demonstrate REM sleep in awake users with hallucinations (e.g. Koukkous and Lehmann, 1976).	Anecdotal evidence of new insights (Gauther, 1846) and creativity. Increased verbal creativity in users (Bliem et al., 2013). Increased divergent thinking (measure of creativity) in those of lower creativity (Minor et al., 2014)	THC acts on the cannabinoid receptor CB1 for which the endogenous ligand (arachidonoylglycerol) in the brain is part of the cannabinoid system associated with mood (euphoria) and range of cognitive processes (perceptual, social, memory).

Figure 44.11 *Imaginative effects of cannabis.*

Plant or chemical	Active ingredient(s)	Hallucinatory effect: anecdotal and scientific studies	Effect on imagination / creativity: anecdotal and scientific studies	Relevant neurobiological mechanisms involving neuromodulatory systems
Dopaminergic drugs used to treat Parkinson's disease	Dopamine precursor, l- dopa and/or dopamine receptor agonists such as pramipexole.	Drug-induced excessive dopamine, (especially in disorders with low cholinergic activity), induces mainly visual hallucinations, often complex (people or animals for example) (Collerton, Perry, and McKeith, 2005).	Enhances creative thinking in people with Parkinson's disease (e.g. Lhommée et al., 2014); one study indicates the drugs increase the drive to create as opposed to creative behavior itself (Canesi et al., 2016).	Drugs increase levels of, or effect of, dopamine in mesolimbic brain areas; dopamine playing a major role in reward-motivated behavior and in perception and experience of pleasure.

Figure 44.12 *Imaginative effects of dopamine active hallucinogens.*

rarely discussed between prescribers and patients, patients being reluctant to mention them (Tan and Gan, 2016). While opium, morphine, and its derivatives act on all three opiate receptor subtypes involved in euphoria and addiction, the plant, *Salvia divinorum* (divine sage), acts only on the kappa subtype and is not addictive. The terpene, salvinorin A, extracted from the plant is the most potent hallucinogen known: one hundred times more so than LSD (Cruz et al., 2017). The sage plant and the chemical itself trigger radical alterations in consciousness with the introduction of new concepts and altered perspectives. Although not yet investigated for effects on creative cognition, cognitive changes potentially relevant to the topic are reported. For example, after inhaling combusted sage, healthy individuals reported changes in auditory and visual sensory input as well as losing normal awareness of themselves and their surroundings (Addy et al., 2015). The kappa opioid receptor is implicated in regulating sensory perception and interoception, based on the subjective effects of salvinorin A in healthy volunteers (Maqueda et al., 2015). In primates, a kappa-selective synthetic agonist is sedative and cognitive-impairing at analgesic doses (Davis et al., 1992). Being nonaddictive as well as legal, this psychedelic lends itself to future studies on imagination and creative cognition.

Neuromodulators of Imagination?

Neuroscientific research on human imagination or creativity includes only a few studies in people who do not use hallucinogens of any of the hallucination-

Plant or chemical	Active ingredient(s)	Hallucinatory effect(s): anecdotal and scientific studies	Effect on imagination / creativity: anecdotal and scientific studies	Relevant neurobiological mechanisms involving neuro-modulatory systems
Opium and laudanum	Contained in latex from the seed head of the opium poppy (*Papaver somniferum*), usually smoked. Containing the alkaloids morphine, codeine, thebaine, and papaverine. Laudanum is an alcoholic extract.	Dreamlike, fantastic visions reported during narcotic trances though complex hallucinations are rare (hypnagogic hallucinations an exception). Hallucinations reported by adult males taking opium tea (Klusonová, Vlková, and Visnovský, 2005).	Many examples of writers and musicians who claimed their creativity was enhanced by opium (e.g. Berlioz, De Quincy, Coleridge, Keats, and Cocteau [e.g. Vickers, 2015]) but no systematic studies.	Acting on opiate receptors in the brain (delta – analgesia and addiction, mu – analgesia, addiction and euphoria, and kappa – analgesic and hallucinatory), for which endogenous opiates (e.g. endophins and encephalins) are the natural ligands. The endogenous opiate system in the brain controls perception of pain and pleasure.
Morphine	Alkaloid extracted from the opium poppy used as a medical and recreational drug.	Hallucinations, including visual and auditory, occasionally reported as side effect of analgesia.	Effects on dreaming but no reported studies on creativity.	As for opium.
Heroin	Synthetic derivative of morphine used medically and recreationally as a euphoric.	Occasional anecdotal reports of hallucinations in users.	Users describe altered concentration – paying attention to what is usually ignored. Reported studies are focused on addiction, not creativity.	As for opium.
Divine sage (*Salvia divinorum*)	Terpene (non nitrogen containing chemical), salvinorin A, the most potent hallucinogen known.	Plant used in Mexican shamanism to induce visions. Salvinorin A induces visual and auditory hallucinations as well as altered body image (e.g. Maqueda et al., 2015).	Anecdotally the chemical stimulates imagination. Studies of effects on imagination/ creativity not reported. Dissociative effects, blocking extrasensory perception (Maqueda et al., 2015) and delusions (Addy et al., 2015) may contribute to novel cognition.	Salvinorin A acts on the kappa opioid receptor sub-type, implicated in regulation of sensory perception and interoception (sense of body physiology). Kappa activates dopamine neurons and behavioral disinhibition (Abraham et al., 2018). No actions on 5HT receptors.

Plant or chemical	Active ingredient(s)	Hallucinatory effect(s): anecdotal and scientific studies	Effect on imagination / creativity: anecdotal and scientific studies	Relevant neurobiological mechanisms involving neuro-modulatory systems
Other morphine-like drugs such as recreational mephedrone, analgesics such as methadone, and fentanyl	Drugs, based on opioid structures, synthesized to enhance euphoric or analgesic effects of morphine. Fentanyl is 50-100x more potent as an analgesic than morphine.	Mephedrone ("bath salts") can induce visual, auditory and kinaesthetic hallucinations (e.g. Buckenberg et al. 2016). Occasional hallucinations also reported on fentanyl (dosage being controlled for analgesia as opposed to altered consciousness).	Anecdotally effects are primarily euphoric rather than affecting creativity though users report increased alertness and sense of connectivity.	As for opium.

Figure 44.13 *Imaginative effects of opioids.*

associated neurotransmitters under discussion here. For 5HT, positive correlations are to be found in control subjects between creative ability and 5-HT1 receptor availability in functional imaging of gray matter (Varrone et al., 2015). Polymorphisms of the serotonin transporter and 1A receptor genes have been associated with verbal creativity (Volf et al., 2009) and creative dance ability (Bachner-Melman et al., 2005). There is less evidence for other neurotransmitters: Boot et al. (2017), reviewing previous studies linking creative ideation and divergent thinking to polymorphisms in dopamine receptor genes as well as to markers and manipulations of the dopaminergic system (the last including clinical populations with dopaminergic dysfunction) suggest that moderate (neither low nor high) levels of striatal dopamine enhance creative cognition by facilitating flexibility, and that moderate levels of prefrontal dopamine promote persistence-driven creativity. De Dreu, Bass, and Boot (2015), reviewing genetics and other observational studies on oxytocin, concluded that there is an association between oxytocin and creativity, that oxytocin enables cognitive flexibility pathways more than persistent information processing, and that the oxytocin effect is via dopaminergic activity.

In conclusion of this section on hallucinogenic drugs, 5-HT and its 1A and 1B receptors appear to head the list for involvement of hallucinogens in creative cognition and, by inference, imagination. There is scope for further research on dopaminergic D2 and D3, the opiate kappa and the cannabinoid CB1 receptors based on supportive, though limited, evidence on other neuromodulators involved in hallucinations. How activation of any of these receptors facilitates imagination is far from clear. The 5-HT1A receptor, for example, is the most widely distributed of the 5-HT receptors, concentrated in the cerebral cortex, hippocampus, amygdala, and raphe nucleus. The 5-HT2A is by contrast higher in frontal, parietal, and sensory cortical areas. More specific studies of cognitive function in people using hallucinogenic drugs who experience changed creativity, as well as chemical and functional neuroimaging of subjects using hallucinogens as they experience stimulated imagination, are needed to discover more about how hallucinogens affect imagination.

Hallucinations and an Overactive Imagination

A third line of evidence that links hallucinations with imagination comes from those clinical disorders in which hallucinations are frequent: particularly delirium, psychosis, and neurodegenerative disorders (Collerton, Perry, and McKeith, 2005). These disorders are also notable for high rates of delusions: idiosyncratic, strongly held, beliefs that resist challenge by compelling evidence to the contrary – or what we could call overly imaginative interpretations of experiences. Beliefs that hallucinations are real, significant, and personally relevant are features of all these disorders, and are a potent contribution to distress and disability (Holroyd, Currie, and Wooten, 2001; van Os et al., 2009; Webster and Holroyd, 2000).

However, not all people with hallucinations develop delusionary explanations of their perceptions, with rates being particularly high in psychosis and particularly low in sensory disorders – suggesting that other factors must influence the link between the experience and the interpretation, akin perhaps to the indirect links between hallucinations and artistic responses. Quite which factors these are, and why they appear to be more active in some people and some disorders than others are not known. In psychosis, where the evidence is strongest, emotional state, cognitive style, and past experience may all be relevant (e.g. Freeman 2007), consistent with the examples of artistic responses to hallucinations that suggest that reactions are highly personal.

Imagination and Hallucination: A Synthesis?

From the evidence that we review above, there is a close relationship between some aspects of hallucinatory and imaginary perceptions in the sense that both are internal representations of external things, differing probably only in non-perceptual aspects and their relationship to top-down expectation and sensory information. Linking imagination in its other, artistic senses to hallucinations at the brain level is, however, on much more uncertain ground.

Moving from neuronal activity controlled by transmitters acting on synaptic receptors to network connectivity involves a leap across a wide gap in knowledge, but connectivity is clearly implicated in psychedelic actions and creativity. According to Martin and Nichols (2017: 147) psychedelics alter brain network connectivity and "facilitate a disintegration of the default mode network, producing a hyperconnectivity between brain regions that allow centres that do not normally communicate with each other to do so." Supporting the idea of psychedelic-induced altered connectivity, Leichti (2017) noted in a review of functional imaging evidence on LSD effects in healthy adults that the drug increased connectivity between networks that normally are more dissociated. There was also increased functional thalamocortical connectivity and functional connectivity of the primary visual cortex with other brain areas, both of which correlated with subjective hallucinations. De Araujo et al. (2012: 8), investigating the effects of ayahuasca in human subjects using functional imaging, concluded that there was activation of an extensive net-work linking vision, memory, and intention. They noted that "activity of cortical areas BA30 and BA37 (temporal and cingulate areas), known to be involved with episodic memory and the processing of contextual associations, was also potentiated by ayahuasca intake during imagery," and that there was positive modulation of frontal BA 10, an "area involved with intentional prospective imagination, working memory and the processing of information from internal sources." Kaelen et al. (2016) later observed, again using functional imaging, increased parahippocampal-visual cortex functional connectivity in LSD users, which correlated with ratings of enhanced eyes-closed visual imagery. In an overview of twenty-five imaging studies of users of ayahuasca, DMT, psilocybin, LSD, and mescaline, Dos Santos et al. (2016) concluded that acute effects involve excitation of frontal (lateral and medial),

medial temporal and occipital cortices, whereas long-term use is associated with thinning of the posterior cingulate and thickening of the anterior cingulate cortex.

Conclusions

Are there any systematic links between hallucinations and wider aspects of imagination – or at least greater than those between imagination and anything else: sunsets, or wine, or the infinite, or any of the other great sources of human inspiration? The evidence is mostly absent, and equivocal where it exists. And yet many individuals have believed that there is a direct link between hallucinations and their imagination and have sought out ways of stimulating both; cultures have systematically used hallucinogens to link themselves to other places and times; clinical hallucinations are often associated with an overactive delusionary imagination; and there are overlaps between the brain areas and neurotransmitters that underlie both. For the relationships between these two aspects of human life to become clearer needs more investigation.

A recurrent theme in this chapter has been the variety of concepts attached to the word imagination. The relationship that hallucinations, in themselves a fuzzy concept with indistinct boundaries, have with each of these notions varies widely, so one challenge for the future will be to be much clearer about operational definitions of imagination (and hallucinations), so that the interplay of these concepts can be investigated more systematically. Clear conceptual frameworks will allow relationships between different modalities of hallucinations with different aspects of imagination to be tested using methods aimed at different levels of these phenomena in terms of models, phenomenology, consequences, and brain activity – akin to those used to study visual hallucinations (e.g. Collerton, Mosimann and Perry, 2015). No single method is likely to give unequivocal results since these are complex phenomena; converging combined approaches will give stronger evidence. There is an argument for the value of responsible research on psychedelic drug effects for further understanding creative aspects of human imagination and their links to hallucinations, analogous to recent new initiatives studying their potential applications in the treatment of depression, addiction, and anxiety (see Kyzar et al., 2017, for example).

This is an exciting time to be investigating hallucinations and imagination.

References

Abraham, A. D., Fontaine, H. M., Song, A. J., et al. (2018). κ-Opioid Receptor Activation in Dopamine Neurons Disrupts Behavioural Inhibition. *Neuropsychopharmacology*, *43*(2), 362–372.

Addy, P. H., Garcia-Romeu, A., Metzger, M., and Wade, J. (2015). The Subjective Experience of Acute, Experimentally-Induced Salvia Divinorum Inebriation. *Journal of Psychopharmacology*, *29*(4), 426–435.

Akers, B. P., Ruiz, J. F., Piper, A., and Ruck C. A. P. (2011) A Prehistoric Mural in Spain Depicting Neurotropic *Psilocybe* Mushrooms? *Economic Botany, 65*(2), 121–128.

Aleman, A., and Larøi, F. (2008). *Hallucinations: The Science of Idiosyncratic Perception.* Washington, DC: American Psychological Association.

de Araujo, B., Ribeiro, S., Cecchi, G. A., et al. (2012) Seeing with the Eyes Shut: Neural Basis of Enhanced Imagery Following Ayahuasca Ingestion. *Human Brain Mapping, 33* (11), 2550–2560.

Bachner-Melman, R., Dina, C., Zohar, A. H., et al. (2005). AVPR1a and SLC6A4 Gene Polymorphisms Are Associated with Creative Dance Performance. *PLoS Genetics,* 1(3), e42.

Bliem, B., Unterrainer, H. F., Papousek, I., Weiss, E. M., and Fink, A. (2013). Creativity in Cannabis-Users and in Drug Addicts in Maintenance Treatment and in Rehabilitation. *Neuropsychiatry, 27*(1), 2–10.

Block, R. I., and Wittenborn, J. R. (1984). Marijuana Effects on Visual Imagery in a Paired-Associate Task. *Perceptual and Motor Skills, 58*(3), 759–766.

Blom, J. D. (2015). Defining and Measuring Hallucinations and their Consequences – What Is Really the Difference between a Veridical Perception and a Hallucination? Categories of Hallucinatory Experiences. In D. Collerton, U. Mosimann, and E. Perry (eds.), *The Neuroscience of Visual Hallucinations.* West Sussex, UK: John Wiley & Sons, 23–45.

Boot, N., Baas, M., van Gaal, S., et al. (2017). Creative Cognition and Dopaminergic Modulation of Fronto-Striatal Networks: Integrative Review and Research Agenda. *Neuroscience & Biobehavioural Reviews, 78,* 13–23.

Canesi, M., Rusconi, M. L., Moroni, F., et al. (2016). Creative Thinking, Professional Artists, and Parkinson's Disease. *Journal of Parkinson's Disease, 6*(1), 239–246.

Caruncho, M. V., and Fernández, F. B. (2011). The Hallucinations of Frédéric Chopin. *Medical Humanities, 37*(1), 5–8.

Collerton, D., Mosimann, U. P., and Perry, E. K. (eds.) (2015). *The Neuroscience of Visual Hallucinations.* West Sussex, UK; Hoboke, NJ: John Wiley & Sons.

Collerton, D., Perry, E., and McKeith, I. (2005). Why People See Things That Are Not There: A Novel Perception and Attention Deficit Model for Recurrent Complex Visual Hallucinations. *Behavioral and Brain Sciences, 28*(6), 737–757.

Collerton, D., Taylor, J. P., Tsuda, I., et al. (2016). How Can We See Things That Are Not There? Current Insights into Complex Visual Hallucinations. *Journal of Consciousness Studies, 23*(7–8), 195–227.

Cruz, A., Domingos, S., Gallardo, E., and Martinho, A. (2017). A Unique Natural Selective Kappa-Opioid Receptor Agonist, Salvinorin A, and Its Roles in Human Therapeutics. *Phytochemistry, 137,* 9–14.

Davis, R. E., Callahan, M. J., Dickerson, M., and Downs, D. A. (1992). Pharmacologic Activity of CI-977, a Selective Kappa Opioid Agonist, in Rhesus Monkeys. *Journal of Pharmacology and Experimental Therapeutics, 261*(3), 1044–1049.

De Dreu, C. K., Baas, M., and Boot, N. C. (2015). Oxytocin Enables Novelty Seeking and Creative Performance through Upregulated Approach: Evidence and Avenues for Future Research. *Wiley Interdisciplinary Reviews: Cognitive Science, 6*(5), 409–417.

De Quincy, T. (1821) Confessions of an English Opium-Eater. *London Magazine,* IV(xxii), 353–379.

Dittrich, A., Bickel, P., Schöpf, J., and Zimmer, D. (1976). Comparison of Altered States of Consciousness Induced by the Hallucinogens (–)-Delta9-Trans-Tetrahydrocannabinol (Delta9-THC) and N,N-Dimethyltryptamine (DMT). *Archiv für Psychiatrie und Nervenkrankheiten, 223*(1), 77–87.

Dos Santos, R. G., Osório, F. L., Crippa, J. A. S., and Hallak, J. E. C. (2016). Classical Hallucinogens and Neuroimaging: A Systematic Review of Human Studies: Hallucinogens and Neuroimaging. *Neuroscience & Biobehavioural Reviews, 71*, 715–728.

Dudley, R., Wood, M., Spencer, H., et al. (2012). Identifying Specific Interpretations and Use of Safety Behaviours in People with Distressing Visual Hallucinations: An Exploratory Study. *Behavioural and Cognitive Psychotherapy, 40*(3), 367–375.

Ellis, H. (1898). Mescal: A New Artificial Paradise. *The Contemporary Review, 73*, 130–141.

Faust-Socher, A., Kenett, Y. N., Cohen, O. S., Hassin-Baer, S., and Inzelberg, R. (2014). Enhanced Creative Thinking under Dopaminergic Therapy in Parkinson Disease. *Annals of Neurology, 75*(6), 935–942.

Ffytche, D. H., Howard, R. J., Brammer, M. J., et al. (1998). The Anatomy of Conscious Vision: An fMRI Study of Hallucinations. *Nature Neuroscience, 1*(8), 738–742.

Finegersh, A., Rompala, G. R., Martin, D. I., and Homanics, G. E. (2015). Drinking beyond a Lifetime: New and Emerging Insights into Paternal Alcohol Exposure on Subsequent Generations. *Alcohol, 49*(5), 461–470.

Finkelstein, H. (1975). Dali's Paranoia-Criticism or the Exercise of Freedom. *Twentieth Century Literature, 21*(1), 59–71.

Freeman, D. (2007). Suspicious Minds: The Psychology of Persecutory Delusions. *Clinical Psychology Review, 27*(4), 425–457.

Frucht, S. J., and Bernsohn, L. (2002). Visual Hallucinations in PD. *Neurology, 59*(12), 1965.

Gallimore, A. R. (2015). Restructuring Consciousness – The Psychedelic State in Light of Integrated Information Theory. *Frontiers in Human Neuroscience, 9*, 346.

Gallimore, A. R., and Strassman, R. J. (2016). A Model for the Application of Target-Controlled Intravenous Infusion for a Prolonged Immersive DMT Psychedelic Experience. *Frontiers in Pharmacology, 7*, 211.

Gauther, T. (1846) Le Club des Haschischins. *Revue des Deux Mondes*, période initiale, 13 (1846), 520–535.

Goetz, C. G., Vaughan, C. L., Goldman, J. G., and Stebbins, G. T. (2014). I Finally See What You See: Parkinson's Disease Visual Hallucinations Captured with Functional Neuroimaging. *Movement Disorders, 29*(1), 115–117.

Heller, R. H. (1972) *Edvard Munch: The Scream*. New York, NY: Viking Press.

Holm-Hadulla, R. M., and Bertolino, A. (2014). Creativity, Alcohol and Drug Abuse: The Pop Icon Jim Morrison. *Psychopathology, 47*(3), 167–173.

Holroyd, S., Currie, L., Wooten, G. F. (2001). Prospective Study of Hallucinations and Delusions in Parkinson's Disease. *Journal of Neurology, Neurosurgery & Psychiatry, 70*, 734–738.

Howe, J. (2001). *Edvard Munch: Psyche, Symbol and Expression*. Boston, MA: Boston College, McMullen Museum of Art.

Huxley, A. (1954/2004). *The Doors of Perception*. London, UK: Vintage Books.

Inzelberg, R. (2013). The Awakening of Artistic Creativity and Parkinson's Disease. *Behavioral Neuroscience, 127*(2), 256–261.

Iwaki, H., and Nomoto, M. (2014). The Adverse Effects of Anticholinergic Drugs. *Brain and Nerve, 66*(5), 551–560.

Janiker, O., and Dobkin de Rios, M. (1989). LSD and Creativity. *Journal of Psychoactive Drugs*, *21*(1), 129–134.

Kaelen, M., Roseman, L., Kahan, J., et al. (2016). LSD Modulates Music-Induced Imagery via Changes in Parahippocampal Connectivity. *European Neuropsychopharmacology*, *26*(7), 1099–1109.

Kennaway, J. (2017). "Those Unheard Are Sweeter." Musical Hallucinations in Nineteenth-Century Medicine and Culture. *Terrain: Anthropologie & Sciences Humaines*, 68, doi : 10.4000/terrain.16426.

Kenney, S. (1975). Two Endings: Virginia Woolf's Suicide and *Between the Acts*. *University of Toronto Quarterly*, *44*(4), 265–289.

Klusonová, H., Vlková, J., and Visnovský, P. (2005). Natural Opium as One of the Possibilities for Drug Abusers. *Biomedical Papers of the Medical Faculty of the University Palacky, Olomouc, Czechoslovakia*, *149*(2), 481–483.

Kometer, M., Schmidt, A., Jäncke, L., and Vollenweider, F. X. (2013). Activation of Serotonin 2A Receptors Underlies the Psilocybin-Induced Effects on α Oscillations, N170 Visual-Evoked Potentials, and Visual Hallucinations. *Journal of Neuroscience, 33* (25), 10544–10551.

Koukkou, M., and Lehmann, D. (1976). Human EEG Spectra before and during Cannabis Hallucinations. *Biological Psychiatry*, *11*(6), 663–677.

Kowal, M. A., Hazekamp, A., Colzato, L. S., et al. (2015). Cannabis and Creativity: Highly Potent Cannabis Impairs Divergent Thinking in Regular Cannabis Users. *Psychopharmacology*, *232*(6), 1123–1134.

Kulig, K. (1990). LSD. *Emergency Medicine Clinics of North America*, *8*(3), 551–558.

Kuypers, K. P., Riba, J., de la Fuente Revenga, M., et al. (2016). Ayahuasca Enhances Creative Divergent Thinking while Decreasing Conventional Convergent Thinking. *Psychopharmacology*, *233*(18), 3395–3403.

Kyzar, E. J., Nichols, C. D., Gainetdinov, R. R., Nichols, D. E., and Kalueff, A. V. (2017). Psychedelic Drugs in Biomedicine. *Trends in Pharmacological Sciences*, *38*(11), 992–1005.

LaFrance, E. M., and Cuttler, C. (2017). Inspired by Mary Jane? Mechanisms underlying Enhanced Creativity in Cannabis Users. *Consciousness and Cognition*, *56*, 68–76.

Landon, M., and Fischer, R. (1970). On Similar Linguistic Structures in Creative Performance and Psilocybin-Induced Experience. *Confinia Psychiatrica*, *13*(2), 115–138.

Leichti, M. E. (2017). Modern Clinical Research on LSD. *Neuropsychopharmacology, 42* (11), 2114–2127.

Leikin, J. B., Krantz, A. J., Zell-Kanter, M., Barkin, R. L., and Hryhorczuk, D. O. (1989). Clinical Features and Management of Intoxication due to Hallucinogenic Drugs. *Medical Toxicology and Adverse Drug Experience*, *4*(5), 324–350.

Lhommée, E., Batir, A., Quesada, J. L., et al. (2014). Dopamine and the Biology of Creativity: Lessons from Parkinson's Disease. *Frontiers in Neurology*, *5*, 55.

Liu, J., Li, J., Feng, L., et al. (2014). Seeing Jesus in Toast: Neural and Behavioral Correlates of Face Pareidolia. *Cortex*, *53*, 60–77.

Maqueda, A. E., Valle, M., Addy, P. H., et al. (2015). Salvinorin-A Induces Intense Dissociative Effects, Blocking External Sensory Perception and Modulating Interoception and Sense of Body Ownership in Humans. *International Journal of Neuropsychopharmacology*, *18*(12), pyv065.

Martin, D. A., and Nichols, C. D. (2017). The Effects of Hallucinogens on Gene Expression. *Current Topics in Behavioural Neurosciences, 36,* 1–22.

McKenna, T. (1999). *Food of the Gods: The Search for the Original Tree of Knowledge. A Radical History of Plants, Drugs and Human Evolution.* London, UK: Random House.

McNorgan, C. (2012). A Meta-Analytic Review of Multisensory Imagery Identifies the Neural Correlates of Modality-Specific and Modality-General Imagery. *Frontiers in Human Neuroscience, 6,* 285.

Minor, K. S., Firmin, R. L., Bonfils, K. A., et al. (2014). Predicting Creativity: The Role of Psychometric Schizotypy and Cannabis Use in Divergent Thinking. *Psychiatry Research, 220*(1–2), 205–210.

Naselaris, T., Olman, C. A., Stansbury, D. E., Ugurbil, K., and Gallant, J. L. (2015). A Voxel-Wise Encoding Model for Early Visual Areas Decodes Mental Images of Remembered Scenes. *Neuroimage, 105,* 215–228.

Nielsen, T. A. (1992). A Self-Observational Study of Spontaneous Hypnagogic Imagery Using the Upright Napping Procedure. *Imagination, Cognition and Personality, 11*(4), 353–366.

Novak, S. J. (1997). LSD Before Leary. Sidney Cohen's Critique of 1950s Psychedelic Drug Research. *Isis: An International Review Devoted to the History of Science and Its Cultural Influences, 88*(1), 87–110.

O'Craven, K. M., and Kanwisher, N. (2000). Mental Imagery of Faces and Places Activates Corresponding Stimulus-Specific Brain Regions. *Journal of Cognitive Neuroscience, 126,* 1013–1023.

Orsolini, L., Papanti, G. D., de Berardis, D., et al. (2017). The "Endless Trip" Among the NPS Users: Psychopathology and Psychopharmacology in the Hallucinogen-Persisting Perception Disorder. A Systematic Review. *Frontiers in Psychiatry, 8,* 240.

Osborne, A. L., Solowij, N., and Weston-Green, K. (2017). A Systematic Review of the Effect of Cannabidiol on Cognitive Function: Relevance to Schizophrenia. *Neuroscience and Biobehavioural Reviews, 72,* 310–324.

Ostwald, P. F. (1987). *Schumann: The Inner Voices of a Musical Genius.* Boston, MA: Northeastern University Press.

Palhano-Fontes, F., Andrade, K. C., Tofoli, L. F., et al. (2015). The Psychedelic State Induced by Ayahuasca Modulates the Activity and Connectivity of the Default Mode Network. *PLoS One, 10*(2), e0118143.

Perry, E. K., and Perry, R. H. (1995). Acetylcholine and Hallucinations: Disease-Related Compared to Drug-Induced Alterations in Human Consciousness. *Brain and Cognition, 28*(3), 240–258.

Perry, N., and Perry, E. (2018). *Botanic Brain Balms.* London, UK: Filbert Press.

Prado, V. F., Janickova, H., Al-Onaizi, M. A., and Prado, M. A. (2017). Cholinergic Circuits in Cognitive Flexibility. *Neuroscience, 345,* 130–141.

Riley, S. C., and Blackman, G. (2008). Between Prohibitions: Patterns and Meanings of Magic Mushroom Use in the UK. *Substance Use and Misuse, 43*(1), 55–71.

Rothenberg, A. (2001). Bipolar Illness, Creativity, and Treatment. *Psychiatric Quarterly, 72*(2), 131–147.

Sessa, B. (2008). Is It Time to Revisit the Role of Psychedelic Drugs in Enhancing Human Creativity? *Psychopharmacology, 22*(8), 821–827.

Shine, J. M., Keogh, R., O'Callaghan, C., et al. (2015). Imagine That: Elevated Sensory Strength of Mental Imagery in Individuals with Parkinson's Disease and Visual

Hallucinations. *Proceedings of the Royal Society of London B: Biological Sciences*, *282*(1798), 2014–2047.

Sireteanu, R., Oertel, V., Mohr, H., Linden, D., and Singer, W. (2008). Graphical Illustration and Functional Neuroimaging of Visual Hallucinations during Prolonged Blindfolding: A Comparison to Visual Imagery. *Perception*, *37*, 1805–1821.

Slotnick, S.D., Thompson. W.L., and Kosslyn, M. (2005). Visual Mental Imagery Induces Retinotopically Organised Activation of Early Visual Areas. *Cerebral Cortex*, *15*, 1570–1583.

Sweat, N. W., Bates, L. W., and Hendricks, P. S. (2016). The Associations of Naturalistic Classic Psychedelic Use, Mystical Experience, and Creative Problem Solving. *Journal of Psychoactive Drugs*, *48*(5), 344–350.

Takahashi, K., and Watanabe, K. (2013). Gaze Cueing by Pareidolia Faces. *i-Perception*, *4*, 490–492.

Tan, M., and Gan, T. J. (2016). Opioid-Induced Hallucination: Distressful or Sought After? *Anaesthesia and Analgesia*, *123*(4), 818–819.

Teaktong, T., Piggott, M. A., Mckeith, I. G., et al. (2005). Muscarinic M2 and M4 Receptors in Anterior Cingulate Cortex: Relation to Neuropsychiatric Symptoms in Dementia with Lewy Bodies. *Behavioural Brain Research*, *161*(2), 299–305.

ten Berge, J. (2002). Jekyll and Hyde Revisited: Paradoxes in the Appreciation of Drug Experiences and Their Effects on Creativity. *Journal of Psychoactive Drugs*, *34*(3), 249–262.

Thirion, B., Duchesnay, E., Hubbard, E., et al. (2006). Inverse Retinotopy: Inferring the Visual Content of Images from Brain Activation Patterns. *Neuroimage*, *33*, 1104–1116.

Thomson, C., Wilson, R., Collerton, D., Freeston, M., and Dudley, R. (2017). Cognitive Behavioural Therapy for Visual Hallucinations: An Investigation using a Single-Case Experimental Design. *The Cognitive Behaviour Therapist*, 10.

Uchiyama, M., Nishio, Y., Yokoi, K., et al. (2012). Pareidolias: Complex Visual Illusions in Dementia with Lewy Bodies. *Brain*, *135*, 2458–2469.

(2015). Pareidolia in Parkinson's Disease without Dementia: A Positron Emission Tomography Study. *Parkinsonism and Related Disorders*, *21*, 603–609.

van Os, J., Linscott, R. J., Myin-Germeys, I., Delespaul, P., and Krabbendam, L. (2009). A Systematic Review and Meta-Analysis of the Psychosis Continuum: Evidence for a Psychosis Proneness–Persistence–Impairment Model of Psychotic Disorder. *Psychological Medicine*, *39*(2), 179–195.

Varrone, A., Svenningsson, P., Marklund, P., et al. (2015). 5-HT1B Receptor Imaging and Cognition: A Positron Emission Tomography Study in Control Subjects and Parkinson's Disease Patients. *Synapse*, *69*(7), 365–374.

Vickers, N. (2015). Opium as a Literary Stimulant: The Case of Samuel Taylor Coleridge. *International Review Neurobiology*, *120*, 327–338.

Volf, N. V., Kulikov, A. V., Bortsov, C. U., and Popova, N. K. (2009). Association of Verbal and Figural Creative Achievement with Polymorphism in the Human Serotonin Transporter Gene. *Neuroscience Letters*, *463*(2), 154–157.

Vollenweider, F. X., Vontobel, P., Hell, D., and Leenders, K. L. (1999). 5-HT Modulation of Dopamine Release in Basal Ganglia in Psilocybin-Induced Psychosis in Man – a PET study with [11 C]raclopride. *Neuropsychopharmacology*, *20*(5), 424–433.

Waters, F., Collerton, D., Ffytche, D. H., et al. (2014). Visual Hallucinations in the Psychosis Spectrum and Comparative Information from Neurodegenerative Disorders and Eye Disease. *Schizophrenia Bulletin*, *40*(suppl 4), S233–S245.

Webster, R., and Holroyd, S. (2000). Prevalence of Psychotic Symptoms in Delirium. *Psychosomatics, 41*(6), 519–522.

Wiebe, T. H., Sigurdson, E. S., and Katz, L. Y. (2006). Angel's Trumpet (*Datura stramonium*) Poisoning and Delirium in Adolescents in Winnipeg, Manitoba: Summer 2006. *Paediatrics and Child Health, 13*(3), 193–196.

Wood, L. D. (2010). Clinical Review and Treatment of Select Adverse Effects of Dopamine Receptor Agonists in Parkinson's Disease. *Drugs & Aging, 27*(4), 295–310.

Yokoi, K., Nishio, Y., Uchiyama, M., et al. (2014). Hallucinators Find Meaning in Noises: Pareidolic Illusions in Dementia with Lewy Bodies. *Neuropsychologia, 56*(1), 245–254.

45 The Psychiatry of Imagination

Bernard J. Crespi

> "*Absolutely everything around us that was created by the hand of mankind, the entire world of human culture, is the product of human imagination and of creation based on this imagination*".
>
> Vygotsky (2004: 9)

If everything around us springs ultimately from the imaginations of humans, where does the imagination come from? What is it for, and with what psychological phenotypes is it associated, positively and negatively? At extremes of the continuous psychological axes that underlie imagination, do we find psychiatric pathologies? If so, what forms and symptoms, and why? In this chapter, I focus on the primary unresolved question of to what degree, and in what ways, extremes of imagination manifest in, and mediate, psychiatric disorders and their phenotypes.

First, I discuss what I do and do not mean by "imagination." I also discuss what imagination is not – its conceptual boundaries, and its apparent antithesis to intelligence.

Second, I introduce the psychiatric disorders to be considered here, explain their causes and meanings, and provide them with cognitive-affective architectures grounded in psychology, neuroscience, and evolutionary theory. I focus predominantly on autism and psychotic-affective disorders (mainly schizophrenia, bipolar disorder, and depression, and the disorders associated with the continua connecting them with typical cognition and mood). The range of disorders discussed here with regard to the imagination is motivated mainly by theoretical considerations regarding how autism and psychotic-affective disorders are associated with aspects of typical cognition, with aspects of imagination, and with one another.

Third, I guide the reader through sets of diverse literature bearing on the dimensions of imagination in autism and psychotic-affective conditions. This literature and question have previously been reviewed by Crespi et al. (2016); here, I extend, deepen, and sharpen their analysis.

Finally, I contrast imagination with intelligence, in general and in the context of autism spectrum and psychotic-affective spectrum disorders, and make suggestions for future work.

What Imagination Can Be Imagined to Be, and Not to Be

On one hand, we have a simple linear definition of imagination, from the Oxford English Dictionary (en.oxforddictionaries.com, July 2018):

The faculty or action of forming new ideas, or images or concepts of external objects not present to the senses.

This definition is valuable conceptually, in capturing a one-dimensional essence of a meaning of imagination, but it has limited applicability with regard to its empirical study, which requires quantification and comparison. For these purposes, on the other hand, we can unpack a set of interrelated concept-dimensions for imagination, each of which can be studied scientifically and associated with phenomena that differ but are more or less closely allied (Figure 45.1). This definition of imagination is less succinct than the first one, but it can be made to dovetail directly with the four-tiered scheme developed by Abraham (Chapter 1), as shown in Figure 45. 2.

Our definitional landscape of imagination is inherently neurological, in that in principle each of its components is subserved by modules, regions, circuitries, or networks in the brain that have been characterized to some degree. The elucidation of such modules and networks has been achieved on a large scale for imagination, predominantly in the context of the so-called "default mode" or "task-negative" network, which comprises a set of brain regions that are preferentially activated when the brain is engaged with internally directed, rather than externally directed, cognitive and affective processes (Figure 45.3). We will consider this set of correlated brain activations as the "imagination network," based on the evidence linking imagination-related functions with the core neural structures of the region. As such, the default mode network represents the primary neurological system subserving imagination and creativity (Jauk et al., 2015). Three aspects of the imagination network are especially important for the purposes of this article.

First, the imagination network is anticorrelated (inversely related) in its activation with the so-called "task-positive" network, which is activated upon engagement with external stimuli involving attentional and executive-functional cognitive activities, such as gathering salient information, manipulating it within the brain, and solving

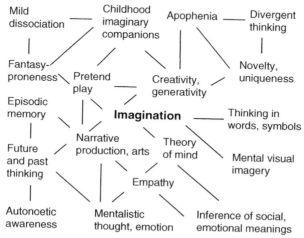

Figure 45.1 *Imagination as a set of related phenomena in neurotypical cognition, associated with core functions of the human brain related to self-related and social cognition.*

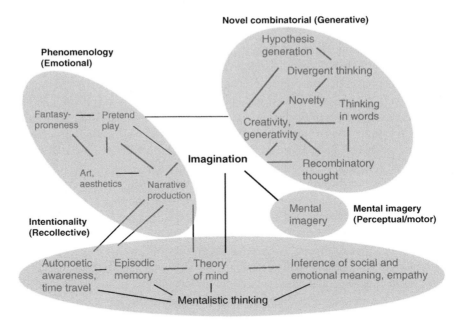

Figure 45.2 *Four primary domains of imagination. Shown here with four gray-shaded shapes, as described in Figure 1.3.*

specific problems (Figure 45.4). To a first approximation, then, the task-positive network can be considered as a neural system subserving intelligence, that involves integration of frontal with parietal regions, in conjunction with more or less efficient deactivation of the imagination network, and in accordance with the "P-FIT" (Parieto-Frontal Integration Theory) model for intelligence (Jung and Haier, 2007). These observations suggest that, in their purest neurological and philosophical forms, imagination and intelligence can be hypothesized as orthogonal if not functionally opposite to one another, or arranged at extremes of a "paradoxical simplex" (DeYoung,

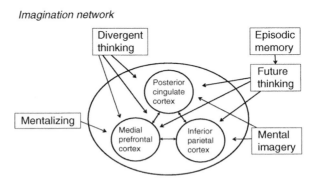

Figure 45.3 *The human imagination (default mode) network. Comprised of three main regions, the posterior cingulate cortex (PCC) (including the precuneus), the medial prefrontal cortex (mPFC), and the inferior parietal lobe (IPL), which includes the temporal-parietal junction.*

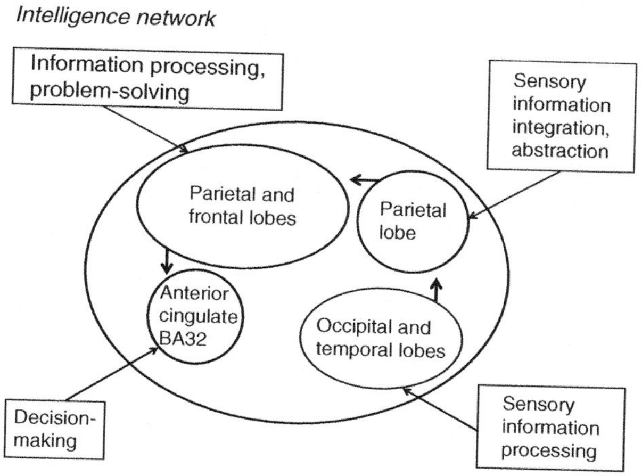

Intelligence network

Information processing, problem-solving

Sensory information integration, abstraction

Parietal and frontal lobes

Parietal lobe

Anterior cingulate BA32

Occipital and temporal lobes

Decision-making

Sensory information processing

Figure 45.4 *The human intelligence network. This represents a set of neural regions spanning from parietal to frontal areas that sequentially engage in functions that instantiate components of intelligence-related cognition.*

Grazioplene, and Peterson, 2012). Perhaps most importantly, intelligence tells us most clearly what imagination is not: it is specifically not, like intelligence is, a system for precise perception, focused external attention, exacting salience determination, learning, acquiring and applying knowledge, comprehending complex ideas, or finding patterns, systems, causes and truths where they exist (Figure 45.5).

Second, the imagination network overlaps broadly with the "social brain" network set of regions, the distributed yet integrated set of neural structures specialized for the processing of different aspects of social information (Meyer et al., 2019). Human imagination is thus most commonly explicitly social. These considerations also highlight the strong evolutionary comparative evidence that social selective pressures have been especially important in brain elaboration and expansion among the human lineage.

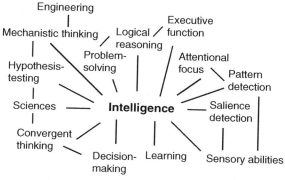

Figure 45.5 *Intelligence as a set of related phenomena in neurotypical cognition. Associated with core functions of the human brain related to "real" phenomena, logical operations, mechanistic cognition, and problem-solving.*

Third, the imagination network is defined and described here in an iconic and platonic idealized form, while in neurological reality it is expected to vary among individuals in aspects of structure and function to degrees that remain largely unknown. A given region may thus be especially likely to differ in its role and functioning between individuals with different sorts of psychiatric disorders – especially those that involve alterations to imagination. For example, in autism the imagination network may function less for social daydreaming and episodic thinking, and more for visual-pictorial thinking or a focus on one's specialized nonsocial interests (Crespi et al., 2016).

Psychiatric Disorders of Imagination

Having described what imagination is (for our purposes), and what it specifically is not, we have set the scene for analyzing our primary question of what "imagination disorders" are, and how they map onto our current classifications of named psychiatric disorders. Given that all biological systems vary in two directions, from smaller to larger, less to more, slower to faster, and so on, we can, most generally and simply, conceive of two sets of disorders: (1) too little imagination, and (2) too much imagination, with typical, "normal" levels of imagination in between. By our two-dimensional landscape structure of imagination's components (Figures 45.1 and 45.2), the low/high bidirectionality can apply across the landscape as a whole, more to some spatially autocorrelated regions than to others, and to specific components.

What, then, are human disorders of imagination? I develop and test the hypothesis that autism spectrum disorder traits represent manifestations of reduced imagination (and imagination functions reduced relative to intelligence-related functions) and that psychotic-affective spectrum disorder traits represent manifestations of pathologically increased imagination (and relatively reduced intelligence). A hypothesis of autism centrally involving reduced imagination and schizophrenia involving expansion of imagination via conflating it with beliefs, has been described by Currie and Ravenscroft (2002), and parallels aspects of the exposition provided here.

The autism spectrum can be conceptualized by two main threads, leading back to Kanner and Asperger: underdeveloped social cognition, and the presence of especially restricted interests and repetitive behavior. The psychotic-affective spectrum is more diverse, encompassing the DSM categories of schizophrenia, bipolar disorder, major depression, borderline and schizotypal personality disorders, and related diagnoses. All of these psychotic-affective diagnoses partially yet substantially overlap in their arrays of symptoms, their genetic underpinnings where known, and their neurological correlates (e. g. Crespi and Badcock 2008).

I apply three sets of analyses to evaluate the hypothesis of the autism spectrum and psychotic-affective spectrum as diametric disorders of imagination relative to intelligence. First, I interpret the major psychological and cognitive phenotypes (symptoms) associated with autism, and with the psychotic-affective spectrum, in the contexts of imagination and intelligence. Second, I take the reverse approach, addressing in turn each of the components of imagination shown in Figure 45.1, and comparing their patterns of expression mainly between autism and schizophrenia, the psychotic-affective disorder with the most information available. This analysis takes the form of a narrative literature review, and represents an extension of Crespi et al. (2016). Third, I consider the imagination disorders hypothesis in the context of the genetic bases of the autism spectrum and psychotic-affective spectrum, drawing on evidence from recent genome-wide studies, polygenic risk scores that provide a metric of overall genetic risk, and studies of genetic correlations, which indicate the degree to which expression of a pair of traits, such as autism risk and imagination, or schizophrenia and intelligence, is jointly mediated by similar alleles – and thus represents the same phenotype from a polygenic perspective.

Imaginative Dimensions of the Autism Spectrum and the Psychotic-Affective Spectrum

To what extent are the symptoms of the autism spectrum interpretable in terms of underdeveloped imagination, and the psychotic-affective spectrum as its overdeveloped opposite?

The two main traditional facets of autism – social-communicative deficits as well as restrictive interests and repetitive behavior – can each be considered as sequelae to reduced imagination. Sociality and communication thus centrally involve the social brain, social imagination, and the brain's imagination network, the functions of which revolve around theory (imagination) of mind in others, inference (imagination) of emotions and intentions in others, and language as combinatorial, recursive imagination, generation, encoding, and sharing of mental ideas. Restrictive interests and repetitive behavior, and inflexibility to change and insistence on sameness, can likewise be conceptualized as following from reduced imaginative cognition, in that they represent opposites to the core novelties, diversities, and generativities of imagination, in nonsocial contexts. The primacy of imagination-related traits in autism spectrum disorders is also supported by the observation that Baron-Cohen's Autism Quotient, a primary metric for autism traits, shows a strong male bias only for its Imagination Subscale, a subscale that reflects social imagination (Crespi et al., 2016).

Psychotic-affective disorders involve both psychosis (reality distortions, mainly hallucinations and delusions) and affective (mood) alterations, most notably in mania, hypomania, and depression. Hallucinations thus represent imaginary perceptions (or, more precisely, extremes of the imagined component of perception), and delusions are imagined narratives that transform into beliefs; both are most frequently social in their content or involve animated, personified inanimate objects (e.g. Birchwood et al., 2000).

While psychosis can be considered in terms of reality-incongruent perception and cognition, mania and depression, as in bipolar disorder and depression, can be conceptualized as forms of reality-incongruent forms of mood, in this way imagined as better, worse, or different. Within this context, mania, which involves varying degrees of euphoria, grandiosity, and increased energy, irritability, and distractability, can be considered to represent a manifestation of intensified, risky, and dysregulated goal-seeking, driven by increased mood-directed motivation (Johnson et al., 2012). The goals are more or less conscious internal images or concepts, and are thus imagined via future thinking in concert with the alterations to mood. Mania and psychosis occur together (by definition) in bipolar I disorder, whereby intensified mood and mental imagery contribute to the reality distortions of psychosis; hypomania (in so-called bipolar II disorder), by contrast, involves mania phenotypes that are sufficiently less-pronounced and contribute, in some individuals, to remarkable episodes of imagination-fueled creativity (e.g., Simeonova et al., 2005). In the setting of goal-seeking, depression can, by contrast, be seen to commonly center on inability to give up on unattainable and unrealistic imagined goals (Nesse, 2000).

Diametric and Extreme Aspects of Imagination

Pretend Play

Pretend play in children can be considered as a paradigmatic manifestation of imagination, in that it centers on fantasy, novelty, mild forms of dissociation (mental detachment from immediate physical surroundings and social circumstances) and made-up social narratives. As initially described by Kanner (1943), pretend play is reduced in children with autism (review in Jarrold, 2003) and, in such children, solitary and repetitive behavior focused on objects takes its place (Kasari, Chang, and Patterson, 2013; Wolfberg, 2009).

The overall intensity of childhood pretend play has not been quantified in relation to the development, in childhood or later, of psychotic-affective disorders. Anecdotal reports, however, support the hypothesis of high levels of forms of hallucinatory play in childhood schizophrenia, as in the case of Jani, who "required constant stimulation and had few friends, preferring the company of a cast of imaginary rats, cats, dogs and little girls" (Elsworth, 2013).

What specific forms of pretend play might, then, be indicative of high intensity, such that they should be elevated in the context of psychotic-affective traits and conditions, but lower on the autism spectrum? Jani's childhood imaginary companions, noted above, represent a possible manifestation of especially highly developed pretend and social play; imaginary companions are present in up to about half to two-thirds of children (Carlson, Tahiroglu, and Taylor, 2008), and their presence has been linked with: (1) relatively vivid mental imagery (Gleason, Jarudi, and Cheek, 2003), (2) increased tendency to hallucinate (Pignon et al., 2018), (3) high scores on measures of dissociation (Carlson, Tahiroglu, and Taylor, 2008; Dierker, Davis, and Sanders, 1995), (4) high levels of paranoia, and psychoticism (Bonne et al., 1999); (5) a preference for fantasy-based over reality-based toys (Acredolo, Goodwyn, and Fulmer, 1995); (6) higher creativity (Hoff, 2005) and (7) better theory of mind abilities (Carlson, Mandell, and Williams, 2004; Taylor and Carlson, 1997); the former six of these correlates show established positive associations with the psychotic-affective spectrum (Crespi et al., 2016).

Considered together, this set of findings suggests that high levels of some manifestations of pretend play, expressed as imaginary companions, are associated with a higher incidence of psychotic-affective symptoms and traits (Crespi et al., 2016). By contrast, Davis et al. (2018) have demonstrated a greatly reduced prevalence of imaginary companions among children with autism (16 percent, compared to 45 percent in controls), as expected under the hypothesis that imagination is reduced on the autism spectrum (also see Chapter 23).

Creativity

Creativity can be considered as a function of imagination plus usefulness or application, be it functional or aesthetic, real or unreal; in all cases, some thing or entity is generated in the mind and then the world. Creativity shows consistent evidence of reduction in autism (Dichter et al., 2009; Jarrold, Boucher, and Smith, 1996), with specific impairment in the imagining of unreal things (Scott and Baron-Cohen, 1996). As such, creativity, and its imaginational basis in autism, tends to be reality-based (Craig and Baron-Cohen, 1999; Craig, Baron-Cohen, and Scott, 2000), structure-guided (Mottron, Dawson, and Soulières, 2009), and focused on specific areas of nonsocial interest (Ten Eycke & Müller, 2015). At the level of personality variation, autistic traits are associated with low levels of openness to experience, extraversion, and novelty-seeking, each of which shows positive associations with creativity (e.g., Batey and Furnham, 2006; Kunihira et al., 2006).

In contrast to autism, large bodies of research have established links of creativity with phenotypes and disorders on the psychotic-affective spectrum, such that increased divergent thinking, magical thinking, openness, novelty-seeking, hypomania, positive schizotypy, and goal-seeking, as well as reduced latent inhibition (more diffuse and distractable attention, as opposed to more focused attention in autism) are connected with enhanced creative accomplishments (e.g. Acar, Chen, and Cayirdag, 2018; Taylor 2017). Such creativity and psychopathological symptoms on the psychotic-affective spectrum often center on people and other animate beings (e.g., Collerton, Perry, and McKeith, 2005), in contrast to real, nonanimate things in autism; psychotic-affective creativity thus appears to be mainly social-imagination based, as in most forms of magical ideation (Brugger and Mohr, 2008).

The relationship of psychotic-affective disorders, symptoms, and correlates with measures of creativity is not necessarily linear and positive, in that more severe disorder expression (e.g. on the schizophrenia spectrum), and "negative symptoms" appear to involve reductions in creativity (Acar, Chen, and Cayirdag, 2017; Baas et al., 2016). Indeed, according to Carson's (2011) "shared vulnerability" model, creativity and psychotic-affective conditions overlap only partially with respect to neurological and psychological traits that contribute to both; moreover, in relatively extreme form, or in association with deleterious phenotypes such as childhood trauma, creativity-increasing phenotypes can raise liability to psychotic-affective disorders.

Narrative and the Arts

Studies of story-writing and narrative comprehension among individuals with autism show that they exhibit reduced capacities in both areas, especially with regard to social themes, fantasy, conceptual novelty, and acquiring the "big picture" of a narrative as opposed to its local details (Barnes and Baron-Cohen, 2012; Bottema-

Beutel and White, 2016). Comparably, art by individuals with autism tends to be either reality-based (e.g. highly realistic drawing) or derive from rule-based systems for filling space (Roth, 2007; Snyder and Thomas, 1997). Autism is indeed associated with technical, nonartistic professions, such as engineering, mathematics, and science (Campbell and Wang, 2012; Dickerson et al., 2014; Spek and Velderman, 2013). By contrast, schizotypy, schizophrenia, bipolar disorder, and depression are notably associated with the production of poetry, literature (fiction), visual and creative arts, and the humanities (e.g. Kyaga, 2014; MacCabe et al., 2018; Power et al., 2015; Taylor 2017). The default mode (imagination) network has indeed been considered as the "seat of literary creativity," based on evidence from functional imaging (Wise and Braga, 2014).

Although psychotic-affective disorders have been linked with artistic and literary imagination and creativity, their relatively severe forms are by no means conducive to such endeavors; as opined by Sylvia Plath (Wagner-Martin 1987: 112): "when you are insane, you are busy being insane – all the time," and thus cannot create. Extreme, pathological imaginative phenotypes involve hallucinations, delusions, and confabulations that commonly take narrative, "social story," and mentalistically based forms (e.g. Currie, 2000; Currie and Jureidini, 2003; Nettle, 2001), even if personal narrative identity is reduced (e.g. in schizophrenia; Raffard et al., 2010). Social narrative production and appreciation, and technical compared to literary and artistic professions, represent striking contrasts between the autism spectrum and the psychotic-affective spectrum, that bear directly on reductions vs. enhancements of social imagination. In this framework, narrative production is especially important because it connects imagination with socially oriented creativity, mental imagery, autobiographical memory, future thinking, the self, and mentalizing most generally.

Mental Past and Futures

Episodic memory, future thinking, and autonoetic awareness (thinking about one's past or future self) have all been reported as decreased in autism (Cooper and Simons, 2019; Ferretti et al., 2018; Hanson and Atance, 2014; Terrett et al., 2013); autobiographical memory has also been reported as over-general (less specific) among individuals with Asperger syndrome (Tanweer, Rathbone, and Souchay, 2010). These findings are consistent with reduced imagination in autism, given that imaginative and future-oriented cognition are directly dependent on recruiting components of thought from episodic and autobiographical memories (Schacter et al., 2012), which may be reduced in autism in association with a reduced sense of the self. Indeed, reduced autobiographic memory in Asperger syndrome has been attributed to an underdeveloped sense of self (Goddard et al., 2007), which appears to be a general feature of the autism spectrum.

Episodic memory and future thinking are also reduced in schizophrenia, bipolar disorder, and depression, with memory tending to be overgeneral (Hach, Tippett, and Addis, 2014; King et al., 2011), and reduced autonoetic awareness has been reported among individuals with high schizotypy (Arzy et al., 2011) or with schizophrenia (de Oliveira et al., 2009; Raffard et al., 2010). In contrast to these results, higher autonoetic awareness has been found among individuals with elevated positive schizotypy, with regard to mental time travel (Winfield and Kamboj, 2010); positive schizotypy has also been associated with a stronger sense of presence (in autonoetic awareness) and perceived similarity of imagined events to past episodes (Raffard et al., 2010). Moreover, high levels of intrusive episodic memories are characteristic of depression, bipolar, schizophrenia, schizotypy, and dissociation (Brewin and Soni, 2011; Jones and Steel, 2012), especially as sequelae to trauma and adversity.

Reductions in episodic memory and future thinking, and over-general memory, have thus been demonstrated in both autism and psychotic-affective conditions. Whether the causes of such reductions are the same in both sets of disorders remains unclear.

Salience

Under the "weak central coherence" model, which can be traced back to Happé and Frith (Frith, 2012; Happé and Frith, 2006), autism involves a reduced drive to discern and imagine meanings, represented as global, "big picture" wholes, due to enhanced perceptual functioning, detail- and parts-focused attention, mechanistic cognition, restricted interests, and increased focus on predictable patterns and "systemizing" (interest in rule-based mechanistic and inanimate systems) (Baron-Cohen and Lombardo, 2017). As such, this model, in the context of salience, can help to unify cognitive theories of autism.

Reduced drive for meaning, and increased "meanings" found in rule-based systems and patterns in autism, contrast directly with overdeveloped drive for meaning, salience hypersensitivity, arbitrariness, and inappropriateness, and apophenia (tendency to infer and imagine meaningful patterns and connections where none exist); these traits are characteristic of psychotic-affective conditions, especially schizotypy, schizophrenia, and psychosis more generally (DeYoung, Grazioplene, and Peterson, 2012; Fyfe et al., 2008). Schizophrenia has indeed been considered as "salience syndrome" (e.g. van Os, 2009), due to excessive, promiscuous, and inappropriate assignment of meaning, with meaning most commonly involving imagined scenarios (delusions) and percepts (hallucinations), confabulations, or unacknowledged fantasy, usually with animate and social content (Jensen and Kapur, 2009).

As an example of the "salience spectrum" in autism and psychosis, consider someone (e.g. the author) viewing a city scene at his train stop. First-level *nonsalience* would be represented by the pixel pattern on his iPhone camera, bereft of interpretation. At the second level we find *hyposalience*, where small, piecemeal nonsocial functional parts or units – a car wheel, a shop window, or a crane hook, are perceived and understood only in terms of their highly local purposes, such as a wheel for spinning. These first two levels appear characteristic of the autism spectrum (Happé and Frith, 2006), involving specifically enhanced perceptual functions and thinking in pictures (including memories thereof), and weak central coherence. Third, *normosalience*, under typical cognition, centers on viewing and interpreting the entire scene, and its meanings, through integration of parts into wholes. Imagination can also be applied to the scene – for example, the crane and worksite being run and overrun by ants set on world domination – but the fantasy remains as such, with conscious insight into its narrative-based salience and fantasy. Fourth, and finally, we find *hyper-salience*, and imagination without insight into its unreality: delusions, hallucinations, and paranoia concerning alien ants controlling my mind; people in storefronts secretly watching me, humanity's only possible savior, and so on – a scene imbued with too strong central coherence and fantastical meaning.

Mental Imagery and Sensory Systems

Mental imagery is important because it provides raw material for the imagination, in the forms of internally generated patterns and parts that may coalesce to produce a novel form. Mental imagery among individuals with autism has been described as thinking in realistic, photographic pictures drawn from memory (Grandin, 1995, 2009). Indeed, Boucher (2007) suggested that imagination in autism may be "limited to rerunning images on the visuospatial scratchpad." Such descriptions are concordant with documented enhancements of some visual and spatial abilities in autism, and highly realistic drawing and spatial memory abilities as autism-associated islets of exceptional ability (Sahyoun et al., 2010; Soulières et al., 2009), although they remain largely anecdotal.

Especially vivid mental imagery, and enhanced abilities at some mental imagery tasks, have been demonstrated in schizotypy, schizophrenia, bipolar disorder, and dissociation (Ivins et al., 2014; Matthews et al., 2014). Mental imagery also mediates striving and goal achievement among individuals with bipolar disorder (Conway, Meares, and Standart, 2004; Meyer, Finucane, and Jordan, 2011), and it is strongly positively associated with hypomanic traits, in healthy population (McGill and Moulds, 2014). In psychosis, hallucinations involve confusion between mental imagery and perception (Brébion et al., 2008; Currie, 2000). Psychotic-affective conditions also commonly involve intrusive, involuntary, and negative mental imagery (Brewin and Soni, 2011; Jones and Steel, 2012) as major features leading to their negative mental effects.

Visual mental imagery and visual perception are closely associated because they use broadly overlapping brain regions, with information flow within and between them (Dentico et al., 2014; Slotnick, Thompson, and Kosslyn, 2012). As such, perceptual and sensory systems become directly relevant to the imagination, given that sharply and deeply perceived reality (in whatever form) should mitigate against novel image generation, while more abstract and ambiguous perceptions promote or allow it.

Sensory functions, which are directed externally, are inversely associated with internally directed default mode functions (e. g. Greicius and Menon, 2004). A large body of evidence, centered on the enhanced perceptual function (Mottron et al., 2006) and intense world (Markram and Markram, 2010) theories of autism, indicates that sensory abilities tend to be increased in autism (Mottron, Dawson, and Soulières, 2009; Tavassoli et al., 2014). Baron-Cohen (2009) has, indeed, suggested that increased sensory abilities in autism contribute to a detail-focused and systemizing cognitive style, which may reduce imaginative cognition to the extent that detail-oriented and rule-based thought diminish the generation of cognitive novelty.

In contrast to autism, a considerable suite of studies demonstrates reduced sensory function and abilities in schizophrenia (Javitt, 2009a, 2009b). In schizophrenia, psychotic symptoms have been considered as due to misinterpretation of imagination as perception, mediated in part by degradation of sensory functions; thus, hallucinations are associated with impaired sensory processing (Javitt, 2009a, 2009b), and at an extreme, sensory deprivation induces aspects of psychosis (Daniel and Mason, 2015). Reduced sensory abilities in schizophrenia may also potentiate apophenia and psychotic symptoms due to confusion between poorly perceived reality and imagination (Brébion et al., 2008; Javitt, 2009a, 2009b).

The Imagination Network and Its Components in Autism and Psychotic-Affective Disorders

The components of the imagination analyzed above appear to be closely associated with one another (Figure 45.6), as would be expected given their joint links with imagination itself. A key question thus becomes to just what degree imagination is "fractionable" or behaves as a unified construct? Ferretti et al. (2018) found that both narrative abilities and episodic future thinking were impaired in a subset of children with autism spectrum disorders, suggesting that these two aspects of imagination are causally related. Similarly, Joliffe and Baron-Cohen (1999) linked narrative deficits with reduced central coherence in autism. Further such tests would be useful, especially for linking the psychological architecture of imagination with its neurological bases.

Most generally, default system activation appears to be reduced in autism, in association with lower levels of self-referential and imaginative cognition (Buckner, Andrews-Hanna, and Schacter, 2008; Kennedy and Courchesne, 2008). Reduced connectivity has also been reported within the default mode in autism (Neufeld et al.,

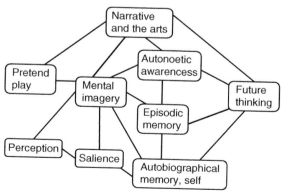

Figure 45.6 *The major components of human imagination are interconnected with one another.*

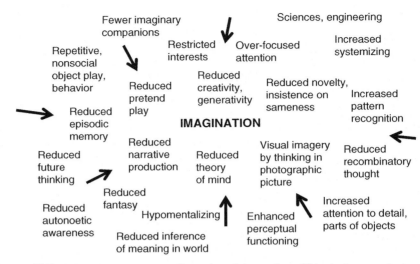

Figure 45.7 *Imagination is generally reduced in autism. This is in association with reductions in its components as shown here by "implosion" of a large set of imagination-related constructs.*

2017), and the temporal-parietal junction (which overlaps parts of the default mode, and mediates imaginative mentalizing) (Wible, 2012a, 2012b) also shows lower activation in autism (Kana et al., 2014). Finally, reduced deactivation of the default mode has been reported in autism, upon task initiation (Spencer et al., 2012).

How do these results compare to similar studies of schizophrenia? The default system shows some evidence of overactivation in schizophrenia, in association with reality distortion and increased imaginative cognition (Buckner, Andrews-Hanna, and Schacter, 2008; Guo et al., 2017); there is also less deactivation of this system upon external-task initiation (Alonso-Solís et al., 2015; Landin-Romero et al., 2014), as in autism. Reduced task-induced deactivation in the default mode region of the precuneus has also been reported in schizophrenia and schizotypy; this same activation pattern has also been linked with measures of higher creativity (Fink et al., 2014; Takeuchi et al., 2011). Finally, increased connectivity within the default mode network has been associated with schizophrenia (Clark et al., 2018; Peeters et al., 2015).

Taken together, these studies are consistent with some degree of opposite patterns of functional activation of the default mode in autism compared with schizophrenia, as also described in several reviews (Broyd et al., 2009; Karbasforoushan and Woodward, 2012). However, there is considerable heterogeneity in findings across studies, and very few analyses have considered autism and schizophrenia together using the same protocols.

Figures 45.7 and 45.8 provide pictorial summaries of the apparent alterations to imagination found in autism and psychotic-affective conditions (especially schizophrenia), with implosive reduction of imagination's components in autism, and pathological expansions in schizophrenia. These figures represent integrative hypotheses of central roles for imagination in both sets of disorders, brought about, ultimately, by the evolution of greatly enhanced imagination along the human lineage.

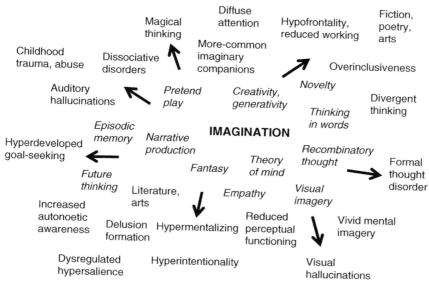

Figure 45.8 *Imagination is generally increased on the psychotic-affective spectrum. This is in association with increases in its components as shown here by "explosion" of a large set of imagination-related constructs.*

Imagination and Intelligence

As defined here, imagination and intelligence are essentially opposite to one another, with imagination involving generation of the unreal, and intelligence involving analysis and comprehension of the real. This opposite relationship is abstract but grounded in neurological anticorrelation of functional brain activations for the imagination (default, task-negative mode) network and the intelligence (task-positive) network (e.g. Buckner, Andrews-Hanna, and Schacter, 2008). The relationship of this pair of networks is not, however, necessarily a symmetrical toggling between them: The strength of the negative correlation between the two networks' activation is indeed positively associated with fluid intelligence (Santarnecchi, Emmendorfer, and Pascual-Leone, 2017), suggesting that the neurological basis of variation in intelligence extends brainwide to include the functional efficiency of switching network modes, as well as such factors as neural signal transmission speed and signal-to-noise ratios (Crespi, 2016a).

Given that imagination and intelligence, like virtually all traits, evolve genetically, is there evidence of a genetic basis to these phenotypes and their association, in relation to the autism spectrum and psychotic-affective spectrum? This question can be addressed using polygenic risk scores, scores for each individual of how many "risk" or "high phenotype" alleles they have across hundreds or thousands of loci, and genetic correlations, which measures the degree to which two traits are genetically the same due to overlap in the loci that make up their genetic bases (i.e. pleiotropy, whereby multiple traits are affected by the same locus or loci). The main results of such analyses are threefold: First, across multiple studies, autism genetic risk is positively genetically correlated with intelligence, such that alleles "for" autism overlap broadly with alleles "for" higher intelligence (review in Crespi, 2016a; Coleman et al., 2018). These findings also fit with the set of "high-intelligence" phenotypic traits associated with autism, as described by Crespi (2016a). Genetic risk for schizophrenia is, in contrast to autism, negatively genetically correlated with intelligence, such that alleles "for" schizophrenia overlap broadly with alleles "for" relatively low intelligence (Crespi, 2016a; Coleman et al., 2018).

Second, polygenic risk scores for schizophrenia and bipolar disorder have been positively associated with creativity, measured in terms of engaging in a successful artistic profession (Power et al., 2015), as well as with the Autism Quotient subscale of Imagination, such that higher risk scores involve higher self-reported imaginative abilities (Krapohl et al., 2016; Crespi et al., 2016). By construction of the Autism Quotient, one of the main metrics for autism in nonclinical populations, a higher level of autism traits involves lower self-report imagination; in principle, autism polygenic risk scores are also expected to be associated with metrics of reduced imagination. These studies are also supported, at the phenotypic level, by higher rates of schizophrenia, bipolar disorder, and depression among individuals who studied artistic subjects at university (MacCabe et al., 2018), and by higher rates of autism among siblings of individuals who studied science, engineering, or mathematics (Campbell and Wang, 2012).

Third, autism shows a significant negative genetic correlation with self-reported empathy, while schizophrenia shows a significant positive one (Warrier et al., 2018). Considering empathy as affective imagination of someone else's feelings or thoughts, these findings further support a diametric relation between autism and schizophrenia in this regard.

Taken together, these analyses support the idea of opposite extremes of imagination-intelligence trade-offs in autism vs. schizophrenia. What is not yet clear, however, is how different components of imagination are related to intelligence, phenotypically or genetically, in typical populations and among individuals high on autism spectrum or psychotic-affective spectrum traits.

Conclusions

Human psychological variation, expressed as dimensional mental disorders with special emphasis on autism spectrum and psychotic-affective conditions, represents a uniquely useful window into increasing our understanding of the imagination. In this context, interdisciplinary approaches that integrate across fields from genetics, to neuroscience, to psychology, psychiatry, and evolutionary biology, are especially important, because they forge causal biological links rather than simply describing patterns within single levels of organization.

How can the ideas and results from this chapter motivate future data collection, beyond a call for increased integration from theory to data, and across empirical fields? Specific suggestions for future work include:

(1) studies of the genetic basis of imagination, its components, and its neural instantiations, to better define its genetic architecture and relate it genetically to other phenotypes;

(2) analyses of how different measures of imagination are related to fluid intelligence, in the framework of both psychometric and neural models of these constructs; and

(3) more direct comparisons between disorders, especially autism and psychosis, with regard to the components and functioning of the imagination, and its neural basis as reflecting, in part, trade-offs between cognitive functions.

Such studies will help not just in better understanding imagination, but also in learning to enhance it, in conjunction with its handmaiden of creativity, and also apply its modification in therapies for autism (Woodard, Chung, and Korn, 2014) and psychotic-affective disorders (Choi-Kain and Gunderson, 2008). The upshot will be yet more Vygotskian creations of human culture, which we can hardly begin to imagine.

References

Acar, S., Chen, X., and Cayirdag, N. (2018). Schizophrenia and Creativity: A Meta-Analytic Review. *Schizophrenia Research, 195,* 23–31.

Acredolo, L., Goodwyn, S., and Fulmer, A. (1995). *Why Some Children Create Imaginary Companions: Clues from Infant and Toddler Play Preferences.* Poster presented at the biennial meetings of the Society for Research in Child Development, Indianapolis, IN.

Alonso-Solís, A., Vives-Gilabert, Y., Grasa, E., et al. (2015). Resting-State Functional Connectivity Alterations in the Default Network of Schizophrenia Patients with Persistent Auditory Verbal Hallucinations. *Schizophrenia Research, 161,* 261–268.

Arzy, S., Mohr, C., Molnar-Szakacs, I., and Blanke, O. (2011). Schizotypal Perceptual Aberrations of Time: Correlation between Score, Behavior and Brain Activity. *PLoS One, 6,* e16154.

Baas, M., Nijstad, B. A., Boot, N. C., and de Dreu, C. K. (2016). Mad Genius Revisited: Vulnerability to Psychopathology, Biobehavioral Approach-Avoidance, and Creativity. *Psychological Bulletin, 142*(6), 668.

Barnes, J. L., and Baron-Cohen, S. (2012). The Big Picture: Storytelling Ability in Adults with Autism Spectrum Conditions. *Journal of Autism and Developmental Disorders, 42,* 1557–1565.

Baron-Cohen, S. (2009). Autism: The Empathizing-Systemizing (E-S) Theory. *Annals of the New York Academy of Sciences, 1156,* 68–80.

Baron-Cohen, S., and Lombardo, M. V. (2017). Autism and Talent: The Cognitive and Neural Basis of Systemizing. *Dialogues in Clinical Neuroscience, 19*(4), 345.

Batey, M., and Furnham, A. (2006). Creativity, Intelligence, and Personality: A Critical Review of the Scattered Literature. *Genetic, Social, and General Psychology Monographs, 132*(4), 355–429.

Birchwood, M., Meaden, A., Trower, P., Gilbert, P., and Plaistow, J. (2000). The Power and Omnipotence of Voices: Subordination and Entrapment by Voices and Significant Others. *Psychological Medicine, 30,* 337–344.

Bonne, O., Canetti, L., Bachar, E., De-Nour, A. K., and Shalev, A. (1999). Childhood Imaginary Companionship and Mental Health in Adolescence. *Child Psychiatry and Human Development*, *29*, 277–286.

Bottema-Beutel, K., and White, R. (2016). By the Book: An Analysis of Adolescents with Autism Spectrum Condition Co-Constructing Fictional Narratives with Peers. *Journal of Autism and Developmental Disorders*, *46*(2), 361–377.

Boucher, J. (2007). Memory and Generativity in Very High Functioning Autism: A Firsthand Account, and an Interpretation. *Autism*, *11*(3), 255–264.

Brébion, G., Ohlsen, R. I., Pilowsky, L. S., and David, A. S. (2008). Visual Hallucinations in Schizophrenia: Confusion between Imagination and Perception. *Neuropsychologia*, *22*, 383.

Brewin, C. R., and Soni, M. (2011). Gender, Personality, and Involuntary Autobiographical Memory. *Memory*, *19*, 559–565.

Broyd, S. J., Demanuele, C., Debener, S., et al. (2009). Default-Mode Brain Dysfunction in Mental Disorders: A Systematic Review. *Neuroscience and Biobehavioral Reviews*, *33*, 279–296.

Brugger, P., and Mohr, C. (2008). The Paranormal Mind: How the Study of Anomalous Experiences and Beliefs May Inform Cognitive Neuroscience. *Cortex*, *44*, 1291–1298.

Buckner, R. L., Andrews-Hanna, J. R., and Schacter, D. L. (2008). The Brain's Default Network. *Annals of the New York Academy of Sciences*, *1124*, 1–38.

Campbell, B. C., and Wang, S. S. (2012). Familial Linkage between Neuropsychiatric Disorders and Intellectual Interests. *PloS One*, *7*, e30405.

Carlson, S. M., Mandell, D. J., and Williams, L. (2004). Executive Function and Theory of Mind: Stability and Prediction From Ages 2 to 3. *Developmental Psychology*, *40*, 1105.

Carlson, S. M., Tahiroglu, D., and Taylor, M. (2008). Links between Dissociation and Role Play in a Nonclinical Sample of Preschool Children. *Journal of Trauma Dissociation*, *9*, 149–171.

Carson, S. H. (2011). Creativity and Psychopathology: A Shared Vulnerability Model. *Canadian Journal of Psychiatry*, *56*, 144–153.

Choi-Kain, L. W., and Gunderson, J. G. (2008). Mentalization: Ontogeny, Assessment, and Application in the Treatment of Borderline Personality Disorder. *American Journal of Psychiatry*, *165*, 1127–1135.

Clark, S. V., Mittal, V. A., Bernard, J. A., et al. (2018). Stronger Default Mode Network Connectivity Is Associated with Poorer Clinical Insight in Youth at Ultra High Risk for Psychotic Disorders. *Schizophrenia Research*, *193*, 244–250.

Coleman, J. R., Bryois, J., Gaspar, H. A., et al. (2018). Biological Annotation of Genetic Loci Associated with Intelligence in a Meta-Analysis of 87,740 Individuals. *Molecular Psychiatry*, 1.

Collerton, D., Perry, E., and McKeith, I. (2005). Why People See Things That Are Not There: A Novel Perception and Attention Deficit Model for Recurrent Complex Visual Hallucinations. *The Behavioral and Brain Sciences*, *28*, 737–757.

Conway, M., Meares, K., and Standart, S. (2004). Images and Goals. *Memory*, *12*, 525–531.

Cooper, R. A., and Simons, J. S. (2019). Exploring the Neurocognitive Basis of Episodic Recollection in Autism. *Psychonomic Bulletin & Review*, *26*(1), 163–181. doi:10.3758/s13423-018-1504-z.

Craig, J., and Baron-Cohen, S. (1999). Creativity and Imagination in Autism and Asperger Syndrome. *Journal of Autism and Developmental Disorders, 29,* 319–326.

Craig, J., Baron-Cohen, S., and Scott, F. (2000). Story-Telling Ability in Autism: A Window into the Imagination. *Israel Journal of Psychiatry, 37,* 64–70.

Crespi, B. J. (2016a). Autism as a Disorder of High Intelligence. *Frontiers in Neuroscience, 10,* 300.

(2016b). The Evolutionary Etiologies of Autism Spectrum and Psychotic Affective Spectrum Disorders. In A. Alvergne, C. Jenkinson, and C. Faurie (eds.), *Evolutionary Thinking in Medicine: From Research to Policy and Practice.* Cham, Switzerland: Springer International Publishing AG, 299–327.

Crespi, B., and Badcock, C. (2008). Psychosis and Autism as Diametrical Disorders of the Social Brain. *The Behavioral and Brain Sciences, 31,* 241–261.

Crespi, B., Leach, E., Dinsdale, N., Mokkonen, M., and Hurd, P. (2016). Imagination in Human Social Cognition, Autism, and Psychotic-Affective Conditions. *Cognition, 150,* 181–199.

Currie, G. (2000). Imagination, Delusion and Hallucinations. *Mind & Language, 15,* 168–183.

Currie, G., and Jureidini, J. (2003). Art and Delusion. *The Monist, 86*(4), 556–578.

Currie, G., and Ravenscroft, I. (2002). *Recreative Minds: Imagination in Philosophy and Psychology.* Oxford, UK: Oxford University Press.

Daniel, C., and Mason, O. J. (2015). Predicting Psychotic-Like Experiences during Sensory Deprivation. *BioMed Research International, 2015,* 439379.

Davis, P. E., Simon, H., Meins, E., and Robins, D. L. (2018). Imaginary Companions in Children with Autism Spectrum Disorder. *Journal of Autism and Developmental Disorders, 48*(8), 2790–2799.

de Oliveira, H., Cuervo-Lombard, C., Salamé, P., and Danion, J. (2009). Autonoetic Awareness Associated with the Projection of the Self into the Future: An Investigation in Schizophrenia. *Psychiatry Research, 169,* 86–87.

Dentico, D., Cheung, B. L., Chang, J., et al. (2014). Reversal of Cortical Information Flow during Visual Imagery as Compared to Visual Perception. *NeuroImage, 100,* 237–243.

DeYoung, C. G., Grazioplene, R. G., and Peterson, J. B. (2012). From Madness to Genius: The Openness/Intellect Trait Domain as a Paradoxical Simplex. *Journal of Research in Personality, 46*(1), 63–78.

Dichter, G. S., Lam, K. S. L., Turner-Brown, L. M., et al. (2009). Generativity Abilities Predict Communication Deficits but not Repetitive Behaviors in Autism Spectrum Disorders. *Journal of Autism and Developmental Disorders, 39,* 1298–1304.

Dickerson, A. S., Pearson, D. A., Loveland, K. A., et al. (2014). Role of Parental Occupation in Autism Spectrum Disorder Diagnosis and Severity. *Research in Autism Spectrum Disorders, 8,* 997–1007.

Dierker, L. C., Davis, K. F., and Sanders, B. (1995). The Imaginary Companion Phenomenon: An Analysis of Personality Correlates and Developmental Antecedents. *Dissociation, 4,* 220–228.

Elsworth, C. (2013). We Did Not Know That Our Schizophrenic Daughter January Schofield's Imaginary Friends Were Hallucinations. The Telegraph, January 27. www.telegraph.co.uk/news/health/children/9828583/We-did-not-know-that-our-

schizophrenic-daughter-January-Schofields-imaginary-friends-were-hallucina
tions.html.

Ferretti, F., Adornetti, I., Chiera, A., et al. (2018). Time and Narrative: An Investigation of Storytelling Abilities in Children with Autism Spectrum Disorder. *Frontiers in Psychology*, *9*, 944.

Fink, A., Weber, B., Koschutnig, K., et al. (2014). Creativity and Schizotypy from the Neuroscience Perspective. *Cognitive, Affective & Behavioral Neuroscience*, *14*, 378–387.

Frith, U. (2012). Why We Need Cognitive Explanations of Autism. *The Quarterly Journal of Experimental Psychology*, *65*, 2073–2092.

Fyfe, S., Williams, C., Mason, O. J., and Pickup, G. J. (2008). Apophenia, Theory of Mind and Schizotypy: Perceiving Meaning and Intentionality in Randomness. *Cortex*, *44*, 1316–1325.

Gleason, T. R., Jarudi, R. N., and Cheek, J. M. (2003). Imagination, Personality, and Imaginary Companions. *Social Behavior and Personality*, *31*, 721–737.

Goddard, L., Howlin, P., Dritschel, B., and Patel, T. (2007). Autobiographical Memory and Social Problem-Solving in Asperger Syndrome. *Journal of Autism and Developmental Disorders*, *37*, 291–300.

Grandin, T. (1995). *Thinking in Pictures*. New York, NY: Vintage Press Random House.
  (2009). How Does Visual Thinking Work in the Mind of a Person with Autism? A Personal Account. *Philosophical Transactions of the Royal Society of London. Series B, Biological Sciences*, *364*, 1437–1442.

Greicius, M. D., and Menon, V. (2004). Default-Mode Activity during a Passive Sensory Task: Uncoupled from Deactivation but Impacting Activation. *Journal of Cognitive Neuroscience*, *16*, 1484–1492.

Guo, W., Liu, F., Chen, J., et al. (2017). Hyperactivity of the Default-Mode Network in First-Episode, Drug-Naive Schizophrenia at Rest Revealed by Family-Based Case-Control and Traditional Case-Control Designs. *Medicine*, *96*(13).

Hach, S., Tippett, L. J., and Addis, D. R. (2014). Neural Changes Associated with the Generation of Specific Past and Future Events in Depression. *Neuropsychologia*, *65*, 41–55.

Hanson, L. K., and Atance, C. M. (2014). Brief Report: Episodic Foresight in Autism Spectrum Disorder. *Journal of Autism and Developmental Disorders*, *44*, 674–684.

Happé, F., and Frith, U. (2006). The Weak Coherence Account: Detail-Focused Cognitive Style in Autism Spectrum Disorders. *Journal of Autism and Developmental Disorders*, *36*, 5–25.

Hoff, E. V. (2005). Imaginary Companions, Creativity, and Self-Image in Middle Childhood. *Creativity Research Journal*, *17*, 167–180.

Ivins, A., Di Simplicio, M., Close, H., Goodwin, G. M., and Holmes, E. (2014). Mental Imagery in Bipolar Affective Disorder versus Unipolar Depression: Investigating Cognitions at Times of "Positive" Mood. *Journal of Affective Disorders*, *166*, 234–242.

Jarrold, C. (2003). A Review of Research into Pretend Play in Autism. *Autism*, *7*, 379–390.

Jarrold, C., Boucher, J., and Smith, P. K. (1996). Generativity Deficits in Pretend Play in Autism. *British Journal of Developmental Psychology*, *14*, 275–300.

Jauk, E., Neubauer, A. C., Dunst, B., Fink, A., and Benedek, M. (2015). Gray Matter Correlates of Creative Potential: A Latent Variable Voxel-Based Morphometry Study. *NeuroImage*, *111*, 312–320.

Javitt, D. C. (2009a). When Doors of Perception Close: Bottom-Up Models of Disrupted Cognition in Schizophrenia. *Annual Review of Clinical Psychology, 5*, 249–275.

(2009b). Sensory Processing in Schizophrenia: Neither Simple nor Intact. *Schizophrenia Bulletin, 35*, 1059–1064.

Jensen, J., and Kapur, S. (2009). Salience and Psychosis: Moving from Theory to Practise: A Commentary on: "Do Patients with Schizophrenia Exhibit Aberrant Salience?" by Roiser et al. (2008). *Psychological Medicine, 39*(2), 197–198.

Johnson, S. L., Edge, M. D., Holmes, M. K., and Carver, C. S. (2012). The Behavioral Activation System and Mania. *Annual Review of Clinical Psychology, 8*, 243–267.

Jolliffe, T., and Baron-Cohen, S. (1999). A Test of Central Coherence Theory: Linguistic Processing in High-Functioning Adults with Autism or Asperger Syndrome: Is Local Coherence Impaired? *Cognition, 71*, 149–185.

Jones, V., and Steel, C. (2012). Schizotypal Personality and Vulnerability to Involuntary Autobiographical Memories. *Journal of Behavior Therapy and Experimental Psychiatry, 43*, 871–876.

Jung, R. E., and Haier, R. J. (2007). The Parieto-Frontal Integration Theory (P-FIT) of Intelligence: Converging Neuroimaging Evidence. *Behavioral and Brain Sciences, 30*(2), 135–154.

Kana, R. K., Libero, L. E., Hu, C. P., Deshpande, H. D., and Colburn, J. S. (2014). Functional Brain Networks and White Matter Underlying Theory-of-Mind in Autism. *Social Cognitive and Affective Neuroscience, 9*, 98–105.

Kanner, L. (1943). Autistic Disturbances of Affective Contact. *The Nervous Child, 2*, 217–250. Reprinted (1968) in *Acta Paedopsychiatrica, 35*, 100–136.

Karbasforoushan, H., and Woodward, N. D. (2012). Resting-State Networks in Schizophrenia. *Current Topics in Medicinal Chemistry, 12*, 2404–2414.

Kasari, C., Chang, Y. C., and Patterson, S. (2013). Pretending to Play or Playing to Pretend: The Case of Autism. *American Journal of Play, 6*(1), 124.

Kennedy, D. P., and Courchesne, E. (2008). Functional Abnormalities of the Default Network during Self- and Other-Reflection in Autism. *Social Cognitive and Affective Neuroscience, 3*, 177–190.

King, M. J., Williams, L., MacDougall, A. G., et al. (2011). Patients with Bipolar Disorder Show a Selective Deficit in the Episodic Simulation of Future Events. *Consciousness and Cognition, 20*, 1801–1807.

Krapohl, E., Euesden, J., Zabaneh, D., et al. (2016). Phenome-Wide Analysis of Genome-Wide Polygenic Scores. *Molecular Psychiatry, 21*(9), 1188.

Kunihira, Y., Senju, A., Dairoku, H., Wakabayashi, A., and Hasegawa, T. (2006). "Autistic" Traits in Non-Autistic Japanese Populations: Relationships with Personality Traits and Cognitive Ability. *Journal of Autism and Developmental Disorders, 36*(4), 553–566.

Kyaga, S. (2014). *Creativity and Mental Illness: The Mad Genius in Question*. Hampshire, UK: Palgrave Macmillan.

Landin-Romero, R., McKenna, P. J., Salgado-Pineda, P., et al. (2014). Failure of Deactivation in the Default Mode Network: A Trait Marker for Schizophrenia? *Psychological Medicine, 45*(6), 1315–1325.

MacCabe, J. H., Sariaslan, A., Almqvist, C., et al. (2018). Artistic Creativity and Risk for Schizophrenia, Bipolar Disorder and Unipolar Depression: A Swedish Population-

Based Case–Control Study and Sib-Pair Analysis. *The British Journal of Psychiatry, 212*(6), 370–376.

Markram, K., and Markram, H. (2010). The Intense World Theory – A Unifying Theory of the Neurobiology of Autism. *Frontiers in Human Neuroscience*, 4: 224.

Matthews, N.L., Collins, K. P., Thakkar, K. N., and Park, S. (2014). Visuospatial Imagery and Working Memory in Schizophrenia. *Cognitive Neuropsychiatry, 19*, 17–35.

McGill, B., and Moulds, M. L. (2014). Characteristics of Autobiographical Memories and Prospective Imagery across a Spectrum of Hypomanic Personality Traits. *Memory, 22*, 1139–1148.

Meyer, M. L., Davachi, L., Ochsner, K. N., and Lieberman, M. D. (2019). Evidence that Default Network Connectivity during Rest Consolidates Social Information. *Cerebral Cortex, 29*(5), 1910–1920. doi.org/10.1093/cercor/bhy071.

Meyer, T. D., Finucane, L., and Jordan, G. (2011). Is Risk for Mania Associated with Increased Daydreaming as a Form of Mental Imagery? *Journal of Affective Disorders, 135*, 380–383.

Mottron, L., Dawson, M., and Soulières, I. (2009). Enhanced Perception in Savant Syndrome: Patterns, Structure and Creativity. *Philosophical Transactions of the Royal Society of London. Series B, Biological Sciences, 364*, 1385–1391.

Mottron, L., Dawson, M., Soulières, I., Hubert, B., and Burack, J. A. (2006). Enhanced Perceptual Functioning in Autism: An Update, and Eight Principles of Autistic Perception. *Journal of Autism and Developmental Disorders, 36*, 27–43.

Mullally, S. L., and Maguire, E. A. (2013). Memory, Imagination, and Predicting the Future: A Common Brain Mechanism? *Neuroscientist, 20*, 220–234.

Nesse, R. M. (2000). Is Depression an Adaptation? *Archives of General Psychiatry, 57*(1), 14–20.

Nettle, D. (2001). *Strong Imagination: Madness, Creativity and Human Nature.* New York, NY: Oxford University Press.

Neufeld, J., Kuja-Halkola, R., Mevel, K., et al. (2017). Alterations in Resting State Connectivity Along the Autism Trait Continuum: A Twin Study. *Molecular Psychiatry* [Epub ahead of print]. doi:10.1038/mp.2017.160.

Peeters, S. C., van de Ven, V., Gronenschild, E. H., et al. (2015). Default Mode Network Connectivity as a Function of Familial and Environmental Risk for Psychotic Disorder. *PLoS One, 10*, e0120030.

Pignon, B., Geoffroy, P. A., Gharib, A., et al. (2018). Very Early Hallucinatory Experiences: A School-Based Study. *Journal of Child Psychology and Psychiatry, 59*(1), 68–75.

Power, R. A., Steinberg, S., Bjornsdottir, G., et al. (2015). Polygenic Risk Scores for Schizophrenia and Bipolar Disorder Predict Creativity. *Nature Neuroscience, 18* (7), 953.

Raffard, S., D'Argembeau, A., Lardi, C., et al. (2010). Narrative Identity in Schizophrenia. *Consciousness and Cognition, 19*, 328–340.

Roth, I. (2007). Autism and the Imaginative Mind. In I. Roth (ed.), *Proceedings of the British Academy: Imaginative Minds.* Oxford, UK: Oxford University Press, 277–306.

Sahyoun, C. P., Belliveau, J. W., Soulières, I., Schwartz, S., and Mody, M. (2010). Neuroimaging of the Functional and Structural Networks Underlying Visuospatial vs. Linguistic Reasoning in High-Functioning Autism. *Neuropsychologia, 48*, 86–95.

Santarnecchi, E., Emmendorfer, A., and Pascual-Leone, A. (2017). Dissecting the Parieto-Frontal Correlates of Fluid Intelligence: A Comprehensive ALE Meta-Analysis Study. *Intelligence, 63*, 9–28.

Schacter, D. L., Addis, D. R., Hassabis, D., et al. (2012). The Future of Memory: Remembering, Imagining, and the Brain. *Neuron, 76*, 677–694.

Scott, F. J., and Baron-Cohen, S. (1996). Imagining Real and Unreal Things: Evidence of a Dissociation in Autism. *Journal of Cognitive Neuroscience, 8*, 371–382.

Simeonova, D. I., Chang, K. D., Strong, C., and Ketter, T. A. (2005). Creativity in Familial Bipolar Disorder. *Journal of Psychiatric Research, 39*(6), 623–631.

Slotnick, S. D., Thompson, W. L., and Kosslyn, S. M. (2012). Visual Memory and Visual Mental Imagery Recruit Common Control and Sensory Regions of the Brain. *Cognitive Neuroscience, 3*, 14–20.

Snyder, A. W., and Thomas, M. (1997). Autistic Artists Give Clues to Cognition. *Perception, 26*, 93–96.

Soulières, I., Dawson, M., Samson, F., et al. (2009). Enhanced Visual Processing Contributes to Matrix Reasoning in Autism. *Human Brain Mapping, 30*, 4082–4107.

Spek, A. A., and Velderman, E. (2013). Examining the Relationship between Autism Spectrum Disorders and Technical Professions in High Functioning Adults. *Research in Autism Spectrum Disorders, 7*, 606–612.

Spencer, M. D., Chura, L. R., Holt, R. J., et al. (2012). Failure to Deactivate the Default Mode Network Indicates a Possible Endophenotype of Autism. *Molecular Autism, 3*, 1–9.

Takeuchi, H., Taki, Y., Hashizume, H., et al. (2011). Failing to Deactivate: The Association between Brain Activity during a Working Memory Task and Creativity. *NeuroImage, 55*, 681–687.

Tanweer, T., Rathbone, C. J., and Souchay, C. (2010). Autobiographical Memory, Autonoetic Consciousness, and Identity in Asperger Syndrome. *Neuropsychologia, 48*(4), 900–908.

Tavassoli, T., Miller, L. J., Schoen, S. A., Nielsen, D. M., and Baron-Cohen, S. (2014). Sensory Over-Responsivity in Adults with Autism Spectrum Conditions. *Autism, 18*(4), 428–432.

Taylor, C. L. (2017). Creativity and Mood Disorder: A Systematic Review and Meta-Analysis. *Perspectives on Psychological Science, 12*(6), 1040–1076.

Taylor, E. H. (1998). Advances in the Diagnosis and Treatment of Children with Serious Mental Illness. *Child Welfare, 77*(3), 311–332.

Taylor, M., and Carlson, S. M. (1997). The Relation between Individual Differences in Fantasy and Theory of Mind. *Child Development, 68*, 436–455.

Ten Eycke, K. D., and Müller, U. (2015). Brief Report: New Evidence for a Social-Specific Imagination Deficit in Children with Autism Spectrum Disorder. *Journal of Autism and Developmental Disorders, 45*, 213–220.

Terrett, G., Rendell, P. G., Raponi-Saunders, S., et al. (2013). Episodic Future Thinking in Children with Autism Spectrum Disorder. *Journal of Autism and Developmental Disorders, 43*, 2558–2568.

van Os, J. (2009). "Salience Syndrome" Replaces "Schizophrenia" in DSM-V and ICD-11: Psychiatry's Evidence-Based Entry into the 21st Century? *Acta Psychiatrica Scandinavica, 120*, 363–372.

Vygotsky, L. S. (2004). Imagination and Creativity in Childhood. *Journal of Russian and East European Psychology, 42*, 7–97.

Wagner-Martin, L. (1987). *Sylvia Plath: A Biography.* New York, NY: St. Martin's Griffin.

Warrier, V., Toro, R., Chakrabarti, B., et al. (2018). Genome-Wide Analyses of Self-Reported Empathy: Correlations with Autism, Schizophrenia, and Anorexia Nervosa. *Translational Psychiatry, 8*(1), 35.

Wible, C. G. (2012a). Schizophrenia as a Disorder of Social Communication. *Schizophrenia Research and Treatment, 2012*, 920485.

(2012b). Hippocampal Temporal-Parietal Junction Interaction in the Production of Psychotic Symptoms: A Framework for Understanding the Schizophrenic Syndrome. *Frontiers in Human Neuroscience*, 6.

Winfield, H., and Kamboj, S. K. (2010). Schizotypy and Mental Time Travel. *Consciousness and Cognition, 19*, 321–327.

Wise, R. J. S., and Braga, R. M. (2014). Default Mode Network: The Seat of Literary Creativity? *Trends in Cognitive Sciences, 18*, 116–117.

Wolfberg, P. J. (2009). *Play and Imagination in Children with Autism*. Shawnee Mission, KS: AAPC Publishing.

Woodard, C. R., Chung, J., and Korn, M. (2014). A Pilot Study of the Meta-Play Method: A Novel Play Intervention for Toddlers with Autism. *Journal of Autism, 1*, 3.

46 Meditation and Imagination

Sthaneshwar Timalsina

Rather than simply exploring what imagination is, or providing a taxonomy of imagination, meditation manuals and their philosophical accounts describe a different domain of imagination: identifying imagination as one of the mental faculties that needs to be cultivated and trained with an underlying premise that imaginal accculturation has an enormous role to play in the subject's mental health and his[1] interaction with society. Unfortunately, extant philosophical investigations of imagination in light of yogic and tantric materials has been overshadowed by the text-historical and scientific approaches, with the first focusing on the emergence of practice and its sociocultural boundaries, and the latter focusing on meditation and its relation to health. Historically, issues such as imagination or emotion have been neglected topics even in Western intellectual discourse. Classical texts written in Sanskrit come in contrasting flavors, with both positive and negative depictions of imagination. While a romantic understanding of imagination is vivid in literature and aesthetics, philosophical texts attribute a dubious role to imagination, with *kalpanā* (imagination) consistently being depicted, whether in Hindu or Buddhist philosophical texts, as a hindrance for recognizing reality or for veridical perception (Timalsina, 2013). In this latter presentation, *kalpanā* is equated with the monstrous power of *māyā* or illusion that projects the world that is not even there, and traps beings in their delirious slumber. This trend is changing, though, with new studies bringing to discourse the constructive role of imagination, particularly in contemplative practices.[2] Visualization, primarily by means of playing with images, appears to dominate substantial space in the literature of meditation, and it also appears that since classical times, imagination has been identified by philosophers as a faculty to explore the nature of consciousness. Rather than these practices seeking to draw a line between fantasy and reality, they appear to use fantasy in order to reconstitute commonsense reality. This paper explores the extent to which these practices envision those possibilities. At the same time, this paper also identifies a conceptual framework for pursuing such an investigation. I engage with contemporary theories of imagination in order to contextualize some of the archaic practices of imagination and the justifications behind such practices.

Meditation practice, any form of contemplative exercise among different cultures oriented toward altered mental and/or psychosomatic states, involves a substantial amount of imagination in its course. The insights derived from such practices can help

---

1 This chapter uses "he" and "his" throughout, but the author intends "she" and "her" as well.
2 For example, see Crangle (1994), Hayes (2006, 2013), Shulman (2012), and Timalsina (2005, 2006, 2015a, 2015b, 2017).

us ground the ways in which imagination and creativity have been understood across cultures. In particular, it can open up a space for conversation across disciplines on the overlap between conceptualizing imagination and linking imagination with other modes of consciousness such as memory or perception, or with the potency of consciousness such as in the context of creativity. With a focus on excerpts from two tantric philosophers, Abhinavagupta (eleventh century), and Maheśvarānanda (fourteenth century), I demonstrate on the one hand how a productive role is given to imagination, and on the other how the practices harnessed in contemplation aim to ultimately transform the subject's assessment and response to lived events. This essay in essence explores how interacting creatively with fantastic images can be used as a device to reconstitute not only the subject's self-assessment or the way a subject recognizes himself and his role in his community, but also the way he reacts to natural stimuli. These excerpts and the philosophical corpus that interprets them share a voice regarding the overlap between playing with images, the role simple imagination or *kalpanā* has in creativity (*pratibhā*), and the role imagination plays in grounding human creativity. The interplay between the fantastic and the real, one of the recurring themes of Abhinavagupta's philosophy, also deserves special attention, as his is not the philosophy of subjective idealism, and at the same time, he also rejects the vertical split between the mental and the physical. By exploring the taxonomy of imagination in his literature, I also intend to make some connections with the ways imagination has been explained in our own times. In particular, Abhinavagupta is exemplary for his use of imagination as a mechanism to understand his philosophy, one that allows subjects to transform their horizon of consciousness by means of some fantastic games that he uses for deconstructing the predisposed order of conceptualization. Before initiating a global dialogue upon imagination by offering Abhinavagupta's philosophical exposition upon esoteric experiences that are sometimes given in liturgical fashion, I would like to begin the conversation on the structures of consciousness by analyzing examples of Abhinavagupta's use of imagination in transforming reality and elevating awareness.

Maheśvarānanda's text falls under the same philosophical paradigm. I am using his case for extending the scope of imagination in daily ritual practice. Unique to Maheśvarānanda is the maṇḍala ritual that anticipates a transformed somatosensory experience. Imagination in this account is not directed toward the past, which would therefore constitute some form of episodic memory that is heavily constructed and edited by the faculty of imagination; neither is this directed toward the future in simple play with fantastic images. Ritual imagination is directed here toward the present moment, unleashing imagination to creatively fill in the mode of experience. Here, imagination stands alone as the luminous power of consciousness, able both to reflexively gaze upon its own modifications and to curb and manipulate distinctive states in order to edit and control the horizons of experience.

Abhinavagupta's Ritual Fantasy

The visualizations outlined by Abhinavagupta are derived from the manuals on Goddess worship, with the most prominent practice connecting the triadic deities identified as Parā, Parāparā, and Aparā with three different modes of consciousness in its most introverted, extroverted, and intermediate grounds. Tantric visualization practices – whether they are focused on any of the deities, their maṇḍalas, or the specific mantras – or this specific practice focused on the triadic goddesses all seek to internalize the external rituals by replacing real objects with mental imagery or, in other words, replacing corporeal processes with exercise of the vital force (*prāṇa*) and mental acts of blending imagery. The course of practice involves deciphering metaphors, making metonymic connections, and shifting from one image to the other – all of which culminate in transforming the subject's experience of himself and his surroundings.

Abhinavagupta outlines this particular course of visualization as follows (Shastri, 1918: 199–200):

> [The aspirant] should first imagine the unity of the vital force, consciousness, and the body since there is no need for the acts of [ritual] bathing etc., as [he] has been purified merely by having rested in complete bliss [the conceptual state that envelops all modes of conceptualization]. And because pure consciousness is of the character of absolute subjectivity (*paramaśiva*) . . . he should [mentally] tie the [metaphoric] tuft of consciousness in the form of the mind and the vital force by a mere visualization (lit. articulation, *uccāra*) [of absolute subjectivity] so that [the mind,] tied to absolute subjectivity (*paramaśiva*), does not wander around. Having pierced through the complex of sensory faculties that depend on the mind, [he] should transform the ritual objects, [the ritual] site, and the directional bases in front [of him] into pure consciousness {*tat*}. [He] should [mentally] fill and worship the libation pot with the same permeation [used in the process] of bonding the tuft [by visualizing pure consciousness enveloping the objects]. He should [then mentally] worship the altar with drops of pure consciousness {*tat*}, and worship and libate the circle of mantras within the body complex with the fluid of pure consciousness {*tad*} by connecting the left ring finger with the thumb [to control the breath]. And then [he] should imagine his seat [first] to the extent of breath, and then in the altar, shaped as a trident and culminating with three potencies [constituting transcendence, transcendence while immanent, and immanence, by means of Parā, Parāparā, and Aparā]. [He] should imagine [his] seat extending up to the category of *māyā* [the limiting factor that gives rise to subjectivity and externality] with [the visualization of] the phoneme "*sa*," and extending up to the three potencies [or Goddesses] while [visualizing] the phoneme "*au*." In the order of {*evaṃ*} the categories up to *māyā* located within the phoneme "*sa*," culminating with three potencies in the phoneme of "*au*," and the potency in the form of reflexive consciousness (*vimarśa*) that is to be worshipped as located on top of the triad {*tad*}, [the aspirant] should [mentally] install the foundation and what is founded upon it by a single articulation [of the phoneme "*sauḥ*"]. After completing [this course], [the aspirant] should visualize the world located within consciousness that has been objectified, and also [visualize] that this [world] is comprised of consciousness. In this way there is a circumscription (*saṃpuṭa*) of the world by consciousness and of consciousness by the world. It is because the world emerges from consciousness and dissolves back into it, and because consciousness emerges from the objects to be cognized and [the world] rests there as well, the essence of consciousness having these modalities (*etāvattva*) is gained by means of a twofold circumscription.[3]

---

3 *tatra   snānādikartavyatānapeṣayaiva   pūrṇānandaviśrāntyaiva   labdhaśuddhiḥ   prathamaṃ prāṇasaṃviddehaikībhāvaṃ bhāvayitvā saṃvidaś ca paramaśivarūpatvāt … saṃvidagneḥ śikhāṃ*

The passage cited above needs some unpacking, particularly in light of our discussion on imagination. First of all, there is a rich play with images, as every ritual object, the deities being worshipped, and the mechanism or the process of ritual, are all fantasies. In this hour-long visualization, a real ritual with external objects, a real altar with trident and lotuses drawn upon it, with deities situated in each tine of the trident, each with a lotus as their base, and the supreme divinity, all are replaced with mental images. Breath and select phonemes are used as the signposts in this ritual substitution of external objects with the imagined objects. The aspirant's own bodily assessment, his central nervous system, and his sensory faculties are accordingly supplanted by the projected imagery. The sequence of mental substitution culminates with the external world being subsumed within consciousness: The world of everyday experience compresses to yet another layer of imagery. The complex categories (thirty-six categories within this system) are all replaced with the imagery selectively envisioned and successively dissolved into the higher categories. The deities invoked in the *maṇḍala* such as Parā, Parāparā, and Aparā, and the supreme Śiva with his consort Śakti, are all merged within pure consciousness. By reducing the external world to mental images and those to pure consciousness, and by eventually seeing an identity between the world and consciousness, the aspirant discovers his identity with pure consciousness, and at the same time his oneness with the world. At this juncture, the subject wakes up with his altered personality: He no longer experiences himself as fragmented and separate from the rest of the reality but as one and woven within the system that constitutes his being in the world, identical the recurring and concurring events. In this transformed experience, the world is not "out there," but within himself, with the phenomenal subject discovering his identity with the absolute subjectivity, the supreme Śiva.

Next, the vocabulary Abhinavagupta uses in the mechanism of visualization is worth considering: "having formed or shaped" *bhāvayitvā* (the causative of becoming, in the sense of constructing something), "having articulated" (*uccārya*), "should perform" (*kuryāt*), "should remake" (*kuryāt*), "should imagine" (*kalpayet*), and "should visualize" (*paśyet*). All these terms are used here as interchangeable, as they are all prescribing the course of visualization, either in the context of creating the imagery or in manipulating the images. The imagining captures both the objects and the subject: Mental objects are to be shaped according to the external objects so that the externals can be replaced, and the subject is first supposed to engage in a ritual act, and eventually transform his subjective horizon. Moreover, in Abhinavagupta's language, real construction with words such as *bhāvanā* are

buddhiprāṇarūpāṃ sakṛduccāramātreṇaiva baddhāṃ kuryāt — yena paramaśiva eva pratibaddhā tadvyatiriktaṃ na kiñcid abhidhāvati, tathāvidhabuddhadhiṣṭhita-karaṇacakrānuvedhena purovartino yāgadravyagṛhadigādhārādīn api tanmayībhūtān kuryāt | tato 'rghapātram api śikhābandhavyāptyaiva pūrayet pūjayec ca | tadviprudbhiḥ staṇḍilāny api tadrasena vāmānāmaṅguṣṭhayogād dehacakreṣu mantracakraṃ pūjayet tarpayec ca, tataḥ prāṇāntas tataḥ sthiṇḍile triśūlātmakaṃ śaktitrayāntam āsanaṃ kalpayet, māyāntaṃ hi sārṇa aukāre ca śaktitrayāntam āsanaṃ kalpayet | māyāntaṃ hi sārṇa aukāre ca śaktitrayāntaṃ tadupari yājyā vimarśarūpā śaktiḥ — ity evaṃ sakṛduccāreṇaivādhārādheyanyāsaṃ kṛtvā tatraivādheyabhūtāyām api saṃvidi viśvaṃ paśyet| tad api ca saṃvinmayam ity evaṃ viśvasya saṃvidā tena ca tasyāḥ saṃpuṭībhāvo bhavati saṃvida uditaṃ tatraiva paryavasitaṃ yataḥ viśvaṃ, vedyāc ca saṃvid udeti tatraiva ca viśrāmyati – iti etāvattvaṃ saṃvittattvaṃ saṃpuṭībhāvadvayāl labhyate | Tantrasāra of Abhinavagupta, see Shastri (1918, Chapter 22, 199–200). The translation is mine.

interchangeably used with fantasy consciousness, *kalpanā*. Even the word for veridical perception, *paśyati*, is blurred, by it being used for visualization. Abhinavagupta's is a monistic philosophy of *saṃvid*, consciousness. Although the term is translated as consciousness, this is not what it means in common English usage, as the term refers to pre-subjective/objective potential for being conscious of something. Abhinavagupta views this as the core for the emergence of subjectivity and objective reality. And, interestingly, he finds teleology to be guided by imagination, as it is by means of fantasy that he explores the possibility of encountering reality. In this meditation, not only can fantasy replace the real-world materials, but Abhinavagupta also implies that fantasy consciousness can reshape our biologically and culturally conditioned parameters of experiencing reality and help us return to the ground of pure consciousness that has not yet expressed itself in terms of the inner and outer, real and fantastic, and the sacred and profane. This is not a mere fantasy, though. For Abhinavagupta, imagination enjoys the absolute power to reconstitute reality, to deconstruct the habit patterns or psychosomatic predispositions (saṃskāra), by means of which the subject can not only alter his experience in response to the external stimuli, but can also reshape his own self-assessment. This thesis is further buttressed if we explore the terminology where Abhinavagupta identifies the creative force embedded with being identical with reflexive consciousness, with terms such as creativity (*pratibhā*) being used as synonymous with fantasy (*kalpanā*).

Maheśvarānanda on Ritual Visualization

The following paragraph sums up the visualization practice within the Kaula system that considers engagement with the world and bodily enjoyment as essential to self-awareness. In the passage cited below, we find a meticulous sequence of imagining that constitutes the body of the ritual, with what is projected eventually replacing what is real. Just as in the case of Abhinavagupta's visualization, this also aims toward transforming the external ritual domain with the mental objects and uses philosophy as a mechanism to establish correlations. According to Maheśvarānanda (see Dvivedi 1992, verses 42–47),

> Visualization [lit. observation (*nibhālana*)] is a reflection upon one's own potency, and this is very rare in the world. Liquor, betel leaves, fragrance, and flowers are easily accessed to offer to the divine. Regulating breath implies the suspension of [the mind and the sensory faculties from] the engagement [with the externals] (*vṛttānta*), even when the expansive forces (*vibhava*) that are oriented towards action are held motionless in order to reflexively cognize the essential being of oneself. [The ritual act of] desiccation is removing the polluting factors (*mala*), and [the ritual act of] burning [negative karma] is cutting off the predispositions. Soaking the body [ritual bathing] is the purification carried out with an immersion into the nectar of wisdom. Harnessing the body is reflecting upon the collection of conceptual constructs as empty of constructions. Libation is engaging with the objects of cognition. The entities that nourish the self-nature are the flowers. The complete libation of the bodily drops (*kulabindu*) purified with the marking of the

mantras is the offering of the sprouts of all the mental constructions into the source of complete I-consciousness. Whatever is the mental state (*bhāva*) of [meditating subject], that alone is his divinity. Deity images grant whatever is desired if they are visualized [by the subject that has] the identical mental states.[4]

In this highly cryptic passage, Maheśvarānanda has outlined that every single aspect of tantric ritual worship can be transformed into sustained visualization. In so doing, he borrows inputs from two different domains: Śākta liturgies and Trika and Pratyabhijñā philosophies.[5] Imagination plays multiple roles in this process:

(1) Project a ritual even in its physical absence.
(2) Substitute the projected ritual with the corresponding mental objects for each of the components of the ritual.
(3) Cultivate an altered state of consciousness by subverting what is given and use philosophy for this justification.
(4) Transforming subjective awareness, wherein the yogin imagines himself to be the absolute, the totality of beings and things.
(5) Bring this projected consciousness back into conventional reality and act appropriately in the social sphere with this transformed gaze.

The passage requires further unpacking. Kaula rituals are comprised of four basic elements: following the rules, having the appropriate mental state, preparing the required substances for food and drink for the deities, and making the specific gestures as the means to invoke the deities while making the offerings. Among these constituents, Maheśvarānanda views the second, the mental state, as primary, and he identifies the ritual as a process wherein the aspirant transforms his own mental state to recognize his true identity.[6] One of the preparatory steps toward the ritual worship is the regulation of breath, which is generally conducted with recitation of specific phonemes. Instead, Maheśvarānanda recommends this to be the step of gazing upon the emerging stage of sensory engagement, tapping them even before the imagined objects are fully manifest in the mind in order to complement the external objects. The aspirant in this stage directs his attention toward the imagined

---

4   *nijabalanibhālanam eva varivasyā sā ca durlabhā loke|*
    sulabhāni viśvapater āsavatāmbūlagandhapuṣpāṇi ||
    vimraṣṭuṃ nijasattvaṃ vibhave kāryonmukhe stimite 'pi |
    bāhyavṛttāntānāṃ bhaṅgaḥ prāṇasya saṃyamo jñeyaḥ ||
    śoṣo malasya nāśo dāha etasya vāsanocchedaḥ |
    āplāvanaṃ tanūnāṃ jñānasudhāsekanirmitā śuddhiḥ ||
    avikalpatayā marśo vikalpavargasyāṅgasannāhaḥ |
    arghyaṃ vedyavilāsaḥ puṣpāṇi svabhāvapṣakā bhāvāḥ ||
    pūrṇāhantāyā mukhe viśvavikalpāṅkurāṇāṃ vikṣepam |
    mantrollekhaviśuddhaṃ pūrṇaṃ kulabindutarpaṇaṃ bhaṇāmaḥ ||
    yo yasya bhāvayogas tasya khalu sa eva devatā bhavati |
    tadbhāvabharitā abhilaṣitaṃ tathā phalanti pratimāḥ || Mahārthamañjarī, verses 42–47.

    The translation of these passages in the body is mine.
5   I have extensively addressed the literature and philosophy of tantric visualization in Timalsina 2015a and Timalsina 2015b.
6   *tasmāt svasvarūpaparāmarśa eva paramā pūjā | Parimala* upon MM 42.

objects that are used in this ritual worship. What Maheśvarānanda is demanding is not to preclude the emergence of objectivity, or to dwell in some thought-free state, but rather to gaze upon thoughts as they emerge from the core of being. At the same time, Maheśvarānanda anticipates that the subject is not swept aside by the tide of thoughts but is able to regulate them by allowing only the assigned imageries to come to the screen of the mind. Accordingly, mental projection replaces the purificatory rites and the mantric gaze allows the subject to accept his newly emerged form that is free from impurities. This transformation is a catalyst for the subject's rediscovery of himself as the higher subjectivity enveloping the totality. Specific corporeal gestures are used in tantric rites for installation of particular mantras in different corporeal limbs. Maheśvarānanda exploits this act by metaphorically projecting this to the reflexive consciousness expunged of all forms of mental constructions. At the same time, he is also endorsing the engagement with the objects of consciousness and cultivating the sense of contentment as a reward. Tantric rituals demand the offering of various substances. He sums up this offering in terms of dissolving the emerging thoughts into pure consciousness where the gaze, having suspended the process of the emergence of thought, returns to its origins and reaches the state without any conceptual turmoil. He outlines his philosophy in the last verse in this sequence (MM, verse 47), where the deity being worshipped is identified as the particular mental state of the aspirant.

In this monistic paradigm, there is no deity other than the very consciousness manifest in distinctive emotional states and conceptual conditions. After all, it is the subject's mental state that matters in determining his engagement with the world. This is what Maheśvarānanda means by materialization. In other words, the subject's mental states can be ritually altered and this transformation can directly affect our socially constructed reality. Maheśvarānanda is giving power to imagination in this reframing of the reality, making it the ultimate tool for achieving absolute freedom. Ritual, for him, is therefore a sustained practice of imagination: In his philosophy, the self and his world are created by the habits and mental conditions of the very subject. The subject, accordingly, is always free to alter the conditioning factors, and rituals are directed toward cultivating the power of imagination.

Interface between Meditation and Imagination

From the tantric perspective, the above exercises are not "fantasies" in the literal sense, as the aspirant would not say, "let me imagine," or "let me fantasize." However, the texts do repeatedly use the terms that translate in English with acts related to imagination (*bhāvayet, kalpayet, cintayet, dhyāyet*, etc.). At the same time, the texts mix up the process with terms that relate to the acts linked with memory (*smaret, anusmaraṇa*). In practice, a big part of visualization does borrow inputs from memory. The foremost challenge for us is the taxonomy of imagination, identifying where these types of imagination would fit, if they even qualify to be categorized as such. Indeed, not all the cognitive activities involved in the above visualizations do qualify as acts of imagination. Some of them are beliefs (I am Śiva or Bhairava [an aspect of the god], consciousness permeates the world, etc.). Others are desires or wishes (physical cleanliness without bathing, ritual offering without substances, etc.). In all accounts, it is consistent that the types of imagination we have at hand are distinct from daydreaming, as these imaginings have a distinctive goal; there is a consistent meta-gaze upon what has been fantasized; there is a regulation of the entities that are allowed to be imagined, etc.

Moreover, the above two examples of visualization from Abhinavagupta and Maheśvarānanda demonstrate multiple types of imagination at play:

(1) Projecting the objects of libation, for instance, is imagining things that are spatiotemporally real.
(2) Merging into the fluid of consciousness is not spatiotemporally possible.
(3) There is a clear play of the ability to form beliefs about objects, for instance, that the objects of experience are manifestations of consciousness.
(4) This involves the ability to evaluate things in an altered domain, such as experiencing oneself as circumscribing the totality.
(5) The course of visualization aims to reconstitute the subjective state, and actualize a transformed vision of oneself, including one's role in a wider community.

While these varieties of imagination resemble to some extent the ones outlined by Stevenson (2003) and Abraham (2016), I am modifying the taxonomy of imagination based on the above two ritual accounts:

(1) Playing with images: In propositional form, this type of imagination always has directionality; it is always intentional. The ritualized imagination borrows all forms of mental imagery; there are objects to see, smell, touch, taste, and hear.
(2) Sensory imagination: Rather than playing with images, this type of imagination involves a sensory presence; subjects report having some sort of sensory experience of the imagined object. For example, in the ritualized imagination, rather than imagining the phonemes, the subject hears those phonemes being articulated in his heart. In the screen of his mind, the subject in the imagined ritual sphere sees himself engaged in *maṇḍala* worship. This is akin to the moment of orgasmic union with what is being fantasized, where the subject actually experiences the amorous embrace of his partner.
(3) Imagining things as imagined as such vs. imagining them as real: In some cases, subjects report imagining things while imagining, and their mode of consciousness is actively imagining while the content is given as the content of imagination. In other instances, subjects are interpreting the contents as experienced but they are in fact fantasizing those objects.
(4) Guided vs. spontaneous imagination: We involuntarily imagine things and events. However, we can also direct our minds toward imagining an intended course of events. Ritualized imagination is a key example for guided imagination.
(5) Synthetic imagination: Different inputs from multiple domains are simultaneously imagined.
(6) Episodic imagination: Subjects can imagine encountering deities (or ghosts for that matter) and summon them, forming an episodic memory. On other

occasions, the entire complex (presentation and representation, giving presence in the form of images and remembering these images) can be a simultaneous act.

(7) Transformative imagination: With a complex play of images, with a sustained act of guided imagination, and by means of recreating episodic memory-type of imagination, the subject becomes transformed, with his subjective assessment and his response to the objective world being altered. The subject actually experiences the instances of fantasy as real events from the past.

As is evident from the list above, I am reading imagination as a gradually progressing ability, a potency, and for this reason, it cannot be categorized based on its contents alone. It is not possible for those who are not accustomed to guided imagination to suspend other cognitive modes and engage in pure imagination for a prolonged period. The final anticipated outcome of this sustained course of imagination is a total transformation of the somatosensory and mental response to the stimuli. Based on the intensity of visualization, subjects are capable of sustaining their altered state of experience for a varying duration of time. The ultimate goal of these practices is to deconstruct the existing modes of constructed experience that have both the biological and sociocultural underpinning. However, not all imaginations can lead to the same liberated state of consciousness, and some courses of imaginations can have a negative side-effect. Tantric texts are particularly wary of the misuse of visualization and recommend readers to undertake such practices only with the supervision of a highly trained mentor. When the transformation by means of visualization is firm and the subjects are capable of shifting their focus at will from ordinary consciousness to the realm of fantasy and back to everyday experience, they acquire a new gaze and a transformed vision of bliss. Aspirants report this as a liberating experience as it gives them a sense of freedom from both biological and social constraints. All in all, the act that begins as imagining culminates with creating, with a singular goal of subjective transformation. Subjects also report as a consequence being able to mirror others' conditions, empathize with others' pain, or altruistically act upon others' suffering. Based on these accounts, imagination is one of the cognitive faculties that can be cultivated and transformed.

In her introduction to *The Routledge Handbook of Philosophy of Imagination,* Amy Kind (2016: 4) identifies that some imaginations are prompted by initial suggestions. The type of imagination I have discussed in this chapter does borrow prompts from a real-life ritual paradigm. She also makes a distinction between voluntary and involuntary forms of imagining. While all forms of visualization are voluntary, an urge for an involuntary presence of the fantasy objects underlies the subjects' aspiration to "directly encounter" the deity or enter into the visualized mental space. Accordingly, tantric visualizations demonstrate both the presence and absence of the props: In some instances there are props such as the body of the aspirant visualized as the maṇḍala while in other instances subjects simply visualize the intended object. Kind also identifies "collaboration" as an additional factor. In our context, if the ritual visualization involves masses, visualization may involve collaboration. However, tantric visualizations are predominantly practiced in isolation and are hardly collaborative. The final identifying factor in Kind's taxonomy involves "forms," that some imaginations have a propositional structure (subjects imagine that A is B) while in other instances they lack a propositional attitude (subjects simply imagine A). The examples of visualization identified above demonstrate both the tendencies. When subjects dive deeper in their fantasy zone, they seem to have less of a propositional attitude and their subjective horizon seems to be gradually occupied by the field of visualization. In congruence with Kind's thesis that some imaginations borrow "props," various imaginations prescribed in the course of visualization borrow supports, for instance by using phonemes to guide the flow of vital energies so that it gradually surges upward in the body. In her taxonomy, Kind does not address sustained forms of imagination. The conversation on visualization in this chapter can fill this lacuna. In a prolonged ritualized visualization, for instance in various forms of guided meditation and in altered states of consciousness, subjects not only cultivate intended forms of experiences, they also surrender their subjective consciousness, with them reporting being "empty" (śūnya) or being expunged of their subjectivity. Sustained imagination is supported in the course of visualization by means of the ritual manuals that are often memorized by the aspirants and used in their course of visualization. Yet another distinction needs to be made: What occurs during the mode of imagination is not just imagination. While tantric aspirants are predominantly imagining in the course of visualization, they are also borrowing imagery from their memory while at the same time remaining actively aware of their immediate presence. These subjects, while brooded in their fantasy zone, are constantly integrating aspects from their memory while also attentively gazing upon their own present modes of consciousness. Also noteworthy are the circumstances when we are in the mode of imagination and all that occurs is not just imagination. It is an active mode of consciousness and, in addition to the act of imagining, we are also playing with images borrowed from our memory, are perceptively aware of the surroundings, are using sensory stimuli as a component to enhance our imagination, and are combining our beliefs and thoughts in the act of imagination.

Central elements in this progression toward complex acts of imagination involve playing with different inputs while exercising different cognitive faculties. Metaphoric thinking, metonymic linking of two domains, and cognitive blending of the inputs from two or more sources are ubiquitous in both the exercises outlined above. Select metaphors can explain the role metaphor plays in the course of visualization: CONSCIOUSNESS IS FLUID (drops of consciousness), BLISS IS A SEAT (resting on a blissful state of mind), CONSCIOUSNESS IS A THREAD (to tie the tuft of consciousness), SUBJECT IS SPEECH (articulation of absolute subjectivity), COGNITION IS PIERCING INTO OBJECTS (penetrate the sensory faculties, as if the act of reversing the gaze of consciousness is a physical process that actually pierces through the sensory complex), PHILOSOPHICAL CATEGORIES ARE THE SEATS (making a seat atop māyā, sitting on top of the triad that signify volition, cognition, and action), MENTAL ACTS ARE PHYSICAL ACTS (mental energy to sustain visualization for a prolonged period of time is identified as vigor), HAPPINESS IS BLOSSOMING (the mind blossoms when visualization reaches to higher states), etc. In fact, the very fabric of tantric language is woven with metaphors, with a surplus of meaning, something additional imparted by means of general speech (Timalsina 2007).

The final insights that can be derived from this conversation relate to images: Are instances of imagination always accompanied by images? Philosophers such as Descartes or Hume maintained that for any mental episode to be considered as imagination, it needs to be accompanied by images.[7] There are some serious objections to the claim that every episode of imagination is necessarily accompanied by mental images (Gregory, 2016). Imagining negative facts, for instance, cannot be supported by the presence of any images. This objection anticipates the premise that the image that is present in the mind corresponds to or is the very content of imagination. The course of visualization has something else to offer. When we entertain negative facts, for example, "David did not attend the conference," or "Round squares are nonexistent," what is presumed according to the objection is that there is a content of imagination that corresponds to what we are imagining. However, even in imagining the negative facts, we can be occupied with images: a person, a circle, or a square. There is no correspondence required between what we fantasize and what is present in our mind during the mode of imagination. While negating, we can still have the presence of the object in our mind. And whether in affirmation or in negation, the object can be partially present. When we miss someone, we are mentally presenting the person. Therefore, it is wrong to assume that negative facts have no images in the mode of imagination. What is missing in the above argument is that the presence of images does not constitute imagination. My argument is that it is not the thing (content) but the act itself that constitutes imagination. As has been said earlier, not everything that happens in the mode of imagination is actually an act of imagination, and just like other cognitive modes, imagining is yet another mode that is saturated with distinctive cognitive faculties. In the above examples, most of the components that constitute visualization contain images. However, there is no image to correspond to the affective roles, such as the devotional attitude toward the deity. Emotional states based on imagined objects can overpower the subjects, giving a semblance of emotion. It is noteworthy that there is a clear distinction between the state and the object. Accordingly, there is also no imagery possible for the absolute, pure bliss, or concepts such as infinity, eternity, and so on. Finally, multiple aspects of visualization invoke the formless, the very texts repeatedly address that what is being visualized is devoid of images, and so it is counterintuitive to impose images in these accounts.

The intricate connection of image with imagination also has a linguistic aspect. If we return to the Sanskrit language, acts of imagination are derived from the verbs √kṛpu, the root for *kalpayati*, which means both "imagines" and "creates." The words derived from it do not intrinsically say anything about images, unlike the English term "imagination." If we extend the scope further, no word used in describing visualization makes images necessary: Most of the words in this application are derived from √dhyai = to think, the causative use of √bhū = to be, in the sense of "to make it happen," √smṛ = to remember, or √cint = to think. Apparently, the

---

7 For further discussion of mental imagery in the context of imagination, see Gregory, 2016, 97–110.

discussion of whether thoughts are like images (for example, Fodor 1975, Kosslyn 1980) or like description (for example, Dennett 1978, Pylyshyn 1978) never made headway in discussing the culture that is suffused with images. Arguably, this was due to their primary focus on utilizing the potentials of imagination in transforming everyday experience rather than defining it. This lacuna has left the ground open for discussion, as the texts that describe visualization do use images but also stress that images are applicable only in the initial steps. The manuals on visualization use propositional attitudes in addressing imagination, while at the same time seeking to ground the experience that is expunged of both the subjective and objective horizons. The literature on meditation repeatedly stresses that the reality we share is a construction, whether collective or personal and is always subject to alteration.

What Can Meditation Reveal about Imagination?

Meditation practices come in many forms. Some cause the practitioner to recognize his bodily and cognitive limitations by means of forcing him to see with the eyes of his mind what he tends to generally block, forget, or pretend is not there, like an awareness of his own mortality. Others suspend all forms of conceptualization, giving the subject a much-needed pause from sustained episodes of imagination. What I have highlighted in this chapter is a different type of meditation that utilizes imagination in an exploration of its parameters by providing multiple modalities, for instance, emotional and conceptual contents to sustain a course of imagination. The meditation practices outlined above use imagination as a tool or a mechanism to alter our everyday perception, to enhance some of our experiences, to ground the subject in the midst of other subjects, and to create a new intersubjective domain. This all stems from the breach between the mental and physical that is underscored in all forms of contemplative practices.

All our cognitive faculties, including daydreaming, counterfactual imagining, and empathic response, appear to have a real biological and social role. Further studies on these areas may guide us in unravelling the domains of imagination and their relation to transforming negative emotions. Meditative practices appear to focus on the subject's self-assessment. Any transformation in personality demands that the person reflect or develop a meta-gaze to evaluate himself among other selves and things. While the course of meditation repeatedly seeks to alter the subjective domain, the extent to which this interacts with the socially and biologically cultivated personality is yet to be analyzed. In the above examples of visualization, philosophy appears as a tool to deconstruct the given horizon of somatosensory experiences and a mechanism to transform subjectivity. Philosophy, in this light, is therapeutic and transformative, rather than descriptive or analytical. The issues that need further investigation involve the role contemplative practices play in subjective transformation and in creating empathic beings. How our belief systems affect imagination and personality is yet another issue. Accordingly, whether these sustained acts of imagination can help individuals in recognizing their place in the collectively shared social reality is also an issue for further study.

References

Abraham, A. (2016). The Imaginative Mind. *Human Brain Mapping*, *37*(11), 4197–4211. doi .org/10.1002/hbm.23300.

Crangle, E. F. (1994). *The Origin and Development of Early Indian Contemplative Practices.* Wiesbaden, Germany: Otto Harrassowitz Verlag.

Dennett, D. (1978). Two Approaches to Mental Images. In *Brainstorms: Philosophical Essays on Mind and Psychology.* Cambridge, MA: MIT Press.

Dvivedi, V. V. (ed.). (1992). *Mahārthamañjarī* of Maheśvarānanda. With the *Auto- Commentary, Parimala.* Varanasi, India: Sampurnananda University.

Fodor, J. (1975). Imagistic Representation. In N. Block (ed.), *The Language of Thought.* Cambridge, MA.: Harvard University Press, 63–86.

Gregory, D. (2016). Imagination and Mental Imagery. In A. Kind (ed.), *The Routledge Handbook of Philosophy of Imagination.* London, UK; New York, NY: Routledge, 97–110.

Hayes, G. A. (2006). The Guru's Tongue: Metaphor, Imagery, and Vernacular Language in Vaiṣṇava Sahajiyā Traditions. *Pacific World: Journal of the Institute of Buddhist Studies*, *3*(8), 41–71.

(2013). Possible Selves, Body Schemas, and *Sādhana*: Using Neuroscience in the Study of Medieval Vaiṣṇava Hindu Tantric Texts. *Religions*, *2014*(5), 684–699. doi:10.3390/ rel5030684.

Kind, A. (2016). Introduction. *The Routledge Handbook of Philosophy of Imagination.* London, UK; New York, NY: Routledge, 1–11.

Kosslyn, S. M. (1980). *Image and Mind.* Cambridge, MA: Harvard University Press.

Pylyshyn, Z. (1978). Imagery and Artificial Intelligence. In C. Wade Savage (ed.), *Perception and Cognition: Issues in the Foundation of Psychology.* Minneapolis, MN: University of Minnesota Press, 19–56.

Shastri, M. R. (ed.) (1918). *Tantrasāra* of Abhinavagupta. Bombay, India: Nirnaya Sagar Press.

Shulman, D. (2012). *More than Real: A History of the Imagination in South India.* Cambridge, MA: Harvard University Press.

Stevenson, L. (2003). Twelve Conceptions of Imagination. *The British Journal of Aesthetics*, *43*(3), 238–259. doi.org/10.1093/bjaesthetics/43.3.238.

Timalsina, S. (2005). Meditating Mantras: Meaning and Visualization in Tantric Literature. In K. A. Jacobsen (ed.), *Theory and Practice of Yoga: Essays in Honour of Gerard James Larson.* Leiden, Netherlands: Brill, 213–236.

(2006). *Seeing and Appearance: History of the Advaita Doctrine of Dṛṣṭisṛṣṭi.* Indo-Halle Series 10. Aachen, Germany: Shaker Verlag.

(2007). Metaphors, *Rasa*, and *Dhvani*: Suggested Meaning in Tantric Esotericism. *Method and Theory in the Study of Religion*, *19*(1–2), 134–162.

(2013). Gauḍapāda on Imagination. *Journal of Indian Philosophy*, *41*(6), 591–602.

(2015a). *Tantric Visual Culture: A Cognitive Approach.* London, UK: Routledge.

(2015b). *Language of Images: Visualization and Meaning in Tantras.* New York, NY: Peter Lang.

(2017). Visualization in Hindu Practice. *Oxford Research Encyclopedia of Religion.*

47 Flow in Performance and Creative Cognition – An Optimal State of Task-Based Adaptation

Örjan de Manzano

The term *flow* originates from the work of psychologist Mihály Csíkszentmihályi, who in the 1960s began studying the creative process of fine art students (Csíkszentmihályi, 2014). He was intrigued by the observation that when painting was going well, the artists kept on working single-mindedly, disregarding hunger, fatigue, and discomfort – yet seemed to lose interest in the artistic creations once they had been completed. This phenomenon inspired further studies on chess players, rock climbers, dancers, composers and others (Csíkszentmihályi, 1997). It became clear, that for many individuals it was primarily the rewarding experience they felt when they were involved in the activity that motivated them, not external rewards such as money or fame. The activities seemed intrinsically motivating or autotelic (*auto* = self, *telos* = goal), that is, worthwhile in and of themselves. Moreover, the subjective experience of being immersed in them was described in almost identical terms across individuals, across play and work settings, and did not vary much by culture, gender, or age. This form of optimal experience is what Csíkszentmihályi has termed *flow*, based on many of the respondents describing the feeling as an almost automatic, effortless, yet highly focused state of consciousness (Csíkszentmihályi, 1997).

Elements of Flow

Based on an extensive set of qualitative interviews, Csíkszentmihályi and colleagues identified nine elements that characterize the flow experience (Csíkszentmihályi, 1990):

(1) **Challenge-skill balance.** Task difficulty needs to match the person's peak ability. A task that is too easy will create boredom; a task that is too difficult will induce feelings of stress and anxiety. The space between boredom and anxiety forms the *flow channel*, where optimal experience may emerge.

(2) **Action-awareness merging.** Total immersion in an activity can give the experience that every action is a natural extension of the mind. For instance, a tool can be perceived as an extension of the body. Actions feel automatic and require little conscious effort.

(3) **Clear goals.** The person has a clear sense of what he or she wants to achieve.

(4) **Unambiguous feedback.** There is a clear and immediate relation between thoughts, actions, and their implications.

(5) **High concentration.** Attention is completely focused on the task. Distractions do not enter consciousness. Nonetheless, the feeling is that little conscious effort is required to maintain attention on the task.

(6) **Sense of control.** There is an experience of being in total control of what is going on.

(7) **Loss of self-consciousness.** Self-reflective thoughts, worry, and fear of social evaluation are absent.

(8) **Transformation of time.** The sense of time may be lost as there is total focus on the present. After the activity, time may seem to have moved faster or slower than usual.

(9) **Autotelic experience.** Flow is associated with positive affect and a sense of reward that sometimes comes only afterward, when attention is no longer focused on the activity.

When operationalizing and examining flow, the elements of the flow experience are usually transformed into dimensions that load equally on a composite flow score (Jackson and Eklund, 2004). Flow is consequently not measured as an all-or-nothing peak experience, but rather treated as a continuous variable that can be used to characterize the experiential quality of any activity. Even so, flow is often described as an alternate state of consciousness in first-person accounts (Csíkszentmihályi, 1990), presumably based on the unique experience of *effortless attention*, that is, when high-level cognitive processing and performance is coupled with action-awareness merging and reward (Ullén et al., 2010).

While the flow elements give a general idea of the required conditions and subjective experience of being in flow, the importance of each element will naturally vary to some degree across activities. Elements can also be present in a more or less abstract form. The goal of an activity can be highly concrete, as in the case of climbing a mountain, but also quite abstract, for instance manifesting as the curiosity and desire to explore and/or discover something new. Abstract goals are common in many creative activities, which involve imagining and formulating problems as much as solving them (Csíkszentmihályi and Getzels, 1970). Feedback also does not have to be in the form of concrete external stimuli, but can be "self-administered," so to speak, based on internalized criteria (e.g. an artist's cultural definition of beauty). Thus, there is a certain domain-specificity to the dimensions of the flow experience, which may also influence how flow is operationalized within a given activity.

Further, sense of agency (the experience that "I am in control of my actions") and actual behavioral control are not always perfectly related. Visual artists, musicians, writers, and others have often described themselves as bearing witness to their own performance when in flow, as if it is "really the fingers that are doing it and not the brain" (Csíkszentmihályi, 1997: 118). Vuorre and Metcalfe (2016) studied flow and agency in an experiment employing a computer game paradigm, in which participants had to click on visual stimuli appearing on the screen using a computer mouse, at different game speeds, and then report agency and flow on visual analogue scales. The results showed a clear dissociation between the sense of agency and the experience of flow. Specifically, the sense of agency decreased as the task became more difficult, whereas the feeling of flow peaked at middle values of difficulty, where participants presumably were in the flow channel.

Flow, Expertise and Effortless Attention

Perhaps the most distinguishing feature of flow is the feeling of totally focused yet effortless attention, which may seem like a contradiction in terms. Attention is generally understood to require cognitive control, which is accompanied by a subjective sense of mental effort (Kahneman, 1973). Under normal circumstances, the expectation is consequently that an increased demand on attentional resources will increase subjective effort. Nevertheless, a flow state is uniquely characterized by a subjective experience of total yet unforced concentration despite high demand. How is that possible? Three crucial factors will be discussed here – automaticity, imagery, and the subjective experience of effortless attention.

Central to theories about flow, particularly with regard to action-awareness merging, is the observation that mental effort associated with an activity is reduced with practice (Willingham, 1998). This most typically reflects a decreased demand on executive cognitive control for organizing behavior and an increased demand on storage and processing in task-specific areas. Petersen et al. (1998) have explained this in terms of a "scaffolding-storage" framework. For unskilled task performance, top-down cognitive control processes supported by working memory are engaged to organize behavior in relation to novel goals and external constraints (e.g. stimuli). After practice, processes or associations are more efficiently stored and accessed, i.e. there is an increase in automaticity, and the scaffolding network falls away. This process is underpinned by neural plasticity, i.e. functional and structural reorganization of the brain, which results in optimized performance and reduced mental effort (Doyon and Benali, 2005). Neuroimaging studies have shown that there can be extensive differences in regional brain anatomy in both gray and white matter structure as a function of expertise (reviewed in Ullén, Hambrick, and Mosing, 2016)[1]. For example, we recently compared brain structure between adult monozygotic (identical) twin siblings who differed substantially in piano practice using magnetic resonance imaging (de Manzano and Ullén, 2018). The analyses revealed that the more musically trained twins had greater cortical thickness in the auditory-motor network of the left hemisphere, more developed white matter microstructure in relevant tracts in both hemispheres, and increased gray matter volume in a region of the left cerebellum associated with fine hand motor tasks. Importantly, since monozygotic twin siblings have the same genes, these effects were presumably due to a causal influence of practice. Functional reorganizations, which refer to

---

1 Animal studies suggest that these differences could arise from various expertise-dependent adaptations including increased synapse numbers, modified synapse morphology, and increased myelination of relevant fiber tracts (reviewed in Markham and Greenough, 2004).

changes in brain activation patterns after practicing an activity, also occur (Herholz et al., 2016). These include both altered functional properties of specific brain regions and changes in connectivity patterns between regions. Similar adaptations presumably serve to augment performance, optimize retrieval, maintenance and processing of domain-specific information, and increase automaticity, which in turn alleviates executive control processes and reduces mental effort. Importantly, structural and functional plasticity also constitute a neural substrate for expertise-related imagery and mental simulations (Abraham, 2016).

One functional adaptation that is particularly interesting with regard to automaticity and effortless attention is *action-perception coupling*, by which a representation of a perceptual effect can trigger the movement necessary to produce the effect itself (Novembre and Keller, 2014). Such sensorimotor associations can be established through training. For example, Lahav, Saltzman, and Schlaug (2007) trained nonmusicians to play a novel melody on the piano over a period of five days, and then studied their brain activity using functional magnetic resonance imaging (fMRI) while they were listening to the trained melody as well as novel melodies. The results showed that listening to the trained melody, as compared to the novel melodies, induced additional activity in premotor regions that are involved in action planning. This suggests that acquiring action sequences with an audible output creates sensorimotor associations between the sound of those actions and the corresponding motor representations. This naturally requires the task to involve fairly consistent mappings between sensory information and action outcomes (unambiguous feedback).

Action-perception coupling can greatly reduce the need for executive cognitive control of performance. In the case of learned reflexes, certain external stimuli will automatically trigger the associated response even before the person is made aware (e.g. emergency braking of a vehicle). Even with less automaticity, perception can be gradually tuned to contextually relevant information that then generates expectations and imagery, which in turn can be used to plan and prepare actions ahead of time. For example, Keller and colleagues have shown that action-perception coupling associated with musical training enables musicians to plan their actions by imagining the auditory sequences in an anticipatory fashion (reviewed in Novembre and Keller, 2014). Similarly, cricket players do not always keep their eyes on the ball, but rely on brief visual cues and an experience-based model to imagine ball trajectories, which in turn trigger anticipatory eye-movements to where the ball is expected to bounce (Land and McLeod, 2000). Action-perception coupling and auditory anticipatory imaging can further enhance timing accuracy and economical force control through the optimization of movement kinematics (Keller, Dalla Bella, and Koch, 2010).

Thus, with a high degree of action-perception coupling, fewer attentional resources are needed for information filtering, action selection, setting movement parameters and so on, and resources can instead be focused on higher level aspects, such as preparing and imagining the optimal sequence of actions and predicted outcomes ahead of time. Presumably, this is an important factor in what creates a feeling of control, that is, the subjective experience of knowing what will happen and how to respond to it at every instant. This ability to plan ahead creates a buffer to the present that allows for fluent performance. One might say that consciousness exists in a virtual near-future state. As long as performance can be maintained at the challenge-skill equilibrium, and sensory feedback continues to meet expectations in reference to the goal of the task, action and perception act much like a closed-loop system, boosted by processes of imagination – in other words, a stable state of total concentration on task, but with little associated conscious effort, as characteristic of flow.

The stability of cognitive processing enabled by action-perception coupling and automaticity may itself contribute to the experience of effortlessness. McGuire and Botvinick (2010) have argued that cognitive control should be viewed as an ongoing process and that subjective mental effort is associated with a change in that process rather than with the process itself. Their thesis, which has found much empirical support, is that the anterior cingulate cortex on the medial wall of the brain monitors and signals unmet demand for cognitive control and that this signal also helps encode the costliness of mental effort (McGuire and Botvinick, 2010). The magnitude of this signal, for instance in response to an error in performance, has been found to correlate with reactive executive cognitive control of behavior as well as with subjective mental effort. If task demand or even a conflict-inducing event is well anticipated, however, there will be a preparatory upregulation of control, which means that unmet demand will remain low. Mental effort can therefore be dissociated from cognitive control, such that a demanding but well-anticipated situation can involve strong control without a negative effort-related experience. This links back to the anticipatory planning discussed above, which could thus promote cognitive control of high-level performance without a concomitant increase in perceived mental effort, thereby contributing to the experience of flow. Another factor that could potentially dissociate perceived effort from cognitive control is the intrinsic motivation and enjoyment that accompanies flow. We have previously suggested that this can occur as a result of an interaction between positive valence and attention (de Manzano et al., 2010), as positive valence can distract from negative and even painful stimuli (Roy, Peretz, and Rainville, 2008). A task of great attentional load may consequently be experienced as less effortful in a state of positive affect.

As explained, action-perception coupling can obviate executive control of lower-level processing. In fact, once the neural system has reached a certain level of automaticity, attending to the components of a well-learned skill can impair concurrent performance (Beilock et al., 2002; Gray, 2004). That is, when not all attentional resources are required for micromanaging performance, they are preferably directed elsewhere. Wulf and colleagues have studied various sports activities and illustrated that shifting the focus of attention from conscious control of movements (internal focus) to the outcome of an action (external focus), often results in more effective performance (Wulf and Lewthwaite, 2010). In golf, for instance, focusing on the swing of the club instead of on the swing of the arms was found to improve the accuracy of pitch shots (Wulf and Su, 2007). It was suggested that an external focus causes greater coherence between the predicted (imagined) action outcome and actual sensory feed-back, which allows the motor system to adjust more adaptively to task demands. Focusing on the desired movement effect allows for a more automatic mode of control, with the anticipated outcome almost as a by-product. Moreover, the enhanced outcome seems to be achieved with less effort. Again, this leads back to the notion of functional networks created through skill-learning, which underpin optimal performance, effortless attention, and flow.

As described above, individuals who persist in trying to consciously control their movements appear to interfere with automatic control processes. One potential source of such interference is self-consciousness, which is likely one main reason why loss of self-consciousness is an element of flow (cf. *Elements of Flow*). Self-focus and social anxiety can lead to self-evaluation and activate self-regulatory processes in attempts to manage thoughts and affective responses. Wulf and colleagues refer to this as *microchoking* (Wulf and Lewthwaite, 2010). They have illustrated that negative self-focus, which is reflected in higher anxiety and fear levels and lower levels of self-efficacy, is associated with more widespread, inefficient activation of the muscular system, disruption of automaticity, and the use of more conscious control over ongoing movement. Again, practice seems an important factor, as greater experience and preparation usually reduces anxiety and the need to engage in active suppression of negative thoughts and emotional reactions.

Training-dependent changes in cognitive processing can also affect *flow-proneness*, that is, the tendency to experience flow more often. Heller, Bullerjahn, and von Georgi (2015) found that the more singers practiced, the more likely they were to have flow experiences. Marin and Bhattacharya (2013) similarly showed that in a group of pianists flow-proneness was predicted by their amount of daily practice. Based on a web-survey with more than 4,500 individuals, Butković, Ullén, and Mosing (2015) revealed that proneness to flow experience during music-playing predicts music practice much better than both the creativity-related personality trait openness to experience and IQ ($r = .41$, $r = .19$ and $r = .04$, respectively). Interestingly, general flow-proneness (combining work, leisure-time activities and household maintenance tasks) was unrelated to musical practice. These findings together illustrate that the tendency to experience flow in an activity – much like expertise – develops with practice and does not readily transfer to other activities.

One general conclusion that can be drawn at this point, supported by a number of independent observations from different research groups working on different topics, is that effortless attention appears dependent on a certain level of domain-specific expertise that matches skills with challenges, enables enough automaticity of behavior to free executive systems from micromanaging sensorimotor processing, allows attentional resources to focus on action planning and more qualitative aspects of performance, and helps to minimize negative self-referential thought. This conclusion further suggests something very interesting – that training-dependent changes in cognitive processing and flow to some extent share neural substrates. Given what has been described here about optimization of perception and action and expertise-related neural plasticity, it appears plausible that those shared mechanisms would involve the functional characteristics of information exchange within domain-specific brain networks. This will be elaborated further in the section on *The Neural Correlates of Flow*.

Flow and Creativity

As mentioned at the beginning of this chapter, the study of flow came out of observations of artists at work, and ever since, flow has been associated with creative performance. In view of the literature, which has until now been based mostly on qualitative studies, I suggest that there are at least three ways in which flow might be related to creativity. The first hypothesis is that the experience of flow can play a causal role as a motivating factor that supports commitment and, in the long term, achievement in practically any domain. The second hypothesis is that flow signals immersion, which is presumably beneficial for task performance in any activity. The relation between flow and creativity might then be purely correlational. The third hypothesis is that creative thinking relies on certain cognitive processes and possibly a certain state of mind that is intimately linked to the experience of flow.

The most discussed association between flow and creativity concerns how flow may lead to intrinsic motivation, which in turn promotes practice and expertise. Knowledge and expertise are essential for creativity because (1) more knowledge means increased complexity of the associative network and a greater number of mental elements to form new concepts, and (2) knowledge provides a framework by which those concepts can be identified as novel and useful. Thus, perhaps the most reliable way to think out of the box is to fill it with knowledge until it begins to leak new ideas. Getting to that stage can, however, be quite hard and that is why flow is believed to be important. Besides enabling intrinsic motivation and allowing a person to become "hooked" on a particular activity, flow also naturally leads to engaging with ever greater complexity. This is because to keep enjoying the activity, that is to remain in the flow channel, a person needs to keep discovering new challenges in order to avoid boredom, and to improve skills in order to avoid anxiety (Csíkszentmihályi, 1997). The studies presented earlier in this chapter on the relation between flow-proneness and musical practice clearly indicate a significant role for flow in skill acquisition and creative achievement (Butković, Ullén, and Mosing, 2015; Heller, Bullerjahn, and von Georgi, 2015; Marin and Bhattacharya, 2013). It is remarkable that domain-specific flow is a better predictor of practice than personality and cognitive ability combined (Butković, Ullén, and Mosing, 2015). Another aspect of creative work is that external rewards can be rare, particularly when going against the mainstream. In such situations, intrinsic motivation can be the motor that pushes work forward. This suggests that intrinsic motivation may play a particularly important role for eminent creative achievements (hypothesis 1).

Flow has already been mentioned in the context of several creative activities. Nonetheless, it might seem counterintuitive to associate flow with originality of thought. The flow state is supposedly more easily achieved in situations that are predictable, controllable, and low-risk. Creative work, on the other hand, is inherently unpredictable, uncontrollable, and high-risk. One answer, as discussed earlier, is that the subjective experience of these conditions can depend on the focus of attention. For example, even though the goal or end product might not be easily envisioned, the actions that will inevitably lead you to it can seem to follow naturally from one another. Thus, even in a creative task that from a certain perspective would appear daunting (e.g. a writing task that could induce "blank page anxiety"), a flow state might nonetheless be enabled by breaking up the goal into subgoals and focusing on the immediate performance. Complete immersion in the activity and the present moment might then promote associative thinking, imaginative cognition, and perhaps even creative ideas. Note that the latter does not necessitate a unique relation between flow and creativity. It does, however, require a certain level of automaticity of creative thinking. To automate creativity, which is typically defined as producing something that is at the same time novel and useful, might seem rather impossible. Automation typically requires very stable and predictable relations between input, output, and feedback, which is uncharacteristic of open-ended problem-solving.

In order to look more closely at the role of automaticity in creative cognition, we have examined brain activity in a sample of pianists with a wide range of improvisation experience, while each of them played short musical improvisations on a small keyboard during fMRI (Pinho et al., 2014). Pianists who were more trained specifically in improvisation had lower activity in the frontoparietal working memory network, as well as greater effective functional connectivity among prefrontal, premotor, and motor areas during improvisation.[2] In other words, pianists with greater expertise in improvisation showed lower demands on executive control and a more efficient information exchange within the network of domain-specific brain regions. It therefore appears that long-term training can indeed lead to an automation of task-specific cognitive processes involved in creative performance. We suggest that once sufficient knowledge has been acquired, a reduced explicit control over generative processes, in favor of more automated implicit processing, becomes a viable and efficient cognitive strategy. This is because free association in the context of well-developed long-term memory structures will result in spontaneous yet relevant responses at high fluency. A similar strategy will not work for novices, because their responses will presumably be either too simplistic or too random. The novice is instead better off engaging deliberate top–down control processes that can guide retrieval and action planning. This indicates that individuals with more domain-specific knowledge and practice in being creative are also more likely to experience flow, along the lines discussed previously. Thus, the relation between flow and optimal creative performance could be an analog to that between flow and optimal performance in general (hypothesis 2).

The third hypothesis concerning how flow might relate to creativity assumes that creative thinking involves a specific mode of cognitive processing that is intimately linked to the flow state. This might seem highly unlikely, at least in a strict sense, given the simple observations that flow can be experienced in noncreative tasks and that creative cognition does not necessarily induce flow. Nonetheless there are several elements of flow that relate to cognition that are also important for creative thinking, such as self-confidence, an emotional state of moderate arousal and positive affect, and arguably effortless attention. Positive affect has been shown to

---

2 Effective functional connectivity in this context means that activity levels correlated more highly across the involved regions specifically during improvisation.

improve performance in tasks that require cognitive flexibility (Nijstad et al., 2010), i.e. set shifting and updating of working memory and broader access to remote semantic associates. Cognitive flexibility is often assumed to indicate creative potential, as creative potential is often operationalized as the number of switches between semantic categories and/or the originality of responses in divergent thinking tests.[3] Both positive affect and cognitive flexibility are furthermore underpinned by the release of the neurotransmitter dopamine, which is known to influence gating thresholds and the filtering and regulation of information flow (Yasuno et al., 2004). It has been suggested that dopamine release in certain brain regions may place networks of cortical neurons in a more reactive state, which allows them to switch more easily between representations and process multiple stimuli across a wider association range (Seamans and Yang, 2004). We have also found that individuals with high flow-proneness have higher dopamine D2-receptor availability in the subcortical region striatum (de Manzano et al., 2013), which indicates low impulsiveness, stable emotion, and positive affect.

The increase in cognitive flexibility mediated by positive affect typically comes at the cost of impaired performance on tasks requiring focused attention and filtering of distracting information (Goschke and Bolte, 2014). Thus, positive affect appears to shift balance from robust maintenance in working memory and proactive control toward a "diffuse mental state" characterized by less gating of information and reactive control (Vanlessen et al., 2016). This resonates to some degree with early psychological theories of creativity that relate creative thinking to a certain state of mind – characterized as dreamlike, associative, inclusive, and separate from reality-oriented cognition (Martindale, 1999). Modern neuroimaging could also be said to support some version of these notions, as many recent findings indicate that creative cognition involves a unique functional combination of executive control systems and the *default mode network* (Beaty et al., 2018). The default mode network involves several interconnected regions that are typically engaged during rest and are involved in various forms of imagination, daydreaming, mind-wandering, remembering the past, and planning for the future (Raichle, 2015).

However, this general finding does not account for the fact that real-life creative performance is often a highly dynamic activity that can involve the use of different cognitive strategies. In the case of musical improvisation, for instance, Clarke (1988) described three main principles or strategies: (1) current behavior may be part of a hierarchical structure, to some extent worked out in advance, and to some extent constructed online; (2) current behavior may be part of an associative chain of actions; and (3) current behavior may be selected from a number of actions contained within the performer's repertoire. Clarke also asserts that in practice these principles are usually intermingled throughout performance. The quality of creative output might not differ between them, but cognition and neural processing presumably does.

---

3 Divergent thinking tests typically involve generating a multitude of novel and meaningful responses to open-ended questions. In the classical Guilford's alternate uses test, for instance, participants are instructed to propose different uses for certain artifacts, such as a brick, within a limited time period (Guilford et al., 1960).

In order to explore the implications of using different cognitive strategies on brain activity during creative performance, we performed another fMRI study with the same sample of pianists as mentioned previously. This time we were able to show that creative cognition can be biased toward at least two general cognitive strategies or control modes that differ with regard to the involved brain networks (Pinho et al., 2016). When the pianists were given an instruction to play only on certain keys (focus on the pitch set), they engaged an *extrospective* network characterized by activity in working-memory regions and the lateral prefrontal cortex exerting top-down control of behavior. When the pianists were instead given the instruction to convey a certain emotion (happy/fearful), they engaged an *introspective* free-associative network, in which largely automated processes in specialized brain systems, including the default mode network, are organized under the influence of the medial and inferior prefrontal cortices. This latter network corresponds to that previously described in relation to creative thinking. Based on these outcomes, two points can be made concerning creative cognition and flow. First, there is not one single mode of creative thinking and second, some creative activities are perhaps more likely to be associated with flow than others. Artistic activities, for example, often benefit from cognitive flexibility, allow for a certain level of automaticity and action-perception coupling, and involve longer episodes of continuous performance. Compared to scientific creativity for instance, artistic activities also rely heavily on spontaneous associations, emotional involvement, and the expression of affect (Eysenck, 1995; Feist, 1999). Overall, this indicates that artistic creativity predominantly involves "implicit" problem-solving strategies that are underpinned by information exchange in the introspective network. When it comes to such strategies, one might argue that flow is not just a signal of immersion but more intimately associated with a certain state of mind that is particularly conducive to creative thinking (hypothesis 3).

All these discussions beg the question of whether the quality of creative output is indeed improved by being in flow. Unfortunately, there are not many studies to date that have addressed this question experimentally. Cseh, Phillips, and Pearson (2015) administered a creative mental synthesis task (originally designed to explore mental imagery in creativity) to a sample of nonartist participants. They collected a post-task measure of state flow, pre- and post-task mood measures, and performance ratings by participants and external raters. Their findings showed that the experience of flow was related to more positive affect during the task, and to higher self-perceived performance. However, there was no relation to the externally rated measures of task performance. The authors therefore concluded that flow is more likely to increase motivation than to provide direct cognitive enhancement. In another study, MacDonald, Byrne, and Carlton (2006) explored whether flow in music students working in groups of three during a music composition task was associated with the quality of creative output, as rated by lecturers and postgraduate students. The compositions belonging to the groups in which individuals on average reported higher flow was also rated as more creative by the lecturers. It is clear that more research is needed to fully understand whether flow can actually contribute to the quality of real-time creative performance.

The Neural Correlates of Flow

It is important to note that even though fluent creative performance appears related to processing in the introspective network, this does not necessarily mean that the flow experience has to be tied exclusively to processing in this network. Although it is tempting to hypothesize that a deactivation of the extrospective network in favor of automatic and implicit processing in the introspective network would be a general mechanism for flow (Dietrich, 2004), there are more things to consider. Flow can be experienced in a wide range of tasks that presumably differ substantially with regard to involved neural systems. In addition, when executive systems and attentional resources are freed from micromanaging behavior they are, as noted, usually employed in higher-level cognitive processing. Therefore, flow should be related to optimal processing in whatever network is most suitable for a certain activity. In line with this reasoning, flow has been associated with *more* activity in the extrospective network and *less* activity in default mode regions when solving mental arithmetic tasks (Ulrich, Keller, and Gron, 2016) and there is also evidence to suggest a moderate increase of activity in prefrontal regions more generally during flow (Harmat et al., 2015).

Rather than trying to localize flow to processing in a certain brain region, Weber et al. (2009) have formulated a hypothesis in which flow is described as a state of optimal synchronization and information exchange between attentional and reward systems. They have also suggested a methodological approach to index flow by measuring functional connectivity between regions involved in attention and motivation during performance of a task (Weber et al., 2018). This seems like a promising avenue for continued research on the neural basis of the flow experience.

Concluding Remarks and Future Directions

In this chapter, three hypotheses were presented for how flow might be related to creativity: as a source of motivation, as an epiphenomenon to optimal (creative) performance, or as intimately related to a creative state of mind, which implies a shared neural substrate. These hypotheses are not necessarily mutually exclusive and it could be argued that they rather indicate different aspects of flow that may all be related to creative cognition and creative achievement, but through different mechanisms.

Little is known about why individuals experience flow in the first place, but one suggestion, which is relevant to the first hypothesis (flow as a source of motivation), is that flow functions as a reward signal indicating to the brain that the biological system has been successfully optimized for a certain task (de Manzano et al., 2010). The reward signal could both motivate the brain to remember and return to the same system configuration on subsequent occasions and facilitate this process. Even consciously, the memory of flow could be used as an abstract goal or target state, that is, an abstract representation of a potentially very complex mode of processing that needs to be (re)established. From an evolutionary perspective, and given the fact that expertise is pivotal for both the individual and society (particularly when it comes to creative achievements), it makes sense for humans to be endowed with a mechanism that rewards long-term skill acquisition. Considering the relation between flow-proneness and domain-specific practice (Butković, Ullén, and Mosing, 2015), intrinsic motivation resulting from flow experiences might very well be a key component in such a mechanism. Further research on how the concept of flow could be implemented successfully in training and education could potentially have broad and important implications for training and education as well as creative achievement.

There is currently only weak support for the second and third hypotheses given the extremely limited number of studies and diverse findings regarding state flow and immediate creative output. Nonetheless, this chapter provides the outlines of a mechanistic model for how the experience of flow could result from cognitive processing during performance, building on psychological and neuroscientific empirical research centering on expertise and attention. This tentative model predicts that high-state flow during creative cognition is contingent on optimized information exchange within an expertise-specific functional network formed around a core brain network for imaginative cognition (the default mode network). Consequently, within the context of a creative task, flow could conceivably be a reward signal that indicates an optimal state of domain-relevant imaginative cognition and implicit problem-solving. It could be hypothesized that such states, in particular, underpin truly eminent creative achievements.

References

Abraham, A. (2016). The Imaginative Mind. *Human Brain Mapping*, *37*(11), 4197–4211.

Beaty, R. E., Kenett, Y. N., Christensen, A. P., et al. (2018). Robust Prediction of Individual Creative Ability from Brain Functional Connectivity. *Proceedings of the National Academy of Sciences of the United States of America*, *115*(5), 1087–1092.

Beilock, S. L., Carr, T. H., MacMahon, C., and Starkes, J. L. (2002). When Paying Attention becomes Counterproductive: Impact of Divided versus Skill-Focused Attention on Novice and Experienced Performance of Sensorimotor Skills. *Journal of Experimental Psychology-Applied*, *8*(1), 6–16.

Butković, A., Ullén, F., and Mosing, M. A. (2015). Personality and Related Traits as Predictors of Music Practice: Underlying Environmental and Genetic Influences. *Personality and Individual Differences*, *74*, 133–138.

Clarke, E. F. (1988). Generative Principles in Music Performance. In J. A. Sloboda (ed.), *Generative Processes in Music: The Psychology of Performance, Improvisation, and Composition*. New York, NY: Clarendon Press/Oxford University Press, 1–26.

Cseh, G. M., Phillips, L. H., and Pearson, D. G. (2015). Flow, Affect and Visual Creativity. *Cognition & Emotion*, *29*(2), 281–291.

Csíkszentmihályi, M. (1990). *Flow: The Psychology of Optimal Experience*. New York, NY: Harper & Row.

(1997). *Creativity: Flow and the Psychology of Discovery and Invention*. New York, NY: HarperPerennial.

(2014). *The Systems Model of Creativity: The Collected Works of Mihaly Csikszentmihalyi.* New York, NY: Springer.

Csíkszentmihályi, M., and Getzels, J. W. (1970). Concern for Discovery – An Attitudinal Component of Creative Production. *Journal of Personality, 38*(1), 91–105.

de Manzano, Ö., Cervenka, S., Jucaite, A., et al. (2013). Individual Differences in the Proneness to Have Flow Experiences Are Linked to Dopamine D2-Receptor Availability in the Striatum. *NeuroImage, 67,* 1–6.

de Manzano, Ö., Theorell, T., Harmat, L., and Ullén, F. (2010). The Psychophysiology of Flow during Piano Playing. *Emotion, 10*(3), 301–311.

de Manzano, Ö., and Ullén, F. (2018). Same Genes, Different Brains: Neuroanatomical Differences between Monozygotic Twins Discordant for Musical Training. *Cerebral Cortex, 28*(1), 387–394.

Dietrich, A. (2004). Neurocognitive Mechanisms Underlying the Experience of Flow. *Consciousness and Cognition, 13*(4), 746–761.

Doyon, J., and Benali, H. (2005). Reorganization and Plasticity in the Adult Brain during Learning of Motor Skills. *Current Opinion in Neurobiology, 15,* 161–167.

Eysenck, H. J. (1995). *Genius. The Natural History of Creativity.* Volume 12. Cambridge, UK: Cambridge University Press.

Feist, G. J. (1999). The Influence of Personality on Artistic and Scientific Creativity. In R. J. Sternberg (ed.), *Handbook of Creativity.* Cambridge, UK: Cambridge University Press, 273–296.

Goschke, T., and Bolte, A. (2014). Emotional Modulation of Control Dilemmas: The Role of Positive Affect, Reward, and Dopamine in Cognitive Stability and Flexibility. *Neuropsychologia, 62,* 403–423.

Gray, R. (2004). Attending to the Execution of a Complex Sensorimotor Skill: Expertise Differences, Choking, and Slumps. *Journal of Experimental Psychology-Applied, 10*(1), 42–54.

Guilford, J. P., Christensen, P. R., Merrifield, P. R., and Wilson, R. C. (1960). *Alternate Uses Manual.* Menlo Park, CA: Mind Garden Inc.

Harmat, L., de Manzano, Ö., Theorell, T., et al. (2015). Physiological Correlates of the Flow Experience during Computer Game Playing. *International Journal of Psychophysiology, 97,* 1–7.

Heller, K., Bullerjahn, C., and von Georgi, R. (2015). The Relationship between Personality Traits, Flow-Experience, and Different Aspects of Practice Behavior of Amateur Vocal Students. *Frontiers in Psychology, 6,* 1901.

Herholz, S. C., Coffey, E. B., Pantev, C., and Zatorre, R. J. (2016). Dissociation of Neural Networks for Predisposition and for Training-Related Plasticity in Auditory-Motor Learning. *Cerebral Cortex, 26*(7), 3125–3134.

Jackson, S. A., and Eklund, R. C. (2004). *The Flow Scales Manual.* Morgantown, WV: Publishers Graphics.

Kahneman, D. (1973). *Attention and Effort.* Englewood, NJ: Prentice-Hall.

Keller, P. E., Dalla Bella, S., and Koch, I. (2010). Auditory Imagery Shapes Movement Timing and Kinematics: Evidence from a Musical Task. *Journal of Experimental Psychology: Human Perception and Performance, 36*(2), 508–513.

Lahav, A., Saltzman, E., and Schlaug, G. (2007). Action Representation of Sound: Audiomotor Recognition Network while Listening to Newly Acquired Actions. *Journal of Neuroscience, 27*(2), 308–314.

Land, M. F., and McLeod, P. (2000). From Eye Movements to Actions: How Batsmen Hit the Ball. *Nature Neuroscience, 3*(12), 1340–1345.

MacDonald, R., Byrne, C., and Carlton, L. (2006). Creativity and Flow in Musical Composition: An Empirical Investigation. *Psychology of Music, 34*(3), 292–306.

Marin, M. M., and Bhattacharya, J. (2013). Getting into the Musical Zone: Trait Emotional Intelligence and Amount of Practice Predict Flow in Pianists. *Frontiers in Psychology, 4*, 853.

Markham, J. A., and Greenough, W. T. (2004). Experience-Driven Brain Plasticity: Beyond the Synapse. *Neuron Glia Biology, 1*, 351–363.

Martindale, C. (1999). Biological Bases of Creativity. In R. J. Sternberg (ed.), *Handbook of Creativity*. Cambridge, UK: Cambridge University Press, 137–152.

McGuire, J. T., and Botvinick, M. M. (2010). The Impact of Anticipated Cognitive Demand on Attention and Behavioral Choice. In B. Bruya (ed.), *Effortless Attention: A New Perspective in the Cognitive Science of Attention and Action*. Cambridge, MA: MIT Press, 103–120.

Nijstad, B. A., de Dreu, C. K. W., Rietzschel, E. F., and Baas, M. (2010). The Dual Pathway to Creativity Model: Creative Ideation as a Function of Flexibility and Persistence. *European Review of Social Psychology, 21*, 34–77.

Novembre, G., and Keller, P. E. (2014). A Conceptual Review on Action-Perception Coupling in the Musician's Brain: What Is It Good For? *Frontiers in Human Neuroscience, 8*, 603.

Petersen, S. E., van Mier, H., Fiez, J. A., and Raichle, M. E. (1998). The Effects of Practice on the Functional Anatomy of Task Performance. *Proceedings of the National Academy of Sciences of the United States of America, 95*(3), 853–860.

Pinho, A. L., de Manzano, Ö., Fransson, P., Eriksson, H., and Ullén, F. (2014). Connecting to Create – Expertise in Musical Improvisation Is Associated with Increased Functional Connectivity between Premotor and Prefrontal Areas. *Journal of Neuroscience, 34*(18), 6156–6163.

Pinho, A. L., Ullén, F., Castelo-Branco, M., Fransson, P., and de Manzano, Ö. (2016). Addressing a Paradox: Dual Strategies for Creative Performance in Introspective and Extrospective Networks. *Cerebral Cortex, 26*(7), 3052–3063.

Raichle, M. E. (2015). The Brain's Default Mode Network. *Annual Review of Neuroscience, 38*, 433–447.

Roy, M., Peretz, I., and Rainville, P. (2008). Emotional Valence Contributes to Music-Induced Analgesia. *Pain, 134*(1–2), 140–147.

Seamans, J. K., and Yang, C. R. (2004). The Principal Features and Mechanisms of Dopamine Modulation in the Prefrontal Cortex. *Progress in Neurobiology, 74*(1), 1–58.

Ullén, F., de Manzano, Ö., Theorell, T., and Harmat, L. (2010). The Physiology of Effortless Attention. In B. Bruya (ed.), *Effortless Attention: A New Perspective in the Cognitive Science of Attention and Action*. Cambridge, MA: MIT Press, 205–218.

Ullén, F., Hambrick, D. Z., and Mosing, M. A. (2016). Rethinking Expertise: A Multi-Factorial Gene-Environment Interaction Model of Expert Performance. *Psychological Bulletin, 142*(4), 427–446.

Ulrich, M., Keller, J., and Gron, G. (2016). Neural Signatures of Experimentally Induced Flow Experiences Identified in a Typical fMRI Block Design with BOLD Imaging. *Social Cognitive and Affective Neuroscience, 11*(3), 496–507.

Vanlessen, N., de Raedt, R., Koster, E. H. W., and Pourtois, G. (2016). Happy Heart, Smiling Eyes: A Systematic Review of Positive Mood Effects on Broadening of Visuospatial Attention. *Neuroscience & Biobehavioral Reviews*, *68*, 816–837.

Vuorre, M., and Metcalfe, J. (2016). The Relation between the Sense of Agency and the Experience of Flow. *Consciousness and Cognition*, *43*, 133–142.

Weber, R., Alicea, B., Huskey, R., and Mathiak, K. (2018). Network Dynamics of Attention during a Naturalistic Behavioral Paradigm. *Frontiers in Human Neuroscience*, *12*, 182.

Weber, R., Tamborini, R., Westcott-Baker, A., and Kantor, B. (2009). Theorizing Flow and Media Enjoyment as Cognitive Synchronization of Attentional and Reward Networks. *Communication Theory*, *19*, 397–422.

Willingham, D. B. (1998). A Neuropsychological Theory of Motor Skill Learning. *Psychological Review*, *105*(3), 558–584.

Wulf, G., and Lewthwaite, R. (2010). Effortless Motor Learning?: An External Focus of Attention Enhances Movement Effectiveness and Efficiency. In B. Bruya (ed.), *Effortless Attention: A New Perspective in the Cognitive Science of Attention and Action*. Cambridge, MA: MIT Press, 75–101.

Wulf, G., and Su, J. (2007). An External Focus of Attention Enhances Golf Shot Accuracy in Beginners and Experts. *Research Quarterly for Exercise and Sport*, *78*(4), 384–389.

Yasuno, F., Suhara, T., Okubo, Y., et al. (2004). Low Dopamine D(2) Receptor Binding in Subregions of the Thalamus in Schizophrenia. *American Journal of Psychiatry*, *161*(6), 1016–1022.

48 The Force of the Imagination

Anna Abraham

What shines through the contributions featured in this volume is our collective understanding that many different and vital aspects of our mental life belong to the vastness that is the imagination. While each chapter emphasizes one or another facet of the imagination, it is clear that this preference is largely due to the academic traditions that typify specific disciplines, and the choice on the part of scholars to zone in on a particular focus of interest within those traditions.[1] So what can we glean about the imagination in general from these assorted perspectives? This final chapter briefly considers some of the implications that can be derived from these accounts of the nature of the imagination.

Imagination is Emergent, Fluid, and Dynamic

One needs to be able to stand before one can walk. But once walking becomes a virtually effortless capacity, we are able to run, leap, and dance, traversing physical space. Fantastic feats of physical prowess, such as a basketball player springing in the air to land a slam dunk or a ballet dancer executing series of fouettés, are only possible following the development of a good sense of balance in early childhood. Acquiring a well-functioning system of balance, then, provides the necessary physiological scaffolding that allows us to push and perturb the limits of the balance system. Stability emerges from instability, and from that stability emerges the capacity to engage functionally in designed or engineered temporary instability. So the capacities we acquire for a given purpose are utilized beyond their original context in novel ways.

This manner of functional "exaptation" is a useful way to think about the imagination. Our capacity to imagine is the means by which we can bring images and ideas to mind in the absence of external input. Implicit within this action is the ability to (1) invoke, construct, and integrate concrete and abstract ideations, (2) draw on knowledge reserves that we acquire through life experience for the same, and (3) distance one's focus from the pressures of the current context. The last enables us to move beyond the confines of a reactive space to that of a proactive realm.

Engaging beyond the limits of the active present and the ability to detach oneself from the immediacy of the now enable a wide range of corollaries, ranging from the

---

1 Chapters 2–11

predictable[2] to the fantastical,[3] from the stable to the precarious. I can imagine my impressions and experiences of persons, objects, and events from seconds, minutes, hours, days, weeks, years, and decades ago.[4] Roaming the retrospective spaces of "what was" frees me to explore prospective spaces of "what can be" seconds later, minutes later, hours later, and so on, as well as adjoining temporal possibility spaces of "what might have been."[5] Contemplating hypotheticals and higher order meta-representations opens up the exploration of atemporal spaces of "what could be" and "what if" beyond one's own reality.[6]

The fidelity of my imaginings to any given reality can range from low to high depending on the level of accuracy, abstraction, and richness of the experience. My imaginings can vary enormously in their manifestation by being sparse, unimodal, and one-dimensional in some contexts and rich, crossmodal, and multidimensional in others. Regardless of how transitory or enduring the imaginings, they can evoke emotional responses, action tendencies, and conceptual insights, which are instantiated in the present, in the here and the now.[7] We are thus brought full circle. The point of departure begins with distancing from the present, and the point of arrival in the canvas of the imagination can extend in any direction, to any extent and even right back to (and encroaching on) the present.

This is not a new observation and has in fact been voiced in a similar form as far back as 1970 by Jean Starobinski in his extraordinary essay on the imagination (Starobinski, 2001):[8]

> Insinuated in perception itself, embroiled with the operations of memory, opening around us the horizon of the possible, escorting the will, hope, fear and conjecture, the imagination is much more than an image-making faculty that re-creates the world that we perceive directly: it is a power of departure, thanks to which we represent to ourselves the things that are distant, and distance ourselves from present realities. Hence this ambiguity that we find everywhere: the imagination, because it anticipates and predicts, serves action, draws before us the configuration of the doable before it is done. In this first sense, the imagination cooperates with 'the function of the real', because our adaptation to the world demands that we leave the present moment, that we go beyond the data of the immediate world, in order to grasp in thought a future of indistinct borders. But, turning our back on the tangible universe that the present rallies around us, the imagining consciousness can also give itself space and project its fables in a direction in which it does not have to take into account a possible clashing with the event itself: in this second sense, the imagination is fiction, play, or dream; a more or less deliberate error, pure fascination. Far from contributing to 'the function of the real', it proclaims our existence in leading it into the region of fantasies. Thus, it contributes step by step towards an extension of our practical domination of the real, or works to loosen the restraints that link us to it. And what complicates matters even further is that nothing guarantees the success

---

2 Chapters 12–18 3 Chapters 44 and 45 4 Chapters 19–22 5 Chapters 8, 26, 27 6 Chapters 9, 21–25, 28–33 7 Chapters 7, 30, 34–39, 46 and 47 8 Unpublished translation by William Glover (reproduced with

of the anticipatory imagination: it always runs the risk of not receiving the confirmation that it expects, and to have produced nothing more than a vain image of our collective hope. On the other hand, we must recognise that the most delirious imagination always retains its own reality, the same that to which all psychic activities can lay claim. It is a fact among facts. If there is necessarily, in all practical life, an imagination of the real, we see in the greatest disordering of images a reality of the imaginary.

The latter reflections highlight how the imagination can change shape or be biased under conditions of disinhibition, immaturity, instruction, and injury.[9] And the association between the particularities of these conditions and the type of the distortions in our imaginings (be it temporary or permanent, specific or generalized) speak to the flow and power of the imagination. The essence of imagination is this: It is fluid, it is dynamic, and it is emergent.

Issues to Bear in Mind Within this Discourse

The manner in which the chapter contributors positioned their argument sometimes diverged in interesting ways and occasionally in relation to factors held to be critical or central to understanding the nature of the human imagination. Some of the noteworthy points that beg further consideration are briefly mentioned:

(i) **Focusing on the inner world ≠ Ignoring the outer world:** The undeniable relevance of societal, cultural, political, and historical contexts to the patterns and directions of our imaginings was frequently highlighted.[10] While the social is often implicit in our understanding of the workings of the imagination, there is a clear need to emphasize and study these relations more explicitly.

(ii) **Distinctions between imaginative and non-imaginative thought:** The viewpoints put forward tended to differ in this respect, with some emphasizing the separateness or differences between the two[11] and others highlighting how intricately interwoven they are.[12]

(iii) **Flexibility in the forms and processes of the imagination:** The categories of imagination framework (Figure 1.3), as it stands, suggests that the nature of the representation form (e.g. visual image, episodic memory trace) determines patterns of processes that are afforded in relation to that form (e.g. visualization, constructive simulation). However, such default relations may not necessarily hold and/or can be overridden in contexts in which a novel perspective is being forged.[13]

(iv) **The impact of the ever-changing environment on the imagination:** The world as we perceive it and act within it is in constant flux owing to political, sociocultural, and technological developments.[14] An awareness needs to be

9 Chapters 40–45 10 Chapters 1–3, 10, 37–39 11 For example, Chapters 5, 8 and 47 12 For example, Chapters 6, 7, 21 and 27 13 Chapters 9 and

cultivated of how changes in these respects within the outer world influence our day-to-day imaginings.

Concluding Note: A Metaphor that Captures the Imagination

Metaphors are a useful semantic tool to wield in order to grasp, represent, and communicate our ideas about complex phenomena. And there can scarcely be any doubt that our understanding of a construct as complex as the imagination would be abetted by the same. So which metaphor would fit this context?

An apt one to apply may be that of water, owing to the somewhat uncanny similarities between the features, forms, and forces of the human imagination and the properties of water. Imagination can manifest in wildly different forms from the tangible to the intangible. Its workings range from calm and predictable to volatile and unpredictable. It is a fundamental part of our physiological make-up, permeating our very being, and it is essential to our mental life. It is nourishing and constructive yet can also be overwhelming and destructive. It is quiet. It is dogged. It shapes. It wields. It fits. It flows. It pushes against fault lines. It breaks away. It lacks definition, yet it is formidable.

This is what we have been granted as a species. A true force of nature within ourselves. The force of imagination.

Bibliography

Starobinski, J. (2001). *La relation critique*. Paris, France: Editions Gallimard.

Name Index

Subject Index